CHAPTER	FOCUS COMPANY	MANAGERIAL FOCUS	CONTRAST COMPANIES	KEY RATIOS
8	Reporting and Interpreting Cost of Sales and Inventory	**DANIER** Danier Leather Inc. (Clothing Manufacturer)	Manufacturing management		**Inventory Turnover**
9	Reporting and Interpreting Property, Plant, and Equipment; Natural Resources; and Intangibles	**WESTJET** WestJet Airlines Ltd. (Major Canadian airline)	Planning productive capacity	Southwest Airlines Ryanair	**Fixed Asset Turnover**
10	Reporting and Interpreting Current Liabilities	**BAUER** Performance Sports Ltd. Bauer Performance Sports (Manufacturing, distribution, and sale of sports equipment)	Capital structure		**Current Ratio Trades Payable Turnover**
11	Reporting and Interpreting Non-Current Liabilities	**BCE** Bell Canada Enterprises Inc. (Communications company)	Long-term debt financing	Rogers Communications Telus	**Financial Leverage Times Interest Earned**
12	Reporting and Interpreting Owners' Equity	**BCE** Bell Canada Enterprises Inc. (Communications company)	Corporate ownership	Rogers Communications Telus	**Earnings per Share Dividend Yield**
13	Analyzing Financial Statements	 Canadian Tire Corporation Limited (Household goods and automotive supplies)	Financial statement analysis	Home Depot RONA	**Ratio Summary**
14	Reporting and Interpreting Investments in Other Corporations (online)	EMPIRE COMPANY LIMITED Empire Company Limited (Grocery retailer (Sobeys))	Investment strategies		

FINANCIAL
ACCOUNTING

FIFTH CANADIAN EDITION

Robert Libby

Cornell University

Patricia A. Libby

Ithaca University

Daniel Short

Texas Christian University

George Kanaan

Concordia University

Maureen Gowing

University of Windsor

Financial Accounting
Fifth Canadian Edition

The Internet addresses listed in the text were accurate at the time of publication.
The inclusion of a Web site does not indicate an endorsement by the authors or
McGraw-Hill Ryerson, and McGraw-Hill Ryerson does not guarantee the accuracy
of the information presented at these sites.

ISBN-13: 978-0-07-133946-9
ISBN-10: 0-07-133946-9

1 2 3 4 5 6 7 8 9 10 TCP 1 9 8 7 6 5 4

Printed and bound in Canada

Care has been taken to trace ownership of copyright material contained in this text;
however, the publisher will welcome any information that enables them to rectify any
reference or credit for subsequent editions.

Director of Product Management: *Rhondda McNabb*
Product Manager: *Keara Emmett*
Executive Marketing Manager: *Joy Armitage Taylor*
Product Developer: *Amy Rydzanicz*
Senior Product Team Associate: *Christine Lomas*
Supervising Editor: *Graeme Powell*
Photo/Permissions Researcher: *Steve Rouben,* Photo Affairs, Inc.
Copy Editor: *Julie van Tol*
Proofreader: *Julia Cochrane*
Production Coordinator: *Scott Morrison*
Manufacturing Production Coordinator: *Emily Hickey*
Cover Design: *Dave Murphy*
Cover Image: *Maciej Frolow/GettyImages (RM)*
Interior Design: *Dave Murphy*
Page Layout: *Laserwords Private Limited*
Printer: *Transcontinental Printing Group*

Library and Archives Canada Cataloguing in Publication

Financial accounting / Robert Libby, Patricia A. Libby, Daniel Short,

George Kanaan, Maureen Gowing.—Fifth Canadian edition.

Includes bibliographical references and index.

ISBN 978-0-07-133946-9

1. Accounting—Textbooks. 2. Corporations—Accounting—Textbooks.

3. Financial statements—Textbooks. I. Libby, Robert, author

HF5636.F54 2014   657   C2013-906032-4

Robert Libby

Robert Libby is the David A. Thomas Professor of Management at the Johnson Graduate School of Management at Cornell University, where he teaches the introductory financial accounting course. He has previously taught at the University of Illinois, Pennsylvania State University, University of Texas at Austin, University of Chicago, and University of Michigan. He received his B.S. from Pennsylvania State University and his M.A.S. and Ph.D. from the University of Illinois; he is also a CPA. Bob is a widely published author specializing in behavioural accounting.

Patricia A. Libby

Patricia Libby is Chair of the Department of Accounting and Associate Professor of Accounting at Ithaca College, where she teaches the undergraduate financial accounting course. She has previously taught graduate and undergraduate financial accounting at Eastern Michigan University and the University of Texas. Before entering academe, she was an auditor with Price Waterhouse (now PricewaterhouseCoopers) and a financial administrator at the University of Chicago. She received her B.S. from Pennsylvania State University, her M.B.A. from DePaul University, and her Ph.D. from the University of Michigan; she is also a CPA. Pat conducts research on using cases in the introductory course and other parts of the accounting curriculum.

Daniel G. Short

Daniel Short is Professor of Accounting and Dean of the M.J. Neeley School of Business at Texas Christian University in Fort Worth, Texas. Formerly, he was Dean at the Richard T. Farmer School of Business at Miami University (Ohio) and the College of Business at Kansas State University. Prior to that, he was Associate Dean at the University of Texas at Austin, where he taught the undergraduate and graduate financial accounting courses. He has also taught at the University of Michigan and the University of Chicago. Dan received his undergraduate degree from Boston University and his M.B.A. and Ph.D. from the University of Michigan. He has won numerous awards for his outstanding teaching abilities, and has published articles.

George Kanaan

George Kanaan is Associate Professor of Accountancy and Associate Dean at the John Molson School of Business at Concordia University, where he teaches the introductory financial accounting course. George previously taught undergraduate and graduate courses at other universities in Canada, China, and Lebanon. He received his B.A. from the Lebanese University, his M.A. from Southern Illinois University at Carbondale, and his Ph.D. from the University of Wisconsin–Madison. He has conducted research on disclosures related to pension accounting, deferred income taxes, and the effects of changing prices. George's research has been published in *The Journal of Accounting, Auditing and Finance,* and *Managerial Finance.*

Maureen Gowing

Maureen Gowing is Associate Professor of Accounting at the Odette School of Business at the University of Windsor. She has developed and taught Ph.D. research seminars, MBA, and undergraduate courses in both managerial and financial accounting. She acquired extensive experience in valuation working as a financial analyst in the oil and securities industries, and did forensic work at the Vancouver Stock Exchange. Maureen obtained her B.A. from Carleton University, her M.B.A. from the University of Toronto, and her Ph.D. from Queen's University. She is also a CMA. Maureen is a member of the Academic Advisory Committee of the Canadian Institute of Chartered Accountants (CICA) and a member of the editorial board of Contemporary Accounting Research. She has conducted research on the effects of personal values on ethical reasoning, and has published in academic journals such as the *Journal of Business Ethics* and *Business Ethics: A European Review.* She is also a co-author of a managerial accounting text.

Contents in Brief

Contents

CHAPTER **THREE**

Operating Decisions and the Statement of Earnings   104

CHAPTER **SIX**

Communicating and Interpreting Accounting Information   291

FOCUS COMPANY: THOMSON REUTERS CORPORATION—COMMUNICATING FINANCIAL INFORMATION AND CORPORATE STRATEGY

CHAPTER **SEVEN**

Reporting and Interpreting Sales Revenue, Receivables, and Cash   344

FOCUS COMPANY: GILDAN ACTIVEWEAR INC.—BUILDING BRANDS TO BUILD GROSS PROFIT: MANAGING PRODUCT DEVELOPMENT, PRODUCTION, AND WORKING CAPITAL

CHAPTER **EIGHT**

Reporting and Interpreting Cost of Sales and Inventory   409

FOCUS COMPANY: DANIER LEATHER INC.—DESIGNING AND MANUFACTURING HIGH-QUALITY FASHIONABLE LEATHER PRODUCTS

CHAPTER **NINE**

Reporting and Interpreting Property, Plant, and Equipment; Natural Resources; and Intangibles 465

FOCUS COMPANY: WESTJET AIRLINES—
MANAGING EARNINGS THROUGH CONTROL OF
PRODUCTIVE CAPACITY

CHAPTER **TEN**

Reporting and Interpreting Current Liabilities 534

CHAPTER **ELEVEN**

Reporting and Interpreting Non-current Liabilities 588

CHAPTER **FOURTEEN**

Reporting and Interpreting Investments in Other Corporations   (Online)

FOCUS COMPANY: EMPIRE COMPANY LIMITED—
INVESTMENT STRATEGIES AND DIVERSIFICATION

Since it was first published, *Financial Accounting* has grown to be the market-leading financial accounting textbook on which both students and instructors rely. The authors of the Fifth Canadian Edition continue to make financial accounting more relevant and interesting to students. How? By helping the instructor and student become partners in learning, using a remarkable learning approach that keeps students engaged and involved in the material from the first day of class.

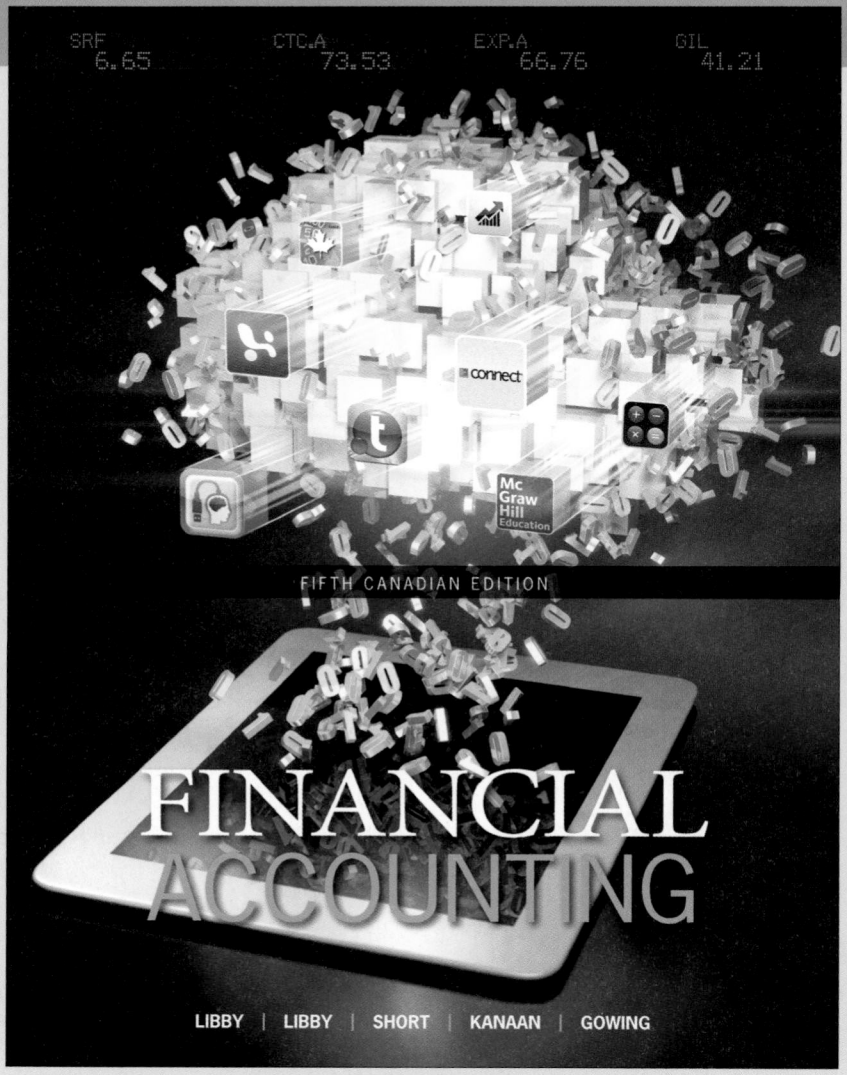

FINANCIAL ACCOUNTING

FIFTH CANADIAN EDITION

LIBBY | LIBBY | SHORT | KANAAN | GOWING

Financial Accounting's distinctive focus-company approach motivates students by involving them in the business decisions of a real company and demonstrating how financial accounting makes a difference in the success of a firm. That, combined with pedagogical features and technology tools that serve a variety of learning styles, makes *Financial Accounting* the textbook that both students and instructors agree is the best of its kind on the market today.

For Both Students and Instructors

Financial Accounting maintains its leadership by focusing on

CURRENCY. *Financial Accounting* keeps your students' learning up to date, preparing them for the courses and jobs they will have in the future. International Financial Reporting Standards (IFRS) are completely integrated within each chapter (or throughout the text), and an Accounting Standards for Private Enterprises box concludes each chapter. In addition, the annual reports, financial data, and articles used in both the instruction and the problem material continue to be updated.

RELEVANCE—THE PIONEERING FOCUS-COMPANY

APPROACH. The authors first introduced their focus-company approach as the best method for helping students understand financial statements and real-world implications of financial accounting for future managers. This approach shows how relevant accounting is and motivates students by explaining accounting in a real-world context. Throughout each chapter, the material focuses on a familiar company, its decisions, and its financial statements. This provides the perfect setting for discussing the importance of accounting and how businesses use accounting information. Furthering the real-world applicability, the end-of-chapter cases tie directly to the financial statements of the Canadian Tire Corporation, conveniently located in Appendix A, and to the annual report of RONA Inc., available online. These reports give students valuable practice reading and interpreting real financial data. In addition, real-world excerpts expand on topics, with insight into how real firms use financial accounting to their competitive advantage.

CLARITY. Do students complain that their textbook is hard to read? They don't if they're reading *Financial Accounting*. It is the proven choice for presenting financial accounting with a clear, relevant approach that keeps students engaged throughout the course. To continue to meet the changing needs of financial accounting instructors and students, the organization of the material has been refined to ensure maximum readability for students and flexibility for instructors.

TECHNOLOGY—POWERFUL TOOLS FOR
TEACHING AND STUDY. Today's students have diverse learning

styles and conflicting time commitments, so they need technology tools that will help them study more efficiently and effectively. Every new copy of the text includes access to *Connect*, a web-based assignment and assessment platform that gives students the opportunity to better connect with their coursework. *Connect* also includes a fully integrated eBook, access to LearnSmart, and other study tools that will help them maximize their study time and make their learning experience more enjoyable. The powerful course management tool on *Connect* also offers a wide range of exclusive features that help instructors spend less time managing and more time teaching.

Inside the Textbook

Financial Accounting offers a host of pedagogical tools that complement the way you like to teach and the ways your students like to learn. Some offer information and tips that help you present a complex subject, while others highlight issues relevant to what your students read online and in the papers, or see on TV. Either way, *Financial Accounting*'s pedagogical support will make a real difference in your course and in your students' learning.

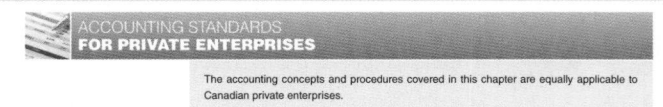

ACCOUNTING STANDARDS FOR PRIVATE ENTERPRISES

Not all companies are public, and not all students will end up working in one. Because of this, and because private enterprises are not required to use IFRS, this box was developed. **Accounting Standards for Private Enterprises** addresses the differences between the two types of reporting, such as why a statement of changes in equity isn't necessary or what details aren't reported in financial statements and related notes.

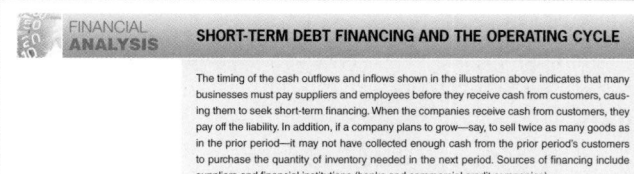

INTERNATIONAL PERSPECTIVE

The **International Perspective** sections make students aware of differences in accounting methods used in various countries. Financial statements and real-world excerpts related to international companies are included in the end-of-chapter material as well.

FINANCIAL ANALYSIS

These features tie important chapter concepts to real-world decision-making examples. They also highlight alternative viewpoints, and add to the critical thinking and decision-making focus of the text.

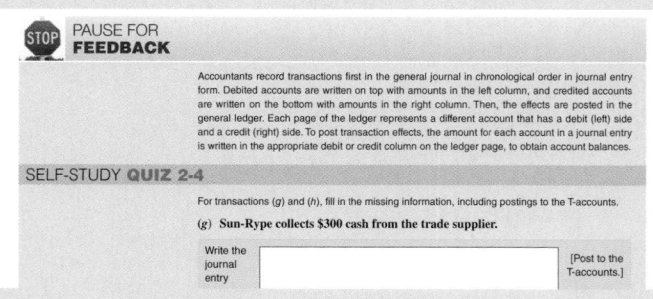

PAUSE FOR FEEDBACK AND SELF-STUDY QUIZ

Research shows that students learn best when they are actively engaged in the learning process. This active-learning feature engages the student, provides interactivity, and promotes efficient learning. These quizzes ask students to pause at strategic points throughout each chapter to ensure they understand key points before moving ahead.

A Complete Learning System

FOCUS ON CASH FLOWS

The early and consistent coverage of cash flows encourages students to think more critically about the decisions they will face as managers, and the impact those decisions will have on the company's cash flow. Each of Chapters 2 through 12 includes a discussion and analysis of changes in the cash flow of the focus company, and an exploration of the decisions that caused those changes.

FOCUS ON CASH FLOWS

CASH FLOW FROM OPERATIONS, NET EARNINGS, AND THE QUALITY OF EARNINGS

As presented in the previous chapters, the statement of cash flows explains the difference between the ending and beginning balances in the cash account during the accounting period. Put simply, the statement of cash flows is a categorized list of all transactions of the period that affected the cash account. The three categories are operating, investing, and financing activities. Since the adjustments made in this chapter did not affect cash, the components of the statement of cash flows presented in Chapters 2 and 3 have not changed.

Many standard financial analysis texts warn analysts to look for unusual deferrals and accruals when they attempt to predict future periods' earnings. They often suggest that wide disparities between net earnings and cash flow from operations are a useful warning sign. For example, Subramanyan suggests the following:

Accounting accruals determining net income rely on estimates, deferrals, allocations, and valuations. These considerations sometimes allow more subjectivity than do the factors determining cash flows. For this reason we often relate cash flows from operations to net income in assessing its quality. *Some users consider earnings of higher quality when the ratio of cash flows from operations divided by net income is greater.* This derives from a concern with revenue recognition or expense accrual criteria yield-

KEY RATIO ANALYSIS

Students will be better prepared to use financial information if they understand how to evaluate elements of financial performance while learning how to measure and report them. For this reason, we include relevant key ratios in the **Key Ratio Analysis** sections. Each box presents a ratio analysis for the chapter's focus company as well as for comparative companies. Cautions are also provided to help students understand the limitations of certain ratios.

KEY RATIO ANALYSIS

THE CURRENT RATIO

Users of financial information compute a number of ratios when analyzing a company's past performance and financial condition as input in predicting its future potential. The change in ratios over time and how they compare to the ratios of the company's competitors or industry averages provide valuable information about a company's strategies for its operating, investing, and financing activities.

We introduce here the first of many ratios that will be presented throughout the rest of this textbook, with a final summary of ratio analysis in Chapter 13. In Chapters 2, 3, and 4, we present four ratios that provide information about management's effectiveness at managing short-term debt (current ratio), controlling revenues and expenses (net profit margin), and utilizing assets (total asset turnover ratio and return on assets), all for the purpose of enhancing returns to shareholders. The remaining chapters discuss other ratios that provide valuable information to assess a company's strategies, strengths, and areas of concern.

As we discussed earlier in the chapter, companies raise large amounts of money to acquire additional assets by issuing shares to investors and borrowing funds from creditors. These additional

A QUESTION OF ACCOUNTABILITY

The more students are exposed to ethical situations, the more likely they will be to consider the effects their choices will have on others. These boxes appear throughout the text, conveying to students the importance and consequences of acting responsibly in business practice.

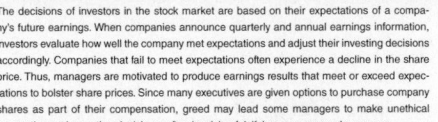

MANAGEMENT'S INCENTIVES TO VIOLATE ACCOUNTING RULES

A QUESTION OF ACCOUNTABILITY

The decisions of investors in the stock market are based on their expectations of a company's future earnings. When companies announce quarterly and annual earnings information, investors evaluate how well the company met expectations and adjust their investing decisions accordingly. Companies that fail to meet expectations often experience a decline in the share price. Thus, managers are motivated to produce earnings results that meet or exceed expectations to bolster share prices. Since many executives are given options to purchase company shares as part of their compensation, greed may lead some managers to make unethical accounting and reporting decisions, often involving falsifying revenues and expenses.

Fraud is a criminal offense for which managers may be sentenced to jail. Samples of fraud cases, a few involving faulty revenue and expense accounting, are shown below. Just imagine what it must have been like to be 65-year-old Bernie Ebbers or 21-year-old Barry Minkow, both sentenced to 25 years in prison for accounting fraud.

A Complete Learning System

ORGANIZATION OF THE CHAPTER

This framework, at the beginning of each chapter, provides a powerful visual schematic of the content and of what questions will be answered.

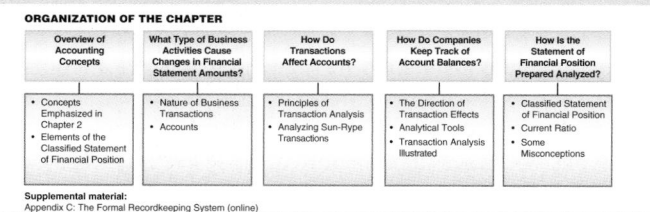

ALL JOURNAL ENTRIES TIED TO THE ACCOUNTING EQUATION

In early chapters, all journal entries marked with (A), (L), (SE), (R), (E), or (X)—if a contra account—and with + and – signs assist students in transaction analysis. All journal entries end with a summary of the effects of each transaction on the fundamental accounting equation.

T-accounts (when appropriate) in the margin show the effect a transaction has on cash and net earnings.

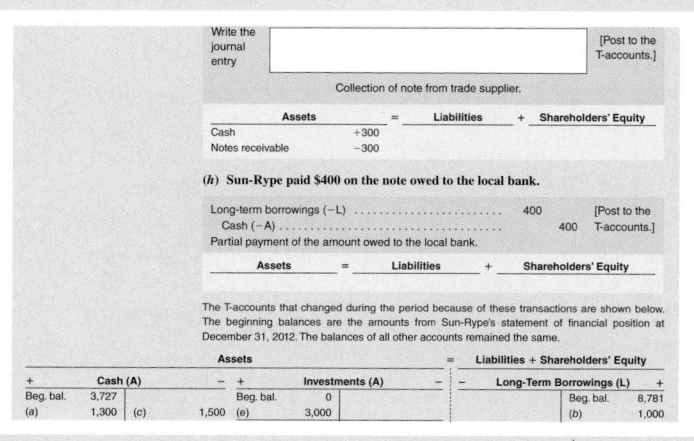

REAL WORLD EXCERPT

These excerpts appear throughout the text and include annual report information from focus companies and others, news articles, analysts' reports, and press releases.

ICONS

Easily identifiable margin icons indicate what types of skills are being addressed in the end-of-chapter material.

 International coverage

 An ethical dilemma

 Cash flow analysis

 Ratio analysis

 Written work, for developing communication skills
eXcel Exercises to be solved using the Excel template provided

 Problems and cases requiring analysis, for developing the ability to use financial information to guide business decisions.

Flexible End-of-Chapter Content and Organization

Each chapter is followed by an extensive selection of end-of-chapter material that examines and integrates multiple concepts presented in the chapter. To maintain the real-world emphasis, they are often based on real Canadian, U.S., and international companies, and require analysis, conceptual thought, calculation, and written communication. Assignments suitable for written individual or group projects and oral presentations are also included.

Chapter Take-Aways   Bulleted end-of-chapter summaries complement the learning objectives outlined at the beginning of the chapter.

Key Ratios   Summary of the key ratios presented in the chapter.

Finding Financial Information   Highlights where to find the financial data discussed in the chapter in an easy-to-review graphic.

Questions   Allow students and faculty to ensure that chapter concepts have been grasped.

Exercises   Assignments that cover multiple learning objectives from the chapter.

Problems   Detailed assignments that integrate various topics discussed in the chapter. Cross-references to the Alternate Problems appear in blue.

Alternate Problems   Similar in level and content to the end-of-chapter problems, and include cross-references to the Problems in blue.

Cases and Projects   This section includes Finding and Interpreting Financial Information, Financial Reporting and Analysis Cases, Critical Thinking Cases, and Financial Reporting and Analysis Team Project.

Annual Reports   The annual reports of two dynamic companies, the Canadian Tire Corporation and RONA Inc., are referenced in the text's problem material. Excerpts from the annual report for the Canadian Tire Corporation appear in Appendix A in the text, and RONA's annual report is available online.

What's New in the Fifth Canadian Edition?

Based on market feedback, the primary goals of the fifth edition are to

- Simplify explanations of complex topics.
- Provide a better match of end-of-chapter material to instructor and student needs.
- Accurately reflect the exciting changes taking place in the accounting environment.
- Provide real-world excerpts from financial statements of Canadian and international companies prepared in conformity with International Financial Reporting Standards.
- Provide instructors with more flexibility in key topical coverage.

As a result, the authors have made the detailed revisions noted in the following sections:

Chapter One

- Changed the focus company to Sun-Rype Products Ltd.
- Simplified the financial statements presented in this chapter.
- Updated the section related to the professional accounting organizations to reflect the current efforts to unify the accounting profession in Canada.
- Revised the section "Accounting Standards for Private Enterprises" for improved clarity in all chapters.
- Substantially revised the end-of-chapter exercises, problems, and cases, and added new exercises, problems, and annual report cases.

Chapter Two

- Changed the focus company to Sun-Rype Products Ltd.
- Simplified the statement of financial position presented in the chapter.
- Expanded on the qualitative characteristics of accounting information.
- Added a new Financial Analysis feature.
- Changed the Key Ratio feature to current ratio (moved debt-to-equity ratio to Chapter 12).
- Substantially revised the end-of-chapter exercises, problems, and cases, and added new exercises, problems, and annual report cases.

Chapter Three

- Changed the focus company to Sun-Rype Products Ltd.
- Simplified the statement of earnings presented in the chapter.
- Revised the discussion related to non-operating items.
- Updated and revised the sample of revenue recognition policies in Exhibit 3.2.
- Repositioned and expanded the feature "A Question of Accountability."
- Revised the Transaction Analysis Rules.
- Revised the Key Ratio Analysis feature.
- Substantially revised the end-of-chapter exercises, problems, and cases, and added new exercises, problems, and annual report cases.

Chapter Four

- Changed the focus company to Sun-Rype Products Ltd.
- Revised the steps in the adjustment process to be systematic and for improved clarity.
- Illustrated new three-step analysis for adjusting entries.
- Relocated the discussion of accounting for the use of property and equipment.
- Revised the Focus on Cash Flows feature.
- Deleted the Supplemental Cash Flow information.

- Substantially revised the end-of-chapter exercises, problems, and cases, and added new exercises, problems, and annual report cases.
- Added two new comprehensive cases.

Chapter Five

- Changed the focus company to Danier Leather Inc.
- Added a table comparing the direct and indirect methods of preparing cash flow from operations.
- Added two columns for revenue and expenses in Exhibit 5.4.
- Added an illustration of cash flow patterns.
- Revised the discussion "Additional Cash Flow Disclosure."
- Revised Appendix 5C (online).
- Substantially revised the end-of-chapter exercises, problems, and cases, and added new exercises, problems, and annual report cases.

Chapter Six

- Updated focus and comparison companies.
- Expanded on the coverage of the qualitative characteristics of accounting information.
- Added a general classification of accounts in the statement of financial position.
- Shortened the section on the statement of comprehensive income.
- Updated Demonstration Case.
- Substantially revised the end-of-chapter exercises, problems, and cases, and added new exercises, problems, and annual report cases.

Chapter Seven

- Updated focus and comparison companies.
- Expanded on the discussion of accounting for bad debts.
- Eliminated the discussion of the percentage of credit sales method.
- Repositioned the Key Ratio Analysis feature.

- Reorganized the steps needed to prepare bank reconciliation.
- Deleted the instalment method from Appendix 7A.
- Substantially revised the end-of-chapter exercises, problems, and cases, and added new exercises, problems, and annual report cases.

Chapter Eight

- Changed the focus company to Danier Leather Inc.
- Added Exhibit 8.5 to highlight the flow of units and costs over time.
- Repositioned various exhibits so they are closely aligned with the related narrative.
- Substantially revised the end-of-chapter exercises, problems, and cases, and added new exercises, problems, and annual report cases.

Chapter Nine

- Updated focus and comparison companies.
- Added brief discussion of the componentization of property, plant, and equipment.
- Explained that IFRS permits companies to use either the cost model or the revaluation model to report the value of long-lived assets.
- Revised the Key Ratio Analysis feature.
- Substantially revised the end-of-chapter exercises, problems, and cases, and added new exercises, problems, and annual report cases.

Chapter Ten

- Changed the focus company to Bauer Performance Sports Ltd.
- Replaced the current ratio with the quick ratio.
- Added a new section on working capital management.
- Added Appendix 10B on present value concepts, which is a revised version of Appendix 11A from the fourth Canadian edition.
- Substantially revised the end-of-chapter exercises, problems, and cases, and added new exercises, problems, and annual report cases.

Chapter Eleven

- Changed the focus company to Bell Canada Enterprises Inc.
- Added discussion of notes payable.
- Revised the discussion related to leases and employee retirement benefits.
- Added a Financial Analysis box on zero-coupon bonds.
- Changed the Key Ratio feature to debt-to-equity ratio (moved financial leverage ratio to Chapter 13).
- Substantially revised the end-of-chapter exercises, problems, and cases, and added new exercises, problems, and annual report cases.

Chapter Twelve

- Updated focus and comparison companies.
- Substantially revised the end-of-chapter exercises, problems, and cases, and added new exercises, problems, and annual report cases.

Chapter Thirteen

- Changed the focus company to Canadian Tire Corporation.
- Added percentage component analysis to the statement of financial position.
- Substantially revised the end-of-chapter exercises, problems, and cases, and added new exercises, problems, and annual report cases.

Chapter Fourteen (Online)

- Changed the focus company to Empire Company Limited.
- Incorporated updates of the relevant IAS and IFRS.
- Simplified accounting for passive investments by directly adjusting the investments account to fair value.
- New Pause for Feedback feature added to the self-study quizzes.
- New content for the A Question of Accountability feature.
- New Key Ratio feature on the economic return to investing.
- Substantially revised the end-of-chapter exercises, problems, and cases, and added new exercises, problems, and annual report cases.

Teaching and Learning with Technology

McGraw-Hill Connect™ is a web-based assignment and assessment platform that gives students the means to better connect with their coursework, with their instructors, and with the important concepts that they will need to know for success now and in the future.

With Connect, instructors can deliver assignments, quizzes, and tests online. Nearly all the questions from the text are presented in an auto-gradeable format and tied to the text's learning objectives. Instructors can edit existing questions and author entirely new problems. Track individual student performance—by question, assignment, or in relation to the entire class—with detailed grade reports. Integrate grade reports easily with Learning Management Systems (LMS) such as WebCT and Blackboard.

By choosing Connect, instructors are providing their students with a powerful tool for improving academic performance and truly mastering course material. Connect allows students to practise important skills at their own pace and on their own schedule. Importantly, students' assessment results and instructors' feedback are all saved online—so students can continually review their progress and plot their course to success. Connect also provides 24/7 online access to an eBook—an online edition of the text—to aid them in successfully completing their work, wherever and whenever they choose.

KEY FEATURES

SIMPLE ASSIGNMENT MANAGEMENT

With Connect, creating assignments is easier than ever, so you can spend more time teaching and less time managing.
- Create and deliver assignments easily with selectable end-of-chapter questions and testbank material to assign online.
- Streamline lesson planning, student progress reporting, and assignment grading to make classroom management more efficient than ever.
- Go paperless with the eBook and online submission and grading of student assignments.

SMART GRADING

When it comes to studying, time is precious. Connect helps students learn more efficiently by providing feedback and practice material when they need it, where they need it.
- Automatically score assignments, giving students immediate feedback on their work and side-by-side comparisons with correct answers.
- Access and review each response; manually change grades or leave comments for students to review.
- Reinforce classroom concepts with practice tests and instant quizzes.

INSTRUCTOR LIBRARY

The Connect Instructor Library is your course creation hub. It provides all the critical resources you'll need to build your course, just how you want to teach it.
- Assign eBook readings and draw from a rich collection of textbook-specific assignments.
- Access instructor resources, including ready-made PowerPoint presentations and media to use in your lectures.
- View assignments and resources created for past sections.
- Post your own resources for students to use.

eBOOK

Connect reinvents the textbook learning experience for the modern student. Every Connect subject area is seamlessly integrated with Connect eBooks, which are designed to keep students focused on the concepts key to their success.
- Provide students with a Connect eBook, allowing for anytime, anywhere access to the textbook.
- Merge media, animation, and assessments with the text's narrative to engage students and improve learning and retention.
- Pinpoint and connect key concepts in a snap using the powerful eBook search engine.
- Manage notes, highlights, and bookmarks in one place for simple, comprehensive review.

Services and Support

LEARNSMART

No two students are alike. Why should their learning paths be? LearnSmart uses revolutionary adaptive technology to build a learning experience unique to each student's individual needs. It starts by identifying the topics a student knows and does not know. As the student progresses, LearnSmart adapts and adjusts the content based on his or her individual strengths, weaknesses, and confidence, ensuring that every minute spent studying with LearnSmart is the most efficient and productive study time possible.

SMARTBOOK

As the first and only adaptive reading experience, SmartBook is changing the way students read and learn. SmartBook creates a personalized reading experience by highlighting the most important concepts a student needs to learn at that moment in time. As a student engages with SmartBook, the reading experience continuously adapts by highlighting content based on what each student knows and doesn't know. This ensures that he or she is focused on the content needed to close specific knowledge gaps, while it simultaneously promotes long-term learning.

Lyryx Assessment

Available as an option to package with the Libby text at a small additional cost, Lyryx Assessment Financial Accounting contains algorithmic problems tied to the Libby text, unlimited opportunity for students to practise, and automatic grading with extensive feedback for both students and instructors.

INSTRUCTOR SUPPORT

The following resources are available online to support instructors:

- **Instructor's Manual.** Includes a chapter outline, detailed lecture notes, suggested activities, and a reading list for each chapter.
- **Solutions Manual.** Provides solutions for end-of-chapter questions, exercises, problems, and cases.
- **PowerPoint® Presentations.** These slides for use in your classroom are completely customized for the fifth Canadian edition of *Financial Accounting*.
- **Computerized Test Bank.** Includes more than 1,800 True/False, Multiple Choice, and Essay questions.
- **Instructor's Excel® Template Solutions.** These Excel template solutions accompany the templates available to students online.

SUPERIOR LEARNING SOLUTIONS AND SUPPORT

The McGraw-Hill Ryerson team is ready to help you assess and integrate any of our products, technology, and services into your course for optimal teaching and learning performance. Whether it's helping your students improve their grades, or putting your entire course online, the McGraw-Hill Ryerson team is here to help you do it. Contact your Learning Solutions Consultant today to learn how to maximize all of McGraw-Hill Ryerson's resources!

For more information on the latest technology and Learning Solutions offered by McGraw-Hill Ryerson and its partners, please visit us online: **www.mcgrawhill.ca/he/solutions**.

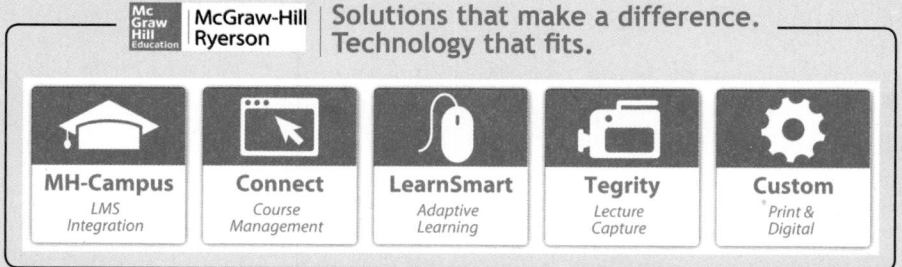

Acknowledgements

Writing and adapting a successful textbook requires a team effort and we have enjoyed working with excellent teammates. Throughout the process of writing this textbook, many people stepped forward with tremendous efforts that enabled us to accomplish our goals. First and foremost, we are deeply indebted to Robert Libby, Patricia Libby, and Daniel Short, authors of the U.S. edition, for developing the pedagogical approach used in this text. Their approach helped us tremendously in shaping this fifth Canadian edition.

We would like to recognize the sincere and devoted efforts of the many people who added their input to the process of developing this book. We received invaluable advice and suggestions during the manuscript development and revision process. For this assistance, we thank the following colleagues:

FIFTH EDITION REVIEWERS

Robert Collier, *University of Ottawa*
Han Donker, *University of Northern British Columbia*
Allan Forester, *Wilfrid Laurier University*
Larry Goldsman, *McGill University*
Donna Gunn, *St. Francis Xavier University*
Duane Kennedy, *University of Waterloo*
Shiraz S. Kurji, *Mount Royal University*
Camillo Lento, *Lakehead University*
Amy MacFarlane, *University of Prince Edward Island*
Marie Madill-Payne, *George Brown College*
Debbie Musil, *Kwantlen Polytechnic University*
Scott Sinclair, *University of British Columbia*
Vicki Sweeney, *University of Western Ontario*
Gilles Valade, *Thompson Rivers University*
Peggy Wallace, *Trent University*

We also received invaluable input and support through the years from present and former colleagues and students. We are indebted to the following individuals who helped adapt, critique, and shape the ancillary package for the Canadian market: Susan Cohlmeyer, Memorial University of Newfoundland; Robert Ducharme, University of Waterloo; Ian Feltmate, Acadia University; Allan Foerster, Wilfrid Laurier University; Richard Michalski, McMaster University.

The extraordinary efforts of a talented group of individuals at McGraw-Hill Ryerson made all of this come together. We especially thank Rhondda McNabb for her involvement in the planning stage of this project; Keara Emmett for her guidance throughout this project; Suzanne Simpson Millar, Christopher Cullen, and Amy Rydzanicz for tirelessly following the development process through various stages of the final product; Jessica Barnoski who managed the final production of this book, and all the marketing and sales people who helped bring this book to both instructors and students. We also thank all those who worked behind the scenes to ensure the successful completion of this book. Special thanks to Julie van Tol who edited our work and Julia Cochrane for proofreading the entire manuscript.

We thank the Canadian Tire Corporation and RONA Inc. for permitting us to use their financial statements to provide students with real-world examples of financial statements and accompanying notes. We are also grateful to all the focus companies that allowed us to use excerpts from their financial statements and notes to illustrate the main ideas in each chapter.

Special thanks go to our families for their support, patience, and understanding while we worked on completing this fifth Canadian edition of the book. We dedicate the book to them.

George Kanaan
Maureen Gowing

To Our Student Readers

This book is aimed at two groups of readers:

1. *Future managers,* who will need to interpret and use financial statement information in business decisions.

2. *Future accountants,* who will prepare financial statements for those managers.

Future managers need a firm basis for using financial statement information in their careers in marketing, finance, banking, manufacturing, human resources, sales, information systems, or other areas of management. Future accountants need a solid foundation for further professional study.

Both managers and accountants must understand how to *use financial statements in making real business decisions* to perform their duties successfully. The best way to learn this is to study accounting in real business contexts. This is the key idea behind our focus-company approach, which we introduce in the first chapter. Each chapter's material is integrated with a focus company, its decisions, and its financial statements. The focus companies are drawn from different industries, providing you with a broad range of experience in realistic business and financial accounting practices. In each chapter, you *will actually work with these real companies' statements* and with those of additional contrast companies.

When you complete this course, you will be able to read and understand financial statements of real companies. We help you achieve this goal by

1. Selecting learning objectives and content based on the way that seasoned managers use financial statements in modern businesses. We emphasize the topics that count.

2. Recognizing that students using this book have no previous exposure to accounting and financial statements and often little exposure to the business world. We take you through the financial statements three times, at increasing levels of detail (in Chapter 1, Chapters 2 through 5, and Chapters 6 through 13). This is the secret to our "building-block approach."

3. Helping you "learn how to learn" by teaching efficient and effective approaches for learning the material. Keep these learning hints in mind throughout.

4. Providing regular feedback in Self-Study Quizzes, which occur throughout each chapter. Complete the quizzes before you move on. Check your answers against the solutions at the end of the chapter. If you are still unclear about any of the answers, refer back to the chapter material before moving on.

5. Repeating the key terms and their definitions in the margins. A handy index is provided on Connect.

6. Introducing the Key Financial Ratios used to assess different elements of financial performance at the same time you are learning how to measure and report those elements. These will show you what kinds of accounting information managers use and how they interpret it.

7. At the end of each chapter, test what you have learned by working through the Demonstration Cases. *Working problems is one of the keys to learning accounting.*

Good luck in your financial accounting course.

George Kanaan
Maureen Gowing

Financial Statements and Business Decisions

After studying this chapter, you should be able to do the following:

LEARNING OBJECTIVES

LO1 Recognize the information conveyed in each of the four basic financial statements and how it is used by different decision makers (investors, creditors, and managers).

LO2 Identify the role of International Financial Reporting Standards (IFRS) in determining the content of financial statements.

LO3 Identify the roles of managers and auditors in the accounting communication process.

LO4 Appreciate the importance of ethics, reputation, and legal liability in accounting.

FOCUS COMPANY: **Sun-Rype Products Ltd.**

VALUING AN INVESTMENT USING FINANCIAL STATEMENT INFORMATION

Sun-Rype Products Ltd.(www.sunrype.com), based in Kelowna, British Columbia, was founded in 1946 by the British Columbia Fruit Growers' Association to produce pure apple juice made from apples grown in the Okanagan Valley. This product, called SunRype, was followed by other related products, such as apple sauce, dehydrated apples, and pie filling. In 1959, the company's original name, BC Fruit Processors Ltd., was changed to Sun-Rype Products Ltd. in recognition of the popularity of the SunRype brand name.

Sun-Rype Products Ltd. (Sun-Rype) has grown over the years through innovation and the acquisition of another company. It has expanded the list of products it manufactures and sells to include a wide variety of fruit juices and cocktails, as well as fruit snacks such as Fruit to Go, FruitSource, Mini Bites, and FunBites.

Sun-Rype became a public company in 1996. Its shares currently trade on the Toronto Stock Exchange (TSX). Anyone who has invested in Sun-Rype will have taken into consideration the value of the company's economic resources, its debts to others, its ability to sell goods for more than the cost of producing them, and its ability to generate the cash necessary to pay its current bills. Much of this assessment was based on financial information that Sun-Rype provided to investors in the form of financial statements.

UNDERSTANDING THE BUSINESS

THE PLAYERS

The success story of Sun-Rype began in 1946 when the British Columbia Fruit Growers' Association invested a major portion of its funds into the business, thereby becoming the company's founder and sole owner. As is common in new businesses, the founder also functioned as manager of the business (it was *owner-manager*).

When the association started the company, Sun-Rype needed additional money to build manufacturing facilities and to develop the business. It borrowed money from a local bank and other lenders, or *creditors*, and used these funds to expand the business. Sun-Rype's leadership in producing pure apple juice and subsequent expansion into other fruit juices and fruit snacks helped the company become the leading manufacturer and marketer of fruit-based food and beverage products in western Canada.

Individuals who buy small percentages of large corporations are called *investors*. They hope to gain from their investment in two ways: they expect to receive a portion of what the company earns in the form of cash payments called *dividends*, and they hope to eventually sell their share of the company at a higher price than they paid.

Creditors lend money to a company for a specific length of time. They gain by charging interest on the money they lend. The exchanges of money between Sun-Rype and its lenders and owners are called *financing activities*. Sun-Rype's purchases or sales of property, such as roasting equipment used in producing coffee products, are called *investing activities*.

THE BUSINESS OPERATIONS

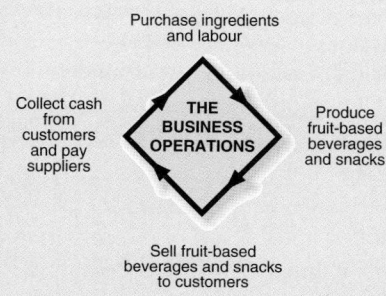

To understand any company's financial statements, you must first understand its operations. As noted, Sun-Rype produces and markets fruit juices and nutritious snacks for personal consumption. Sun-Rype's products are manufactured from natural ingredients. To produce the fruit juices and nutritious snacks for sale, Sun-Rype needs raw materials such as fresh fruits and grains. Sun-Rype purchases these ingredients and accessories from other companies, referred to as *suppliers*.

Sun-Rype distributes its many products through its own distribution network throughout Canada and selected regions of the United States. It sells its products to retail stores, or *customers*, through wholesale distributors.

THE ACCOUNTING SYSTEM

LO¹

Recognize the information conveyed in each of the four basic financial statements and how it is used by different decision makers (investors, creditors, and managers).

ACCOUNTING is a system that collects and processes (analyzes, measures, and records) financial information about an organization and reports that information to decision makers.

Accounting is a system that collects and processes (analyzes, measures, and records) financial information about an organization and reports that information to decision makers. Like all businesses, Sun-Rype has an accounting system that collects and processes its financial information and reports it to decision makers. Sun-Rype's managers (often called *internal decision makers*) and parties outside the firm (often called *external decision makers*), such as the investors in Sun-Rype's shares and the bank's loan officer, use reports produced by this system. Exhibit 1.1 outlines the two parts of the accounting system. Internal managers typically require continuous detailed information because they must plan and manage the day-to-day operations of the organization. Developing accounting information for internal decision makers is called *managerial* or *management accounting* and is the subject of a separate accounting course. The focus of this text is accounting for external decision makers, called *financial accounting*, and the four basic financial statements and related disclosures that are the output of that system.

We begin this process with a brief but comprehensive overview of the four basic financial statements and the people and organizations involved in their preparation and use. This overview provides you with a context in which you can learn the more detailed material that is presented in the following chapters. In particular, we focus on how two primary users of the statements, investors (owners) and creditors (lenders), relied on each of Sun-Rype's four basic financial statements in their decisions to invest in or lend money to Sun-Rype. Later in the chapter, we discuss a broader range of

Exhibit **1.1**
The Accounting System and
Decision Makers

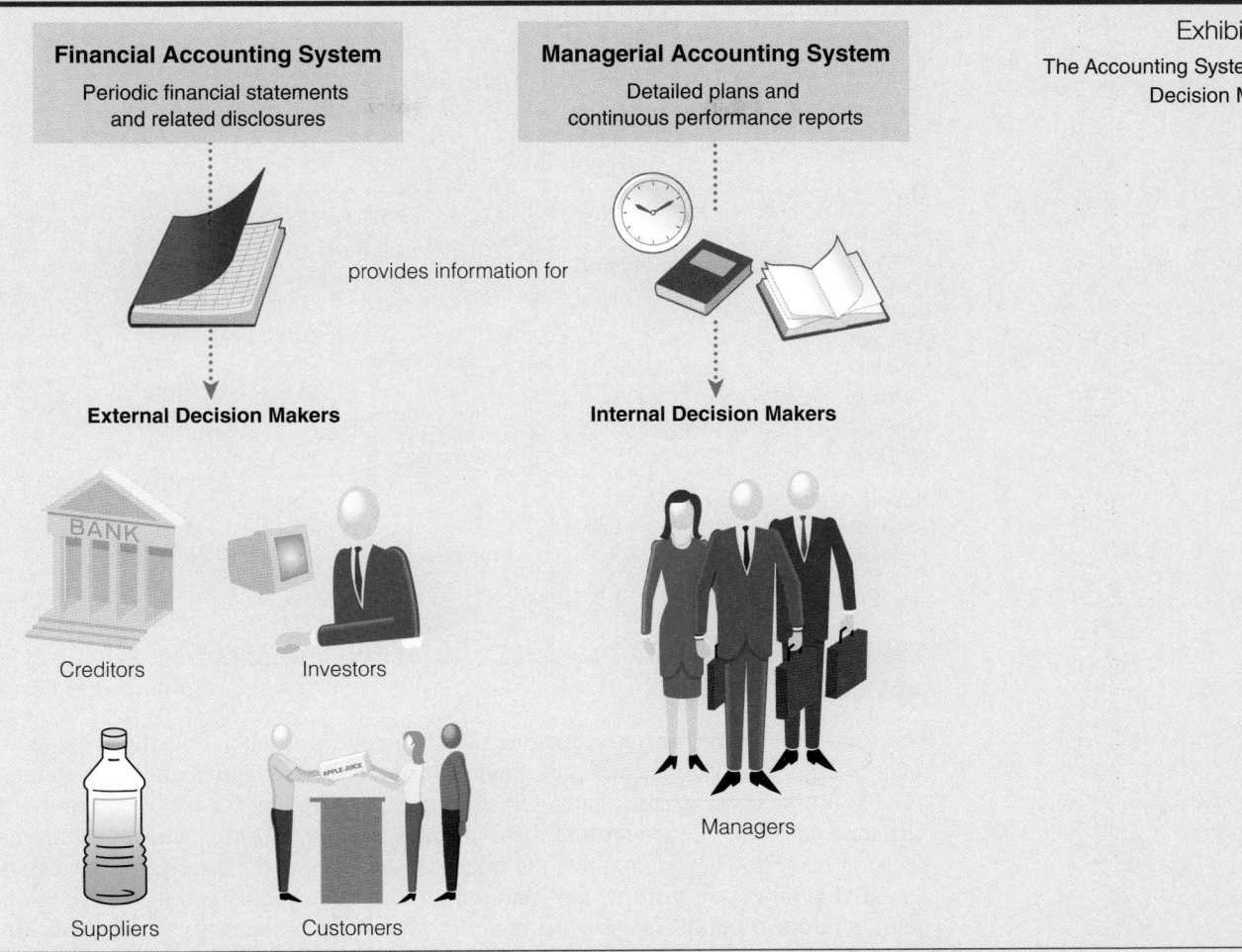

uses of financial statement data in marketing, management, human resources, and other business contexts.

To understand the way investors and creditors use Sun-Rype's financial statements in their decisions, we must first understand what specific information is presented in the four basic financial statements for a company such as Sun-Rype. *Instead of trying to memorize the definitions of every term used in this chapter, focus your attention on learning the general structure and content of the statements.* Specifically, you should focus on these questions:

1. What categories of items (often called *elements*) are reported on each of the four statements? (What type of information does a statement convey, and where can you find it?)

2. How are the elements within a statement related? These *relationships* are usually described by an equation that tells you how the elements fit together.

3. Why is each element important to managers', owners', or creditors' decisions? (How important is the information to decision makers?)

The pause for feedback/self-study quizzes that occur throughout the chapter will test your ability to answer these questions. Remember that since this chapter is an overview, each concept discussed in this chapter will be discussed again in Chapters 2 through 5.

ORGANIZATION OF THE CHAPTER

The Four Basic Financial Statements: An Overview	Responsibilities for the Accounting Communication Process
• The Statement of Financial Position • The Statement of Comprehensive Income • The Statement of Changes in Equity • The Statement of Cash Flows • Relationships among the Four Financial Statements • Notes to Financial Statements	• International Financial Reporting Standards (IFRS) • Management Responsibility and the Demand for Auditing • Ethics, Reputation, and Legal Liability

Supplemental material:
Appendix 1A: Types of Business Entities
Appendix 1B: Employment in the Accounting Profession Today

THE FOUR BASIC FINANCIAL STATEMENTS: AN OVERVIEW

The four basic financial statements are the statement of financial position, the statement of comprehensive income, the statement of changes in equity, and the statement of cash flows. These are the statements normally prepared by for-profit corporations. The statements are intended primarily to inform investors, creditors, and other external decision makers. They summarize the financial activities of the business. They can be prepared at any point in time and can apply to any time span (such as one year, one quarter, or one month). Like most companies, Sun-Rype prepares financial statements for investors and creditors at the end of each quarter (known as *quarterly reports*) and at the end of the year (known as *annual reports*).

The Statement of Financial Position[1]

> A **STATEMENT OF FINANCIAL POSITION (BALANCE SHEET)** reports the financial position (assets, liabilities, and shareholders' equity) of an accounting entity at a point in time.

The purpose of the **statement of financial position (balance sheet)** is to report the financial position (amount of assets, liabilities, and shareholders' equity) of an accounting entity at a particular point in time. We can learn a lot about what the statement of financial position reports just by reading the statement from the top. The statement of financial position of Sun-Rype is shown in Exhibit 1.2.

Structure   The *heading* of the statement of financial position identifies four significant items related to the statement:

1. *name of the entity*—Sun-Rype Products Ltd.
2. *title of the statement*—Statement of Financial Position
3. *specific date of the statement*—At December 31, 2012
4. *unit of measure*—(in thousands of Canadian dollars)

> An **ACCOUNTING ENTITY** is the organization for which financial data are to be collected.

The organization for which financial data are to be collected and reported is called an **accounting entity**. The accounting entity must be precisely defined and is often called the business or the corporation. On the statement of financial position, the accounting entity itself, not the business owners, is viewed as owning its debts and the resources it uses.

The heading of the statement indicates the time dimension of the report. The statement of financial position is like a financial snapshot clearly stating the entity's financial position *at a specific point in time*—in this case, December 31, 2012—which is

Exhibit **1.2**

Statement of Financial Position

SUN-RYPE PRODUCTS LTD. Statement of Financial Position At December 31, 2012 (in thousands of Canadian dollars)			
Assets			
Cash			$ 3,727
Trade receivables			14,047
Inventories			29,149
Prepayments			502
Property, plant, and equipment			42,041
Goodwill			1,061
Other assets			446
Total assets			$90,973
Liabilities			
Trade payables		$25,672	
Short-term borrowings		3,646	
Provisions		1,687	
Long-term borrowings		8,781	
Other liabilities		4,151	
Total liabilities			$43,937
Shareholders' Equity			
Contributed capital		$18,421	
Retained earnings		28,681	
Other components		(66)	
Total shareholders' equity			47,036
Total liabilities and shareholders' equity			$90,973

The notes are an integral part of these financial statements.

This statement is an adaptation of Sun-Rype's actual statement of financial position. A more detailed statement of financial position is presented in Chapter 2.

Source: Sun-Rype Products Ltd., Annual Report, 2012.

Name of the entity	*Title of the statement*
Accounting period	
Unit of measure	

Amount of cash in the company's bank accounts
Amounts owed by customers from prior sales
Fruit-based juices, snack products, and production materials
Rent and insurance paid in advance
Factories and production equipment
Economic resource that lacks physical substance
A variety of assets that are covered in future chapters

Amounts owed to suppliers for prior purchases
Amounts owed to lenders within one year
Estimated liabilities whose amounts and timing of payment are not known with certainty
Amounts owed on written debt contracts after one year
A variety of liabilities that are covered in future chapters

Amounts invested in the business by shareholders
Past earnings not distributed to shareholders
Adjustments to assets and liabilities that are explained in future chapters

stated clearly on the statement. Financial reports are normally denominated in the currency of the country in which the entity is legally required to report its financial results. In this case, Sun-Rype reports in Canadian dollars. Similarly, U.S. companies report in U.S. dollars and Mexican companies in Mexican pesos. Medium-sized companies such as Sun-Rype often report their financial figures in thousands; that is, they round the last three digits to the nearest thousand. The inventories amount of $29,149 on Sun-Rype's statement of financial position actually means $29,149,000. The amounts shown in the rest of this chapter are in thousands of Canadian dollars, except where otherwise noted.

Sun-Rype's statement of financial position lists the company's assets first. Assets are economic resources controlled by the entity. Assets are followed by liabilities and shareholders' equity. These are the sources of financing or claims against the company's economic resources. Financing provided by creditors creates a liability. Financing provided by owners creates owners' equity. Because Sun-Rype is a corporation, its owners' equity is designated shareholders' equity.[2] Since each asset must have a source of financing, a company's assets must, by definition, equal the sum of its liabilities and shareholders' equity. The **basic accounting equation** is written as

BASIC ACCOUNTING EQUATION Assets = Liabilities + Shareholders' Equity

Statement of Financial Position

Assets = Liabilities + Shareholders' Equity

Assets	=	**Liabilities + Shareholders' Equity**
Economic resources		Sources of financing for the economic resources
(e.g., cash, inventory)		Liabilities: from creditors
		Shareholders' Equity: from shareholders

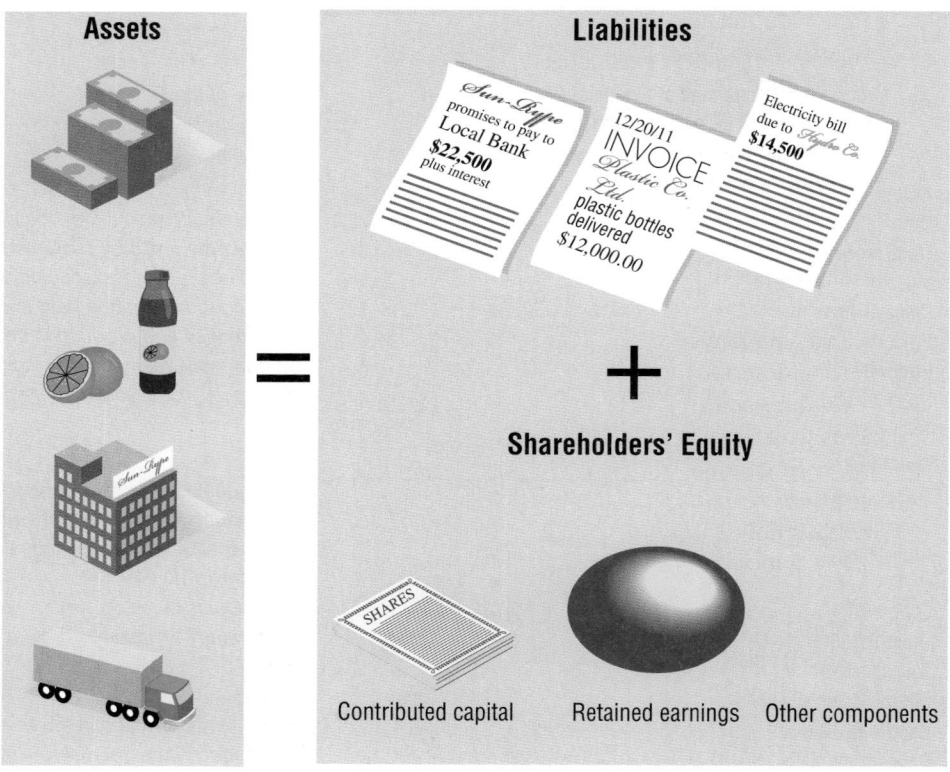

The basic accounting equation shows what we mean when we refer to a company's *financial position*: the economic resources that the company owns and the sources of financing for those resources.

Elements   *Assets* are economic resources controlled by the entity as a result of past business events, and from which future economic benefits can be obtained. Sun-Rype lists seven items under the category *assets*. The specific items listed as assets on a company's statement of financial position depend on the nature of its operations. But these are common names used by many companies. The seven items listed by Sun-Rype are the economic resources needed to manufacture and sell food and beverage products through major channels of distribution. Each of these economic resources is expected to provide future benefits to the company. To prepare for the production process, Sun-Rype first needed *cash* to purchase *land* on which to build manufacturing facilities and install production machinery (*plant and equipment*). Sun-Rype needs to have insurance to protect its resources against potential losses; advance payment of any insurance premiums gave rise to *prepayments* that reflect future economic benefits (i.e., insurance protection). Sun-Rype then began making its fruit-based juices and snacks, which led to the value assigned to *inventories*. When Sun-Rype sells its food and beverage products to retailers and wholesalers, it often sells them on credit and receives promises to pay, called *trade receivables*, which are collected in cash later. Sun-Rype's profitable operations led to expansion of its business activities by acquiring other businesses, including assets that are not easily identifiable or measured. These assets are known as *goodwill* and include such items as customer loyalty, quality products, and reputation for good service. Because of the complexity of its operations, Sun-Rype's resources include *other assets*, which are explained in future chapters.

Every asset on the statement of financial position is initially measured at the total cost incurred to acquire it. Subsequent to acquisition, assets are reported on the statement of financial position at values that reflect the benefits the company expects to realize from these assets through use or sale.

Liabilities are the entity's obligations that result from past business events. They arise primarily from the purchase of goods or services on credit and through cash borrowings to finance the business.

There are five types of liabilities listed on Sun-Rype's statement of financial position. *Trade payables* arise from the purchase of goods and services from suppliers on credit, without a formal written contract (or note). *Short-term borrowings* represent amounts borrowed from banks and other creditors, to be repaid in the near future. *Provisions* are estimated amounts payable in the future, but the exact amount and timing of the payment depend on future events. *Long-term borrowings* result from cash borrowings based on formal written debt contracts with lending institutions, such as banks. Sun-Rype is a medium-size company that incurs *other liabilities*, which are identified and described in future chapters.

Shareholders' equity indicates the amount of financing provided by owners of the business, as well as earnings over time. Shareholders' equity arises from three sources: (1) *contributed capital*, or the investment of cash and other assets in the business by the owners; (2) *retained earnings*, or the amount of earnings reinvested in the business (and thus not distributed to shareholders in the form of dividends); and (3) *other components*, which essentially reflect changes in the values of specific assets and liabilities over time.

In Exhibit 1.2, the Shareholders' Equity section reports three items. The contributions by Sun-Rype's shareholders are reported as contributed capital. Sun-Rype's net earnings less all dividends paid to the shareholders since formation of the corporation equal $28,681 at December 31, 2012, and is reported as retained earnings. Total shareholders' equity is the sum of contributed capital, retained earnings, and the valuation adjustments to specific assets and liabilities at year-end.

INTERPRETING ASSETS, LIABILITIES, AND SHAREHOLDERS' EQUITY ON THE STATEMENT OF FINANCIAL POSITION

FINANCIAL ANALYSIS

Assessment of Sun-Rype's assets is important to its creditors and to its owners because assets provide a basis for judging whether the company has sufficient resources available to operate the business. Assets are also important because they could be sold for cash if Sun-Rype goes out of business.

Creditors are interested in Sun-Rype's liabilities because of their concern as to whether or not the company has sufficient sources of cash to pay its debts. Sun-Rype's debts are also relevant to its bankers' decisions to lend money to the company, because existing creditors share the bankers' claims against Sun-Rype's assets. Legal ownership of assets remains with the creditors to secure Sun-Rype's repayment of debt. If a business does not pay its creditors, they may force the sale of assets sufficient to meet their claims. In some situations, the sale of assets may not cover all of the company's debts; thus, creditors often take a loss. This is because the assets were acquired with the intent of producing benefits to Sun-Rype in the normal course of its operations. These assets may not be valued by external parties as having the same potential benefits for them as the assets had for Sun-Rype. Thus, creditors may not be able to sell the assets for the amount of the debt.

Sun-Rype's shareholders' equity, or net worth, is important to creditors because, legally, their claims for repayment of obligations must be settled before those of the owners. If Sun-Rype goes out of business and its assets are sold, the proceeds of that sale must be used to pay back creditors before the shareholders receive any money. Shareholders provide resources for the company to use in the future, with no promise of any future repayment. They are entitled to what is left only after creditors' claims have been settled. Thus, creditors consider shareholders' equity a protective cushion.

A Note on Format A few additional formatting conventions are worth noting here. Assets may be listed on the statement of financial position in either increasing or decreasing order of their convertibility to cash. Most Canadian companies, like Sun-Rype, list their assets beginning with the most-liquid asset, cash, and ending with the least-liquid assets, which are not readily convertible to cash, such as goodwill. In contrast, many international companies, like the Benetton Group, list their least-liquid assets first and most-liquid assets last. Similarly, liabilities may be listed by either increasing or decreasing order of maturity (due date). International Accounting Standard 1 allows companies to use either format to report their assets and liabilities.

Most financial statements include the monetary unit sign (in Canada, $) beside the first amount in a group of items (e.g., contributed capital in shareholders' equity). Also, it is common to place a single underline below the last item in a group before a total or subtotal (e.g., Other assets). A double underline is also placed below group totals (e.g., Total assets). The same conventions are followed in all four basic financial statements.

PAUSE FOR FEEDBACK

We just learned that the statement of financial position reports dollar amounts for a company's assets, liabilities, and shareholders' equity at a specific point in time. These elements are related in the basic accounting equation: Assets = Liabilities + Shareholders' Equity. Before you move on, complete the following questions to test your understanding of these concepts.

SELF-STUDY QUIZ 1-1

1. Sun-Rype's *assets* are listed in one section and *liabilities* and *shareholders' equity* in another. Notice that the two sections balance, in conformity with the basic accounting equation. In the following chapters, you will learn that the accounting equation is the basic building block for the entire accounting process. Your task here is to verify that total assets ($90,973) is correct, using the numbers for liabilities and shareholders' equity presented in Exhibit 1.2.

2. Learning which items belong in each of the categories on the statement of financial position is an important first step in understanding their meaning. Mark each item in the following list as an asset (A), a liability (L), or shareholders' equity (SE), without referring to Exhibit 1.2.

_____ Trade payables		_____ Inventories	
_____ Trade receivables		_____ Bank borrowings	
_____ Cash		_____ Provisions	
_____ Contributed capital		_____ Retained earnings	
_____ Property, plant, and equipment			

After you complete your answers, check them with the solutions at the end of the chapter.

The Statement of Comprehensive Income

The **STATEMENT OF COMPREHENSIVE INCOME** reports the change in shareholders' equity during a period from business activities, excluding exchanges with shareholders.

Structure The **statement of comprehensive income** reports the change in shareholders' equity during a period from business activities other than investments by shareholders (such as the issuance of shares) or distributions to shareholders (such as dividends). The statement of comprehensive income has two parts. The first part reports the accountant's primary measure of a company's performance: revenues generated less expenses incurred during the accounting period. Accountants label this measure of performance "net earnings."[3] The second part reports other comprehensive income, which comprises other items that are not recognized in the statement of earnings.

The **STATEMENT OF EARNINGS** reports the revenues and expenses of the accounting period.

Companies can present all items of income and expenses either in one statement of comprehensive income or in two related statements—a **statement of earnings** (or income statement[4]) reporting the revenues and expenses of the accounting period that have already affected net earnings, and a statement of comprehensive income reporting additional income and expense items that will affect net earnings in the future. Sun-Rype uses the one-statement approach. For simplicity, we assume that Sun-Rype uses the two-statement approach and focus our attention in this chapter on the statement of earnings. The statement of comprehensive income will be covered in Chapters 6 and 12.

A quick reading of Sun-Rype's statement of earnings (Exhibit 1.3) provides an indication of its purpose and content. The heading of the statement, again, identifies the name of the entity, title of the statement, and unit of measure used in the statement. Unlike the statement of financial position, which reports financial information as of a certain date, the statement of earnings reports information for a *specified period of time* (e.g., for the year ended December 31, 2012). The time period covered by the financial statements (one year in this case) is called an **accounting period**.

Notice that Sun-Rype's statement of earnings has three major captions: revenues, expenses, and net earnings. The statement of earnings equation that describes this relationship is

The ACCOUNTING PERIOD is the time period covered by the financial statements.

Revenues   –   **Expenses**   =   **Net earnings**

Exhibit **1.3**
Statement of Earnings and Statement of Comprehensive Income

SUN-RYPE PRODUCTS LTD. Statement of Earnings For the Year Ended December 31, 2012 (in thousands of Canadian dollars, except for EPS)		
Revenues		
Net sales		$152,795
Expenses		
Cost of sales	$125,474	
Sales and marketing	11,699	
Distribution	6,813	
General and administrative	5,987	
Finance costs	708	
Total pretax expenses		150,681
Earnings before income taxes		2,114
Income tax expense		847
Net earnings for the year		$ 1,267
Earnings per share		$ 0.12

Name of the entity
Title of the statement
Accounting period
Unit of measure

Revenue earned from sale of food and beverage products

Cost to produce food and beverage products that have been sold
Expenses related to marketing and promotion of Sun-Rype's products
Expenses related to distribution of Sun-Rype's products
Expenses related to administration of the company's business activities
Interest and other costs that an entity incurs in connection with the borrowing of funds

Income taxes related to the period's pretax earnings

SUN-RYPE PRODUCTS LTD. Statement of Comprehensive Income For the Year Ended December 31, 2012 (in thousands of Canadian dollars)	
Net earnings for the year	$1,267
Other comprehensive income (loss)	
Foreign currency translation differences for foreign operations	(13)
Total comprehensive income (loss) for the year	$1,254

Name of the entity
Title of the statement
Accounting period
Unit of measure

Effect of changes in exchange rates on Sun-Rype's investments in U.S. companies

The notes are an integral part of these financial statements.

This statement is an adaptation of Sun-Rype's actual statement of comprehensive income for 2012.

Source: Sun-Rype Products Ltd., Annual Report, 2012.

Elements   Companies earn *revenues* from the sale of goods or services to customers (in Sun-Rype's case, from the sale of fruit-based beverages and snacks). Revenues are normally reported on the statement of earnings when the goods or services are sold to customers, *whether or not they have been paid for*. Retail stores, such as Tim Hortons and Dollarama, often receive cash at the time of sale. However, when Sun-Rype sells its food and beverage products to wholesale distributors, it receives a promise of future payment called a trade receivable, which is collected in cash at a later date. In either case, the business recognizes the total of cash and credit sales made during a specific accounting period as revenue for that period. Various terms are used in financial statements to describe different sources of revenue (e.g., provision of services, sale of goods, rental of property). Sun-Rype lists only one source of revenue, net sales, resulting from selling fruit juices and snack products.

Expenses represent the monetary value of resources the entity used up, or consumed, to earn revenues during the period. Sun-Rype lists six items as expenses on the statement of earnings. The *cost of sales* (or *cost of goods sold*) is Sun-Rype's total cost to produce the food and beverage products sold to customers during the year. These include the costs of ingredients, wages paid to the factory workers, and even a portion of the cost of buildings, equipment, and tools used (called *depreciation*) to produce the goods that were sold. *Sales and marketing expenses* include items such as the salaries of marketing personnel and promotion of the company's products through print and electronic media. *Distribution expenses* include a variety of expenses such as the salaries of sales personnel and expenses related to the distribution of the company's products. *General and administrative expenses* include items such as the salaries of management personnel, rental of office space, insurance, utilities, plus other general costs of operating the company not directly related to production. The *finance costs* reflect interest and other costs that Sun-Rype incurred in connection with the funds it borrowed from creditors. Finally, as a corporation, Sun-Rype must pay income tax to the government based on its pretax earnings. Sun-Rype's *income tax expense* for 2012 is approximately 40 percent of its pretax earnings.

Expenses may require immediate payment of cash, payment of cash at a future date, or use of some other resource, such as an inventory item, that may have been paid for in a previous period. For accounting purposes, the expense reported in one accounting period may actually be paid for in cash in another accounting period. Nevertheless, the company recognizes all expenses (cash and credit) incurred during a specific accounting period, regardless of the timing of the cash payment. For example, let us assume that Sun-Rype owes $50,000 in sales commissions to salespeople who sold food and beverage items to retailers in December 2012, but it did not pay the $50,000 until January 2013. In this case, the sales commissions would be recognized as expenses for the accounting period ending on December 31, 2012. This is because the salespeople exerted effort during December 2012, which resulted in commissions for successfully selling the company's various products.

Net earnings (also called *net income* or *profit*) is the excess of total revenues over total expenses incurred to generate revenue during a specific period. Sun-Rype's net earnings for the year measures its success in selling fruit-based snacks and beverages for more than it cost to generate those sales. If total expenses exceed total revenues, a loss is reported. (Losses are normally noted by parentheses around the reported figure.) When revenues and expenses are equal for the period, the business has operated at breakeven.

We noted earlier that revenues are not necessarily the same as collections from customers, and expenses are not necessarily the same as payments to suppliers. As a result, the amount of net earnings normally *does not equal* the net cash generated by operations. This latter amount is reported on the statement of cash flows discussed later in the chapter.

ANALYZING THE STATEMENT OF EARNINGS: BEYOND THE BOTTOM LINE

FINANCIAL ANALYSIS

Investors and creditors closely monitor a firm's net earnings because they reflect the firm's ability to sell goods and services for more than the cost to produce and deliver them. Investors buy the company's shares when they believe that net earnings will improve and lead to a higher share price. Lenders also rely on future earnings to provide the resources to repay loans. The details of the statement are also important. For example, Sun-Rype had to sell $152,795 (all dollar amounts in thousands) worth of food and beverage products in 2012 to earn $1,267. If a competitor were to lower its prices by just 10 percent, forcing Sun-Rype to do the same in order to retain its market share, or if Sun-Rype had to triple marketing expenses to catch up to a competitor, its net earnings could be reduced significantly and might turn into a loss. In fact, Sun-Rype reported a loss in 2011, caused primarily by increased commodity prices, which resulted in total expenses exceeding the revenues generated in that year. These and other factors help investors and creditors estimate the company's future net earnings based on past information.

Exhibit 1.3 also shows Sun-Rype's statement of comprehensive income, which consists of net earnings for the year adjusted downward by $13 to represent the effect of changes in the exchange rate between the U.S. and Canadian dollars on the company's operations in the United States during 2012. This adjustment is reported in other comprehensive income instead of net earnings because Sun-Rype's investment in the U.S. companies is expected to continue in the foreseeable future.

PAUSE FOR FEEDBACK   STOP

As noted above, the statement of earnings reports revenues, expenses, and net earnings for a stated period of time. To practise your understanding of these concepts, complete the following questions.

SELF-STUDY QUIZ 1-2

1. Learning which items belong in each of the statement of earnings categories is an important first step in understanding their meaning. Mark each statement of earnings item in the following list as either a revenue (R) or an expense (E), without referring to Exhibit 1.3.
   _____ Cost of sales
   _____ Sales
   _____ General and administrative

2. During 2012, Sun-Rype delivered food and beverage products to customers for which the customers paid, or promised to pay in the future, amounts totalling $152,795. During the same

period, it collected $152,181 in cash from its customers. Without referring to Exhibit 1.3, indicate which of the two amounts will be shown on Sun-Rype's statement of earnings as sales revenue for 2012. Explain.

3. During the year 2012, Sun-Rype produced food and beverage items with a total production cost of $128,119. During the same period, it delivered to customers goods that had cost a total of $125,474 to produce. Without referring to Exhibit 1.3, indicate which of the two amounts will be shown on Sun-Rype's statement of earnings as cost of sales for 2012. Explain.

After you complete your answers, check them with the solutions at the end of the chapter.

The Statement of Changes in Equity

The STATEMENT OF CHANGES IN EQUITY reports all changes to shareholders' equity during the accounting period.

Structure The **statement of changes in equity** reports all changes to shareholders' equity during the accounting period. Sun-Rype prepares a separate statement of changes in equity, shown in Exhibit 1.4 in a condensed format.[5] The heading identifies the name of the entity, title of the statement, and unit of measure used. Like the statement of comprehensive income, the statement of changes in equity covers a specific period of time, which in this case is one year. This statement reports the way that net earnings, distribution of net earnings (dividends), and other changes to shareholders' equity affected the company's financial position during the accounting period. We focus on retained earnings in this chapter and discuss the other components of equity in later chapters.

RETAINED EARNINGS reflect the net earnings that have been generated since the creation of the company but not distributed yet to shareholders as dividends.

Retained earnings reflect the net earnings that have been generated since the creation of the company but not distributed yet to shareholders as dividends. Net earnings achieved during the year increases the balance of retained earnings. The declaration of dividends to the shareholders decreases retained earnings.[6] The retained earnings equation that describes these relationships is

$$\textbf{Beginning Retained Earnings} + \textbf{Net Earnings} - \textbf{Dividends} = \textbf{Ending Retained Earnings}$$

Exhibit **1.4**

Statement of Changes in Equity

Name of the entity
Title of the statement
Accounting period
Unit of measure

SUN-RYPE PRODUCTS LTD.
Statement of Changes in Equity
For the Year Ended December 31, 2012
(in thousands of Canadian dollars)

	Contributed Capital	Retained Earnings	Accumulated Other Comprehensive Income
Balance as at Jan. 1, 2012	$18,518	$27,914	(53)
Net earnings for the year		1,267	
Other comprehensive income (loss)			(13)
Repurchase and cancellation of shares	(97)		
Distribution of dividends		(500)	
Balance as at Dec. 31, 2012	$18,421	$28,681	$(66)

Last-period ending balances
Net earnings reported on the statement of earnings
Foreign currency translation differences for foreign operations
Repurchase and cancellation of shares previously issued by Sun-Rype
Dividends declared during the period
Ending balances reported on the statement of financial position

The notes are an integral part of these financial statements.

This statement is an adaptation of Sun-Rype's actual statement of changes in equity for 2012.

Source: Sun-Rype Products Ltd., Annual Report, 2012.

Elements The statement begins with Sun-Rype's balances to contributed capital, retained earnings, and other equity components at January 1, 2012 (the beginning of the accounting period). The net earnings reported on the statement of earnings for the current period is added to (subtracted from) the beginning balance of retained earnings, and dividends declared during the year are subtracted from this amount. During 2012, Sun-Rype reported net earnings of $1,267, as shown in Exhibit 1.3. Also during 2012, Sun-Rype declared and paid a total of $500 in dividends to its shareholders.[7] The net result is that retained earnings at December 31, 2012 (the end of the accounting period), increased by $767 (= $1,267 − $500).

The ending retained earnings amount of $28,681 is the same as that reported in Exhibit 1.2 on Sun-Rype's statement of financial position. The ending balances of contributed capital and other components are also reported on the statement of financial position. Thus, the statement of changes in equity shows how the statement of comprehensive income and the statement of financial position are linked through specific components of shareholders' equity.

Statement of Changes in Equity

Equity, beginning of the period
+ Net earnings for the year
+ Other comprehensive income
− Dividends
+/− Other changes, net
Equity, end of the period

INTERPRETING RETAINED EARNINGS

FINANCIAL ANALYSIS

Reinvestment of net earnings, or retained earnings, is an important source of financing for Sun-Rype, representing about one-third of its financing. Creditors closely monitor a firm's retained earnings because the firm's policy on dividend payments to its shareholders affects its ability to repay its debts. Every dollar Sun-Rype pays to shareholders as a dividend is not available for use in paying back its debt to creditors. The reverse is also true; every dollar used to repay creditors is unavailable either for distribution to investors as dividends or for retention and reinvestment in the company's future growth. Investors examine retained earnings to determine whether the company is reinvesting a sufficient portion of net earnings to support future growth.

PAUSE FOR FEEDBACK

The statement of retained earnings explains changes to the retained earnings balance caused by net earnings and dividends during the reporting period. Check your understanding of these relationships by completing the following question.

SELF-STUDY QUIZ 1-3

Sun-Rype's retained earnings reflects the way that the net earnings and distribution of dividends affected the financial position of the company during the accounting period. In a prior period, Sun-Rype's financial statements reported the following amounts: beginning retained earnings, $29,089; total assets, $82,318; dividends, $2,382; cost of sales, $104,867; and net earnings, $4,503. Without referring to Exhibit 1.4, compute ending retained earnings.

After you complete your answer, check it with the solutions at the end of the chapter.

The Statement of Cash Flows

Structure The **statement of cash flows** reports cash inflows and outflows that are related to operating, investing, and financing activities during the accounting period. Sun-Rype's statement of cash flows, presented in Exhibit 1.5, divides Sun-Rype's cash inflows (receipts) and outflows (payments) into three primary categories of cash flows in a typical business: cash flows from operating, investing, and financing activities.

The **STATEMENT OF CASH FLOWS** reports cash inflows and outflows that are related to operating, investing, and financing activities during the accounting period.

Exhibit **1.5**

Statement of Cash Flows

	SUN-RYPE PRODUCTS LTD.	
	Statement of Cash Flows	
	For the year ended December 31, 2012	
	(in thousands of Canadian dollars)	
Name of the entity		
Title of the statement		
Accounting period		
Unit of measure		
Directly related to earnings from operations	**Cash flows from operating activities**	
	Cash collected from customers	$152,181
	Cash paid to trade suppliers	(111,202)
	Cash paid for operating expenses	(23,907)
	Cash paid for interest	(826)
	Cash received for taxes (income tax refund)	1,690
	Net cash flow from operating activities	$17,936
Purchase/sale of financial and productive assets	**Cash flows from investing activities**	
	Cash paid to purchase property, plant, and equipment	(1,418)
	Net cash flow used for investing activities	(1,418)
From investors and creditors	**Cash flows from financing activities**	
	Cash received from borrowings	1,502
	Repayment of borrowings	(14,264)
	Repurchase of own shares	(97)
	Cash paid for dividends	(500)
	Net cash flow used for financing activities	(13,359)
Change in cash during the period	**Net increase in cash during the year**	3,159
Last period's ending cash balance	**Cash at beginning of year**	571
	Effect of exchange rate changes on cash	(3)
Ending cash on the statement of financial position	**Cash at end of year**	$ 3,727

The notes are an integral part of these financial statements.

This statement is an adaptation of Sun-Rype's actual statement of cash flows.

Source: Sun-Rype Products Ltd., Annual Report, 2012.

The heading identifies the name of the entity, the title of the statement, and the unit of measure used. Like the statement of earnings, the statement of cash flows covers a specified period of time, which in this case is one year.

As discussed earlier in this chapter, reported revenues do not always equal cash collected from customers because some sales may be on credit. Also, expenses reported on the statement of earnings may not be equal to cash paid out during the period because expenses may be incurred in one period and paid for in another. As a result, net earnings (revenues minus expenses) does *not* usually equal the amount of cash received minus the amount paid during the period. Because the statement of earnings does not provide any information concerning cash flows, accountants prepare the statement of cash flows to report inflows and outflows of cash.

The statement of cash flows equation describes the causes of the change in cash reported on the statement of financial position from the end of the last period to the end of the current period:

+/− **Cash flows from operating activities**
+/− **Cash flows from investing activities**
+/− **Cash flows from financing activities**
Change in cash

Note that each of the three cash flow sources can be either positive or negative.

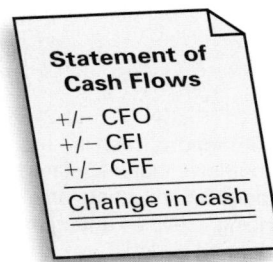

Elements   *Cash flows from operating activities (CFO)* are cash flows that are directly related to generating earnings. For example, when retailers pay Sun-Rype for the food and beverage products it delivered to them, Sun-Rype lists the amounts collected as cash collected from customers. When Sun-Rype pays salaries or bills received for materials, it includes the amounts in cash paid to employees and trade suppliers.[8]

Cash flows from investing activities (CFI) include cash flows related to the acquisition or sale of the company's productive assets. This year, Sun-Rype had one cash outflow for investing activities: purchase of additional property, plant, and equipment to meet the growing demand for its products.

Cash flows from financing activities (CFA) are directly related to the financing of the company itself. They involve both receipts and payments of cash to investors and creditors. During 2012, Sun-Rype borrowed $1,502 from banks and other creditors, and it paid $14,264 to banks for previous loans that became due during the year. It also paid $97 to repurchase its own shares from shareholders, as well as $500 in dividends to the company's shareholders.

INTERPRETING THE STATEMENT OF CASH FLOWS

FINANCIAL
ANALYSIS

Many analysts believe that the statement of cash flows is particularly useful for predicting future cash flows that may be available for payment of debt to creditors and dividends to investors. Bankers often consider the operating activities section to be the most important, because it indicates the company's ability to generate cash from sales to meet its current cash needs. Any amount left can be used to repay debt or expand the company.

Shareholders will invest in a company if they believe that it will eventually generate more cash from operations than it uses, so that cash will become available to pay dividends and to expand. The investing activities section shows that Sun-Rype has invested in new manufacturing capacity, a good sign if demand continues to increase. The financing activities section indicates that Sun-Rype was able to borrow funds from banks and other creditors but had to pay back debt that became due. It also paid cash dividends to shareholders and repurchased shares for cash. The cash generated from operations was sufficient to cover the company's cash needs for both investing and financing activities.

PAUSE FOR
FEEDBACK STOP

The statement of cash flows reports inflows and outflows of cash for a stated period of time classified into three categories: operating, investing, and financing activities. Answer the following questions to test your understanding of the concepts involved.

SELF-STUDY **QUIZ 1-4**

1. During the period 2012, Sun-Rype delivered food and beverage products to customers that paid, or promised to pay in the future, amounts totalling $152,795. During the same period, it collected $152,181 in cash from its customers. Without referring to Exhibit 1.5, indicate which of the two numbers will be shown on Sun-Rype's statement of cash flows for 2012.

2. Learning which items belong in each category on the statement of cash flows is an important first step in understanding their meaning. Mark each item in the following list as a cash flow from operating activities (O), investing activities (I), or financing activities (F), without referring to Exhibit 1.5. Also, place parentheses around the letter only if it is a cash *outflow.*

   _____ Cash paid for dividends   _____ Cash paid to purchase property, plant,
   _____ Cash paid for interest   and equipment
   _____ Cash received from bank borrowings   _____ Cash collected from customers
   _____ Cash paid for taxes

After you complete your answers, check them with the solutions at the end of the chapter.

Relationships among the Four Financial Statements

Our discussion of the four basic financial statements focused on the different elements reported on each of the statements, how the elements are related through the equation for each statement, and how the elements are important to the decisions of investors, creditors, and other external users. We have also discovered how the statements, all of which are outputs from the same system, are related to one another. In particular, we learned that

1. Net earnings from the statement of earnings results in an increase in ending retained earnings on the statement of changes in equity.
2. Ending retained earnings from the statement of changes in equity is one of the three components of shareholders' equity on the statement of financial position.
3. The change in cash on the statement of cash flows added to the cash balance at the beginning of the year equals the balance of cash at the end of the year, which appears on the statement of financial position.

Thus, as external users, we can think of the statement of earnings (and the statement of comprehensive income) as explaining, through the statement of changes in equity, how the operations of the company changed its financial position during the year. The statement of cash flows explains how the operating, investing, and financing activities of the company affected the cash balance on the statement of financial position during the year. These relationships are illustrated in Exhibit 1.6 for Sun-Rype's financial statements.

Exhibit **1.6**

Relationships among Sun-Rype's
Statements

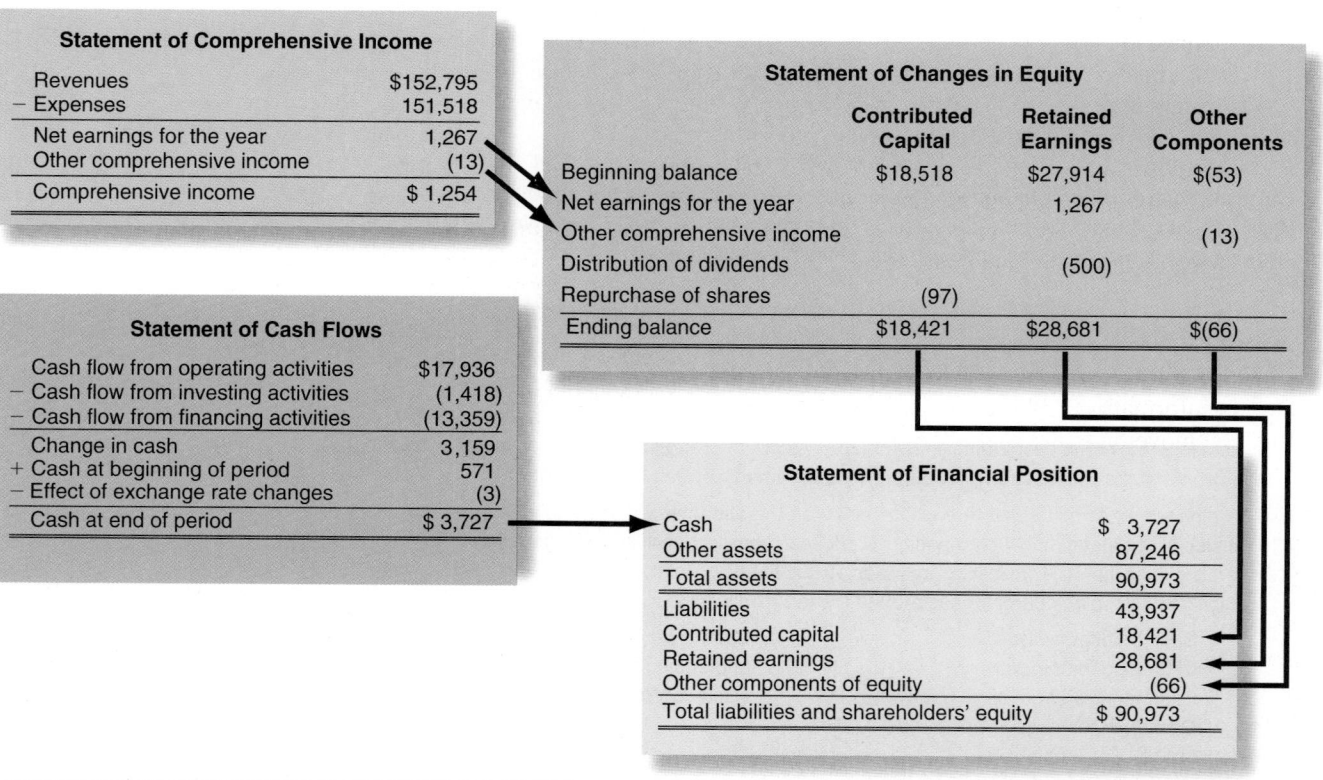

Statement of Comprehensive Income

Revenues	$152,795
− Expenses	151,518
Net earnings for the year	1,267
Other comprehensive income	(13)
Comprehensive income	$ 1,254

Statement of Changes in Equity

	Contributed Capital	Retained Earnings	Other Components
Beginning balance	$18,518	$27,914	$(53)
Net earnings for the year		1,267	
Other comprehensive income			(13)
Distribution of dividends		(500)	
Repurchase of shares	(97)		
Ending balance	$18,421	$28,681	$(66)

Statement of Cash Flows

Cash flow from operating activities	$17,936
− Cash flow from investing activities	(1,418)
− Cash flow from financing activities	(13,359)
Change in cash	3,159
+ Cash at beginning of period	571
− Effect of exchange rate changes	(3)
Cash at end of period	$ 3,727

Statement of Financial Position

Cash	$ 3,727
Other assets	87,246
Total assets	90,973
Liabilities	43,937
Contributed capital	18,421
Retained earnings	28,681
Other components of equity	(66)
Total liabilities and shareholders' equity	$ 90,973

MANAGERIAL USES OF FINANCIAL STATEMENTS

FINANCIAL ANALYSIS

In our discussion of financial analysis thus far, we have focused on the perspectives of investors and creditors. In addition, managers within the firm often make direct use of financial statements. For example, Sun-Rype's marketing managers and credit managers use customers' financial statements to decide whether to extend credit to them for their purchases of Sun-Rype products. Sun-Rype's purchasing managers analyze financial statements of suppliers to judge whether the suppliers have the resources to meet Sun-Rype's demand for fresh fruits and other ingredients for their products. Both Sun-Rype's human resource managers and the employees' union use the company's financial statements as a basis for contract negotiations over pay rates. The net earnings figure even serves as a basis for computing employee bonuses.

When Sun-Rype's managers examine the financial statements of the company's customers and suppliers, they rely on these statements as the best source of financial information available to external users because they do not have access to internal financial information produced by their customers and their suppliers. However, when they make internal decisions regarding Sun-Rype's operations, they rely on more-detailed financial information obtained through the company's managerial accounting system.

Notes to Financial Statements

At the bottom of each of the four basic financial statements you will typically find the following statement: "The notes are an integral part of these financial statements." This is the accounting equivalent of the nutritional content on pre-packaged food. It warns users that failure to read the notes to these financial statements will result in incomplete knowledge of the company's financial health. **Notes** provide supplemental information about the financial condition of a company, without which the financial statements cannot be fully understood.

There are three basic types of notes. The first type provides descriptions of the accounting rules applied in the company's statements. The second presents additional detail about a line on the financial statements. For example, Sun-Rype's inventory note indicates the costs of raw materials and supplies used for production purposes as well as finished products that are ready for sale to customers. The third type of note presents additional financial disclosures about items not listed on the statements themselves. For example, Sun-Rype is exposed to significant risks; the risks related to credit and fluctuations in exchange rates are disclosed in a note. We will discuss many note disclosures throughout the book because understanding their content is critical to understanding the company.[9]

NOTES provide supplemental information about the financial condition of a company, without which the financial statements cannot be fully understood.

Summary of the Four Basic Financial Statements

We learned a lot about the content of the four basic statements. Exhibit 1.7 summarizes this information. Take a few minutes to review the information in the exhibit before you move on to the next section of the chapter.

RESPONSIBILITIES FOR THE ACCOUNTING COMMUNICATION PROCESS

Effective communication means that the recipient understands what the sender intends to convey. For decision makers to use the information in Sun-Rype's financial statements effectively, they have to understand what information each statement conveys. Understandability is the foundation of effective communication.

They also need to know that the amounts reported in the statements fairly represent what is claimed. Financial statements that do not represent what they claim to are meaningless and cannot be used effectively to make decisions. For example, if the

LO2

Identify the role of International Financial Reporting Standards (IFRS) in determining the content of financial statements.

Exhibit **1.7**

Summary of Four Basic Financial
Statements

Financial Statement	Purpose	Structure	Examples of Content
Statement of Financial Position	Reports the financial position (economic resources and sources of financing) of an accounting entity *at a point in time*.	**Statement of Financial Position** Assets = Liabilities + Shareholders' Equity	Cash, trade receivables, plant and equipment, notes payable, contributed capital
Statement of Comprehensive Income (including the Statement of Earnings)	Reports the net earnings achieved *during the accounting period*, as well as income and expense items that are not recognized in net earnings.	**Statement of Comprehensive Income** Revenues – Expenses Net earnings + Other comprehensive income Comprehensive income	Sales revenue, cost of sales, selling expense, interest expense
Statement of Changes in Equity	Reports the way that elements of comprehensive income, dividends, and changes to contributed capital affected the financial position of the company *during the accounting period*.	**Statement of Changes in Equity** Equity, beginning of the period + Net earnings + Other comprehensive income – Dividends +/– Other changes, net Equity, end of the period	Retained earnings, elements of comprehensive income, distributions of dividends, increase in contributed capital
Statement of Cash Flows	Reports inflows (receipts) and outflows (payments) of cash *during the accounting period* in the operating, investing, and financing categories.	**Statement of Cash Flows** +/– CFO +/– CFI +/– CFF Change in cash	Cash collected from customers, cash paid to suppliers, cash paid to purchase equipment, cash borrowed from banks

statement of financial position lists $2,000,000 for a factory that does not exist, that part of the statement does not convey useful information.

Decision makers also need to understand the *measurement rules* applied in computing the numbers on the statements. A swim coach would never try to evaluate a swimmer's time in the "100 freestyle" without first asking whether the time was for a race in metres or in yards. Likewise, a decision maker should never attempt to use accounting information without first understanding the measurement rules that were used to develop the information. The measurement rules used to develop the information in financial statements are based on **International Financial Reporting Standards (IFRS)**. These encompass broad principles, specific rules, practices, and conventions of general application that are used by organizations to record transactions and report financial statement information to interested users.

INTERNATIONAL FINANCIAL REPORTING STANDARDS (IFRS) are guidelines for the measurement rules used to develop the information in financial statements.

International Financial Reporting Standards (IFRS)

How Are Accounting Standards Determined?   The accounting system that we use today has a long history. Its foundations are normally traced back to the works of an Italian monk and mathematician, Fr. Luca Pacioli. In 1494, he described an approach developed by Italian merchants to account for their activities as owner-managers of business ventures. Many others wrote works on accounting after Pacioli, but prior to 1933, each company's management largely determined its own financial reporting practices. Thus, little uniformity in practice existed among companies.

Following the dramatic stock market decline of 1929, the *Securities Act* of 1933 and the *Securities Exchange Act* of 1934 were passed into law by the U.S. Congress. These acts created the **Securities and Exchange Commission (SEC)**, the U.S. government agency that determines the financial statements that public companies must provide to shareholders and the measurement rules that they must use in producing those statements. In Canada, provincial securities legislation created securities commissions, most notably the **Ontario Securities Commission (OSC)**, which is the most influential Canadian regulator of the flow of financial information provided by publicly traded companies whose shares trade on Canadian stock exchanges, such as the Toronto Stock Exchange. Similar to the SEC, the OSC plays an influential role in the promotion, surveillance, and enforcement in sound accounting practices by publicly traded companies. The OSC is one of 13 securities regulators in Canada's provinces and territories. These regulators have formed the Canadian Securities Administrators, which coordinates and harmonizes regulation of the Canadian capital markets among them.

Since their establishment, these securities commissions have worked with organizations of professional accountants to form groups that work toward establishing generally accepted accounting principles. In Canada, the **Accounting Standards Board (AcSB)** is the private-sector body given the primary responsibility to set the detailed rules that become accepted accounting standards. The AcSB is responsible for establishing standards of accounting and reporting by publicly accountable enterprises, private enterprises, government organizations, and not-for-profit organizations. These standards or recommendations, which are published in the *CICA Handbook,* have expanded over time because of the increasing diversity and complexity of business practices. The OSC performs surveillance and enforcement functions for legal requirements arising from standards in the *CICA Handbook.*

In January 2006, the AcSB decided to move to a single set of globally accepted high-quality standards and concluded that this is best accomplished by converging Canadian generally accepted accounting principles with IFRS. The AcSB implemented its plan by requiring all publicly accountable enterprises to use IFRS in reporting their financial statements for fiscal years (annual accounting periods) that started on or after January 1, 2011. As a result, Canadian publicly accountable enterprises currently prepare their financial statements in accordance with IFRS.

International Financial Accounting Standards are produced by the **International Accounting Standards Board (IASB)**, which is an independent standard-setting board responsible for the development and publication of IFRS. It consists of 15 members from 12 countries and co-operates with national accounting standard setters to achieve convergence in accounting standards around the world.[10] The IASB initially issued International Accounting Standards (IAS). New IASs are known as IFRS.

This book focuses on the accounting and financial reporting by publicly accountable enterprises. The accounting and financial reporting standards used by other types of organizations are covered in advanced accounting courses. Differences between the accounting standards applicable to Canadian publicly accountable enterprises and Canadian private enterprises are highlighted at the end of each chapter.

Most managers do not need to learn all of the details included in all accounting standards. Our approach is to focus on those standards appropriate to an introductory course that have the greatest effect on the numbers presented in financial statements.

Why Are Accounting Standards Important to Managers and External Users? Accounting standards are of great interest to the companies that must prepare the statements and to the readers of these statements. IFRS provide guidance to

The **SECURITIES AND EXCHANGE COMMISSION (SEC)** is the U.S. government agency that determines the financial statements that public companies must provide to shareholders and the measurement rules that they must use in producing those statements.

The **ONTARIO SECURITIES COMMISSION (OSC)** is the most influential Canadian regulator of the flow of financial information provided by publicly traded companies in Canada.

The **ACCOUNTING STANDARDS BOARD (AcSB)** is the private-sector body given the primary responsibility to set the detailed rules that become accepted accounting standards.

The **INTERNATIONAL ACCOUNTING STANDARDS BOARD (IASB)** is an independent standard-setting board that is responsible for the development and publication of International Financial Reporting Standards.

companies in selecting the accounting methods that best reflect the results of their operations and financial situation. These globally accepted accounting standards also prevent managers from deliberately manipulating and reporting values that serve their personal interests by using accounting practices not in conformity with IFRS. Widely divergent accounting practices reduce the comparability of financial information from different companies operating in the same line of business. IFRS enhance the comparability by limiting the number of acceptable alternative accounting methods across companies and over time. Furthermore, understanding IFRS enables external users to assess the quality of the information presented in the financial statements and related notes.

Companies, their managers, and their owners are most directly affected by the information presented in the financial statements. Companies incur the cost of preparing the statements and bear the major economic consequences of their publication. These economic consequences include, among others,

1. changes to the selling price of a company's shares,
2. changes to the amount of bonuses received by management and employees, and
3. loss of competitive advantage over other companies.

INTERNATIONAL PERSPECTIVE

THE INTERNATIONAL ACCOUNTING STANDARDS BOARD AND GLOBAL CONVERGENCE OF ACCOUNTING STANDARDS

REAL-WORLD EXCERPT

Deloitte IAS Plus Website

(WWW.IASPLUS.COM)

Financial accounting standards and disclosure requirements are set by national regulatory agencies and standard-setting bodies. However, since 2002, there has been a substantial movement toward the adoption of International Financial Reporting Standards (IFRS) issued by the International Accounting Standards Board (IASB). Examples of jurisdictions currently requiring the use of IFRS include the following:

All countries in the European Union

Australia and New Zealand

Hong Kong (S.A.R. of China), China, India, Malaysia, and South Korea

Israel and Turkey

Argentina, Brazil, and Chile

Canada and Mexico

In the United States, the SEC allows foreign companies whose shares are traded on U.S. exchange markets to use IFRS and is considering allowing the same for domestic companies in the future.

Source: May 2013. Deloitte IAS PLUS website. For information, contact Deloitte Touche Tohmatsu Limited.

Sun-Rype's share price can be determined in part based on the net earnings computed in compliance with IFRS. This presents the possibility that changes in accounting standards can affect the price buyers are willing to pay for companies. Employees who receive part of their pay based on reaching stated net earnings targets are directly concerned with any changes in how the net earnings figure is determined. Managers and owners are often concerned that publishing more information in financial statements will give away trade secrets to other companies that compete with them. As a consequence of these and other concerns, changes in accounting standards are actively debated, political lobbying often takes place, and the accounting standards that are eventually issued are often a compromise among the conflicting wishes of interested parties.

Management Responsibility and the Demand for Auditing

Who is responsible for the accuracy of the numbers in Sun-Rype's financial statements? Primary responsibility lies with management, as represented by the highest officer of the company and its highest financial officer.[11] Companies take three important steps to assure investors that the company's records are accurate: (1) they develop and maintain a system of internal controls over both the records and the assets of the company, (2) they hire outside independent auditors to attest to the fairness of the statement presentations, and (3) they form a committee of the board of directors to oversee the integrity of these two safeguards. These responsibilities are often reiterated in a formal **report to management (management certification)**, which indicates management's primary responsibility for financial statement information and the steps to ensure the accuracy of the company's records. The three safeguards outlined above and management certification are required for all Canadian companies with publicly traded shares. Managers of companies that prepare fraudulent financial statements are subject to criminal and civil penalties.

The **REPORT TO MANAGEMENT (MANAGEMENT CERTIFICATION)** indicates management's primary responsibility for financial statement information and the steps to ensure the accuracy of the company's records.

Three steps to ensure the accuracy of records:

System of Controls   External Auditors   Board of Directors

The role of the independent auditor is described in more detail in the **audit report (report of independent auditors)**, which describes the auditor's opinion of the fairness of the financial statements and the evidence gathered to support that opinion (see Exhibit 1.8). It is important to note that the main difference between the report of management and the report of the independent auditors concerns the responsibility for the financial information included in the company's annual report. As the report of the independent auditors indicates, the auditor's responsibility is to express an opinion on Sun-Rype's financial statements that have been prepared by its accounting personnel and reviewed by the *audit committee* of the *board of directors*, which assumes responsibility for the quality of the content of these financial statements.[12]

The **AUDIT REPORT (REPORT OF INDEPENDENT AUDITORS)** describes the auditors' opinion of the fairness of the financial statement presentations and the evidence gathered to support that opinion.

In Canada, professional accountants have been designated as *Chartered Accountant (CA), Certified General Accountant (CGA),* or *Certified Management Accountant (CMA).* A concerted effort to unify the Canadian accounting profession started in 2011 with the objective of merging the three professional accounting designations into one designation: *Chartered Professional Accountant (CPA).* These efforts have resulted in the unification of the accounting profession in Quebec in 2012 and the establishment of Chartered Professional Accountants of Canada (CPA Canada) effective January 1, 2013. At the time of the writing of this text, continuing discussions among various provincial and national professional accounting organizations will likely result in one professional accounting designation in the near future.[13] The CPA designation is granted on completion of the CPA professional educational program and practical experience requirements.[14] Professional accountants can offer various accounting services to the public, as indicated in Appendix 1B.

Exhibit **1.8**

Auditors' Report
Source: Sun-Rype Products Ltd.,
Annual Report, 2012.

REAL-WORLD EXCERPT

Sun-Rype Products Ltd.

ANNUAL REPORT

INDEPENDENT AUDITORS' REPORT

To the Shareholders of Sun-Rype Products Ltd.

We have audited the accompanying consolidated financial statements of Sun-Rype Products Ltd., which comprise the consolidated statements of financial position as at December 31, 2012 and 2011, and the consolidated statements of comprehensive income, changes in equity and cash flows for the years then ended, 2010, and notes, comprising a summary of significant accounting policies and other explanatory information.

Management's Responsibility for the Consolidated Financial Statements

Management is responsible for the preparation and fair presentation of these consolidated financial statements in accordance with International Financial Reporting Standards as issued by the International Accounting Standards Board, and for such internal control as management determines is necessary to enable the preparation of consolidated financial statements that are free from material misstatement, whether due to fraud or error.

Auditors' Responsibility

Our responsibility is to express an opinion on these consolidated financial statements based on our audits. We conducted our audits in accordance with Canadian generally accepted auditing standards. Those standards require that we comply with ethical requirements and plan and perform the audit to obtain reasonable assurance about whether the consolidated financial statements are free from material misstatement.

An audit involves performing procedures to obtain audit evidence about the amounts and disclosures in the consolidated financial statements. The procedures selected depend on our judgment, including the assessment of the risks of material misstatement of the consolidated financial statements, whether due to fraud or error. In making those risk assessments, we consider internal control relevant to the entity's preparation and fair presentation of the consolidated financial statements in order to design audit procedures that are appropriate in the circumstances, but not for the purpose of expressing an opinion on the effectiveness of the entity's internal control. An audit also includes evaluating the appropriateness of accounting policies used and the reasonableness of accounting estimates made by management, as well as evaluating the overall presentation of the consolidated financial statements.

We believe that the audit evidence we have obtained in our audits is sufficient and appropriate to provide a basis for our audit opinion.

Opinion

In our opinion, the consolidated financial statements present fairly, in all material respects, the consolidated financial position of Sun-Rype Products Ltd. as at December 31, 2012 and 2011, and its consolidated financial performance and its consolidated cash flows for the years then ended in accordance with International Financial Reporting Standards as issued by the International Accounting Standards Board.

KPMG LLP

Chartered Accountants
Vancouver, Canada
March 6, 2013

An **AUDIT** is an examination of the financial reports to ensure that they represent what they claim and conform to IFRS.

An **audit** is an examination of the financial reports to ensure that they represent what they claim and conform to IFRS. In performing an audit, the independent auditor examines the underlying transactions and the accounting methods used to account for these transactions. Because of the enormous number of transactions that total billions of dollars each year for a major enterprise, such as Air Canada, the auditor does not examine each transaction. Rather, professional approaches are used to ascertain beyond reasonable doubt that transactions were measured and reported properly.[15]

Many opportunities exist for managers to intentionally prepare misleading financial reports. An audit performed by an independent auditor is the best protection available to the public. When that protection fails, however, the independent auditor is sometimes found liable for losses incurred by those who rely on the statements. In this regard, the Canadian Public Accountability Board was created in 2003 to provide public oversight for auditors of public companies.

Ethics, Reputation, and Legal Liability

If financial statements are to be of any value to decision makers, users must have confidence in the fairness of the information. These users will have greater confidence in the information if they know that the people who were associated with auditing the financial statements were required to meet professional standards of ethics and competence.

The Canadian accounting profession requires its members to adhere to professional codes of ethics. These broad principles are supported by specific rules governing the performance of audits by members of professional accounting organizations. These organizations stress how important it is for each member to behave in ways that enhance the reputation of the profession by voluntarily complying with codes of ethical conduct. For example, CPA Canada places professional and ethical behaviour as the most important of the enabling competencies possessed by its members.[16]

Failure to comply with professional rules of conduct can result in serious penalties for professional accountants, including rescinding the professional designation of an offending member. The potential economic effects of damage to reputation and malpractice liability, however, provide even stronger incentives to abide by professional standards. Thus, the profession recognizes that its members' reputations for ethical conduct and competence are their most important assets. Finally, recent changes in laws and securities regulation permit the assessment of personal financial penalties on professional accountants who are found guilty of non-compliance, and they must compensate for the financial harm done to others.

Financial statement fraud is a fairly rare event, due in part to the diligent efforts of practising professional accountants. In fact, many such frauds are first identified by the firm's accounting staff or its external auditors, who advise regulatory authorities of possible wrongdoing. In doing so, these "whistle blowers" place the interest of the public at large ahead of their own interests and act accordingly. However, in case of malpractice, independent auditors may be held liable for losses suffered by those who relied on the audited financial statements.

It is important to note that the vast majority of managers and owners do act in an honest and responsible manner. However, when the top officers in an organization collude to deceive other parties, they may temporarily succeed. In many cases, even the most diligent audit may not immediately uncover the results of fraud involving collusion of the top officers of a corporation, such as occurred in a number of well-publicized cases involving companies such as Livent Inc. and SNC-Lavalin Group Inc. in Canada, American Investment Group Inc. (AIG) in the United States, Siemens AG in Germany, and Parmalat S.p.A. in Italy. However, those who were involved in fraudulent behaviour were eventually identified and were sanctioned by the appropriate legal authorities.

Misrepresentations by managers highlight the importance of ensuring the integrity of the financial reporting system by the public accounting profession. Disclosure of financial information that does not conform to existing accounting standards imposes significant costs on the shareholders, creditors, and employees of companies affected by fraudulent activities. Recent reforms of the accounting profession and the imposition of new government regulations both in Canada and in the United States make it more difficult and costly for company managers to engage in fraudulent activities.

LO4

Appreciate the importance of ethics, reputation, and legal liability in accounting.

ACCOUNTING STANDARDS
FOR PRIVATE ENTERPRISES

The use of IFRS is required of all Canadian publicly accountable enterprises. However, corporations that do not have their shares traded on organized exchange markets and other private for-profit enterprises (proprietorships and partnerships) are not required to use IFRS. Instead, Canadian private enterprises may prepare their financial statements in accordance with a set of Canadian accounting standards that exclude inappropriate financial reporting complexities.[17]

The AcSB's decision to allow Canadian private enterprises to use accounting standards that deviate from IFRS recognizes that the information needs of external users of the financial statements of private enterprises differ from the information needs of users of the financial statements of publicly accountable enterprises. The major difference between the two types of enterprises is that external users of the private enterprise's financial statements do not include the many individual investors that typically purchase shares of publicly accountable enterprises. Hence, lenders are often the major external stakeholders in private enterprises and may obtain additional information from these companies upon request.

The financial statements prepared by both types of companies are based on the same conceptual foundations, but they may differ with respect to the details that are reported in the financial statements and related notes. Differences related to the basic financial statements are highlighted below. Other differences between IFRS and accounting standards for private enterprises (ASPE) will be highlighted in future chapters.

Financial Reporting Issue	IFRS	ASPE
Basic financial statements	The four basic financial statements are	The four basic financial statements are
	1. *Statement of comprehensive income.* This statement includes all revenues, expenses, gains, and losses reported in the statement of earnings as well as income and loss items that are not included in the computation of net earnings, such as gains and losses resulting from the measurement of specific financial assets and liabilities at fair value.	1. *Income statement.* This statement includes all revenues, expenses, gains, and losses for the period. Private enterprises are not required to report comprehensive income or loss.
	2. *Statement of changes in equity.* This statement reports the changes to various components of equity, including contributed capital, retained earnings, and accumulated other comprehensive income or loss.	2. *Statement of retained earnings.* This statement reports the changes to retained earnings during the period, which result primarily from net earnings and dividends.
	3. *Statement of financial position.* Some publicly accountable enterprises have continued to use the title "balance sheet" after adopting IFRS.	3. *Balance sheet*
	4. *Statement of cash flows*	4. *Statement of cash flows*
	Publicly accountable enterprises must use IFRS for external reporting.	Private enterprises may use IFRS for external reporting. They may also choose to follow neither IFRS nor ASPE, particularly if they are not dependent on significant external sources of financing for their operations.

DEMONSTRATION **CASE**

At the end of most chapters, one or more demonstration cases are presented. These cases provide an overview of the primary issues discussed in the chapter. Each demonstration case is followed by a recommended solution. You should read the case carefully and then prepare your own solution before you study the recommended solution. *This self-evaluation is highly recommended.* The introductory case presented here reviews the elements reported on the statement of earnings and statement of financial position and how the elements within each are related.

Shoppers Drug Mart Corporation is Canada's leading drugstore chain, with more than 1,250 licensed drugstores operating under the name Shoppers Drug Mart (Pharmaprix in Quebec). Following is a list of the financial statement items and amounts adapted from recent statements of earnings and financial position. The numbers are presented in millions of dollars for the year ended December 29, 2012.

Cash	$ 105	Property and equipment	$ 1,734
Cost of sales	6,609	Retained earnings	2,881
Goodwill	2,913	Sales revenues	10,782
Income tax expense	215	Contributed capital	1,442
Income tax payable	65	Short-term borrowings	421
Interest expense	58	Total assets	7,474
Inventories	2,148	Total pretax expenses	9,959
Long-term borrowings	871	Total liabilities	3,151
Net earnings	608	Total liabilities and shareholders'	
Operating and administrative	3,292	equity	7,474
expenses	62	Total shareholders' equity	4,323
Other assets	587	Trade payables	1,207
Other long-term liabilities	42	Trade receivables	470
Prepayments			

Required:

1. Prepare a statement of financial position and a statement of earnings for the year, following the formats in Exhibits 1.2 and 1.3.

2. Specify what information these two statements provide.

3. Indicate the other two statements that would be included in Shoppers Drug Mart's annual report.

4. Securities regulations require that the financial statements of Shoppers Drug Mart be subject to an independent audit. Suggest why Shoppers Drug Mart might voluntarily subject its financial statements to an independent audit if there were no such requirement.

SUGGESTED **SOLUTION**

1.

SHOPPERS DRUG MART CORPORATION
Statement of Earnings
For the Year Ended December 29, 2012
(in millions of Canadian dollars)

Sales revenues	$10,782
Expenses	
Cost of sales	6,609
Operating and administrative expenses	3,292
Interest expense	58
Total pretax expenses	9,959
Earnings before income tax	823
Income tax expense	(215)
Net earnings	$ 608

SHOPPERS DRUG MART CORPORATION
Statement of Financial Position
At December 29, 2012
(in millions of Canadian dollars)

Assets	
Cash	$ 105
Trade receivables	470
Inventories	2,148
Prepayments	42
Property and equipment	1,734
Goodwill	2,913
Other assets	62
Total assets	$7,474
Liabilities	
Trade payables	1,207
Short-term borrowings	421
Income tax payable	65
Long-term borrowings	871
Other long-term liabilities	587
Total liabilities	3,151
Shareholders' equity	
Contributed capital	1,442
Retained earnings	2,881
Total shareholders' equity	4,323
Total liabilities and shareholders' equity	$7,474

2. The statement of financial position reports the amount of assets, liabilities, and shareholders' equity of an accounting entity at a point in time. The statement of earnings reports the accountant's primary measure of performance of a business, revenues less expenses, during the accounting period.

3. Shoppers Drug Mart Corporation would also present a statement of changes in equity and a statement of cash flows.

4. Users will have greater confidence in the accuracy of financial statement information if they know that the people who audited the statements were required to meet professional standards of ethics and competence.

Epilogue: Shoppers Drug Mart Corporation was acquired by Loblaw Companies Limited in 2013.

APPENDIX 1A: TYPES OF BUSINESS ENTITIES

This textbook emphasizes *accounting for profit-making business entities.* The three main types of business entities are sole proprietorship, partnership, and corporation. Specific aspects of the three types of business entities are compared in Exhibit 1.9. A *sole proprietorship* is an unincorporated business owned by one person; it is usually small in size and is common in the service, retailing, and farming industries. Often the owner is the manager. Legally, the business and the owner are not separate entities. However, accounting views the business as a separate entity that must be accounted for separately from its owner.

A *partnership* is an unincorporated business owned by two or more persons known as *partners.* Some partnerships are large in size (e.g., international public accounting firms and law firms). The agreements between the owners are specified in a partnership contract that deals with matters such as division of profit among partners and distribution of resources of the business on termination of its operations. A partnership is not legally separate from its owners. Legally, each partner in a general partnership is responsible for the debts of the business (each general partner has *unlimited liability*). The partnership, however, is a separate business entity to be accounted for separately from its several owners.

A *corporation* is a business incorporated federally under the *Canada Business Corporations Act* or provincially under similar provincial acts. The owners are called shareholders or stockholders. Ownership is represented by shares of capital that usually can be bought and sold freely. When an approved application for incorporation is filed by the organizers, a charter is issued by either the federal or the provincial government. This charter gives the corporation the right to operate as a legal entity, separate from its owners. The shareholders enjoy *limited liability.* Shareholders cannot lose more than they paid for their shares. The corporate charter specifies the types and amounts of share capital that can be issued. Most provinces require a minimum of two shareholders and a minimum amount of resources to be contributed at the time of organization. The shareholders elect a governing board of directors, which in turn employs managers and exercises general supervision of the corporation.

Exhibit **1.9**

Comparison of Three Types of
Business Entities

	Proprietorship	Partnership	Corporation
Number of owners	One owner	Two or more owners	Many owners
Legal status of entity	Not separate from that of its owner	Not separate from that of its owners	Separate legal entity
Responsibility of owners for debts of business entity	Unlimited legal liability	Unlimited legal liability	Owners' liability limited to their investment
Accounting status	Each entity is separate from its owners for accounting purposes.		

Members of the board of directors, executives, and officers of companies, as well as employees do not enjoy limited liability for any damage caused by their willful wrong-doing. Because a corporation is considered a legally separate entity, directors and executives may find themselves being sued for damages by their employer. Accounting also views the corporation as a separate business entity that must be accounted for separately from its owners.

In terms of economic importance, the corporation is the dominant form of business organization in Canada. This dominance is caused by the many advantages of the corporate form: (1) limited liability for the shareholders, (2) continuity of life, (3) ease in transferring ownership (shares), and (4) opportunities to raise large amounts of money by selling shares to a large number of people. The primary disadvantages of a corporation are (1) loss of control by shareholders, (2) complex reporting procedures for a variety of government agencies, and (3) potential for double taxation of earnings (they are taxed when they are earned and again when they are distributed to shareholders as dividends). In this textbook, we emphasize the corporate form of business. Nevertheless, the accounting concepts and procedures that we discuss also apply to other types of businesses. The main differences among these three types of entities appear in the equity section of the statement of financial position.

APPENDIX 1B: EMPLOYMENT IN THE ACCOUNTING PROFESSION TODAY

Since 1900, accounting has attained the stature of professions such as law, medicine, engineering, and architecture. As with all recognized professions, accounting is subject to professional competence requirements, is dedicated to service to the public, requires a high level of academic study, and rests on a common body of knowledge. As indicated earlier, the Canadian accounting designations are granted only on completion of requirements specified by the respective professional accounting organizations. Although specific requirements vary among the professional organizations, they include a university degree with a specified number of accounting courses, good character, a minimum of two years of relevant professional experience, and successful completion of a professional examination. Currently, all accountants must be licensed by the government to engage in professional practice, and they must meet ongoing tests of competence to retain their licence. Similar accounting designations exist in other countries, most notably the Certified Public Accountant (CPA) in the United States.

Accountants are usually engaged in professional practice or employed by businesses, government entities, and not-for-profit organizations. The accounting profession is continuously changing. While many accountants still provide traditional accounting and tax services to businesses, individual clients, and government organizations, other areas of practice have become increasingly common in the accounting profession today. Demand for value-added accounting services (e.g., financial analysis, evaluation and implementation of new information technology and business processes, management advisory and consulting services, forensic accounting, and environmental accounting) is reshaping the nature of educational programs that prepare students to become professional accountants.[18]

Practice of Public Accounting

Although an individual may practise public accounting, usually two or more individuals organize an accounting firm in the form of a partnership (in many cases, a limited liability partnership, or LLP). Accounting firms vary in size from a one-person office to regional firms to the "Big Four" firms (Deloitte & Touche, Ernst & Young, KPMG, and PricewaterhouseCoopers), which have hundreds of offices worldwide. Accounting firms usually render three types of services: audit or assurance services, management consulting services, and tax services.

Audit or Assurance Services Audit or assurance services are independent professional services that improve the quality of information or its context for decision makers. The most important assurance service performed by professional accountants in public practice is financial statement auditing. The purpose of an audit is to lend credibility to the financial reports, that is, to ensure that they fairly represent what they claim. An audit involves an examination of the financial reports (prepared by the management of the entity) to ensure that they conform to the applicable accounting standards. Other areas of assurance services include integrity and security of electronic commerce and reliability of information systems.

Management Consulting Services Many independent accounting firms offer management consulting services. These services are usually accounting based and encompass such activities as the design and installation of accounting, data processing, and profit-planning and control (budget) systems; financial advice; forecasting; internal controls; cost-effectiveness studies; and operational analysis. To maintain their independence, professional accountants are prohibited from performing certain consulting services for the public companies that they audit.

Tax Services Accountants in public practice usually provide income tax services to their clients. These services include both tax planning as a part of the decision-making process and the determination of the income tax liability (reported on the annual income tax return). Because of the increasing complexity of provincial and federal tax laws, a high level of competence is required, which accountants specializing in taxation can provide. The accountant's involvement in tax planning is often quite significant. Most major business decisions have significant tax impacts; in fact, tax-planning considerations often govern certain business decisions.

Employment by Organizations

Many accountants, including CAs, CGAs, CMAs, and CPAs, are employed by profit-making, not-for-profit, and government organizations. An organization, depending on its size and complexity, may employ from a few to hundreds of accountants. In a business enterprise, the chief financial officer (usually a vice-president or controller) is a member of the management team. This responsibility usually entails a wide range of management, financial, and accounting duties.

In a business entity, accountants are typically engaged in a wide variety of activities, such as general management, general accounting, cost accounting, profit planning and control (budgeting), internal auditing, and computerized data processing. A primary function of the accountants in organizations is to provide data that are useful for internal managerial decision making and for controlling operations. The functions of external reporting, tax planning, control of assets, and a host of related responsibilities are normally also performed by accountants in industry.

Employment in the Public and Not-for-Profit Sectors

The vast and complex operations of governmental units, from the local to the international level, create a need for accountants. The same holds true for other not-for-profit organizations, such as charitable organizations, hospitals, and universities. Accountants employed in the public and not-for-profit sectors perform functions similar to those performed by their counterparts in private organizations.

A survey of positions occupied by accounting professionals and related salaries is available at www.accountemps.com.

CHAPTER **TAKE-AWAYS**

1. **Recognize the information conveyed in each of the four basic financial statements and how it is used by different decision makers (investors, creditors, and managers).**

   The *statement of financial position* reports financial values for assets, liabilities, and shareholders' equity at a specific point in time.

   The *statement of comprehensive income* reports the net earnings (revenues minus expenses) for a period, as well as changes in equity during that period, except those resulting from exchanges with owners.

   The *statement of changes in equity* reports the way that net earnings, the distribution of net earnings (dividends), and other changes to shareholders' equity affected the company's financial position during a specific period.

   The *statement of cash flows* reports inflows and outflows of cash for a specific period.

   The statements are used by investors and creditors to evaluate different aspects of the firm's financial position and performance.

2. **Identify the role of International Financial Reporting Standards (IFRS) in determining the content of financial statements.**

   IFRS are the broad principles, specific rules, and practices used to develop and report the information in financial statements. Knowledge of IFRS is necessary to accurately interpret the numbers in financial statements.

3. **Identify the roles of managers and auditors in the accounting communication process.**

   Management has primary responsibility for the accuracy of a company's financial information. Auditors are responsible for expressing an opinion on the fairness of the financial statement presentations based on their examination of the reports and records of the company.

4. **Appreciate the importance of ethics, reputation, and legal liability in accounting.**

   Users will have confidence in the accuracy of financial statement numbers only if the people associated with their preparation and audit have reputations for ethical behaviour and competence. Management and auditors can also be held legally liable for fraudulent financial statements and malpractice.

   In this chapter, we studied the basic financial statements that communicate financial information to external users. Chapters 2, 3, 4, and 5 will provide a more detailed look at financial statements and examine how to translate data about business transactions into these statements. Learning the relationship between business transactions and financial statements is the key to using financial statements in planning and decision making. Chapter 2 begins our discussion of how the accounting function collects data about business transactions and processes the data to provide periodic financial statements, with emphasis on the statement of financial position. To accomplish this purpose, Chapter 2 discusses key accounting concepts, the accounting model, transaction analysis, and analytical tools. We examine typical business activities of Sun-Rype to demonstrate the concepts in Chapters 2, 3, and 4.

FINDING **FINANCIAL INFORMATION**

STATEMENT OF FINANCIAL POSITION

Assets = Liabilities + Shareholders' Equity

STATEMENT OF COMPREHENSIVE INCOME

$$\begin{array}{r} \text{Revenues} \\ -\quad \text{Expenses} \\ \hline \text{Net earnings} \\ +/-\quad \text{Other comprehensive income/loss} \\ \hline \text{Comprehensive income (loss)} \end{array}$$

STATEMENT OF CHANGES IN EQUITY

$$\begin{array}{r} \text{Equity, beginning of the period} \\ +\quad \text{Net earnings} \\ +/-\quad \text{Other comprehensive income/loss} \\ -\quad \text{Dividends} \\ +/-\quad \text{Other changes, net} \\ \hline \text{Equity, end of the period} \end{array}$$

STATEMENT OF CASH FLOWS

$$\begin{array}{r} +/-\quad \text{Cash flows from operating activities} \\ +/-\quad \text{Cash flows from investing activities} \\ +/-\quad \text{Cash flows from financing activities} \\ \hline \text{Change in Cash} \end{array}$$

connect GLOSSARY

Review key terms and definitions on *Connect.*

QUESTIONS

1. Define *accounting.*
2. Briefly distinguish financial accounting from managerial accounting.
3. The accounting process generates financial reports for both internal and external users. Identify some of the groups of users.
4. Briefly distinguish investors from creditors.
5. What is an accounting entity? Why is a business treated as a separate entity for accounting purposes?
6. What information should be included in the heading of each of the four primary financial statements?
7. What are the purposes of (a) the statement of earnings, (b) the statement of financial position, (c) the statement of cash flows, and (d) the statement of changes in equity?
8. Explain why the statement of earnings and statement of cash flows are dated, e.g.,"For the Year Ended December 31, 2014," whereas the statement of financial position is dated, e.g., "At December 31, 2014."
9. Briefly explain the importance of assets and liabilities to the decisions of investors and creditors.
10. Briefly define *net earnings* and *net loss.*
11. Explain the accounting equation for the statement of earnings. Define the three major items reported on the statement of earnings.
12. Explain the accounting equation for the statement of financial position. Define the three major components reported on the statement of financial position.
13. Explain the accounting equation for the statement of cash flows. Explain the three major components reported on the statement.
14. Explain the accounting equation for retained earnings. Explain the major items that affect the ending balance of retained earnings.
15. Financial statements discussed in this chapter are aimed at *external* users. Briefly explain how a company's *internal* managers in different functional areas (e.g., marketing, purchasing, human resources) might use financial statement information from their own or other companies.
16. Briefly describe how accounting standards are determined in Canada, including the roles of the ACSB and the OSC.
17. Briefly explain the responsibility of company management, the board of directors, and the independent auditors in the internal control and financial reporting process.
18. (Appendix 1A) Briefly differentiate among a sole proprietorship, a partnership, and a corporation.
19. (Appendix 1B) List and briefly explain the three primary services that accountants in public practice provide.

connect EXERCISES

■ LO1

E1–1

Leon's Furniture Ltd.

Preparing a Statement of Financial Position

Leon's Furniture Ltd. is one of Canada's largest retailers, selling a wide range of merchandise, including furniture, major appliances, and home electronics. A recent statement of financial position contained the following items (in millions). Prepare a statement of financial position as at December 31, 2012, solving for the missing amount.

Cash and cash equivalents	$ 75
Dividends payable	7
Intangible assets and goodwill	14
Inventories	86
Net property, plant, and equipment	218
Noncurrent liabilities	18
Other assets	11
Other current assets	152
Other current liabilities	35
Retained earnings	425
Contributed capital	27
Total assets	586
Total liabilities and shareholders' equity	?
Trade receivables	30
Trade and other payables	74

E1–2 Completing a Statement of Financial Position and Inferring Net Earnings   ▌LO1

Terry Lloyd and Joan Lopez organized Read More Store as a corporation; each contributed $50,000 cash to start the business and received 4,000 shares of capital. The store completed its first year of operations on December 31, 2014. On that date, the following financial items were determined: cash on hand and in the bank, $48,900; amounts due from customers from sales of books, $25,000; unused portion of store and office equipment, $49,000; amounts owed to publishers for books purchased, $7,000; one-year note for $3,000, signed on January 15, 2014, and payable to a local bank. No dividends were declared or paid to the shareholders during the year.

Required:

1. Complete the following statement of financial position as at December 31, 2014.
2. What was the amount of net earnings for the year?

	Assets		**Liabilities**	
Cash	$_____	Trade payables	$_____	
Trade receivables	_____	Note payable	_____	
Store and office equipment	_____	Interest payable	120	
		Total liabilities		$_____
		Shareholders' Equity		
		Contributed capital	$_____	
		Retained earnings	12,780	
		Total shareholders' equity	_____	
		Total liabilities and shareholders' equity		
Total assets	$_____			$_____

E1–3 Analyzing Revenues and Expenses and Preparing a Statement of Earnings   ▌LO1

Assume that you are the owner of The University Shop, which specializes in items that interest students. At the end of September 2015, you find (for September only) the following:

a. Sales, per the cash register tapes, of $119,000, plus one sale on credit (a special situation) of $1,000.

b. With the help of a friend (who majored in accounting), you determined that all of the goods sold during September had cost $40,000 to purchase.

c. During the month, according to the cheque book, you paid $38,000 for salaries, rent, supplies, advertising, and other expenses; however, you have not yet paid the $600 monthly utilities for September.

Required:

On the basis of the data given, what was the amount of net earnings for September (disregard income taxes)? Show computations. (*Hint:* A convenient form to use has the following major side captions: Revenue from Sales, Expenses, and the difference—Net Earnings for the period.)

■ **LO1**

Corus Entertainment Inc.

E1–4   **Preparing a Statement of Earnings and Inferring Missing Values**

Corus Entertainment Inc. is a Canadian integrated media and entertainment company that delivers engaging, interactive, and informative content to millions of people every day. Its television services include YTV, Teletoon, and the Oprah Winfrey Network (Canada). It also owns many radio stations in the major Canadian markets. A recent annual statement of comprehensive income contained the following items (in thousands of Canadian dollars). Solve for the missing amounts and prepare a condensed statement of earnings for the year ended August 31, 2012. (*Hint:* First order the items as they would appear on the statement of earnings and then solve for the missing values.)

Cost of sales	$417,015
Interest expense	52,269
Net earnings	156,151
Revenues	?
General and administrative expenses	135,282
Depreciation expense	25,639
Income tax expense	57,242
Total expenses excluding income taxes	?
Earnings before income tax	?

■ **LO1**

E1–5   **Analyzing Revenues and Expenses and Completing a Statement of Earnings**

Home Realty Inc. has been operating for three years and is owned by three investors. J. Doe owns 60 percent of the 9,000 shares that are outstanding and is the managing executive in charge. On December 31, 2014, the following financial items for the entire year were determined: commissions earned and collected in cash, $150,000; rental service fees earned and collected, $15,000; expenses paid including salaries, $62,000; commissions, $35,000; payroll taxes, $2,500; rent, $2,200; utilities, $1,600; promotion and advertising, $8,000; income taxes, $18,500; and miscellaneous expenses, $500. At December 31, $16,000 of commissions were earned but not collected, and the rent for December ($200) was not paid. Complete the following statement of earnings:

_____		
_____		
_____		
Revenues		
Commissions	$ _____	
Rental service fees	_____	
Total revenues		$ _____
Expenses		
Salaries	$ _____	
Commission	_____	
Payroll tax	_____	
Rent	_____	
Utilities	_____	
Promotion and advertising	_____	
Miscellaneous	_____	
Total expenses (excluding income taxes)		_____
Earnings before income taxes		$ _____
Income tax expense		_____
Net earnings		$ _____

E1–6 Inferring Values by Using the Statement of Earnings and Statement of Financial Position Equations ■ LO1

Review the chapter explanations of the statement of earnings and the statement of financial position equations. Apply these equations in each independent case to compute the two missing amounts for each case. Assume that it is the end of 2013, the first full year of operations for the company.

(*Hint:* Organize the listed items as they are presented in the statement of financial position and statement of earnings equations and then compute the missing amounts.)

Independent Cases	Total Revenues	Total Expenses	Net Earnings (Loss)	Total Assets	Total Liabilities	Shareholders' Equity
A	$91,700	$76,940		$140,200	$69,000	
B		74,240	$14,740	107,880		$79,010
C	69,260	76,430		97,850	69,850	
D	58,680		21,770		17,890	78,680
E	84,840	78,720			25,520	79,580

E1–7 Preparing a Statement of Earnings and a Statement of Financial Position ■ LO1

Ducharme Corporation was organized by five individuals on January 1, 2014. At the end of January 2014, the following monthly financial data are available:

Total revenues	$299,000
Total expenses (excluding income taxes)	189,000
Income tax expense (all unpaid as at January 31)	34,500
Cash balance, January 31, 2014	65,150
Receivables from customers (all considered collectible)	34,500
Merchandise inventory (by inventory count at cost)	96,600
Payables to suppliers for merchandise purchased from them (will be paid during February 2014)	26,450
Contributed capital (2,600 shares)	59,800
No dividends declared in January 2014	

Required:

1. Prepare a summarized statement of earnings for the month of January 2014.
2. Prepare a statement of financial position at January 31, 2014.

E1–8 Computing Ending Balance of Retained Earnings ■ LO1

Sultan Inc. was organized on January 1, 2014. It reported the following for its first two years of operations:

Net earnings for 2014	$ 31,000
Dividends for 2014	14,200
Total shareholders' equity at end of 2014	130,000
Net earnings for 2015	42,000
Dividends for 2015	18,700
Total shareholders' equity at end of 2015	250,000

Required:

Compute the ending balance of retained earnings for Sultan Inc. as at December 31, 2015. Show computations.

■ LO1

E1–9 **Analyzing and Interpreting a Statement of Earnings**

Pest Away Corporation was organized by three individuals on January 1, 2014, to provide insect extermination services. At the end of 2014, the following statement of earnings was prepared:

PEST AWAY CORPORATION
Statement of Earnings
For the Year Ended December 31, 2014

Revenues		
Service revenue (cash)	$192,000	
Service revenue (credit)	24,000	
Total revenues		$216,000
Expenses		
Salaries	$ 76,000	
Rent	21,000	
Utilities	12,000	
Advertising	14,000	
Supplies	25,000	
Interest	8,000	
Total expenses		156,000
Earnings before income tax		$ 60,000
Income tax expense		21,000
Net earnings for the year		$ 39,000

Required:

1. What was the average amount of monthly revenue?
2. What was the amount of monthly rent?
3. Explain why supplies are reported as an expense.
4. Explain why interest is reported as an expense.
5. What was the average income tax rate for Pest Away Corporation?
6. Can you determine how much cash the company had on December 31, 2014? Explain.

■ LO1

Saputo Inc.

E1–10 **Focusing on Cash Flows: Matching Cash Flow Items to Categories**

Saputo Inc. is a Canadian company that produces, markets, and distributes a wide variety of products to customers in over 50 countries. Its products include cheese, fluid milk, yogurt, dairy ingredients, and snack cakes. The following items were taken from its recent statement of cash flows. Note that different companies use slightly different titles for the same item. Without referring to Exhibit 1.5, mark each item in the list as a cash flow from operating activities (O), investing activities (I), or financing activities (F). Place parentheses around the letter only if it is a cash outflow.

_____ (1) Cash paid to suppliers

_____ (2) Cash received from customers

_____ (3) Dividends paid

_____ (4) Issuance of share capital

_____ (5) Interest paid

_____ (6) Proceeds from disposal of investment

_____ (7) Purchases of property, plant, and equipment

_____ (8) Repurchase of share capital

■ LO1

E1–11 **Preparing a Statement of Cash Flows**

NITSU Manufacturing Corporation is preparing the annual financial statements for its shareholders. A statement of cash flows must be prepared. The following data on cash flows were developed for the entire year ended December 31, 2014: cash inflow from operating revenues, $270,000; cash expended for operating expenses, $180,000; sale of unissued NITSU shares for cash, $30,000; cash dividends declared and paid to shareholders during the year, $22,000; and payments on long-term borrowings,

$80,000. During the year, a tract of land was sold for $15,000 cash (which was the same price that NITSU had paid for the land in 2013), and $38,000 cash was expended for two new machines. The machines were used in the factory. The beginning-of-the-year cash balance was $63,000.

Required:

Prepare a statement of cash flows for 2014. Follow the format illustrated in the chapter.

PROBLEMS

P1–1 Preparing a Statement of Earnings and a Statement of Financial Position (AP1–1)

■ LO1

Assume that you are the president of Nuclear Company. At December 31, 2014, the end of the first year of operations, the following financial data for the company are available:

Cash	$ 25,000
Receivables from customers (all considered collectible)	12,000
Inventory of merchandise (based on physical count and priced at cost)	90,000
Equipment owned, at cost less used portion	45,000
Payables to suppliers of merchandise	47,370
Salary payable for 2014 (on December 31, 2014, this was owed to an employee, but the amount was not paid until January 10, 2015)	2,000
Total sales revenue	140,000
Expenses, including the cost of the merchandise sold (excluding income taxes)	89,100
Income taxes expense (at 30% of pretax earnings); all paid during 2014	?
Contributed capital, 7,000 shares outstanding	87,000
No dividends were declared or paid during 2014.	

Required (show computations):

1. Prepare a summarized statement of earnings for the year ended December 31, 2014.
2. Prepare a statement of financial position at December 31, 2014.

P1–2 Analyzing a Student's Business, and Preparing a Statement of Earnings and a Statement of Financial Position (AP1–2)

■ LO1

Upon graduation from high school, William Nitter accepted a job as a plumber's assistant for a large local plumbing company. After three years of hard work, William received a plumbing licence and decided to start his own business. He had saved $24,000, which he invested in the business. His lawyer had advised him to start as a corporation. First, he transferred the $24,000 from his savings account to a business bank account for William's Plumbing Services Inc. and was issued shares. He then purchased a used panel truck for $18,000 cash and second-hand tools for $3,000, rented space in a small building, inserted an advertisement in the local paper, and opened his business on July 1, 2014. Immediately, William was very busy; after one month, he employed an assistant.

Although William knew practically nothing about the financial side of the business, he realized that a number of reports were required and that expenses and collections from clients had to be controlled carefully. At December 31, 2014, prompted in part by concern about his income tax situation, William recognized the need for financial statements. His wife, Jennifer, developed some financial statements for the business. On December 31, 2014, with the help of a friend, she gathered the following data for the six months just ended. Bank account deposits of collections for plumbing services totalled $64,000. The following cheques had been written: plumber's assistant, $17,000; payroll taxes, $750; oil, gas, and maintenance for the truck, $2,400; rent, $2,500; supplies purchased and used on jobs, $17,100; utilities and telephone, $1,850; insurance, $700 for the past six months; and miscellaneous expenses (including advertising), $900. Also, uncollected invoices to customers for plumbing services amounted to $6,000. The $500 rent for December had not been paid. William estimated the cost of using the truck and tools (depreciation) during the three months to be $2,400. The average income tax rate for income from his business is 30 percent.

Required:

1. Prepare a statement of earnings for William's Plumbing Services Inc. for the six months of July through December 2014. Use the following main captions: Revenue from services, Expenses, Earnings before income taxes, and Net earnings.

2. Prepare a statement of financial position for William's Plumbing Services Inc. as at December 31, 2014.

3. Do you think that William may have a need for one or more additional financial reports for 2014 and thereafter? Explain.

■ LO1

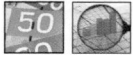

P1–3 **Comparing Net Earnings with Cash Flow (A Challenging Problem)** (AP1–3)

Choice Chicken Company was organized on January 1, 2014. At the end of the first quarter (three months) of operations, the owner prepared a summary of its activities as shown in the first row of the following tabulation:

Summary of Transactions	Computation of	
	Net earnings	Cash
a. Services performed for customers, $85,000, of which $15,000 remained uncollected at the end of the quarter.	+$85,000	+$70,000
b. Cash borrowed from the local bank, $25,000 (one-year note).		
c. Small service truck purchased at the end of the quarter to be used in the business for two years starting the next quarter: cost, $8,000 cash.		
d. Wages earned by employees, $36,000, of which one-sixth remained unpaid at the end of the quarter.		
e. Service supplies purchased for use in the business, $4,000 cash, of which $1,000 were unused (still on hand) at the end of the quarter.		
f. Other operating expenses, $31,000, of which one-half remained unpaid at the end of the quarter.		

Based only on these transactions, compute the following for the quarter:
  Net earnings (or loss)
  Cash inflow (or outflow)		

Required:

1. For each of the six transactions given in this tabulation, enter what you consider the correct amounts. Enter a zero when appropriate. The first transaction is illustrated.

2. For each transaction, explain the basis for your responses.

■ LO1

P1–4 **Evaluating Data to Support a Loan Application (A Challenging Problem)**

On January 1, 2016, three individuals organized West Company as a corporation. Each individual invested $10,000 cash in the business. On December 31, 2016, they prepared a list of resources owned (assets) and a list of debts (liabilities) to support the company's request for a loan of $70,000 submitted to a local bank. None of the three investors had studied accounting. The two lists prepared were as follows:

Company resources	
Cash	$ 12,000
Service supplies inventory (on hand)	7,000
Service trucks (four practically new)	68,000
Personal residences of organizers (three houses)	190,000
Service equipment used in the business (practically new)	30,000
Amounts due from customers (for services already completed)	15,000
Total	$322,000
Company obligations	
Unpaid wages to employees	$ 19,000
Unpaid taxes	8,000
Owed to suppliers	10,000
Owed on service trucks and equipment (to a finance company)	50,000
Loan from organizer	15,000
Total	$102,000

Required:

Prepare a short memo indicating the following:

1. Which of these items do not belong on the statement of financial position (bear in mind that the company is considered to be separate from the owners)?

2. What additional questions would you raise about measurement of items on the lists? Explain the basis for each question.

3. If you were advising the local bank on its loan decision, which amounts on the lists would create special concerns? Explain the basis for each concern and include any recommendations that you have.

4. In view of your responses to (1) and (2), calculate the amount of shareholders' equity as at December 31, 2016. Show your computations.

P1–5 Using Financial Reports: Applying the Accounting Equation to Liquidate a Company   ■ LO1

On June 1, 2015, Bland Corporation prepared a statement of financial position just prior to going out of business. The totals for the three main components showed the following:

Assets (no cash)	$90,000
Liabilities	50,000
Shareholders' equity	40,000

Shortly thereafter, all of the assets were sold for cash.

Required:

1. How would the statement of financial position appear immediately after the sale of the assets for cash for each of the following cases? Use the format given here.

	Cash Received for the Assets	Assets	–	Liabilities	=	Shareholders' Equity
			Balances Immediately after Sale			
Case A	$ 90,000	$ _____	$ _____			$ _____
Case B	80,000	$ _____	$ _____			$ _____
Case C	100,000	$ _____	$ _____			$ _____
Case D	35,000	$ _____	$ _____			$ _____

2. How should the cash be distributed in each separate case? (*Hint:* Creditors must be paid in full before owners receive any payment.) Use the format given here:

	To Creditors	To Shareholders	Total
Case A	$ _____	$ _____	$ _____
Case B	$ _____	$ _____	$ _____
Case C	$ _____	$ _____	$ _____
Case D	$ _____	$ _____	$ _____

ALTERNATE PROBLEMS

AP1–1 Preparing a Statement of Earnings and a Statement of Financial Position (P1–1)   ■ LO1

Assume that you are the president of McClaren Corporation. At June 30, 2015, the end of the first year of operations, the following financial data for the company are available:

Cash	$13,150
Receivables from customers (all considered collectible)	9,500
Inventory of merchandise (based on physical count and priced at cost)	57,000
Equipment owned, at cost less used portion	36,000
Payables to suppliers of merchandise	31,500
Salary payable for 2015 (on June 30, 2015, this was owed to an employee, but the amount was not paid until July 7, 2015)	1,500
Total sales revenue	90,000
Expenses, including the cost of the merchandise sold (excluding income taxes)	60,500
Income taxes expense (at 30% of pretax earnings); all paid during 2015	?
Contributed capital, 5,000 shares outstanding	?
No dividends were declared or paid during 2015.	

Required (show computations):

1. Prepare a summarized statement of earnings for the year ended June 30, 2015.
2. Prepare a statement of financial position as at June 30, 2015.

LO1

AP1–2   **Analyzing a Student's Business, and Preparing a Statement of Earnings and a Statement of Financial Position (P1–2)**

While pursuing his undergraduate studies, Bruno Clarke needed to earn sufficient money for the coming academic year. Unable to obtain a job with a reasonable salary, he decided to try the lawn care business for three months during the summer. After a survey of the market potential, Bruno bought a used pick-up truck on June 1 for $3,000. On each door he painted "Bruno's Lawn Service, Tel: 555-9623." He also spent $1,800 for mowers, trimmers, and tools. To acquire these items, he borrowed $5,000 cash by signing a note payable, promising to pay the $5,000 plus interest of $150 at the end of the three months (ending August 31).

At the end of the summer, Bruno realized that he had done a lot of work, and his bank account looked good. This fact prompted him to become concerned about how much profit the business had earned.

A review of the cheque stubs showed the following: bank deposits of collections from customers totalled $25,200. The following cheques had been written: gas, oil, and lubrication, $1,840; mower repair, $150; helpers, $9,500; payroll taxes, $400; truck repairs, $410; payment for assistance in preparing payroll tax forms, $50; insurance, $240; telephone, $210; miscellaneous supplies used, $160; and $5,150 to pay off the note, including interest (on August 31). A notebook kept in the truck, plus some unpaid bills, reflected that customers still owed him $1,250 for lawn services rendered and that he owed $200 for gas and oil (credit card charges). He estimated that the cost for use of the truck and the other equipment (depreciation) for three months amounted to $1,000.

Required:

1. Prepare a quarterly statement of earnings for Bruno's Lawn Service for the months of June, July, and August 2014. Use the following main captions: Revenues from services, Expenses, and Net earnings. Because this is a sole proprietorship, the company will not be subject to income tax.
2. Prepare a statement of financial position for Bruno's Lawn Service as at August 31, 2014. Bruno's business is a proprietorship with one equity item: Bruno Clarke, capital.
3. Do you see a need for one or more additional financial reports for this business for 2014 and thereafter? Explain.

LO1

AP1–3   **Comparing Net Earnings with Cash Flow (A Challenging Problem) (P1–3)**

New Delivery Company was organized on January 1, 2015. At the end of the first quarter (three months) of operations, the owner prepared a summary of its operations as shown in the first row of the following tabulation:

	Computation of	
Summary of Transactions	**Net Earnings**	**Cash**
a. Services performed for customers, $66,000, of which one-sixth remained uncollected at the end of the quarter.	$66,000	$55,000
b. Cash borrowed from the local bank, $45,000 (one-year note).		
c. Small service truck purchased at the end of the quarter to be used in the business for two years starting the next quarter: cost, $9,500; paid 20% down, balance on credit.		
d. Wages earned by employees, $21,000, of which one-half remained unpaid at the end of the quarter.		
e. Service supplies purchased for use in the business, $3,800 cash, of which one-fifth were unused (still on hand) at the end of the quarter.		
f. Other operating expenses, $36,000, of which one-sixth remained unpaid at the end of the quarter.		
Based only on the above transactions, compute the following for the quarter: Net earnings (or loss) Cash inflow (or outflow)	_____	_____

Required:

1. For each of the six transactions given in this tabulation, enter what you consider to be the correct amounts. Enter a zero when appropriate. The first transaction is illustrated.
2. For each transaction, explain the basis for your responses.

CASES AND PROJECTS

FINDING AND INTERPRETING FINANCIAL INFORMATION

CP1–1 Finding Financial Information

Refer to the financial statements of Canadian Tire Corporation in Appendix A at the end of this book.

■ LO1, 3

Canadian Tire
Corporation

Required:

Look at the statement of earnings, statement of financial position, and statement of cash flows closely and attempt to infer the types of information they report. Then answer the following questions based on the report.

1. On what day of the year does Canadian Tire's fiscal year end?
2. For how many years does it present complete
   a. statements of financial position (balance sheets)?
   b. statements of earnings (or income)?
   c. statements of cash flows?
3. Are its financial statements audited by independent accountants? How do you know?
4. Did its total assets increase or decrease over the last year?
5. What was the balance of merchandise inventories at the end of the most current year?
6. Write out its basic accounting equation in Canadian dollars at year-end.

CP1–2 Finding Financial Information

Go to *Connect* for the financial statements of RONA Inc. and related notes.

■ LO1, 3

RONA Inc.

Required:

1. What is the amount of net earnings (net income) for the current fiscal year?
2. What amount of revenue was earned in the current fiscal year?
3. How much inventory does the company have at the end of the current fiscal year?
4. By what amount did cash and cash equivalents* change during the year?
5. Who is the auditor for the company?

*Cash equivalents are short-term investments that are readily convertible into cash and whose value is unlikely to change.

CP1–3 Comparing Companies

Refer to the financial statements and the accompanying notes of Canadian Tire Corporation given in Appendix A and of RONA Inc. on *Connect*.

■ LO1

Canadian Tire
Corporation vs.
RONA Inc.

Required:

1. Total assets is a common measure of the size of a company. Which company had the higher total assets at the end of the most recent year?
2. Net sales is also a common measure of the size of a company. Which company had the higher net sales for the most recent year?
3. Growth during a period is calculated as

   Growth Rate = [(Ending Amount − Beginning Amount)/Beginning Amount] × 100

   Which company had the higher growth rate in total assets during the most recent year? Which company had the higher growth rate in net sales during the most recent year?

FINANCIAL REPORTING AND ANALYSIS CASE

■ **LO1**

CP1–4   **Using Financial Reports: Identifying and Correcting Deficiencies in a Statement of Earnings and a Statement of Financial Position**

Performance Corporation was organized on January 1, 2014. At the end of 2014, the company had not yet employed an accountant; however, an employee who was "good with numbers" prepared the following statements at that date:

Performance Corporation December 31, 2014	
Income from sales of merchandise	$175,000
Total amount paid for goods sold during 2014	(90,000)
Selling costs	(25,000)
Depreciation (on service vehicles used)	(10,000)
Income from services rendered	52,000
Salaries and wages paid	(62,000)

Performance Corporation December 31, 2014		
Resources		
Cash		$ 32,000
Merchandise inventory (held for resale)		42,000
Service vehicles		50,000
Retained earnings (net earnings of 2014)		30,000
Grand total		$154,000
Debts		
Payable to suppliers		$ 22,000
Note owed to bank		25,000
Due from customers		13,000
Total		$ 60,000
Supplies on hand (to be used in rendering services)	$ 15,000	
Accumulated depreciation* (on service vehicles)	10,000	
Contributed capital, 6,500 shares	65,000	
Total		90,000
Grand total		$150,000

*Accumulated depreciation represents the cost related to the used portion of the asset and should be subtracted from the asset balance.

Required:

1. List all of the deficiencies that you can identify in these statements. Give a brief explanation of each one.

2. Prepare a proper statement of earnings for Performance Corporation for 2014 (correct net earnings is $30,000) and a proper statement of financial position at December 31, 2014 (correct total assets are $142,000).

CRITICAL THINKING CASES

■ **LO1, 3**

CP1–5   **Making Decisions as a Manager: Reporting the Assets and Liabilities of a Business**

Emmanuel Lucas owns and operates Emmanuel's Shop (a sole proprietorship). An employee prepares a financial report for the business at each year-end. This report lists all of the resources (assets) owned by Emmanuel, including such personal items as the home he owns and occupies. It also lists all of the debts of the business, but not his personal debts.

Required:

1. From an accounting point of view, do you disagree with what is being included in and excluded from the report of business assets and liabilities? Explain.

2. Upon questioning, Emmanuel responded, "Don't worry about it; we use it only to support a loan from the bank." How would you respond to this comment?

CP1–6 Making Decisions as an Owner: Deciding about a Proposed Audit

You are one of three partners who own and operate Sam's Cleaning Service. The company has been operating for 10 years. One of the other partners has always prepared the company's annual financial statements. Recently you proposed that the statements be audited each year because it would benefit the partners and preclude possible disagreements about the division of net earnings. The partner who prepares the statements proposed that his nephew Roger, who has a lot of financial experience, can do the job and at little cost. Your other partner remained silent.

Required:

1. What position would you take on the proposal? Justify your response.
2. What would you strongly recommend? Give the basis for your recommendation.

CP1–7 Evaluating an Ethical Dilemma: Ethics and Auditor Responsibilities

A key factor that an auditor provides is independence. The *codes of professional conduct* typically state that a member in public practice should be independent in fact and appearance when providing auditing and other attestation service.

Required:

Do you consider the following circumstances to suggest a lack of independence? Justify your position. (Use your imagination. Specific answers are not provided in the chapter.)

1. James Slater is a partner with a large audit firm and is assigned to the CGI audit. James owns 10 shares of CGI.
2. Maria Tsoukas has invested in a mutual fund company that owns 100,000 shares of Sears Canada Inc. She is the auditor of Sears.
3. Bob Fisher is a clerk/typist who works on the audit of the Bank of Montreal. He has just inherited 70,000 shares of the Bank of Montreal. (Bob enjoys his work and plans to continue despite his new wealth.)
4. Nancy Chen worked on weekends as the controller for a small business that a friend started. Nancy quit the job in midyear and now has no association with the company. She works full-time for a large accounting firm and has been assigned to do the audit of her friend's business.
5. Sylvia Bertone borrowed $100,000 for a home mortgage from First City National Bank. The mortgage was granted on normal credit terms. Sylvia is the partner in charge of the First City audit.

FINANCIAL REPORTING AND ANALYSIS TEAM PROJECT

CP1–8 Team Project: Examining an Annual Report

As a team, select an industry to analyze. A list of companies classified by industry can be obtained by accessing **www.fpinfomart.ca** and then choosing "Companies by Industry." You can also find a list of industries and companies within each industry via **http://ca.finance.yahoo.com/investing**. A list of industries can be obtained by clicking on "Order Annual Reports" under "Tools."

Each group member should acquire the annual report for one publicly traded company in the industry, with each member selecting a different company. (Library files, the SEDAR service at **www.sedar.com**, and the company's website are good sources.)

Required:

On an individual basis, each group member should write a short report answering the following questions about the selected company. Discuss any patterns that you observe as a team. Then, as a team, write a short report comparing and contrasting your companies, using the six attributes listed below.

1. What types of products or services does it sell?
2. On what day of the year does its fiscal year end?
3. For how many years does it present complete
   a. statements of financial position (or balance sheets)?
   b. statements of earnings and statements of comprehensive income?
   c. statements of cash flows?
4. Are its financial statements audited by independent auditors? If so, by whom?
5. Did its total assets increase or decrease over the last year?
6. Did its net earnings increase or decrease over the last year?

SOLUTIONS TO SELF-STUDY QUIZZES

Self-Study Quiz 1-1 (all amounts are in thousands of dollars)

1. Assets ($90,973) − Liabilities ($43,937) = Shareholders' Equity ($47,036).

2. L, A, A, SE, A, A, L, L, SE (reading down the columns).

Self-Study Quiz 1-2

1. E, R, E (reading down the columns).

2. Sales revenue in the amount of $152,795 is recognized because sales revenue is normally reported on the statement of earnings when the goods or services have been delivered to customers who have either paid or promised to pay for them in the future.

3. Cost of sales is $125,474 because expenses are the dollar amount of resources used up to earn revenues during the period. Only the food and beverage products that have been delivered to customers are used up. The fruits, grains, and plastic bottles still on hand are part of the asset inventory.

Self-Study Quiz 1-3

Ending Retained Earnings = Beginning Retained Earnings + Net Earnings − Dividends
                          = $29,089 + 4,503 − 2,382 = $31,210

Self-Study Quiz 1-4

1. An amount of $152,181 is recognized on the statement of cash flows because this number represents the actual cash collected from customers related to current and prior years' sales.

2. (F), (O), F, (O), (I), O.

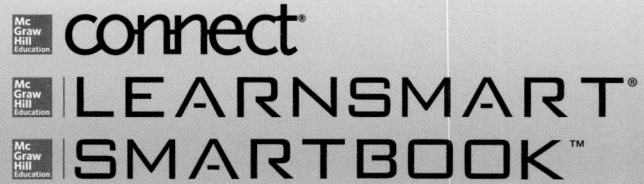

Investing and Financing Decisions and the Statement of Financial Position

After studying this chapter, you should be able to do the following:

LO1 Understand the objective of financial reporting, the qualitative characteristics of accounting information, and the related key accounting assumptions and principles.

LO2 Define the elements of a classified statement of financial position.

LO3 Identify what constitutes a business transaction, and recognize common account titles used in business.

LO4 Apply transaction analysis to simple business transactions in terms of the accounting model: Assets = Liabilities + Shareholders' Equity.

LO5 Determine the impact of business transactions on the statement of financial position by using two basic tools: journal entries and T-accounts.

LO6 Prepare a classified statement of financial position and analyze it by using the current ratio.

LO7 Identify investing and financing transactions and demonstrate how they are reported on the statement of cash flows.

FOCUS COMPANY: **Sun-Rype Products Ltd.**

EXPANSION STRATEGY IN THE FRUIT-BASED BEVERAGE INDUSTRY

Sun-Rype (www.sunrype.com), founded in 1946, produces and markets a wide assortment of fruit juices and nutritious fruit snacks. Its products are sold throughout Canada and in selected regions in the United States.

Sun-Rype has continued to grow over time to become the leading manufacturer and marketer of fruit-based food and beverage products in western Canada. The company achieved its growth through product innovation, marketing, and geographic expansion of sales. Expanding the company's sales required the acquisition of productive capacity, which was financed by both shareholders and creditors. The company's growth over time is highlighted through the increase in its assets, liabilities, and shareholders' equity, as reported on its statement of financial position at December 31, 2012, and compared to December 31, 2000. The amounts below and throughout this chapter are in thousands of Canadian dollars, except where noted.

	Assets	=	Liabilities	+	Shareholders' Equity
December 31, 2012	$91,473		$43,937		$47,536
December 31, 2000	35,231		11,433		23,798
Change	$56,242		$32,504		$23,738

Year	Sales	Total Assets
2000	94,670	35,266
2001	101,092	43,534
2002	104,071	48,764
2003	111,248	56,002
2004	115,214	60,670
2005	125,411	68,253
2006	130,641	59,447
2007	135,134	56,884
2008	125,368	73,622
2009	147,696	60,968
2010	138,185	68,375
2011	147,529	95,639
2012	152,795	91,473

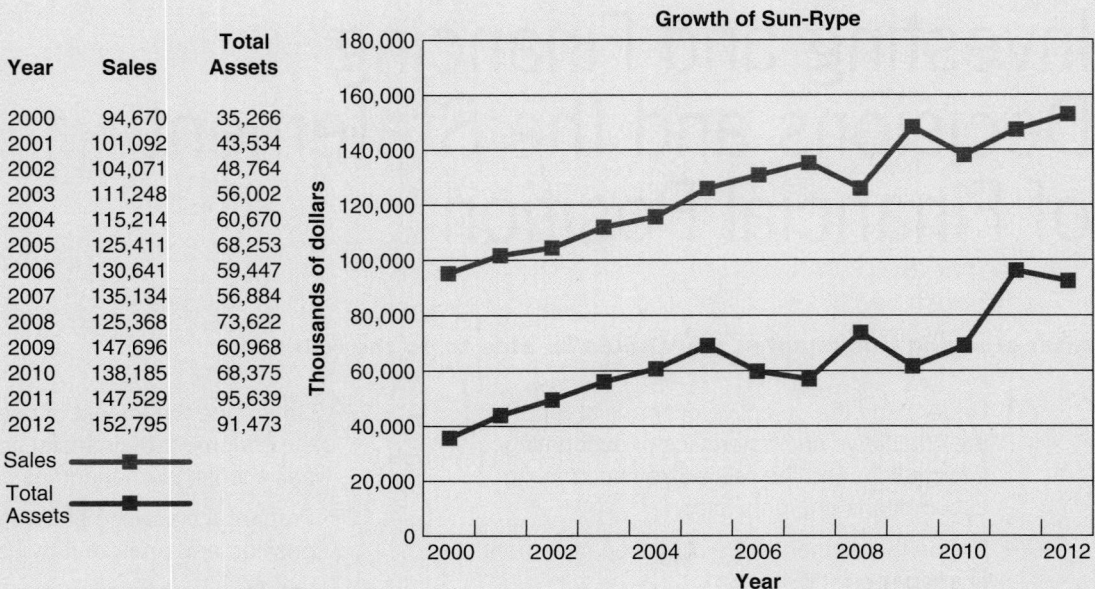

Source: Annual reports of Sun-Rype Products Ltd.

The company's annual growth in sales and total assets since 2000 are plotted on the graph.

UNDERSTANDING THE BUSINESS

Nutrition, health, and wellness are issues that concern all people. Individuals strive to get proper nutrition and be healthy for as long as possible. Governments also put effort into helping their citizens get proper nutrition so they can be productive members of society. For these reasons, nutrition, health, and wellness have attracted the attention of many businesses worldwide. A large number of companies have emerged over time to meet the needs of people seeking basic nutrition and healthy lifestyles. Although Sun-Rype is not as large as other companies that compete in the food and beverage industry, its focus on fruit-based foods and beverages has been well received by its customers.

Sun-Rype relies on a strategy of quality for both its products and its services, focusing on research and development to bring innovative products to consumers. The company's financial performance, reported in its audited financial statements, helps users to understand how well Sun-Rype has implemented its strategy in the past, and to evaluate future growth potential.

Financial statements are intended to communicate the economic facts, measured in monetary units, in a standardized, formal way. Therefore, by applying accounting principles consistently, accountants formally communicate comparable estimates that faithfully represent important economic facts about companies like Sun-Rype and its competitors. As explained in Chapter 1, financial statements include four components: the statement of financial position, the statement of comprehensive income, the statement of changes in equity, and the statement of cash flows. In this chapter, we focus on the statement of financial position, and we examine how this financial statement communicates the results or consequences of Sun-Rype's strategy by answering the following questions:

- What type of business activities cause changes in amounts reported on the statement of financial position from one period to the next?
- How do specific activities affect each of these amounts?
- How do companies keep track of these amounts?

Once we have answered these questions, we will be able to use the information on the statement of financial position to perform two key analytical tasks:

1. Analyze and predict the effects of business decisions on a company's financial statements.

2. Use the financial statements of other companies to identify and evaluate the activities that managers engaged in during a past period. This is a key task in *financial statement analysis.*

In this chapter, we focus on typical asset acquisition activities (often called *investing activities*) in which Sun-Rype engages, along with the related *financing activities*, such as borrowing funds from creditors and receiving funds from investors to acquire the assets. We examine only those activities that affect amounts reported on the statement of financial position. Operating activities that affect amounts reported on both the statement of earnings and the statement of financial position are covered in Chapters 3 and 4. Although these activities are all related, we separate them initially to aid your understanding. To begin, let us return to the basic concepts introduced in Chapter 1.

ORGANIZATION OF THE CHAPTER

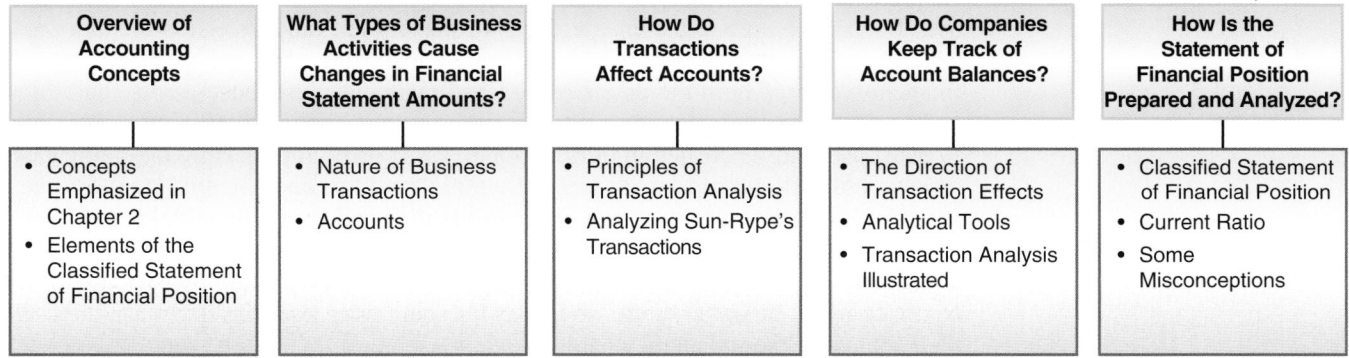

Overview of Accounting Concepts	What Types of Business Activities Cause Changes in Financial Statement Amounts?	How Do Transactions Affect Accounts?	How Do Companies Keep Track of Account Balances?	How Is the Statement of Financial Position Prepared and Analyzed?
• Concepts Emphasized in Chapter 2 • Elements of the Classified Statement of Financial Position	• Nature of Business Transactions • Accounts	• Principles of Transaction Analysis • Analyzing Sun-Rype's Transactions	• The Direction of Transaction Effects • Analytical Tools • Transaction Analysis Illustrated	• Classified Statement of Financial Position • Current Ratio • Some Misconceptions

Supplemental material:
Appendix C: The Formal Recordkeeping System (on *Connect*)

OVERVIEW OF ACCOUNTING CONCEPTS

The key accounting terms and concepts we defined in Chapter 1 are part of a theoretical framework developed over many years. The framework prescribes the nature, function, and limitations of both financial accounting and financial statements. The essential elements of this framework are embodied in the IASB *Framework for the Preparation and Presentation of Financial Statements,*[1] which identifies concepts that form the foundation for financial reporting. This framework is the subject of a major project undertaken jointly by the IASB and the Financial Accounting Standards Board (FASB) of the United States. The first phase of this project was completed in 2010, and work continues on the remaining phases.[2] This conceptual framework establishes the concepts that underlie the estimates and judgments embodied in financial statements. It also provides guidance to accounting standard setters in developing new accounting standards and in revising existing standards. Exhibit 2.1 presents an overview of the key concepts discussed in the next five chapters. An understanding of the accounting concepts will be helpful as you study because learning and remembering *how* the accounting process works is much easier if you know *why* it works a certain way. A clear understanding of these concepts will also help you in future chapters as we examine more-complex business activities.

Concepts Emphasized in Chapter 2

Objective of Financial Reporting   The **primary objective of external financial reporting** is to provide financial information about a business to help external parties, primarily investors and creditors, make sound financial decisions in their capacity

LO1

Understand the objective of financial reporting, the qualitative characteristics of accounting information, and the related key accounting assumptions and principles.

The **PRIMARY OBJECTIVE OF EXTERNAL FINANCIAL REPORTING** is to provide financial information about a business to help external parties make sound financial decisions.

Exhibit **2.1**

Financial Accounting and
Reporting—Conceptual Framework

*Concepts in red are discussed
in Chapters 1 and 2. Those in
black will be discussed in future
chapters.*

Objective of External Financial Reporting:

To provide useful economic information to external users for decision making

Qualitative characteristics of accounting information:
- Fundamental characteristics: **relevance, faithful representation**
- Enhancing characteristics: **comparability, verifiability, timeliness, understandability**

Elements to be Measured and Reported:
- **Assets, Liabilities, Equity,** Revenues, Expenses, Gains, Losses

Concepts for Measuring and Reporting Information:
- **Assumptions: Separate-Entity, Unit-of-Measure, Continuity,** Periodicity
- **Principles:** **Historical Cost,** Revenue Recognition, Full Disclosure
- **Constraints:** Cost

as capital providers. The users of accounting information are identified as *decision makers*. These decision makers include average investors, creditors, and experts who provide financial advice. They are all expected to have a reasonable understanding of accounting concepts and procedures (this may be one of the reasons you are studying accounting). Of course, as we discussed in Chapter 1, many other groups, such as suppliers and customers, also use external financial statements. To achieve this objective, financial reports must enable decision makers not only to assess the amounts, timing, and uncertainty of future cash inflows and outflows but also to understand the financial value of both the assets owned and claims against those assets (liabilities and equity).

Most users are interested in information to assist them in projecting the future cash inflows and outflows of a business. For example, creditors and potential creditors need to assess an entity's ability to pay interest over time and repay the initial amount borrowed, called the *principal*. Investors and potential investors want to assess the entity's ability to pay dividends in the future. They also want to evaluate how successful the company might be in the future, so that as the share price rises, investors can then sell their shares for more than they paid.

Qualitative Characteristics of Accounting Information   To fulfill the primary objective of providing useful information, the conceptual framework provides guidance on the essential characteristics that determine the usefulness of accounting information. There are two fundamental qualitative characteristics—relevance and faithful representation—supported by four enhancing qualitative characteristics: comparability, verifiability, timeliness, and understandability.[3] Accounting information that embodies the best balance of these characteristics will be of high quality to external decision makers. These six characteristics are presented in Exhibit 2.2 and discussed below along with important constraints on accounting measurement.[4]

Exhibit **2.2**

Qualitative Characteristics of
Accounting Information

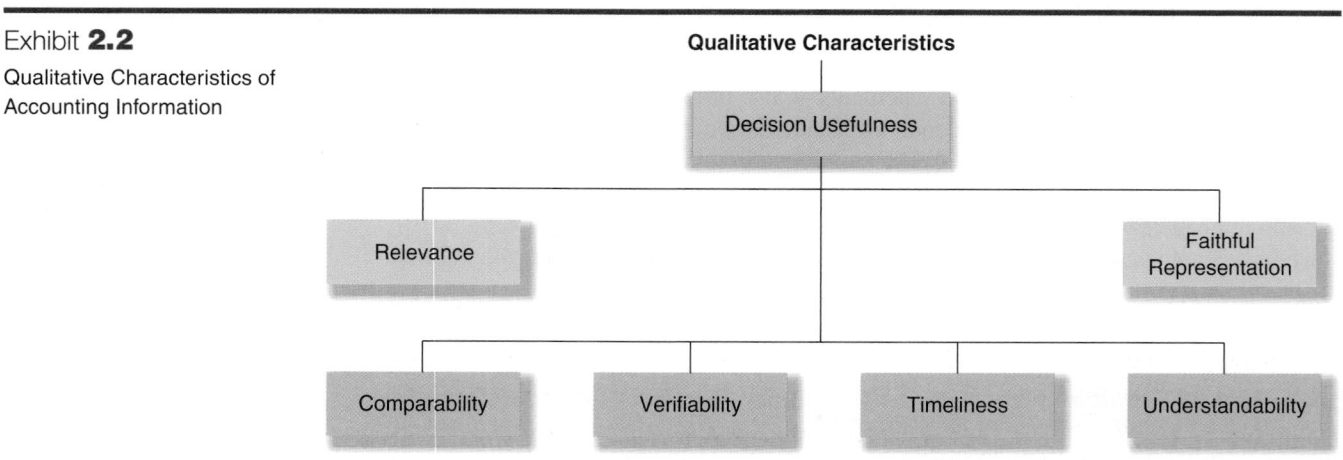

Qualitative Characteristics

Relevance   Information disclosed in financial statements is relevant if it can influence users' decisions. **Relevant information** has predictive and/or confirmatory value. For example, net earnings is a relevant piece of information if it helps users predict future net earnings. It is also relevant if it confirms or changes prior expectations based on previous evaluations.

While all transactions affecting an entity must be accounted for, items that are of low significance do not have to conform precisely to specified accounting guidelines or be separately reported if they would not influence reasonable decisions. Accountants usually designate such items as *immaterial*. **Material amounts** are amounts that are large enough to influence a user's decision. Determining material amounts is often very subjective and is viewed as an *entity-specific aspect of relevance*.

Faithful Representation   To be useful for decision making, information provided in financial statements must be a **faithful representation** of the economic phenomena it is supposed to represent, thus reflecting the substance of the underlying transactions, which may differ from their legal form. The information must be complete, neutral (unbiased), and free from material error. For instance, the inventory account of a company that sells computer equipment would include items that are held for sale to customers. If inventory also included desktop and laptop computers used by employees in their daily work, then the inventory balance would not be a faithful representation of the merchandise available for sale.

Comparability   **Comparability** of accounting information across businesses is enhanced when similar accounting methods have been applied. This enables users to identify similarities and differences between two items reported by two different companies or by the same company in different accounting periods. Comparability of financial statement items is enhanced if the same methods are used on a consistent basis to measure and report these items.

Verifiability   Information presented in financial statements is **verifiable** if independent accountants can agree on the nature and amount of a transaction. Verifiability enhances the usefulness of accounting information by helping to assure users that the economic phenomena that underlie the company's activities are faithfully represented in the financial statements.

Timeliness   Information should be available to decision makers in time to be considered in making decisions. **Timely** information enhances the information's ability to predict future values and to confirm past values. The relevance of accounting information for decision making declines as time passes.

Understandability   To make proper use of accounting information, users are expected to have a reasonable understanding of business and economic activities and be willing to analyze the information in a diligent manner. **Understandability** is the quality of information that enables users to comprehend its meaning. Clear and concise classification and presentation of information enhances its understandability.

The Cost Constraint of Accounting Measurement   The **cost constraint** suggests that information should be produced only if the perceived benefits of increased decision usefulness exceed the expected costs of providing that information. Companies produce and disseminate accounting information to users with the expectation that the benefits to users from such information exceed the cost of producing it by the company as well as the cost users incur to interpret and analyze the information. For example, the company's managers may decide that voluntary disclosure of information about specific aspects of the company's operations would be beneficial to users. In such cases, the costs of information disclosure and subsequent processing by users should not exceed the expected benefits. In this context, the cost constraint plays an important role in determining whether new information should be produced and communicated to users.

RELEVANT INFORMATION can influence a decision; it has predictive and/or confirmatory value.

MATERIAL AMOUNTS are amounts that are large enough to influence a user's decision.

FAITHFUL REPRESENTATION suggests that information provided in financial statements must reflect the substance of the underlying transactions, which may differ from their legal form.

COMPARABILITY of accounting information across businesses is enhanced when similar accounting methods have been applied.

Information is **VERIFIABLE** if independent accountants can agree on the nature and amount of a transaction.

TIMELY information enhances the information's ability to predict future values and to confirm past values.

UNDERSTANDABILITY is the quality of information that enables users to comprehend its meaning.

The **COST CONSTRAINT** suggests that information should be produced only if the perceived benefits of increased decision usefulness exceed the expected costs of providing that information.

The **SEPARATE-ENTITY ASSUMPTION** states that the activities of each business must be accounted for separately from the activities of its owners.

The **UNIT-OF-MEASURE ASSUMPTION** states that accounting information should be measured and reported in the national monetary unit.

The **CONTINUITY (GOING-CONCERN) ASSUMPTION** states that businesses are assumed to continue to operate into the foreseeable future.

The **HISTORICAL COST PRINCIPLE** requires assets to be recorded at the historical cash-equivalent cost, which is cash paid plus the current monetary value of all non-cash considerations also given on the date of the exchange.

Accounting Assumptions   Three of the four basic assumptions that underlie accounting measurement and reporting relate to the statement of financial position. They were discussed in Chapter 1. The **separate-entity assumption** states that the activities of each business must be accounted for separately from the activities of its owners, all other persons, and other entities. Separation of the owners' resources (and obligations) from those of the business entity is necessary for a proper evaluation of the entity's results of operations and its financial position. For example, a building purchased by the owner of a real estate development and management company for personal use should not be mixed with buildings owned by the company. The **unit-of-measure assumption** states that accounting information should be measured and reported in the national monetary unit (Canadian dollars in Canada, euros in countries that use it, pesos in Mexico, etc.), even if the entity has business operations in many countries.

The use of a specific unit of measure allows for meaningful aggregation of financial amounts. Furthermore, accountants assume that the unit of measure has a stable value over time, even though we recognize that the price we pay to purchase a specific item, such as a chocolate bar, tends to increase over time. Sun-Rype's statement of financial position includes many assets purchased in different years and measured in Canadian dollars. The unit-of-measure assumption allows accountants to combine dollar amounts from various years, even though the purchasing power of the monetary unit has changed over time.

For accounting purposes, a business is normally assumed to continue operating long enough to carry out its objectives and to meet contractual commitments. The **continuity (going-concern) assumption** states that businesses are assumed to continue to operate into the foreseeable future. Violation of this assumption means that assets and liabilities should be valued and reported on the statement of financial position as if the company were to be liquidated (i.e., discontinued, with all assets sold and all debts paid). In all future chapters, unless indicated otherwise, we assume that businesses meet the continuity assumption.

The fourth assumption, periodicity, provides guidance on measuring revenues and expenses, and will be discussed in Chapter 3.

Basic Accounting Principle   The **historical cost principle** requires assets to be recorded at the historical cash-equivalent cost, which is cash paid plus the current monetary value of all non-cash considerations (any assets, privileges, or rights) also given on the date of the exchange. One advantage of this approach is that many assets are acquired according to legal contracts that clearly state the acquisition cost. For example, if Sun-Rype trades an old delivery van for a new delivery van, the cost of the new van is equal to the cash paid plus the market value of the old van. Thus, in most cases, cost is relatively easy to determine and can be verified. A disadvantage of this approach is that, subsequent to the date of acquisition, the continued reporting of historical cost on the statement of financial position does not reflect any change in market value, usually because market value is a less verifiable measure than historical cost.

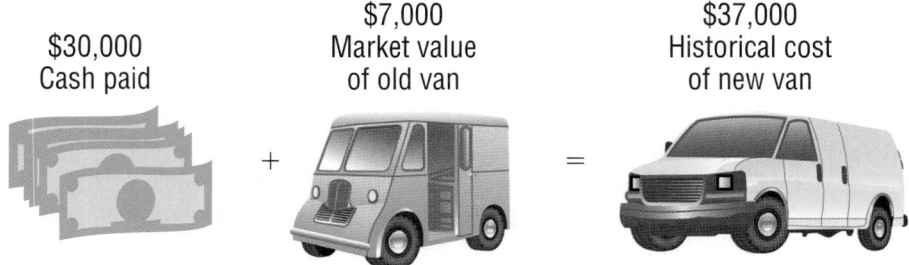

| $30,000 Cash paid | + | $7,000 Market value of old van | = | $37,000 Historical cost of new van |

Sun-Rype owns land that it acquired several years ago and reports it on the statement of financial position at historical cost. Although the market price or economic value of the land has risen over time, its recorded value remains unchanged at its original cost because this amount is a verifiable measure based on an actual exchange that occurred in the past. It would be desirable to show on the statement of financial position the land's fair value, that is, the price at which it could be sold instead of its outdated historical cost. However, the land's fair value may not be reliable if different real estate appraisers produce different values for the same piece of land. Accountants continue, therefore, to rely on historical cost measures for reporting purposes because they are factual, although they may not be useful for specific decision-making purposes. Furthermore, as long as Sun-Rype remains a going concern it is unlikely to sell the land at its fair value. The land retains usefulness, often referred to as the asset's value-in-use, to Sun-Rype. If Sun-Rype has no intent to sell the land, then its fair value is not specifically relevant to understanding the financial health of the company. The use of alternative measurement bases for asset valuation will be discussed in Chapter 9.

Assets, liabilities, and equity are the key elements of a corporation's statement of financial position, as we learned in Chapter 1. Let us examine the definitions in more detail.

Elements of the Classified Statement of Financial Position

Assets are economic resources controlled by an entity as a result of past transactions or events and from which future economic benefits may be obtained. These are the resources that the entity has and can use in its future operations. When Sun-Rype purchases an asset, it acquires the right for future benefits to be derived from that asset, as well as any future risks and obligations arising from control of the asset. External users of Sun-Rype's financial statements care about its assets because they embody future financial benefits. For lenders, Sun-Rype's assets and their productivity are the basis upon which they can generate forecasts about how readily the company can repay its financial obligations. For Sun-Rype's shareholders, the increase in the value of their investment will depend in large part on the realized future benefits arising from assets under the company's control.

To make financial statements more useful to investors, creditors, and analysts, specific *classifications* of information are included on the statements. Various classifications are used in practice, and you should not be confused when you notice slightly different formats used by different companies.

Let us explore Sun-Rype's simplified statement of financial position, presented in Exhibit 2.3. First, notice the title of the statement: Consolidated Statement of Financial Position. *Consolidated* means that the classified elements of Sun-Rype's statement of financial position are combined with those of other companies under its control (e.g., Naumes Concentrates Inc.).[5] For convenience, the amounts for the various elements of the statement of financial position are shown in thousands of Canadian dollars. Two amounts are shown for each element: one at December 31, 2012, and the other at December 31, 2011, one year earlier. This system allows investors to compare, at a glance, the value of each classified element from year to year, and then analyze these changes to understand whether the company's financial position has improved or deteriorated over time.

Sun-Rype's statement of financial position is shown in *column* or *report* format, with assets listed first, followed by liabilities, and then shareholders' equity. Other companies may choose an account format with the assets listed on the left-hand side and liabilities and shareholders' equity listed on the right. Both formats are standard ways of communicating the same information. We now explain the various elements that appear on Sun-Rype's statement of financial position.

Exhibit 2.3 presents Sun-Rype's statement of financial position, with amounts rounded to the nearest thousand dollars. Notice that Sun-Rype's fiscal year ends on December 31. The choice of year-ends will be discussed in Chapter 4.

Typically, the assets of a company include the following:

1. Current assets (short term)
    a. Cash
    b. Short-term investments
    c. Trade and other receivables
    d. Inventories

LO²

Define the elements of a classified statement of financial position.

ASSETS are economic resources controlled by an entity as a result of past transactions or events and from which future economic benefits may be obtained.

Exhibit **2.3**

Sun-Rype's Statement of Financial
Position

Amount of cash in the company's bank accounts

Amounts owed by customers from prior sales

Food and drink products, raw materials, and supplies

Rent and insurance paid in advance

A variety of assets that are covered in future chapters

Factories and production equipment

An intangible asset that results from the acquisition of another business

Amounts owed to suppliers for prior purchases

Estimated liabilities whose amounts and timing of payment are not
known with certainty

Amount of taxes owed to the government

Amounts owed to lenders within one year

Amounts owed on written debt contracts after one year

Amount of taxes deferred to future periods

Amounts invested in the business by shareholders

Past earnings not distributed to shareholders

Adjustments to assets and liabilities that are explained in future chapters

SUN-RYPE PRODUCTS LTD.
Consolidated Statement of Financial Position
As at December 31
(in thousands of Canadian dollars)

Assets	2012	2011
Current assets		
Cash	$ 3,727	$ 571
Trade and other receivables	14,047	13,672
Inventories	29,149	31,794
Prepayments	502	579
Other current assets	446	2,244
Total current assets	**47,871**	**48,860**
Non-current assets		
Property, plant, and equipment	42,041	46,195
Goodwill	1,061	1,084
Total non-current assets	**43,102**	**47,279**
Total assets	**$90,973**	**$96,139**
Liabilities and Equity		
Current liabilities		
Trade and other payables	$25,672	$19,479
Provisions	1,687	1,297
Income taxes payable	116	–
Short-term borrowings	3,646	12,926
Total current liabilities	**31,121**	**33,702**
Non-current liabilities		
Long-term borrowings	8,781	12,636
Deferred tax liabilities	4,035	3,422
Total non-current liabilities	**12,816**	**16,058**
Total liabilities	**43,937**	**49,760**
Equity		
Contributed capital	18,421	18,518
Retained earnings	28,681	27,914
Other components	(66)	(53)
Total equity	**47,036**	**46,379**
Total liabilities and equity	**$90,973**	**$96,139**

Note: This statement is an adaptation of Sun-Rype's
actual statement of financial position. Some of the
elements of the actual statement were combined for
illustrative purposes.

Source: Sun-Rype Products Ltd., Annual Report 2012.

    e. Prepayments (i.e., expenses paid in advance of use)

    f. Other current assets

  2. Non-current assets (long term)

    a. Property, plant, and equipment (at cost less accumulated depreciation)

    b. Financial assets

    c. Goodwill

    d. Intangible assets

    e. Other (miscellaneous) assets

Sun-Rype lists its assets *in order of liquidity*, which means how soon an asset is expected by management to be transformed into cash. Notice that several of Sun-Rype's assets are categorized as current assets. **Current assets** are those economic resources that Sun-Rype will typically transform into cash or use within the next year or the operating business cycle of the company, whichever is longer. Under current assets, *cash* appears first because it is the most liquid asset. *Short-term investments* represent the reported values for shares of other companies and other financial assets purchased as investments of excess cash.

CURRENT ASSETS are assets that will be used or turned into cash, normally within one year. Inventory is always considered to be a current asset, regardless of the time needed to produce and sell it.

Any *receivable* represents an amount of money owed to Sun-Rype. *Trade and other receivables* consist primarily of *trade receivables*, which are amounts owed by customers who purchased products and services on credit. These amounts are normally collected within one year of the statement's date.

Inventories refers to goods that (1) are held for sale to customers in the normal course of business or (2) are used to produce goods or services for sale. Inventory is always considered to be a current asset, no matter how long it takes to produce and sell. Sun-Rype's inventory would include a variety of fruit-based foods and beverages not yet sold to customers; fruits, nutrients, and other ingredients purchased but not yet used for production purposes; and partially completed products. *Prepayments* (e.g., insurance premiums and rent paid in advance for use of a building) reflect available benefits (e.g., monthly insurance protection, office space) that the company will use within one year. *Other current assets*, when reported, will include a number of assets with smaller balances that are combined.

ANALYSIS OF CHANGES IN INVENTORY AND TRADE RECEIVABLES

FINANCIAL ANALYSIS

Investors analyze the financial statements of a company to decide whether or not to purchase its shares or to lend it money. One important decision factor is how easily a company can access cash to pay both debts to its creditors and dividends to its shareholders. In a normal business cycle, Sun-Rype would produce fruit-based beverages and fruit snacks for sale to distributors such as Sobeys and Loblaw. These products, called *inventories*, are stored in warehouses until they are sold. The faster these products are sold to customers, the faster these assets are transformed into cash. Let us examine the company's ability to access cash, assuming for simplicity that Sun-Rype's inventories consist of products held for sale.

Notice that the balance of trade receivables increased from $13,672 at December 31, 2011, to $14,047 at December 31, 2012, indicating that the amount of sales on credit exceeded the cash collected from customers. An investor would also observe that cash increased from $571 at December 31, 2011, to $3,727 at December 31, 2012. Investors would examine the statement of cash flows to gain clearer insight on how events in the past year resulted in the change in cash (see Chapter 5). For the moment, this brief analysis would reassure an investor that the first two elements reported on the statement of financial position are relevant to answering an important question about how easily Sun-Rype can access cash to pay its debts to creditors and dividends to shareholders.

Following the current assets section, Sun-Rype reports a number of non-current assets. **Non-current assets** are considered to be long term because they will be used or turned into cash over a period longer than the next year. *Property, plant, and equipment* includes all land, buildings, machinery, and equipment such as tools, furniture, and other fixtures that will be used for the production, packaging, and storage of Sun-Rype's foods and drinks. These are also called *fixed assets* or *capital assets*—they have a physical form you can touch, and therefore each asset is *tangible*.

NON-CURRENT ASSETS are considered to be long term because they will be used or turned into cash over a period longer than the next year.

Goodwill is an intangible asset that arises when a company purchases another business to control its operating, investing, and financing decisions. Often, the purchase price of a business exceeds the fair value of all of the identifiable assets owned by the business minus all of the identifiable liabilities owed to others. Goodwill reflects assets that are not easily identifiable or measured, such as customer confidence, quality of products, reputation for good service, and financial standing of the acquired business. The amount of $1,061 that Sun-Rype reported at December 31, 2012, resulted from the acquisition of Naumes Concentrates Inc. in 2011. *Intangible assets* have no physical substance but have a long life. They are usually not acquired for resale but are directly related to the operations of the business. Intangible assets include such items as franchises, patents, trademarks, and copyrights. Their values arise from the *legal rights* and *privileges* of ownership, which are recognized if they are purchased from external parties or as a result of internal development. Sun-Rype did not report any intangible assets on its statement of financial position at December 31, 2012. Intangible assets, including goodwill, are discussed in more detail in Chapter 9.

Other assets, when reported, will include a number of assets that are combined because of their relatively small values.

FINANCIAL ANALYSIS

UNRECORDED BUT VALUABLE ASSETS

Many very valuable intangible assets, such as trademarks, patents, and copyrights that are developed inside a company (not purchased), are not reported on the statement of financial position. For example, Tim Hortons' statement of financial position or related notes do not report any value for its trademark because it was developed internally over time through research, development, and advertising (it was not purchased). Likewise, the Coca-Cola Company does not report any asset for its patented Coke formulas, although it does report more than US$6 billion in various trademarks that it has purchased.

LIABILITIES are present debts or obligations of the entity that result from past transactions and that will be paid with assets or services.

Liabilities are present debts or obligations of the entity that result from past transactions and that will be paid with assets or services. They represent future outflows of assets (mainly cash) or services to the *creditors* that provided the corporation with the resources needed to conduct its business. When the corporation borrows money, creditors receive not only full payment of the amount owed to them but also interest on the borrowed amount.

Typically, the liabilities of a company include the following:

1. Current liabilities (short term)
   a. Trade and other payables
   b. Short-term borrowings
   c. Income taxes payable
   d. Accrued liabilities
   e. Provisions
   f. Other current liabilities
2. Non-current liabilities (long term)
   a. Long-term borrowings
   b. Deferred income tax liabilities
   c. Provisions
   d. Other liabilities

CURRENT LIABILITIES are obligations that will be paid in cash (or other current assets) or satisfied by providing service within the coming year.

Just as assets are reported in order of liquidity, liabilities are usually listed by order of time to maturity (how soon an obligation must be paid). **Current liabilities** are obligations that will be paid in cash (or other current assets) or satisfied by providing service within the coming year. Normally, the cash from converting current assets is used to pay current liabilities.

Any *payable* represents an amount of money that Sun-Rype must pay. *Trade and other payables* consist primarily of *trade payables*, which are amounts owed to suppliers of materials that Sun-Rype used in producing and packaging its products for sale. The second current liability, *short-term borrowings*, represents short-term loans from banks. Bank loans are common when the company does not have a sufficient amount of cash to pay its creditors. The third liability, *income taxes payable*, is simply an estimate of the amount of taxes Sun-Rype is expected to pay to taxation authorities. *Accrued liabilities* represent the total amount owed to suppliers for various types of services, such as payroll, rent, and other obligations. Sun-Rype did not report any accrued liabilities on its statement of financial position at December 31, 2012. *Provisions* are estimated liabilities that are expected to be paid within one year, but the exact amount and date of payment are not known with certainty. *Other current liabilities*, when reported, will include a number of liabilities with relatively small amounts that are combined.

ANALYSIS OF CHANGE IN CURRENT LIABILITIES

FINANCIAL
ANALYSIS

Using both current assets and current liabilities for Sun-Rype, we can improve our analysis of the availability of cash to repay debts to creditors and dividends to shareholders.

Sun-Rype's statement of financial position shows that the company owes $2,581 less in current liabilities at December 31, 2012, than it did at December 31, 2011. As investors, we would tentatively conclude that the company has reduced its reliance on suppliers and other creditors to finance its current assets. However, investors must learn far more about the business cycle for beverage and nutrition products, Sun-Rype's main competitors, and the outlook for the industry sectors in which Sun-Rype operates before coming to a firm conclusion.

At the beginning of this chapter, we stated that investors are most interested in relevant information that helps them predict future cash inflows and outflows. From this very preliminary analysis, investors can predict that, because Sun-Rype has decreased its current liabilities by $2,581, a smaller amount of cash is needed in the year 2013 to repay the outstanding debt to creditors compared to the amount of $33,702 that was settled during the year 2012.

Non-current liabilities are a company's debts that have maturities extending beyond one year from the date of the statement of financial position. They include *long-term borrowings* from banks and other lenders; *deferred income tax liabilities*, which arise from temporary differences between the net earnings measured in accordance with IFRS and taxable income that is determined in conformity with applicable tax laws; *provisions*, which are estimated liabilities characterized by uncertainty about the exact amount to be paid and the timing of the payment; and *other liabilities*, which include a number of other liabilities. These various types of non-current liabilities will be covered in future chapters.

NON-CURRENT LIABILITIES are a company's debts that have maturities extending beyond one year from the date of the statement of financial position.

ENVIRONMENTAL LIABILITIES—THE GREENING OF ACCOUNTING STANDARDS

A QUESTION
OF ACCOUNTABILITY

For many years, companies faced growing pressure to estimate and disclose environmental liabilities such as the cleanup of hazardous waste. IFRS require Canadian publicly accountable enterprises to report their best estimate of probable liabilities, including environmental liabilities, in notes to the financial statements. For example, Suncor Energy Inc., which mines oil from the tar sands of northern Alberta, reported environmental liabilities exceeding $4,293 million in its 2012 financial statements, representing approximately 11.5 percent of its total liabilities at December 31, 2012. It is estimated, however, that a significant percentage of companies under-report or fail to report such liabilities, often because of the way disclosure rules are applied.

A key economic concern for many Canadian companies is how to manage their resources in an economically sustainable way. Sun-Rype, like many Canadian companies, is subject to environmental regulation, and has disclosed the following information in its annual information form for 2012:*

Environmental Protection

Sun-Rype maintains an active environmental program that reflects responsible policies and a respect for the environment. Internal audits are conducted annually and every third year by an external environmental auditor to ensure that appropriate management policies and practices towards waste management, recycling and reuse of products are maintained. Sun-Rype is subject to environmental regulation by federal, provincial and local authorities. There are currently no environmental orders outstanding or pending against Sun-Rype.

Other companies, such as Suncor Energy Inc. and Bombardier Inc., publish detailed reports on environmental sustainability or corporate social responsibility, which include both financial and non-financial performance indicators that measure their progress toward meeting sustainable development targets.

Source: Sun-Rype Products Ltd., Annual Information Form, 2013.

SHAREHOLDERS' EQUITY (OWNERS' EQUITY or STOCKHOLDERS' EQUITY) is the financing provided by the owners and the operations of the business.

Shareholders' equity (owners' equity or **stockholders' equity)** is the financing provided to the corporation by both its owners and the operations of the business. One key difference between shareholders and creditors is that creditors are entitled to settlement of their legal claims on the corporation's assets before the shareholders receive a penny, even if this consumes all of the corporation's assets. Consequently, shareholders have a residual claim on the corporation's assets.

Shareholders *invest* in a company because they expect to receive two types of cash flow: dividends, which are a distribution of the corporation's earnings (a return on shareholders' investment), and gains from selling their investment in the corporation for more than they paid (known as *capital gains*).

Typically the shareholders' equity of a corporation includes the following:

1. Contributed capital
2. Retained earnings (accumulated earnings that have not been declared as dividends)
3. Other components

CONTRIBUTED CAPITAL results from shareholders providing cash (and sometimes other assets) to the business.

Contributed capital results from shareholders providing cash (and sometimes other assets) to the business. Sun-Rype's contributed capital of $18,421 at December 31, 2012, has resulted from contributions by shareholders at different points in the company's history.

Most companies that operate profitably retain part of their earnings for reinvestment in their business. The other part is distributed as dividends to shareholders. Earnings that are not distributed to shareholders but instead are reinvested in the business by management are called **retained earnings**. Sun-Rype's retained earnings equalled $28,681 at December 31, 2012, and represent the amount of earnings that have not been distributed to shareholders since the company was incorporated. Sun-Rype's growth over time has been financed by a substantial reinvestment of retained earnings. In addition to contributed capital and retained earnings, shareholders' equity includes other components that are explained in Chapter 6.

RETAINED EARNINGS refers to the accumulated earnings of a company that are not distributed to the shareholders and are reinvested in the business.

We just learned the elements of the statement of financial position (assets, liabilities, and share-holders' equity) and how assets and liabilities are usually classified (current or non-current). Current assets (including inventory) are expected to be used or transformed into cash within the next 12 months, and current liabilities are expected to be paid or settled within the next 12 months with cash, services, or other current assets.

SELF-STUDY **QUIZ 2-1**

The following is a list of items from a recent statement of financial position for Tim Hortons Inc. Indicate on the line provided whether each of the following is categorized on the statement of financial position as a current asset (CA), a non-current asset (NCA), a current liability (CL), a non-current liability (NCL), or shareholders' equity (SE).

_____ Accrued liabilities	_____ Long-term debt	_____ Property and equipment
_____ Inventories	_____ Retained earnings	_____ Notes receivable (due in five years)
_____ Trade receivables	_____ Trade payables	_____ Cash

After you have completed your answers, check them with the solutions at the end of the chapter.

Now that we have reviewed several of the basic accounting concepts and terms, we need to understand the economic activities of a business that result in changes in amounts reported in financial statements and the process used in generating the financial statements.

WHAT TYPES OF BUSINESS ACTIVITIES CAUSE CHANGES IN FINANCIAL STATEMENT AMOUNTS?

LO3

Identify what constitutes a business transaction, and recognize common account titles used in business.

Nature of Business Transactions

Accounting focuses on specific events that have an economic impact on the entity. Those events that are recorded as a part of the accounting process are called transactions. The first step in translating the results of business events to financial statement amounts is determining which events to include. As the definitions of assets and liabilities indicate, only economic resources and debts *resulting from past transactions* are recorded on the statement of financial position. A **transaction** is either of two types of events:

A TRANSACTION is (1) an exchange between a business and one or more external parties to a business or (2) a measurable internal event, such as adjustments for the use of assets in operations.

1. *External events* are *exchanges* of assets, goods, or services by one party for assets, services, or promises to pay (liabilities) by one or more other parties. Examples include the purchase of a machine from a supplier, the sale of merchandise to customers, borrowing of cash from a bank, and investment of cash in the business by the owners. Transactions that affect elements of the statement of financial position are discussed in this chapter, and those that affect elements of the statement of earnings will be covered in Chapter 3.

2. *Internal events* include certain events that are not exchanges between the business and other parties but nevertheless have a direct and measurable effect on the accounting entity. Examples include using up insurance paid in advance and using buildings and equipment over several years. Accounting for internal events will be discussed in Chapter 4.

Throughout this textbook, the word "transaction" will be used in the broad sense to include both types of events.

Some important events that have an economic impact on the company, however, are *not* reflected in Sun-Rype's statements. In most cases, signing a contract is not considered to be a transaction because it involves *the exchange only of promises*, not of assets such as cash, goods, services, or property. For example, assume that Sun-Rype signs an employment contract with a new regional manager. From an accounting perspective, no transaction has occurred because no exchange of assets, goods, or services has been made. Each party to the contract has exchanged promises; the manager agrees to work and Sun-Rype agrees to pay the manager for work rendered. For each day the new manager works, however, the exchange of services for pay results in a transaction that Sun-Rype must record. Because of their importance, long-term employment contracts, leases, and other commitments may need to be disclosed in notes to the financial statements.

How does the accounting staff at Sun-Rype record external and internal events that cause changes in the amounts reported on the company's statement of financial position? The recording of transactions has evolved over time. Advances in computer hardware and software technology have paved the way for efficient recording of transactions and instantaneous preparation of financial statements. However, the basic system of recording transactions has withstood the test of time and has been in use for more than 500 years. The basic tenets of manual and computerized recording systems are discussed in this chapter and elaborated on further in Chapters 3 and 4.

Accounts

An **ACCOUNT** is a standardized format that organizations use to accumulate the monetary effects of transactions on each financial statement item.

An **account** is a standardized record that organizations use to accumulate the monetary effects of transactions on each financial statement item. The cumulative result of all transactions that affect a specific account, or its ending balance, is then reported on the appropriate financial statement. To facilitate the recording of transactions, each company establishes a *chart of accounts*, a list of accounts and their unique numeric codes. The chart of accounts is organized by financial statement element, with asset accounts listed first (by order of liquidity), followed by liabilities (by order of time to maturity), shareholders' equity, revenue, and expense accounts, in that order. In formal recordkeeping systems, including computerized accounting systems, use of appropriate account numbers is essential if the monetary effects of similar transactions are to be grouped correctly. Exhibit 2.4 lists account titles that are quite common and used by most companies. This list is helpful when you are completing assignments and are unsure of an account title.

You have probably already noticed some patterns in how accounts are named:

1. Accounts with "receivable" in the title are always assets; they represent amounts owed to the corporation by (receivable from) customers and others, to be collected in the future.

2. Accounts with "payable" in the title are always liabilities; they represent amounts owed by the corporation to be paid to others in the future.

3. The prepayments account is an asset; it represents amounts paid by the corporation to others for future benefits, such as future insurance coverage, rental of property, or advertising.

4. Accounts with "deferred" in the title are always liabilities, representing amounts paid in the past to the corporation by others who expect future goods or services from the corporation.

Every company creates its own chart of accounts to fit the nature of its business activities. For example, a small lawn care service may have an asset account called Lawn-Mowing Equipment, but a large corporation such as the Royal Bank of Canada is unlikely to report such an account. These differences will become more apparent as we examine the statements of financial position of various companies. Because each company has a different chart of accounts, you should *not* try to memorize a typical chart of accounts, but you should understand the nature of each typical account. Then

Exhibit **2.4**
Typical Account Titles

Exhibit **2.4**
Typical Account Titles

Accounts with "receivable" in the title are always assets; they represent amounts owed to the corporation by (receivable from) customers and others, to be collected in the future.

Accounts with "payable" in the title are always liabilities; they represent amounts owed by the corporation to be paid to others in the future.

The prepayments account is an asset; it represents amounts paid by the corporation to others for future benefits, such as future insurance coverage, rental of property, or advertising.

Accounts with "deferred" in the title are always liabilities, representing amounts paid in the past to the corporation by others who expect future goods or services from the corporation.

Assets	Liabilities	Shareholders' Equity	Revenues	Expenses
Cash	Trade payables	Contributed capital	Sales revenue	Cost of sales
Short-term investments	Accrued liabilities	Retained earnings	Fee revenue	Wages expense
Trade receivables	Notes payable		Interest revenue	Rent expense
Notes receivable	Taxes payable		Rent revenue	Interest expense
Inventory (to be sold)	Deferred revenue		Service revenue	Depreciation expense
Supplies	Bonds payable			Advertising expense
Prepayments				Insurance expense
Long-term investments				Repair expense
Equipment				Income tax expense
Buildings				
Land				
Intangibles				

when you see a company that uses a slightly different title, you will understand what it means. For example, some companies use the term Trade Accounts Receivable (same as Trade Receivables) or Merchandise Inventory (same as Inventory). *When you prepare homework problems, you will either be given the company's account names or be expected to select appropriate descriptive names, similar to the ones in Exhibit 2.4.* Once a name is selected for an account, you must use that exact name in all transactions affecting that account.

The accounts you see in the financial statements are actually summations (or aggregations) of a number of specific accounts in a company's recordkeeping system. For example, Sun-Rype keeps separate accounts for the different beverages and snacks it produces and sells but combines them as *Inventories* on the statement of financial position. Equipment, buildings, and land are also combined into an account called *Property, plant, and equipment*. Since our aim is to understand financial statements of actual companies, we focus on aggregated accounts.

UNDERSTANDING FINANCIAL STATEMENTS OF FOREIGN COMPANIES

INTERNATIONAL PERSPECTIVE

The adoption of IFRS by many countries has made it easier to read foreign companies' financial statements. GlaxoSmithKline, the pharmaceutical giant in the United Kingdom, prepares its financial statements under IFRS. However, there are still some differences in the structure of the statements and account titles that may cause confusion. For example, many European companies place non-current assets before current assets and list shareholders' equity before liabilities. Companies in the United States do not use the term "provision" to report estimated liabilities; they do recognize such liabilities, however, under different titles. The key to avoiding confusion is to pay attention to the subheadings in the financial statements and read the notes related to specific financial statement elements.

LO4

Apply transaction analysis to simple business transactions in terms of the accounting model: Assets = Liabilities + Shareholders' Equity.

HOW DO TRANSACTIONS AFFECT ACCOUNTS?

Managers make business decisions that often result in transactions affecting financial statements. For example, the decisions to expand the number of stores, advertise a new product, change an employee benefit package, and invest excess cash would all affect the financial statements. Sometimes these decisions have unintended consequences as well. For example, the decision to purchase additional inventory for cash in anticipation of a major sales initiative will increase inventory and decrease cash. But, if there is no demand for the additional inventory, the lower cash balance will also reduce the company's ability to pay its other obligations.

Because business decisions often involve an element of risk, business managers should understand how transactions impact the accounts on the financial statements. The process for determining the effects of transactions is called *transaction analysis*.

Principles of Transaction Analysis

TRANSACTION ANALYSIS is the process of studying a transaction to determine its economic effect on the entity in terms of the accounting equation.

Transaction analysis is the process of studying each transaction to determine its economic effect on the entity in terms of the accounting equation (A = L + SE, also known as the *fundamental accounting model*). We outline the process in this section of the chapter and create a visual tool representing the process (the transaction analysis model). The basic accounting equation and two fundamental concepts are the foundation for this model. Recall from Chapter 1 that the accounting equation for a business that is organized as a corporation is as follows:

$$\text{Assets (A)} = \text{Liabilities (L)} + \text{Shareholders' Equity (SE)}$$

The two concepts underlying the transaction analysis process follow:

1. Every transaction affects at least two accounts; it is critical to correctly identify the accounts affected and the direction of the effect (increase or decrease).
2. The accounting equation must remain in balance after each transaction.

Success in performing transaction analysis depends on a clear understanding of how the transaction analysis model is constructed, based on these concepts. *Study this material well. You should not move on to a new concept until you understand and can apply all prior concepts.*

Dual Effects   The idea that every transaction has *at least two effects* on the basic accounting equation is known as the *dual effects* concept.[6] Most transactions with external parties involve an *exchange* by which the business entity both receives something and gives up something in return. For example, suppose that Sun-Rype purchased some office supplies for cash. In this exchange, Sun-Rype would receive supplies (an increase in an asset) and in return would give up cash (a decrease in an asset):

Transaction	Sun-Rype Received	Sun-Rype Gave
Purchased paper for cash	Supplies (increased)	Cash (decreased)

In analyzing this transaction, we determined that the accounts affected were office supplies and cash. As we discussed in Chapter 1, however, most supplies are purchased on credit (i.e., money is owed to suppliers). In that case, Sun-Rype would engage in *two* transactions:

1. The purchase of an asset on credit

   In the first transaction, Sun-Rype would receive office supplies (an increase in an asset) and would give in return a promise to pay later, called accounts payable (an increase in a liability).

2. The eventual payment

   In the second transaction, Sun-Rype would eliminate or receive back its promise to pay (a decrease in the accounts payable liability) and would give up cash (a decrease in an asset).

Transaction	Sun-Rype Received	Sun-Rype Gave
1. Purchased paper for credit	Office supplies (increased)	Accounts payable (increased) [a promise to pay]
2. Paid on its accounts payable	Accounts payable (decreased) [a promise was eliminated]	Cash (decreased)

As noted earlier, not all important business events result in a transaction that affects the financial statements. Most important, signing a contract involving *the exchange of promises to perform a future business transaction does not result in a transaction* that is recorded. For example, if Sun-Rype sent an order to its paper supplier for more paper without making any payment, and the supplier accepted the order but did not fill it immediately, then no transaction has taken place for accounting purposes because Sun-Rype and the paper supplier have exchanged only promises.[7] From the supplier's perspective, the same holds true. No transaction has taken place, so the supplier's financial statements are not affected. As soon as the paper is shipped to Sun-Rype, however, the supplier gives up inventory in exchange for a promise from Sun-Rype to pay for the paper it receives, and Sun-Rype exchanges its promise to pay for the paper it receives. Because a *promise* has been exchanged for *goods*, a transaction has taken place, and the financial statements of both Sun-Rype and the supplier will be affected.

Balancing the Accounting Equation   The accounting equation must remain in balance after each transaction. Total assets (resources) must equal total liabilities plus shareholders' equity (claims to resources). If the correct accounts have been identified and the appropriate direction of the effect on each account has been determined, then the equation should remain in balance. A systematic transaction analysis includes the following steps, in this order:

Step 1: **Identify and classify accounts and effects.**

- **Identify the accounts affected (by their titles)**, making sure that at least two accounts change. Ask yourself, what is received and what is given?

- **Classify each by type of account.** Was each account an asset (A), a liability (L), or shareholders' equity (SE)?

- **Determine the direction of the effect.** Did the account increase [+] or decrease [−]?

Step 2: **Verify that the accounting equation, A = L + SE, remains in balance.**

Analyzing Sun-Rype's Transactions

To illustrate the use of the transaction analysis process, let us consider typical Sun-Rype transactions that are also common to most businesses. This chapter presents transactions affecting accounts reported on the statement of financial position. Assume that Sun-Rype engaged in the following transactions during January 2013, the month following the statement of financial position in Exhibit 2.3. The month will end on January 31. For simplicity, account titles are based on that statement of financial position. Note that monetary amounts are usually preceded by the symbol of the currency used in the exchange transactions (e.g., $ for Canadian dollars, € for euros). In the following illustration, all amounts are in thousands of Canadian dollars.

(*a*) **Sun-Rype issues shares to new investors in exchange for $1,300 in cash.**

Step 1: **Identify and classify accounts and effects.**

Received: Cash (+A) $1,300   **Given:** Additional share certificates, Contributed capital (+SE) $1,300

Step 2: **Is the accounting equation in balance?**

Yes. The left side increased by $1,300 and the right side increased by $1,300.

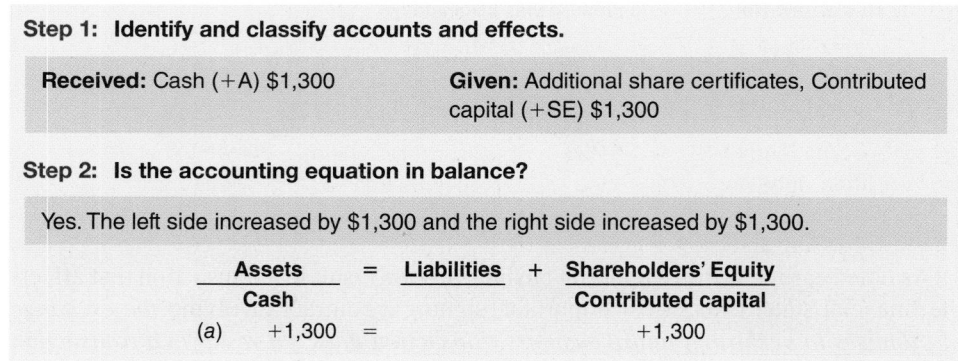

	Assets	=	**Liabilities**	+	**Shareholders' Equity**
	Cash				Contributed capital
(*a*)	+1,300	=			+1,300

(*b*) **The company borrows $1,000 from its local bank, signing a note to be paid in two years.**

Step 1: **Identify and classify accounts and effects.**

Received: Cash (+A) $1,000   **Given:** Written promise to bank, Long-term borrowings (+L) $1,000

Step 2: **Is the accounting equation in balance?**

Yes. The left side increased by $1,000 and the right side increased by $1,000.

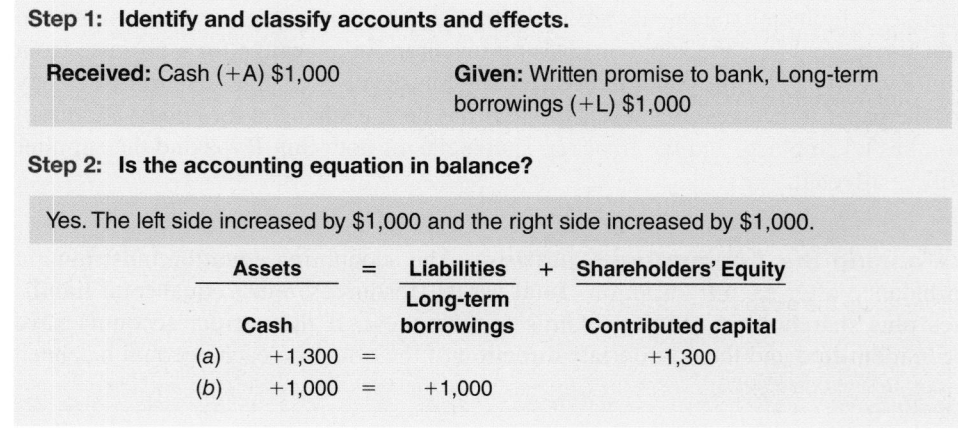

	Assets	=	**Liabilities**	+	**Shareholders' Equity**
			Long-term		
	Cash		borrowings		Contributed capital
(*a*)	+1,300	=			+1,300
(*b*)	+1,000	=	+1,000		

Transactions (*a*) and (*b*) are *financing* transactions. Companies that need cash for *investing* purposes (to buy or build additional facilities as part of their plans for growth) often seek funds by selling shares to investors, as in transaction (*a*), or borrowing from creditors, usually banks, as in transaction (*b*).

(*c*) **For expansion, Sun-Rype opened a new production facility. The company purchased $2,200 of new processing and packaging equipment and storage tanks, paying $1,500 in cash and signing a note for $700, payable to the equipment manufacturer in two years.**

Step 1: Identify and classify accounts and effects.

Received: Property, plant, and equipment (+A) $2,200

Given: (1) Cash (−A) $1,500 and a written promise to pay the manufacturer, Long-term borrowings (+L) $700

Step 2: Is the accounting equation in balance?

Yes. The left side increased by $700 and the right side increased by $700.

	Assets		=	Liabilities	+	Shareholders' Equity
	Cash	Property, plant, and equipment		Long-term borrowings		Contributed capital
(*a*)	+1,300		=			+1,300
(*b*)	+1,000		=	+1,000		
(*c*)	−1,500	+2,200	=	+700		

Notice that more than two accounts were affected by transaction (*c*).

The analysis of transactions (*d*) through (*f*) follows. The effects are listed in the chart at the end of Self-Study Quiz 2-2. Space is left in the chart for your answers to the quiz, transactions (*g*) and (*h*), which follow transaction (*f*).

(*d*) **Sun-Rype lends $450 to a trade supplier in financial difficulty. The trade supplier signs notes agreeing to repay the amount borrowed in six months.**

Step 1: Identify and classify accounts and effects.

Received: Written promise from the trade supplier, Notes receivable (+A) $450

Given: Cash (−A) $450

Step 2: Is the accounting equation in balance?

Yes. The equation remains in balance because assets increase and decrease by the same amount: $450.

(*e*) **Sun-Rype purchases shares issued by another company as a long-term investment, paying $3,000 in cash. The number of shares purchased allows Sun-Rype to exert significant influence over decisions made by that company.**

Step 1: Identify and classify accounts and effects.

Received: Share certificates from the other company, Investments (+A) $3,000

Given: Cash (−A) $3,000

Step 2: Is the accounting equation in balance?

Yes. The equation remains in balance because assets increase and decrease by the same amount: $3,000.

(*f*) **Sun-Rype's board of directors declares cash dividends of $200 for shareholders. The dividends are paid immediately.**

Step 1: Identify and classify accounts and effects.

Received: Earnings retained in the business distributed to investors, Retained earnings (−SE) $200   **Given:** Cash (−A) $200

Step 2: Is the accounting equation in balance?

Yes. The left side decreased by $200 and the right side decreased by $200.

 PAUSE FOR
FEEDBACK

Transaction analysis involves identifying (by title) accounts affected in a transaction, recognizing that at least two accounts are affected, classifying the accounts (asset, liability, or shareholders' equity), and determining the direction of the effect on the account (increase or decrease). If all accounts and effects are correct, then the fundamental accounting equation (A = L + SE) will remain in balance. *The most effective way to develop your transaction analysis skills is to practice with many transactions.*

SELF-STUDY QUIZ 2-2

Review the analysis in transactions (*a*) through (*f*) and complete the transaction analysis steps in the chart following the transactions (*g*) and (*h*). *Repeat the steps until they become a natural part of your thought process.*

(*g*) **Sun-Rype collects $300 cash on notes receivable from the trade supplier.** (*Hint:* **Think about what is received and what is given.**)

Step 1: Identify and classify accounts and effects.
Step 2: Is the accounting equation in balance?

(*h*) **Sun-Rype paid $400 on the note owed to the local bank.**

Step 1: Identify and classify accounts and effects.
Step 2: Is the accounting equation in balance?

Include these effects on the following chart.

			Assets		=	Liabilities	+	Shareholders' Equity	
	Cash	Notes receivable	Investments	Property, plant, and equipment		Long-term borrowings		Contributed capital	Retained earnings
(*a*)	1,300				=			+1,300	
(*b*)	+1,000				=	+1,000			
(*c*)	−1,500			+2,200	=	+700			
(*d*)	−450	+450			=				
(*e*)	−3,000		+3,000		=				
(*f*)	−200				=				−200
(*g*)					=				
(*h*)					=				

After you complete your answers, check them with the solutions at the end of the chapter.

(*i*) **Sun-Rype's board of directors approved the construction of a new production plant at a meeting in January 2013 and the borrowing of $2,000 from the local bank to finance the construction of the new plant in February 2013.**

Unlike transactions (*a*) through (*h*), which reflect exchanges between Sun-Rype and external parties, these two decisions of the board of directors are not transactions because no exchanges have taken place yet. The company's board of directors made commitments that will likely translate into actions in February 2013. Specific statement of financial position accounts will be affected only when the actual exchanges occur in February 2013. However, to improve on the representational faithfulness of financial statements, such commitments will normally be disclosed in a financial statement note.

HOW DO COMPANIES KEEP TRACK OF ACCOUNT BALANCES?

LO⁵

Determine the impact of business transactions on the statement of financial position by using two basic tools: journal entries and T-accounts.

For most organizations, recording transaction effects and keeping track of account balances in the manner just presented is impractical. To handle the multitude of daily transactions that businesses generate, companies establish accounting systems, usually computerized, that follow a cycle. The accounting cycle, illustrated in Exhibit 2.5, highlights the primary activities performed during the accounting period to analyze, record, and post transactions. In Chapters 2 and 3, we will illustrate these activities *during the period*. In Chapter 4, we will complete the accounting cycle by discussing and illustrating activities *at the end of the period* to adjust the records, prepare financial statements, and close the accounting records.

During the accounting period, transactions that result in exchanges between the company and other external parties are analyzed and recorded in the *general journal* in chronological order, and the related accounts are updated in the *general ledger*. These formal records are based on two very important tools used by accountants: journal entries and T-accounts. From the standpoint of accounting systems design, these analytical tools are more efficient mechanisms for reflecting the effects of transactions and for determining account balances for financial statement preparation. *As future business managers, you should develop your understanding and use of these tools in financial analysis. For those studying accounting, this knowledge is the foundation for understanding the accounting system and future accounting coursework.* After we explain how to perform transaction analysis by using these tools, we illustrate their use in financial analysis.

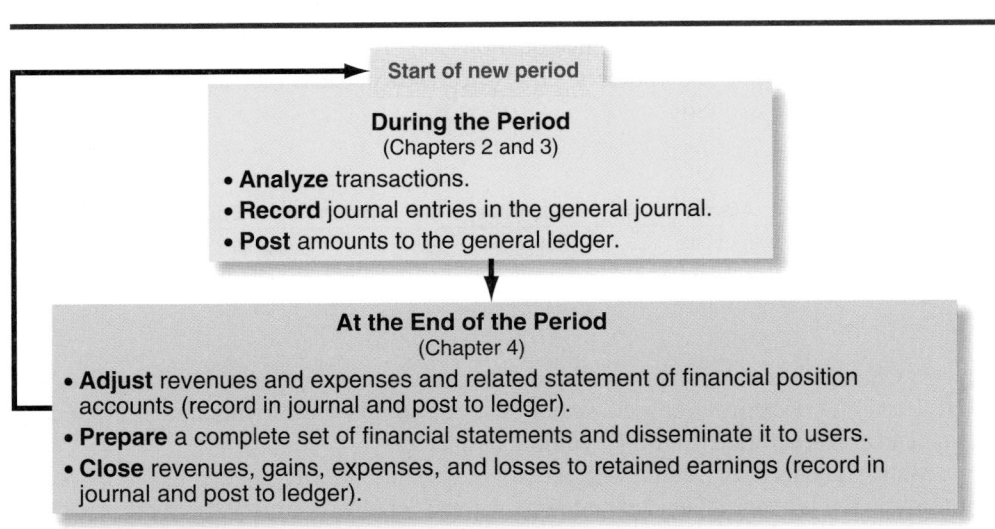

Exhibit **2.5**

The Accounting Cycle

Exhibit **2.6**

Transaction Analysis Model

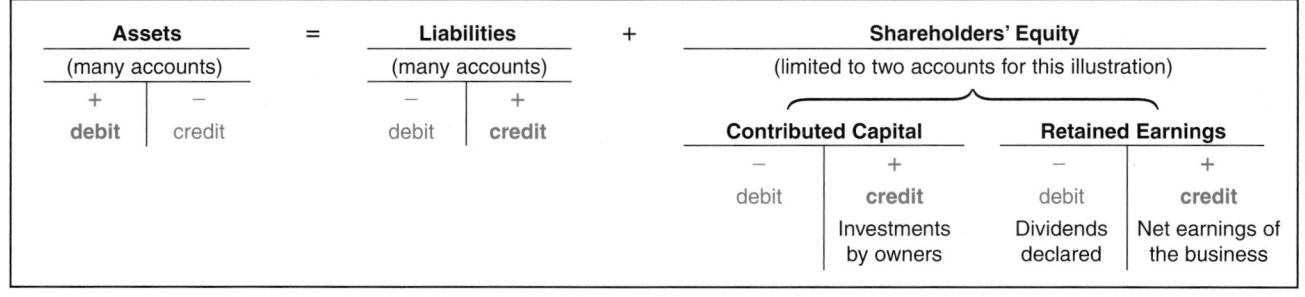

The Direction of Transaction Effects

As we saw earlier, transactions change the balances of assets, liabilities, and shareholders' equity accounts. To reflect these effects efficiently, we need to structure the transaction analysis model in a manner that shows the *direction* of the effects. One very useful tool for summarizing the transaction effects and determining the balances for individual accounts is a **T-account**, as shown in Exhibit 2.6. Notice the following:

The **T-ACCOUNT** is a tool for summarizing transaction effects for each account, determining balances, and drawing inferences about a company's activities.

- Each T-account has two sides: a left side, known as the debit side, and a right side, known as the credit side.
- The increase symbol, +, is located on the left side of the T for accounts that appear on the left side of the accounting equation (assets), and on the right side of the T for accounts that are on the right side of the equation (liabilities and shareholders' equity).

DEBIT (dr) is on the left side of an account.

- The term **debit** (dr for short) is always written on the left side of each account, and the term **credit** (cr for short) is always written on the right side.

CREDIT (cr) is on the right side of an account.

From this transaction analysis model, we can observe the following:

- Asset accounts increase on the left (debit) side. They have debit balances. It would be highly unusual for an asset account, such as inventories, to have a negative (credit) balance.
- Liabilities and shareholders' equity accounts increase on the right (credit) side, creating credit balances.

To remember which accounts are increased by debit and which accounts are increased by credit, recall that a debit (left) increases asset accounts, because assets are on the left side of the accounting equation (A − L + SE). Similarly, a credit (right) increases liability and shareholders' equity accounts because they are on the right side of the accounting equation.

In summary,

Assets	=	Liabilities	+	Shareholders' Equity
↑ with debits		↑ with credits		↑ with credits
Accounts have		Accounts have		Accounts have
debit balances		credit balances		credit balances

In Chapter 3, we will add revenue and expense account effects. Until then, as you are learning to perform transaction analysis, you should refer to this model often until you can construct it on your own without assistance.

Many students have trouble with accounting because they forget that the term "debit" is simply the left side of an account and the term "credit" is simply the right side of an account. Perhaps someone once told you that you were a credit to your school or your family. As a result, you may think that credits are good and debits are bad. Such is not the case. Just remember that *debit is on the left* and *credit is on the right*.

If you have identified the correct accounts and effects through transaction analysis, the accounting equation will remain in balance. Moreover, *the total monetary value of all debits equals the total monetary value of all credits* in a transaction. For an extra measure of assurance, add this equality check (debits = credits) to the transaction analysis process.

PAUSE FOR FEEDBACK

From Exhibit 2.6, we learned that each account can increase and decrease. In the transaction analysis model, the effect of a transaction on each element can be represented with a T, with one side increasing and the other side decreasing. The balances of asset accounts that appear on the left side of the accounting equation are increased on the left side of the T. The balances of liability and shareholders' equity accounts that are on the right side of the accounting equation are increased on the right side of the T. In accounting, the left side of the T is called the debit side and the right side is called the credit side. Most accounts have a balance on the positive side.

SELF-STUDY QUIZ 2-3

The following is a list of items from a recent statement of financial position for Tim Hortons Inc. Indicate on the line provided whether each of the following accounts usually has a debit (dr) or a credit (cr) balance.

_____ Accrued liabilities	_____ Long-term debt	_____ Property and equipment
_____ Inventories	_____ Retained earnings	_____ Notes receivable (due in five years)
_____ Trade receivables	_____ Trade payables	_____ Cash

After you have completed your answers, check them with the solutions at the end of the chapter.

Analytical Tools

The Journal Entry   In a bookkeeping system, transactions are initially recorded in chronological order in a *general journal* (see Appendix C, available on *Connect*, for a detailed illustration of formal recordkeeping procedures). After analyzing the business documents (such as purchase invoices, receipts, and cash register tapes) that describe a transaction, the bookkeeper prepares the formal journal entry and enters the effects on the accounts by using debits and credits. The **journal entry**, then, is an accounting method for expressing the effects of a transaction on various accounts, using the double-entry bookkeeping system explained previously. The journal entry for transaction (*c*) in the Sun-Rype illustration is written as follows:

A JOURNAL ENTRY is an accounting method for expressing the effects of a transaction on various accounts, using the double-entry bookkeeping system.

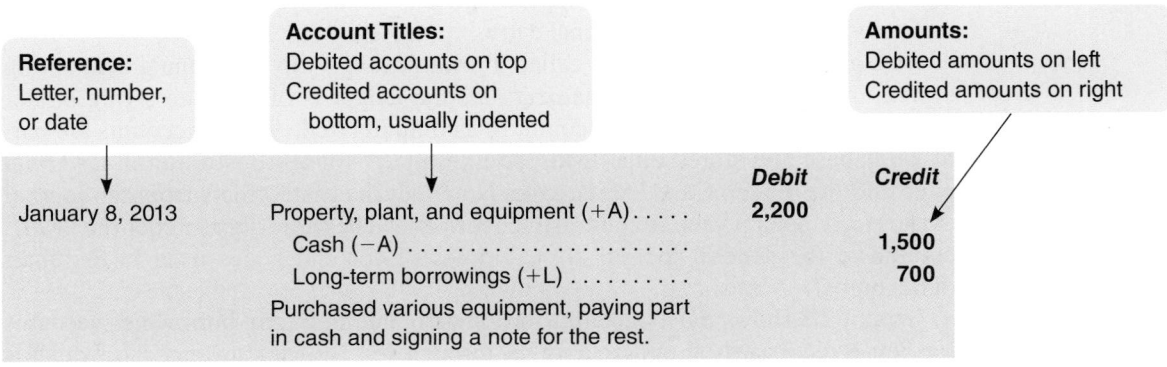

Reference:
Letter, number, or date

Account Titles:
Debited accounts on top
Credited accounts on bottom, usually indented

Amounts:
Debited amounts on left
Credited amounts on right

		Debit	Credit
January 8, 2013	Property, plant, and equipment (+A).	2,200	
	Cash (−A)		1,500
	Long-term borrowings (+L)		700
	Purchased various equipment, paying part in cash and signing a note for the rest.		

Notice the following:

- It is useful to include a date or some form of reference for each transaction. The debited accounts are written first (on top) with the amounts recorded in the left column. The credited accounts are written below the debits and are indented to the right in manual records; the credited amounts are written in the right column. The order of the debited accounts or credited accounts does not matter, as long as the debits are on top and the credits are on the bottom and indented to the right.
- Total debits ($2,200) equal total credits ($1,500 + $700).
- Three accounts are affected by this transaction. Any journal entry that affects more than two accounts is called a *compound entry*. Although this is the only transaction in the preceding illustration that affects more than two accounts, many transactions in subsequent chapters will require compound journal entries.

Recording external transactions in the journal is based on legal documents that highlight the contractual commitments between Sun-Rype and other parties. For example, Sun-Rype signed a contract with a manufacturer to purchase equipment for $2,200. It issued a cheque for $1,500 to transfer cash to the manufacturer and promised to pay $700 in two years. Consequently, the effects of this transaction are recorded in the journal and reflected in Sun-Rype's financial statements. The equipment manufacturer retains legal control of the equipment until it is fully paid after two years. For accounting purposes, however, Sun-Rype has control of and will use this resource to generate revenue over the next two years. This highlights the focus on the economic substance of a transaction rather than its legal form in reporting information to financial statement users. While recording external transactions in the journal requires legal documents, some legal contracts, such as signing a contract to hire a new employee, are not reflected in the financial statements.

While you are learning to perform transaction analysis, use the symbol A, L, or SE next to each account title, as in the preceding journal entry, for all homework problems. Specifically identifying accounts as assets (A), liabilities (L), or shareholders' equity (SE) clarifies the transaction analysis and makes journal entries easier to write. For example, if Cash is to be increased, we will write Cash (+A). Throughout subsequent chapters, we include the direction of the effect along with the symbol to help you understand the effects of each transaction on the financial statements.

Many students try to memorize journal entries without understanding or using the transaction analysis model. The task becomes increasingly difficult as more detailed transactions are presented in subsequent chapters. In the long run, *memorizing, understanding, and using the transaction analysis model* presented here will save you time and prevent confusion.

The T-Account   By themselves, journal entries do not provide the balances in accounts. After the journal entries have been recorded, the bookkeeper posts (transfers) the monetary values to each account affected by the transaction to determine the new account balances. In most computerized accounting systems, this happens automatically upon recording the journal entry.

As a group, the accounts are called a *general ledger*. In the manual accounting system used by some small organizations, the ledger is often a three-ring binder with a separate page for each account. In a computerized system, accounts are part of a database and stored on a disk. See Exhibit 2.7 for an illustration of a journal page and the related Cash ledger page. Note that the cash effects from the journal entries have been posted to the Cash ledger page. The three digits under the "Ref." column in the general journal are examples of account codes used in the chart of accounts.

Exhibit 2.8 shows the T-accounts for the cash and long-term borrowings accounts for Sun-Rype, based on transactions (*a*) through (*h*). Notice that for Cash, which is

Exhibit **2.7**

Posting Transaction Effects from
the Journal to the Ledger

General Journal   Page G1

Date	Account Titles and Explanation (in thousands)	Ref.	Debit	Credit
Jan. 2	Cash	101	1,300	
	Contributed capital			1,300
	Investment by shareholders.			
Jan. 6	Cash	101	1,000	
	Long-term borrowings	201		1,000
	Borrowed from bank.			
Jan. 8	Property and equipment	140	**2,200**	
	Cash	101		**1,500**
	Long-term borrowings	201		**700**
	Purchased equipment paying part cash			
	and the rest due on a note payable.			

General Ledger			**Cash**		101
Date	Explanation	Ref.	Debit	Credit	Balance
	Balance				3,727
Jan. 2		G1	1,300		5,027
Jan. 6		G1	1,000		6,027
Jan. 8		G1		1,500	4,527

General Ledger			**Property, Plant, and Equipment**		140
Date	Explanation	Ref.	Debit	Credit	Balance
	Balance				42,041
Jan. 8		G1	2,200		44,241

General Ledger			**Long-Term Borrowings**		201
Date	Explanation	Ref.	Debit	Credit	Balance
	Balance				8,781
Jan. 6		G1		1,000	9,781
Jan. 8		G1		700	10,481

Exhibit **2.8**

T-Accounts Illustrated

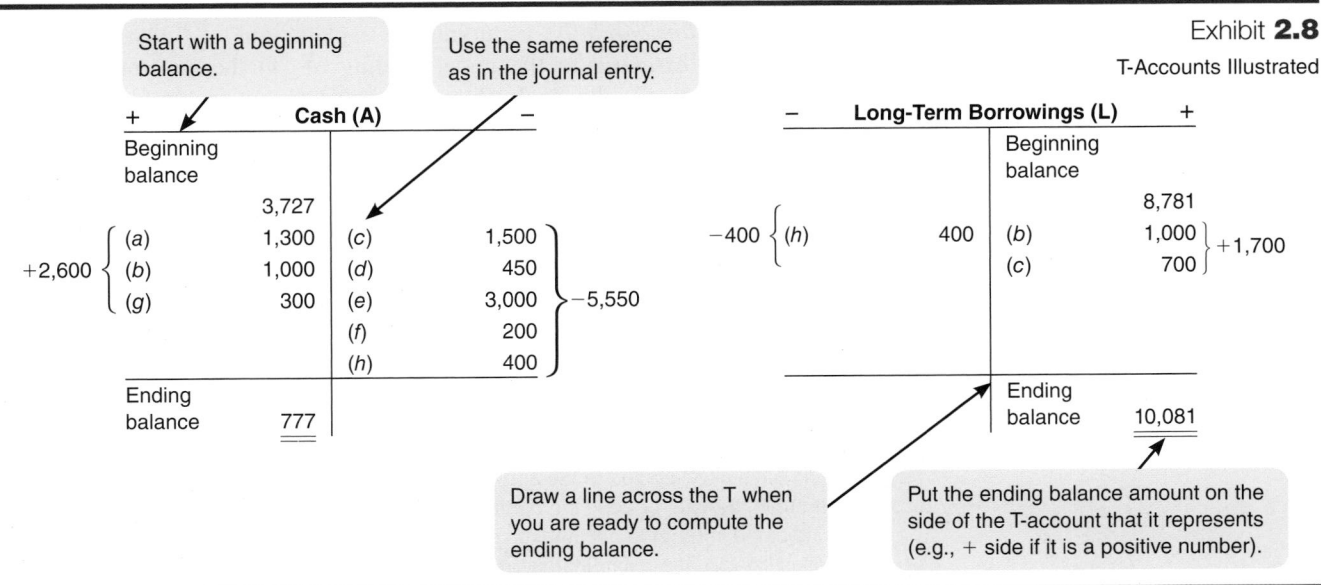

Start with a beginning
balance.

Use the same reference
as in the journal entry.

	+	Cash (A)	−	
	Beginning balance			
	3,727			
	(a) 1,300	(c)	1,500	
+2,600	(b) 1,000	(d)	450	
	(g) 300	(e)	3,000	−5,550
		(f)	200	
		(h)	400	
	Ending balance	777		

	−	Long-Term Borrowings (L)	+	
−400	(h)	400	Beginning balance	
			8,781	
			(b) 1,000	+1,700
			(c) 700	
			Ending balance 10,081	

Draw a line across the T when
you are ready to compute the
ending balance.

Put the ending balance amount on the
side of the T-account that it represents
(e.g., + side if it is a positive number).

an asset, increases are shown on the left and decreases are on the right side of the T-account. For long-term borrowings, however, increases are shown on the right and decreases on the left since notes payable is a liability. Some small businesses still use handwritten or manually maintained accounts in this T-account format. Computerized systems retain the concept but not the format of the T-account.

In Exhibit 2.8, notice that the ending balance is indicated on the positive side with a double underline. To find the account balances, we can express the T-accounts as equations:

	Cash	Long-Term Borrowings
Beginning balance	$ 3,727	$8,781
+ "+" side	+2,600	+1,700
− "−" side	−5,550	−400
Ending balance	$ 777	$10,081

A word on terminology: the words "debit" and "credit" are used as verbs, nouns, and adjectives. For example, we can say that Sun-Rype's Cash account was debited (verb) when shares were issued to investors, meaning that the amount was entered on the left side of the T-account. Or we can say that a credit (noun) was entered on the right side of an account. Borrowings may be described as a credit account (adjective). These terms will be used instead of "left" and "right" throughout the rest of the textbook.

The next section illustrates the steps to follow in analyzing the effects of transactions, recording the effects in journal entries, and determining account balances by using T-accounts.

Transaction Analysis Illustrated

In this section, we will use the monthly transactions of Sun-Rype that were presented earlier to demonstrate transaction analysis and the use of journal entries and T-accounts. We analyze each transaction, checking to make sure that the accounting equation remains in balance and that debits equal credits. The amounts from Sun-Rype's statement of financial position at January 1, 2013, have been inserted as the beginning balances in the T-accounts, located together at the end of the illustration. After reviewing or preparing each journal entry, trace the effects to the appropriate T-accounts by using the transaction letters (*a*) to (*h*) as a reference. The first transaction has been highlighted for you.

Study this illustration carefully, including the explanations of transaction analysis. Careful study is *essential* to the understanding of (1) the accounting model, (2) transaction analysis, (3) the dual effects of each transaction, and (4) the dual-balancing system. *The most effective way to learn these critical concepts that affect material throughout the rest of the textbook is to practise, practise, practise.*

(*a*) **Sun-Rype issues shares to new investors in exchange for $1,300 in cash.**

Cash (+A)   1,300
   Contributed capital (+SE)   1,300
Issued contributed capital for cash.

Assets		=	Liabilities	+	Shareholders' Equity	
Cash	+1,300				Contributed capital	+1,300

These effects have been posted to the appropriate T-accounts at the end of the illustration. To post the amounts, transfer or copy the debit or credit amount on each line to the appropriate T-account indicated in order to accumulate balances for each account. For example, the $1,300 debit is listed in the debit (increase) column of the Cash T-account.

(*b*) **The company borrows $1,000 from its local bank, signing a note to be paid in two years.**

Cash (+A) 1,000
   Long-term borrowings (+L) 1,000
Borrowed money from the local bank, payable in two years.

Assets		=	Liabilities		+	Shareholders' Equity
Cash	+1,000		Long-term borrowings	+1,000		

(*c*) **For expansion, Sun-Rype opened a new production facility. The company purchased $2,200 of new processing and packaging equipment and storage tanks, paying $1,500 in cash and signing a note for $700, payable to the equipment manufacturer in two years.**

Property, plant, and equipment (+A) 2,200
   Cash (−A) 1,500
   Long-term borrowings (+L) 700
Purchased various equipment, paying part in cash and signing
a note for the rest, payable in two years.

Assets		=	Liabilities		+	Shareholders' Equity
Property, plant, and equipment	+2,200		Long-term borrowings	+700		
Cash	−1,500					

(*d*) **Sun-Rype lends $450 to a trade supplier in financial difficulty. The trade supplier signs notes agreeing to repay the amount borrowed within six months.**

Notes receivable (+A) 450
   Cash (−A) 450
Lent money to a trade supplier; to be repaid within six months.

Assets		=	Liabilities	+	Shareholders' Equity
Cash	−450				
Notes receivable	+450				

(*e*) **Sun-Rype purchases shares issued by another corporation as a long-term investment, paying $3,000 in cash.**

Investments (+A) 3,000
   Cash (−A) 3,000
Purchased shares in another corporation as a long-term investment.

Assets		=	Liabilities	+	Shareholders' Equity
Cash	−3000				
Investments	+3000				

(*f*) **Sun-Rype's board of directors declares cash dividends of $200 for shareholders. The dividends are paid immediately.**

Retained earnings (−SE) 200
   Cash (−A) 200
Declared and paid dividends to shareholders.

Assets		=	Liabilities	+	Shareholders' Equity	
Cash	−200				Retained earnings	−200

PAUSE FOR FEEDBACK

Accountants record transactions first in the general journal in chronological order in journal entry form. Debited accounts are written on top with amounts in the left column, and credited accounts are written on the bottom with amounts in the right column. Then the effects are posted in the general ledger. Each page of the ledger represents a different account, which has a debit (left) side and a credit (right) side. To post transaction effects, the amount for each account in a journal entry is written in the appropriate debit or credit column on the ledger page, to obtain account balances.

SELF-STUDY QUIZ 2-4

For transactions (g) and (h), fill in the missing information, including postings to the T-accounts.

(g) Sun-Rype collects $300 cash from the trade supplier.

Write the journal entry.

[Post to the T-accounts.]

Collection of note from trade supplier.

Assets		=	Liabilities	+	Shareholders' Equity
Cash	+300				
Notes receivable	−300				

(h) Sun-Rype paid $400 on the note owed to the local bank.

Long-term borrowings (−L) 400   [Post to the
   Cash (−A) 400   T-accounts.]
Partial payment of the amount owed to the local bank.

Assets	=	Liabilities	+	Shareholders' Equity

The T-accounts that changed during the period because of these transactions are shown below. The beginning balances are the amounts from Sun-Rype's statement of financial position at December 31, 2012 (Exhibit 2.3). The balances of all other accounts remained the same.

Assets = **Liabilities + Shareholders' Equity**

+	Cash (A)		−
Beg. bal.	3,727		
(a)	1,300	(c)	1,500
(b)	1,000	(d)	450
(g)	☐	(e)	3,000
		(f)	200
		(h)	☐
End. bal.	777		

+	Property, Plant, and Equipment (A)	−
Beg. bal.	42,041	
(c)	2,200	
End. bal.	44,241	

+	Investments (A)		−
Beg. bal.	0		
(e)	3,000		
End. bal.	3,000		

+	Notes Receivable (A)		−
Beg. bal.	0		
(d)	450	(g)	☐
End. bal.	150		

−	Long-Term Borrowings (L)		+
		Beg. bal.	8,781
		(b)	1,000
(h) ☐		(c)	700
		End. bal.	10,081

−	Contributed Capital (SE)		+
		Beg. bal.	18,421
		(a)	1,300
		End. bal.	19,721

−	Retained Earnings (SE)		+
		Beg. bal.	28,681
(f)	200		
		End. bal.	☐

You can verify that you posted the entries properly by adding the increase side and subtracting the decrease side and then comparing your answer to the ending balance for each T-account. Check your answers with the solutions at the end of the chapter.

INFERRING BUSINESS ACTIVITIES FROM T-ACCOUNTS

FINANCIAL
ANALYSIS

T-accounts are useful primarily for instructional and analytical purposes. In many cases, we will use T-accounts to determine what transactions a company engaged in during a period. For example, the primary transactions affecting trade payables for a period are purchases of assets on account and cash payments to suppliers. If we know the beginning and ending balances of trade payables and all of the amounts that were purchased on credit during a period, we can determine the amount of cash paid, p. A T-account will include the following:

–	Trade Payables (L)		+
	Beg. bal.	600	
Cash payments to suppliers ?	Purchases on account	1,500	
	End. bal.	300	

Solution:

Beginning balance	+	Purchases on account	–	Cash payments to suppliers	=	Ending balance
$600	+	$1,500	–	p	=	$300
		$2,100	–	p	=	$300
				p	=	$1,800

HOW IS THE STATEMENT OF FINANCIAL POSITION PREPARED AND ANALYZED?

LO6

Prepare a classified statement of financial position and analyze it by using the current ratio.

As discussed in Chapter 1, a statement of financial position is one of the financial statements that will be communicated to users, especially those external to the business. It is possible to prepare a classified statement of financial position at any point in time from the balances in the accounts.

Classified Statement of Financial Position

The statement of financial position in Exhibit 2.9 was prepared by using the new balances shown in the T-accounts in the preceding Sun-Rype illustration. The accounts that have changed since December 31, 2012, are highlighted (shaded lines in the exhibit). Notice several additional features in Exhibit 2.9:

- The assets and liabilities are classified into two categories: *current* and *non-current*. Current assets are those to be used or transformed into cash within the upcoming year, whereas non-current assets are those that will last longer than one year. Current liabilities are those obligations to be paid or settled within the next 12 months with current assets.

- Dollar signs are indicated at the top and bottom of both the asset section and the liabilities and shareholders' equity section.

- The statement includes comparative data. That is, it compares the account balances at January 31, 2013, with those at December 31, 2012. When multiple periods are presented, the most recent statement of financial position amounts are usually listed on the left.

At the beginning of the chapter, we presented the changes in Sun-Rype's total assets from 2000 to 2012. We questioned what made the accounts change and what the process was for reflecting the changes. Now we can see that the assets have changed again in one month, along with liabilities and shareholders' equity, because of the transactions illustrated in this chapter:

	Assets	=	Liabilities	+	Shareholders' Equity
January 31, 2013	93,373		45,237		48,136
December 31, 2012	90,973		43,937		47,036
Change	+ 2,400		+ 1,300		+ 1,100

Exhibit **2.9**

Sun-Rype's Statement of Financial Position

SUN-RYPE PRODUCTS LTD.
Consolidated Statement of Financial Position
(in thousands of Canadian dollars)

Assets	January 31, 2013	December 31, 2012
Current assets		
Cash	$ 777	$ 3,727
Trade and other receivables	14,047	14,047
Notes receivable	150	–
Inventories	29,149	29,149
Prepayments	502	502
Other current assets	446	446
Total current assets	**45,071**	**47,871**
Non-current assets		
Investments	3,000	–
Property, plant, and equipment	44,241	42,041
Goodwill	1,061	1,061
Total non-current assets	**48,302**	**43,102**
Total assets	**$93,373**	**$90,973**
Liabilities and Equity		
Current liabilities		
Trade and other payables	$25,672	$25,672
Provisions	1,687	1,687
Income taxes payable	116	116
Short-term borrowings	3,646	3,646
Total current liabilities	**31,121**	**31,121**
Non-current liabilities		
Long-term borrowings	10,081	8,781
Deferred tax liabilities	4,035	4,035
Total non-current liabilities	**14,116**	**12,816**
Total liabilities	**45,237**	**43,937**
Equity		
Contributed capital	19,721	18,421
Retained earnings	28,481	28,681
Other components	(66)	(66)
Total equity	**48,136**	**47,036**
Total liabilities and equity	**$93,373**	**$90,973**

KEY RATIO ANALYSIS

THE CURRENT RATIO

Users of financial information compute a number of ratios when analyzing a company's past performance and financial condition as input in predicting its future potential. The change in ratios over time and how they compare to the ratios of the company's competitors or industry averages provide valuable information about a company's strategies for its operating, investing, and financing activities.

We introduce here the first of many ratios that will be presented throughout the rest of this textbook, with a final summary of ratio analysis in Chapter 13. In Chapters 2, 3, and 4, we present four ratios that provide information about management's effectiveness at managing short-term debt (current ratio), controlling revenues and expenses (net profit margin), and utilizing assets (total asset turnover ratio and return on assets), all for the purpose of enhancing returns to shareholders. The remaining chapters discuss other ratios that provide valuable information to assess a company's strategies, strengths, and areas of concern.

As we discussed earlier in the chapter, companies raise large amounts of money to acquire additional assets by issuing shares to investors and borrowing funds from creditors. These additional assets are used to generate more earnings. However, since debt must be repaid, taking on increasing amounts of debt carries increased risk. Information about current liabilities is very important to managers and analysts because these obligations must be paid in the near future. Analysts say that a company has liquidity if it has the ability to pay its current obligations. Companies that do not settle their current obligations in a timely manner quickly find that suppliers of goods and services may not be prepared to grant them credit for their purchases, potentially forcing them to seek short-term financing through banks. The current ratio provides one measure for analysts to examine the company's financing strategy.

ANALYTICAL QUESTION → Does the company currently have the resources to pay its short-term debt?

RATIO AND COMPARISONS → Analysts use the *current ratio* as an indicator of the amount of current assets available to satisfy current liabilities. It is computed as follows:

Current Ratio = Current Assets ÷ Current Liabilities

The 2012 ratio for Sun-Rype is

$$\$47{,}871 \div \$31{,}121 = 1.54$$

<table>
<tr><th colspan="3">Comparisons over Time</th><th colspan="2">Comparisons with Competitors</th></tr>
<tr><th colspan="3">Sun-Rype</th><th>Lassonde Industries Inc.</th><th>Leading Brands Inc.*</th></tr>
<tr><th>2010</th><th>2011</th><th>2012</th><th>2012</th><th>2012</th></tr>
<tr><td>1.97</td><td>1.52</td><td>1.54</td><td>2.01</td><td>1.06</td></tr>
</table>

*The fiscal year of Leading Brands ended on February 28, 2013.

INTERPRETATIONS

In General → The current ratio is a very common ratio. Creditors and security analysts use the current ratio to measure the ability of the company to pay its short-term obligations with short-term assets. Generally, the higher the ratio, the more cushion a company has to pay its current obligations if future economic conditions take a downturn. While a high ratio normally suggests good liquidity, too high a ratio suggests inefficient use of resources. An old guideline was that companies should have a current ratio between 1.0 and 2.0. Today, many strong companies use sophisticated management techniques to minimize funds invested in current assets and, as a result, have current ratios below 1.0.

Focus Company Analysis → Sun-Rype's current ratio for 2012 indicates that the company has $1.54 for each $1.00 in current liabilities. The ratio decreased in 2011 primarily because of an increase in short-term borrowings to pay for the acquisition of Naumes Concentrates Inc. in June 2011 as part of the company's growth strategy. In some cases, analysts would be concerned about both the level and the trend, but the situation is understandable when considering the reason for the decline in the ratio. Sun-Rype's ratio is between those of its competitors, Lassonde Industries Inc. and Leading Brands Inc. Since all three companies have ratios exceeding 1.0, this suggests that they have sufficient liquidity to meet their short-term obligations.

A Few Cautions → The current ratio may be a misleading measure of liquidity if significant funds are tied up in assets that are not easily converted into cash. A company with a high current ratio might still have liquidity problems if the majority of its current assets are slow-moving inventory. Analysts recognize that managers can manipulate the current ratio by engaging in particular types of transactions just before the close of the fiscal year. For example, the current ratio can be improved by paying creditors immediately prior to the preparation of financial statements.

SELECTED FOCUS COMPANY CURRENT RATIOS—2012

Danier Leather Inc. 5.19

Gildan Activewear Inc. 3.57

WestJet Airlines Ltd. 1.38

Lassonde Industries Inc. is a leading North American company that develops, manufactures, and sells innovative and distinctive lines of fruit and vegetable juices and drinks marketed under recognized brands such as Everfresh, Fairlee, Fruité, Oasis, and Rougemont.

Leading Brands Inc. is a fully integrated Canadian company that specializes in beverage bottling, distribution, sales, merchandising, brand development, brand licensing, and brand management of beverage products. Its products are distributed to customers across Canada, the western United States, and Asia.

As you can see, using the relevant financial information from financial statements to calculate a single ratio is only the first step toward understanding whether a company is healthy enough to merit your investment money. The real challenges are discovering why the ratios have changed over time, comparing the ratios with competitors' ratios, developing a keen understanding of the industry and businesses, and using all this knowledge to predict the future for a company.

PAUSE FOR FEEDBACK

We just learned that the current ratio measures a company's ability to pay short-term obligations with short-term assets—a liquidity measure. It is computed by dividing current assets by current liabilities. A ratio between 1.0 and 2.0 is normally considered good, although some companies may need a higher ratio, while other companies with good cash management systems can have a ratio below 1.0 (i.e., more current liabilities than current assets).

SELF-STUDY QUIZ 2-5

Dollarama Inc. is the leading dollar store operator in Canada, with more than 700 locations across the country. The company offers a broad assortment of everyday consumer products, general merchandise, and seasonal items. It reported the following balances on its recent statements of financial position (in millions). Compute Dollarama's current ratio for the three years.

	Current Assets	Current Liabilities	Current Ratio
January 29, 2012	$396	$143	
January 30, 2011	319	137	
February 1, 2010	338	159	

What does this ratio suggest about Dollarama's liquidity in the current year and over time?

After you complete your answers, check them with the solutions at the end of the chapter.

FOCUS ON CASH FLOWS

INVESTING AND FINANCING ACTIVITIES

LO7

Identify investing and financing transactions and demonstrate how they are reported on the statement of cash flows.

Recall from Chapter 1 that companies report cash inflows and outflows over a period in their statement of cash flows. This statement divides all transactions that affect cash into three categories: operating, investing, and financing activities. Investing and financing activities are covered in this chapter, whereas operating activities are covered in Chapter 3.

The eight transactions we have analyzed for Sun-Rype are issuing shares, borrowing from a bank, purchasing equipment, lending to trade suppliers, purchasing shares in other companies, declaring and paying dividends, collecting cash on a note receivable, and paying down a bank loan (see Exhibit 2.10). All of these transactions affected cash. Four of the eight transactions relate to investment activities, and the other four relate to financing activities.

The first set includes one transaction that increased cash inflow and three transactions that decreased cash. The collection on notes receivable increased cash by $300. On the other hand, the payment of $1,500 in cash for the purchase of equipment, the short-term loan to trade suppliers for $450, and the investment in shares of other companies for $3,000 resulted in a total cash outflow of $4,950. The net change to cash from investment activities is an outflow of *$4,650.*

The second set of transactions relates to financing activities and includes two transactions that increased cash and two transactions that decreased cash. The issuance of shares for $1,300 and borrowing $1,000 from the bank increased cash by $2,300. In contrast, payment of dividends of $200 and partial repayment on a bank loan of $400 decreased cash by $600 during the same period. The net change to cash from financing activities is an inflow of *$1,700.* In summary, the change in the cash balance from $3,727 at December 31, 2012, to $777 at January 31, 2013, can be explained as follows:

Cash from (used for) investment activities	$(4,650)
Cash from (used for) financing activities	1,700
Net change in cash flow	(2,950)
Cash at beginning of month	3,727
Cash at end of month	$ 777

Exhibit **2.10**

Sun-Rype's Statement of Cash Flows

SUN-RYPE PRODUCTS LTD.
Consolidated Statement of Cash Flows
For the Month Ended January 31, 2013
(in thousands of Canadian dollars)

Operating Activities		
(none in this chapter)		*Items are referenced to events (a) through (h) illustrated in this chapter.*
Investing Activities		
Purchased equipment (*c*)	$(1,500)	*Also called capital expenditures*
Purchased long-term investments (*e*)	(3,000)	
Lent funds to trade supplier (*d*)	(450)	
Received payment on loans to trade supplier (*g*)	300	
Net cash used in investing activities	**(4,650)**	
Financing Activities		
Issued shares (*a*)	1,300	
Borrowed from banks (*b*)	1,000	
Repaid loan from bank (*h*)	(400)	
Paid dividends (*f*)	(200)	
Net cash provided by financing activities	**1,700**	
Net decrease in cash	**(2,950)**	
Cash at beginning of month	3,727	*Agrees with the cash balance*
Cash at end of month	**$ 777** ←	*reported on the statement of financial position*

The statement of cash flows provides information that not only shows the sources and uses of cash but also helps both investors and creditors predict future cash flows for Sun-Rype and make appropriate financial decisions. The pattern of cash flows shown in Exhibit 2.10 (net cash outflows for investing activities and net cash flows from financing activities) is typical of Sun-Rype's past several annual statements of cash flows. Companies seeking to expand usually report cash outflows for investing activities.

PAUSE FOR **FEEDBACK**

As we discussed, every transaction affecting cash can be classified as an operating (discussed in Chapter 3), an investing, or a financing activity. Investing activities relate to purchasing/selling investments or property and equipment or lending funds to/receiving repayment from others. Financing activities relate to borrowing or repaying banks, issuing shares to investors, repurchasing shares from investors, or paying dividends to investors.

SELF-STUDY **QUIZ 2-6**

Lance Inc. manufactures and sells snack products. Indicate whether the following transactions from a recent statement of cash flows were investing (I) or financing (F) activities, and show the direction of the effect on cash (+ means increases cash; − means decreases cash):

Transaction	Type of Activity (I or F)	Effect on Cash Flows (+ or −)
1. Paid dividends		
2. Sold property		
3. Repaid debt		
4. Purchased vending machines		
5. Issued new shares		

After you complete your answers, check them with the solutions at the end of the chapter.

Some Misconceptions

Some people confuse bookkeeping with accounting. In effect, they confuse a part of accounting with the whole. Bookkeeping involves routine data entry, a clerical task that requires only minimal knowledge of accounting. A bookkeeper may record the repetitive and uncomplicated transactions in most businesses and may maintain the simple records of a small business. In contrast, the accountant is a highly trained professional, competent in the design of information systems, analysis of complex transactions, financial reporting, interpretation of financial data, auditing, taxation, and management consulting.

Another prevalent misconception is that all transactions are subject to precise and objective measurement, and that the accounting results reported in the financial statements are exactly what happened during that period. In reality, accounting numbers are influenced by estimates, as subsequent chapters will illustrate. Some people believe that financial statements report the entity's market value (including its assets), but they do not. To understand and interpret financial statements, you must be aware of their limitations as well as their usefulness. You should understand what the financial statements do and do not try to accomplish.

Finally, financial statements are often thought to be inflexible because of their quantitative nature. As you study accounting, you will learn that it requires considerable *professional judgment* on the part of the accountant to capture the economic essence of complex transactions. Accountants develop professional judgment after years of experience in analyzing business transactions and in applying accounting principles and financial reporting standards in preparing and auditing financial reports. Accounting is stimulating intellectually; it is not a cut-and-dried subject. It calls on your intelligence, analytical ability, creativity, and judgment. Accounting is a communication process involving an audience (users) with a wide diversity of knowledge, interest, and capabilities; therefore, it will call on your ability as a communicator. The language of accounting uses concisely written phrases and symbols to convey information about the resource flows measured for specific organizations.

To understand financial statements, you must have a certain level of knowledge of the concepts and the measurement procedures used in the accounting process. You should learn what accounting is really like and appreciate the reasons for using certain procedures. This level of knowledge cannot be gained by reading a list of the concepts and a list of the misconceptions. Neither can a generalized discussion of the subject matter suffice. A certain amount of involvement, primarily problem solving (similar to the requirement in mathematics courses), is essential in the study of accounting focused on the needs of the user. Therefore, we provide problems aimed at the desirable knowledge level for the user as well as the preparer of financial statements.

ACCOUNTING STANDARDS
FOR PRIVATE ENTERPRISES

As noted in Chapter 1, the accounting standards applicable for the reporting of financial information by private enterprises may differ from IFRS, especially the accounting for complex transactions and the extent of detail reported in the notes to the financial statements. Differences in the application of accounting standards may lead to different values for assets, liabilities, and equity, which are reported on the statement of financial position. A few differences are highlighted below.

Financial Reporting Issue	IFRS	ASPE
Presentation of assets, liabilities, and shareholders' equity	Publicly accountable enterprises have a choice between two ways of presenting their assets and liabilities. The choice depends upon which method provides the most relevant information. Companies may list their assets in increasing order of liquidity, with the least-liquid assets listed at the top of the assets. Hence, non-current assets are presented before current assets. IFRS similarly emphasize longer-term financing sources by listing equity before liabilities and, within liabilities, by listing non-current liabilities before current liabilities (decreasing time to maturity). However, assets should be reported by decreasing order of liquidity and liabilities by increasing time to maturity if such classification provides more relevant information to users of financial statements.	Private enterprises report their assets in a decreasing order of liquidity, with the most-liquid asset (cash) presented first. Similarly, liabilities are reported in order of time to maturity. Current assets are presented before non-current assets, and current liabilities appear before non-current liabilities.
Asset valuation	Publicly accountable enterprises may choose to report their assets using either the cost model or the revaluation model. For example, property, plant, and equipment can be reported at fair value (e.g., net sales price) provided that the company uses this method consistently over time. This allows the company to record increases and decreases in the values of these assets.	Private enterprises are required to report assets at historical cost and are not permitted to record increases in these assets over time.

DEMONSTRATION **CASE**

On April 1, 2014, three ambitious college students started Terrific Lawn Maintenance Corporation. Completed transactions (summarized) through April 30, 2014, for Terrific Lawn Maintenance Corporation follow:

a. Issued 1,500 shares in exchange for $9,000 cash. Each investor received 500 shares.
b. Acquired rakes and other hand tools (equipment) with a list price of $690 for $600; paid the hardware store $200 cash and signed a note for the balance with the hardware store.
c. Ordered three lawn mowers and two edgers from Lawn Supply Inc. for $4,000.
d. Purchased four acres of land as a future site of a storage garage. Paid cash, $5,000.
e. Received the mowers and edgers that had been ordered, signing a note to pay Lawn Supply in full, in 30 days.
f. Sold one acre of land to the city for a park. The city paid Terrific Lawn Maintenance Corp. $1,250, the cost of the land in cash.
g. One of the owners borrowed $3,000 from a local bank for personal use.

Required:

1. Set up T-accounts for cash, equipment (for hand tools and mowing equipment), land, short-term notes payable (to equipment supply companies), and contributed capital. Indicate beginning balances of $0 in the T-accounts. Analyze each transaction by using the process outlined in the chapter. Prepare journal entries in chronological order. Enter the effects of the transactions in the appropriate T-accounts. Identify each amount with its letter in the preceding list. Use the following transaction analysis model:

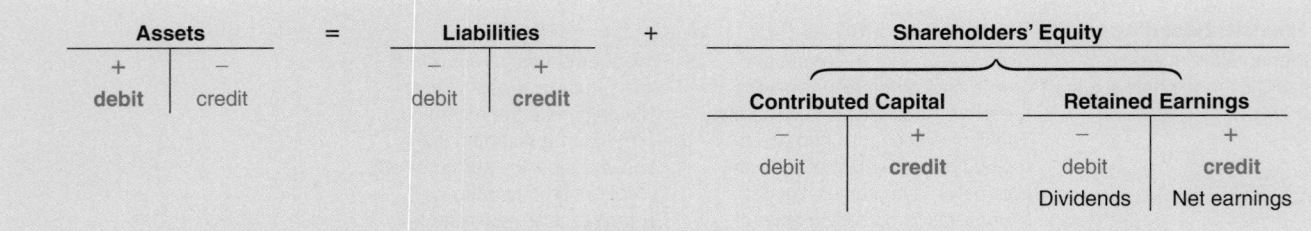

Assets		=	Liabilities		+	Shareholders' Equity			
+	−		−	+		**Contributed Capital**		**Retained Earnings**	
debit	credit		debit	**credit**		−	+	−	+
						debit	**credit**	debit	**credit**
								Dividends	Net earnings

2. Use the amounts in the T-accounts developed in (1) to prepare a classified statement of financial position for Terrific Lawn Maintenance Corporation at April 30, 2014. Show the account balances for all assets, liabilities, and shareholders' equity.

3. Prepare the investing and financing sections of the statement of cash flows.

We strongly recommend that you prepare your own answers to these requirements and then check your answers with the following solution.

SUGGESTED **SOLUTION**

1. Transaction analysis, journal entries, and T-accounts:

(**a**) Cash (+A) 9,000
        Contributed capital (+SE) 9,000

Assets		=	Liabilities	+	Shareholders' Equity	
Cash	+9,000				Contributed capital	+9,000

(**b**) Equipment (+A) 600
        Cash (−A) 200
        Short-term notes payable (+L) 400

Assets		=	Liabilities		+	Shareholders' Equity
Equipment	+600		Short-term notes			
Cash	−200		payable	+400		

The historical cost principle states that assets should be recorded at the amount paid on the date of the transaction. This is $600, not the list price of $690.

(**c**) This is not a transaction; no exchange has taken place. No accounts are affected.

(**d**) Land (+A) 5,000
        Cash (−A) 5,000

Assets		=	Liabilities	+	Shareholders' Equity
Land	+5,000				
Cash	−5,000				

(**e**) Equipment (+A) 4,000
        Short-term notes payable (+L) 4,000

Assets		=	Liabilities		+	Shareholders' Equity
Equipment	+4,000		Short-term notes			
			payable	+4,000		

(**f**) Cash (+A) 1,250
        Land (−A) 1,250

Assets		=	Liabilities	+	Shareholders' Equity
Cash	+1,250				
Land	−1,250				

(*g*) This is not a transaction that involves the company. The separate-entity assumption states that transactions of the owners are separate from transactions of the business.

	Assets							=		Liabilities + Shareholders' Equity	
+	**Cash (A)**		**−**	**+**	**Equipment (A)**		**−**		**−**	**Short-Term Notes Payable (L)**	**+**
Beg. bal.	0			Beg. bal.	0					Beg. bal.	0
(*a*)	9,000	(*b*)	200	(*b*)	600					(*b*)	400
(*f*)	1,250	(*d*)	5,000	(*e*)	4,000					(*e*)	4,000
				End. bal.	4,600					End. bal.	4,400
End. bal.	5,050										
									−	**Contributed (SE) Capital**	**+**
+	**Land (A)**		**−**							Beg. bal.	0
Beg. bal.	0									(*a*)	9,000
(*d*)	5,000	(*f*)	1,250							End. bal.	9,000
End. bal.	3,750										

2. Statement of financial position:

TERRIFIC LAWN MAINTENANCE CORPORATION
Statement of Financial Position
At April 30, 2014

Assets		Liabilities	
Current Assets		*Current Liability*	
Cash	$ 5,050	Short-term notes payable	$ 4,400
Total current assets	5,050		
Equipment	4,600	**Shareholders' Equity**	
Land	3,750	Contributed capital	9,000
Total assets	$13,400	Total liabilities and shareholders' equity	$13,400

   Notice that the statement of financial position presented earlier in the text listed assets on the top and liabilities and shareholders' equity on the bottom. It is also acceptable practice to prepare a statement of financial position with assets on the left side and liabilities and shareholders' equity on the right side, as in the preceding example.

3. Investing and financing effects of the statement of cash flows:

TERRIFIC LAWN MAINTENANCE CORPORATION
Statement of Cash Flows
For the Month Ended April 30, 2014

Operating Activities	
(none in this case)	
Investing Activities	
Purchased land (*d*)	$(5,000)
Purchased equipment (*b*)	(200)
Sold land (*f*)	1,250
Net cash used in investing activities	**(3,950)**
Financing Activities	
Issued shares (*a*)	9,000
Net cash provided by financing activities	**9,000**
Change in cash	**5,050**
Beginning cash balance	0
Ending cash balance	**$ 5,050**

CHAPTER TAKE-AWAYS

1. **Understand the objective of financial reporting, qualitative characteristics of accounting information, and the related key accounting assumptions and principles.**
   - The primary objective of external financial reporting is to provide financial information about a business to help external parties, primarily investors and creditors, make sound financial decisions.
   - To be useful, financial information must have specific characteristics. These include two fundamental qualitative characteristics, relevance and faithful representation, and four enhancing qualitative characteristics: comparability, verifiability, timeliness, and understandability.
   - Key accounting assumptions and principles are as follows:
     a. Separate-entity assumption—transactions of the business are accounted for separately from transactions of the owner.
     b. Unit-of-measure assumption—financial information is reported in the national monetary unit.
     c. Continuity (going-concern) assumption—a business is expected to continue to operate into the foreseeable future.
     d. Historical cost principle—financial statement elements should be recorded at their cash-equivalent cost on the date of the transaction.

2. **Define the elements of a classified statement of financial position.**
   - Elements of the statement of financial position are as follows:
     a. Assets—these are probable future economic benefits owned by the entity as a result of past transactions.
     b. Liabilities—these are present debts or obligations of the entity as a result of past transactions, which will be paid with assets or services.
     c. Shareholders' equity—this is the financing provided by the owners and the operations of the business.

3. **Identify what constitutes a business transaction, and recognize common account titles used in business.**
   A transaction includes the following:
   - An exchange between a business and one or more external parties to a business
   or
   - A measurable internal event such as adjustments for the use of assets in operations.
   An account is a standardized format that organizations use to accumulate the dollar effects of transactions of each financial statement item. Typical account titles include the following:
   - Assets—cash, trade receivables, inventory, prepayments, and property and equipment.
   - Liabilities—trade payables, notes payable, accrued liabilities, and taxes payable.
   - Shareholders' equity—contributed capital and retained earnings.

4. **Apply transaction analysis to simple business transactions in terms of the accounting model: Assets = Liabilities + Shareholders' Equity.**
   To determine the economic effect of a transaction on the entity in terms of its accounting equation, each transaction is analyzed as to the accounts (at least two) that are affected. In an exchange, the company receives something and gives something. If the accounts, direction of the effects, and amounts are correctly analyzed, the accounting equation must stay in balance. The transaction analysis model is as follows:

Assets	=	**Liabilities**	+	**Shareholders' Equity**			
+ | −		− | +		**Contributed Capital**		**Retained Earnings**	
debit | credit		debit | **credit**		− | +		− | +	
				debit | **credit**		debit | **credit**	
						Dividends | Net earnings	

5. **Determine the impact of business transactions on the statement of financial position by using two basic tools: journal entries and T-accounts.**
   - Journal entries express the effects of a transaction on accounts by using the debit-credit framework. The accounts and amounts to be debited are listed first. Then the accounts and amounts to be credited are listed below the debits and indented, resulting in debits on the left and credits on the right. A brief description of the transaction is then included for future reference:

(date or reference)	Property, plant, and equipment	2,200	
	Cash (−A)		1,500
	Long-term borrowings (+L)		700

- T-accounts summarize transaction effects for each account. These tools can be used to determine balances and draw inferences about a company's activities.

+	Assets	−		−	Liabilities and Shareholders' Equity	+
Beginning balance					Beginning balance	
Increases		Decreases		Decreases		Increases
Ending balance					Ending balance	

6. **Prepare a classified statement of financial position and analyze it by using the current ratio.**
   Classified statements of financial position are structured as follows:
   - Assets are categorized as "current assets" (those to be used or turned into cash within the year, with inventory always considered to be a current asset) and "non-current assets," such as long-term investments, property and equipment, and intangible assets.
   - Liabilities are categorized as "current liabilities" (those that will be paid within the next year or the operating cycle, whichever is longer) and non-current liabilities.
   - Shareholders' equity accounts are listed as contributed capital first, followed by retained earnings and other components. The current ratio (current assets ÷ current liabilities) measures a company's liquidity, that is, the ability of the company to pay its short-term obligations with current assets.

7. **Identify investing and financing transactions and how they are reported on the statement of cash flows.**
   A statement of cash flows reports the sources and uses of cash for the period by the type of activity that generated the cash flow: operating, investing, or financing. Investing activities are purchasing and selling long-term assets, making loans, and receiving payment from loans to others. Financing activities are borrowing and repaying loans to banks, issuing and repurchasing shares, and paying dividends.

In this chapter, we discussed the fundamental accounting model and transaction analysis. Journal entries and T-accounts were used to record the results of transaction analysis for investing and financing decisions that affect specific accounts. In Chapter 3, we continue our detailed look at financial statements, in particular the statement of earnings. The purpose of Chapter 3 is to build on your knowledge by discussing concepts for the measurement of revenues and expenses and by illustrating transaction analysis for operating decisions.

KEY **RATIO**

The current ratio measures the ability of the company to pay its short-term obligations with current assets. Although a ratio between 1.0 and 2.0 indicates that sufficient current assets are available to meet obligations when they become due, many companies with sophisticated cash management systems have ratios below 1.0. The ratio is computed as follows:

$$\textbf{Current Ratio} = \frac{\textbf{Current Assets}}{\textbf{Current Liabilities}}$$

FINDING **FINANCIAL INFORMATION**

STATEMENT OF FINANCIAL POSITION

Current Assets	**Current Liabilities**
Cash	Bank borrowings
Trade receivables	Trade payables
Notes receivable	Notes payable
Inventory	Accrued liabilities
Prepayments	**Non-current Liabilities**
Non-current Assets	Long-term
Investments	borrowings
Property, plant,	**Shareholders' Equity**
and equipment	Contributed capital
Goodwill	Retained earnings

STATEMENT OF CASH FLOWS
Under Investing Activities
 + Sales of non-current assets for cash
 − Purchases of non-current assets for cash
 − Loans to others
 + Receipt of cash on loans to others
Under Financing Activities
 + Borrowing from banks
 − Repayment of loans from banks
 + Issuance of shares
 − Repurchase of shares
 − Payment of dividends

STATEMENT OF EARNINGS
To be presented in Chapter 3

NOTES
To be discussed in future chapters

Review key terms and definitions on *Connect*.

QUESTIONS

1. What is the primary objective of financial reporting for external users?
2. Define the following:
   a. Asset
   b. Current asset
   c. Liability
   d. Current liability
   e. Contributed capital
   f. Retained earnings
3. Explain why information must be relevant and representationally faithful to be useful.
4. Explain what the following assumptions and principle mean in accounting:
   a. Separate-entity assumption
   b. Unit-of-measure assumption
   c. Continuity assumption
   d. Cost principle
5. Why is it important to have accounting assumptions?
6. How is the current ratio computed and how is it interpreted?
7. For accounting purposes, what is an account? Explain why accounts are used in an accounting system.
8. What are the limitations of using the historical cost principle as a basis for valuation of assets subsequent to acquisition?
9. What is the fundamental accounting model?
10. Define a business transaction in the broad sense and give examples of the two different kinds of transactions.
11. Explain what debit and credit mean.
12. Briefly explain what is meant by transaction analysis. What are the two steps in transaction analysis?
13. What two equalities in accounting must be maintained in transaction analysis?
14. What is a journal entry?
15. What is a T-account? What is its purpose?
16. What transactions are classified as investing activities in a statement of cash flows? What transactions are classified as financing activities?
17. What is the difference between a bookkeeper and an accountant?

LO1, 2, 3, 4   **E2–1**   **Matching Definitions with Terms**

Match each definition with its related term by entering the appropriate letter in the space provided. There should be only one definition per term (that is, there are more definitions than terms).

Term	Definition
_____ (1) Transaction	A. Economic resources to be used or turned into cash within one year.
_____ (2) Continuity assumption	
_____ (3) Statement of financial position	B. Reports assets, liabilities, and shareholders' equity.
_____ (4) Liabilities	
_____ (5) Assets = Liabilities + Shareholders' Equity	C. Business transactions are separate from the transactions of the owners.
_____ (6) Note payable	D. Increase assets; decrease liabilities and shareholders' equity.
_____ (7) Historical cost principle	
_____ (8) Account	E. An exchange between an entity and other parties.
_____ (9) Dual effects	F. The concept that businesses will operate into the foreseeable future.
_____ (10) Retained earnings	
_____ (11) Current assets	G. Decrease assets; increase liabilities and shareholders' equity.
_____ (12) Separate-entity assumption	
_____ (13) Debits	H. The concept that assets should be recorded at the amount paid on the exchange date.
_____ (14) Trade receivables	
_____ (15) Unit-of-measure assumption	I. A standardized format used to accumulate data about each item reported on financial statements.
_____ (16) Shareholders' equity	
	J. Amounts owed from customers.

Term	Definition
	K. The fundamental accounting model.
	L. The account that is credited when money is borrowed from a bank.
	M. The concept that states that accounting information should be measured and reported in the national monetary unit.
	N. Cumulative earnings of a company that are not distributed to the owners.
	O. Probable debts or obligations to be paid with assets or services.
	P. Every transaction has at least two effects.
	Q. Financing provided by owners and by business operations.
	R. Probable economic resources expected to be used or turned into cash beyond the next 12 months.

E2–2 Qualitative Characteristics of Accounting Information　　　　　　　■ LO1

Match each qualitative characteristic of useful accounting information with the related definition by entering the appropriate letter in the space provided. There should be only one definition per term (that is, there are more definitions than terms).

Qualitative Characteristics	Definitions
_____ (1) Relevance	A. Application of the same accounting methods over time.
_____ (2) Confirmatory value	B. Agreement between what really happened and the disclosed information.
_____ (3) Verifiability	C. The information is available prior to the decision.
_____ (4) Faithful representation	D. The information helps reduce the uncertainty in the future.
_____ (5) Predictive value	E. The information provides input to evaluate previous expectations.
_____ (6) Comparability	F. The information allows the evaluation of one alternative against another alternative.
	G. The information has a bearing on a specific decision.
	H. Implies that qualified persons working independently arrive at similar conclusions.

E2–3 Identifying Events as Accounting Transactions　　　　　　　■ LO3

Which of the following events results in an exchange transaction for O'Brien Company (Y for yes and N for no)?

_____ (1) O'Brien purchased a machine and signed a note payable, payable in six months.

_____ (2) Six investors in O'Brien Company sold their shares to another investor.

_____ (3) The company lent $150,000 to a member of the board of directors.

_____ (4) O'Brien Company ordered supplies from Office Max to be delivered next week.

_____ (5) The founding owner, Meaghan O'Brien, purchased additional shares in another company.

_____ (6) The company borrowed $1,000,000 from a local bank.

E2–4 Identifying Account Titles　　　　　　　■ LO1, 3

The following are independent situations.

a. A company purchases a piece of land for $100,000 cash. An appraiser for the buyer valued the land at $105,000.

b. A telecommunications company purchases the patent (an intangible asset) on a software application for its wireless communication system. The company paid $250,000 cash and signed a note for $550,000, payable in one year at an annual interest rate of 5 percent.

c. A company orders and receives five laptops for office use for which it signs a note promising to pay $12,000 within three months.

d. A company makes a cash payment of $5,400 for prepaid services.

e. A manufacturing company signs a contract for the construction of a new warehouse for $500,000. At the signing, the company writes a cheque for $50,000 as a deposit on the future construction.

f. A publishing firm purchases the copyright (an intangible asset) to a manuscript for an introductory accounting text from the author for $40,000.

g. A company purchases a new delivery truck that has a list, or sticker, price of $35,000 for $32,000 cash.

h. A company purchases on account women's clothing for sale to customers. The supplier's invoice of $2,430 is payable within 30 days.

i. A new company is formed and sells 2,000 shares for $22 per share to investors.

j. A company purchases 400 shares of Sun-Rype Products Ltd. for $2,432 cash.

k. A local company is a sole proprietorship (one owner); its owner buys a car for $10,000 for personal use. Answer from the company's point of view.

l. A manufacturing firm pays dividends of $100,000 to shareholders in cash.

m. A company pays $1,500 principal on its note payable.

Required:

1. Indicate the appropriate elements on the classified statement of financial position (use account titles), if any, that are affected in each of the preceding events. Consider what is given and what is received.
2. At what amount would you record the land in (*a*)? The truck in (*g*)? What measurement principle are you applying?
3. What accounting concept did you apply for situation (*k*)?

■ **LO3, 5**   **E2–5**   **Classifying Accounts and Their Usual Balances**

WestJet Airlines

As described in a recent annual report, WestJet Airlines provides quality travel services to many destinations in North America.

Required:

For each of the following accounts from WestJet's recent statement of financial position, complete the following chart by indicating whether the account is classified as a current asset (CA), a non-current asset (NCA), a current liability (CL), a non-current liability (NCL), or shareholders' equity (SE), and whether the account usually has a debit or a credit balance.

Account	Statement of Financial Position Classification	Debit or Credit Balance
1. Advance ticket sales (deferred revenue)		
2. Cash and cash equivalents		
3. Contributed capital		
4. Intangible assets		
5. Inventory		
6. Long-term borrowings		
7. Prepayments		
8. Property and equipment		
9. Retained earnings		
10. Trade payables		
11. Trade receivables		

■ **LO4**   **E2–6**   **Identifying Effects on Elements of the Statement of Financial Position**

Complete the following table by entering either "increases" or "decreases" in columns (1) and (2), and either "debit" or "credit" in columns (3) and (4).

	(1) Debit	(2) Credit	(3) Increases	(4) Decreases
Assets				
Liabilities				
Shareholders' equity				

■ **LO4**   **E2–7**   **Determining Financial Statement Effects of Several Transactions**

The following events occurred for Mitka Ltd.:

a. Received investment of $32,000 cash by organizers.

b. Purchased land for $18,000 in land; paid $6,000 in cash and signed a mortgage note with a local bank for the balance (due in five years).

c. Borrowed cash from a bank and signed a note for $11,000.

d. Lent $300 to an employee who signed a note due in three months.

e. Paid the bank the amount borrowed in (c).

f. Purchased $8,000 of equipment, paying $4,000 in cash and signing a note due to the manufacturer.

Required:
For each of the events (a) through (f), perform transaction analysis and indicate the account, amount, and direction of the effects (+ for increase and − for decrease) on the accounting equation. Check that the accounting equation remains in balance after each transaction. Use the following headings:

Event	Assets	=	Liabilities	+	Shareholders' Equity

E2–8 Determining Financial Statement Effects of Several Transactions ■ **LO4**

Tim Hortons Inc. is one of the largest quick-service restaurants in North America. The company operates a chain of coffee and doughnut shops across Canada and the United States specializing in fresh coffee, baked goods, and homestyle lunches. The following activities occurred during a recent year. The amounts are rounded to millions of dollars.

Tim Hortons Inc.

a. Purchased additional property and equipment for $186.7 in cash.

b. Repurchased its own shares for $225.2 cash. The shares were originally sold for the same amount.

c. Declared $110.2 in dividends and paid $130.5 during the year.

d. Several investors in Tim Hortons shares sold their shares to other investors on the stock exchange for $3.5.

e. Repaid $7.7 in principal on long-term debt obligations.

f. Paid $175.9 in income taxes.

Required:
For each of these events, perform transaction analysis and indicate the account, amount, and direction of the effects on the accounting equation. Check that the accounting equation remains in balance after each transaction. Use the following headings:

Event	Assets	=	Liabilities	+	Shareholders' Equity

E2–9 Recording Investing and Financing Activities ■ **LO5**

Refer to E2–7.

Required:
For each of the events in E2–7, prepare journal entries, checking that debits equal credits.

E2–10 Analyzing the Effects of Transactions in T-Accounts ■ **LO5**

Grady Service Company Inc. was organized by Chris Grady and five other investors. The following events occurred during the year:

a. Received $63,000 cash from the investors; each was issued 1,400 shares.

b. Purchased equipment for use in the business at a cost of $16,000; one-fourth was paid in cash, and the company signed a note for the balance, payable in six months.

c. Signed an agreement with a cleaning service to pay it $200 per week for cleaning the corporate offices.

d. Lent $2,500 to one of the investors, who signed a note due in six months.

e. Issued shares to additional investors, who contributed $6,000 in cash and a lot of land valued at $15,000.

f. Paid the amount of the note payable in (b).

g. Conor Mulkeen borrowed $10,000 for personal use from a local bank and signed a note payable in one year.

Required:

1. Prepare journal entries for each transaction. If an event does not require a journal entry, explain the reason. Use the account titles listed in (2).

2. Create T-accounts for the following accounts: cash, note receivable, equipment, land, note payable, and contributed capital. Beginning balances are zero. For each of the preceding transactions, record the effects of the transaction in the appropriate T-accounts. Include good referencing and totals for each T-account.

3. Using the balances in the T-accounts, fill in the following amounts for the accounting equation:

Assets $_____ = Liabilities $_____ + Shareholders' Equity $_____

LO4, 6   **E2–11**   **Inferring Investing and Financing Transactions, and Preparing a Statement of Financial Position**

During its first week of operations ending January 7, 2014, FastTrack Sports Inc. completed six transactions with the dollar effects indicated in the following schedule:

Accounts	Dollar Effect of Each of the Six Transactions						Ending Balance
	1	2	3	4	5	6	
Cash	$15,000	$75,000	$(5,000)	$(4,000)	$(9,500)		
Note receivable (short term)				4,000			
Store fixtures					9,500		
Land			16,000			$4,000	
Note payable (due in three months)		75,000	11,000			4,000	
Contributed capital	15,000						

Required:

1. Write a brief explanation of each transaction. Explain any assumptions that you made.

2. Compute the ending balance in each account and prepare a classified statement of financial position for FastTrack Sports Inc. on January 7, 2014.

LO6   **E2–12**   **Inferring Investing and Financing Transactions, and Preparing a Statement of Financial Position**

During its first month of operations, March 2015, Faye's Fashions Inc. completed seven transactions with the dollar effects indicated in the following T-accounts:

	Cash		
(a)	50,000	4,000	(b)
(f)	2,000	4,000	(c)
		6,000	(d)
		3,000	(e)

	Short-Term Investments		
(d)	6,000	2,000	(f)

	Short-Term Note Receivable	
(c)	4,000	

	Computer Equipment	
(g)	4,000	

	Delivery Truck	
(b)	25,000	

	Long-Term Note Payable		
(e)	3,000	21,000	(b)

	Contributed Capital	
	50,000	(a)
	4,000	(g)

Required:

1. Write a brief explanation of transactions (*a*) through (*g*). Explain any assumptions that you made.

2. Compute the ending balance in each account and prepare a classified statement of financial position for Faye's Fashions Inc. at the end of March 2015.

LO5   **E2–13**   **Recording Journal Entries**

BMW Group

BMW Group, headquartered in Munich, Germany, manufactures several automotive brands, including BMW, MINI, and Rolls-Royce. Financial information is reported in euros (€), using IFRS as applicable to the European Union. The following transactions were adapted from the annual report of the BMW Group; amounts are in millions of euros:

a. Declared €937 in dividends to be paid next month.

b. Issued additional shares for €19 cash.

c. Paid €1,516 in dividends declared in prior months.

d. Borrowed €7,977 and signed long-term notes, payable in the distant future.

e. Lent €27 to trade suppliers, who signed notes to repay the loans in three months.

f. Purchased equipment for €6,890, paying €5,236 in cash and signing a note for the balance.

g. Purchased investments for €2,073 cash.

Required:
Prepare journal entries for each transaction. Be sure to use good referencing, and categorize each account as an asset (A), a liability (L), or shareholders' equity (SE). If a transaction does not require a journal entry, explain the reason.

E2–14 **Analyzing the Effects of Transactions by Using T-Accounts, Preparing a Statement of Financial Position, and Interpreting the Current Ratio as a Manager of the Company**   ■ **LO5, 6**

Massimo Company has been operating for one year (2013). You are a member of the management team investigating expansion ideas, all of which will require borrowing funds from banks. At the start of 2014, Massimo's T-account balances were as follows:

Assets:

Cash		Short-Term Investments		Property and Equipment	
1,000		2,000		2,500	

Liabilities:

Short-Term Notes Payable		Long-Term Notes Payable	
	2,200		300

Shareholders' Equity:

Contributed Capital		Retained Earnings	
	1,000		2,000

Required:
1. Using the data from these T-accounts, complete the accounting equation on January 1, 2014:

   Assets $_____ = Liabilities $_____ + Shareholders' Equity $_____

2. Enter in the T-accounts the following transactions that occurred in 2014:
   a. Paid one-half of the principal on the long-term note payable.
   b. Sold $1,000 of the investments for $1,000 cash.
   c. Sold one-half of the property and equipment for $1,250 cash.
   d. Borrowed $2,000 from the bank and signed a note promising to pay the principal and interest at an annual rate of 5 percent in three years.
   e. Paid $500 in dividends to shareholders.

3. Compute ending balances in the T-accounts to complete the statement of financial position on December 31, 2014:

   Assets $_____ = Liabilities $_____ + Shareholders' Equity $_____

4. Using the ending balances in the T-accounts, prepare a classified statement of financial position at December 31, 2014, in good form.

5. Calculate the current ratio at December 31, 2014. If the industry average for the current ratio is 1.50, what does your computation suggest to you about Massimo Company? Would you support expansion by borrowing? Why or why not?

E2–15 **Explaining the Effects of Transactions on Specific Accounts by Using T-Accounts**   ■ **LO5**

Heavey and Lovas Furniture Repair Service, a company with two shareholders, began operations on June 1, 2014. The following T-accounts indicate the activities for the month of June.

Cash (A)				Notes Receivable (A)				Tools and Equipment (A)			
(a)	17,000	(b)	10,000	(c)	1,500	(d)	500	(a)	3,000	(f)	800
(d)	500	(c)	1,500								
(f)	800	(e)	1,000								

Building (A)				Notes Payable (L)				Contributed Capital (SE)			
(b)	50,000			(e)	1,000	(b)	40,000			(a)	20,000

Required:

Explain transactions (*a*) through (*f*), which resulted in the entries in the T-accounts; that is, what activity made the account increase or decrease?

■ LO5   **E2–16**   **Inferring Typical Investing and Financing Activities in Accounts**

The following T-accounts indicate the effects of normal business transactions:

Equipment			Note Receivable			Notes Payable		
1/1	500		1/1	150			100	1/1
	250	?		?	225	?	170	
31/12	100		31/12	170			180	31/12

Required:

1. Describe the typical investing and financing transactions that affect each T-account; that is, what economic events made these accounts increase or decrease?
2. For each T-account, compute the missing amounts.

■ LO7   **E2–17**   **Identifying Investing and Financing Activities Affecting Cash Flows**

Bauer Performance
Sports Ltd.

Bauer Performance Sports Ltd. is a leading developer and manufacturer of ice hockey, roller hockey, and lacrosse equipment as well as related apparel. The company holds the top market share position in both ice and roller hockey. Its products are marketed under the Bauer Hockey, Mission Roller Hockey, Maverik Lacrosse, and Cascade Sports brand names. The following are several of Bauer's investing and financing activities that were reflected in a recent annual statement of cash flows:

a. Issuance of shares

b. Purchase of property, plant, and equipment

c. Issuance of long-term debt

d. Principal repayment of long-term debt

e. Purchase of investments

f. Repurchase of shares

g. Proceeds from disposition of property, plant, and equipment

Required:

For each of these, indicate whether the activity is investing (I) or financing (F), and indicate the direction of the effect on cash flows (+ = increases cash; − = decreases cash).

■ LO7   **E2–18**   **Preparing the Investing and Financing Section of the Statement of Cash Flows**

Hilton Hotels
Corporation

Hilton Hotels Corporation constructs, operates, and franchises domestic and international hotel and hotel-casino properties. Information from the company's recent annual statement of cash flows indicates the following investing and financing activities during that year (simplified):

Payment of debt principal	$ 24
Purchase of investments	139
Sale of property (assume sold at cost)	230
Issuance of shares	60
Purchase and renovation of properties	370
Additional borrowing from banks	992
Receipt of principal payment on a note receivable	125

Required:

Prepare the investing and financing sections of the statement of cash flows for Hilton hotels. Assume that the company's year-end is December 31, 2014.

PROBLEMS

P2–1 **Identifying Accounts on a Classified Statement of Financial Position and Their Normal Debit or Credit Balances** (AP2–1)

LO2, 5

Saputo Inc.

Saputo Inc. is Canada's leading processor of dairy products. The company produces, markets, and distributes a wide array of products of the utmost quality, including cheese, fluid milk, yogurt, dairy ingredients, and snack-cakes. Saputo's products are distributed in many countries, primarily in Canada, the United States, and Argentina. The following are several of the accounts that appeared on the company's recent statement of financial position:

Account	Statement of Financial Position Classification	Debit or Credit Balance
1. Cash and cash equivalents		
2. Deferred income tax liabilities		
3. Retained earnings		
4. Income taxes payable		
5. Prepayments		
6. Contributed capital		
7. Trademarks and other intangibles		
8. Trade payables		
9. Accrued liabilities		
10. Bank loans (short term)		
11. Property, plant, and equipment		
12. Long-term investments		
13. Trade receivables		
14. Long-term borrowings		

Required:
For each account, indicate how it normally should be categorized on a classified statement of financial position. Use CA for current asset, NCA for non-current asset, CL for current liability, NCL for non-current liability, and SE for shareholders' equity. Also indicate whether the account normally has a debit or a credit balance.

P2–2 **Determining Financial Statement Effects of Various Transactions, and Interpreting the Current Ratio** (AP2–2)

LO3, 4, 6

eXcel

East Hill Home Healthcare Services was organized on January 1, 2013, by four friends. Each organizer invested $10,000 in the company and, in turn, was issued 8,000 shares. To date, they are the only shareholders. At the end of 2014, the accounting records reflected total assets of $700,000 ($50,000 cash, $500,000 land, $50,000 equipment, and $100,000 buildings), total liabilities of $200,000 (short-term notes payable of $100,000 and long-term notes payable of $100,000), and shareholders' equity of $500,000 ($100,000 contributed capital and $400,000 retained earnings). The following summarized events occurred during January 2015:

a. Sold 9,000 additional shares to the original organizers for a total of $90,000 cash.

b. Purchased a building for $60,000, equipment for $15,000, and four acres of land for $14,000; paid $9,000 in cash and signed a note for the balance (due in 15 years). (*Hint*: Five different accounts are affected.)

c. Sold one acre of land acquired in (*b*) for $3,500 cash to another company.

d. Purchased short-term investments for $18,000 cash.

e. One shareholder reported to the company that he sold 300 East Hill shares to another shareholder for $3,000 cash.

f. Lent $5,000 to one of the shareholders for moving costs, receiving a signed six-month note from the shareholder.

Required:

1. Was East Hill Home Healthcare Services organized as a sole proprietorship, a partnership, or a corporation? Explain the basis for your answer.

2. During January 2015, the records of the company were inadequate. You were asked to prepare the summary of the preceding transactions. To develop a quick assessment of their economic effects

on East Hill Home Healthcare Services, you have decided to complete the tabulation that follows and to use plus (+) for increases and minus (−) for decreases for each account. The first event is used as an example.

		Assets					=	Liabilities		+	Shareholders' Equity	
	Cash	Short-Term Investments	Notes Receivable	Land	Building	Equipment		Short-Term Notes Payable	Long-Term Notes Payable		Contributed Capital	Retained Earnings
Beg.	50,000			500,000	100,000	50,000	=	100,000	100,000	+	100,000	400,000
(a)	+90,000										+90,000	

3. Did you include the transaction between the two shareholders—event (*e*)—in the tabulation? Why or why not?

4. Based only on the completed tabulation, provide the following amounts at January 31, 2015 (show computations):

    a. Total assets

    b. Total liabilities

    c. Total shareholders' equity

    d. Cash balance

    e. Total current assets

5. Compute the current ratio at January 31, 2015. What does this suggest about the company?

■ LO6

P2–3   **Recording Transactions in T-Accounts, Preparing a Statement of Financial Position, and Evaluating the Current Ratio (AP2–3)**

Injection Plastics Company has been operating for three years. At December 31, 2014, the accounting records reflected the following:

Cash	$21,000	Intangibles	$ 3,000
Investments (short term)	2,000	Trade payables	15,000
Trade receivables	3,000	Accrued liabilities	2,000
Inventories	24,000	Short-term borrowings	7,000
Notes receivable (long term)	1,000	Notes payable (long-term)	48,000
Equipment	48,000	Contributed capital	90,000
Factory building	90,000	Retained earnings	30,000

During the year 2015, the following summarized transactions were completed:

a. Purchased equipment that cost $18,000; paid $6,000 cash and signed a one-year note for the balance.

b. Issued 2,000 additional shares for $12,000 cash.

c. Lent $7,000 to a manager, who signed a two-year note.

d. Purchased short-term investments for $9,000 in cash.

e. Paid $5,000 on the note in transaction (*a*).

f. Borrowed $12,000 cash on December 31, 2015, from the bank and signed a note, payable June 30, 2016.

g. Purchased a patent (an intangible asset) for $3,000 cash.

h. Built an addition to the factory for $25,000; paid $9,000 in cash and signed a three-year note for the balance.

i. Hired a new president at the end of the year. The contract was for $85,000 per year plus options to purchase company shares at a set price based on company performance.

j. Returned defective equipment to the manufacturer, receiving a cash refund of $1,000.

Required:

1. Create a T-account for each of the accounts on the statement of financial position and enter the balances at the end of 2014 as beginning balances for 2015.

2. Record each of the transactions for 2015 in a T-account (including referencing) and determine the ending balances.

3. Explain your response to transaction (*i*).

4. Prepare a classified statement of financial position at December 31, 2015.

5. Compute the current ratio at December 31, 2015. What does this ratio suggest about Injection Plastics Company?

P2–4 **Identifying Effects of Transactions on the Statement of Cash Flows** (AP2–4)
Refer to P2–3.

■ **LO7**

Required:
Using the transactions (*a*) through (*j*) in P2–3, indicate whether each transaction is an investing (I) or financing (F) activity for the year and the direction of the effect on cash flows (+ for increase and − for decrease). If there is no effect on cash flows, write NE.

P2–5 **Recording Transactions, Preparing Journal Entries, Posting to T-Accounts, Preparing a Statement of Financial Position, and Evaluating the Current Ratio** (AP2–5)
Bayer AG, with headquarters in Leverkusen, Germany, is an international, research-based group of companies active in health care, nutrition, and high-tech materials. Popular products include ASPIRIN, Alka-Seltzer, and One-A-Day vitamins. The following is Bayer's (simplified) statement of financial position as at September 30, 2012:

■ **LO5, 6**

Bayer AG

eXcel

BAYER AG Statement of Financial Position At September 30, 2012 (in millions of euros)	
ASSETS	
Current assets	
Cash and cash equivalents	€ 3,181
Receivables	8,644
Inventories	6,539
Other assets	1,514
	19,878
Non-current assets	
Investments	319
Property, plant, and equipment	9,480
Intangible assets	19,477
Other assets	2,767
	32,043
Total assets	**€51,921**
LIABILITIES AND SHAREHOLDERS' EQUITY	
Current liabilities	
Trade accounts payable	€ 3,397
Financial liabilities	3,721
Provisions	4,593
Other short-term liabilities	1,502
	13,213
Non-current liabilities	
Provisions	7,524
Deferred income taxes	2,401
Financial liabilities	7,521
Other liabilities	2,254
	19,700
Shareholders' equity	
Contributed capital	8,284
Retained earnings	10,724
	19,008
Total liabilities and shareholders' equity	**€51,921**

Assume that the following transactions occurred in the last quarter of 2012:

a. Issued additional shares for €60 in cash.

b. Borrowed €615 from banks due in two years.

c. Declared and paid €1,160 in dividends to shareholders.

d. Purchased additional intangibles for €64 cash.

e. Purchased property, plant, and equipment; paid €1,514 in cash and €5,410 with additional long-term bank loans.

f. Acquired additional investments; paid €623 in cash.

g. Lent €125 to an associated company that signed a six-month note.

h. Sold investments costing €461 for the same amount in cash.

Required:

1. Prepare a journal entry for each transaction.
2. Create a T-account for each financial statement account and include the September 30, 2012, balances. Post each journal entry to the appropriate T-accounts.
3. Prepare a statement of financial position for Bayer based on the T-account ending balances at December 31, 2012.
4. Compute Bayer's current ratio at December 31, 2012. What does this suggest about the company?

LO7

Bayer AG

P2–6 **Preparing the Investing and Financing Sections of a Statement of Cash Flows** (AP2–6)

Refer to P2–5.

Required:

Based on the transactions that occurred in 2012, prepare the investing and financing sections of the statement of cash flows of Bayer for the fourth quarter of 2012.

LO6

Danier Leather Inc.

P2–7 **Using Financial Reports: Preparing a Classified Statement of Financial Position, and Analyzing the Current Ratio** (AP2–7)

The accounts below, in alphabetical order, are adapted from Danier Leather Inc.'s recent statement of financial position (amounts in thousands of dollars):

	Current Year	Prior Year		Current Year	Prior Year
Accounts payable and accrued liabilities	$10,161	$11,024	Income taxes payable	$ –	$ 278
			Inventories	24,891	28,964
Accounts receivable	517	385	Non-current liabilities	1,373	1,318
			Prepaid expenses and other current assets	1,225	901
Cash	34,332	28,698			
Contributed capital	15,965	16,094			
			Property and equipment, net	15,738	15,458
Deferred income tax asset	1,909	1,678			
Deferred revenue	1,587	1,536			
			Retained earnings	49,526	45,834

Required:

1. Prepare, in good form, a classified statement of financial position (with two years reported) for Danier Leather Inc. Assume a fiscal year-end of June 30.
2. Compute the company's current ratio for the current year. How would you interpret this ratio for Danier Leather?

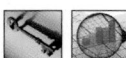

LO5, 6

P2–8 **Analyzing the Effects of Transactions Using T-Accounts, Preparing a Statement of Financial Position, and Interpreting the Current Ratio over Time as a Bank Loan Officer** (AP2–8)

Lee Delivery Company Inc. was organized at the beginning of 2014. The following transactions occurred during 2014 (the company's first year of operations):

a. Received $40,000 cash from the organizers in exchange for shares in the new company.

b. Purchased land for $16,000 and signed a one-year note (at a 6 percent annual interest rate).

c. Bought two used delivery trucks for operating purposes at the start of the year at a cost of $10,000 each; paid $5,000 cash and signed a promissory note for the balance, payable over the next three years (at an annual interest rate of 7 percent).

d. Sold one-fourth of the land for $4,000 to Birkins Moving, which promised to pay in six months.

e. Paid $2,000 cash to a truck repair shop for a new motor for one of the trucks. (*Hint:* Increase the account you used to record the purchase of the trucks since the usefulness of the truck has been improved.)

f. Traded the other truck and $6,000 cash for a new one. The old truck's fair value is $10,000.

g. Shareholder Jonah Lee paid $27,500 cash for a vacant lot (land) for his personal use.

h. Collected the amount of the note due from Birkins Moving in (d).

i. Paid one-third of the principal of the note due for the delivery trucks in (c).

Required:

1. Set up appropriate T-accounts with beginning balances of $0 for Cash, Short-term notes receivable, Land, Equipment, Short-term notes payable, Long-term notes payable, and Contributed capital. Using the T-accounts, record the effects of these transactions on Lee Delivery Company.

2. Prepare a classified statement of financial position for Lee Delivery Company at the end of 2014. Compute the current ratio at that date.

3. At the end of the next two years, Lee Delivery Company reported the following amounts on its statements of financial position:

	December 31, 2015	December 31, 2016
Current assets	$52,000	$ 47,000
Non-current assets	38,000	73,000
Total assets	**90,000**	**120,000**
Short-term notes payable	23,000	40,000
Long-term notes payable	17,000	20,000
Total liabilities	**40,000**	**60,000**
Shareholders' equity	**50,000**	**60,000**

Compute the company's current ratio for 2014, 2015, and 2016. What is the trend and what does this suggest about the company?

4. At the beginning of 2017, Lee Delivery Company applied to your bank for a $50,000 short-term loan to expand the business. The vice-president of the bank asked you to review the information and make a recommendation on lending the funds based solely on the results of the current ratio. What recommendation would you make to the bank's vice-president about lending the money to Lee Delivery Company?

ALTERNATE PROBLEMS

AP2–1 **Identifying Accounts on a Classified Statement of Financial Position and Their Normal Debit or Credit Balances (P2–1)**

■ LO2, 5

Celestica Inc.

According to a recent annual report of Celestica Inc., the company is a "key player in the new technology-driven global economy." The company provides a broad range of services, including "design, prototyping, assembly, testing, product assurance, supply chain management, worldwide distribution, and after-sales service." The following are several of the accounts from a recent statement of financial position:

(1) Trade accounts receivable

(2) Short-term borrowings

(3) Contributed capital

(4) Long-term debt

(5) Prepaid expenses and other assets

(6) Intangible assets

(7) Property, plant, and equipment

(8) Retained earnings

(9) Trade accounts payable

(10) Cash and short-term investments

(11) Accrued liabilities

(12) Other long-term liabilities

(13) Inventories

(14) Income taxes payable

Required:

Indicate how each account normally should be categorized on a classified statement of financial position. Use CA for current asset, NCA for non-current asset, CL for current liability, NCL for non-current liability, and SE for shareholders' equity. Also indicate whether the account normally has a debit or a credit balance.

■ **LO3, 4**   **AP2–2**   **Determining Financial Statement Effects of Various Transactions, and Interpreting the Current Ratio (P2–2)**

Adamson Inc. is a small manufacturing company that makes model trains to sell to toy stores. It has a small service department that repairs customers' trains for a fee. The company has been in business for five years. At December 31, 2013 (the company's fiscal year-end), the accounting records reflected total assets of $500,000 (cash, $120,000; equipment, $70,000; buildings, $310,000), total liabilities of $200,000 (short-term notes payable, $140,000; long-term notes payable, $60,000), and total shareholders' equity of $300,000 (contributed capital, $220,000; retained earnings, $80,000). During the current year, 2014, the following summarized events occurred:

a. Borrowed $110,000 cash from the bank and signed a 10-year note.

b. Purchased equipment for $30,000, paying $3,000 in cash and signing a note due in six months for the balance.

c. Issued 10,000 shares for $100,000 cash.

d. Purchased a delivery truck (equipment) for $10,000; paid $5,000 cash and signed a short-term note payable for the remainder.

e. Lent $2,000 cash to the company president, Clark Adamson, who signed a note promising to pay the amount and annual interest at the rate of 10 percent in one year.

f. Built an addition on the factory for $200,000 and paid cash to the contractor.

g. Purchased $85,000 in long-term investments.

h. Returned a $3,000 piece of equipment purchased in (b) because it proved to be defective; received a reduction of the note payable equal to the value of the defective equipment.

i. A shareholder sold $5,000 of his shares in Adamson Incorporated to her neighbour for $6,400.

Required:

1. Prepare a summary of the preceding transactions. To develop a quick assessment of the transaction effects on Adamson Incorporated, you have decided to complete the tabulation that follows and to use plus (+) for increases and minus (−) for decreases for each account. The first transaction is used as an example.

			Assets			=	Liabilities	+	Shareholders' Equity	
	Cash	Notes Receivable	Long-Term Investments	Equipment	Building	Short-Term Notes Payable	Long-Term Notes Payable		Contributed Capital	Retained Earnings
Beg.	120,000			70,000	310,000 =	140,000	60,000	+	220,000	60,000
(a)	+110,000						+110,000			

2. Did you include all transactions in the tabulation? If not, which one did you exclude and why?

3. Based on beginning balances plus the completed tabulation, calculate the following amounts at the end of 2014 (show computations):
   a. Total assets
   b. Total liabilities
   c. Total shareholders' equity
   d. Cash balance
   e. Total current assets

4. Compute the company's current ratio at the end of the year. What does this ratio suggest to you about Adamson Incorporated?

AP2–3 Recording Transactions in T-Accounts, Preparing a Statement of Financial Position, and Evaluating the Current Ratio (P2–3)

■ LO5, 6

Gildan Activewear Inc.

Gildan Activewear Inc. specializes in manufacturing and selling T-shirts, sport shirts, and fleece. The following is adapted from a recent statement of financial position dated September 30, 2012. Amounts are in thousands of dollars:

Cash and cash equivalents	$70,410	Accounts payable and accrued liabilities	$ 256,442
Accounts receivable	260,948	Long-term debt	181,000
Inventories	553,068	Long-term provisions	13,042
Prepaid expenses	14,451	Other long-term liabilities	19,612
Other current assets	16,723		
Property, plant, and equipment, net	552,437	Contributed capital	101,113
Intangible assets	259,981	Retained earnings	1,306,724
Goodwill	141,933		
Other non-current assets	26,486	Other components of equity	18,504

Assume that the following transactions occurred in the first quarter of fiscal year 2013, ended on December 31, 2012:

a. Received $630 on sale of intangibles at cost.

b. Paid $14,000 in principal on long-term debt.

c. Purchased $3,400 in non-current investments for cash.

d. Sold equipment at its cost for $600 cash.

e. Purchased additional intangibles for $5,400 cash.

f. Issued additional shares for $1,500 in cash.

g. Purchased property, plant, and equipment; paid $12,450 in cash and $9,400 with additional long-term bank loans.

h. Sold other non-current assets at cost for $310 cash.

i. Declared and paid $9,000 in dividends to shareholders.

Required:

1. Create a T-account for each of the accounts on the statement of financial position; enter the balances at September 30, 2012.

2. Record each of the transactions for the first quarter ended December 31, 2012, in a T-account (including referencing) and determine the ending balances.

3. Prepare a classified statement of financial position at December 31, 2012.

4. Compute the current ratio at December 31, 2012. What does this suggest about Gildan Activewear?

AP2–4 Identifying Effects of Transactions on the Statement of Cash Flows (P2–4)

■ LO7

Gildan Activewear Inc.

Refer to AP2–3.

Required:

Using transactions (*a*) through (*i*) in AP2–3, indicate whether each transaction is an investing (I) or financing (F) activity for the year and the direction of the effect on cash flows (+ for increase and − for decrease). Indicate no effect on cash flows related to investing or financing with NE.

AP2–5 Recording Transactions, Preparing Journal Entries, Posting to T-Accounts, Preparing a Statement of Financial Position, and Evaluating the Current Ratio (P2–5)

■ LO5, 6

Dell Inc.

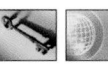

e**X**cel

Dell Inc. is a leading global provider of computer products and services for both the consumer and enterprise markets. Dell offers a full line of desktop and notebook PCs, network servers, workstations, storage systems, printers, handheld computers, digital music players, LCD and plasma televisions, and projectors. The following is Dell's (simplified) statement of financial position from a recent year:

DELL INC.
Statement of Financial Position
At February 3, 2012
(in millions of U.S. dollars)

ASSETS	
Current assets	
Cash and cash equivalents	$13,852
Short-term investments	966
Receivables	9,803
Inventories	1,404
Other assets	3,423
Total current assets	**29,448**
Non-current assets	
Property, plant, and equipment, net	2,124
Long-term investments	3,404
Long-term receivables	1,372
Goodwill	5,838
Other non-current assets	2,347
Total assets	**$44,533**
LIABILITIES AND SHAREHOLDERS' EQUITY	
Current liabilities	
Short-term borrowings	$ 2,867
Accounts payable	11,656
Deferred services revenue	3,544
Accrued liabilities	3,934
Total current liabilities	**22,001**
Non-current liabilities	
Long-term borrowings	6,387
Deferred services revenue	3,836
Other liabilities	3,392
Total liabilities	**35,616**
Shareholders' equity	**8,917**
Total liabilities and shareholders' equity	**$44,533**

Assume that the following transactions (in millions of dollars) occurred in fiscal year 2013 (ending on February 2, 2013):

a. Issued additional shares for $200 in cash.

b. Borrowed $300 from banks; due in two years.

c. Purchased additional investments for $7,500 cash; one-fifth were long term and the rest were short term.

d. Purchased property, plant, and equipment; paid $4,650 in cash and $850 with additional long-term bank loans.

e. Lent $250 to associated companies that signed a six-month note.

f. Sold short-term investments costing $5,000 for $5,000 cash.

Required:

1. Prepare a journal entry for each transaction.
2. Create a T-account for each item on the statement of financial position and include the February 3, 2012 balances. Post each journal entry to the appropriate T-account.
3. Prepare a statement of financial position for Dell based on the T-account ending balances at February 2, 2013.
4. Compute Dell's current ratio for fiscal year 2013. What does this suggest about the company?

AP2–6   Preparing the Investing and Financing Sections of a Statement of Cash Flows (P2–6)
Refer to AP2–5.

■ **LO7**

Dell Inc.

Required:

Based on the transactions that occurred in fiscal year 2013, prepare the investing and financing sections of Dell's statement of cash flows for that year.

AP2–7   Using Financial Reports: Preparing a Classified Statement of Financial Position, and Analyzing the Current Ratio (P2–7)

■ **LO6**

The accounts below, in alphabetical order, are adapted from a recent statement of financial position for Big Burgers Inc. (amounts are in thousands of dollars):

	Current Year	Prior Year		Current Year	Prior Year
Accounts and notes receivable	$ 795.9	$ 745.5	Long-term debt	$ 8,937.4	$ 8,357.3
Accrued liabilities	2,344.2	2,144.0	Notes payable (short term)	544.0	–
Cash and cash equivalents	4,260.4	1,379.8	Other long-term liabilities	1,869.0	1,758.2
Contributed capital	2,814.2	2,202.6	Other non-current assets	1,245.0	1,338.4
Current maturities of long-term debt	658.7	862.2	Prepaid expenses and other current assets	646.4	585.0
Intangible assets, net	1,950.7	1,828.3	Property and equipment, net	20,108.0	20,903.1
Inventories	147.0	147.5	Retained earnings	12,331.9	11,998.9
Long-term investments	1,035.4	1,109.9	Trade payables	689.4	714.3

Required:

1. Construct, in good form, a classified statement of financial position (with two years reported) for Big Burgers Inc.
2. Compute the company's current ratio at the end of the current year. How do you interpret this ratio for Big Burgers?

AP2–8   Analyzing the Effects of Transactions by Using T-Accounts, Preparing a Statement of Financial Position, and Interpreting the Current Ratio as a Bank Loan Officer (P2–8)

■ **LO5, 6**

Chu Delivery Company Inc. was organized in 2015. The following transactions occurred during 2015:

a. Received $40,000 cash from organizers in exchange for shares in the new company.

b. Purchased land for $12,000, signing a one-year note.

c. Bought two used delivery trucks for operating purposes at the start of the year at a cost of $10,000 each; paid $4,000 cash and signed a note due in three years for the rest (ignore interest).

d. Sold one-fourth of the land for $3,000 to Pablo Moving, which signed a six-month note.

e. Paid $1,000 cash to a truck repair shop for a new motor for one of the trucks. (*Hint:* Increase the account you used to record the purchase of the trucks since the productive life of the truck has been improved.)

f. Shareholder Jingbi Chu paid $27,600 from her personal savings to purchase a vacant lot (land) for her personal use.

Required:

1. Set up appropriate T-accounts with beginning balances of zero for Cash, Short-term notes receivable, Land, Equipment, Short-term notes payable, Long-term notes payable, and Contributed capital. Using the T-accounts, record the effects of these transactions by Chu Delivery Company.
2. Prepare a classified statement of financial position for Chu Delivery Company at December 31, 2015.

3. At the end of the next two years, Chu Delivery Company reported the following amounts on its statements of financial position:

	December 31, 2016	December 31, 2017
Current assets	$42,000	$ 47,000
Non-current assets	38,000	53,000
Total assets	80,000	100,000
Short-term notes payable	23,000	40,000
Long-term notes payable	17,000	10,000
Total liabilities	40,000	50,000
Shareholders' equity	40,000	50,000

Compute the company's current ratio for 2015, 2016, and 2017. What is the trend and what does this suggest about the company?

4. At the beginning of 2018, Chu Delivery Company applied to your bank for a $100,000 loan to expand the business. The vice-president of the bank asked you to review the information and make a recommendation on lending the funds based solely on the results of the current ratio. What recommendation would you make to the bank's vice-president about lending the money to Chu Delivery Company?

CASES AND PROJECTS

FINDING AND INTERPRETING FINANCIAL INFORMATION

■ LO1, 2, 3, 4, 7 **CP2–1**

Canadian Tire Corporation

Finding Financial Information

Refer to the financial statements and the accompanying notes of Canadian Tire Corporation in Appendix A at the end of this book.

Required:

1. Is the company a corporation, a partnership, or a proprietorship? How do you know?
2. Use the company's statement of financial position to determine the amounts in the accounting equation (A = L + SE).
3. The company shows on the statement of financial position that inventories are reported at $1,503.3 million. Does this amount represent the expected selling price? Why or why not?
4. What is the company's fiscal year-end? Where did you find the exact date?
5. What are the company's non-current liabilities?
6. Compute the company's current ratio, and explain its meaning.
7. How much cash did the company spend on purchasing property, plant, and equipment each year (capital expenditures)? Where did you find the information?

■ LO1, 2, 3, 4, 7 **CP2–2**

RONA Inc.

Finding Financial Information

Go to *Connect* for the financial statements of RONA Inc. and related notes.

Required:

1. Use the company's statement of financial position to determine the amounts in the accounting equation (A = L + SE) as at December 30, 2012.
2. If the company were liquidated at the end of the current year (December 30, 2012), are the shareholders guaranteed to receive $1,883,576,000?
3. What are the company's non-current liabilities?
4. What is the company's current ratio?
5. Did the company have a cash inflow or outflow from investing activities? How much?

■ LO3, 7   **CP2–3**

Canadian Tire Corporation vs. RONA Inc.

Comparing Companies within an Industry

Refer to the financial statements and the accompanying notes of Canadian Tire Corporation (Appendix A) and RONA Inc. (*Connect*) and the Industry Ratio Report (Appendix B) on *Connect*.

Required:

1. Which company is larger in terms of total assets?

2. Compute the current ratio for both companies. Compared to the industry average (from the Industry Ratio Report), are these two companies more or less able to satisfy short-term obligations with current assets? Explain.

3. In the most recent year, how much cash, if any, was spent buying back (repurchasing) each company's own common shares?

4. How much did each company pay in dividends for the most recent year?

5. What account title does each company use to report any land, buildings, and equipment it may have?

FINANCIAL REPORTING AND ANALYSIS CASES

CP2–4 Broadening Financial Research Skills: Locating Financial Information on the SEDAR Database

■ LO6, 7

The Securities Commissions regulate companies that issue shares on the stock market. They receive financial reports from public companies electronically under a system called *SEDAR* (System for Electronic Document Analysis and Retrieval). Using the Internet, anyone may search the database for the reports that have been filed.

Using your Web browser, access the SEDAR database at **www.sedar.com**. To search the database, select "English," then "Company Profiles"; click on the letter T under Public Companies to get a list of all company names that start with T. Select Thomson Reuters Corporation (TRC), then click on "View this company's public documents" at the lower left corner of the next screen.

Required:

1. Look at SEDAR filings by clicking on the most recent Interim financial statements/report—English. Then locate the statement of financial position.

   a. What was the amount of TRC's total assets at the end of the most recent quarter reported?

   b. Did long-term debt increase or decrease for the quarter?

   c. Compute the current ratio. What does this suggest about the company?

2. Look at the statement of cash flow in the interim report.

   a. What amount did TRC spend on capital expenditures for the most recent quarter reported?

   b. What was the total amount of cash flows from (used in) financing activities for the most recent quarter reported?

CP2–5 Using Financial Reports: Evaluating the Reliability of a Statement of Financial Position

■ LO1, 2, 6

Betsey Jordan asked a local bank for a $50,000 loan to expand her small company. The bank asked Betsey to submit a financial statement of the business to supplement the loan application. Betsey prepared the following statement of financial position:

Statement of Financial Position At June 30, 2014	
Assets	
Cash and investments	$ 9,000
Inventory	30,000
Equipment	46,000
Personal residence (monthly payments, $2,800)	300,000
Other assets	20,000
Total assets	**$405,000**
Liabilities	
Short-term debt to suppliers	$ 62,000
Long-term debt on equipment	38,000
Total debt	100,000
Shareholders' equity	**305,000**
Total liabilities and shareholders' equity	**$405,000**

Required:

1. The statement of financial position has several flaws. However, there is at least one major deficiency. Identify it and explain its significance.
2. As a bank manager, would you lend the company money? Explain.

CP2–6   Using Financial Reports: Analyzing the Statement of Financial Position
Smiley Corp. and Tsang Inc. were organized in 2005. Both companies operate in the same line of business. The statements of financial position of the two companies at December 31, 2014, are as follows:

Smiley Corp. Statement of Financial Position December 31, 2014		Tsang Inc. Statement of Financial Position December 31, 2014	
Assets		**Assets**	
Cash	$ 17,000	Cash	$ 7,200
Trade receivables	30,000	Trade receivables	14,400
Inventory	16,000	Inventory	7,600
Property, plant, and equipment	117,600	Property, plant, and equipment	244,400
Total	$180,600	Total	$273,600
Liabilities and Shareholders' Equity		**Liabilities and Shareholders' Equity**	
Liabilities:		Liabilities:	
Notes payable (short-term)	$ 18,600	Notes payable (short-term)	$ 33,600
Trade payables	14,400	Trade payables	64,800
Total liabilities	33,000	Total liabilities	98,400
Shareholders' equity:		Shareholders' equity:	
Contributed capital	90,000	Contributed capital	108,000
Retained earnings	57,600	Retained earnings	67,200
Total shareholders' equity	147,600	Total shareholders' equity	175,200
Total	$180,600	Total	$273,600

Required:

1. Eric Frechette wants to invest in one of these two companies by purchasing all of its shares. As a financial adviser to Mr. Frechette, which company would you select as an investment? Provide justification for your selection.
2. Each company applied to Development Bank for a loan of $20,000, payable in four months. As a bank loan officer, would you lend each company the requested amount? Explain.

CRITICAL THINKING CASES

CP2–7   Making a Decision as a Financial Analyst: Preparing and Analyzing a Statement of Financial Position
Your best friend from home writes you a letter about an investment opportunity that has come her way. A company is raising money by issuing shares and wants her to invest $20,000 (her recent inheritance from her great-aunt's estate). Your friend has never invested in a company before and, knowing that you are a financial analyst, asks that you look over the statement of financial position and send her some advice. An *unaudited* statement of financial position, in only moderately good form, is enclosed with the letter:

DEWEY, CHEETUM, AND HOWE INC.
Statement of Financial Position
For the Year Ending December 31, 2015

Trade receivables	$ 8,000
Cash	1,000
Inventory	8,000
Furniture and fixtures	52,000
Delivery truck	12,000
Buildings (estimated market value)	98,000
Total assets	**$179,000**
Trade payables	$ 16,000
Payroll taxes payable	13,000
Long-term notes payable	15,000
Mortgage payable	50,000
Total liabilities	94,000
Contributed capital	80,000
Retained earnings	5,000
Total shareholders' equity	85,000
Total liabilities and shareholders' equity	**$179,000**

There is only one footnote, and it states that the building was purchased for $65,000, has been depreciated by $5,000 on the books, and still carries a mortgage (shown in the liability section). The footnote further states that, in the opinion of the company president, the building is "easily worth $98,000."

Required:

1. Draft a new statement of financial position for your friend, correcting any errors you note. (If any of the account balances need to be corrected, you may need to adjust the balance of retained earnings accordingly.) If no errors or omissions exist, say so.

2. Write a letter to your friend explaining the changes you made to the statement of financial position, if any, and offer your comments on the company's apparent financial condition based only on this information. Suggest other information your friend might want to review before coming to a final decision on whether to invest.

CP2–8 Manipulating Financial Statements: Ethical Considerations

■ LO3, 4, 6

Technology N Motion is a publicly traded company that is facing financial difficulties. To survive, the company needs large new bank loans. As the chief financial officer of the company, you approached several banks, but each has asked for your audited financial statements for 2014, the most recent fiscal year. You called for a meeting with other corporate officers to discuss how the financial statements could be improved. The suggestions made by your colleagues include the following:

a. We owe $20 million to our suppliers. We could show half this amount as a liability on our statement of financial position and report the other half as contributed capital. This will improve our financial position.

b. We own land that is worth at least $8 million in today's market, but it cost us only $3 million when we bought it. Why not show the land at $8 million on the company's statement of financial position, which increases both the total assets and shareholders' equity by $5 million?

c. We owe FirstRate Software $2 million, due in 30 days. I can ask their chief financial officer to let us delay the payment of this debt for a year, and our company could sign him a note that pays 8 percent interest.

Required:

Evaluate each of these three proposals to improve Technology N Motion's financial statements by considering both accounting and ethical issues.

CP2–9   **Evaluating an Ethical Dilemma: Analyzing Management Incentives**

Nortel Networks Corporation (Nortel), based in Brampton, Ontario, is a global supplier of networking solutions and services. In 2005, the company released the findings of an independent review as a result of continuing problems with its accounting. The review revealed that three former company executives, the chief executive officer, the chief financial officer, and the controller, used accounting practices that increased reported earnings from late 2002 to mid-2003. Through Nortel's internal investigation, several problems had become known, not the least of which was $900 million of inappropriately reported liabilities and approximately $250 million of overstated net earnings. This mattered to the executives who received a bonus if earnings before tax exceeded specific levels.

In April 2004, Nortel issued a news release announcing the appointment of its new chief executive officer (CEO), Mr. William Owens, and the termination of its previous CEO, for cause. The previous CEO left his position on April 28 and left the company's board of directors on May 21, 2004. Neither the chairman of the board of directors nor the new CEO would comment on the termination. A month earlier the chief financial officer and the controller had been placed on paid leave of absence and they too were fired. A day later, the U.S. Securities and Exchange Commission announced that it was investigating Nortel, and then the Ontario Securities Commission launched its own investigation. But the worst was yet to come.

In May 2004, a U.S. federal grand jury subpoenaed Nortel for accounting records and other documents prepared for the previous four years during which the previous CEO, an accountant, had served as chief financial officer. A few days later the Ontario Public Service Employees Union Pension Trust filed a class action lawsuit to recover losses arising from its investment in Nortel shares between April 2003 and 2005, based on fraudulent financial information. By August 2004, the Royal Canadian Mounted Police began a Canadian criminal investigation into the former CEO's activities. The cost to Nortel has been over $2.4 billion in cash awarded to the Ontario pension fund in April 2005, and the company sued the former CEO to recover this money from him personally. Pursuant to the independent review, 12 senior executives agreed to repay a total of $8.6 million in bonuses they received from the company in the past.

Required:

1. Describe the parties that were harmed or helped by this fraud.
2. Explain how greed may have contributed to this fraud.
3. Why do you think the independent auditors failed to catch the fraud?

FINANCIAL REPORTING AND ANALYSIS TEAM PROJECT

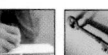

CP2–10   **Team Project: Analyzing the Statement of Financial Position and Ratios**

As a team, select an industry to analyze. A list of companies classified by industry can be obtained by accessing **www.fpinfomart.ca** and then choosing "Companies by Industry" on the left-hand side. You can also find a list of industries and companies within each industry via **http://ca.finance.yahoo.com/investing**. A list of industries can be obtained by clicking on "Order Annual Reports" under "Tools."

Each group member should acquire the annual report for a different publicly traded company in the industry. (Library files, the SEDAR service at **www.sedar.com**, and the company's website are good sources.)

Required:

Each team member should write a short report answering the following questions about the selected company. Discuss any patterns that you as a team observe. Then, as a team, write a short report comparing and contrasting your companies.

1. For the most recent year, what are the top three asset accounts by size? What percentage is each account of the total assets (Calculated as Asset A ÷ Total Assets)?
2. What are the major investing and financing activities (by dollar size) for the most recent year? (Look at the statement of cash flows.)
3. Perform a ratio analysis.

    a. What does the current ratio measure in general?
    b. Compute the current ratio for the last three years. (You may find prior years' information in the section in the annual report called "Selected Financial Information," or search for prior years' annual reports.)
    c. What do your results suggest about the company?
    d. If available, find the industry ratio for the most recent year, compare it to your results, and discuss why you believe your company differs from or is similar to the industry ratio.

SOLUTIONS TO SELF-STUDY QUIZZES

Self-Study Quiz 2-1
Column 1: CL; CA; CA. Column 2: NCL; SE; CL. Column 3: NCA; NCA; CA.

Self-Study Quiz 2-2
(g) Cash (A) is received +300. The trade supplier's written promise to pay is "given back" (paid off); Notes receivable (A) –300. The equation remains the same because assets increase and decrease by the same amount.

(h) Cash (A) is given –400. Sun-Rype's written promise to the bank is "given back" (paid off); Long-term notes payable –400. There is a $400 decrease on the left side of the equation and a $400 decrease on the right side.

If your answers did not agree with these, go back and make sure that you have completed each of the steps for each transaction.

Self-Study Quiz 2-3
Column 1: cr; dr; dr. Column 2: cr; cr; cr. Column 3: dr; dr; dr.

Self-Study Quiz 2-4
(g) Journal entry:

Cash (+A)   300
   Notes receivable (−A)   300

(h) Effects on the Accounting Equation:

Assets		=	Liabilities		+	Shareholders' Equity
Cash	−400		Long-term borrowings	−400		

Posting to Ledger Accounts:

Cash: (g) 300; (h) 400   Notes receivable: (g) 300   Long-term borrowings: (h) 400

Ending balance of Retained earnings = $28,481

Self-Study Quiz 2-5
Current Ratio:

January 29, 2012	$396 ÷ $143 = 2.77
January 30, 2011	$319 ÷ $137 = 2.33
February 1, 2010	$338 ÷ $159 = 2.13

Dollarama has a high level of liquidity, which has increased over the three years. It is a cash-oriented business with a strong cash management system. However, its increasing ratio may indicate a build-up in its inventories, which may be a cause for concern.

Self-Study Quiz 2-6
1. F −
2. I +
3. F −
4. I −
5. F +

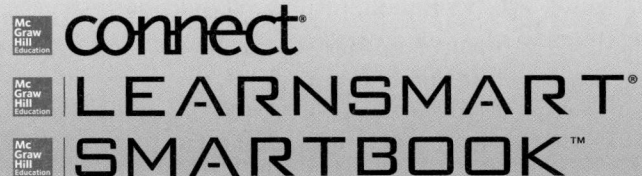

Operating Decisions and the Statement of Earnings

After studying this chapter, you should be able to do the following:

FOCUS COMPANY: **Sun-Rype Products Ltd.**

OFFERING PRODUCTS TAILORED TO CLIENTS' NEEDS

Sun-Rype (www.sunrype.com) is a leading Canadian provider of fruit-based juices and snack products. To achieve and maintain its success, Sun-Rype has to produce beverages and food items that cater to the needs of a wide variety of customers with different cultural backgrounds, tastes, social status, and financial means.

The company's plants, located in Kelowna, British Columbia, and Saleh and Wapato in the state of Washington, receive and process fruit to produce 100 percent pure apple juice and apple purée, which is used in fruit snack production and in both concentrated and single-strength juices. Sun-Rype also produces a broad range of juices, juice blends, and drinks from purchased fruit concentrates and other ingredients.

Sun-Rype has grown over time through product innovation, marketing, and geographic expansion of sales. Its research and development department continuously improves and develops new products and new packaging. The company's dedicated food scientists, microbiologists, and industrial engineers strive to maintain a continuous flow of new and revitalized products. They work closely with marketing personnel to develop new product offerings to meet consumer demands. The company recognizes that the market potential for some of its products extends beyond its in-house capabilities and builds strong manufacturing and distribution partnerships with other companies to meet its customers' needs.

Sun-Rype employs approximately 450 people both in Canada and the United States, with sales exceeding $140 million annually.

UNDERSTANDING THE BUSINESS

To become a leading Canadian provider of fruit-based foods and beverages, Sun-Rype's executives develop strategies, plans, and measurable indicators of progress toward their goals. In developing operating and growth strategies, companies such as Sun-Rype plan their companywide operations in terms of the elements of the statement of earnings (specific revenues and expenses). These strategies are most often disclosed in the management discussion and analysis section of the annual report.

Financial analysts develop their own set of expectations about Sun-Rype's future performance. The published statement of earnings provides the primary basis for comparing analysts' projections to the actual results of operations. We discuss these comparisons and the stock market's reactions to Sun-Rype's results throughout this chapter as we learn about income recognition and measurement. To understand how business plans and the results of operations are reflected on the statement of earnings, we need to answer the following questions:

1. How do business activities affect the statement of earnings?
2. How are these activities recognized and measured?
3. How are these activities reported on the statement of earnings?

In this chapter, we focus on Sun-Rype's operating activities, which include sales of its many products to consumers through various distribution channels, such as grocery stores, club stores, mass merchandisers, and drug stores. The results of these activities are reported on the statement of earnings.

ORGANIZATION OF THE CHAPTER

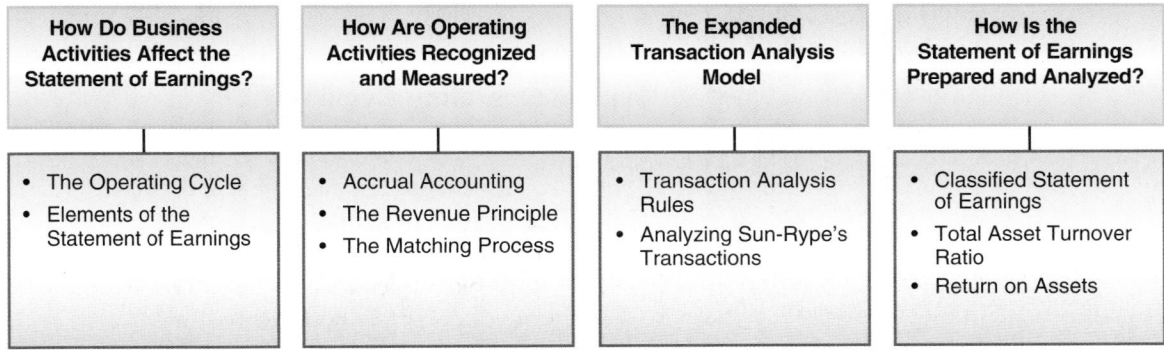

How Do Business Activities Affect the Statement of Earnings?	How Are Operating Activities Recognized and Measured?	The Expanded Transaction Analysis Model	How Is the Statement of Earnings Prepared and Analyzed?
• The Operating Cycle • Elements of the Statement of Earnings	• Accrual Accounting • The Revenue Principle • The Matching Process	• Transaction Analysis Rules • Analyzing Sun-Rype's Transactions	• Classified Statement of Earnings • Total Asset Turnover Ratio • Return on Assets

Supplemental material:
Appendix C: The Formal Recordkeeping System (on *Connect*)

HOW DO BUSINESS ACTIVITIES AFFECT THE STATEMENT OF EARNINGS?

The Operating Cycle

The long-term objective for any business is *to turn cash into more cash*. For companies to stay in business, this excess cash must be generated from operations (i.e., from the activities for which the business was established), not from borrowing money or selling non-current assets.

Companies acquire inventory and the services of employees and then sell inventory or services to customers. The **operating (or cash-to-cash) cycle** begins when a company receives goods to sell (or, in the case of a service company, has employees work), pays for them, and sells to customers; it ends when customers pay cash to the company. The length of time for completion of the operating cycle depends on the nature of the business.

LO¹

Describe a typical business operating cycle and explain the necessity for the periodicity assumption.

The **OPERATING (CASH-TO-CASH) CYCLE** is the time it takes for a company to pay cash to suppliers, sell goods and services to customers, and collect cash from customers.

The operating cycle for Sun-Rype is relatively short. It spends cash to purchase ingredients used in the preparation and packaging of its many products according to its own blends and recipes; sells these products through distribution channels that reach consumers at home, work, and play; and then collects cash from customers. In some companies, inventory is paid for well before it is sold. Toys "R" Us, for example, builds its inventory for months prior to the year-end holiday season. It borrows funds from banks to pay for the inventory and repays the loans with interest when cash is received from customers. In other companies, cash is received from customers well after a sale takes place. For example, car dealerships often sell cars over time, with monthly payments from customers due over several years. Companies attempt to shorten the operating cycle by creating incentives to encourage customers to buy sooner or pay faster, in order to improve the company's cash flows.

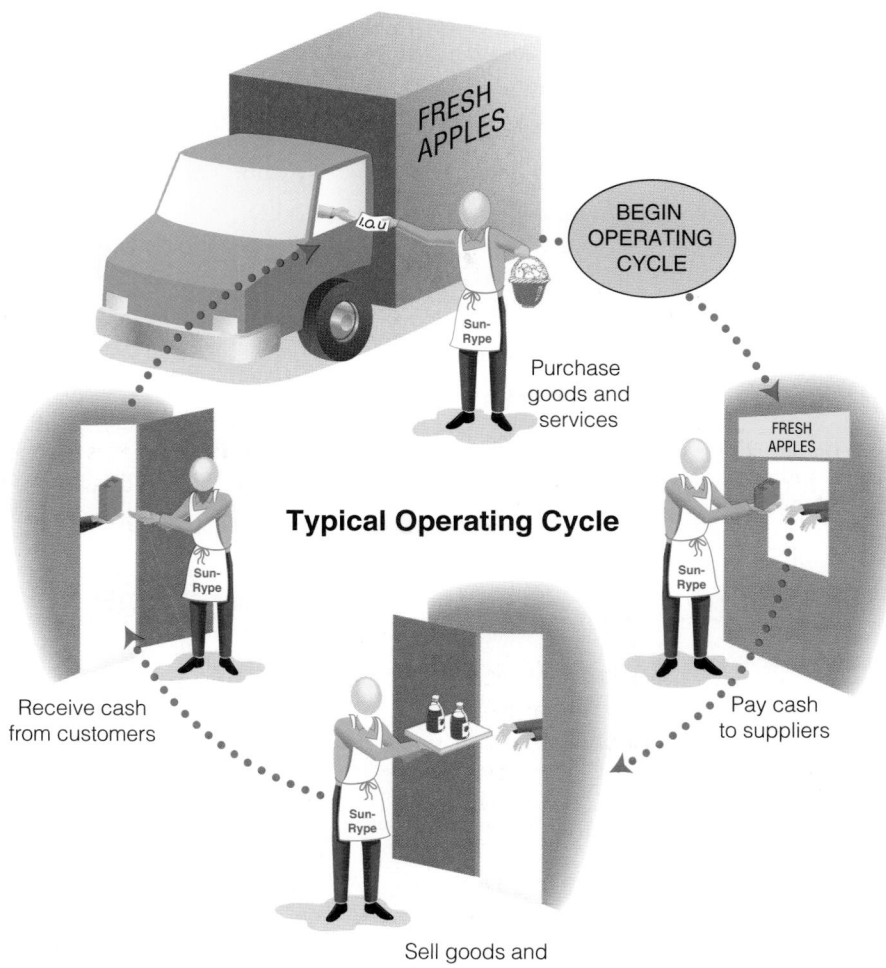

Typical Operating Cycle

SHORT-TERM DEBT FINANCING AND THE OPERATING CYCLE

The timing of the cash outflows and inflows shown in the illustration above indicates that many businesses must pay suppliers and employees before they receive cash from customers, causing them to seek short-term financing. When the companies receive cash from customers, they pay off the liability. In addition, if a company plans to grow—say, to sell twice as many goods as in the prior period—it may not have collected enough cash from the prior period's customers to purchase the quantity of inventory needed in the next period. Sources of financing include suppliers and financial institutions (banks and commercial credit companies).

Managers know that reducing the time needed to turn cash into more cash (i.e., shortening the operating cycle) means higher net earnings and faster growth. Managers may purchase additional inventory or other assets for growth or repay debt with the excess cash, or they may distribute it to owners.

Until a company ceases activities, the operating cycle is repeated continuously. However, decision makers require periodic information about the financial condition and performance of a business. To measure net earnings for a specific period of time, accountants follow the **periodicity assumption**, which assumes that the long life of a company can be reported in shorter time periods, such as months, quarters, and years.[1] Two types of issues arise in reporting periodic net earnings to users:

The PERIODICITY ASSUMPTION means that the long life of a company can be reported in shorter periods.

1. Recognition issues: *When* should the effects of operating activities be recognized (recorded)?

2. Measurement issues: *What amounts* should be recognized?

Before we examine the rules accountants follow as they resolve these issues, let us review the elements of financial statements that are affected by operating activities.

Elements of the Statement of Earnings

Exhibit 3.1 shows a recent statement of earnings for Sun-Rype. As we indicated in Chapter 1, the statement of earnings is the main part of a statement of comprehensive income. We continue to focus our attention on the statement of earnings in this chapter, postponing the discussion of comprehensive income to Chapters 6 and 12.

The statement of earnings has multiple subtotals, such as *earnings from operations* and *earnings before income taxes.* This *multiple-step* format is very common.[2] Classification of the various elements of the statement of earnings helps financial statement users assess the company's operating performance and predict its future profitability.

LO2

Explain how business activities affect the elements of the statement of earnings.

Exhibit **3.1**

Statement of Earnings

CONSOLIDATED STATEMENT OF EARNINGS
Years Ended December 31
(in thousands of Canadian dollars, except for earnings per share)

	2012	2011	
Sales	$ 152,795	$ 147,529	
Cost of sales	(125,474)	(126,311)	
Gross profit	27,321	21,218	
Operating expenses			← Operating activities (central focus of business)
Sales and marketing	(11,699)	(14,721)	
Distribution	(6,813)	(7,352)	
General and administrative	(5,987)	(6,410)	← Includes insurance, repairs, utilities, and fuel expenses
Total operating expenses	(24,499)	(28,483)	
Earnings (loss) from operations	2,822	(7,265)	← Subtotal of operating revenues minus operating expenses
Other income (expenses and losses)			
Finance costs	(708)	(714)	
Loss on disposal of property, plant, and equipment	–	(57)	← Peripheral activities (not the main focus of the business)
Earnings (loss) before income taxes	2,114	(8,036)	← Subtotal of all income minus all expenses except income taxes
Income tax recovery (expense)	(847)	2,349	
Net earnings (loss) for the year	$ 1,267	$ (5,687)	
Earnings (loss) per share	$ 0.12	$ (0.53)	← Net earnings divided by weighted average number of shares outstanding

Note: This statement of earnings is an adaptation of Sun-Rype's actual consolidated statement of earnings.

The statement of earnings includes three major sections:

1. Results of continuing operations
2. Results of discontinued operations

Net earnings (the sum of 1 and 2)

3. Earnings per share

All companies report information for sections 1 and 3, while some companies report information in section 2, depending upon their particular circumstances. The bottom line, net earnings, is the sum of sections 1 and 2. First, we will focus on the most common and most relevant section, continuing operations.

Continuing Operations   This section of the statement of earnings presents the results of continuing operations. As we discuss the elements of the statement of earnings, it is useful to refer to the conceptual framework outlined in Exhibit 2.1 in Chapter 2.

Operating Revenues   **Revenues** are defined as increases in assets or settlements of liabilities from *ongoing operations* of the business. Operating revenues result from the sale of goods or services. Sun-Rype earns revenue when it sells goods and renders services to customers. It recognizes revenue in the statement of earnings when the significant risks and rewards of ownership have been transferred to the buyer, which is mainly upon delivery of goods or services. When revenues are earned, assets, usually cash or trade receivables, often increase. Sometimes, a company receives cash in exchange for a promise to provide goods or services in the future. At that point, revenue is not earned, but a liability account, Deferred Revenue, is created. When the company provides the promised goods or services to the customer, revenue is recognized and the liability is settled.

Operating Expenses   **Expenses** are decreases in assets or increases in liabilities from ongoing operations and are incurred to generate revenues during the period. Some students confuse the terms "expenditures" and "expenses." An expenditure is any outflow of cash for any purpose, whether to buy equipment, pay off a bank loan, or pay employees their wages. An expense is more narrowly defined; it will only result when an asset, such as equipment or supplies, is *used to generate revenue during a period*, or when an amount is *incurred to generate revenues during a period*, such as using electricity, even if the amount will be paid in the future. Therefore, *not all expenditures are expenses*, and *expenses are necessary to generate revenues*.

Sun-Rype pays employees to produce and sell fruit-based beverages and snacks, uses electricity to operate equipment and light facilities, advertises the goods it sells, and uses a wide variety of supplies in its production processes. Without incurring these expenses, Sun-Rype could not generate revenues. Although some of the expenses may result from expenditures of cash at the time they are incurred, some expenses may be incurred after cash was paid, in the past, while other expenses may be incurred before cash is paid, in the future. When an expense occurs, assets such as Supplies Inventory decrease (are used up) *or* liabilities such as Salaries Payable or Utilities Payable increase.

The following are Sun-Rype's primary operating expenses:

1. *Cost of sales* is the cost of products sold to customers. For example, when Sun-Rype purchases fresh fruits from local suppliers, it pays for transport and handling, in addition to the purchase price. All of these costs are included in the cost of the asset "inventories." As inventories are used to produce and package the squeezed fruits, they become an expense, called cost of sales. In companies with a manufacturing or merchandising focus, the cost of sales (also called cost of goods sold) is usually the most significant expense. The cost of sales for Sun-Rype is $125,474 and represents about 82.1 percent of the sales for 2012.[3] The difference between sales—net of sales discounts, returns and allowances—and cost of sales is known as **gross profit** or **gross margin**.[4]

REVENUES are increases in assets or settlements of liabilities from ongoing operations.

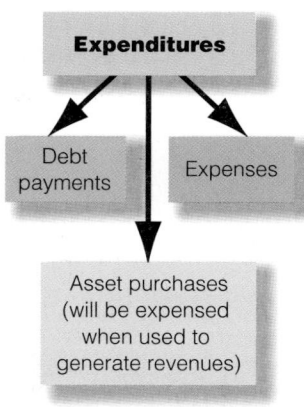

EXPENSES are decreases in assets or increases in liabilities to generate revenues during the period.

GROSS PROFIT (or GROSS MARGIN) is net sales less cost of sales.

2. *Operating expenses* are the usual expenses, other than cost of sales, that are incurred in operating a business during a specific accounting period. The expenses reported will depend on the nature of the company's operations. International Accounting Standard 1 requires companies to classify their expenses either by function—such as marketing and promotion, distribution, and administrative—or by nature of the expense. Classification by nature includes the three main costs of production: materials, labour, and property and equipment use.

Sun-Rype, like most companies, classifies its expenses by function.[5] *Sales and marketing* expenses include the salaries of marketing personnel and those who support the sales effort, such as legal counsel, accountants, and computer technicians. They may also include promotion of the company's products through various print and electronic media. *Distribution* expenses include a variety of expenses related to the distribution of the company's products to its customers, such as the wages earned by distribution personnel and depreciation of delivery vehicles. *General and administrative* expenses relate to salaries of administrative personnel, rental of office space, insurance, and utilities, plus other general operating expenses not directly related to production, sales, and distribution of the company's products. Another subtotal, **earnings from operations**, also called operating income, equals net sales less cost of sales and other operating expenses.

EARNINGS FROM OPERATIONS (operating income) equals net sales less cost of sales and other operating expenses.

Non-operating Items   Not all activities affecting a statement of earnings are central to continuing operations. Any revenues, expenses, gains, or losses that result from these other activities are not included as part of earnings from operations, but are instead categorized as other income or expenses. Typically, these include the following:

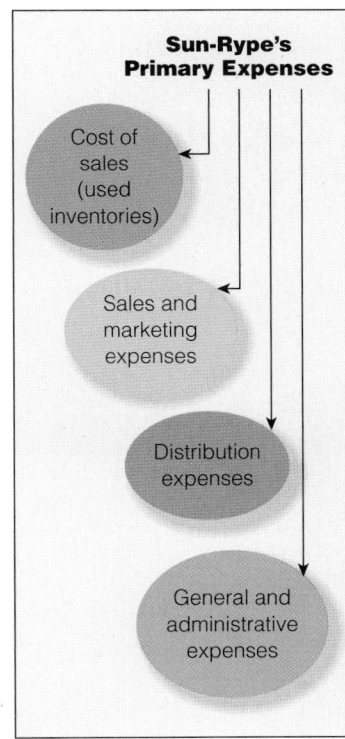

Sun-Rype's Primary Expenses

- *Investment income* (or *Investment, Interest,* or *Dividend revenue*). Using excess cash to purchase shares in other corporations is an investing activity for Sun-Rype, not a central operation (producing and selling fruit-based beverages and snacks). Therefore, any interest or dividends earned on the investment are not included as operating revenue.

- *Financing costs.* Likewise, since borrowing money is a financing activity, any cost of using that money (called interest) is not an operating expense. In addition to interest expense, Sun-Rype incurs other financing costs when other currencies, such as the U.S. dollar, are the basis for purchase or sale transactions. Except for financial institutions, incurring interest expense or earning investment income is *not* part of the central operations of most businesses, including Sun-Rype. We say these are peripheral (normal but not central) transactions.

- *Gains (or losses) on disposal of assets.* Companies dispose of (either sell or abandon) property, plant, and equipment from time to time to maintain modern facilities. Selling land for more than the original purchase price does not result in earning revenue because the transaction is not the central operating focus for the business. **Gains** (with an account called *Gain on disposal of assets*) are increases in assets or decreases in liabilities from *peripheral* transactions. **Losses** are decreases in assets or increases in liabilities from *peripheral* transactions. Abandoning or getting rid of property, plant, and equipment results in losses to the company. In 2011, Sun-Rype disposed of old assets and recognized a loss of $57.

GAINS are increases in assets or decreases in liabilities from peripheral transactions.

LOSSES are decreases in assets or increases in liabilities from peripheral transactions.

The non-operating items that are subject to income taxes are added to or subtracted from earnings from operations to obtain the **earnings before income taxes** (or pretax earnings).

EARNINGS BEFORE INCOME TAXES (pretax earnings) equals revenues minus all expenses except income tax expense.

Income Tax Expense   Income tax expense is the last expense listed on the statement of earnings. All for-profit corporations are required to compute income taxes owed to federal, provincial, and foreign governments. Income tax expense is calculated as a percentage of earnings before income taxes, reflecting the difference between income, which includes revenues and gains, and expenses and losses; it is determined by using applicable tax rates. Sun-Rype's effective tax rate in 2012 was 40 percent (income tax expense ÷ earnings before income taxes). This indicates that for every dollar of earnings before income taxes that Sun-Rype incurred in 2012, the company incurred $0.40 in income taxes.

Discontinued Operations   Companies may dispose of a major line of business or a geographical area of operations during the accounting period, or decide to discontinue a specific operation in the near future. When the decision is made to discontinue a major component of a business, the net earnings or loss from that component, as well as any gain or loss on subsequent disposal, are disclosed separately on the statement of earnings as *discontinued operations*. Because of their non-recurring nature, the financial results of discontinued operations are not useful in predicting future recurring net earnings; hence, they are presented separately from the results of continuing operations.

Earnings per Share   Corporations are required to disclose earnings per share on the statement of earnings or in the notes to the financial statements. This ratio is widely used in evaluating the operating performance and profitability of a company. At this introductory level, we can compute earnings per share simply as net earnings divided by the average number of shares outstanding during the period. Please note, however, that the calculation of the ratio is actually more complex and beyond the scope of this course.

Sun-Rype earned $0.12 per share in 2012 compared to a loss of $0.53 per share in 2011. Although this appears to be bad news, investors would want to learn why the company realized a loss in 2011 and check the historical trend of earnings per share for a period of five years. More important, investors need to compare Sun-Rype's performance to that of its competitors during the same period. Regardless, overreliance on this ratio for investment decisions can lead to inadvisable decisions.

FINANCIAL ANALYSIS

STOCK MARKET REACTIONS TO ACCOUNTING ANNOUNCEMENTS

Stock market analysts and investors use accounting information to make investment decisions. The stock market, which is based on investors' expectations about future company performance, often reacts negatively when a company does not meet previously specified operating results. A company can experience difficulty even if it does not report a loss. Any unexpected deviation of actual performance from the operating plan, such as lower than expected quarterly earnings, needs to be explained.

On November 8, 2012, Sun-Rype announced the results of its third quarter ending September 30, 2012. On the day of the announcement, the price per share closed at $5.80, an increase of $0.04 over the closing price on the previous day.* Sun-Rype reported net earnings of $0.05 per share for the third quarter of 2012 compared to a net loss of $0.28 for the third quarter of 2011, which reflects an improvement in its operating performance. Prior to the earnings announcement, investors had built expectations of the company's performance based on available information. The increase in share price on the day of the earnings announcement suggests that investors were pleased with the company's results and reacted positively when the reported earnings per share figure exceeded their expectations.

This is a clear example of how external users react to information. Accounting information has a pervasive effect on all forms of corporate decision making, as well as on the economic decisions that investors and creditors make.

*Source: Sun-Rype's website, accessed on April 11, 2013; http://www.sunrype.com.

HOW ARE OPERATING ACTIVITIES RECOGNIZED AND MEASURED?

You probably determine your personal financial position by the balance in your bank account. Your financial performance is measured as the difference between your account balance at the end of the period and the balance at the beginning of the period (i.e., whether you end up with more or less cash). If you have a higher account balance, cash receipts exceeded cash disbursements for the period. Many local retailers and other small businesses use **cash basis accounting**, which records revenues when cash is received and expenses when cash is paid, regardless of when the revenues are earned or the expenses incurred. This basis is often quite adequate for these organizations, which usually do not have to report to external users.

CASH BASIS ACCOUNTING records revenues when cash is received and expenses when cash is paid.

Accrual Accounting

Net earnings measured on a cash basis can be misleading. For example, a company using a cash basis can report higher net earnings in one period simply because (1) a customer paid cash in advance of receiving a good or service or (2) the company postponed the payment of utility bills until the next period. In the first case, the company has not performed the service or delivered the promised goods to earn revenue. In the second case, the company has already used gas, electricity, and phone service to generate revenues (creating an expense), but the expense is not recorded because payment will occur in the next period.

LO3

Explain the accrual basis of accounting and apply the revenue principle and matching process to measure net earnings.

Financial statements created under cash basis accounting normally postpone or accelerate recognition of revenues and expenses long after or before goods and services are produced and delivered. They also do not necessarily reflect all assets and liabilities of a company on a particular date. For these reasons, cash basis financial statements are not very useful to external decision makers. Therefore, IFRS require accrual basis accounting for financial reporting purposes.

In **accrual basis accounting**, revenues and expenses are recognized when the transaction that causes them occurs, not necessarily when cash is received or paid. *Revenues are recognized when they are earned and expenses when they are incurred.* The *revenue principle* and the *matching process* determine when revenues and expenses are to be recorded under accrual basis accounting.

ACCRUAL BASIS
Income Measurement

Revenues (when earned)
− Expenses (when incurred)

Net earnings

ACCRUAL BASIS ACCOUNTING records revenues when earned and expenses when incurred, regardless of the timing of cash receipts or payments.

The Revenue Principle

Companies engage in a series of events that lead to the recognition of revenue. For example, after purchasing the raw materials, such as fresh fruits, Sun-Rype places them into a production process that culminates in finished products, including Sun-Rype Fruit Plus, Smoothies, Fruit to Go, and many other products. The finished products are then stored in the company's warehouses and marketed to consumers through various media before they are sold to customers either for cash or on credit. Each activity (purchase of raw materials, production, promotion, sale, and collection from customers) contributes to the recognition of revenue. It is difficult, however, to estimate and recognize the value each activity adds to the amount eventually recognized as revenue. Instead, accountants attempt to identify the most critical event that leads to a flow of future benefits to Sun-Rype from all of these activities.

To guard against identification of critical events that may favour earlier recognition of revenue and increase net earnings, the following five conditions must be met for revenue to be recognized, according to the **revenue principle**. If any of the following conditions are not met, revenue is normally not recognized and cannot be recorded:[6]

a. *The entity has transferred to the buyer the significant risks and rewards of ownership of the goods.* In most cases, the transfer of the risks and rewards of ownership coincides with the transfer of the legal title or the passing of possession to the buyer.

The **REVENUE PRINCIPLE** states that revenues are recognized when the significant risks and rewards of ownership are transferred to the buyer, it is probable that future economic benefits will flow to the entity, and the benefits and the costs associated with the transaction can be measured reliably.

b. *The entity retains neither continuing managerial involvement to the degree usually associated with ownership nor effective control over the goods sold.* If the entity retains significant risks of ownership, the transaction is not a sale and revenue is not recognized. An entity may retain a significant risk of ownership in a number of ways. For example, if the buyer has the right to rescind the purchase for a reason specified in the sales contract and the entity is uncertain about the probability of return, then revenue cannot be recognized at the point of sale.

c. *The amount of revenue can be measured reliably.* There are no uncertainties as to the amount to be collected.

d. *It is probable that the economic benefits associated with the transaction will flow to the entity.* The consideration received for the sale of goods is either cash or the customer's promise to pay cash in the future. For cash sales, collection is not an issue since it is received on the date of the exchange. For sales on credit, the company reviews the customer's ability to pay. If the customer is considered creditworthy, collecting cash from the customer is reasonably likely.

e. *The costs incurred or to be incurred with respect to the transaction can be measured reliably.* Companies that provide service after sale may incur additional costs related to the sale transaction. In general, the costs to be incurred after the shipment of the goods can normally be measured reliably when the other conditions for the recognition of revenue have been satisfied. However, revenue cannot be recognized when the expenses cannot be measured reliably.

If *any* of the previous conditions are *not* met, revenue is normally *not* recognized and should not be recorded. For most businesses, these conditions are met at the point of delivery of goods or services.[7]

Companies usually disclose their revenue recognition practices in a note to the financial statements. The following excerpt from Sun-Rype's note describes how it recognizes its revenue:

Sun-Rype Products Ltd.
Notes to Consolidated Financial Statements

3. Significant Accounting Policies

(j) Revenue
Revenue from the sale of goods in the normal course of activities is measured at the fair value of the consideration received or receivable, net of returns, trade discounts and volume rebates. Revenue is recognized when persuasive evidence exists, usually in the form of executed sales documents, that the significant risks and rewards of ownership have been transferred to the customer, recovery of the consideration is probable, the associated costs and possible return of the goods can be estimated reliably, there is no continuing management involvement in the goods, and the amount of revenue can be measured reliably. Generally this recognition occurs upon shipment. The value of promotional incentives, trade discounts and volume rebates provided to customers are estimated using historical trends and are recognized at the time of sale as a reduction in revenue. In subsequent periods, the Company makes any required adjustments to both revenue and promotional incentive accruals based on actual costs.

Exhibit 3.2 shows excerpts from the revenue recognition policies used by other companies that offer different types of products and services. Note that the point in time when revenue should be recognized depends on the nature of the products sold and services provided by the company.

Although businesses expect to receive cash in exchange for their goods and services at the time of delivery, the timing of cash receipts from customers does not dictate when businesses report revenues. Instead, the key to determining when to report revenues is whether or not the business has done what it promised to do. Thus, cash can

Exhibit **3.2**

Timing of Revenue Recognition

Company Name	Typical Timing of Revenue Recognition
WestJet Airlines *Air transportation*	**(i) Guest** Guest revenue, including the air component of vacation packages, are recognized when air transportation is provided. Tickets sold but not yet used are reported in the consolidated statement of financial position as advance ticket sales. **(ii) Other** Other revenue includes charter revenue, cargo revenue, net revenue from the sale of the land component of vacation packages, ancillary revenue and other. Revenue for the land component of vacation packages is generated from providing agency services equal to the amount paid by the guest for products and services, less payment to the travel supplier, and is reported at the net amount received. Revenue from the land component is deferred as advance ticket sales and recognized in earnings on completion of the vacation. Ancillary revenue is recognized when the services and products are provided to the guests. Included in ancillary revenue are fees associated with guest itinerary changes or cancellations, baggage fees, buy-on-board sales, pre-reserved seating fees and ancillary revenue from the WestJet Rewards Program. **(iii) WestJet Rewards Program** The Corporation has a rewards program that allows guests to accumulate credits to be used towards flights and vacation packages. Revenue received in relation to credits issued is deferred as a liability at fair value until the credit is utilized and air transportation is provided, at which time it is recognized in guest revenue. Revenue associated with credits expected to expire (breakage) is recognized in other revenue at the time the revenue is expected to be received.
Danier Leather Inc. *Clothing (leather and suede products)*	Revenue includes sales of merchandise, alteration services, and gift cards to customers through stores operated by the Company and sales of incentive and promotional product merchandise to a third party distributor. Revenue is measured at the fair value of consideration received net of sales tax, returns and discounts. Sales of merchandise to customers through stores operated by the Company are recognized when the significant risks and rewards of ownership have been transferred to the buyer, which is the time the customer tenders payment for and takes possession of the merchandise. Alteration revenue is recorded based on the percentage of completion method. Due to alteration revenue representing less than one percent of merchandise revenue, the short time required to complete an alteration and that at any point in time there is an immaterial amount of partially processed alterations, alteration revenue is recorded at the same time as the customer tenders payment for and takes possession of the merchandise. Sales to third-party distributors are recorded when the significant risks and rewards of ownership have been transferred to the buyer, which is at the time the distributor ships the merchandise to their customer. Gift cards sold are recorded as deferred revenue and revenue is recognized at the time of redemption or in accordance with the Company's accounting policy for breakage. Breakage income represents the estimated value of gift cards that is not expected to be redeemed by customers where the unredeemed balance is more than two years old from the date of issuance. Historically, breakage has not been material.
Bell Canada Enterprises Inc. *Telecommunications*	We recognize revenues from the sale of products or the rendering of services when they are earned; specifically when all the following conditions are met: • the significant risks and rewards of ownership are transferred to customers and we retain neither continuing managerial involvement nor effective control • there is clear evidence that an arrangement exists • the amount of revenue and related costs can be measured reliably • it is probable that the economic benefits associated with the transaction will flow to the company. In particular, we recognize: • fees for local, long distance and wireless services when we provide the services • other fees, such as network access fees, licence fees, hosting fees, maintenance fees and standby fees, over the term of the contract • subscriber revenues when customers receive the service • advertising revenue, net of agency commissions, when advertisements are aired or delivered on the Internet • revenues from the sale of equipment when the equipment is delivered and accepted by customers • revenues on long-term contracts as services are provided, equipment is delivered and accepted, and contract milestones are met.

Sources: WestJet, Annual Report 2012; Danier Leather, Annual Report 2012; BCE, Annual Report 2012.

be received (1) *before* the goods or services are delivered, (2) at the *same* time as the goods or services are delivered, or (3) *after* the goods or services are delivered, as shown in Exhibit 3.3.

Exhibit **3.3**

Recording Revenues versus
Cash Receipts

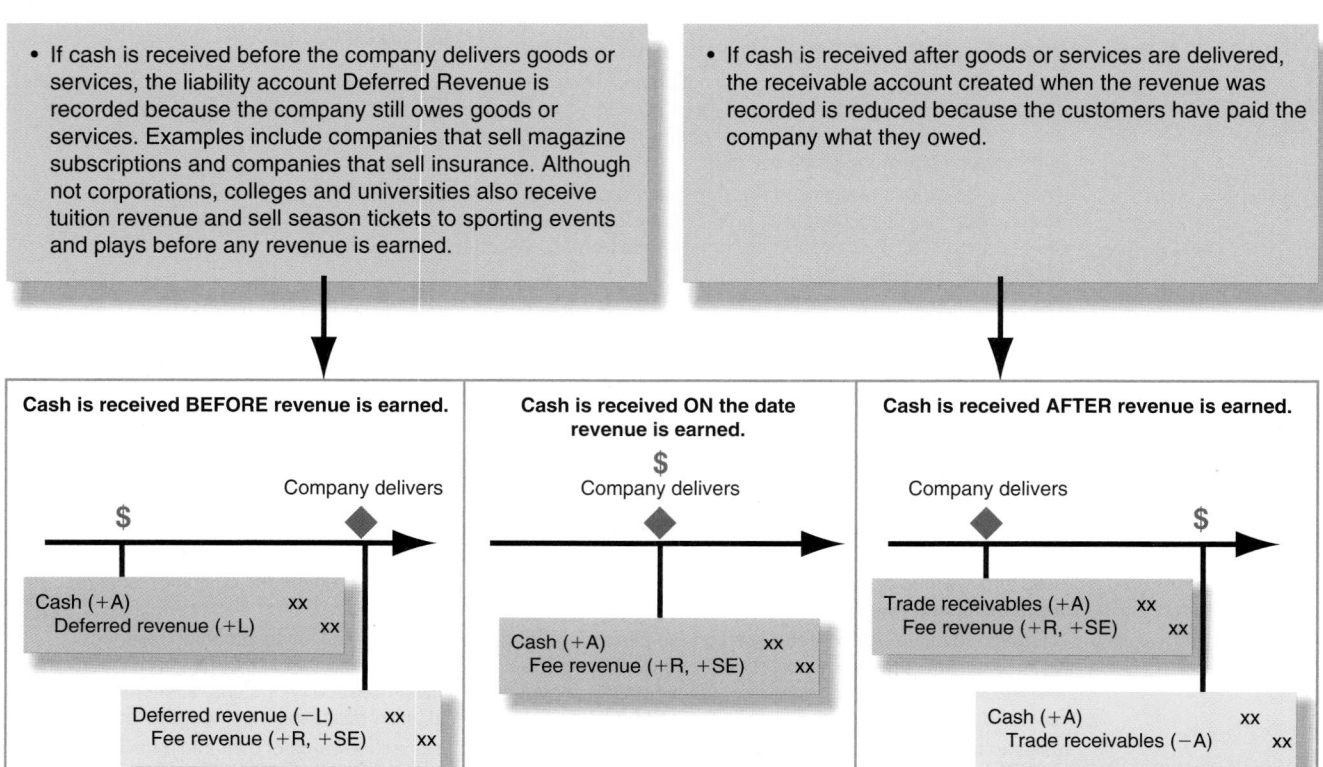

- If cash is received before the company delivers goods or services, the liability account Deferred Revenue is recorded because the company still owes goods or services. Examples include companies that sell magazine subscriptions and companies that sell insurance. Although not corporations, colleges and universities also receive tuition revenue and sell season tickets to sporting events and plays before any revenue is earned.

- If cash is received after goods or services are delivered, the receivable account created when the revenue was recorded is reduced because the customers have paid the company what they owed.

Cash is received BEFORE revenue is earned.

Company delivers

Cash (+A)   xx
    Deferred revenue (+L)   xx

Deferred revenue (−L)   xx
    Fee revenue (+R, +SE)   xx

Cash is received ON the date revenue is earned.

Company delivers

Cash (+A)   xx
    Fee revenue (+R, +SE)   xx

Cash is received AFTER revenue is earned.

Company delivers

Trade receivables (+A)   xx
    Fee revenue (+R, +SE)   xx

Cash (+A)   xx
    Trade receivables (−A)   xx

PAUSE FOR FEEDBACK

The revenue principle's five recognition criteria are as follows: (1) the significant risks and rewards of ownership are transferred to customers, (2) the company retains neither continuing managerial involvement nor effective control over the goods sold, (3) the amount of revenue can be measured reliably, (4) it is probable that the economic benefits associated with the transaction will flow to the company, and (5) the costs related to the transaction can be measured reliably. Regardless of when cash is received, revenue is earned and recorded when these criteria are met.

SELF-STUDY QUIZ 3-1

This self-study quiz allows you to practise applying the revenue principle under accrual accounting. Complete this quiz now to make sure you can apply this principle. The following transactions are samples of typical monthly operating activities of Sun-Rype.

1. Indicate the account titles that are affected and the type of account for each (A for asset, L for liability, and R for revenue).

2. Identify the amount of revenue that is recognized in January, the revenue that has been earned in December, and the revenue that will be earned in future periods (deferred revenue).

3. Compute the revenue recognized in January and compare it to the amount of cash received in January.

4. Which amount—revenue recognized in January or cash received in January—is a better measure of Sun-Rype's operating performance? Explain.

Refer to Sun-Rype's statement of earnings presented in Exhibit 3.1 for account titles. All amounts are in thousands of dollars.

Activity	Accounts Affected and Type of Account	Cash Received in January	Amount of Revenue Earned in		Deferred Revenue
			December	January	
(a) In January, Sun-Rype sold fruit-based beverages to customers for $3,520 cash.					
(b) In January, Sun-Rype sold fruit snacks to retail outlets for $3,020, of which $2,020 was in cash and the rest was on account.					
(c) In January, Sun-Rype received $345 in cash from customers, of which $75 related to December sales.					
(d) In January, Sun-Rype signed contracts with new clients and received $50 in cash. The company provided $40 in services to these clients during January; the remainder of the services will be provided over the next three months.					
(e) In January, retail outlets paid $120 on account to Sun-Rype. This amount covers sales of various products in December.					
Totals					

After you complete your answers, check them with the solutions at the end of the chapter.

The Matching Process

The **matching process** requires that expenses be recorded when incurred in earning revenue. In other words, all of the resources consumed in earning revenues during a specific period must be recognized in that same period, *a matching of costs with benefits.* The costs of generating revenue include expenses incurred, such as the following:

The **MATCHING PROCESS** requires that expenses be recorded when incurred in earning revenue.

- Salaries to employees who *worked during the period* (wages expense)
- Utilities for the electricity *used during the period* (utilities expense)
- Fruits, plastic containers, and other ingredients used to produce fruit-based beverages and foods that are *sold during the period* (cost of sales)
- Facilities *rented during the period* (rent expense)
- *Use* of buildings and equipment for production purposes *during the period* (depreciation expense)

Some of these expenses are matched directly to sales revenue, such as the cost of sales and sales commissions. Other expenses, such as utilities, rent of facilities, insurance, and interest, may not be identifiable with specific sources of revenue but need to be incurred in order to generate revenue during the period.

As with revenues and cash receipts, expenses are recorded as incurred, *regardless of when cash is paid.* Cash may be paid before, during, or after an expense is incurred, as shown in Exhibit 3.4. An entry will be made on the date the expense is incurred and another one on the date of the cash payment, if at different times.

Exhibit **3.4**

Recording Expenses versus
Cash Payments

- For example, fresh fruits and packaging supplies are acquired prior to their use. These items are recorded as inventory, an asset, when they are purchased, but are not expensed until they are used. Similarly, companies usually pay for rent in advance of using rental property and record the cash outlay in the Prepayments asset account, representing future benefits to the company. This asset is allocated over time to Rent expense as the property is used. In addition, part of the cost of long-term assets, such as equipment used in operations, needs to be matched with the revenues generated in the period. The portion of the assets that was used up is recognized as depreciation expense.

- In some cases, resources are used to generate revenues prior to a cash outlay. Sun-Rype's payroll expense represents the amount earned by managers and employees who prepare the products for sale to customers. It is an expense for that period. While employees are usually paid after they provide their services, wages expense and wages payable should be recorded when the service is provided by the employees.

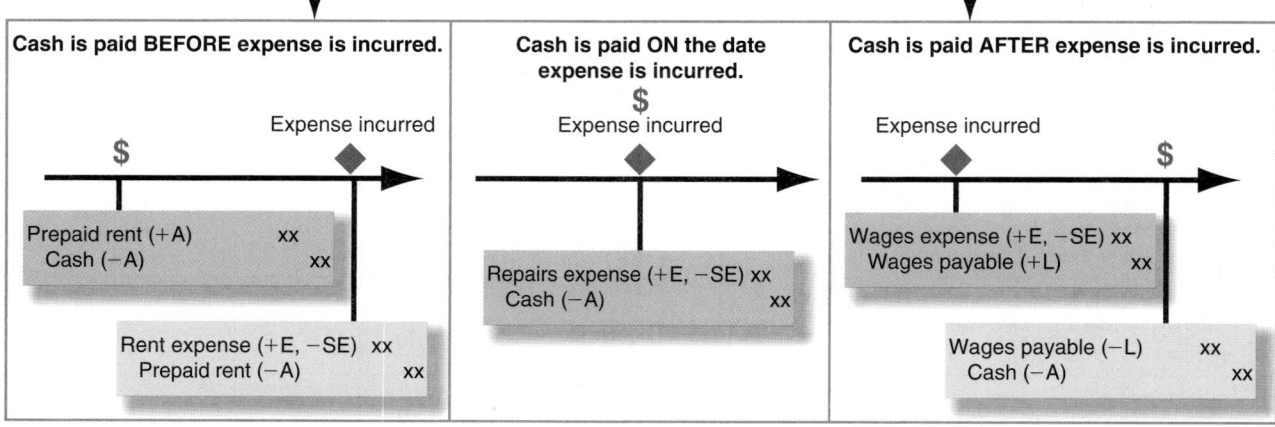

Cash is paid BEFORE expense is incurred.	**Cash is paid ON the date expense is incurred.**	**Cash is paid AFTER expense is incurred.**

Prepaid rent (+A)   xx
    Cash (−A)   xx
	Repairs expense (+E, −SE) xx
	    Cash (−A) xx
		Wages expense (+E, −SE) xx
		    Wages payable (+L) xx

Rent expense (+E, −SE) xx
    Prepaid rent (−A)   xx
		Wages payable (−L) xx
		    Cash (−A) xx

PAUSE FOR FEEDBACK

The *matching process* requires that costs incurred to generate revenues be recognized in the same period—that costs be matched with revenues. Regardless of when cash is paid, expense is recorded when incurred.

SELF-STUDY QUIZ 3-2

This self-study quiz allows you to practise applying the *matching process* under accrual accounting. It is important to complete this quiz now to make sure you can apply this process.

The following transactions are samples of typical monthly operating activities of Sun-Rype.

1. Indicate the account titles that are affected and the type of account for each (A for asset, L for liability, and E for expense).

2. If an expense is to be recognized in January, indicate the amount. If an expense is not to be recognized in January, indicate why.

3. Compute the amount of expenses recognized in January and compare this amount to the cash paid in January.

Refer to Sun-Rype's statement of earnings presented in Exhibit 3.1 for account titles. All amounts are in thousands of dollars.

Activity	Accounts Affected and Type of Account	Cash Paid in January	Amount of Expense Incurred in January OR Why an Expense Is Not Recognized
(a) In January, Sun-Rype paid $1,000 to suppliers on account for raw materials received in December. These raw materials were not yet used in the production process.			
(b) In January, the cost of fruit snacks sold to retail outlets was $1,400.			
(c) In January, Sun-Rype paid $450 for rent of warehousing facilities for January, February, and March.			
(d) In January, the cost of fruit-based beverages sold to customers was $1,960. These items were produced in previous months.			
(e) In late January, Sun-Rype received a utility bill for $50 payable in February for electricity used in January.			
Totals			

After you complete your answers, check them with the solutions at the end of the chapter.

MANAGEMENT'S INCENTIVES TO VIOLATE ACCOUNTING RULES

A QUESTION OF ACCOUNTABILITY

The decisions of investors in the stock market are based on their expectations of a company's future earnings. When companies announce quarterly and annual earnings information, investors evaluate how well the company met expectations and adjust their investing decisions accordingly. Companies that fail to meet expectations often experience a decline in the share price. Thus, managers are motivated to produce earnings results that meet or exceed expectations to bolster share prices. Since many executives are given options to purchase company shares as part of their compensation, greed may lead some managers to make unethical accounting and reporting decisions, often involving falsifying revenues and expenses.

Fraud is a criminal offense for which managers may be sentenced to jail. Samples of fraud cases, a few involving faulty revenue and expense accounting, are shown below. Just imagine what it must have been like to be 65-year-old Bernie Ebbers or 21-year-old Barry Minkow, both sentenced to 25 years in prison for accounting fraud.

The CEO	The Fraud	Conviction/Plea	The Outcome
Bernard Madoff, 71 Madoff Investment Securities	Scammed $50 billion from investors in a Ponzi scheme in which investors receive "returns" from money paid by subsequent investors.	Confessed, December 2008	Sentenced to 150 years
Bernie Ebbers, 65 Worldcom	Recorded $11 billion in operating expenses as if they were assets.	Convicted, July 2005	Sentenced to 25 years
Sanjay Kumar, 44 Computer Associates	Recorded sales in the wrong accounting period.	Pleaded guilty, April 2006	Sentenced to 12 years
Martin Grass, 49 Rite Aid Corporation	Recorded rebates from drug companies before they were earned.	Pleaded guilty, June 2003	Sentenced to 8 years
Barry Minkow, 21 ZZZZ Best	Made up customers and sales to show profits when, in reality, the company was a sham.	Convicted, December 1988	Sentenced to 25 years
Garth Drabinsky, 60 **Myron Gotlieb**, 67 Livent Inc.	Defrauded investors of $500 million through false invoices and kickbacks.	Convicted, March 2009	Sentenced to 5 and 4 years, respectively

Many others are affected by fraud. Shareholders lose the value of their share holdings, employees may lose their jobs (and pension funds, as in the case of Enron), and customers and suppliers may become wary of dealing with a company operating under the cloud of fraud. As a manager, you may face an ethical dilemma in the workplace. The ethical choice is the decision you will be proud of 20 years later.

LO⁴

Apply transaction analysis to examine and record the effects of operating activities on the financial statements.

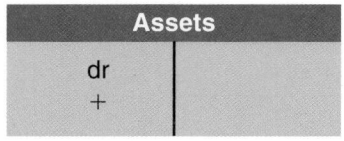

Assets	
dr +	

Liabilities	
	cr +

Shareholders' Equity Accounts	
	cr +

Revenue and Gains	
	cr +

Expenses and Losses	
dr +	

THE EXPANDED TRANSACTION ANALYSIS MODEL

We have seen the variety of business activities affecting the statement of earnings and how they are measured. Now we need to determine how these business activities are recorded in the accounting system and reflected in the financial statements. Chapter 2 covered investing and financing activities affecting assets, liabilities, and contributed capital. We now expand the transaction analysis model presented in that chapter to include operating activities.

Transaction Analysis Rules

The complete transaction model presented in Exhibit 3.5 includes all five elements: assets, liabilities, shareholders' equity, revenues, and expenses. Recall that the retained earnings account is the accumulation of all past revenues and expenses minus any earnings distributed as dividends to shareholders (i.e., earnings not retained in the business). Retained earnings increase when net earnings are realized and decrease when a loss occurs.

Some students attempt to memorize journal entries in the introductory accounting course. However, they are often overwhelmed by the number and complexity of transactions as the course progresses. To avoid this pitfall, you should instead be able to construct the transaction analysis model in Exhibit 3.5 on your own and use it to analyze transactions. It will be very beneficial in completing assignments and analyzing more complex transactions in future chapters. Now let us study Exhibit 3.5 carefully to remember how the model is constructed and to understand the impact of operating activities on both the statement of financial position and the statement of earnings:

- All accounts can increase or decrease, although revenues and expenses tend to increase throughout a period. For accounts on the left side of the accounting equation, the increase symbol, +, is written on the left side of the T-account. For accounts on the right side of the accounting equation, the increase symbol, +, is written on the right side of the T-account, *except for expenses, which increase on the left side of the T-account.*

- Debits (dr) are written on the left side of each T-account and credits (cr) are written on the right.

- Every transaction affects at least two accounts.

These relationships among financial statement elements are summarized in the upper part of Exhibit 3.5.

Before illustrating the use of the expanded transaction analysis model, we want to emphasize the following:

1. Revenues increase net earnings, retained earnings, and shareholders' equity. Therefore, revenues have *credit* balances; that is, to increase a revenue account, you credit it, which increases net earnings and retained earnings. Recording revenue results in either increasing an asset (such as cash or trade receivables) or decreasing a liability (such as deferred subscriptions revenue).

2. Expenses decrease net earnings, thus decreasing retained earnings and shareholders' equity. Therefore, expenses have *debit* balances (opposite of the balance in retained earnings); that is, to increase an expense, you debit it, which decreases net earnings and retained earnings. Recording an expense results in either decreasing an asset (such as supplies when used) or increasing a liability (such as wages payable when money is owed to employees).

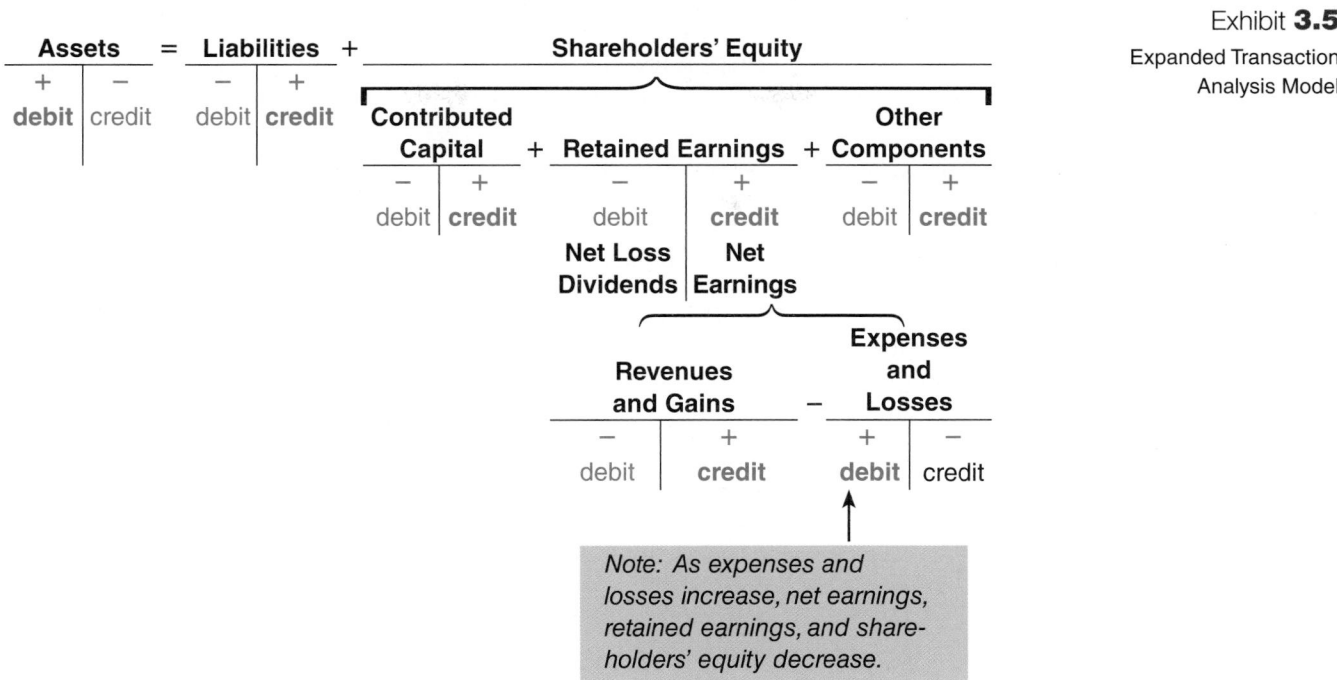

Exhibit **3.5**
Expanded Transaction
Analysis Model

3. When revenues exceed expenses, the company reports net earnings, increasing retained earnings and shareholders' equity. However, when expenses exceed revenues, a loss results that decreases retained earnings and, thus, shareholders' equity.

The steps to follow in analyzing transactions presented in Chapter 2 are now modified to determine the effects of earning revenues and incurring expenses.

Step 1: Identify and classify accounts and effects.

- **Identify the accounts (by title) affected,** making sure that at least two accounts change.

     Ask yourself: Was revenue earned (if so, then what was received)?

          Was an expense incurred (if so, then what was given)?

          If no revenue or expense was affected, what was received and given?

- **Classify the accounts by type.** Was each account an asset (A), a liability (L), shareholders' equity (SE), a revenue (R), or an expense (E)?

- **Determine the direction of the effect.** Did the account increase [+] or decrease [−]?

Step 2: Verify that the accounting equation (A = L + SE) remains in balance.

When a transaction occurs, ask the following questions:

- *Is a revenue earned (i.e., did the company perform or deliver to customers)?* If the answer is yes, then a revenue account is increased (credited). Then identify what the company received in the exchange and the other accounts affected.

- *Is an expense incurred (i.e., did the company incur an expense to generate the revenue)?* If the answer is yes, then an expense is increased (debited). Then identify what the company gave in the exchange and the other accounts affected.

- *If a revenue was not earned or an expense was not incurred, what was received and what was given?*

You should refer to the expanded transaction analysis model until you can construct it on your own without assistance. Study the following illustration carefully to make sure that you understand the impact of operating activities on both the statement of financial position and the statement of earnings.

Analyzing Sun-Rype's Transactions

Now we continue activities for Sun-Rype, building on the company's statement of financial position presented at the end of Chapter 2. It included only the effects of the investing and financing transactions that occurred during the month of January 2013. We analyze, record, and post to the T-accounts the effects of this chapter's operating activities that also occurred during the same accounting period. In Chapter 4, we will complete the accounting cycle with the activities at the end of the period (January 31). All amounts are in thousands of Canadian dollars, and the effects are posted to the appropriate T-accounts at the end of the illustration.

(a) **Sun-Rype sold fruit-based beverages and snacks to customers for $3,520 in cash. The cost of these sales was $1,960. (***Note:*** This requires two entries, one for the revenue earned and one for the expense incurred in generating the revenue.)**

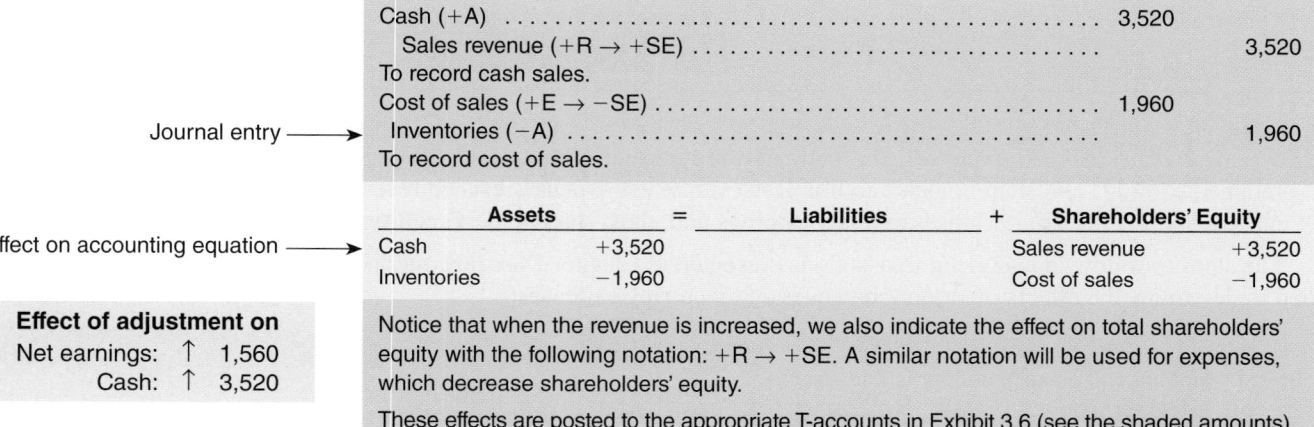

Journal entry ⟶

Cash (+A) 3,520
   Sales revenue (+R → +SE) 3,520
To record cash sales.
Cost of sales (+E → −SE) 1,960
   Inventories (−A) 1,960
To record cost of sales.

	Assets	=	Liabilities	+	Shareholders' Equity	
Cash	+3,520				Sales revenue	+3,520
Inventories	−1,960				Cost of sales	−1,960

Effect on accounting equation ⟶

Effect of adjustment on
Net earnings: ↑ 1,560
Cash: ↑ 3,520

Notice that when the revenue is increased, we also indicate the effect on total shareholders' equity with the following notation: +R → +SE. A similar notation will be used for expenses, which decrease shareholders' equity.

These effects are posted to the appropriate T-accounts in Exhibit 3.6 (see the shaded amounts).

Recall that revenues are recognized when Sun-Rype sells goods and renders services regardless of the timing of cash receipts, and expenses are recognized when incurred regardless of the timing of cash payments. To highlight the difference between accrual basis accounting and cash basis accounting, we show in the margin the net effect of each transaction on net earnings and on cash.

(b) **Sun-Rype sold food and beverage products to retail outlets for $3,020; $2,020 was received in cash and the rest was due from the outlets. The cost of products sold was $1,400.**

Effect of transaction on
Net earnings: ↑ 1,620
Cash: ↑ 2,020

Cash (+A) 2,020
Trade receivables (+A) 1,000
   Sales revenue (+R → +SE) 3,020
To record sales, partly for cash and the rest on account.
Cost of sales (+E → −SE) 1,400
   Inventories (−A). 1,400
To record cost of sales.

	Assets	=	Liabilities	+	Shareholders' Equity	
Cash	+2,020				Sales revenue	+3,020
Trade receivables	+1,000				Cost of sales	−1,400
Inventories	−1,400					

(*c*) **Sun-Rype received $345 from retail outlets for prior sales made on account.**

Cash (+A)	. . . .	345	
Trade receivables (−A)	. . . .		345
To record collection from customers.			

Assets		=	Liabilities	+	Shareholders' Equity
Cash	+345				
Trade receivables	−345				

Effect of transaction on
Net earnings: No effect
Cash: ↑ 345

(*d*) **Sun-Rype signed contracts with a new client and received $50 cash. The company earned $40 immediately by performing services for this client; the rest will be earned in February.**

Cash (+A)	. . . .	50	
Service revenue (+R → +SE)	. . . .		40
Deferred service revenue (+L)	. . . .		10
To record the receipt of cash for current and future services.			

Assets		=	Liabilities		+	Shareholders' Equity	
Cash	+50		Deferred service revenue	+10		Service revenue	+40

Effect of transaction on
Net earnings: ↑ 40
Cash: ↑ 50

(*e*) **At the beginning of January, Sun-Rype paid $740 in advance for the following: $160 for insurance covering the next four months beginning January 1, $450 for rent of warehousing facilities for the next three months beginning January 1, and $130 for advertising to be run in February.**

Prepayments (+A)	. . . .	740	
Cash (−A)	. . . .		740
To record payment of cash for insurance, rent, and advertising.			

Assets		=	Liabilities	+	Shareholders' Equity
Cash	−740				
Prepayments	+740				

Effect of transaction on
Net earnings: No effect
Cash: ↓ 740

(*f*) **Sun-Rype paid $731 for utilities, repairs, and fuel for delivery vehicles, all considered distribution expenses.**

Distribution expenses (+E → −SE)	. . . .	731	
Cash (−A)	. . . .		731
To record payment for various expenses.			

Assets		=	Liabilities	+	Shareholders' Equity	
Cash	−731				Distribution expenses	−731

Effect of transaction on
Net earnings: ↓ 731
Cash: ↓ 731

(*g*) **Sun-Rype ordered and received $2,900 in supplies inventories; $900 was paid in cash and the rest was on account with suppliers.**

Inventories (+A)	. . . .	2,900	
Cash (−A)	. . . .		900
Trade payables (+L)	. . . .		2,000
To record purchase of supplies with partial payment.			

Effect of transaction on
Net earnings: No effect
Cash: ↓ 900

Assets		=	Liabilities		+	Shareholders' Equity
Cash	−900		Trade payables	+2,000		
Inventories	+2,900					

(*h*) **Sun-Rype paid $1,350 in cash to employees for work in January: $400 to personnel associated with distribution activities and $950 for employees in the corporate headquarters, considered as administrative expenses.**

Effect of transaction on

Net earnings: ↓ 1,350
Cash: ↓ 1,350

Distribution expenses (+E → −SE)	400	
General and administrative expenses (+E → −SE)	950	
Cash (−A)		1,350
To record payment to employees.		

Assets		=	Liabilities	+	Shareholders' Equity	
Cash	−1,350				Distribution expenses	−400
					General and administrative expenses	−950

PAUSE FOR **FEEDBACK**

We just illustrated the steps in analyzing and recording transactions, including those involving earning revenue and incurring expenses. Now it is your turn.

SELF-STUDY **QUIZ 3-3**

For transactions (*i*) through (*k*), fill in the missing information. Be sure to post journal entries to the T-accounts in Exhibit 3.6.

(*i*) **Sun-Rype received $105 in cash: $5 in interest earned on notes receivable and $100 in payments made on notes receivable from customers.**

Write the journal entry, post the effects to the T-accounts, and show the effects on net earnings and cash.

Effect of transaction on

Net earnings: _____
Cash: _____

Assets		=	Liabilities	+	Shareholders' Equity	
Cash	+105				Interest revenue	+5
Notes receivable	−100					

(*j*) **Sun-Rype paid $1,000 on accounts owed to suppliers.**

Write the journal entry; post the effects to the T-accounts.

Show the effects on the accounting equation and on net earnings and cash.

Effect of transaction on

Net earnings: _____
Cash: _____

Assets	=	Liabilities	+	Shareholders' Equity

(k) **Sun-Rype sold land for $350. The cost of the land is $50.**

Show the effects on the accounting equation, on net earnings, and on cash.

Cash (+A) 350
  Property, plant, and equipment (−A) 50
  Gain on sale of land (Gain → +SE). 300
To record sale of land at a gain.

Assets	=	Liabilities	+	Shareholders' Equity

Effect of transaction on
Net earnings: _____
Cash: _____

After you complete your answers, check them with the solutions at the end of the chapter.

Exhibit 3.6 shows the T-accounts that changed during the period because of transactions (*a*) through (*k*). The balances of all other accounts remained the same. The amounts from Sun-Rype's statement of financial position at the end of Chapter 2 have been included as the beginning balances in Exhibit 3.6 for the assets, liabilities, and shareholders' equity accounts. However, the accounts that are reported on the statement of earnings have zero beginning balances so that the effects of transactions on revenue and expense accounts can be accumulated over the period.

You can verify that you posted the entries for transactions (*i*) through (*k*) properly by adding the increase side and subtracting the decrease side, and then comparing your answer to the ending balance given in each of the T-accounts.

HOW IS THE STATEMENT OF EARNINGS PREPARED AND ANALYZED?

LO⁵

Prepare a statement of earnings and understand the difference between net earnings and cash flow from operations.

Classified Statement of Earnings

Based on the January transactions that have just been posted in the T-accounts, we can now prepare a statement of earnings reflecting the operating activities for January.

SUN-RYPE PRODUCTS LTD.
Consolidated Statement of Earnings
For the Month Ended January 31, 2013
(in thousands of Canadian dollars)

Revenues	
Sales revenue	$6,540
Service revenue	40
Total revenues	6,580
Cost of sales	(3,360)
Gross profit	3,220
Operating expenses	
Distribution	1,131
General and administrative	950
Total operating expenses	2,081
Earnings from operations	1,139
Other revenues and gains (expenses and losses)	
Interest revenue	5
Gain on sale of land	300
Earnings before income taxes	$1,444

Exhibit **3.6**

T-Accounts

The beginning balances of financial statement accounts are taken from Exhibit 2.9.

ASSETS

+	Cash (A)		−
Beg. bal.	777		
(a)	3,520	(e)	740
(b)	2,020	(f)	731
(c)	345	(g)	900
(d)	50	(h)	1,350
(i)			
(k)	350	(j)	
End. bal.	2,446		

+	Trade Receivables (A)		−
Beg. bal.	14,047		
(b)	1,000	(c)	345
End. bal.	14,702		

+	Inventories (A)		−
Beg. bal.	29,149	(a)	1,960
		(b)	1,400
(g)	2,900		
End. bal.	28,689		

+	Prepayments (A)		−
Beg. bal.	502		
(e)	740		
End. bal.	1,242		

+	Notes Receivable (A)		−
Beg. bal.	150		
		(i)	
End. bal.	50		

+	Property, Plant, and Equipment, net (A)		−
Beg. bal.	44,241	(k)	50
End. bal.	44,191		

LIABILITIES

−	Deferred Service Revenue (L)		+
		(d)	10
		End. bal.	10

−	Trade Payables (L)		+
		Beg. bal.	25,672
(j)		(g)	2,000
		End. bal.	26,672

REVENUES AND GAINS

−	Sales Revenue (R)		+
		(a)	3,520
		(b)	3,020
		End. bal.	6,540

−	Service Revenue (R)		+
		(d)	40
		End. bal.	40

−	Interest Revenue (R)		+
		(i)	
		End. bal.	5

−	Gain on Sale of Land (G)		+
		(k)	300
		End. bal.	300

EXPENSES

+	Cost of Sales (E)		−
(a)	1,960		
(b)	1,400		
End. bal.	3,360		

+	Distribution Expenses (E)		−
(f)	731		
(h)	400		
End. bal.	1,131		

+	General and Administrative Expenses (E)		−
(h)	950		
End. bal.	950		

This statement of earnings does not at this point reflect all revenues earned or expenses incurred in January. For example:

- The Prepayments account includes rent and insurance covering January and future months, but the expenses are not yet recorded for the amounts used in January. This is true of the equipment used during the month as well. Until adjusted, assets are overstated and expenses are understated.

- We have not calculated income taxes for the amount incurred in January and owed within the next quarter. Thus, both expenses and liabilities are understated.

- Deferred revenue (a liability account) has not been updated for any amount of service revenue earned in January. In this case, liabilities are overstated and revenues are understated.

Chapter 4 will describe the adjustment process to update the accounting records. After the adjustments are made, the amount of income tax expense will be determined and the statements will reflect IFRS following accrual basis accounting.

REPORTING MORE DETAILED FINANCIAL INFORMATION IN THE NOTES

FINANCIAL
ANALYSIS

Many companies, especially very large ones, operate in more than one geographic area. These companies are often called *multinationals*. A consolidated statement of earnings that is based on aggregated data may not prove as useful to investors seeking to assess possible risks and returns from companies operating in foreign markets. This is also true if a company operates in more than a single business. For example, a manufacturing operation in a South American country suffering from political unrest is riskier than a manufacturing facility located in Ontario. Therefore, many companies provide additional information about geographic and business segments in notes to the financial statements.[8] An excerpt from Sun-Rype's 2012 financial statements provides information on its geographic segments:

REAL-WORLD EXCERPT

Sun-Rype Products Ltd.

2012 FINANCIAL STATEMENTS

Extracts from Note 25: Operating Segments
(in thousands of dollars)

Geographic Segment	Sales	Non-current Assets
Canada	$111,867	$29,166
United States	40,928	12,875
	$152,795	$42,041

OPERATING ACTIVITIES

FOCUS ON
CASH FLOWS

In Chapter 2, we presented Sun-Rype's statement of cash flows for the investing and financing activities for the month of January. Recall that investing activities relate primarily to transactions affecting non-current assets. Financing activities are those from bank borrowings, issuance of shares, and dividend payments to shareholders.

In this chapter, we focus on cash flows from operating activities, which essentially reflects cash basis accounting. This section of the statement of cash flows reports *cash from* operating sources, primarily customers, and *cash to* suppliers and others involved in operations. The accounts most often associated with operating activities are current assets, such as trade receivables, inventories, and prepayments, and current liabilities, such as trade payables, wages payable, and deferred revenue.

We present the cash flows from operating activities section of the statement of cash flows by using the *direct method*—cash receipts and cash disbursements. However, most companies report cash from operations by using the *indirect method*, which will be discussed in Chapter 5 and later chapters.

			Effect on Cash Flows
Operating activities			
Cash received:	from customers		+
Cash paid:	to suppliers		−
	to employees		−
	for interest on borrowings*		−
	for income taxes		−
Investing activities (from Chapter 2)			
Financing activities (from Chapter 2)			

*Although interest relates to borrowing, a financing activity, interest paid may be classified as an operating activity because it enters into the determination of net earnings or loss (IAS 7—Statement of Cash Flows, para. 33).

When a transaction affects cash, it is included on the statement of cash flows. When a transaction does not affect cash, such as when acquiring a building with a long-term mortgage note payable or selling goods on account to customers, it is not included on the statement. *If you see cash in a transaction, it will be reflected on the statement of cash flows.* Therefore, when preparing the cash flows from operating activities section of the statement of cash flows by using the direct method, the easiest way is to look at the activities in the cash T-account:

		+	**Cash (A)**	−		
	Bal.	777				
From customers	(a)	3,520	740	(e)	To suppliers of services
From customers	(b)	2,020	731	(f)	To suppliers of services
From customers	(c)	345	900	(g)	To trade suppliers
From customers	(d)	50	1,350	(h)	To employees
From customers	(i)	105	1,000	(j)	To trade suppliers
From investing activity	(k)	350			
	Bal.	2,446			

Operating activities contributed $1,314 in cash during January. This amount represents the increase of $1,669 (= $2,446 − $777) in the cash account, minus the cash received from the sale of land ($350) and the interest received on the note receivable ($5), which are investing activities.[9] The cash flow from operating activities is different from earnings from operations of $1,409 that is based on accrual accounting. Note that the gain of $300 on the sale of land and the interest revenue are not included because they do not relate to operating transactions. The difference between $1,409 and $1,314 is because revenue is recognized when earned, regardless of when cash is received, and expenses are recognized when incurred, regardless of when cash is paid.

We presented above, in the margin, the effects of each operating transaction on both net earnings and cash. If you compute the net effect of all transactions on net earnings, you will get $1,409, the same net earnings figure that appears in the statement of earnings. You should not be surprised by this result because the statement of earnings reflects the net effects of all operating transactions during a period. Similarly, the net effect of the same operating transactions on cash is $1,314, which equals the net cash flow from operating activities on the statement of cash flows.

To remain in business in the long run, companies must generate positive cash flows from operations. Cash is needed to pay suppliers and employees. When cash from operations is negative over a period of time, the only other ways to obtain the necessary funds are to (1) sell non-current assets, which reduces future productivity; (2) borrow from creditors at increasing interest rates to compensate for the increased risk of default on the debt; and (3) issue additional shares, where investor expectations about poor future performance drive the stock price down. There are clearly negative implications associated with generating funds through sources not directly related to operating activities.

Sun-Rype experienced net inflow of cash as well as net outflow of cash from operating activities over the five-year period 2008–2012, as shown below. Furthermore, the cash flow from operations differs from the reported net earnings. These differences are the result of using accrual basis accounting, where the reported revenues differ from cash receipts and the reported expenses differ from cash payments for operating purposes.

	2008	2009	2010	2011	2012
Cash flow from operations	$(26,836)	$22,576	$10,178	$(5,726)	$17,072
Net earnings	(11,673)	6,767	4,503	(5,687)	1,267

PAUSE FOR FEEDBACK

Every transaction affecting cash can be classified as an operating, an investing, or a financing effect.

Operating effects relate to receipts of cash from customers and payments to suppliers (employees, utilities, and other suppliers of goods and services for operating the business).

Investing effects relate to purchasing/selling investments or property and equipment or lending funds to/receiving repayment from others.

Financing effects relate to borrowing or repaying banks, issuing shares to investors, repurchasing shares from investors, or paying dividends to investors.

SELF-STUDY QUIZ 3-4

Canadian Tire Corporation Limited offers a range of retail goods and services, including general merchandise, apparel, sporting goods, petroleum, and financial services throughout Canada. The transactions below relate to typical activities of the corporation. Indicate whether the transaction affected cash flow as an operating (O), investing (I), or financing (F) activity, and indicate the direction of the effect on cash (+ for increases; − for decreases):

Canadian Tire Corporation Limited

Transactions	Type of Activity (O, I, or F)	Effect on Cash Flows (+ or −)
1. Payment of dividends to shareholders		
2. Receipt of cash from customers		
3. Purchase of property and equipment for cash		
4. Payment of income taxes		
5. Payment of cash to suppliers		
6. Repayment of long-term borrowings		
7. Receipt of interest on investments		
8. Cash proceeds of long-term borrowings		
9. Issuance of shares		
10. Payment of interest on borrowings		
11. Payment of cash to employees		
12. Sale of property for cash		

After you complete your answers, check them with the solutions at the end of the chapter.

KEY RATIO ANALYSIS

TOTAL ASSET TURNOVER RATIO AND RETURN ON ASSETS

LO⁶

Compute and interpret the total asset turnover ratio and the return on assets.

In Chapter 2, we discussed the current ratio, a tool to evaluate the company's ability to pay its short-term obligations with current assets—a liquidity measure. We now introduce two ratios to assess managers' use of assets in total to improve net earnings. These two ratios focus on the use of assets to generate revenue and net earnings, respectively. As we will see in other chapters, similar analysis of the use of specific types of assets provides additional information for decision makers.

TOTAL ASSET TURNOVER RATIO

ANALYTICAL QUESTION → How effective is management at generating sales from assets (resources)?

RATIO AND COMPARISONS → The total asset turnover ratio is useful in answering this question. It is computed as follows:

$$\text{Total Asset Turnover Ratio} = \frac{\text{Sales (or Operating) Revenues}}{\text{Average Total Assets*}}$$

*Average Total Assets = (Beginning total assets + Ending total assets) ÷ 2

The 2012 ratio for Sun-Rype is

$$\frac{\$152,795}{(\$96,139 + \$91,473) \div 2} = 1.63$$

Comparisons over Time			Comparisons with Competitors	
Sun-Rype			Lassonde Industries Inc.	Leading Brands Inc.*
2010	2011	2012	2012	2012
1.93	1.65	1.63	3.48	1.26

*The fiscal year of Leading Brands ends on February 28, 2013.

INTERPRETATIONS

In General → The total asset turnover ratio measures the sales generated per dollar of assets. A high total asset turnover ratio signifies efficient management of assets; a low total asset turnover ratio signifies less efficient management. A company's products and business strategy contribute significantly to its total asset turnover ratio. However, when competitors are similar, management's ability to control the firm's assets is vital in determining its success. Stronger financial performance improves the total asset turnover ratio.

Creditors and security analysts use this ratio to assess a company's effectiveness at controlling current and non-current assets. In a well-run business, creditors expect the ratio to fluctuate because of seasonal upswings and downturns. For example, as inventory is built up prior to a high-sales season, companies need to borrow funds. The total asset turnover ratio declines with this increase in assets. Eventually, the season's high sales provide the cash needed to repay the loans. The total asset turnover ratio then rises with the increased sales.

Focus Company Analysis → Sun-Rype's total asset turnover ratio decreased from 2010 to 2012, suggesting a decrease in management's effectiveness in using assets to generate sales. Its assets increased during this three-year period, but its sales did not keep pace with the increased assets.

Compared to its competitors, Sun-Rype's 2012 total asset turnover ratio falls in the middle. The difference in ratios is due in part to differences in operating strategy: Lassonde Industries markets a wider variety of products than Sun-Rype, including specialty food products and selected wines from various countries. This wider selection of products allows for better utilization of the company's assets. However, Leading Brands is smaller than Sun-Rype. Its focus on producing and marketing a small variety of fruit-based beverages may have limited its ability to generate more revenues from its assets.

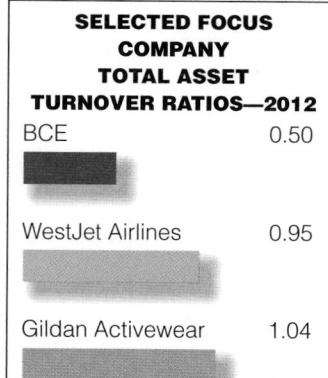

SELECTED FOCUS COMPANY TOTAL ASSET TURNOVER RATIOS—2012	
BCE	0.50
WestJet Airlines	0.95
Gildan Activewear	1.04

A Few Cautions → The total asset turnover ratio may decrease because of seasonal fluctuation, but a declining ratio may also be caused by changes in corporate policies leading to a rising level of assets. Examples include relaxing credit policies for new customers and reducing collection efforts in trade receivables. A detailed analysis of the changes in the key components of assets is needed to determine the causes of a change in the total asset turnover ratio, and thus in management's decisions. Remember that any one ratio is not sufficient as a basis for investment decisions.

RETURN ON ASSETS (ROA)

ANALYTICAL QUESTION → How well has management used the total invested capital provided by debtholders and shareholders during the period?

RATIO AND COMPARISONS → Analysts refer to the rate of return on assets (ROA) as a useful measure in addressing this issue. It is computed as follows:

$$\text{Return on Assets} = \frac{\text{Net Earnings} + \text{Interest Expense (net of tax)}}{\text{Average Total Assets}}$$

Both the total asset turnover ratio and the return on assets measure management's effectiveness at utilizing the company's resources: the first in generating revenue during the period, the second in generating after-tax return on the use of assets.

The return on assets takes into consideration the resources contributed by both shareholders and creditors. For this reason, the return to shareholders or net earnings is augmented by the return to creditors, which is interest expense. Interest expense is measured net of income tax because it represents the net cost of the funds provided by the creditors to the corporation. The returns to both shareholders and creditors are measured net of tax in the numerator of this ratio.

The 2012 ratio for Sun-Rype is

$$\frac{\$1,267 + \$847^* \times (1 - 0.40)^{**}}{(\$96,139 + 91,473) \div 2} = 0.019 \text{ (or 1.9\%)}$$

*As disclosed in Note 17 to Sun-Rype's financial statements.

**For simplicity, this illustration assumes a corporate tax rate of 40 percent. The income tax rate can be computed, however, as the ratio of income tax expense to earnings before income tax.

Comparisons over Time			Comparisons with Competitors	
Sun-Rype			Lassonde Industries Inc.	Leading Brands Inc.*
2010	2011	2012	2012	2012
5.9%	−6.1%	1.9%	7.9%	4.1%

*The fiscal year of Leading Brands ends on February 28, 2013.

INTERPRETATIONS

In General → ROA measures how much the firm earned from the use of its assets. It is the broadest measure of profitability and management effectiveness, independent of financing strategy. ROA allows investors to compare management's investment performance against alternative investment options. Firms with higher ROA are doing a better job of selecting new investments, all other things being equal. Company managers often compute the measure on a division-by-division basis and use it to evaluate division managers' relative performance.

Focus Company Analysis → The decrease in the ratio from 2010 to 2011 was mainly due to a significant increase in the cost of certain raw materials, including apples and fruit concentrates, which resulted in significantly higher cost of sales and a net loss for 2011. A business acquisition on June 30, 2011, resulted in increased sales in 2012. In addition, marketing and general and administrative expenses decreased in 2012. The increased revenues and reduced expenses

SELECTED FOCUS COMPANY COMPARISONS: RETURN ON ASSETS—2012	
WestJet Airlines	7.7%
Gildan Activewear	8.2%
BCE	9.2%

allowed the company to end the year with a relatively small amount of net earnings. Its competitors achieved higher ratios in 2012, indicating more effective utilization of their assets to generate return to both shareholders and debtholders.

A Few Cautions → Effective analysis of ROA requires an understanding of why ROA differs from prior levels and from the ROA of the company's competitors. Analysis of the differences in ROA over time and across companies can be facilitated by a decomposition of this ratio into two other ratios, as shown later in Chapter 13.

PAUSE FOR
FEEDBACK

The total asset turnover ratio measures management's effectiveness in utilizing the company's resources to generate revenue during the period, while the return on assets measures management's effectiveness at utilizing total assets in generating after-tax return for both creditors and shareholders. We just illustrated the computation of both ratios for Sun-Rype and explained how these ratios should be interpreted. Now it is your turn to compute and interpret these ratios for another company.

SELF-STUDY QUIZ 3-5

Sears Canada

Sears Canada is one of the biggest Canadian retailers. It operates a large number of department stores, which sell home fashions, appliances, apparel, home electronics, and garden products. It also sells merchandise online. Selected information about the company's resources and operations are presented below (amounts in millions of Canadian dollars):

	2012	2011	2010	2009	2008	2007
Total assets	$2,479	$2,834	$3,072	$3,405	$3,265	$3,002
Total revenue	4,301	4,619	4,939	5,201	5,733	6,326
Net earnings	101	(60)	115	235	289	306
Interest expense	13	9	17	25	10	13
Tax rate	26%	14%	34%	32%	31%	33%

Required:

1. Complete the following table by computing the total asset turnover ratio and the return on assets for 2009 and 2008.

	2012	2011	2010	2009	2008
Total asset turnover ratio	1.62	1.56	1.53		
Return on assets (ROA)	4%	−2%	4%		

2. What conclusion can you draw from these ratios about the company's effectiveness in managing the economic resources under its control?

After you complete your answers, check them with the solutions at the end of the chapter.

ACCOUNTING STANDARDS
FOR PRIVATE ENTERPRISES

The accounting concepts and procedures covered in this chapter are equally applicable to Canadian private enterprises.

DEMONSTRATION **CASE**

This case is a continuation of the Terrific Lawn Maintenance Corporation case introduced in Chapter 2. The company was established with supplies, property, and equipment purchased ready for business. The statement of financial position at April 30, 2014, based on investing and financing activities, is as follows:

TERRIFIC LAWN MAINTENANCE CORPORATION
Statement of Financial Position
As at April 30, 2014

Assets		Liabilities	
Cash	$ 5,050	Notes payable	$ 4,400
Equipment	4,600		
Land	3,750	**Shareholders' Equity**	
		Share capital	9,000
Total assets	$13,400	Total liabilities and shareholders' equity	$13,400

The following completed activities occurred during April 2014:

a. Purchased and used gasoline for mowers and edgers, paying $90 in cash at a local gas station.
b. In early April, received from the city $1,600 cash in advance for lawn maintenance service for April through July ($400 each month). The entire amount was recorded as deferred revenue.
c. In early April, purchased insurance costing $300 covering six months, April through September. The entire payment was recorded as prepayment.
d. Mowed lawns for residential customers who are billed every two weeks. A total of $5,200 of service was billed in April.
e. Residential customers paid $3,500 on their accounts.
f. Paid wages every two weeks. Total cash paid in April was $3,900.
g. Received a bill for $320 from the local gas station for additional gasoline purchased on account and used in April.
h. Paid $100 on trade payables.

Required:

1. a. On a separate sheet of paper, set up T-accounts for cash, trade receivables, equipment, land, prepayments, trade payables, deferred revenue, notes payable, share capital, mowing revenue, fuel expense, and wages expense. Beginning balances for asset, liability, and equity accounts should be taken from the preceding statement of financial position. Beginning balances for operating accounts are $0. Indicate these balances on the T-accounts.
   b. Analyze each transaction using the steps outlined in Chapter 2. Please refer to the expanded transaction analysis model presented in this chapter.
   c. On a separate sheet of paper, prepare journal entries to record the transactions above in chronological order and indicate their effects on the accounting model (Assets = Liabilities + Shareholders' Equity) as well as their effects on net earnings and cash. Verify that the accounting equation is in balance.
   d. Enter the effects of each transaction in the appropriate T-accounts. Identify each amount with its letter in the list of activities.
   e. Compute balances in each of the T-accounts.
2. Use the amounts in the T-accounts to prepare a statement of earnings for the month ended April 30, 2014. (Adjustments to accounts will be presented in Chapter 4.)

We strongly recommend that you prepare your own answers to these requirements and then check your answers with the following solution.

SUGGESTED **SOLUTION**

1. Transaction analysis, journal entries, effects on accounting equation, effects on net earnings and cash, and T-accounts:

Effect of transaction on
Net earnings: ↓ 90
Cash: ↓ 90

(a) Fuel expense (+E → −SE)		90	
Cash (−A)			90

Assets		=	**Liabilities**	+	**Shareholders' Equity**	
Cash	−90				Fuel expense	−90

Effect of transaction on
Net earnings: No effect
Cash: ↑ 1,600

(b) Cash (+A)		1,600	
Deferred revenue (+L)			1,600

Assets		=	**Liabilities**		+	**Shareholders' Equity**	
Cash	+1,600		Deferred revenue	+1,600			

Effect of transaction on
Net earnings: No effect
Cash: ↓ 300

(c) Prepayments (+A)		300	
Cash (−A)			300

Assets		=	**Liabilities**	+	**Shareholders' Equity**	
Cash	−300					
Prepayments	+300					

Effect of transaction on
Net earnings: ↑ 5,200
Cash: No effect

(d) Trade receivables (+A)		5,200	
Mowing revenue (+R → +SE)			5,200

Assets		=	**Liabilities**	+	**Shareholders' Equity**	
Trade receivables	+5,200				Mowing revenue	+5,200

Effect of transaction on
Net earnings: No effect
Cash: ↑ 3,500

(e) Cash (+A)		3,500	
Trade receivables (−A)			3,500

Assets		=	**Liabilities**	+	**Shareholders' Equity**	
Cash	+3,500					
Trade receivables	−3,500					

Effect of transaction on
Net earnings: ↓ 3,900
Cash: ↓ 3,900

(f) Wage expense (+E → −SE)		3,900	
Cash (−A)			3,900

Assets		=	**Liabilities**	+	**Shareholders' Equity**	
Cash	−3,900				Wages expense	−3,900

Effect of transaction on
Net earnings: ↓ 320
Cash: No effect

(g) Fuel expense (+E → −SE)		320	
Trade payables (+L)			320

Assets		=	**Liabilities**		+	**Shareholders' Equity**	
			Trade payables	+320		Fuel expense	−320

Effect of transaction on
Net earnings: No effect
Cash: ↓ 100

(h) Trade payables (−L)		100	
Cash (−A)			100

Assets		=	**Liabilities**		+	**Shareholders' Equity**	
Cash	−100		Trade payables	−100			

T-Accounts

The beginning balances of the statement of financial position accounts are taken from the solutions to the demonstration case in Chapter 2.

ASSETS

+	Cash (A)		–
Beg. bal.	5,050		
(b)	1,600	(a)	90
(e)	3,500	(c)	300
		(f)	3,900
		(h)	100
End. bal.	5,760		

+	Trade Receivables (A)		–
(d)	5,200	(e)	3,500
End. bal.	1,700		

+	Equipment (A)		–
Beg. bal.	4,600		
End. bal.	4,600		

+	Prepayments (A)		–
(c)	300		
End. bal.	300		

+	Land (A)		–
Beg. bal.	3,750		
End. bal.	3,750		

LIABILITIES

–	Trade Payables (L)		+
(h)	100	(g)	320
		End. bal.	220

–	Deferred Revenue (L)		+
		(b)	1,600
		End. bal.	1,600

–	Notes Payables (L)		+
		Beg. bal.	4,400
		End. bal.	4,400

SHAREHOLDERS' EQUITY

–	Share Capital (SE)		+
		Beg. bal.	9,000
		End. bal.	9,000

REVENUES

+	Mowing Revenue (R)		–
		(d)	5,200
		End. bal.	5,200

EXPENSES

+	Wages Expense (E)		–
(f)	3,900		
End. bal.	3,900		

+	Fuel Expense (E)		–
(a)	90		
(g)	320		
End. bal.	410		

2.

TERRIFIC LAWN MAINTENANCE CORPORATION
Statement of Earnings
For the Month Ended April 30, 2014

Revenues	
Mowing revenue	$5,200
Operating Expenses	
Fuel expense	410
Wages expense	3,900
	4,310
Earnings before income tax	890
Income tax expense	0 ◄──────*To be discussed in Chapter 4*
Net earnings	$ 890
Earnings per share for the month	$ 0.59*

*890/1,500 shares.

CHAPTER **TAKE-AWAYS**

1. **Describe a typical business operating cycle and explain the necessity for the periodicity assumption.**
   - The operating cycle, or the cash-to-cash cycle, is the time it takes to purchase goods or services from suppliers, sell the goods or services to customers, and collect cash from customers.
   - The periodicity assumption means that we can measure and report financial information periodically by assuming that the long life of the company can be cut into shorter periods.

2. **Explain how business activities affect the elements of the statement of earnings.**
   Elements on the classified statement of earnings are as follows:
   a. Revenues are increases in assets or settlements of liabilities from ongoing operations.
   b. Expenses are decreases in assets or increases in liabilities from ongoing operations.
   c. Gains are increases in assets or settlements of liabilities from peripheral activities.
   d. Losses are decreases in assets or increases in liabilities from peripheral activities.

3. **Explain the accrual basis of accounting and apply the revenue principle and matching process to measure net earnings.**
   When applying accrual accounting concepts, revenues are recognized (recorded) when earned and expenses are recognized when incurred to generate the revenues.
   - By the revenue principle, we recognize revenues when the earnings process is complete or nearly complete, an exchange has taken place, and collection is probable.
   - By the matching process, we recognize expenses when incurred in earning revenue.

4. **Apply transaction analysis to examine and record the effects of operating activities on the financial statements.**
   The expanded transaction analysis model includes revenues and expenses:

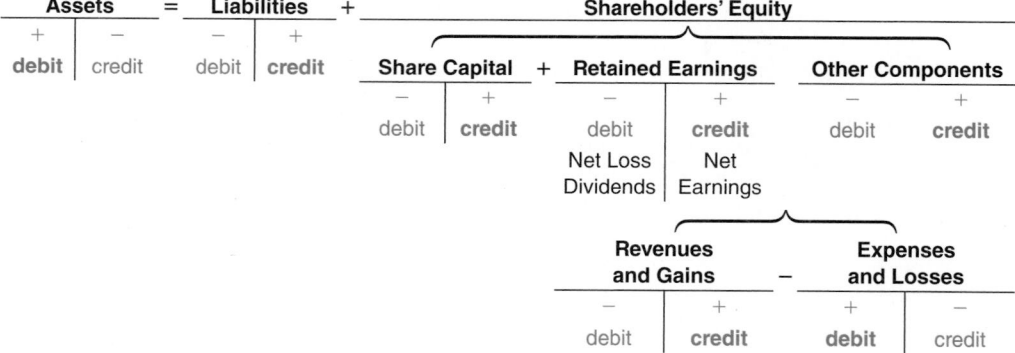

5. **Prepare a statement of earnings and understand the difference between net earnings and cash flow from operations.**
   The statement of earnings reports the revenues generated during the period and the related expenses. Net earnings is the difference between revenues and expenses, whereas cash flow from operations equals the difference between cash receipts and cash payments related to operations. Net earnings differs from cash flow from operations because the revenue principle and matching process result in the recognition of revenues and related expenses that are independent of the timing of cash receipts and payments.

6. **Compute and interpret the total asset turnover ratio and the return on assets.**
   The total asset turnover ratio (sales ÷ average total assets) measures the sales generated from the use of assets. The higher the ratio, the more efficient the company is at managing assets. The return on assets (ROA) measures how much the company earned from the use of assets. It provides information on profitability and management's effectiveness in utilizing assets. An increasing ROA over time suggests increased efficiency. ROA is computed as the sum of net earnings and interest expense (net of tax) divided by average total assets.

In this chapter, we discussed the operating cycle and accounting concepts relevant to income determination: the periodicity assumption, definitions for the statement of earnings elements (revenues, expenses, gains, and losses), the revenue principle, and the matching process. These accounting principles are defined in accordance with the accrual basis of accounting, which requires revenues to be recorded when earned and expenses to be recorded when incurred in generating revenues during the period. We expanded the transaction analysis model introduced in Chapter 2 by adding revenues and expenses. In Chapter 4, we discuss the activities at the end of the accounting period: the adjustment process, the preparation of adjusted financial statements, and the closing process.

KEY **RATIOS**

The total asset turnover ratio measures the sales generated from the use of assets. A high ratio suggests that the company is managing its assets (resources used to generate revenues) efficiently. It is computed as follows:

$$\text{Total Asset Turnover Ratio} = \frac{\text{Sales (or Operating) Revenues}}{\text{Average Total Assets*}}$$

The return on assets measures how much the company earned from the use of assets during the period. A high ratio suggests that the company is managing its assets efficiently. It is computed as follows:

$$\text{Return on Assets (ROA)} = \frac{\text{Net Earnings} + \text{Interest Expense (net of tax)}}{\text{Average Total Assets*}}$$

*(Beginning Total Assets + Ending Total Assets) ÷ 2

FINDING **FINANCIAL INFORMATION**

STATEMENT OF FINANCIAL POSITION

Current Assets	**Current Liabilities**
Cash	Trade payables
Trade and notes receivable	Notes payable
	Accrued liabilities
Inventories	**Non-current**
Prepayments	**Liabilities**
Non-current Assets	Long-term
Long-term investments	borrowings
	Provisions
Property, plant, and equipment	**Shareholders' Equity**
Intangibles	Share capital
	Retained earnings

STATEMENT OF EARNINGS
Revenues
  Sales (from various operating activities)
    Investment income
Expenses
  Cost of sales, rent, wages, interest, depreciation, insurance, etc.
Pretax Earnings
  Income tax expense
Net Earnings

STATEMENT OF CASH FLOWS
Under Operating Activities
  + Cash from customers
  + Cash from interest
  − Cash to suppliers
  − Cash to employees
  − Cash for interest
  − Cash for income taxes

NOTES
Under Summary of Significant Accounting Policies
  Description of company's revenue recognition policy

Mc Graw Hill Education **connect** GLOSSARY

Review key terms and definitions on *Connect*.

QUESTIONS

1. Assume that you have just opened a small gift store that specializes in gift items imported from Asia. Explain the typical business operating cycle for your store.
2. Explain what the periodicity assumption means in accounting.
3. Write the statement of earnings equation and define each element.
4. Explain the difference between
   a. revenues and gains
   b. expenses and losses
5. Define *accrual accounting* and contrast it with *cash basis accounting*.
6. What conditions must normally be met for revenue to be recognized under the accrual basis of accounting?
7. Explain the matching process.
8. Explain why shareholders' equity is increased by revenues and decreased by expenses.
9. Explain why revenues are recorded as credits and expenses as debits.
10. Complete the following matrix by entering either "debit" or "credit" in each cell:

Item	Increase	Decrease
Revenues		
Expenses		
Gains		
Losses		

11. Complete the following matrix by entering either "increase" or "decrease" in each cell:

Item	Debit	Credit
Revenues		
Expenses		
Gains		
Losses		

12. Identify whether each of the following transactions results in a cash flow effect from operating, investing, or financing activities, and indicate the effect on cash (+ for increase and − for decrease). If there is no cash flow effect, write "none":

Transaction	Operating, Investing, or Financing Effect	Direction of the Effect
Cash paid to suppliers		
Sale of goods on account		
Cash received from customers		
Purchase of investments for cash		
Cash paid for interest		
Issuance of shares for cash		

13. State the equation for the total asset turnover ratio, and explain how it is interpreted.
14. State the equation for the return on assets and explain how it is interpreted.

EXERCISES

■ connect

E3–1 Inferring Statement of Earnings Values   ■ LO2

Supply the missing dollar amounts for the 2014 statement of earnings of Ultimate Style Company for each of the following independent cases:

	Case A	Case B	Case C	Case D	Case E
Sales revenue	$900	$700	$410	$?	$?
Selling expense	?	150	80	400	250
Cost of sales	?	380	?	500	310
Income tax expense	?	30	20	40	30
Gross profit	400	?	?	?	440
Earnings before income tax	200	90	?	190	?
Administrative expense	150	?	60	100	80
Net earnings	170	?	50	?	80

E3–2 Preparing a Statement of Earnings   ■ LO2

The following data were taken from the records of Village Corporation at December 31, 2014:

Sales revenue	$70,000
Gross profit	24,500
Selling (distribution) expense	8,000
Administrative expense	?
Earnings before income tax	10,000
Income tax rate	30%
Number of shares outstanding	4,000

Required:

Prepare a complete statement of earnings for the company (showing both gross profit and earnings from operations). Show all computations. (*Hint:* Set up the side captions starting with sales revenue and ending with earnings per share; use the amounts and percentages given to infer missing values.)

E3–3 Reporting Cash Basis versus Accrual Basis Earnings   ■ LO3

Mostert Music Company had the following transactions in March:

a. Sold instruments to customers for $15,000; received $10,000 in cash and the rest on account.

b. Determined that the cost of the instruments sold was $9,000.

c. Purchased $3,000 of new instruments inventory; paid $1,000 in cash and the rest on account.

d. Paid $750 in wages for the month.

e. Received a $200 bill for utilities that will be paid in April.

f. Received $3,000 from customers as deposits on orders of new instruments to be sold to customers in April.

Complete the following statements:

Cash Basis Statement of Earnings		Accrual Basis Statement of Earnings	
Revenues	$	Revenues	$ . . . .
Cash sales	. . . .	Sales to customers	. . . .
Customer deposits			
Expenses		Expenses	
Inventory purchases	. . . .	Cost of sales	. . . .
Wages paid	. . . .	Wages expense	. . . .
		Utilities expense	. . . .
Net earnings		Net earnings	

Does the cash basis or the accrual basis of accounting provide a better indication of the operating performance of Mostert Music Company in March? Explain.

LO2, 3

E3–4 **Identifying Revenues**

Revenues are normally recognized when the entity has transferred to the buyer the significant risks and rewards of ownership of the goods, it retains neither continuing managerial involvement to the degree usually associated with ownership nor effective control over the goods, it is probable that future economic benefits will flow to the company, and the benefits from and costs associated with the transaction can be measured reliably. The amount recorded is the cash-equivalent sales price. Assume that the following events and transactions occurred in September 2014:

a. A customer purchases a ticket from WestJet for $435 cash to travel the following January. Answer from WestJet's standpoint.

b. General Motors issues $26 million in new shares.

c. Hall Construction Company signs a contract with a customer for the construction of a new $500,000 warehouse. At the signing, Hall receives a cheque for $50,000 as a deposit on the future construction. Answer from Hall's standpoint.

d. On September 1, 2014, a bank lends $10,000 to a company. The loan carries a 6 percent annual interest rate, and the principal and interest are due in a lump sum on August 31, 2015. Answer from the bank's standpoint.

e. A popular ski magazine company receives a total of $1,800 from subscribers on September 30, the last day of its fiscal year. The subscriptions begin in the next fiscal year. Answer from the magazine company's standpoint.

f. Sears Canada sells a $100 lamp to a customer who charges the sale on his store credit card. Answer from the standpoint of Sears.

g. A customer orders and receives 10 personal computers from Dell Inc.; the customer promises to pay $20,000 within three months. Answer from Dell's standpoint.

h. Sam Shell Dodge sells a truck with a list, or sticker, price of $24,000 for $21,000 cash.

i. The Hudson's Bay Company orders 1,000 men's shirts from Gildan Activewear Inc. at $18 each for future delivery. The terms require payment in full within 30 days of delivery. Answer from Gildan's standpoint.

j. Gildan Activewear completes production of the shirts described in (i) and delivers the order. Answer from Gildan's standpoint.

k. Gildan receives payment from the Hudson's Bay Company for the order described in (i). Answer from Gildan's standpoint.

Required:
For each of the September transactions,
1. Indicate the account titles that are affected and the type of each account (A for asset, L for liability, SE for shareholders' equity, and R for revenue).
2. If revenue is to be recognized in September, indicate the amount. If revenue is not to be recognized in September, indicate which of the revenue recognition criteria are not met.

Use the following headings in structuring your solution:

Event or Transaction	Accounts Affected and Type of Account	Amount of Revenue Earned in September OR Revenue Criteria Not Met

LO2, 3

E3–5 **Identifying Expenses**

Revenues are normally recognized when goods or services have been provided and payment or promise of payment has been received. Expense recognition is guided by an attempt to match the costs associated with the generation of those revenues to the same time period. Assume that the following events and transactions occurred in January 2014:

a. A new grill is installed at a McDonald's restaurant. On the same day, payment of $14,000 is made in cash.

b. On January 1, 2014, Carousel Mall has janitorial supplies costing $1,000 in storage. An additional $600 worth of supplies is purchased during January. At the end of January, $900 worth of janitorial supplies remains in storage.

c. A Concordia University employee works eight hours, at $15 per hour, on January 31; however, payday is not until February 3. Answer from the university's point of view.

d. Wang Company pays $3,600 for a fire insurance policy on January 2. The policy covers the current month and the next 11 months. Answer from Wang's point of view.

e. Amber Incorporated has its delivery van repaired in January for $280 and charges the amount on account.

f. Ziegler Company, a farm equipment company, receives its phone bill at the end of January for $230 for January calls. The bill has not been paid to date.

g. Spina Company receives and pays in January a $2,100 invoice from a consulting firm for services received in January.

h. Felicetti's Taxi Company pays a $600 invoice from a consulting firm for services received and recorded in Accounts Payable in December.

i. Dell Inc. pays its computer service technicians $85,000 in salary for the two weeks ended January 7. Answer from Dell's standpoint.

j. Turner Construction Company pays $4,500 in workers' compensation insurance for the first three months of the year.

k. McGraw-Hill Ryerson Limited uses $1,200 worth of electricity and natural gas in its headquarters building for which it has not yet been billed.

l. Gildan Activewear Inc. completes production of 500 men's shirts ordered by Bon Ton Department Store at a cost of $9 each and delivers the order. Answer from Gildan's standpoint.

m. The campus bookstore receives 500 accounting textbooks at a cost of $70 each. The terms indicate that payment is due within 30 days of delivery.

n. During the last week of January, the campus bookstore sells 450 accounting textbooks received in (*m*) at a sales price of $100 each.

o. Sam Shell Dodge pays its salespeople $3,500 in commissions related to December automobile sales. Answer from Sam Shell Dodge's standpoint.

p. On January 31, Sam Shell Dodge determines that it will pay its salespeople $4,200 in commissions related to January sales. The payment will be made in early February. Answer from Sam Shell Dodge's standpoint.

Required:

For each of the January transactions,

1. Indicate the account titles that are affected and the type of each account (A for asset, L for liability, SE for shareholders' equity, and E for expense).

2. If an expense is to be recognized in January, indicate the amount. If an expense is not to be recognized in January, indicate why.

Use the following headings in structuring your solution:

Event or Transaction	Accounts Affected and Type of Account	Amount of Expense Incurred in January OR Why an Expense Is Not Recognized

E3–6 Identifying Revenues and Expenses

   ■ **LO**2, 3, 5

Peter's Bowling Inc. operates several bowling centres for games and equipment sales. The transactions on the following page occurred in October 2014.

Required:

1. For each transaction, indicate in the appropriate column the account titles that are affected and the type of account (A for asset, L for liability, R for revenue, and E for expense), and the amount of cash received or paid.

2. If a revenue or expense is to be recognized in October, indicate the amount. If a revenue or expense is not to be recognized in October, indicate why.

3. Explain why the difference between revenues and expenses is not equal to the net cash flow during October 2014.

Activity	Account Affected and Type of Account	Cash Received (Paid) in October	Amount of Revenue Earned or Expense Incurred in October OR Why a Revenue or an Expense Is Not Recognized
(a) The bowling leagues gave Peter's a deposit of $2,600 for the upcoming fall season.			
(b) Peter's received $2,500 from customers on account who purchased merchandise in September.			
(c) Peter's paid $1,900 for the September electricity bill and received the October bill for $2,200, which will be paid in November.			
(d) Peter's sold bowling equipment inventory for $7,000; received $3,000 in cash and the rest on account; cost of sales is $4,200.			
(e) Peter's collected $13,000 from customers for games played in October.			
(f) Peter's paid $1,400 to plumbers for repairing a broken pipe in the washrooms.			
(g) Peter's paid $4,700 to employees for work in October.			
(h) Peter's purchased and paid for $1,800 in insurance for coverage from October 1 to December 31.			
Totals			

LO3

E3–7   Timing of Revenue Recognition

Modern Equipment Corp. manufactures special-purpose machines for use in the mining industry. In late April, the company received an order from Kross Mining Company (KMC) for a special-purpose machine to be delivered in two months. The specific events related to the production of this machine are shown below.

April 29	KMC placed an order for a special-purpose machine to be manufactured and delivered in two months.
May 3	Raw materials and components are ordered so that the machine can be manufactured.
May 4	Modern Equipment receives written confirmation of the order from KMC.
May 12	Manufacture of the machine is completed.
May 13	The machine is shipped to KMC.
May 14	KMC receives the machine.
May 15	Modern Equipment receives written confirmation that the machine was delivered to KMC.
May 16	An invoice is sent to KMC.
June 16	KMC receives free after-sales service for the machine.
June 19	A cheque is received from KMC in full payment.
June 25	The cheque is cleared by the bank.

Required:

When should Modern Equipment Corp. recognize revenue from the sale of the machine? Explain.

LO4

E3–8   Determining the Financial Statement Effects of Operating Activities

Peter's Bowling Inc. operates several bowling centres (for games and equipment sales). For each of the transactions below, complete the tabulation, indicating the amount and effect (+ for increase and − for decrease) of each transaction. (Remember that A = L + SE, R − E = NE, and NE affects SE through retained earnings.) Write "N" if there is no effect. The first transaction is provided as an example.

	Statement of Financial Position			Statement of Earnings		
Transaction	**Assets**	**Liabilities**	**Shareholders' Equity**	**Revenues**	**Expenses**	**Net Earnings**
(a) Peter's collected $13,000 from customers for games played in October.	+13,000	N	+13,000	+13,000	N	+13,000
(b) Peter's sold $7,000 in bowling equipment inventory; received $3,000 in cash and the rest on account; cost of sales is $4,200.						
(c) Peter's received $2,500 from customers on account who purchased merchandise in September.						
(d) The bowling leagues gave Peter's a deposit of $2,600 for the upcoming fall season.						
(e) Peter's paid $1,900 for the September electricity bill and received the October bill for $2,200 to be paid in November.						
(f) Peter's paid $4,700 to employees for work in October.						
(g) Peter's purchased $1,800 in insurance for coverage from October 1 to December 31.						
(h) Peter's paid $1,400 to plumbers for repairing a broken pipe in the washrooms.						

E3–9 Preparing a Statement of Earnings   ■ LO4, 5

Refer to the transactions in E3–8 (including the example), and prepare a statement of earnings for Peter's Bowling Inc. for the month of October 2014. Use an income tax rate of 40 percent.

E3–10 Determining Financial Statement Effects of Various Transactions   ■ LO4

The following transactions occurred during a recent year:

a. Issued shares to organizers for cash (example).

b. Borrowed cash from the local bank.

c. Purchased equipment on credit.

d. Earned revenue; collected cash.

e. Incurred expenses on credit.

f. Earned revenue; billed the customer.

g. Paid cash on account.

h. Incurred expenses; paid cash.

i. Earned revenue; collected three-fourths in cash and the rest on credit.

j. Experienced theft of $100 cash.

k. Declared and paid cash dividends.

l. Collected cash from customers on account.

m. Incurred expenses; paid four-fifths in cash and the rest on credit.

n. Paid income tax expense for the period.

Required:

Complete the tabulation below for each of the transactions, indicating the effect (+ for increase and − for decrease) of each transaction. (Remember that A = L + SE, R − E = NE, and NE affects SE through retained earnings.) Write "N" if there is no effect. The first transaction is provided as an example.

	Statement of Financial Position			Statement of Earnings		
Transaction	**Assets**	**Liabilities**	**Shareholders' Equity**	**Revenues**	**Expenses**	**Net Earnings**
(a) (example)	+	N	+	N	N	N

E3–11 Determining Financial Statement Effects of Various Transactions   ■ LO4

Saputo Inc. produces, markets, and distributes a wide variety of products, including cheese, fluid milk, yogurt, dairy ingredients, and snack cakes. It is the largest dairy processor in Canada and serves customers in over 50 countries.

Saputo Inc.

The following transactions occurred during a recent year. Amounts are in millions of dollars.

a. Issued $25 in shares to investors (example).

b. Purchased $119 of additional property, plant, and equipment for cash.

c. Incurred $249 in selling expenses with two-thirds paid in cash and the rest on account.

d. Purchased on account $4,947 of raw materials used in processing various dairy products.

e. Earned $2 interest on investments; received 50 percent in cash.

f. Paid $7 on bank loans.

g. Sold $6,930 of products to customers on account; the cost of the products sold was $5,013.

h. Incurred $3 in interest expense (not yet paid).

i. Declared and paid cash dividends of $147.

Required:
Complete the tabulation below for each of the transactions, indicating the effect (+ for increase and − for decrease) of each transaction. (Remember that A = L + SE, R − E = NE, and NE affects SE through retained earnings.) Write "N" if there is no effect. The first transaction is provided as an example.

	Statement of Financial Position			Statement of Earnings		
Transaction	Assets	Liabilities	Shareholders' Equity	Revenues	Expenses	Net Earnings
(a) (example)	+25	N	+25	N	N	N

LO4

Sysco

E3–12   **Recording Journal Entries**
Sysco, formed in 1969, is the largest U.S. marketer and distributor of food service products, serving nearly 250,000 restaurants, hotels, schools, hospitals, and other institutions. The following summarized transactions are typical of those that occurred in a recent year:

a. Borrowed $745 million from financial institutions, signing long-term notes.

b. Provided $42.4 billion in service to customers during the year, with $32.4 billion on account and the rest received in cash.

c. Purchased plant and equipment for $784.5 million in cash.

d. Purchased $33.7 billion inventory on account.

e. Paid $2.9 billion in salaries during the year.

f. Received $29.8 billion on account paid by customers.

g. Purchased and used fuel of $749 million in delivery vehicles during the year (paid for in cash).

h. Declared and paid $622.8 million in dividends for the year.

i. Paid $31.5 billion cash on trade payables.

j. Incurred $56 million in utility usage during the year; paid $44 million in cash and the rest on account.

Required:
Prepare a journal entry to record each of the transactions. Determine whether the accounting equation remains in balance and debits equal credits after each entry.

LO4, 5

E3–13   **Analyzing the Effects of Transactions in T-Accounts**
Lisa Fruello and Emilie Dumont had been operating a catering business for several years. In March 2014, the partners were planning to expand by opening a retail sales shop and decided to form the business as a corporation called Travelling Gourmet Inc. The following transactions occurred in March 2014:

a. Received $80,000 cash from each of the two shareholders to form the corporation, in addition to $2,000 in accounts receivable, $5,300 in equipment, a van (equipment) appraised at a fair market value of $13,000, and $1,200 in supplies.

b. Purchased a vacant store for sale in a good location for $360,000, making a $72,000 cash down payment and signing a 10-year mortgage from a local bank for the rest.

c. Borrowed $50,000 from the local bank and signed a 5 percent, one-year note.

d. Purchased for $10,830 cash food and paper supplies that were used in March.

e. Catered four parties in March for $4,200; $1,600 was billed, and the rest was received in cash.

f. Made and sold food at the retail store for $11,900 cash.

g. Received a $420 telephone bill for March to be paid in April.

h. Paid $363 in gas for the van in March.

i. Paid $6,280 in wages to employees who worked in March.

j. Paid a $300 dividend from the corporation to each owner.

k. Paid $50,000 in exchange for equipment (refrigerated display cases, cabinets, tables, and chairs) and renovated and decorated the new store for $20,000 cash (added to the cost of the building).

Required:

1. Set up appropriate T-accounts for cash, accounts receivable, supplies, equipment, building, accounts payable, note payable, mortgage payable, contributed capital, retained earnings, food sales revenue, catering sales revenue, supplies expense, utilities expense, wages expense, and fuel expense.

2. Record in the T-accounts the effects of each transaction for Travelling Gourmet Inc. in March. Identify the amounts with the letters starting with (*a*). Compute ending balances.

3. Show the effects (direction and amount) of each transaction on net earnings and cash.

E3–14 Recording Journal Entries   ■ LO4, 5

Rowland & Sons Air Transport Service Inc. has been in operation for three years. The following transactions occurred in February:

February	1	Paid $1,900 for rent of hangar space in February.
	2	Purchased fuel costing $450 on account for the next flight to Winnipeg.
	4	Received customer payment of $950 to ship several items to Montreal next month.
	7	Flew cargo from Ottawa to Edmonton; the customer paid $1,240 for the air transport.
	10	Paid pilot $4,000 in wages for flying in January.
	14	Paid $600 for an advertisement in the local paper, to run on February 19.
	18	Flew cargo for two customers from Regina to Calgary for $1,800; one customer paid $500 cash and the other asked to be billed.
	25	Purchased spare parts for the planes costing $1,350 on account.
	27	Declared a $1,300 cash dividend to be paid in March.

Required:

1. Prepare a journal entry to record each transaction. Be sure to categorize each account as an asset (A), a liability (L), shareholders' equity (SE), a revenue (R), or an expense (E).

2. Show the effects (direction and amount) of each transaction on net earnings and cash.

E3–15 Analyzing the Effects of Transactions in T-Accounts, and Computing Cash Basis versus   ■ LO3, 4, 5, 6
Accrual Basis Earnings

Sbrocchi's Piano Rebuilding Company has been operating for one year (2013). At the start of 2014, its statement of earnings accounts had zero balances and the account balances on its statement of financial position were as follows:

Cash	$10,000	Trade payables	$16,000
Trade receivables	50,000	Deferred revenue (deposits)	6,400
Supplies	2,400	Note payable (due in three years)	80,000
Equipment	16,000	Share capital	16,000
Land	12,000	Retained earnings	36,000
Building	64,000		

Required:

1. Create T-accounts for the accounts reported on the statement of financial position and for these additional accounts: rebuilding fees revenue, rent revenue, wages expense, and utilities expense. Enter the beginning balances.

2. Enter the following January 2014 transactions in the T-accounts, using the letter of each transaction as the reference:

   a. Received a $600 deposit from a customer who wanted her piano rebuilt.

   b. Rented a part of the building to a bicycle repair shop; received $820 for rent in January.

   c. Rebuilt and delivered five pianos to customers who paid $18,400 in cash.

   d. Received $7,200 from customers as payment on their accounts.

   e. Received an electric and gas utility bill for $520 to be paid in February.

   f. Ordered $960 in supplies.

   g. Paid $2,140 on account to suppliers.

    h. Received from Ella Sbrocchi, the major shareholder, a $920 tool (equipment) to use in the business in exchange for the company's shares.

    i. Paid $15,000 in wages to employees for work in January.

    j. Declared and paid a cash dividend of $2,600.

    k. Received and paid for the supplies ordered in (*f*).

3. Using the data from the T-accounts, calculate the amounts for the following on January 31, 2014:
Revenues, $_____ − Expenses, $_____ = Net earnings, $_____
Assets, $_____ = Liabilities, $_____ + Shareholders' Equity, $_____

4. Calculate the company's net earnings for January by using the cash basis of accounting. Why does this differ from the net earnings in (3) above?

5. Calculate the return on assets for January 2014. If the company had a return on assets of 6 percent in December 2013 and 5 percent in November 2013, what does your computation suggest to you about Sbrocchi's Piano Rebuilding Company? What would you state in your report?

■ **LO4**

E3–16   **Analyzing the Effects of Transactions on the Statement of Cash Flows**
Refer to E3–15.

Required:
Use the following chart to identify whether each of the transactions in E3–15 results in a cash flow effect from operating (O), investing (I), or financing (F) activities, and indicate the direction and the effect on cash (+ for increase and − for decrease). If there is no cash flow effect, write "none." The first transaction is provided as an example.

Transaction	Operating, Investing, or Financing Effect	Direction and Amount of the Effect
(a)	O	+600

■ **LO4**

E3–17   **Preparing a Statement of Earnings and a Partial Statement of Cash Flows**
Refer to E3–15.

Required:

1. Use the ending balances in the T-accounts in E3–15 to prepare the following:
    a. A statement of earnings for January 2014, in good form.
    b. The operating activities section of the statement of cash flows for January 2014, in good form.

2. Explain the difference between the net earnings and the cash flow from operating activities computed in (1).

■ **LO2, 3, 4, 5**

E3–18   **Inferring Operating Transactions and Preparing a Statement of Earnings and a Statement of Financial Position**
Kiernan Kite Company (a corporation) sells and repairs kites from manufacturers around the world. Its stores are located in rented space in malls and shopping centres. During its first month of operations ended April 30, 2015, Kiernan Kite Company completed eight transactions with the dollar effects indicated in the following schedule:

Accounts	Dollar Effect of Each of the Eight Transactions								Ending Balance
	(a)	(b)	(c)	(d)	(e)	(f)	(g)	(h)	
Cash	$50,000	$(10,000)	$(5,000)	$ 7,000	$(2,000)	$(1,000)		$3,000	
Trade receivables				3,000					
Inventory			20,000	(3,000)				(300)	
Prepayments					1,500				
Store fixtures		10,000							
Trade payables			15,000				1,200		
Deferred revenue								2,000	
Share capital	50,000								
Sales revenue				10,000				1,000	
Cost of sales				3,000				(300)	
Wages expense						1,000			
Rent expense					500				
Utilities expense							1,200		

Required:

1. Write a brief explanation of transactions (*a*) through (*h*). Explain any assumptions that you made.
2. Compute the ending balance in each account and prepare a statement of earnings for the company for April 2015 and a classified statement of financial position as at April 30, 2015.

E3–19 **Computing and Explaining the Total Asset Turnover Ratio**

The following data are from annual reports of Justin's Jewellery Company:

	2014	2013	2012
Total assets	$ 60,000	$ 50,000	$ 40,000
Total liabilities	12,000	10,000	5,000
Total shareholders' equity	48,000	40,000	35,000
Sales	154,000	144,000	130,000
Net earnings	5,000	3,800	25,000

Required:

Compute Justin's total asset turnover ratio and its return on assets for 2013 and 2014. What do these results suggest to you about Justin's Jewellery Company?

E3–20 **Analyzing the Effects of Transactions by Using T-Accounts and Interpreting the Total Asset Turnover Ratio as a Financial Analyst**

LO4, 6

Internet Marketing Inc. (IMI), which has been operating for three years, provides marketing consulting services worldwide for online companies. You are a financial analyst assigned to report on the effectiveness of IMI's management team at managing its assets. At the start of 2014 (its fourth year), IMI's T-account balances were as follows. Amounts are in thousands of dollars.

ASSETS

Cash		Trade Receivables		Long-Term Investments	
3,200		8,000		6,400	

LIABILITIES

Trade Payables		Deferred Revenue		Long-Term Borrowings	
	2,400		5,600		1,600

SHAREHOLDERS' EQUITY

Contributed Capital		Retained Earnings	
	4,800		3,200

REVENUES

Consulting Fee Revenue		Investment Income	

EXPENSES

Wages Expense		Travel Expense		Utilities Expense	

Rent Expense	

Required:

1. Using the data from these T-accounts, complete the accounting equation on January 1, 2014.

   Assets, $_____ = Liabilities, $_____ + Shareholders' Equity, $_____

2. Enter the following 2014 transactions in the T-accounts:

   a. Provided $58,000 in services to clients; received $48,000 in cash and the rest on account.

   b. Received $5,600 cash from clients on account.

    c. Received $400 in cash as income on investments.

    d. Paid $36,000 for wages, $12,000 for travel, $7,600 in rent, and $1,600 on trade payables.

    e. Received $1,600 in cash from clients in advance of services that IMI will provide next year.

    f. Received a utility bill for $800 for services used in 2014.

    g. Paid $480 in dividends to shareholders.

3. Compute ending balances in the T-accounts to determine the missing amounts on December 31, 2014:

    Revenues, $_____ − Expenses, $_____ = Net earnings, $_____

    Assets, $_____ = Liabilities, $_____ + Shareholders' Equity, $_____

4. Calculate the total asset turnover ratio for 2014. If the company had a total asset turnover ratio of 2.00 in 2013 and of 1.80 in 2012, what does your computation suggest to you about IMI? What would you state in your report?

LO4   **E3–21**   **Inferring Transactions and Computing Effects by Using T-Accounts**

A recent annual report of a leading business and financial news company included the following accounts. Amounts are in millions of dollars.

Trade Receivables			Prepayments			Deferred Revenue		
1/1	313		1/1	25			240	1/1
	2,573	?		43	?	?	328	
31/12	295		31/12	26		31/12	253	

Required:

1. Describe the typical transactions that affect each T-account (i.e., the economic events that occur to make these accounts increase and decrease).

2. Compute the missing amounts for each T-account.

LO6   **E3–22**   **Computing and Interpreting the Total Asset Turnover Ratio and the Return on Assets**

Bianca Corp. and Uzma Inc. operate in the same industry. The companies' total assets, revenue, and net earnings for the years 2013–2016 are provided below. All amounts are in thousands of dollars.

Bianca Corp.	2016	2015	2014	2013
Total assets	$ 40,000	$ 50,000	$ 60,000	$ 65,000
Revenue	130,000	144,000	154,000	150,000
Net earnings	25,000	3,800	5,000	4,800
Interest expense, net of tax	1,000	800	700	800
Uzma Inc.				
Total assets	$ 65,000	$ 60,000	$ 50,000	$ 40,000
Revenue	150,000	154,000	144,000	130,000
Net earnings	4,800	5,000	3,800	25,000
Interest expense, net of tax	400	500	400	300

Required:

1. Compute the total asset turnover ratio and the return on assets for each company for each of the years 2014, 2015, and 2016.

2. Based on the two sets of ratios that you computed, which company was more efficient in managing its assets during the 2013–2016 period? Explain.

P3–4 Analyzing the Effects of Transactions on the Statement of Cash Flows (AP3–4)
Refer to P3–3.

■ **LO4**

Required:
Use the following chart to identify whether each of the transactions in P3–3 results in a cash flow effect from operating (O), investing (I), or financing (F) activities, and indicate the direction and the effect on cash (+ for increase and − for decrease). If there is no cash flow effect, write "none." The first transaction is provided as an example.

Transaction	Operating, Investing, or Financing Effect	Direction and Amount of the Effect
(a)	F	+60,000

P3–5 Analyzing the Effects of Transactions by Using T-Accounts, Preparing Financial Statements, and Evaluating the Total Asset Turnover Ratio and the Return on Assets (AP3–5)

■ **LO4, 5, 6**

*e**X**cel*

The following are the summary account balances from a recent statement of financial position of Modern Sportswear Inc. The accounts are followed by a list of transactions for the month of January 2015. All amounts are shown in millions of dollars:

Cash	$ 635	Trade payables	$1,822
Long-term borrowings	2,229	Income tax payable	300
Trade receivables	1,503	Prepayments	16
Inventories	551	Retained earnings	4,266
Deferred income taxes (credit)	2,518	Other non-current assets	1,126
Property and equipment, net	10,759	Share capital	3,455

The accounts have normal debit or credit balances, but they are not necessarily listed in good order.

The following additional information is also available:

a. Purchased new equipment costing $150 by issuing long-term debt.

b. Received $900 on trade receivables.

c. Received and paid the telephone bills for $1.

d. Earned $500 in sales to customers on account; the cost of sales was $300.

e. Paid employees $100 for wages earned in January.

f. Paid half of the income taxes payable.

g. Purchased inventory for $223 on account.

h. Prepaid rent for February for a warehouse for $12.

i. Paid $10 of long-term borrowings and $1 in interest on the debt.

j. Purchased a patent (an intangible asset) for $8 cash.

Required:
1. Set up T-accounts for the preceding list and enter the respective balances. (You will need additional T-accounts for statement of earnings accounts.)
2. For each transaction, record the effects in the T-accounts. Label each by using the letter of the transaction. Compute ending balances.
3. Show the effects (direction and amount) of each transaction on net earnings and cash.
4. Prepare in good form a statement of earnings for the month of January 2015 and a classified statement of financial position as at January 31, 2015.
5. Prepare the operating activities section of the statement of cash flows for January 2015, and explain the difference between the cash flow from operating activities and the net earnings computed in (3).
6. Compute the company's total asset turnover ratio. What does this ratio suggest to you about Modern Sportswear Inc.?

P3–6 Determining and Interpreting the Effects of Transactions on Statement of Earnings Categories and Return on Assets (AP3–6)

■ **LO4, 6**

Apple Inc,

Apple Inc. popularized both the personal computer and the easy-to-use graphic interface. Today it competes against many companies that rely on the Windows and Android operating systems. The company's statement of earnings for a recent year is presented below (in millions of U.S. dollars):

Net sales	$156,508
Cost of sales	87,846
Gross profit	68,662
Operating expenses:	
Research and development	3,381
Selling, general, and administrative	10,040
Total operating expenses	13,421
Earnings from operations	55,241
Other income and expense:	
Interest expense	(38)
Other income, net	560
Earnings before provision for income taxes	55,763
Provision for income taxes	14,030
Net earnings	$ 41,733

Required:

1. Compute the return on assets based on the information presented in the statement of earnings. Apple's total assets averaged $146,218 million for that year.

2. Assume that the following hypothetical *additional* transactions occurred during the fiscal year. Complete the following tabulation, indicating the sign and amount of the effect of each additional transaction (+ for increase, − for decrease, and "N" for no effect). Consider each item independently and ignore income taxes.

   a. Recorded sales on account of $700 and related cost of sales of $475.

   b. Incurred additional research and development expense of $100, which was paid in cash.

   c. Issued additional shares for $350 cash.

   d. Declared and paid dividends of $90.

Transaction	Gross Profit	Earnings from Operations	Return on Assets
a.			
b.			
c.			
d.			

■ LO5, 6   **P3–7**   **Computing and Analyzing the Total Asset Turnover Ratio and the Return on Assets** (AP3–7)

Barrick Gold

WestJet Airlines

Le Groupe Jean Coutu

A summary of selected historical results is presented below for three Canadian companies: Barrick Gold, WestJet Airlines, and Le Groupe Jean Coutu. Each of these companies has grown in size over time by acquiring assets and investing in other companies. (Amounts are in millions of dollars.)

	2012	2011	2010	2009	2008	2007
Barrick Gold						
Total assets	$47,282	$48,884	$34,367	$26,924	$24,161	$21,951
Total revenue	14,547	14,312	11,001	8,136	7,913	6,332
Net earnings (loss)	(677)	4,537	3,630	(4,274)	785	1,119
Interest expense, net of tax	462	360	290	84	16	85
Operating cash flow	5,439	5,315	4,585	(2,322)	2,206	1,732
WestJet Airlines						
Total assets	3,747	3,474	3,384	3,350	3,279	2,984
Total revenue	3,427	3,072	2,607	2,281	2,549	2,127
Net earnings	242	149	90	98	178	193
Interest expense, net of tax	36	40	44	44	53	57
Operating cash flow	722	506	419	319	461	541
Le Groupe Jean Coutu						
Total assets	1,393	1,073	1,060	996	1,949	2,337
Total revenue	2,740	2,733	2,613	2,543	1,676	13,265
Net earnings (loss)	558	230	183	113	(251)	163
Interest expense, net of tax	0.6	2	2	2	4	195
Operating cash flow	224	245	214	203	146	192

Required:

1. Complete the following table by computing the total asset turnover ratio and the return on assets for each company for each of the years 2011 and 2012.

	2012	2011	2010	2009	2008
Barrick Gold					
Total asset turnover ratio			0.36	0.32	0.34
Return on assets (ROA)			12.8%	−16.4%	3.47%
WestJet Airlines					
Total asset turnover ratio			0.77	0.69	0.81
Return on assets (ROA)			3.98%	4.28%	7.38%
Le Groupe Jean Coutu					
Total asset turnover ratio			2.54	1.73	0.78
Return on assets (ROA)			18.0%	7.81%	−11.53%

2. Based on the computed ratios, rank these companies from most successful to least successful in implementing their growth strategies and effectively utilizing their assets.

3. Which of these three companies appears to be in the best position at the end of 2012 to pay off its short-term liabilities? What additional information would help you provide a more definite answer to this requirement? Explain.

P3–8 Recording Journal Entries and Identifying Effects on the Total Assets Turnover Ratio

■ **LO4, 6**

Cedar Fair

Cedar Fair L.P. (Limited Partnership) is one of the largest amusement park operators in the world, owning 11 amusement parks, 5 outdoor water parks, 1 indoor water park, and 6 hotels. Parks in the United States include Cedar Point in Ohio; Valleyfair near Minneapolis/St. Paul; Dorney Park and Wildwater Kingdom near Allentown, Pennsylvania; Worlds of Fun/Oceans of Fun in Kansas City; and Great America in Santa Clara, California. It also operates Canada's Wonderland, near Toronto. The following are summarized transactions similar to those that occurred in a recent year (amounts in thousands of dollars):

a. Guests at the parks paid $566,266 cash in admissions.

b. The primary operating expenses (such as employee wages, utilities, and repairs and maintenance) for the year were $450,967, with $412,200 paid in cash and the rest on account.

c. Interest paid on long-term borrowings was $58,962.

d. The parks sell food and merchandise and operate games. The cash received during the year for these combined activities was $355,917. The cost of merchandise sold during the year was $90,626.

e. Cedar Fair purchased and built additional buildings, rides, and equipment during the year, paying $83,481 in cash.

f. Guests may stay in some of the parks at accommodations owned by the company. During the year, accommodations revenue was $74,049; $72,910 was paid by the guests in cash and the rest was on account.

g. Cedar Fair paid $125,838 on notes payable.

h. The company purchased $146,100 in food and merchandise inventory for the year, paying $118,000 in cash and the rest on account.

i. The selling, general, and administrative expenses (such as the president's salary and advertising for the parks, those not classified as operating expenses) for the year were $131,882; $125,500 was paid in cash and the rest was on account.

j. Cedar Fair paid $9,600 on trade payables during the year.

Required:

1. Prepare a journal entry to record each of these transactions. Use the letter of each transaction as its reference.

2. Show the effects (direction and amount) of each transaction on net earnings and cash.

3. Indicate the direction of the effect (increase, decrease, or no effect) of each of the transactions (*a*) through (*j*) on the total asset turnover ratio, and provide an explanation for your answer. Cedar Fair's total asset turnover ratio was 0.56 in the previous year. For example, transaction (*a*) increases the ratio. Both sales and total assets would increase. Since the ratio is less than 1.0, the increase in sales (the numerator) is proportionally higher than the increase in total assets (the denominator).

■ LO6

P3–9   **Analyzing the Effects of Transactions on the Statement of Cash Flows**
Refer to P3–8, and use the following chart to identify whether each transaction in P3–8 results in a cash flow effect from operating (O), investing (I), or financing (F) activities, and indicate the direction and amount of the effect on cash (+ for increase and − for decrease). If there is no cash flow effect, write "none." The first transaction is provided as an example.

Transaction	Operating, Investing, or Financing Effect	Direction and Amount of the Effect
(a)	O	+566,266

ALTERNATE PROBLEMS

■ LO4, 5

AP3–1   **Preparing a Statement of Earnings and a Partial Statement of Financial Position, and Evaluating the Total Asset Turnover Ratio and the Return on Assets (P3–1)**
You were recently offered a position as an intern in the accounting firm Faitou and Dowal LLP. On your first day at work, your supervisor wanted to test your knowledge of accounting. She gave you the following list of accounts and related balances of New Look Corp. as at December 31, 2015, and asked you to complete the requirements below.

(Amounts in thousands of dollars)	Debit	Credit
Accumulated depreciation—furniture and fixtures		$ 90
Cash	$ 410	
Contributed capital (10,000 shares)		500
Cost of sales	2,600	
Depreciation expense	10	
Deferred revenue		30
Furniture and fixtures	370	
Interest receivable	10	
Interest revenue		10
Merchandise inventory	860	
Note receivable, due on September 30, 2017	240	
Other operating expenses	400	
Prepayments	15	
Retained earnings, January 1, 2015		1,400
Salaries expense	295	
Salaries payable		15
Sales revenue		3,500
Trade payables		190
Trade receivables	525	
Total	$5,735	$5,735

Required:

1. Prepare the statement of earnings for New Look Corp. for the year ended December 31, 2015. The company is subject to an income tax rate of 40 percent and pays its income taxes within three months.

2. By how much would net earnings change if depreciation expense was omitted in the preparation of the statement of earnings?

3. Prepare the liabilities and shareholders' equity sections of a classified statement of financial position for New Look Corp. as at December 31, 2015.

4. Compute the total asset turnover ratio and the return on assets based on your answers to the previous requirements, and explain the meaning of each ratio. Assume that the company reported total assets of $2,150 at December 31, 2014.

AP3–2 Recording Journal Entries (P3–2)

■ LO4

Sandro Spina is the president of TemPro Inc., a company that provides temporary employees for not-for-profit companies. TemPro has been operating for five years; its revenues are increasing with each passing year. You have been hired to help Sandro in analyzing the following transactions for the first two weeks of April:

April 1   Purchased office supplies for $2,600 on account.

3   Received the April telephone bill for $1,950 to be paid in May.

5   Billed the local United Way $23,500 for temporary services provided.

8   Paid $3,005 for supplies purchased and recorded on account last period.

8   Placed an advertisement in the local paper for $1,400 cash.

9   Purchased a new computer for the office costing $2,300 cash.

10   Paid employee wages of $11,900. Of this amount, $3,800 had been earned and recorded in the wages payable account in the prior period.

11   Received $12,500 on account from the local United Way office for services provided on April 5.

12   Purchased land as the site of a future office for $50,000. Paid $10,000 down and signed a note payable for the balance. The note is due in five years and has an annual interest rate of 10 percent.

13   Issued 3,000 additional shares for cash at $45 per share in anticipation of building a new office.

14   Billed Family & Children's Service $14,500 for services rendered.

Required:

1. Prepare a journal entry to record each of the transactions. Be sure to categorize each account as an asset (A), a liability (L), shareholders' equity (SE), a revenue (R), or an expense (E).

2. Complete the tabulation below for each of the transactions, indicating the effect (+ for increase and − for decrease) of each transaction. The first transaction is provided as an example. (Remember that A = L + SE, R − E = NE, and NE affects SE through retained earnings.) Write "N" if there is no effect.

| | **Statement of Financial Position** | | | **Statement of Earnings** | | |
Date	Assets	Liabilities	Shareholders' Equity	Revenues	Expenses	Net Earnings
April 2	+$2,600	+$2,600	N	N	N	N

AP3–3 Analyzing the Effects of Transactions by Using T-Accounts, Preparing a Statement of Earnings, and Evaluating the Total Asset Turnover Ratio and the Return on Assets as a Manager (P3–3)

■ LO4, 5, 6

Nina Prada, a connoisseur of fine chocolate, opened Nina's Chocolates Inc. in Valleytown on March 1, 2014. The shop specializes in a selection of gourmet chocolates and a line of gourmet ice cream. You have been hired as manager. Your duties include maintaining the store's financial records. The following transactions occurred in March 2014, the first month of operations:

a. Received contributions of $30,000 in total from four shareholders to form the corporation.

b. Paid store rent for three months at $1,600 per month (recorded as prepayment).

c. Purchased supplies for $800 cash.

d. Purchased chocolates on account for $10,000, due in 60 days.

e. Issued additional shares to new investors for $20,000 cash.

f. Used the money from (*e*) to purchase a computer for $4,000 (for recordkeeping and inventory tracking). The rest was used to buy furniture and fixtures for the store.

g. Placed a grand-opening advertisement in the local paper for $850 cash.

h. Sold chocolates for $3,600; $3,050 was in cash and the rest on accounts. The cost of the chocolates sold was $2,000.

i. Made a $1,000 payment on trade payables.

j. Incurred and paid employee wages of $2,520.

k. Collected trade receivables of $100 from customers.

l. Made a repair on one of the display cases for $268 cash.

m. Made cash sales of $5,200 during the rest of the month. The cost of the goods sold was $2,800.

Required:

1. Set up appropriate T-accounts for cash, trade receivables, supplies, merchandise inventory, prepaid rent, equipment, furniture and fixtures, trade payables, notes payable, interest payable, contributed capital, sales revenue, cost of sales, advertising expense, wages expense, repair expense, and interest expense. All accounts begin with zero balances.

2. Record in the T-accounts the effects of each transaction for Nina's Chocolates Inc. in March, referencing each transaction in the accounts with the transaction letter. Show the ending balances in the T-accounts.

3. Prepare a statement of earnings for March 2014.

4. Write a short memo to Nina offering your opinion on the results of operations during the first month of business.

5. After three years in business, you are being evaluated for a salary increase. One measure is how efficiently you managed the assets of the business. The following data are available:

	2016*	2015	2014
Total assets	$112,000	$63,000	$49,000
Total liabilities	63,000	28,000	21,000
Total shareholders' equity	49,000	35,000	28,000
Total sales	119,000	105,000	70,000
Net earnings	28,000	14,000	5,600

*At the end of 2016, Nina decided to open a second store, requiring loans and inventory purchases prior to the opening in early 2017.

Compute the total asset turnover ratio and the return on assets for 2015 and 2016, and evaluate the results. Do you think your salary should be increased? Why? The company is subject to an income tax rate of 30 percent.

LO4

AP3–4   Analyzing the Effects of Transactions on the Statement of Cash Flows (P3–4)
Refer to AP3–3.

Required:
Use the following chart to identify whether each of the transactions in AP3–3 results in a cash flow effect from operating (O), investing (I), or financing (F) activities, and indicate the direction and the effect on cash (+ for increase and − for decrease). If there is no cash flow effect, write "none." The first transaction is provided as an example.

Transaction	Operating, Investing, or Financing Effect	Direction and Amount of the Effect
(a)	F	+30,000

LO4, 5, 6

Canada Post

AP3–5   Analyzing the Effects of Transactions by Using T-Accounts, Preparing Financial Statements, and Evaluating the Total Asset Turnover Ratio and the Return on Assets (AP3–5)
The following are several December 31, 2011, account balances (in millions of dollars) from a recent annual report of Canada Post Corporation, followed by several typical transactions. The corporation's vision is described in the annual report as follows:

> Canada Post will be a world leader in providing innovative physical and electronic delivery solutions, creating value for our customers, employees, and all Canadians.

Account	Balance	Account	Balance
Property, plant, and equipment, net	$2,379	Equity	$1,353
Trade payables	255	Receivables	718
Prepayments	115	Other non-current assets	1,866
Accrued liabilities	130	Cash	1,113
Long-term borrowings	1,111	Investments (long-term)	553
Deferred revenues	129	Other non-current liabilities	3,766

These accounts have normal debit or credit balances, but are not necessarily in good order. The following hypothetical transactions (in millions of dollars) occurred the next month (from January 1, 2012, to January 31, 2012):

a. Provided delivery service to customers, receiving $564 in trade receivables and $60 in cash.

b. Purchased new equipment costing $540; signed a long-term note.

c. Paid $74 in cash to rent equipment, with $64 for rental this month and the rest for rent for the first few days in February.

d. Spent $396 in cash to maintain and repair facilities and equipment during the month.

e. Collected $675 from customers on account.

f. Borrowed $90 by signing a long-term note (ignore interest).

g. Paid employees $279 earned during the month.

h. Purchased for cash and used $49 in supplies.

i. Paid $184 on trade payables.

j. Ordered $72 in spare parts and supplies.

Required:

1. Set up T-accounts for the preceding list and enter the respective balances. (You will need additional T-accounts for statement of earnings accounts.)

2. For each transaction, record the effects in the T-accounts. Label each by using the letter of the transaction. Compute ending balances.

3. Show the effects (direction and amount) of each transaction on net earnings and cash.

4. Prepare in good form a statement of earnings for January 2012.

5. Prepare in good form a classified statement of financial position as at January 31, 2012.

6. Prepare the operating activities section of the statement of cash flows for January 2012, and explain the difference between the cash flow from operating activities and the net earnings computed in (4).

7. Compute the company's total asset turnover ratio and its return on assets. What do these ratios suggest to you about Canada Post? Assume that the long-term note of $90 was signed on January 31, and that interest has not accrued yet.

AP3–6 **Determining and Interpreting the Effects of Transactions on Statement of Earnings Categories and Return on Assets** (P3–6)

■ **LO**4, 6

Barnes & Noble Inc.

Barnes & Noble Inc. revolutionized bookselling by making its stores public spaces and community institutions where customers may browse, find a book, relax over a cup of coffee, talk with authors, and join discussion groups. Today it is fighting increasing competition not only from traditional sources but also from online booksellers. Presented here is a recent statement of earnings (in millions of dollars):

Net sales	$5,121
Cost of sales	3,540
Gross margin	1,581
Operating expenses:	
Selling and administrative	1,251
Depreciation and amortization	174
Pre-opening expenses	13
Total operating expenses	1,438
Earnings from operations	143
Other income and expenses:	
Interest expense	2
Earnings before provision for income taxes	141
Provision for income taxes	56
Net earnings	$ 85

Required:

Assume that the following hypothetical *additional* transactions occurred during the fiscal year: (*a*) recorded and received interest income of $14, (*b*) purchased $95 of additional inventory on open account, (*c*) recorded and paid additional advertising expense of $19, and (*d*) issued additional common shares for $90 cash.

Complete the following tabulation, indicating the sign of the effect of each *additional* transaction (+ for increase, − for decrease, and NE for no effect). Assume that the company's return on assets is less than one prior to these transactions. Consider each item independently and ignore income taxes.

Transaction	Earnings (Loss) from Operations	Net Earnings	Return on Assets
(a)			
(b)			
(c)			
(d)			

■ **LO5, 6**

Gildan Activewear

Research In Motion

Andrew Peller

AP3–7   **Computing and Analyzing the Total Asset Turnover Ratio and the Return on Assets** (P3–7)

A summary of selected historical results is presented below for three Canadian companies: Gildan Activewear, Research In Motion (renamed BlackBerry in February 2013), and Andrew Peller. Each of these companies has grown in size over time by acquiring assets and investing in other companies. (Amounts are in millions of dollars.)

	2012	2011	2010	2009	2008
Gildan Activewear					
Total assets	$1,896	$1,890	$1,328	$1,075	$1,102
Total revenue	1,948	1,726	1,311	1,038	1,250
Net earnings	148	240	198	95	145
Interest expense, net of tax	7.3	3.3	0.5	1.8	5.8
Research In Motion					
Total assets	13,165	13,731	12,875	10,205	5,511
Total revenue	11,073	18,435	19,907	14,953	4,914
Net earnings	(646)	1,164	3,411	2,457	1,294
Interest expense, net of tax	0	0	0	0	0.3
Andrew Peller					
Total assets	297	286	268	265	260
Total revenue	289	277	265	263	237
Net earnings	15	13	11	22	11
Interest expense, net of tax	3.6	3.8	4.5	6	4

Required:

1. Complete the following table by computing the total asset turnover ratio and the return on assets for each company for each of the years 2011 and 2012.

	2012	2011	2010	2009
Gildan Activewear				
Total asset turnover ratio			1.09	0.95
Return on assets (ROA)			16.5%	8.9%
Research In Motion				
Total asset turnover ratio			1.73	1.90
Return on assets (ROA)			29.6%	31.3%
Andrew Peller				
Total asset turnover ratio			0.99	1.00
Return on assets (ROA)			5.8%	10.7%

2. Based on the computed ratios, comment on the companies' success in implementing their growth strategies and effectively utilizing their assets to generate revenue and net earnings.

3. Assuming that you are interested in investing in one of these three companies, which company would you choose? Write a brief report to justify your choice.

CASES AND PROJECTS

FINDING AND INTERPRETING FINANCIAL INFORMATION

CP3–1 Finding Financial Information

Refer to the financial statements and the accompanying notes of Canadian Tire Corporation in Appendix A.

Required:

1. State the amount of the largest expense on the statement of earnings for 2012 and describe the transaction represented by the expense.

2. Assuming that all net sales are on credit, how much cash did Canadian Tire Corporation collect from customers? (*Hint:* Use a T-account for Trade and other receivables and Loans receivable to infer collections.)

3. A shareholder has complained that "more dividends should be paid because the company had net earnings of $499.2 million in 2012. Since this amount is all cash, more of it should go to the shareholders." Explain why the shareholder's assumption that net earnings equal net cash inflow is not valid. If you believe that the assumption is valid, state so and support your position concisely.

4. Describe and contrast the purpose of a statement of earnings versus a statement of financial position.

5. Compute the company's total asset turnover ratio and its return on assets for 2012. Explain their meaning.

■ **LO**2, 4, 6

Canadian Tire Corporation

CP3–2 Finding Financial Information

Go to *Connect* for the financial statements of RONA Inc.

Required:

1. What is the company's revenue recognition policy? (*Hint:* Look in the notes to the financial statements.)

2. How much inventory did the company buy during the year? (*Hint:* Refer to Note 6 to the financial statements, and use a T-account for Inventories to infer how much was purchased.)

3. Refer to Note 5.1 to the financial statements and compute the ratio of Selling, general and administrative expenses to revenues for the years ended December 30, 2012, and December 25, 2011. By what percentage did these expenses increase or decrease from fiscal year 2011 to 2012? (*Hint:* Percentage Change = [Current-Year Amount − Prior-Year Amount]/Prior-Year Amount.)

4. Compute the company's total asset turnover ratio for the year ended December 30, 2012, and explain its meaning.

■ **LO**2, 4, 6

RONA Inc.

CP3–3 Comparing Companies within an Industry

Refer to the financial statements of Canadian Tire Corporation (Appendix A) and RONA Inc. (on *Connect*), and the Industry Ratio Report (Appendix B on *Connect*).

Required:

1. What title does each company give its statement of earnings? Explain what the term "consolidated" means.

2. Which company had higher net earnings at the end of its fiscal year?

3. Compute the total asset turnover ratio and the return on assets for each company for the most recent year. Which company is utilizing assets more effectively to generate sales and net earnings? Explain.

4. Compare the total asset turnover ratio and the return on assets for both companies to the industry average. On average, are these two companies utilizing assets to generate sales and net earnings better or worse than their competitors?

■ **LO**2, 3, 5

Canadian Tire Corporation vs. RONA Inc.

5. How much cash was provided by operating activities by each company during the most recent year? What was the percentage change in operating cash flows for each company during the most recent year? (*Hint:* Percentage Change = [Current-Year Amount − Prior-Year Amount] ÷ Prior-Year Amount.)

6. How much did each company pay in income taxes during the last fiscal year reported in the financial statements? Where did you find this information?

7. What segments does Canadian Tire report in the notes to its financial statements? What does RONA report about segments?

LO4, 5   **CP3–4** **FINANCIAL REPORTING AND ANALYSIS CASE**

Using Financial Reports: Analyzing Changes in Accounts and Preparing Financial Statements
Pete's Painting Service was organized as a corporation on January 20, 2014, by three individuals, each receiving 5,000 shares of capital from the new company. The following is a schedule of the *cumulative* account balances immediately after each of the first 10 transactions ending on January 31, 2014.

	CUMULATIVE BALANCES									
Accounts	**(a)**	**(b)**	**(c)**	**(d)**	**(e)**	**(f)**	**(g)**	**(h)**	**(i)**	**(j)**
Cash	$75,000	$70,000	$85,000	$71,000	$61,000	$64,000	$60,000	$49,000	$44,000	$60,000
Trade receivables			12,000	12,000	12,000	26,000	26,000	26,000	26,000	10,000
Office fixtures		22,000	22,000	22,000	22,000	22,000	22,000	22,000	22,000	22,000
Land				18,000	18,000	18,000	18,000	18,000	18,000	18,000
Accounts payable					3,000	3,000	3,000	10,000	5,000	5,000
Note payable (long term)		17,000	17,000	21,000	21,000	21,000	21,000	21,000	21,000	21,000
Contributed capital	75,000	75,000	75,000	75,000	75,000	75,000	75,000	75,000	75,000	75,000
Retained earnings							(4,000)	(4,000)	(4,000)	(4,000)
Paint revenue			27,000	27,000	27,000	44,000	44,000	44,000	44,000	44,000
Supplies expense					5,000	5,000	5,000	8,000	8,000	8,000
Wages expense					8,000	8,000	8,000	23,000	23,000	23,000

Required:

1. Analyze the changes in this schedule for each transaction, and then explain the transaction. Transaction (*a*) is an example:

    a. Cash increased $75,000, and Contributed capital (shareholders' equity) increased $75,000. Therefore, transaction (*a*) was an issuance of shares of the corporation for $75,000 cash.

2. Based only on the preceding schedule after transaction (*j*), prepare a statement of earnings, a statement of shareholders' equity, and a statement of financial position.

3. For each of the transactions, indicate the type of effect on cash flows (O for operating, I for investing, or F for financing) and the direction (+ for increase and − for decrease) and amount of the effect. If there is no effect, write "none." The first transaction is provided as an example.

Transaction	Operating, Investing, or Financing Effect	Direction and Amount of the Effect
(*a*)	F	+75,000

LO3, 6   **CP3–5** **CRITICAL THINKING CASES**

Making a Decision as a Bank Loan Officer: Analyzing and Restating Financial Statements That Have Major Deficiencies (A Challenging Case)
Tom Martinez started and operated a small boat repair service company during 2015. He is interested in obtaining a $100,000 loan from your bank to build a dry dock to store boats for

customers in the winter months. At the end of the year, he prepared the following statements based on information stored in a large filing cabinet:

MARTINEZ COMPANY

Profit for 2015

Service fees collected during 2015		$ 55,000
Cash dividends received		10,000
Total		65,000
Expense for operations paid during 2015	$22,000	
Cash stolen	500	
New tools purchased during 2015 (cash paid)	1,000	
Supplies purchased for use on service jobs (cash paid)	3,200	
Total		26,700
Net earnings		$ 38,300

Assets Owned at the End of 2015

Cash in chequing account	$ 29,300
Service garage (at current market value)	32,000
Tools and equipment	18,000
Land (at current market value)	30,000
Shares in ABC Industrial	130,000
Total	$239,300

The following is a summary of completed transactions:

a. Received the following contributions to the business from the owner when it was started in exchange for 1,000 shares in the new company:

Building	$21,000	Land	$20,000
Tools and equipment	17,000	Cash	1,000

b. Earned service fees during 2015 of $87,000; of the cash collected, $20,000 was for deposits from customers on work to be done by Martinez during 2016.

c. Received the cash dividends on shares of ABC Industrial purchased by Tom as a personal investment six years earlier.

d. Incurred expenses during 2015, $61,000.

e. Determined amount of supplies on hand (unused) at the end of 2015, $700.

Required:

1. Did Tom prepare the statement of earnings on a cash basis or on an accrual basis? Explain how you can tell. Which basis should be used? Explain why.

2. Reconstruct the correct entries under accrual accounting principles and post the effects to T-accounts.

3. Prepare an accrual-based statement of earnings for 2015 and a statement of financial position at the end of 2015. Explain (using footnotes) the reason for each change that you make to the statement of earnings.

4. What additional information would assist you in formulating your decision regarding the loan to Tom?

5. Based on the revised statements and additional information needed, write a letter to Tom explaining your decision at this time regarding the loan.

CP3–6 Proper Measurement of Net Earnings ■ LO3

Paula Manolakos purchased La Forêt Inc., a bakery, from Gianni Fiori. The purchase agreement included a provision that required Paula to pay Gianni 25 percent of the bakery's net earnings in each of the next five years. The agreement stated that the bakery's net earnings would be measured in a "fair and reasonable manner," but did not state that it would be measured in accordance with the applicable financial reporting standards. Neither Paula nor Gianni was familiar with accounting concepts.

In measuring net earnings, Paula used the following accounting policies:

a. Revenue was recognized when cash was received from customers. Because of the nature of the business, most customers paid in cash, but a few customers purchased merchandise on account and were allowed to pay in 30 days.

b. Paula set her annual salary at $60,000, which Gianni has agreed was reasonable. She also paid $30,000 per year to her spouse and to each of her two teenage children. These family members did not work in the business on a regular basis, but they did help during busy periods.

c. Weekly expenditures for eggs, milk, flour, and other supplies were charged directly to supplies expense, as were the weekly groceries for Paula's family.

d. The bakery had modern baking equipment valued at $50,000 at the time Paula purchased the company. The statement of earnings for the first year included a $50,000 equipment expense related to these assets.

e. Income taxes expense included the amount paid by the corporation (which was computed correctly), as well as the personal income taxes paid by various members of Paula's family on the salaries they earned for working in the business.

Gianni was disappointed, however, when Paula reported net earnings for the first year that was far below his expectations.

Required:

1. Discuss the fairness and reasonableness of Paula's accounting policies. Identify the accounting principle or assumption that may have been violated.

2. Do you think that the net cash flow from operations (cash receipts minus cash payments) is higher or lower than the net earnings reported by Paula? Explain.

3. What advice would you give Gianni to ensure that the bakery's net earnings would be measured properly in future years?

■ **LO3**

CP3–7 **Evaluating an Ethical Dilemma**

Mike Kruk is the manager of a Vancouver regional office for an insurance company. As the regional manager, his compensation package comprises a base salary, commissions, and a bonus when the region sells new policies in excess of its quota. Mike has been under enormous pressure lately, stemming largely from two factors. First, he is experiencing mounting personal debt because of a family member's illness. Second, compounding his worries, the region's sales of new policies have dipped below the normal quota for the first time in years.

You have been working for Mike for two years, and like everyone else in the office, you consider yourself lucky to work for such a supportive boss. You also feel great sympathy for his personal problems over the last few months. In your position as accountant for the regional office, you are only too aware of the drop in new policy sales and the impact this will have on the manager's bonus. While you are working late at year-end, Mike stops by your office.

Mike asks you to change the manner in which you have accounted for a new property insurance policy for a large local business. A cheque for the premium, substantial in amount, came in the mail on December 31, the last day of the reporting year. The premium covers a period beginning on January 5. You deposited the cheque and correctly debited cash and credited a *deferred revenue* account. Mike says, "Hey, we have the money this year, so why not count the revenue this year? I never did understand why you accountants are so picky about these things anyway. I'd like you to change the way you have recorded the transaction. I want you to credit a *revenue* account. And anyway, I've done favours for you in the past, and I am asking for such a small thing in return." With that, he leaves for the day.

Required:

1. How should you handle this situation?

2. What are the ethical implications of Mike's request?

3. Who are the parties who would be helped or harmed if you complied with the request?

4. If you fail to comply with his request, how will you explain your position to him in the morning?

FINANCIAL REPORTING AND ANALYSIS TEAM PROJECT

■ **LO2, 3, 5, 6**   **CP3–8**   **Team Project: Analyzing Statement of Earnings and Ratios**

As a team, select an industry to analyze. A list of companies classified by industry can be obtained by accessing **www.fpinfomart.ca** and then choosing "Companies by Industry" on the left-hand side. You can also find a list of industries and companies within each industry via **http://ca.finance. yahoo.com/investing** (click on "Order Annual Reports" under "Tools").

Each team member should acquire the annual report for a different publicly traded company in the industry. (Library files, the SEDAR service at **www.sedar.com**, and the company's website are good sources.)

Required:

On an individual basis, each team member should write a short report that answers the following questions about the selected company. Discuss any patterns across the companies that you as a team observe. Then, as a team, write a short report comparing and contrasting your companies.

1. For the most recent year, what is/are the major revenue account(s)? What percentage is each of total operating revenues (computed as Revenue A ÷ Total Revenues)?

2. For the most recent year, what is/are the major expense account(s)? What percentage is each of total operating expenses (computed as Expense A ÷ Total Expenses)?

3. Perform a ratio analysis:

   a. What do the total asset turnover ratio and the return on assets measure in general?

   b. Compute these ratios for the last three years.

   c. What do your results suggest about the company?

   d. If available, find the industry ratios for the most recent year, compare them with your results, and discuss why you believe your company's ratios differ from or are similar to the industry ratios.

4. Describe the company's revenue recognition policy, if reported. (Usually found in note 2 to the financial statements, titled Significant Accounting Policies.)

5. Cash from operating activities as a percentage of net earnings measures how liberal (i.e., speeding up revenue recognition or delaying expense recognition) or conservative (i.e., taking care not to record revenues too early or expenses too late) a company's management is in choosing among various revenue and expense recognition policies. A ratio above 1.0 suggests more conservative policies, and a ratio below 1.0 suggests more liberal policies. Compute the percentage for the last three years. What do your results suggest about the company's choice of accounting policies?

SOLUTIONS TO SELF-STUDY QUIZZES

Self-Study Quiz 3-1

Accounts Affected and Type of Account	Amount of Cash Received	Amount of Revenue Earned in		Deferred Revenue
		December	January	
(a) Cash (A)	$3,520			
Sales (R)			$3,520	
(b) Cash (A)	2,020			
Trade Receivables (A)				
Sales (R)			3,020	
(c) Cash (A)	345			
Sales (R)			270	
Trade Receivables (A)		$ 75		
(d) Cash (A)	50			
Sales (R)			40	
Deferred Revenue (L)				$10
(e) Cash (A)	120			
Trade Receivables (A)		120		
Totals	**$6,055**	**$195**	**$6,850**	**$10**

The total cash received in January, $6,055, is not equal to the amount of revenue recognized for January, $6,850. The cash received in January includes two amounts for revenue recorded for December and $10 for revenue to be recognized in the future. On the other hand, the revenues for January include $1,000 to be collected at a later date. Revenues reflect the efforts made in January, not earlier or later, and are therefore a better measure of operating performance than cash receipts.

Self-Study Quiz 3-2

Accounts Affected and Type of Account	Cash Paid in January	Amount of Expense Recognized in January OR Why an Expense Is Not Recognized
(a) Cash (A) Trade Payables (L)	$1,000	December purchase, paid in January; supplies expensed when used or sold.
(b) Inventories (A) Cost of Sales (E)		$1,400 (of used inventory).

(c) Cash (A)
    General and Administrative Expense (E)
    Prepayments (A)
	450	$150 incurred in January. $300 not incurred until future months.

(d) Inventories (A) Cost of Sales (E)		$1,960 (of used inventory).
(e) Trade Payables (L) General and Administrative Expense (E)		$50 incurred in January to be paid in the future.
Totals	**$1,450**	**$3,560—Expenses for January.**

If your answers did not agree with ours, we recommend that you go back to each transaction to make sure that you have completed each of the steps for each transaction.

Self-Study Quiz 3-3

Effect of transaction on
Net earnings: ↑   5
Cash: ↑   105

(i)   Cash (+A)   105
      Interest revenue (+R → +SE).........................   5
      Notes receivable (−A)   100
(j)   Trade payables (−L)   1,000
      Cash (−A)   1000

Effect of transaction on
Net earnings: No effect
Cash: ↓   1,000

Assets		=	Liabilities		=	Shareholders' Equity
Cash	−1,000		Trade payables	−1,000		

(k)

Assets		=	Liabilities	=	Shareholders' Equity
Cash	+350				Gain on sale of land

Effect of transaction on
Net earnings: ↑   300
Cash: ↑   350

Property, plant, and equipment	−50			+300

Self-Study Quiz 3-4

1. F −,   2. O +,   3. I −,   4. O −,   5. O −,   6. F −,   7. I or O +,   8. F +,   9. F +, 10. F or O −,   11. O −,   12. I +.

Self-Study Quiz 3-5

1.

	2012	2011	2010	2009	2008
Total Asset Turnover Ratio	1.62	1.56	1.53	1.56	1.83
Return on Assets (ROA)	0.04	−0.02	0.04	0.08	0.09

2. The total asset turnover ratio decreased in 2009, remained stable over the next three years, and increased slightly in 2012. This indicates that Sears has recently improved on using its total assets to generate revenues. The company's sales decreased steadily from $6,326 in 2007 to $4,301 in 2012. Its total assets also decreased over the period from 2008 to 2012. The decline in sales, which is due to the economic downturn that started in 2008, has resulted in declining net earnings over the period from 2007 to 2010, and resulted in a net loss in 2011. Consequently, the return on assets dropped significantly from 2008 to 2011. The results of 2012 reflect an effort by Sears' management to improve on the utilization of its assets to generate revenues and earnings.

Adjustments, Financial Statements, and the Quality of Earnings

After studying this chapter, you should be able to do the following:

LEARNING OBJECTIVES

LO1 Explain the purpose of adjustments and analyze the adjustments necessary at the end of the period to update statement of financial position and statement of earnings accounts.

LO2 Use a trial balance to prepare financial statements.

LO3 Prepare a statement of earnings with earnings per share, a statement of changes in equity, and a statement of financial position.

LO4 Compute and interpret the net profit margin ratio and the return on equity.

LO5 Explain the closing process at the end of the period.

FOCUS COMPANY: **Sun-Rype Products Ltd.**
ESTIMATING REVENUES AND EXPENSES AT YEAR-END

The end of the accounting period is a very busy time for Sun-Rype (**www.sunrype.com**). The last day of the fiscal year for Sun-Rype falls on December 31 of each year.[1] The financial statements, however, are not distributed to users on that day. They are released only after management and the external auditors make many critical evaluations.

- Management must ensure that the correct amounts are reported on the statement of financial position and the statement of earnings. This often requires estimations, assumptions, and judgments about the timing of revenue and expense recognition, and values for assets and liabilities.

- The auditors have to (1) assess the strength of the controls established by management to safeguard the company's assets and ensure the accuracy of the financial records, and (2) evaluate the appropriateness of estimates and accounting principles used by management in determining revenues and expenses.

Managers of most companies understand the need to present financial information fairly so as not to mislead users. This is one reason why external auditors examine the company's records on a test, or sample, basis. To maximize the chance of detecting any errors significant enough to affect users' decisions, auditors allocate more of their testing to transactions most likely to be in error. End-of-period adjustments are the most complex portion of the annual recordkeeping process; they are prone to unintentional error. Typical end-of-period adjustment errors include failure to provide adequate provision for product warranty, failure to include items that should be expensed, and end-of-period transactions recorded in the wrong period (called *cut-off errors*). These adjustments receive much attention from the auditors.

For 2012, Sun-Rype's year-end estimation and auditing process took until March 6, 2013, the date on which the auditor KPMG, SA completed the audit work and signed its audit opinion. At that point, the financial statements were made available to the public.

UNDERSTANDING THE BUSINESS

Managers are responsible for preparing financial statements that are useful to investors, creditors, and others. Financial information is most useful for analyzing the past and predicting the future when it is considered by users to be of *high quality*. High-quality information is relevant (i.e., important in the analysis and available in a timely manner) and faithfully represents the substance of the underlying transactions (i.e., complete, neutral, and free from material error).

Users expect revenues and expenses to be reported in the proper period, based on the revenue principle and matching process discussed in Chapter 3. Revenues must be recorded when earned, and expenses must be recorded when incurred, regardless of when cash is received or paid. Many operating activities take place over one accounting period or over several periods, such as prepaying insurance or owing salaries to employees for past work. Because recording these and similar activities daily is often very costly, most companies wait until the end of the period to record *adjustments* to revenue and expense accounts to reflect the proper amounts in the correct period. These entries update the records and are the focus of this chapter.

In this chapter, we emphasize the use of the analytical tools introduced in Chapters 2 and 3 (journal entries and T-accounts) to help you understand how the necessary adjustments are analyzed and recorded at the end of the accounting period. Then we prepare financial statements by using adjusted account balances. Finally, we illustrate how we prepare the accounting records for the next accounting period by performing a process called "closing the books."

ORGANIZATION OF THE CHAPTER

Adjusting Revenues and Expenses	**Preparing Financial Statements**	**Closing the Books**
• Accounting Cycle • Purpose of Adjustments • Types of Adjustments • Adjustment Process • Materiality and Adjusting Entries	• Statement of Earnings • Statement of Changes in Equity • Statement of Financial Position • Net Profit Margin Ratio • Return on Equity	• End of the Accounting Cycle • Post-closing Trial Balance

Supplemental material:

Appendix 4A: An Operational Recordkeeping Efficiency
Appendix C: The Formal Recordkeeping System (on *Connect*)

ADJUSTING REVENUES AND EXPENSES

Accounting Cycle

The **ACCOUNTING CYCLE** is the process used by entities to analyze and record transactions, adjust the records at the end of the period, prepare financial statements, and prepare the records for the next cycle.

The **accounting cycle** is the process used by entities to analyze and record transactions, adjust the records at the end of the period, prepare financial statements, and prepare the records for the next cycle. *During* the accounting period, transactions that result in exchanges between the company and other external parties are analyzed and recorded in the general journal in chronological order (journal entries), and the related accounts are updated in the general ledger (T-accounts), similar to our Sun-Rype illustrations in Chapters 2 and 3. In this chapter, we examine the *end-of-period* steps that

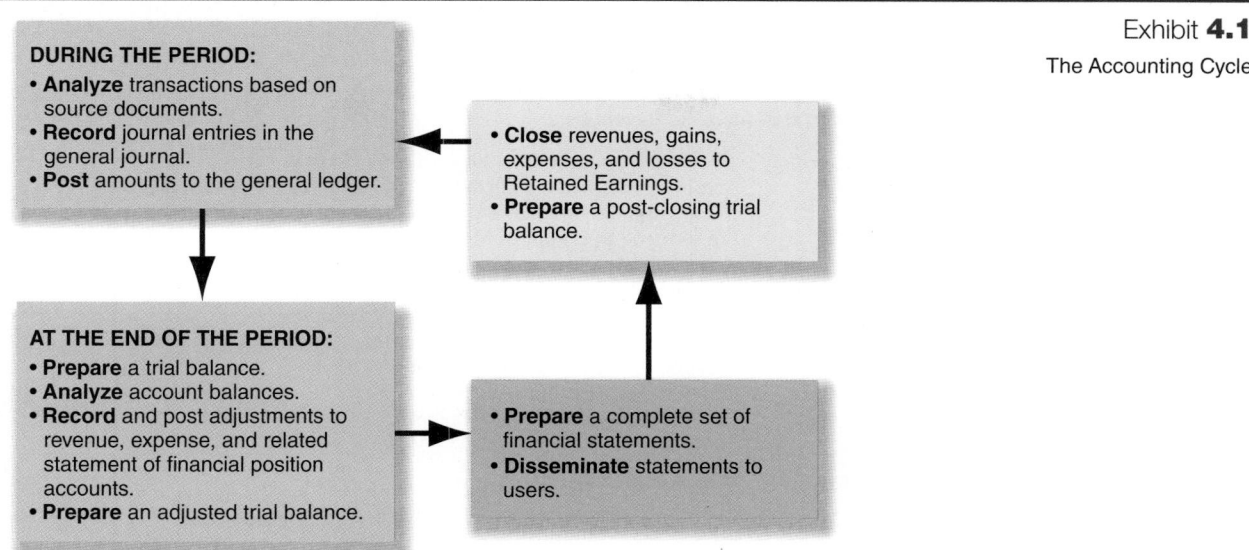

Exhibit **4.1**
The Accounting Cycle

DURING THE PERIOD:
- **Analyze** transactions based on source documents.
- **Record** journal entries in the general journal.
- **Post** amounts to the general ledger.

- **Close** revenues, gains, expenses, and losses to Retained Earnings.
- **Prepare** a post-closing trial balance.

AT THE END OF THE PERIOD:
- **Prepare** a trial balance.
- **Analyze** account balances.
- **Record** and post adjustments to revenue, expense, and related statement of financial position accounts.
- **Prepare** an adjusted trial balance.

- **Prepare** a complete set of financial statements.
- **Disseminate** statements to users.

focus primarily on adjustments to record revenues and expenses in the proper period and to update the statement of financial position accounts for reporting purposes. Exhibit 4.1 presents the fundamental steps in the accounting cycle.

Purpose of Adjustments

Accounting systems are designed to record most recurring daily transactions, particularly those involving cash. As cash is received or paid, it is recorded in the accounting system. In general, this focus on cash works well, especially when cash receipts and payments occur in the same period as the activities that produce revenues and expenses. However, cash is not always received in the period in which the company earns revenue; likewise, cash is not always paid in the period in which the company incurs an expense.

How does the accounting system record revenues and expenses when one transaction is needed to record a cash receipt or payment and another transaction is needed to record a revenue when it is earned or an expense when it is incurred? The solution to the problem created by such differences in timing is to record **adjusting entries** at the end of every accounting period, so that

- Revenues are recorded when earned (the *revenue principle*).

- Expenses are recorded when they are incurred to generate revenue during the same period (the *matching process*).

- *Assets* are reported at amounts that represent the probable future benefits remaining at the end of the period.

- *Liabilities* are reported at amounts that represent the probable future sacrifices of assets or services owed at the end of the period.

Companies wait until *the end of the accounting period* to adjust their accounts because adjusting the records daily would be very costly and time-consuming. Adjusting entries are required every time a company wants to prepare financial statements for external users.

Types of Adjustments

Exhibit 4.2 describes the four types of adjustments (two in which cash was already received or paid and two in which cash will be received or paid). Each of these types of adjustments involves two entries:

1. One entry to record the cash receipt or payment during the period, and
2. One entry to record the revenue or expense in the proper period through an adjusting entry prepared at the end of the period.

LO1

Explain the purpose of adjustments and analyze the adjustments necessary at the end of the period to update statement of financial position and statement of earnings accounts.

ADJUSTING ENTRIES are entries necessary at the end of the accounting period to identify and record all revenues and expenses of that period.

Exhibit **4.2**

Four Types of Adjustments

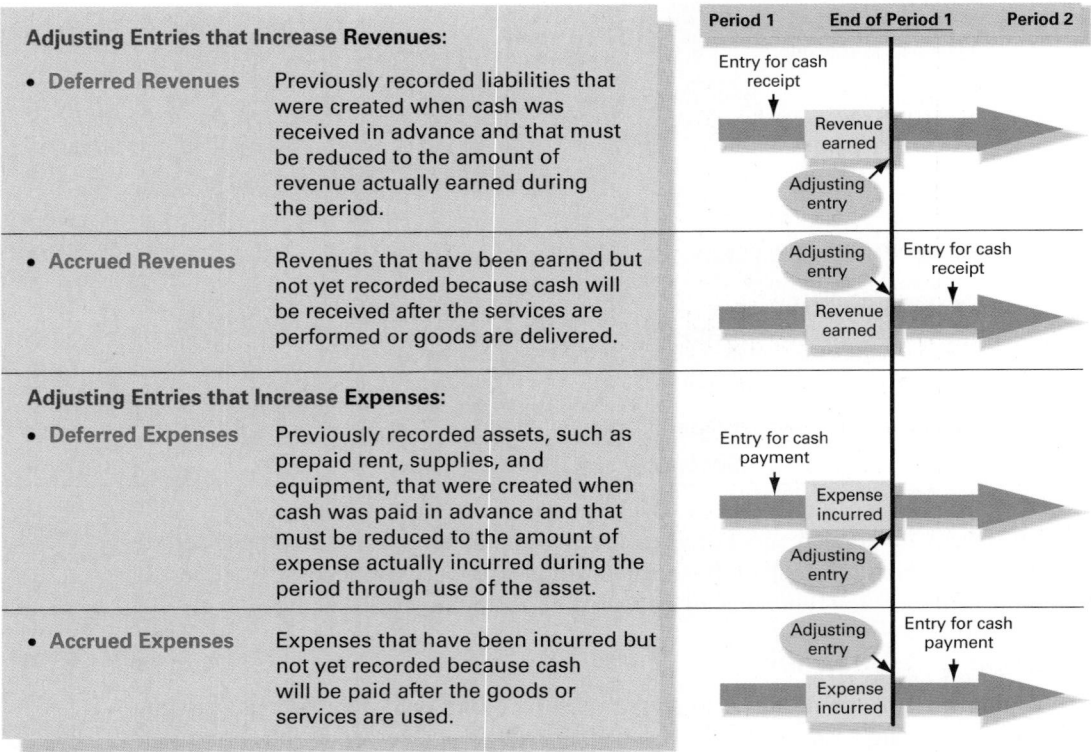

In practice, almost every account could require an adjustment. Rather than trying to memorize an endless list of specific examples, you should focus instead on learning the general types of adjustments that are needed and the process that is used to determine how to adjust the accounts. We will illustrate the process involved in analyzing and adjusting the accounts by reviewing all the adjustments needed for Sun-Rype before preparing January's financial statements based on adjusted balances.

When a customer pays for goods or services before the company delivers them, the company records the amount of cash received in a deferred revenue account. **Deferred revenue** is a liability representing the company's promise to perform or deliver the goods or services in the future. Recognition of (recording) the revenue is deferred (postponed) until the company meets its obligation.

Sometimes companies perform services or provide goods (i.e., earn revenue) before customers pay. Because the cash that is owed for these goods has not yet been received, the revenue that was earned has not been recorded. Revenues that have been earned but have not yet been recorded at the end of the accounting period are called **accrued revenues**.

Exhibit 4.3 summarizes the process involved in adjusting deferred revenues and accrued revenues, using deferred fees and interest revenue as examples. The first column indicates the classification of the revenue, either deferred or accrued. The remaining columns indicate the timing and type of journal entry required. AJE in the exhibit refers to "adjusting journal entry." Note that in both cases, the goal is the same—to record revenues in the proper period. Also note that adjusting entries affect one account on the statement of financial position and one account on the statement of earnings, but *cash is never adjusted*. Cash was recorded when received prior to the end of the period, or will be recorded when collected in a future period.

DEFERRED REVENUES are previously recorded liabilities that need to be adjusted at the end of the accounting period to reflect the amount of revenues earned.

EXAMPLES:
- Deferred ticket revenue
- Deferred subscription revenue

ADJUSTING ENTRY:
↓ Liability and ↑ Revenue

ACCRUED REVENUES are previously unrecorded revenues that need to be recorded at the end of the accounting period to reflect the amount earned and its related receivable account.

EXAMPLES:
- Interest receivable
- Rent receivable

ADJUSTING ENTRY:
↑ Asset and ↑ Revenue

	During the period	End of period	Next period
	Entry when **cash is received before** the company performs (earns revenue)	AJE needed because the company has performed (earned a revenue) during the period	Entry when **cash is received after** the company performs (earns revenue)
Deferred Revenues	Cash (+A) 　Deferred fee revenue (+L)	Deferred fee revenue (−L) 　Fee revenue (+R, +SE)	
Accrued Revenues		Interest receivable (+A) 　Interest revenue (+R, +SE)	Cash (+A) 　Interest receivable (−A)

Revenues recorded
in the proper period

Exhibit **4.3**

Illustration of Adjusting Deferred
and Accrued Revenues

Assets represent resources with probable future benefits to the company. Many assets are used over time to generate revenues, including supplies, prepaid rent, prepaid insurance, buildings, equipment, and intangible assets such as patents and copyrights. These assets are **deferred expenses**. At the end of every period, an adjustment must be made to record the amount of the asset that was used during the period.

Numerous expenses are incurred in the current period without being paid for until the next period. Common examples include interest expense incurred on debt, wages expense for the wages owed to employees, and utilities expense for water, gas, and electricity used during the period for which the company has not yet received a bill. These **accrued expenses** accumulate (accrue) over time but are not recognized until the end of the period in an adjusting entry.

Exhibit 4.4 summarizes the process involved in adjusting deferred expenses and accrued expenses, using prepaid insurance and wages expense as examples. AJE refers, again, to "adjusting journal entry." Note that in both cases, the goal is to record expenses in the proper period. In addition, note that the adjusting journal entry involves one account on the statement of financial position and one account on the statement of earnings, and cash is never affected. Cash was recorded when paid prior to the end of the period or will be recorded in a future period.

Adjustment Process

Throughout the rest of the text, you will discover that nearly every account, except cash, on a company's statement of financial position will need to be adjusted, often requiring management to make judgments and estimates. In this chapter, we will

DEFERRED EXPENSES are previously acquired assets that need to be adjusted at the end of the accounting period to reflect the amount of expense incurred in using the assets to generate revenue.

EXAMPLES:
- Supplies
- Prepayments (e.g., rent, insurance)
- Buildings and equipment

ADJUSTING ENTRY:
↑ Expense and ↑ Asset

ACCRUED EXPENSES are previously unrecorded expenses that need to be recorded at the end of the accounting period to reflect the amount incurred and its related payable account.

EXAMPLES:
- Interest payable
- Wages payable
- Property taxes payable

ADJUSTING ENTRY:
↑ Expense and ↓ Liability

	During the period	End of period	Next period
	Entry when **cash is paid before** the company incurs an expense	AJE needed because the company has incurred an expense during the period	Entry when **cash is paid after** the company incurs an expense
Deferred Expenses	Prepaid insurance (+A) 　Cash (−A)	Insurance expense (+E, −SE) 　Prepaid insurance (−A)	
Accrued Expenses		Wages expense (+E, −SE) 　Wages payable (+L)	Wages payable (−L) 　Cash (−A)

Expenses recorded
in the proper period

Exhibit **4.4**

Illustration of Adjusting Deferred
and Accrued Expenses

illustrate common adjusting entries. In analyzing adjustments at the end of the period, there are three steps:

Step 1: Ask: Was revenue earned or an expense incurred that has not yet been recorded?

If the answer is YES, the revenue or expense account must be increased—credit the revenue account or debit the expense account in the adjusting entry.

Step 2: Ask: Was the related cash received or paid in the past or will it be received or paid in the future?

If cash was received in the past (creating a deferred revenue [liability] account in the past) → reduce the liability account (usually deferred revenue) that was recorded when cash was received, because the entire liability or part of it has been settled since then.

If cash will be received in the future → increase the receivable account (such as interest receivable or rent receivable) to record what is owed by others to the company (creates accrued revenue).

If cash was paid in the past (creating a deferred expense account [asset] in the past) → reduce the asset account (such as supplies or prepayments) that was recorded in the past because the entire asset or part of it has been used since then.

If cash will be paid in the future → increase the payable account (such as interest payable or wages payable) to record what is owed by the company to others (creates an accrued expense).

Step 3: Compute the amount of revenue earned or expense incurred, and record the adjusting entry.

Sometimes the amount is given or known, sometimes it must be computed, and sometimes it must be estimated.

What are the adjustments needed for Sun-Rype at the end of January 2013? We start by preparing and reviewing the unadjusted trial balance.

LO²

Use a trial balance to prepare financial statements.

A **TRIAL BALANCE** is a list of all accounts with their balances that provides a check on the equality of the debits and credits.

Unadjusted Trial Balance   Before adjusting the accounting records, managers normally review an unadjusted trial balance. A **trial balance** is a list of all accounts with their balances that provides a check on the equality of the debits and credits. In spreadsheet form, it lists the names of individual accounts in one column, usually in financial statement order, with their ending debit or credit balances in the next two columns. Debit balances are indicated in the left column and credit balances are indicated in the right column. Then the two columns are totalled to provide a check on the equality of the debits and credits. However, if wrong accounts and/or amounts are used in the journal entries, then a computer-generated trial balance will have errors even though debits equal credits.[2] Once equality is established, the accounts on the trial balance can be reviewed to determine whether any adjustments need to be recorded.

A trial balance is a schedule prepared for internal purposes and is not considered to be a financial statement for external users. Exhibit 4.5 presents an unadjusted trial balance for Sun-Rype at January 31, 2013, based on the balances of the T-accounts illustrated in Chapters 2 and 3, plus other accounts that may be needed but currently have zero balances. Several common adjustments are indicated in the margin of Exhibit 4.5 and will be illustrated in this chapter.

Exhibit **4.5**

Trial Balance for Sun-Rype
Products Ltd.

SUN-RYPE PRODUCTS LTD.
Trial Balance
At January 31, 2013
(in thousands of Canadian dollars)

| | | Unadjusted Trial Balance | |
		Debit	Credit
Assets	Cash and cash equivalents	$ 2,446	
	Trade and other receivables	14,702	
	Notes receivable	50	
	Inventories	28,689	
	Prepayments	1,242	
	Other current assets	446	
	Property, plant, and equipment	69,678	
	Accumulated depreciation		$ 25,487
	Investments	3,000	
	Goodwill	1,061	
Liabilities	Trade and other payables		26,672
	Accrued liabilities		–
	Provisions		1,687
	Income taxes payable		116
	Short-term borrowings		3,646
	Deferred service revenue		10
	Long-term borrowings		10,081
	Deferred tax liabilities		4,035
Shareholders' Equity	Contributed capital		19,721
	Retained earnings		28,681
	Accumulated other comprehensive income	66	
	Dividends declared*	200	
Revenues and Gains	Sales revenue		6,540
	Service revenue		40
	Interest revenue		5
	Gain on sale of land		300
Expenses and Losses	Cost of sales	3,360	
	Sales and marketing	–	
	Distribution expenses	1,131	
	General and administrative expenses	950	
	Depreciation expense	–	
	Interest expense	–	
	Income taxes expense	–	
	Totals	**$127,021**	**$127,021**

*The dividends declared account is added for illustrative purposes.

May need an accrual for any amount earned from customers but not yet recorded

May need an adjustment for the amount of insurance, rent, and advertising used during the period

Represents the historical cost of property, plant, and equipment

Represents the portion of the cost of property, plant, and equipment used in the past

For reporting purposes:
Property, plant, and equipment (at cost) $69,678
– Accumulated depreciation (used cost) 25,487
Carrying amount (unused cost) $44,191

May need an accrual for any wages, utilities, and interest incurred

Needs an accrual for the amount of income tax expense incurred during the period

May need an adjustment for the amount earned during the period

Represents the beginning balance of retained earnings

Revenue from selling food products and beverages
Revenue from services provided to customers
Revenue earned during the period on note receivable

Summary expense for many operating expenses, including advertising and salaries of marketing personnel
Summary expense for many operating expenses, including salaries of distribution personnel
Summary expense for many operating expenses, including insurance, rent, utilities, and salaries
Expense for property, plant, and equipment used during the period
Expense for interest incurred on borrowings during the period
Expense for income taxes incurred during the period
Debits = Credits

Sun-Rype's trial balance in Exhibit 4.5 lists several accounts that suggest adjusting entries are necessary. Note that you can identify them as deferrals or accruals by whether cash is received or paid in the past or the future.

Account	Cash Received or Paid in the Past		Revenue Earned or Expense Incurred (during the month)		Cash to Be Received or Paid in the Future
Deferred service revenue	Deferred revenue	→	All or a portion may have been earned by month-end.		
Trade receivables			Customers may owe Sun-Rype for merchandise delivered but not recorded.	→	Accrued revenue
Prepayments	Deferred expense	→	All or a portion of the prepaid rent, insurance, and advertising may have been used by month-end.		
Property, plant, and equipment	Deferred expense	→	These non-current assets have been used during the month to generate revenues. A portion of their historical cost is recorded as an expense.		
Accrued liabilities			Sun-Rype owes (1) amounts due for utilities used during the month but not yet billed and (2) wages to employees for work during the last week of January. Neither has yet been recorded as an expense.	→	Accrued expense
Borrowings			Sun-Rype owes interest on borrowed funds.	→	Accrued expense
Income taxes payable			Income tax expense needs to be recorded for the period.	→	Accrued expense

We will now use the adjustment process to record adjusting entries for Sun-Rype at the end of January.[3] Study the following illustration carefully to understand the steps in the adjustment process, paying close attention to the computation of the amounts in the adjustment and the effects on the account balances. First, we adjust the deferred revenues and accrued revenues and then the deferred expenses and accrued expenses, using the three-step adjustment process.

For each of the following adjustments, we shorten the term "adjusting journal entry" to AJE for ease of labelling. Also, as you learned in Chapters 2 and 3, it is important to continue to check that debits equal credits in each entry and that the accounting equation remains in balance. In the following adjustments, all entries and the accounting equation are in balance.

Deferred Revenues

(AJE 1) Deferred Service Revenue   Sun-Rype provided additional services in January for $10 to new clients that had previously paid initial fees to Sun-Rype.

Step 1: Was revenue earned that is not yet recorded? YES. Because Sun-Rype provided services to clients, the company has earned service revenue that is not yet recorded. Record an increase in the revenue account.

Step 2: Was the related cash received in the past or will it be received in the future? Sun-Rype received cash IN THE PAST from clients for future services and recorded the amount received in the deferred service revenue liability account. At January 31, the liability account must be reduced by $10 because Sun-Rype performed the services during the current period.

Step 3: Compute the amount of revenue earned. The amount of the revenue that was earned is given as $10. The adjusting journal entry reflects the changes to the accounts.

31/1—AJE 1

Deferred service revenue (−L)   10
    Service revenue (+R, → + SE)   10

Assets	=	Liabilities		+	Shareholders' Equity	
		Deferred service revenue	−10		Service revenue	+10

Deferred Service Revenue (L)				Service Revenue (R)		
		Ch. 3 bal.	10		Ch. 3 bal.	40
*AJE 1	10				AJE 1	10
		End. bal.	0		End. bal.	50

Effect of adjustment on
Net earnings: ↑ 10
Cash: No effect

For other companies, additional examples of deferred revenues include magazine subscriptions; season tickets to sporting events, plays, and concerts; airline tickets sold in advance; and rent paid in advance by renters. Each of these requires an adjusting entry at the end of the accounting period to report the amount of revenue earned during the period.

Accrued Revenues

(AJE 2) Trade Receivables Sun-Rype sold merchandise on account for $900 on January 31, but the sales invoices had not been recorded yet.

Step 1: Was revenue earned that is not yet recorded? YES. Revenue has been earned during January, but cash will be received in the future, requiring an *accrual of revenue.* Record an increase in the revenue account.

Step 2: Was the related cash received in the past or will it be received in the future? Sun-Rype will receive payment from clients for past sales. Because cash will be received IN THE FUTURE, a receivable needs to be increased. Increase trade receivables.

Step 3: Compute the amount of revenue earned. The amount of the revenue that was earned is given as $900. The adjusting journal entry reflects the changes to the accounts.

31/1 — AJE 2		
Trade receivables[4] (+A)	900	
Sales revenue (+R, → + SE)		900

Assets		=	Liabilities	+	Shareholders' Equity	
Trade receivables	+900				Sales revenue	+900

Trade Receivables (A)				Sales Revenue (R)		
Ch. 3 bal.	14,702				Ch. 3 bal.	6,540
AJE 2	900				AJE 2	900
End. bal.	15,602				End. bal.	7,440

Effect of adjustment on
Net earnings: ↑ 900
Cash: No effect

Deferred Expenses

(AJE 3) Prepayments At the beginning of January 2013, Sun-Rype paid a total of $740 for future expenses, including insurance ($160), rent ($450), and advertising ($130). The payment for insurance covers four months: one month has passed (January), and three months of future insurance benefits remain. The payment for rent covers three months: one month has passed, and two months of future rent benefits remain. The payment for advertising relates to February 2013 and has not been used yet. In addition to the payment of $740 in January, Sun-Rype has paid an amount of $502 prior to January 2013 to cover future expenses as reflected on its statement of financial position at January 1, 2013. For illustrative purposes, we assume that this amount relates entirely to prepaid advertising expenses, and that $472 was used in January.

Step 1: Was expense incurred that is not yet recorded? YES. The company used insurance coverage for one month, rental space for one month, and advertising during January, but no entry has been made to record expenses in the appropriate accounts. Record an increase in insurance expense, rent expense, and advertising expense.

Step 2: Was the related cash paid in the past or will it be paid in the future? IN THE PAST. At the beginning of January, Sun-Rype acquired insurance coverage for the next four months and prepaid rent for the next three months. It had also paid for advertising in future periods. The payments were recorded in the Prepayments account, which must now be reduced at month-end because insurance, rent, and advertising have been used during the month. Reduce Prepayments.

Step 3: Compute the amount of expense incurred. One month has expired for the prepaid amounts for insurance and rent, and part of the amount prepaid for advertising has been used:

(1) Insurance: $160 ÷ 4 months = $40 used in January

(2) Rent: $450 ÷ 3 months = $150 used in January

(3) Advertising: $472 (given)

Three expense accounts are affected by the adjustment—insurance expense, rent expense, and advertising expense. The first two expense accounts are categorized as general and administrative expenses, and advertising expense is part of marketing expenses. The adjusting journal entry reflects the changes to the accounts.

31/1—AJE 3

General and administrative expenses (+E, −SE).....................	190	
Sales and marketing expenses (+E, −SE).........................	472	
Prepayments (−A)...		662

Assets		=	Liabilities	+	Shareholders' Equity	
Prepayments	−662				General and administrative expenses	−190
					Sales and marketing expenses	−472

Prepayments (A)				General and Administrative Expenses (E)				Sales and Marketing Expenses (E)		
Ch. 2 bal.	502			Ch. 3 bal.	950			Ch. 3 bal.	0	
Purchased	740	Used	662	AJE 3	190			AJE 3	472	
End. bal.	580			End. bal.	1,140			End. bal.	472	

Effect of adjustment on

Net earnings: ↓ 662

Cash: No effect

(AJE 4) Property, Plant, and Equipment Before illustrating the adjustment process, notice that the property, plant, and equipment account is stated at the original cost of $69,678 in the trial balance but was stated at $44,191 (original cost minus the portion allocated to past operations) in previous chapters. Unlike supplies that are purchased and then used over a relatively short period, property, plant, and equipment represents deferred expenses that will be used over many years. Property, plant, and equipment increases when assets are *acquired* and decreases when they are *sold*. However, these assets are also *used* over time to generate revenue. Thus, a part of their cost should be expensed in the same period (the matching process). Accountants say that these assets depreciate over time as they are used. In accounting, depreciation is an allocation of an asset's cost over its estimated useful life to the company.

To keep track of the asset's historical cost, the amount that has been used is not subtracted directly from the asset account. Instead, it is accumulated in a new kind of account called a contra account. A **contra account** is an account that is an offset to, or reduction of, the primary account. It is *directly related to another account, but has a balance on the opposite side of the T-account.* As a contra account increases, the net amount (the account balance less the contra account balance) decreases. For property, plant, and equipment, the contra account is called *accumulated depreciation*.[5] This is the first of several contra accounts you will learn about throughout the text. We will designate contra accounts with an X in front of the type of account to which it is related (e.g., accumulated depreciation [XA] for contra asset).

Since assets have debit balances, accumulated depreciation has a credit balance. On the statement of financial position, the amount that is reported for property, plant, and

A CONTRA ACCOUNT is an account that is an offset to, or reduction of, the primary account.

equipment is its **carrying amount (book value or net book value)**, which equals the ending balance in the property, plant, and equipment account minus the ending balance in the accumulated depreciation account. For Sun-Rype, accumulated depreciation has a credit balance of $25,487:

The **CARRYING AMOUNT (BOOK VALUE**, or **NET BOOK VALUE)** of an asset is the difference between its acquisition cost and accumulated depreciation, its related contra account.

+	**Property, Plant, and Equipment (A)**	–	–	**Accumulated Depreciation (XA)**	+
Beginning bal.	Sell			Beginning bal.	
Buy				Used	
Ending balance		–		Ending balance	= **Carrying amount**

↑
Amount reported
on the statement
of financial position

Depreciation is discussed in much greater detail in Chapter 9. Until then, we will give you the amount of depreciation estimated by the company for the period. Sun-Rype estimates depreciation to be $4,800 per year.

Step 1: Was expense incurred that is not yet recorded? YES. The company used buildings and equipment during January. Record an increase in the depreciation expense account.

Step 2: Was the related cash paid in the past or will it be paid in the future? Sun-Rype purchased property and equipment IN THE PAST to be used over several years to generate revenue. The acquisitions were recorded in the property, plant, and equipment asset account. The carrying amount must now be reduced to record the depreciation for January. Reduce the carrying value by increasing the accumulated depreciation contra account.

Step 3: Compute the amount of expense incurred. The property, plant, and equipment has been used to generate revenues for one month. Thus, we need to calculate depreciation expense for one month:

Monthly depreciation = $4,800 ÷ 12 months = $400 per month

31/1—AJE 4
Depreciation expense (+E, −SE) 400
    Accumulated depreciation—Property, plant, and equipment (+XA → −A). . .   400

Assets		=	**Liabilities**	+	**Shareholders' Equity**	
Accumulated depreciation—					Depreciation expense	−400
Property, plant, and equipment	−400					

Note that increasing the contra-asset account decreases total assets.

Depreciation Expense (E)			**Accumulated Depreciation—Property, Plant, and Equipment (XA)**		
Ch. 3 bal.	0			Ch. 3 bal.	25,487
AJE 4	400			AJE 4	400
End. bal.	400			End. bal.	25,887

Effect of adjustment on
Net earnings: ↓ 400
Cash: No effect

Accrued Expenses

(AJE 5) Accrued Expenses (Salaries, Utilities, and Interest) By January 31, Sun-Rype owed the following amounts: (1) $50 for use of natural gas and electricity (utilities) during January; (2) $310 to its employees for the last week in January: $150 for distribution and $160 for administrative employees working at its headquarters; and (3) interest on both short-term and long-term borrowings.

Step 1: Was expense incurred that is not yet recorded? YES. During January, the company used gas and electricity, employees' labour, and money borrowed from creditors, but by the end of January, not all of these expenses had been recorded. Record an increase in each of the following expense accounts: general and administrative expenses (for the utilities and the salaries of administrative employees), distribution expenses (for the salaries of distribution employees), and interest expense.

Step 2: Was the related cash paid in the past or will it be paid in the future? IN THE FUTURE. Each of the expenses will need to be paid in the next period, but no liability has yet been recorded. Thus, liabilities on the statement of financial position need to be increased. Although individual liability accounts such as utilities payable, salaries payable, and interest payable could be increased, Sun-Rype records all of these accrued expenses in one account, accrued liabilities. Increase the liability.

Step 3: Compute the amount of expense incurred. Each of the amounts is computed or estimated by Sun-Rype at the end of January. These amounts are as follows:

(1) Utilities: Amount given as $50, which is estimated by Sun-Rype based on reviewing prior utility bills.

(2) Salaries: $150 for distribution employees and $160 for administrative employees.

(3) Interest on borrowings: $102 computed by Sun-Rype based on the total amount borrowed and the interest rate that Sun-Rype is required to pay to creditors for the debt.

31/1—AJE 5

General and administrative expenses (+E, −SE)...................... 210	
Distribution expenses (+E, −SE) 150	
Interest expense (+E, −SE) 102	
Accrued liabilities (+L)	462

Assets	=	Liabilities	+	Shareholders' Equity	
		Accrued liabilities +462		General and administrative expenses	−210
				Distribution expenses	−150
				Interest expense	−102

General and Administrative Expenses (E)				Distribution Expenses (E)		
Bal. from				Ch. 3 bal.	1,131	
AJE 3	1,140					
AJE 5	210			AJE 5	150	
End. bal.	1,350			End. bal.	1,282	

Interest Expense (E)				Accrued Liabilities (L)		
Ch. 3 bal.	0			Ch. 2 bal.		0
AJE 5	102			AJE 5		462
End. bal.	102			End. bal.		462

Effect of adjustment on
Net earnings: ↓ 462
Cash: No effect

(AJE 6) Income Taxes Payable   The final adjusting journal entry is to record the accrual of income taxes that will be paid in the next quarter (an unrecorded expense). This adjusting entry is recorded last because all other adjustments should be incorporated in computing earnings before income taxes (i.e., balances from the unadjusted trial balance plus the effects of all the previous adjustments):

	Revenues and Gains	Expenses and Losses	
Unadjusted totals	$6,885	$5,441	From Exhibit 4.5
AJE 1	10		
AJE 2	900		
AJE 3		662	
AJE 4		400	
AJE 5		462	
	$7,795	− $6,965	= $830 Pretax earnings

Sun-Rype's average income tax rate is 40 percent.

Step 1: Was expense incurred that is not yet recorded? YES. Companies incur taxes on earnings. Hence, income tax expense must be recorded at the end of the period based on all adjusted revenues, gains, expenses, and losses. Record an increase in the income tax expense account.

Step 2: Was the related cash paid in the past or will it be paid in the future? IN THE FUTURE. Income taxes are due at the end of each quarter. So the tax liabilities on the statement of financial position must be increased. Increase the income tax payable liability account.

Step 3: Compute the amount of expense incurred. Income taxes are computed on the pretax earnings after all other adjustments have been made:

$830 pretax earnings × 0.40 = $332 income tax expense for January

31/1—AJE 6
Income tax expense (+E, −SE) 332
 Income taxes payable (+L)..................................... 332

Assets	=	Liabilities	+	Shareholders' Equity
		Income taxes payable +332		Income tax expense −332

Income Tax Expense (E)				Income Tax Payable (L)	
Ch. 3 bal.	0			Ch. 3 bal.	116
AJE 6	332			AJE 6	332
End. bal.	332			End. bal.	448

Effect of adjustment on
Net earnings: ↓ 332
Cash: No effect

In all the adjustments we completed, you may have noticed that *the cash account was never adjusted.* The cash has already been received or paid by the end of the period, or will be received or paid after the end of the period. Adjustments are required to record revenues and expenses in the proper period because the cash part of the transaction occurs at a different point in time. In addition, *each adjusting entry always included one account on the statement of earnings and one account on the statement of financial position.* Now it is your turn to practise the adjustment process.

PAUSE FOR **FEEDBACK**

Adjustments are necessary at the end of the accounting cycle to record all revenues and expenses in the proper period and to reflect the proper valuation for assets and liabilities.

• *Deferred revenues* (liabilities) have balances at the end of the period because cash was received before it was earned. If all or part of the liability has been satisfied by the end of the period, revenue needs to be recorded and the liability reduced.

- *Accrued revenue* adjustments are necessary when the company has earned revenue, but the cash will be received in the next period. Since nothing has yet been recorded, revenue needs to be recognized and an asset (a receivable) increased.

- *Deferred expenses* (assets) have balances at the end of the period because cash was paid in the past by the company for the assets. If all or part of the asset has been used to generate revenues in the period, an expense needs to be recorded and the asset reduced.

- *Accrued expense* adjustments are necessary when the company has incurred an expense but the cash will be paid in the next period. Since nothing has yet been recorded, an expense needs to be recognized and a liability (a payable) increased.

SELF-STUDY QUIZ 4-1

For practice, complete the following adjustments using the three-step process outlined in the chapter: (1) Determine if a revenue was earned or an expense incurred, (2) determine if cash was received or paid in the past or will be received or paid in the future, and (3) compute the amount.

B.C. Flippers, a scuba diving and instruction business, completed its first year of operations on December 31, 2014. For each of the following adjustments, identify the type of adjustment, determine the amount of the adjustment, and record the adjusting journal entry.

AJE 1: B.C. Flippers received $6,000 from customers on November 15, 2014, for diving trips in December and January. The $6,000 was recorded in deferred revenue on that date. By the end of December, one-third of the diving trips had been completed.

AJE 2: On December 1, 2014, B.C. Flippers provided advanced diving instruction to 10 customers who will pay the business $800 in January. No entry was made when the instruction was provided.

AJE 3: On September 1, 2014, B.C. Flippers paid $24,000 for insurance for the 12 months beginning on September 1. The amount was recorded as prepaid insurance on September 1.

AJE 4: On March 1, 2014, B.C. Flippers borrowed $300,000 at a 6 percent annual interest rate. Interest totalling $15,000 has accrued until December 31, 2014, but is payable on March 1, 2015.[6]

	(1) Revenue Earned or Expense Incurred?	(2) Cash Received/Paid in the Past or Cash to Be Received/Paid in the Future?	(3) Amount	Adjustment Journal Entry Accounts	Debit	Credit
AJE 1						
AJE 2						
AJE 3						
AJE 4						

After you complete your answers, check them with the solutions at the end of the chapter.

Materiality and Adjusting Entries

MATERIALITY suggests that minor items that would not influence the decisions of financial statement users are to be treated in the easiest and most convenient manner.

The term "materiality" describes the relative significance of financial statement information in influencing economic decisions made by financial statement users. **Materiality** suggests that minor items that would not influence the decisions of financial statement users are to be treated in the easiest and most convenient manner. An item of information, or an aggregate of items, is material if it is probable that its omission or misstatement would influence or change a decision. It is a practical concept that provides scope for accountants to be cost effective when they record the effects of transactions and prepare financial disclosure. The concept of materiality allows accountants to estimate amounts and even to ignore specific accounting principles if the results of their actions do not have a material effect on the financial statements. This concept is also of particular importance to the audit process. Auditors use professional judgment to decide whether both individual transactions and aggregated small transactions will result in a *material* misstatement of the financial position of the company.

The process of making adjusting entries can be simplified if we account for immaterial items in the easiest and most convenient manner. For example, businesses purchase many assets that provide benefits for a long period of time. Some of these assets have a very low cost, such as pencil sharpeners and wastebaskets. The proper accounting treatment for such assets is to depreciate their acquisition cost to expense over their useful lives. However, the cost of such assets can be directly charged to expense accounts rather than to asset accounts, in accordance with the materiality concept, thus eliminating the need for an adjusting entry to record periodic depreciation expense. Furthermore, adjusting entries to record accrued expenses or revenues may be ignored if the monetary amounts are immaterial.

The accountant's decision to treat a specific item as immaterial depends on a number of considerations and is a matter of professional judgment. Traditional guidelines in the auditing profession imply that an item is material if it exceeds 1 to 1.5 percent of total assets or sales, or 5 to 10 percent of net earnings. Materiality depends on the nature of the item and its monetary value. If an employee has been stealing small amounts of money systematically, these amounts should not be judged as immaterial because they indicate a weakness in the company's internal control system that should be corrected.[7] Accountants must also consider the combined effect of numerous immaterial events. While each item may be immaterial when considered by itself, the combined effect of many items may be material.

ADJUSTMENTS AND INCENTIVES

A QUESTION
OF ACCOUNTABILITY

Owners and managers of companies are most directly affected by the information presented in financial statements. If the financial performance and condition of the company appear strong, the company's share price rises. Shareholders usually receive dividends, and the value of their investment increases. Managers often receive bonuses based on the strength of a company's financial performance, and many in top management are compensated with options to buy their company's shares at prices below market.* The higher the market value, the more compensation they earn. When actual performance lags behind expectations, managers and owners may be tempted to manipulate accruals and deferrals to make up part of the difference. For example, managers may record cash received in advance of being earned as revenue in the current period or may fail to accrue certain expenses at year-end.

Evidence from studies of large samples of companies indicates that some do engage in such behaviour. This research is borne out by enforcement actions of the securities commissions against companies and sometimes against their auditors. These enforcement actions most often relate to accrual of revenue and receivables that should be deferred to future periods. In many of these cases, the firms involved, their managers, and their auditors are penalized for such actions. Furthermore, owners suffer because the company's share price is affected negatively by news of an investigation by a securities commission.

For example, in June 2004, the Ontario Securities Commission (OSC) charged four top management personnel of Atlas Cold Storage Income Trust with misleading investors after the warehouse operator restated two years of earnings. The OSC indicated that, in preparing Atlas Cold's financial statements, the four executives understated some costs and expenses and recorded some expenses in the wrong periods. These errors resulted in overstatements of net earnings for 2001, 2002, and the second quarter of 2003. The restatement (correction) of the company's financial results erased a total of $42.6 million of net earnings for 2001 and 2002, widened the loss for the third quarter of 2003, and caused suspension of payments to investors.

In September 2006, the OSC reached a settlement agreement with Ronald Perryman, the company's vice-president of finance, who "demonstrated a lack of due diligence that contributed, in part, to the presentation of an improved picture of the financial performance of Atlas for the period including the financial years 2001, 2002, and the first two reporting periods of 2003." Perryman agreed (a) to resign all positions as an officer or director of any issuer, (b) not to become or act as a director or officer of any issuer for 10 years, (c) to be reprimanded, and (d) to pay the sum of $20,000 in respect of the costs of the investigation and hearing in this matter.**

*M. Nelson, J. Elliott, and R. Tarpley. "How Are Earnings Managed? Examples from Auditors," *Accounting Horizons,* Supplement 2003, pp. 17–35.

**In the Matter of the Securities Act, R.S.O. 1990, c. S.5, as Amended and in the Matter of Patrick Gouveia, Andrew Peters, Ronald Perryman, and Paul Vickery,* Ontario Securities Commission website. Accessed May 18, 2013.

PREPARING FINANCIAL STATEMENTS

Based on the transactions that have been recorded during January and the adjustments that were recorded at January 31, 2013, we can now prepare financial statements reflecting the operating activities for January. Recall from prior chapters what the four statements are and how they relate to each other:

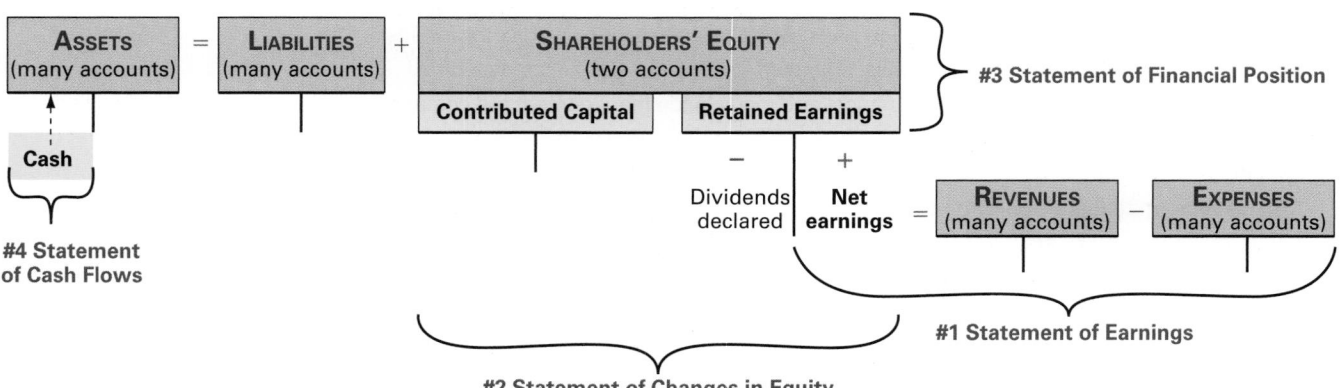

Because net earnings is a component of retained earnings on the statement of financial position, it is necessary to compute net earnings first by preparing the statement of earnings (#1). The statement of changes in equity (#2) is then prepared because it reports the changes and ending balances in contributed capital and retained earnings, providing the connection to the statement of financial position (#3). Finally, the sources and uses of cash are reported on the statement of cash flows (#4), and the ending balance for cash on the statement equals the cash balance on the statement of financial position:

Statement	Formula
#1 Statement of Earnings	Revenues − Expenses = Net Earnings
#2 Statement of Changes in Equity	Beginning Retained Earnings + Net Earnings − Dividends Declared = Ending Retained Earnings Beginning Contributed Capital + Share Issuances − Share Repurchases = Ending Contributed Capital Ending Shareholders' Equity
#3 Statement of Financial Position	Assets = Liabilities + Shareholders' Equity (includes Cash)
#4 Statement of Cash Flows	Cash provided by (or used in) operating activities +/− Cash provided by (or used in) investing activities +/− Cash provided by (or used in) financing activities Change in Cash + Beginning Cash Ending Cash

As you learned in Chapter 1, these four financial statements are interrelated; that is, the numbers from one statement flow into the next statement as indicated in the coloured financial statement elements above. Thus, if a number on the statement of earnings changes or is in error, it will affect other statements. Although shareholders' equity includes three main elements, we report changes to both contributed capital and retained earnings in this chapter, and discuss changes to other components of equity in future chapters. Refer to Exhibit 1.6 of Chapter 1 for an alternative way of presenting the relationships among the four financial statements.

Before we prepare a complete set of financial statements, let us update the trial balance to reflect the adjustments and to provide us with adjusted balances for the statements.[8] In Exhibit 4.6, four new columns are added. Two are used to reflect the adjustments in each of the accounts. The other two are the updated balances, determined by adding (or subtracting) across each row. Again, we note that the total debits equal the total credits in each of the columns. It is from these adjusted balances that we will prepare a statement of earnings, a statement of changes in equity, and a statement of financial position.

Statement of Earnings

The statement of earnings is prepared first, because net earnings is a component of retained earnings. The January statement of earnings for Sun-Rype is based on transactions in Chapters 2 and 3 and adjustments in this chapter. Note that a few of the expense accounts have been combined into specific categories on the statement of earnings.

You will note that the earnings per share (EPS) ratio is reported on the statement of earnings (Exhibit 4.7). It is widely used in evaluating the operating performance and profitability of a company and is the only ratio required to be disclosed on the statement or in the notes to the financial statements. The actual computation of the ratio is quite complex and appropriate for advanced accounting courses. We simplify the earnings per share computation:[9]

LO³

Prepare a statement of earnings with earnings per share, a statement of changes in equity, and a statement of financial position.

$$\text{Earnings per Share} = \frac{\textbf{Net Earnings Available to the Common Shareholders}}{\textbf{Weighted-Average Number of Common Shares Outstanding during the Period}}$$

Exhibit **4.6**

Adjusted Trial Balance for Sun-Rype Products Ltd.

SUN-RYPE PRODUCTS LTD.
Trial Balance
At January 31, 2013
(in thousands of dollars)

	Unadjusted Trial Balance		Adjustments				Adjusted Trial Balance	
	Debit	Credit	Debit		Credit		Debit	Credit
Assets								
Cash and cash equivalents	2,446						2,446	
Trade receivables	14,702		AJE 2	900			15,602	
Notes receivable	50						50	
Inventories	28,689						28,689	
Prepayments	1,242				AJE 3	662	580	
Other current assets	446						446	
Property, plant, and equipment	69,678						69,678	
Accumulated depreciation		25,487			AJE 4	400		25,887
Investments	3,000						3,000	
Goodwill	1,061						1,061	
Liabilities								
Trade payables		26,672						26,672
Provisions		1,687						1,687
Income taxes payable		116			AJE 6	332		448
Short-term borrowings		3,646						3,646
Accrued liabilities					AJE 5	462		462
Deferred revenue		10	AJE 1	10				0
Long-term borrowings		10,081						10,081
Deferred tax liabilities		4,035						4,035
Shareholders' Equity								
Contributed capital		19,721						19,721
Retained earnings		28,681						28,681
Accumulated other comprehensive income	66						66	
Dividends declared	200						200	
Revenues and Gains								
Sales revenue		6,540			AJE 2	900		7,440
Service revenue		40			AJE 1	10		50
Interest revenue		5						5
Gain on sale of land		300						300
Expenses and Losses								
Cost of sales	3,360						3,360	
Sales and marketing expenses			AJE 3	472			472	
Distribution expenses	1,131		AJE 5	150			1,281	
General and administrative expenses	950		AJE 3	190				
			AJE 5	210			1,350	
Depreciation expense			AJE 4	400			400	
Interest expense			AJE 5	102			102	
Income taxes expense			AJE 6	332			332	
Totals	127,021	127,021		2,766		2,766	129,115	129,115

Effects of the adjusting entries

To compute the adjusted balances, add or subtract across each row.

The denominator is the average number of shares outstanding (the number at the beginning of the period, plus the number at the end of the period, divided by two). For Sun-Rype, we use 10,799,000, the average number of shares outstanding as disclosed in its 2012 annual report.

$$\text{Earnings per Share} = \$498{,}000 \text{ net earnings} \div 10{,}799{,}000 \text{ shares}$$
$$= \$0.05 \text{ for January 2013}$$

Exhibit **4.7**

Consolidated Statement of Earnings

SUN-RYPE PRODUCTS LTD.
Consolidated Statement of Earnings
For the Month Ended January 31, 2013
(in thousands of Canadian dollars)

Revenues	
Sales revenue	$7,440
Service revenue	50
Total revenues	7,490
Cost of sales	3,360
Gross profit	4,130
Operating expenses	
Sales and marketing	472
Distribution	1,281
General and administrative	1,350
Depreciation expense	400
Total operating expenses	3,503
Earnings from operations	627
Other non-operating items	
Interest revenue	5
Interest expense	(102)
Gain on sale of land	300
Earnings before income taxes	830
Income taxes expense	332
Net earnings	$ 498
Earnings per share	$ 0.05

As was indicated in Chapter 1, Sun-Rype and all Canadian publicly accountable enterprises are required to prepare a statement of comprehensive income that can be combined with the statement of earnings. The preparation of such a statement is beyond the scope of this textbook.

Statement of Changes in Equity

The final amount from the statement of earnings, net earnings, is carried forward to the retained earnings column of the statement of changes in equity. Dividends declared during January 2013 are deducted to arrive at the ending balance at January 31, 2013. The issuance of additional shares (from Chapter 2) is added to the beginning balance of contributed capital. Other components of equity are unchanged for this illustration:

SUN-RYPE PRODUCTS LTD.
Statement of Changes in Equity
For the Month Ended January 31, 2013
(in thousands of Canadian dollars)

	Contributed Capital	Retained Earnings	Accumulated Other Comprehensive Income	Shareholders' Equity	
Beginning balance	$18,421	$28,681	$(66)	$47,036	
Issuance of shares	1,300			1,300	◄—— From event (a) in Chapter 2
Net earnings		498		498	◄—— From the statement of earnings
Distribution of dividends		(200)		(200)	◄—— From event (f) in Chapter 2
Ending balance	$19,721	$28,979	$(66)	$48,634	◄—— Included in the statement of financial position

Statement of Financial Position

The ending balances for contributed capital, retained earnings, and accumulated other comprehensive income from the statement of changes in equity are included on the statement of financial position. You will notice that the contra-asset account accumulated depreciation has been subtracted from the property, plant, and equipment account to reflect its carrying amount (or net book value) at month-end for financial reporting purposes. Also, recall that assets are listed in order of liquidity, while liabilities are listed in order of time to maturity. Current assets are those used or turned into cash within one year. Current liabilities are obligations to be settled within one year.

In addition to preparing the basic financial statements, companies provide further information about specific elements of these statements in notes that follow the statements. The additional details supporting the reported numbers facilitate analysis of the company's operating performance and financial condition. A closer look at note disclosures related to financial statements is provided in Chapter 6.

SUN-RYPE PRODUCTS LTD. Consolidated Statement of Financial Position At January 31, 2013 (in thousands of Canadian dollars)	
Assets	
Current assets	
Cash and cash equivalents	$ 2,446
Trade receivables	15,602
Notes receivable	50
Inventories	28,689
Prepayments	580
Other current assets	446
Total current assets	47,813
Property, plant, and equipment	43,791
Investments	3,000
Goodwill	1,061
Total assets	**$95,665**
Liabilities and Shareholders' Equity	
Current liabilities	
Trade payables	$26,672
Provisions	1,687
Income taxes payable	448
Short-term borrowings	3,646
Accrued liabilities	462
Total current liabilities	32,915
Long-term borrowings	10,081
Deferred income tax liabilities	4,035
Total liabilities	47,031
Shareholders' equity	
Contributed capital	19,721
Retained earnings	28,979
Accumulated other comprehensive income	(66)
Total shareholders' equity	48,634
Total liabilities and shareholders' equity	**$95,665**

CASH FLOW FROM OPERATIONS, NET EARNINGS, AND THE QUALITY OF EARNINGS

FOCUS ON
CASH FLOWS

As presented in the previous chapters, the statement of cash flows explains the difference between the ending and beginning balances in the cash account during the accounting period. Put simply, the statement of cash flows is a categorized list of all transactions of the period that affected the cash account. The three categories are operating, investing, and financing activities. Since the adjustments made in this chapter did not affect cash, the components of the statement of cash flows presented in Chapters 2 and 3 have not changed.

Many standard financial analysis texts warn analysts to look for unusual deferrals and accruals when they attempt to predict future periods' earnings. They often suggest that wide disparities between net earnings and cash flow from operations are a useful warning sign. For example, Subramanyan suggests the following:

> Accounting accruals determining net income rely on estimates, deferrals, allocations, and valuations. These considerations sometimes allow more subjectivity than do the factors determining cash flows. For this reason we often relate cash flows from operations to net income in assessing its quality. *Some users consider earnings of higher quality when the ratio of cash flows from operations divided by net income is greater* [emphasis added]. This derives from a concern with revenue recognition or expense accrual criteria yielding high net income but low cash flows.*

The cash flows from operations to net earnings ratio is illustrated and discussed in more depth in Chapter 13.

*K. Subramanyan, *Financial Statement Analysis* (New York, McGraw-Hill/Irwin, 2009), p. 412.

NET PROFIT MARGIN RATIO AND RETURN ON EQUITY

KEY RATIO
ANALYSIS

LO4

Compute and interpret the net profit margin ratio and the return on equity.

Evaluating company performance is the primary goal of financial statement analysis. Company managers, as well as competitors, use financial statements to better understand and evaluate a company's business strategy. Analysts, investors, and creditors use these same statements to evaluate performance as part of their share valuation and credit evaluation judgments. In Chapter 3, we introduced the return on assets to examine managers' effectiveness at using assets to generate earnings. We now discuss two other measures of profitability. The net profit margin ratio compares net earnings to the revenues generated during the period, and the return on equity relates net earnings to shareholders' investment in the business.

NET PROFIT MARGIN RATIO

ANALYTICAL QUESTION → How effective is management at controlling revenues and expenses to generate more earnings?

RATIO AND COMPARISONS → The net profit margin ratio is useful in answering this question. It is computed as follows:

$$\text{Net Profit Margin Ratio} = \frac{\text{Net Earnings}}{\text{Net Sales (or Operating Revenues)*}}$$

*Net sales is sales revenue less any returns from customers, and other reductions. For companies in the service industry, total operating revenues equals net sales.

The 2012 ratio for Sun-Rype is

$$\$1,267/\$152,795 = 0.008\ (0.8\%)$$

Comparisons over Time			Comparisons with Competitors	
Sun-Rype			Lassonde Industries Inc.	Leading Brands Inc.*
2010	2011	2012	2012	2012
3.3%	−3.9%	0.8%	4.4%	3.4%

*The fiscal year of Leading Brands ends on February 28, 2013.

INTERPRETATIONS

In General → The net profit ratio margin measures how much profit is earned as a percentage of revenues generated during the period. A rising net profit margin ratio signals more efficient management of sales and expenses. Differences among industries result from the nature of the products or services provided and the intensity of competition. Differences among competitors in the same industry reflect how each company responds to changes in competition (and demand for the product or the service) and changes in managing sales volume, sales price, and costs. Financial analysts expect well-run businesses to maintain or improve their net profit margin ratio over time.

Focus Company Analysis → Sun-Rype's net profit margin ratio dropped to a negative value in 2011 and then recovered to a positive value in 2012. The decrease in 2011 is due to a significant increase in the cost of certain raw materials, including apples and fruit concentrates, in 2011 relative to 2010, which increased the cost of sales and reduced the gross profit significantly, resulting in a loss for the year. Compared with its competitors, Sun-Rype did not perform as well as Lassonde Industries or Leading Brands in 2012 as it was recovering from the loss it incurred in 2011. Despite the return to profitability in 2012, Sun-Rype's management should analyze the various expense items in an effort to better control these costs and continue to improve on its performance.

A Few Cautions → The decisions that management makes to maintain the company's net profit margin ratio in the current period may have negative long-run implications. Analysts should perform additional analysis of the ratio to identify trends in each component of revenues and expenses. This involves dividing each line on the statement of earnings by net sales. Statements presented with these percentages are called *common-sized statements of earnings*, as discussed in Chapter 13. Changes in the percentages of the individual components of net earnings provide information on shifts in management's strategies.

> **SELECTED FOCUS COMPANY NET PROFIT MARGIN RATIOS—2012**
>
> Danier Leather 2.7
>
>
> Canadian Tire 4.4
>
>
> Gildan 7.6

RETURN ON EQUITY

ANALYTICAL QUESTION → How well has management used shareholder investment to generate net earnings during the period?

RATIO AND COMPARISONS → The return on equity (ROE) helps in answering this question. It is computed as follows:

$$\text{Return on Equity} = \frac{\text{Net Earnings}}{\text{Average Shareholders' Equity*}}$$

*Average Shareholders' Equity = (Beginning Shareholders' Equity + Ending Shareholders' Equity) ÷ 2

The 2012 ratio for Sun-Rype is

$$\frac{\$1,267}{(\$46,379 + \$47,536) \div 2} = 0.027\ (2.7\%)$$

Comparisons over Time			Comparisons with Competitors	
Sun-Rype			Lassonde Industries Inc.	Leading Brands Inc.*
2010	2011	2012	2012	2012
9.0%	−5.8%	2.7%	7.7%	4.9%

*The fiscal year of Leading Brands ends on February 28, 2013.

INTERPRETATIONS

In General → ROE measures how much the firm earned as a percentage of shareholders' invest-ment. In the long run, firms with higher ROE are expected to have higher share prices than firms with lower ROE, all other things being equal. Managers, analysts, and creditors use this ratio to assess the effectiveness of the company's overall business strategy (its operating, investing, and financing strategies).

Focus Company Analysis → Sun-Rype's ROE dropped to a negative value in 2011 because its expenses, mainly cost of sales, increased proportionately more than the increase in its rev-enues. This parallels the decrease in its net profit margin over the same period. The company returned to profitability in 2012 and achieved a positive ROE. However, Sun-Rype's ROE for 2012 is significantly lower than those of its competitors. This indicates that Sun-Rype's utilization of resources has generated a lower level of return on shareholders' investment than the managers of Lassonde Industries and Leading Brands were able to achieve.

A Few Cautions → An increasing ROE can also indicate that a manufacturing company is failing to invest in research and development or in modernization of plant and equipment. While such a strategy will decrease expenses and thus increase ROE in the short run, it normally results in future declines in ROE as the company's products, plant, and equipment reach the end of their life cycles. As a consequence, experienced decision makers evaluate ROE in the context of a company's business strategy.

More detailed analysis of ROE and its relationship to other financial ratios is covered in Chapter 13.

SELECTED FOCUS COMPANY RETURNS ON EQUITY—2012

Danier Leather Inc. 6.3

Canadian Tire 10.9

Gildan 10.9

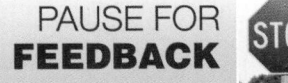

PAUSE FOR FEEDBACK STOP

Adjustments are necessary at the end of the accounting cycle to ensure that all revenues and expenses are recorded in the proper period and to reflect the proper valuation for assets and liabilities. If adjustments are omitted, the reported amounts for assets, liabilities, equity, revenues, expenses, and net earnings will be incorrect and the related ratios are likely to be misleading.

SELF-STUDY QUIZ 4-2

Refer to Exhibit 4.6. Compute the net profit margin for Sun-Rype based on information disclosed in (1) the unadjusted trial balance and (2) the adjusted trial balance. Why are the two ratios different? Is the difference between the two ratios significant? Explain.

After you complete your answers, check them with the solutions at the end of the chapter.

CLOSING THE BOOKS

End of the Accounting Cycle

The statement of financial position accounts are updated continuously throughout the accounting period, and the ending balance for the current period becomes the beginning account balance for the next period. The balances in these accounts,

LO5

Explain the closing process at the end of the period.

PERMANENT (REAL) ACCOUNTS are the statement of financial position accounts whose ending balances are carried into the next accounting period.

TEMPORARY (NOMINAL) ACCOUNTS are statement of earnings (and sometimes dividends declared) accounts that are closed to retained earnings at the end of the accounting period.

CLOSING ENTRIES transfer balances in temporary accounts to retained earnings and establish zero balances in temporary accounts.

INCOME SUMMARY is a temporary account used only during the closing process to facilitate closing temporary accounts.

called **permanent (real) accounts**, are not reduced to zero at the end of the accounting period. For example, the ending cash balance of one accounting period must be the beginning cash balance of the next accounting period. The only time a permanent account has a zero balance is when the item represented is no longer owned or owed.

In contrast, revenue, expense, gain, loss, and dividend accounts are used to accumulate transaction effects for the *current accounting period only*; they are called **temporary (nominal) accounts**. The final step in the accounting cycle, closing the books, is done to prepare statement of earnings accounts for the next accounting cycle. Therefore, at the end of each period, the balances in the temporary accounts are transferred, or closed, to the retained earnings account by recording **closing entries**.

The closing entries have two purposes:

1. To transfer the balances in the temporary accounts to retained earnings.
2. To establish a zero balance in each of the temporary accounts to start the accumulation in the next accounting period.

The special summary account, called **income summary**, is a temporary account used only during the closing process to facilitate closing temporary accounts. It is used to close the revenue, gain, expense, and loss accounts. Accounts with credit balances are closed by debiting the total amount to income summary, and accounts with debit balances are closed by crediting the total amount to income summary. The balance of the income summary account reflects the net earnings (or loss) and is then closed to retained earnings. In this way, the statement of earnings accounts are again ready for their temporary accumulation function for the next period.

Closing entries are dated the last day of the accounting period, entered in the usual format in the journal, and immediately posted to the ledger (or T-accounts). *Temporary accounts with debit balances are credited and accounts with credit balances are debited.* We illustrate the closing process by preparing the closing entries for Sun-Rype at January 31, 2013, although in practice companies close their records only at the end of the fiscal year:

Sales Revenue (R)

Closing	7,440	Sales in January	7,440
		End. Bal.	0

Income Summary (T)

Cost of sales in January	3,360	Sales in January	7,440
...		...	
...		...	
Closing	660		
		End. Bal.	0

Cost of Sales (E)

Cost of sales in January	3,360	Closing	3,360
		End. Bal.	0

Dividends Declared (SE)

Dividends declared in January	200	Closing	200
		End. Bal.	0

Retained Earnings (SE)

		Ch. 3 bal.	28,681
Dividends declared	200	Net earnings	498
		End. Bal.	28,979

Sales revenue (−R)	7,440	
Service revenue (−R)	50	
Interest revenue (−R)	5	
Gain on sale of land (−R)	300	
Income summary (+T)		7,795
To close the revenue accounts to Income Summary.		
Income summary (−T)	7,297	
Cost of sales (−E)		3,360
Distribution expenses (−E)		1,281
General and administrative expenses (−E)		1,350
Depreciation expense (−E)		400
Interest expense (−E)		102
Income tax expense (−E)		332
To close the expense accounts to Income Summary.		
Income summary (−T)	498	
Retained earnings (+SE)		498
To close the Income Summary account to Retained Earnings.		
Retained earnings (−SE)	200	
Dividends declared (+SE)		200
To close the Dividends Declared account to Retained Earnings.		

Post-closing Trial Balance

After the closing process is complete, all of the statement of earnings accounts have a zero balance. These accounts are then ready for recording revenues and expenses in the new accounting period. The ending balance in retained earnings is now up to date (matches the amount on the statement of financial position) and is carried forward as the beginning balance for the next period. A **post-closing trial balance** should be prepared as the last step of the accounting cycle to check that debits equal credits and that all temporary accounts have been closed.

The **POST-CLOSING TRIAL BALANCE** should be prepared as the last step of the accounting cycle to check that debits equal credits and that all temporary accounts have been closed.

ACCRUALS AND DEFERRALS: JUDGING EARNINGS QUALITY

FINANCIAL
ANALYSIS

Most of the adjustments discussed in this chapter, such as the allocation of prepaid insurance or the determination of accrued interest revenue, involve direct calculations and require little judgment on the part of the company's management. In later chapters, we will discuss many other adjustments that involve difficult and complex estimates about the future. These include, for example, estimates of customers' ability to make payments to the company for purchases on account, the useful lives of new machines, and future amounts that a company may owe on warranties of products sold in the past. Each of these estimates and many others can have significant effects on the stream of net earnings that companies report over time.

When attempting to value firms based on their statement of financial position and statement of earnings information, analysts also evaluate the estimates that form the basis for the adjustments. Managers who make relatively pessimistic estimates that reduce current net earnings are judged to be *prudent* in deciding on financial reporting strategies, and the financial reports they produce are given more credence. The resulting net earnings numbers are often said to be of *higher quality* because they are less influenced by management's natural optimism. Firms that consistently make optimistic estimates that result in reporting higher net earnings, however, are judged to be *aggressive*. Analysts judge these companies' operating performance to be of lower quality.

ACCOUNTING STANDARDS FOR PRIVATE ENTERPRISES

The accounting concepts and procedures related to adjusting and closing the appropriate accounts are equally applicable to private enterprises.

DEMONSTRATION **CASE**

We take our final look at the accounting activities of Terrific Lawn Maintenance Corporation by illustrating the activities at the end of the accounting cycle: the adjustment process, financial statement preparation, and the closing process. Chapter 2 presented investing and financing activities, and Chapter 3 presented operating activities. No adjustments had been made to the accounts to reflect all revenues earned and expenses incurred in April, however. The trial balance for Terrific Lawn on April 30, 2014, based on the unadjusted balances in Chapter 3, is as follows:

TERRIFIC LAWN MAINTENANCE CORPORATION
Unadjusted Trial Balance
At April 30, 2014

	Debit	Credit
Cash	5,760	
Trade receivables	1,700	
Prepayments	300	
Equipment	4,600	
Accumulated depreciation		0
Land	3,750	
Trade payables		220
Deferred revenue		1,600
Notes payable		4,400
Utilities payable		0
Wages payable		0
Interest payable		0
Income tax payable		0
Contributed capital		9,000
Retained earnings		0
Mowing revenue		5,200
Fuel expense	410	
Wages expense	3,900	
Insurance expense	0	
Utilities expense	0	
Depreciation expense	0	
Interest expense	0	
Income tax expense	0	
Totals	20,420	20,420

Additional information is as follows:

a. One-fourth of the $1,600 cash received from the city at the beginning of April for future mowing service has been earned in April. The $1,600 in deferred revenue represents four months of service (April through July).

b. Insurance costing $300, providing coverage for six months (April through September), was paid by Terrific Lawn at the beginning of April and has been partially used in April.

c. Mowers, edgers, rakes, and hand tools (equipment) have been used to generate revenue. They have a total cost of $4,600. Depreciation expense is estimated at $456 per year.

d. Wages have been paid through April 29. Wages earned in April by the employees but not yet paid accrue at $130 per day.

e. An extra telephone line was installed in April at an estimated cost of $52, including hook-up and usage charges. The bill will be received and paid in May.

f. Interest accrues on the outstanding notes payable at an annual rate of 6 percent. The $4,400 in principal has been outstanding all month.

g. The estimated income tax rate for Terrific Lawn is 35 percent for both federal and provincial income taxes.

Required:

1. Using the process outlined in this chapter, (1) identify the type of adjustment related to each transaction, (2) determine the amount for the adjustment, (3) record the adjusting journal entries for April, and (4) record the effect of the adjustment on net earnings and cash.

2. Prepare an adjusted trial balance.

3. Prepare a statement of earnings, a statement of changes in equity, and a statement of financial position based on the amounts in the adjusted trial balance. Include earnings per share on the statement of earnings. The company issued 1,500 shares.

4. Prepare the closing entry for April 30, 2014.

5. Compute the company's net profit margin ratio and the return on equity for the month.

6. For each of the items (a), (b), and (c) above, indicate the effect of omitting the required adjustment on the elements of the statement of financial position and statement of earnings. Use O for overstatement, U for understatement, and N for no effect. Ignore the effects of income taxes on overstatements or understatements of revenues and expenses.

	Statement of Financial Position			Statement of Earnings		
Transaction	Assets	Liabilities	Shareholders' Equity	Revenues	Expenses	Net Earnings
(a)						
(b)						
(c)						

We strongly recommend that you prepare your own answers to these requirements and then check your answers with the following solution.

SUGGESTED **SOLUTION**

1. Analysis of deferrals and accruals, and adjusting entries:

(a) *One fourth of the $1,600 cash received from the city at the beginning of April for future mowing service has been earned in April. The $1,600 in deferred revenues represents four months of service (April through July).*

Step 1: Was revenue earned that is not yet recorded? YES. Because the company provided mowing services to clients, the company has earned mowing revenue that is not yet recorded. Record an increase in the revenue account.

Step 2: Was the related cash received in the past or will it be received in the future? The company received cash IN THE PAST from clients for future mowing services and recorded the amount received in the deferred revenue liability account. At January 31, the liability account must be reduced because the company performed the services during the current period.

Step 3: Compute the amount of revenue earned. The amount of the revenue that was earned is $400 (= $1,600 × 1/4). The adjusting journal entry reflects the changes to the accounts.

30/4—AJE a
Deferred revenue (−L) 400
   Mowing revenue (+R, → + SE).   400

Assets	=	Liabilities		+	Shareholders' Equity	
		Deferred revenue	−400		Mowing revenue	+400

Deferred Revenue (L)				Mowing Revenue (R)		
		Ch. 3 bal.	−400		Ch. 3 bal.	5,200
*AJE a	400				AJE a	400
		End. bal.	1,200		End. bal.	5,600

Effect of adjustment on
Net earnings: ↑ 400
Cash: No effect

(b) *Insurance costing $300, providing coverage for six months (April through September), was paid by Terrific Lawn at the beginning of April and has been partially used in April.*

Step 1: Was expense incurred that is not yet recorded? YES. The company used insurance coverage for one month during April but no entry has been made to record the expense. Record an increase in insurance expense.

Step 2: Was the related cash paid in the past or will it be paid in the future? IN THE PAST. At the beginning of April, the company acquired insurance coverage for the next six months. The payment was recorded in the Prepayments account, which must now be reduced at month-end because insurance has been used during the month. Reduce Prepayments.

Step 3: Compute the amount of expense incurred. One month has expired for the prepaid insurance:

(1) Insurance: $300 ÷ 6 months = $50 used in April

30/4—AJE b

Insurance expense (+E, −SE) 50
   Prepayments (−A) 50

Assets	=	Liabilities	+	Shareholders' Equity	
Prepayments	−50			Insurance expense	−50

Effect of adjustment on

Net earnings: ↓ 50

Cash: No effect

Insurance Expense (E)			Prepayments (A)		
Ch. 3 bal.	0		Ch. 3 bal.	300	
AJE b	50				AJE b 50
End. bal.	50		End. bal.	250	

(c) *Mowers, edgers, rakes, and hand tools (equipment) have been used to generate revenue. The company estimates $456 in depreciation each year.*

Step 1: Was expense incurred that is not yet recorded? YES. The company used the equipment during April. Record an increase in the depreciation expense account.

Step 2: Was the related cash paid in the past or will it be paid in the future? The company purchased equipment IN THE PAST to be used over several years to generate revenue. The acquisitions were recorded in the property, plant, and equipment asset account. The carrying amount must now be reduced to record the depreciation for April. Reduce the carrying value by increasing the accumulated depreciation contra account.

Step 3: Compute the amount of expense incurred. The equipment has been used to generate revenues for one month. Thus, we need to calculate depreciation expense for one month:

Monthly depreciation = $456 ÷ 12 months = $38 per month

30/4—AJE c

Depreciation expense (+E, −SE) 38
   Accumulated depreciation—Equipment (+XA → −A)................. 38

Assets	=	Liabilities	+	Shareholders' Equity	
Accumulated depreciation—					
Equipment	−38			Depreciation expense	−38

Note that increasing the contra-asset account decreases total assets.

Effect of adjustment on

Net earnings: ↓ 38

Cash: No effect

Depreciation Expense (E)			Accumulated Depreciation—Equipment (XA)		
Ch. 3 Bal.	0			Ch. 3 bal.	0
AJE c	38			AJE c	38
End. bal.	38			End. bal.	38

(d) *Wages have been paid through April 29. Wages earned in April by the employees but not yet paid accrue at $130 per day.*

Step 1: Was expense incurred that is not yet recorded? YES. The company used employees' labour during April, but the related expense has not been recorded yet. Record an increase in wages expense.

Step 2: Was the related cash paid in the past or will it be paid in the future? IN THE FUTURE. The wages earned by the employees in April will need to be paid in the next period, but no liability has yet been recorded. Thus, liabilities on the statement of financial position need to be increased. Increase the wages payable liability account.

Step 3: Compute the amount of expense incurred. The employees worked for one day, earned $130, but were not paid.

AJE d

Wages expense (+E, −SE)	130	
Wages payable (+L)		130

Assets	=	Liabilities		+	Shareholders' Equity	
		Wages payable	+130		Wages expense	−130

Wages Expense (E)			Wages Payable (L)		
Ch. 3 bal.	3,900		Ch. 3 bal.		0
AJE d	130		AJE d		130
End. bal.	4,030		End. bal.		130

Effect of adjustment on
Net earnings: ↓ 130
Cash: No effect

(e) *An extra telephone line was installed in April at an estimated cost of $52, including hook-up and usage charges. The bill will be received and paid in May.*

Step 1: Was expense incurred that is not yet recorded? YES. The company installed a new telephone line and used it during April, but the related expense has not been recorded yet. Record an increase in utilities expense.

Step 2: Was the related cash paid in the past or will it be paid in the future? IN THE FUTURE. The cost of the new telephone line and related charges will need to be paid in the next period, but no liability has yet been recorded. Increase the utilities payable liability account.

Step 3: Compute the amount of expense incurred. $52 is estimated as incurred in April.

AJE e

Utilities expense (+E, −SE)	52	
Utilities payable (+L)		52

Assets	=	Liabilities		+	Shareholders' Equity	
		Utilities payable	+52		Utilities expense	−52

Utilities Expense (E)			Utilities Payable (L)		
Ch. 3 bal.	0		Ch. 3 bal.		0
AJE e	52		AJE e		52
End. bal.	52		End. bal.		52

Effect of adjustment on
Net earnings: ↓ 52
Cash: No effect

(f) *The note payable of $4,400 has been outstanding all month. Interest on this note is calculated at an annual rate of 6 percent, and an amount of $22 has accrued during April.*

Step 1: Was expense incurred that is not yet recorded? YES. The company used in April funds that it borrowed from creditors in the past. The cost of using the amount of $4,400 during April has not been recorded yet. Record an increase in interest expense.

Step 2: Was the related cash paid in the past or will it be paid in the future? The cost of borrowed funds accumulates over time and will need to be paid IN THE FUTURE, but no liability has yet been recorded. Increase the interest payable liability account.

Step 3: Compute the amount of expense incurred. The amount of interest that accrued was given as $22. It is equal to $4,400 \times 0.06 \times 1/12$.

AJE f		
Interest expense (+E, −SE)	22	
Interest payable (+L)		22

Assets	=	Liabilities	+	Shareholders' Equity
		Interest payable +22		Interest expense −22

Interest Expense (E)			Interest Payable (L)	
Ch. 3 bal.	0		Ch. 3 bal.	0
AJE f	22		AJE f	22
End. bal.	22		End. bal.	22

Effect of adjustment on
Net earnings: ↓ 22
Cash: No effect

(g) *The estimated income tax rate for Terrific Lawn is 35 percent for both federal and provincial income taxes.*

Step 1: Was expense incurred that is not yet recorded? YES. The company incurs taxes on earnings. Hence, income tax expense must be recorded at the end of April based on all adjusted revenues and expenses. Record an increase in the income tax expense account.

Step 2: Was the related cash paid in the past or will it be paid in the future? Income taxes will need to be paid IN THE FUTURE. So the tax liabilities on the statement of financial position must be increased. Increase the income tax payable liability account.

Step 3: Compute the amount of expense incurred. Income taxes are computed on the pretax earnings after all other adjustments have been made. Pretax earnings are computed as follows:

	Revenues	Expenses	
Unadjusted totals	$5,200	$4,310	From trial balance
a	400		
b		50	
c		38	
d		130	
e		52	
f		22	
	$5,600	− $4,602	= **$998 Pretax earnings**

Income tax expense = Pretax earnings ($998) × Income tax rate (0.35) = $349 (rounded)

AJE g
Income tax expense (+E, −SE) 349
   Income taxes payable (+L) 349

Assets	=	Liabilities	+	Shareholders' Equity	
		Income taxes payable	+349	Income tax expense	−349

Income Tax Expense (E)			Income Tax Payable (L)		Effect of adjustment on
Ch. 3 Bal.	0		Ch. 3 bal.	0	Net earnings: ↓ 349
AJE f	349		AJE f	349	Cash: No effect
End. bal.	349		End. bal.	349	

Note that all the adjustments affected net earnings because the revenue and expense accounts had to be increased to record all the revenues earned and the expenses incurred during the period. These adjustments affected specific asset and liability accounts, but none of the adjustments affected the cash account, because adjustments are internal transactions that do not involve an exchange with an outside party.

2. Adjusted trial balance:

TERRIFIC LAWN MAINTENANCE CORPORATION
Trial Balance
At April 30, 2014
(in thousands of dollars)

	Unadjusted Trial Balance		Adjustments				Adjusted Trial Balance	
	Debit	Credit	Debit		Credit		Debit	Credit
Cash	5,760						5,760	
Trade receivables	1,700						1,700	
Prepayments	300			(b)	50		250	
Equipment	4,600						4,600	
Accumulated depreciation		0		(c)	38			38
Land	3,750						3,750	
Trade payables		220						220
Deferred revenue		1,600	(a)	400				1,200
Notes payable		4,400						4,400
Utilities payable		0		(e)	52			52
Wages payable		0		(d)	130			130
Interest payable		0		(f)	22			22
Income taxes payable		0		(g)	349			349
Contributed capital		9,000						9,000
Retained earnings		0						0
Mowing revenue		5,200		(a)	400			5,600
Fuel expense	410						410	
Wages expense	3,900		(d)	130			4,030	
Insurance expense	0		(b)	50			50	
Utilities expense	0		(e)	52			52	
Depreciation expense	0		(c)	38			38	
Interest expense	0		(f)	22			22	
Income tax expense	0		(g)	349			349	
Totals	20,420	20,420	1,041		1,041		21,011	21,011

3. Financial statements:

**TERRIFIC LAWN MAINTENANCE
CORPORATION**
Statement of Earnings
For the Period Ended April 30, 2014

Revenues:		
Mowing revenue	$5,600	
Total revenues	5,600	
Expenses:		
Fuel	410	
Wages	4,030	
Insurance	50	
Utilities	52	
Depreciation	38	
Interest	22	
Total expenses	4,602	
Earnings before income taxes	998	
Income tax expense	349	
Net earnings	$ 649	
Earnings per share	$0.433	← $649 Net earnings ÷ 1,500 shares outstanding

TERRIFIC LAWN MAINTENANCE CORPORATION
Statement of Changes in Equity
For the Period Ended April 30, 2014

	Contributed Capital	Retained Earnings	Total
Balance, April 1, 2014	$ 0	$ 0	$ 0
Issuance of shares	9,000		9,000
Net earnings		649	649
Dividends			0
Balance, April 30, 2014	$9,000	$649	$9,649

TERRIFIC LAWN MAINTENANCE CORPORATION
Statement of Financial Position
At April 30, 2014

Assets			Liabilities	
Current Assets:			**Current Liabilities:**	
Cash		$ 5,760	Trade payables	$ 220
Trade receivables		1,700	Deferred revenue	1,200
Prepayments		250	Wages payable	130
Total current assets		7,710	Utilities payable	52
Equipment	$4,600		Interest payable	22
Less: Accumulated depreciation	38	4,562	Income taxes payable	349
Land		3,750	Notes payable	4,400
			Total current liabilities	6,373
			Shareholders' Equity	
			Contributed capital	9,000
			Retained earnings	649
			Total shareholders' equity	9,649
Total assets		$16,022	Total liabilities and shareholders' equity	$16,022

4. Closing entries:

Mowing revenue (−R)	5,600	
Income summary (+T)		5,600
Income summary (−T)	4,951	
Fuel expense (−E)		410
Wages expense (−E)		4,030
Insurance expense (−E)		50
Utilities expense (−E)		52
Depreciation expense (−E)		38
Interest expense (−E)		22
Income tax expense (−E)		349
Income summary (−T)	649	
Retained earnings (+SE)		649

5. Net profit margin ratio for April:

$$\frac{\text{Net Earnings}}{\text{Net Sales}} = \$649 \div \$5{,}600 = 0.1159 \text{ or } 11.59\%$$

Return on equity for April:

$$\frac{\text{Net Earnings}}{\text{Average Shareholders' Equity}} = \frac{\$649}{(\$9{,}000 + \$9{,}649) \div 2} = 0.0696 \text{ or } 6.96\%$$

6.

	Statement of Financial Position			**Statement of Earnings**		
Transaction	**Assets**	**Liabilities**	**Shareholders' Equity**	**Revenues**	**Expenses**	**Net Earnings**
(a)	N	O, $400	U, $400	U, $400	N	U, $400
(b)	O, $50	N	O, $50	N	U, $50	O, $50
(c)	O, $38	N	O, $38	N	U, $38	O, $38

APPENDIX 4A: AN OPTIONAL RECORDKEEPING EFFICIENCY

In the demonstration case, cash received or paid prior to revenue or expense recognition was recorded in a statement of financial position account. This approach is consistent with accrual accounting, since, on the transaction date, either an asset or a liability exists. Payments or receipts are often recorded, however, as expenses or revenues on the transaction date. This is done to simplify recordkeeping, since revenues or expenses are frequently earned or incurred by the end of the accounting period. When the full amount is not completely incurred or earned, an adjustment is necessary in these cases as well. Note that, regardless of how the original entry is recorded, the same correct ending balances in the deferred revenue and mowing revenue accounts result after the adjustment. The adjusting entry is different, however, in each case.

For example, the company received $1,600 in cash from the city at the beginning of April for mowing service covering four months, April through July. The original entry could have been recorded in a revenue account as follows:

Cash (+A)	1,600	
Mowing revenue (+R, +SE)		1,600

If the company's fiscal year ends on April 30, then an adjusting entry must be made at that date to recognize the portion of the revenue that has not been earned yet. The company provided mowing service for one month and earned only $400 ($1,600 ÷ 4 months). The remaining amount, $1,200, has not been earned yet. Mowing revenue should be reduced by $1,200, and a liability, deferred revenue, should be increased by the same amount.

The adjusting entry and transaction effects follow:

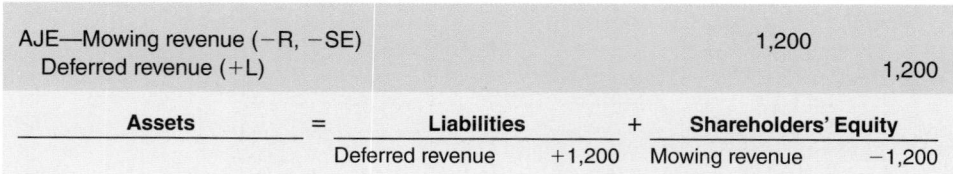

| AJE—Mowing revenue (−R, −SE) | 1,200 | |
| Deferred revenue (+L) | | 1,200 |

Assets	=	Liabilities	+	Shareholders' Equity	
		Deferred revenue	+1,200	Mowing revenue	−1,200

If the company's fiscal year ends on December 31, then no adjustment to the first journal entry is required because the full amount of $1,600 would have been earned during the fiscal year.

CHAPTER **TAKE-AWAYS**

1. **Explain the purpose of adjustments and analyze the adjustments necessary at the end of the period to update statement of financial position and statement of earnings accounts.**
   - Adjusting entries are necessary at the end of the accounting period to measure earnings properly, correct errors, and provide for adequate valuation of financial statement accounts. There are four types of adjustments:
     - Deferred revenues—previously recorded liabilities created when cash was received in advance that must be adjusted for the amount of revenue earned during the period.
     - Accrued revenues—revenues that were earned during the period but have not yet been recorded (cash will be received in the future).
     - Deferred expenses—previously recorded assets (prepaid rent, supplies, and equipment) that must be adjusted for the amount of expense incurred during the period.
     - Accrued expenses—expenses that were incurred during the period but have not yet been recorded (cash will be paid in the future).

   The analysis involves the following steps:

   Step 1: Determine if revenue was earned or an expense was incurred. Record an increase in the revenue or expense account.

   Step 2: Determine whether cash was received or paid in the past or will be received or paid in the future. If in the past, the existing asset or liability is overstated and needs to be reduced. If in the future, the related receivable or payable account needs to be increased.

   Step 3: Compute the amount of revenue earned or expense incurred in the period.
   - Recording adjusting entries has no effect on the cash account.

2. **Use a trial balance to prepare financial statements.**
   A trial balance is a list of all accounts with their debit or credit balances indicated in the appropriate column to provide a check on the equality of the debits and credits. The trial balance may be
   - Unadjusted—before adjustments are made.
   - Adjusted—after adjustments are made.
   - Post-closing—after revenues, expenses, gains, and losses are closed to retained earnings.

3. **Prepare a statement of earnings with earnings per share, a statement of changes in equity, and a statement of financial position.**
   Adjusted account balances are used in preparing the following financial statements:
   - Statement of Earnings: Revenues − Expenses = Net Earnings (including earnings per share computed as net earnings divided by the weighted-average number of common shares outstanding during the period).
   - Statement of Changes in Equity: (Beginning Contributed Capital + Issuance of Shares − Repurchase of Shares) + (Beginning Retained Earnings + Net Earnings − Dividends Declared) = Ending Shareholders' Equity.
   - Statement of Financial Position: Assets = Liabilities + Shareholders' Equity.
   - Statement of Cash Flows—Since adjustments never affect cash, the statement of cash flows is not changed.

4. **Compute and interpret the net profit margin ratio and the return on equity.**
   The net profit margin ratio (net earnings ÷ net sales) measures how much profit is earned as a percentage of revenues generated during the period. A rising net profit margin ratio signals more

efficient management of revenues and expenses. The return on equity measures how well management used shareholders' investment to generate revenue during the period. Managers, analysts, and creditors use this ratio to assess the effectiveness of the company's overall business strategy (its operating, investing, and financing strategies).

5. **Explain the closing process at the end of the period.**

Temporary accounts (revenues, expenses, gains, and losses) are closed to a zero balance at the end of the accounting period to allow for the accumulation of these items in the following period. To close these accounts, debit each revenue and gain account, credit each expense and loss account, and record the difference to retained earnings.

Each year, many companies report healthy net earnings but file for bankruptcy. Some investors consider this situation to be a paradox, but sophisticated analysts understand how this situation can occur. The statement of earnings is prepared under the accrual concept (revenue is reported when earned and the related expense is reported when incurred). The statement of earnings does not report cash collections and cash payments. Troubled companies usually file for bankruptcy because they cannot meet their cash obligations (e.g., they cannot pay their suppliers or meet their required interest payments). The statement of earnings does not help analysts assess the cash flows of a company. The statement of cash flows discussed in Chapter 5 is designed to help statement users evaluate a company's cash inflows and outflows.

KEY **RATIOS**

The net profit margin ratio measures how much each sales dollar generated in net earnings during the period. A high or rising ratio suggests that the company is managing its sales and expenses efficiently. It is computed as follows:

$$\text{Net Profit Margin Ratio} = \frac{\text{Net Earnings}}{\text{Net Sales (or Operating Revenues)}}$$

Return on equity measures how much the firm earned for each dollar of shareholders' investment. It is computed as follows:

$$\text{Return on Equity} = \frac{\text{Net Earnings}}{\text{Average Shareholders' Equity}}$$

FINDING **FINANCIAL INFORMATION**

STATEMENT OF FINANCIAL POSITION

Current Assets	Current Liabilities
Accruals include	Accruals include
Interest receivable	Interest payable
Rent receivable	Wages payable
Deferrals include	Utilities payable
Inventory	Income tax payable
Prepayments	Deferrals include
Non-current Assets	Deferred revenue
Deferrals include	
Property and equipment	
Intangibles	

STATEMENT OF EARNINGS

Revenues
  Include end-of-period adjustments
Expenses
  Include end-of-period adjustments
Earnings before Income Taxes
  Income tax expense
Net earnings

STATEMENT OF CASH FLOWS
  Adjusting Entries Do Not Affect Cash

NOTES
In Various Notes, if Not on the Financial Statements
  Details of accrued liabilities
  Interest paid, interest and dividends
    received, income taxes paid, significant
    non-cash transactions (if not reported on
    the statement of cash flows)

☰connect GLOSSARY

Review key terms and definitions on *Connect*.

QUESTIONS

1. Explain the accounting information processing cycle.
2. Identify, in sequence, the phases of the accounting information processing cycle.
3. Briefly explain adjusting entries. List the four types of adjusting entries, and give an example of each type.
4. What is a trial balance? What is its purpose?
5. What is a contra asset? Give an example of one.
6. Explain why adjusting entries are entered in the journal on the last day of the accounting period and then are posted to the ledger.
7. Explain how the financial statements relate to each other.
8. What is the equation for each of the following: (*a*) statement of earnings, (*b*) the retained earnings component of the statement of changes in equity, (*c*) statement of financial position, and (*d*) statement of cash flows?
9. Explain the effect of adjusting entries on cash.
10. How is earnings per share computed and interpreted?
11. Contrast an unadjusted trial balance with an adjusted trial balance. What is the purpose of each?
12. Why does net earnings differ from cash flow from operations? Explain.
13. What is the practical importance of the concept of materiality to preparers, auditors, and users of financial statements?
14. What is meant by the "quality of earnings"?
15. What is the purpose of closing entries? Why are they recorded in the journal and posted to the ledger?
16. Differentiate among permanent, temporary, real, and nominal accounts.
17. Why are the statement of earnings accounts closed, but the statement of financial position accounts are not?
18. What is a post-closing trial balance? Is it a useful part of the accounting information processing cycle? Explain.
19. How is the net profit margin ratio computed and interpreted?
20. How is the return on equity computed and interpreted?

☰connect EXERCISES

■ **LO2**

E4–1   Preparing a Trial Balance

Swanson Company has the following adjusted accounts and balances at year-end (June 30, 2014):

Accrued expenses payable	150	Income taxes expense	110	Prepayments	40
Accumulated depreciation	250	Income taxes payable	30	Rent expense	400
Buildings and equipment	1,400	Interest expense	80	Retained earnings	170
Cash	120	Interest income	50	Salaries expense	660
Contributed capital	300	Inventories	610	Sales revenue	2,400
Cost of sales	820	Land	200	Trade payables	200
Deferred fees	100	Long-term debt	1,300	Trade receivables	400
Depreciation expense	110				

All of these accounts have normal debit or credit balances.

Required:
Prepare an adjusted trial balance in good form for the Swanson Company at June 30, 2014.

■ **LO1, 2**

E4–2   Identifying Adjusting Entries from an Unadjusted Trial Balance

As stated in its annual report, Unik Computer Corporation is an information technology company, developing and marketing hardware, software, solutions, and services. The following trial balance lists accounts that Unik uses. Assume that the balances are unadjusted at the end of the fiscal year ended December 31, 2015:

UNIK COMPUTER CORPORATION
Unadjusted Trial Balance
At December 31, 2015
(millions of dollars)

	Debit	Credit
Cash	$ 10,200	
Short-term investments	100	
Trade receivables	19,300	
Inventories	7,900	
Prepayments	14,400	
Property, plant, and equipment	18,900	
Accumulated depreciation		$ 8,100
Intangible assets	50,700	
Trade payables		24,200
Accrued liabilities		17,300
Income taxes payable		6,200
Deferred revenue		900
Long-term borrowings		24,700
Contributed capital		14,000
Retained earnings		17,800
Product revenue		91,700
Services revenue		26,300
Interest revenue		400
Cost of products sold	69,300	
Cost of services sold	20,300	
Interest expense	300	
Research and development costs	3,600	
Other operating expenses	14,500	
Income tax expense	2,100	
	$231,600	$231,600

Required:

1. Based on the information in the unadjusted trial balance, list the deferred accounts that may need to be adjusted at December 31 and the related statement of earnings account in each case (no computations are necessary).

2. Based on the information in the unadjusted trial balance, list the accrual accounts that may need to be recorded at December 31 and the related statement of earnings account in each case (no computations are necessary).

3. Which accounts should be closed at the end of the year? Why?

E4–3 **Recording Adjusting Entries and Determining Financial Statement Effects (Deferral Accounts)** ■ LO1
Consider the following transactions for Liner Company:

a. Collected $2,400 rent for the period December 1, 2014, to April 1, 2015, which was credited to deferred rent revenue on December 1, 2014.

b. Paid $1,800 for a one-year insurance premium on July 1, 2014; debited prepaid insurance for that amount.

c. Purchased a machine for $10,000 cash on January 1, 2013. The company estimated annual depreciation of $2,000.

Required:

1. Prepare the adjusting entries required for the year ended December 31, 2014, using the process illustrated in the chapter.

2. For each of the transactions above, indicate the amount and direction of the effects of the adjusting entry on the elements of the statement of financial position and the statement of earnings. Use the following format: + for increase, − for decrease, and "N" for no effect.

	Statement of Financial Position			Statement of Earnings		
Transaction	Assets	Liabilities	Shareholders' Equity	Revenues	Expenses	Net Earnings
(a)						
(b)						
(c)						

■ LO1   **E4–4   Recording Adjusting Entries and Determining Financial Statement Effects (Accrual Accounts)**
Consider the following transactions for Liner Company:

a. Received a $220 utility bill for electricity usage in December to be paid in January 2015.

b. Owed wages to 10 employees who worked three days at $150 each per day at the end of December 2014. The company will pay employees at the end of the first week of January 2015.

c. On September 1, 2014, lent $3,000 to an officer who will repay the loan in one year at an annual interest rate of 6 percent.

Required:

1. Prepare the adjusting entries required for the year ended December 31, 2014, using the process illustrated in the chapter.

2. For each of the transactions above, indicate the amount and direction of the effects of the adjusting entry on the elements of the statement of financial position and statement of earnings. Use the following format: + for increase, − for decrease, and "N" for no effect.

	Statement of Financial Position			Statement of Earnings		
Transaction	Assets	Liabilities	Shareholders' Equity	Revenues	Expenses	Net Earnings
(a)						
(b)						
(c)						

■ LO1   **E4–5   Recording Adjusting Entries**
Evans Company completed its first year of operations on December 31, 2014. All of the 2014 entries have been recorded, except for the following:

a. At year-end, employees earned wages of $6,000, which will be paid on the next payroll date, January 6, 2015.

b. At year-end, the company had earned interest revenue of $3,000. The cash will be collected March 1, 2015.

Required:

1. What is the annual reporting period for this company?

2. Identify whether each transaction above is a deferral or an accrual. Using the process illustrated in the chapter, prepare the required adjusting entry for transactions (a) and (b). Include appropriate dates and write a brief explanation of each entry.

3. Why are these adjustments made?

■ LO1   **E4–6   Recording Adjusting Entries and Reporting Balances in Financial Statements**
Dion Ltée is making adjusting entries for the year ended December 31, 2015. In developing information for the adjusting entries, the accountant learned the following:

a. Paid a one-year insurance premium of $1,800 on October 1, 2015, for coverage beginning on that date.

b. At December 31, 2015, obtained the following data relating to shipping supplies. The company uses a large amount of shipping supplies that are purchased in volume, stored, and used as needed:

Shipping supplies on hand, January 1, 2015	$24,000
Purchases of shipping supplies during 2015	72,000
Shipping supplies on hand, per inventory December 31, 2015	22,000

Required:

1. What amount should be reported on the 2015 statement of earnings for insurance expense? for shipping supplies expense?

2. What amount should be reported on the December 31, 2015, statement of financial position for prepaid insurance? for shipping supplies inventory?

3. Using the process illustrated in the chapter, record the adjusting entry for insurance at December 31, 2015, assuming that the bookkeeper debited the full amount paid on October 1, 2015, to prepaid insurance.

4. Using the process illustrated in the chapter, record the adjusting entry for shipping supplies at December 31, 2015, assuming that the purchases of shipping supplies were debited in full to shipping supplies inventory.

E4–7   Recording Seven Typical Adjusting Entries   ■ LO1

Divtek's Variety Store is completing the accounting process for the year just ended on December 31, 2014. The transactions during 2014 have been journalized and posted. The following data with respect to adjusting entries are available:

a. Wages earned by employees during December 2014, unpaid and unrecorded at December 31, 2014, amounted to $2,700. The last payroll was December 28; the next payroll will be January 11, 2015.

b. Office supplies inventory at January 1, 2014, was $450. Office supplies purchased and debited to office supplies inventory during the year amounted to $500. The year-end count showed $275 of supplies on hand.

c. One-fourth of the basement space is rented to Heald's Specialty Shop for $560 per month, payable monthly. On December 31, 2014, the rent for November and December 2014 had not been collected or recorded. Collection is expected January 10, 2015.

d. The store used delivery equipment that cost $60,500; the estimated depreciation for 2014 was $12,100.

e. On July 1, 2014, a two-year insurance premium amounting to $2,400 was paid in cash and debited in full to prepaid insurance. Coverage began on July 1, 2014.

f. The remaining basement space of the store is rented for $1,600 per month to another merchant, M. Carlos Inc. Carlos sells compatible, but not competitive, merchandise. On November 1, 2014, the store collected six months' rent in the amount of $9,600 in advance from Carlos; it was credited in full to deferred rent revenue when collected.

g. Divtek's Variety Store operates a repair shop to meet its own needs. The shop also does repairs for M. Carlos. At the end of December 31, 2014, Carlos had not paid $800 for completed repairs. This amount has not yet been recorded as repair shop revenue. Collection is expected during January 2015.

Required:

1. Identify each of these transactions as a deferred revenue, a deferred expense, an accrued revenue, or an accrued expense.

2. Using the process illustrated in the chapter, prepare for each situation the adjusting entry that should be recorded for Divtek's Variety Store at December 31, 2014.

■ LO1

E4–8 **Determining Financial Statement Effects of Seven Typical Adjusting Entries**
Refer to E4–7.

Required:

For each of the transactions in E4–7, indicate the amount and direction of the effects of the adjusting entry on the elements of the statement of financial position and statement of earnings. Use the following format: + for increase, − for decrease, and "N" for no effect.

	Statement of Financial Position			**Statement of Earnings**		
Transaction	**Assets**	**Liabilities**	**Shareholders' Equity**	**Revenues**	**Expenses**	**Net Earnings**
a.						
b.						
c.						
etc.						

■ LO1

E4–9 **Recording Seven Typical Adjusting Entries**

Cardon's Boat Yard Inc. repairs, stores, and cleans boats for customers. It is completing the accounting process for the year just ended on November 30, 2015. The transactions during 2015 have been journalized and posted. The following data with respect to adjusting entries are available:

a. Cardon's winterized (cleaned and covered) three boats for customers at the end of November, but did not prepare the bill of $2,700 for the service it provided until December.

b. On October 1, 2015, Cardon's paid $1,200 to the local newspaper for an advertisement to run every Thursday for 12 weeks. All ads have been run except for three Thursdays in December to complete the 12-week contract.

c. On April 1, 2015, Cardon's borrowed $300,000 at an annual interest rate of 4 percent to expand its boat storage facility. The loan requires Cardon's to pay the interest quarterly until the note is repaid in three years. Cardon's paid quarterly interest on July 1 and October 1, 2015.

d. The Kwan family paid Cardon's $4,500 on November 1, 2015, to store its sailboat for the winter until May 1, 2016. Cardon's credited the full amount to deferred storage revenue on November 1.

e. Cardon's used boat-lifting equipment that cost $220,000; the estimated depreciation for fiscal year 2015 is $22,000.

f. Boat repair supplies on hand at December 1, 2014, totalled $16,500. Repair supplies purchased and debited to Supplies Inventory during the year amounted to $46,000. The year-end inventory count showed $12,400 of the supplies remaining on hand.

g. Wages earned by employees during November 2015, unpaid and unrecorded at November 30, 2015, amounted to $3,800. The next payroll date will be December 5, 2015.

Required:

1. Identify each of these transactions as a deferred revenue, a deferred expense, an accrued revenue, or an accrued expense.

2. Using the process illustrated in the chapter, prepare for each situation the adjusting entry that should be recorded for Cardon's at November 30, 2015.

■ LO1

E4–10 **Determining Financial Statement Effects of Seven Typical Adjusting Entries**
Refer to E4–9.

Required:

For each of the transactions in E4–9, indicate the amount and direction of the effects of the adjusting entry on the elements of the statement of financial position and statement of earnings. Use the following format: + for increase, − for decrease, and "N" for no effect.

	Statement of Financial Position			Statement of Earnings		
Transaction	Assets	Liabilities	Shareholders' Equity	Revenues	Expenses	Net Earnings
(a)						
(b)						
(c)						
etc.						

E4–11 Determining Financial Statement Effects of Three Adjusting Entries   ■ LO1, 3

Terbish Company started operations on January 1, 2014. It is now December 31, 2014, the end of the fiscal year. The part-time bookkeeper needs your help to analyze the following three transactions:

a. During 2014, the company purchased office supplies that cost $1,600. At the end of 2014, office supplies of $400 remained on hand.

b. On January 1, 2014, the company purchased a special machine for cash at a cost of $12,000. The machine's cost is estimated to depreciate at $1,200 per year.

c. On July 1, 2014, the company paid cash of $600 for a one-year premium on an insurance policy on the machine; coverage begins on July 1, 2014.

Required:

Complete the following schedule of the amounts that should be reported for 2014:

Selected Statement of Financial Position Amounts at December 31, 2014	Amount to Be Reported
Assets	
Equipment	$_____
Accumulated depreciation	_____
Carrying amount of equipment	_____
Office supplies inventory	_____
Prepaid insurance	_____
Selected Statement of Earnings Amounts for the Year Ended December 31, 2014	
Expenses	
Depreciation expense	$_____
Office supplies expense	_____
Insurance expense	_____

E4–12 Inferring Transactions   ■ LO1

Deere & Company is the world's leading producer of agricultural equipment; a leading supplier of a broad range of industrial equipment for construction, forestry, and public works; a producer and marketer of a broad line of lawn and grounds care equipment; and a provider of credit, managed health care plans, and insurance products for businesses and the general public. The following information is taken from an annual report (in millions of dollars):

Deere & Company

Income Taxes Payable				Dividends Payable				Interest Payable		
	Beg. bal.	71			Beg. bal.	43			Beg. bal.	45
(a) ?	(b)	332	(c) ?		(d)	176	(e) 297	(f)		?
	End. bal.	80			End. bal.	48			End. bal.	51

Required:

1. Identify the nature of each of the transactions (a) through (f). Specifically, what activities cause the accounts to increase and decrease?

2. Compute the amounts of transactions (a), (c), and (f).

■ **LO1**

E4–13   **Analyzing the Effects of Errors on Financial Statement Items**

Cohen & Boyd Inc., publishers of movie and song trivia books, made the following errors in adjusting the accounts at year-end (December 31):

a. Did not accrue $1,400 owed to the company by another company renting part of the building as a storage facility.

b. Did not record $15,000 depreciation on equipment costing $115,000.

c. Failed to adjust the deferred fee revenue account to reflect that $1,500 was earned by the end of the year.

d. Recorded a full year of accrued interest expense on a $17,000, 9 percent note payable that has been outstanding only since November 1 of the current year.

e. Failed to adjust prepaid insurance to reflect that $650 of insurance coverage has been used.

Required:

1. For each error, prepare (*a*) the adjusting journal entry that was made, if any; (*b*) the entry that should have been made at year-end; and (*c*) the entry to correct the error.

2. Using the following headings, indicate the effect of each error and the amount of the effect (i.e., the difference between the entry that was or was not made and the entry that should have been made). Use O if the effect overstates the item, U if the effect understates the item, and NE if there is no effect.

	Statement of Financial Position			Statement of Earnings		
Transaction	Assets	Liabilities	Shareholders' Equity	Revenues	Expenses	Net Earnings
(*a*)						
(*b*)						
(*c*)						
etc.						

3. Explain the concept of materiality and how it might affect the adjusting entries you prepared in (1).

■ **LO1, 3**

E4–14   **Analyzing the Effects of Adjusting Entries on the Statement of Earnings and Statement of Financial Position**

On December 31, 2014, Mica Company prepared a statement of earnings and a statement of financial position but failed to take into account four adjusting entries. The statement of earnings, prepared on this incorrect basis, reflected pretax earnings of $30,000. The statement of financial position (before the effect of income taxes) reflected total assets, $90,000; total liabilities, $40,000; and shareholders' equity, $50,000. The data for the four adjusting entries follow:

a. Depreciation of $9,000 for the year on equipment that cost $75,000 was not recorded.

b. Wages amounting to $17,000 for the last three days of December 2014 were not paid and not recorded (the next pay date is January 10, 2015).

c. An amount of $9,600 was collected on December 1, 2014, for rental of office space for the period December 1, 2014, to February 28, 2015. The $9,600 was credited in full to deferred rent revenue when collected.

d. Income taxes were not recorded. The income tax rate for the company is 30 percent.

Required:

Complete the following tabulation to correct the financial statements for the effects of the four errors (indicate deductions with parentheses):

Items	Net Earnings	Total Assets	Total Liabilities	Shareholders' Equity
Balances reported	$30,000	$90,000	$40,000	$50,000
Effect of depreciation	_____	_____	_____	_____
Effect of wages	_____	_____	_____	_____
Effect of rent revenue	_____	_____	_____	_____
Adjusted balances	_____	_____	_____	_____
Effect of income taxes	_____	_____	_____	_____
Correct balances	======	======	======	======

E4–15 Reporting a Correct Statement of Earnings with Earnings per Share to Include the Effects of Adjusting Entries and Evaluating the Net Profit Margin Ratio as an Auditor   **LO1, 3, 4**

Barton Inc. completed its first year of operations on December 31, 2014. Because this is the end of the fiscal year, the company bookkeeper prepared the following tentative statement of earnings:

Statement of Earnings, 2014		
Rental revenue		$114,000
Expenses:		
Salaries and wages expense	$28,500	
Maintenance expense	12,000	
Rent expense (on location)	9,000	
Utilities expense	4,000	
Gas and oil expense	3,000	
Miscellaneous expenses (items not listed elsewhere)	1,000	
Total expenses		57,500
Net earnings		$ 56,500

You are an independent accountant hired by the company to audit its accounting systems and review its financial statements. In your audit, you developed additional data as follows:

a. Unpaid wages for the last three days of December amounting to $310 were not recorded.

b. The unpaid $400 telephone bill for December 2014 has not been recorded.

c. Depreciation on rental cars, amounting to $23,000 for 2014, was not recorded.

d. Interest on a $20,000, one-year, 10 percent note payable dated October 1, 2014, was not recorded. The full amount of interest is payable on the maturity date of the note.

e. The deferred rental revenue account has a balance of $4,000 as at December 31, 2014, which represents rental revenue for the month of January 2015.

f. Maintenance expense includes $1,000, which is the cost of maintenance supplies still on hand at December 31, 2014. These supplies will be used in 2015.

g. The income tax expense is $7,000. Payment of income tax will be made in 2015.

Required:

1. For each item, (*a*) through (*g*), what adjusting entry, if any, do you recommend that Barton should record at December 31, 2014? If none is required, explain why.

2. Prepare a correct statement of earnings for 2014 in good form, including earnings per share, assuming that 7,000 shares are outstanding. Show computations.

3. Compute the net profit margin ratio based on the corrected information. What does this ratio suggest? If the industry average for net profit margin ratio is 18 percent, what might you infer about Barton?

■ LO3

E4–16   **Evaluating the Effect of Adjusting Deferred Subscriptions on Cash Flows and Performance as a Manager**

You are the regional sales manager for Weld News Company. Weld is making adjusting entries for the year ended March 31, 2015. On September 1, 2014, $12,000 cash was received from customers in your region for two-year magazine subscriptions beginning on that date. The magazines are published and mailed to customers monthly. These were the only subscription sales in your region during the year.

Required:

1. What amount should be reported as cash from operations on the 2015 statement of cash flows?
2. What amount should be reported on the 2015 statement of earnings for subscriptions revenue?
3. What amount should be reported on the March 31, 2015, statement of financial position for deferred subscriptions revenue?
4. Prepare the adjusting entry at March 31, 2015, assuming that the subscriptions received on September 1, 2014, were recorded for the full amount in deferred subscriptions revenue.
5. The company expects your region's annual revenue target to be $4,000.

   a. Evaluate your region's performance, assuming that the revenue target is based on cash sales.

   b. Evaluate your region's performance, assuming that the revenue target is based on accrual accounting.

■ LO1, 3, 5

E4–17   **Recording Adjusting Entries, Completing a Trial Balance, Preparing Financial Statements, and Recording Closing Entries**

Cayuga Ltd. prepared the following trial balance at the end of its first year of operations ending December 31, 2015. To simplify the case, the amounts given are in thousands of dollars. Other data not yet recorded at December 31, 2015, are as follows:

a. Insurance expired during 2015, $4.

b. Depreciation expense for 2015, $4.

c. Wages payable, $8.

d. Income tax expense, $9.

Account Title	Unadjusted Debit	Unadjusted Credit	Adjustments Debit	Adjustments Credit	Adjusted Debit	Adjusted Credit
Cash	38					
Trade receivables	9					
Prepaid insurance	6					
Machinery (20-year life, no residual value)	80					
Accumulated depreciation		8				
Trade payables		9				
Wages payable						
Income taxes payable						
Contributed capital (4,000 shares)		68				
Retained earnings (deficit)	4					
Revenues (not detailed)		84				
Expenses (not detailed)	32					
Totals	169	169				

Required:

1. Prepare the adjusting entries for 2015.
2. Show the effects (direction and amount) of the adjusting entries on net earnings and cash.
3. Complete the trial balance Adjustments and Adjusted columns.
4. Using the adjusted balances, prepare a statement of earnings, a statement of changes in equity, and a statement of financial position.

5. What is the purpose of "closing the books" at the end of the accounting period?
6. Using the adjusted balances, prepare the closing entries for 2015.

E4–18 Preparing Financial Statements, Closing Entries, and Analyzing the Net Profit Margin Ratio and Return on Equity

■ LO3, 4, 5

Liner Company has the following adjusted trial balance at December 31, 2014. No dividends were declared; however, 400 additional shares were issued during the year for $2,000:

	Debit	Credit
Cash	$ 2,700	
Trade receivables	3,000	
Interest receivable	120	
Prepayments	600	
Notes receivable	3,000	
Equipment	12,000	
Accumulated depreciation		$ 2,000
Trade payables		1,600
Accrued liabilities		3,820
Income taxes payable		2,900
Deferred rent revenue		600
Contributed capital (500 shares)		2,400
Retained earnings		1,000
Sales revenue		45,000
Interest revenue		120
Rent revenue		300
Wages expense	20,600	
Depreciation expense	2,000	
Utilities expense	1,220	
Insurance expense	600	
Rent expense	10,000	
Income tax expense	3,900	
Total	$59,740	$59,740

Required:
1. Prepare a statement of earnings in good form for 2014. Include earnings per share.
2. Prepare closing entries and post the effects to the appropriate ledger accounts.
3. Prepare a statement of financial position in good form at December 31, 2014.
4. Compute Liner Company's net profit margin ratio and return on equity for the year. What do these ratios mean?

E4–19 Analyzing and Evaluating Return on Equity from a Security Analyst's Perspective

■ LO4

Papa John's International is one of the fastest-growing pizza delivery and carry-out restaurant chains. Selected statement of earnings and statement of financial position amounts (in thousands) for two recent years are presented below:

Papa John's
International

	Current Year	Prior Year
Net earnings	$ 55,655	$ 51,940
Average shareholders' equity	212,711	196,118

Required:
1. Compute the return on equity for the current and prior years and explain the meaning of the change.
2. Would security analysts more likely increase or decrease their estimates of share value on the basis of this change? Explain.

■ LO4

Telus Corp.

E4–20 **Evaluating Profitability by Using the Net Profit Margin Ratio and Return on Equity**

Telus Corp. is a leading Canadian telecommunications company. It provides a wide range of communications products and services including data, Internet protocol (IP), voice, wireless, entertainment, and video. Selected information about the company's resources and operations for fiscal year 2008–2012 are presented below (amounts in millions of Canadian dollars):

	2012	2011	2010	2009	2008
Total shareholders' equity	$ 7,686	$ 7,513	$7,781	$7,355	$7,108
Total revenue	10,921	10,325	9,792	9,606	9,653
Net earnings	1,318	1,215	1,052	1,002	1,131

Required:

1. Compute the net profit margin ratio and the return on equity for 2009 to 2012.
2. As a potential investor, how do you interpret these ratios?
3. What additional information would you require before deciding whether or not to invest in Telus's shares?

■ LO1

E4–21 **(Appendix 4A) Recording Adjusting Entries**

Consider each of the following independent cases and prepare the adjusting journal entry at year-end.

1. On June 30, 2014, Able Ltd. paid $18,000 for a two-year insurance policy. Insurance coverage started on July 1, 2014. The company's bookkeeper debited insurance expense and credited cash, $18,000. Able's fiscal year ends on January 31, 2015.
2. On August 1, 2014, Landlord Inc. received $6,400 from a tenant representing payment of rent in advance for eight months (including August). Landlord's bookkeeper debited cash and credited rent expense for $6,400. Landlord's fiscal year ends on December 31, 2014.
3. The accountant for Jung Corp. computed the income tax expense for the year 2014 to be $12,200. Before recording the journal entry, she noticed that the unadjusted trial balance at December 31, 2014 (the company's fiscal year-end), included prepaid income taxes of $3,400 and a zero balance for income tax expense.
4. On June 1, 2015, the supplies inventory account for Katz Ltd. showed a debit balance of $4,400. During June 2015, miscellaneous supplies totalling $1,800 were purchased on account and recorded as follows:

Supplies expense	1,800	
Trade payables		1,800

A physical count of supplies available at June 30, 2015, showed that $2,600 of supplies were still on hand. Katz's fiscal year ends on June 30, 2015.

connect PROBLEMS

■ LO2

MEGA Brands Inc.

P4–1 **Preparing a Trial Balance** (AP4–1)

MEGA Brands Inc. designs, manufactures, and markets high-quality toys and stationery products. The company has manufacturing facilities or distribution centres in 14 countries. Its products are marketed worldwide in over 100 countries under leading brands such as MEGA BLOKS, ROSE ART, and BOARD DUDES. The following is a list of accounts and amounts reported in the company's financial statements for 2012. The accounts have normal debit or credit balances and their balances are rounded to the nearest thousand dollars. The company's fiscal year ends on December 31.

Accumulated other comprehensive income	$ 4,745	Long-term debt	113,198
Cash and cash equivalents	8,018	Marketing and advertising expenses	16,937
Cost of sales	262,452	Prepaid expenses	9,370
Current portion of long-term debt	8,023	Property, plant, and equipment	39,817
Financial assets (current)	113	Research and development expenses	16,218
Financial expenses	17,647	Retained earnings (deficit), January 1, 2012	?
Goodwill	30,000	Sales revenue	420,271
Income tax expense	1,642	Selling, distribution, and administrative expenses	87,830
Income taxes payable	5,631	Contributed capital	460,400
Intangibles	22,771	Trade and other payables	62,638
Inventories	45,779	Trade and other receivables	130,541

Required:

Prepare an adjusted trial balance at December 31, 2012. List the accounts in the following order: assets, liabilities, shareholders' equity, revenues, and expenses. How did you determine the amount for retained earnings (deficit)?

P4–2 **Recording Adjusting Entries and Determining Their Financial Statement Effects** (AP4–2)   ■ LO1, 3

Chandra Company's fiscal year ends on June 30. It is June 30, 2015, and all of the 2015 entries have been made, except the following adjusting entries:

a. On March 30, 2015, Chandra paid $3,200 for a six-month premium for property insurance starting on that date. Cash was credited and prepaid insurance was debited for this amount.

b. At June 30, 2015, wages of $900 were earned by employees but not yet paid. The employees will be paid on the next pay date, July 15, 2015.

c. On June 1, 2015, Chandra collected maintenance fees of $450 for two months. At that date, Chandra debited cash and credited deferred maintenance revenue for $450.

d. Depreciation must be recognized on a service truck that cost $19,000 on July 1, 2014. Depreciation of the truck was estimated at $4,000 per year.

e. Cash of $4,200 was collected on May 1, 2015, for services to be rendered evenly over the next year, beginning on May 1 (deferred service revenue was credited).

f. On February 1, 2015, the company borrowed $16,000 from a local bank and signed a 9 percent note for that amount. The principal and interest are payable on January 31, 2013.

g. On June 15, 2015, the company received from the city a tax bill for $500, covering property taxes on land for the first half of 2015. The amount is payable during July 2015.

h. The company earned service revenue of $2,000 on a special job that was completed on June 29, 2015. Collection will be made during July 2015; no entry has been recorded.

Required:

1. Indicate whether each transaction relates to a deferred revenue, a deferred expense, an accrued revenue, or an accrued expense.
2. Prepare the adjusting entry required for each transaction at June 30, 2015.
3. Show the effects (direction and amount) of the adjusting entries on net earnings and cash.

P4–3 **Recording Adjusting Entries and Determining Their Financial Statement Effects** (AP4–3)   ■ LO1, 3

Lamorte Towing Company is at the end of its fiscal year, December 31, 2014. The following data that must be considered were developed from the company's records and related documents:

a. On January 1, 2014, the company purchased a new hauling van at a cash cost of $24,600. Depreciation estimated at $4,000 for the year has not been recorded for 2014.

b. During 2014, office supplies amounting to $1,000 were purchased for cash and debited to supplies inventory. At the end of 2013, the inventory of supplies remaining on hand (unused) was $400. The inventory of supplies on hand at December 31, 2014, was $250.

c. On December 31, 2014, the company completed repairs on one of its trucks at a cost of $1,200; the amount is not yet recorded and, by agreement, will be paid during January 2015.

d. On December 31, 2014, property taxes on land owned during 2014 were estimated at $1,500. The taxes have not been recorded, and will be paid in 2015 when billed.

e. On December 31, 2014, the company completed a contract for another company for $6,000 payable by the customer within 30 days. No cash has been collected, and no journal entry has been made for this transaction.

f. On July 1, 2014, a one-year insurance premium on equipment in the amount of $1,200 was paid and debited in full to prepaid insurance on that date. Coverage began on July 1.

g. On October 1, 2014, the company borrowed $11,000 from the local bank on a one-year, 6 percent note payable. The principal plus interest is payable on September 30, 2015.

h. Earnings before any of the adjustments or income taxes equalled $30,000. The company's income tax rate is 40 percent. (*Hint:* Compute adjusted pretax earnings based on transactions (*a*) through (*g*) to determine the income tax expense for 2014.)

Required:

1. Indicate whether each transaction relates to a deferred revenue, a deferred expense, an accrued revenue, or an accrued expense.
2. Prepare the adjusting entry required for each transaction at December 31, 2014.
3. Using the following headings, indicate the effect of each adjusting entry and the amount of each. Use + for increase, − for decrease, and "N" for no effect.

	Statement of Financial Position			Statement of Earnings		
Transaction	Assets	Liabilities	Shareholders' Equity	Revenues	Expenses	Net Earnings
(a)						
(b)						
(c)						
etc.						

P4–4 **Computing Amounts on Financial Statements and Finding Financial Information (AP4–4)**

The following transactions and events are provided by the records of South Hill Apartments (a corporation) at the end of its fiscal year, December 31, 2014:

Revenue
a. Rent revenue collected in cash during 2014 for occupancy in 2014 $512,000
b. Rent revenue earned for occupancy in December 2014; not collected until 2015   16,000
c. Rent collected in December 2014 in advance of occupancy in January 2015   12,000

Salaries
d. Cash payment in January 2014 for employee salaries earned in December 2013   4,000
e. Salaries incurred and paid during 2014   62,000
f. Salaries earned by employees during December 2014 that will be paid in January 2015   3,000
g. Cash advance to employees in December 2014 for salaries that will be earned in January 2015   1,500

Supplies
h. Maintenance supplies inventory on January 1, 2014 (balance on hand)   3,000
i. Maintenance supplies purchased for cash during 2014   8,000
j. Maintenance supplies inventory on December 31, 2014   1,700

Required:
For each of the following accounts, compute the balance that should be reported in South Hill's 2014 financial statements, indicate on which financial statement the item will be reported, and indicate the effect (direction and amount) on cash flows (+ for increase, − for decrease, and "N" for no effect). (*Hint:* Create T-accounts to determine account balances.)

Account	2014 Balance	Financial Statement	Effect on Cash Flows
1. Rent revenue			
2. Salary expense			
3. Maintenance supplies expense			
4. Rent receivable			
5. Receivables from employees			
6. Maintenance supplies inventory			
7. Deferred rent revenue			
8. Salaries payable			

P4–5 Inferring Year-End Adjustments, Computing Earnings per Share and Net Profit Margin Ratio, and Recording Closing Entries (AP4–5) ■ LO1, 2, 4, 5

Savory Ltd. is completing the information-processing cycle at its fiscal year-end, December 31, 2015. Following are the correct account balances at December 31, 2015, both before and after the adjusting entries for 2015:

	Trial Balance, December 31, 2015						
	Before Adjusting Entries		Adjustments		After Adjusting Entries		
Items	Debit	Credit	Debit	Credit	Debit	Credit
a. Cash	$ 12,600				$ 12,600	
b. Service revenue receivable					560	
c. Prepaid insurance	840				560	
d. Equipment	168,280				168,280	
e. Accumulated depreciation, equipment		$ 42,100				$ 54,000
f. Accrued advertising payable						6,580
g. Contributed capital		112,000				112,000
h. Retained earnings, January 1, 2015		19,600				19,600
i. Service revenue		64,400				64,960
j. Salary expense	56,380				56,380	
k. Depreciation expense					11,900	
l. Insurance expense					280	
m. Advertising expense					6,580	
	$238,100	$238,100			$257,140	$257,140

Required:

1. Compare the amounts in the columns before and after the adjusting entries to reconstruct the adjusting entries made in 2015. Explain each adjustment.
2. Compute the amount of net earnings, assuming that it is based on the amounts (*a*), before adjusting entries, and (*b*), after adjusting entries. Which net earnings amount is correct? Explain.
3. Compute the earnings per share, assuming that 4,000 shares are outstanding.
4. Compute the net profit margin ratio and the return on equity, assuming that contributed capital did not change during the year. What do the computed ratios suggest to you about the company?
5. Prepare the closing entries at December 31, 2015.

■ LO1, 2, 3, 5   **P4–6**   **Recording Adjusting and Closing Entries and Preparing a Statement of Earnings, Including Earnings per Share, and a Statement of Financial Position** (AP4–6)

Mitakis Inc., a small service repair company, keeps its records without the help of an accountant. After much effort, an outside accountant prepared the following unadjusted trial balance as at the end of the company's fiscal year, December 31, 2015:

Account Titles	Debit	Credit
Cash	$19,600	
Trade receivables	7,000	
Supplies inventory	1,300	
Prepaid insurance	900	
Equipment (five-year life, no residual value)	27,000	
Accumulated depreciation, equipment		$12,000
Other assets	5,100	
Trade payables		2,500
Note payable (two years; 7% each December 31)		5,000
Contributed capital (4,000 shares)		16,000
Retained earnings		10,300
Service revenue		48,000
Other expenses, excluding income tax	32,900	
Totals	$93,800	$93,800

Data not yet recorded at December 31, 2015, include the following:

a. Depreciation expense for 2015, $3,000.

b. Insurance expired during 2015, $450.

c. Wages earned by employees not yet paid on December 31, 2015, $1,100.

d. Supplies inventory on December 31, 2015, reflecting $600 remaining on hand.

e. Income tax expense, $2,950.

Required:

1. Prepare the adjusting entries at December 31, 2015.
2. Show the effects (direction and amount) of the adjusting entries on net earnings and cash.
3. Prepare a statement of earnings for 2015 and a statement of financial position at December 31, 2015. Include the effects of transactions (*a*) through (*e*).
4. Compute the net earnings for the year, assuming that you did not make an adjustment to the balance of the supplies inventory account. Does this error cause a material change to net earnings? Explain.
5. Prepare the closing entries at December 31, 2015.

■ LO3, 4, 5   **P4–7**   **Preparing Both a Statement of Earnings and a Statement of Financial Position from a Trial Balance and Closing Entries** (AP4–7)

Juan Real Estate Company (organized as a corporation on April 1, 2013) has completed the accounting cycle for the second year, ended March 31, 2015. Juan has also completed a correct trial balance as follows:

<table>
<tr><td colspan="3" align="center">**JUAN REAL ESTATE COMPANY**
Adjusted Trial Balance
At March 31, 2015</td></tr>
<tr><td>**Account Titles**</td><td align="right">**Debit**</td><td align="right">**Credit**</td></tr>
<tr><td>Cash</td><td align="right">$ 53,000</td><td></td></tr>
<tr><td>Trade receivables</td><td align="right">44,800</td><td></td></tr>
<tr><td>Office supplies inventory</td><td align="right">300</td><td></td></tr>
<tr><td>Automobiles (company cars)</td><td align="right">30,000</td><td></td></tr>
<tr><td>Accumulated depreciation, automobiles</td><td></td><td align="right">$ 10,000</td></tr>
<tr><td>Office equipment</td><td align="right">3,000</td><td></td></tr>
<tr><td>Accumulated depreciation, office equipment</td><td></td><td align="right">1,000</td></tr>
<tr><td>Trade payables</td><td></td><td align="right">20,250</td></tr>
<tr><td>Salaries and commissions payable</td><td></td><td align="right">1,500</td></tr>
<tr><td>Note payable, long term</td><td></td><td align="right">30,000</td></tr>
<tr><td>Contributed capital (30,000 shares)</td><td></td><td align="right">35,000</td></tr>
<tr><td>Retained earnings (on April 1, 2014)</td><td></td><td align="right">7,350</td></tr>
<tr><td>Dividends declared</td><td align="right">8,000</td><td></td></tr>
<tr><td>Sales commissions earned</td><td></td><td align="right">77,000</td></tr>
<tr><td>Management fees earned</td><td></td><td align="right">13,000</td></tr>
<tr><td>Operating expenses (detail omitted to conserve your time)</td><td align="right">48,000</td><td></td></tr>
<tr><td>Depreciation expense (including $500 on office equipment)</td><td align="right">5,500</td><td></td></tr>
<tr><td>Interest expense</td><td align="right">2,500</td><td></td></tr>
<tr><td>Totals</td><td align="right">$195,100</td><td align="right">$195,100</td></tr>
</table>

Required:

1. Prepare a statement of earnings for the reporting year ended March 31, 2015. Include income tax expense, assuming a 30 percent tax rate. Use the following major captions: revenues, expenses, earnings before income taxes, income tax, net earnings, and earnings per share (list each item under these captions as appropriate).

2. Prepare the journal entry to record income taxes for the year (not yet paid).

3. Prepare a statement of financial position at the end of the reporting year, March 31, 2015. Use the following captions (list each item under these captions as appropriate):

Assets
Current assets
Non-current assets

Liabilities
Current liabilities
Non-current liabilities

Shareholders' Equity
Contributed capital
Retained earnings

4. Compute the net profit margin ratio and the return on equity. What do these ratios suggest?

5. Prepare the closing entries at March 31, 2015.

P4–8 **Recording Adjusting and Closing Entries, Preparing a Statement of Earnings Including**   ■ LO1, 2, 3, 4, 5
Earnings per Share, and Preparing a Statement of Financial Position (AP4–8)
It is your first day on the job as a trainee for an entry position in the accounting department of Alimex Inc., a merchandising company. The company controller provides you with the following *unadjusted* trial balance as at December 31, 2014, with accounts listed in alphabetical order:

	Debit	Credit
Accumulated depreciation, equipment		$ 9,000
Cash	$ 11,000	
Contributed capital (15,000 shares)		60,000
Cost of sales	129,000	
Deferred revenue		11,240
Equipment, at cost	60,000	
Merchandise inventory	18,200	
Other operating expenses	1,400	
Note receivable, due December 31, 2015	24,000	
Prepaid income taxes	1,040	
Prepaid rent	16,800	
Rent expense	11,000	
Retained earnings, January 1, 2014		70,000
Sales revenue		301,000
Trade payables		33,000
Trade receivables	100,000	
Wages expense	111,800	
	$484,240	$484,240

Additional information is as follows:

a. Wages owed to employees totalled $8,000 as at December 31, 2014.

b. The note receivable was obtained by Alimex on September 1, 2014. The note carries an annual interest rate of 5 percent, payable to Alimex at maturity only.

c. The balance in prepaid rent represents a payment August 1, 2014, for 12 months of rent, beginning on that date.

d. The equipment has a useful life of 20 years. Depreciation expense for 2014 was estimated at $3,000.

e. Cash dividends of $1 per share were declared on December 31, 2014, payable on January 25, 2015.

f. The company is subject to an income tax rate of 20 percent. Income taxes are due March 15, 2015.

Journal entries related to these transactions have not been recorded yet.

Required:

1. Prepare in proper form the adjusting journal entries as at December 31, 2014, for items (*a*) through (*f*) above. Create new accounts, if necessary. (*Hint:* Complete (2) before making the adjusting entry related to item (*f*).)

2. Show the effects (direction and amount) of the adjusting entries on net earnings and cash.

3. Prepare a multiple-step statement of earnings for the year ended December 31, 2014. Alimex did not issue or repurchase any shares during 2014.

4. Prepare a classified statement of financial position as at December 31, 2014.

5. Prepare the closing entries at December 31, 2014.

6. Compute the net profit margin ratio and total asset turnover for 2014, and explain the meaning of each ratio. Total assets equalled $200,000 at January 1, 2014.

■ LO4   **P4–9**   **Using Financial Reports: Evaluating Profitability by Using the Net Profit Margin Ratio and Return on Equity**

The Jean Coutu Group

Metro Inc.

Shoppers Drug Mart Corporation

A summary of selected historical results is presented below for three Canadian companies: The Jean Coutu Group, Metro Inc., and Shoppers Drug Mart Corporation, which was acquired by Loblaw Companies Limited in 2013. Each of these companies has grown in size over time by acquiring assets and investing in other companies. (Amounts are in millions of dollars.)

	2012	2011	2010	2009
The Jean Coutu Group				
Total shareholders' equity	$ 1,111	$ 1,073	$ 1,060	$ 996
Total revenue	2,740	2,733	2,613	
Net earnings	558	230	183	
Operating cash flow	224	245	214	
Metro Inc.				
Total shareholders' equity	2,545	2,399	2,443	2,264
Total revenue	12,011	11,396	11,343	
Net earnings	489	393	392	
Operating cash flow	780	744	548	
Shoppers Drug Mart Corporation				
Total shareholders' equity	4,323	4,268	4,103	3,712
Total revenue	10,782	10,459	10,193	
Net earnings	608	614	592	
Operating cash flow	917	974	828	

Required:

1. Compute the net profit margin ratio and the return on equity for each company for each of the years 2010–2012 using the table below:

	2012	2011	2010
The Jean Coutu Group			
Net profit margin			
Return on equity (ROE)			
Quality of earnings			
Metro Inc.			
Net profit margin			
Return on equity (ROE)			
Quality of earnings			
Shoppers Drug Mart Corporation			
Net profit margin			
Return on equity (ROE)			
Quality of earnings			

2. Based on the computed ratios, rank these companies from most successful to least successful in generating net earnings for shareholders.

3. Assume that you are interested in investing in one of these three companies. Which company would you choose? Write a brief report to justify your choice.

4. Analysts examine both net earnings and cash flow from operating activities in evaluating a company. One measure that relates these two numbers is the quality of earnings ratio, which equals cash flow from operations divided by net earnings. The higher the ratio, the higher the quality of earnings. Compute this ratio for 2010–2012, and rank the three companies from highest to lowest, based on the quality of their earnings.

P4–10 Recording Journal Entries and Inferring Adjustments   ■ LO1

Stay'N Shape was started by Jennifer Long several years ago to provide physical fitness services to its customers. The following balances were extracted from the company's general ledger as at the following dates:

	May 31, 2014	April 30, 2014
Deferred revenue	$ 4,500	$ 3,000
Trade receivables	44,000	59,000
Prepaid rent	?	4,900
Prepaid insurance	?	1,200
Notes payable	20,000	20,000
Supplies inventory	?	7,200
Supplies expense	17,200	

Additional information about several transactions that occurred in May is provided below:

a. Some customers pay for services in advance. The remaining customers are sent invoices for services used and are allowed one month to pay their invoices. During May, the company received from customers a total of $62,000 in cash, including an amount of $7,000 that was paid by customers in advance.

b. At the end of April, the company paid rent for the next five months and recorded the amount as prepaid rent.

c. The balance of prepaid insurance at April 30 represents the cost of insuring the company's premises and equipment for one month. In May, the company received an invoice from the insurance company for a renewal of the company's insurance policy for one year. The insurance premium was increased by 10 percent over the amount of the premium of the previous year because the company filed a few insurance claims. The company paid the one-year insurance premium.

d. The note payable carries annual interest of 6 percent and is due on June 30, 2014, along with accrued interest. The company recognizes interest expense on a monthly basis.

e. An invoice for $780 pertaining to advertising work done during May was received on May 2.

f. Supplies amounting to $17,200 were purchased on account during May and debited to the supplies expense account. A physical count of supplies on hand on May 31 valued the inventory at $11,500.

Required:
Prepare journal entries to record the following transactions and events:
1. The receipt of cash from customers and the recognition of all revenues earned in May.
2. Rent expense for May.
3. Payment of the premium for the new insurance policy.
4. Interest expense that accrued in May.
5. The invoice for advertising work, received on May 2.
6. The adjustment to the supplies inventory account.

ALTERNATE PROBLEMS

■ **LO2**

AP4–1   **Preparing a Trial Balance** (P4–1)

Starbucks Corporation

Starbucks Corporation purchases and roasts high-quality, whole-bean coffees and sells them along with fresh-brewed coffees, Italian-style espresso beverages, a variety of pastries and confections, coffee-related accessories and equipment, and a line of premium teas. In addition to sales through its company-operated retail stores, Starbucks also sells coffee and tea products through other distribution channels. The following is a simplified list of accounts and amounts reported in financial statements. The accounts have normal debit or credit balances and the dollars are rounded to the nearest million. Assume the year ended on September 30, 2012.

Accrued liabilities	$1,174	Goodwill	399	Other operating expenses	430
Cash and cash equivalents	1,189	Income tax expense	674	Prepayments	196
Contributed capital	68	Interest expense	33	Property, plant, and	
Cost of sales	5,813	Interest revenue	305	equipment, net	2,659
Deferred income tax assets	239	Inventories	1,242	Retained earnings,	
Depreciation and		Long-term investments	576	beginning of year	?
amortization expense	550	Long-term debt	549	Short-term investments	848
Deferred revenue	678	Net sales revenues	13,300	Store operating expenses	3,918
General and administrative		Other assets	386	Trade payables	398
expenses	801	Other long-term liabilities	345	Trade receivables	486

Required:
Prepare an adjusted trial balance at September 30, 2012. How did you determine the amount for retained earnings?

■ **LO1, 3**

AP4–2   **Recording Adjusting Entries and Determining Their Financial Statement Effects** (P4–2)

eXcel

Zumra Company's annual accounting year ends on December 31. It is December 31, 2015, and all of the 2015 entries have been made, except the following adjusting entries:

a. On September 1, 2015, Zumra collected six months' rent of $8,400 on storage space. At that date, Zumra debited cash and credited deferred rent revenue for $8,400.

b. On October 1, 2015, the company borrowed $18,000 from a local bank and signed a 5 percent note for that amount. The principal and interest are payable on the maturity date, September 30, 2016.

c. Depreciation of $2,500 must be recognized on a service truck purchased on July 1, 2015, at a cost of $15,000.

d. Cash of $3,000 was collected on November 1, 2015, for services to be rendered evenly over the next year beginning on November 1. Deferred service revenue was credited when the cash was received.

e. On November 1, 2015, Zumra paid a one-year premium for property insurance, $9,000, for coverage starting on that date. Cash was credited and prepaid insurance was debited for this amount.

f. The company earned service revenue of $4,000 on a special job that was completed December 29, 2015. Collection will be made during January 2016. No entry has been recorded.

g. At December 31, 2015, wages earned by employees totalled $14,000. The employees will be paid on the next payroll date, January 15, 2016.

h. On December 31, 2015, the company estimated it owed $500 for 2015 property taxes on land. The tax will be paid when the bill is received in January 2016.

Required:

1. Indicate whether each transaction relates to a deferred revenue, a deferred expense, an accrued revenue, or an accrued expense.
2. Prepare the adjusting entry required for each transaction at December 31, 2015.
3. Show the effects (direction and amount) of the adjusting entries on net earnings and cash.

AP4–3 **Recording Adjusting Entries and Determining Their Financial Statement Effects** (P4–3)   ■ LO1, 3
Bill's Catering Company is at its accounting year-end, December 31, 2015. The following data that must be considered were developed from the company's records and related documents:

a. During 2015, office supplies amounting to $1,200 were purchased for cash and debited in full to supplies inventory. At the beginning of 2015, the supplies on hand amounted to $450. The inventory of supplies at December 31, 2015 was $400.

b. On December 31, 2015, the company catered an evening gala for a local celebrity. The $7,500 bill was payable by the end of January 2016. No cash has been collected, and no journal entry has been made for this transaction. (Ignore cost of sales.)

c. On October 1, 2015, a one-year insurance premium on equipment in the amount of $1,200 was paid and debited in full to prepaid insurance on that date. Coverage began on November 1.

d. On December 31, 2015, repairs on one of the company's delivery vans were completed at a cost estimate of $600; the amount has not yet been paid or recorded. The repair shop will bill Bill's Catering at the beginning of January 2016.

e. In November 2015, Bill's Catering signed a lease for a new retail location, providing a down payment of $2,100 in rent for the first three months. The amount was debited to prepaid rent. The lease began on December 1, 2015.

f. On July 1, 2015, the company purchased new refrigerated display counters at a cash cost of $18,000. Depreciation of $2,600 has not been recorded for 2015.

g. On November 1, 2015, the company lent $4,000 to one of its employees on a one-year, 3 percent note. The principal plus interest is payable by the employee on October 31, 2016.

h. Earnings before any of the adjustments or income taxes totalled $22,400. The company's income tax rate is 30 percent. Compute the adjusted net earnings, taking into consideration transactions (a) through (g) to determine the income tax expense for 2015.

Required:

1. Indicate whether each transaction relates to a deferred revenue, a deferred expense, an accrued revenue, or an accrued expense.
2. Prepare the adjusting entries required at December 31, 2015, for transactions (a) through (g).
3. Using the following headings, indicate the effect of each adjusting entry and the amount of each. Use + for increase, − for decrease, and "N" for no effect:

	Statement of Financial Position			Statement of Earnings		
Transaction	Assets	Liabilities	Shareholders' Equity	Revenues	Expenses	Net Earnings
(a)						
(b)						
(c)						
etc.						

■ LO1

AP4–4   **Computing Amounts on Financial Statements and Finding Financial Information** (P4–4)

The following transactions and events are provided by the records of Deerfield Cleaning (a corporation) at the end of its fiscal year, December 31, 2015:

Cash Receipts and Revenue

a. Cash collected in January 2015 for the only cleaning contracts completed in past years that were not yet paid by customers .... $ 11,000

b. Service revenue collected in cash during 2015 for cleaning contracts in 2015 213,000

c. Service revenue earned for contracts in December 2015 but not collected until 2016 14,000

d. Amount collected in advance in December 2015 for service to be provided in January 2016 19,000

Salaries

e. Cash payment made in January 2015 for employee salaries earned in 2014; no other amounts were due to employees for past periods 1,500

f. Salaries incurred and paid during 2015 78,000

g. Salaries earned by employees during December 2015 that will be paid in January 2016 1,900

Supplies

h. Cleaning supplies inventory on January 1, 2015 1,800

i. Cleaning supplies purchased for cash during 2015 14,500

j. Cleaning supplies inventory on December 31, 2015 2,700

Required:

For each of the following accounts, compute the balance that should be reported in Deerfield's 2015 financial statements, indicate on which financial statement the item will be reported, and report the effect (direction and amount) on cash flows (+ for increase, − for decrease, and "N" for no effect). (*Hint:* Create T-accounts to determine account balances.)

Account	2015 Balance	Financial Statement	Effect on Cash Flows
1. Service revenue			
2. Cleaning supplies expense			
3. Trade receivables			
4. Wages expense			
5. Cleaning supplies inventory			
6. Deferred revenue			
7. Wages payable			

■ LO1, 2, 4, 5   **AP4–5**   **Inferring Year-End Adjustments, Computing Earnings per Share and the Net Profit Margin Ratio, and Recording Closing Entries** (P4–5)

Gilca Ltd. is completing the information-processing cycle at the end of its fiscal year, December 31, 2014. The correct account balances at December 31, 2014, both before and after the adjusting entries for 2014, are shown below:

| | Trial Balance, December 31, 2014 | | | | | |
| | Before Adjusting Entries | | Adjustments | | After Adjusting Entries | |
Items	Debit	Credit	Debit	Credit	Debit	Credit
a. Cash	$ 18,000				$ 18,000	
b. Service revenue receivable					1,500	
c. Prepayments	1,200				800	
d. Property, plant, and equipment	210,000				210,000	
e. Accumulated depreciation, PP&E		$ 52,500				$ 70,000
f. Income taxes payable						6,500
g. Deferred revenue		16,000				8,000
h. Contributed capital		110,000				110,000
i. Retained earnings, January 1, 2014		21,700				21,700
j. Service revenue		83,000				92,500
k. Salary expense	54,000				54,000	
l. Depreciation expense					17,500	
m. Rent expense					400	
n. Income tax expense					6,500	
	$283,200	$283,200			$308,700	$308,700

Required:

1. Compare the amounts in the columns before and after the adjusting entries to reconstruct the adjusting entries made in 2014. Explain each adjustment.

2. Compute the net earnings for 2014, assuming that it is based on the amounts (*a*) before adjusting entries and (*b*) after adjusting entries. Which net earnings amount is correct? Explain.

3. Compute the earnings per share, assuming that 5,000 shares are outstanding.

4. Compute the net profit margin ratio and the return on equity, assuming that contributed capital did not change during the year. What do the computed ratios suggest to you about the company?

5. Prepare the closing entries at December 31, 2014.

AP4–6 Recording Adjusting and Closing Entries, Preparing a Statement of Earnings Including Earnings per Share, and Preparing a Statement of Financial Position (P4–6)   ■ LO1, 2, 3, 5

Sutton Inc., a small service company, keeps its records without the help of an accountant. After much effort, an outside accountant prepared the following unadjusted trial balance as at the end of the company's fiscal year, December 31, 2014:

Account Titles	Debit	Credit
Cash	$ 60,000	
Trade receivables	13,000	
Service supplies inventory	800	
Prepaid insurance	1,000	
Service trucks (five-year life, no residual value)	20,000	
Accumulated depreciation, service trucks		$ 12,000
Other assets	11,200	
Trade payables		3,000
Note payable (three years; 5% each December 31)		20,000
Contributed capital (5,000 shares outstanding)		28,200
Retained earnings		7,500
Service revenue		77,000
Other expenses, excluding income tax	41,700	
Totals	$147,700	$147,700

Data not yet recorded at December 31, 2014, were as follows:

a. Supplies inventory on December 31, 2014, reflecting $200 remaining on hand.

b. Insurance expired during 2014, $400.

c. Depreciation expense for 2014, $4,000.

d. Wages earned by employees not yet paid on December 31, 2014, $1,100.

e. Income tax expense, $7,350.

Required:

1. Prepare the adjusting entries at December 31, 2014.

2. Show the effects (direction and amount) of the adjusting entries on net earnings and cash.

3. Prepare a statement of earnings for 2014 and a statement of financial position at December 31, 2014, including the effects of transactions (*a*) through (*e*).

4. Assume that you forgot to adjust the balance of the service supplies inventory account. How would this error affect the amount of net earnings for the year? Does this error lead to a material effect on net earnings? Explain.

5. Prepare the closing entries at December 31, 2014.

■ LO3, 4, 5   **AP4–7**   **Preparing Both a Statement of Earnings and a Statement of Financial Position from a Trial Balance (P4–7)**

ACME Pest Control Services (organized as a corporation on September 1, 2012) has completed the accounting cycle for the second year, ended August 31, 2014. ACME Pest Control has also completed a correct trial balance as follows:

ACME PEST CONTROL SERVICES Trial Balance At August 31, 2014		
Account Titles	**Debit**	**Credit**
Cash	$ 26,000	
Trade receivables	30,800	
Supplies inventory	1,300	
Service vehicles (company vans)	60,000	
Accumulated depreciation, automobiles		$ 20,000
Equipment	14,000	
Accumulated depreciation, equipment		4,000
Trade payables		16,700
Salaries payable		1,100
Note payable, long term		34,000
Contributed capital (10,000 shares)		40,000
Retained earnings (on September 1, 2013)		4,300
Dividends declared	2,000	
Sales revenue		38,000
Maintenance contract revenue		17,000
Operating expenses (detail omitted to conserve your time)	27,000	
Depreciation expense (including $2,000 on equipment)	12,000	
Interest expense	2,000	
Totals	$175,100	$175,100

Required:

1. Prepare a statement of earnings for the reporting year ended August 31, 2014. Include income tax expense, assuming a 30 percent tax rate. Use the following major captions: revenues, expenses, net earnings before income tax, income tax, net earnings, and earnings per share (list each item under these captions as appropriate).

2. Prepare the journal entry to record income taxes for the year (not yet paid).

3. Prepare a statement of financial position at the end of the reporting year, August 31, 2014. Use the following captions (list each item under these captions as appropriate):

Assets

Current assets

Non-current assets

Liabilities

Current liabilities

Non-current liabilities

Shareholders' Equity

Contributed capital

Retained earnings

4. Compute the net profit margin ratio and the return on equity. What do these ratios suggest?

5. Prepare the closing entries at August 31, 2014.

AP4–8 Recording Adjusting and Closing Entries, Preparing a Statement of Earnings Including Earnings per Share, and Preparing a Statement of Financial Position (P4–8)

■ LO1, 2, 3, 4, 5

Claudia Pederzolli is enrolled in a co-op program in accounting that provides an opportunity for alternating study and work terms. For her second work term, Claudia was offered a position at the local branch of a CPA firm. After three weeks on the job, she was asked to assist her supervisor in preparing the financial statements of Sakura Ltd., a long-time client of the CPA firm. Claudia was provided with the following *unadjusted* trial balance for Sakura Ltd. as at December 31, 2014, as well as additional information to prepare the required financial statements:

	Debit	Credit
Cash	$ 247,000	
Trade receivables	485,000	
Note receivable	60,000	
Property, plant, and equipment	500,000	
Accumulated depreciation		$ 140,625
Trade payables		70,400
Note payable		30,000
Deferred rent revenue		6,000
Contributed capital (100,000 shares)		620,000
Retained earnings—January 1, 2014		165,000
Sales revenue		999,000
Cost of sales	502,000	
Salaries expense	222,000	
Other operating expenses	15,025	
	$2,031,025	$2,031,025

Additional information is as follows:

a. The company lent $60,000 to an employee on October 1, 2014, and recorded the note receivable. According to the terms of the note, interest at an annual rate of 5 percent will be paid when the note matures on March 15, 2016.

b. The company borrowed $30,000 on December 1, 2014, and signed a note, payable at December 31, 2015. Interest on the note is 4 percent per year and is payable at the beginning of each month, starting January 1, 2015.

c. A portion of the building was rented to Senecal Inc. on November 1, 2014, for three months for a total amount of $6,000. Sakura received the amount in cash from Senecal on that date and recorded it as deferred rent revenue.

d. Depreciation on the property, plant, and equipment was estimated at $15,625 for 2014.

e. Dividends of $0.60 per share were declared in December 2014, payable January 15, 2015.

f. Sakura Ltd. is subject to an income tax rate of 30 percent. The company will pay income taxes on March 15, 2015.

Journal entries related to these events have not been recorded yet.

Required:

Assume the role of Claudia Pederzolli and answer the following requirements:

1. Prepare the adjusting journal entries as at December 31, 2014, for items (*a*) through (*f*) above. Create new accounts, if necessary. (*Hint:* Complete (2) before making the adjusting entry related to item (*f*).)

2. Show the effects (direction and amount) of the adjusting entries on net earnings and cash.

3. Prepare a multiple-step statement of earnings for the year ended December 31, 2014. Sakura Ltd. did not issue or repurchase any shares during 2014.

4. Prepare a classified statement of financial position as at December 31, 2014.

5. Prepare the closing entries at December 31, 2014.

6. Compute the net profit margin ratio and the return on equity for 2014, and explain the meaning of each ratio.

COMPREHENSIVE PROBLEMS (CHAPTERS 1–4)

■ **LO**1, 2, 3, 4, 5

COMP4–1

Recording Transactions (Including Adjusting and Closing Entries), Preparing a Complete Set of Financial Statements, and Performing Ratio Analysis

Brothers Anthony and Christopher Gaber began operations of their tool and die shop (A & C Tools Inc.) on January 1, 2013. The company's fiscal year ends on December 31. The trial balance on January 1, 2014, was as follows:

Account No.	Account Titles	Debit	Credit
01	Cash	$ 3,000	
02	Trade receivables	5,000	
03	Service supplies inventory	12,000	
04	Land		
05	Equipment	60,000	
06	Accumulated depreciation (equipment)		$ 6,000
07	Other assets (not detailed, to simplify)	4,000	
11	Trade payables		5,000
12	Notes payable		
13	Wages payable		
14	Interest payable		
15	Income taxes payable		
21	Contributed capital (65,000 shares)		65,000
31	Retained earnings		8,000
35	Service revenue		
40	Depreciation expense		
41	Income tax expense		
42	Interest expense		
43	Other expenses		
	Totals	$84,000	$84,000

Transactions and events during 2014 are as follows:

a. Borrowed $10,000 cash on a 12 percent note payable, dated March 1, 2014.

b. Purchased land for future building site; paid cash, $9,000.

c. Earned revenues for 2014 of $160,000, including $50,000 on credit.

d. Sold 3,000 additional shares for $1 cash per share.

e. Recognized other expenses for 2014, $85,000, including $20,000 on credit.

f. Collected trade receivables, $24,000.

g. Purchased additional assets, $10,000 cash (debit other assets account).

h. Paid trade payables, $13,000.

i. Purchased service supplies on account, $18,000 (debit to Account No. 03).

j. Signed a $25,000 service contract to start February 1, 2015.

k. Declared and paid cash dividend, $15,000.

Data for adjusting entries are as follows:

l. Service supplies inventory on hand at December 31, 2014, $12,000 (debit other expenses account).

m. Depreciation on the equipment estimated at $6,000 per year.

n. Accrued interest on notes payable (to be computed).

o. Wages earned since the December 24 pay date but not yet paid, $15,000.

p. Income tax expense for 2014 payable in 2015, $8,000.

Required:

1. Set up T-accounts for the accounts on the trial balance and enter their beginning balances.

2. Record transactions (*a*) through (*k*) and post them to the T-accounts.

3. Record and post the adjusting entries (*l*) through (*p*).

4. Prepare a statement of earnings (including earnings per share), a statement of changes in equity for 2014, and a statement of financial position at December 31, 2014.

5. Record and post the closing entries.

6. Prepare a post-closing trial balance.

7. Compute the following ratios for 2014 and explain what they mean:

   a. current ratio

   b. total asset turnover ratio

   c. net profit margin ratio

   d. return on equity

OMP4–2 **Recording Transactions (Including Adjusting and Closing Entries), Preparing a Complete Set of Financial Statements, and Performing Ratio Analysis**   ■ LO1, 2, 3, 4, 5

Serena and Bill Davis began operations of their furniture repair shop, Rumours Furniture Inc., on January 1, 2013. The company's fiscal year ends December 31. The trial balance on January 1, 2014, was as follows (in thousands of dollars):

Account No.	Account Titles	Debit	Credit
01	Cash	$ 5	
02	Trade receivables	4	
03	Supplies inventory	2	
04	Small-tools inventory	6	
05	Equipment		
06	Accumulated depreciation (equipment)		
07	Other assets (not detailed to simplify)	9	
11	Trade payables		7
12	Notes payable		
13	Wages payable		
14	Interest payable		
15	Income taxes payable		
16	Deferred revenue		
21	Contributed capital (15,000 shares)		15
31	Retained earnings		4
35	Service revenue		
40	Depreciation expense		
41	Income tax expense		
42	Interest expense		
43	Other expenses		
	Totals	$26	$26

Transactions during 2014 (summarized in thousands of dollars) follow:

a. Borrowed $25 cash on July 1, 2014, on an 8 percent note, payable on June 30, 2015.

b. Purchased equipment for $18 cash on July 1, 2014.

c. Sold 5,000 additional shares for $1 cash per share.

d. Earned revenues for 2014: $74, including $15 on credit.

e. Recognized other expenses for 2014: $35, including $9 on credit.

f. Purchased additional small-tools inventory, $3 cash.

g. Collected trade receivables, $8.

h. Paid trade payables, $11.

i. Purchased supplies on account, $10 (debit to Account No. 03).

j. Received a $3 deposit on work to start January 15, 2015.

k. Declared and paid cash dividend, $12.

Data for adjusting entries are as follows:

l. Service supplies inventory of $4 and small-tools inventory of $9 on hand at December 31, 2014 (debit other expenses account).

m. Depreciation on the equipment estimated at $4 per year.

n. Accrued interest on notes payable (to be computed).

o. Wages earned since the December 24 pay date but not yet paid, $4.

p. Income tax expense payable in 2015, $4.

Required:

1. Set up T-accounts for the accounts on the trial balance and enter their beginning balances.
2. Record transactions (*a*) through (*k*) and post them to the T-accounts.
3. Record and post the adjusting entries (*l*) through (*p*).
4. Prepare a statement of earnings (including earnings per share) for 2014, a statement of changes in equity for 2014, and a statement of financial position at December 31, 2014.
5. Record and post the closing entries.
6. Prepare a post-closing trial balance.
7. Compute the following ratios for 2014 and explain what they mean:
   a. current ratio
   b. total asset turnover ratio
   c. net profit margin ratio
   d. return on equity

CASES AND PROJECTS

FINDING AND INTERPRETING FINANCIAL INFORMATION

■ **LO1, 3, 4, 5**   **CP4–1**   **Finding Financial Information**

Canadian Tire Corporation

Refer to the financial statements of Canadian Tire Corporation in Appendix A at the end of this book.

Required:

1. How much did the company pay in interest for the 2012 fiscal year? Where did you find this information?
2. To what account is accumulated depreciation related?
3. What company accounts would not appear on a post-closing trial balance?
4. Prepare the closing entry for inventories.
5. What is the company's basic earnings per share for the two years reported?
6. Compute the company's net profit margin ratio for 2011 and 2012 based on information reported on the statement of earnings. How would you interpret the results?

■ **LO3, 4, 5**   **CP4–2**   **Finding Financial Information**

RONA Inc.

Go to *Connect* for the financial statements of RONA Inc.

Required:

1. What is the balance of the prepaid expenses account at the end of the most recent year? Where did you find this information?
2. What is the difference between prepaid rent and deferred rent revenue?
3. Describe in general terms what accrued liabilities are.
4. What would generate the finance income that is reported in Note 25 to the financial statements?
5. Which company accounts would not have balances on a post-closing trial balance?
6. Give the closing entry, if any, for prepaid expenses.
7. What is the company's earnings per share (basic only) for the two years reported?
8. Compute the company's net profit margin ratio for the two years reported. What do the results suggest to you about RONA Inc.?

CP4–3 Comparing Companies over Time

Refer to the financial statements of Canadian Tire Corporation (Appendix A) and RONA Inc. (on *Connect*), and the Industry Ratio Report (Appendix B on *Connect*).

Required:

1. What was the cost of sales for each company's most recent fiscal year? Where did you find the information?

2. Compute the percentage of cost of sales to sales for each company if possible. Compute the same ratio for the previous two fiscal years and comment on the results.

3. Compute each company's net profit margin ratio for the years shown in its annual report. What do your results suggest about each company over the two-year period?

4. Compute each company's return on equity for the most recent year. Which company is more profitable? Explain.

5. Compare each company's net profit margin ratio and return on equity for the most recent year to the industry averages for both ratios in the Industry Ratio Report. Were these two companies performing better or worse than the average company in the industry?

■ LO2, 5

Canadian Tire Corporation

vs. RONA Inc.

FINANCIAL REPORTING AND ANALYSIS CASES

CP4–4 Analyzing the Effects of Adjustments

Seneca Land Company, a closely held corporation, invests in commercial rental properties. Seneca's fiscal year ends on December 31. At the end of each year, numerous adjusting entries must be made because many transactions completed during the current and prior years have economic effects on the financial statements of the current and future years. Assume that the current year is 2014.

■ LO1

Required:

This case concerns four transactions that have been selected for your analysis. Answer the questions for each.

Transaction (*a*): On July 1, 2013, the company purchased office equipment costing $14,000 for use in the business. The company estimates that the equipment will have a useful life of 10 years and no residual value.

1. Over how many accounting periods will this transaction directly affect Seneca's financial statements? Explain.

2. Assuming that depreciation expense is $1,400 per year, how much depreciation expense was reported on the 2013 and 2014 statements of earnings?

3. How should the office equipment be reported on the statement of financial position at December 31, 2015?

4. Would Seneca make an adjusting entry at the end of each year during the life of the equipment? Explain your answer.

Transaction (*b*): On September 1, 2014, Seneca collected $24,000 for rent of office space. This amount represented rent for a six-month period, September 1, 2014, through February 28, 2015. Deferred rent revenue was increased (credited), and cash was increased (debited) for $24,000.

1. Over how many accounting periods will this transaction affect Seneca's financial statements? Explain.

2. How much rent revenue on this office space should Seneca report on the 2014 statement of earnings? Explain.

3. Did this transaction create a liability for Seneca as of the end of 2014? Explain. If yes, how much?

4. Should Seneca make an adjusting entry on December 31, 2014? Explain. If your answer is yes, prepare the adjusting entry.

Transaction (*c*): On December 31, 2014, Seneca owed wages of $7,500 to employees because they worked the last three days in December 2014. The next payroll date is January 5, 2015.

1. Over how many accounting periods does this transaction affect Seneca's financial statements? Explain.

2. How would this $7,500 amount affect Seneca's statement of earnings for 2014 and the statement of financial position at December 31, 2014?

3. Should Seneca make an adjusting entry on December 31, 2014? Explain. If your answer is yes, prepare the adjusting entry.

Transaction (d): On January 1, 2014, Seneca agreed to supervise the planning and subdivision of a large tract of land for a customer, J. Ray. This service job involves four separate phases. By December 31, 2014, three phases had been completed to Ray's satisfaction. The remaining phase will be done during 2015. The total price for the four phases (agreed on in advance by both parties) was $60,000. Each phase involves about the same amount of services. On December 31, 2014, Seneca had not collected any cash for the services already performed.

1. Should Seneca record any service revenue on this job for 2014? Explain. If yes, prepare the adjusting entry to record the revenue.

2. What entry will Seneca make when it completes the last phase, assuming that the full contract price is collected on the completion date, February 15, 2015?

LO1, 2, 4, 5   CP4–5   Using Financial Reports: Inferring Adjusting and Closing Entries and Answering Analytical Questions

Rowland Company was organized on January 1, 2013. At the end of the first year of operations, December 31, 2013, the bookkeeper prepared the following trial balances (amounts in thousands of dollars):

Account No.	Account Titles	Unadjusted Trial Balance Debit	Unadjusted Trial Balance Credit	Adjustments		Adjusted Trial Balance Debit	Adjusted Trial Balance Credit
11	Cash	40				40	
12	Trade receivables	17				17	
13	Prepaid insurance	2				1	
14	Rent receivable					2	
15	Property, plant, and equipment	46				46	
16	Accumulated depreciation						11
17	Other assets	6				6	
18	Trade payables		27				27
19	Wages payable						3
20	Income taxes payable						5
21	Deferred rent revenue						4
22	Note payable (10%; dated January 1, 2013)		20				20
23	Contributed capital (1,000 shares)		30				30
24	Retained earnings	3				3	
25	Revenues (total)		105				103
26	Expenses (total including interest)	68				83	
27	Income tax expense					5	
	Totals	182	182			203	203

Required:

1. Based on inspection of the two trial balances, prepare the 2013 adjusting entries recorded by the bookkeeper (provide brief explanations).

2. Based on these data, prepare the 2013 closing entries with brief explanations.

3. Answer the following questions (show computations):

   a. How many shares were outstanding at year-end?

   b. What was the amount of interest expense included in the total expenses?

   c. What was the balance of retained earnings on December 31, 2013?

   d. What was the average income tax rate?

   e. How would the rent receivable and deferred rent revenue accounts be reported on the statement of financial position?

   f. Explain why cash increased by $40,000 during the year even though net earnings was comparatively very low.

   g. What was the amount of earnings per share for 2013?

   h. What was the average selling price of the shares?

   i. When was the insurance premium paid and over what period of time did the coverage extend?

   j. What was the net profit margin ratio for the year?

   k. What was the return on equity for the year?

CP4–6 Using Financial Reports: Analyzing Financial Information in a Sale of a Business (A Challenging Case)

■ LO1, 3

Robert Brissette, a local massage therapist, decided to sell his practice and retire. He has had discussions with a therapist from another province who wants to relocate. The discussions are at the complex stage of agreeing on a price. The financial statements of Robert's practice, Brissette Stress Reduction, played an important role in this process. Robert's secretary, Kelsey Doucette, maintained the records, under his direction. Each year, Kelsey developed a statement of net earnings on a cash basis from the records she maintained but she did not prepare a statement of financial position. Upon request, Robert provided the other therapist with the following statements for 2015 prepared by Kelsey:

BRISSETTE STRESS REDUCTION		
Statement of Earnings 2015		
Therapy fees collected		$130,000
Expenses paid:		
Rent for office space	$19,500	
Utilities expense	360	
Telephone expense	2,200	
Office salaries expense	23,500	
Office supplies expense	900	
Miscellaneous expenses	1,400	
Total expenses		47,860
Net earnings		$ 82,140

Upon agreement of the parties, you have been asked to examine the financial figures for 2015. The other therapist said, "I question the figures because, among other things, they appear to be on a 100 percent cash basis." Your investigations revealed the following additional data at December 31, 2015:

a. Of the $130,000 in therapy fees collected in 2015, $30,000 was for services performed prior to 2015.

b. At the end of 2015, therapy fees of $6,000 for services performed during the year were uncollected.

c. Office equipment owned and used by Brissette Stress Reduction cost $8,000. It is depreciated at a rate of $800 per year.

d. An inventory of office supplies at December 31, 2015, reflected $400 worth of items purchased during the year that were still on hand. Also, the records for 2014 indicate that the supplies on hand at the end of that year were about $250.

e. At the end of 2015, Kelsey, whose salary is $24,000 per year, had not been paid for the last week of December because the next payday is January 8, 2016.

f. The $140 phone bill for December 2015 was not paid until January 11, 2016.

g. The payment for office rent was for 13 months, including January 2016.

Required:

1. Prepare a correct statement of earnings for 2015 based on the information above. Show your computations for any amounts changed from those in the statement prepared by Kelsey. (*Hint:* Use four column headings: Item, Cash Basis per Brissette's Statement, $; Explanation of Changes; and Corrected Basis, $.)

2. Write a memo to support your schedule prepared in (1). The purpose should be to explain the reasons for your changes and to suggest other important items that should be considered in the pricing decision.

CP4–7 Using Financial Reports: Preparing Statements of Earnings for Different Periods

■ LO1, 3

Wong's Insurance Agency adjusts its accounts at the end of each month. The adjusted balances of the revenue and expense accounts at two different dates of the year appear below. The company's fiscal year starts on January 1:

	September 30, 2015	June 30, 2015
Commissions earned	$72,000	$45,000
Salaries expense	18,000	12,000
Rent expense	11,250	7,500
Depreciation expense	1,350	900
Advertising expense	14,000	7,500

The company is subject to an income tax rate of 40 percent.

Required:

Prepare statements of earnings for two separate time periods: the quarter ending September 30, 2015, and the nine-month period ending September 30, 2015. Explain how you determined the amounts for each time period and show supporting computations.

LO1, 3   **CP4–8**   **Using Financial Reports: Analyzing Financial Information from Real Financial Statements**

WestJet Airlines

The current liabilities of WestJet Airlines include the advance ticket sales account. The company's recent annual reports show the following trend in the balance of this account over a three-year period:

	2012	2011	2010
Advance ticket sales (in thousands)	$480,947	$432,186	$336,926

The first note to the company's financial statements, titled *Significant accounting policies*, includes the following disclosure about revenue recognition:

> Guest revenues, including the air component of vacation packages, are recognized when air transportation is provided. Tickets sold but not yet used are included in the consolidated balance sheet as advance ticket sales.

Required:

1. What does the balance in the advance ticket sales account represent?
2. Why does WestJet recognize guest revenue when transportation is provided, rather than when cash is received?
3. How does WestJet Airlines normally settle this liability?
4. Should WestJet recognize flight expenses, such as jet fuel, salaries of flight crew, and cost of food and beverage, in the period when the flights occur or during the period when tickets are sold? Explain.
5. Explain the most probable reason for the increase in the amount of this liability from 2010 to 2012.
6. Based on the trend in the amount of this liability, would you expect the annual amounts of guest revenue to increase, decrease, or remain stable over the three-year period? Explain.

LO1, 3   **CP4–9**   **Using Financial Reports: Analyzing Financial Information from Real Financial Statements**

Andrew Peller Ltd.

Andrew Peller Ltd. is a leading producer and marketer of quality wines in Canada. Selected information from the company's financial statements for the year ended March 31, 2012, is provided below (in thousands of dollars):

	March 31, 2012	March 31, 2011
Statement of Financial Position		
Trade receivables	$ 24,937	$ 23,390
Prepayments	1,338	818
Accrued liabilities	8,654	10,599
Dividends payable	1,252	1,148
Income taxes payable	40	1,000
Long-term debt	41,456	42,720
Other information		
Sales for fiscal year 2012	276,883	$265,420
Income taxes paid during the year	5,801	896

Required:

1. Compute the amount of cash collected from customers during the year. Assume that all sales for fiscal year 2012 were on credit.
2. Prepayments represent the net amount of a number of accounts, including prepaid insurance. The company had $818 in prepaid insurance at March 31, 2011, and $1,338 at March 31, 2012. It also paid $2,345 in June 2011 to renew its insurance policies. Prepare the adjusting journal entry on March 31, 2012, to record the amount of insurance expense for fiscal year 2012. The payment of $2,345 was debited to the insurance expense account.

3. Explain the nature of the accrued liabilities account. What would have caused the account balance to decrease during the year?

4. The company's board of directors declared dividends of $4,905 during the year. Prepare a summary journal entry to record the amount of dividends paid during the year.

5. The company is required to pay income taxes in advance on a quarterly basis even though the exact amount of income taxes expense is not calculated until the end of the fiscal year. Compute the amount of income taxes expense for 2012 and prepare the related adjusting journal entry at March 31, 2012.

6. The company's long-term debt includes a long-term bank loan for $6,000. The company signed for this loan on October 31, 2011, to be repaid on October 31, 2012. Interest on the loan, at an annual rate of 8 percent, is payable each year on October 31. Prepare the adjusting journal entry that should be made on March 31, 2012, to recognize interest expense for fiscal year 2012.

7. Assume that the company's accountant did not record the journal entry you prepared for (6) above. What would be the effect of this error (overstatement, understatement, no effect) on the following:

   a. Total assets at March 31, 2012.

   b. Net earnings for the year 2012, assuming that the company is subject to an income tax rate of 40 percent.

   c. Current liabilities at March 31, 2012.

CRITICAL THINKING CASES

CP4–10 Using Financial Reports: Evaluating Financial Information as a Bank Loan Officer

■ LO1, 3, 4

Magliochetti Moving Corp. has been in operation since January 1, 2014. It is now December 31, 2014, the end of the company's fiscal year. The company has not done well financially during the first year, although revenue has been fairly good. The three shareholders manage the company, but they have not given much attention to recordkeeping. In view of a serious cash shortage, they have applied to your bank for a $20,000 loan. You requested a complete set of financial statements. The following annual financial statements for 2014 were prepared by a clerk and then were given to the bank:

eXcel

MAGLIOCCHETTI MOVING CORP.

Statement of Earnings		Statement of Financial Position	
For the Period Ended December 31, 2014		At December 31, 2014	
Transportation revenue	$85,000	**Assets**	
Expenses:		Cash	$ 2,000
Salaries expense	17,000	Receivables	3,000
Maintenance expense	12,000	Inventory of maintenance supplies	6,000
Other expenses	18,000	Equipment	40,000
Total expenses	$47,000	Prepayments	4,000
Net earnings	$38,000	Other assets	27,000
		Total assets	$82,000
		Liabilities	
		Trade payables	$ 9,000
		Shareholders' Equity	
		Contributed capital (10,000 shares outstanding)	35,000
		Retained earnings	38,000
		Total liabilities and shareholders' equity	$82,000

After briefly reviewing the statements and looking into the situation, you requested that the statements be redone (with some expert help) to "incorporate depreciation, accruals, inventory counts, income taxes, and so on." As a result of a review of the records and supporting documents, the following additional information was developed:

a. The inventory of maintenance supplies of $6,000 shown on the statement of financial position has not been adjusted for supplies used during 2014. An inventory count of the maintenance supplies on hand (unused) on December 31, 2014, showed $1,800. Supplies used should be debited to maintenance expense.

b. The insurance premium paid in 2014 was for 2014 and 2015; therefore, the prepaid insurance at December 31, 2014, amounted to $2,000. The total insurance premium was debited to prepaid insurance when paid in 2014.

c. The equipment cost $40,000 when purchased January 1, 2014. Depreciation expense of $5,000 has not been recorded for 2014.

d. Unpaid (and unrecorded) salaries at December 31, 2014, amounted to $2,200.

e. At December 31, 2014, transportation revenue collected in advance amounted to $7,000. This amount was credited to transportation revenue when the cash was collected.

f. The company is subject to an income tax rate of 30 percent.

Required:

1. Record the six adjusting entries required on December 31, 2014, based on the preceding additional information.

2. Recast the preceding statements after taking into account the adjusting entries. Use the following format for the solution:

Items	Amounts Reported	Changes Plus	Minus	Correct Amounts
(List here each item from the two statements)				

3. Omission of the adjusting entries caused the following:
    a. Net earnings to be overstated or understated (select one) by $_____.
    b. Total assets to be overstated or understated (select one) by $_____.
    c. Total liabilities to be overstated or understated (select one) by $_____.

4. Use both the unadjusted and adjusted balances to calculate the following ratios for the company: (*a*) earnings per share, (*b*) net profit margin ratio, and (*c*) return on equity. Explain the causes of the differences and the impact of the changes on the financial analysis.

5. Write a letter to the company explaining the results of the adjustments, your analysis, and your decision regarding the loan.

■ LO1, 3   **CP4–11**   **Making a Decision as an Auditor: Effects of Errors on Net Earnings, Assets, and Liabilities**
Megan Company was careless about its financial records during its first year of operations, 2013. It is December 31, 2013, the end of the company's fiscal year. An external auditor examined the records and discovered numerous errors, all of which are described below. Assume that each error is independent of the others.

		Effect on				
	Net Earnings		**Assets**		**Liabilities**	
Independent Errors	**2013**	**2014**	**2013**	**2014**	**2013**	**2014**
(a) Depreciation expense for 2013, not recorded in 2013, $950.	O $950	N	O $950	O $950	N	N
(b) Wages earned by employees during 2013, not recorded in 2013, but will be paid in 2014, $500.						
(c) Revenue earned during 2013 but not collected or recorded until 2014, $600; will be collected in 2014.						
(d) Amount paid in 2013 and recorded as expense in 2013, but it is not an expense until 2014, $200.						
(e) Revenue collected in 2013 and recorded as revenue in 2013, but it is not earned until 2014, $900.						
(f) Sale of services for cash in 2013. Recorded as a debit to cash and as a credit to trade receivables, $300.						
(g) On December 31, 2013, bought land on credit for $8,000, but did not record the transaction until payment was made on February 1, 2014.						

Required:

Analyze each error and indicate its effect on 2013 and 2014 net earnings, assets, and liabilities if not corrected. Do not assume any other errors. Use these codes to indicate the effect of each dollar amount: O = overstated, U = understated, and N = no effect. Write an explanation of your analysis of each transaction to support your response.

A sample explanation of analysis of errors that are not corrected is provided below, using the first error as an example:

a. Failure to record depreciation in 2013 caused depreciation expense to be too low; therefore, net earnings was overstated by $950. Accumulated depreciation is also too low by $950, which causes assets to be overstated by $950 until the error is corrected.

CP4–12 **Making Decisions as a Manager: Evaluating the Effects of Business Strategy on Return on Equity**

■ **LO4**

Sony

Sony is a world leader in the manufacture of consumer and commercial electronics as well as the entertainment and insurance industries.

Required:

Using the table below, indicate the most likely effect of each of the following changes in business strategy on Sony's return on equity for the current period and future periods (+ for increase, − for decrease, and NE for no effect), assuming all other things are unchanged. Explain your answer for each. Treat each item independently.

a. Sony decreases its investment in research and development aimed at products to be brought to market in more than one year.

b. Sony begins a new advertising campaign for a movie to be released during the next year.

c. Sony issues additional shares for cash, the proceeds to be used to acquire other high-technology companies in future periods.

Strategy Change	Current-Period ROE	Future Periods' ROE
(a)		
(b)		
(c)		

FINANCIAL REPORTING AND ANALYSIS TEAM PROJECT

CP4–13 **Team Project: Analyzing Accruals, Earnings per Share, Net Profit Margin Ratio, and Return on Equity**

■ **LO1, 3, 4**

As a team, select an industry to analyze. A list of companies classified by industry can be obtained by accessing **www.fpinfomart.ca** and then choosing "Companies by Industry." You can also find a list of industries and companies within each industry via **http://ca.finance.yahoo.com/investing** (click on "Order Annual Reports" under "Tools").

Each group member should acquire the annual report for a different publicly traded company in the industry. (Library files, the SEDAR service at **www.sedar.com**, and the company's website are good sources.)

Required:

On an individual basis, each team member should write a short report answering the following questions about the selected company. Discuss any patterns across the companies that you as a team observe. Then, as a team, write a short report comparing and contrasting your companies.

1. From the statement of earnings, what are the company's earnings per share for the last three years?

2. Perform a ratio analysis:
    a. What does the net profit margin measure in general?
    b. What does the return on equity measure in general?
    c. Compute these ratios for the last three years.
    d. What do your results suggest about the company? (You may refer to the Management Discussion and Analysis section of the annual report to learn about the company's stated reasons for any change over time.)
    e. If available, find the industry ratio for the most recent year, compare it to your results, and discuss why you believe the ratio for your company differs from or is similar to the industry ratio.

3. List the accounts and amounts of accrued liabilities on the most recent statement of financial position. (You may find the detail in the notes to the statements.) What is the ratio of the total accrued liabilities to the total liabilities?

SOLUTIONS TO SELF-STUDY QUIZZES

Self-Study Quiz 4-1

	(1) Revenue Earned or Expense Incurred?	(2) Cash Received/Paid in the Past or Cash to Be Received/Paid in the Future?	(3) Amount	Adjusting Journal Entry		
				Accounts	Debit	Credit
AJE 1	Trip Revenue earned	Received in past: *Deferred Revenue*	$6,000 × 1/3 = $2,000 earned	Deferred Revenue (−L) Trip Revenue (+R, +SE)	2,000	2,000
AJE 2	Instruction Revenue earned	To be received: *Accrued Revenue*	$800 earned (given)	Trade Receivable (+A) Instruction Revenue (+R, +SE)	800	800
AJE 3	Insurance Expense incurred	Paid in past: *Prepaid Expense*	$24,000 ÷ 12 = $2,000 per month $2,000 × 4 months = $8,000 used	Insurance Expense (+E, −SE) Prepaid Insurance (−A)	8,000	8,000
AJE 4	Interest Expense incurred	To be paid: *Accrued Expense*	$300,000 × 0.06 × 10/12 = $15,000 incurred and owed	Interest Expense (+E, −SE) Interest Payable (+L)	15,000	15,000

Self-Study Quiz 4-2

Net profit margin ratio based on the unadjusted trial balance:

   Earnings before income taxes = $1,444

   Income tax expense = $1,444 × 40% = $576 (rounded); Net earnings = $1,444 − $576 = $868

   Net profit margin = $868 ÷ ($6,540 + $40) = 0.132 or 13.2%

   Net profit margin based on the adjusted trial balance:

   Net profit margin = $498 ÷ ($7,540 + $50) = 0.066 or 6.6%

The difference between the two ratios is due to the end-of-period adjustments, which increased revenues by $910 and increased expenses by $1,856, thus lowering net earnings significantly from $1,444 to $498. The difference between the two ratios is 6.6%. It is certainly a material difference. Clearly, if adjustments to the revenue and expense accounts are not made, net earnings will be overstated as well as the net profit margin ratio. Inaccurate information is not useful for decision making. Thus, what appears to be a set of very intricate procedures, when properly executed, actually contributes to the decision usefulness of financial statements.

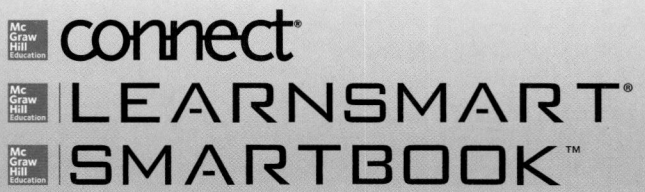

Reporting and Interpreting Cash Flows

After studying this chapter, you should be able to do the following:

LO1 Classify cash flow items into cash flows from operating, investing, and financing activities.

LO2 Report and interpret cash flows from operating activities by using the indirect method.

LO3 Analyze and interpret the quality of earnings ratio.

LO4 Report and interpret cash flows from investing activities.

LO5 Analyze and interpret the capital expenditures ratio.

LO6 Report and interpret cash flows from financing activities.

LO7 Understand the format of the statement of cash flows and additional cash flow disclosures.

FOCUS COMPANY: **Danier Leather Inc.**

PRODUCING VALUE FOR CUSTOMERS AND CASH FLOWS TO SHAREHOLDERS

Danier Leather Inc. (**www.danier.com**) was founded in 1972 as a manufacturer of suede and leather apparel sold directly to individuals and large Canadian department stores. Twenty-six years later, the company's success had led to an increase in the number of its retail outlets, expansion of its product lines, and pursuit of international growth opportunities. In 1998, shares were issued to the public to obtain the funds needed to implement the company's expansion strategy. Over the next 14 years, the company continued to grow and expand its business and markets to become the leading Canadian designer, manufacturer, and retailer of quality leather and suede garments for women and men. By 2012, the company's annual sales of coats, jackets, blazers, pants, skirts, handbags, and other accessories exceeded $148 million.

Although it may be puzzling, profitable operations do not always ensure positive cash flow. As we have seen in earlier chapters, this occurs because the timing of revenues and expenses does not always match cash inflows and outflows. As a consequence, Danier Leather Inc. must carefully manage cash flows as well as net earnings. For the same reasons, financial analysts must consider the information provided in Danier Leather's statement of cash flows in addition to information reported on its statement of financial position and its statement of earnings.

UNDERSTANDING THE BUSINESS

Net earnings is an important indicator of performance, but cash flow is also critical to a company's success. Cash flow permits a company to expand its operations, replace worn assets, take advantage of new investment opportunities, pay its creditors, and pay dividends to its owners. Some financial analysts go as far as saying that "cash flow is king." Both managers and analysts need to understand the various sources and uses of cash that are associated with business activity.

The statement of cash flows focuses attention on a firm's ability to generate cash internally, its management of current assets and current liabilities, and the details of its investments and external financing. It is designed to help both managers and analysts answer important cash-related questions such as these:

- Will the company have enough cash to pay its short-term debts to suppliers, employees, taxation authorities, and other creditors without additional borrowing?
- Is the company adequately managing its trade receivables, inventory, and other current assets?
- Has the company made necessary investments in new productive capacity?
- Did the company generate enough cash flow internally to finance necessary investments, or did it rely on external financing?
- Is the company changing the proportion of debt and equity in its capital structure?

We begin our discussion with an overview of the statement of cash flows. Then, we examine the information reported in each section of the statement in depth. The chapter ends with a discussion of additional cash flow disclosures.

ORGANIZATION OF THE CHAPTER

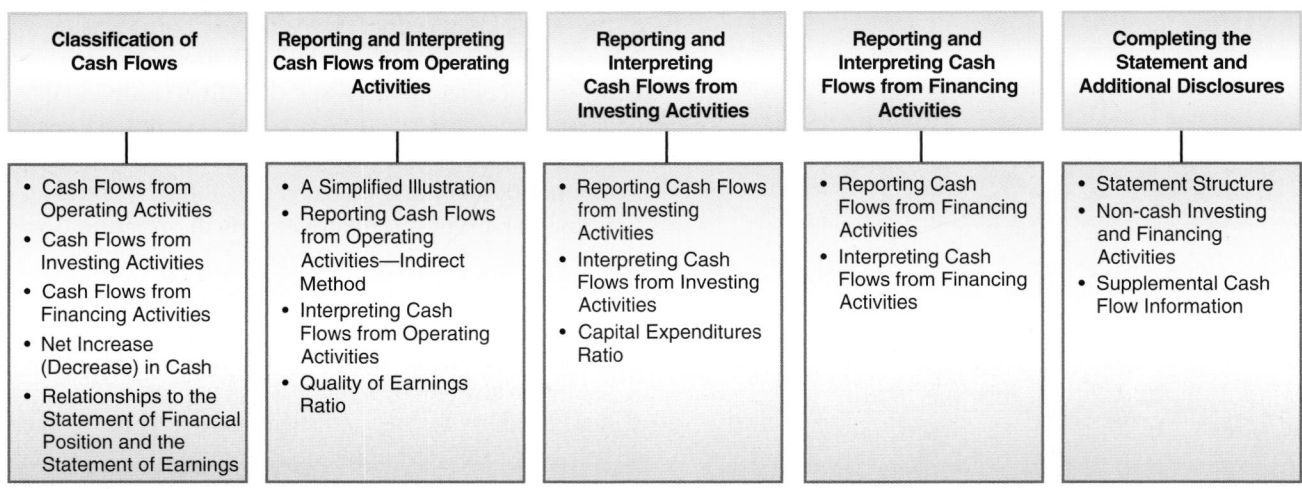

Supplemental material:
Appendix 5A: Adjustment for Gains and Losses on the Sale of Long-Lived Assets—Indirect Method
Appendix 5B: Reporting Cash Flows from Operating Activities—Direct Method
Appendix 5C: Spreadsheet Approach—Statement of Cash Flows: Indirect Method (on *Connect*)

LO¹

Classify cash flow items into cash flows from operating, investing, and financing activities.

A CASH EQUIVALENT is a short-term, highly liquid investment with an original maturity of less than three months, and subject to an insignificant risk of changes in value.

CLASSIFICATION OF CASH FLOWS

Basically, the statement of cash flows explains how the cash balance at the beginning of the period changed to another cash balance at the end of the period. For the purpose of this statement, the definition of cash includes cash and cash equivalents. **Cash equivalents** are short-term, highly liquid investments that are both

1. readily convertible to known amounts of cash, and
2. less than three months to their maturity and subject to an insignificant risk of changes in value.

Generally, an investment qualifies as a cash equivalent only when it has an original maturity of three months or less from the date of acquisition.[1] Examples of cash equivalents are treasury bills (a form of short-term government debt), money market funds,

Exhibit **5.1**
Consolidated Statement of Cash
Flows

REAL-WORLD EXCERPT

Danier Leather Inc.

ANNUAL REPORT

DANIER LEATHER INC.
Consolidated Statements of Cash Flows
For the Year Ended June 30, 2012*
(in thousands of Canadian dollars)

Operating activities

Net earnings	$ 4,028
Items not affecting cash:	
Depreciation of property and equipment	3,366
Amortization[2] of computer software	380
Deferred income taxes	(657)
Net change in non-cash working capital items related to operations	3,008**
Cash flows from operating activities	10,125
Investing activities	
Acquisition of property and equipment	(3,974)
Acquisition of computer software	(52)
Cash flows used in investing activities	(4,026)
Financing activities	
Issuance of shares	99
Repurchase of shares	(219)
Payment of dividends	(1,124)
Cash flows used in financing activities	(1,244)
Increase in cash and cash equivalents	4,855
Cash and cash equivalents, beginning of period	28,698
Cash and cash equivalents, end of period	$33,553

The balances of certain accounts have been adjusted to simplify the presentation.

*Danier Leather's fiscal year ends on the last Saturday in June each year.
**Changes in non-cash operating working capital items:

Increase in trade receivables	$ (132)
Decrease in inventories	4,073
Decrease in prepayments	102
Decrease in trade payables	(1,073)
Increase in accrued liabilities	316
Decrease in income tax payable	(278)
	$ 3,008

Source: Danier Leather, Annual Report 2012.

and commercial paper (short-term notes payable issued by large corporations). Danier Leather Inc. defines its cash and cash equivalents as cash on hand, bank balances, and money market investments with maturities of three months or less.

As you can see in Exhibit 5.1, the statement of cash flows reports cash inflows and outflows based on three broad categories: (1) operating activities, (2) investing activities, and (3) financing activities. Together, these three cash flow categories explain the change in cash from the beginning balance to the ending balance on the statement of financial position. To improve comparability, International Accounting Standard 7—Statement of Cash Flows defines each category included in the required statement. These definitions (with explanations) are presented in the following sections.

Cash Flows from Operating Activities

Cash flows from operating activities (cash flows from operations) are the cash inflows and cash outflows that directly relate to revenues and expenses from normal

CASH FLOWS FROM
OPERATING ACTIVITIES are
cash inflows and outflows
directly related to earnings from
normal operations.

operations. There are two alternative approaches for presenting the operating activities section of the statement:

1. The **direct method** of presenting the operating activities section of the statement of cash flows reports the components of cash flows from operating activities listed as gross receipts and gross payments:

Inflows	Outflows
Cash received from	Cash paid for
Customers	Purchase of goods for resale and services (electricity, etc.)
Dividends and	Salaries and wages
interest on investments	Income taxes
	Interest on borrowings

The difference between the inflows and outflows is called the *net cash inflow (outflow) from operating activities*. Danier Leather experienced a net cash inflow of $10,125 from its operations for fiscal year 2012. Although IAS 7 encourages companies to report cash flows from operating activities by using the direct method, it is rarely seen in Canada. Many financial executives have reported that they do not use it because it is more expensive to implement than the indirect method. Attempts by standard setters to require use of the direct method are usually met with intense opposition from the preparer community.

2. The **indirect method** of presenting the operating activities section of the statement of cash flows starts with net earnings for the period and then eliminates non-cash items to arrive at net cash inflow (outflow) from operating activities:

Net earnings
+/−Adjustments for non-cash items
Net cash inflow (outflow) from operating activities

Notice in Exhibit 5.1 that Danier Leather reported net earnings of $4,028 but generated positive cash flows from operating activities of $10,125. Why do net earnings and cash flows from operating activities differ? Recall that the statement of earnings is prepared under the accrual concept, whereby revenues are recorded when earned without regard to when the related cash is collected. Similarly, expenses are recorded in the same period as the revenues without regard to when the related cash payments are made.

For now, the most important thing to remember about the two methods is that they are simply alternative ways to compute the same amount. The total amount of *cash flows from operating activities is always the same* (an inflow of $10,125 in Danier Leather's case), *whether it is computed by using the direct or the indirect method*, as illustrated below:

Direct		Indirect	
Cash collected from customers	$148,087	Net earnings	$ 4,028
		Depreciation of property and	
Cash payments to suppliers	(68,325)	equipment	3,366
Cash payments for other		Amortization of computer	
expenses	(67,158)	software	380
Cash payments for interest	(20)	Deferred income taxes	(657)
		Changes in current assets and	
Cash payments for income taxes	(2,459)	liabilities	3,008
Net cash provided by operating		Net cash provided by operating	
activities	$ 10,125	activities	$10,125

Cash Flows from Investing Activities

Cash flows from investing activities are cash inflows and outflows related to the acquisition or sale of long-term productive assets and investments in the securities of other companies. Typical cash flows from investing activities include the following:

Inflows	Outflows
Cash received from	*Cash paid for*
Sale or disposal of property, plant, and equipment	Purchase of property, plant, and equipment
Sale or maturity of investments in securities	Purchase of investments in securities

CASH FLOWS FROM INVESTING ACTIVITIES are cash inflows and outflows related to the acquisition or sale of productive facilities and investments in the securities of other companies.

The difference between these cash inflows and outflows is called *net cash inflow (outflow) from investing activities.*

For Danier Leather, this amount was an outflow of $4,026 for fiscal year 2012. The investing activities section of the statement shows Danier Leather's long-term investment strategy. The management discussion and analysis (MD&A) section of the report indicates that the company was continuing to invest in expanding the number of stores in shopping malls and in renovating existing stores.

Cash Flows from Financing Activities

Cash flows from financing activities are cash inflows and outflows related to external sources (owners and creditors) to finance the enterprise and its operations. Usual cash flows from financing activities include the following:

Inflows	Outflows
Cash received from	*Cash paid for*
Borrowing on notes, mortgages, bonds, etc., from creditors	Repayment of principal to creditors
Issuing shares to shareholders	Interest on borrowings if it is classified as a financing activity
	Repurchasing shares from owners
	Dividends to shareholders

CASH FLOWS FROM FINANCING ACTIVITIES are cash inflows and outflows related to external sources of financing (owners and creditors) for the enterprise.

The difference between these cash inflows and outflows is called *net cash inflow (outflow) from financing activities.*

For Danier Leather, this amount was an outflow of $1,244 for fiscal year 2012. The financing activities section of the statement shows that Danier Leather issued new common shares for $99, repurchased shares (that it issued previously) for $219, and paid cash dividends of $1,124 to shareholders.[3]

Net Increase (Decrease) in Cash

The combination of the net cash flows from operating activities, investing activities, and financing activities must equal the net increase (decrease) in cash for the reporting period. For fiscal year 2012, Danier Leather reported a net increase of $4,855, which explains the change in cash and cash equivalents on the statement of financial position from the beginning balance of $28,698 to the ending balance of $33,553:

	(in thousands)
Net cash provided by operating activities	$10,125
Net cash used in investing activities	(4,026)
Net cash used in financing activities	(1,244)
Net increase in cash and cash equivalents	4,855
Cash and cash equivalents at beginning of period	28,698
Cash and cash equivalents at end of period	$33,553

Beginning and ending balances from the statement of financial position

The three main sections of the statement of cash flows are Cash Flows from Operating Activities, which are related to generating earnings from normal operations; Cash Flows from Investing Activities, which are related to the acquisition and sale of productive assets; and Cash Flows from Financing Activities, which are related to external financing of the enterprise. The net cash inflow or outflow for the year is the same amount as the increase or decrease in cash and cash equivalents for the year on the statement of financial position. To make sure you understand the appropriate classifications of the different cash flows, answer the following questions before you move on.

SELF-STUDY QUIZ 5-1

Canadian Tire Corporation

Canadian Tire Corporation is a network of businesses engaged in retail, financial services, and petroleum. A listing of some items that are reported on its statement of cash flows follows. Without referring to Exhibit 5.1, indicate whether each item is disclosed in the operating activities (O), investing activities (I), or financing activities (F) section of the statement.

_____ a. Purchase of short-term investments   _____ f. Change in inventories
_____ b. Net earnings   _____ g. Change in accrued liabilities
_____ c. Change in trade receivables   _____ h. Depreciation and amortization
_____ d. Additions to property, plant, and equipment   _____ i. Issuance of shares
_____ e. Change in prepayments and other   _____ j. Change in trade payables
current assets

After you complete your answers, check them with the solutions at the end of the chapter.

To give you a better understanding of the statement of cash flows, we now discuss in more detail Danier Leather's statement and the way that it relates to the statement of financial position and the statement of earnings. Then, we examine the way that each section of the statement describes a set of important decisions that Danier Leather management made. We also discuss the way financial analysts use each section to evaluate the company's performance.

Relationships to the Statement of Financial Position and the Statement of Earnings

Preparing and interpreting the statement of cash flows require analyzing the accounts that are reported on both the statement of financial position and the statement of earnings. As we discussed in previous chapters, accountants record transactions as journal entries that are posted to specific ledger accounts. The accounts' balances are then used to prepare the statement of earnings and the statement of financial position. Companies cannot prepare the statement of cash flows by using amounts recorded in the specific accounts because these amounts are based on accrual accounting. Instead, accountants must analyze the amounts recorded under the accrual basis and adjust them to a cash basis. To prepare the statement of cash flows, they need the following data:

1. *Comparative statements of financial position*, which are used to compute the cash flows from all activities (operating, investing, and financing).

2. A *complete statement of earnings*, which is used primarily to identify cash flows from operating activities.

3. *Additional details* concerning selected accounts that reflect different types of transactions and events. Analysis of individual accounts is necessary, because often the net change in an account balance during the year does not reveal the underlying nature of the cash flows.

Our approach to preparing and understanding the statement of cash flows focuses on the changes in the accounts that are reported on the statement of financial position. It relies on a simple algebraic manipulation of the accounting equation:

$$\text{Assets} = \text{Liabilities} + \text{Shareholders' Equity}$$

First, assets can be split into cash and non-cash assets:

$$\text{Cash} + \text{Non-cash Assets} = \text{Liabilities} + \text{Shareholders' Equity}$$

If we move the non-cash assets to the right side of the equation, then

$$\text{Cash} = \text{Liabilities} + \text{Shareholders' Equity} - \text{Non-cash Assets}$$

Given this relationship, the change in cash (Δ) between the beginning and end of the period must equal the changes (Δ) in the amounts on the right side of the equation during the same period:

$$\Delta\text{Cash} = \Delta\text{Liabilities} + \Delta\text{Shareholders' Equity} - \Delta\text{Non-cash Assets}$$

Thus, *any transaction that changes cash must be accompanied by a change in liabilities, shareholders' equity, or non-cash assets.*

In general, increases in cash are associated with decreases in non-cash asset accounts and increases in liability and shareholders' equity accounts. In contrast, cash decreases when non-cash assets increase, and when liabilities or shareholders' equity decrease:

Decrease in Non-cash Assets
Increase in Liabilities and Shareholders' Equity → **Cash Inflow**

Increase in Non-cash Assets
Decrease in Liabilities and Shareholders' Equity → **Cash Outflow**

Exhibit 5.2 illustrates this concept along with a sample of cash transactions that affect different asset, liability, and equity accounts.

Next, we will compute the change in each account on the statement of financial position (ending balance − beginning balance) and classify each change as relating to operating (O), investing (I), or financing (F) activities, based on Danier Leather's financial statements.

Exhibit 5.3 shows Danier Leather's comparative statements of financial position at the end of fiscal years 2011 and 2012, and its statement of earnings for fiscal year 2012. *The financial position accounts related to generating earnings (operating items) should be marked with an O.* These accounts include the following:

- most current assets (other than short-term investments that relate to investing activities);[4]
- most current liabilities (other than amounts owed to investors and financial institutions,[5] all of which relate to financing activities);
- retained earnings, because it increases by the amount of net earnings, which is the starting point of the operating section. (Retained earnings also decreases by the amount of dividends declared, which is a financing outflow noted by an F.)

Category	Transaction	Effect on Cash	Other Account Affected
Operating	Collect trade receivables	+Cash	−Trade receivables (A)
	Pay trade payables	−Cash	−Trade payables (L)
	Prepay rent	−Cash	+Prepaid rent (A)
	Pay interest	−Cash	−Retained earnings (SE)
	Sell for cash	+Cash	+Retained earnings (SE)
Investing	Purchase equipment for cash	−Cash	+Equipment (A)
	Sell investment securities for cash	+Cash	−Investments
Financing	Pay back debt to bank	−Cash	−Notes payable—Bank (L)
	Issue shares for cash	+Cash	+Contributed capital (SE)

Exhibit **5.2**

Selected Cash Transactions and Their Effects on Other Statement of Financial Position Accounts

In Exhibit 5.3, all of the relevant current assets and liabilities have been marked with an O. These items include trade receivables, inventories, prepayments, trade payables, and accrued liabilities. As we have noted, retained earnings is also relevant to operations.

Exhibit **5.3**

Danier Leather Inc.: Comparative Statements of Financial Position and Current Statement of Earnings

Related Cash Flow Section		**DANIER LEATHER INC.** **Consolidated Statements of Financial Position** **(in thousands of Canadian dollars)**			
Change in Cash			**June 30, 2012**	**June 25, 2011**	**Change**
	Assets				
	Current assets				
	Cash and cash equivalents		$33,553	$28,698	$4,855
O	Trade receivables		517	385	132
O	Inventories		24,891	28,964	−4,073
O	Prepayments		799	901	−102
	Total current assets		59,760	58,948	
I*	Property and equipment (net)		15,012	14,404	608
I*	Computer software		726	1,054	−328
O	Deferred income tax asset		2,335	1,678	−657
	Total assets		$77,833	$76,084	
	Liabilities				
	Current liabilities				
O	Trade payables		8,137	9,210	−1,073
O	Accrued liabilities		4,984	4,668	316
O	Income tax payable		–	278	−278
F	Dividends payable		708	–	708
	Total current liabilities		13,829	14,156	
	Total liabilities		13,829	14,156	
	Shareholders' Equity				
F	Contributed capital		15,040	15,160	−120
O and F	Retained earnings		48,964	46,768	2,196
	Total shareholders' equity		64,004	61,928	
	Total liabilities and shareholders' equity		$77,833	$76,084	

The balances of certain accounts have been adjusted to simplify the presentation.
*The accumulated depreciation/amortization accounts are also related to operations because depreciation and amortization expenses are added back to net earnings.

DANIER LEATHER INC. **Consolidated Statement of Earnings** **(in thousands of Canadian dollars)**	
	Year ended **June 30, 2012**
Net sales	$148,219
Cost of sales	71,325
Gross profit	76,894
Selling, general, and administrative	67,576
Depreciation of property and equipment	3,366
Amortization of computer software	380
Operating profit	5,572
Interest expense	20
Earnings before income taxes	5,552
Provision for income taxes	1,524
Net earnings	$ 4,028

The balances of certain accounts have been adjusted to simplify the presentation.
Source: Danier Leather, Annual Report 2012.

The financial position accounts related to investing activities should be marked with an I. These include all of the remaining assets on the statement of financial position. In Exhibit 5.3, these are property and equipment and computer software.

The financial position accounts related to financing activities should be marked with an F. These include all of the remaining liability and shareholders' equity accounts on the statement of financial position. In Exhibit 5.3, these accounts include contributed capital and retained earnings (for decreases resulting from dividends declared).

In the next sections of this chapter, we use this information to prepare each section of the statement of cash flows.

REPORTING AND INTERPRETING CASH FLOWS FROM OPERATING ACTIVITIES

The operating activities section can be prepared in one of two formats: the direct method and the indirect method. The next section presents a comparison of the direct and indirect methods by using a simplified illustration. Then we reconstruct the operating activities section of Danier Leather's statement of cash flows by using the indirect method.

A Simplified Illustration

The simplified example below illustrates the difference between the computation of cash flows from operating activities using the *direct* versus the *indirect* method. We first show the effects of a series of summary transactions on the accounting equation and the statement of cash flows. Then we show how the transaction effects on operating activities can be grouped to prepare the operating activities section of the statement of cash flows.

Sample Corporation reported the following account balances at December 31, 2013:

LO²

Report and interpret cash flows from operating activities by using the indirect method.

SAMPLE CORPORATION
Statement of Financial Position
At December 31, 2013

Assets		
Cash		$ 19,200
Trade receivables		22,000
Merchandise inventory		75,000
Prepayments		15,000
Property, plant, and equipment	$113,500	
Less: Accumulated depreciation	20,000	93,500
Total assets		$224,700
Liabilities and Shareholders' Equity		
Liabilities		
Trade payables		$ 14,000
Salaries payable		1,500
Income tax payable		4,500
Long-term borrowings		54,000
Total liabilities		74,000
Shareholders' equity		
Contributed capital	$126,000	
Retained earnings	24,700	150,700
Total liabilities and shareholders' equity		$224,700

The following summary transactions occurred during 2014:

1. Purchased merchandise for $62,000 on account, and paid $59,000 to various suppliers.

2. Sold merchandise on account for $140,000, and collected $145,000 in cash from customers. The cost of merchandise sold was $69,000.

3. Salaries expense totalled $28,000, but only $27,000 was paid to employees during the year.

4. Interest expense of $5,000 was paid in full.

5. Other operating expenses totalled $15,800, including expenses of $5,000 that were prepaid and $10,800 that were paid during the year.

6. Purchased a new building for $20,000 and issued shares in full payment.

7. Declared and paid cash dividend of $6,000.

8. Depreciation expense was $7,000 for the year.

9. Income tax expense for 2014 totalled $9,000; the company paid $10,500 to the tax authorities.

The effects of these transactions on the accounting equation and cash flows are shown in Exhibit 5.4. Note that some of the accounts we use, such as prepayments; property, plant and equipment; accrued liabilities; and retained earnings, are groupings of many accounts. The main ideas that we present in this illustration do not change with the addition of more detailed accounts.

Study Exhibit 5.4 carefully, particularly the amounts entered in the revenues and expenses columns, comparing them to the amounts shown under the effects on cash flows, operating activities column.

The detailed transaction effects in Exhibit 5.4 can be used to prepare the operating activities section of the statement of cash flows by listing the cash receipts and cash payments related to operations:

SAMPLE CORPORATION
Statement of Cash Flows (Partial)
For the Year Ended December 31, 2014
(Direct Method)

Operating Activities		
Collections from customers		$145,000
Payments:		
to suppliers	$59,000	
to employees	27,000	
for interest	5,000	
for other operating expenses	10,800	
for income taxes	10,500	
Total payments		112,300
Net cash flows from operating activities		$ 32,700

These amounts appear in the Operating Activities column in Exhibit 5.4.

Let us now turn our attention to the reporting of cash flow from operations under the indirect method. The starting point of the computation is net earnings, which is the difference between revenues (including gains) and expenses (including losses). We know that the revenues earned by the company in 2014 do not necessarily result in an equal amount of cash collections from customers during the year. In fact, the amount of cash received from customers during the year could be equal to, lower than, or higher than the amount of revenues. Similarly, the amount of expenses incurred during the year may not equal the amount of cash payments for these expenses. Given that revenues and expenses include both cash and non-cash components, we need to remove the non-cash revenues and non-cash expenses from net earnings in order to obtain the cash components. Exhibit 5.5 shows how we can decompose the revenues and expenses into cash and non-cash components.

The amounts in column A are taken from the revenues and expenses columns in Exhibit 5.4, and the amounts in column B are the corresponding cash receipts or payments that appear in the operating activities column of the same exhibit. The earnings from operations, $6,200, is made up of a $32,700 cash component and a $26,500 non-cash component.

Exhibit **5.4**

Effects of Summary Transactions on the Accounting Equation

	Assets					=	Liabilities				+	Shareholders' Equity					Effect on Cash Flows		
Transaction	Cash	Trade Receivables	Merchandise Inventory	Prepaid Expenses	Property, Plant, and Equipment (net)		Trade Payables	Salaries Payable	Income Tax Payable	Long-Term Borrowings		Common Shares	Retained Earnings	Revenues	Expenses	Description of Item	Operating Activities	Investing Activities	Financing Activities
Balance, January 1, 2014	19,200	22,000	75,000	15,000	93,500		14,000	1,500	4,500	54,000		126,000	24,700						
1a. Purchase of merchandise			62,000				62,000												
1b. Payment to suppliers	(59,000)						(59,000)										(59,000)		
2a. Credit sales		140,000												140,000		Sales			
2b. Cost of merchandise sold			(69,000)												(69,000)	Cost of sales			
2c. Collection from customers	145,000	(145,000)															145,000		
3a. Salaries expense								28,000							(28,000)	Salaries			
3b. Payments to employees	(27,000)							(27,000)									(27,000)		
4. Payment of interest	(5,000)														(5,000)	Interest	(5,000)		
5. Other operating expenses	(10,800)			(5,000)											(15,800)	Other expenses	(10,800)		
6. Purchase of building					20,000							20,000							
7. Payment of dividends	(6,000)														(6,000)	Dividends			(6,000)
8. Depreciation/ amortization expense					(7,000)										(7,000)	Depreciation			
9a. Income tax expense for the year									9,000						(9,000)	Income tax			
9b. Payment of income taxes	(10,500)								(10,500)								(10,500)		
Balance, December 31, 2014	45,900	17,000	68,000	10,000	106,500		17,000	2,500	3,000	54,000		146,000	24,700	140,000	(139,800)		32,700	—	(6,000)

Exhibit 5.5

Decomposition of Revenues and Expenses into Cash and Non-Cash Components

Transaction	A Operating Revenue or Expense (Accrual Amount)	−	B Cash Component	=	C Difference (Non-cash Component)
Sales	$140,000		$145,000		$ (5,000)
Cost of sales	(69,000)		(59,000)		(10,000)
Salaries expense	(28,000)		(27,000)		(1,000)
Interest expense	(5,000)		(5,000)		-0-
Other operating expenses	(15,800)		(10,800)		(5,000)
Depreciation expense	(7,000)		-0-		(7,000)
Income tax expense	(9,000)		(10,500)		1,500
Cash/accrual earnings from operations	$ 6,200		$ 32,700		$(26,500)

The non-cash components of revenue and expense accounts are reflected in related accounts on the statement of financial position. For example, salary expense totalled $28,000 for 2014, but the company paid only $27,000. The unpaid amount of $1,000 is a liability, salary payable, which must be paid in the future. Hence, it increases the balance of salaries payable from $1,500 to $2,500.

As indicated previously, the direct method focuses on the cash elements of net earnings by computing cash receipts and cash payments for operating purposes, reporting the details found in column B of Exhibit 5.5 to arrive at net cash flows from operating activities. In contrast, the indirect method starts with net earnings and eliminates the non-cash elements reported in column C of Exhibit 5.5 to arrive at the same result. In general,

Net Earnings = Cash Elements +/− Non-cash Elements
Cash Elements = Net Earnings +/− Non-cash Elements

Hence, the net cash flows from operating activities can be computed indirectly as

Net Cash Flows from Operating Activities = $6,200 + $26,500 = $32,700

The decomposition of net earnings into cash and non-cash components, as presented in Exhibit 5.5, requires a reconstruction of all the transactions that occurred during the year. Such details are not publicly available. But because transactions that affect revenue or expense accounts also affect primarily the current asset or current liability accounts, we can use the changes in the statement of financial position accounts to compute the non-cash components of net earnings, which are identified in column C of Exhibit 5.5. This process, which is explained in detail in the next section, leads to an alternative way of computing and reporting the net cash flows from operating activities:

SAMPLE CORPORATION
Statement of Cash Flows (Partial)
For the Year Ended December 31, 2014
(Indirect Method)

Operating Activities

Net earnings from operations		$6,200
Add (deduct) items not affecting cash:		
Depreciation expense	$ 7,000	
Decrease in trade receivables	5,000	
Decrease in merchandise inventory	7,000	
Decrease in prepayments	5,000	
Increase in trade payables	3,000	
Increase in salaries payable	1,000	
Decrease in income tax payable	(1,500)	
Net adjustments		26,500
Net cash flows from operating activities		$32,700

Notice that the adjustments listed above are the same amounts that appear in column C in Exhibit 5.5, except they show the non-cash component of the cost of sales ($10,000) as the result of a decrease in merchandise inventory by $7,000 and an increase in trade payables by $3,000.

Before proceeding further, remember the following:

1. Cash flow from operating activities is always the same regardless of whether it is computed by using the direct method or the indirect method.

2. The investing and financing sections are always presented in the same manner, regardless of the format of the operating section.

Reporting Cash Flows from Operating Activities—Indirect Method

The indirect method of reporting cash flows from operating activities starts with net earnings and eliminates the non-cash components of revenues and expenses. The general structure of the operating activities section is as follows:

> Operating Activities
> Net earnings
> Add/subtract items not affecting cash:
> + Depreciation expense
> + Decreases in non-cash current assets
> − Increases in non-cash current assets
> + Increases in current liabilities
> − Decreases in current liabilities
> Net Cash Flows from Operating Activities

To keep track of all the additions and subtractions made to convert net earnings to cash flows from operating activities, it is helpful to set up a schedule to record the computations. We construct such a schedule for Danier Leather in Exhibit 5.6.

We begin our schedule presented in Exhibit 5.6 with net earnings of $4,028, taken from Danier Leather's statement of earnings (Exhibit 5.3). Completing the operating section by using the indirect method involves two steps:

Step 1:   Adjust net earnings for the effect of depreciation and amortization expenses. Recording depreciation and amortization expenses does not affect the cash account (or any other current asset or liability). It affects a non-current asset (such as property, plant, and equipment, net or intangible assets). *Since depreciation and amortization expenses are subtracted in computing net earnings, but do not affect cash, we always add them back* to convert net earnings to cash flows from operating activities.[6] In the case of Danier Leather, we need to remove the effect of depreciation and amortization expenses by adding back $3,366 and $380 to net earnings (see Exhibit 5.6).[7]

Step 2:   Adjust net earnings for changes in current assets and current liabilities marked as operating (O). Each *change* in operating current assets (other than cash and short-term investments) and liabilities (other than amounts owed to owners and financial institutions) causes a difference between net earnings and cash flows from operating activities.[8] When converting net earnings to cash flows from operating activities, apply the following general rules:

  • Add the change when a current asset decreases or a current liability increases.

  • Subtract the change when a current asset increases or a current liability decreases.

Understanding what makes these current assets and current liabilities increase and decrease is the key to understanding the logic of these additions and subtractions.

Exhibit **5.6**

Danier Leather Inc.: Schedule for
Net Cash Flows from Operating
Activities, Indirect Method (in
thousands of dollars)

Conversion of net earnings to net cash flows from operating activities:

Item	Amount	Explanation
Net earnings, accrual basis	$ 4,028	From statement of earnings.
Add (subtract) to convert to cash basis:		
Depreciation of property and equipment	+3,366	Add because depreciation expense is a non-cash expense.
Amortization of computer software	+380	Add because amortization expense is a non-cash expense.
Deferred income taxes	−657	Subtract because deferred income taxes do not affect cash.
Increase in trade receivables	−132	Subtract because cash collected from customers is less than accrual basis revenues.
Decrease in inventories	+4,073	Add because cost of sales is more than purchases.
Decrease in prepayments	+102	Add because accrual basis expenses are more than cash prepayments for expenses.
Decrease in trade payables	−1,073	Subtract because purchases on account (due to suppliers) are less than cash payments to suppliers.
Increase in accrued liabilities	+316	Add because cash payments for expenses are less than accrual basis expenses.
Decrease in income tax payable	−278	Subtract because cash payments for income tax are more than income tax expense.
Net cash inflow from operating activities	$10,125	Reported on the statement of cash flows.

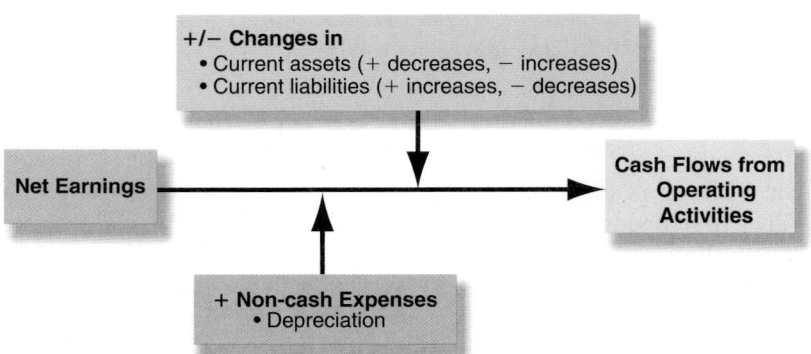

Change in Trade Receivables   We illustrate this logic with the first operating item (O) listed on Danier Leather's statement of financial position (Exhibit 5.3), trade receivables. Remember that the statement of earnings reflects sales revenue, but the statement of cash flows must reflect cash collections from customers. As the following trade receivables T-account illustrates, when sales revenues are recorded, trade receivables increase, and when cash is collected from customers, trade receivables decrease:

	Trade Receivables (A)			
Change	Beginning balance	385		
+132	Sales revenue (on account)	148,219	Collections from customers	148,087
	Ending balance	517		

In the Danier Leather example, the amount of trade receivables at the beginning of the fiscal year 2012 ($385) is normally collected from customers during that fiscal year. In addition, most of the sales made during that fiscal year are collected in cash from customers. However, customers who purchase the company's products on account toward the end of the fiscal year will likely pay the amounts due during the next fiscal year. This is reflected in the ending balance of trade receivables ($517). Hence, the amount of cash collections from customers is $148,087 (= $385 + $148,219 − $517). The cash received is lower than sales revenue. As a result, sales revenue must be decreased to determine the amount of cash collected from customers during the year.

This can also be determined by adjusting sales revenue for the change in trade receivables during the year. The increase in trade receivables ($517 − $385 = $132) is subtracted from sales revenue.[9] In contrast, a decrease in trade receivables signals that the cash collected from customers exceeds the sales revenue. Hence, the decrease in trade receivables is added to sale revenue.

This same underlying logic is used to determine adjustments for the other current assets and liabilities.

To summarize, the statement of earnings reflects revenues of the period, but cash flows from operating activities must reflect cash collections from customers. Sales on account increase the balance in trade receivables, and collections from customers decrease the balance:

Trade Receivables (A)		
Beg. bal.	385	
Increase	132	
End. bal.	517	

The statement of financial position for Danier Leather indicates an *increase* in trade receivables of $132 for the period, which means cash collected from customers is less than revenue. To convert net earnings to cash flows from operating activities, the amount of the increase in trade receivables must be *subtracted* from net earnings in Exhibit 5.6. A decrease in trade receivables is added to net earnings.

Change in Inventory The statement of earnings reflects merchandise sold for the period, whereas cash flows from operating activities must reflect cash purchases.

Both the change in inventory and the change in trade payables (borrowing from suppliers) determine the magnitude of this difference. It is easiest to think about the change in inventory in terms of the simple case in which the company pays cash to trade suppliers. We address the added complexity involved when purchases are made on account when we discuss the adjustment for the change in trade payables.

As shown in the inventories T-account, purchases of goods increase the balance in inventory, and recording the cost of sales decreases the balance in inventory. Therefore, the change in inventory is the difference between purchases and cost of sales:

Inventories (A)		Inventories (A)			
Beg. bal.		Beg. bal.	28,964		
Purchases	Cost of sales			Decrease	4,073
End. bal.		End. bal.	24,891		

Danier Leather's statement of financial position indicates that inventory *decreased* by $4,073, which means that the cost of purchases is less than the cost of merchandise sold. The decrease must be *added* to net earnings to convert to cash flows from operating activities in Exhibit 5.6. (An increase is subtracted from net earnings.)

Change in Prepayments The statement of earnings reflects expenses of the period, but cash flows from operating activities must reflect the cash payments. Cash paid in advance increases the prepayments balance, and expenses recognized during the period decrease the balance:

Prepayments (A)		Prepayments (A)			
Beg. bal.		Beg. bal.	901		
Purchases	Services used (expense)			Decrease	102
End. bal.		End. bal.	799		

Danier Leather's statement of financial position indicates that prepayments *decreased* by $102 during the year, which means that new cash prepayments are less than the amount of expenses. The decrease (the lower prepayments) must be *added* to net earnings in Exhibit 5.6. (An increase is subtracted from net earnings.)

Change in Trade Payables Cash flow from operations must reflect cash purchases, but not all purchases are for cash. Purchases on account increase trade payables, and cash paid to suppliers decreases trade payables:

Trade Payables (L)		Trade Payables (L)	
	Beg. bal.		Beg. bal. 9,210
Cash payments	Purchases on account	Decrease 1,073	
	End. bal.		End. bal. 8,137

Danier Leather's trade payables *decreased* by $1,073, indicating that cash payments were more than purchases on account, and this decrease (the extra payments) must be *subtracted* from net earnings in Exhibit 5.6. (An increase is added to net earnings.)

Change in Accrued Liabilities The statement of earnings reflects all accrued expenses, but the statement of cash flows must reflect actual payments for those expenses. Recording accrued expenses increases the accrued liabilities balance, and cash payments for the expenses decrease it:

Accrued Liabilities (L)		Accrued Liabilities (L)	
	Beg. bal.		Beg. bal. 4,668
Payment of accruals	Accrued expenses		Increase 316
	End. bal.		End. bal. 4,984

Danier Leather's accrued liabilities *increased* by $316, which indicates that cash paid for the expenses is less than accrual basis expenses. The increase must be *added* to net earnings in Exhibit 5.6. (A decrease is subtracted from net earnings.)

Change in Income Tax Payable Cash flow from operations must reflect cash payments to the tax authorities, but the statement of earnings must reflect income tax expense based on accrual basis accounting. Recognition of income tax expense increases income tax payable, and cash paid to the tax authorities decreases it:

Income Tax Payable (L)		Income Tax Payable (L)	
	Beg. bal.		Beg. bal. 278
Cash payments	Income tax expense	Decrease 278	
	End. bal.		End. bal. 0

Danier Leather's income tax payable *decreased* by $278, indicating that cash payments were more than income tax expense, and this decrease must be *subtracted* from net earnings in Exhibit 5.6. (An increase is added to net earnings.)

Summary We can summarize the typical additions and subtractions that are required to reconcile net earnings with cash flows from operating activities as follows:

Item	Additions and Subtractions to Reconcile Net Earnings to Cash Flows from Operating Activities	
	When Item Increases	When Item Decreases
Depreciation and amortization	+	NA
Trade receivables	−	+
Inventory	−	+
Prepayments	−	+
Trade payables	+	−
Accrued liabilities	+	−
Income tax payable	+	−

Notice in this table that an increase in a current asset or a decrease in a current liability is always subtracted to reconcile net earnings to cash flows from operating activities. A decrease in a current asset or an increase in a current liability is always added to reconcile net earnings to cash flows from operating activities. The statement of cash flows for Danier Leather (Exhibit 5.1) shows the same additions and subtractions to reconcile net earnings to cash flows from operating activities described in Exhibit 5.6.

It is important to note again that the net cash inflow or outflow from operating activities is the same regardless of whether the direct or indirect method of presentation is used (in this case, an inflow of $10,125). The two methods differ only in terms of the details reported on the statement. We show in Appendix 5B how cash flows from operations can be computed by using the direct method.

AUSTRALIAN PRACTICES

INTERNATIONAL PERSPECTIVE

REAL-WORLD EXCERPT

Domino's Pizza Enterprises Ltd.

ANNUAL REPORT

Domino's Pizza Enterprises Ltd. is the largest pizza chain in Australia. It is also the largest franchisee for the Domino's Pizza brand in the world. Australian companies prepare their financial statements in accordance with Australian Accounting Standards, which are based on IFRS. As we noted before, IAS 7 encourages companies to report their cash flows from operations using the direct method. But Australian Accounting Standards require Australian companies to use the direct method. Hence, Domino's cash flow from operations is presented as follows:

STATEMENT OF CASH FLOWS
For the Year Ended 1 July, 2012
(in millions of Australian dollars)

Cash Flows from Operating Activities	
Receipts from customers	295.1
Payments to suppliers and employees	(250.8)
Interest received	1.8
Interest and other costs of finance paid	(0.5)
Income taxes paid	(8.0)
Net cash generated by operating activities	37.6

Note that Domino's combines payments to suppliers and employees, but other companies report these items separately. Like Canadian companies that choose the direct method, Domino's reports the indirect presentation in a note to the financial statements.

PAUSE FOR **FEEDBACK** STOP

The indirect method for reporting cash flows from operating activities reports a conversion of net earnings to net cash flow from operating activities. The conversion involves additions and subtractions for (1) expenses (such as depreciation expense) and revenues that do not affect current assets or current liabilities, and for (2) changes in each of the individual current assets (other than cash and short-term investments) and current liabilities (other than short-term debt to financial institutions and current maturities of long-term debt, which relate to financing). This is done to reflect differences in the timing of accrual basis net earnings and cash flows. To test whether you understand these concepts, answer the following questions before you move on.

SELF-STUDY **QUIZ 5-2**

Sun-Rype Products Ltd.

Indicate which of the following items taken from the statement of cash flows of Sun-Rype Products Ltd. would be added (+), subtracted (−), or not included (0) in the reconciliation of net earnings to cash flow from operations.

_____   *a.* Increase in inventories   _____   *d.* Decrease in trade receivables
_____   *b.* Repayment of loans and borrowings   _____   *e.* Increase in trade and other payables
_____   *c.* Depreciation expense   _____   *f.* Increase in prepayments

After you complete your answers, check them with the solutions at the end of the chapter.

LO³

Analyze and interpret the quality of earnings ratio.

Interpreting Cash Flows from Operating Activities

The operating activities section of the statement of cash flows focuses attention on the firm's ability to generate cash internally through operations, and its management of working capital (current assets minus current liabilities). Many analysts regard this as the most important section of the statement because, in the long run, operations are the only sustainable source of cash. Investors should not invest in a company if they believe that it will not be able to pay them dividends or make reinvestments with cash generated from operations. Similarly, creditors should not lend money if they believe that cash generated from operations will not be available to pay back the loan. For example, many Internet-based companies crashed when investors lost faith in their ability to turn business ideas into cash from operations.

A common rule followed by financial and credit analysts is to avoid firms with rising net earnings but falling cash flow from operations. Rapidly rising inventories require the use of cash until goods are sold. Similarly, rapidly rising trade receivables reflect a delay in the collection of cash. Rising inventories and trade receivables often predict a slump in net earnings as revenues fall. This increases the need for external financing as overall cash inflows from operations decline. A true understanding of the meaning of the difference between net earnings and cash flow from operations requires a detailed understanding of its causes.

In fiscal year 2012, Danier Leather reported net earnings of $4,028, which was lower than its cash flow from operations of $10,125. What caused this relationship? To answer this question, we must carefully analyze how Danier Leather's operating activities are reported in its statement of cash flows. To properly interpret this information, we must also learn more about the leather industry. Danier Leather normally reports higher cash flow from operations than net earnings because of the effect of depreciation and amortization expenses, which reduce net earnings but do not require cash outflows. At the same time, it carefully manages the assets and liabilities that relate to operating activities, keeping the total changes in these assets and liabilities to a minimum. Many analysts compute the quality of earnings ratio as a general sign of the ability to generate cash through operations.

KEY RATIO ANALYSIS

QUALITY OF EARNINGS RATIO

ANALYTICAL QUESTION → How much cash does each dollar of net earnings generate?
RATIO AND COMPARISONS → The quality of earnings ratio is useful in answering this question. It is computed as follows:

$$\text{Quality of Earnings Ratio} = \frac{\text{Cash Flows from Operating Activities}}{\text{Net Earnings}}$$

Danier Leather's ratio for the year 2012 is

$$\$10,125/\$4,028 = 2.51$$

Comparisons over Time				Comparisons with Competitors	
Danier Leather				**Coach Inc.**	**G-III Apparel Group**
2010	2011	2012		2012	2012
1.94	0.58	2.51		1.17	0.96

SELECTED FOCUS COMPANY COMPARISONS—2012

		6.58
	2.97	
1.63		
Gildan	Canadian Tire	Sun-Rype

INTERPRETATIONS

In General → The quality of earnings ratio measures the portion of earnings that was generated in cash. All other things being equal, a higher quality of earnings ratio indicates a greater ability to finance operating and other cash needs from operating cash inflows.[10] A higher ratio also indicates that it is less likely that the company is using aggressive revenue recognition policies to increase net earnings. When this ratio does not equal 1.0, analysts must establish the source of the difference to determine the significance of the findings. There are four potential causes of any difference:

1. **The corporate life cycle (growth or decline in sales).** When sales are increasing, receivables and inventory normally increase faster than trade payables. This often reduces operating cash flows below the reported net earnings, which, in turn, reduces the ratio. When sales are declining, the opposite occurs and the ratio increases.
2. **Seasonality.** Seasonal (from quarter to quarter) variations in sales and purchases of inventory can cause the ratio to deviate from 1.0 during particular quarters.
3. **Changes in revenue and expense recognition.** Aggressive revenue recognition or failure to accrue appropriate expenses will inflate net earnings and reduce the ratio.
4. **Changes in management of operating assets and liabilities.** Inefficient management will increase operating assets and decrease liabilities, which will reduce operating cash flows and reduce the ratio. More efficient management will have the opposite effect.

Focus Company Analysis → Danier Leather's quality of earnings ratio dropped from 1.94 to 0.58 in 2011 and increased to 2.51 in 2012. In comparison with its competitors, Danier Leather has a much higher quality of earnings ratio than both Coach Inc. and G-III Apparel Group for fiscal year 2012. Danier Leather's higher ratio would prompt financial analysts to read the management's discussion and analysis sections of the annual reports of the three companies to determine the causes of such differences.

A Few Cautions → The quality of earnings ratio can be interpreted only based on an understanding of the company's business operations and strategy. For example, a low ratio can be due simply to normal seasonal changes. However, it can also indicate obsolete inventory, slowing sales, or failed expansion plans. To test for these possibilities, analysts often analyze this ratio in tandem with the trade receivables turnover and inventory turnover ratios.

FRAUD AND CASH FLOWS FROM OPERATIONS

A QUESTION OF ACCOUNTABILITY

The statement of cash flows often gives outsiders the first hint that financial statements may contain errors and irregularities. The importance of this indicator as a predictor is receiving more attention following corporate scandals. For example, *Investors Chronicle* reported on an accounting fraud at a commercial credit company, suggesting that

> . . . a look at Versailles's cash flow statement—an invaluable tool in spotting creative accounting—should have triggered misgivings. In the company's last filed accounts . . . Versailles reported operating profits of . . . $25 million but a cash outflow from operating activities of $24 million . . . such figures should . . . have served as a warning. After all, what use is a company to anyone if it reports only accounting profits which are never translated into cash?*

As noted in earlier chapters, unethical managers sometimes attempt to reach earnings targets by manipulating accruals and deferrals of revenues and expenses to inflate net earnings. Since these adjustments do not affect the cash account, they have no effect on the statement of cash flows. As a consequence, a growing difference between net earnings and cash flow from operations can be a sign of such manipulations. This could be an early warning sign of operating and financial difficulties that may lead to bankruptcy.

*Source: James Chapman, "Creative Accounting: Exposed!" *Investor's Chronicle.*

REPORTING AND INTERPRETING CASH FLOWS FROM INVESTING ACTIVITIES

Reporting Cash Flows from Investing Activities

Preparing this section of the statement of cash flows requires analyzing the accounts related to property, plant, and equipment; intangible assets; and investments in the securities of other companies. Normally, the relevant statement of financial position accounts include short-term investments and non-current asset accounts, such as long-term investments and property, plant, and equipment. The following relationships are the ones that you will encounter most frequently:

Investing Activity	Related Statement of Financial Position Account(s)	Cash Flow Effect
Purchase of property, plant, and equipment or intangible assets for cash	Property, plant, and equipment and intangible assets (e.g., patents)	Outflow
Sale of property, plant, and equipment or intangible assets for cash		Inflow
Purchase of investment securities for cash	Short- or long-term investments in shares and bonds issued by other companies	Outflow
Sale (maturity) of investment securities for cash		Inflow

Typical investing activities include the following:

1. Cash expenditures that include the acquisition of tangible productive assets, such as buildings and equipment, or intangible assets, such as trademarks and patents. *Only purchases paid for with cash or cash equivalents are included.*

2. Cash proceeds from the sale of productive assets or intangible assets. This is the amount of cash that was received from the sale of assets, regardless of whether the assets were sold at a gain or a loss.

3. Purchase of short- or long-term investments for cash. These investments can include shares or bonds issued by other companies, guaranteed investment certificates, or government securities with maturities of more than three months. (Remember that securities with maturities of three months or less are cash equivalents.)

4. Cash proceeds from the sale or maturity of short- or long-term investments. Again, this is the amount of cash that was received from the sale, regardless of whether the assets were sold at a gain or a loss.

In the case of Danier Leather, the analysis of changes in the statement of financial position (shown in Exhibit 5.3) indicates that two non-current assets (noted with an I) have changed during the period: property and equipment (net), and intangible assets. To determine the causes of changes in these assets, accountants need to search the related company records.

Property and Equipment (Net) The company's property and equipment (PE) account increased by an amount of $608, net of accumulated depreciation. Typically, the net change in PE is the result of three main changes: (1) purchase of new assets, (2) disposal of old assets, and (3) periodic depreciation of these assets. The purchase of assets increases the balance of PE, the disposal of assets decreases the balance by the carrying amount (original cost − accumulated depreciation) of the assets disposed of, and the periodic depreciation increases the accumulated depreciation, which in turn reduces the balance of PE.

During fiscal year 2012, Danier Leather purchased new property and equipment for cash in the amount of $3,974, which is a cash outflow. This amount less the depreciation expense of $3,366, which is added to the net earnings in the operations section of the statement of cash flows, explains the net increase in PE of $608:

Property and Equipment (net)

Beg. bal.	14,404	Depreciation	3,366
Purchases	3,974		
End. bal.	15,012		

Cash purchases and sales of property and equipment are listed separately on the statement of cash flows.

Computer Software   Danier Leather's records indicate that it purchased computer software for cash in the amount of $52, which is a cash outflow. This amount less the amortization expense of $380, which is added to the net earnings in the operations section of the statement of cash flows, explains the net decrease in computer software of $328:

Computer Software (A)

Beg. bal.	1,054	Amortization	380
Purchase	52		
End. bal.	726		

These investing items are listed in the schedule of investing activities in Exhibit 5.7 and result in a cash outflow of $4,026.

Items from Statement of Financial Position and Account Analysis	Cash Inflow (Outflows)	Explanation
Additions to property and equipment	($3,974)	Payment in cash for property and equipment.
Additions to computer software	(52)	Payment in cash for computer software.
Net cash inflow (outflow) from investing activities	($4,026)	Reported on the statement of cash flows.

Exhibit **5.7**

Danier Leather: Schedule for Net Cash Flow from Investing Activities (in thousands of dollars)

Interpreting Cash Flows from Investing Activities

Two common ways of assessing a company's ability to finance its expansion needs from internal sources are the capital expenditures ratio and free cash flow.

LO5

Analyze and interpret the capital expenditures ratio.

CAPITAL EXPENDITURES RATIO

KEY RATIO
ANALYSIS

ANALYTICAL QUESTION → To what degree was the company able to finance purchases of property and equipment, intangibles, and other businesses with cash provided by operating activities?

RATIO AND COMPARISONS → Since capital expenditures for property and equipment, intangibles, and acquisition of other businesses often vary greatly from year to year, this ratio is often computed over longer periods of time than one year. It is computed as follows:

$$\text{Capital Expenditures Ratio} = \frac{\text{Cash Flow from Operating Activities}}{\text{Cash Paid for Capital Expenditures}}$$

Danier Leather's ratio for 2012 is

$$\$10,125/\$4,026 = 2.51$$

Comparisons over Time			Comparisons with Competitors	
Danier Leather			**Coach Inc.**	**G-III Apparel Group**
2010	**2011**	**2012**	**2012**	**2012**
5.24	2.03	2.51	5.18	0.60

SELECTED FOCUS COMPANY COMPARISONS—2012

WestJet Airlines 2.68

Gildan 3.40

Canadian Tire 6.68

INTERPRETATIONS

In General → The capital expenditures ratio reflects the portion of purchases of property and equipment; intangible assets; and acquisition of other businesses financed from operating activities without the need for outside debt or equity financing or the sale of property, plant, and equipment; intangibles; or other investments. A high ratio indicates less need for outside financing for current and future expansion. This provides the company with opportunities for strategic acquisitions, avoids the cost of additional debt, and reduces the risks of bankruptcy that come with additional leverage (see Chapter 11).

Focus Company Analysis → Danier Leather's ratio dropped from 5.24 in 2010 to 2.51 in 2012. Although Danier Leather generates more than sufficient cash to meet its investing needs, its ratio for fiscal year 2012 is lower than the ratio of Coach Inc. but higher than that of G-III Apparel Group, which made a major acquisition in that year. To many, the tangible nature of property and equipment may suggest that it is a low-risk investment. When companies in an industry build more productive capacity than is necessary to meet customer demand, however, the costs of maintaining and financing an idle plant can drive a company to ruin. For this reason, Danier Leather and its competitors, without compromising on product quality, outsource the manufacturing of their products partially to suppliers in other countries where the cost of production is relatively low.

A Few Cautions → Since the needs for investment in both tangible and intangible assets differ dramatically across industries (e.g., airlines versus pizza delivery restaurants), a particular firm's ratio should be compared only with its prior years' figures or with other firms in the same industry. Also, a high ratio may indicate a failure to upgrade a company's productive capacity, which can limit its ability to compete in the future.

FINANCIAL ANALYSIS

FREE CASH FLOW

FREE CASH FLOW = Cash Flows from Operating Activities − Dividends − Capital Expenditures

Managers and analysts also often calculate **free cash flow**[11] as a measure of the firm's ability to pursue long-term investment opportunities. It is normally calculated as follows:

$$\text{Free Cash Flow} = \text{Cash Flows from Operating Activities} - \text{Dividends} - \text{Capital Expenditures}$$

Any positive free cash flow is available for additional capital expenditures, investments in other companies, and mergers and acquisitions, without the need for external financing. While free cash flow is considered a positive sign of financial flexibility, it can also represent a hidden cost to shareholders. Sometimes, managers use free cash flow to pursue unprofitable investments just for the sake of growth or for perquisites for management use (such as fancy offices and corporate jets). In these cases, the shareholders would be better off if free cash flow were paid as additional dividends or used to repurchase the company's shares in the open market.

LO6

Report and interpret cash flows from financing activities.

REPORTING AND INTERPRETING CASH FLOWS FROM FINANCING ACTIVITIES

Reporting Cash Flows from Financing Activities

Financing activities are associated with generating capital from creditors and owners. This section reflects changes in two current liabilities, *notes payable to financial institutions* (often called *short-term borrowings*) and *current portion of long-term borrowings*, as well as changes in *non-current liabilities and shareholders' equity accounts*.

These financial position accounts relate to the issuance and retirement of debt, repurchase of shares, and payment of dividends. The following relationships are the ones that you will encounter most frequently:

Related Statement of Financial Position Account(s)	Cash Flow Financing Activity	Effect
Short-term borrowings	Borrowing cash from bank or other financial institution	Inflow
	Repayment of loan principal	Outflow
Long-term borrowings	Long-term borrowings for cash	Inflow
	Repayment of principal on long-term borrowings	Outflow
Contributed capital	Issuance of shares for cash	Inflow
	Repurchase (retirement) of shares for cash	Outflow
Retained earnings	Payment of cash dividends	Outflow

Financing activities are associated with generating capital from creditors and owners. Typical financing activities include the following:

1. **Proceeds from issuance of short- and long-term borrowings.** This represents cash received from borrowing from banks and other financial institutions, and from issuance of long-term debt (e.g., notes) to the public. *If the debt is issued for other than cash* (e.g., issued directly to a supplier of equipment to pay for a purchase), *it is not included in the statement.*

2. **Principal payments on short- and long-term borrowings.** Cash outflows associated with debt include the periodic repayment of principal as well as interest payments. Cash repayments of principal are listed as cash flows from financing activities.

3. **Proceeds from the issuance of shares.** This represents cash received from the sale of shares to investors. *If the shares are issued for other than cash* (e.g., issued directly to an employee as part of salary), *the amount is not included in the statement.*

4. **Purchase of shares for retirement.** This cash outflow includes cash payments for repurchase of the company's own shares from shareholders.

5. **Interest and dividends.** Cash flows from interest and dividends received and paid should be classified in a consistent manner from period to period as operating, investing, or financing activities. Cash dividends are usually reported as a financing activity because they are payments to shareholders. Alternatively, dividends paid may be classified as a component of cash flows from operating activities in order to assist users to determine the ability of an entity to pay dividends out of operating cash flows.

   Dividends received may be classified as investing cash flows because they represent returns on investments. Alternatively, they may be classified as operating cash flows because they enter into the determination of net earnings or net loss.

   Interest paid may be classified as financing cash flow because it is a cost of obtaining financial resources, and interest received may be classified as investing cash flow because it is a return on investments. Alternatively, they may be classified as operating cash flows because they enter into the determination of net earnings or net loss.

To compute cash flows from financing activities, you should review changes in debt and shareholders' equity accounts. In the case of Danier Leather, analysis of changes in the account balances on the statement of financial position indicates that dividends payable, contributed capital, and retained earnings changed during the period (noted with an F in Exhibit 5.3).

	Item from Statement of Financial Position and Account Analysis	Cash Inflow (Outflow)	Explanation
Exhibit 5.8	Net proceeds from issuance of shares	$99	Cash proceeds from issue of shares
Danier Leather: Schedule for Net Cash Flow from Financing Activities (in thousands)	Repurchase of shares	(219)	Cash payments to repurchase outstanding shares
	Payment of dividends	(1,124)	Payment of cash dividends to shareholders
	Net cash inflow from financing activities	$(1,244)	Reported on the statement of cash flows

Contributed Capital   Danier Leather's change in contributed capital resulted from two decisions. First, Danier Leather issued common shares to employees for $99 in cash, which is a cash inflow.[12] The company also repurchased outstanding shares for $219 cash, which is a cash outflow.[13] These two amounts are listed in the schedule of financing activities in Exhibit 5.8:

Contributed Capital (SE)			
		Beg. bal.	15,160
Repurchased	219	Issued	99
		End. bal.	15,040

Retained Earnings   The change in retained earnings resulted from the addition of net earnings and the declaration of dividends:[14]

Retained Earnings (SE)			
		Beg. bal.	46,768
Dividends declared	1,832	Net earnings	4,028
		End. bal.	48,964

Dividends Payable   Companies usually pay dividends on a quarterly basis, and cash payments to shareholders are typically made within three or four weeks from the date of dividend declaration. The dividends declared during fiscal year 2012 were not all paid in that year:

Dividends Payable (L)			
		Beg. bal.	0
Payment to shareholders	1,124	Dividends declared	1,832
		End. bal.	708

Short- or Long-Term Borrowings   If Danier Leather had borrowed or repaid principal on short- or long-term borrowings during the period, these would also be listed in this section. The appropriate amounts would be determined by analyzing the short- and long-term borrowings accounts:

Short- or Long-Term Debt (L)		
	Beg. bal.	
Retire (repay)	Issue (borrow)	
	End. bal.	

Interpreting Cash Flows from Financing Activities

The long-term growth of a company is normally financed from three sources: internally generated funds (cash from operating activities), the issuance of shares, and money borrowed on a long-term basis. As we discuss in Chapter 11, companies can adopt a number of different capital structures (the balance of debt and equity). The financing sources that management uses to fund growth will have an important impact on the firm's risk and return characteristics. The statement of cash flows shows how management has elected to fund its growth. This information is used by analysts who wish to evaluate the capital structure and growth potential of a business.

INTERPRETATION OF CASH FLOW PATTERNS

FINANCIAL
ANALYSIS

The statement of cash flows depicts the relationships among the operating, investing, and financing activities. Throughout this chapter, we have illustrated the reporting and interpretation of Danier Leather's cash flows for fiscal year 2012. These cash flows are specific to one company for a specified time period. To generalize, the table below shows the eight possible patterns of cash flows generated from (used for) operating, investing, and financing activities. A general explanation for each observed pattern is also provided:

Analysis of Cash Flow Patterns

	1	2	3	4	5	6	7	8
Cash Flow from Operating	+	+	+	+	−	−	−	−
Cash Flow from Investing	+	−	+	−	+	−	+	−
Cash Flow from Financing	+	−	−	+	+	+	−	−

A general explanation of each pattern follows:

1. The company is using cash generated from operations, from the sale of non-current assets, and from financing to build its cash reserves. This is a very liquid company, possibly looking for acquisitions. This pattern is very unusual.

2. The company is using cash generated from operations to buy non-current assets and to reduce its debt or distribute cash dividends to shareholders. This pattern reflects a mature, successful firm.

3. The company is using cash from operations and from the sale of non-current assets to reduce its debt or distribute cash dividends to shareholders. It is actually downsizing its operations.

4. The company is using cash from operations and from borrowing (or from equity investment) to expand. This pattern is typical of many growing companies.

5. The company's operating cash flow problems are covered by the sale of non-current assets and by borrowing or shareholder contributions. The company is selling its non-current assets to stay in business, and the fact that investors are willing to supply the financing indicates that they apparently expect a turnaround in operating cash flows.

6. The company is experiencing a shortfall in cash flow from operations and from investing activities. The deficiency in cash is financed by long-term borrowings or investments by shareholders. This pattern is most typical of a young, fast-growing company.

7. The company is financing operating cash flow shortages, paying its debtholders and/or its shareholders via the sale of non-current assets. The company is actually shrinking.

8. The company is using cash reserves to finance operations, pay long-term creditors and/or investors, and acquire new non-current assets. This unusual scenario is possible only if cash previously accumulated is being used to meet these cash outflows.

Source: Adapted from M. T. Dugan, B. E. Gup, and W. D. Samson, "Teaching the Statement of Cash Flows," *Journal of Accounting Education,* Vol. 9, 1991, pp. 33–52.

Danier Leather's statement of cash flows for fiscal years 2008–2012 showed the following pattern of cash flows (in thousands of dollars):

	2012	2011	2010	2009	2008
Net cash provided by (used in) operating activities	$10,125	$4,523	$14,003	$10,773	$ 5,750
Net cash provided by (used in) investing activities	(4,026)	(2,390)	(2,672)	(3.576)	(3,891)
Net cash provided by (used in) financing activities	(1,244)	(1,140)	(9,396)	(2,451)	(2,556)

In each of these five years, Danier Leather used cash generated from operations to invest in non-current assets and to repurchase outstanding shares or distribute cash dividends to shareholders. This pattern of cash flows reflects a mature, successful company.

PAUSE FOR FEEDBACK

Cash flows can be generated from or used in operating, investing, and financing activities. The sources and uses of cash flows provide an indication of the phase that the company is experiencing in its life cycle. For example, successful companies generate cash flows from operations for use in investing and financing activities, but companies that sell their long-lived assets to finance their operations and pay their creditors may not survive for long. Check your understanding of the different patterns of cash flows by answering the following questions before you move on.

SELF-STUDY QUIZ 5-3

American International Group Inc.

American International Group Inc. (AIG) is a leading international insurance organization with operations in more than 130 countries and jurisdictions. Its statement of cash flows for three recent years included the following summary:

Years Ended December 31 (in millions of U.S. dollars)			
	Year 3	Year 2	Year 1
Net cash provided by (used in) operating activities	$ 35	$ 16,910	$ 18,584
Net cash provided by (used in) investing activities	36,322	(10,225)	5,778
Net cash provided by (used in) financing activities	(36,926)	(9,261)	(28,997)

What conclusions can you derive by examining the pattern of the company's cash flows during these three years?

After you complete your answers, check them with the solutions at the end of the chapter.

LO7

Understand the format of the statement of cash flows and additional cash flow disclosures.

COMPLETING THE STATEMENT AND ADDITIONAL DISCLOSURES

Statement Structure

Refer to the formal statement of cash flows for Danier Leather that is shown in Exhibit 5.1. As you can see, it is a simple matter to construct the statement after the detailed analysis of the accounts and transactions have been completed (shown in Exhibits 5.6, 5.7, and 5.8). Exhibit 5.9 summarizes the general structure of the statement for companies that use the indirect method. As you can see, the *net increase or decrease in cash and cash equivalents* is added to the cash and cash equivalents reported on the statement of financial position at the beginning of the period, and the result equals the cash and cash equivalents reported on the same statement at the end of the period. Companies that use the direct method for computing cash flow from operations usually present a reconciliation of net earnings to cash flow from operations (the indirect method as presented in Exhibit 5.6) as a supplemental schedule. Companies must also provide two other disclosures related to the statement of cash flows.

Non-cash Investing and Financing Activities

NON-CASH INVESTING AND FINANCING ACTIVITIES are transactions that do not have direct cash flow effects; they are reported as a supplement to the statement of cash flows in narrative or schedule form.

Certain transactions are important investing and financing activities but have no cash flow effects. These are called **non-cash investing and financing activities**; they are reported as a supplement to the statement of cash flows in narrative or schedule form. For example, the purchase of a $100,000 building with a $100,000 mortgage given by the former owner does not cause either an inflow or an outflow of cash. As a result,

	Exhibit **5.9**
Statement of Cash Flows (Indirect Method)	
Operating Activities:	Structure of the Statement of Cash Flows (Indirect Method)

Statement of Cash Flows (Indirect Method)

Operating Activities:

Net earnings

\+ Depreciation and amortization expense

− Gain on sale of long-lived asset

\+ Loss on sale of long-lived asset

\+ Decreases in operating assets

\+ Increases in operating liabilities

− Increases in operating assets

− Decreases in operating liabilities

Net Cash Flow from Operating Activities

Investing Activities:

− Purchase of property, plant, and equipment or intangible assets

\+ Sale of property, plant, and equipment or intangible assets

− Purchase of investment securities

\+ Sale (maturity) of investment securities

Net Cash Flow from Investing Activities

Financing Activities:

\+ Borrowing from bank or other financial institution

− Repayment of loan principal

\+ Issuance of long-term debt for cash

− Repayment of principal on long-term debt

\+ Issuance of shares

− Repurchase (retirement) of shares

− Payment of (cash) dividends

Net Cash Flow from Financing Activities

Net Increase or Decrease in Cash and Cash Equivalents

Cash and cash equivalents at beginning of period

Cash and cash equivalents at end of period

these non-cash activities are not listed in the three main sections of the statement of cash flows. IAS 7 requires supplemental disclosure of these transactions in either narrative or schedule form. Danier Leather's statement of cash flows does not list any non-cash investing and financing activities. The following excerpt from the 2012 annual report of Gildan Activewear Inc. provides examples of these non-cash transactions:

REAL-WORLD EXCERPT

Gildan Activewear

ANNUAL REPORT

Supplemental cash flow disclosure (in thousands of U.S. dollars)			
	2012	**2011**	**2010**
Non-cash transactions			
Additions to property, plant, and equipment included in trade payables and accrued liabilities	(1,295)	5,026	2,099
Proceeds on disposal of long-lived assets included in other assets	—	—	427

Supplemental Cash Flow Information

Companies that use the indirect method of presenting cash flows from operations must also disclose the amounts of interest and dividends received and paid during the period, as well as cash paid for income taxes. These are normally listed in the operating activities section of the statement or in the notes.

ACCOUNTING STANDARDS
FOR PRIVATE ENTERPRISES

The requirements for the reporting of cash flow information by Canadian private enterprises (Section 1540 of the *CICA Handbook*) are practically the same as the requirements for Canadian publicly accountable enterprises (IAS 7). One notable difference is the classification of interest and dividends received and paid:

Financial Reporting Issue	IFRS	ASPE
Classification of cash flows from interest and dividends		
• Interest paid	Cash payments for interest are classified as either operating or financing activities.	Cash payments for interest are classified as an operating activity if they are included in the determination of net earnings.
• Dividends paid	Dividend payments to shareholders are classified as either operating or financing activities.	Dividend payments to shareholders are classified as an operating activity.
• Interest and dividends received	Cash flows from interest and dividends received are classified as either operating or investing activities.	Cash flows from interest and dividends received are classified as operating activities.

DEMONSTRATION **CASE**

During the year ended December 31, 2014, Old Style Brewery, a craft brewer, reported net earnings of $3,182 (all numbers in thousands) and cash and cash equivalents of $472 at the beginning and $24,676 at the end of the year. It also engaged in the following activities:

a. Paid $18,752 in principal on long-term borrowings.
b. Received $46,202 in cash from initial public offering of shares.
c. Incurred other non-current accrued operating expenses of $857.
d. Paid $18,193 in cash for purchase of property, plant, and equipment.
e. Trade receivables increased by $881.
f. Borrowed $16,789 from various lenders.
g. Refundable deposits payable increased by $457.
h. Inventories increased by $574.
i. Made cash deposits on equipment of $5,830.
j. Income tax refund receivable decreased by $326.
k. Sold (issued) shares to employees for $13 in cash.
l. Trade payables decreased by $391.
m. Received $4 from other investing activities.
n. Accrued liabilities increased by $241.
o. Prepayments increased by $565.
p. Recorded depreciation of $1,324.
q. Paid $5 cash for other financing activities.

Required:
Based on this information, prepare the statement of cash flows for the year ended December 31, 2014. Use the indirect method to compute the cash flows from operating activities.

We strongly recommend that you prepare your own answer to this requirement and then check it with the following solution.

SUGGESTED **SOLUTION**

OLD STYLE BREWERY
Statement of Cash Flows
For the Year Ended December 31, 2014
(in thousands)

Operating activities	
Net earnings	$ 3,182
Add (deduct) items not affecting cash:	
Depreciation	1,324
Other non-current accrued expenses	857
Increase in trade receivables	(881)
Increase in inventories	(574)
Decrease in income taxes receivable	326
Increase in prepayments	(565)
Decrease in trade payables	(391)
Increase in accrued liabilities	241
Increase in refundable deposits payable	457
Net cash flows from operating activities	3,976
Investing activities	
Expenditures for property, plant, and equipment	(18,193)
Deposits on equipment	(5,830)
Other investing activities	4
Net cash flow from investing activities	(24,019)
Financing activities	
Proceeds from debt	16,789
Repayment of debt	(18,752)
Proceeds from sale of shares (IPO)	46,202
Proceeds from sale of shares (options)	13
Other financing activities	(5)
Net cash flow from financing activities	44,247
Increase in cash and cash equivalents	24,204
Cash and cash equivalents:	
Beginning of year	472
End of year	$24,676

APPENDIX 5A: ADJUSTMENT FOR GAINS AND LOSSES ON THE SALE OF LONG-LIVED ASSETS— INDIRECT METHOD

The operating activities section of the statement of cash flows prepared under the indirect method may include an adjustment for gains and losses on the sale of long-lived assets reported on the statement of earnings. The transactions that cause gains and losses should be classified on the statement of cash flows as operating, investing, or financing activities, depending on their dominant characteristics. For example, if the sale of a productive asset (e.g., a delivery truck) produced a gain, it would be classified as an investing activity.

An adjustment must be made in the operating activities section to avoid double counting of the gain or the loss. To illustrate, if Danier Leather sells for $8,000 cash a delivery truck with an original cost of $10,000 and accumulated depreciation of $4,000, the following entry is made:[15]

Cash (+A)	8,000	
Accumulated depreciation (−XA, +A)	4,000	
Property and equipment (−A)		10,000
Gain on sale of assets (+Gain, +SE) ($8,000 − $6,000)		2,000

Assets		=	Liabilities	+	Shareholders' Equity	
Cash	+8,000				Gain on sale of assets	+2,000
Accumulated depreciation	+4,000					
Property and equipment	−10,000					

The $8,000 inflow of cash is an investing cash inflow, but the gain of $2,000 is also reported on the statement of earnings. Because the gain is included in the computation of net earnings, it is necessary to remove (subtract) the $2,000 gain from the operating activities section of the statement to avoid double counting:

Cash flows from operating activities	
Net earnings	$4,028
Adjustments to reconcile net earnings to cash flow from operating activities:	
. . .	. . .
Gain on disposal of property and equipment	(2,000)
. . .	. . .
Net cash flow provided by operating activities	. . .
Cash flows from investing activities	
Purchases of property and equipment	. . .
Proceeds from disposal of property and equipment	8,000
. . .	. . .
Net cash used in investing activities	. . .

If the company had sold the same asset for $5,000 cash, the following entry would have been made:

Cash (+A)	5,000	
Accumulated depreciation (−XA, +A)	4,000	
Loss on sale of assets (−Loss, −SE) ($5,000 − $6,000)	1,000	
Property and equipment (−A)		10,000

Assets		=	Liabilities	+	Shareholders' Equity	
Cash	+ 5,000				Loss on sale of assets	−1,000
Accumulated depreciation	+ 4,000					
Property and equipment	−10,000					

On the statement of cash flows, the loss of $1,000 must be removed (added to net earnings) in the computation of cash flows from operating activities, and the total cash collected of $5,000 must be shown in the investing activities section of the statement:

Cash flows from operating activities	
Net earnings	$4,028
Adjustments to reconcile net earnings to cash flow from operating activities:	
. . .	. . .
Loss on disposal of property and equipment	1,000
. . .	. . .
Net cash flow provided by operating activities	. . .
Cash flows from investing activities	
Purchases of property and equipment	. . .
Proceeds from disposal of property and equipment	5,000
. . .	. . .
Net cash used in investing activities	. . .

APPENDIX 5B: REPORTING CASH FLOWS FROM OPERATING ACTIVITIES—DIRECT METHOD

Exhibit 5.3 shows Danier Leather's comparative statements of financial position at the end of fiscal years 2012 and 2011 and its statement of earnings for the year 2012. Recall that the direct method reports gross cash receipts and gross cash payments related to operating activities. It presents a summary of all operating transactions that resulted in either a debit or a credit to cash.

Cash Flows from Operating Activities

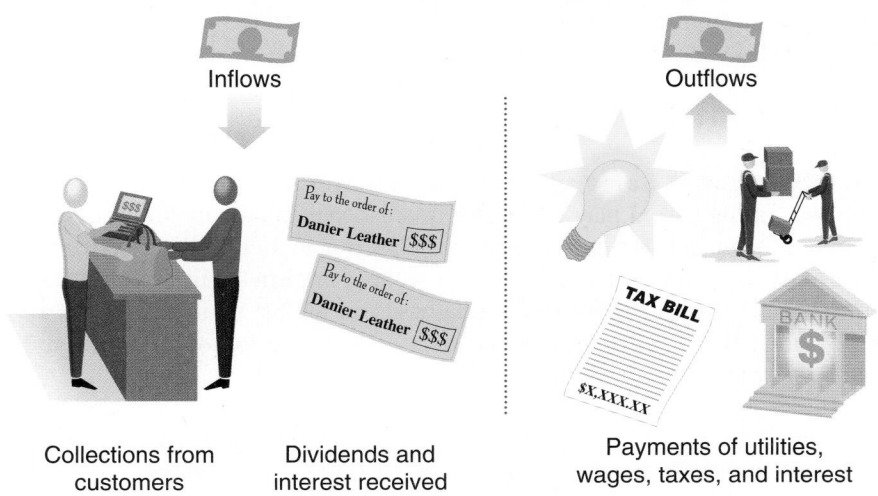

Inflows		Outflows
Collections from customers	Dividends and interest received	Payments of utilities, wages, taxes, and interest

The computation of cash receipts and payments requires adjusting each item on the statement of earnings from an accrual basis to a cash basis. To facilitate this process, the asset, liability, and equity accounts in Exhibit 5.3 that relate to operating activities have been marked with an O. These items include trade receivables, inventories, prepayments, trade payables, accrued liabilities, deferred revenue, income tax payable, deferred income tax asset, and retained earnings.

Converting Revenue and Expense Items from an Accrual Basis to a Cash Basis   The computation of cash receipts and payments requires adjusting each item on the statement of earnings from an accrual basis. To facilitate this process, we analyze the change in the balance of each current asset and current liability account by examining the type of transactions that affect the account. This process helps us determine the amount of cash received or paid during the accounting period.

We will use the following relation to analyze the changes in each current asset and liability account:

Converting Revenues to Cash Inflows   When sales are recorded, trade receivables increase, and when cash is collected, trade receivables decrease. Hence, the change from the beginning balance of trade receivables to the ending balance can be represented as follows:

In general	Danier Leather's example
Trade receivables, beginning (known)	$ 385
+ Sales revenue (known)	148,219
− Cash collections from customers (computed)	A
= Trade receivables, ending (known)	$ 517

The beginning and ending balances of trade receivables are reported on the statement of financial position, and sales revenue is reported on the statement of earnings. However, the amount collected from customers is not reported on either statement, but can be derived from the relation above.

The beginning balance of trade receivables increases the cash received from customers on the assumption that all amounts owed to the company at the beginning of the period are collected during the period. In contrast, the ending balance of trade receivables is deducted from sales revenue, because these receivables have already been included in sales revenue but have not yet been collected from customers.

Using information from Danier Leather's statement of earnings and statement of financial position presented in Exhibit 5.3, we can compute the cash collected from customers as follows:[16]

Trade Receivables

Beg. bal.	385		
Sales	148,219	Collections	**148,087**
End. bal.	517		

$$\text{Cash collections} = \$385 + \$148,219 - \$517 = \$148,087$$

Converting Cost of Sales to Cash Paid to Suppliers   The cost of sales during the accounting period may be greater or smaller than the amount of cash paid to suppliers of merchandise during the period. The computation of the cash paid to suppliers is a two-stage process. First, we analyze the change in the inventories account to determine the amount of merchandise purchases during the period, and then we analyze the change in the trade payables account to compute the amount of cash payments to suppliers by using the following relations:

In general	Danier Leather's example
Inventories, beginning (known)	$28,964
+ Merchandise purchases (computed)	+ A
− Cost of sales (known)	− 71,325
= Inventories, ending (known)	= $24,891

In general	Danier Leather's example
Trade payables, beginning (known)	$9,210
+ Merchandise purchases (computed)	+ A
− Cash payments to suppliers (computed)	− B
= Trade payables, ending (known)	= $8,137

The beginning and ending balances of inventory and trade payables are reported on the statement of financial position, and the cost of sales is reported on the statement of earnings. However, the amount of merchandise purchases and the payments to suppliers are not reported on either statement, but can be derived from the relations above.

The ending balance of inventory is added to cost of sales to determine the cost of goods that were available for sale during the period. Given that part of the merchandise was available at the beginning of the period, it is deducted from the goods available to determine the amount of purchases during the period.

Using information from Danier Leather's statement of earnings and statement of financial position presented in Exhibit 5.3, we can compute the cash paid to suppliers in two steps as follows:

Inventories

Beg. bal.	28,964		
Purchases	**67,252**	Cost of sales	71,325
End. bal.	24,891		

$$\text{Merchandise Purchases} = \$71,325 + \$24,891 - \$28,964 = \$67,252$$

The beginning balance of trade payables is added to merchandise purchases to determine the total amount payable to suppliers. The ending balance of trade payables is then deducted from that total because this amount has not been paid to suppliers yet:[17]

Trade Payables

		Beg. bal.	9,210
Cash payments	**68,325**	Purchases	67,252
		End. bal.	8,137

$$\text{Cash Payments to Suppliers} = \$67,252 + \$9,210 - \$8,137 = \$68,325$$

Converting Other Operating Expenses to a Cash Outflow The total amount of any operating expense on the statement of earnings may differ from the cash payment for that expense during the accounting period. Some expenses are paid before they are recognized as expenses (e.g., prepaid rent). When prepayments are made, the balance in the prepayments asset account increases; when prepayments are used up and recognized as expenses for the period, the account balance decreases. Other expenses are paid for after they are recognized in the same or previous periods. In this case, when expenses are recorded, the balance in the accrued liabilities account increases; when payments are made, the account balance decreases. The computation of the cash paid for operating expenses is therefore a two-stage process. First, we analyze the change in the prepayments account to determine the amount of cash paid during the period, and then we analyze the change in the accrued liabilities account to compute the amount of cash that was paid during the period for various other expenses, as shown in the following relations:

In general	Danier Leather's example
Prepayments, beginning (known)	$901
+ Cash payments for future (deferred) expenses (unknown)	+ A
− Prepayments that were used up during the period (unknown)	− B
= Prepayments, ending (known)	= $799

In general	Danier Leather's example
Accrued liabilities, beginning (known)	$4,668
+ Expenses accrued during the period (unknown)	+ C
− Cash payments for accrued expenses (unknown)	− D
= Accrued liabilities, ending (known)	= $4,984

The beginning and ending balances of prepayments and accrued liabilities are reported on the statement of financial position. But the prepayments (B) that were used up during the period are not reported separately on the statement of earnings. Hence, we cannot compute the amount of cash (A) paid for future expenses. Similarly, the expenses (C) that accrued during the period are not reported separately on the statement of earnings, which makes it difficult to compute the amount of cash (D) paid during the period to settle accrued expenses. However, the amounts B and C are reported together on the statement of earnings as operating expenses (or selling, general, and administrative expenses). By combining the two relations, we can then compute the sum of A and D, which represents the payments made for other expenses.

Using information from Danier Leather's statement of earnings and statement of financial position presented in Exhibit 5.3, we can compute the cash paid for other expenses as follows:

Cash Paid for Other Expenses = $67,576 (general, selling, and administrative expenses, reflecting prepayments that expired during the fiscal year and accrued expenses)

	+ 799	(prepayments, end of fiscal year)
	− 901	(prepayments, beginning of fiscal year)
	+ 4,668	(accrued liabilities, beginning of fiscal year)
	− 4,984	(accrued liabilities, end of fiscal year)
	= $67,158	

Prepayments

Beg. bal.	901		
Cash payments unknown		Prepayments that expired	unknown
End. bal.	799		

Accrued Liabilities

		Beg. bal.	4,668
Cash payments unknown		Unpaid expenses	unknown
		End. bal.	4,984

Similar analysis can be applied to computing the cash payments for interest and income taxes. Danier Leather reports interest expense of $20. Since there is no interest payable balance, interest paid must be equal to interest expense.

Danier Leather's income tax expense equals $1,524. This expense usually consists of two components: an amount that is currently payable to the federal and provincial taxation authorities and another amount labelled "deferred income taxes." Deferred income taxes result from temporary differences that exist between amounts reported on the financial statements in accordance with IFRS and amounts included in tax reports in conformity with tax rules that must be used by corporations. These differences relate to the timing of recognition of revenues and expenses for financial reporting (i.e., based on accrual accounting) compared to taxation rules that essentially use a cash basis of accounting.

The computation of cash paid for income taxes takes into consideration changes in two accounts: income taxes payable and deferred income taxes. The general computation of income tax payments follows:

Income tax expense	$1,524
+ Income taxes payable, beginning	278
− Income taxes payable, ending	0
	1,802
+ Decrease in deferred income tax asset	657
Cash payments for income taxes	$2,459

The operating cash inflows and outflows are accumulated in Exhibit 5.10.

To summarize, the following adjustments must commonly be made to convert statement of earnings items to the related operating cash flow amounts:

Statement of Earnings Account	+/− Change in Statement of Financial Position Account(s)	= Operating Cash Flow
Sales revenue	+ Beginning trade receivables − Ending trade receivables	= Collections from customers
Cost of sales	− Beginning inventory + Ending inventory + Beginning trade payables − Ending trade payables	= Payments to suppliers of inventory
Other operating expenses	− Beginning prepayments + Ending prepayments + Beginning accrued liabilities − Ending accrued liabilities	= Payments to suppliers of services (e.g., rent, utilities, wages)
Interest expense	+ Beginning interest payable − Ending interest payable	= Payments for interest
Income tax expense	+ Beginning income taxes payable − Ending income taxes payable +/− Changes in deferred incomes tax assets and liabilities	= Payments for income taxes

Exhibit **5.10**

Danier Leather Inc.: Schedule of Net Cash Flows from Operating Activities, Direct Method (in thousands of dollars)

Cash flows from operating activities		
Cash collected from customers		$148,087
Cash payments		
• to suppliers	$68,325	
• for other operating expenses	67,158	
• for interest	20	
• for income taxes	2,459	137,962
Net cash provided by operating activities		$ 10,125

PAUSE FOR
FEEDBACK

The direct method for reporting cash flows from operating activities reports gross cash receipts and gross cash payments related to operating activities. To test your understanding of this method relative to the indirect method, answer the following questions.

SELF-STUDY **QUIZ 5-4**

Indicate which of the following items taken from the statement of cash flows would be added (+), subtracted (−), or not included (0) in the cash flow from operations section when the direct method is used:

_____ *a.* Increase in inventories
_____ *b.* Payment of dividends to shareholders
_____ *c.* Cash collections from customers
_____ *d.* Purchase of property, plant, and equipment for cash
_____ *e.* Payment of interest to debtholders
_____ *f.* Payment of taxes to the taxation authorities

After you complete your answers, check them with the solutions at the end of the chapter.

Available on *Connect*: APPENDIX 5C: SPREADSHEET APPROACH— STATEMENT OF CASH FLOWS: INDIRECT METHOD

CHAPTER **TAKE-AWAYS**

1. **Classify cash flow items into cash flows from operating, investing, and financing activities.**
   The statement has three main sections: cash flows from operating activities, which are related to earning revenue from normal operations; cash flows from investing activities, which are related to the acquisition and sale of productive assets; and cash flows from financing activities, which are related to external financing of the enterprise. The net cash inflow or outflow for the year is the same amount as the increase or decrease in cash and cash equivalents for the year. Cash equivalents are highly liquid investments with original maturities of less than three months.

2. **Report and interpret cash flows from operating activities by using the indirect method.**
   The indirect method for reporting cash flows from operating activities presents a conversion of net earnings to net cash flows from operating activities. The conversion involves additions and subtractions for (1) non-current accruals, including expenses (such as depreciation expense) and revenues that do not affect current assets or current liabilities, and (2) changes in each of the individual current assets (other than cash and short-term investments) and current liabilities (other than short-term borrowings from financial institutions and current portion of long-term borrowings, which relate to financing) that reflect differences in the timing of accrual basis earnings and cash flows.

3. **Analyze and interpret the quality of earnings ratio.**
   The quality of earnings ratio (Cash flows from operating activities ÷ Net earnings) measures the portion of net earnings that was generated in cash. A higher quality of earnings ratio indicates greater ability to finance operating and other cash needs from operating cash inflows. A higher ratio also indicates that it is less likely that the company is using aggressive revenue recognition policies to increase net earnings.

4. **Report and interpret cash flows from investing activities.**
   Investing activities reported on the statement of cash flows include cash payments to acquire property, plant, and equipment, and short- and long-term investments. They also include cash proceeds from the sale of these assets.

5. **Analyze and interpret the capital expenditures ratio.**
   The capital expenditures ratio (Cash flows from operating activities ÷ Cash paid for capital expenditures) reflects the portion of purchases of property, plant, and equipment; intangible assets; and acquisition of other businesses that are financed from operating activities without the need

for outside debt or equity financing or the sale of other investments or other non-current assets. A high ratio is beneficial because it provides the company with opportunities for strategic acquisitions.

6. **Report and interpret cash flows from financing activities.**
   Cash inflows from financing activities include cash proceeds from issuance of short- and long-term borrowings and contributed capital. Cash outflows include principal payments on short- and long-term borrowings, cash paid for the repurchase of the company's shares, and dividend payments. Cash payments associated with interest relate to operating activities.

7. **Understand the format of the statement of cash flows and additional cash flow disclosures.**
   The statement of cash flows splits transactions that affect cash into three categories: operating, investing, and financing activities. The operating section is most often prepared using the indirect method, which begins with net earnings and adjusts the amount to eliminate non-cash transactions. Non-cash investing and financing activities are investing and financing activities that do not involve cash. They include, for example, purchases of non-current assets with long-term borrowings or shares, exchanges of non-current assets, and exchanges of debt for shares. These transactions are disclosed only as supplemental disclosures to the statement of cash flows along with cash paid for taxes and interest under the indirect method.

Chapters 1 through 5 discussed the important steps in the accounting process that lead to the preparation of the four basic financial statements. This end to the internal portions of the accounting process, however, is just the beginning of the process of communicating accounting information to external users.

In the next chapter, we discuss the important players in this communication process; the many statement format choices available; the additional note disclosures required for publicly accountable enterprises; and the process, manner, and timing of the transmission of this information to users. At the same time, we discuss common uses of the information in investment analysis, debt contracts, and management compensation decisions. These discussions will help you consolidate much of what you have learned about the financial reporting process from previous chapters. It will also preview many of the important issues we will address later in the book.

KEY **RATIOS**

The quality of earnings ratio indicates what portion of net earnings was generated in cash. It is computed as follows:

$$\text{Quality of Earnings Ratio} = \frac{\text{Cash Flows from Operating Activities}}{\text{Net Earnings}}$$

The capital expenditures ratio measures the ability to finance purchases of property, plant, and equipment, intangibles, and other businesses from operations. It is computed as follows:

$$\text{Capital Expenditures Ratio} = \frac{\text{Cash Flows from Operating Activities}}{\text{Cash Paid for Capital Expenditures}}$$

FINDING **FINANCIAL INFORMATION**

STATEMENT OF FINANCIAL POSITION
Changes in Assets, Liabilities, and Shareholders' Equity

STATEMENT OF EARNINGS
Net Earnings and Accruals

STATEMENT OF CASH FLOWS
Cash Flows from Operating Activities
Cash Flows from Investing Activities
Cash Flows from Financing Activities
Separate Schedule (or note)
    Non-cash investing and financing
        activities
    Interest and taxes paid
    Interest, dividends, and taxes received

NOTES
Under Summary of Significant Accounting Policies
    Definition of cash equivalents
Under Separate Note
    If not listed on statement of cash flows:
    Non-cash investing and financing activities
    Interest and taxes paid
    Interest, dividends, and taxes received

GLOSSARY

Review key terms and definitions on *Connect.*

QUESTIONS

1. Compare the purposes of the statement of earnings, the statement of financial position, and the statement of cash flows.
2. What information does the statement of cash flows report that is not reported on the other required financial statements? How do investors and creditors use that information?
3. What are cash equivalents? How are purchases and sales of cash equivalents reported on the statement of cash flows?
4. What are the major categories of business activities reported on the statement of cash flows? Define each of these activities.
5. What are the typical cash inflows from operating activities? What are the typical cash outflows for operating activities?
6. Under the indirect method, depreciation expense is added to net earnings to compute cash flows from operating activities. Does depreciation cause an inflow of cash?
7. Explain why cash paid during the period for purchases and for salaries is not specifically reported as cash outflows on the statement of cash flows under the indirect method.
8. Explain why a $50,000 increase in inventory during the year must be included in developing cash flows for operating activities under the indirect method.
9. Compare the two methods of reporting cash flows from operating activities in the statement of cash flows.
10. What are the typical cash inflows from investing activities? What are the typical cash outflows for investing activities?
11. What are the typical cash inflows from financing activities? What are the typical cash outflows for financing activities?
12. What are non-cash investing and financing activities? Give two examples. How are they reported on the statement of cash flows?
13. A company used cash for both operating and investing activities, but had positive cash flow from financing activities. What does this cash flow pattern suggest about this company?

EXERCISES

E5–1 Matching Items Reported to Statement of Cash Flow Categories (Indirect Method)

Lassonde Industries Inc. is a Canadian company that develops, manufactures, and sells innovative and distinctive lines of fruit and vegetable juices and drinks that are marketed under recognized brand names such as Everfresh, Fairlee, and Oasis. Some of the items included in its recent annual consolidated statement of cash flows, presented using the indirect method, are listed below.

Indicate whether each item is disclosed in the operating activities (O), investing activities (I), or financing activities (F) section of the statement, or write not applicable (NA) if the item does not appear on the statement.

_____ 1. Dividends paid.

_____ 2. Repayment of long-term debt.

_____ 3. Depreciation and amortization.

_____ 4. Proceeds from the issuance of shares.

_____ 5. Change in trade payables and accrued liabilities.

_____ 6. Sale of intangible assets.

_____ 8. Net earnings.

_____ 9. Acquisition of property, plant, and equipment.

_____ 10. Change in inventories.

■ **LO1**

Lassonde Industries Inc.

E5–2 Determining the Effects of Transactions on the Statement of Cash Flows

Leon's Furniture Limited is an Ontario-based retailer of home furnishings. For each of the following first-quarter transactions, indicate whether net cash inflows (outflows) from operating activities (O), investing activities (I), or financing activities (F) are affected and whether the effect is an inflow (+) or an outflow

■ **LO1**

Leon's Furniture Limited

(−), or write NE if the transaction has no effect on cash. (*Hint:* Determine the journal entry recorded for the transaction. The transaction affects net cash flows if, and only if, the cash account is affected.)

_____ 1. Paid cash to purchase new equipment.

_____ 2. Purchased raw materials inventory on account.

_____ 3. Collected cash from customers.

_____ 4. Recorded an adjusting entry to record an accrued salaries expense.

_____ 5. Recorded and paid interest on notes payable.

_____ 6. Repaid principal on credit loan from the bank.

_____ 7. Paid rent for the following period.

_____ 8. Sold land for cash at its carrying amount.

_____ 9. Made payments to suppliers.

_____ 10. Declared and paid cash dividends to shareholders.

■ **LO1**

Dell Inc.

E5–3   **Determining the Effects of Transactions on the Statement of Cash Flows**

Dell Inc. is a leading manufacturer of personal computers and servers for the business and home markets. For each of the following transactions, indicate whether net cash inflows (outflows) from operating activities (O), investing activities (I), or financing activities (F) are affected and whether the effect is an inflow (+) or an outflow (−), or write NE if the transaction has no effect on cash. (*Hint:* Determine the journal entry recorded for the transaction. The transaction affects net cash flows if, and only if, the cash account is affected.)

_____ 1. Recorded and paid income taxes to the federal government.

_____ 2. Issued shares for cash.

_____ 3. Paid rent for the following period.

_____ 4. Recorded an adjusting entry for expiration of a prepayment.

_____ 5. Paid cash to purchase new equipment.

_____ 6. Borrowed cash and signed notes payable in five years.

_____ 7. Collected cash from customers.

_____ 8. Purchased raw materials inventory on account.

_____ 9. Recorded and paid salaries to employees.

_____ 10. Purchased new equipment by signing a three-year note.

■ **LO2**

E5–4   **Interpreting Depreciation Expense from a Management Perspective**

QuickServe, a chain of convenience stores, was experiencing some serious cash flow difficulties because of rapid growth. The company did not generate sufficient cash from operating activities to finance its new stores, and creditors were not willing to lend money because the company had not produced any profit for the previous three years. The new controller for QuickServe proposed a reduction in the estimated life of store equipment to increase depreciation expense, saying, "We can improve cash flows from operating activities because depreciation expense is added back on the statement of cash flows." Other executives were not sure that this was a good idea because the increase in depreciation would make it more difficult to have positive earnings: "Without profit, the bank will never lend us money."

Required:

What action would you recommend for QuickServe? Why?

■ **LO2**

E5–5   **Reporting and Interpreting Cash Flows from Operating Activities from an Analyst's Perspective (Indirect Method)**

Capaz Company completed its statement of earnings and statement of financial position for 2015 and provided the following information:

Statement of Earnings for 2015		
Service revenue		$53,000
Expenses		
Salaries	$41,000	
Depreciation	7,000	
Amortization of copyrights	200	
Other expenses	9,700	57,900
Net loss		$ (4,900)

Partial Statement of Financial Position	2015	2014
Trade receivables	$ 8,000	$15,000
Salaries payable	15,000	1,000
Other accrued liabilities	1,000	5,100

In addition, Capaz bought a small service machine for $5,000.

Required:

1. Present the operating activities section of the statement of cash flows for Capaz Company using the indirect method.
2. What were the major reasons that Capaz was able to report a net loss but positive cash flow from operations? Why are the reasons for the difference between cash flow from operations and net income important to financial analysts?

E5–6 **Inferring Statement of Financial Position Changes from the Statement of Cash Flows**

A statement of cash flows for Mega Brands reported the following information (in millions of U.S. dollars):

Operating Activities	Current Year
Net earnings	$8,330
Cash effect of changes in	
Receivables	(3,265)
Inventories	(18,524)
Payables	9,067
Other current assets	7,311
Net cash provided by operations	$ 2,919

Required:

Based on the information reported on the statement of cash flows for Mega Brands, determine whether the following accounts increased or decreased during the year: receivables, inventories, payables, and other current assets.

E5–7 **Inferring Statement of Financial Position Changes from the Statement of Cash Flows (Indirect Method)**

A recent statement of cash flows for Colgate-Palmolive reported the following information (in millions of U.S. dollars):

Operating Activities	
Net earnings	$ 1,957.2
Depreciation	347.6
Cash effect of changes in	
Receivables	(69.8)
Inventories	(134.7)
Other current assets	(31.0)
Payables	125.2
Other current liabilities	43.8
Net cash provided by operations	$2,238.3

Required:

Based on the information reported on the statement of cash flows for Colgate-Palmolive, determine whether the following accounts increased or decreased during the period: receivables, inventories, other current assets, and payables.

E5–8 **Analyzing Cash Flows from Operating Activities; Interpreting the Quality of Earnings Ratio**

An annual report for PepsiCo contained the following information (in millions of U.S. dollars):

Net earnings	$6,214
Depreciation and amortization	2,689
Decrease in trade receivables	250
Decrease in inventories	144
Decrease in prepayments	89
Increase in trade payables	548
Decrease in taxes payable	97
Cash dividends paid	3,305
Repurchase of shares	3,226

Required:

1. Compute the cash flows from operating activities for PepsiCo by using the indirect method.
2. Compute the quality of earnings ratio.
3. What were the major reasons that Pepsi's quality of earnings ratio did not equal 1.0?

■ **LO4, 6**   **E5–9**   **Reporting Cash Flows from Investing and Financing Activities**

Pan American Silver Corp.

Pan American Silver Corp. is a mining company based in British Columbia. In a recent quarter, it reported the following activities:

Net earnings	$354,146
Purchase of property, plant, and equipment	123,579
Shares issued for cash	4,453
Dividends paid	10,732
Cash collection from customers	828,735
Depreciation and amortization	82,756
Income taxes paid	58,736
Payments for products and services	305,528
Proceeds from sale of short-term investments	1,297

Required:

1. Based on this information, present the investing and financing activities sections of the statement of cash flows.
2. Compute the capital expenditures ratio. What does the ratio tell you about the company's ability to finance purchases of property, plant, and equipment with cash provided by operating activities?

■ **LO4, 6**   **E5–10**   **Reporting and Interpreting Cash Flows from Investing and Financing Activities with Discussion of Management Strategy**

Empire Company Limited

Empire Company Limited owns or franchises more than 1,300 corporate and franchised stores in all 10 provinces under retail banners that include Sobeys, Foodland, FreshCo, Safeway, IGA, IGA Extra, and Price Chopper. In a recent year, the Empire Company Limited reported the following activities (in millions of Canadian dollars):

Net earnings	$265.7
Purchases of property and equipment	431.0
Increase in trade payables and accrued liabilities	138.7
Issue of shares	129.1
Depreciation and amortization	324.8
Proceeds from sale of discontinued operations	78.0
Repayment of long-term borrowings	307.7
Increase in trade receivables	27.6
Payment of dividends	46.1

Required:

1. Based on this information, prepare the investing and financing activities sections of the statement of cash flows.
2. What do you think was management's plan for the use of the cash generated by the sale of discontinued operations?

■ **LO5**   **E5–11**   **Analyzing and Interpreting the Capital Expenditures Ratio**

Boston Beer Company

A recent annual report for Boston Beer Company contained the following data for the three most recent years (in millions of U.S. dollars):

	2012	2011	2010
Cash flow from operating activities	$95.3	$72.8	$67.8
Cash flow from investing activities	(67.3)	(19.6)	(13.6)
Cash flow from financing activities	(3.0)	(52.7)	(60.7)

Assume that all investing activities involved acquisition of new property, plant, and equipment.

Required:

1. Compute the capital expenditures ratio for the three-year period in total.
2. What portion of Boston Beer's investing activities was financed from external sources or pre-existing cash balances during the three-year period?

E5–12 **Reporting Non-cash Transactions on the Statement of Cash Flows; Interpreting the Effect on the Capital Expenditures Ratio** ■ **LO7**

An analysis of Martin Corporation's operational asset accounts provided the following information:

a. Acquired a large machine that cost $26,000, paying for it by signing a $15,000, 12 percent interest-bearing note due at the end of two years, and issuing 500 shares with a market value of $22 per share.

b. Acquired a small machine that cost $8,700. Full payment was made by transferring a tract of land that had a carrying amount of $8,700.

Required:

1. Show how this information should be reported on the statement of cash flows.
2. What would be the effect of these transactions on the capital expenditures ratio? How might these transactions distort interpretation of the ratio?

E5–13 **(Appendix 5A) Reporting and Interpreting Cash Flows from Operating Activities with Loss on Sale of Equipment (Indirect Method)** ■ **LO2**

New Vision Company completed its statement of earnings and statement of financial position for 2015 and provided the following information:

Statement of Earnings for 2015		
Service revenue		$66,000
Expenses:		
Salaries	$42,000	
Depreciation	7,300	
Utilities	7,000	
Loss on sale of equipment	1,700	58,000
Net earnings		$ 8,000

Partial Statement of Financial Position	2015	2014
Trade receivables	$12,000	$24,000
Salaries payable	19,000	10,000
Other accrued liabilities	5,000	9,000
Land	52,000	57,000

Required:

Present the operating activities section of the statement of cash flows for New Vision Company using the indirect method. Assume a December 31 fiscal year-end.

E5–14 **(Appendix 5A) Computing and Reporting Cash Flow Effects of Sale of Property, Plant, and Equipment** ■ **LO2, 4**

Perez Construction Inc. provided the following information about the sale of property, plant, and equipment during two recent years:

	Year 1	Year 2
Property, plant, and equipment (at cost)	$75,000	$13,500
Accumulated depreciation on equipment disposed of	40,385	3,773
Gain (loss) on sale	(16,751)	2,436

Required:

1. Determine the cash flow from the sale of equipment that would be reported in the investing activities section of the statement of cash flows for each year.
2. Perez uses the indirect method for the operating activities section of the statement of cash flows. What amounts related to the sale of equipment would be added or subtracted in the computation of net cash flows from operating activities for each year?

E5–15

BHP Billiton

(Appendix 5B) Matching Items Reported on the Statement of Cash Flows to Specific Categories (Direct Method)

The Australian company BHP Billiton is one of the world's biggest mining companies. Some of the items included in its annual consolidated statement of cash flows, presented using the direct method, are listed below.

Indicate whether each item is disclosed in the operating activities (O), investing activities (I), or financing activities (F) section of the statement, or write NA if the item does not appear on the statement:

_____ 1. Dividends paid.

_____ 2. Income taxes paid.

_____ 3. Interest received.

_____ 4. Net earnings.

_____ 5. Payments for property, plant, and equipment.

_____ 6. Payments in the course of operations.

_____ 7. Proceeds from ordinary share issues.

_____ 8. Proceeds from the sale of property, plant, and equipment.

_____ 9. Receipts from customers.

_____ 10. Repayment of loans.

E5–16

(Appendix 5B) Comparing Net Earnings and Cash Flows from Operations

Paul's Painters, a service organization, prepared the following special report for the month of January 2015:

Service Revenue, Expenses, and Net Earnings		
Service revenue		
Cash services (per cash register tape)	$105,000	
Credit services (per charge bills; not yet collected by end of January)	30,500	
		$135,500
Expenses		
Salaries and wages expense (paid by cheque)	$ 50,000	
Salaries for January not yet paid	3,000	
Supplies used (taken from stock, purchased for cash during December)	2,000	
Estimated cost of using company-owned truck for the month (depreciation)	500	
Other expenses (paid by cheque)	26,000	81,500
Earnings before income tax		54,000
Income tax expense (not yet paid)		13,500
Net earnings for January		$ 40,500

Required:

1. The owner (who knows little about the financial part of the business) asked you to compute the amount by which cash had increased in January 2015 from the operations of the company. You decided to prepare a detailed report for the owner with the following major captions: cash inflows (collections), cash outflows (payments), and the difference—net increase (or decrease) in cash.

2. Reconcile the difference—net increase (or decrease) in cash—you computed in (1) with the net earnings for January 2015 by filling in the following chart:

Reconciliation with net earnings:	
Net earnings	$40,500
Deduct: Non-cash services	(?)
Add: Non-cash expenses	?
Net increase (decrease) in cash	$29,000

E5–17 **(Appendix 5B) Reporting and Interpreting Cash Flows from Operating Activities from an Analyst's Perspective (Direct Method)**

Refer to the following summarized statement of earnings and additional selected information for Huanca Inc.:

Statement of Earnings	
Revenues	$146,500
Cost of sales	55,500
Gross profit	91,000
Salary expense	56,835
Depreciation and amortization	33,305
Other expenses	7,781
Net loss	$ (6,921)
Other information:	
Decrease in trade receivables	$ 170
Decrease in inventories	643
Increase in prepayments	664
Increase in trade payables	2,282
Decrease in accrued liabilities	1,142

Required:

1. Based on this information, compute cash flow from operating activities using the direct method. Assume that prepayments and accrued liabilities relate to other expenses.

2. What were the major reasons that Huanca was able to report positive cash flow from operations despite a net loss? Why are the reasons for the difference between cash flows from operations and net earnings important to financial analysts?

PROBLEMS

■ LO1, 2, 3

P5–1 **Analyzing the Effects of Transactions on Earnings and Cash Flows, and Reporting Cash Flows from Operating Activities (Indirect Method)** (AP5–1)

The following are the summary account balances from the statement of financial position of Granger Inc. as at October 31, 2014. The accounts are followed by a list of transactions for the month of November 2014. The following accounts have normal debit or credit balances. The amounts shown are in millions of dollars:

Cash	$ 88	Trade payables	$ 315
Trade receivables	192	Income tax payable	6
Inventories	576	Long-term borrowings	204
Prepayments	21	Deferred income taxes (credit)	37
Property, plant, and equipment, net	982	Retained earnings	1,210
Other non-current assets	13	Contributed capital	100

The following transactions occurred in November 2014:

a. Purchased new equipment costing $50 by issuing long-term debt.

b. Received $90 on trade receivables.

c. Received and paid the telephone bills for $1.

d. Earned $100 in sales to customers on account; the cost of sales was $60.

e. Paid employees $10 for salaries earned in November.

f. Paid half of the income taxes payable.

g. Purchased inventory for $23 on account.

h. Prepaid rent for December for a warehouse for $12.

i. Paid $10 of long-term borrowings and $1 in interest on the debt.

j. Purchased a patent (an intangible asset) for $8 cash.

Required:

1. Prepare a spreadsheet similar to Exhibit 5.4. Show the effects of the November 2014 transactions on the appropriate accounts, and on the three cash flow categories.

2. Prepare a table similar to Exhibit 5.5 showing both the cash and non-cash components of revenues and expenses for November 2014.

3. Prepare the operating activities section of the statement of cash flows for Granger Inc. for November 2014 using the indirect method.

4. Compute the quality of earnings ratio for November 2014, and explain why it is different from 1.0.

■ **LO**1, 2, 3, 5, 7   **P5–2**   **Preparing the Statement of Cash Flows (Indirect Method)** (AP5–2)

Selected financial information for Frank Corporation is presented below:

Selected 2014 transactions are as follows:

a. Purchased investment securities for $5,000 cash.

b. Borrowed $15,000 on a two-year, 8 percent interest-bearing note.

c. During 2014, sold machinery for its carrying amount; received $11,000 in cash.

d. Purchased machinery for $50,000; paid $9,000 in cash and signed a four-year note payable to the dealer for $41,000.

e. Declared and paid a cash dividend of $10,000 on December 31, 2014.

Selected account balances at December 31, 2013 and 2014 are as follows:

	December 31	
	2014	**2013**
Cash	$76,000	$21,000
Trade receivables	17,000	12,000
Inventory	52,000	60,000
Trade payables	7,000	10,000
Accrued wages payable	800	1,000
Income taxes payable	5,000	3,000

One-fourth of the sales and one-third of the purchases were made on credit.

FRANK CORPORATION
Statement of Earnings
For the Year Ended December 31, 2014

Sales revenue		$400,000
Cost of sales		268,000
Gross profit		132,000
Expenses		
Salaries and wages	$51,000	
Depreciation	9,200	
Rent (no accruals)	5,800	
Interest (no accruals)	12,200	
Income tax	$11,800	
Total expenses		90,000
Net earnings		$ 42,000

Required:

1. Prepare a statement of cash flows for the year ended December 31, 2014. Use the indirect method to compute the cash flows from operating activities. Include any additional required note disclosures.

2. Compute and explain the quality of earnings ratio and the capital expenditures ratio.

P5–3 **Preparing a Statement of Cash Flows (Indirect Method)** (AP5–3)

The comparative statements of financial position of Mikos Inc. as at December 31, 2014 and 2015, and its statement of earnings for the year ended December 31, 2015, are presented below:

■ LO2, 7

MIKOS INC.
Comparative Statements of Financial Position
December 31

	2015	2014
Assets		
Cash	$ 9,000	$ 17,000
Short-term investments	45,000	20,000
Trade receivables	68,000	26,000
Inventories, at cost	54,000	40,000
Prepayments	4,000	6,000
Land	45,000	70,000
Property, plant, and equipment, net	280,000	179,000
Intangible assets	24,000	28,000
	$529,000	$386,000
Liabilities and Shareholders' Equity		
Trade payables	$ 17,000	$ 40,000
Income tax payable	6,000	1,000
Accrued liabilities	10,000	-0-
Long-term notes payable	110,000	150,000
Contributed capital	200,000	60,000
Retained earnings	186,000	135,000
	$529,000	$386,000

MIKOS INC.
Statement of Earnings
For the Year Ended December 31, 2015

Sales		$850,000
Cost of sales	$430,000	
Amortization expense—intangible assets	4,000	
Depreciation expense—property, plant, and equipment	33,000	
Operating expenses	221,000	
Interest expense	12,000	700,000
Earnings before income taxes		150,000
Income tax expense		45,000
Net earnings		$105,000

Additional information is as follows:

a. Land was sold for cash at its carrying amount.

b. The short-term investments will mature in February 2016.

c. Cash dividends were declared and paid in 2015.

d. New equipment with a cost of $166,000 was purchased for cash, and old equipment was sold at its carrying amount.

e. Long-term notes of $10,000 were paid in cash, and notes of $30,000 were converted to shares.

Required:

1. Prepare a statement of cash flows for Mikos Inc. for the year ended December 31, 2015. Use the indirect method to report cash flows from operating activities.

2. Assume the role of a bank loan officer who is evaluating this company's cash flow situation. Analyze the statement of cash flows you prepared in (1).

3. What additional information does the statement of cash flows provide that is not available on either the statement of financial position or the statement of earnings? Explain.

■ **LO2**

Pan American Silver
Corp.

P5–4 **Comparing Cash Flows from Operating Activities (Indirect Method)** (AP5–4)

The accountants of Pan American Silver Corp. completed the statement of financial position at June 30, 2012, and the statement of earnings for the quarter ended on that date, and have provided the following information (in thousands of dollars):

Statement of Earnings		
Sales revenue		$200,597
Gain on sale of assets		11,220
		211,817
Expenses		
Cost of sales	$113,959	
Depreciation and amortization	24,324	
Royalties	6,018	
Exploration and project development	10,976	
General and administration	6,107	
Other (income) loss	(19,369)	
Interest and financing	1,446	
Income tax	24,315	167,776
Net earnings		$ 44,041

Selected Statement of Financial Position Accounts		
	June 30, 2012	**March 31, 2012**
Short-term investments	$161,376	$228,321
Trade receivables	119,509	103,343
Inventories	263,657	135,696
Prepayments	9,247	9,343
Trade payables	45,740	30,879
Accrued liabilities	30,689	13,199
Income taxes payable	15,254	74,366

Required:

1. Prepare the operating activities section of the statement of cash flows. Use the indirect method.

2. Companies that use the direct method to report cash flows from operations are also required to disclose in the notes a reconciliation of net earnings to cash flows from operating activities. What additional information does this disclosure requirement provide to users of financial statements? Explain.

■ **LO2, 3, 5**

P5–5 **(Appendix 5A) Preparing the Statement of Cash Flows with Sale of Equipment (Indirect Method)** (AP5–5)

The following information has been reported by Laporte Inc. on its statements of financial position at December 31, 2013 and 2014, and on its statement of earnings for the year ended December 31, 2014. Amounts are in millions of dollars:

Statements of Financial Position

	2014	2013
Cash	$ 90	$ 68
Trade receivables	34	24
Merchandise inventory	28	32
Long-term investments	–	18
Property, plant, and equipment	196	154
Accumulated depreciation	(78)	(96)
Total assets	$270	$200
Trade payables	$ 24	38
Income taxes payable	3	4
Long-term borrowings	80	20
Contributed capital	115	100
Retained earnings	48	38
Total liabilities and shareholders' equity	$270	$200

Statement of Earnings

Sales	$140
Cost of sales	(84)
Gross profit	56
Depreciation expense	(10)
Other operating expenses	(34)
Earnings from operations	12
Gain on sale of investments	6
Loss on sale of equipment	(2)
Earnings before income tax	16
Income tax expense	4
Net earnings	$ 12

Additional information is as follows:

a. Old equipment was sold for cash during 2014. It had an original cost of $40 and an accumulated depreciation of $28.

b. A new building was acquired during the year in exchange for a long-term note for $60, payable in five years. In addition, new equipment was purchased for cash.

Required:

1. Prepare the operating activities section of the statement of cash flows for Laporte Inc. for the year ended December 31, 2014. Use the indirect method to report the cash flow from operations.

2. Prepare the investing activities section of the statement of cash flows for Laporte Inc. for the year ended December 31, 2014.

3. Compute and explain each of the following for the year 2014: (*a*) quality of earnings ratio, (*b*) capital expenditures ratio, and (*c*) free cash flow.

4. Based on your answers to (1) and (2) above, determine the net cash flow from financing activities. (*Hint:* This can be done without preparing the financing activities section of the statement.)

5. The president of Laporte Inc., Tanya Turcotte, was provided with a copy of the operating activities section of the statement of cash flows that you prepared in (1), and made the following comment: "This report is supposed to show operating cash inflows and outflows during the year, but I don't see how much cash Laporte Inc. received from customers and how much it paid to trade suppliers and for income taxes. Please ask whoever prepared this statement to provide me with these numbers." Based on Tanya's comment, compute the following amounts for 2014:

a. Cash collected from customers.

b. Cash paid to trade suppliers.

c. Cash paid for income taxes.

P5–6   **(Appendices 5A and 5B) Preparing the Statement of Cash Flows with Sale of Equipment (Direct Method)** (AP5–6)

Refer to the information for Laporte Inc. in P5–5.

Required:

1. Prepare a statement of cash flows for Laporte Inc. for the year ended December 31, 2014. Use the direct method to report cash flows from operating activities.

2. What additional information does the statement of cash flows provide that is not available on either the statement of financial position or the statement of earnings?

P5–7   **(Appendix 5B) Preparing a Statement of Cash Flows (Direct Method)** (AP5–7)

Refer to the information for Granger Inc. in P5–1.

Required:

1. Prepare a spreadsheet similar to Exhibit 5.4. Show the effects of the November 2014 transactions on the appropriate accounts, and on the three cash flow categories.

2. Prepare a table similar to Exhibit 5.5 showing both the cash and non-cash components of revenues and expenses for November 2014.

3. Prepare the operating activities section of the statement of cash flows for Granger Inc. for November 2014 using the direct method.

4. As a user of financial statements, would you prefer to see the cash flow from operating activities reported using the direct method or the indirect method? Justify your answer.

P5–8   **(Appendix 5B) Preparing a Statement of Cash Flows (Direct Method)** (AP5–8)

Refer to the information for Frank Corporation in P5–2.

Required:

1. Prepare a statement of cash flows for the year ended December 31, 2014. Use the direct method to compute the cash flows from operating activities. Include any additional required note disclosures.

2. Is the direct method of reporting cash flows from operating activities easier to prepare than the indirect method? Explain.

3. Is the direct method of reporting cash flows from operating activities easier to understand than the indirect method? Explain.

ALTERNATE PROBLEMS

■ **LO1, 2, 3**

Canada Post
Corporation

eXcel

AP5–1   **Analyzing the Effects of Transactions on Earnings and Cash Flows, and Reporting Cash Flows from Operating Activities (Indirect Method)** (P5–1)

The following are several December 31, 2012, account balances (in millions of dollars) from the 2012 annual report of Canada Post Corporation, followed by several typical transactions:

Account	Balance	Account	Balance
Non-current assets	$4,798	Equity of Canada	$1,533
Trade payables	482	Trade receivables	662
Short-term investments	842	Supplies inventory	171
Accrued liabilities	732	Cash	271
Long-term borrowings	1,127	Provisions	75
Deferred revenue	129	Other non-current liabilities	2,666

These accounts have normal debit or credit balances, but are not necessarily in good order. The following hypothetical transactions (in millions of dollars) occurred in January 2013:

a. Provided delivery service to customers, receiving $720 in trade receivables and $60 in cash.

b. Purchased new equipment costing $816; paid $116 and signed a long-term note for the remainder.

c. Paid $74 cash to rent equipment, with $64 for rental this month and the rest for rent for the first few days in February.

d. Spent $126 cash to maintain and repair facilities and equipment during the month.

e. Collected $652 from customers on account.

f. Borrowed $90 by signing a long-term note.

g. Paid employees $180 for work during the month.

h. Purchased $9 of supplies on account.

i. Paid $184 on trade payables.

j. Ordered $72 in spare parts and supplies.

k. Received a bill for $6 for utilities services, payable in February.

l. Used supplies during the month totalling $65.

Required:

1. Prepare a spreadsheet similar to Exhibit 5.4. Show the effects of the January transactions on the appropriate accounts, and on the three cash flow categories.

2. Prepare a table similar to Exhibit 5.5 showing both the cash and non-cash components of revenues and expenses for January 2013.

3. Prepare the operating activities section of the statement of cash flows for Canada Post Corporation for January 2013 using the indirect method.

4. Compute the quality of earnings ratio for January 2013, and explain why it is different from 1.0.

AP5–2 **Preparing the Statement of Cash Flows (Indirect Method) (P5–2)**   ■ LO1, 2, 3, 5, 7
Stonewall Company was organized on January 1, 2015. During the year ended December 31, 2015, the company provided the following data:

Statement of Earnings	
Sales revenue	$ 80,000
Cost of sales	(35,000)
Depreciation expense	(4,000)
Other expenses	(32,000)
Net earnings	$ 9,000
Statement of Financial Position	
Cash	$ 48,000
Trade receivables	18,000
Merchandise inventory	15,000
Machinery (net)	25,000
Total assets	$106,000
Trade payables	$ 10,000
Accrued liabilities	21,000
Dividends payable	2,000
Note payable, short term	15,000
Contributed capital	54,000
Retained earnings	4,000
Total liabilities and shareholders' equity	$106,000

Analysis of selected accounts and transactions follows:

a. Issued 3,000 shares for cash, at $18 per share.

b. Borrowed $15,000 on a one-year, 8 percent interest-bearing note; the note was dated June 1, 2015.

c. Paid $29,000 to purchase machinery.

d. Purchased merchandise for resale at a cost of $50,000; paid $40,000 cash and the balance on account.

e. Exchanged plant machinery with a carrying amount of $2,000 for office machines with a market value of $2,000.

f. Declared a cash dividend of $5,000 on December 15, 2015, payable to shareholders on January 15, 2016.

g. Because this is the first year of operations, all account balances are zero at the beginning of the year; therefore, the changes in the account balances are equal to the ending balances.

Required:

1. Prepare a statement of cash flows for the year ended December 31, 2015. Use the indirect method to report cash flows from operating activities.

2. Compute and explain the quality of earnings ratio and the capital expenditures ratio.

■ LO2, 3

AP5–3   **Preparing the Statement of Cash Flows (Indirect Method)** (P5–3)

The comparative statements of financial position for Marwa Ltd. at December 31, 2015 and 2014, are presented below:

Comparative Statements of Financial Position As at December 31		
	2015	**2014**
Cash	$ 10,000	$ 56,500
Trade receivables	35,000	20,000
Merchandise inventory	10,000	17,500
Prepayments	4,000	5,000
Property, plant, and equipment, net	1,062,000	646,000
Total Assets	$1,121,000	$745,000
Trade payables	$ 23,500	$ 19,500
Income taxes payable	6,000	14,000
Note payable, due Nov. 1, 2016	22,500	52,500
Contributed capital	180,000	150,000
Retained earnings	889,000	509,000
Total Liabilities and Shareholders' Equity	$1,121,000	$745,000

The statement of earnings for 2015 showed the following information:

Sales	$2,000,000
Gross profit	1,300,000
Operating expenses (includes depreciation of $45,000)	600,000
Interest expense	15,000
Income tax expense	160,000

As well, property, plant, and equipment were acquired for $475,000 cash during 2015. Also during 2015, property, plant, and equipment were sold at their carrying amount in exchange for cash.

Required:

1. Prepare a complete statement of cash flows for Marwa Ltd. for the year 2015. Use the indirect method for the operating section.

2. Compute the following amounts:

   a. Cash collected from customers in 2015.

   b. Cash paid to suppliers of merchandise inventory in 2015.

3. Calculate and briefly explain (*a*) the quality of earnings ratio, and (*b*) free cash flow.

AP5–4 Comparing Cash Flows from Operating Activities (Indirect Method) (P5–4)   ■ LO2

Zena Company's accountants just completed the financial statements for the year and have provided the following information (in thousands):

Statement of Earnings for 2014

Sales revenue		$20,600
Expenses and losses:		
Cost of sales	$9,000	
Depreciation	2,000	
Salaries	5,000	
Rent	2,500	
Insurance	800	
Utilities	700	
Interest	600	20,600
Net earnings		$ 0

Selected Statement of Financial Position Accounts

	2014	2013
Merchandise inventory	$ 82	$ 60
Trade receivables	380	450
Trade payables	240	210
Salaries payable	29	20
Rent payable	2	6
Prepaid rent	2	7
Prepaid insurance	14	5

In addition, the company signed long-term notes for $20,000 during the year.

Required:

1. Prepare the operating activities section of the statement of cash flows for 2014 by using the indirect method.

2. As a financial analyst, would you prefer to see the cash flow from operations reported using the direct method or the indirect method? Justify your answer.

3. As the accountant who prepares the company's statement of cash flows, would you prefer to use the direct or the indirect method to report the cash flow from operations? Explain.

AP5–5 (Appendix 5A) Preparing the Statement of Cash Flows with Sale of Equipment   ■ LO2, 3, 4, 5
(Indirect Method) (P5–5)

Mary Wong, the sole shareholder and manager of Kitchenware Inc., has approached you and asked you to prepare a statement of cash flows for her company. The company sells kitchen utensils that are used in most households. Mary is worried about the meeting that she has scheduled in two weeks with a lending officer of her bank. It is time for a review of the company's loan from the bank.

Mary provided you with the following condensed financial statements for the fiscal years ended December 31, 2013 and 2014. She assures you that the financial statements are free of any omissions or misstatements, and that they conform to IFRS.

KITCHENWARE INC.
Statements of Financial Position as at December 31
(in thousands of dollars)

	2014	2013
Assets		
Current assets		
Cash	$ 1,000	$ 3,400
Short-term investments	2,000	8,000
Trade accounts receivable	56,300	10,600
Inventories	10,000	30,000
Furniture and fixtures, at cost	59,000	26,000
Less: Accumulated depreciation	(24,000)	(12,000)
Investments	2,000	3,000
Total assets	$106,300	$69,000
Liabilities and Shareholders' Equity		
Current liabilities		
Bank loan	$ 18,000	$ 8,000
Trade accounts payable	17,000	13,100
Dividends payable	-0-	600
Total current liabilities	35,000	21,700
Non-current liabilities		
Mortgage notes payable	28,000	-0-
Total liabilities	63,000	21,700
Shareholders' equity		
Contributed capital	24,000	22,000
Retained earnings	19,300	25,300
Total shareholders' equity	43,300	47,300
Total liabilities and shareholders' equity	$106,300	$69,000

KITCHENWARE INC.
Statement of Earnings
For the Years Ended December 31

	2014	2013
Sales revenue	$980,000	$880,000
Cost of sales	(640,000)	(560,000)
Gross profit	340,000	320,000
Operating expenses:		
Depreciation	(15,200)	(12,000)
Selling and general	(298,800)	(288,000)
Earnings from operations	26,000	20,000
Interest expense	(9,600)	(3,200)
Loss on sale of furniture	(1,200)	-0-
Gain on sale of investments	800	-0-
Earnings before income taxes	16,000	16,800
Income tax expense (@25%)	(4,000)	(4,200)
Net earnings	$ 12,000	$ 12,600

Additional information is as follows:

a. During 2014, the company sold old furniture with an original cost of $5,000 and $3,200 of accumulated depreciation up to the date of sale.

b. During 2014, the company sold one of the non-current investments that had cost $1,000. The gain on this sale is reported on the statement of earnings.

c. The company considers short-term investments as cash equivalents.

Required:

1. Prepare a partial statement of cash flows for Kitchenware Inc. showing the operating activities section for the year ended December 31, 2014. The company uses the indirect method to report cash flows from operations.

2. Compute the following amounts:

    a. Cash collected from customers, assuming that 90 percent of the sales are on credit.

    b. Cash paid to trade suppliers of merchandise.

    c. Cash received for sale of old furniture.

3. Prepare the investing activities section of the statement of cash flows for Kitchenware Inc. for the year ended December 31, 2014.

4. Compute and explain (*a*) the quality of earnings ratio, and (*b*) free cash flow.

5. In an effort to improve the company's financial performance, Mary proposed that the furniture and fixtures be depreciated over a longer period. This change will decrease depreciation expense by $2,000 in 2013 and by $4,000 in 2014. As a professional accountant, would this proposed change be acceptable to you? Explain.

AP5–6 **(Appendices 5A and 5B) Preparing the Statement of Cash Flows with Sale of Equipment (Direct Method)** (P5–6)
Refer to the information for Kitchenware Inc. in AP5–5.

Required:

1. Prepare a statement of cash flows for Kitchenware Inc. for the year ended December 31, 2015. Use the direct method to report cash flows from operating activities.

2. Discuss the importance of the statement of cash flows to users of financial statements. What additional information does it provide that is not reported in the other financial statements? Explain by referring to the statement that you prepared in (1) above.

AP5–7 **(Appendix 5B) Preparing a Statement of Cash Flows (Direct Method)** (P5–7)
Refer to the information for Canada Post in AP5–1.

Canada Post
Corporation

e**X**cel

Required:

1. Prepare a spreadsheet similar to Exhibit 5.4. Show the effects of the January 2013 transactions on the appropriate accounts, and on the three cash flow categories.

2. Prepare a table similar to Exhibit 5.5 showing both the cash and non-cash components of revenues and expenses for January 2013.

3. Prepare the operating activities section of the statement of cash flows for Canada Post for January 2013 using the direct method.

4. As a user of financial statements, would you prefer to see the cash flow from operating activities reported using the direct method or the indirect method? Justify your answer.

AP5–8 **(Appendix 5B) Preparing a Statement of Cash Flows (Direct Method)** (P5–8)
Refer to the information for Stonewall Company in AP5–2.

Required:

1. Prepare a statement of cash flows for the year ended December 31, 2015. Use the direct method to compute the cash flows from operating activities. Include any additional required note disclosures.

2. Is the direct method of reporting cash flows from operating activities easier to prepare than the indirect method? Explain.

3. Is the direct method of reporting cash flows from operating activities easier to understand than the indirect method? Explain.

CASES AND PROJECTS

FINDING AND INTERPRETING FINANCIAL INFORMATION

CP5–1 **Finding Financial Information**
Go to *Connect* for the financial statements of RONA Inc. and related notes.

■ **LO**2, 4, 6

RONA Inc.

Required:

1. Which of the two basic reporting approaches for the cash flows from operating activities did the company adopt?

2. What amount of cash did the company pay for taxes during the current year?

3. Refer to Note 5.2 to the financial statements. Explain why the depreciation of property, plant, and equipment ($69,561) and amortization of intangible assets ($26,867) were added in the reconciliation of net earnings to net cash provided by operating activities in the statement of cash flows.

4. Has the company paid cash dividends during the last two years? How do you know?

5. What was the amount of free cash flow for the year ended December 30, 2012?

■ LO2, 4, 6   **CP5–2**   **Finding Financial Information**

Canadian Tire
Corporation

Refer to the financial statements of Canadian Tire Corporation and related notes given in Appendix A of this book.

Required:

1. What were the three largest adjustments to reconcile net earnings from operations to the net cash provided by operating activities? Explain the direction of the effect of each adjustment in the reconciliation.

2. What were Canadian Tire Corporation's major uses of cash over the years 2011 and 2012? What were its major sources of cash for these activities?

3. What was the amount of free cash flow for the year ended December 29, 2012? What does this imply about the company's financial flexibility?

4. Canadian Tire reported a large amount of cash and cash equivalents at December 29, 2012. What type of assets does the company consider as cash equivalents?

■ LO3, 5   **CP5–3**   **Comparing Companies within an Industry**

Canadian Tire
Corporation

vs. RONA Inc.

Refer to the financial statements of Canadian Tire Corporation (Appendix A) and RONA Inc. (on *Connect*), and to the Industry Ratio Report (Appendix B on *Connect*).

Required:

1. Compute the quality of earnings ratio for both companies for the current year. How might the difference in their sales growth rates explain the difference in the ratio? Sales growth rate = (Current year's sales − Prior year's sales) ÷ Prior year's sales.

2. Compare the quality of earnings ratio for both companies to the industry average. Are these companies producing more or less cash from operating activities relative to net earnings than the average company in the industry?

3. Compute the capital expenditures ratio for both companies for the current year. Compare their abilities to finance purchases of property, plant, and equipment; acquisition of intangible assets; and acquisition of other businesses with cash provided by operating activities.

FINANCIAL REPORTING AND ANALYSIS CASES

■ LO2, 3, 4, 5, 6   **CP5–4**

Sun-Rype Products
Ltd.

Using Financial Reports: Analyzing the Statement of Cash Flows of Sun-Rype Products Ltd.
Sun-Rype Products Ltd. is a Canadian juice and fruit snack company based in Kelowna, British Columbia. Its statements of cash flows for fiscal years 2012, 2011, and 2010 are shown below:

SUN-RYPE PRODUCTS LTD.			
Consolidated Statements of Cash Flows			
For the years ended December 31			
(in thousands of Canadian dollars)			
	2012	**2011**	**2010**
Cash flows from operating activities			
Net income (loss) for the year	$ 1,267	$ (5,687)	$ 4,503
Adjustments for:			
Depreciation	5,166	4,745	3,881
Impairment loss	164	293	—
Loss on disposal of property, plant, and equipment	—	57	—
Unrealized foreign exchange loss (gain)	69	(552)	188
Interest expense	826	608	163
Income tax expense (recovery)	847	(2,349)	1,779

SUN-RYPE PRODUCTS LTD.
Consolidated Statements of Cash Flows
For the years ended December 31
(in thousands of Canadian dollars)

	2012	2011	2010
	8,339	(2,885)	10,514
Change in trade and other receivables	(324)	890	1,977
Change in inventories	2,510	(6,122)	(1,482)
Change in prepayments	73	(125)	173
Change in trade and other payables	6,077	1,865	(1,150)
Change in provisions	397	651	146
Cash generated from operating activities	17,072	(5,726)	10,178
Interest paid	(826)	(608)	(163)
Income tax paid	1,690	(276)	(4,251)
Net cash from (used in) operating activities	17,936	(6,610)	5,764
Cash flows from investing activities			
Business acquisitions	–	(9,087)	(5,537)
Acquisition of property, plant, and equipment	(1,418)	(3,929)	(1,852)
Net cash used in investing activities	(1,418)	(13,016)	(7,389)
Cash flows from financing activities			
Advances of loans and borrowings	1,502	18,551	7,260
Repayment of loans and borrowings	(14,264)	(1,282)	(4,867)
Repurchase of own shares	(97)	–	(180)
Net cash from financing activities	(12,859)	17,269	2,213
Net increase (decrease) in cash	3,659	(2,357)	588
Cash position, beginning of year	571	2,928	2,411
Effect of exchange rate changes on cash	(3)	–	(71)
Cash position, end of year	$ 4,227	$ 571	$ 2,928

Required:

1. The cash flows from operating activities show that depreciation is added to net income (loss) for the year. Is depreciation a source of cash? Explain.

2. Was the cash collected from customers during fiscal year 2012 higher or lower than Sun-Rype's sales revenue for that year? Explain.

3. Did Sun-Rype expand during 2011 and 2012? If so, how did the company pay for its expansion? Explain.

4. Compute and analyze Sun-Rype's quality of earnings ratio, capital expenditures ratio, and free cash flow for 2011 and 2012.

5. Analyze the company's pattern of cash flows from operating, investing, and financing activities over the three years. What conclusion can you draw from the changing pattern of cash flows? Explain.

6. Obtain a copy of Sun-Rype's statement of cash flows for the year 2013 through the company's website (www.sunrype.com) or the SEDAR service (www.sedar.com). Did the company's cash flow situation in 2013 improve or deteriorate relative to previous years? Explain.

7. As a potential investor in Sun-Rype's shares, what additional information would you need before making your decision as to whether or not to invest in this company's shares?

CP5–5 **Using Financial Reports: Analyzing Research In Motion's Statement of Cash Flows**

Research In Motion (RIM) (now called Blackberry) is a leading designer, manufacturer, and marketer of innovative wireless solutions for the worldwide mobile communications market. Its products are used around the world and include the BlackBerry wireless platform, software development tools, and software/hardware licensing agreements. RIM's statement of cash flows for fiscal years 2012, 2011, and 2010 are shown on the next page.

■ **LO2, 3, 4, 5, 6**

Research In Motion

RESEARCH IN MOTION LIMITED
Consolidated Statements of Cash Flows
(U.S. dollars, in millions)

	For the Year Ended		
	March 3, 2012	February 26, 2011	February 27, 2010
Cash flows from operating activities			
Net income	$ 1,164	$ 3,411	$ 2,457
Adjustments to reconcile net income to net cash provided by operating activities:			
Amortization	1,523	927	616
Deferred income taxes	(5)	92	51
Income taxes payable	(21)	2	5
Stock-based compensation	97	72	58
Impairment of goodwill	355	–	–
Other	9	1	9
Net changes in working capital items	(210)	(496)	(161)
Net cash provided by operating activities	2,912	4,009	3,035
Cash flows from investing activities			
Acquisition of long-term investments	(355)	(784)	(863)
Proceeds on sale or maturity of long-term investments	376	893	473
Acquisition of property, plant, and equipment	(902)	(1,039)	(1,009)
Acquisition of intangible assets	(2,217)	(557)	(421)
Business acquisitions, net of cash acquired	(226)	(494)	(143)
Acquisition of short-term investments	(250)	(503)	(477)
Proceeds on sale or maturity of short-term investments	550	786	970
Net cash used in investing activities	(3,024)	(1,698)	(1,470)
Cash flows from financing activities			
Issuance of shares	9	67	30
Tax benefits (deficiencies) related to stock-based compensation	(2)	(1)	2
Purchase of treasury stock	(156)	(76)	(94)
Repurchase of shares	–	(2,077)	(775)
Repayment of debt	–	–	(6)
Net cash provided by (used in) financing activities	(149)	(2,087)	(843)
Effect of foreign exchange gain (loss) on cash and cash equivalents	(3)	16	(6)
Net increase (decrease) in cash and cash equivalents for the year	(264)	240	716
Cash and cash equivalents, beginning of year	1,791	1,551	835
Cash and cash equivalents, end of year	1,527	1,791	1,551

See notes to consolidated financial statements

SUPPLEMENTAL INFORMATION

(a) Cash flows resulting from net changes in working capital items are as follows:

	For the year ended		
	March 3, 2012	February 26, 2011	February 27, 2010
Accounts receivable	$ 898	$(1,352)	$ (481)
Other receivables	(168)	(117)	(45)
Inventories	(409)	42	48
Income taxes receivable	(135)	–	–
Other current assets	(143)	54	(40)
Accounts payable	(90)	216	167
Accrued liabilities	(135)	539	442
Income taxes payable	(179)	82	(266)
Deferred revenue	151	40	14
	$(210)	$ (496)	$ (161)
Interest paid during the year	$ –	$ –	$ –
Income taxes paid during the year	$ 684	$ 1,053	$1,082

Required:

1. Have RIM's accounts receivable increased or decreased during fiscal year 2012? By how much have its accounts receivable changed during the past three years? Explain.

2. How does the change in inventory during fiscal year 2012 affect cash? Explain.

3. What conclusions can you derive by examining the pattern of the company's cash flows during these three years?

4. How did the company finance the acquisition of non-current assets during fiscal years 2011 and 2012? Explain.

5. What additional information does the statement of cash flows provide that is not available on either the statement of financial position or the statement of earnings?

CRITICAL THINKING CASE

CP5–6 **Ethical Decision Making: A Real-Life Example**

■ **LO**1, 2, 6

Enron

Enron Corporation was a major U.S. energy company. Its executives engaged in a systematic accounting fraud that resulted in the company's bankruptcy in 2001. In a February 19, 2004, press release, the U.S. Securities and Exchange Commission described a number of fraudulent transactions that Enron executives concocted in an effort to meet the company's financial targets. One particularly well-known scheme was called the "Nigerian barge" transaction, which took place in the fourth quarter of 1999. According to court documents, Enron arranged to sell three electricity-generating power barges moored off the coast of Nigeria. The "buyer" was the investment banking firm Merrill Lynch. Although Enron reported this transaction as a sale in its statement of earnings, it turns out this was no ordinary sale. Merrill Lynch didn't really want the barges and had only agreed to buy them because Enron guaranteed, in a secret side deal, that it would arrange for the barges to be bought back from Merrill Lynch within six months of the initial transaction. In addition, Enron promised to pay Merrill Lynch a hefty fee for doing the deal. In an interview on National Public Radio on August 17, 2002, Carl Levin, a Senator from Michigan, declared, "[T]he case of the Nigerian barge transaction was, by any definition, a loan."

Required:

1. Discuss whether the Nigerian barge transaction should have been considered a loan rather than a sale. As part of your discussion, consider the following questions. Doesn't the Merrill Lynch payment to Enron at the time of the initial transaction automatically make it a sale, not a loan? Which aspects of the transaction are similar to a loan? Which aspects suggest that the criteria for revenue recognition (discussed in Chapter 3) were not fulfilled?

2. The effect of recording the transaction as a sale rather than a loan is fairly clear: Enron was able to boost its revenues and net earnings. What is somewhat less obvious, but nearly as important, are the effects on the statement of cash flows. Describe how recording the transaction as a sale rather than as a loan would change the statement of cash flows.

3. How would the two different statements of cash flows (described in your response to (2)) affect financial statement users?

FINANCIAL REPORTING AND ANALYSIS TEAM PROJECT

CP5–7 **Team Project: Analyzing Cash Flows**

■ **LO**1, 2, 3, 4, 5, 6

As a team, select an industry to analyze. A list of companies classified by industry can be obtained by accessing **www.fpinfomart.ca** and then choosing "Companies by Industry." You can also find a list of industries and companies within each industry via **http://ca.finance.yahoo.com/investing** (click on "Order Annual Reports" under "Tools").

Each group member should acquire the annual report for a different publicly traded company in the industry. (Library files, the SEDAR service at **www.sedar.com**, and the company's website are good sources.)

Required:

On an individual basis, each team member should write a short report answering the following questions about the selected company. Discuss any patterns across the three companies that your team observes. Then, as a team, write a short report comparing and contrasting your companies.

1. Which of the two basic reporting approaches for cash flows from operating activities did the company adopt?
2. What is the quality of earnings ratio for the most current year? What were the major causes of differences between net earnings and cash flow from operations?
3. What is the capital expenditures ratio for the three-year period presented in total? How is the company financing its capital expenditures?
4. What portion of the cash from operations in the current year is being paid to shareholders in the form of dividends?

SOLUTIONS TO SELF-STUDY QUIZZES

Self-Study Quiz 5-1

a. I, *b.* 0, *c.* 0, *d.* I, *e.* 0, *f.* 0, *g.* 0, *h.* 0, *i.* F, *j.* 0.

Self-Study Quiz 5-2

a. −, *b.* 0, *c.* +, *d.* +, *e.* +, *f.* −.

Self-Study Quiz 5-3

AIG's pattern of cash flows in year 1 is similar to pattern 3, which indicates that the company is downsizing. In year 2, the company's cash flows are similar to pattern 2, suggesting that AIG is a mature, successful firm that is using cash generated from operations to buy non-current assets and to reduce its debt or distribute cash dividends to shareholders. Finally, the pattern of cash flows in year 3 (pattern 3) indicates that the company has downsized its operations.

Self-Study Quiz 5-4

a. NA, *b.* NA, *c.* +, *d.* NA, *e.* −, *f.* −.

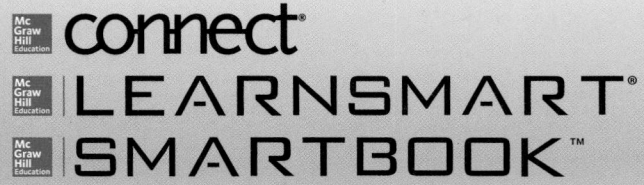

Communicating and Interpreting Accounting Information

After studying this chapter, you should be able to do the following:

LEARNING OBJECTIVES

LO1 Recognize the people involved in the accounting communication process (regulators, managers, board of directors, auditors, information intermediaries, and users), their roles in the process, and the guidance they receive from legal and professional standards.

LO2 Identify the steps in the accounting communication process, including the issuance

of press releases, annual reports, quarterly reports, and documents filed with securities commissions, as well as the guiding principles in communicating useful information.

LO3 Recognize and apply the different financial statement and disclosure formats used by companies in practice.

FOCUS COMPANY: **Thomson Reuters Corporation**

COMMUNICATING FINANCIAL INFORMATION

AND CORPORATE STRATEGY

Thomson Reuters Corporation (**thomsonreuters .com**) is the result of the Thomson Corporation's acquisition of Reuters Group PLC in 2008. The Thomson Corporation originated in 1934 when Roy Thomson acquired his first newspaper in Canada, *The Timmins Press*, in Ontario. Reuters Group PLC dated back to 1850 when Paul Julius Reuter started a business that transmitted news and stock price information between Aachen, Germany, and Belgium, using a combination of carrier pigeons and telegraph cables. These two companies grew to become the world's leading source of intelligent information for businesses and professionals.

The growth of Thomson Reuters has partially been the result of numerous acquisitions of other businesses over the years.[1] When corporations offer shares to the public, they gain access to capital markets. Capital markets provide corporations with funds necessary to pursue strategies such as expansion of the business. Thomson Reuters combines industry expertise with innovative technology to deliver essential information to leading decision makers in the financial and risk, legal, tax and accounting, intellectual property and science, and media markets.

As a publicly traded company listed on the Toronto Stock Exchange and the New York Stock Exchange, Thomson Reuters is required to provide detailed information in regular filings with the Ontario Securities Commission, other Canadian securities regulatory authorities, and the U.S. Securities and Exchange Commission (SEC). As the certifying officers of the company, James C. Smith, president and chief executive officer, and Stephane Bello, executive vice-president and chief financial officer, are responsible for the accuracy of the filings. The board of directors and auditors monitor the integrity of the system that produces the disclosures. Integrity in communicating with investors and other users of financial statements is key to maintaining relationships with providers of capital. Furthermore, clear and timely communication of the company's financial situation enables Thomson Reuters to comply with exchange rules and securities commission regulations. It also informs the company's customers, investors, creditors, and other users of financial statements of the company's success in implementing its business strategy.

UNDERSTANDING THE BUSINESS

Thomson Reuters Corporation provides intelligent information for businesses and professionals throughout the world. The company's operations are influenced by external, market-driven factors, such as demand for information in specific sectors of the economy and competition from other companies. These external factors influence both management decisions concerning the breadth of the products and services offered and its plans for acquisition of additional companies to help grow the business.

As Thomson Reuters strives to maintain its leading position in the industry, it continues to look for opportunities to innovate in response to its customers' needs. Successful companies such as Thomson Reuters ensure that their financial reporting reflects their business strategies. Thomson Reuters' investments in new businesses; the results of operating, investing, and financing activities; and the company's financial condition are communicated to shareholders, creditors, and other interested parties through press releases, conference calls with shareholders, financial analysts together with the media, and periodic reporting of financial information.

When investors lose faith in the truthfulness of a firm's accounting numbers, they also normally punish the company's stock. Disclosure of an accounting fraud causes, on average, a 20 percent drop in the price of a company's shares. The accounting scandals that occurred in recent years at large corporations such as Sino-Forest Corporation, Livent Inc., and Parmalat S.p.A. caused these companies' shares to become worthless.

CORPORATE GOVERNANCE refers to the procedures designed to ensure that the company is managed in the interests of the shareholders.

Thomson Reuters is committed to high standards of **corporate governance**, the procedures designed to ensure that the company is managed in the interests of the shareholders. Its corporate governance practices are generally consistent with the best-practice guidelines of the Canadian securities regulatory authorities and the SEC.[2] Good corporate governance can ease a company's access to capital, lowering both the cost of borrowing (interest rates) and the perceived riskiness of investment in its shares.

In an attempt to restore investor confidence following the scandals at Enron and WorldCom, the U.S. Congress passed the *Public Accounting Reform and Investor Protection Act* (the *Sarbanes-Oxley Act*), which strengthens financial reporting and corporate governance provisions for public companies. Compliance with the provisions of this Act has also affected Canadian companies that are publicly traded on U.S. stock exchanges. In light of the U.S. experience, the Canadian Securities Administrators, which coordinates and harmonizes regulation of the Canadian capital markets among the 13 securities regulators of Canada's provinces and territories, has imposed requirements on all publicly traded companies to bolster investors' confidence in financial reporting by Canadian companies. Even with these added safeguards, the wisdom of famed analyst Jack Ciesielski's warning to financial statement users is still evident:

One usual answer to the question "why does accounting matter?" is that it helps to avoid "blow-ups": the unpleasant outcome when a stock crashes because the firm's management engaged in accounting chicanery that subsequently becomes visible. . . . the analyst who understands accounting matters will know precisely where the "soft spots" are in financial reporting, the ones that can be manipulated in order to meet an expected earnings target or avoid breaking a loan covenant.

Source: Analyst's Accounting Observer, www.accountingobserver.com.

Chapters 2 through 5 focused on the mechanics of preparing the statement of financial position, statement of earnings, statement of changes in equity, and statement of cash flows. In these chapters, we explained the importance of IFRS in generating the information disclosed in these statements. You learned to compute and interpret some financial ratios to understand how creditors and investors use the information to justify their credit and investment decisions.

In this chapter, we will take a more detailed look at the people involved in the regulations that govern the process that conveys accounting information to statement users in the Internet age. We will also take a look at disclosures provided in financial reports to help you learn how to find relevant information.

ORGANIZATION OF THE CHAPTER

Players in the Accounting Communication Process	The Disclosure Process	A Closer Look at Financial Statements and Notes
• Regulators (CSA, AcSB, AASB, Stock Exchanges) • Managers (CEO, CFO, and Accounting Staff) • Board of Directors (Audit Committee) • Auditors • Information Intermediaries: Analysts and Information Services • Users: Institutional and Private Investors, Creditors, and Others	• Press Releases • Annual Reports • Quarterly Reports • Reports to Securities Commissions • Guiding Principles for Communicating Useful Information • Constraints of Accounting Measurement	• Overview of Thomson Reuters' Financial Statements • Classified Statement of Financial Position • Classified Statement of Earnings • Earnings Measurement • Statement of Comprehensive Income • Statement of Changes in Equity • Statement of Cash Flows • Notes to Financial Statements • Voluntary Disclosures

Supplemental material:
Appendix 6A: Canadian Capital Markets (on *Connect*)

PLAYERS IN THE ACCOUNTING COMMUNICATION PROCESS

Exhibit 6.1 summarizes the major actors involved in the integrity of the financial reporting process.

Regulators (CSA, AcSB, AASB, Stock Exchanges)

The financial information reported by Canadian companies is subject to strict regulations and standards issued by government regulators and private standard-setting organizations. Canadian publicly traded corporations must comply with provincial securities regulations that are coordinated by the Canadian Securities Administrators (CSA). The CSA is a forum for the 13 securities regulators of Canada's provinces and territories that was established to harmonize regulation of the Canadian capital markets. The CSA's mission is to protect investors from unfair, improper, or fraudulent practices and to foster fair, efficient, and vibrant capital markets. However, provincial or territorial regulators handle all complaints regarding securities violations in their respective jurisdictions and have legal authority to enforce provincial regulations concerning the timeliness and quality of financial disclosure.[3]

Securities regulators work closely with the Accounting Standards Board (AcSB), which is responsible for establishing standards of accounting and reporting by Canadian companies. External auditors ensure that companies prepare their financial

LO1

Recognize the people involved in the accounting communication process (regulators, managers, board of directors, auditors, information intermediaries, and users), their roles in the process, and the guidance they receive from legal and professional standards.

Exhibit **6.1**

Ensuring the Integrity of Financial Position

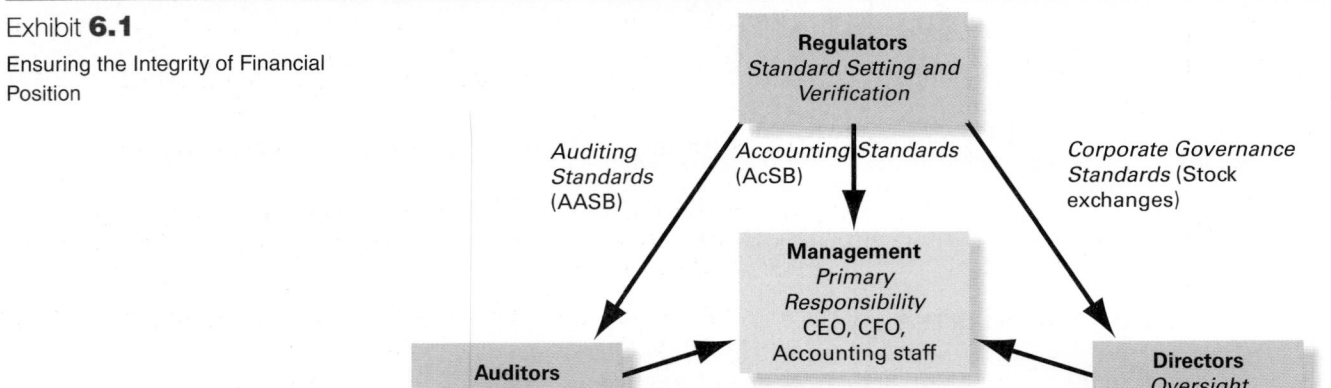

reports in accordance with these standards, and their audit work is guided by International Standards on Auditing, which have been adopted by the Canadian Auditing and Assurance Standards Board (AASB) as Canadian Auditing Standards.

Stock exchanges also provide an essential quality assurance service to listed companies by undertaking ongoing surveillance of their reporting and trading activities. When they suspect non-compliance with accounting standards, the stock exchanges undertake independent investigations and share information with securities commissions; the Canada Revenue Agency (CRA), which collects income taxes from corporations; and other law enforcement agencies, such as the Royal Canadian Mounted Police (RCMP). As intermediaries, the stock exchanges may also enforce their rules through penalties ranging from temporary cease-trade orders to fines and delisting of companies.

Managers (CEO, CFO, and Accounting Staff)

As noted in Chapter 1, the primary responsibility for the information in Thomson Reuters' financial statements and related disclosures lies with management as represented by the highest officer in the company, often called the chief executive officer (CEO), and the highest officer associated with the financial and accounting side of the business, often called the chief financial officer (CFO). These two officers must sign the statement of management responsibility that is included in the annual report. In all Canadian publicly accountable enterprises, these two officers must personally certify the following on an annual basis:

- Based on his or her knowledge, having exercised reasonable diligence, the annual filings do not contain any untrue statement of a material fact or omit to state a material fact, and the annual financial information together with other financial information included in the annual filings fairly presents, in all material respects, the financial condition, financial performance, and cash flows of the company.

- They have disclosed to the auditors and the audit committee of the board all significant deficiencies and material weaknesses in the design or operation of internal controls over financial reporting that are reasonably likely to adversely affect the company's ability to record, process, summarize, and report financial information.

- They have disclosed to the auditors, the board, and the audit committee of the board any fraud involving management or other employees who have a significant role in the company's internal control over financial reporting.

The members of the *accounting staff* who actually prepare the details of the reports also have professional responsibility for the accuracy of this information, although their legal responsibility is smaller. However, their future professional success depends heavily on their reputations for honesty and competence. Accounting managers responsible for financial statements with material errors are routinely dismissed from their positions—subject to professional review and sanction, which may include permanent curtailment of their license to practice—and often have difficulty finding other employment.

Board of Directors (Audit Committee)

The **board of directors**, elected by the shareholders to represent their interests, is responsible for maintaining the integrity of the company's financial reports. Thomson Reuters' corporate governance guidelines state that the board of directors is responsible for reviewing and overseeing the integrity of Thomson Reuters with respect to its compliance with applicable audit, accounting, and financial reporting requirements. The audit committee of the board, which must be composed of non-management (independent) directors with financial literacy, is responsible for hiring the company's independent auditors. They also meet separately with the auditors to discuss management's compliance with their financial reporting responsibilities. This structure complies with both U.S. and Canadian best practices.

Recent changes to securities regulations have increased the burden of responsibility for accurate financial disclosure on company executives and external auditors. If any company listed on a stock exchange is found guilty of knowingly violating any disclosure regulation, not only the company but also members of its board of directors and audit committee can be sued. If experts such as accountants or financial analysts who relied on the company's financial reports also issued disclosure that misrepresented the company, they too may be individually sued by users who seek to recover some or all of their financial losses, which may have resulted from relying on such misleading information. With the recent acceptance of class action lawsuits in Canada, investors who may have been unable individually to endure the costs of legal action may now pool their resources to undertake civil legal action. It is not necessary for corporate employees and executives to be found guilty of any criminal offense in order for class action lawsuits to be successful.

Auditors

The provincial securities commissions require publicly traded companies to have their statements audited by professional independent accountants following International Standards on Auditing. Many privately owned companies also have their statements audited. An **unqualified (clean) audit opinion** is the auditors' declaration that the financial statements are fair presentations in all material respects in conformity with IFRS. By signing an unqualified audit opinion, the audit firm assumes part of the financial responsibility for the fairness of the financial statements and related presentations. This opinion, which adds credibility to the statements, is also often required by agreements with lenders and private investors.[4] Subjecting the company's statements to independent verification reduces the risk that the company's condition is misrepresented in the statements. As a consequence, rational investors and lenders should lower the rate of return (interest) they charge for providing capital.

PricewaterhouseCoopers is currently Thomson Reuters' auditor. KPMG, Deloitte & Touche, Ernst & Young, and PricewaterhouseCoopers are the largest audit firms, employing thousands of professional accountants practising in offices throughout the world. They audit the great majority of publicly traded companies and many privately held companies. Some public companies and most private companies are audited by audit firms of smaller size. A list of well-known companies and their auditors at the time this chapter was written follows:

The **BOARD OF DIRECTORS**, elected by the shareholders to represent their interests, is responsible for maintaining the integrity of the company's financial reports.

An **UNQUALIFIED (CLEAN) AUDIT OPINION** is the auditors' declaration that the financial statements are fair presentations in all material respects in conformity with IFRS.

Company	Industry	Auditor
Nestlé, S.A. (Switzerland)	Health and nutrition	KPMG
Singapore Airlines (Singapore)	Airline	Ernst & Young
Tim Hortons (Canada)	Fast food	PricewaterhouseCoopers
Royal Bank of Canada	Financial services	Deloitte & Touche

A QUESTION OF ACCOUNTABILITY   **WHERE WERE THE AUDITORS?**

Most professional accountants act in an honest and ethical manner, abiding by the codes of ethics developed by the professional accounting organizations. Nevertheless, a few accountants act in their own interest and disregard ethical conduct. They even become accomplices in spectacular fraud cases and subsequent company bankruptcies. For example, Enron Corp., a U.S. energy trading company, intentionally inflated its net earnings by hiding assets and related debts from 1997 to 2001. Throughout this period, the audit firm Arthur Andersen LLP, a global accounting services company with revenues in excess of $500 million, should have known that the financial statements issued by Enron's management were fraudulent.

The collapse of Enron, the largest unexpected bankruptcy in U.S. history at that time, caused tremendous losses to the company's shareholders, creditors, employees, and other stakeholders. Furthermore, Enron's bankruptcy in December 2001 caused the collapse of Arthur Andersen. More than 300 clients left the firm within 90 days, taking $250 million of potential revenue with them to other audit firms. This audit failure led to calls for improved accountability by managers and auditors, thereby generating considerable discussion among securities regulators, financial analysts, investors, and creditors for stricter regulation of the accounting profession.

The *Sarbanes-Oxley Act* (*SOX*), approved by the U.S. Congress in July 2002, was a direct response to the Enron scandal and others that occurred in the United States. This law has set higher standards of responsibility for the officers and directors of publicly listed companies as well as for auditors. Canadian companies that are listed on U.S. stock exchanges must also comply with the *SOX* requirements.

Information Intermediaries: Analysts and Information Services

Students often view the communication process between companies and financial statement users as a simple process of mailing the report to individual shareholders who read the report and then make investment decisions based on what they have learned. This simple picture is far from today's reality. Now most investors rely on sophisticated financial analysts and information services to gather and analyze information. Exhibit 6.2 summarizes this process.

Financial Analysts   Financial analysts receive accounting reports and other information about the company from electronic information services. They also gather information through conversations with company executives and visits to company facilities and competitors. The results of their analyses are combined into analysts' reports.

Analysts' reports normally include forecasts of share price and future quarterly and annual earnings per share; a buy, sell, or hold recommendation for the company shares; and explanations for these judgments. In making these **earnings forecasts**, predictions of earnings for future accounting periods, the analysts rely heavily on their knowledge of how the accounting system translates business events into the numbers

EARNINGS FORECASTS are predictions of earnings for future accounting periods.

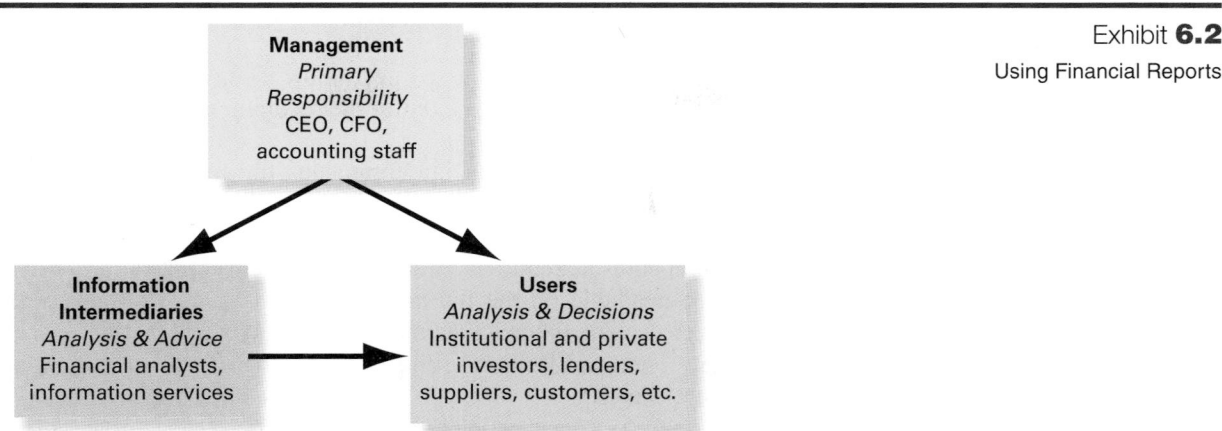

Exhibit **6.2**
Using Financial Reports

on a company's financial statements, which are the subject matter of this text. Individual analysts often specialize in particular industries (such as sporting goods or energy companies). Analysts are regularly evaluated based on the accuracy of their forecasts, as well as the profitability of their stock picks.

Analysts often work in the research departments of brokerage and investment banking houses such as RBC Dominion Securities, mutual fund companies such as the Investors Group, and investment advisory services such as Standard & Poor's, which sell their advice to others. Through their reports and recommendations, analysts transfer their knowledge of accounting, the company, and the industry to others who lack this expertise. Many believe that investment decisions, which are based on analysts' advice, cause stock market prices to react quickly to information in financial statements. A quick, unbiased reaction to information is called *market efficiency* in finance. It is highly unlikely that unsophisticated investors can glean more information from financial statements than what the sophisticated analysts have already learned. Careful analysis does not lead all analysts to the same conclusions, however. These differences of opinion are reflected in the following earnings (per share) forecasts for Thomson Reuters Corporation and stock recommendations made by a number of analysts at the date indicated below:

REAL-WORLD EXCERPT

Thomson-Reuters Corporation

ANALYSTS' EARNINGS
FORECASTS

THOMSON REUTERS CORPORATION

Analysts' Earnings Forecasts (as of August 8, 2013)

	For fiscal 2013	For fiscal 2014
Average forecast	$ 1.84	$ 2.00
Lowest forecast	1.80	1.78
Highest forecast	1.89	2.17
Number of analysts	19	19

Reprinted with permission of Thomson Reuters.

Analysts make recommendations to buy, hold, or sell a company's shares based on their earnings forecasts. In the case of Thomson Reuters, the analysts' recommendations at the time of writing this chapter were "buy" (3 analysts), "outperform" (1 analyst), "hold" (15 analysts), "underperform" (2 analysts), and "sell" (0 analyst).

Company managers provide analysts with information for their analysis. Optimistic earnings forecasts, however, put additional pressure on management to meet and even exceed analysts' forecasts to please investors. The drive to meet analysts' earnings expectations has led the management of some companies to adopt accounting policies that result in premature recognition of revenue or deferral of expenses, or both, to increase reported earnings.

The information services discussed next allow investors to gather their own information about the company and to monitor the recommendations of analysts.

Information Services   Canadian companies file financial statements and other securities-related forms electronically with SEDAR (System for Electronic Document Analysis and Retrieval), which is the official site for the filing of documents by public companies as required by securities laws in Canada.[5] SEDAR is currently a free service available on the Internet at **www.sedar.com**.[6] Many companies also provide access to their financial statements and other information over the Internet. You can view Thomson Reuters' filings by clicking on Investor Relations at **www. thomsonreuters.com**.

Financial analysts and other sophisticated users obtain much of the information they use from the wide variety of commercial online information services. Services such as *Lexis-Nexis* (**lexisnexis.ca**); *S&P Capital IQ* (**capitaliq.com**); *Westlaw Business*, which is owned by Thomson Reuters (**business.westlaw.com**); and *CanWest Interactive Inc.* (**fpinfomart.ca**) provide broad access to financial statements and related news information. They also allow users to search the database by keyword, including various financial statement terms.

More general information services include Factiva (**dowjones.com/factiva**), Bloomberg (**bloomberg.com**), and Thomson Reuters Eikon (**thomsonreuterseikon. com**), as well as the financial sections of national newspapers such as *The Globe and Mail* and the *National Post*. Factiva provides access to news stories about companies and company press releases, including the initial announcements of annual and quarterly financial results. The Bloomberg service and Thomson Reuters Eikon also provide the ability to combine these sources of information in sophisticated analyses.

A growing number of other resources offer a mixture of free and fee-based information regarding many companies on the Internet. These include **reuters.com, hoovers. com, finance.yahoo.com**, and **money.msn.com**.

FINANCIAL ANALYSIS   INFORMATION SERVICES AND JOB SEARCHES

Information services have become the primary tool for professional analysts who use them. Information services are an important source of information for job seekers; potential employers expect top job applicants to demonstrate knowledge about their companies during an interview, and electronic information services are an excellent source of company information. The best place to learn about your potential employers is their websites. Be sure to read the material in the employment section and the investor relations section of the site. To learn more about electronic information services, contact the business or reference librarian at your college or university library, or explore some of the websites mentioned earlier.

Users: Institutional and Private Investors, Creditors, and Others

INSTITUTIONAL INVESTORS are managers of pension funds, mutual funds, endowment funds, and other funds that invest on behalf of others.

Institutional investors include private pension funds (associated with unions and employees of specific companies); public pension funds (for provincial and municipal employees); mutual funds; and endowment, charitable foundation, and trust funds (such as the endowment of your college or university). These institutional shareholders usually employ their own analysts who also rely on the information intermediaries just discussed. Institutional shareholders control the majority of publicly traded shares of Canadian companies. For example, at the time of writing this book, institutional investors, such as Royal Bank of Canada and Jarislowsky Fraser Ltd., owned approximately 38 percent of Thomson Reuters' outstanding shares.

Private investors include individuals who purchase shares in companies, for example, individuals making large investments, as well as small retail investors who, like most individuals, buy a relatively small number of shares of publicly traded companies through brokers such as BMO Nesbitt Burns. Private investors normally lack the expertise to understand financial statements and the resources to gather data efficiently. As a consequence, they often rely on the advice of information intermediaries or turn their money over to the management of mutual and pension funds (institutional investors).

Lenders, or **creditors**, include suppliers, banks, commercial credit companies, and other financial institutions that lend money to companies. Lending officers and financial analysts in these organizations use these same public sources of information. In addition, when companies borrow money from financial institutions, they often agree to provide additional financial information (e.g., monthly statements) as part of the lending contract. Lenders are often the primary external user group for financial statements of private companies. Institutional and private investors also become creditors when they buy a company's publicly traded bonds and debentures.[7]

Financial statements play an important role in the relationships between customers and suppliers. Customers evaluate the financial health of suppliers to determine whether they will be reliable, up-to-date sources of supply. Suppliers evaluate their customers to estimate their future needs and ability to pay debts. Competitors also attempt to learn useful information about a company from its statements. The potential loss of competitive advantage is one of the costs to the preparer of public financial disclosures. Accounting regulators consider these costs as well as the direct costs of preparation when they require new disclosures.

THE DISCLOSURE PROCESS

As noted in our discussion of information services and information intermediaries, the accounting communication process includes more steps and participants than one would envision in a world in which annual and quarterly reports are simply mailed to shareholders.

Press Releases

To provide timely information to external users and to limit the possibility of selective leakage of information, Thomson Reuters and most public companies announce quarterly and annual earnings through a **press release**: a written public news announcement normally distributed to major news services as soon as the figures are available. Thomson Reuters normally issues its annual earnings press releases about five weeks after the end of the accounting period. The announcements are sent electronically to the major print and electronic news services, including Reuters and Bloomberg, which make them immediately available to subscribers. Exhibit 6.3 shows an excerpt of a typical quarterly press release for Thomson Reuters that includes key financial figures and an invitation to interested parties to access a live webcast concerning the company's quarterly results. The press release also includes condensed unaudited financial statements that form part of the formal quarterly report to shareholders, distributed after the press release.

Many companies, including Thomson Reuters, follow these press releases with a webcast conference call at which senior managers (often the CEO and/or CFO) present the results and then answer questions from analysts about the results. These calls are open to the investing public. Listening to these calls (which are often archived on a company's website for a period of time afterwards) is a good way to learn about a company's business strategy and its expectations for the future, as well as key factors that analysts consider when they evaluate a company.

PRIVATE INVESTORS include individuals who purchase shares in companies.

LENDERS (CREDITORS) include suppliers and financial institutions that lend money to companies.

LO2

Identify the steps in the accounting communication process, including the issuance of press releases, annual reports, quarterly reports, and documents filed with securities commissions, as well as the guiding principles in communicating useful information.

A **PRESS RELEASE** is a written public news announcement normally distributed to major news services.

Exhibit **6.3**

Earnings Press Release for
Thomson Reuters Corporation

REAL-WORLD EXCERPT

*Thomson Reuters
Corporation*

PRESS RELEASE

THOMSON REUTERS REPORTS FIRST-QUARTER 2013 RESULTS

NEW YORK – Thomson Reuters (TSX / NYSE: TRI), the world's leading source of intelligent information for businesses and professionals, today reported results for the first quarter ended March 31, 2013. The company reported revenues from ongoing businesses of $3.1 billion, a 2% increase before currency. Adjusted EBITDA declined 2% and the corresponding margin was 24.4% versus 25.1% in the prior-year period. Underlying operating profit decreased 7% and the corresponding margin was 14.9% versus 16.2% in the prior-year period.

First-quarter adjusted earnings per share (EPS) were $0.38, down $0.01 from the prior-year period.

"The first-quarter performance was consistent with our full-year expectations and I am pleased with the positive trajectory of the business as we begin the year," said James C. Smith, chief executive officer of Thomson Reuters.

"We are executing more effectively, launching better products, simplifying our systems and processes and managing with more rigor and discipline, which is why our confidence continues to build and we can affirm our full-year 2013 Outlook."

. . .

Thomson Reuters will webcast a discussion of its first-quarter 2013 results today beginning at 8:30 a.m. Eastern Daylight Time (EDT). You can access the webcast by visiting the "Investor Relations" section of http://thomsonreuters.com. An archive of the webcast will be available following the presentation.

Source: www.thomsonreuters.com.

FINANCIAL ANALYSIS

HOW DOES THE STOCK MARKET REACT TO EARNINGS ANNOUNCEMENTS?

For actively traded shares such as those of Thomson Reuters, most of the stock market reaction (share price increases and decreases from investor trading) to the news in the press release usually occurs quickly. Recall that a number of analysts follow Thomson Reuters and regularly predict the company's earnings. When the actual earnings are published, the market reacts not to the amount of earnings but to the difference between actual earnings and expected earnings. This amount is called unexpected earnings.

Companies such as Thomson Reuters issue press releases concerning other important events, including announcements of new services or the material acquisition of new companies. Press releases related to annual earnings often precede the issuance of the annual report by 15 to 45 days. This time is necessary to prepare the additional detail and to print and distribute those reports. The time difference between quarterly earnings press releases and the filing of quarterly reports is usually a shorter period.

Annual Reports

For privately held companies, *annual reports* are relatively simple documents photo-copied on white paper. They normally include the following:

1. Basic financial statements: statement of earnings, statement of financial position, statement of changes in equity, and statement of cash flows.

2. Related notes.

3. Report of independent accountants (auditor's opinion).

The annual reports of public companies are significantly more elaborate, both because of additional reporting requirements imposed on these companies by securities commissions and because many companies use their annual reports as public relations tools to communicate non-accounting information to shareholders, customers, the press, and others.

The annual reports of public companies are normally split into two sections. The first, *non-financial*, section usually includes a letter to shareholders from the chairperson and CEO, along with descriptions of the company's management philosophy, products, successes (and occasionally failures), and exciting prospects and challenges for the future. Beautiful photographs of products, facilities, and personnel are often included. The second, *financial*, section includes the core of the report. Securities regulators set minimum disclosure standards for the financial section of the annual reports of public companies. The principal components of the financial section follow:

1. Summarized financial data.
2. Management's discussion and analysis, covering financial condition and results of operations.
3. The basic financial statements.
4. Notes to the financial statements.
5. Report of Independent Accountants (Auditor's Opinion) and the Management Report.

The order of these components varies.

Most of these components, except for management's discussion and analysis (MD&A), have been discussed in earlier chapters. This component includes management's discussion and explanation of key figures in the financial statements and risks the company faces in the future. The MD&A section contains important non-financial and strategic information to help users interpret the financial statements. Unlike the annual financial statements and related notes, information in the MD&A section is not audited. The securities commissions in Canada and the United States have noted that the intent of the MD&A is to clearly convey an interpretation of how all of the important factors combined to generate the reported results of a company. Readers should feel as if they were at a meeting of the company's board of directors where the results were reported and discussed. Well-established firms committed to high-quality disclosure, such as Thomson Reuters, include comparisons of their previous year's forecast to actual outcomes. Many companies devote a sizeable portion of their annual reports to the MD&A section. For example, Thomson Reuters devoted 53 pages of its 2012 annual report to a detailed analysis of the company's results of operations and its various business segments. Thomson Reuters' MD&A section also includes a review of the company's liquidity, capital resources, and contractual obligations. The complete annual reports of Thomson Reuters for previous years back to 1999, which include all of these sections, are available on the company's website.

Quarterly Reports

Quarterly reports normally begin with a short letter to shareholders. This is followed by a condensed statement of earnings for the quarter, which often shows less detail than the annual statement of earnings, and a condensed statement of financial position dated at the end of the quarter (e.g., March 31 for the first quarter). These condensed financial statements are not audited and so are marked "unaudited." Often, the statement of cash flows, the statement of changes in equity, and some notes to the financial statements are omitted. Private companies also normally prepare quarterly reports for lenders. Companies issue their quarterly reports about five weeks after the end of each quarter.

Reports to Securities Commissions

Public companies must also file periodic reports with the OSC and other provincial securities commissions. These reports include the annual report, quarterly reports, an annual information form, and an information circular.

The annual information form provides a more-detailed description of the business, including such items as the company's corporate structure, the industry in which it operates, the products and services it offers, product and project development, sales and marketing, manufacturing, and competition. The form also lists the properties owned and leased by the company, and significant contracts that the company has signed.

The information circular is a legal document that is forwarded to the company's shareholders prior to the annual general or special meeting of shareholders. It provides information about the items that the shareholders will be asked to consider and vote on during the meeting, including election of new directors, appointment of independent auditors, and other matters of a legal nature. The circular also provides details of the compensation of the CEO, CFO, and other key executive officers as well as information about the company's corporate governance practices.

In addition to these periodic reports, companies file other types of reports as the need arises. These include a short-form prospectus providing details of the equity and/or debt securities that they plan to issue to investors, and press releases concerning new developments. The SEDAR website, **www.sedar.com**, lists all of the reports, documents, and news items that Thomson Reuters and other corporations have filed.[8]

Guiding Principles for Communicating Useful Information

Information presented in financial reports is useful if it makes a difference in the context of making a decision. A number of qualitative characteristics of accounting information have been included in conceptual frameworks developed by the FASB and the IASB and adopted by other standard-setting organizations. The desirable qualities of accounting information are part of a joint IASB/FASB project to revisit the conceptual framework for financial reporting. This first phase of the conceptual framework identifies relevance and faithful representation as the two fundamental qualitative characteristics, supported by four enhancing qualitative characteristics: comparability, verifiability, timeliness, and understandability.[9] These six characteristics were introduced in Chapter 2 (Exhibit 2.2) and are presented in more detail in Exhibit 6.4.

Exhibit **6.4**

Qualitative Characteristics of Accounting Information

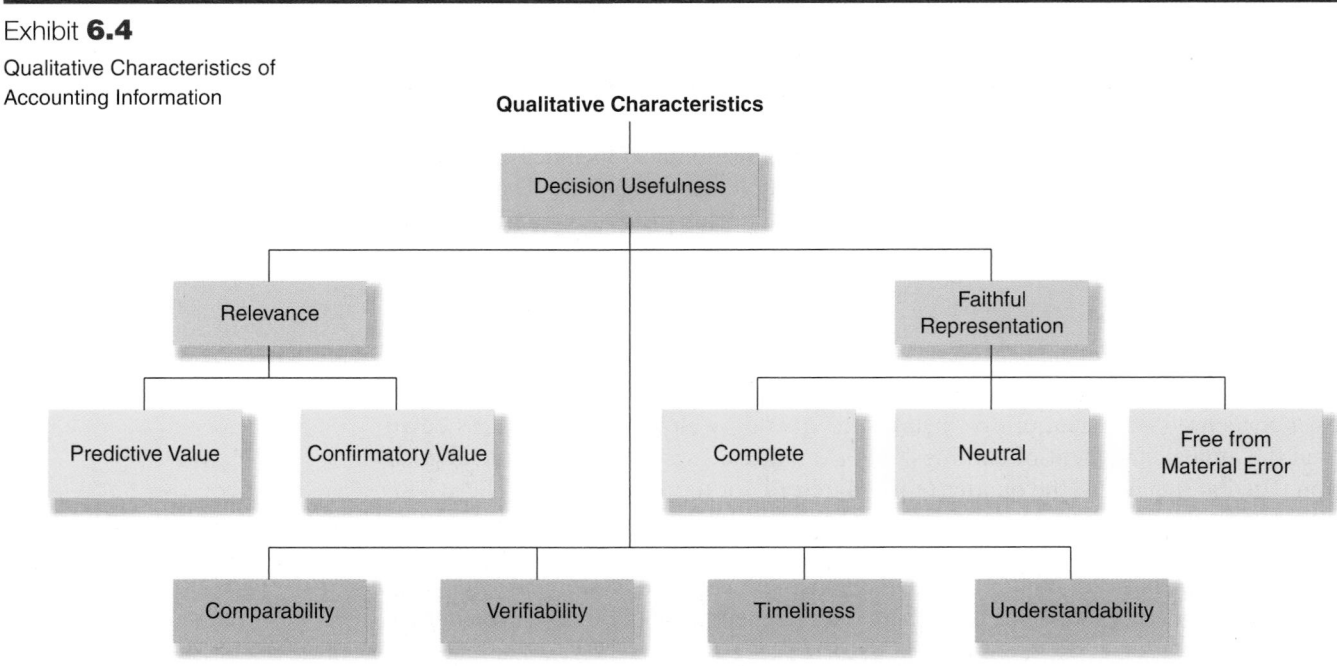

Relevance Information disclosed in financial statements is **relevant** if it can influence users' decisions by helping them assess the economic effect of past activities and/or predict future events. For example, the various elements of a statement of earnings have predictive value if they help users predict future levels of net earnings or its subcomponents, such as earnings from operations. The *predictive value* of the statement of earnings is enhanced if non-recurring items are presented separately on a multiple-step statement of earnings, because these items are transient in nature. Similarly, information presented on the statement of earnings has *confirmatory value* if it confirms or changes prior expectations based on previous evaluations. Comparison of predicted results with actual results is helpful in improving the quality of the prediction process.

Faithful Representation To be useful for decision making, information provided in financial statements must be a **faithful representation** of the economic phenomena it is supposed to represent, thus reflecting the substance of the underlying transactions. The information must be complete, neutral, and free from material error. For example, deferred revenue that is recognized prematurely as revenue for the period overstates the amount of revenue reported on the statement of earnings, causing a lack of faithful representation of current-period revenues.

The usefulness of accounting information is enhanced when it is neutral, that is, free from bias in its measurement and presentation. Bias in measurement occurs when the item being measured is consistently understated or overstated. For example, a consistent understatement of depreciation expense leads to a biased higher amount of net earnings. In this context, the development of accounting standards for measurement and reporting of transaction effects should not result in favouring one group of users over others. The measurement and reporting of liabilities, for example, should not result in consistent underreporting of liabilities on the statement of financial position, because this would favour owners over creditors and may influence investment and credit decisions of financial statement users.

Information that faithfully represents the underlying transactions should reflect the economic substance of the transactions and how they affect the economic condition of the company rather than their legal form. For example, when a company leases equipment, the monthly or annual payment represents an expense that is reported on the statement of earnings. However, the specific provisions of the lease contract may indicate that it is essentially a purchase of an asset, which is financed by the seller. Regardless of the legal form of the lease contract, if the underlying substance of the transaction reflects a purchase transaction, then accountants must classify the transaction as a purchase and account for the equipment as an asset and the future lease payments as a liability.

Comparability **Comparability** of accounting information across businesses is enhanced when similar accounting methods have been applied. It enables users to identify similarities and discrepancies between two sets of financial reports produced by two different companies. This quality is also important when comparing information provided by the same company over time. The comparability of financial reports is enhanced if consistent information is made available by using the same accounting methods over time as well. Changes in accounting methods reduce the comparability of information and necessitate disclosure of the effects of the change in order to maintain comparability.

Verifiability Information presented in financial statements is **verifiable** if independent accountants can agree on the nature and amount of the transaction. For example, the historical cost of a piece of land that is reported on a company's statement of financial position at year-end is usually highly verifiable. The cost of acquisition is based on the purchase price and related costs that result from actual exchanges with external parties. However, the appraised market value of the land at that date is a subjective estimate that reflects the appraiser's past experience. It is not verifiable because it is not based on an actual exchange transaction. However, if a company is considering the sale of land, its market value would be relevant for that decision even though it is less verifiable than the land's historical cost.[10]

Timeliness   Information that is not available to users in a timely manner loses its relevance because it cannot be considered in making decisions. **Timely** information enhances both its predictive and confirmatory values. The relevance of accounting information for decision making declines as time passes. For this reason, companies produce quarterly reports and issue press releases to convey timely information to investors, creditors, and other user groups.

Understandability   Information cannot be useful if it is not properly understood. **Understandability** is the quality of information that enables users to comprehend its meaning. It is assumed that users of accounting information have a reasonable knowledge of business and economic activities as they are reflected in financial reports. It is also assumed that users are willing to study the information with reasonable diligence.[11] In this context, the classification and presentation of information within the financial statements and related notes enhance its understandability.

Constraints of Accounting Measurement

Accurate interpretation of financial statements requires that the statements' reader be aware of important constraints of accounting measurement.

Cost   Companies produce and disseminate accounting information to users with the expectation that the benefits to users of such information exceed the cost of producing it. The **cost constraint** suggests that information should be produced only if the perceived benefits of increased decision usefulness exceed the expected costs of providing that information. Such benefits may be difficult to measure, but the costs of producing additional information can be estimated with reasonable accuracy. When standard setters, such as the AcSB, require companies to disclose specific information, known as *mandatory* disclosure, they have determined implicitly that the benefits to users exceed the costs the company will incur to produce the information. For example, the regulation introduced by the CSA concerning internal control over financial reporting imposed additional costs on companies to evaluate the effectiveness of internal control procedures put in place to discourage corporate fraud by managers and other employees.[12] The perceived benefits of this new regulation include increased verifiability and decision usefulness of the accounting information disclosed in financial statements. While the cost of improving internal control procedures can be estimated, the related benefits to users of financial statements may be difficult to measure.

In other cases, the company's managers may decide that *voluntary* disclosure of information about specific aspects of the company's operations would be beneficial to users. In such cases, the costs of disclosure should not exceed the expected benefits. In this context, the cost constraint plays an important role in determining whether new information should be produced and communicated to users.

Prudence   **Prudence** requires that special care be taken to avoid (1) overstating assets and revenues and (2) understating liabilities and expenses. Users of financial statements often want to know about possible sources of trouble for the company. For example, creditors need to know how secure their investments will be if the company's fortunes deteriorate, but they may not be interested in whether the company might do exceptionally well. They care more about the downside risk than the upside potential. For this reason, financial statements that show assets at historical cost but reduce these amounts when current values are significantly lower help satisfy the needs of creditors. This lower-of-cost-or-market guideline attempts to offset managers' natural

TIMELY information enhances both its predictive and confirmatory values.

UNDERSTANDABILITY is the quality of information that enables users to comprehend its meaning.

The COST CONSTRAINT suggests that information should be produced only if the perceived benefits of increased decision usefulness exceed the expected costs of providing that information.

PRUDENCE suggests that care should be taken not to overstate assets and revenues or understate liabilities and expenses.

optimism about their business operations, which sometimes creeps into the financial reports that they prepare. More companies have perished through excessive optimism than through excessive caution. Prudence is viewed as a constraint rather than a desirable quality of accounting information, because the prudent reporting of accounting information contradicts the concept of neutrality and is likely to result in bias in the values reported on financial statements.

In summary, the usefulness of accounting information depends on many players, each contributing his or her share in the process of preparing and disseminating information that is credible. Credibility of the information conveyed in financial reports depends on those who establish accounting standards, those who are responsible for the preparation of financial reports, and those responsible for ensuring compliance with the accounting standards. The standard-setting process alone, no matter how meticulous, cannot establish and sustain trust. Compliance in practice; appropriate audit procedures; and professional codes of conduct, oversight, and public disciplinary procedures all work together to enhance the credibility of those who are legally responsible for the periodic production and communication of accounting information to a variety of users.

GLOBAL DIFFERENCES IN ACCOUNTING STANDARDS

INTERNATIONAL PERSPECTIVE

Financial accounting standards and disclosure requirements are set by national regulatory agencies and standard-setting bodies. Many countries have already adopted IFRS issued by the International Accounting Standards Board (IASB). However, the Financial Accounting Standards Board (FASB) and the U.S. Securities and Exchange Commission (SEC) are still considering when and how U.S. companies should prepare their financial statements using accounting standards that are based on IFRS. Despite efforts by the IASB and the FASB to harmonize U.S. accounting standards with IFRS, there are still several important differences at the time of writing this chapter. A partial list of the differences and the chapter in which these issues are addressed is presented below:

Difference*	U.S. GAAP	IFRS	Chapter
Extraordinary items	Permitted	Prohibited	3
Last-in, first-out method for inventory	Permitted	Prohibited	8
Reversal of inventory write-downs	Prohibited	Permitted	8
Basis of property, plant, and equipment	Historical cost	Fair value or historical cost	9

*Source: US GAAP versus IFRS: The basics, Ernst & Young, November 2012.

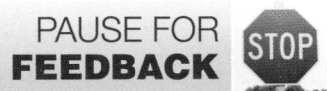
PAUSE FOR FEEDBACK STOP

In this section, you learned the roles of different parties in the accounting communication process and the guidance they receive from legal and professional standards. Management of the reporting company decides the appropriate format and level of detail to present in its financial reports. Independent audits increase the credibility of the information. Directors monitor managers' compliance with reporting standards and hire the auditor. Financial statement announcements from public companies are usually first transmitted to users through electronic information services. Staff of securities commissions review the public financial reports for compliance with legal and professional standards and punish violators. Analysts play a major role in making financial statement and other information available to average investors through their stock recommendations and earnings forecasts. Before you move on, complete the following exercise to test your understanding of these concepts.

SELF-STUDY QUIZ 6-1

Match the players involved in the accounting communication process with their roles, or the guiding principles for communicating information with their definitions.

1. Relevant information

2. CEO and CFO

3. Financial analyst

4. External auditor

5. Cost constraint

a. Management primarily responsible for accounting information.

b. An independent party that provides an opinion that the financial statements are presented fairly and in accordance with IFRS.

c. Information that influences users' decisions.

d. Only information that provides benefits in excess of costs should be reported.

e. An individual who analyzes financial information and provides advice.

After you complete your answers, check them with the solutions at the end of the chapter.

A CLOSER LOOK AT FINANCIAL STATEMENTS AND NOTES

LO3

Recognize and apply the different financial statement and disclosure formats used by companies in practice.

To make financial statements more useful to investors, creditors, and analysts, specific *classifications* of information are included in the statements. Various classifications are used in practice. You should not be confused when you notice different formats used by different companies. You will find that each format is consistent with the principles discussed in this text.

Overview of Thomson Reuters' Financial Statements

Exhibits 6.5 to 6.9 show the financial statements of Thomson Reuters for the fiscal year 2012. Note that Thomson-Reuters calls its statement of earnings the income statement, which is the term more commonly used in the United States.

Classified Statement of Financial Position

Exhibit 6.5 shows the December 31, 2012, statement of financial position for Thomson Reuters. This statement looks very similar to the structure of the statements of financial position for Sun-Rype Products Ltd. and Danier Leather Inc. presented in previous chapters. The statement of financial position is classified as follows:

Assets (by order of liquidity)
Current assets (short term)
Non-current assets
Total assets
Liabilities (by order of time to maturity)
Current liabilities (short term)
Non-current liabilities
Total liabilities
Shareholders' equity (by source)
Contributed capital (by owners)
Retained earnings (accumulated earnings minus accumulated dividends declared)
Accumulated other comprehensive income (loss)
Total shareholders' equity
Total liabilities and shareholders' equity

Exhibit **6.5**

Thomson Reuters' Consolidated
Statement of Financial Position

REAL-WORLD EXCERPT

*Thomson Reuters
Corporation*

ANNUAL REPORT

THOMSON REUTERS CORPORATION
Consolidated Statement of Financial Position

(millions of U.S. dollars)	Notes	December 31, 2012	December 31, 2011	December 31, 2010
ASSETS				
Cash and cash equivalents	11	1,301	422	864
Trade and other receivables	12	1,835	1,984	1,809
Other financial assets	19	72	100	74
Prepaid expenses and other current assets	13	641	641	912
Assets held for sale	14	302	767	—
Current assets		4,151	3,914	3,659
Computer hardware and other property, net	15	1,423	1,509	1,567
Computer software, net	16	1,682	1,640	1,613
Other identifiable intangible assets, net	17	8,135	8,471	8,714
Goodwill	18	16,256	15,932	18,892
Other financial assets	19	360	425	460
Other non-current assets	20	515	535	558
Deferred tax	23	50	50	68
Total assets		32,572	32,476	35,531
LIABILITIES AND EQUITY				
Liabilities				
Current indebtedness	19	1,008	434	645
Payables, accruals, and provisions	21	2,633	2,675	2,924
Deferred revenue		1,224	1,379	1,300
Other financial liabilities	19	95	81	142
Liabilities associated with assets held for sale	14	35	35	—
Current liabilities		4,995	4,604	5,011
Long-term indebtedness	19	6,223	7,160	6,873
Provisions and other non-current liabilities	22	2,514	2,513	2,217
Other financial liabilities	19	37	27	71
Deferred tax	23	1,305	1,422	1,684
Total liabilities		15,074	15,726	15,856
Equity				
Capital	24	10,371	10,288	10,284
Retained earnings		8,311	7,633	10,518
Accumulated other comprehensive (loss) income		(1,537)	(1,516)	(1,480)
Total shareholders' equity		17,145	16,405	19,322
Non-controlling interests		353	345	353
Total equity		17,498	16,750	19,675
Total liabilities and equity		32,572	32,476	35,531

Contingencies (note 29)

The related notes form an integral part of these consolidated financial statements.

These financial statements were approved by the Company's board of directors on March 6, 2013.

Reprinted with permission of Thomson Reuters.
Source: Thomson Reuters' Annual Report 2012, www.sedar.com, posted 11 March 2012.

Alternatively, assets may be reported by increasing order of liquidity, starting with the least-liquid asset and ending with the most-liquid asset. On the financing side, the equity section would be presented before liabilities, with non-current liabilities listed before current liabilities. This presentation format has been adopted by many European companies and is consistent with IFRS.

Classified Statement of Earnings

As we have seen in previous chapters, the statement of earnings includes a number of sections and subtotals to aid the user in identifying the company's earnings from operations (operating profit) for the year, and to highlight the effect of other items on net earnings.

Most manufacturing and merchandising companies use the following basic structure:

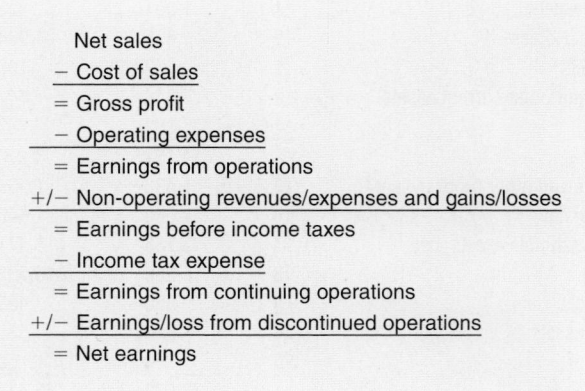

The operating expenses consist mainly of distribution costs, administrative expenses, and other operating expenses.[13] When a corporation controls less than 100 percent of the voting shares of other corporations, net earnings is allocated between the company's shareholders that hold a controlling interest and other shareholders that have a non-controlling interest.

Thomson Reuters is a service company. Consequently, its statement of earnings (income statement, Exhibit 6.6) does not include the subtotal "gross profit." In addition, the company reports the depreciation and amortization expense separately from other operating expenses.

Earnings Measurement

The measurement of earnings continues to be a subject of debate. Accountants have attempted over the years to estimate the true earnings that an entity achieves during a specific period. Until recently, the dominant approach to earnings measurement has focused on measurement of revenues and expenses. The principles of revenue recognition, matching, and historical cost were predominant in measuring revenues, expenses, gains, and losses that are reported on the statement of earnings. Consequently, the values of assets and liabilities reported on the statement of financial position did not necessarily reflect their current values but the values that resulted from the application of these accounting principles. For example, depreciation of property and equipment reflects an allocation of historical acquisition costs instead of a decline in the current value of these assets over time.

More recently, the desire to provide more relevant information for decision-making purposes has focused the attention of accounting standard setters toward measuring the current values of assets and liabilities. While the measurement of assets and liabilities at their current values is consistent with economic theory and leads to an estimation of economic earnings, the actual determination of current value is not a simple task. Different measures of current value have been proposed over time and are currently used in determining the values reported on the statement of financial position. Ideally, companies should measure their assets and liabilities at fair value or exit value, which is defined as "the price that would be received to sell an asset or paid to transfer a liability in an orderly transaction between market participants at the measurement date."[14] Because of practical difficulties in determining a price for an asset or liability in the absence of an active market, accounting standard setters have provided guidance to accountants for the measurement of fair value under different circumstances.

Exhibit **6.6**
Statement of Earnings of Thomson
Reuters Corporation

THOMSON REUTERS CORPORATION
Consolidated Income Statement

(millions of U.S. dollars, except per share amounts)	Notes	Year ended December 31 2012	2011
Revenues		13,278	13,807
Operating expenses	5	(9,762)	(9,997)
Depreciation		(429)	(438)
Amortization of computer software		(700)	(659)
Amortization of other identifiable intangible assets		(619)	(612)
Goodwill impairment	18	–	(3,010)
Other operating gains, net	6	883	204
Operating (loss) profit		2,651	(705)
Finance costs, net:			
Net interest expense	7	(390)	(396)
Other finance (costs) income	7	40	(15)
Other non-operating charge			
(Loss) income before tax and equity method investees		2,301	(1,116)
Share of post-tax earnings in equity method investees	8	(23)	13
Tax expense	9	(157)	(293)
Earnings (loss) from continuing operations		2,121	(1,396)
Earnings from discontinued operations, net of tax		2	4
Net earnings (loss)		2,123	(1,392)
Earnings (loss) attributable to:			
Common shareholders		2,070	(1,390)
Non-controlling interests		53	(2)
Earnings (loss) per share	10		
Basic earnings (loss) per share:			
From continuing operations		$2.50	($1.68)
From discontinued operations		–	0.01
Basic earnings (loss) per share		$ 2.50	($1.67)
Diluted earnings (loss) per share:			
From continuing operations		$ 2.49	($1.68)
From discontinued operations		–	0.01
Diluted earnings (loss) per share		$ 2.49	($1.67)

The related notes form an integral part of these consolidated financial statements.

Reprinted with permission of Thomson Reuters.
Source: Thomson Reuters' Annual Report 2012, **www.sedar.com**, posted 11 March 2012.

REAL-WORLD EXCERPT

Thomson Reuters
Corporation
ANNUAL REPORT

DIFFERENT EARNINGS FOR DIFFERENT PURPOSES

FINANCIAL
ANALYSIS

In recent years, many companies reported different measures of earnings in addition to net earnings, as determined by IFRS. Thomson Reuters uses certain non-IFRS financial measures as supplemental indicators of its operating performance and financial position and for internal planning purposes. The company has stated that it reports non-IFRS financial measures because it believes their use provides more insight into and understanding of its performance.

For example, in discussing its annual and quarterly results of operations, Thomson Reuters' management focuses investors' and analysts' attention on revenues; operating profit from ongoing businesses; and underlying operating profit, which they define as operating profit excluding the impact of items that distort the performance of the company's operations such as amortization of other identifiable intangible assets, impairment charges, and other operating gains and losses.

Comparison of the revenue, operating profit, and underlying operating profit for the years 2010–2012 shows clearly why investors and analysts should be cautious about interpreting non-IFRS measures of profit (amounts in millions of dollars):

	2012	2011	2010
Revenue	13,278	$13,807	$13,070
Operating (loss) profit	2,651	(705)	1,419
Underlying operating profit	2,405	2,541	2,356

Both revenue and underlying operating profit increased from 2010 to 2011, but declined in 2012. In contrast, operating profit turned into a loss in 2011 before recovering in 2012. In 2011, Thomson Reuters recorded a non-cash goodwill impairment charge of $3.0 billion. The impairment was due to weaker than expected performance by its former Markets division, which consisted largely of businesses now in its Financial and Risk segment. The impairment charge was included in Thomson Reuters' IFRS financial measures for 2011, but excluded from its non-IFRS financial measures. Because the non-recurring impairment charge significantly distorted the results of its ongoing business, management of Thomson Reuters wanted to draw analysts' and users' attention to underlying operating profit as an alternative, non-IFRS measure of profit.

Most companies, including the focus companies used in this book, report one or more supplemental measure of operating performance. The most common measure is EBITDA (earnings before interest, taxes, depreciation, and amortization), which excludes interest expense, income tax expense, and depreciation and amortization expense from the computation of net earnings. Another measure of performance is adjusted net earnings, which excludes from net earnings any costs related to acquisitions of other businesses.

The lack of active markets for many assets and liabilities has resulted in the use of different valuation approaches, ranging from historical cost to exit value. The following table summarizes the valuation bases that are currently permitted by IFRS for the reporting of asset and liability values on the statement of financial position:

Asset or Liability Group	Valuation Basis
Financial assets (e.g., investment in shares of other corporations, trade receivables, notes receivable)	Amortized cost or fair value
Inventories	Lower of cost and net realizable value
Property, plant, and equipment	Depreciated cost or recoverable amount
Investment properties (e.g., commercial real estate properties)	Depreciated cost or fair value
Intangible assets	Amortized cost or fair value
Financial liabilities	Amortized cost or fair value

Because end-of-period valuations are not based on actual exchange transactions between the company and outside parties, the gains and losses that result from such valuations are usually reported separately in a statement of comprehensive income and distinguished from gains and losses that have been realized through actual transactions. This also leads to the preparation of a statement of changes in equity that reconciles the values reported on the statement of financial position to those reported on the statement of comprehensive income. The effects of the various asset and liability valuation methods on the values reported on financial statements are discussed in later chapters.[15]

Statement of Comprehensive Income

The statement of earnings includes the results of operations for a specific accounting period as well as the effects of discontinued operations. Over the years, accounting academics and standard setters have debated whether the statement of earnings should include additional elements reflecting unrealized changes in the values of specific assets and liabilities. Hence, publicly accountable enterprises are now required to disclose additional information in a statement of comprehensive income. The additional components of income reflect the financial effect of events that cause changes in shareholders' equity, other than investments by shareholders or distributions to shareholders. The additional components of income, or *other comprehensive income*, include unrealized gains and losses on certain financial instruments, as well as other items discussed in advanced accounting courses. The net earnings and other comprehensive income totals are then combined to create a final total called comprehensive income (the bottom line for this statement).

The statement of comprehensive income for Thomson Reuters for the year ended December 31, 2012 (Exhibit 6.7), includes specific adjustments to net earnings. Measurement of the various components of other comprehensive income (loss) is rather complex and is covered in advanced accounting courses.

Statement of Changes in Equity

The statement of changes in equity shows a summary of the changes to the various components of equity that occurred during the period because of transactions with shareholders (issuance of additional shares, repurchase of shares, declaration of dividends); the net earnings or loss that the company realized from its operating, investing, and financing activities; and the adjustments to asset and liability values that are not reflected in the net earnings or loss for the year. This statement reconciles the beginning and ending values for each component of equity and indicates the nature of the changes that occurred to

---

Exhibit 6.7
Thomson Reuters' Consolidated Statement of Comprehensive Income

REAL-WORLD EXCERPT

Thomson-Reuters Corporation
ANNUAL REPORT

THOMSON REUTERS CORPORATION
Consolidated Statement of Comprehensive Income

(millions of U.S. dollars)	Notes	Year ended December 31 2012	2011
Net (loss) earnings		2,123	(1,392)
Other comprehensive income (loss):			
Cash flow hedges adjustments to earnings	19	(57)	62
Cash flow hedges adjustments to equity		23	(41)
Foreign currency translation adjustments to equity		13	(59)
Foreign currency translation adjustments to earnings		–	2
Net actuarial losses on defined benefit pension plans, net of tax[1]	26	(234)	(262)
Other comprehensive income (loss)		(255)	(298)
Total comprehensive income (loss)		1,868	(1,690)
Comprehensive income (loss) for the period attributable to:			
Common shareholders		1,815	(1,688)
Non-controlling interests		53	(2)

[1] The related tax benefit was $120 million and $126 million for the years ended December 31, 2012 and 2011, respectively.

The related notes form an integral part of these consolidated financial statements.

Reprinted with permission of Thomson Reuters.
Source: Thomson Reuters' Annual Report 2012, www.sedar.com, posted 11 March 2012.

Exhibit **6.8**

Thomson Reuters' Consolidated
Statement of Changes in Equity

THOMSON REUTERS CORPORATION

Consolidated Statement of Changes in Equity

(millions of U.S. dollars)	Stated share capital	Contributed surplus	Total capital	Retained earnings	Unrecognized gain (loss) on cash flow hedges	Foreign currency translation adjustments	Total accumulated other comprehensive loss ("AOCL")	Non-controlling interests	Total
Balance, December 31, 2011	10,134	154	10,288	7,633	(22)	(1,494)	(1,516)	345	16,750
Comprehensive income (loss)(1)	–	–	–	1,836	(34)	13	(21)	53	1,868
Distributions to non-controlling interest	–	–	–	–	–	–	–	(45)	(45)
Dividends declared on preference shares	–	–	–	(3)	–	–	–	–	(3)
Dividends declared on common shares	–	–	–	(1,059)	–	–	–	–	(1,059)
Shares issued under Dividend Reinvestment Plan ("DRIP")	38	–	38	–	–	–	–	–	38
Repurchases of common shares	(72)		(72)	(96)					(168)
Stock compensation plans	101	16	117	–	–	–	–	–	117
Balance, December 31, 2012	10,201	170	10,371	8,311	(56)	(1,481)	(1,537)	353	17,498

(1)Retained earnings for the year ended December 31, 2012 includes net actuarial losses of $234 million, net of tax (2011 – $262 million).

The related notes form an integral part of these consolidated financial statements.

Reprinted with permission of Thomson Reuters.

Source: Thomson Reuters' Annual Report 2012, www.sedar.com, posted 11 March 2012.

each of these components. For example, in Exhibit 6.8, the increase in retained earnings from $7,633 to $8,311 has resulted from an addition of $1,836 based on the statement of comprehensive income; reductions of $3 and $1,056 for dividends declared on preferred and common shares, respectively; and repurchase of common shares.

Statement of Cash Flows

Lastly, Thomson Reuters' statement of cash flows (Exhibit 6.9) shows the sources and uses of cash that resulted from its operating, investing, and financing activities during the years ended December 31, 2011 and 2012.

We introduced the three classifications of cash flows in prior chapters:

Cash Flows from Operating Activities. This section reports cash flows associated with operations.

Cash Flows from Investing Activities. Cash flows in this section are associated with the purchase and sale of (1) productive assets (other than inventory) and (2) investments in other companies.

Cash Flows from Financing Activities. These cash flows are related to financing the business through borrowing and repaying loans, issuances and repurchases of shares, and dividend payments.

Such a classification of the cash flows is important, especially for those cash flows resulting from operating activities. Companies cannot survive for a long time without generating positive cash flows from their operations.

The cash flows from operating activities can be reported by using either the *direct* or the *indirect* method, as illustrated in Chapter 5. For Thomson Reuters, the first section is reported by using the indirect method, which presents a reconciliation of net earnings (profit) on an accrual basis to cash flows from operations.

Exhibit **6.9**

Statement of Cash Flows of the
Thomson Reuters Corporation

REAL-WORLD EXCERPT

*Thomson Reuters
Corporation*

ANNUAL REPORT

THOMSON REUTERS CORPORATION
Consolidated Statement of Cash Flow

(millions of U.S. dollars)	Notes	Year ended December 31	
		2012	2011
Cash provided by (used in):			
Operating Activities			
Net earnings (loss)		2,123	(1,392)
Adjustments for:			
Depreciation		429	438
Amortization of computer software		700	659
Amortization of other identifiable intangible assets		619	612
Goodwill impairment		–	3,010
Net gains on disposals of businesses and investments		(829)	(388)
Deferred tax	23	(118)	(202)
Other	27	(61)	139
Changes in working capital and other items	27	(159)	(279)
Net cash provided by operating activities		2,704	2,597
Investing Activities			
Acquisitions, net of cash acquired	28	(1,301)	(1,286)
Proceeds from other disposals, net of taxes paid		1,901	415
Capital expenditures, less proceeds from disposals		(977)	(1,041)
Other investing activities		13	49
Investing cash flows from continuing operations		(364)	(1,863)
Investing cash flows from discontinued operations		90	56
Net cash used in investing activities		(274)	(1,807)
Financing Activities			
Proceeds from debt	19	–	349
Repayments of debt	19	(2)	(648)
Net borrowings under short-term loan facilities		(422)	400
Repurchases of common shares	24	(168)	(326)
Dividends paid on preference shares		(3)	(3)
Dividends paid on common shares	24	(1,021)	(960)
Other financing activities		65	(39)
Net cash used in financing activities		(1,551)	(1,227)
Translation adjustments on cash and cash equivalents		–	(5)
Decrease in cash and cash equivalents		879	(442)
Cash and cash equivalents at beginning of period	11	442	864
Cash and cash equivalents at end of period	11	1,301	442

Supplemental cash flow information is provided in note 27.

Interest paid		(419)	(399)
Interest received		5	9
Total income taxes paid		(446)	(511)

Amounts paid and received for interest are reflected as operating cash flows. Interest paid is net of debt-related hedges.
Amounts paid and received for income taxes are reflected as either operating cash flows or investing cash flows depending on the nature of the underlying transaction.

The related notes form an integral part of these consolidated financial statements.

**FOCUS ON
CASH FLOWS**

OPERATING ACTIVITIES (INDIRECT METHOD)

The operating activities section prepared by using the indirect method helps the analyst understand the *causes of differences* between a company's net earnings and cash flows. Net earnings and cash flows from operating activities can be quite different. Remember that the statement of earnings is prepared under the accrual concept. Revenues are recorded when earned, without regard to when the related cash flow occurs. Likewise, expenses are recorded when incurred in the same period, without regard to when the related cash flows occur.

In the indirect method, the operating activities section starts with net earnings computed under the accrual concept and then eliminates non-cash items, leaving cash flows from operating activities:

$$
\begin{array}{r}
\text{Net earnings} \\
\underline{+/-\ \text{Adjustment for non-cash items}} \\
=\ \text{Cash provided by operating activities}
\end{array}
$$

The items listed between net earnings and cash flow from operations identify the sources of the difference. For example, since no cash is paid during the current period for Thomson Reuters' depreciation expense of $429, this amount is added back to net earnings in the conversion process. Similarly, increases and decreases in certain current assets and liabilities (also known as non-cash elements of working capital) also account for some of the difference between net earnings and cash flow from operations. As we cover different portions of the statement of earnings and the statement of financial position in more detail in Chapters 7 to 12, we will also review the relevant sections of the statement of cash flows that are covered in Chapter 5.

Notes to Financial Statements

While the amounts reported on the various financial statements provide important information, users require additional details to facilitate their analysis. Standard-setting organizations, such as the AcSB, and securities commissions, such as the OSC, require public companies to provide a minimum set of detailed information to assist the users of financial statements in making informed investment and credit decisions. In addition, companies may provide other information voluntarily if management believes that such information will reflect positively on the company. In general, management refrains from disclosing information that may have a negative effect on the company's future profitability and financial condition—hence the need for a minimum set of disclosures that are typically provided in notes to financial statements. Thomson Reuters included 31 notes to its financial statements for 2012, covering both mandatory and voluntary disclosures.

Notes to financial statements include three types of information:

1. Description of the key accounting policies (rules) applied to the company's statements.

2. Additional details supporting reported amounts in the financial statements.

3. Relevant financial information not disclosed in the statements.

Excerpts from Thomson Reuters' notes are illustrated below, along with our discussion of selected elements of the company's financial statements.

Accounting Policies Applied in the Company's Statements The first or second note is typically a summary of significant accounting policies. As you will see in your study of subsequent chapters, IFRS permit companies to select from alternative methods for measuring the effects of transactions. The summary of significant accounting policies tells the user which accounting methods the company has adopted. For example, Thomson Reuters' accounting policy for computer hardware and other property is as follows:

NOTES TO CONSOLIDATED FINANCIAL STATEMENTS

Note 1: Summary of Business and Significant Accounting Policies

Computer hardware and other property

Computer hardware and other property are recorded at cost and depreciated on a straight-line basis over their estimated useful lives as follows:

Computer hardware	3–5 years
Buildings and building improvements	5–40 years
Furniture, fixtures, and equipment	3–10 years

Residual values and useful lives are reviewed at the end of each reporting period and adjusted if appropriate.

Reprinted with permission of Thomson Reuters.
Source: Thomson Reuters' Annual Report 2012, www.sedar.com, posted 11 March 2012.

Without an understanding of the various accounting methods used, it is impossible to analyze a company's financial results effectively.

ALTERNATIVE ACCOUNTING METHODS AND IFRS

FINANCIAL ANALYSIS

Many people mistakenly believe that IFRS permit only one accounting method to be used to compute each value in the financial statements (e.g., inventories). Actually, IFRS often allow the selection of an accounting method from a menu of acceptable methods. This permits a company to choose the methods that most closely reflect its particular economic circumstances. This flexibility complicates the financial statement users' task. Users must understand how the company's choice of accounting methods affects its financial statement presentations.

For example, before analyzing two companies' statements prepared by using different accounting methods, one company's statements must be converted to the other's methods to make them comparable. Otherwise, the reader is in a situation similar to comparing distances in kilometres and miles without conversion to a common scale. In Chapters 8 and 9, we discuss alternative accounting methods and their effects on financial statements.

Additional Detail Supporting Reported Amounts The second category of notes provides supplemental information concerning the data shown in the financial statements. Among other information, these notes may show revenues broken down by geographic region of business segments, describe unusual transactions, or offer expanded detail on a specific classification. For example, in Note 5 on the next page, Thomson Reuters indicates the make-up of its operating expenses for 2012. It lists the different types of expenses that make up the total amount of operating expenses reported on the statement of earnings. Details indicate that staff costs make up about 55 percent of the operating expenses.

NOTES TO CONSOLIDATED FINANCIAL STATEMENTS

Note 5: Operating Expenses

The components of operating expenses include the following (in millions of U.S. dollars):

	Year ended December 31	
	2012	**2011**
Salaries, commissions, and allowances	4,998	5,132
Share-based payments	101	87
Post-employment benefits	261	242
Total staff costs	5,360	5,461
Goods and services[(1)]	2,256	2,487
Data	1,027	1,044
Telecommunications	589	628
Real estate	494	526
Fair value adjustments[(2)]	36	(149)
Total operating expenses	9,762	9,997

[(1)]Goods and services include professional fees, consulting services, contractors, technology-related expenses, selling and marketing, and other general and administrative costs.

[(2)]Fair value adjustments primarily represent the impact from embedded derivatives and certain share-based awards.

Reprinted with permission of Thomson Reuters.
Source: Thomson Reuters' Annual Report 2012, www.sedar.com, posted 11 March 2012.

Relevant Financial Information Not Disclosed on the Statements   The final category of notes includes information that impacts the company financially but is not shown on the financial statements. Examples include information on legal matters and any material event that occurred subsequent to year-end but before the financial statements are published. In Note 29, Thomson Reuters disclosed information related to lawsuits and legal claims.

NOTES TO CONSOLIDATED FINANCIAL STATEMENTS

Note 29: Contingencies, Commitments and Guarantees

Lawsuits and legal claims

In November 2009, the European Commission initiated an investigation relating to the use of the Company's Reuters Instrument Codes (RIC symbols). RIC symbols are specifically designed to help financial professionals retrieve news and information on financial instruments (such as prices and other data on stocks, bonds, currencies and commodities) from Thomson Reuters financial data services. In December 2012, the European Commission announced that it accepted the Company's proposal in response to the investigation without any finding of infringement of European Union competition law by the Company. In line with the Company's agreement with the European Commission, the Company will offer its customers rights to continue to use its RICs with data from an alternative consolidated data feed provider to which they have moved.

In addition to the matter described above, the Company is engaged in various legal proceedings, claims, audits and investigations that have arisen in the ordinary course of business. These matters include but are not limited to intellectual property infringement claims, employment matters and commercial matters. The outcome of all of the matters against the Company is subject to future resolution, including the uncertainties of litigation. Based on information currently known to the Company and after consultation with outside legal counsel, management believes that the probable ultimate resolution of any such matters, individually or in the aggregate, will not have a material adverse effect on the financial condition of the Company, taken as a whole.

Reprinted with permission of Thomson Reuters.
Source: Thomson Reuters' Annual Report 2012, www.sedar.com, posted 11 March 2012.

Voluntary Disclosures

IFRS and securities regulations set only a minimum level of required financial disclosures. Many companies, including Thomson Reuters, provide important disclosures beyond those required. Such voluntary disclosures may appear in the annual report, in documents filed with securities commissions, in press releases, or on the company's website.

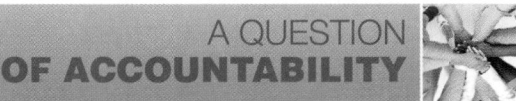

ACCOUNTING AND SUSTAINABLE DEVELOPMENT

A QUESTION
OF ACCOUNTABILITY

A growing area of voluntary disclosures in North America is sustainability reporting. Publicly accountable enterprises are under increasing pressure to disclose information about the social and environmental impacts of their activities, particularly if they operate in the mining, chemical, and resource extraction industries, which engage in activities that affect the sustainability of the resources used for production purposes. Many international organizations have voiced their concerns about sustainable development and developed specific frameworks for sustainability reporting, such as the Global Reporting Initiative (GRI). A recent research report by the Canadian Financial Executives Research Foundation indicates the following:

> Significant research has been undertaken over the past 20 years by professional accounting bodies and international standards setting organizations to develop best practices and meaningful, comparative disclosure and reporting of sustainability performance by companies. Against this backdrop, senior financial executives in Canada also recognize the need for enterprises to measure and report on their sustainability performance in a transparent manner. However, concerns remain over the comparability of disclosure between companies and industries as well as ongoing measurement challenges related to environment and social responsibility reporting in general.

Source: Canadian Financial Executives Institute of Canada, *Corporate Sustainability Reporting in Canada*, March 2009, p. 2.

REAL-WORLD EXCERPT

*Corporate
Sustainability
Reporting in Canada*

Despite these difficulties, reporting on social and environmental sustainability is required in some countries for companies that wish to list their shares on their stock exchanges. Such reports are voluntary disclosures in Canada. However, many believe that managing a company in the interests of a wider group of stakeholders and reporting on these efforts is an ethical imperative.

ACCOUNTING STANDARDS
FOR PRIVATE ENTERPRISES

Accounting standard setting is a long process of consultation among the users, the preparers, and the standard-setting boards. The AcSB, after careful consideration of the information provided by preparers and users, decided to proceed with a set of accounting standards for private enterprises that are simpler than the IFRS applicable to publicly accountable enterprises.

While IFRS and the accounting standards for private enterprises are based on the same conceptual framework, the main differences relate to the extent of disclosures required for the two types on enterprises:

Financial Reporting Issue	IFRS	ASPE
Extent of required disclosures	Shareholders and creditors of publicly accountable enterprises do not generally have direct access to the entity's financial information. Management is therefore required to disclose the necessary information that would assist these financial statement users in making informed decisions.	For private enterprises, shareholders have access to the entity's financial information; hence, the disclosures are intended primarily for the other user groups.

DEMONSTRATION **CASE**

Canadian Tire Corporation is an interrelated network of businesses across Canada that sell home, car, sports, and leisure products, as well as work clothes and casual attire. In addition, Canadian Tire is the country's largest independent gasoline retailer through its Canadian Tire Petroleum subsidiary, which sells fuel and related products at many outlets in most provinces. Canadian Tire's financial statements for the years 2011 and 2012 are shown below:

CANADIAN TIRE CORPORATION
Consolidated Statements of Financial Position

As at (Dollars in millions)	December 29, 2012	December 31, 2011
ASSETS		
Cash and cash equivalents (Note 9)	$ 1,015.5	$ 325.8
Short-term investments (Note 10)	168.9	196.4
Trade and other receivables (Note 11)	750.6	829.3
Loans receivable (Note 12)	4,265.7	4,081.7
Merchandise inventories	1,503.3	1,448.6
Prepaid expenses and deposits	39.1	44.3
Assets classified as held for sale (Note 13)	5.5	30.5
Total current assets	7,748.6	6,956.6
Long-term receivables and other assets (Note 14)	681.2	668.9
Long-term investments	182.7	128.2
Goodwill and intangible assets (Note 15)	1,089.9	1,110.0
Investment property (Note 16)	95.1	72.4
Property and equipment (Note 17)	3,343.5	3,365.9
Deferred income taxes (Note 18)	40.4	36.8
Total assets	$13,181.4	$12,338.8
LIABILITIES		
Bank indebtedness (Note 9)	$ 86.0	$ 124.8
Deposits (Note 19)	1,311.0	1,182.3
Trade and other payables (Note 20)	1,631.3	1,640.9
Provisions (Note 21)	185.8	191.9
Short-term borrowings (Note 23)	118.9	352.6
Loans payable (Note 24)	623.7	628.7
Income taxes payable	5.5	3.9
Current portion of long-term debt (Note 25)	661.9	27.9
Total current liabilities	4,624.1	4,153.0
Long-term provisions (Note 21)	54.8	55.1
Long-term debt (Note 25)	2,336.0	2,347.7
Long-term deposits (Note 19)	1,111.8	1,102.2
Deferred income taxes (Note 18)	77.7	66.1
Other long-term liabilities (Note 26)	213.4	205.7
Total liabilities	8,417.8	7,929.8
SHAREHOLDERS' EQUITY		
Share capital (Note 28)	688.0	710.5
Contributed surplus	2.9	1.1
Accumulated other comprehensive income (loss)	(1.7)	11.0
Retained earnings	4,074.4	3,686.4
Total shareholders' equity	4,763.6	4,409.0
Total liabilities and shareholders' equity	$13,181.4	$12,338.8

The related notes form an integral part of these consolidated financial statements.

Consolidated Statements of Earnings

For the years ended (Dollars in millions except per share amounts)	December 29, 2012	December 31, 2011
Revenue (Note 31)	$11,427.2	$10,387.1
Cost of producing revenue (Note 32)	(7,929.3)	(7,326.4)
Gross margin	3,497.9	3,060.7
Other income	5.7	18.4
Operating expenses		
Distribution costs	(356.2)	(368.7)
Sales and marketing expenses	(1,636.4)	(1,307.9)
Administrative expenses	(707.6)	(640.4)
Total operating expenses (Note 33)	(2,700.2)	(2,317.0)
Operating income	803.4	762.1
Finance income	18.1	23.0
Finance costs	(144.3)	(155.2)
Net finance costs (Note 34)	(126.2)	(132.2)
Income before income taxes	677.2	629.9
Income taxes (Note 35)	(178.0)	(162.9)
Net income	$ 499.2	$ 467.0
Basic earnings per share	$ 6.13	$ 5.73
Diluted earnings per share	$ 6.10	$ 5.71
Weighted average number of Common and Class A Non-voting shares outstanding (Note 29):		
Basic	81,435,218	81,447,398
Diluted	81,805,594	81,803,786

The related notes form an integral part of these consolidated financial statements.

Consolidated Statements of Cash Flows

For the years ended (Dollars in millions)	December 29, 2012	December 31, 2011
Cash generated from (used for):		
Operating activities		
Net income	$ 499.2	$ 467.0
Adjustments for:		
Gross impairment loss on loans receivable (Note 12)	323.7	352.0
Depreciation on property and equipment and investment property (Note 33)	248.9	229.8
Income tax expense	178.0	162.9
Net finance costs	126.2	132.2
Amortization of intangible assets (Note 33)	86.2	66.3
Changes in fair value of derivative instruments	(7.7)	(3.1)
Deferred income taxes	16.5	(6.4)
Other	13.7	9.8
Gain on revaluation of shares (Note 8)	–	(10.4)
	1,484.7	1,400.1
Changes in working capital and other (Note 36)	(434.0)	219.6
Cash generated from operating activities before interest and income taxes	1,050.7	1,619.7
Interest paid	(155.3)	(176.6)
Interest received	8.9	26.1
Income taxes paid	(161.3)	(63.7)
Cash generated from operating activities	743.0	1,405.5
Investing activities		
Acquisition of FGL Sports (Note 8)	–	(739.9)
Acquisition of short-term investments	(264.0)	(334.8)
Acquisition of long-term investments	(130.0)	(123.1)

(continued)

Additions to property and equipment and investment property	(222.3)	(230.5)
Additions to intangible assets	(64.3)	(128.9)
Long-term receivables and other assets	17.6	(3.2)
Proceeds from the disposition of long-term investments	4.7	18.1
Proceeds from the maturity and disposition of short-term investments	360.7	364.0
Proceeds on disposition of property and equipment, investment property and assets held for sale	45.0	21.0
Other	(8.9)	(4.1)
Cash used for investing activities	(261.5)	(1,161.4)
Financing activities		
Net (repayment) issuance of short-term borrowings	(233.7)	10.1
Issuance of loans payable	235.3	129.3
Repayment of loans payable	(240.3)	(187.6)
Issuance of share capital (Note 28)	12.4	11.6
Repurchase of share capital (Note 28)	(33.1)	(11.9)
Issuance of long-term debt	637.4	–
Repayment of long-term debt and finance lease liabilities	(30.1)	(355.6)
Dividends paid	(97.7)	(89.6)
Payment of transaction costs related to long-term debt	(3.2)	–
Cash generated from (used for) financing activities	247.0	(493.7)
Cash generated (used) in the year	728.5	(249.6)
Cash and cash equivalents, net of bank indebtedness, beginning of year	201.0	450.9
Effect of exchange rate fluctuations on cash held	–	(0.3)
Cash and cash equivalents, net of bank indebtedness, end of the year (Note 9)	$929.5	$ 201.0

The related notes form an integral part of these consolidated financial statements.

Source: Canadian Tire Corporation Limited, Annual Report 2012.

Required:

1. Examine Canadian Tire's statements of financial position. Identify the six largest changes in the carrying amount of assets, liabilities, and shareholders' equity between the statement dates. Based on what you have learned so far, what type of transactions could have caused the changes in the carrying amount of these items?

2. Access Note 17 to the financial statements of Canadian Tire Corporation in Appendix A at the end of this book, and identify the specific changes to the property and equipment account.

3. Compute the following ratios for fiscal years 2011 and 2012: total asset turnover, return on assets, return on equity, and net profit margin. Use the results of your computations to comment on the company's financial situation and the profitability of its operations in both years. Canadian Tire's total assets and shareholders' equity at the beginning of fiscal year 2010 amounted to $11,048.5 million and $4,004.9 million, respectively.

4. Canadian Tire's operations generated significant amounts of cash during fiscal years 2011 and 2012. The company also made significant investments in long-term assets in fiscal year 2012. How did the company finance the investment in these assets?

5. Compute and interpret the quality of earnings ratio and the capital expenditures ratio for fiscal years 2011 and 2012.

6. Access reuters.com and search for Canadian Tire Corporation and then "Financials" followed by "Analysts." What are the consensus analysts' estimates of Canadian Tire's earnings per share (EPS) for fiscal years 2013 and 2014? Do analysts expect Canadian Tire's EPS to increase or decrease in the future? What information did the analysts take into consideration in computing their EPS estimates for the next two years?

We strongly recommend that you prepare your own answers to these requirements and then check your answers with the following solution.

SUGGESTED **SOLUTION**

1. The six statements of financial position items that had the largest changes in their carrying amounts on the statements of financial position and the typical reasons for these changes are summarized below (amounts in millions of dollars):

Statement of Financial Position Item	Change	Typical Reasons for Change
Cash and cash equivalents	$689.7	Increase in investments in highly liquid assets such as certificates of deposit and commercial paper.
Loans receivable	184.0	Increase in the amount of loans to customers, net of collections.
Deposits (short term)	128.7	Increase in deposits made by customers for future delivery of merchandise and service.
Current portion of long-term debt	634.0	Increase in the long-term borrowings that are payable within a year.
Merchandise inventories	54.7	Increase in merchandise inventories due to purchase of merchandise for resale to customers.
Retained earnings	388.0	Net earnings for the year minus dividends declared during the year.

2. Note 17 to the financial statements shows that Canadian Tire's property and equipment includes land, buildings, fixtures and equipment, leasehold improvements, assets under finance lease, and construction in progress. The cost of these assets increased by $179.4 million during 2012. At the same time, accumulated depreciation and impairment of the buildings, fixtures and equipment, leasehold improvements, and assets under finance lease increased by $201.8 million during the year, which reduced the carrying amounts of these assets.

3.

Ratio	2012	2011
Total Asset Turnover = Net Sales ÷ Average Total Assets	0.90	0.89
Return on Assets = $\dfrac{\text{Net Earnings} + \text{Interest Expense, Net of Tax}}{\text{Average Total Assets}}$	4.7%	5.0%
Return on Equity = Net Earnings ÷ Average Shareholders' Equity	10.9%	11.1%
Net Profit Margin = Net Earnings ÷ Net Sales	4.4%	4.5%

Computations:

2012

Total asset turnover ratio = $11,427.2 ÷ [($13,181.4 + $12,338.8)/2] = 0.90
Return on assets = [$499.2 + 144.3 × (1 − 0.26*)] ÷ [($12,338.8 + $13,181.4)/2] = 0.047
Return on equity = $499.2 ÷ [($4,409.0 + 4,763.6)/2] = 0.109
Net profit margin ratio = $499.2 ÷ $11,427.2 = 0.044

*Tax rate = $178.0/$677.2 = 0.26

2011

Total asset turnover ratio = $10,387.1 ÷ [($11,048.5 + $12,338.8)/2] = 0.89
Return on assets = [$467.0 + 155.2 × (1 − 0.26**)] ÷ [($11,048.5 + $12,338.8)/2] = 0.050
Return on equity = $467.0 ÷ [($4,004.9 + $4,409)/2] = 0.111
Net profit margin ratio = $467.0 ÷ $10,387.1 = 0.045

**Tax rate = $162.9/$629.9 = 0.26

The total asset turnover ratio has not changed significantly, suggesting the same efficiency in the utilization of the company's assets to generate revenue. The three profitability ratios— return on assets, return on equity, and net profit margin—decreased slightly relative to the previous year, because both total assets and equity increased at slightly higher rate than the increase in net earnings. This suggests that management needs to monitor its expenses in order to improve on its utilization of the company's resources and generate relatively higher earnings in the future.

4. Canadian Tire's statement of cash flows shows that the company used a net amount of $261.40 on investing activities during 2012. Both the operating and financing activities contributed posi- tive cash flows, which financed the investing activities.

5. Quality of Earnings Ratio $= \dfrac{\text{Cash Flow from Operating Activities}}{\text{Net Earnings}}$

2011: $1,405.5 \div $467.0 = 3.01$
2012: $743.0 \div $499.2 = 1.49$

The ratios indicate that the quality of the company's earnings dropped in 2012 relative to 2011, but the ratio exceeds 1.0. This indicates that Canadian Tire's management is prudent in adopting financial reporting strategies that result in good quality of the reported earnings.

Capital Expenditures Ratio $= \dfrac{\text{Cash Flow from Operating Activities}}{\text{Cash Paid for Capital Acquisitions}}$

2011: $1,405.5 \div $1,099.3 = 1.28$
2012: $743.0 \div $286.6 = 2.59$

In both years, the company generated enough cash from its operations to cover the payments needed for the additional investments in property and equipment, intangible assets, and acquisitions of other businesses. The acquisition of FGL Sports in 2011 caused an increased in capital expenditures and a relatively lower ratio.

6. Canadian Tire's basic EPS for fiscal year 2012 is $6.13, as disclosed in its statement of earnings. The average analyst's estimate of Canadian Tire's EPS was $6.64 for fiscal year 2013 and $7.02 for fiscal year 2014, at the time of writing this text. These average EPS estimates are based on individual estimates from 12 analysts.

Analysts use a variety of information sources to arrive at their EPS estimates. First, they need to develop a very good understanding of the industry and Canadian Tire's role in it. Their information sources would include the company's financial statements, population trends and expectations of future demand for the company's products, the company's strategies and future plans, conversations with company executives, and information about the company's competitors.

Appendix 6A: The Canadian Capital Markets (Online)

CHAPTER **TAKE-AWAYS**

1. **Recognize the people involved in the accounting communication process (regulators, managers, board of directors, auditors, information intermediaries, and users), their roles in the process, and the guidance they receive from legal and professional standards.**
   Management of the reporting company must decide on the appropriate format (categories) and level of detail to present in its financial reports. Independent audits increase the credibility of the information. Financial statement announcements from public companies are usually first transmitted to users through electronic information services. The securities commission staff review public reports for compliance with legal and professional standards, investigate irregularities, and punish violators. Analysts play a major role in making financial statements and other information available to average investors through their stock recommendations and earnings forecasts.

2. **Identify the steps in the accounting communication process, including the issuance of press releases, annual reports, quarterly reports, and documents filed with securities commissions, as well as the guiding principles in communicating useful information.**
   Earnings are first made public in press releases. Companies follow these announcements with annual and quarterly reports containing statements, notes, and additional information. Public companies must also file additional reports, containing more details about the company, with the securities commissions (e.g., OSC, SEC).

3. **Recognize and apply the different financial statement and disclosure formats used by companies in practice.**
   Most statements are classified and include subtotals that are relevant to analysis. On the statement of financial position, the most important distinctions are between current and

non-current assets and liabilities. On the statement of earnings and statement of cash flows, the separation of operating and non-operating items is most important. The notes to the statements describe the accounting rules applied and give more information about items disclosed in the statements, as well as information about economic events not disclosed in the statements.

In Chapter 7 we begin our in-depth discussion of financial statements. We will begin with two of the most liquid assets, cash and trade receivables, and transactions that involve revenues and certain selling expenses. Accuracy in revenue recognition and the related recognition of cost of sales (discussed in Chapter 8) are the most important determinants of the accuracy and, thus, the usefulness of financial statement presentations. We will also introduce concepts related to the management and control of cash and receivables, which is a critical business function. A detailed understanding of these topics is crucial to future managers, accountants, and financial analysts.

FINDING **FINANCIAL INFORMATION**

STATEMENT OF FINANCIAL POSITION
Key Classifications
  Current and non-current assets
    and liabilities
  Contributed capital and retained earnings

STATEMENT OF EARNINGS
Key Subtotals
  Gross profit
  Earnings from operations
  Net earnings
  Earnings per share

STATEMENT OF CASH FLOWS
Under Operating Activities (indirect method)
  Net earnings
  ± Items not affecting cash
  = Cash provided by operating activities

NOTES
Key Classifications
  Descriptions of accounting rules applied in
    the statements
  Additional detail supporting reported
    numbers
  Relevant financial information not disclosed
    on the statements

GLOSSARY

Review key terms and definitions on *Connect.*

QUESTIONS

1. Describe the roles and responsibilities of management, the board of directors, and independent auditors in the financial reporting process.
2. Define the following three users of financial accounting disclosures and the relationships among them: *financial analysts*, *private investors*, and *institutional investors*.
3. Briefly describe the role of information services in the communication of financial information.
4. Explain why information must be relevant and representationally faithful to be useful.
5. Identify the constraints of accounting measurement and their role in the reporting of accounting information.
6. What basis of accounting (accrual or cash) does IFRS require on (*a*) the statement of earnings, (*b*) the statement of financial position, and (*c*) the statement of cash flows?
7. Briefly explain the normal sequence and form of financial reports produced by private companies in a typical year.
8. Briefly explain the normal sequence and form of financial reports produced by public companies in a typical year.
9. What are the major subtotals on the statement of earnings, and what purpose do they serve?
10. List the six major classifications reported on a statement of financial position.
11. What are the three major classifications on a statement of cash flows?
12. What are the three major categories of notes or footnotes presented in annual reports? Cite an example of each.

■ LO1

E6–1 **Matching Players in the Accounting Communication Process with Their Definitions**
Match each player with the related definition by entering the appropriate letter in the space provided.

Players
_____ (1) Financial analyst
_____ (2) Creditor
_____ (3) Independent auditor
_____ (4) Private investor
_____ (5) CSA
_____ (6) Information service
_____ (7) Institutional investor
_____ (8) CEO and CFO

Definitions
A. Financial institution or supplier that lends money to the company.
B. Chief executive officer and chief financial officer, who have primary responsibility for the information presented in financial statements.
C. Manager of pension, mutual, and endowment funds who invests on behalf of others.
D. Canadian Securities Administrators, which harmonizes securities regulations in the Canadian capital markets.
E. Company that gathers, combines, and transmits (paper and electronic) financial and related information from various sources.
F. Adviser who analyzes financial and other economic information to make forecasts and stock recommendations.
G. Individual who purchases shares in companies.
H. Independent CPA who examines financial statements and attests to their fairness.

■ LO2

E6–2 **Finding Financial Information: Matching Information Items to Financial Reports**
Following are information items included in various financial reports. Match each information item with the report(s) where it would most likely be found by entering the appropriate letter(s) in the space provided.

Information Item	Report
_____ (1) Summarized financial data for 5- or 10-year period.	A. Annual report
_____ (2) Initial announcement of quarterly earnings.	B. Annual information form
_____ (3) Complete quarterly statement of earnings, statement of financial position, and statement of cash flows.	C. Press release
_____ (4) Basic financial statements for the year.	D. Quarterly report
_____ (5) Detailed discussion of the company's competition.	E. None of the above
_____ (6) Notes to financial statements.	
_____ (7) Identification of those responsible for the financial statements.	
_____ (8) Initial announcement of hiring of new vice-president of sales.	

■ LO2

Le Château

E6–3 **Understanding the Disclosure Process through the Le Château Website**
Using your Web browser, access Le Château at **http://lechateau.com/style/company/links/ investor.jsp**. Examine the most recent quarterly earnings press release and the related interim report.

Required:
Based on the information provided on the site, answer the following questions:
1. What were the release dates of the quarterly earnings press release and the interim report?
2. What additional information was provided in the interim report that was not reported in the earnings press release?

E6–4 Researching Information Provided on Company Websites

Using your Web browser, visit Canadian Tire Corporation at **www.corp.canadiantire.ca**.

Required:

Based on the information provided on the site, answer the following questions:

1. Which document(s) provided the most recent information on quarterly earnings?

2. For the most recent quarter, what was the change in sales revenue compared with the same quarter one year earlier? What was management's explanation for the change (if any)?

3. What were the annual earnings per share and stock price per share on the day of the most recent fourth-quarter earnings press release?

E6–5 Understanding Earnings per Share and Stock Prices

The following news story appeared on Yahoo! finance on July 24, 2012, after Apple Inc., the maker of iMac, iPod, iPad and iPhone products, released its results of operations for the third quarter of fiscal year 2012:

LO2, 3

Canadian Tire Corporation

LO1

Apple Inc.

REAL-WORLD EXCERPT

www.finance. yahoo.ca

Apple sags in 3Q as iPhone gets cheaper

By Peter Svensson, Associated Press – Tuesday, July 24, 2012, 6:47 PM EDT

NEW YORK (AP)—Consumers are buying cheaper Apple products. That's a disappointment for investors who thought the company would keep boosting profits and revenues at its previous breakneck pace.

On Tuesday, Apple Inc. revealed that both revenue and net income posted increases of just over 20 percent—cause for celebration at most companies, but meager by Apple standards.

The growth was the slowest in more than two years, and failed to meet analyst expectations.

. . .

Net income in Apple's fiscal third quarter was $8.8 billion, or $9.32 per share. That was up 21 percent from $7.3 billion, or $7.79 per share, a year ago.

Analysts polled by FactSet were expecting earnings of $10.37 per share.

Revenue at the Cupertino, Calif., company was $35 billion, up 23 percent. Analysts were expecting $37.5 billion.

Apple shares fell $29.82, or 5 percent, to $571.10 in after-hours trading, after the release of the results.

. . .

Required:

The earnings of Apple Inc. increased from $7.79 per share for the third quarter of 2011 to $9.32 per share a year later, but its share price dropped by $30 after the announcement of the quarterly result. Explain why the price per share decreased even though the company announced an increase in its earnings per share.

E6–6 Understanding Earnings per Share and Share Prices

Research In Motion Limited (RIM), which was renamed Blackberry in 2013, reported on September 27, 2012, a net loss of $238 million for the second quarter of its 2013 fiscal year, compared to net earnings of $329 million for the same quarter of 2012. Its revenues dropped from $4.2 billion in the second quarter of 2012 to $2.9 billion in the second quarter of 2013 due to increased competition from makers of smartphones and the streamlining of the company's operations. The company's share price closed at $7.50 on September 28 compared to $7.14 on September 27, prior to the announcement of its quarterly results.

LO1

Research in Motion Limited

Required:

1. Identify the direction and amount of the change in net earnings for the second quarter of 2013 compared with the same quarter of 2012.

2. Identify the direction and amount of the change in RIM's share price after the release of the second-quarter results.

3. Explain why RIM's share price changed in the opposite direction from the change in its earnings.

LO2

E6–7   **Guiding Principles for Communicating Useful Information**

Match each qualitative characteristic of useful accounting information with the related definition by entering the appropriate letter in the space provided.

Qualitative Characteristics	Definitions
_____ (1) Relevance	A. Application of the same accounting methods over time.
_____ (2) Timeliness	B. Agreement between what really happened and the disclosed information.
_____ (3) Predictive value	C. The information is available prior to the decision.
_____ (4) Confirmatory value	D. The accounting information does not favour a particular group.
_____ (5) Verifiability	E. The information helps reduce uncertainty in the future.
_____ (6) Faithful representation	F. The information provides input to evaluate previous expectations.
_____ (7) Neutrality	G. The information allows the evaluation of one alternative against another alternative.
_____ (8) Comparability	H. The information has a bearing on a specific decision.
_____ (9) Consistency	I. The information can be depended upon.
	J. Implies that qualified persons working independently arrive at similar conclusions.

LO2

E6–8   **Assessing the Relevance and Faithful Representation of Information**

Paula Romanov is the credit manager of Pinnacle Inc. She is considering whether to extend credit to Mak Inc., a new customer. Pinnacle sells most of its goods on credit but is very careful in extending credit to new customers. Tim Mak, the owner of Mak Inc., provided the following documents to Paula to assist her in her evaluation:

1. A detailed analysis of the sales revenue and earnings that Mak Inc. expects to achieve within the next 12 months.
2. Projections of the company's sales during the next five years.
3. The company's monthly bank statements for the past three years.
4. A report of the company's credit history prepared by Mak's employees.
5. A letter signed by all four company officers indicating that they are prepared to personally guarantee the amount of credit that Pinnacle approves.
6. Brief resumés of the four company officers along with descriptions of the functions they perform in the company.
7. Eight letters of reference from close friends and relatives of the four company officers.

Required:

Analyze each of the items above with respect to the characteristics of relevance (predictive value and confirmatory value) and faithful representation (complete, neutral, and free from material error). Explain whether or not each item possesses these characteristics.

LO3

E6–9   **Finding Financial Information: Matching Financial Statements with the Elements of Financial Statements**

Match each financial statement with the items presented in it by entering the appropriate letter in the space provided.

Elements of Financial Statements	Financial Statements
_____ (1) Liabilities	A. Statement of earnings
_____ (2) Cash from operating activities	B. Statement of financial position
_____ (3) Losses	C. Statement of cash flows
_____ (4) Assets	D. None of the above
_____ (5) Revenues	
_____ (6) Cash from financing activities	
_____ (7) Shareholders' equity	
_____ (8) Expenses	
_____ (9) Assets owned by a shareholder	

E6–10 Ordering the Classifications on a Typical Statement of Financial Position

■ LO3

A list of classifications on the statement of financial position is shown below. Number the classifications in the order in which they normally appear on a statement of financial position.

No.	Title
_____	Current liabilities
_____	Non-current liabilities
_____	Long-term investments
_____	Intangible assets
_____	Property, plant, and equipment
_____	Current assets
_____	Retained earnings
_____	Share capital
_____	Other non-current assets

E6–11 Finding Financial Information as a Potential Investor

■ LO3

You are considering investing the cash gifts you received for graduation in shares of various companies. You visit the websites of major companies, searching for relevant information.

Required:

For each of the following, indicate where you would locate the information in an annual report. (*Hint:* The information may be in more than one location.)

1. The detail on major classifications of non-current assets.
2. The accounting method(s) used for financial reporting purposes.
3. Whether the company has had any capital expenditures for the year.
4. Net amount of property, plant, and equipment.
5. Policies on amortizing intangibles.
6. Depreciation expense.
7. Any significant gains or losses on disposals of property, plant, and equipment.
8. Accumulated depreciation of property, plant, and equipment at the end of the last fiscal year.

E6–12 Inferring Share Issuances and Cash Dividends from Changes in Shareholders' Equity

■ LO3

Power Corporation

Power Corporation recently reported the following December 31 balances in its shareholders' equity accounts (in millions of dollars):

	Current Year	Prior Year
Share capital	$1,350	$1,332
Retained earnings	8,119	7,559
Reserves	356	541
Total shareholders' equity	$9,825	$9,430

During the current year, Power Corp. reported earnings of $1,116 million. Assume that the only other transactions that affected share capital and retained earnings during the current year were the issuance of shares and the declaration and payment of cash dividends.

Required:

Recreate the two journal entries reflecting the issuance of shares and the declaration and payment of dividends.

E6–13 Inferring Statement of Earnings Values

■ LO3

Supply the missing dollar amounts for the 2014 statement of earnings of BGT Company for each of the following independent cases. (*Hint:* Organize each case in the format of a classified or multistep statement of earnings. Rely on the amounts given to infer the missing values.)

	Case A	Case B	Case C	Case D	Case E
Sales revenue	$770	$?	$?	$600	$1,050
Pretax earnings	?	?	150	130	370
Income tax expense	65	210	60	45	?
Cost of sales	?	320	125	250	?
Gross profit	?	880	?	?	630
Selling expenses	90	275	45	70	?
Net earnings	115	275	?	?	240
Administrative expenses	200	120	80	?	175

■ connect PROBLEMS

■ **LO1, 2**   **P6–1**   **Matching Transactions with Concepts**

The concepts of accounting covered in Chapters 2 through 6 are shown below. Match each transaction with its related concept by entering the appropriate letter in the space provided. Use only one letter for each blank space:

Concepts	Transactions
Concepts	**Transactions**
_____ (1) Users of financial statements	A. Recorded a $1,000 sale of merchandise on credit.
_____ (2) Objective of financial statements	B. Counted (inventoried) the unsold items at the end of the period and valued them in dollars.
Qualitative Characteristics	C. Acquired a vehicle for use in operating the business.
_____ (3) Relevance	D. Reported the amount of depreciation expense because it will likely affect important decisions of statement users.
_____ (4) Verifiability	
_____ (5) Materiality	E. Identified as the investors, creditors, and others interested in the business.
Assumptions	F. Used special accounting approaches because of the uniqueness of the industry.
_____ (6) Separate entity	G. Issued notes payable of $1 million.
_____ (7) Continuity	H. Paid a contractor for an addition to the building with $10,000 cash and $20,000 market value of the company's shares ($30,000 was deemed to be the cash equivalent price).
_____ (8) Unit of measure	
_____ (9) Periodicity	
Elements of Financial Statements	I. Engaged an outside independent accountant to audit the financial statements.
_____ (10) Revenues	J. Sold merchandise and rendered services for cash and on credit during the year; then determined the cost of those goods sold and the cost of rendering those services.
_____ (11) Expenses	
_____ (12) Gains	K. Established an accounting policy that sales revenue shall be recognized only when ownership of the goods sold passes to the customer.
_____ (13) Losses	
_____ (14) Assets	L. To design and prepare the financial statements to assist the users in making decisions.
_____ (15) Liabilities	
_____ (16) Accounting equation	M. Established a policy not to include in the financial statements the personal financial affairs of the owners of the business.
Principles and Related Concepts	N. Sold an asset at a loss that was a peripheral or incidental transaction.
_____ (17) Cost	O. The value to users of a special financial report exceeds the cost of preparing it.
_____ (18) Revenue recognition	P. Valued an asset, such as inventory, at lower than its purchase cost because its market value is lower.
_____ (19) Matching	
_____ (20) Full disclosure	Q. Dated the statement of earnings "For the Year Ended December 31, 2014."
Constraints of Accounting	R. Used services from outsiders—paid cash for some and the remainder on credit.
_____ (21) Cost	S. Acquired an asset (a pencil sharpener that will have a useful life of five years) and recorded it as an expense when purchased for $2.99.
_____ (22) Prudence	
_____ (23) Industry peculiarities	
	T. Disclosed in the financial statements all relevant financial information about the business; necessitated the use of notes to the financial statements.
	U. Sold an asset at a gain that was a peripheral or incidental transaction.
	V. Assets of $500,000 − Liabilities of $300,000 = Shareholders' equity of $200,000.
	W. Accounting and reporting assume a "going concern."

P6–2 Matching Definitions with Terms Related to the Statement of Financial Position   ■ **LO3**

Selected terms related to the statement of financial position, which were discussed in Chapters 2 through 5, are listed below. Match each definition with its related term by entering the appropriate letter in the space provided.

Terms

_____ (1) Retained earnings   _____ (10) Carrying amount

_____ (2) Current liabilities   _____ (11) Contributed surplus

_____ (3) Liquidity   _____ (12) Liabilities

_____ (4) Contra-asset account   _____ (13) Non-current assets

_____ (5) Accumulated depreciation   _____ (14) Shareholders' equity

_____ (6) Intangible assets   _____ (15) Current assets

_____ (7) Other assets   _____ (16) Assets

_____ (8) Shares outstanding   _____ (17) Non-current liabilities

_____ (9) Normal operating cycle

Definitions

A. A miscellaneous category of assets.

B. Amount of contributed capital for which shares were not issued.

C. Total assets minus total liabilities.

D. Nearness of assets to cash (in time).

E. Assets expected to be collected in cash within one year or the operating cycle, if longer.

F. Same as book value; cost less accumulated depreciation to date.

G. Accumulated earnings minus accumulated dividends.

H. Asset offset account (subtracted from asset).

I. Balance of the common shares account divided by the issue price per share.

J. Assets that do not have physical substance.

K. Probable future economic benefits owned by the entity from past transactions.

L. Liabilities expected to be paid out of current assets, normally within the next year.

M. The average cash-to-cash time involved in the operations of the business.

N. Sum of the annual depreciation expense on an asset from the date of its acquisition to the current date.

O. All liabilities not classified as current liabilities.

P. Property, plant, and equipment.

Q. Debts or obligations from past transactions to be paid with assets or services.

R. None of the above.

P6–3 Preparing a Statement of Financial Position and Analyzing Some of Its Parts (AP6–1)   ■ **LO3**

         *e*X*cel*

Gold Jewellers Inc. is developing its annual financial statements for 2015. The following amounts were correct at December 31, 2015: cash, $58,000; trade receivables, $71,000; merchandise inventory, $154,000; prepaid insurance, $1,000; investment in shares of Z Corporation (long term), $36,000; store equipment, $67,000; used store equipment held for disposal, $9,000; accumulated depreciation, store equipment, $13,000; trade payables, $58,000; long-term note payable, $42,000; income taxes payable, $9,000; retained earnings, $164,000; and common shares, 100,000 shares outstanding (originally issued at $1.10 per share).

Required:

1. Based on these data, prepare the company's statement of financial position at December 31, 2015. Use the following major captions (list the individual items under these captions):

   a. Assets: current assets; long-term investments; property, plant, and equipment; and other assets.

   b. Liabilities: current liabilities and non-current liabilities.

   c. Shareholders' equity: share capital and retained earnings.

2. What is the carrying amount of store equipment? Explain what this value means.

■ **LO2, 3**

WestJet Airlines Ltd.

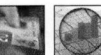

P6–4 Using Financial Reports: Interpreting Financial Statement Information and Analyzing and Interpreting Ratios (AP6–2)

WestJet Airlines Ltd. was founded in 1996 by a team of Calgary entrepreneurs and, as of December 31, 2012, has grown from serving five western Canadian destinations with three aircraft to serving

81 destinations in North America, Central America, and the Caribbean with 100 aircraft. WestJet's financial statements for 2012 and 2011 and excerpts from selected notes to its financial statements are shown below:

CONSOLIDATED STATEMENTS OF FINANCIAL POSITION
WestJet Airlines Ltd.
December 31, 2012 and 2011
(stated in thousands of Canadian dollars)

	Note	2012	2011
Assets			
Current assets:			
Cash and cash equivalents	5	1,408,199	1,243,605
Restricted cash	6	51,623	48,341
Accounts receivable	19	37,576	34,122
Prepaid expenses, deposits, and other	19	101,802	66,936
Inventory	19	35,595	31,695
		1,634,795	1,424,699
Non-current assets:			
Property and equipment	7	1,985,599	1,911,227
Intangible assets	8	50,808	33,793
Other assets	19	75,413	103,959
Total assets		3,746,615	3,473,678
Liabilities and shareholders' equity			
Current liabilities:			
Accounts payable and accrued liabilities	19	460,003	307,109
Advance ticket sales	19	480,947	432,186
Non-refundable guest credits	19	47,859	43,485
Current portion of long-term debt	10	164,909	158,832
Current portion of maintenance provisions	9	34,135	245
		1,187,853	941,857
Non-current liabilities:			
Maintenance provisions	9	145,656	151,645
Long-term debt	10	574,139	669,880
Obligations under finance leases		–	3,174
Other liabilities	19	9,914	10,449
Deferred income tax	11	356,748	326,456
Total liabilities		2,274,310	2,103,461
Shareholders' equity:			
Share capital	12	614,899	630,408
Equity reserves		69,856	74,184
Hedge reserves		(5,746)	(3,353)
Retained earnings		793,296	668,978
Total shareholders' equity		1,472,305	1,370,217
Total liabilities and shareholders' equity		3,746,615	3,473,678

The accompanying notes are an integral part of the consolidated financial statements.

Source: WestJet Airlines Ltd., Annual Report 2012.

CONSOLIDATED STATEMENTS OF EARNINGS
WestJet Airlines Ltd.
Years Ended December 31, 2012 and 2011
(stated in thousands of Canadian dollars, except per share amounts)

	Notes	2012	2011
Revenues:			
Guest		3,133,492	2,790,299
Other		293,917	281,241
		3,427,409	3,071,540
Expenses:			
Aircraft fuel		992,787	915,878
Airport operations		454,114	421,561
Flight operations and navigational charges		366,871	344,442
Sales and distribution		313,082	296,954
Marketing, general, and administration		208,620	186,290
Depreciation and amortization		185,401	174,751
Aircraft leasing		173,412	165,571
Inflight		156,411	139,478
Maintenance		154,406	146,260
Employee profit share		46,585	23,804
		3,051,689	2,814,989
Earnings from operations		375,720	256,551
Non-operating income (expense):			
Finance income	15	18,391	15,987
Finance costs	15	(48,900)	(60,911)
Gain on foreign exchange		1,061	2,485
Gain (loss) on disposal of property and equipment		469	(54)
Loss on fuel derivatives	16	(6,512)	(6,052)
		(35,491)	(48,545)
Earnings before income taxes		340,229	208,006
Income tax expense:			
Current		66,230	1,236
Deferred		31,607	58,068
	11	97,837	59,304
Net earnings		242,392	148,702
Earnings per share:			
Basic		$1.79	$1.06
Diluted		$1.78	$1.06

The accompanying notes are an integral part of the consolidated financial statements.

Source: WestJet Airlines Ltd., Annual Report 2012.

CONSOLIDATED STATEMENTS OF CASH FLOWS
WestJet Airlines Ltd.
Years Ended December 31, 2012 and 2011
(stated in thousands of Canadian dollars)

	Notes	2012	2011
Operating activities			
Net earnings		242,392	148,702
Items not involving cash:			
Depreciation and amortization		185,401	174,751
Change in long-term maintenance provisions		34,426	38,522
Change in other liabilities		(383)	(313)
Amortization of hedge settlements		1,400	1,400
Loss on fuel derivatives		6,512	6,052
(Gain) loss on disposal of property and equipment		(469)	54
Stock-based payment expense		12,815	12,553
Deferred income tax expense		31,607	58,068
Finance income		(18,391)	(15,987)
Finance cost		48,900	60,911
Unrealized foreign exchange (gain) loss		(1,487)	1,453
Change in non-cash working capital		173,563	89,739
Change in restricted cash		(3,282)	(19,758)
Change in other assets		(6,894)	(4,344)
Cash interest received		17,780	14,631
Cash taxes (paid) received		(950)	26
Purchase of shares pursuant to compensation plans		(1,306)	–
		721,634	566,460
Investing activities:			
Aircraft additions		(218,116)	(61,265)
Other property and equipment and intangible additions		(51,191)	(57,108)
		(269,307)	(118,373)
Financing activities			
Increase in long-term debt		72,995	–
Repayment of long-term debt		(162,678)	(199,225)
Decrease in obligations under capital leases		(75)	(108)
Shares repurchased	12	(112,065)	(74,570)
Dividends paid		(37,549)	(35,000)
Issuance of shares pursuant to compensation plans	13	198	34
Cash interest paid		(43,055)	(51,722)
Change in non-cash working capital		(5,825)	(2,084)
		(288,054)	(362,675)
Cash flow from operating, investing, and financing activities		164,273	85,412
Effect of foreign exchange on cash and cash equivalents		321	(1,123)
Net change in cash and cash equivalents		164,594	84,289
Cash and cash equivalents, beginning of year		1,243,605	1,159,316
Cash and cash equivalents, end of year		1,408,199	1,243,605

The accompanying notes are an integral part of the consolidated financial statements.

Source: WestJet Airlines Ltd., Annual Report 2012.

NOTES TO CONSOLIDATED FINANCIAL STATEMENTS
1. Statement of significant accounting policies:

. . .

(d) Revenue recognition
(i) Guest revenue, including the air component of vacation packages, are recognized when air transportation is provided. Tickets sold but not yet used are reported in the consolidated statement of financial position as advance ticket sales.

. . .

Source: WestJet Airlines Ltd., Annual Report 2012.

Required:

1. Examine WestJet's statements of financial position. The company's assets increased in 2012. Which asset shows the largest increase?

2. WestJet's current liabilities include the advance ticket sales account with a balance of $480,947. What does this account represent, and what type of transactions would cause an increase or a decrease in the account balance? Explain.

3. Compute the total asset turnover ratio, return on assets, return on equity, and net profit margin ratio for both 2011 and 2012. Comment on the profitability of WestJet's operations in both years. WestJet's total assets and shareholders' equity at December 31, 2010, amounted to $3,383,980 and $1,304,233, respectively.

4. WestJet's operations generated significant amounts of cash during both 2011 and 2012. The company also made significant investments in new aircraft in 2012. How did the company finance the acquisition of additional aircraft?

5. Compute and interpret the quality of earnings ratio and the capital expenditures ratio for both 2011 and 2012. (*Note:* Include property and equipment and intangible assets in your computation of the ratio.)

6. Access one of the online information services listed in the chapter, search for WestJet Airlines Ltd. (WJA.TO), and look for earnings estimates. What is the average analysts' estimate of WestJet's earnings per share (EPS) for the next two fiscal years? Do analysts expect WestJet's EPS to increase or decrease in the future? What information did the analysts take into consideration in computing their EPS estimates for the next two years?

P6–5 Using Financial Reports: Interpreting Financial Statement Information and Analyzing and Interpreting Ratios (AP6–3)

◾ LO2, 3

Danier Leather Inc.

Danier Leather Inc. is one of the largest publicly traded specialty leather apparel retailers in the world. It designs, manufactures, and sells high-quality fashionable leather clothing and accessories to customers. Its products are sold in stores at shopping malls, through its corporate sales division, and online through its website, **www.danier.com**. Since entering the retail business in 1974, the company has produced a strong, long-term track record of growth and earnings from continuing operations. Danier's financial statements for 2011 and 2012 are shown on the next few pages.

Required:

1. Examine Danier's statements of financial position. Identify the four largest changes in the carrying amount of assets, liabilities, and shareholders' equity between the statement of financial position dates. What type of transactions could have caused the changes in the carrying amounts of these items?

2. The carrying amounts of the assets and liabilities reported on the company's statements of financial position reflect a mix of historical acquisition costs, amortized costs, and fair values. Refer to the notes to the company's financial statements for fiscal year 2012, which are available on the company's website (**www.danier.com**), and identify the valuation bases used by the company for financial reporting purposes.

3. Using information from the company's statements of financial position and statement of earnings for 2012, can you determine the amount of cash flow generated from operations? If not, where can you find such information?

4. Compute the following ratios for fiscal years 2011 and 2012: total asset turnover ratio, return on assets, return on equity, and net profit margin ratio. Use the results of your computations to comment on the company's financial situation and profitability of its operations in both years. Danier's total assets and shareholders' equity at June 24, 2010, amounted to $73,581 and $54,265, respectively.

5. Suppose that you are evaluating Danier's financial statements for a potential investment in the company's shares. To what extent is the information contained in these financial statements relevant for your decision? What additional information would you require before making your decision?

Danier Leather Inc.
Consolidated Statements of Financial Position
(thousands of dollars)

	June 30, 2012	June 25, 2011
Assets		
Current Assets		
Cash and cash equivalents (Note 4)	$34,332	$28,698
Accounts receivable	517	385
Income taxes recoverable	426	–
Inventories (Note 5)	24,891	28,964
Prepaid expenses	799	901
	60,965	58,948
Non-current Assets		
Property and equipment (Note 6)	15,012	14,404
Computer software (Note 7)	726	1,054
Deferred income tax asset (Note 13)	1,909	1,678
	$78,612	$76,084
Liabilities		
Current Liabilities		
Payables and accruals (Note 9)	$10,161	$11,024
Deferred revenue	1,463	1,489
Sales return provision (Note 10)	124	47
Income tax payable	–	278
	11,748	12,838
Non-current liabilities		
Deferred lease inducements and rent liability	1,373	1,318
	13,121	14,156
Shareholders' Equity		
Share capital (Note 11)	15,040	15,160
Contributed surplus	925	934
Retained earnings	49,526	45,834
	65,491	61,928
	$78,612	$76,084

See accompanying notes to the consolidated financial statements.

Source: Danier Leather, Annual Report 2012.

Danier Leather Inc.
Consolidated Statements of Earnings and Comprehensive Earnings
(thousands of dollars, except per share amounts)

	For the Years Ended	
	June 30, 2012	June 25, 2011
Revenue	$148,219	$157,621
Cost of sales (Note 12)	71,513	71,352
Gross profit	76,706	86,269
Selling, general, and administrative expenses (Note 12)	71,357	75,618
Interest income	(229)	(160)
Interest expense	51	103
Earnings before income taxes	5,527	10,708
Provision for income taxes (Note 13)	1,524	3,140
Net earnings and comprehensive earnings	$ 4,003	$ 7,568
Net earnings per share:		
Basic	$ 0.86	$ 1.62
Diluted	$ 0.83	$ 1.55
Weighted average number of shares outstanding:		
Basic	4,638,829	4,673,944
Diluted	4,794,355	4,889,053
Number of shares outstanding at period end	4,646,902	4,678,135

See accompanying notes to the consolidated financial statements.

Source: Danier Leather, Annual Report 2012.

ALTERNATE PROBLEMS

AP6–1 Preparing a Statement of Financial Position and Analyzing Some of Its Parts (P6–3) ■ LO3

The Java House is developing its annual financial statements for 2014. The following amounts were correct at December 31, 2014: cash, $58,800; investment in shares of PAX Corporation (long term), $36,400; store equipment, $67,200; trade receivables, $71,820; carpet inventory, $154,000; prepaid rent, $1,120; used store equipment held for disposal, $9,800; accumulated depreciation, store equipment, $13,440; income taxes payable, $9,800; long-term note payable, $42,000; trade payables, $58,800; retained earnings, $165,100; and common shares (100,000 shares outstanding, originally sold and issued at $1.10 per share).

Required:

1. Based on these data, prepare the company's statement of financial position at December 31, 2014. Use the following major captions (list the individual items under these captions):

   a. Assets: current assets; long-term investments; property, plant, and equipment; and other assets.

   b. Liabilities: current liabilities and long-term liabilities.

   c. Shareholders' equity: share capital and retained earnings.

2. What is the carrying amount of the store equipment? Explain what this value means.

AP6–2 Using Financial Reports: Interpreting Financial Statement Information and Analyzing and Interpreting Ratios (P6–4) ■ LO2, 3

RONA Inc. (**www.rona.ca**), founded in 1939, is Canada's leading distributor and retailer of hardware, home improvement, and gardening products. It has a network that exceeds 600 stores across Canada. Its sales grew from $478 million in 1993 to $4,884 million in 2012. Its financial statements for 2011 and 2012 are shown on the next few pages.

RONA Inc.

Required:

1. Examine RONA's balance sheets. Why did the company's assets increase significantly in 2012? Which sections of the annual reports would include information that helps the reader answer this question? Which assets show the largest increases, and how did the company finance the increase in these assets?

2. RONA's current assets include a prepaid expenses account with a balance of $20,162. What does this account represent, and what type of transactions would cause an increase or a decrease in the account balance? Explain.

3. Compute the total asset turnover ratio, return on assets, return on equity, and net profit margin ratio for both 2011 and 2012. Comment on the profitability of RONA's operations in both years. RONA's total assets and shareholders' equity at December 26, 2010, amounted to $2,921,620 and $1,911,697, respectively.

4. RONA's operations generated significant amounts of cash during both 2011 and 2012. The company also made significant investments in 2012. How did the company finance these investments?

5. Compute and interpret the quality of earnings ratio for both 2011 and 2012.

6. Access one of the online information services listed in the chapter, search for RONA Inc. (RON.TO), and look for analyst estimates. What is the average analysts' estimate of RONA's earnings per share (EPS) for the next two years? Do analysts expect RONA's EPS to increase or decrease in the future? What information did the analysts take into consideration in computing their EPS estimates for the next two years?

RONA Inc.
Consolidated Statements of Financial Position
December 30, 2012 and December 25, 2011
(in thousands of dollars)

	2012	2011
Assets		
Current		
Cash	$ 21,006	$ 17,149
Trade and other receivables (Note 10)	363,152	370,094
Other financial assets (Note 11)	1,440	1,468
Current tax assets	15,145	7,616
Inventory (Note 6)	890,437	840,287
Prepaid expenses	20,162	20,836
Current assets	1,311,342	1,257,450
Non-current		
Other financial assets (Note 11)	15,045	13,617
Property, plant, and equipment (Note 12)	813,901	874,246
Non-current assets held for sale (Note 13)	22,898	10,455
Goodwill (Note 14)	428,180	426,968
Intangible assets (Note 15)	143,725	126,968
Other non-current assets (Note 16)	5,114	5,435
Deferred tax assets (Note 7)	66,253	65,239
Total assets	$2,806,458	$2,780,378
Liabilities		
Current		
Bank loans	$ 11,332	$ 4,377
Trade and other payables	495,698	487,864
Dividends payable	2,258	2,527
Current tax liabilities	–	–
Derivative financial instruments (Note 25)	3,553	691
Provisions (Note 20)	16,335	6,947
Instalments on long-term debt (Note 18)	11,683	20,257
Current liabilities	540,859	522,663
Non-current		
Long-term debt (Note 18)	305,020	232,073
Other non-current liabilities (Note 19)	34,741	33,653
Provisions (Note 20)	17,712	3,606
Deferred tax liabilities (Note 7)	24,550	32,759
Total liabilities	922,882	824,754

(continued)

RONA Inc.
Consolidated Statements of Financial Position
December 30, 2012 and December 25, 2011
(in thousands of dollars)

	2012	2011
Equity		
Share capital (Note 22)	$ 764,882	$ 793,416
Retained earnings	1,071,426	1,115,801
Contributed surplus	12,521	11,386
Accumulated other comprehensive income	(2,597)	(505)
Total equity attributable to owners of RONA Inc.	1,846,232	1,920,098
Non-controlling interests	37,344	35,526
Total equity	1,883,576	1,955,624
Total liabilities and equity	$2,806,458	$2,780,378

The accompanying notes are an integral part of the consolidated financial statements.

Source: RONA, Annual Report 2012.

RONA Inc.
Consolidated Income Statements
Years ended December 30, 2012 and December 25, 2011
(in thousands of dollars, except per share amounts)

	2012	2011
Revenues (Note 4)	$4,884,016	$4,804,584
Operating profit before impairment and restructuring costs, impairment of non-financial assets and other charges (Note 5.1)	85,563	156,900
Goodwill impairment (Note 14)	–	(117,000)
Restructuring costs, impairment of non-financial assets and other charges (Notes 5.4)	(44,268)	(71,343)
Operating profit (loss)	41,295	(31,443)
Finance income (Note 25)	5,333	5,262
Finance costs (Note 25)	(20,576)	(34,729)
	(15,243)	(29,467)
Income (loss) before income tax expense	26,052	(60,910)
Income tax expense (Note 7)	(6,969)	(13,863)
Net income (loss)	$ 19,083	$ (74,773)
Net income (loss) attributable to:		
Owners of RONA Inc.	$ 17,297	$ (78,382)
Non-controlling interests	1,786	3,609
	$ 19,083	$ (74,773)
Net income (loss) per share attributable to owners of RONA Inc. (Note 29)		
Basic	$0.07	$(0.66)
Diluted	$0.07	$(0.66)

The related notes form an integral part of these consolidated financial statements.

Source: RONA, Annual Report 2012.

RONA Inc.
Consolidated Statements of Cash Flows
Years Ended December 30, 2012, and December 25, 2011
(in thousands of dollars)

	2012	2011
Operating activities		
Income (loss) before income tax expense	$ 26,052	$(60,910)
Adjustments:		
Depreciation, amortization and impairment of non-financial assets (Note 5.2)	115,735	149,736
Change in provision for restructuring costs	23,135	–
Change in fair value of derivative financial instruments	(628)	(159)
Net gain on disposal of assets	(3,973)	(1,123)
Goodwill impairment (Note 14)	–	117,000
Stock-based compensation expense (recovery) (Note 23)	3,676	(2,684)
Difference between amounts paid for post-employment benefits and current year expenses	(3,036)	(2,855)
Other	(1,223)	3,308
	159,738	202,313
Net change in working capital (Note 8)	(14,877)	66,682
	144,861	268,995
Interest received	3,825	3,898
Income taxes paid	(23,139)	(42,648)
Cash flows from operating activities	125,547	230,245
Investing activities		
Business acquisitions (Note 9)	(11,808)	(47,707)
Acquisition of property, plant, and equipment (Note 12)	(37,971)	(70,198)
Acquisition of intangible assets (Note 15)	(48,403)	(39,225)
Acquisition of other financial assets	(2,968)	(6,049)
Proceeds on disposal of property, plant, and equipment	16,498	10,216
Proceeds on disposal of other financial assets	2,612	4,765
Interest received	813	1,365
Cash flows from investing activities	(81,227)	(146,833)
Financing activities		
Bank loans	4,073	(326)
Other long-term debt	80,912	92,112
Financing costs	(80)	(2,541)
Repayment of other long-term debt	(19,991)	(33,886)
Repurchase of debentures	–	(283,171)
Proceeds from issue of common shares	5,676	4,406
Proceeds from issue of preferred shares	–	172,500
Fees related to issue to preferred shares	–	(5,484)
Repurchase of common shares (Note 22)	(66,767)	(31,768)
Cash dividends paid by a subsidiary to non-controlling interests	–	(3,920)
Dividends on common shares	(17,191)	(18,253)
Dividends on preferred shares	(9,062)	(5,458)
Interest paid	(18,033)	(26,051)
Cash flows from financing activities	(40,463)	(141,840)
Net increase (decrease) in cash	3,857	(58,428)
Cash, beginning of year	17,149	75,577
Cash, end of year	$ 21,006	$ 17,149

The related notes form an integral part of these consolidated financial statements.

Source: RONA, Annual Report 2012.

■ LO2, 3   **AP6–3**   **Using Financial Reports: Interpreting Financial Statement Information and Analyzing and**
Leon's Furniture   **Interpreting Ratios** (P6–5)
Limited   Leon's Furniture Limited is a leading Canadian full-line furniture retailer. The company sells home
furnishings, major appliances, and home electronics through more than 75 company-owned and
franchised stores across Canada. Its sales grew from $289 million when it became a public company
in 1996 to $682 million in 2012. Leon's financial statements for 2011 and 2012 are shown on the
next few pages.

Required:

1. Examine Leon's statements of financial position. Identify the four largest changes in the carrying amount of assets, liabilities, and shareholders' equity between the statements of financial position dates. What type of transactions could have caused the changes in the carrying amount of these items?

2. The carrying amounts of the assets and liabilities reported on the company's statements of financial position reflect a mix of historical acquisition costs, amortized costs, and fair values. Refer to the notes to the company's financial statements for fiscal year 2012 that are available on its website (**www.leons.ca/investorrelations.aspx**) and identify the valuation bases used by the company for financial reporting purposes.

3. Using information from the company's statements of financial position and statement of earnings for 2012, can you determine the amount of cash flow generated from operations? If not, where can you find such information? The company's notes to its financial statements indicate that depreciation of property, plant, and equipment and for investment properties for 2012 is $14,020 and that amortization of intangible assets totalled $866.

4. Compute the following ratios for fiscal years 2011 and 2012: total asset turnover ratio, return on assets, return on equity, and net profit margin ratio. Use the results of your computations to comment on the company's financial situation and profitability of its operations in both years. Leon's total assets and shareholders' equity at December 31, 2010, amounted to $566,674 and $410,286, respectively.

5. Suppose that you are evaluating Leon's financial statements for a potential investment in the company's shares. To what extent is the information contained in these financial statements relevant for your decision? What additional information would you require before making your decision?

LEON'S FURNITURE INC.
Consolidated Statements of Financial Position
As at December 31
(thousands of dollars)

	2012	2011
ASSETS		
Current		
Cash and cash equivalents (Notes 5 and 7)	$ 74,949	$ 72,505
Available-for-sale financial assets (Notes 5 and 18(e))	146,735	149,318
Trade receivables (Note 5)	30,245	28,937
Income taxes recoverable	3,644	5,182
Inventories (Note 4)	86,057	87,830
Deferred financing costs (Note 21)	1,317	–
Total current assets	342,947	343,772
Other assets	1,273	1,431
Property, plant, and equipment, net (Note 8)	218,146	214,158
Investment properties (Note 9)	8,315	8,366
Intangible assets, net (Note 10)	3,101	3,958
Goodwill (Note 10)	11,282	11,282
Deferred income tax assets (Note 16)	528	1,444
	$585,592	$584,411
LIABILITIES AND SHAREHOLDERS' EQUITY		
Current		
Trade and other payables (Notes 5 and 11)	$ 73,542	$ 86,357
Customers' deposits	20,386	19,157
Dividends payable (Note 13)	7,055	17,457
Deferred warranty plan revenue	14,743	16,152
Total current liabilities	115,726	139,123
Deferred warranty plan revenue	17,251	19,445
Redeemable share liability (Notes 5 and 12)	428	382
Total liabilities	133,405	158,950
Commitments and contingencies (Note 18)		
Shareholders' equity		
Common shares (Note 13)	26,693	20,918
Accumulated other comprehensive income (loss)	2,395	(104)
Retained earnings	423,099	404,647
Total shareholders' equity	452,187	425,461
	$585,592	$584,411

The accompanying notes are an integral part of these consolidated financial statements.

Source: Leon's Furniture, Annual Report 2012.

LEON'S FURNITURE INC.
Consolidated Statements of Income
Years Ended December 31
(thousands of dollars)

	2012	2011
Revenue (Note 14)	$ 682,163	$ 682,836
Cost of sales	398,704	394,099
Gross profit	283,459	288,737
Operating expenses (Note 15)		
General and administrative	99,346	96,038
Sales and marketing	83,479	78,387
Occupancy	34,289	32,731
Other	6,012	6,239
	223,126	213,395
Operating profit	60,333	75,342
Finance income	3,350	3,506
Profit before income taxes	63,683	78,848
Income tax expense (Note 16)	16,901	22,182
Profit for the year attributable to the shareholders of the company	$ 46,782	$ 56,666
Weighted average number of common shares outstanding		
Basic	70,032,721	69,969,417
Diluted	72,317,598	72,305,424
Earnings per share (Note 17)		
Basic	$ 0.67	$ 0.81
Diluted	$ 0.65	$ 0.78

The accompanying notes are an integral part of these consolidated financial statements.
Source: Leon's Furniture, Annual Report 2012.

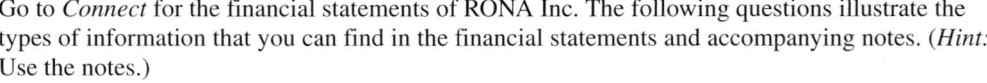

CASES AND PROJECTS

FINDING AND INTERPRETING FINANCIAL INFORMATION

LO2, 3

Canadian Tire
Corporation

CP6–1 **Finding Financial Information**

Refer to the financial statements of Canadian Tire Corporation given in Appendix A at the end of this book. The following questions illustrate the types of information that you can find in the financial statements and accompanying notes.

Required:
1. What items were included as non-current assets on the statement of financial position (balance sheet)?
2. What is the carrying amount of equipment the company owned at December 29, 2012?
3. The company spent $98 million on capital expenditures in 2012. Were operating activities or financing activities the major source of cash for these expenditures?
4. What was the company's largest asset (net) at December 29, 2012?
5. What was the amount of interest expense for 2012?

LO2, 3

RONA Inc.

CP6–2 **Finding Financial Information**

Go to *Connect* for the financial statements of RONA Inc. The following questions illustrate the types of information that you can find in the financial statements and accompanying notes. (*Hint:* Use the notes.)

Required:
1. What subtotals does the company report in its statement of earnings?
2. Over what useful life are buildings depreciated?
3. What portion of property and equipment is composed of land and parking lots?
4. The company reported cash flow from operating activities of $125.6 million for fiscal year 2012. However, its cash and cash equivalents increased by $3.9 million during the same year. Explain how that happened.

CP6–3 Comparing Companies within an Industry

Refer to the financial statements of Canadian Tire Corporation (Appendix A) and RONA Inc. (on *Connect*) and the Industry Ratio Report (Appendix B on *Connect*).

■ LO3

Canadian Tire Corporation

RONA Inc.

Required:

1. Compute the following ratios for the most recent year for each company: total asset turnover ratio, return on assets, return on equity, and net profit margin ratio. Use the results of your computations to comment on each company's financial situation and profitability of its operations for that year.

2. Compare the ratios you computed for each company in (1) to the industry average. Are these two companies doing better or worse than the industry average? Explain.

FINANCIAL REPORTING AND ANALYSIS CASE

CP6–4 Using Financial Reports: Financial Statement Inferences

The following amounts were selected from the annual financial statements for Genesis Corporation at December 31, 2015 (end of the third year of operations):

■ LO2, 3

From the 2015 statement of earnings:	
Sales revenue	$ 275,000
Cost of sales	(170,000)
All other expenses (including income tax)	(95,000)
Net earnings	$ 10,000
From the December 31, 2015, statement of financial position:	
Current assets	$ 90,000
All other assets	212,000
Total assets	302,000
Current liabilities	40,000
Non-current liabilities	66,000
Common shares*	100,000
Contributed surplus	16,000
Retained earnings	80,000
Total liabilities and shareholders' equity	$ 302,000

*10,000 shares issued and outstanding throughout the year.

Required:

Analyze the data on the 2015 financial statements of Genesis by answering the questions that follow. Show computations.

1. What was the gross margin on sales?
2. What was the amount of earnings per share?
3. If the income tax rate was 25 percent, what was the amount of pretax earnings?
4. What was the average issuance price per common share?
5. Assuming that no dividends were declared or paid during 2015, what was the beginning balance (January 1, 2015) of retained earnings?

CRITICAL THINKING CASES

CP6–5 Assessing the Relevance and Verifiability of Information

Intrawest is a world leader in destination resorts and leisure travel. The company's success formula starts with a resort and then builds an animated village with shops, hotels, convention facilities, and restaurants. Intrawest's development of real estate properties has resulted in a significant portfolio of real estate holdings.

■ LO2

Intrawest

By June 30, 2005, Intrawest's assets included resort properties with a carrying amount of US$791.8 million, representing the costs incurred by the company to acquire land and build its resort properties. In contrast, financial analysts estimated the market value of these properties at amounts ranging from US$1.12 billion to US$1.70 billion. In fact, analyst Michael Smith of National Bank Financial estimated the market value of Intrawest's real estate at US$1.12 billion compared to an estimate of US$1.45 billion by Pirate Capital. However, both of these estimates were lower than a third estimate by Mark Hill of JMP Securities, who values these properties at US$1.70 billion.

Required:

1. Assume the role of an auditor of Intrawest's financial statements. Which of these four values would you advise the company's management to report on its statement of financial position at June 30, 2005? Justify your reasoning.

2. Assume the role of an investment broker who is advising a client about the purchase of Intrawest's resort properties. Which value would you use as a basis for your recommendation to your client and why?

■ **LO1, 3**   **CP6–6**   **Evaluating an Ethical Dilemma: Management Incentives and Fraudulent Financial Statements**

Sino-Forest
Corporation

Sino-Forest Corporation was a Chinese company that produced fibre boards for residential and commercial use. It made an initial public offering on the Alberta Stock exchange in 1994, and it listed its shares on the Toronto Stock Exchange (TSX) in 1995. The company's revenue grew from $3 million in 1994 to $395.4 million in 2010. It became the largest forestry company on the TSX with a market capitalization in excess of $6 billion. According to the company, it generated revenue by purchasing and selling forestry plantations in China.

On June 2, 2011, allegations of fraudulent misrepresentation were levelled against Sino-Forest by the Ontario Securities Commission. The OSC suspended trading of the company's shares by September 2011 and laid charges on May 22, 2013, against co-founder Allen Chen and four other men who had been senior executives.

These actions were undertaken after allegations made by a firm called Muddy Waters LLC, which accused Sino-Forest of falsely reporting both the value of its forestry assets and its revenue from sale of those assets. Muddy Waters, a Hong Kong company, published data it had gathered during a private investigation in China of Sino-Forest. The findings of Muddy Waters indicated that Sino-Forest never purchased timber in 2007 and therefore deliberately misled investors by overstating the value of its assets. Therefore, the sale of these assets in 2010 could not have occurred. It was alleged that Sino-Forest's revenue for 2012 was overstated by 52 percent, or $157.8 million.

Sino-Forest filed for bankruptcy protection on March 30, 2012. Its corporate restructuring included a proposed settlement of a class-action lawsuit against Ernst & Young, which provides assurance, tax, transaction, and advisory services. A group of investors opposed the proposed restructuring because it included the settlement whereby Ernst & Young agreed to pay $117 million into a fund to compensate shareholders whose shares rapidly became worthless.

Many articles were written about the alleged Sino-Forest fraud in the news media. Access some of these articles to answer the following questions.

Required:

1. Identify the important events related to Sino-Forest Corporation that occurred between June 2, 2011, when Muddy Waters published its allegations, and May 22, 2013, when the OSC laid formal charges against Sino-Forest's former CEO and executives.

2. What role did the auditing firm Ernst & Young play in this situation?

3. If you were a leader at Ernst &Young, what recommendations would you make to avoid the same type of situation in the future?

4. What role may have been played by the Chinese government, which made the situation worse for shareholders, during the investigation by the OSC?

FINANCIAL REPORTING AND ANALYSIS TEAM PROJECT

■ **LO2, 3**   **CP6–7**   **Team Project: Analyzing the Accounting Communication Process**

As a team, select an industry to analyze. A list of companies classified by industry can be obtained by accessing **www.fpinfomart.ca** and then choosing "Companies by Industry." You can also find a list of industries and companies within each industry via **http://ca.finance.yahoo.com/investing** (click on "Order Annual Reports" under "Tools").

Each group member should acquire the annual report for a different publicly traded company in the industry. (Library files, the SEDAR service at **www.sedar.com**, and the company's website are good sources.)

Required:

On an individual basis, each team member should write a short report answering the following questions about the selected company. Discuss any patterns across the companies that you as a team observe. Then, as a team, write a short report comparing and contrasting your companies.

1. What formats are used to present the each of the following?
   a. Statements of financial position.
   b. Statement of earnings.
   c. Operating activities section of the statement of cash flows.
2. Find a footnote for each of the following and describe its contents in brief:
   a. An accounting rule applied in the company's statements.
   b. Additional detail about a reported financial statement number.
   c. Relevant non-numeric financial information reported in the financial statements.
3. Using electronic sources, find one article reporting the company's annual earnings announcement. When is it dated and how does that date compare to the statement of financial position date?
4. Using electronic sources, find two analysts' reports for your company.
   a. Give the date, name of the analyst, and his or her recommendation from each report.
   b. Discuss why the recommendations are similar or different. Look at the analysts' reasoning for their respective recommendations.

SOLUTION TO SELF-STUDY QUIZ

Self-Study Quiz 6-1

1. *c,*   2. *a,*   3. *e,*   4. *b,*   5. *d.*

Reporting and Interpreting Sales Revenue, Receivables, and Cash

After studying this chapter, you should be able to do the following:

FOCUS COMPANY: **Gildan Activewear Inc.**

BUILDING BRANDS TO BUILD GROSS PROFIT: MANAGING PRODUCT DEVELOPMENT, PRODUCTION, AND WORKING CAPITAL

Over the past several years, casual wear has become increasingly acceptable in the workplace as employers adopt flexible dress codes. Gildan Activewear Inc. (www.gildan.com), based in Montréal, Québec, took advantage of this trend and became a significant producer and marketer of high-quality casual wear, including T-shirts, sports shirts, and sweatshirts. In 2006, Gildan expanded its product line to include underwear and basic athletic socks. Starting in 2012, Gildan began managing its business as two operating segments. The first segment, Printwear, focuses on designing, manufacturing, and distributing undecorated activewear products in large quantities primarily to wholesale distributors in North America, Europe, and the Asia-Pacific region. The second operating segment, Branded Apparel, includes socks, underwear, and activewear products that are marketed primarily to U.S. retailers. Gildan's markets are essentially high-volume, basic, and frequently replenished non-fashion apparel that can be purchased in retail stores and at corporate, tourist, entertainment, and sports events.

Gildan started as a family operation and grew to become a publicly traded company in both Canada and the United States. Gildan's competitive strengths include its expertise in building and operating large-scale, vertically integrated, and strategically located manufacturing hubs. Gildan is successful in part because of its ongoing investments in manufacturing, which allow it to operate efficiently to reduce costs and offer competitive pricing, consistent product quality, and a reliable supply chain to service replenishment programs with short production/delivery cycle times. Gildan has developed a significant manufacturing infrastructure in two main hubs in Central America (primarily Honduras) and the Caribbean Basin (Dominican Republic), where it has built modern textile and sock manufacturing facilities and has established sewing operations. More recently, the company acquired a smaller manufacturing facility for the production of activewear in Bangladesh, which mainly serves its international markets. Gildan sources its yarn primarily from U.S. third-party yarn suppliers, as well as from its own yarn-spinning facilities in Georgia and North Carolina. With control over every important element in its supply chain, Gildan effectively profits from reliable and on-time delivery of consistent-quality products at a low cost.

Gildan's sales grew from US$224 million for fiscal year 1999 to US$1,948.3 million for its fiscal year ended September 30, 2012.[1] Such growth in sales could not happen if the company did not pursue specific business strategies to produce quality products and market them effectively to targeted customers. The company's focus on low-cost manufacturing of premium-quality casual wear and its marketing philosophy of controlled distribution have been important factors in its success. The company's management recognized that its dedication to being the lowest-cost producer and leading marketer of branded basic casual wear is based on a growth strategy that comprises specific objectives, such as (1) maximizing printwear market penetration and opportunities, (2) penetrating the U.S. retail market as a full-line supplier of branded family apparel, (3) generating manufacturing and distribution cost reductions, and (4) reinvesting in capital projects and complementary strategic acquisition opportunities. These objectives and related action plans are aimed at increasing net sales and/or decreasing the cost of sales, thereby increasing gross profit.

UNDERSTANDING THE BUSINESS

The success of each element of Gildan's strategy can be seen in the information presented in the statement of earnings excerpt in Exhibit 7.1. Net sales (revenue) is reported first, and cost of sales (cost of goods sold, cost of products sold) is set out separately from the remaining expenses. The statement of earnings then reports *gross profit (gross margin)*, which is net sales minus cost of sales.

Planning Gildan's growth strategy requires careful coordination of sales and production activities, as well as cash collection from customers. Much of this coordination involves judicious use of credit card and sales discounts, as well as prudent management of sales returns and bad debts.[2] These activities affect *net sales revenue* on the statement of earnings and *cash* and *trade accounts receivable* on the statement of financial position, which are the focus of this chapter. We will introduce the gross profit percentage as a basis for evaluating changes in gross profit, as well as the receivables turnover ratio as a measure of the efficiency of credit granting and collection activities. But the cash collected from customers is a tempting target for fraud and embezzlement; therefore, we will discuss some common controls integral to most accounting systems to minimize these misdeeds.

Lenders, shareholders, and analysts carefully monitor net sales and receivables because of their importance as predictors of the success of companies. Their importance is supported by the fact that the majority of shareholder lawsuits and enforcement actions by securities regulators against companies for misleading financial statements relate to these accounts.

CONSOLIDATED STATEMENTS OF EARNINGS AND COMPREHENSIVE INCOME Years ended September 30, 2012, October 2, 2011, and October 3, 2010 (in thousands of U.S. dollars)			
	2012	2011	2010
Net sales	$1,948,253	$1,725,712	$1,311,463
Cost of sales	1,552,128	1,288,106	947,206
Gross profit	396,125	437,606	364,257

Source: Gildan Activewear, Annual Report 2012.

Exhibit **7.1**
Net Sales and Gross Profit on the Statement of Earnings
REAL-WORLD EXCERPT
Gildan Activewear
ANNUAL REPORT

ORGANIZATION OF THE CHAPTER

Accounting for Sales Revenue	**Measuring and Reporting Receivables**	**Reporting and Safeguarding Cash**
• Sales to Consumers • Sales Discounts to Businesses • Sales Returns and Allowances • Reporting Net Sales • Gross Profit Percentage	• Classifying Receivables • Accounting for Bad Debts • Reporting Trade Receivables • Estimating Bad Debts • Receivables Turnover Ratio • Internal Control and Management Responsibility • Control over Trade Receivables	• Cash and Cash Equivalents Defined • Cash Management • Internal Control of Cash • Reconciliation of the Cash Accounts and the Bank Statements

Supplemental material:

Appendix 7A: Applying the Revenue Principle in Special Circumstances
Appendix 7B: Recording Discounts and Returns

LO¹

Apply the revenue principle to determine the accepted time to record sales revenue for typical retailers, wholesalers, manufacturers, and service companies.

ACCOUNTING FOR SALES REVENUE

As indicated in Chapter 3, the *revenue principle* requires that revenues be recorded when the following conditions are met: (1) the entity has transferred to the buyer the significant risks and rewards of ownership of the goods, (2) the entity retains neither continuing managerial involvement to the degree usually associated with ownership nor effective control over the goods sold, (3) the amount of revenue can be measured reliably, (4) it is probable that the economic benefits associated with the transaction will flow to the entity, and (5) the costs incurred or to be incurred with respect to the transaction can be measured reliably.[3] For sellers of goods, these criteria are most often met and sales revenue recorded when title and risks of ownership pass to the buyer. The point at which title (ownership) changes hands is determined by the shipping terms in the sales contract. When goods are shipped *FOB (free on board) shipping point*, title changes hands at shipment, and the buyer normally pays for shipping. When they are shipped *FOB destination point*, title changes hands on delivery, and the seller normally pays for shipping. Revenues from goods sold FOB shipping point are normally recognized at shipment. Revenues from goods sold FOB destination point are normally recognized at delivery.

Service companies most often record sales revenue when they have provided services to the buyer. Companies disclose the specific revenue recognition rules they follow in the note to their financial statements titled "Significant Accounting Policies." Gildan reported the following in its accounting policies:

REAL-WORLD EXCERPT

Gildan Activewear

ANNUAL REPORT

NOTES TO CONSOLIDATED FINANCIAL STATEMENTS

1. Significant Accounting Policies

(s) Revenue recognition:

Revenue is recognized upon shipment of products to customers, since title passes upon shipment, and to the extent that the selling price is fixed or determinable. At the time of sale, estimates are made for customer price discounts and volume rebates based on the terms of existing programs. Sales are recorded net of these program costs and estimated sales returns, which are based on historical experience, current trends and other known factors, and exclude sales taxes. New programs which relate to prior sales are recognized at the time the new program is introduced.

Source: Gildan Activewear, Annual Report 2012.

Like Gildan, many manufacturers, wholesalers, and retailers recognize revenue at shipment. This is when the title and risks of ownership pass to the buyer. Auditors expend a lot of effort to ensure that revenue recognition rules are applied consistently and revenues are recognized in the proper period.

The appropriate *amount* of revenue to record is the *cash-equivalent sales price*. Sales practices differ depending on whether sales are made to businesses or consumers. Gildan sells its products primarily through wholesale distributors, a strategy that enables the company to use a small sales force. Gildan sells its products to a network of distributors in Canada, the United States, Mexico, Europe, and Asia, which in turn resell the products to retailers and garment decorators. Consumers ultimately purchase the company's products in such venues as sports, entertainment, and corporate events as well as travel and tourism destinations. Gildan also sells its product line of active-wear, underwear, and athletic socks to Canadian and U.S. retailers. Gildan recognizes revenue when its sells its products to its customers (wholesalers and retailers), not to the ultimate consumer of its products.

ACCELERATED REVENUE RECOGNITION IS A MATTER OF JUDGMENT

A QUESTION OF ACCOUNTABILITY

Until recently, the premature recognition of revenue was one of the most common reasons the U.S. Securities and Exchange Commission (SEC) would pursue fraud enforcement action against corporations. The issue arises because companies report revenue before it has been earned.

The proposed new revenue recognition standard, however, does not strictly prohibit accelerated revenue recognition on consumer contracts. A familiar example is the sale of extended warranties on consumer products. A retailer will often offer the customer extended service for two or three years on a product such as a laptop. If the retailer provides the service, then the amount received for the extended warranty cannot be recognized until it has been earned. If a third party, for example, the product's manufacturer, is expected to provide the service in the future, then the retailer may recognize at that time the revenue it has earned for selling the extended warranty contract to the customer. This simple example illustrates why accounting standards are subject to change and highlights the importance of the professional judgment that accountants must exercise when deciding upon the timing of revenue recognition.

Gildan uses a variety of methods to motivate its customers, both businesses and consumers, to buy its products and make payment for their purchases. The principal methods include (1) allowing all customers to use credit cards to pay for purchases, (2) providing business customers direct credit and discounts for early payment, and (3) allowing returns from all customers under specific circumstances. These methods, in turn, affect the way we compute *net sales revenue*.

Sales to Consumers

Sales to consumers are for cash or credit card (mainly Visa, MasterCard, and American Express). The seller accepts credit cards as payment for a variety of reasons:

1. Increasing customer traffic at its stores.
2. Avoiding the costs of providing credit directly to customers, including for record-keeping and bad debts (discussed later).
3. Lowering losses due to bad cheques.
4. Avoiding losses from fraudulent credit card sales. (Normally, the credit card company absorbs any losses if the seller follows the credit card company's verification procedure.)

LO2

Analyze the impact of credit card sales, sales discounts, and sales returns on the amounts reported as net sales.

5. Receiving money faster. (Since credit card receipts can be directly deposited in its bank account, the seller receives cash payments faster than it would if it provided credit directly to consumers.)

The credit card company charges a fee for the service it provides. For example, when a seller processes the credit card payment, it might receive credit for an amount equal to only 97 percent of the sales price. The fee charged by the credit card company for its services is the **credit card discount**, 3 percent in this case. If daily credit card sales were $3,000, Gildan would report the following:[4]

A **CREDIT CARD DISCOUNT** is the fee charged by the credit card company for its services.

Sales revenue	$3,000
Less: Credit card discounts (0.03 × $3,000)	90
Net sales (reported on the statement of earnings)	$2,910

Sales Discounts to Businesses

Most of Gildan's sales to businesses are credit sales on open account; that is, there is no formal written promissory note indicating the amount owed to Gildan by the customer. When Gildan sells T-shirts to wholesalers on credit, credit terms are printed on each sales document and invoice (bill) sent to the customer. Often credit terms are abbreviated, using symbols. For example, if the full amount of the invoice is due within 30 days of the invoice date, the credit terms would be noted as *n/30*. Here, the *n* means the sales amount *net* of, or less, any sales returns.

A **SALES (OR CASH) DISCOUNT** is a cash discount offered to encourage prompt payment of a trade account receivable.

A **sales (or cash) discount** is a cash discount offered to encourage prompt payment of a trade account receivable.[5] For example, Gildan may offer standard credit terms of 2/10, n/30, which means that the customer may deduct 2 percent from the invoice amount if cash payment is made within 10 days of the date of sale. If cash payment is not made within the 10-day discount period, the full invoice amount (less any returns) is due within a maximum of 30 days.

Early Payment Incentive

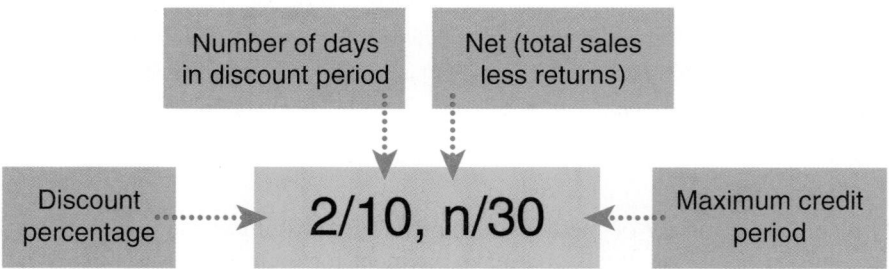

Gildan offers this sales discount to encourage customers to pay more quickly. This provides two benefits to Gildan:

1. Prompt receipt of cash from customers reduces the necessity of borrowing money to meet operating needs.
2. Since customers tend to pay invoices providing discounts first, a sales discount also decreases the likelihood that the customer will run out of funds before Gildan's invoice is paid.

Companies commonly record sales discounts taken by subtracting the discount from sales if payment is made within the discount period (the usual case).[6] For example, if credit sales are recorded with terms 2/10, n/30 and payment of $980 (= $1,000 × 0.98) is made within the discount period, net sales of the following amount would be reported:

Sales revenue	$1,000
Less: Sales discounts (0.02 × $1,000)	20
Net sales (reported on the statement of earnings)	$980

If the payment is made after the discount period, the full $1,000 is reported as net sales.

Note that both the purpose of and accounting for both sales discounts and credit card discounts are similar. Both sales discounts and credit card discounts provide an attractive service to customers and promote faster receipt of cash, thereby reducing recordkeeping costs and minimizing bad debts. Accounting for sales discounts is discussed in more detail in Appendix 7B.

TO TAKE OR NOT TO TAKE THE DISCOUNT, THAT IS THE QUESTION

FINANCIAL
ANALYSIS

Customers usually pay within the discount period because the savings are substantial. With terms 2/10, n/30, 2 percent is saved by paying 20 days early (the 10th day instead of the 30th), which is equivalent to an annual interest rate of 37 percent. This annual interest rate is obtained by first computing the interest rate for the discount period. When the 2 percent discount is taken, the customer pays only 98 percent of the gross sales amount. For example, on a $100 sale with terms 2/10, n/30, $2 would be saved and $98 would be paid 20 days early. The interest rate for the 20 day discount period is

(Amount Saved ÷ Amount Paid) = Interest Rate for 20 Days

($2 ÷ $98) = 2.04% for 20 days or 0.102% per day

Given that there are 365 days in a year, the annual interest rate is then computed in the following manner:

Annual Interest Rate = 0.102% × 365 days = 37.23%

Credit customers would save a lot of money even if they had to borrow cash from a bank at a high rate such as 15 percent to take advantage of cash discounts. Normally, the bank's interest rate is less than the high interest rate associated with failing to take cash discounts.

STRETCHING OUT THE PAYABLES

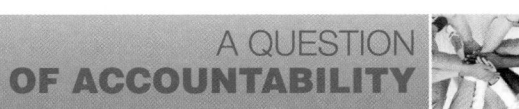

A QUESTION
OF ACCOUNTABILITY

Hoffa Shoes has been incurring significant interest charges (10 percent) on short-term borrowing from its bank.* Hoffa normally purchases shoes from suppliers on terms 1/10, n/30. The annual rate of interest earned by taking the discount is 18.43 percent, computed as follows:

(Amount Saved ÷ Amount Paid) = Interest Rate for 20 Days

($1 ÷ $99) = 1.01% for 20 days or 0.0505 per day

Annual Interest Rate = 0.0505% × 365 days = 18.43%

Hoffa's policy had been to take all purchase discounts even if it had to borrow at 10 percent to make the early payment. Management reasoned that the company earned 8.43 percent more than it paid in interest (18.43 percent − 10 percent).

A new employee suggested a new plan. Records indicated that, even though the terms of Hoffa's agreement with its suppliers (1/10, n/30) required payment of the full amount within a maximum of 30 days, the suppliers would not complain as long as payment was made within 55 days of the purchase date, since they normally did not send out a second bill until 60 days after the purchase date. She reasoned that Hoffa would be better off forgoing the discount and paying on the 55th day after the purchase date. She argued that, since Hoffa would now be paying within 55 days instead of 10 days of the purchase, not taking the discount would be borrowing for 45 days, not the 20 days used in the former analysis. The analysis supporting the proposal is as follows:

$$\text{(Amount Saved} \div \text{Amount Paid)} = \text{Interest Rate for 45 Days}$$
$$(\$1 \div \$99) = 1.01\% \text{ for 45 days or } 0.02244\%$$
$$\text{Annual Interest Rate} = 0.02244\% \times 365 \text{ days} = 8.19\%$$

In effect, her plan allows Hoffa to borrow from suppliers at 8.19 percent instead of the bank's rate of 10 percent, saving 1.81 percent. When she presented this plan to the management for discussion, the purchasing manager agreed with the arithmetic presented but objected nonetheless. Since the plan violated its agreement with suppliers, the purchasing manager thought it was unethical. Many ethical dilemmas in business involve trade-offs between monetary benefits and potential violations of moral values.

*Hoffa Shoes is a fictitious company, but most companies face this dilemma.

Sales Returns and Allowances

For Gildan, prompt delivery of exactly what the customer ordered is key to maintaining good relations with the customers to whom it sells. Delivery of incorrect or damaged merchandise may cost the customer sales and can destroy these relationships. When this occurs, the customers have a right to return unsatisfactory or damaged merchandise and receive a refund or an adjustment to their bill.

SALES RETURNS AND ALLOWANCES is a reduction of gross sales revenues for return of or allowances for unsatisfactory goods.

Sales returns and allowances is a reduction of gross sales revenues for return of or allowances for unsatisfactory goods. Such returns are often accumulated in a separate account called sales returns and allowances and must be deducted from gross sales revenue in determining net sales. This account informs Gildan's management of the volume of returns and allowances, providing an important measure of the quality of customer service. Assume, for example, that a customer bought 40 dozen T-shirts from Gildan for $2,000 on account. Before paying for the T-shirts, the customer discovered that 10 dozen T-shirts were not the colour ordered and returned them to Gildan.[7] Gildan would compute net sales as follows:

Sales revenue	$2,000
Less: Sales returns (0.25 × $2,000)	500
Net sales (reported on the statement of earnings)	$1,500

The cost of sales related to the 10 dozen T-shirts would also be reduced.

Based on past experience, Gildan's management knows that some customers that purchased socks, underwear, and activewear products during the current year may return the purchased merchandise or be granted an allowance for potentially defective products in the following year. Because the expected product returns relate to sales made during the current year, Gildan estimates the potential sales returns for the year and establishes a provision for sales returns.

LO3

Compute and interpret the gross profit percentage.

Reporting Net Sales

On the company's books, credit card discounts, sales discounts, and sales returns and allowances are accounted for separately to allow managers to monitor the costs of credit card use, sales discounts, and returns. Using the numbers in the preceding examples, the amount of net sales reported on the statement of earnings is computed in the following manner:[8]

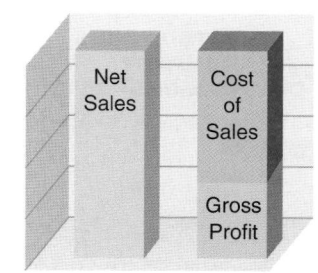

Sales revenue	$6,000
Less: Credit card discounts (a contra revenue)	90
Sales discounts (a contra revenue)	20
Sales returns and allowances (a contra revenue)	500
Net sales (reported on the statement of earnings)	$5,390

Gildan indicates in its revenue recognition note that its revenues are reported net of returns, discounts, and allowances. Companies rarely disclose the determinants of net sales in the annual report, so it is often difficult to determine the effects of these items, even for well-educated external users. As we noted earlier, net sales less cost of sales equals the subtotal *gross profit* or *gross margin*. Analysts often examine gross profit as a percentage of net sales, called the *gross profit* or *gross margin percentage.*

GROSS PROFIT PERCENTAGE

KEY RATIO ANALYSIS

ANALYTICAL QUESTION → How effective is management at selling goods and services for more than the costs to purchase or produce them?

RATIO AND COMPARISONS → The gross profit percentage is helpful in answering this question. It is computed as follows:

$$\text{Gross Profit Percentage} = \frac{\text{Gross Profit}}{\text{Net Sales}}$$

The 2012 ratio for Gildan is

$$\$396{,}125 \div \$1{,}948{,}253 = 0.203 \ (20.3\%)$$

Comparisons over Time			Comparisons with Competitors	
Gildan			Hanesbrands Inc.	Delta Apparel Inc.
2010	2011	2012	2012	2012
27.8%	25.4%	20.3%	31.4%	17.1%

INTERPRETATIONS

In General → The gross profit percentage measures how much gross profit is generated from every sales dollar. It reflects the ability to charge premium prices and produce goods and services at low cost. All other things being equal, a higher gross profit results in higher net earnings.

Business strategy, as well as competition, affects the gross profit percentage. Companies pursuing a product-differentiation strategy use research and development and product promotion activities to convince customers of the superiority or distinctiveness of the company's products. This allows them to charge premium prices, producing higher gross profit percentages. Companies following a low-cost strategy rely on more efficient management of production to reduce costs and increase the gross profit percentage. Managers, analysts, and creditors use this ratio to assess the effectiveness of the company's product development, marketing, and production strategy.

Focus Company Analysis → Gildan's gross profit percentage decreased steadily between 2010 and 2012, dropping from 27.8 to 20.3 percent. Gildan's ratio slightly surpassed the ratio for Delta Apparel, but it fell significantly below the ratio achieved by Hanesbrands. At the beginning of the chapter, we discussed key elements of Gildan's business strategy that focused on vertical integration and low-cost manufacturing of premium-quality products in Central America, its marketing philosophy, and its distribution strategy. According to Gildan's annual report for fiscal

SELECTED FOCUS COMPANY COMPARISONS—2012

Sun-Rype Products 17.9%

Canadian Tire 30.6%

Danier Leather 51.8%

year 2012, the decline in the gross profit percentage was primarily due to higher cotton costs, lower average net selling prices for Printwear, manufacturing inefficiencies, and shutdown costs during the year. The company also noted that gross profit in the second half of 2012 improved significantly compared to gross profit in the first half of the fiscal year as the company used inventory with increasingly lower cost cotton compared to the first half of fiscal 2012.

A Few Cautions → To assess the company's ability to sustain its gross margins, you must understand the sources of any change in its gross profit percentage. For example, an increase in margin resulting from increases in seasonal sales of high-margin products is less likely to be sustainable than one resulting from introducing new products. Also, higher prices must often be sustained with higher research and development and advertising expenses, which may reduce the operating and net profit substantially. This is why, if operating expenses do not decrease too, a small decrease in gross profit percentage can lead to a large decrease in net earnings.

STOP PAUSE FOR FEEDBACK

Credit card sales, sales discounts, and sales returns all reduce the amounts reported as net sales. Both credit card discounts and sales or cash discounts promote faster receipt of cash. Sales returns and allowances include refunds and adjustments to customers' bills for defective or incorrect merchandise.

The gross profit percentage measures the ability to charge premium prices and produce goods and services at lower cost. Managers, analysts, and creditors use this ratio to assess the effectiveness of the company's product development, marketing, and production strategy.

Before you move on, complete the following questions to test your understanding of these concepts.

SELF-STUDY QUIZ 7-1

1. Assume that Sportswear Inc. sold $30,000 worth of T-shirts to various retailers with terms 1/10, n/30, and half of that amount was paid within the discount period. Gross sales at company-owned stores were $5,000 for the same period, 80 percent being paid using credit cards with a 3 percent discount and the rest in cash. Compute net sales for the period.

2. During the first quarter of fiscal year 2014, the company's net sales were $150,000 and cost of sales was $110,000. Verify that its gross profit percentage was 26.66 percent.

After you complete your answers, check them with the solutions at the end of the chapter.

MEASURING AND REPORTING RECEIVABLES

Classifying Receivables

Receivables may be classified in three common ways. First, receivables may be classified as trade or non-trade receivables. **Trade receivables** are open accounts owed to the business by trade customers and are created in the normal course of business when there is a sale of merchandise or services on credit. A *non-trade receivable* arises from transactions other than the normal sale of merchandise or services. For example, if Gildan lent money to key employees to assist them in financing the purchase of their first homes, the loans would be classified as non-trade receivables.

Second, the receivable may be either an account receivable or a note receivable. An account receivable is created when there is a sale of products and services on open account to customers or when a company expects to receive payments from

TRADE RECEIVABLES are open accounts owed to the business by trade customers.

other parties, such as collection from an insurance company following an unfortunate accident. A **note receivable** is a written promise made by another party (e.g., a customer) to pay the company (1) a specified amount of money, called the *principal*, at a definite future date, known as the *maturity date*, and (2) a specified amount of interest at one or more future dates. Interest is the amount charged for use of the principal. A note receivable is also classified as a financial asset, reflecting the contractual right to receive cash from debtors in the future. We discuss the computation of interest when we discuss notes payable in Chapter 10.

Third, in a classified statement of financial position, receivables are also classified as either *current* or *non-current* (short term or long term), depending on when the cash is expected to be collected.

Different combinations of these classifications are possible. For example, a current trade accounts receivable indicates that merchandise was sold on account and the amount is expected to be received in the near future. Canadian companies use different titles to report current receivables. Most companies use the title *trade and other receivables*. Some companies use the title *accounts receivable*, which consists mostly of trade accounts receivable. Gildan uses the title *trade accounts receivable*, which clearly indicates that its accounts receivable are the result of trading transactions with customers. In this book, we focus our attention on trade accounts receivable, but we will continue to use the account title "trade receivables" for convenience.

> A NOTE RECEIVABLE is a written promise that requires another party to pay the business under specific conditions (amount, time, interest).

FOREIGN CURRENCY RECEIVABLES

INTERNATIONAL PERSPECTIVE

Export (international) sales are a growing part of the Canadian economy. For example, international sales amounted to 96.5 percent of Gildan's revenues in 2012, particularly sales to the U.S. market. As is the case with domestic sales to other businesses, most export sales to businesses are on credit. When the buyer has agreed to pay in its local currency instead of Canadian dollars, Gildan cannot add trade receivables that are denominated in a foreign currency directly to trade receivables denominated in Canadian dollars.* Gildan's accountants must first convert the trade receivable denominated in foreign currencies into Canadian dollars by using the end-of-period exchange rate between the two currencies. For example, if a European distributor purchased goods from Gildan for €20,000 on August 31, 2012, and each euro was worth CDN$1.24 on that date, Gildan would add $24,800 to its trade receivables on that date. If Gildan has not collected the €20,000 by September 30, 2012, the end of its fiscal year, then the receivable should be adjusted for the change in the value of the euro, and an exchange gain or loss should be reported on the statement of earnings.

*Gildan has reported its financial statements in U.S. dollars since 2004. The use of Canadian dollars here is for illustrative purposes only.

Selected Foreign Currency Exchange Rates (in CDN$) (as at October 11, 2013)
Mexican Peso $0.079
Chinese Yuan $0.170
American Dollar $1.035

Accounting for Bad Debts

As we noted before in the discussion of sales discounts and allowances, Gildan allows its customers (wholesalers and retailers) to purchase goods on open account because it believes that providing this service will increase sales, but it also has a cost. Gildan must pay to maintain a credit granting and collection system, because some customers may not pay their debts. Credit policies should be based on the *trade-off* between profit on additional sales and any additional bad debts. If the credit policy is too restrictive, it will result in a low rate of bad debts, but the company will turn away many good credit customers, causing a loss of sales revenue. On the other hand, if Gildan's credit policy is too liberal, then net sales will increase, but bad debts will likely increase as well, because more customers will likely default on their payments, causing a write-off of trade receivables.

LO4

Estimate, report, and evaluate the effects of uncollectible trade receivables (bad debts) on financial statements.

For billing and collection purposes, Gildan keeps a separate account for each of the retailers and wholesalers that buy its products. Changes in the accounts of individual customers are recorded in a *subsidiary ledger*, which provides details of the total amount of trade receivables reported on the statement of financial position. When Gildan extends credit to its customers, it knows that a certain amount of credit sales may not be collected in the future. The matching process requires the recording of bad debt expense in the *same* accounting period as the one in which the related sales are made. This presents an important accounting problem. Gildan may not learn which particular customers will not pay until the *next* accounting period. So, at the end of the period of sale, it normally does not know which customers' trade receivables are bad debts.

Gildan resolves this problem by using the **allowance method**, which bases bad debt expense on an estimate of uncollectible accounts. There are two primary steps in applying the allowance method: (1) estimating and recording bad debts expense and (2) writing off specific accounts determined to be uncollectible during the period. The estimation of bad debts is an example of prudence, whereby Gildan deducts the estimated amount of bad debts from the ending balance of trade receivables and reports the net realizable value of trade receivables on the statement of financial position. Gildan accounting policy regarding trade accounts receivable is stated in Note 3 to its financial statements for 2012:

> The **ALLOWANCE METHOD** bases bad debt expense on an estimate of uncollectible accounts.

REAL-WORLD EXCERPT

Gildan Activewear

ANNUAL REPORT

3. SIGNIFICANT ACCOUNTING POLICIES

. . .

(d) Trade accounts receivable:
Trade accounts receivable consist of amounts due from our normal business activities. An allowance for doubtful accounts is maintained to reflect expected credit losses. Bad debts are provided for based on collection history and specific risks identified on a customer-by-customer basis. Uncollected accounts are written off through the allowance for doubtful accounts.

Source: Gildan Activewear, Annual Report 2012.

Gildan reported the following changes to its Allowance for Doubtful Accounts for fiscal years 2011 and 2012 in Note 7 to its financial statements:

REAL-WORLD EXCERPT

Gildan Activewear

ANNUAL REPORT

Note 7: Trade Accounts Receivable:
The movement in the allowance for doubtful accounts in respect of trade receivables was as follows:

	2012	2011
Balance, beginning of year	$4,106	$ 6,969
Bad debt expense (recovery)	(401)	632
Write-off of trade accounts receivable	(648)	(3,757)
Increase due to business acquisitions (note 5)	1,438	262
Balance, end of year	$4,495	$ 4,106

Source: Gildan Activewear, Annual Report 2012.

The various transactions that affected the Allowance for Doubtful Accounts are explained below.

> **BAD DEBT EXPENSE (DOUBTFUL ACCOUNTS EXPENSE)** is the expense associated with estimated uncollectible trade receivables.

Recording Bad Debt Expense Estimates   **Bad debt expense (doubtful accounts expense)** is the expense associated with estimated uncollectible trade receivables. It is recorded through an *adjusting journal entry at the end of the accounting period*. For the year ended October 2, 2011, Gildan estimated bad debt expense to be $632 and made the following adjusting entry:

Bad debt expense (E)	632	
Allowance for doubtful accounts (XA)		632

Assets	=	Liabilities	+	Shareholders' Equity
Allowance for doubtful accounts −632				Bad debt expense −632

Gildan includes the bad debt expense in the category "Selling, general and administrative" expenses on the statement of earnings. Bad debt expense decreases net earnings and shareholders' equity. Trade Receivables could not be credited in the journal entry, because it is difficult to know at that date which customers may not pay in the future. The credit is made, instead, to the account called **Allowance for Doubtful Accounts (Allowance for Doubtful Receivables** or **Allowance for Doubtful Debts)**, a contra-asset account containing the estimated uncollectible trade receivables. As a contra asset, the balance in Allowance for Doubtful Accounts is always subtracted from the balance of the asset Trade Receivables. Thus, the entry decreases the net realizable value of trade receivables and total assets.

For fiscal year 2012, Gildan's experience with collection from its customers resulted in a reduction in the balance of the Allowance account by a net amount of $401.

ALLOWANCE FOR DOUBTFUL ACCOUNTS (ALLOWANCE FOR DOUBTFUL RECEIVABLES, ALLOWANCE FOR DOUBTFUL DEBTS) is a contra-asset account containing the estimated uncollectible trade receivables.

Impaired Receivables—Writing Off Specific Uncollectible Accounts *Throughout the year*, when it is determined that a customer will not pay its debt (e.g., due to bankruptcy), the receivable is considered impaired. The write-off of that individual receivable is recorded through a journal entry. When a specific trade receivable has been identified as uncollectible, it must be removed from the appropriate Trade Receivables account. At the same time, the previously established allowance for such a doubtful receivable is no longer needed and should be removed from the Allowance for Doubtful Accounts.

The following journal entry summarizes the write-off of $648 in trade receivables during fiscal year 2012:

Allowance for doubtful accounts (XA)	648	
Trade receivables (A)		648

Assets		=	Liabilities	+	Shareholders' Equity
Allowance for doubtful accounts	+648				
Trade receivables	−648				

Notice that this journal entry *did not affect any statement of earnings accounts*. The estimated bad debt expense was already recorded with an adjusting entry in the period of sale. Also, the entry *did not change the carrying amount of trade receivables*, since the decrease in the asset account (Trade Receivables) was offset by an equal decrease in the contra-asset account (Allowance for Doubtful Accounts). Thus, it did not affect total assets.

Recovery of Accounts Previously Written Off When a customer makes a payment on an account previously written off, the initial journal entry to write off the account is reversed for the amount that is collected, and another journal entry is made to record the collection of cash. For illustrative purposes, assume that Gildan recovered $10 from customers that had their accounts written off previously. The journal entries and transaction effects related to the recovery of bad debts are shown below:

Trade receivables (A)	10	
Allowance for doubtful accounts (XA)		10
Cash (A)	10	
Trade receivables (A)		10

Assets		=	Liabilities	+	Shareholders' Equity
Trade receivables	+10				
Allowance for doubtful accounts	−10				
Cash	+10				
Trade receivables	−10				

Notice that the net effect of the recovered amount on trade receivables is zero. The recovered amount is first recorded in Trade Receivables to reinstate the amount in the customers' accounts and show that the customers have honoured their previous commitments to pay Gildan $10.

In addition to the above transactions, Gildan increased the balance of the Allowance for Doubtful Accounts by $262 in 2011 and $1,438 in 2012 because it acquired other businesses, and a portion of their trade receivables is potentially uncollectible as well.

Summary of the Accounting Process It is important to remember that accounting for bad debts is a three-step process:

Step	Timing	Accounts Affected		Financial Statement Effects	
1. Record estimated bad debts adjustment	End of period in which sales are made	Bad debt expense (E)	↑	Net earnings	↓
		Allowance for doubtful accounts (XA)	↑	Assets (Trade receivables, net)	↓
2. Identify and write off actual bad debts	Throughout period as bad debts become known	Trade receivables (A)	↓	Net earnings	
		Allowance for doubtful accounts (XA)	↓	Assets (Trade receivables, net)	No effect
3. Record recovery of bad debts that were written off previously	Throughout period as bad debts are recovered	Trade receivables (A)	↑↓	Net earnings	No effect
		Allowance for doubtful accounts (XA)	↓	Assets (Trade receivables, net)	↓
		Cash (A)	↑	Cash	↑

Gildan's accounting for bad debts for fiscal years 2011 and 2012 can now be summarized in terms of the changes in Trade Accounts Receivable (gross) and the Allowance for Doubtful Accounts:[9]

Trade Accounts Receivable (gross) (A)

Balance at Oct. 4, 2010	152,653		
Sales on account	1,725,712	Collections on account	1,678,908
		Write-offs	3,757
Balance at Oct. 2, 2011	195,700		
Sales on account	1,948,253	Collections on account	1,878,215
		Write-offs	648
Balance at Sept. 30, 2012	265,090		

Allowance for Doubtful Accounts (XA)

		Balance at Oct. 4, 2010	6,969
Write-offs	3,757	Bad debt expense adjustment	632
		Increase due to business acquisitions	262
		Balance at Oct. 2, 2011	4,106
Write-offs	648	Increase due to business acquisitions	1,438
Bad debt recovery	401		
		Balance at Sept. 30, 2012	4,495

Trade Accounts Receivable (gross) includes the total trade accounts receivable, both collectible and uncollectible. The balance in the Allowance for Doubtful Accounts is the portion of the trade accounts receivable balance the company estimates to be uncollectible. Trade Accounts Receivable (net) reported on the statement of financial position

CONSOLIDATED STATEMENT OF FINANCIAL POSITION
September 30, 2012, and October 2, 2011
(in thousands of dollars)

	2012	2011
Assets		
Current assets:		
Cash and cash equivalents (Note 6)	$ 70,410	$ 82,025
Trade accounts receivable (Note 7)	260,595	191,594
Income taxes receivable	353	515
Inventories (Note 8)	553,068	568,311
Prepaid expenses and deposits	14,451	10,827
Assets held for sale (Note 19)	8,029	13,142
Other current assets	8,694	9,228

Source: Gildan Activewear, Annual Report 2012.

is the portion of the accounts the company expects to collect (or its estimated net realizable value). These details are useful to external users of financial statements for assessing the quality of the company's receivables.

Reporting Trade Receivables

Analysts who want information on Gildan's receivables will find Trade Accounts Receivable, net of allowance for doubtful accounts (the *carrying amount*), of $260,595 and $191,594 for fiscal years 2012 and 2011, respectively, reported on the statement of financial position (Exhibit 7.2).

Gildan disclosed details of the changes to the Allowance for Doubtful Accounts in Note 7 to its financial statement for 2012 as indicated above.

PAUSE FOR
FEEDBACK

When receivables are material, companies must employ the allowance method to account for doubtful accounts. These are the steps in the process:

a. Prepare an adjusting entry at the end of the accounting period to record the estimated bad debt expense and increase the allowance for doubtful accounts.

b. Write off specific accounts that are determined to be uncollectible during the period. This eliminates the specific uncollectible trade account receivable and reduces the allowance for doubtful accounts.

The adjusting entry reduces net earnings as well as net trade accounts receivable. The write-off affects neither. Before you move on, complete the following questions to test your understanding of these concepts.

SELF-STUDY QUIZ 7-2

In a recent year, Delta Apparel Inc., a Gildan competitor, had a beginning credit balance in the Allowance for Doubtful Accounts of $2,136 (all numbers in thousands of U.S. dollars). It wrote off trade receivables totalling $9,167 during the year and made a bad debt expense adjustment of $8,813 for the year.

1. Prepare the adjusting journal entry that Delta made to record bad debt expense at the end of the year.

2. Prepare the journal entry summarizing Delta's total write-offs of bad debts during the year.

3. Compute the balance in the Allowance for Doubtful Accounts at the end of the year.

After you complete your answers, check them with the solutions at the end of the chapter.

Estimating Bad Debts

The bad debt expense recorded in the end-of-period adjusting entry is often estimated based on an aging of trade receivables.

The AGING OF TRADE RECEIVABLES METHOD estimates uncollectible accounts based on the age of each trade receivable.

Aging of Trade Receivables Method   The **aging of trade receivables method** estimates uncollectible accounts based on the age of each trade receivable. It relies on the fact that, as trade receivables become older and overdue, they are usually less likely to be collectible. For example, a receivable that is due in 30 days but has not been paid after 60 days is more likely to be collected, on average, than a similar receivable that still remains unpaid after 120 days.

Suppose that Amer and Ciero (a hypothetical company) split its receivables into five age categories, as presented in Exhibit 7.3. Management of the company might then *estimate* the following probable bad debt rates: 1 percent of receivables not yet due, 3 percent of receivables that are past due by 1 to 30 days, 6 percent of receivables that are past due by 31 to 60 days, and so on. The total of the amounts estimated to be uncollectible under the aging method is the balance that *should be* in the Allowance for Doubtful Accounts at the end of the period. This is called the *estimated ending balance.* From this, the adjustment to record Bad Debt Expense (and an increase in the allowance for doubtful accounts) for 2014 is computed.

This computation can also be illustrated in T-account form. The current credit balance in the allowance account, before the end-of-period adjustment, is $188. We insert the new ending balance from the aging schedule and then solve for the current amount of bad debt expense:

Allowance for Doubtful Accounts (XA)			
		2014 Beginning balance	1,455
Write-offs (throughout the year)	1,267		
		Unadjusted balance	188
Step 2: Adjustment inferred	→	2014 Bad debt expense (adjustment)	1,344
Step 1: Ending balance estimated from aging of trade receivables	→	2014 Ending balance	1,532

The end-of-period adjusting entry to Bad Debt Expense and Allowance for Doubtful Accounts is made on December 31 for $1,344.

The amount written off throughout the year may sometimes exceed the beginning balance of the Allowance for Doubtful Accounts, which indicates that the company underestimated the amount that is potentially uncollectible. If the total amount written off equals $1,567, the Allowance account will have an unadjusted *debit* balance of $112, and the bad debt expense will equal $1,644.

Gildan disclosed the aging of its trade receivables in the management's discussion and analysis section of its annual report, as shown in Exhibit 7.4. If these receivables

Exhibit **7.3**

Aging Analysis of Trade Receivables

AMER AND CIERO Analysis of Aged Trade Receivables December 31, 2011						
Customer	**Not Yet Due**	**1–30 Days Past Due**	**31–60 Days Past Due**	**61–90 Days Past Due**	**Over 90 Days Past Due**	**Total**
Adams, Inc.	$ 600					$ 600
Baker Stores	300	$ 900	$ 100			1,300
Cox Co.			400	$ 900	$ 100	1,400
Zoe Stores	2,000		1,000			3,000
Total	$17,200	$12,000	$8,000	$1,200	$1,600	$40,000
Estimated % uncollectible	1%	3%	6%	10%	25%	
Estimated uncollectible accounts	$ 172	$ 360	$ 480	$ 120	$ 400	$ 1,532

Exhibit **7.4**

Aging of Trade Receivables

REAL-WORLD EXCERPT

Gildan Activewear

ANNUAL REPORT

The aging of trade receivable balances was as follows as at

(in $ millions)	September 30, 2012	October 2, 2011
Not past due	226.6	166.9
Past due 0–30 days	32.9	21.0
Past due 31–60 days	3.0	2.8
Past due 61–120 days	1.2	1.4
Past due over 121 days	1.4	3.6
Trade receivables	265.1	195.7
Less: Allowance for doubtful accounts	(4.5)	(4.1)
Total trade receivables	260.6	191.6

Source: Gildan Activewear, Annual Report 2012.

were due within 30 days, then the longer the receivable remains uncollected, the lower the likelihood it will be collected. Beyond 90 days, collectibility is very doubtful. The percentage of receivables past due decreased slightly from 14.7 percent in 2011 to 14.4 percent in 2012, which is an encouraging signal. The decrease in the Allowance for Doubtful Accounts from $7.0 million at October 4, 2010, to $4.5 million at September 30, 2011, reflects management's confidence that fewer customers may default on their debts to Gildan. These details help shareholders, lenders, and analysts estimate future impairments of trade receivables.

Actual Write-Offs Compared with Estimates   The amount of uncollectible accounts actually written off seldom equals the estimated amount previously recorded. This error in estimating bad debts is taken into consideration in determining the bad debt expense at the end of the next accounting period. *When estimates are found to be incorrect, financial statement values for prior annual accounting periods are not corrected.*

SALES VERSUS COLLECTIONS: THE MARKETING–FINANCIAL MANAGEMENT CONFLICT

FINANCIAL ANALYSIS

Company managers often forget that while extending credit increases sales volume, it may also increase the volume of bad debts if proper credit checks of the customers are not made, or if the company relaxes its credit policy too much. Marketing-oriented companies that emphasize sales without monitoring the collection of credit sales will soon find much of their current assets tied up in trade receivables. On the other hand, the absence of bad debts may be the result of a very tight credit policy that reduces both sales and net earnings.

In the last decade, the leading domestic automotive companies, such as General Motors and DaimlerChrysler (now Daimler AG), contributed to sales growth by providing short- and medium-term financing to their dealers and distributors in order to encourage them to purchase their products. Financing of sales by the seller, called *vendor financing*, had become common industry practice until the risks of vendor financing came to light when demand for automobiles and auto parts weakened. Dealers and distributors started to default on their debts, and vendors were forced to absorb credit losses and increase their allowances for doubtful accounts.

When credit losses are relatively high because of vendor financing, financial analysts should be cautious in their analysis of companies' sales growth.

LO5

Compute and interpret the receivables turnover ratio and the effects of trade receivables on cash flows.

Prudence in the Valuation of Trade Receivables   Creditors and analysts prefer that companies follow financial strategies that result in reporting lower amounts for net earnings and assets, and higher amounts for liabilities. Accountants and auditors are also cautious about reporting optimistic values that overstate the company's operating performance and its financial position. For Trade Receivables, the amount reported on the statement of financial position should reflect the amount expected to be collected from customers. In this context, prudence suggests that the allowance for doubtful accounts be commensurate with the creditworthiness of the company's customers. A prudent measure of trade receivables means a larger amount of bad debt expense and a larger allowance for doubtful accounts. It is better to err on the side of having a larger allowance than having a smaller one that may not be adequate to cover future bad debts.

To assess the effectiveness of overall credit granting and collection activities, managers and analysts often compute the receivables turnover ratio.

KEY RATIO ANALYSIS

RECEIVABLES TURNOVER RATIO

ANALYTICAL QUESTION → How effective are credit granting and collection activities?

RATIO AND COMPARISONS → An answer to this question is provided by the receivables turnover ratio, which is computed as follows:

$$\text{Receivables Turnover Ratio} = \frac{\text{Net Credit Sales*}}{\text{Average Net Trade Receivables**}}$$

*Since the amount of net credit sales is normally not reported separately, most analysts use net sales in this equation.

**Average Net Trade Receivables = (Beginning Net Trade Receivables + Ending Net Trade Receivables) ÷ 2

The 2012 ratio for Gildan is

$$\frac{\$1,948,253}{(\$191,594 + \$260,595) \div 2} = 8.62$$

If Gildan's trade receivables are turned over 8.62 times per year or 365 days, how many days would be needed, on average, to turn these receivables over once? This is known as the *average collection period* or *average days' sales in receivables* and is computed by dividing the receivables turnover ratio into 365 days:

$$\text{Average Collection Period} = \frac{365}{\text{Receivables Turnover Ratio}} = \frac{365}{8.62} = 42.3 \text{ days}$$

Gildan's average collection period is consistent with its credit policy, as most sales are billed to customers with credit terms of between 30 and 60 days.

Comparisons over Time			Comparisons with Competitors	
Gildan			Hanesbrands Inc.	Delta Apparel
2010	2011	2012	2012	2012
8.59	10.24	8.62	9.45	6.55

INTERPRETATIONS

In General → The receivables turnover ratio reflects how many times average trade accounts receivable are recorded and collected during the period. The higher the ratio, the faster the collection of receivables. A higher ratio benefits the company because it can invest the cash collected to earn interest income, or reduce borrowings to reduce interest expense. Overly generous payment schedules and ineffective collection methods keep the receivables turnover ratio low. Analysts and creditors watch this ratio because a sudden decline may mean that a company is extending payment deadlines in an attempt to prop up lagging sales, or even recording sales that will later be returned by customers. Many managers and analysts compute the average collection period, which indicates the average time it takes a customer to pay the amounts due.

Focus Company Analysis → Gildan's receivables turnover ratio increased from 8.59 in 2010 to 10.24 in 2011, then decreased to 8.62 in 2012. This indicates that the company did not turn over its trade receivables in 2012 as quickly as it did in 2011. Its average collection period increased from 35.6 days in 2011 to 42.3 days in 2012. Gildan's ratio is higher than Delta Apparel's ratio, but slightly lower than Hanesbrands'. Gildan's customers are faster at paying their bills than Delta Apparel's customers. Alternatively, Gildan may have a more effective collections practice or different receivables contracts with shorter credit terms.

A Few Cautions → Since differences across industries and between firms in the manner in which customer purchases are financed can cause dramatic differences in the ratio, a particular firm's ratio should be compared only with its own prior years' figures or with other firms in the same industry following the same financing practices.

Selected Industry Comparisons: Receivables Turnover Ratio—2012

Retailing 107.78

Food, Beverage, and Tobacco 14.40

Paper and Forest Products 11.59

PAUSE FOR FEEDBACK

When using the *aging of trade receivables method*, compute the estimated ending balance in the allowance account and solve for the bad debt expense. This process involves multiplying the amount in each age category by the estimated percentage uncollectible to produce the estimated ending balance in the allowance for doubtful accounts. The difference between the estimated ending balance and the balance in the allowance account before the adjustment becomes the bad debt expense for the year. Before you move on, answer the following questions to test your understanding of this method.

SELF-STUDY QUIZ 7-3

1. Assume that Kleer Company reported beginning and ending balances in the allowance for doubtful accounts of $723 and $904, respectively. It also reported that write-offs of bad debts amounted to $648 (all numbers in thousands). Assuming that the company did not collect any amounts that were written off previously, what amount did the company record as bad debt expense for the period? (*Hint:* Use the allowance for doubtful accounts T-account to solve for the missing value.)

   Allowance for Doubtful Accounts (XA)

2. Kleer Company reported an increase in trade receivables for the period. Was that increase added to or subtracted from net earnings in the computation of cash flow from operations? Explain your answer.

3. Explain whether *granting longer payment deadlines* (e.g., 60 days instead of 30 days) will most likely *increase* or *decrease* the receivables turnover ratio.

After you complete your answers, check them with the solutions at the end of the chapter.

TRADE RECEIVABLES

FOCUS ON CASH FLOWS

The change in trade receivables can be a major determinant of a company's cash flow from operations. The statement of earnings reflects the revenues earned during the period, whereas the cash flow from operating activities reflects the cash collections from customers for the same period. Since sales on account increase the balance in trade receivables, and cash collections from customers decrease the balance in trade receivables, the change in trade receivables from the beginning to the end of the period is the difference between sales and cash collections.

Exhibit **7.5**

Receivables on the Statement of Cash Flows

GILDAN ACTIVEWEAR INC.

Consolidated Statements of Cash Flows

Years ended September 30, 2012, and October 2, 2011

(in thousands of U.S. dollars)

	2012	2011
Cash flows from (used in) operating activities:		
Net earnings	$148,464	$234,156
Adjustments to reconcile net earnings to cash flows from operating activities (Note 23(a)):	94,221	47,917
	242,685	282,073
Changes in non-cash working capital balances:		
Trade accounts receivable	(36,660)	(18,861)
Income taxes receivable	2,440	(5,341)
Inventories	77,111	(177,821)
Prepaid expenses and deposits	(1,828)	(569)
Other current assets	(2,368)	1,553
Accounts payable and accrued liabilities	(61,798)	82,605
	$219,582	$163,639

Source: Gildan Activewear, Annual Report 2012.

EFFECT ON STATEMENT OF CASH FLOWS

In General → When a net *decrease in trade receivables* for the period occurs, the amount of cash collected from customers exceeds revenue; thus, the decrease must be *added* to revenue or to net earnings (since revenue is a component of net earnings) in computing cash flows from operations. When a net *increase in trade receivables* occurs, cash collected from customers is less than revenue; thus, the increase must be *subtracted* from net earnings in computing cash flows from operations.

	Effect on Cash Flows
Operating activities (indirect method)	
Net earnings	$xxx
Adjusted for	
Decrease in trade receivables	+
or	
Increase in trade receivables	–

Focus Company Analysis → Exhibit 7.5 is the operating activities section of Gildan's statement of cash flows. The increase in sales during 2012 has resulted in an increase in Gildan's balance in trade accounts receivable. This increase is subtracted from net earnings in the computation of Gildan's cash flow from operations, because revenues are higher than cash collected from customers during 2012. When trade receivables decrease, the amount of the decrease is added back to net earnings in determining the cash flow from operating activities, because cash collected from customers exceeds the amount of revenues.

INTERNAL CONTROL refers to the process by which the company's board of directors, management, and other personnel provide reasonable assurance regarding the reliability of the company's financial reporting, the effectiveness and efficiency of its operations, and its compliance with applicable laws and regulations.

Internal Control and Management Responsibility

The term **internal control** refers to the process by which a company's board of directors, audit committee, management, and other personnel provide reasonable assurance that the accounting system minimizes the risk of material misstatement of reported financial information.[10] In addition, the system must assure the effectiveness and efficiency of the company's operations, and its compliance with all laws and regulations. A well-designed system of internal control prevents inadvertent errors and removes opportunities for individuals to steal, misrepresent, defraud, or embezzle assets from a company. Canadian legislation prevents top executives and members of the board of directors from ignoring their management responsibility to design, supervise, and implement appropriate internal control systems.

Canadian scandals such as those involving Nortel Networks Corp. and Livent Inc. led the Canadian Securities Administrators to enact regulations regarding internal control systems, including National Instrument (NI) 52-109, which requires the corporation's chief executive officer and chief financial officer to sign form 52-109F1 (certification of annual filings), a legal document that certifies the quality of the internal control system.[11] In particular, for corporations listed on the Toronto Stock Exchange, the two officers certify the reliability of financial reporting in accordance with applicable accounting standards. Executives must also attest to the effectiveness of the internal control and financial reporting system. The annual report must disclose any deficiencies in the disclosure controls and procedures, the related risks, and any plans to remedy these deficiencies. No audit is necessary, but auditors would find it unusual if an executive certified a deficient system. Auditors must correct or refuse to attest to all audited disclosure, including false claims made on form 52-109F1.

ETHICS AND THE NEED FOR INTERNAL CONTROL

A QUESTION OF ACCOUNTABILITY

Some people are bothered by the recommendation that all well-run companies should have strong internal control procedures. These people believe that control procedures suggest that the company's management does not trust its employees. Although the vast majority of employees are trustworthy, employee theft costs businesses billions of dollars each year. Interviews with convicted felons indicate that, in many cases, they stole from their employers because they thought that it was easy and that no one cared (internal control procedures were not present).

A recent survey of global economic crime (which includes asset misappropriations, accounting fraud, bribery, cybercrime, money laundering, and illegal insider trading) revealed that these activities continue to be serious issues affecting many organizations in many countries. This is particularly true during difficult economic times, when the reduction of the workforce also affects accounting staff, who are responsible for internal control of operations. The survey indicated that asset misappropriation, accounting fraud, corruption and bribery, and cybercrime (resulting from our increasing dependence on information and communications technologies) are the most prevalent types of economic crime. It also revealed that internal control was not effective in detecting the fraud. In fact, internal audit procedures were identified as the primary source of fraud detection in fewer than 15 percent of the cases.[12] This explains the continued emphasis by securities regulators on the validation of internal control over financial reporting.

Many companies have a formal code of ethics that requires high standards of behaviour in dealing with customers, suppliers, fellow employees, and the company's assets. Although each employee is ultimately responsible for his or her own ethical behaviour, internal control procedures can be thought of as important value statements from management. Preventing theft through strong internal control prevents people from destroying their lives if they steal and are subsequently caught and penalized for their unethical behaviour.

Control over Trade Receivables

The internal control system must respond to different sets of activities with different types of control. Controlling and protecting cash to prevent embezzlement, for example, will be different from controlling the security and accuracy of the information system.

Many managers forget that although extending credit will increase sales volume, the related receivables do not increase net earnings unless they are collected. Companies that emphasize sales without monitoring the collection of credit sales will soon find much of their current assets tied up in trade receivables. By guarding against extending credit to non-worthy customers, the following practices can help minimize bad debts:

1. Require approval of customers' credit history by a person independent of the sales and collection functions.

2. Monitor the age of trade receivables periodically, and contact customers with overdue payments.

3. Reward both sales and collection personnel for speedy collections so that they work as a team.

REPORTING AND SAFEGUARDING CASH

Cash and Cash Equivalents Defined

CASH is money or any instrument that banks will accept for deposit and immediate credit to the company's account, such as a cheque, money order, or bank draft.

Cash is defined as money or any instrument that banks will accept for deposit and immediate credit to the company's account, such as a cheque, money order, or bank draft. Cash is usually divided into three categories: cash on hand, cash deposited in banks, and other instruments that meet the definition of cash.

International Accounting Standard 7—Statement of Cash Flows defines **cash equivalents** as short-term, highly liquid investments that are readily convertible to known amounts of cash and that are subject to an insignificant risk of change in value. Typical instruments included as cash equivalents are bank certificates of deposit and treasury bills issued by the government to finance its activities.

CASH EQUIVALENTS are short-term, highly liquid investments that are readily convertible to known amounts of cash and that are subject to an insignificant risk of change in value.

Even though a company may have several bank accounts and several types of cash equivalents, all cash accounts and cash equivalents are usually combined as one amount for financial reporting purposes. Gildan reports a single account, Cash and Cash Equivalents, with a balance of $70.4 million at September 30, 2012. The company clearly specifies cash equivalents as all liquid investments with maturities of three months or less from the date of acquisition.

Cash Management

Many businesses receive a large amount of cash, cheques, and credit card receipts from their customers each day. Anyone can spend cash, so management must develop procedures to safeguard the cash it uses in the business. Effective cash management involves more than protecting cash from theft, fraud, or loss through carelessness. Other cash management responsibilities include the following:

1. Accurate accounting so that reports of cash flows and balances may be prepared.

2. Controls to ensure that enough cash is on hand to meet (*a*) current operating needs, (*b*) maturing liabilities, and (*c*) unexpected emergencies.

3. Prevention of the accumulation of excess amounts of idle cash. Idle cash earns no revenue; therefore, it is often invested in securities to earn revenue (return) until it is needed for operations.

Internal Control of Cash

Because cash is the asset most vulnerable to theft and fraud, a significant number of internal control procedures should focus on cash. You have already observed internal control procedures for cash, although you may not have known it at the time. At most movie theatres, one employee sells tickets and another employee collects them. It would be less expensive to have one employee do both jobs, but it would also be easier for that single employee to steal cash and admit a patron without issuing a ticket. If different employees perform the tasks, a successful theft requires the participation of both.

Effective internal control of cash should include the following:

1. **Separation of duties related to cash handling and recordkeeping.**

   a. Complete separation of the tasks of receiving cash and disbursing cash ensures that the individual responsible for depositing cash has no authority to sign cheques.

   b. Complete separation of the procedures of accounting for cash receipts and cash disbursements ensures, for example, that those handling sales returns do not create fictitious returns to conceal cash shortages.

   c. Complete separation of the physical handling of cash and all phases of the accounting function ensures that those either receiving or paying cash have no authority to make accounting entries.

   The following diagram illustrates how the separation of duties contributes to strong internal control:

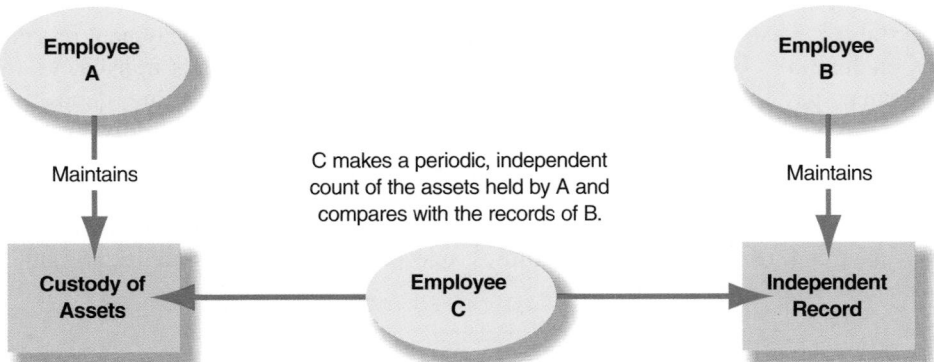

   The separation of individual responsibilities deters theft, because the collusion of two or more persons is needed to steal cash and then conceal the theft in the accounting records.

2. **Prescribed policies and procedures.**

   Specific policies and procedures should be established so that the work done by one individual is compared with the results reported by other individuals. Exhibit 7.6 provides a summary of typical policies and procedures to control cash.

Exhibit **7.6**

Typical Internal Controls for Cash

Internal Control Component	Prescribed Policies or Procedures
Cash budget	Prepare a monthly forecast of cash receipts, disbursements, and balances for the year, and require managers to document and justify any deviations from the budget each month.
Cash receipts	Prepare a listing of cash receipts on a daily basis. In practice, this often takes the form of cash register receipts or a descriptive list of incoming cheques. Require that all cash receipts be deposited in a bank daily. Keep any cash on hand under strict control.
Cash payments	Require separate approval of the purchases and other expenditures and separate approval of the actual cash payments. Assign the cash payment approval and the actual cheque-signing responsibilities to different individuals. Use pre-numbered cheques and pay special attention to payments by electronic funds transfers, since the bank does not process controlled documents (cheques).
Independent internal verification	Require comparison, by an independent supervisor, of cash receipts to bank deposits and cheques issued to invoices. Require monthly reconciliation of bank accounts with the cash accounts on the company's books (discussed in detail in the next section).
Rotation of duties	Require that employees take vacations, and rotate their duties.

When procedures similar to those described in Exhibit 7.6 are followed, concealing a fraudulent cash disbursement is difficult without the collusion of two or more persons. Reconciliation of cash accounts with bank statements provides an additional control on disbursements. The level of internal control, which is reviewed by the outside independent auditor, increases the reliability of the financial statements of the business.

Reconciliation of the Cash Accounts and the Bank Statements

LO⁷

Reconcile cash accounts and bank statements.

A **BANK STATEMENT** is a monthly report from a bank that shows deposits recorded, cheques cleared, other debits and credits, and a running bank balance.

Content of a Bank Statement Proper use of the bank accounts of a business can be an important internal control procedure for cash. Each month, the bank provides the company (the depositor) with a **bank statement** that lists (1) each deposit recorded by the bank during the period, (2) each cheque cleared by the bank during the period, (3) other debits and credits, and (4) the running balance in the company's account. The bank statement also shows the bank charges or deductions (such as service charges) made directly to the company's account by the bank. A typical bank statement is shown in Exhibit 7.7.

Exhibit 7.7 lists four items that need explanation. Notice that the payment of salaries on June 3 is coded EFT.[13] This is the code for electronic funds transfer. Many companies pay salaries to their employees by using electronic chequing, depositing electronic payments directly into the employees' bank accounts instead of issuing paper cheques. When a company orders the electronic payment, it records this item on its books in the same manner as a paper cheque, so no additional entry is needed. Electronic funds transfer has become common among companies and individuals as they use this form of payment for utilities, telecommunication, insurance, and other recurring expenses.

Exhibit **7.7**

Example of a Bank Statement

			CB Canadian Bank 123 Bank Street Anytown, ON L5Z 2M7		STATEMENT OF ACCOUNT	

DATE	BRANCH NUMBER	ACCOUNT TYPE	ACCOUNT NUMBER	PAGE NO.
30 06 2013	1379	Chequing	79253	1 OF 1

J. Doe Company
10945 Long Road
Anytown, ON
L5X 3L5

Date	Code	Description	Debits	Credits	Balance
		Balance Forward			7,762.40
1-6	CK	Cheque No. 53	500.00		7,262.40
1-6	CK	Cheque No. 48	153.49		7,108.91
3-6	EFT	Payment of salaries	2,572.50		4,536.41
5-6	MD	Deposit		3,000.00	7,536.41
5-6	CK	Cheque No. 55	56.00		7,480.41
9-6	CK	Cheque No. 49	682.27		6,797.14
11-6	CK	Cheque No. 54	400.00		6,397.14
12-6	MD	Deposit		1,000.00	7,397.14
14-6	CK	Cheque No. 50	289.50		7,107.64
16-6	CK	Cheque No. 56	735.00		6,372.64
20-6	NSF	Cheque returned—not sufficient funds	204.76		6,167.88
20-6	SC	Service charge—cheque returned	10.00		6,157.88
21-6	MD	Deposit		1,500.00	7,657.88
22-6	CK	Cheque No. 58	1,583.00		6,074.88
24-6	CK	Cheque No. 61	79.50		5,995.38
24-6	CK	Cheque No. 57	192.25		5,803.13
26-6	CK	Cheque No. 62	573.00		5,230.13
29-6	MD	Deposit		4,500.00	9,730.13
30-6	CK	Cheque No. 59	936.00		8,794.13
30-6	INT	Interest earned		25.37	8,819.50

Code:
CK—Cheque
INT—Interest
EFT—Electronic funds transfer
MD—Merchant deposit
NSF—Not sufficient funds
SC—Service charge

Please check this statement and report any errors or omissions within 30 days of its delivery.
Please notify your branch of any change of address.

Notice that on June 20, listed under debits, there is a deduction for $204.76 coded NSF. A cheque for $204.76 was received from a customer, R. Smith, and deposited by J. Doe Company with its bank, the Canadian Bank. The bank processed the cheque through banking channels to Smith's bank. Smith's account did not have sufficient funds to cover it; therefore, Smith's bank returned it to the Canadian Bank, which then charged it back to J. Doe Company. This type of cheque is often called an *NSF cheque* (not sufficient funds). The company needs to collect the amount of the cheque again from the customer. The NSF cheque is now a receivable; consequently, J. Doe Company must make a journal entry to debit Trade Receivables (R. Smith) and credit Cash for the $204.76.

Notice the $10 listed under debits on June 20 and coded SC. This is the code for bank service charges. The bank statement included a memo by the bank explaining this service charge (which was not documented by a cheque). J. Doe Company must make a journal entry to reflect the $10 decrease in the bank balance as a debit to a relevant expense account, such as bank service expense, and a credit to cash.

Notice the $25.37 listed on June 30 under credits and the code INT for interest earned. The bank pays interest on chequing account balances, which increased J. Doe Company's account for interest earned during the period. The company must record the interest by making a journal entry to debit cash and credit interest revenue for the $25.37.

Need for Reconciliation A **bank reconciliation** is the process of comparing (reconciling) and verifying the accuracy of both the ending cash balance in the company's records and the ending cash balance reported by the bank on the monthly bank statement. A bank reconciliation should be completed for each separate chequing account (i.e., for each bank statement received from each bank) at the end of each month.

A **BANK RECONCILIATION** is the process of verifying the accuracy of both the bank statement and the cash accounts of a business.

Usually, the ending cash balance as shown on the bank statement does not agree with the ending cash balance shown by the related Cash ledger account on the books of the company. For example, the Cash ledger account of J. Doe Company showed the following at the end of June (Doe has only one chequing account):

Cash

June 1 balance	6,637.14	Cheques written in June	8,714.45
June deposits	11,800.00		
Ending balance	9,722.69		

The $8,819.50 ending cash balance shown on the bank statement (Exhibit 7.7) is different from the $9,722.69 ending balance of cash shown on the books of J. Doe Company. This difference exists because (1) some transactions affecting cash were shown on the bank statement but had not been recorded in the books of the J. Doe Company, (2) some transactions were recorded in the books of J. Doe Company but were not shown on the bank statement, and (3) errors occurred in recording transactions.

The flow of documents that have not reached either the company or the bank by the end of the accounting period is illustrated below:

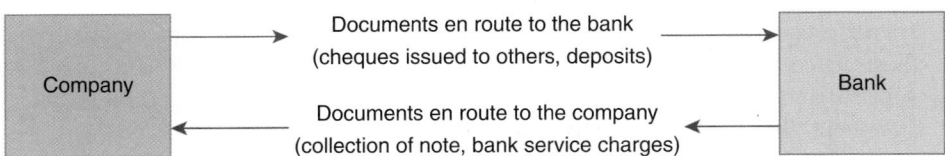

The most common causes of differences between the ending bank balance and the ending book balance of cash are as follows:

1. **Bank service charges.** An expense for bank services listed on the bank statement. This expense is not recorded on the company's books.

2. **NSF cheques.** A "bad cheque" or "bounced cheque" that was deposited but must be deducted from the company's cash account and recorded as a receivable.

3. **Interest.** The interest paid by the bank to the company on its bank balance.

4. **Deposits in transit.** These are deposits sent to the bank by the company and recorded in the company's ledger as debits to the Cash account. The bank has not recorded these deposits (they are not shown on the bank statement as an increase in the bank balance). Deposits in transit usually happen when deposits are made one or two days before the close of the period covered by the bank statement. Deposits in transit are determined by comparing the deposits listed on the bank statement with the copies of the deposit slips retained by the company or other company records.

5. **Outstanding cheques.** These are cheques written by the company and recorded in the company's ledger as credits to the Cash account that have not cleared the bank (they are not shown on the bank statement as a deduction from the bank balance). The outstanding cheques are identified by comparing the cancelled cheques that the bank returned with the record of cheques (such as cheque stubs or a journal) maintained by the company.

6. **Errors.** Both the bank and the company may make errors, especially when the volume of cash transactions is large.

Bank Reconciliation Illustrated   The company should make a bank reconciliation immediately after receiving each bank statement. The general format for the bank reconciliation follows:

Ending cash balance per books	$xxx	Ending cash balance per bank statement	$xxx
+ Collections by bank	xx	+ Deposits in transit	xx
− NSF cheques/Service charges	xx	− Outstanding cheques	xx
± Company errors	xx	± Bank errors	xx
Ending correct cash balances	$xxx	Ending correct cash balance	$xxx

J. Doe Company followed these steps in preparing the bank reconciliation:

1. **Identify bank charges and credits not recorded on the company's books.** Examination of the bank statement in Exhibit 7.7 and the company's records indicate the following:

   a. The bank deducted $204.76 for a cheque by R. Smith that was returned to the company because of insufficient funds. This amount has not been recorded on the company's books.

   b. The bank deducted $10.00 as a service charge for the returned cheque. The service charge has not been recorded on the company's books.

   c. The bank added $25.37 to the company's account as interest on the amount deposited in the bank during June. This interest revenue has not been recorded by the company yet.

When these amounts are recorded in the company's books, the revised balance in the cash account will decrease to $9,533.30 ($9,722.69 − $204.76 − $10.00 + $25.37).

2. **Identify the deposits in transit.** A comparison of the deposit slips on hand with those listed on the bank statement revealed that a deposit of $1,800.00 made on June 30 and recorded in the company's Cash account was not listed on the bank statement. It will be added by the bank when it records the deposit.

3. **Identify the outstanding cheques.** A comparison of the cancelled cheques returned by the bank with the company's records of all cheques drawn showed the following cheques still outstanding (not cleared) at the end of June:

Cheque No.	Amount
60	$ 145.00
63	815.00
64	117.20
Total	$1,077.20

The amounts of the three cheques have already been recorded in the company's Cash account but have not been entered on the bank statement, because those who received the cheques from the company have not yet presented them to the bank for clearance.

When the bank records the deposit in transit and the outstanding cheques in the company's account, the revised bank balance will equal $9,542.30 ($8,819.50 − $1,077.20 + $1,800.00). The revised bank balance differs from the revised cash balance by $9 ($9,542.30 − $9,533.30).

4. **Determine the impact of errors.** Because the difference in the revised bank and book balances is divisible by 9, a transposition of numbers was suspected. (A transposition, such as writing 27 for 72, will always cause an error that is exactly divisible by 9.) Comparison of the cancelled cheques returned by the bank with the company's records of all cheques issued to others revealed that a cheque written for $56 as per the bank statement was recorded in the company's accounts as $65. Examination of the journal entries showed that the incorrect entry made was a debit to Trade Payables and a credit to Cash for $65 (instead of $56). Therefore, $9 (i.e., $65 − $56) must be added to the Cash account, leading to a revised cash balance of $9,542.30.

Exhibit 7.8 shows the bank reconciliation prepared by J. Doe Company for the month of June to reconcile the ending bank balance ($8,819.50) with the ending book balance ($9,722.69). On the completed reconciliation, the correct cash balance is $9,542.30. This balance is different from both the reported bank and book balances before the reconciliation with the bank statement. This correct balance reflects the amount of cash available to J. Doe Company for use in the future and should be shown in the Cash account after the reconciliation. In this example, it is also the correct amount of cash that should be reported on the statement of financial position (J. Doe Company has only one chequing account and no cash on hand).

Note that in Exhibit 7.8, the two sections of the bank reconciliation now show correct cash balances of $9,542.30. This amount will be reported as cash on a statement of financial position prepared at June 30, 2013.

A bank reconciliation like the one in Exhibit 7.8 accomplishes two major objectives:

1. Checks the accuracy of the bank balance and the company cash records, which involves developing the correct cash balance. The correct cash balance (plus cash on hand, if any) is the amount of cash that is reported on the statement of financial position.

2. Identifies any previously unrecorded transactions or changes that are necessary to cause the company's Cash account(s) to show the correct cash balance. Any transactions or changes on the *company's books side* of the bank reconciliation need journal entries. Therefore, the journal entries on the next page, based on the company's books side of the bank reconciliation, must be entered into the company's records.

Exhibit **7.8**

Bank Reconciliation Illustrated

J. DOE COMPANY
Bank Reconciliation
June 30, 2013

Company's Books		Bank Statement	
Ending cash balance per books	$9,722.69	Ending cash balance per bank statement	$8,819.50
Additions		Additions	
Interest earned	25.37	Deposit in transit	1,800.00
Error in recording cheque No. 55	9.00		
	9,757.06		10,619.50
Deductions		Deductions	
NSF cheque of R. Smith	204.76	Outstanding cheques	1,077.20
Bank service charges	10.00		
Ending correct cash balance	$9,542.30	Ending correct cash balance	$9,542.30

Accounts of J. Doe Company

(a) Cash (A)	25.37	
Interest revenue (R)		25.37
To record interest on chequing account with the bank.		
(b) Trade receivables (A)	204.76	
Cash (A)		204.76
To record NSF cheque received from R. Smith.		
(c) Trade receivables (A)	10.00	
Cash (A)		10.00
To record service fees charged by the bank		
and receivable from R. Smith.		
(d) Cash (A)	9.00	
Trade payables (L)		9.00
To correct error made in recording a cheque payable to a creditor		

Assets	=	Liabilities	+	Shareholders' Equity
Cash (+25.37 − 204.76 −180.39		Trade payables +9.00		
− 10.00 + 9.00)				
Trade receivables +214.76				Interest earned +25.37

The cash account prior to reconciliation was given earlier in this chapter. After the preceding journal entries are posted, the cash account is as follows:

Cash Account of J. Doe Company

Cash			
June 1 Balance	6,637.14	June Cheques written	8,714.45
June Deposits	11,800.00	June 30 NSF cheque*	204.76
June 30 Interest earned*	25.37	June 30 Bank service charge related to NSF cheque*	10.00
June 30 Correcting entry*	9.00		
Correct cash balance	9,542.30		

*Based on the bank reconciliation.

Notice that all of the additions and deductions on the company's books side of the reconciliation need journal entries to update the Cash account. The additions and deductions on the bank statement side do not need journal entries because they will work out automatically when they clear the bank.

PAUSE FOR FEEDBACK

Cash is the most liquid of all assets, flowing continually into and out of a business. As a result, a number of critical control procedures, including the *reconciliation* of bank accounts, should be applied. Also, management of cash may be critically important to decision makers who must have cash available to meet current needs, yet must avoid excess amounts of idle cash that produce no revenue. Answer the following questions to check your understanding of the basics of bank reconciliation before you move on.

SELF-STUDY QUIZ 7-4

Indicate which of the following items discovered while preparing a company's bank reconciliation will result in adjustment of the cash balance on the statement of financial position.

1. Outstanding cheques.

2. Deposits in transit.

3. Bank service charges.

4. NSF cheques that were deposited.

After you complete your answers, check them with the solutions at the end of the chapter.

ACCOUNTING STANDARDS FOR PRIVATE ENTERPRISES

This chapter covered the revenue recognition criteria that are applicable mainly to the sale of merchandise. We discuss in Appendix 7A the revenue recognition methods that are applicable for companies involved in long-term contracts extending beyond one accounting period. Accounting standard setters require companies to use the percentage of completion method to recognize both revenue and expenses on long-term contracts on a gradual basis over the duration of the contract.

Financial Reporting Issue	IFRS	ASPE
Long-term contracts	Canadian publicly accountable enterprises are required to use the percentage of completion method, which is discussed in Appendix 7A.	When the percentage of completion method cannot be used, Canadian private enterprises are required to use the completed contract method, which recognizes revenue and the related expenses in the period of completion of the contract, but not in prior periods.

DEMONSTRATION CASE A

Wholesale Warehouse Stores sold $950,000 in merchandise during 2014: $400,000 was on credit with terms 2/10, n/30 (75 percent of these amounts were paid within the discount period); $500,000 was paid with credit cards (there was a 3 percent credit card discount); and the rest was paid in cash. On December 31, 2014, the Trade Receivables balance was $80,000, and the Allowance for Doubtful Accounts was $3,000 (credit balance).

Required:

1. Compute net sales for 2014, assuming that sales and credit card discounts are treated as contra-revenue accounts.

2. Assume that Wholesale uses the aging of trade receivables method and that it estimates that $10,000 worth of current accounts are uncollectible. Record bad debt expense for 2014.

We strongly recommend that you prepare your own answers to these requirements and then check your answers with the following solution.

SUGGESTED SOLUTION

1. Both sales discounts and credit card discounts should be subtracted from sales revenues in the computation of net sales:

Sales revenue	$950,000
Less: Sales discounts (0.02 × 0.75 × $400,000)	6,000
Credit card discounts (0.03 × $500,000)	15,000
Net sales	$929,000

2. The entry made when using the aging of trade receivables method is the estimated balance minus the unadjusted balance.

Bad debt expense (E) ($10,000 − $3,000)	7,000	
Allowance for doubtful accounts (XA)		7,000

Assets	=	Liabilities	+	Shareholders' Equity
Allowance for doubtful accounts −7,000				Bad debt expense −7,000

DEMONSTRATION **CASE B**

Heather Ann Long, a first-year university student, has just received her first chequing account statement. This was her first chance to attempt a bank reconciliation. She had the following information to work with:

Bank balance, September 1	$1,150
Deposits during September	650
Cheques cleared during September	900
Bank service charge	5
Bank balance, October 1	895

Heather was surprised that the deposit of $50 she made on September 29 had not been posted to her account and was pleased that her rent cheque of $200 had not cleared her account. Her chequebook balance was $750.

Required:

1. Complete Heather's bank reconciliation.
2. Why is it important for individuals such as Heather and businesses to do a bank reconciliation each month?

We strongly recommend that you prepare your own answers to these requirements and then check your answers with the following solution.

SUGGESTED **SOLUTION**

1. Heather's bank reconciliation:

Heather's Books		Bank Statement	
October 1 cash balance	$750	October 1 cash balance	$895
Additions		Additions	
None		Deposit in transit	50
Deductions		Deductions	
Bank service charge	(5)	Outstanding cheque	(200)
Correct cash balance	$745	Correct cash balance	$745

2. Bank statements, whether personal or business, should be reconciled each month. This process helps ensure that a correct balance is reflected in the customer's books. Failure to reconcile a bank statement increases the chance that an error will not be discovered and may result in bad cheques being written. Businesses must reconcile their bank statements for an additional reason: the correct balance that is calculated during reconciliation is reported on the statement of financial position. A bank reconciliation is an important internal control measure.

APPENDIX 7A: APPLYING THE REVENUE PRINCIPLE IN SPECIAL CIRCUMSTANCES

The revenue principle was introduced in Chapter 3. As noted earlier, application of this principle in the case of Gildan and similar companies is fairly straightforward. Such companies record revenue according to their sales contract, which specifies the point at which transfer of ownership occurs. We now expand our discussion of the revenue principle and see how it is applied in business practice by companies other than typical manufacturers, wholesalers, and retailers.

Revenue Recognition before the Earnings Process Is Complete: Long-Term Construction Contracts

An important exception to the usual criteria for revenue recognition exists for companies involved in long-term construction projects, such as building an office complex for a large corporation. These projects may take a number of years to complete. As a result, if the company recorded no revenue or expenses directly related to the project during the years that it worked on the project and then recorded massive amounts of revenue and related expenses in the year that it delivered the product to the customer, the financial statements would not accurately represent the company's economic activities during the period of construction. This method of accounting, which is often referred to as the **completed contract method**, records revenue when the completed product is delivered to the customer and may be used by Canadian private enterprises under specific circumstances.

> The **COMPLETED CONTRACT METHOD** records revenue when the completed product is delivered to the customer.

To deal with this unique problem for long-term construction projects, many companies use the **percentage of completion method**, which records revenue based on a reliable measure of the percentage of work completed during the accounting period, instead of the completed contract method, which records revenue when the completed product is delivered to the customer.

> The **PERCENTAGE OF COMPLETION METHOD** records revenue based on a reliable measure of the percentage of work completed during the accounting period.

Under the percentage of completion method, if the contract revenue and contract costs can be estimated reliably, then both are recognized periodically as revenue and expenses during each period, based on the stage of completion of the contract activity at the end of the reporting period.[14] It also must be probable that the economic benefits of the contract will be collected. Typically, the amount of work accomplished each year is measured by the *percentage of total cost* that was incurred during the year.[15] For example, assume that the total contract price for building a bridge was $50 million and the total cost for construction was $40 million. In 2013, the construction company spent $10 million, which was 25 percent of the contract cost ($10 million ÷ $40 million).[16] This percentage of completion is then multiplied by the total contract revenue to determine the amount of revenue to be reported in 2013 (25% × $50 million = $12.5 million). The amount of expense reported in 2013 is the actual cost incurred, $10 million, and the profit is $2.5 million, the difference between revenue and expense ($12.5 million − $10 million).

Notice that the percentage of completion method does not completely satisfy the first revenue recognition criterion because revenue is reported before the significant risks and rewards of ownership are transferred to the customer. It is an acceptable method, however, because it reflects the economic substance of a company's construction activity throughout the contract period.

When the outcome of a construction contract cannot be estimated reliably, but it is probable that the costs can be collected, the amount of revenue recognized each period is limited to the contract costs that have been incurred in that period, assuming that they are recoverable from the customer. The contract costs are recognized as an expense in that period. This cost recovery method, the **zero profit method**, records revenue that is equal to the actual costs incurred during the accounting period. In the previous example, the revenue that can be recognized is exactly equal to the costs incurred in the first year of the contract. Therefore, the revenue and expenses recognized in 2013 will both equal $10 million, resulting in zero profit in that year.

> The **ZERO PROFIT METHOD** records revenue that is equal to the actual costs incurred during the accounting period.

Revenue Recognition for Service Contracts

Companies that provide services over more than one accounting period often follow revenue recognition policies similar to those followed for long-term construction contracts.[17] They recognize revenue from the completed portion of the services. For example, Federal Express, which provides air delivery service, employs the percentage of completion revenue recognition policy, as indicated in the following note:

FEDERAL EXPRESS CORPORATION AND SUBSIDIARIES

Note 1. Summary of Significant Accounting Policies

Notes to Consolidated Financial Statements

REVENUE RECOGNITION. We recognize revenue upon delivery of shipments for our transportation businesses and upon completion of services for our business services, logistics and trade services businesses. . . . For shipments in transit, revenue is recorded based on the percentage of service completed at the balance sheet date.

For the services in progress at the end of the accounting period, Federal Express uses the percentage of completion method for revenue recognition, recognizing only a percentage of the revenues and related costs of providing the services based on the degree of completion of the service. This method is also called the *proportional performance* method. This form of revenue recognition is very similar to Shaw Communications Inc.'s accounting for its cable and Internet contracts and SNC-Lavalin's accounting for its construction contracts. Each company recognizes revenues and expenses related to the *completed portion* of its contract with the customer. The major difference is that Shaw Communications is paid for the cable and Internet subscriptions in advance, SNC-Lavalin receives progress payments throughout the contract period, and Federal Express receives payment from its business customers after it provides the service.

FINANCIAL ANALYSIS

REVENUE RECOGNITION AND FINANCIAL STATEMENT ANALYSIS

Financial analysts cannot evaluate a company's net earnings if they do not understand how it applied the revenue recognition criteria. As a result, all companies disclose any special revenue recognition issues in the notes to their financial statements. For example, CGI Group Inc., a leading worldwide provider of information technology solutions, business process outsourcing, systems integration, and consulting, states the following in its annual report:

NOTES TO THE CONSOLIDATED FINANCIAL STATEMENTS

3. Summary of Significant Accounting Policies

Revenue recognition

. . .

The Company provides services and products under arrangements that contain various pricing mechanisms. The Company recognizes revenue when the following criteria are met: there is clear evidence that an arrangement exists, the amount of revenue and related costs can be measured reliably, it is probable that future economic benefits will flow to the Company, the stage of completion can be measured reliably where services are delivered and the significant risks and rewards of ownership, including effective control, are transferred to clients where products are sold. Revenue is measured at the fair value of the consideration received or receivable net of discounts, volume rebates and sales related taxes.

. . .

Systems integration and consulting services
Revenue from systems integration and consulting services under time and material arrangements is recognized as the services are rendered, and revenue under cost-based arrangements is recognized as reimbursable costs are incurred.

Revenue from systems integration and consulting services under fixed-fee arrangements where the outcome of the arrangements can be estimated reliably is recognized using the percentage-of-completion method over the service periods. The Company uses the labour costs or labour hours to measure the progress towards completion. This method relies on estimates of total expected labour costs or total expected labour hours to complete the service, which are compared to labour costs or labour hours incurred to date, to arrive at an estimate of the percentage of revenue earned to date. Management regularly reviews underlying estimates of total expected labour costs or hours. Revisions to estimates due to volume variations, changes in technology and other factors which may not be foreseen at inception are reflected in the consolidated statements of earnings in the period in which the facts that gave rise to the revision become known. If the outcome of an arrangement cannot be estimated reliably, revenue is recognized to the extent of arrangement costs incurred that are likely to be recoverable.

Source: CGI Group Inc., Annual Report 2012.

This succinct explanation of the percentage of completion method is adequate for someone who has read this chapter, but it is doubtful that someone who has not studied accounting would understand its meaning. Shareholders, lenders, and analysts must examine the company's accounting policy choices for recognition of long-term contract revenue. This will assist them in understanding whether or not reported net revenues are comparable among companies operating in the same industry. Long-term contract revenue recognition is covered in detail in advanced accounting courses.

DEMONSTRATION **CASE C**

Assume that Landevco Inc., a major land development company, decided to subdivide a large lot of land and develop it into a commercial and residential complex. Landevco contracted with Construk Corp. for the construction of this complex, which will take three years to complete and cost Landevco $400 million, payable in three instalments of $100 million, $150 million, and $150 million at the end of years 1, 2, and 3, respectively. Construk expects to incur $300 million in total costs of construction over the three years. Construk is confident that Landevco will make the promised progress payments on time. The actual costs incurred totalled $90 million, $120 million, and $90 million for years 1, 2, and 3, respectively.

Required:

1. Assume that all the criteria for use of the percentage of completion method are met. Determine the amount that Construk should recognize as profit each year.

2. Assume also that the costs of constructing this project could not be estimated reliably. Use the zero profit method to determine the amount of revenue and profit recognized by Construk each year.

3. Assume that the costs of constructing this project could not be estimated reliably prior to starting the construction. Use the completed contract method to determine the amount of profit that would be recognized each year.

4. Compare the three revenue recognition methods with respect to the recognition of profit each year and for the three-year period as a whole.

We strongly recommend that you prepare your own answers to these requirements and then check your answers with the following solution.

SUGGESTED **SOLUTION**

1., 2., and 3.

	Year 1	Year 2	Year 3	Three-Year Period
Actual costs incurred per year	$90	$120	$90	$300
Percentage of completion method				
Percentage of work completed (= Annual cost ÷ Total costs)	30%	40%	30%	
Revenue (= Contract price × Percentage of work completed)	120	160	120	400
Profit (= Revenue − Actual costs)	30	40	30	100
Zero profit method				
Revenue (= Actual costs)	90	120	190	400
Expenses	90	120	90	300
Profit (= Revenue − Actual costs)	0	0	100	100
Completed contract method				
Revenue	0	0	400	400
Expenses*	0	0	300	300
Profit (= Revenue − Expenses)	0	0	100	100

*The costs incurred each year are accumulated in an asset account until the project is completed. They are recognized as expenses in the year of the completion of the project.

4. The percentage of completion method recognizes each year a proportion of the overall profit based on the percentage of work completed. Neither the completed contract nor the zero profit method recognizes profit during the first two years of the contract period, but both recognize the total amount of profit during the third year. These two methods differ, however, with respect to the amounts of revenue and expense recognized each year. All three methods show the same amount of profit, $100 million, over the three-year period.

APPENDIX 7B: RECORDING DISCOUNTS AND RETURNS

In the chapter, both *credit card discounts* and *cash discounts* have been recorded as contra revenues. For example, if the credit card company charges a 3 percent fee for its service, and credit card sales were $3,000 at a factory store for January 2, the sales transaction is recorded as follows:

Cash (A)	2,910	
Credit card discount (XR or E)	90	
Sales revenue (R)		3,000

Assets		=	Liabilities	+	Shareholders' Equity	
Cash	+2,910				Sales revenue	+3,000
					Credit card discount	−90

Similarly, if credit sales are recorded with terms 2/10, n/30 ($1,000 × 0.98 = $980), and payment is made within the discount period, the selling company records the following:

Trade receivables (A)	1,000	
Sales revenue (R)		1,000

Assets		=	Liabilities	+	Shareholders' Equity	
Trade receivables	+1,000				Sales revenue	+1,000

Cash (A)	980	
Sales discount (XR or E)	20	
Trade receivables (A)		1,000

Assets		=	Liabilities	+	Shareholders' Equity	
Cash	+980				Sales discount	−20
Trade receivables	−1,000					

Sales Returns and Allowances should always be treated as a contra-revenue account. Assume that the T-shirt Company bought 1,000 T-shirts for $6,000 on account. On the date of sale, the selling company makes the following journal entry:

Trade receivables (A)	6,000	
Sales revenue (R)		6,000

Assets		=	Liabilities	+	Shareholders' Equity	
Trade receivables	+6,000				Sales revenue	+6,000

Before paying for the T-shirts, the T-shirt Company discovered that 50 T-shirts were not the colour ordered and returned them to the seller. On that date, the seller records the following:

| Sales returns and allowances (XR) .... | 300 | |
| Trade receivables (A) .... | | 300 |

Assets		=	Liabilities	+	Shareholders' Equity	
Trade receivables	−300				Sales returns and allowances	−300

In addition, the related cost of sales entry for the 50 T-shirts would be reversed and the T-shirts returned to inventory. If the returned merchandise is defective, then it has to be reworked before it can be restored to inventory. Accounting for returned merchandise that is either defective or damaged is discussed in other accounting courses.

CHAPTER **TAKE-AWAYS**

1. **Apply the revenue principle to determine the accepted time to record sales revenue for typical retailers, wholesalers, manufacturers, and service companies.**
   Revenue recognition policies are widely recognized as one of the most important determinants of the fair presentation of financial statements. For most merchandisers and manufacturers, the required revenue recognition point is the time of shipment or delivery of goods. For service companies, it is the time at which services are provided.

2. **Analyze the impact of credit card sales, sales discounts, and sales returns on the amounts reported as net sales.**
   Both credit card discounts and cash discounts can be recorded either as contra revenues or as expenses. When recorded as contra revenues, they reduce net sales. Sales returns and allowances, which should always be treated as contra revenues, also reduce net sales.

3. **Compute and interpret the gross profit percentage.**
   The gross profit percentage measures the ability to charge premium prices and produce goods and services at lower cost. Managers, analysts, and creditors use this ratio to assess the effectiveness of the company's product development, marketing, and production strategy.

4. **Estimate, report, and evaluate the effects of uncollectible trade receivables (bad debts) on financial statements.**
   When receivables are material, companies must employ the allowance method to account for uncollectibles. The steps in the process are as follows:
   1. Prepare the end-of-period adjusting entry to record an estimate of bad debt expense.
   2. Write off specific accounts determined to be uncollectible during the period.
   3. Recover amounts previously written off.
   The adjusting entry reduces net earnings as well as net trade receivables. The write-off of trade receivables affects neither.

5. **Compute and interpret the receivables turnover ratio and the effects of trade receivables on cash flows.**
   The receivables turnover ratio measures the effectiveness of credit granting and collection activities. It reflects how many times average trade receivables were recorded and collected during the period. Analysts and creditors watch this ratio because a sudden decline may mean that a company is extending collection deadlines in an attempt to prop up lagging sales, or is even recording sales that will later be returned by customers. Alternatively, the average collection period indicates the average number of days it takes to collect from customers.
   When a net decrease in trade receivables for the period occurs, cash collected from customers exceeds revenue and cash flows from operations increase. When a net increase in trade receivables occurs, cash collected from customers is less than revenue; thus, the cash flow from operations declines.

6. **Report, control, and safeguard cash.**

   Cash is the most liquid of all assets, flowing continuously into and out of a business. As a result, a number of critical control procedures, including the reconciliation of bank accounts, should be applied. Also, management of cash may be critically important to decision makers who must have cash available to meet current needs, yet must avoid excess amounts of idle cash that produce no revenue.

7. **Reconcile cash accounts and bank statements.**

   A bank reconciliation compares (reconciles) the ending cash balance in the company's records to the ending cash balance reported by the bank on the monthly bank statement. It also identifies the accounts that must be adjusted as a result of this process.

   Closely related to recording revenue is recording the cost of what was sold. Chapter 8 will focus on transactions related to inventory and cost of sales. This topic is important because cost of sales has a major impact on a company's gross profit and net earnings, which are watched closely by investors, analysts, and other users of financial statements. Increasing emphasis on quality, productivity, and costs has further focused production managers' attention on cost of sales and inventory. Since inventory cost figures play a major role in product introduction and pricing decisions, they are also important to marketing and general managers. Finally, since inventory accounting has a major effect on many companies' tax liabilities, this is an important place to introduce the effect of taxation on management decision making and financial reporting.

KEY **RATIOS**

The gross profit percentage measures the excess of sales prices over the costs to purchase or produce the goods or services sold, as a percentage. It is computed as follows:

$$\text{Gross Profit Percentage} = \frac{\text{Gross Profit}}{\text{Net Sales}}$$

The receivables turnover ratio measures the effectiveness of credit granting and collection activities. It is computed as follows:

$$\text{Receivables Turnover Ratio} = \frac{\text{Net Credit Sales}}{\text{Average Net Trade Receivables}}$$

FINDING **FINANCIAL INFORMATION**

STATEMENT OF FINANCIAL POSITION

Under Current Assets

Trade receivables (net of allowance for doubtful accounts)

STATEMENT OF EARNINGS

Revenues

Net sales (sales revenue less discounts, if treated as contra revenues, and sales returns and allowances)

Expenses

Selling expenses (including bad debt expense and discounts if treated as expenses)

STATEMENT OF CASH FLOWS

Under Operating Activities (indirect method)

Net earnings

+ decrease in trade and other receivables (net)

− increase in trade and other receivables (net)

NOTES

Under Summary of Significant Accounting Policies

Revenue recognition policy

GLOSSARY

■ connect

Review key terms and definitions on *Connect*.

QUESTIONS

1. Explain the difference between sales revenue and net sales.
2. What is gross profit or gross margin on sales? How is the gross profit ratio computed? In your explanation, assume that net sales revenue is $100,000 and cost of sales is $60,000.
3. What is a credit card discount? How does it affect amounts reported on the statement of earnings?
4. What is a sales discount? Use credit terms 1/10, n/30 in your explanation.
5. What is the distinction between sales allowances and sales discounts?
6. Differentiate trade receivables from notes receivable.
7. Which basic accounting concept is satisfied by using the allowance method of accounting for bad debts?
8. Using the allowance method, is bad debt expense recognized in (*a*) the period in which sales related to the uncollectible amounts were made or (*b*) the period in which the seller learns that the customer is unable to pay?
9. What is the effect of the write-off of bad debts (using the allowance method) on (*a*) net earnings and (*b*) net trade receivables?
10. Does an increase in the receivables turnover ratio generally indicate faster or slower collection of receivables? Explain.
11. Define cash and cash equivalents in the context of accounting. Indicate the types of items that should be included.
12. Summarize the primary characteristics of an effective internal control system for cash.
13. Trade receivables are typically collected within three months from the date of sale. Can they be considered cash equivalents? Explain.
14. Why should cash-handling and cash-recording activities be separated? How is this separation accomplished?
15. What are the purposes of bank reconciliation? What balances are reconciled?
16. Briefly explain how the total amount of cash reported on the statement of financial position is computed.
17. (Appendix 7A) When is it acceptable to use the percentage of completion method?
18. (Appendix 7B) Under the gross method of recording sales discounts, is the amount of sales discount taken recorded (*a*) at the time the sale is recorded or (*b*) at the time the collection of the account is recorded?

EXERCISES

■ connect

E7–1   Interpreting the Revenue Principle

■ LO1

Identify the most likely point in time when sales revenue should be recorded for each of the listed transactions.

Transaction	Point A	Point B
a. Airline tickets sold by an airline on a credit card.	_____ Point of sale	_____ Completion of flight
b. Computer sold by mail-order company on a credit card.	_____ Shipment	_____ Delivery to customer
c. Sale of inventory to a business customer on open account.	_____ Shipment	_____ Collection from customers

LO2

E7–2 Reporting Net Sales with Credit Sales and Sales Discounts

During the months of January and February, Silver Corporation sold goods to three customers on open account. The sequence of events was as follows:

Jan. 6 Sold goods for $850 to S. Green and billed that amount subject to terms of 2/10, n/30.
    9 Sold goods to M. Munoz for $700 and billed that amount subject to terms of 2/10, n/30.
   14 Collected cash due from S. Green.
Feb. 2 Collected cash due from M. Munoz.
   28 Sold goods for $450 to R. Reynolds and billed that amount subject to terms of 2/10, n/45.

Required:

1. Assuming that sales discounts are treated as contra revenues, compute net sales for the two months ended February 28.
2. Prepare the journal entries to record the transactions that occurred on January 6 and 14.

LO2

E7–3 Reporting Net Sales with Credit Sales, Sales Discounts, and Credit Card Sales

The following transactions were selected from the records of Evergreen Company:

July 12 Sold merchandise to Rami, who charged the $1,000 purchase on his Visa credit card. Visa charges Evergreen a 2 percent credit card fee.
   15 Sold merchandise to Steven at an invoice price of $6,000; terms 2/10, n/30.
   20 Sold merchandise to Tania at an invoice price of $2,000; terms 2/10, n/30.
   23 Collected payment from Steven from July 15 sale.
Aug. 25 Collected payment from Tania from July 20 sale.

Required:

1. Assuming that sales discounts are treated as contra revenues, compute net sales for the two months ended August 31.
2. Prepare the journal entries to record the transactions that occurred on July 12, 15, and 23.

LO2

E7–4 Reporting Net Sales with Credit Sales, Sales Discounts, Sales Returns, and Credit Card Sales

The following transactions were selected from among those completed by Gunzo Wholesalers in 2014:

Nov. 20 Sold two items of merchandise to Brigitte, who charged the $800 sales amount on her Visa credit card. Visa charges Gunzo a 2 percent credit card fee.
   25 Sold 20 items of merchandise to Clara for $5,000; terms 2/10, n/30.
   28 Sold 10 identical items of merchandise to David for $6,000; terms 2/10, n/30.
   30 David returned one of the items purchased on the 28th; the item was defective, and credit was given to the customer.
Dec. 6 David paid the account balance in full.
   30 Clara paid in full the amount due for the purchase on November 25, 2014.

Required:

1. Assuming that sales discounts and credit card discounts are treated as contra revenues, compute net sales for the two months ended December 31, 2014.
2. Prepare the journal entries to record the transactions that occurred on November 20, November 25, and December 30.

LO2

E7–5 Determining the Effects of Credit Sales, Sales Discounts, Credit Card Sales, and Sales Returns and Allowances on Statement of Earnings Categories

Rockland Shoe Company records sales returns and allowances as contra revenues, and sales discounts and credit card discounts as selling expenses. Complete the following tabulation, indicating the effect (+ for increase, − for decrease, and NE for no effect) of each transaction. Do not record the related cost of sales.

July 12 Sold merchandise to Rosa, who charged the $400 purchase on her American Express card. American Express charges a 3 percent credit card fee.
   15 Sold merchandise to Thomas for $6,000; terms 2/10, n/30.
   20 Collected the amount due from Thomas.
   21 Lee returned shoes with an invoice price of $1,000 before he paid for them.

Transaction	Net Sales	Gross Profit	Earnings from Operations
July 12			
July 15			
July 20			
July 21			

E7–6 Evaluating the Effects of Sales Returns and Allowances on Sales

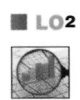

■ LO2

Teen World Inc. sells a wide selection of clothing items for teenage girls. The company imports merchandise from various international suppliers and distributes its merchandise to retail stores in major shopping areas. The company sells merchandise on credit, allows retailers to return incorrect or damaged merchandise within a period of two months, and grants sales allowances under certain circumstances. The company is currently reviewing its sales returns policy and provided you with the following information for the past six quarters:

Quarter	Gross Sales	Cost of Sales	Sales Returns and Allowances
Jan. 1–March 31, 2014	$1,346,300	$ 942,400	$ 53,852
April 1–June 30, 2014	1,474,500	1,042,100	76,674
July 1–Sept. 30, 2014	1,529,100	1,080,300	94,804
Oct. 1–Dec. 31, 2014	1,671,400	1,101,200	140,397
Jan. 1–March 31, 2015	1,708,800	1,103,600	153,792
April 1–June 30, 2015	1,992,700	1,317,500	219,197

Required:

1. Compute the following ratios for each of the six quarters: (*a*) cost of sales to net sales and (*b*) sales return and allowances to gross sales.

2. Comment on the ratios computed in (1) and identify possible reasons for the increase in the amount of sales returns and allowances, and give your recommendations for controlling the amount of sales returns and allowances.

E7–7 Analyzing Gross Profit Percentage on the Basis of a Multiple-Step Statement of Earnings

■ LO3

The following summarized data were provided by the records of Slate Inc. for the year ended December 31, 2014:

Sales of merchandise for cash	$233,000
Sales of merchandise on credit	40,000
Cost of sales	146,000
Selling expenses	47,200
Administrative expenses	20,000
Sales returns and allowances	8,000
Bad debt expense	1,200
Items not included in the above amounts:	
Average income tax rate, 30%	
Number of common shares outstanding, 4,500	

Required:

1. Based on these data, prepare a multiple-step statement of earnings (showing both gross profit and earnings from operations).

2. What was the amount of gross profit? What was the gross profit percentage? Explain what these two numbers mean.

E7–8 Analyzing Gross Profit Percentage on the Basis of a Multiple-Step Statement of Earnings and Within-Industry Comparison

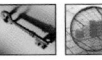

■ LO3

Wood Work Inc. and Modern Furniture Ltd. are two large home furnishing retailers, selling a wide range of furniture, major appliances, and home electronics. The following data were taken from the 2014 annual reports of both companies (amounts in thousands of Canadian dollars):

	Wood Work	Modern Furniture
Sales revenue	$1,341,080	$682,183
Income taxes expense	15,189	16,901
Cash dividends declared	2,443	28,047
Operating expenses	511,897	223,126
Cost of sales	748,047	398,704
Finance expense (income), net	34,272	(3,350)
Other income	2,317	–
Number of common shares outstanding (in millions)	120.8	70.0

Required:

1. Based on these data, prepare a multiple-step statement of earnings for each company for the year ending December 31, 2014 (showing both gross profit and earnings from operations).

2. Compute the gross profit and the gross profit percentage for each company. Explain what these two numbers mean. What do you believe accounts for the difference between the gross profit percentages of both companies?

■ LO4   **E7–9 Computing Bad Debt Expense by Using Aging Analysis**

Brown Cow Dairy uses the aging approach to estimate bad debt expense. The balance of each account receivable is aged on the basis of three time periods as follows: (1) not yet due, $25,000; (2) up to 120 days past due, $10,000; and (3) more than 120 days past due, $5,000. Experience has shown that, for each age group, the average bad debt rates on the receivables at year-end due to uncollectibility are (1) 2 percent, (2) 10 percent, and (3) 30 percent, respectively. At December 31, 2014 (end of the current year), the allowance for doubtful accounts balance was $600 (credit) before the end-of-period adjusting entry was made.

Required:
What amount should be recorded as bad debt expense for the current year?

■ LO4   **E7–10 Computing Bad Debt Expense by Using Aging Analysis and Reporting Trade Receivables**

The Nestlé Group

The Nestlé Group disclosed the following analysis of its trade receivables at December 31, 2012 (amounts in millions of Swiss francs, CHF):

Aged Trade Receivables	Amount
Not past due	10,925
Past due 1–30 days	1,356
Past due 31–60 days	445
Past due 61–90 days	168
Past due 91–120 days	95
Past due more than 120 days	798
	13,787

Assume that the estimated percentages of uncollectible accounts were determined as 1 percent, 5 percent, 10 percent, 20 percent, 30 percent, and 40 percent for the six age groups, respectively. At January 1, 2012, the allowance for doubtful accounts had a balance of CHF372, and a total of CHF95 was written off as uncollectible during 2012. The company recovered CHF15 from customers whose accounts were written off in 2011.

Required:

1. Prepare the journal entries to record the receivables that were written off in 2012, the recovery of receivables written off in 2011, and the bad debt expense for 2012.

2. Show how the information related to trade receivables is presented on the company's statement of financial position as at December 31, 2012.

E7–11 Interpreting Bad Debt Disclosures
■ **LO4**

Daimler AG is a globally leading producer of premium passenger cars and the largest manufacturer of commercial vehicles in the world. Its group of businesses includes Mercedes-Benz Cars, Daimler Trucks, Daimler Financial Services, Mercedes-Benz Vans, and Daimler Buses. In a recent annual report, it disclosed the following information concerning its allowance for doubtful accounts:

Allowances. Changes in the allowance account for receivables from financial service were as follows:			
(in millions of euros)	**2012**	**2011**	**2010**
Balance at January 1	946	1,084	1,168
Charged to costs and expenses	370	394	534
Amounts written off	(235)	(213)	(439)
Reversals	(132)	(299)	(241)
Currency translation and other changes	(11)	(20)	62
Balance at December 31	938	946	1,084
Source: Daimler AG, Annual Report 2012.			

Required:

1. Record summary journal entries related to bad debts for the current year. Ignore the currency translations and other changes.
2. If Daimler had written off an additional €10 million of trade receivables during the period, how would net receivables and net earnings have been affected? Explain.

E7–12 Interpreting Disclosures Related to Credit Card Receivables
■ **LO4**

Wood Work Ltd. sells home furnishings, including a wide range of furniture, major appliances, and home electronics. In a recent annual report, it disclosed the following information concerning its trade receivables.

Aging of trade receivables, and the related impairment allowances, are provided in the following table (in thousands of dollars):

	Doubtful Accounts 2014	
Current	$19,500	$ –
31–60 days	5,000	100
61–90 days	2,300	65
91–120 days	3,400	985
More than 120 days	–	–
	$30,200	$1,150

The changes to the allowance for doubtful trade receivables for 2014 were as follows:

	2014
Balance at beginning of year	$1,200
Impairment losses for unrecoverable receivables	1,300
Amounts written off as uncollectible	(1,150)
Balance at end of year	$1,350

Required:

1. Compute the percentage of uncollectible accounts for each category of receivables that are past due, and comment on the results.
2. How did the company determine the losses due to unrecoverable receivables or bad debt expense?
3. Record summary journal entries related to bad debts for the current year.
4. If Wood Work had written off an amount of an additional $10,000 in trade receivables during the period, how would net trade receivables and net earnings have been affected? Explain.

■ **LO4**

Microsoft

E7–13 **Inferring Bad Debt Write-Offs and Cash Collections from Customers**

Microsoft develops, produces, and markets a wide range of computer software, including the Windows operating system. In a recent annual report, Microsoft reported the following information about trade receivables and net sales revenue:

	Year 2	Year 1
Trade receivables, net of allowances of $333 and $375	$14,987	$13,014
Net revenues	68,643	62,484

According to its annual report, Microsoft recorded bad debt expense of $14 during year 2 and did not reinstate any previously written-off accounts.

Required:

1. What amount of bad debts was written off during year 2?
2. Assuming that all of Microsoft's sales during the period were on open account, compute the amount of cash collected from customers for year 2.

■ **LO4**

Bombardier

E7–14 **Determining the Impact of Uncollectible Accounts on Net Earnings and Working Capital**

An annual report for Bombardier Inc. contained the following information at the end of its fiscal year (in millions of dollars):

	Year 2	Year 1
Trade receivables	$1,559	$1,450
Allowance for uncollectible accounts	(34)	(42)
	$1,525	$1,408

A footnote to the financial statements disclosed that uncollectible accounts of $5 million and $17 million were written off as bad debts during years 1 and 2, respectively. Assume that the tax rate for Bombardier was 30 percent.

Required:

1. Determine the bad debt expense for year 2 based on the preceding facts.
2. Working capital is defined as current assets minus current liabilities. How was Bombardier's working capital affected by the write-off of $17 million in uncollectible accounts during year 2? What impact did the recording of bad debt expense have on working capital in year 2?
3. How was net earnings affected by the $17 million write-off during year 2? What impact did recording bad debt expense have on net earnings for year 2?

■ **LO5**

Dell Inc.

E7–15 **Computing and Interpreting the Receivables Turnover Ratio**

Dell Inc. is a global information technology company that offers its customers a broad range of solutions and services delivered directly by Dell and through other distribution channels. A recent annual report contained the following data:

	(dollars in millions)	
	Current Year	Previous Year
Accounts receivable	$ 6,539	$6,598
Less: Allowance for doubtful accounts	63	95
Accounts receivable, net	$ 6,476	$6,503
Net sales (assume all on credit)	$62,071	

Required:

1. Determine the receivables turnover ratio and average collection period for the current year.
2. Explain the meaning of each number.

E7–16 Analyzing and Interpreting the Receivables Turnover Ratio

The Benetton Group is one of the world's largest manufacturers of casual knitwear and sportswear for men, women, and children. Its annual reports include the following details, reported in thousands of euros:

■ **LO5**

The Benetton Group

Year	2011	2010	2009	2008	2007	2006
Net sales	€2,032,341	€2,053,059	€2,049,259	€2,127,941	€2,085,272	€1,910,975
Net trade receivables	889,330	798,320	786,476	781,458	680,741	610,741

Required:

1. Determine the receivables turnover ratio and average collection period for 2007–2011, and comment on the results.
2. Explain the meaning of the numbers that you calculated in (1).

E7–17 Comparing Receivables Turnover Ratios of Two Companies

Aer Lingus provides passenger and cargo transportation services from Ireland to markets in the United Kingdom, continental Europe, and the United States. It uses the euro as the monetary unit for financial reporting purposes. WestJet Airlines is a Canadian airline that serves more than 65 destinations, mainly in Canada but also in the United States, the Caribbean, and Mexico. The net sales and average balances of trade receivables for Aer Lingus and WestJet Airlines for a recent fiscal year are shown below:

■ **LO5**

Aer Lingus

WestJet Airlines

	Aer Lingus		WestJet Airlines	
	2012	2011	2012	2011
Net revenues	€1,393,284	€1,288,309	$3,427,409	$3,071,540
Trade receivables (net)	42,273	29,138	37,576	34,122

Required:

1. Compute the following for each company for 2012:
   a. The receivables turnover ratio.
   b. The average collection period.
2. Based on your computations for (1), which company's trade receivables appear to be the more "liquid" asset? Explain.
3. The companies use different currencies to prepare their financial statements. Does the use of different currencies affect the interpretation of the receivables turnover ratio and the average collection period? Explain.

E7–18 Interpreting the Effects of Sales Growth and Changes in Receivables on Cash Flow from Operations

Apple Computer Inc. is best known for its iMac, iPod, iPad, and iPhone product lines. Three recent years produced a combination of dramatic increases in sales revenue and net earnings. Cash flows from operations also increased during the period. Contributing to that increasing cash flow was the change in trade receivables. The current- and prior-year statements of financial position reported the following (in millions of U.S. dollars):

■ **LO5**

Apple Computer Inc.

	Current Year	Previous Year
Trade receivables, less allowance for doubtful accounts	$5,369	$5,910

Required:

1. How would the change in trade receivables affect cash flow from operations for the current year? Explain why it would have this effect.
2. Explain how increasing sales revenue often leads to (*a*) increasing trade receivables and (*b*) an excess of sales revenue over collections from customers.
3. The company reported $108,249 million in net sales for the current year. Compute the receivables turnover ratio and the average collection period for the current year. Are the computed numbers useful to an investor? Explain.

■ LO6   **E7–19**   **Identifying Strengths and Weaknesses of Internal Control**

You have been engaged to review the internal control procedures used by Data Flow Inc. During the course of your review, you note the following practices:

a. The credit manager maintains the trade receivables records and handles all collections from customers, because the accounting department personnel are not authorized to handle cash receipts.

b. All cash received from customers is deposited daily in the company's bank account.

c. Employees who handle cash receipts are not permitted to write off trade receivables as uncollectible.

d. Invoices that require payment are first verified by the accounting personnel for accuracy. An accounting clerk stamps them "paid" if they are cleared for payment, and sends them to the treasurer, who issues and signs the cheques.

e. The cheques issued by the company treasurer are not pre-numbered.

f. After preparing the bank reconciliation, any difference between the adjusted cash balance per the company's books and the adjusted balance per the bank statement is debited (or credited) to the cash account.

Required:

Indicate whether each of these six practices reflects a strength or a weakness of the internal control system. Provide justification for your answer.

■ LO6   **E7–20**   **Internal Control over Cash**

Organic Growers Inc. is a successful grower of summer fruits and vegetables. The company has a seasonal business that starts in June and ends in October. The owners use a vast agricultural terrain to grow a variety of vegetables and fruits. They employ four workers to help during the planting season and to pick the vegetables and fruits as they become ready for consumption. To save on the cost of harvesting the produce, the owners allow customers to pick the produce they like from the field and then collect the cash for the goods sold. They also have a small store where they keep small quantities of produce for sale to customers who do not wish to pick the produce themselves. Receipts for the purchased goods are given only to those who ask for them. During the summer, the owners accumulate enough cash to pay for farm supplies at the time they are delivered. They do so to avoid wasting time preparing cheques and balancing the chequebook.

Required:

How can Organic Growers strengthen its internal control over cash and improve on its overall cash management?

■ LO6   **E7–21**   **Reporting Cash and Cash Equivalents When There Are Several Bank Accounts**

Singh Corporation has manufacturing facilities in several cities and has cash on hand at several locations, as well as in several bank accounts. The general ledger at the end of 2014 showed the following accounts:

Cash on hand—Home Office	$ 700	Cash on hand—Location C	$ 200
City Bank—Home Office	58,600	National Bank—Location C	965
Cash on hand—Location A	100	Petty cash fund	300
National Bank—Location A	3,350	Credit Suisse—3-month Certificate of Deposit	5,800
Cash on hand—Location B	200	FransaBank—6-month Certificate of Deposit	4,500
National Bank—Location B	785		

The bank balances given represent the current cash balances as reflected on the bank reconciliations.

Required:

What amount of cash and cash equivalents should be reported on the company's 2014 statement of financial position? Explain the basis for your decisions on any questionable items.

E7–22 Preparing Bank Reconciliation, Entries, and Reporting Cash   ■ LO7

The June 30, 2015, bank statement for Zoltan Company and the June ledger accounts for cash are summarized below:

Bank Statement			
	Cheques	**Deposits**	**Balance**
Balance, June 1, 2015			$ 6,900
Deposits during June		$16,200	23,100
Cheques cleared through June	$17,000		6,100
Bank service charges	40		6,060
Balance, June 30, 2015			6,060

Cash in Bank					
June 1	Balance	6,900	June	Cheques written	19,000
June	Deposits	18,100			

Cash on Hand	
June 30 Balance	300

Required:

1. Reconcile the bank balance to the book balance at June 30, 2015. A comparison of the cheques written with the cheques that have cleared the bank shows outstanding cheques of $2,000. No deposits in transit were carried over from May, but a deposit is in transit at the end of June.
2. Prepare any journal entries that should be made as a result of the bank reconciliation.
3. What is the balance in the cash in bank account after the reconciliation entries?
4. What is the total amount of cash that should be reported on the statement of financial position at June 30, 2015?

E7–23 Preparing Bank Reconciliation, Entries, and Reporting Cash   ■ LO7

The September 30, 2014, bank statement and the September ledger accounts for cash for Russell Company are summarized below:

Bank Statement			
	Cheques	**Deposits**	**Balance**
Balance, September 1, 2014			$ 6,500
Deposits recorded during September		$26,900	33,400
Cheques cleared during September	$27,400		6,000
NSF cheque—Betty Brown	170		5,830
Bank service charges	60		5,770
Balance, September 30, 2014			5,770

Cash in Bank					
Sept. 1	Balance	6,500	Sept.	Cheques written	28,900
Sept.	Deposits	28,100			

Cash on Hand	
Sept. 30 Balance	400

No outstanding cheques and no deposits in transit were carried over from August; however, there are deposits in transit and cheques outstanding at the end of September.

Required:

1. Reconcile the balance in the bank account with the cash balance in the books at September 30, 2014.
2. Prepare any journal entries that should be made as a result of the bank reconciliation.
3. What should be the balance in the cash in bank account after the reconciliation entries?
4. What total amount of cash should the company report on the statement of financial position at September 30, 2014?

■ LO7   **E7–24**   **Preparing Bank Reconciliation, Entries, and Reporting Cash**

The bank statement for the Mini Mart Corporation shows a balance of $1,330 on June 30, but the company's cash in bank account had a balance of $499 on the same date. Comparison of the amounts reported on the bank statement with the company's records indicates (*a*) deposits of $160, representing cash receipts of June 30, that did not appear on the bank statement; (*b*) outstanding cheques totalling $240; (*c*) bank service charges for June amounting to $9; (*d*) collection of a note receivable by the bank on behalf of the company for $800 plus $40 in interest revenue; and (*e*) a cheque for $80 from a customer that was returned with the bank statement and marked NSF.

Required:

1. Prepare a bank reconciliation statement for Mini Mart Corporation as at June 30.
2. Prepare any journal entries that should be made as a result of the bank reconciliation.
3. Why is it important to reconcile the balance in the bank statement with the cash balance in the company's records?
4. What is the amount of cash that the company should report on its statement of financial position at June 30?

E7–25   **(Appendix 7A) Determining Profit for a Construction Contract**

Blanchard Construction Company entered into a long-term construction contract with the government to build a special landing strip at an Air Force base in Saint Hubert, Québec. The project took three years and cost the government $12 million. Blanchard spent the following amounts each year: 2014, $2 million; 2015, $5 million; and 2016, $3 million. The company uses the percentage of completion method. Cost estimates equalled actual costs.

Required:

1. Determine the amount of profit that Blanchard can report each year for this project. Ignore income taxes.
2. Assume that the costs of this project could not be estimated reliably. What amount of profit should the company recognize in each of the three years? Explain.

E7–26   **(Appendix 7B) Recording Credit Sales, Sales Discounts, Sales Returns, and Credit Card Sales**

The following transactions were selected from among those completed by Hailey Retailers in 2014:

Nov. 20	Sold two items of merchandise to Baja, who charged the $450 sales amount on her Visa credit card. Visa charges Hailey a 2 percent credit card fee.
25	Sold 14 items of merchandise to Christine for $2,800; terms 2/10, n/30.
28	Sold 12 identical items of merchandise to Daoud for $7,200; terms 2/10, n/30.
30	Daoud returned one of the items purchased on the 28th; the item was defective, and credit was given to the customer.
Dec. 6	Daoud paid the account balance in full.
30	Christine paid in full the amount due for the purchase on November 25, 2014.

Required:

Prepare the appropriate journal entry for each of these transactions, assuming the company uses the gross method to record sales revenue. Do not record the cost of sales.

■ connect PROBLEMS

■ LO1   **P7–1**   **Applying the Revenue Principle** (AP7–1)

At what point should revenue be recognized in each of the following independent cases? Explain your answers.

Case A. For December holiday gifts, a fast-food restaurant sells coupon books for $10. Each of the $1 coupons in a book may be used in the restaurant at any time during the following 12 months. The customer must pay cash when purchasing the coupon book.

Case B. Howard Land Development Corporation sold a lot to Quality Builders to construct a new home. The price of the lot was $50,000. Quality made a down payment of $10,000 and agreed to pay the balance in six months. After making the sale, Howard learned that Quality Builders often entered into these agreements but refused to pay the balance if it did not find a customer who wanted a house built on the lot.

Case C. Driscoll Corporation has always recorded revenue at the point of sale of its refrigerators. Recently, it has extended its warranties to cover all repairs for a period of seven years. One young accountant with the company now questions whether Driscoll has completed its earning process when it sells the refrigerators. She suggests that the warranty obligation for seven years means that a significant amount of additional work must be performed in the future.

P7–2 **Reporting Net Sales and Expenses with Discounts, Returns, and Bad Debts** (AP7–2)

■ LO2, 4

The following data were selected from the records of Tunga Company for the year ended December 31, 2015:

Balances at January 1, 2015	
Trade receivables (various customers)	$115,000
Allowance for doubtful accounts	4,000

The company sells merchandise for cash and on open account with credit terms 2/10, n/30. Assume a unit sales price of $500 in all transactions, and use the gross method to record sales revenue.

The following transactions occurred during 2015:

a. Sold merchandise for cash, $234,000.

b. Sold merchandise to R. Agostino on open account for $11,500.

c. Sold merchandise to K. Black on open account for $25,000.

d. Two days after purchase, R. Agostino returned one of the units purchased in (b) and received account credit.

e. Sold merchandise to B. Assaf on open account for $26,000.

f. R. Agostino paid his account in full within the discount period.

g. Collected $98,000 cash from customers for credit sales made in 2015, all within the discount periods.

h. K. Black paid the invoice in (c) within the discount period.

i. Sold merchandise to R. Fong on open account for $17,500.

j. Three days after paying the account in full, K. Black returned seven defective units and received a cash refund.

k. Collected $6,000 cash on a trade receivable for sales made in 2014. The amount was received after the discount period.

l. Wrote off an old account of $3,000 after deciding that the amount would never be collected.

m. The company estimates that 4 percent of the trade receivables at December 31, 2015, will be uncollectible in the future.

Required:

1. Using the following categories, indicate the dollar effect (+ for increase, − for decrease, and N for no effect) of each listed transaction, including the write-off of the uncollectible account and the adjusting entry for estimated bad debts (ignore cost of sales). The effects of the first transaction are shown as an example:

Sales Revenue	Sales Discounts (taken)	Sales Returns and Allowances	Bad Debt Expense
a. $234,000	N	N	N

2. Show how the accounts related to the preceding sale and collection activities should be reported on the statement of earnings for 2015. (Treat sales discounts as contra revenues.)

■ **LO3**

eXcel

P7–3 **Understanding the Statement of Earnings Based on the Gross Profit Percentage** (AP7–3)

The following data were taken from the year-end records of Nomura Export Company:

Statement of Earnings Items	Year 1	Year 2
Gross sales revenue	$160,000	$232,000
Sales returns and allowances	?	18,000
Net sales revenue	?	?
Cost of sales	68%	?
Gross profit	?	30%
Operating expenses	18,000	?
Earnings before income taxes	?	20,000
Income tax expense (20%)	?	?
Net earnings	?	?
Earnings per share (10,000 shares outstanding)	2.40	?

Required:

Fill in all of the missing amounts. Show computations.

■ **LO4**

Peet's Coffee and Tea Inc.

P7–4 **Recording Bad Debts and Interpreting Disclosure of Allowance for Doubtful Accounts** (AP7–4)

Peet's Coffee and Tea Inc. is a specialty coffee roaster and marketer of branded fresh whole-bean coffee. It recently disclosed the following information concerning the allowance for doubtful accounts in its annual report (dollars in thousands):

Allowances for Doubtful Accounts	Balance at Beginning of Period	Additions (Charges) to Expense	Write-Offs	Balance at End of Period
Year 3	$283	$?	$201	$124
Year 2	132	187	?	283
Year 1	128	4	–	132

Required:

1. Record summary journal entries related to bad debts for year 1.
2. Supply the missing dollar amounts for year 2 and year 3.

■ **LO4**

P7–5 **Determining Bad Debt Expense Based on Aging Analysis** (AP7–5)

Green Pastures Equipment Company uses the aging approach to estimate bad debt expense at the end of each accounting year. Credit sales occur frequently on terms n/60. The balance of each trade receivable is aged on the basis of three time periods as follows: (1) not yet due, (2) up to one year past due, and (3) more than one year past due. Experience has shown that for each age group, the average bad debt rate on the amounts receivable at year-end due to uncollectibility are (1) 1 percent, (2) 5 percent, and (3) 30 percent, respectively.

At December 31, 2014 (end of the current accounting year), the trade receivables balance was $45,000, and the unadjusted balance of the allowance for doubtful accounts was $1,020 (credit). To simplify, the accounts of only five customers are used; the details of each are given below:

Date	Explanation	Debit	Credit	Balance
	B. Brown—Trade Receivable			
11/3/2013	Sale	$13,000		$13,000
30/6/2013	Collection		$4,000	9,000
31/1/2014	Collection		3,000	6,000
	D. Di Lella—Trade Receivable			
28/2/2014	Sale	22,000		22,000
15/4/2014	Collection		10,000	12,000
30/11/2014	Collection		7,000	5,000
	N. Gidda—Trade Receivable			
30/11/2014	Sale	9,000		9,000
15/12/2014	Collection		2,000	7,000
	S. Kavouris—Trade Receivable			
1/2/2014	Sale	19,000		21,000
1/3/2014	Collection		5,000	16,000
2/3/2012	Sale	5,000		5,000
15/4/2012	Collection		5,000	0
1/9/2013	Sale	10,000		10,000
15/10/2013	Collection		8,000	2,000
31/12/2014	Sale	4,000		20,000
	T. Patel—Trade Receivable			
30/12/2014	Sale	7,000		7,000

Required:

1. Prepare an aging analysis schedule and complete it.
2. Compute the estimated uncollectible amount for each age category and in total.
3. Prepare the adjusting entry for bad debt expense at December 31, 2014.
4. Show how the amounts related to trade receivables should be presented on the statement of earnings for 2014 and the statement of financial position at December 31, 2014.

P7–6 Determining Bad Debt Expense Based on Aging Analysis and Interpreting Ratios (AP7–6)   ■ LO4
IceKreme Inc. makes ice cream machines for sale to ice cream parlours. The following events occurred between April 1 and June 30, 2014:

April 10	Received an order from Peter's Appliances, a wholesaler, for 10 machines.
April 30	Sold 15 machines to Yuri Inc. on credit.
May 1	The purchasing manager of Peter's Appliances visited IceKreme's factory and purchased 12 machines instead of the 10 machines that were previously ordered.
May 5	Yuri Inc. paid for the machines purchased on April 30.
May 7	Sold 10 machines to Cheng Ltd. on credit.
May 10	Wrote off $12,000 of trade receivables that were considered uncollectible. These receivables relate to sales made prior to April 1, 2014.
May 15	Peter's Appliances returned two defective machines and paid the amount due.
June 1	Received $80,000 from Cheng Ltd. on account.
June 30	Recovered $3,000 from the receivables that were written off on May 10.

Additional information is as follows:

- IceKreme sold all machines at $10,000 per unit.

- All of IceKreme's sales were on credit with terms 2/10, n/30.

- IceKreme's records included the following items and their balances as at March 31, 2014:

Trade receivables.	$ 60,000
Allowance of doubtful accounts (credit balance)	15,000
Net sales	600,000

Required:

1. Prepare the journal entries to record the transactions that occurred from April 1 to June 30, 2014.

2. The company uses the *aging of trade receivables* method to determine the amount of bad debt expense. The estimated uncollectible rates for the various age groups are as follows:

| | Age of trade receivables | | | |
	Not yet due	1–30 days past due	31–60 days past due	Over 60 days past due
Estimated % uncollectible	5%	10%	15%	20%

Determine the amount of receivables that may not be collectible in the future, and prepare the journal entry to record bad debt expense at June 30, 2014, the company's fiscal year-end. (*Hint*: Use a time line to keep track of trade receivables in order to determine the age of these receivables.)

3. IceKreme's net trade receivables were $60,000 at June 30, 2013. Calculate IceKreme's average collection period for fiscal year 2014 and explain its meaning.

4. Evaluate IceKreme's average collection period, knowing that two major competitors, Julia Corp. and Pino Ltd., reported average collection periods of 18.3 days and 30.7 days, respectively, for fiscal year 2014.

■ LO3, 4, 5   **P7–7**   **Recording Receivables Transactions, Determining Bad Debt Expense, and Interpreting Ratios** (AP7–7)

At December 1, 2014, Imalda Inc. reported the following information on its statement of financial position:

Trade receivables	$154,000
Allowance for doubtful accounts	4,500 (credit balance)

The following transactions were completed during December 2014:

December 5	Sold merchandise items for $67,000. An amount of $19,000 was received in cash and the rest on account; terms 2/10, n/60. The total cost of sales was $35,000.
December 12	Collected cash for *half* of the credit sales made on December 5.
December 20	Collected $90,000 in cash from customers for credit sales made in November 2014.
December 26	One of Imalda's customers that owed $3,000 to the company experienced financial problems and was forced to close its business in December. The full amount was considered uncollectible.

Imalda uses the aging of trade receivables method to determine bad debt expense. The aging schedule at December 31, 2014, gives the following information about the trade receivables estimated uncollectible:

| | Age of trade receivables | | | |
	Current	1–30 days past due	31–60 days past due	Over 60 days past due
Total	42,000	31,500	5,000	6,500
Estimated % uncollectible	1%	2%	10%	30%

Required:

1. Prepare the journal entries to record the transactions that occurred in December 2014.

2. Using the aging schedule, compute the bad debt expense for December 2014 and prepare the related adjusting entry.

3. Compute the gross profit percentage and the receivables turnover ratio for December 2014 and explain their meaning.

■ LO4   **P7–8**   **Determining Bad Debts and Reporting Trade Receivables** (AP7–8)

The bookkeeper of Vital Inc. has asked you to assist him with the preparation of information about the company's trade receivables for presentation in the statement of financial position at December

31, 2015, the end of the company's fiscal year. The following details have been extracted from the company's files:

	Debit	Credit
Trade receivables, January 1, 2015	$500,000	
Allowance for doubtful accounts, January 1, 2015		$25,000

Sales for 2015 totalled $1,300,000; $300,000 were in cash and the rest on account. The company collected $1,100,000 from credit customers during 2015 and wrote off $30,000 of trade receivables as uncollectible.

Required:

1. Determine the balance of trade receivables at December 31, 2015.

2. Vital estimates that 6 percent of the ending balance of its trade receivables may not be collected in the future. Prepare the journal entries to record the write-off of trade receivables and the bad debt expense for 2015.

3. Show how the information related to trade receivables is presented on the company's statement of financial position as at December 31, 2015.

4. After you finished helping the bookkeeper with the journal entries and the statement of financial position presentation, he said, "These calculations seem to be complicated. Would it not be simpler to treat the $30,000 as bad debt expense when the company is certain that the customers are not able to pay the amount owed? That way, you record the exact amount of bad debt when it happens, and you do not have to estimate an amount of doubtful accounts and risk being incorrect." Prepare a response to the bookkeeper.

P7–9 Preparing a Multiple-Step Statement of Earnings and Computing the Gross Profit Percentage and Receivables Turnover Ratio with Discounts, Returns, and Bad Debts (AP7–9)

■ LO2, 3, 4, 5

e**X**cel

Builders Company Inc. sells heavy-construction equipment. It has 10,000 common shares outstanding and its fiscal year ends on December 31. The adjusted trial balance was taken from the general ledger on December 31, 2014:

Account Titles	Debit	Credit
Cash	$ 33,600	
Trade receivables (net)	14,400	
Inventory, ending	52,000	
Property, plant, and equipment	40,000	
Accumulated depreciation		$ 16,800
Liabilities		24,000
Common shares		72,000
Retained earnings, January 1, 2014		9,280
Sales revenue		145,600
Sales returns and allowances	5,600	
Cost of sales	78,400	
Selling expenses	13,600	
Administrative expenses	14,400	
Bad debt expense	1,600	
Sales discounts	6,400	
Income tax expense	7,680	
Totals	$267,680	$267,680

Required:

1. Prepare a multiple-step statement of earnings (showing both gross profit and net earnings from operations). Treat sales discounts as contra revenues.

2. The beginning balance of trade receivables (net) was $16,000. Compute the gross profit percentage and receivables turnover ratio and explain their meaning.

■ LO**6**

P7–10   Evaluating Internal Controls (AP7–10)

Cripple Creek Company has one trusted employee, who, as the owner said, "handles all of the bookkeeping and paperwork for the company." This employee is responsible for counting, verifying, and recording cash receipts and payments, making the weekly bank deposit, preparing cheques for major expenditures (signed by the owner), making small expenditures from the cash register for daily expenses, and collecting trade receivables. The owner asked the local bank for a $20,000 loan. The bank asked that an audit be performed covering the year just ended. The independent auditor, in a private conference with the owner, presented some evidence of the following activities of the trusted employee during the past year:

a. Cash sales sometimes were not entered in the cash register, and the trusted employee pocketed approximately $50 per month.

b. Cash taken from the cash register (and pocketed by the trusted employee) was replaced with expense memos with fictitious signatures (approximately $12 per day). Cripple Creek is open five days per week throughout the year.

c. A $300 collection on a trade receivable of a valued out-of-town customer was pocketed by the trusted employee and was covered by making a $300 entry as a debit to sales returns and a credit to trade receivables.

d. An $800 collection on a trade receivable from a local customer was pocketed by the trusted employee and was covered by making an $800 entry as a debit to allowance for doubtful accounts and a credit to trade receivables.

Required:

1. What was the approximate amount stolen during the past year?
2. What would be your recommendations to the owner about the company's internal controls?

■ LO**7**

P7–11   Preparing a Bank Reconciliation (AP7–11)

The president of Kostas Fashions Ltd., Joan Kostas, has just received the monthly bank statement for June, which shows a balance of $10,517. She remembers seeing a different balance for cash at June 30 when the company accountant, Peter Wong, presented to her the monthly statement of financial position. She checks the statement of financial position and finds a cash balance of $6,518. She is not sure which amount is correct. She calls Peter and asks him why the two amounts are different. Peter takes the bank statement and related documents and promises to provide her with an explanation within a few hours. He then proceeds to prepare a bank reconciliation report for the month of June.

A review of the documents that accompanied the bank statement shows the following:

a. A credit memorandum for the collection of a note for $2,080, including $80 of interest on the note. The bank charged the company a collection fee of $25.

b. A debit memorandum for an NSF cheque for $286 from customer Rami Cossette.

c. Total service charges for June amounting to $39.

When comparing the bank statement with the company's records, Peter discovered the following discrepancies:

d. A deposit of $1,145 was not recorded on the bank statement.

e. Three cheques had not been presented to the bank for payment yet. The amounts of these cheques are $1,573, $679, and $1,252.

f. A deposit of $2,340 was recorded incorrectly in the books at $2,430.

Required:

1. Explain to Joan why the two balances for cash are not equal, and why it is important to prepare a bank reconciliation statement.
2. Prepare a bank reconciliation statement at June 30 and the related journal entries.

■ LO**7**

P7–12   Preparing a Bank Reconciliation and Related Journal Entries (AP7–12)

The bookkeeper at Hopkins Company has not reconciled the bank statement with the cash account, saying, "I don't have time." You have been asked to prepare a reconciliation and review the procedures with the bookkeeper.

The April 30, 2015, bank statement and the April ledger accounts for cash showed the following (summarized):

Bank Statement			
	Cheques	**Deposits**	**Balance**
Balance, April 1, 2015			$31,000
Deposits during April		$36,100	67,100
Notes collected for company (including $70 interest)		1,180	68,280
Cheques cleared during April	$44,500		23,780
NSF cheque—A. B. Wright	160		23,620
Bank service charges	70		23,550
Balance, April 30, 2015			23,550

Cash in Bank					
Apr. 1	Balance	23,500	Apr.	Cheques written	41,100
Apr.	Deposits	41,500			

Cash on Hand		
Apr. 30	Balance	100

A comparison of cheques written before and during April with the cheques cleared through the bank showed that cheques of $4,100 are still outstanding at April 30. No deposits in transit were carried over from March, but a deposit was in transit at April 30.

Required:

1. Prepare a detailed bank reconciliation at April 30, 2015.
2. Prepare any required journal entries as a result of the reconciliation. Why are they necessary?
3. What were the balances in the cash accounts in the ledger on May 1, 2015?
4. What total amount of cash should be reported on the statement of financial position at April 30, 2015?

P7–13 **(Appendix 7B) Recording Sales, Returns, and Bad Debts**
Use the data presented in P7-2, which was selected from the records of Tunga Company for the year ended December 31, 2015.

Required:

1. Prepare the journal entries for these transactions, including the write-off of the uncollectible account and the adjusting entry for estimated bad debts. Do not record the cost of sales. Show computations for each entry.
2. Show how the accounts related to the preceding sale and collection activities should be reported on the 2015 statement of earnings. (Treat sales discounts as a contra-revenue account.)

ALTERNATE PROBLEMS

AP7–1 **Applying the Revenue Principle** (P7–1)   ■ LO1
Review the revenue recognition practices of the following companies, and indicate at what point in time revenue should be recognized in each of these independent cases. Explain your answer.

Case A. The sales representatives of Computec Corporation are under intense pressure to achieve very high sales levels. To achieve their specific objectives, the sales representatives ask customers to order computer equipment in advance, with payment to be made later. In many cases, the company records sales on the basis of customers' orders, even though the ordered equipment may not have been manufactured yet.

Case B. Scenic Trails Inc. is a campground operator that sells annual memberships to campers. Members are allowed to pay the annual membership fees over a period of six months. The company records revenue from membership fees as soon as a new member signs the membership agreement. Members are allowed 10 days to cancel their memberships, and many members cancel their memberships within days of signing.

Case C. Educational Toys Inc. sells a wide variety of toys to distributors and allows them to return unsold merchandise within a period of three months. The company's policy encourages distributors to buy products and keep them for three months, knowing they could return any unsold merchandise during this period. The company recognizes revenue as soon as it delivers its products to distributors.

■ LO2, 4 **AP7–2** **Reporting Net Sales and Expenses with Discounts, Returns, and Bad Debts** (P7–2)
The following data were selected from the records of Fluwars Company for the year ended December 31, 2014:

Balances at January 1, 2014:	
Trade receivables (various customers)	$116,000
Allowance for doubtful accounts	5,200

The company sold merchandise for cash and on open account with credit terms 1/10, n/30. Assume a unit sales price of $400 in all transactions and use the gross method to record sales revenue.

The following transactions occurred during 2014:

a. Sold merchandise for cash, $228,000.

b. Sold merchandise to Abbey Corp; invoice amount, $12,000.

c. Sold merchandise to Brown Company; invoice amount, $23,600.

d. Abbey paid the invoice in (b) within the discount period.

e. Sold merchandise to Cavendish Inc.; invoice amount, $26,000.

f. Two days after paying the account in full, Abbey returned four defective units and received a cash refund.

g. Collected $89,100 cash from customers for credit sales made in 2014, all within the discount periods.

h. Three days after the purchase date, Brown returned three of the units purchased in (c) and received account credit.

i. Brown paid its account in full within the discount period.

j. Sold merchandise to Decca Corporation; invoice amount, $18,400.

k. Cavendish paid its account in full after the discount period.

l. Wrote off an old account of $2,400 after deciding that the amount would never be collected.

m. The estimated bad debt rate used by the company was 5 percent of trade receivables at December 31, 2014.

Required:

1. Using the following categories, indicate the dollar effect (+ for increase, − for decrease, and N for no effect) of each listed transaction, including the write-off of the uncollectible account and the adjusting entry for estimated bad debts (ignore the cost of sales). The effects of the first transaction are shown as an example.

Sales Revenue	Sales Discounts (taken)	Sales Returns and Allowances	Bad Debt Expense
a. $228,000	N	N	N

2. Show how the accounts related to the preceding sale and collection activities should be reported on the statement of earnings for 2014. (Treat sales discounts as contra revenues.)

AP7–3 Understanding the Statement of Earnings Based on the Gross Profit Percentage (P7–3)   ■ LO3

The following data were taken from the year-end records of Glare Import Company:

Statement of Earnings Items	Year 1	Year 2
Gross sales revenue	$210,000	$255,000
Sales discounts	?	5,000
Net sales revenue	207,000	?
Cost of sales	?	60%
Gross profit	40%	?
Operating expenses	42,800	?
Earnings before income taxes	?	70,000
Income tax expense (30%)	?	?
Earnings before discontinued operations	?	?
Discontinued operations, net of tax	10,000 (loss)	2,500 (gain)
Net earnings	?	?
Earnings per share (8,000 shares outstanding)	?	?

Required:

Fill in all of the missing amounts. Show computations.

AP7–4 Recording Bad Debts and Interpreting Disclosure of Allowance for Doubtful Accounts (P7–4)   ■ LO4

Dorel Industries is a world-class juvenile-products and bicycle company. Dorel reported the following information concerning its allowance for doubtful accounts in recent annual reports (in thousands of dollars):

Dorel Industries Inc.

Allowance for Doubtful Accounts	Balance at Beginning of Period	Charged to Bad Debt Expense	Write-Offs Charged to Allowance	Balance at End of Period
Year 3	$10,364	$2,519	$2,536	?
Year 2	13,554	?	5,239	$10,364
Year 1	11,305	4,758	?	13,554

Required:

1. Supply the missing dollar amounts for year 1, year 2, and year 3.
2. Record summary journal entries related to bad debts for year 1.

AP7–5 Determining Bad Debt Expense Based on Aging Analysis (P7–5)   ■ LO4

Big & Small Engines Inc. uses the aging approach to estimate bad debt expense at the end of each fiscal year. Credit sales occur frequently on terms n/45. The balance of each trade receivable is aged on the basis of four time periods as follows: (1) not yet due, (2) up to 6 months past due, (3) 6 to 12 months past due, and (4) more than one year past due. Experience has shown that for the age groups, the average bad debt rates on the amounts receivable at year-end due to uncollectibility are (1) 1 percent, (2) 5 percent, (3) 20 percent, and (4) 50 percent, respectively.

At December 31, 2014 (end of the current fiscal year), the trade receivables balance was $39,500, and the allowance for doubtful accounts balance was $1,550 (debit). To simplify, the accounts of only five customers are used; the details of each are given below:

Date	Explanation	Debit	Credit	Balance
	R. Aouad—Trade Receivable			
13/3/2014	Sale	$19,000		$19,000
12/5/2014	Collection		$10,000	9,000
30/9/2014	Collection		7,000	2,000
	C. Chronis—Trade Receivable			
01/06/2013	Sale	31,000		31,000
01/11/2013	Collection		20,000	11,000
01/12/2014	Collection		5,000	6,000
	D. McClain—Trade Receivable			
31/10/2014	Sale	12,000		12,000
10/12/2014	Collection		8,000	4,000
	T. Skibinski—Trade Receivable			
02/05/2014	Sale	15,000		15,000
01/06/2014	Sale	10,000		25,000
15/06/2014	Collection		15,000	10,000
15/07/2014	Collection		10,000	0
01/10/2014	Sale	26,000		26,000
15/11/2014	Collection		16,000	10,000
15/12/2014	Sale	4,500		14,500
	H. Wu—Trade Receivable			
30/12/2014	Sale	13,000		13,000

Required:

1. Set up an aging analysis schedule and complete it.
2. Compute the estimated uncollectible amount for each age category and in total.
3. Prepare the adjusting entry for bad debt expense at December 31, 2014.
4. Show how the amounts related to trade receivables should be presented on the statement of earnings for 2014 and the statement of financial position at December 31, 2014.

■ **LO3, 4**   **AP7–6**   **Determining Bad Debt Expense Based on Aging Analysis and Interpreting Ratios** (P7–6)
Modern Machine Shop (MMS) Inc. manufactures special moulds that are used in the production of plastic toys. Below is MMS's trade receivables ledger from October 1 to December 31, 2015:

	General Ledger		Trade Receivables		
Date	Explanation		Debit	Credit	Balance
Oct. 1	Balance				9,500
Oct. 8	Wrote off uncollectible accounts.			1,500	8,000
Oct. 15	Sold 10 moulds to Allen Inc.		5,000		13,000
Oct. 31	Sold 15 moulds to Machinex Ltd.		7,500		20,500
Nov. 5	Received the amount due from Machinex for moulds purchased on October 31.			7,500	13,000
Nov. 7	Sold 20 moulds to Centra Corp.		10,000		23,000
Nov.16	Allen Inc. returned two moulds and paid the amount due for the remaining moulds purchased on October 15.			5,000	18,000
Nov. 25	Centra Corp. returned two moulds purchased on November 7.			1,000	17,000
Nov. 29	Centra Corp. made a partial payment on the moulds purchased on November 7.			5,000	12,000
Dec. 20	Recovered $500 that was written off on October 8.		500	500	12,000

Additional information is as follows:

a. MMS sold its special moulds at $500 each.

b. All sales were on credit with terms 2/10, n/30.

c. MMS's records included the following items and their balances as at September 30, 2015:

Net sales	$100,000
Trade receivables	9,500
Allowance for doubtful accounts (credit balance)	1,300

Required:

1. Prepare the journal entries to record the transactions on October 8, November 5, November 16, and December 20.

2. MMS uses the aging of trade receivables method to determine the amount of receivables that may not be collectible in the future. Its estimated uncollectible rates are as follows:

Age of trade receivables				
	Not yet due	**1–30 days past due**	**31–60 days past due**	**Over 60 days past due**
Estimated % uncollectible	1%	5%	10%	15%

Determine the amount of receivables that may not be collectible in the future, and prepare the journal entry to record bad debt expense on December 31, 2015. Show your calculations. (*Hint:* You may wish to keep track of trade receivables in order to determine the age of these receivables.)

3. MMS's cost of sales is $60,000 for 2015. Compute and evaluate MMS's gross profit percentage for 2015. MMS's gross profit percentages were 35 percent and 40 percent for 2013 and 2014, respectively.

AP7–7 Recording Receivables Transactions, Reporting Trade Receivables, and Interpreting Ratios (P7–7) ■ LO4, 5

Rodamex Inc. reported the following summary transactions during the year ended December 31, 2015:

a. Sold merchandise for $5,000,000, including $500,000 cash and $4,500,000 on account, with terms net/30.

b. Sales returns and allowances, $50,000; 10 percent related to cash sales, and 90 percent related to sales on account.

c. Received $4,200,000 from customers on credit sales.

d. Wrote off $17,000 in uncollectible trade receivables.

e. Recovered $6,000 cash from a customer whose account was previously written off.

Rodamex estimated that doubtful trade receivables represented 2 percent of the trade receivables balance at December 31, 2014, and 2.5 percent at December 31, 2015. The company had $700,000 in trade receivables at December 31, 2014.

Required:

1. Prepare journal entries to record the summary transactions.

2. Show how trade receivables would be presented on the company's comparative statement of financial position as at December 31, 2015.

3. Prepare the adjusting journal entry to record bad debt expense for 2015.

4. Compute the receivables turnover ratio for 2015. What does the result suggest about the company's ability to manage trade receivables during 2015?

5. Compute the gross profit for 2015 assuming that the company's cost of sales averages 40 per cent of its net sales.

AP7–8 Determining Bad Debts and Reporting Trade Receivables (P7–8) ■ LO4

Modern Kitchens Inc. (MKI) is a Montréal-based company that sells imported fancy kitchenware to retailers. Selected account balances as at September 30, 2014, are shown below:

	Debit	Credit
Trade receivables	$119,000	
Allowance for doubtful accounts		$3,000

During October 2014, the following transactions occurred:

a. The company sold merchandise on account to various retailers for a total amount of $76,000, terms 2/10, n/30. A few retailers who purchased merchandise for a gross amount of $40,000 paid the amount due within 10 days. A total of $16,000 of the October sales remained unpaid at October 31, 2014.

b. Customers paid the company $50,000 for merchandise they purchased prior to September 30, 2014. These customers did not pay within the discount period.

c. Two of MKI's customers owed the company a total of $5,000 and were facing financial difficulties during October due to increased competition. They were forced to close their businesses before the end of October 2014. MKI does not expect to receive any money from these two customers and considers their accounts uncollectible.

d. The company received new kitchenware from a Korean supplier, Kim & Sons Ltd., for $40,000. The invoice indicated that the supplier would allow a cash discount of 1 percent if the invoice were paid before the end of October 2014. MKI paid the supplier on November 10, 2014.

MKI estimates that 4 percent of its trade receivables at October 31, 2014, will not be collected in the future.

Required:

1. Prepare the journal entries to record the transactions that occurred in October 2014, and any related adjusting journal entries at October 31, 2014, the end of MKI's fiscal year.

2. Show how the information related to trade receivables is presented on the company's statement of financial position at October 31, 2014.

3. The major shareholder of MKI, Michel Beauregard, was reading through the company's statement of financial position and noticed the account allowance for doubtful accounts. He called Carol Jones, MKI's accountant, and made the following statement: "Carol, I don't think we need to make a provision for doubtful accounts as it will reduce the amount of trade receivables unnecessarily. I think we should wait until we are certain that we cannot collect from our customers before showing a reduction in the trade receivables on the statement of financial position. This way, the trade receivables balance will be more accurate. I would like you to make the necessary change to the financial statements before they are distributed to the other shareholders." Assume the role of Carol and prepare a response to Michel.

4. MKI had an opportunity to get a loan from the Bank of International Trade (BIT) to pay the amount due to Kim & Sons Ltd. The loan would have cost MKI $300 in interest charges. Should MKI have obtained the loan from BIT to pay its debt to Kim & Sons Ltd. before October 31, 2014?

■ **LO2, 3, 5**   **AP7–9**   **Preparing a Multiple-Step Statement of Earnings and Computing the Gross Profit Percentage with Discounts, Returns, and Bad Debts (P7–9)**

Perry Corporation is a local grocery store organized seven years ago as a corporation. At that time, 10,000 common shares were issued to the three organizers. The store is in an excellent location, and sales have increased each year. At the end of 2015, the bookkeeper prepared the following statement (assume that all amounts are correct; note the incorrect terminology and format):

PERRY CORPORATION		
Profit and Loss		
December 31, 2015		
	Debit	**Credit**
Sales		$184,000
Cost of sales	$ 98,000	
Sales returns and allowances	9,000	
Selling expenses	17,000	
Administrative and general expenses	18,000	
Bad debt expense	2,000	
Sales discounts	8,000	
Income tax expense	10,900	
Net earnings	21,100	
Totals	$184,000	$184,000

Required:

1. Beginning with net sales, prepare a multiple-step statement of earnings (showing both gross profit and earnings from operations). Treat sales discounts as a contra-revenue account

2. The beginning and ending balances of trade receivables were $16,000 and $18,000, respectively. Compute the gross profit percentage and receivables turnover ratio and explain their meaning.

AP7–10 Evaluating Internal Controls (P7–10)

■ LO6

Cory Magnum has been working for Matrix Products Inc. for five years and has gained the respect of his peers for his exemplary behaviour and work ethic. His job includes receiving cash and cheques from customers, depositing the cash receipts in the company's account at the local bank, and recording the transactions in the company's computerized accounting program. Cory was faced with personal financial problems and decided to make use of $2,000 of the company's available cash to solve them. He planned to return the money as soon as his financial situation improved. The $2,000 he took was part of the total cash sales to customers during the previous two business days. At the same time, Cory had received a cheque for $2,000 from PLC Ltd. as a partial payment on its trade receivables.

To hide his theft, Cory deposited the cheque instead of the cash into the company's bank account and made the following journal entry:

Cash in bank	2,000	
Cash on hand		2,000

In addition, he recorded the following journal entry to credit the account of PLC Ltd. to avoid any questions from that company in the future:

Sales returns and allowances	2,000	
Trade receivables—PLC Ltd.		2,000

Required:

1. Assume that Matrix Products prepares financial statements on a monthly basis. Would any items on the statement of earnings or the statement of financial position be incorrect? Explain.

2. Identify the weaknesses that exist in the company's internal control system. What changes should be made to strengthen internal control over cash receipts?

AP7–11 Preparing a Bank Reconciliation and Related Journal Entries (P7–11)

■ LO7

Sergio Lucas worked long hours during the summer and saved enough money to pay his tuition and living expenses to continue his studies at the local university. On September 1, he downloaded from the bank's website his bank statement for August to make sure that the bank had not made any errors related to his bank account. Sergio has had a habit of verifying all the entries in his bank account ever since he discovered that the bank had charged him a service fee for a transaction that was unrelated to his account. After comparing the bank statement with the entries he has made in his chequebook, Sergio found that the bank statement showed a balance of $12,506.60 but his chequebook showed a balance of $12,651.65 on August 31, a difference of $145.05. He decided to compare the entries in his chequebook with those in the bank statement, hoping that the bank owes him this difference.

Sergio's review of the bank statement showed the following:

a. Three cheques (#124, #125, and #126) that he wrote in late August have not been withdrawn from his bank account yet. They totalled $619.35.

b. An automatic deduction of $44.10 was made to pay the hydro bill for August.

c. Another automatic deduction of $55.30 was made to pay for telecommunication services from Telus Corp.

d. He forgot to record in his chequebook two withdrawals from instant teller machines totalling $300.

e. A cheque for $385 that he deposited in the bank the night of August 31 did not appear on the bank statement.

f. Sergio discovered that he recorded cheque #123 as $96.25 but the correct amount that cleared his bank account was $69.25.

g. The bank charged him a service fee of $7 for August transactions.

Required:

1. Assume the role of Sergio and prepare a bank reconciliation at August 31.

2. Which amounts should Sergio enter into his chequebook to avoid making any errors in reconciling his chequebook with the bank statement for September?

■ **LO7**   **AP7–12**   **Computing Outstanding Cheques and Deposits in Transit and Preparing a Bank Reconciliation and Journal Entries** (P7–12)

The August 2014 bank statement for Martha Company and the August 2014 ledger accounts for cash follow:

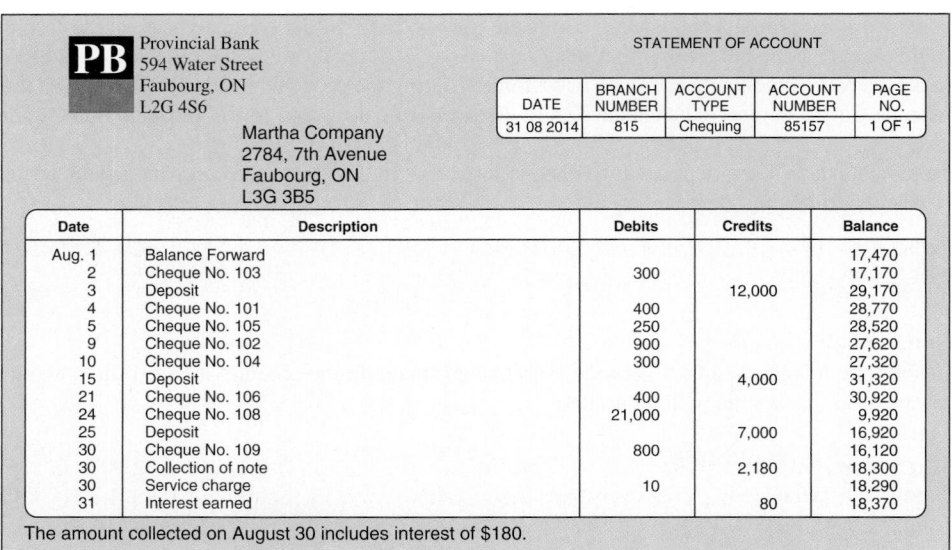

		Provincial Bank			STATEMENT OF ACCOUNT			

PB Provincial Bank, 594 Water Street, Faubourg, ON, L2G 4S6

DATE	BRANCH NUMBER	ACCOUNT TYPE	ACCOUNT NUMBER	PAGE NO.
31 08 2014	815	Chequing	85157	1 OF 1

Martha Company
2784, 7th Avenue
Faubourg, ON
L3G 3B5

Date	Description	Debits	Credits	Balance
Aug. 1	Balance Forward			17,470
2	Cheque No. 103	300		17,170
3	Deposit		12,000	29,170
4	Cheque No. 101	400		28,770
5	Cheque No. 105	250		28,520
9	Cheque No. 102	900		27,620
10	Cheque No. 104	300		27,320
15	Deposit		4,000	31,320
21	Cheque No. 106	400		30,920
24	Cheque No. 108	21,000		9,920
25	Deposit		7,000	16,920
30	Cheque No. 109	800		16,120
30	Collection of note		2,180	18,300
30	Service charge	10		18,290
31	Interest earned		80	18,370

The amount collected on August 30 includes interest of $180.

Cash in Bank

Aug. 1	Balance	16,520	Cheques written		
Deposits			Aug. 2		300
Aug. 2		12,000	4		900
12		4,000	15		290
24		7,000	17		550
31		5,000	18		800
			20		400
			23		21,000

Cash on Hand

Aug. 31	Balance	200	

Outstanding cheques at the end of July were for $250, $400, and $300. No deposits were in transit at the end of July.

Required:

1. Compute the amount of deposits in transit at August 31, 2014.

2. Compute the amount of outstanding cheques at August 31, 2014.

3. Prepare a bank reconciliation at August 31, 2014.

4. Prepare any journal entries that the company should make as a result of the bank reconciliation. Why are they necessary?

5. After the reconciliation journal entries are posted, what balances would be reflected in the cash accounts in the ledger?

6. What total amount of cash should be reported on the August 31, 2014, statement of financial position?

CASES AND PROJECTS

FINDING AND INTERPRETING FINANCIAL INFORMATION

CP7–1 Finding Financial Information

Refer to the financial statements of Canadian Tire Corporation in Appendix A of this book.

■ LO1, 3, 5

Canadian Tire
Corporation

Required:

1. Does the company disclose its revenue recognition policy? What point in time does it use to recognize revenue?

2. Compute the company's gross profit percentage for the most recent two years. Has it risen or fallen? Explain the meaning of the change.

3. Does the company report an allowance for doubtful accounts in the notes to its financial statements? If so, review the details disclosed by the company and explain what they mean.

4. Compute Canadian Tire's receivables turnover ratio for 2012. Is it significantly different from the ratio computed for Gildan in the Key Ratio Analysis section in the chapter? If so, what are some possible reasons for the difference?

5. What does the company include in "cash and cash equivalents"? How close do you think the disclosed amount is to the actual fair market value of these assets?

CP7–2 Finding Financial Information

Go to *Connect* for the financial statements of RONA Inc.

■ LO2, 5

RONA Inc.

Required:

1. The company distributes its products to franchisees and sells directly to consumers. What items would you expect to be subtracted from sales revenue in the computation of net sales?

2. What expenses does RONA subtract from net sales in the computation of earnings before income taxes? How does this differ from Canadian Tire's practice?

3. Compute RONA's receivables turnover ratio for the year ended December 30, 2012. What characteristics of its business might cause it to be so high?

4. What was the change in trade receivables and how did it affect the cash provided by operating activities for 2012?

CP7–3 Comparing Companies within an Industry

Refer to the financial statements of Canadian Tire Corporation (Appendix A) and RONA Inc. (on *Connect*) and the Industry Ratio Report (Appendix B on *Connect*).

■ LO3, 5

Canadian Tire
Corporation

RONA Inc.

Required:

1. Compute the gross profit percentage for both companies for the current year and the previous year. What do the changes in the ratios suggest?

2. Compute the receivables turnover ratio for both companies for fiscal years 2011 and 2012. Canadian Tire had $4,725 in trade receivables (net) at December 31, 2009, and RONA had $299.9 in trade receivables (net) at the same date. What accounts for the change in these ratios?

3. Compare the receivables turnover ratio of each company for 2012 to the industry average. Are these two companies doing better or worse than the industry average? Explain.

FINANCIAL REPORTING AND ANALYSIS CASES

CP7–4 Using Financial Reports: Interpreting Receivables Disclosures

Canadian Tire Corporation is a general retailer with nearly 1,700 retail and gasoline outlets across Canada. Canadian Tire's customers can pay for purchases using a Canadian Tire credit card. The company occasionally offers special promotions that allow customers to purchase merchandise on credit and pay after six months or one year without paying interest on the amount due. Canadian Tire refers

■ LO4

Canadian Tire
Corporation

to credit card receivables as loans receivable. Its annual report for 2012 included the following disclosures related to its loans receivables and the related allowance for credit losses:

12. Loans receivable

Quantitative information about the Company's loans receivable portfolio is as follows:

(in millions of dollars)	Total Principal Amount of Receivables[1]	
	2012	**2011**
Credit card loans	$4,234.3	$4,026.8
Line of credit loans	7.5	8.8
Personal loans[2]	0.5	3.3
Total Financial Services' loans receivable	4,242.3	4,038.9
Dealer loans	623.7	628.7
Other loans[3]	7.7	8.8
Total loans receivable	4,873.7	4,676.4
Less: Long-term portion[4]	608.0	594.7
Current portion of loans receivable	$4,265.7	$4,081.7

1. Amounts shown are net of allowance for loan impairment.
2. Personal loans are unsecured loans that are provided to qualified existing credit card holders for terms of one to five years. Personal loans have fixed monthly payments of principal and interest; however, the personal loans can be repaid at any time without penalty.
3. Dealer loans issued by Franchise Trust (Note 24).
4. The long-term portion of loans receivable is included in long-term receivables and other assets and includes Dealer loans of $601.5 million (2011—$587.5 million).

The gross impairment loss on loans receivable for the year ended December 29, 2012, was $323.7 million (2011, $352.0 million). Recoveries of bad debts for the year ended December 29, 2012, were $58.1 million (2011, $50.0 million).

6.3.3 Allowance for credit losses and past due amounts

In determining the recoverability of a loan receivable, the Company considers any change in the credit quality of the loan receivable from the date credit was initially granted up to the end of the reporting period. The concentration of credit risk is limited due to the customer base being large and unrelated.

The Company's allowances for credit losses are maintained at levels that are considered adequate to absorb future credit losses.

A continuity of the Company's allowances for loans receivable is as follows:

(in millions of dollars)	**2012**	**2011**
Balance, beginning of year	$ 118.7	$ 117.7
Impairment for credit losses	265.6	302.0
Recoveries	58.1	50.0
Write-offs	(331.7)	(351.0)
Balance, end of year	$ 110.7	$ 118.7

. . .

Credit card and line of credit loan balances are written off when a payment is 180 days in arrears. Line of credit loans are considered impaired when a payment is over 90 days in arrears and are written off when a payment is 180 days in arrears. Personal loans are considered impaired when a payment is over 90 days in arrears and are written off when a payment is 365 days in arrears.

Source: Canadian Tire Corporation, Annual Report 2012.

Required:

1. What amounts did Canadian Tire report as loans receivables on its statement of financial position at the end of 2012?

2. Prepare summary journal entries to record the transactions related to loans receivable in 2012. These include the write-off of receivables, recovery of receivables written off, and bad debt expense.

CP7–5 Canadian Banks

The global economic downturn that started in 2007 affected most sectors in the Canadian economy, particularly the financial sector, including the banking industry. For example, the common shares of Toronto Dominion Bank decreased from $68.12 per share on January 2, 2011, to $32.80 per share on February 23, 2012, before they started climbing up in March 2012 onward. Because banks lend money to individuals and companies, one would expect the banks to experience some difficulty in collecting money from their customers during an economic downturn.

Go to the websites and consult the annual reports of Scotiabank, Canadian Imperial Bank of Commerce, and Royal Bank of Canada for fiscal year 2012.

Required:

1. What is the amount of the provision for credit losses that each bank reported on its statement of earnings for both 2011 and 2012?
2. Compute the ratio Provision for credit losses/Net interest income for both 2011 and 2012. Did the ratio increase from 2011 to 2012 for each of these banks? If so, what could have caused the increase? Explain.
3. What is the amount of the allowance for loan losses that each bank reported on its statement of financial position (balance sheet) at the end of its 2012 fiscal year?
4. Compute the ratio Allowance for loan losses/Total loans receivable for both 2011 and 2012, and comment on the change in the ratio from 2011 to 2012.

CRITICAL THINKING CASES

CP7–6 Making Decisions as an Independent Accountant

Lane Manufacturing Company is a relatively small local business that specializes in the repair and renovation of antique furniture. The owner is an expert craftsperson. Although a number of skilled workers are employed, there is always a large backlog of work to be done. A long-time employee who serves as clerk-bookkeeper handles cash receipts, keeps the records, and writes cheques for disbursements. The owner signs the cheques. The clerk-bookkeeper pays small amounts in cash, subject to a month-end review by the owner. Approximately 80 regular customers are extended credit that typically amounts to less than $1,000. Although credit losses are small, in recent years the clerk-bookkeeper had established an allowance for doubtful accounts, and all write-offs were made at year-end. During January 2014 (the current year), the owner decided to start as soon as possible the construction of a building for the business that would provide many advantages over the currently rented space and would allow space to expand facilities. As a part of the considerations in financing, the financing institution asked for 2013 audited financial statements. The company statements had never been audited. Early in the audit, the independent accountant found numerous errors, and one combination of amounts in particular, that caused concern.

There was some evidence that a $2,500 job completed by Lane had been recorded as a receivable (from a new customer) on July 15, 2013. The receivable was credited for a $2,500 cash collection a few days later. The new account was never active again. The auditor also observed that shortly thereafter, three write-offs of trade receivables balances had been made to allowance for doubtful accounts as follows: Jones, $800; Blake, $750; and Sellers, $950—all of whom were known as regular customers. These write-offs drew the attention of the auditor.

Required:

1. Explain what caused the auditor to be concerned. Should the auditor report the suspicions to the owner?
2. What recommendations would you make with respect to internal control procedures for this company?

CP7–7 Evaluating an Ethical Dilemma: Management Incentives and Valuation of Receivables

E.S. Bankest Capital Corp.

Trade receivables that are reported on a statement of financial position should reflect the amount that is expected to be realized when collecting from customers. As indicated in Chapter 6, accounting information is useful if it is both relevant to a decision context and has representational faithfulness. But what if the trade receivables are deliberately misstated? This was the case for a Florida company called E.S. Bankest Capital Corp. (ESB)

ESB was a factoring company, which means it bought trade receivables from other companies at a discount, undertook cash collection from the companies' customers, and profited from the difference.

The factoring process permits the seller of trade receivables to collect cash immediately and shift the credit risk to the purchaser or factor. Banco Espirito Santo of Lisbon, which controls ESB, lent $140 million to ESB along with a line of credit for $30 million based on the value of ESB's trade receivables. Banco Espirito Santo is the second-largest bank in Portugal.

ESB's management had inflated the value of the trade receivables reported on its statement of financial position in order to obtain the loan. The reported value was $225 million when the actual value was only $5 million. The troublesome part of this fraudulent activity is that ESB's auditor, BDO Seidman, did not suspect any wrongdoing by the company and signed off on ESB's financial statements.

When the ESB fraud was disclosed in 2004, the ex-chairman of the company's board of directors, Eduardo Orlansky, was convicted of fraud, money laundering, and conspiracy and sentenced to 20 years in prison after a trial. An investigation indicated that the money borrowed from Banco Espirito Santo was deposited in various umbrella companies controlled by ESB.

Mr. Orlansky was not the only executive convicted. He was ordered to pay $165 million in restitution to Banco Espirito Santo, but the question was whether the bank would ever collect. ESB declared bankruptcy. Then Banco Espirito Santo sued BDO Seidman USA for failing to detect the fraud. The bank sued for actual losses of $170 million plus punitive damages of $351 million, and won the case in August 2007 for a total cash award of $521 million.

During the course of the trial, it was revealed that BDO Seidman was a strategic partner of one of ESB's factoring clients. BDO claimed it was fooled by ESB and that there was no conflict of interest. Although Banco Espirito Santo won the case, BDO Seidman launched and won an appeal. Ultimately, in May 2011, the two parties entered into a confidential settlement agreement.

Many articles were written about the ESB fraud in the news media. Access some of these articles to answer the following questions.

Required:

1. Preparers and auditors of financial statements are expected to exercise prudence in their valuation of assets and liabilities that are reported on the statement of financial position. Explain how the concept of prudence applies to the valuation of the trade receivables reported by ESB.

2. In your opinion, is a confidential settlement between Banco Espirito Santo and BDO Seidman a positive event for the profession of accounting?

■ **LO5**

CP7–8   **Evaluating the Effects of Credit Policy Changes on the Receivables Turnover Ratio and Cash Flows from Operating Activities**

V. R. Rao and Company has been operating for five years as a software consulting firm specializing in the installation of industry standard products. During this period, it has experienced rapid growth in sales revenue and trade receivables. Ms. Rao and her associates all have computer science backgrounds. This year, the company hired you as its first corporate controller. You have put into place new credit granting and collection procedures that are expected to reduce receivables by approximately one-third by year-end. You have gathered the following data related to the changes (in thousands of dollars):

	Beginning of Year	End of Year (projected)
Trade receivables	$1,000,608	$660,495
Less: Allowance for doubtful accounts	36,800	10,225
Net trade receivables	$ 963,808	$650,270
		Current Year (projected)
Net sales (assume all on credit)		$7,015,069

Required:

1. Compute the receivables turnover ratio based on two different assumptions:

    a. Those presented in the preceding table (a decrease in the balance in trade receivables, net).

    b. No change in the balance of net trade receivables; the balance was $963,808 at year-end.

2. Compute the effect (sign and amount) of the projected change in net trade receivables on cash flow from operating activities for the year.

3. On the basis of your findings in (1) and (2), write a brief memo explaining how an increase in the receivables turnover ratio can result in an increase in cash flow from operating activities. Also explain how this increase can benefit the company.

FINANCIAL REPORTING AND ANALYSIS TEAM PROJECT

CP7–9 Team Project: Analyzing Revenues and Receivables ■ LO1, 4, 5

As a team, select an industry to analyze. A list of companies classified by industry can be obtained by accessing **www.fpinfomart.ca** and then choosing "Companies by Industry." You can also find a list of industries and companies within each industry via **http://ca.finance.yahoo.com/investing** (click on "Order Annual Reports" under "Tools").

Each group member should acquire the annual report for a different publicly traded company in the industry. (Library files, the SEDAR service at **www.sedar.com**, and the company's website are good sources.)

Required:

On an individual basis, each team member should write a short report answering the following questions about the selected company. Discuss any patterns across the companies that you as a team observe. Then, as a group, write a short report comparing and contrasting your companies.

1. If your company lists receivables on its statement of financial position, what percentage is this asset of total assets for each of the last three years? If your company does not list receivables, discuss why this is so.

2. Perform a ratio analysis:

   a. What does the receivables turnover ratio measure in general?

   b. If your company lists receivables, compute the ratio for the last three years.

   c. What do your results suggest about the company?

   d. If available, find the industry ratio for the most recent year, compare it to your results, and discuss why you believe your company differs from or is similar to the industry ratio.

3. If your company lists receivables, determine what additional disclosure is available concerning the allowance for doubtful accounts. If the necessary information is provided, what is bad debt expense as a percentage of sales for the last three years?

4. What is the effect of the change in trade receivables on cash flows from operations for the most recent year—that is, did the change increase or decrease operating cash flows? Explain your answer.

SOLUTIONS TO SELF-STUDY QUIZZES

Self-Study Quiz 7-1

1. Gross Sales		$35,000
Less: Sales discounts (0.01 × 1/2 × $30,000)		150
Credit card discounts (0.03 × 0.8 × $5,000)		120
Net Sales		$34,730

2. Gross profit = $150,000 − $110,000 = $40,000

   Gross profit percentage = $40,000 ÷ $150,000 = 26.66%

Self-Study Quiz 7-2

1. Bad debt expense (+E)	8,813	
Allowance for doubtful accounts (+XA)		8,813
2. Allowance for doubtful accounts (−XA)	9,167	
Trade receivables (−A)		9,167

3. Ending balance = Beginning balance + Bad debt expense − Write-offs
   = $2,136 + $8,813 − $9,167 = $1,782

Self-Study Quiz 7-3

1.

Allowance for Doubtful Accounts (XA)			
		Beginning balance	723
Write-offs	648	Bad debt expense (solve)	829
		Ending balance	904

Beginning balance + Bad debt expense − Write-offs = Ending balance

$723 + X − $648 = $904; X = $829

2. The amount would be subtracted from net earnings because an increase in the trade receivables account indicates that sales revenue was in excess of cash collected from customers for the period.

3. Granting longer payment deadlines will most likely decrease the receivables turnover ratio because later collections from customers will increase the average trade receivables balance (the denominator of the ratio), thus decreasing the ratio.

Self-Study Quiz 7-4

3. Bank service charges are deducted from the company's account; thus, cash must be reduced and an expense must be recorded.

4. NSF cheques that were deposited were recorded on the books as increases in the cash account; thus, cash must be decreased and the related account receivable increased.

Reporting and Interpreting Cost of Sales and Inventory

After studying this chapter, you should be able to do the following:

LO1 Apply the cost principle to identify the amounts that should be included in inventory, and determine the cost of sales for typical retailers, wholesalers, and manufacturers.

LO2 Compare methods for controlling and keeping track of inventory, and analyze the effects of inventory errors on financial statements.

LO3 Report inventory and cost of sales by using three inventory costing methods.

LO4 Decide when the use of different inventory costing methods is beneficial to a company.

LO5 Report inventory at the lower of cost and net realizable value (LCNRV).

LO6 Evaluate inventory management by using the inventory turnover ratio and the effects of inventory on cash flows.

FOCUS COMPANY: **Danier Leather Inc.**

DESIGNING AND MANUFACTURING HIGH-QUALITY FASHIONABLE LEATHER PRODUCTS

If you shopped for a leather jacket recently, you probably considered buying one of the well-known brand names, such as Gucci, Danier, and Coach. Danier Leather designs, manufactures, markets, and sells high-quality, fashionable leather clothing and accessories. It is the leader in leather outerwear and sportswear in Canada, and its products are sold in 90 stores located in many cities across Canada.

Danier Leather carries a large stock of products in its warehouses and stores to meet the needs of its customers. To remain a leader in its industry, Danier Leather must continuously introduce new products that respond to the needs of its customers. It must also control the quality and cost of its inventory to enhance the profitability of its operations. Danier Leather accomplishes this not only by establishing mutually beneficial relationships with its suppliers, but also by developing accounting information systems that provide real-time inventory information. Furthermore, Danier Leather's choice of accounting methods to value and report inventory can affect the amount paid in income taxes.

UNDERSTANDING THE BUSINESS

Concerns about the cost and quality of inventory face all modern manufacturers and merchandisers, turning the reader's attention to *cost of sales* (cost of goods sold, cost of products sold) on the statement of earnings (or income statement) and *inventory* on the statement of financial position (or balance sheet). Exhibit 8.1 presents the relevant excerpts from Danier Leather's financial statements that include these accounts. The cost of sales is subtracted from net sales to produce gross profit on Danier Leather's statement of earnings. Inventory is a current asset on the statement of financial position; it is reported below cash and receivables because it is less liquid than these current assets.

Exhibit **8.1**

Excerpts from Statement of
Earnings and Statement of
Financial Position

REAL-WORLD EXCERPT

*Danier Leather
Corporation*

ANNUAL REPORT

DANIER LEATHER INC.

Consolidated Statement of Earnings (Partial)

(in thousands of dollars)

	YEAR ENDED		
	June 30, 2012	June 25, 2011	June 26, 2010
Net sales	$148,219	$157,621	$164,217
Cost of sales	71,513	71,333	77,438
Gross profit	76,706	86,288	86,779

DANIER LEATHER INC.

Consolidated Statements of Financial Position (Partial)

(in thousands of dollars)

	June 30, 2012	June 25, 2011
	ASSETS	
Current assets:		
Cash and cash equivalents (Note 4)	$34,332	$28,698
Accounts receivable	517	385
Income taxes recoverable	426	–
Inventories (Note 5)	24,891	28,964
Prepaid expenses	799	901
Total current assets	$60,965	$58,948

Source: Danier Leather Inc., Annual Report 2012.

Danier Leather's successful management of both inventory and cost of sales requires a combined effort by human resources managers, engineers, production managers, marketing managers, and accounting and financial managers. It is truly a multidisciplinary task. The primary goals of inventory management are to have sufficient quantities of high-quality inventory available to serve customers' needs while minimizing the costs of carrying inventory (production, storage, obsolescence, and financing). Low quality leads to customer dissatisfaction, returns, and a decline in future sales. Also, purchasing or producing too few units of a hot-selling item causes stock-outs, which mean lost sales revenue and potential customer dissatisfaction. Conversely, purchasing or producing too many units of a slow-selling item increases the storage costs and interest costs on short-term borrowings to finance the production or purchases. It may even lead to losses if the merchandise cannot be sold at normal prices.

To meet its inventory management goals, the multidisciplinary team will forecast expected customer demand for different products, including style, size, and colour. It will also provide feedback on actual outcomes so that adjustments to production or purchasing schedules can be made to control the cost of sales and improve gross profit. Both cost of sales and inventory are such important determinants of a company's success that managers, investors, and financial analysts pay close attention to these financial statement items.

The accounting system plays three roles in the inventory management process. First, the system must provide accurate information necessary for preparation of periodic financial statements and reports to tax authorities.[1] Second, it must provide up-to-date information on inventory quantities and costs to facilitate ordering and manufacturing decisions. Third, because inventories are subject to theft and other forms of misuse, the system must also provide the information necessary to help protect and control these important assets.

First, we discuss the components of inventory costs, the important choices management must make in the financial and tax reporting process, and how these choices affect the financial statements and taxes paid. Then we will briefly discuss how accounting systems are organized to keep track of inventory quantities and costs for decision making and control. This topic will be the principal subject matter of your managerial accounting course. Finally, we discuss how managers, investors, and financial analysts evaluate management's effectiveness at inventory management.

ORGANIZATION OF THE CHAPTER

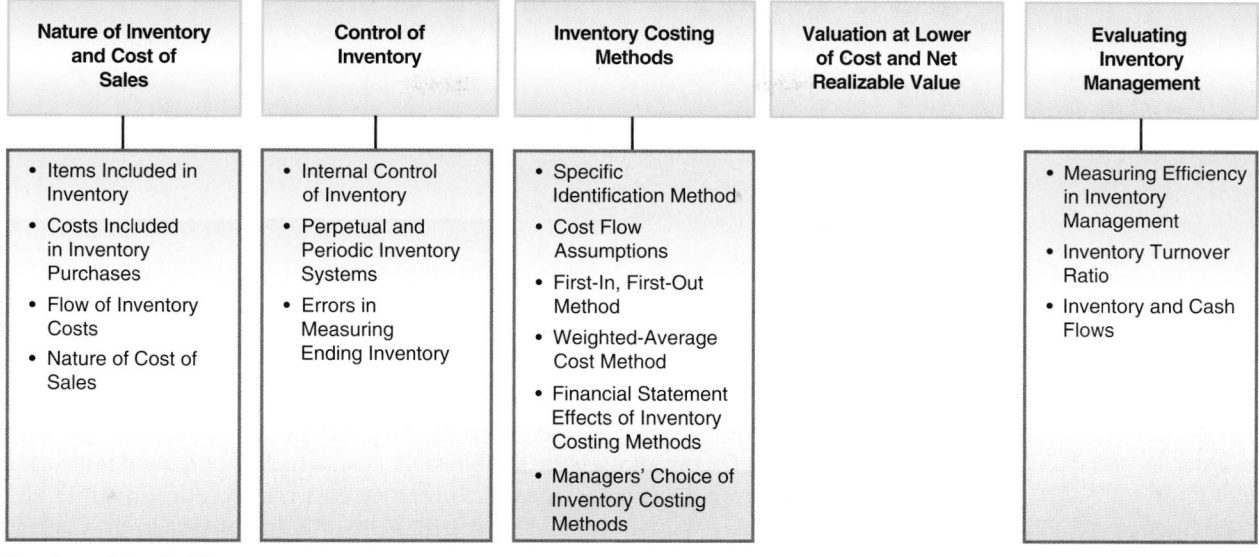

Nature of Inventory and Cost of Sales	Control of Inventory	Inventory Costing Methods	Valuation at Lower of Cost and Net Realizable Value	Evaluating Inventory Management
• Items Included in Inventory • Costs Included in Inventory Purchases • Flow of Inventory Costs • Nature of Cost of Sales	• Internal Control of Inventory • Perpetual and Periodic Inventory Systems • Errors in Measuring Ending Inventory	• Specific Identification Method • Cost Flow Assumptions • First-In, First-Out Method • Weighted-Average Cost Method • Financial Statement Effects of Inventory Costing Methods • Managers' Choice of Inventory Costing Methods		• Measuring Efficiency in Inventory Management • Inventory Turnover Ratio • Inventory and Cash Flows

Supplemental material:

Appendix 8A: Additional Issues in Measuring Purchases

NATURE OF INVENTORY AND COST OF SALES

Items Included in Inventory

Inventory is tangible property that is either (1) held for sale in the normal course of business or (2) used to produce goods or services for sale. Inventory is reported on the statement of financial position as a current asset, because it is normally used or converted into cash within one year or within the next operating cycle of the business, whichever is longer. The types of inventory normally held depend on the characteristics of the business.

Companies that do not manufacture the products they sell, but simply purchase those products and then sell them to customers, are called *merchandisers*. Whole-sale merchandisers distribute products to retail merchandisers for resale to customers through retail stores.

Merchandisers (wholesale or retail businesses) hold the following:

Merchandise inventory. These are goods (or merchandise) held for resale in the normal course of business. The goods are usually acquired in a finished condition and are ready for sale without further processing.

Manufacturing businesses hold the following types of inventory:

Raw materials inventory. This consists of items acquired by purchase, growth (such as food products), or extraction (natural resources) for processing into finished goods. Such items are included in raw materials inventory until used, at which point they become part of work-in-process inventory.

Work-in-process inventory. This includes goods in the process of being manufactured but not yet complete. When complete, work-in-process inventory becomes finished goods inventory.

Finished goods inventory. This consists of manufactured goods that are complete and available for sale.

Danier Leather is both a manufacturer and a merchandiser of leather garments and accessories. It has manufacturing facilities in the Toronto area, but most of the garments that are designed at the company's headquarters in Toronto are produced overseas by independent contractors in the Asia-Pacific area, primarily in China. The products purchased from these contractors are then shipped to Danier Leather's warehouses and stores for sale to customers.

LO1

Apply the cost principle to identify the amounts that should be included in inventory, and determine the cost of sales for typical retailers, wholesalers, and manufacturers.

INVENTORY is tangible property held for sale in the normal course of business or used in producing goods or services for sale.

MERCHANDISE INVENTORY includes goods held for resale in the ordinary course of business.

RAW MATERIALS INVENTORY includes items acquired for the purpose of processing into finished goods.

WORK-IN-PROCESS INVENTORY includes goods in the process of being manufactured.

FINISHED GOODS INVENTORY includes manufactured goods that are complete and available for sale.

Inventories related to Danier Leather's operations are recorded in these accounts. Danier Leather's note on inventories reports the following:

	(in thousands of dollars)	
NOTE 2: Inventories	**June 30, 2012**	**June 25, 2011**
Raw materials	$ 2,644	$ 2,655
Work-in-process	183	265
Finished goods	22,064	26,044
	$24,891	$28,964

Source: Danier Leather Inc., Annual Report 2012.

Costs Included in Inventory Purchases

Goods in inventory are recorded in conformity with the *cost principle.* The primary basis of accounting for inventory is cash-equivalent cost, which is either the price paid or consideration given to acquire an asset. Inventory cost includes, in principle, the sum of the applicable expenditures and charges directly or indirectly incurred in bringing an article to a usable or saleable condition and location.

When Danier Leather purchases raw materials for use in the manufacturing of leather garments, such as jackets, blazers, pants, and handbags, the amount recorded should include the invoice price and indirect expenditures related to the purchase, such as import duties and freight charges to deliver the items to its warehouses (freight-in), as well as inspection and preparation costs. In general, the company should cease accumulating purchase costs either when the raw materials are *ready for use* or when the merchandise inventory is *ready for shipment* to customers. Any additional costs related to selling the merchandise inventory to customers, such as salaries of marketing personnel, should be included in selling and marketing expenses of the period of sale, since they are incurred after the inventory is ready for sale. Direct sales to customers, by telephone or over the Internet, have reduced the need to stock inventory for long periods and reduced inventory storage costs and the cost of obsolescence.

Danier Leather's note on accounting policies included the following:

NOTE 1: Summary of Significant Accounting Policies

(j) Inventories:

. . . For inventories manufactured by the Company, cost includes direct labour, raw materials, manufacturing and distribution centre costs related to inventories and transportation costs that are directly incurred to bring inventories to their present location and condition. For inventories purchased from third party vendors, cost includes the cost of purchase, duty and brokerage, quality assurance costs, distribution centre costs related to inventories and transportation costs that are directly incurred to bring inventories to their present location and condition.

Source: Danier Leather Inc., Annual Report 2012.

FINANCIAL ANALYSIS

APPLYING THE MATERIALITY CONCEPT IN PRACTICE

Incidental costs, such as inspection and preparation costs, are often not very large relative to other costs (see the discussion of materiality in Chapter 4) and do not have to be assigned to the inventory cost. Thus, for practical reasons, many companies use the invoice price, less returns and discounts, to assign a unit cost to raw materials or merchandise and record other indirect expenditures as separate costs that are reported as expenses.

Flow of Inventory Costs

The flow of inventory costs for merchandisers (wholesalers and retailers) is relatively simple, as shown in Exhibit 8.2, Part A. When merchandise is purchased, the merchandise inventory account is increased. When the goods are sold, the merchandise inventory is decreased and the cost of sales is increased.

The flow of inventory costs in a manufacturing environment is more complex, as diagrammed in Exhibit 8.2, Part B. First, *raw materials* (also called *direct materials*) must be purchased. For Danier Leather, these raw materials include lamb leather, calf suede, cow hide, pigskin leathers, zippers, buckles, and buttons, among others. As materials are used in production, their cost is removed from the raw materials inventory and added to the cost of the work-in-process inventory.

Two other components of manufacturing costs, direct labour and factory overhead, are also added to the work-in-process inventory when incurred in the manufacturing process. **Direct labour** cost represents the earnings of employees who work directly on the products being manufactured. **Factory overhead** costs include all other manufacturing costs that are not raw material or direct labour costs. For example, the salary of the factory supervisor and the cost of utilities, security, and material handling are included in factory overhead.

When the leather garments are completed and ready for sale, the related amounts in work-in-process inventory are transferred to finished goods inventory. When the finished goods are sold, cost of sales increases and the costs in the finished goods inventory decreases.

As Exhibit 8.2 indicates, there are three stages to inventory cost flows for both merchandisers and manufacturers. The first involves purchasing and/or production activities. In the second, these activities result in additions to inventory accounts on the statement of financial position. At the third stage, the inventory items are sold and the amounts become cost of sales on the statement of earnings. Since the flows of inventory costs for both merchandise inventory and finished goods into cost of sales are very similar, we will focus the rest of our discussion on merchandising inventory.

DIRECT LABOUR refers to the earnings of employees who work directly on the products being manufactured.

FACTORY OVERHEAD includes manufacturing costs that are not raw material or direct labour costs.

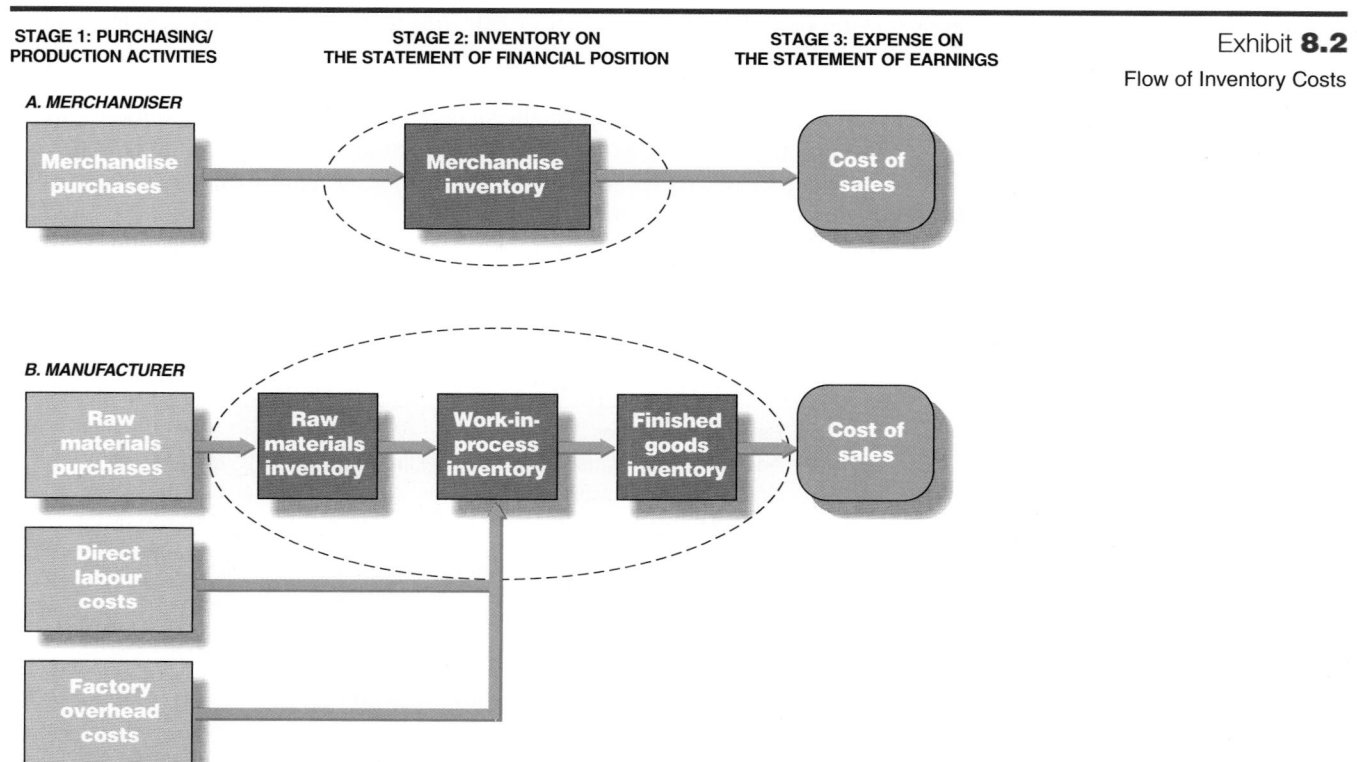

STAGE 1: PURCHASING/ PRODUCTION ACTIVITIES	STAGE 2: INVENTORY ON THE STATEMENT OF FINANCIAL POSITION	STAGE 3: EXPENSE ON THE STATEMENT OF EARNINGS

Exhibit **8.2**

Flow of Inventory Costs

MODERN MANUFACTURING TECHNIQUES AND INVENTORY COSTS

The flows of inventory costs diagrammed in Exhibit 8.2, Part B, represent the keys to manufacturing cost and quality control. The company must pay to finance the purchase and storage of raw materials and purchased parts. This means that minimizing the quantities of these inventories and more closely matching them with projected manufacturing demand are key to an effective process of cost control. Danier Leather must work closely with its suppliers in design, production, and delivery of raw materials and/or finished goods. (This approach to inventory management is called *just-in-time* or *JIT*.) To reduce the costs of work-in-process and finished goods, companies redesign and simplify manufacturing processes and retrain their manufacturing personnel to minimize both direct labour and factory overhead costs. Simplified product design and production processes often lead to higher product quality and reduced scrap and rework costs.

Danier Leather's managerial accounting system is designed to monitor the success of these changes and provide information to allow continuous improvements in manufacturing. The design of such systems is the subject matter of managerial accounting and cost accounting courses.

Nature of Cost of Sales

Cost of sales (COS) is directly related to sales revenue. The amount of sales revenue during an accounting period is the number of units sold multiplied by the sales price. Cost of sales is the same number of units, multiplied by their unit costs; it includes all costs of the merchandise purchased or the finished goods sold during the period.

Let us examine the relationship between cost of sales on the statement of earnings and inventory on the statement of financial position. Danier Leather starts each accounting period with a stock of finished goods inventory called *beginning inventory* (BI). During the accounting period, new *purchases* (P) are added to inventory. The sum of the cost of beginning inventory and the cost of purchases (or additions to finished goods) is the **cost of goods available for sale** during that period. What remains unsold at the end of the period becomes *ending inventory* (EI) of finished goods on the statement of financial position. The portion of the cost of goods available for sale that are actually sold becomes cost of sales on the statement of earnings. The ending inventory for one accounting period then becomes the beginning inventory for the next period. The relationships between these various amounts are brought together in the **cost of sales equation**: $BI + P - EI = COS$.

To illustrate the relationships represented by the cost of sales equation, assume that Danier Leather began the period with $40,000 of women's jackets style #101 in beginning inventory,[2] purchased additional jackets during the period for $55,000, and had $35,000 in inventory at the end of the period. These amounts are combined as follows to compute the cost of sales of $60,000:

THE COST OF GOODS AVAILABLE FOR SALE refers to the sum of the cost of beginning inventory and the cost of purchases (or additions to finished goods) for the period.

COST OF SALES EQUATION:
$BI + P - EI = COS$

Beginning inventory	$40,000
Add: Purchases of merchandise during the year	55,000
Cost of goods available for sale	95,000
Deduct: Ending inventory	−35,000
Cost of sales	$60,000

These same relationships are illustrated in Exhibit 8.3 and can be represented in the merchandise inventory T-account as follows (amounts in millions):

Merchandise Inventory (A)			
Beginning inventory	40,000		
Purchases of inventory	55,000	Cost of sales	60,000
Ending inventory	35,000		

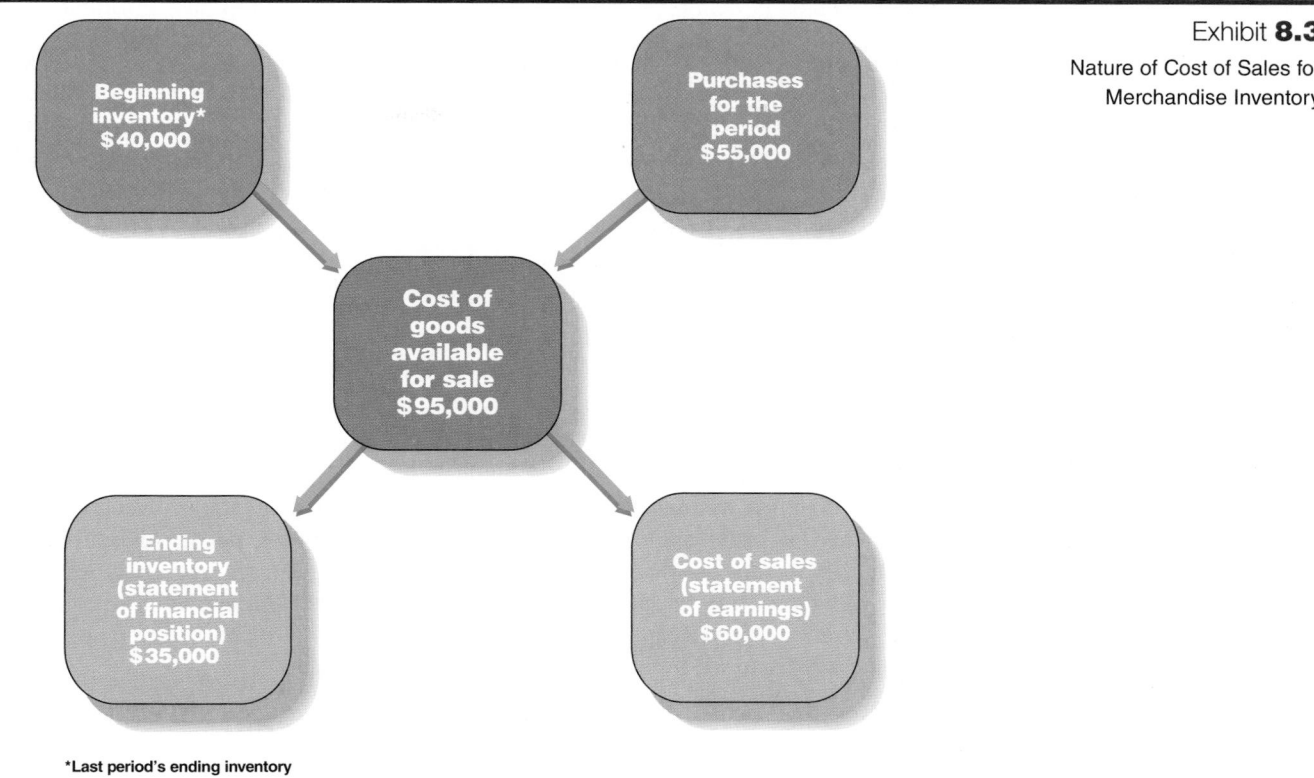

Exhibit **8.3**

Nature of Cost of Sales for
Merchandise Inventory

*Last period's ending inventory

If three of these four amounts are known, either the cost of sales equation or the inventory T-account can be used to solve for the fourth amount.

PAUSE FOR
FEEDBACK

Inventory should include all items owned that are held for resale. Costs flow into inventory when goods are purchased or manufactured. They flow out (as an expense) when they are sold or disposed of. The cost of sales equation describes these flows.

SELF-STUDY **QUIZ 8-1**

Assume the following facts for jacket style #101, which Danier Leather purchased and sold to customers during the year:

Beginning inventory: 200 units at unit cost of $200
Ending inventory: 175 units at unit cost of $200
Sales: 300 units at a sales price of $300 (cost per unit $200)

1. Using the cost of sales equation, compute the cost of purchases of jacket style #101 for the period.

2. Prepare the first three lines of a statement of earnings (showing gross profit) for jacket style #101 for the year.

After you complete your answers, check them with the solutions at the end of the chapter.

CONTROL OF INVENTORY

Internal Control of Inventory

In general, inventory is the asset second-most vulnerable to theft after cash. Efficient management of inventory to avoid cost of stock-outs and overstock situations is also crucial to the profitability of most companies. Consequently, a number of control

LO²

Compare methods for controlling and keeping track of inventory, and analyze the effects of inventory errors on financial statements.

features focus on safeguarding inventories and providing up-to-date information for management decisions. The following are the most important control features:

1. Separation of responsibilities for inventory accounting and physical handling of inventory.
2. Storage of inventory in a manner that protects it from theft and damage.
3. Limiting access to inventory to authorized employees.
4. Maintaining perpetual inventory records (described below).
5. Comparing perpetual records to periodic physical counts of inventory.

Perpetual and Periodic Inventory Systems

To compute cost of sales, three amounts must be known: (1) beginning inventory; (2) purchases of merchandise, or additions to finished goods, during the period; and (3) ending inventory. The amount of purchases for the period is always accumulated in the accounting system. The amounts of cost of sales and ending inventory can be determined by using one of two different inventory systems: perpetual and periodic. To simplify the discussion of how accounting systems keep track of these amounts, we focus this discussion on jacket style #101, which Danier Leather sells. Although the same general principles apply, the more complex details of manufacturing accounting systems are discussed in managerial accounting courses.

In a **PERPETUAL INVENTORY SYSTEM**, a detailed inventory record is maintained, recording each purchase and sale during the accounting period.

Perpetual Inventory System   In a **perpetual inventory system**, a detailed record is maintained for each type of merchandise stocked, showing (1) units and cost of the beginning inventory, (2) units and cost of each purchase, (3) units and cost of the goods for each sale, and (4) units and cost of the goods on hand at any point in time. This up-to-date record is maintained on a transaction-by-transaction basis throughout the period. In a complete perpetual inventory system, the inventory record gives both the cost of ending inventory and the cost of sales at any point in time. Under this system, a physical count must be performed from time to time to ensure that records are accurate in case errors or theft of inventory occur.

All journal entries for purchase and sale transactions discussed in the text so far have been recorded by using a perpetual inventory system. In a perpetual inventory system, purchase transactions are directly recorded in an inventory account. Simultaneously, when each sale is recorded, a companion cost of sales entry is made, decreasing inventory and recording cost of sales. As a result, information on cost of sales and ending inventory is available on a continuous (perpetual) basis.

Whether the accounting system is manual or electronic, the rules for recording and reporting accounting data are the same. The maintenance of a separate inventory record for each type of good stocked on a transaction-by-transaction basis is usually necessary for purchasing, manufacturing, and distribution decisions. Most companies rely heavily on this system and may even share some of this information electronically with their suppliers or customers.[3]

In a **PERIODIC INVENTORY SYSTEM**, ending inventory and cost of sales are determined at the end of the accounting period based on a physical count.

Periodic Inventory System   Under the **periodic inventory system**, companies do *not* maintain an ongoing record of inventory during the year; rather, an actual physical count of the goods remaining on hand is required at the end of each period. The number of units of each type of merchandise on hand is multiplied by their unit cost to compute the total cost of the ending inventory. Cost of sales is calculated by using the cost of sales equation.

Because the amount of inventory is not known until the end of the period when the physical inventory count is taken, the cost of sales cannot be determined reliably until the inventory count is completed. Inventory purchases are debited to a temporary account called purchases. Revenues are recorded at the time of each sale. However, the cost of sales is not recorded until after the inventory count is completed. At all other times, companies using a periodic system must estimate the value of inventory on hand. We briefly discuss the estimation of inventory amounts later in the chapter.

Before affordable computers and bar code readers were available, the primary reason for using the periodic inventory system was its low cost. The primary disadvantage of a periodic inventory system is the lack of timely inventory information. Managers do not receive information quickly about either low stock or overstocked situations. Most modern companies could not survive without this information. As noted at the beginning of the chapter, cost and quality pressures from increasing competition, combined with dramatic declines in the cost of computers, have made sophisticated perpetual inventory systems a minimum requirement at all but the smallest companies.

A perpetual inventory system provides more timely information about inventory quantities and costs. As explained in Chapter 6, timeliness of accounting information enhances its relevance for decision-making purposes. Accordingly, a perpetual inventory system is preferable to a periodic system, because it provides more timely information for inventory management decisions. A perpetual inventory system is also preferred over a periodic system, because internal control procedures have gained more importance in the past few years with recent legislation requiring chief executive officers (CEOs) and chief financial officers (CFOs) of all companies listed on Canadian stock exchanges to certify the quality of internal control systems, as explained in Chapter 7.

Perpetual Inventory Records in Practice The decision to use a perpetual versus a periodic inventory system is based on management's need for timely information for use in operating decisions and on the cost of the perpetual system. Further, the specific manner in which the perpetual system is designed will also be determined with these trade-offs in mind. Many inventory ordering and production decisions require accurate information on inventory quantities but not costs. Quantities on hand provide the information necessary for efficient management of inventory, providing delivery information to dealers, and quality control.

METHODS FOR ESTIMATING INVENTORY—THE GROSS PROFIT METHOD

FINANCIAL ANALYSIS

When a periodic inventory system is used and detailed perpetual inventory records are not kept, the cost of sales and the amount of ending inventory can be directly computed only when a physical inventory count is taken. Because taking a physical inventory count is expensive, it is normally done only once each year. In these circumstances, managers who wish to prepare monthly or quarterly financial statements for internal use often estimate the cost of sales and cost of ending inventory by using the *gross profit method.* The gross profit method uses the historical gross profit percentage (introduced in Chapter 7) to estimate cost of sales.

For example, if Danier Leather's historical gross profit percentage on jacket style #101 is 30 percent and $500,000 worth of this model is sold in January, it will estimate the cost of sales to be $350,000 ($500,000 × [100% − 30%]) for the month. If Danier Leather keeps track of purchases and other additions to inventory, it can then use the cost of sales equation to solve for an estimate of ending inventory. Retailers often take their physical inventory counts based on the retail price instead of cost and then use a similar method (called the *retail method*) to estimate cost. Methods for estimating inventory and cost of sales are discussed in detail in intermediate accounting courses.

Errors in Measuring Ending Inventory

As the cost of sales equation indicates, a direct relationship exists between the cost of ending inventory and the cost of sales, because items not in the ending inventory are assumed to have been sold. Thus, the measurement of ending inventory quantities and costs affects both the statement of financial position (assets) and the statement of earnings (cost of sales, gross profit, and net earnings). The measurement of ending inventory affects not only the net earnings for that period but also the net earnings for the next accounting period. This two-period effect occurs because the ending inventory for one accounting period is the beginning inventory for the next.

Greeting card maker Gibson Greeting Cards (now owned by American Greetings Corporation) had overstated its current-year net earnings by 20 percent, because one division had overstated ending inventory for the year. You can compute the effects of the error on both the current year's and next year's earnings before taxes by using the cost of sales equation. Assume that the ending inventory was inadvertently overstated by $10,000 because of a clerical error that was not discovered. This error would have the following effects in the current year and next year:

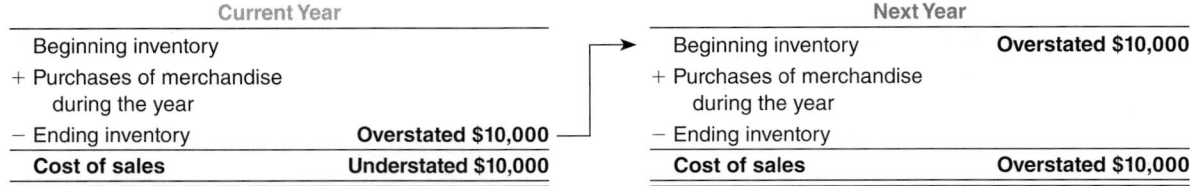

Because the cost of sales was understated, earnings before taxes would be *overstated* by $10,000 in the *current year.* Consequently, income tax expense, income tax payable, and net earnings would be overstated. In addition, since the current year's ending inventory becomes next year's beginning inventory, it would have the following effects: cost of sales would be overstated and earnings before taxes would be *understated* by the same amount in the *next year.* Furthermore, income tax expense, income tax payable, and net earnings would be understated. If there are no other changes, an overstatement during one time period will reverse to an identical understatement in the next.

Each of these errors would flow into retained earnings so that, at the end of the current year, retained earnings would be overstated by $10,000 (less the related income tax expense). This error would be offset in the next year, and retained earnings and inventory at the end of next year would be correct.

Exhibit 8.4 shows how an error that understates the cost of ending inventory affects other elements of financial statements during the year of the error and the following year. An error that overstates ending inventory would have exactly the opposite effects on the financial statement items shown in Exhibit 8.4.

Exhibit **8.4**

Effect of Understatement in Ending Inventory on Selected Financial Statement Items

ERROR: UNDERSTATEMENT OF ENDING INVENTORY

	Year of the Error	Following Year
Beginning inventory	NE*	U
Ending inventory	U	NE
Cost of sales	O	U
Gross profit	U	O
Earnings before income tax	U	O
Income tax expense	U	O
Net earnings	U	O
Retained earnings, end of year	U	NE

*U = Understated; O = Overstated; NE = No Effect

A company can keep track of the ending inventory and cost of sales for the period using (1) the perpetual inventory system, which is based on the maintenance of detailed and continuous inventory records, or (2) the periodic inventory system, which is based on a physical count of ending inventory and use of the cost of sales equation to determine cost of sales. An error in the measurement of ending inventory affects cost of sales on the current period's statement of earnings and ending inventory on the statement of financial position. Because this year's ending inventory becomes next year's beginning inventory, it also affects cost of sales in the following period by the same amount but in the opposite direction. These relationships can be seen through the cost of sales equation (BI + P − EI = COS).

SELF-STUDY QUIZ 8-2

Sarlos Ltd. provided the following summary statement of earnings for fiscal years 2014 and 2015. Assume that an error in the inventory count at December 31, 2014, resulted in an overstatement of ending inventory by $10,000:

| | SARLOS LTD. Statement of Earnings For the Years Ended December 31 | | | |
| | With Inventory Error | | Without Inventory Error | |
	2015	2014	2015	2014
Sales	$600,000	$500,000	$600,000	$500,000
Cost of sales	350,000	300,000	?	?
Gross profit	250,000	200,000	?	?
Selling, general, and administrative expenses	120,000	100,000	?	?
Earnings before income tax	130,000	100,000	?	?
Income tax expense (at 40%)	52,000	40,000	?	?
Net earnings	$ 78,000	$ 60,000	?	?

1. Complete the statement of earnings above for 2014 and 2015, assuming that the inventory error was discovered at the end of 2015.

2. Compute the combined net earnings for both 2014 and 2015. Would the inventory error at December 31, 2014, affect the financial statements for 2016? Explain.

After you complete your answers, check them with the solutions at the end of the chapter.

INVENTORY COSTING METHODS

In the Danier Leather example presented earlier, the cost of all units of jacket style #101 was the same: $200. If inventory costs do not change, this would be the end of our discussion. As we are all aware, the prices of most goods do change. In recent years, the costs of many manufactured items, such as automobiles and motorcycles, have risen gradually. In other high-technology industries, such as the computer industry, however, costs of production have dropped dramatically, along with retail prices.

When inventory costs change, the determination of the cost of sales and the cost of ending inventory can turn net earnings into losses (and vice versa) and cause companies to pay or save millions in taxes. A simple example will illustrate these dramatic effects. Do not let the simplicity of our example mislead you. It applies broadly to actual company practices.

LO3

Report inventory and cost of sales by using three inventory costing methods.

The example is based on the following data for Danier Leather during the first quarter of the current year, assuming for simplicity that Danier Leather purchases and sells only jacket style #101:

Date	Transaction or Event	Number of Jackets	Number of Jackets on Hand	Cost per Jacket	Sale Price per Jacket
January 1	Beginning inventory	800	800	$200	
January 31	Sale to customers	(600)	200		$279
February 5	Purchase	800	1,000	210	
February 28	Sale to customers	(900)	100		295
March 10	Purchase	900	1,000	220	
March 31	Sale to customers	(200)	800		299

Total number of jackets sold = 600 + 900 + 200 = 1,700

Ending inventory = 800 jackets

Note that the cost per jacket increased between January and March. Sales were made on January 31, February 28, and March 31. What amount would the accountant record as cost of sales for each of the sale transactions? The answer depends on which specific goods we assume are sold. Three generally accepted inventory costing methods are available to determine the cost of sales:[4]

1. Specific identification
2. First-in, first-out (FIFO)
3. Weighted average

The three inventory costing methods are alternative ways to assign the total cost of goods available for sale between (1) ending inventory and (2) cost of sales. International Accounting Standard 2 requires only that the inventory costing method used be rational and systematic. The selected inventory costing method should be the one that provides the best correspondence between expenses and revenues. The first method identifies individual items that remain in inventory or are sold. The remaining two methods assume that inventory items follow a certain physical flow. As you proceed through the various illustrations, keep in mind that the three inventory costing methods are simply methods of allocating the total cost of goods available for sale to cost of sales on the statement of earnings and ending inventory on the statement of financial position.

Specific Identification Method

The **SPECIFIC IDENTIFICATION METHOD** identifies the cost of the specific item that was sold.

When the **specific identification method** is used, the cost of each item sold is individually identified and recorded as cost of sales. Without electronic tracking, the method may be manipulated when the units are identical, because one can affect the cost of sales and the ending inventory accounts by picking and choosing from among the several available unit costs. For this reason, IFRS prohibit the use of this method when there are large numbers of inventory items that are interchangeable, such as jackets of the same size and style.

The specific identification method is impractical when large quantities of similar items are kept in stock. It is appropriate, however, when dealing with very expensive items, such as broadband telecommunications systems, aircraft, yachts, fine art objects, buildings, luxury cars, and fine jewellery, because each item tends to differ from the other items. This method requires keeping track of the purchase cost of each item. This is done by either (1) coding the purchase cost on each unit before placing it in stock or (2) keeping a separate record of the unit and identifying it with a serial number.

The technology of bar code scanning and radio frequency identification is a simple and cost-effective method to keep track of inventory items at all times, even for items with low unit costs. The scanner transmits cost and quantity information to a company's central database, thereby creating a perpetual record of inventory costs. This affects the computation of the cost of sales and the cost of ending inventory. To compute the cost of sales, the bar code identifies the specific unit that is sold and matches it to the recorded cost through the scanning process. The recorded cost of all units that remain unsold at March 31 represents the cost of ending inventory.

Cost Flow Assumptions

Most inventory items are accounted for by using one of two cost flow assumptions. The *choice of an inventory costing method is NOT based on the physical flow of goods* on and off the shelves. That is why the methods are called *cost flow assumptions.* A useful visual learning tool for representing inventory cost flows is a stack of inventory units. The different inventory costing methods can then be visualized as flows of inventory in and out of the stack. We use this concept to illustrate inventory cost flow throughout the following sections. We assume first that Danier Leather uses a perpetual inventory system, where the cost of sales is determined at the date of sale. Next, we illustrate the computation of cost of sales and ending inventory when the periodic inventory system is used.

The oldest jackets are placed at the top of the stack because they are typically sold first. The purchase and sale transactions in our example are presented on the time line in Exhibit 8.5, which shows the flow of jackets over time.

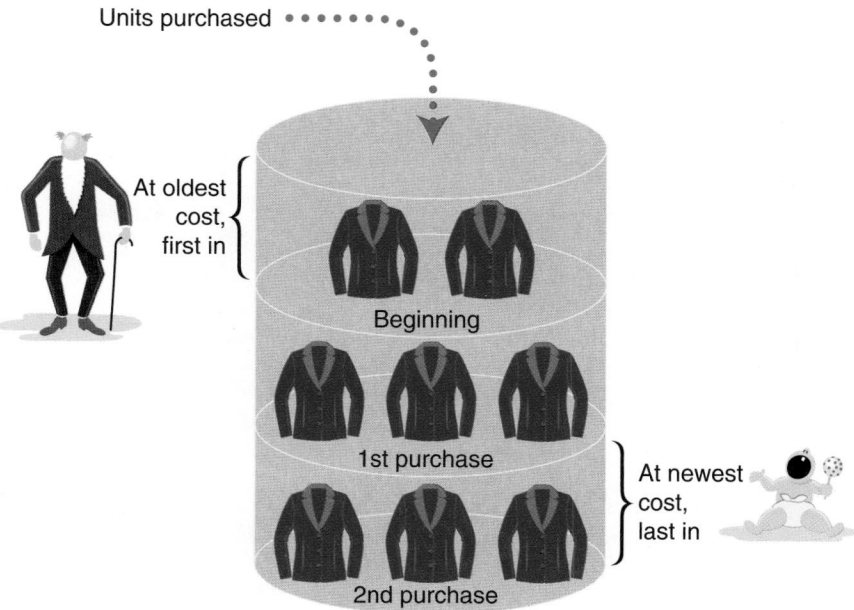

Transaction Date	Jan. 1	Sale Jan. 31	Purchase Feb. 5	Sale Feb. 28	Purchase Mar. 10	Sale Mar. 31
Number of jackets	800	(600)	800	(900)	900	(200)
Cost per jacket purchased	$200		$210		$220	
Sale price per jacket		$279		$295		$299
Cost of jackets sold		?		?		?

Exhibit **8.5**

Flow of Goods over Time

The main objective in this illustration is to determine the cost of jackets sold on each of the three dates.

First-In, First-Out Method

The **FIRST-IN, FIRST-OUT (FIFO) METHOD** assumes that the oldest units (the first costs in) are the first units sold.

The **first-in, first-out (FIFO) method** assumes that the earliest goods purchased (the first ones in) are the first units sold (the first ones out) and the last goods purchased remain in ending inventory. First, each purchase is treated as if it were added to the stack in sequence (800 jackets of beginning inventory at $200 each, followed by a first purchase on February 5 of 800 jackets at $210 each, and a second purchase on March 10 of 900 jackets at $220 each). Each of the 1,700 jackets sold is then removed from the stack in the same sequence it was added (800 units at $200, 800 units at $210, and 100 units at $220); first in is first out. FIFO allocates the oldest unit costs to cost of sales and the newest unit costs to ending inventory. We assume that physical inventory is taken at March 31, the end of the first quarter, to determine the number of jackets unsold, and that the number of jackets in stock is the same under both inventory control systems without any shrinkage or impairment in inventory value.

Perpetual Inventory System   When using the perpetual inventory system, Danier Leather must compute the cost of sales for each sales transaction to continuously update its inventory records. In Exhibit 8.6, the cost of sales is computed after each sales transaction. The graphic depicts the purchase and sale transactions to help you visualize how the cost of sales is computed under this system. The 600 jackets sold on January 31 are taken from the beginning inventory of 800 jackets at a cost of $200 per jacket. When Danier Leather sold 900 jackets on February 28, the company shipped to customers the remaining 200 jackets at a cost of $200 each, plus 700 jackets from the 800 units purchased on February 5 at a cost of $210 each. The remaining 100 jackets were then sold to customers on March 31, along with an additional 100 jackets taken from the 900 jackets purchased on March 10 at a cost of $220 each. This leaves 800 jackets in ending inventory. The total cost of sales is $350,000, and the cost of ending inventory is $176,000.

Exhibit **8.6**

FIFO Inventory Flows—Perpetual Inventory System

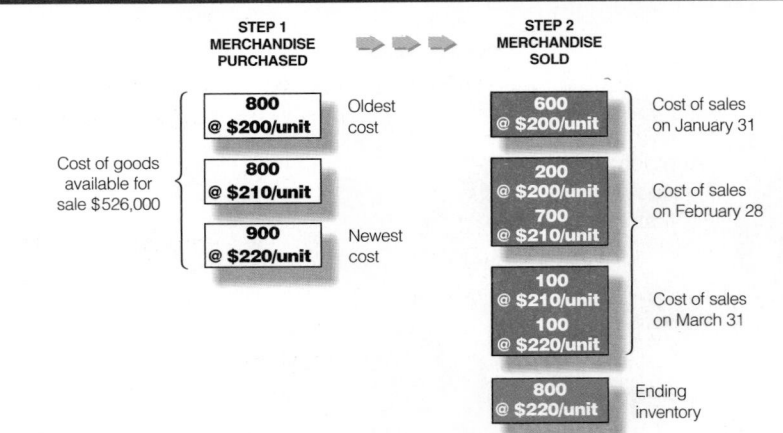

Cost of jackets purchased and sold

Date			Units		Cost		Total
January 1	Beginning inventory	**Oldest cost**	800	×	$200	=	$160,000
January 31	Cost of sales		(600)	×	$200		(120,000)
	Cost of remaining inventory		200	×	$200	=	40,000
February 5	Purchases		800	×	$210	=	168,000
	Cost of goods available for sale		1,000				208,000
February 28	Cost of sales (900 units)		(200)	×	$200		(40,000)
			(700)	×	$210		(147,000)
	Cost of remaining inventory		100	×	$210	=	21,000
March 10	Purchases	**Newest cost**	900	×	$220	=	198,000
	Cost of goods available for sale		1,000				219,000
March 31	Cost of sales (200 units)		(100)	×	$210	=	(21,000)
			(100)	×	$220	=	(22,000)
	Ending inventory		800	×	$220	=	$176,000
	Cost of sales						$350,000

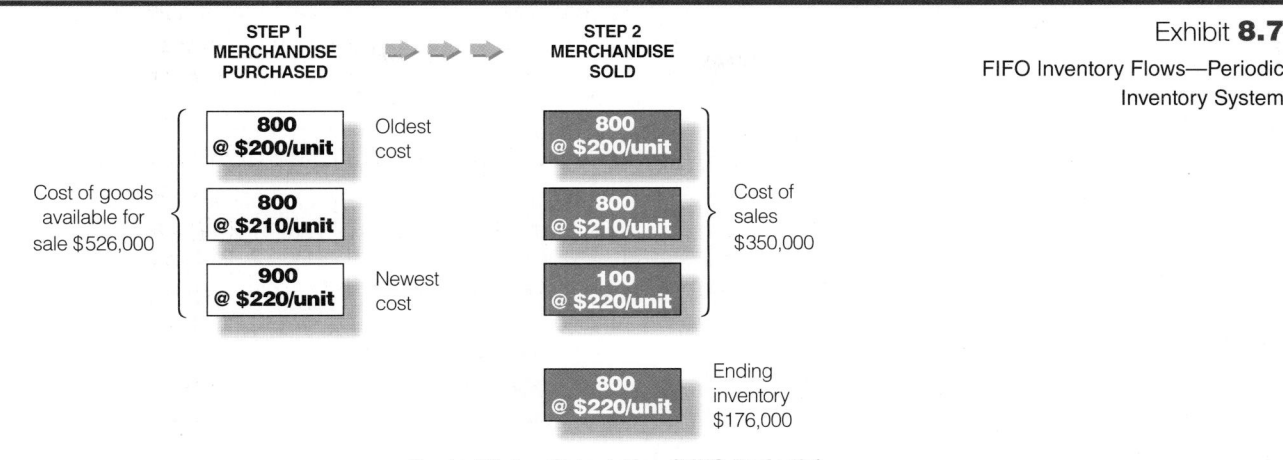

Exhibit **8.7**

FIFO Inventory Flows—Periodic
Inventory System

Cost of Sales Calculation (FIFO Periodic)

Cost of jackets purchased and sold

Date			Units		Cost	Total	
January 1	Beginning inventory	**Oldest cost**	800	×	$200	=	$160,000	
February 5	Purchase		800	×	$210		168,000	
March 10	Purchase	**Newest cost**	900	×	$220		198,000	
	Number of units available for sale		2,500				$526,000	**Cost of goods available for sale**
	Number of units in ending inventory		800	×	$220	=	176,000	**Cost of ending inventory**
	Number of units sold		1,700				$350,000	**Cost of sales**

Periodic Inventory System Would the computation of cost of sales and cost of ending inventory change if Danier Leather used a FIFO periodic inventory system? The answer is no. The only difference is that when a periodic inventory system is used, the cost of sales and the cost of ending inventory are computed at the end of the accounting period. But under FIFO, the order of costs in and out of inventory is identical for both the perpetual and the periodic systems. Therefore, the cost of sales will be the same under both systems. The same applies to the cost of ending inventory. Exhibit 8.7 summarizes the flow of goods. The table at the bottom of Exhibit 8.7 shows the flow of units and costs during the period. Notice that purchases are accumulated until the end of the period when the physical inventory count is taken and the cost of ending inventory is determined. The cost of sales is calculated at that time as the difference between the cost of goods available for sale (beginning inventory plus purchases) and the cost of ending inventory.

The total cost of sales under both systems is $350,000, the same amount computed under the perpetual inventory system. This is not surprising, because the old units that are in inventory at any date are assumed to be sold first before the new units are sold. Under both the perpetual and periodic systems, the 800 units in beginning inventory, the 800 units purchased on February 5, and 100 of the 900 units purchased on March 10 are assumed to be sold.

Comparison of Perpetual and Periodic Systems The differences between the perpetual and periodic inventory systems are highlighted in italics in Exhibit 8.8.

Exhibit **8.8**

Comparison of Perpetual and
Periodic Inventory Systems

Perpetual	**Periodic**
Beginning inventory (carried over from prior period)	Beginning inventory (carried over from prior period)
+ Purchases for the period (accumulated in an *Inventory* account)	+ Purchases for the period (accumulated in a *Purchases* account)
= Cost of goods available for sale	= Cost of goods available for sale
− *Cost of sales (measured at every sale, based on perpetual record)*	− *Ending inventory (measured at end of period, based on physical inventory count)*
= *Ending inventory (perpetual record updated at every sale)*	= *Cost of sales (computed as a residual amount)*

> The recording of the purchase and sales transactions under both inventory control systems are presented in Exhibit 8.9, assuming that all transactions are on account.

Exhibit **8.9**

Comparison of Journal Entries under Both the Perpetual and Periodic Inventory Systems

Perpetual Records (FIFO Costing Method)

1. Record all transactions in chronological order. Purchases should be recorded in the *inventory* account and in a detailed perpetual inventory record. Sales should be recorded in sales revenue, and the cost of sales should be recognized on the date of sale.

January 31:

Trade receivables (A)	167,400	
Sales revenue (R) (600 units × $279)		167,400
Cost of sales (E)	120,000	
Inventory (A) (600 units × $200)		120,000

February 5:

Inventory (A) (800 units × $210)	168,000	
Trade payables (L)		168,000

February 28:

Trade receivables (A)	265,500	
Sales revenue (R) (900 units × $295)		265,500
Cost of sales (E)	187,000	
Inventory (A)		187,000
(200 units × $200 + 700 units × $210)		

March 10:

Inventory (A) (900 units × $220)	198,000	
Trade payables (L)		198,000

March 31:

Trade receivables (A)	59,800	
Sales revenue (R) (200 units × $299)		59,800
Cost of sales (E)	43,000	
Inventory (A)		43,000
(100 units × $210 + 100 units × $220)		

2. At March 31, end of period: Use the cost of sales and inventory amounts. It is not necessary to compute the cost of sales because, under the perpetual inventory system, the cost of sales account is up to date. The balance in the cost of sales account is reported on the statement of earnings. Also, the inventory account shows the ending inventory amount reported on the statement of financial position. A physical inventory count is still necessary to assess the accuracy of the perpetual records and to assess theft and other forms of misuse (called *shrinkage*).

Cost of Sales (E)		
Jan. 31 sale 120,000	
Feb. 28 sale 187,000	
Mar. 31 sale 43,000	
End. 350,000	

March 31:

No entry

Inventory (A)			
Jan. 1 bal. 160,000	Jan. 31 sale 120,000
Feb. 5 purchase 168,000	Feb. 28 sale 187,000
Mar. 10 purchase 198,000	Mar. 31 sale 43,000
End. 176,000	

Periodic Records (FIFO Costing Method)

1. Record all transactions in chronological order. Record all purchases in the *purchases* account and all sales in the sales revenue account.

January 31:

Trade receivables (A)	167,400	
Sales revenue (R) (600 units × $279)		167,400

February 5:

Purchases* (T) (800 units × $210)	168,000	
Trade payables (L)		168,000

*Purchases is a temporary account (T) closed to cost of sales at the end of the period.

February 28:

Trade receivables (A)	265,500	
Sales revenue (R) (900 units × $295)		265,500

March 10:

Purchases (T) (900 units × $220)	198,000	
Trade payables (L)		198,000

March 31:

Trade receivables (A)	59,800	
Sales revenue (R) (200 units × $299)		59,800

2. At March 31, end of period:
   a. Count the number of units on hand.
   b. Compute the cost of the ending inventory.
   c. Compute and record the cost of sales.

Beginning inventory (last period's ending inventory)	$160,000
Add purchases (balance in the Purchases account)	366,000
Cost of goods available for sale	526,000
Deduct ending inventory (physical count—800 units at $220)	176,000
Cost of sales	$350,000

March 31:
Transfer beginning inventory and purchases to the cost of sales account:

Cost of sales (E)	526,000	
Inventory (A) (beginning)		160,000
Purchases (T)		366,000

Transfer the ending inventory amount from the cost of sales account to determine the cost of sales and establish the ending inventory balance:

Inventory (A) (ending)	176,000	
Cost of sales (E)		176,000

Exhibit **8.10**

Weighted-Average Inventory
Flows—Perpetual Inventory System

Cost of Sales Calculation (Weighted-Average Perpetual)

Cost of jackets purchased and sold

Date	Transaction	Units		Cost		Total	
January 1	Beginning inventory	800	×	$200	=	$ 160,000	
January 31	Sale	(600)	×	$200		(120,000)	
		200	×	$200		40,000	
February 5	Purchase	800	×	$210		168,000	
	Number of units available						Cost of goods available
	for sale (NUAS) =	1,000				$208,000	for sale (COGAS)
February 28	Sale	(900)	×	$208		(187,200)	
		100	×	$208		20,800	
March 10	Purchase	900	×	$220		198,000	
	Number of units available						Cost of goods available
	for sale (NUAS) =	1,000				$218,800	for sale (COGAS)
March 31	Sale	(200)	×	$218.8	=	(43,760)	
		800		$218.8	=	175,040	

$$\text{First weighted-average cost per unit} = \frac{\text{COGAS}}{\text{NUAS}} = \frac{\$208,000}{1,000} = \$208$$

$$\text{Second weighted-average cost per unit} = \frac{\text{COGAS}}{\text{NUAS}} = \frac{\$218.800}{1,000} = \$218.8$$

Weighted-Average Cost Method

The **weighted-average cost method** requires computation of the weighted-average unit cost of the goods available for sale.

Perpetual Inventory System   As indicated before, when a perpetual inventory system is used, the inventory records are updated after every purchase and sale transaction in order to keep track of the number of inventory items on hand.

The 600 jackets sold on January 31 are taken from the beginning inventory of 800 jackets at a cost of $200 per unit, for a total cost of $120,000. The cost of the remaining 200 jackets is then added to the cost of the 800 jackets purchased on February 5 to compute a new weighted-average unit cost of $208 per jacket, as shown in Exhibit 8.10.

This average cost is then used to compute the cost of the 900 jackets sold on February 28, that is, 900 × $208, or $187,200. The cost of the remaining 100 jackets is then added to the cost of the 900 jackets purchased on March 10 to compute a third weighted-average cost of $218.80 per jacket. This average cost is then used to compute the cost of the 200 jackets sold on March 31, that is, 200 × $218.80, or $43,760. Since the average cost changed three times, this method is called the *moving weighted-average cost* method. The total cost of sales during the quarter is $350,960 ($120,000 + $187,200 + $43,760), and the cost of ending inventory is $175,040.

Periodic Inventory System   Would the computation of cost of sales and ending inventory change if Danier Leather used a periodic inventory system instead of a perpetual system? As indicated before, when a periodic inventory system is used, the cost of sales and ending inventory are computed at the end of the accounting period. The average cost is calculated by dividing the cost of goods available for sale by the total units available for sale. For our example, the weighted-average unit cost for the quarter is computed as indicated in Exhibit 8.11.

In these circumstances, the cost of sales and the ending inventory are assigned the same weighted-average cost of $210.40 per jacket. The cost of the ending inventory is $168,320 (800 jackets at $210.40 each) compared to $175,040 under the perpetual inventory system, and the cost of sales is $357,680 compared to $350,960 under the

The **WEIGHTED-AVERAGE COST METHOD** uses the weighted-average unit cost of the goods available for sale for both cost of sales and ending inventory.

Exhibit **8.11**

Weighted-Average Inventory
Flows—Periodic Inventory System

Cost of Sales Calculation (Weighted-Average Periodic)

Cost of jackets purchased and sold

Date		Units		Cost		Total	
January 1	Beginning inventory	800	×	$200	=	$160,000	
February 5	Purchase	800	×	$210		168,000	
March 10	Purchase	900	×	$220		198,000	
Number of units available for sale (NUAS):		2,500				$526,000	Cost of goods available for sale (COGAS)
Number of units in ending inventory:		800	×	$210.4	=	168,320	Cost of ending inventory
Number of units sold:		1,700	×	$210.4	=	$357,680	Cost of sales

$$\text{Weighted-average cost per unit} = \frac{\text{COGAS}}{\text{NUAS}} = \frac{\$526,000}{2,500} = \$\,210.40^5$$

perpetual system. The periodic cost of sales is always higher than the perpetual cost of sales in a period of rising prices, because the periodic average cost per unit includes the cost of all units available for sale during the accounting period, whereas the perpetual average cost method considers only the cost of units available for sale at different dates in the accounting period.

The process of recording the purchase and sales transactions during the three-month period and the adjustments at the end of March 31 are similar to those that are presented in Exhibit 8.9, except for the differences in the cost of sales amounts.

Financial Statement Effects of Inventory Costing Methods

Each of the three alternative inventory costing methods is in conformity with IFRS. To understand why managers choose different methods in different circumstances, we must first understand their effects on the statement of earnings and statement of financial position. Exhibit 8.12 summarizes the financial statement effects of the FIFO and weighted-average cost methods using either the perpetual or the periodic inventory system. Remember that the methods differ only in the portion of goods available for sale allocated to cost of sales versus ending inventory. For that reason, the method that gives the highest cost of ending inventory also gives the lowest cost of sales and the highest gross profit, income tax expense, and net earnings amounts, and vice versa.

Exhibit **8.12**

Financial Statement Effects of
Inventory Costing Methods

	Perpetual Inventory System		Periodic Inventory System	
	FIFO	Weighted Average	FIFO	Weighted Average
Cost of Sales Calculation				
Beginning inventory	$160,000	$160,000	$160,000	$160,000
Add: Purchases	366,000	366,000	366,000	366,000
Cost of goods available for sale	526,000	526,000	526,000	526,000
Deduct: Ending inventory (to statement of financial position)	176,000	175,040	176,000	168,320
Cost of sales (to statement of earnings)	$350,000	$350,960	$350,000	$357,680
Effect on the statement of earnings				
Sales	$492,700*	$492,700	$492,700	$492,700
Cost of sales	350,000	350,960	350,000	357,680
Gross profit	$142,700	$141,740	$142,700	$135,020
Effect on the statement of financial position				
Inventory	$176,000	$175,040	$176,000	$168,320

*(600 × $279) + (900 × $295) + (200 × $299)

Notice in Exhibit 8.12 that the cost of sales under FIFO is the same whether Danier Leather uses the perpetual or the periodic inventory system, as previously illustrated. Furthermore, the weighted-average cost of sales is closer to the FIFO cost when a perpetual inventory system is used, because the moving weighted-average cost increased with each new purchase of units, thus approaching the FIFO cost. In the comparison in Exhibit 8.12, unit costs were increasing. *When unit costs are rising, the weighted-average cost method produces lower net earnings and a lower inventory valuation than FIFO. When unit costs are declining, the weighted-average cost method produces higher net earnings and a higher inventory valuation than FIFO.* These effects are summarized in the following table:

| | **Normal Financial Statement Effects of** | | | |
| | **Rising Costs** | | **Declining Costs** | |
	FIFO	**Weighted Average**	**FIFO**	**Weighted Average**
Cost of sales	Lower	Higher	Higher	Lower
Gross profit	Higher	Lower	Lower	Higher
Net earnings	Higher	Lower	Lower	Higher
Ending inventory	Higher	Lower	Lower	Higher

These effects occur because the weighted-average cost method causes the newer unit costs to be reflected in cost of sales on the statement of earnings; FIFO causes the older unit costs to be reflected in cost of sales on the statement of earnings. In contrast, on the statement of financial position, the ending inventory amount under the weighted-average cost method reflects a mix of unit costs, which may be an unrealistic valuation, whereas FIFO ending inventory is based on the newest costs, thus assisting the user in predicting the amount of cash needed to replace the inventory.

DIFFERENT INVENTORY COSTING METHODS AND INTERNATIONAL COMPARISONS

 INTERNATIONAL PERSPECTIVE

While most countries have harmonized or will shortly harmonize their accounting standards with IFRS, the United States has delayed its harmonization process. The Financial Accounting Standards Board (FASB) in the United States permits a fourth method, last-in, first-out (LIFO). LIFO assumes that the most recently purchased items (the last ones in) are sold first and the oldest items are left in inventory. LIFO allocates the newest unit costs to cost of sales and the oldest unit costs to ending inventory. Because, in general, prices rise rather than fall, the effect is to increase cost of sales and therefore decrease taxable income. Reducing income tax payable retains more cash in a corporation to finance future growth or payout to existing debtors and shareholders.

The use of LIFO by U.S. companies for some or all of their inventories creates comparability problems when one attempts to compare companies across international borders. For example, Nissan Motor Company (of Japan) uses FIFO for all inventories, while General Motors uses LIFO to value most of its U.S. inventories, and either average cost or FIFO for non-U.S. inventories. Managers, investors, and financial analysts who read audited financial statements must also carefully read the significant accounting policies that companies use in preparing their financial statements and related note disclosures.

Consistency in Use of Inventory Costing Methods It is important to remember that regardless of the physical flow of goods, a company can use either the weighted-average or the FIFO inventory costing method. Companies are expected to select the most representationally faithful inventory costing method. Therefore, a company is not required to use the same inventory costing method for all inventory items. The justification arises from the pervasive principle of economic substance over form. Each component of inventory value is supposed to reflect most accurately the anticipated benefit that will eventually be realized from either the use or the sale of the inventory. For example, Telestra Corporation uses FIFO cost for valuation of raw materials and weighted-average cost for other inventory items.

To enhance comparability, accounting rules require companies to apply their accounting methods on a consistent basis. A company is not permitted to use FIFO one period, weighted average the next, and then FIFO the next. A change in method is allowed only if the change will improve the measurement of financial results and better report the financial position. Changing from one inventory costing method to another is a significant event. Such a change requires full disclosure about the reason for the change and the accounting effects.

Managers' Choice of Inventory Costing Methods

LO4

Decide when the use of different inventory costing methods is beneficial to a company.

What motivates companies to choose different inventory costing methods? Our discussion in Chapter 6 suggests that management should choose the method that best reflects its economic circumstances for financial reporting purposes. In practice, most managers choose generally accepted accounting methods based on two factors:

1. Effect on net earnings (managers prefer to report higher earnings for their companies).

2. Effect on income taxes (managers prefer to pay the least amount of taxes allowed by law, as late as possible—the *least–latest rule*).

Management must also make a second choice of inventory costing method to use on the company's tax return (for tax purposes). In general, most companies use the same inventory costing method for both financial reporting and tax reporting purposes.

The income tax effects associated with FIFO and weighted average for companies facing rising costs can be illustrated by continuing our simple Danier Leather example. Using the data from Exhibit 8.12 and assuming expenses other than cost of sales are $42,700 and that the tax rate is 25 percent, the following differences in taxes result:

	Perpetual Inventory System		Periodic Inventory System	
	FIFO	Weighted Average	FIFO	Weighted Average
Sales	$492,700*	$492,700	$492,700	$492,700
Cost of sales	350,000	350,960	350,000	357,680
Gross net earnings	142,700	141,740	142,700	135,020
Other expenses	42,700	42,700	42,700	42,700
Net earnings before income taxes	100,000	99,040	100,000	92,320
Income tax expense (at 25%)	25,000	24,760	25,000	23,080
Net earnings	$ 75,000	$ 74,280	$ 75,000	$ 69,240

*(600 × $279) + (900 × $295) + (200 × $299)

For this illustration, the use of the weighted-average cost method produces a lower amount of income taxes than the FIFO method, but the difference in income taxes under the perpetual inventory system is not material. While the lowest amount of income taxes results from the use of weighted-average cost and a periodic inventory system, other important considerations should be taken into account when choosing between a periodic and a perpetual inventory system, such as the cost savings that may result from better control of the inventory flows throughout the year.

Many high-technology companies enjoy declining costs for basic commodities, such as computer chips. In such circumstances, the FIFO method—in which the oldest, most expensive goods become cost of sales—produces the largest cost of sales, the lowest gross profit, and, thus, the lowest income tax liability.

Most Canadian companies use the perpetual inventory system and either FIFO or moving weighted average for inventory costing. The choice of either method affects both the reported cost of inventory on the statement of financial position and net earnings and cash flows. The reported amounts also affect the calculation of several financial ratios. When prices are rising, companies that wish to minimize their income taxes would logically choose weighted-average cost rather than FIFO, because the weighted-average cost method produces lower earnings before income taxes. The lower net earnings reduces profitability and other ratios. However, management may be interested in maximizing net earnings and the reported inventory value to satisfy restrictions imposed by creditors in lending agreements. While companies are expected to adopt the inventory costing method that provides the best representation of the flow of costs during the period, the choice of a specific accounting method is influenced, in some cases, by management's objectives and the effects of the chosen method on the reported results.

INVENTORY COSTING AND CONFLICTS BETWEEN MANAGERS' AND OWNERS' INTERESTS

A QUESTION OF ACCOUNTABILITY

We have seen that the selection of an inventory method can have significant effects on financial statements. Company managers may have an incentive to select a particular method that may not be consistent with the objectives of the owners. For example, the use of weighted-average cost during a period of rising prices may be in the best interests of the owners, because the weighted-average cost method often reduces the company's tax liability. If managers' compensation is tied to reported net earnings, they may prefer FIFO, which typically results in higher net earnings.

A well-designed compensation plan should reward managers for acting in the best interests of the owners, but, unfortunately, this is not always the case. Clearly, a manager who selects an accounting method that is not optimal for the company, solely to increase his or her compensation, has engaged in questionable ethical behaviour.[6]

PAUSE FOR FEEDBACK

Three different inventory costing methods may be used to allocate costs between the units remaining in inventory and the units sold, depending on economic circumstances. The methods are specific identification, FIFO, and weighted-average cost. Each of the inventory costing methods conforms to IFRS. Remember that the cost flow assumption need not match the physical flow of inventory. The following questions test your understanding of the FIFO and weighted-average cost methods.

SELF-STUDY **QUIZ 8-3**

Assume that a company began operations this year. Its purchases for the year were as follows:

January	10 units @ $10 each
May	5 units @ $11 each
November	5 units @ $13 each

During the year, 15 units were sold for $20 each, and other operating expenses totalled $100.

1. Compute cost of sales and pretax earnings for the year under the FIFO and weighted-average cost methods, assuming the use of a periodic inventory system.

2. Which method would you recommend that the company adopt? Why?

After you complete your answers, check them with the solutions at the end of the chapter.

INVENTORY COSTING METHODS AND FINANCIAL STATEMENT ANALYSIS

Critics of multiple inventory valuation methods argue that the existence of alternatives is inconsistent with the comparability characteristic of high-quality, useful accounting information. This quality is needed so that managers, investors, and financial analysts can compare information for a company with that of other companies for the same period. These types of comparisons are more difficult when companies use different accounting methods. Often, it is impossible to convert, for example, a FIFO-based inventory value to a weighted-average cost of inventory because the data needed for the conversion are unavailable. In reality, however, a particular method may result in a better representation of the economic substance of inventory transactions than their legal form might. Absolute standardization based on one inventory costing method could readily result in formal comparability that fails to inform users of the best estimate of either cost of sales or inventory value.

Users of financial statements must be certain that their decisions are based on real differences, not artificial differences created by alternative accounting methods. For this reason, users must be knowledgeable about alternative accounting methods and how they affect financial statements. This is why accounting standards require companies to inform external users when the method of inventory valuation has changed and to restate the prior year's information: not only must a change in method be communicated, but also the reasons the alternative now in place provides an improved reflection of economic substance must be revealed.

VALUATION AT LOWER OF COST AND NET REALIZABLE VALUE

LO5

Report inventory at the lower of cost and net realizable value (LCNRV).

NET REALIZABLE VALUE is the expected sales price less estimated selling costs.

LOWER OF COST AND NET REALIZABLE VALUE (LCNRV) is a valuation method departing from the cost principle; it serves to recognize a loss when the net realizable value drops below cost.

Inventories should be measured at their acquisition cost, in conformity with the cost principle. However, the cost of inventories may not be recoverable if their selling prices have declined, they are damaged, or they have become obsolete. The lower amount should be used as the inventory valuation in compliance with representational faithfulness, which requires the reporting of inventory values that do not exceed the amount that can be obtained from selling the inventory. For the purpose of inventory valuation, market value refers to the **net realizable value** of the inventory, which is essentially an estimate of the amount that a company expects to receive for selling its inventory in the ordinary course of business, net of estimated selling expenses. This valuation rule, a departure from the cost principle, is known as measuring inventories at the **lower of cost and net realizable value (LCNRV)**.

This departure from the cost principle is particularly important for two types of companies: (1) high-technology companies, such as Nokia, that manufacture goods for which the cost of production and the selling price are declining and (2) companies such as Danier Leather that sell seasonal goods such as clothing, the value of which drops dramatically at the end of each selling season (fall or spring).

Under LCNRV, companies recognize a loss in the period in which the net realizable value of an item drops rather than in the period in which the item is sold. The loss is the difference between the purchase cost and the net realizable value and is added to the cost of sales of the period. To illustrate, assume that Danier Leather had the following items in the current period's ending inventory:

Item	Quantity	Cost per Item	Net Realizable Value (NRV) per Item	LCNRV per Item	Total LCNRV
Jackets style #101	1,000	$220	$200	$200	1,000 × $200 = $200,000
Handbags style #305	400	100	210	100	400 × $100 = 40,000

The 1,000 jackets should be recorded in the ending inventory at the net realizable value ($200), which is lower than the cost ($220). Danier Leather makes the following journal entry to record the write-down:[7]

| Cost of sales (E) (1,000 × $20) .... 20,000 | | |
| Allowance for write-down of inventory to NRV (XA) .... | | 20,000 |

Assets	=	Liabilities	+	Shareholders' Equity	
Allowance for write-down of inventory to NRV	−20,000			Cost of sales	−20,000

This allowance account to record the decline in the value of its inventory is similar to using an allowance for doubtful accounts to record the estimated doubtful accounts. Alternatively, the inventory account could have been directly reduced by $20,000.

Since the net realizable value of the handbags ($210) is higher than the original cost ($100), no write-down is necessary. The handbags remain on the books at their cost of $100 per unit ($40,000 in total). Recognition of holding gains on inventory is not permitted by IFRS.

The write-down of the inventory of jackets to net realizable value produces the following financial statement effects:

	Effects of LCNRV Write-Down	
	Current Period	**Period of Sale**
Cost of sales	Increase $20,000	Decrease $20,000
Pretax earnings	Decrease $20,000	Increase $20,000
Ending inventory on statement of financial position	Decrease $20,000	Unaffected

The LCNRV rule accounts for the added expense in the current period, not in the period of sale. Consequently, pretax earnings are reduced by $20,000 in the period in which the net realizable value drops, rather than in the next period when the jackets are sold. Since the cost of sales for the current period increases by $20,000 and the cost of sales for the next period decreases by $20,000, the total cost of sales (and earnings before taxes) for the two periods combined does not change. On the statement of financial position, the $20,000 loss in the current period reduces the amount of inventory reported at year-end.

If the net realizable value of the inventory items that were written down increases in a subsequent accounting period because of changed economic circumstances, then the amount of the write-down is reversed up to the original cost, so that the new carrying amount of the inventory is the lower of the cost and the revised net realizable value. Normally, a reversal of a previous write-down occurs when an inventory item that is carried at net realizable value is still on hand in a subsequent period when its selling price has increased.

Under IFRS, the LCNRV rule must be applied to all inventories, item by item, regardless of the inventory costing methods that a company uses.[8] For example, in the excerpt below, Danier Leather reports the use of the lower of cost (FIFO) and net realizable value rule for financial statement purposes:

REAL-WORLD EXCERPT

Danier Leather Inc.
ANNUAL REPORT

DANIER LEATHER CORPORATION NOTE 1 TO THE CONSOLIDATED FINANCIAL STATEMENTS

NOTE 1. Summary of Significant Accounting Policies

(j) Inventories:

Merchandise inventories are valued at the lower of cost, using the weighted average cost method, and net realizable value. . . . The Company estimates the net realizable value as the amount at which inventories are expected to be sold, taking into account fluctuations in retail prices due to seasonality, age, excess quantities, condition of the inventory, nature of the inventory, and the estimated variable costs necessary to make the sale. Inventories are written down to net realizable value when the cost of inventories is not estimated to be recoverable due to obsolescence, damage or declining selling prices. When circumstances that previously caused inventories to be written down below cost no longer exist, the amount of the write-down previously recorded is reversed.

Source: Danier Leather Inc., Annual Report 2012.

Danier Leather also reports the write-down to its inventories in Note 2 below. These details inform the financial statement users that an additional allowance or loss of $1,746 thousand was made at the end of fiscal year 2012, and an amount of $174 thousand was recovered during the same fiscal year. The amount of the write-downs represents 7 percent of the carrying amount of inventories on that date.

Notes to the consolidated financial statements

NOTE 2: Inventories

	June 30, 2012	June 25, 2011
Cost of inventory recognized as an expense	$70,739	$70,420
Write-downs of inventory due to net realizable value being lower than cost	1,746	1,549
Write-downs recognized in previous periods that were reversed	174	45

Source: Danier Leather Inc., Annual Report 2012.

EVALUATING INVENTORY MANAGEMENT

Measuring Efficiency in Inventory Management

LO6

Evaluate inventory management by using the inventory turnover ratio and the effects of inventory on cash flows.

As noted at the beginning of the chapter, the primary goals of inventory management are to have sufficient quantities of high-quality inventory available to serve customers' needs, while minimizing the costs of carrying inventory (production, storage, obsolescence, and financing). The inventory turnover ratio is an important measure of the company's success in balancing these conflicting goals.

KEY RATIO
ANALYSIS

INVENTORY TURNOVER RATIO

ANALYTICAL QUESTION → How efficient are inventory management activities?

RATIO AND COMPARISONS → The answer to this question is facilitated by the computation of the inventory turnover ratio as follows:

$$\text{Inventory Turnover Ratio} = \frac{\text{Cost of Sales}}{\text{Average Inventory*}}$$

*Average Inventory = (Beginning Inventory + Ending Inventory) ÷ 2

The 2012 inventory turnover ratio for Danier Leather is

$$\frac{\$71,513}{(\$28,964 + \$24,981) \div 2} = 2.65$$

Comparisons over Time			Comparisons with Competitors	
Danier Leather			Coach Inc.	G-III Apparel Group
2010	2011	2012	2012	2012
3.25	2.57	2.65	2.80	3.75

INTERPRETATIONS

In General → The inventory turnover ratio reflects how many times the average inventory was produced and sold during the period. A higher ratio indicates that inventory moves more quickly through the production process to the ultimate customer, reducing storage and obsolescence costs. Because less money is tied up in inventory, the excess can be invested to earn interest income or to reduce borrowings, which reduces interest expense. More efficient purchasing and production techniques, such as just-in-time inventory, as well as high product demand, cause this ratio to be high. Inefficient purchasing and production techniques and declining product demand cause this ratio to be low. Analysts and creditors watch this ratio because a sudden decline may mean that a company is facing an unexpected decline in demand for its products or is becoming sloppy in its production management. Many managers and analysts compute the related number of average days to sell inventory, which, for Danier Leather, is equal to

$$\text{Average Days to Sell inventory} = \frac{365}{\text{Inventory Turnover Ratio}} = \frac{365}{2.65} = 137.7 \text{ days}$$

This number indicates the average time it takes the company to produce and deliver inventory to customers.

Focus Company Analysis → Danier Leather's inventory turnover ratio has decreased during the period 2010–2012. This decrease could reflect the unexpected decline in sales during the recent economic downturn and rising consumer debt levels, which affect consumer disposable income that is spent on non-essential items such as apparel purchases. Danier Leather's inventory turnover ratio is slightly lower than those of its competitors, Coach Inc. and G-III Apparel Group.

A Few Cautions → Differences across industries in purchasing, production, and sales processes cause dramatic differences in the ratio. For example, restaurants such as Pizza Hut, which must turn over their perishable inventory very quickly, tend to have much higher inventory turnover than automakers such as Toyota. A particular firm's ratio should be compared only with its prior years' figures or with other firms in the same industry. Financial statement users need to interpret the ratios carefully because companies may use different accounting methods. For example, both Coach Inc. and G-III Apparel Group use FIFO to value their inventories, whereas Danier Leather uses the weighted-average cost method.

SELECTED FOCUS COMPANY INVENTORY TURNOVER RATIOS—2012

Sun-Rype 2.51

Gildan Activewear 3.47

Canadian Tire 7.74

Inventory and Cash Flows

When companies expand production to meet increases in demand, this increases the amount of inventory reported on the statement of financial position. However, when companies overestimate demand for a product, they usually produce too many units of the slow-moving item. This increases storage costs as well as the interest costs on short-term borrowings that finance the inventory. It may even lead to losses if the excess inventory cannot be sold at normal prices. The statement of cash flows often provides the first sign of such problems.

INVENTORY

FOCUS ON **CASH FLOWS**

As with the change in trade receivables, the change in inventories can be a major determinant of a company's cash flow from operations. The statement of earnings reflects the cost of sales during the period, whereas the statement of cash flows should reflect the cash payments to suppliers for the same period. Cost of sales may be more or less than the amount of cash paid to suppliers during the period. Since most inventory is purchased on open credit (borrowing from suppliers is normally called *trade payables*), reconciling cost of sales with cash paid to suppliers requires consideration of the changes in both the inventory and trade payables accounts.

The simplest way to think about the effects of changes in inventory is to realize that buying (increasing) inventory eventually decreases cash, and selling (decreasing) inventory eventually increases cash. Similarly, borrowing from suppliers, which increases trade payables, increases cash; paying suppliers, which decreases trade payables, decreases cash.

Effect on Statement of Cash Flows

In General → A *decrease in inventory* for the period indicates that the cost of sales exceeded the cost of goods purchased; thus, the decrease in inventory must be *added* to net earnings to reflect the cost of goods purchased.

An *increase in inventory* for the period indicates that the cost of goods purchased exceeded the cost of sales; thus, the increase in inventory must be *subtracted* from net earnings to reflect the cost of goods purchased.

A *decrease in trade payables* for the period indicates that the payments to suppliers exceeded the cost of goods purchased; thus, the decrease in trade payables must be *subtracted* from net earnings in computing cash flows from operations.

An *increase in trade payables* for the period indicates that the cost of goods purchased exceeded the payments to suppliers; thus, the increase in trade payables must be *added* to net earnings in computing cash flows from operations.

	Effect on Cash Flows
Operating activities (indirect method)	
Net earnings	$xxx
Adjusted for	
Add inventory *decrease*	+
Or	
Subtract inventory *increase*	−
Add trade payables *increase*	+
Or	
Subtract trade payables *decrease*	−

Focus Company Analysis → Exhibit 8.13 is the Operating Activities section of Danier Leather's statement of cash flows. When the inventory balance increases during the period, as was the case at Danier Leather for the fiscal years ended June 30, 2012, and June 25, 2011, the company has purchased or produced more inventory than it sold during the period. Thus, the increase in inventory is subtracted from net earnings in the computation of cash flow from operations. Conversely, when the inventory balance decreases during the period, the company has sold more inventory than it purchased or produced, and the decrease in inventory is added to net earnings in the computation of cash flow from operations. When the trade payables balance decreases during the period, as was the case at Danier Leather during 2012, the company has paid more to its suppliers than it purchased on credit. Thus, the decrease is subtracted from net earnings in the computation of cash flow from operations.*

*For companies with foreign currency or business acquisitions/dispositions, the amount of the change reported on the statement of cash flows will not equal the change in the accounts reported on the statement of financial position.

Exhibit 8.13

Inventories on the Statement of Cash Flows

REAL-WORLD EXCERPT

Danier Leather Inc.

ANNUAL REPORT

CONSOLIDATED STATEMENTS OF CASH FLOW
(thousands of Canadian dollars)

	Years Ended	
	June 30, 2012	**June 25, 2011**
	53 weeks	52 weeks
Cash provided by (used in)		
Operating Activities		
Net earnings	$ 4,003	$ 7,568
Adjustments for:		
Amortization of property and equipment	3,300	3,390
Amortization of computer software	380	523
Impairment loss on property and equipment	66	98
Amortization of deferred lease inducement	(175)	(213)
Proceeds from deferred lease inducement	188	155
Straight line rent expense	42	31
Stock-based compensation	25	93
Interest income	(229)	(160)
Interest expense	51	103
Provision for income taxes	1,524	3,140
Changes in working capital (Note 14)	3,198	(3,404)
Interest paid	(12)	(218)
Interest received	223	140
Income taxes paid	(2,459)	(6,723)
Net cash generated from operating activities	10,125	4,523

Source: Danier Leather Inc., Annual Report 2012.

(continued)

14. CHANGES IN WORKING CAPITAL ITEMS:

	June 30, 2012	June 25, 2011
Decrease (increase) in:		
Accounts receivable	(132)	158
Inventories	4,073	(2,425)
Prepaid expenses	69	374
Increase (decrease) in:		
Payables and accruals	(863)	(1,419)
Deferred revenue	(26)	(139)
Sales return provision	77	47
	$3,198	($3,404)

Source: Danier Leather Inc., Annual Report 2012.

PAUSE FOR FEEDBACK

The inventory turnover ratio measures the efficiency of inventory management. It reflects how many times average inventory was produced and sold during the period. Analysts and creditors watch this ratio because a sudden decline may mean that a company is facing an unexpected drop in demand for its products or is becoming sloppy in its production management. Before you move on, complete the following questions to test your understanding of these concepts.

SELF-STUDY QUIZ 8-4

Danier Leather reported the following cost of sales and ending inventory for a recent six-year period (amounts in thousands of dollars):

Year	2012	2011	2010	2009	2008	2007
Cost of sales	$71,513	$71,333	$77,438	$88,589	$87,365	$79,565
Ending inventory	24,891	28,964	26,539	21,045	27,404	28,561

1. Compute the inventory turnover ratios for 2008 through 2012. Is Danier Leather managing its inventory efficiently?

2. If Danier Leather had been able to manage its inventory more efficiently and decreased purchases and ending inventory by $1,000 in 2012, would its inventory turnover ratio for 2012 have increased or decreased? Explain.

3. If Danier Leather had decreased its trade payables, would its cash flow from operations have increased or decreased?

After you complete your answers, check them with the solutions at the end of this chapter.

ACCOUNTING STANDARDS FOR PRIVATE ENTERPRISES

The accounting standards related to measuring and reporting of inventories by Canadian private enterprises are very similar to those included in IAS 2—Inventories, which Canadian publicly accountable enterprises must use.

DEMONSTRATION **CASE A**

This case reviews the application of the inventory costing methods and the inventory turnover ratio. Balent Appliances distributes a number of high-cost household appliances. One product, microwave ovens, has been selected for case purposes. Assume that the following summarized transactions were completed during the accounting period in the order given:

	Units	Unit Cost
a. Beginning inventory	11	$200
b. Inventory purchases	9	220
c. Sales (at $420 per unit)	8	?
d. Inventory purchases	10	210
e. Sales (at $420 per unit)	11	?

Required:

1. Compute the following amounts in accordance with each of the inventory costing methods, assuming that a periodic inventory system is used.

	Ending Inventory		Cost of Sales	
	Units	Dollars	Units	Dollars
a. FIFO				
b. Weighted Average				

2. Compute the inventory turnover ratio for the current period by using each of the inventory costing methods. What does this ratio mean? Which inventory costing method provides the higher ratio? Is this true in all situations? Explain.

3. Will the choice of inventory costing method affect cash flow from operations? Explain.

We strongly recommend that you prepare your own answers to these requirements and then check your answers with the following solution.

SUGGESTED **SOLUTION**

1.

	Ending Inventory		Cost of Sales	
	Units	Dollars	Units	Dollars
a. FIFO	11	$2,320	19	$3,960
b. Weighted Average	11	2,303	19	3,977

Computations
Cost of Goods Available for Sale = Beginning Inventory + Purchases
$$= (11 \text{ units} \times \$200) + (9 \text{ units} \times \$220 + 10 \text{ units} \times \$210)$$
$$= \$6,280$$

FIFO Cost
Ending Inventory = (10 units × $210 + 1 unit × $220) = $2,320
Cost of Sales   = $6,280 − $2,320 = $3,960

Weighted-Average Cost
Average Cost   = $6,280 ÷ 30 units = $209.33
Ending Inventory = 11 units × $209.33 = $2,303
Cost of Sales   = $6,280 − $2,303 = $3,977

2. Inventory Turnover Ratio = Cost of Sales ÷ Average Inventory
   FIFO $3,960 ÷ [($2,200 + $2,320) ÷ 2] = 1.75
   Weighted Average $3,977 ÷ [($2,200 + $2,303) ÷ 2] = 1.77

The inventory turnover ratio reflects how many times the average inventory was purchased and sold during the period. Thus, Balent Appliances purchased and sold its average inventory fewer than two times during the period.

The weighted-average costing method provides the higher inventory turnover ratio. This is generally true when the prices of inventory items increase over time, because the cost of sales reflects more recent, higher prices and ending inventory includes older, lower prices than FIFO.

3. The choice of an inventory costing method does not affect the total amount of purchases and the amount paid to suppliers. It simply allocates the purchases differently between cost of sales and ending inventory. However, the method chosen affects the computation of cost of sales, gross profit, and earnings before income taxes. Hence, the amount of income taxes payable is affected by the inventory costing method.

DEMONSTRATION **CASE B**

Metal Products Inc. has been operating for three years as a distributor of a line of metal products. It is now the end of 2014, and for the first time, the company will undergo an audit by an external auditor. The company uses a periodic inventory system. The annual statements of earnings prepared by the company are as follows:

	For the Year Ended December 31			
	2014		**2013**	
Sales revenue		$800,000		$750,000
Cost of sales				
Beginning inventory	$ 40,000		$ 45,000	
Add purchases	484,000		460,000	
Cost of goods available for sale	524,000		505,000	
Deduct ending inventory	60,000		40,000	
Cost of sales		464,000		465,000
Gross margin on sales		336,000		285,000
Operating expenses		306,000		275,000
Pretax earnings		30,000		10,000
Income tax expense (20%)		6,000		2,000
Net earnings		$ 24,000		$ 8,000

During the early stages of the audit, the external auditor discovered that the ending inventory for 2013 was understated by $15,000.

Required:

1. Based on the preceding statement of earnings amounts, compute the gross profit percentage on sales for each year. Do the results suggest an inventory error? Explain.

2. Correct and reconstruct the two statements of earnings.

3. Answer the following questions:

   a. What are the correct gross profit percentages?

   b. What effect did the $15,000 understatement of the ending inventory have on the pretax earnings for 2013? Explain.

   c. What effect did the inventory error have on the pretax income for 2014? Explain.

   d. How did the inventory error affect the income tax expense?

We strongly recommend that you prepare your own answers to these requirements and then check your answers with the following solution.

SUGGESTED **SOLUTION**

1. The gross profit percentages as reported are as follows:

   2013: $285,000 ÷ $750,000 = 38%

   2014: $336,000 ÷ $800,000 = 42%

   The change in the gross profit percentage from 38% to 42% suggests the possibility of an inventory error in the absence of any other explanation.

2. The corrected statements of earnings follow:

	For the Year Ended December 31			
	2014		**2013**	
Sales revenue		$800,000		$750,000
Cost of sales				
Beginning inventory	$ 55,000*		$ 45,000	
Add purchases	484,000		460,000	
Cost of goods available for sale	539,000		505,000	
Deduct ending inventory	60,000		55,000*	
Cost of sales		479,000		450,000
Gross margin on sales		321,000		300,000
Operating expenses		306,000		275,000
Pretax earnings		15,000		25,000
Income tax expense (20%)		3,000		5,000
Net earnings		$ 12,000		$ 20,000

*Increased by $15,000.

3. *a.* The correct gross profit percentages are as follows:

    2013: $300,000 ÷ $750,000 = 40.0%
    2014: $321,000 ÷ $800,000 = 40.1%

    The inventory error of $15,000 was responsible for the difference in the gross profit percent-ages reflected in (1). The error in the 2013 ending inventory affected the gross margin for both 2013 and 2014 by the same amount, $15,000, but in the opposite direction.
  b. Effect on pretax earnings in 2013: The understatement ($15,000) of ending inventory caused an understatement of pretax earnings by the same amount.
  c. Effect on pretax earnings in 2014: The understatement of beginning inventory (by the same $15,000 since the inventory amount is carried over from the prior period) caused an overstatement of pretax earnings by the same amount.
  d. The total income tax expense for 2013 and 2014 combined was the same ($8,000) regardless of the error. However, there was a shift of $3,000 ($15,000 × 20%) in income tax expense from 2013 to 2014.

OBSERVATION An ending inventory error in one year affects pretax earnings by the amount of the error and in the same direction. It affects pretax earnings again in the following year by the same amount but in the opposite direction.

APPENDIX 8A: ADDITIONAL ISSUES IN MEASURING PURCHASES

Purchase Returns and Allowances

Goods purchased may be returned to the vendor if they do not meet specifications, arrive in damaged condition, or are otherwise unsatisfactory. When the goods are returned or when the vendor makes an allowance because of the circumstances, the effect on the cost of purchases must be measured. The purchaser normally receives a cash refund or a reduction in the liability to the vendor. Assume that Danier Leather returned unsatisfactory software that cost $1,000 to a supplier. The return would be recorded by Danier Leather as follows:

Trade payables (L) (or Cash) 1,000
   Inventory* (A) 1,000

Assets		=	Liabilities		+	Shareholders' Equity
Inventory	−1,000		Trade payables	−1,000		

*Purchase returns and allowances (T) may be credited when the periodic inventory system is used. The ending inventory error is subtracted in the calculation of cost of sales.

Purchase returns and allowances are treated as a reduction in the cost of inventory purchases associated with unsatisfactory goods.

Purchase Discounts

Cash discounts must be accounted for by both the seller and the buyer (accounting by the seller was discussed in Chapter 7). When merchandise is bought on credit, terms such as 2/10, n/30 are sometimes specified. This means that, if payment is made within 10 days from the date of purchase, a 2 percent cash discount for prompt payment of an account, known as the **purchase discount**, is granted. If payment is not made within the discount period, the full invoice cost is due 30 days after the date of purchase. Assume that on January 17, Danier Leather bought goods that had a $1,000 invoice price with terms 2/10, n/30. Assuming that the company uses the gross method, the purchase should be recorded as follows:

Date of Purchase:

| Jan. 17 | Inventory* (A) | 1,000 | |
| | Trade payables (L) | | 1,000 |

Assets		=	Liabilities		+	Shareholders' Equity
Inventory	+1,000		Trade payables	+1,000		

*Purchases (T) is debited when a periodic inventory system is used.

Date of Payment, within the Discount Period:

Jan. 26	Trade payables (L)	1,000	
	Inventory* (A)		20
	Cash (A)		980

Assets		=	Liabilities		+	Shareholders' Equity
Inventory	−20		Trade payables	−1,000		
Cash	−980					

*Purchase discounts (T) is credited when a periodic inventory system is used. Purchase discounts would be reported as a deduction from the cost of purchases in the calculation of cost of sales.

If for any reason Danier Leather did not pay within the 10-day discount period, the following entry would be needed:

| Feb. 1 | Trade payables (L) | 1,000 | |
| | Cash (A) | | 1,000 |

Assets		=	Liabilities		+	Shareholders' Equity
Cash	−1,000		Trade payables	−1,000		

If Danier Leather used the net method instead of the gross method, then the debit to inventory on January 17 would be $980. If payment is made after January 26, then a Discount Lost account is debited for $20, the difference between the cash paid ($1,000) and the amount that Danier Leather would have owed the supplier if it had paid within 10 days. The balance of the Discount Lost account highlights the potential savings from early payments to suppliers that Danier Leather has forgone. The balance of the Discount Lost account is added to Inventory if a perpetual inventory system is used or to Purchases if a periodic inventory system is used.

CHAPTER TAKE-AWAYS

1. **Apply the cost principle to identify the amounts that should be included in inventory, and determine the cost of sales for typical retailers, wholesalers, and manufacturers.**
   Inventory should include all of the items held for resale that the entity owns. Costs flow into inventory when goods are purchased or manufactured and flow out (as an expense) when the goods are sold or otherwise disposed of. In conformity with the matching process, the total cost of sales during the period must be related to the sales revenue earned during the period.

2. **Compare methods for controlling and keeping track of inventory, and analyze the effects of inventory errors on financial statements.**
   A company can keep track of the ending inventory and cost of sales for the period using (1) the perpetual inventory system, which is based on the maintenance of detailed and continuous inventory records for each kind of inventory stocked, or (2) the periodic inventory system, which is based on a physical inventory count of ending inventory and the costing of those goods to determine the proper amounts for cost of sales and ending inventory. An error in the measurement of ending inventory affects the cost of sales on the current period's statement of earnings and ending inventory on the statement of financial position. It also affects the cost of sales in the following period by the same amount, but in the opposite direction, because this year's ending inventory becomes next year's beginning inventory. These relationships can be seen through the cost of sales equation, $BI + P - EI = COS$.

3. **Report inventory and cost of sales by using three inventory costing methods.**
   The chapter discussed three different inventory costing methods and their applications in different economic circumstances. The methods discussed were specific identification, FIFO, and weighted-average cost. Each of the inventory costing methods is in conformity with IFRS. Remember that the cost flow assumption need not match the physical flow of inventory.

4. **Decide when the use of different inventory costing methods is beneficial to a company.**
   The selection of a method of inventory costing is important because it will affect reported net earnings, income tax expense (and, hence, cash flow), and the inventory valuation reported on the statement of financial position. In a period of rising prices, FIFO results in a higher income than does weighted-average cost; in a period of falling prices, the opposite result occurs.

5. **Report inventory at the lower of cost and net realizable value (LCNRV).**
   Ending inventory should be measured based on the lower of actual cost or net realizable value (LCNRV basis). This practice can have a major effect on the statements of companies facing declining costs. Damaged, obsolete, and out-of-season inventory should also be written down to its current estimated net realizable value if that is below cost. The LCNRV adjustment increases cost of sales, decreases net earnings, and decreases reported inventory.

6. **Evaluate inventory management by using the inventory turnover ratio and the effects of inventory on cash flows.**
   The inventory turnover ratio measures the efficiency of inventory management. It reflects how many times the average inventory was produced and sold during the period. Analysts and creditors watch this ratio because a sudden decline in this ratio may mean that a company is facing an unexpected decline in demand for its products or is becoming sloppy in its production management. When a net *decrease in inventory* for the period occurs, sales are more than purchases; thus, the decrease must be *added* to net earnings in computing cash flows from operations. When a net *increase in inventory* for the period occurs, sales are less than purchases; thus, the increase must be *subtracted* from net earnings in computing cash flows from operations.

   In this and previous chapters, we discussed the current assets of a business. These assets are critical for the operations of a business, but in general they produce value only when they are sold. In Chapter 9, we will discuss the property, plant, and equipment; natural resources; and intangibles that are the elements of productive capacity. Many of the capital assets produce value, such as a factory that manufactures cars. These assets present some interesting accounting problems because they benefit a number of accounting periods.

KEY **RATIOS**

The inventory turnover ratio measures the efficiency of inventory management. It reflects how many times the average inventory was produced and sold during the period:

$$\text{Inventory Turnover Ratio} = \frac{\text{Cost of Sales}}{\text{Average Inventory}}$$

FINDING **FINANCIAL INFORMATION**

STATEMENT OF FINANCIAL POSITION
Under Current Assets:
  Inventory

STATEMENT OF EARNINGS
Expenses
  Cost of sales

STATEMENT OF CASH FLOWS
Under Operating Activities (indirect method):
  + decrease in inventory
  − increase in inventory
  + increase in trade payables
  − decrease in trade payables

NOTES
Under Summary of Significant Accounting Policies:
  Description of management's choice of inventory accounting policy (FIFO, weighted-average cost, LCNRV, etc.)
Under a Separate Note:
  If not listed on the statement of financial position, components of inventory (merchandise, raw materials, work-in-process, finished goods)

GLOSSARY

Review key terms and definitions on *Connect*.

QUESTIONS

1. Why is inventory an important item to both internal (management) and external users of financial statements?
2. What are the general guidelines for deciding which items should be included in inventory?
3. Explain the application of the cost principle to an item in the ending inventory.
4. Define cost of goods available for sale. How does it differ from cost of sales?
5. Define beginning inventory and ending inventory.
6. When a perpetual inventory system is used, unit costs of the items sold are known at the date of each sale. In contrast, when a periodic inventory system is used, unit costs are known only at the end of the accounting period. Why are these statements correct?
7. The periodic inventory calculation is BI + P − EI = COS. The perpetual inventory calculation is BI + P − COS = EI. Explain the significance of the difference between these two calculations.
8. The chapter discussed three inventory costing methods. List the three methods and briefly explain each.
9. Explain how net earnings can be manipulated when the specific identification inventory costing method is used.
10. Contrast the effects of weighted average versus FIFO on reported assets (i.e., the ending inventory) when (*a*) prices are rising and (*b*) prices are falling.
11. Contrast the statement of earnings effect of weighted average versus FIFO (i.e., on earnings before income taxes) when (*a*) prices are rising and (*b*) prices are falling.
12. Contrast the effects of weighted average versus FIFO on cash outflow and inflow.
13. Explain briefly the application of the LCNRV concept to the ending inventory and its effect on the statement of earnings and statement of financial position when the net realizable value of inventory is lower than its cost.
14. Explain the difference between a reversal of a write-down and a holding gain.

LO1 **E8–1** **Recording the Cost of Purchases for a Merchandiser**

Elite Apparel purchased 80 new shirts for cash and recorded a total cost of $2,620, determined as follows:

Invoice amount	$2,180
Shipping charges	175
Import taxes and duties	145
Interest paid in advance on loan to finance the purchase	120
	$2,620

Required:

Make the needed corrections in this calculation. Prepare the journal entry or entries to record this purchase in the correct amount, assuming a perpetual inventory system. Show computations.

LO1 **E8–2** **Analyzing Items to Be Included in Inventory**

Boilard Inc. planned to report inventory of $50,000 based on its physical count of inventory in its warehouse at year-end, December 31, 2013. During the audit, the auditor developed the following additional information:

a. Goods from a supplier costing $300 are in transit with Canada Post on December 31, 2013. The terms are F.O.B. shipping point (explained below). Because these goods had not arrived, they were excluded from the physical inventory count.

b. Boilard delivered samples costing $400 to a customer on December 27, 2013, with the understanding that they would be returned to Boilard on January 18, 2014. Because these goods were not on hand, they were excluded from the physical inventory count.

c. On December 31, 2013, goods in transit to customers, with terms F.O.B. shipping point, amounted to $2,000 (the expected delivery date was January 10, 2014). Because the goods had been shipped, they were excluded from the physical inventory count.

d. On December 31, 2013, goods in transit to a customer, F.O.B. destination, amounted to $1,000 and are not expected to arrive at their destination before January 10, 2014. Because the goods had been shipped, they were not included in the physical inventory count.

Required:

Boilard is required to include in inventory all goods for which it has title. Note that the point where title (ownership) changes hands is determined by the shipping terms in the sales contract. When goods are shipped "F.O.B. shipping point," title changes hands at shipment and the buyer normally pays for shipping. When they are shipped "F.O.B. destination," title changes hands on delivery, and the seller normally pays for shipping. Begin with the $50,000 inventory amount, and compute the correct amount for the ending inventory. Explain the basis for your treatment of each of the preceding items. (*Hint:* Set up three columns: item, amount, and explanation.)

LO1 **E8–3** **Inferring Missing Amounts Based on Statement of Earnings Relationships**

Supply the missing dollar amounts for the 2014 statement of earnings of Laurin Retailers for each of the following independent cases:

Case	Sales Revenue	Beginning Inventory	Purchases	Total Available	Ending Inventory	Cost of Sales	Gross Profit	Operating Expenses	Pretax Earnings or (Loss)
A	$1,300	$200	$1,400	$?	$1,000	$?	$?	$400	$?
B	900	200	800	?	?	?	?	150	0
C	?	300	?	?	600	400	800	200	?
D	800	?	600	?	250	?	?	250	100
E	2,000	?	1,800	2,200	?	?	1,000	?	(100)

E8–4 Inferring Missing Amounts Based on Statement of Earnings Relationships

■ **LO1**

Supply the missing dollar amounts for the 2014 statement of earnings of Kwan Company for each of the following independent cases:

	Case A	Case B	Case C
Sales revenue	$ 8,000	$ 6,000	$?
Sales returns and allowances	150	?	275
Net sales revenue	?	?	5,920
Beginning inventory	11,000	6,500	4,000
Purchases	5,000	?	9,420
Transportation-in	?	120	170
Purchase returns	350	600	?
Cost of goods available for sale	?	14,790	13,370
Ending inventory	10,000	10,740	?
Cost of sales	?	?	5,400
Gross profit	?	1,450	?
Expenses (operating)	1,300	?	520
Pretax earnings (loss)	$ 800	$ (500)	$ 0

E8–5 Inferring Merchandise Purchases

■ **LO1**

Le Château Inc. is a Canadian specialty retailer and manufacturer of contemporary fashion apparel, accessories, and footwear for women and men of all ages. Its products are sold in over 200 retail locations across Canada. Assume that you are employed as a stock analyst and your boss has just completed a review of the new annual report. She provided you with her notes, but they are missing some information that you need. Her notes show that the ending inventory for Le Château in the current year was $119,325,000 and in the previous year was $91,773,000. Net sales for the current year were $302,707,000. Gross profit was $206,562,000; net loss was $2,386,000. For your analysis, you determine that you need to know the amount of purchases and the cost of sales for the year.

Le Château Inc.

Required:
Do you need to ask your boss for her copy of the annual report, or can you develop the information from her notes? Explain and show calculations.

E8–6 Analyzing the Effects of an Error in Recording Purchases

■ **LO2**

Garraway Ski Company mistakenly recorded purchases of inventory on account received during the last week of December 2014 as purchases during January of 2015 (this is called a *purchases cut-off error*). Garraway uses a periodic inventory system, and ending inventory was correctly counted and reported each year. Assuming that no correction was made in 2014 or 2015, indicate whether each of the following financial statement amounts will be understated, overstated, or correct:

1. Net earnings for 2014.
2. Net earnings for 2015.
3. Retained earnings at December 31, 2014.
4. Retained earnings at December 31, 2015.

E8–7 Recording Purchases and Sales by Using a Perpetual and a Periodic Inventory System

■ **LO2, 3**

Demski Company reported beginning inventory of 300 units at a unit cost of $20. It engaged in the following purchase and sale transactions during 2014:

Jan. 14 Sold 60 units at unit sales price of $40 on open account.
April 9 Purchased 45 additional units at unit cost of $20 on open account.
Sept. 2 Sold 135 units at sales price of $50 on open account.

At the end of 2014, a physical count showed that Demski Company had 150 units of inventory still on hand.

Required:
Record each transaction, assuming that Demski Company uses (*a*) a perpetual inventory system and (*b*) a periodic inventory system (including any necessary entries at December 31, the end of the accounting period). Demski Company uses the FIFO inventory costing method.

■ LO2

Gibson Greeting
Cards

E8–8 **Analyzing the Effect of an Inventory Error Disclosed in an Actual Note to a Financial Statement**

Several years ago, the financial statements of Gibson Greeting Cards (now owned by American Greetings Corporation) contained the following note:

> On July 1, the Company announced that it had determined that the ending inventory . . . had been overstated . . . The overstatement of inventory . . . was $8,806,000.

Gibson reported net earnings of $25,852,000 for the year in which the error occurred, and its income tax rate was 39.3 percent.

Required:

1. Compute the amount of net earnings that Gibson reported after correcting the inventory error. Show computations.
2. Assume that the inventory error was not discovered. Identify the financial statement accounts that would have been incorrect for the year the error occurred and for the subsequent year. State whether each account was understated or overstated.

■ LO2

E8–9 **Analyzing and Interpreting the Impact of an Inventory Error**

Dalez Corporation prepared the following two statements of earnings (simplified for illustrative purposes):

	First Quarter 2014		Second Quarter 2014	
Sales revenue		$11,000		$18,000
Cost of sales				
Beginning inventory	$4,000		$ 3,800	
Purchases	3,000		13,000	
Cost of goods available for sale	7,000		16,800	
Ending inventory	3,800		9,000	
Cost of sales		3,200		7,800
Gross profit		7,800		10,200
Expenses (operating)		5,000		6,000
Pretax earnings		$ 2,800		$ 4,200

During the third quarter, it was discovered that the ending inventory for the first quarter should have been $4,200.

Required:

1. What effect did this error have on the pretax earnings of each quarter and of the two quarters combined? Explain.
2. Did this error affect the earnings per share amounts for each quarter? (See the discussion of earnings per share in Chapter 6.) Explain.
3. Prepare corrected statements of earnings for each quarter.
4. Set up a schedule with the following headings to reflect the comparative effects of the correct and incorrect amounts on the statement of earnings:

	1st Quarter			2nd Quarter		
Statement of earnings item	Incorrect Amount	Correct Amount	Error (if any)	Incorrect Amount	Correct Amount	Error (if any)

■ LO3

E8–10 **Calculating Ending Inventory and Cost of Sales Under FIFO and Weighted-Average Cost Methods**

Clor Company uses a periodic inventory system. At December 31, 2014, the accounting records provided the following information for Product 1:

	Units	Unit Cost
Inventory, December 31, 2013	3,000	$8
For the year 2014:		
Purchases, March 31	5,000	9
Purchases, August 1	2,000	7
Inventory, December 31, 2014	4,000	

Required:

Compute the cost of sales and the ending inventory under the FIFO and weighted-average costing methods. (*Hint:* Set up adjacent columns for the two methods.)

E8–11 **Analyzing and Interpreting the Financial Statement Effects of the FIFO and Weighted-Average Cost Methods**

LO3, 4

Lunar Company uses a periodic inventory system. The company's accounting records provided the following information for Product 2:

Transactions	Units	Unit Cost
a. Inventory, December 31, 2013	3,000	$12
For the year 2014:		
b. Purchase, April 11	9,000	10
c. Sale, May 1 ($30 each)	5,000	
d. Purchase, June 1	8,000	13
e. Sale, July 3 ($30 each)	6,000	
f. Operating expenses (excluding income tax expense), $85,000		

Required:

1. Prepare a statement of earnings for 2014, through pretax earnings, showing the detailed computation of cost of sales for two cases:

   a. Case A—FIFO

   b. Case B—Weighted average

   For each case, show the computation of the ending inventory. (*Hint:* Set up adjacent columns, one for each case.)

2. Compare the pretax earnings and the ending inventory amounts between the two cases. Explain the similarities and differences.

3. Which inventory costing method may be preferred for income tax purposes? Explain.

4. Prepare journal entries to record transactions (*b*) through (*e*), as well as the cost of sales at December 31, 2014, assuming that Lunar uses FIFO for inventory costing.

E8–12 **Analyzing and Interpreting the Financial Statement Effects of FIFO and Weighted-Average Cost Methods**

LO3, 4

Scoresby Inc. uses a perpetual inventory system. At December 31, 2015, the company's accounting records provided the following information for Product B:

Transactions	Units	Unit Cost
a. Inventory, December 31, 2014	7,000	$ 8
For the year 2015:		
b. Purchase, March 5	19,000	9
c. Sale, June 15 ($29 each)	10,000	
d. Purchase, September 19	8,000	11
e. Sale, November 20 ($31 each)	16,000	
f. Operating expenses (excluding income tax expense), $500,000		

Required:

1. Prepare a statement of earnings for 2015 through pretax earnings, showing the detailed computation of cost of sales for two cases:

   a. Case A—FIFO

   b. Case B—Weighted average

   For each case, show the computation of the ending inventory. (*Hint:* Set up adjacent columns, one for each case.)

2. Compare the two cases with regard to the pretax earnings and the ending inventory amounts. Explain the similarities and differences.

3. Which inventory costing method may be preferred for income tax purposes? Explain.

4. Prepare journal entries to record transactions (*b*) through (*e*), assuming that Scoresby uses FIFO for inventory costing.

LO3, 4

E8–13   **Evaluating the Choice between Two Alternative Inventory Costing Methods Based on Cash Flow and Net Earnings Effects**

Courtney Company uses a periodic inventory system. Data for 2014 are as follows: beginning merchandise inventory (December 31, 2013), 3,000 units at $35; purchases, 12,000 units at $38; operating expenses (excluding income taxes), $213,000; ending inventory per physical count at December 31, 2014, 2,700 units; sales price per unit, $70; and average income tax rate, 30 percent.

Required:

1. Prepare statements of earnings under the FIFO and weighted-average costing methods. Use a format similar to the following:

		Inventory Costing Method	
Statement of Earnings	**Units**	**FIFO**	**Weighted Average**
Sales revenue	_____	$_____	$_____
Cost of sales			
Beginning inventory	_____	_____	_____
Purchases	_____	_____	_____
Cost of goods available for sale	_____	_____	_____
Ending inventory	_____	_____	_____
Cost of sales	_____	_____	_____
Gross profit		_____	_____
Expenses (operating)		_____	_____
Pretax earnings		_____	_____
Income tax expense		_____	_____
Net earnings			

2. Which method, FIFO or weighted-average cost, is preferable in terms of (*a*) net earnings and (*b*) cash flow? Explain.

3. What would be your answer to (2), assuming that prices were falling? Explain.

LO3, 4

E8–14   **Evaluating the Choice between Two Alternative Inventory Costing Methods Based on Cash Flow Effects**

Following is partial information for the statement of earnings of Timber Company under two different inventory costing methods, assuming the use of a periodic inventory system:

	FIFO	**Weighted Average**
Unit sales price, $50		
Cost of sales		
Beginning inventory (400 units)	$13,600	$13,600
Purchases (475 units)	17,100	17,100
Cost of goods available for sale		
Ending inventory (545 units)		
Cost of sales		
Operating expenses	1,700	1,700

Required:

1. Compute the cost of sales under the FIFO and weighted-average inventory costing methods.

2. Prepare a statement of earnings through pretax earnings for each method.

3. Rank the two methods with regard to favourable cash flow, and explain the basis for your ranking.

LO5

E8–15   **Reporting Inventory at Lower of Cost and Net Realizable Value**

Peterson Company is preparing the annual financial statements dated December 31, 2014. Ending inventory information about the five major items stocked for regular sale follows:

	Ending Inventory		
Item	**Quantity on Hand**	**Unit Cost When Acquired (FIFO)**	**Net Realizable Value at Year-End**
A	50	$15	$12
B	80	30	40
C	10	45	52
D	30	25	30
E	350	10	5

Required:

1. Compute the value of the 2014 ending inventory by using the LCNRV rule applied on an item-by-item basis. (*Hint:* Set up columns for item, quantity, total cost, total net realizable value, and LCNRV valuation.)

2. What will be the effect of the write-down of inventory to LCNRV on cost of sales for the year 2014?

3. Assume that 20 units of item E had not been sold by December 31, 2015, and that the net realizable value of that item increased to $7.50 per unit. How would this information be reflected in Peterson's statement of earnings for 2015 and its statement of financial position at year-end? Explain.

E8–16   Reporting Inventory at Lower of Cost and Net Realizable Value   ■ **LO5**
Fine Leather Ltd. had the following inventory at December 31, 2014:

		Per Unit	
Item	**Quantity**	**Cost**	**Net Realizable Value**
Leather jackets			
Model 154	20	$100	$120
Model 160	15	180	168
Model 165	10	250	260
Handbags			
Model 11	60	30	35
Model 12	40	45	42
Model 13	25	65	63

Required:

1. Determine the value of ending inventory that should be reported on the statement of financial position by applying the LCNRV rule to
   a. Each item of inventory
   b. Each major category of inventory
   c. Total inventory

2. Which of the computations in (1) results in the lowest net earnings for 2014? Explain.

3. Which level of inventory aggregation (individual item basis, major categories, or total inventory) is permitted by IFRS? Why are the other levels of aggregation not acceptable? Explain.

E8–17   Interpreting Disclosures Related to Inventory   ■ **LO5**
Le Château Inc. manufactures and sells fashion apparel, accessories, and footwear at various retail locations across Canada. Its annual report for the year ended January 28, 2012, included the following note:

Le Château Inc.

8. INVENTORIES			
(in thousands of dollars)	Jan. 28, 2012	Jan. 29, 2011	Jan. 31, 2010
Raw materials	$ 11,998	$10,443	$ 7,720
Work-in-process	1,039	1,959	1,528
Finished goods	102,656	70,301	47,318
Finished goods in transit	3,632	9,070	4,668
	$119,325	$91,773	$61,234

The cost of inventory recognized as an expense and included in cost of sales for the year ended January 28, 2012, is $96.1 million (2011, $98.3 million), including write-downs recorded of $6.9 million (2011, $6.7 million), as a result of net realizable value being lower than cost. No inventory write-downs recognized in prior periods were reversed.

Required:

1. Explain each of the inventory items listed in the note.

2. Assume that the write-down relates to the values of specific items of raw materials. Prepare the journal entry to record the write-down of inventory costs. Le Château uses a perpetual inventory system.

3. Assume that some of the raw materials that were written down on January 28, 2012, were not used for production purposes by January 27, 2013, the end of its 2013 fiscal year. The inventory items that were written down had an original cost of $2.3 million, and their net realizable value was $1.7 million. Changes in market conditions increased the net realizable value of these items to $2.4 million, which exceeded their original cost. How would this information be reflected in Le Château's statement of earnings for fiscal year 2013 and its statement of financial position as at January 27, 2013? Explain.

■ LO6   **E8–18**

Sony Corporation

Analyzing and Interpreting the Inventory Turnover Ratio

Sony Corporation manufactures and sells cell phones directly to mobile telecommunications service suppliers. The company reported the following amounts for fiscal year 2013 (in billions of yen):

Net sales revenue	6,304
Cost of sales	4,831
Beginning inventory	710
Ending inventory	707

Required:

1. Determine the inventory turnover ratio and the average days to sell inventory for the current year.
2. Explain the meaning of each of the amounts computed in (1).
3. Indicate whether the inventory turnover ratio will increase, decrease, or remain unchanged as a result of the following changes in inventory management. Justify your answers.

    a. Have parts inventory delivered daily by suppliers instead of weekly.
    b. Extend payments for inventory purchases from 30 days to 45 days.
    c. Shorten the production process from 10 days to 8 days.

■ LO6   **E8–19**

Analyzing and Interpreting the Effects of the FIFO/Weighted-Average Choice on the Inventory Turnover Ratio

The records at the end of January 2014 for All Star Company showed the following for a particular kind of merchandise:
Inventory, December 31, 2013, at FIFO: 19 units @ $12 = $228
Inventory, December 31, 2013, at weighted average: 19 units @ $10 = $190

Transactions	Units	Unit Cost	Total Cost
Purchase, January 9, 2014	25	15	$375
Purchase, January 20, 2014	50	16	800
Sale, January 11, 2014 (at $38 per unit)	40		
Sale, January 27, 2014 (at $39 per unit)	28		

Required:

Compute the inventory turnover ratio under the FIFO and weighted-average inventory costing methods and a perpetual inventory system (show computations and round to the nearest dollar). Explain which method you believe is the better indicator of the efficiency of inventory management.

■ LO6   **E8–20**

Bauer Performance
Sports Ltd.

Interpreting the Effect of Changes in Inventories and Trade Payables on Cash Flow from Operations

Bauer Performance Sports Ltd. is a leading developer and manufacturer of ice hockey, roller hockey, and lacrosse equipment as well as related apparel. Its products are marketed under the Bauer Hockey, Mission Roller Hockey, and Maverik Lacrosse brand names throughout the world. A recent annual report included the following on its statement of financial position (amounts in thousands of dollars):

CONSOLIDATED STATEMENTS OF FINANCIAL POSITION		
Item	Current Year	Previous Year
....		
Inventory	91,202	54,211
....	...	...
Trade payables	33,519	16,548

Required:

Explain the effects of the changes in inventory and trade payables on cash flow from operating activities for the current year.

E8–21 (Appendix 8A) Recording Sales and Purchases with Cash Discounts

A. The Cycle Shop sells merchandise on credit terms of 2/10, n/30. Merchandise that cost $900 was sold to Claudette Labelle on February 1, 2014, at $1,600. The company uses the gross method of recording sales discounts.

Required:

1. Prepare the journal entry to record the credit sale. Assume that the company uses the perpetual inventory system.

2. Prepare the journal entry to record the collection of cash from C. Labelle (*a*) on February 9, 2014, and (*b*) on March 2, 2014.

B. On March 4, 2014, the Cycle Shop purchased bicycles and accessories from a supplier on credit for $8,000; the terms were 1/15, n/30. The company uses the net method to record purchases.

Required:

3. Prepare the journal entry to record the purchase on credit. Assume that the company uses the perpetual inventory system.

4. Prepare the journal entry to record the payment of the invoice (*a*) on March 12, 2014, and (*b*) on March 28, 2014.

PROBLEMS

P8–1 Analyzing Items to Be Included in Inventory

LO1

Reggie Company has just completed a physical inventory count at year-end, December 31, 2014. Only the items on the shelves, in storage, and in the receiving area were counted and costed on a FIFO basis. The inventory amounted to $65,000. During the audit, the auditor developed the following additional information:

a. Goods costing $750 were being used by a customer on a trial basis and were excluded from the inventory count at December 31, 2014.

b. Goods costing $900 were in transit to Reggie on December 31, 2014, with terms F.O.B. destination (explained below). Because these goods had not arrived, they were excluded from the physical inventory count.

c. On December 31, 2014, goods in transit to customers, with terms F.O.B. shipping point, amounted to $1,300 (the expected delivery date was January 10, 2015). Because the goods had been shipped, they were excluded from the physical inventory count.

d. On December 28, 2014, a customer purchased goods for $2,650 cash and left them "for pick-up on January 3, 2015." The cost of sales totalled $1,590 and was included in the physical inventory count because the goods were still on hand.

e. On the date of the inventory count, the company received notice from a supplier that goods ordered earlier at a cost of $2,550 had been delivered to the transportation company on December 27, 2014; the terms were F.O.B. shipping point. Because the shipment had not arrived by December 31, 2014, it was excluded from the physical inventory count.

f. On December 31, 2014, the company shipped goods to a customer, F.O.B. destination. The goods, which cost $850, are not expected to arrive at their destination before January 8, 2015. Because the goods were not on hand, they were not included in the physical inventory count.

g. One of the items sold by the company has such a low volume that the management planned to drop it last year. To induce Reggie Company to continue carrying the item, the manufacturer-supplier provided the item on a consignment basis. This means that the manufacturer-supplier retains ownership of the item, and Reggie Company (the consignee) has no responsibility to pay for the items until they are sold to customers. Each month, Reggie Company sends a report to the manufacturer on the number sold and remits cash for the cost. At the end of December 2014, Reggie Company had five of these items on hand; therefore, they were included in the physical inventory count at $950 each.

Required:

Reggie is required to include in inventory all goods for which it has title. Note that the point where title (ownership) changes hands is determined by the shipping terms in the sales contract. When goods are shipped "F.O.B. shipping point," title changes hands at shipment and the buyer normally pays for shipping. When they are shipped "F.O.B. destination," title changes hands on delivery, and the seller normally pays for shipping. Begin with the $65,000 inventory amount and compute the correct amount for the ending inventory. Explain the basis for your treatment of each of the preceding items. (*Hint:* Set up three columns: item, amount, and explanation.)

LO2

eXcel

P8–2 **Analyzing and Interpreting the Effects of Inventory Errors** (AP8–1)

The statements of earnings for Pruitt Company summarized for a four-year period show the following (amounts in thousands of dollars):

	2015	2014	2013	2012
Sales revenue	$2,025	$2,450	$2,700	$2,975
Cost of sales	1,505	1,627	1,782	2,113
Gross profit	520	823	918	862
Operating expenses	490	513	538	542
Pretax earnings	30	310	380	320
Income tax expense (30%)	9	93	114	96
Net earnings	$ 21	$ 217	$ 266	$ 224

An audit revealed that in determining these amounts, the ending inventory for 2013 was understated by $22.

Required:

1. Revise these statements of earnings to reflect the correct amounts.
2. Did the error affect the cumulative net earnings for the four-year period? Explain.
3. What effect did the error have on the income tax expense for 2013 and 2014?

LO3, 4

P8–3 **Analyzing the Effects of Three Alternative Inventory Methods** (AP8–2)

Allsigns Company uses a periodic inventory system. The company's accounting records for the most popular item in inventory showed the following details:

Transactions	Units	Unit Cost
Beginning inventory, January 1, 2015	400	$30
Transactions during 2015:		
a. Purchase, February 20	600	32
b. Sale, April 1 ($46 each)	(700)	
c. Purchase, June 30	500	36
d. Sale, August 1 ($46 each)	(100)	
e. Sales return August 5 (relating to Transaction [d])	20	

Required:

Compute (a) the cost of goods available for sale during 2015, (b) the cost of ending inventory at December 31, 2015, and (c) the cost of sales for 2015, under each of the following inventory costing methods (show computations and round to the nearest dollar):

1. Weighted-average cost.
2. FIFO.
3. Specific identification, assuming that the company is permitted to use it and that two-fifths of the units sold on April 1, 2015, were selected from the beginning inventory and three-fifths were taken from the purchase of February 20, 2015. Assume that the sale of August 1, 2015, was selected from the purchase of June 30, 2015.

As a shareholder, which of these three methods would you prefer?

P8–4 Evaluating Three Alternative Inventory Methods Based on Net Earnings and Cash Flow

■ **LO3, 4**

eXcel

At the end of January 2015, the records of Regina Company showed the following for a particular item that sold at $18 per unit:

Transaction	Units	Amount
Inventory, January 1, 2015	500	$2,500
Sale, January 10	(400)	
Purchase, January 12	600	3,600
Sale, January 17	(300)	
Purchase, January 26	160	1,280

Required:

1. Assuming the use of a perpetual inventory system, prepare a summarized statement through gross profit on sales under each of the following inventory costing methods: (*a*) weighted-average cost, (*b*) FIFO, and (*c*) specific identification, assuming that the company is permitted to use this method. For specific identification, assume that the first sale was out of the beginning inventory and the second sale was out of the January 12 purchase. Show the inventory computations in detail.

2. Which method would result in

   a. the highest pretax earnings?

   b. the lowest income tax expense?

   c. the most favourable cash flow?

   Explain.

3. Prepare journal entries to record the transactions that occurred in January 2015, assuming that FIFO is used for inventory costing.

P8–5 Evaluating the FIFO/Weighted-Average Choice When Costs Are Rising and Falling

■ **LO3, 4**

eXcel

Net earnings is to be evaluated under four different situations as follows:

i. Prices are rising:

   Situation A—FIFO is used.   Situation B—Weighted average is used.

ii. Prices are falling:

   Situation C—FIFO is used.   Situation D—Weighted average is used.

The basic data common to all four situations are sales, 500 units for $15,000; beginning inventory, 300 units; purchases, 400 units; ending inventory, 200 units; and operating expenses, $4,000. The following tabulated statements of earnings for each situation have been set up for analytical purposes:

	Prices Rising		Prices Falling	
	Situation A	Situation B	Situation C	Situation D
Statement of Earnings	**FIFO**	**Weighted Average**	**FIFO**	**Weighted Average**
Sales revenue	$15,000	$15,000	$15,000	$15,000
Cost of sales				
Beginning inventory	3,300	?	?	?
Purchases	4,800	?	?	?
Cost of goods available for sale	8,100	?	?	?
Ending inventory	2,400	?	?	?
Cost of sales	5,700	?	?	?
Gross profit	9,300	?	?	?
Operating expenses	4,000	4,000	4,000	4,000
Pretax earnings	5,300	?	?	?
Income tax expense (30%)	1,590			
Net earnings	$ 3,710	?	?	?

Required:

1. Complete the preceding tabulation for each situation. In Situations A and B (prices rising), assume the following: beginning inventory, 300 units at $11 = $3,300; purchases, 400 units at $12 = $4,800. In Situations C and D (prices falling), assume the opposite; that is, beginning inventory, 300 units at $12 = $3,600; purchases, 400 units at $11 = $4,400. Use periodic inventory procedures.

2. Analyze and discuss the relative effects on pretax earnings and on net earnings as demonstrated by (1) when prices are rising and when prices are falling.

3. Discuss the relative effects, if any, on the cash position for each situation.

4. Would you recommend FIFO or weighted average? Explain.

■ LO2, 4   **P8–6**   **Evaluating the Effects of Inventory Costing Methods on Financial Statement Elements** (AP8–3)
Neverstop Corporation sells item A as part of its product line. Information about the beginning inventory, purchases, and sales of item A are given in the following table for the first six months of 2014. The company uses a perpetual inventory system:

Date	Purchases Number of Units	Unit Cost	Sales Number of Units	Sales Price
January 1 (beginning inventory)	500	$2.50		
January 24			300	$4.00
February 8	600	$2.60		
March 16			560	$4.20
June 11	300	$2.75		

Required:

1. Compute the cost of ending inventory by using the weighted-average costing method.

2. Compute the gross profit for the first six months of 2014 by using the FIFO costing method.

3. Would the gross profit be higher, lower, or the same if Neverstop used the weighted-average costing method rather than the FIFO method? Explain. No calculations are required.

4. Prepare journal entries to record the purchase and sale transactions, as well as the cost of sales, assuming that the weighted-average method is used.

5. Assume that because of a clerical error, the ending inventory is reported to be 440 units rather than the actual number of units (540) on hand. If FIFO is used, calculate the amount of the understatement or overstatement in

   a. the cost of sales for the first six months of 2014.

   b. the current assets at June 30, 2014.

■ LO3, 6   **P8–7**   **Evaluating the Effects of Inventory Costing Methods on Financial Statement Elements** (AP8–4)
Kramer Corp. reported the following sale and purchase transactions related to a specific product in January 2014:

Date	Transaction	Quantity	Unit Cost	Unit Sales Price
Jan. 1	Beginning inventory	5 units	$90	
Jan. 3	Sale on account	3 units		$120
Jan. 6	Purchase on account	11 units	95	
Jan. 8	Sale on account	4 units		120
Jan. 9	Sale on account	5 units		120
Jan. 15	Sales returned due to damage, $240 (two units that were sold on January 9). The units were in very poor condition and were destroyed.			

Kramer Corp. uses a periodic inventory system and the FIFO inventory costing method.

Required:

1. Compute net sales and gross profit for January 2014.

2. Determine the inventory turnover ratio and the average days to sell inventory for January 2014, and explain what the numbers mean.

3. Prepare the journal entries to record the purchase transaction on January 6, the sale transaction on January 8, and the sales return on January 15.

4. Compute the cost of sales for January 2014, assuming for this part only that Kramer uses a perpetual inventory system and the weighted-average cost method.

P8–8 **Evaluating the Statement of Earnings and Cash Flow Effects of Lower of Cost and Net Realizable Value**

LO5

Smart Company prepared its annual financial statements dated December 31, 2014. The company applies the FIFO inventory costing method; however, the company neglected to apply the LCNRV valuation to the ending inventory. The preliminary 2014 statement of earnings follows:

Sales revenue		$280,000
Cost of sales		
Beginning inventory	$ 31,000	
Purchases	184,000	
Cost of goods available for sale	215,000	
Ending inventory (FIFO cost)	46,500	
Cost of sales		168,500
Gross profit		111,500
Operating expenses		62,000
Pretax earnings		49,500
Income tax expense (30%)		14,850
Net earnings		$ 34,650

Assume that you have been asked to restate the 2014 financial statements to incorporate the LCNRV inventory valuation rule. You have developed the following data relating to the ending inventory at December 31, 2014:

Item	Quantity	Acquisition Cost Unit	Acquisition Cost Total	Net Realizable Value
A	3,050	$3	$ 9,150	$4
B	1,500	5	7,500	3.5
C	7,100	1.5	10,650	3.5
D	3,200	6	19,200	4
			$46,500	

Required:

1. Restate the statement of earnings to reflect the valuation of the ending inventory on December 31, 2014, at the LCNRV. Apply the LCNRV rule on an item-by-item basis and show computations.
2. Compare and explain the LCNRV effect on each amount that was changed in (1).
3. What is the conceptual basis for applying LCNRV to merchandise inventories?
4. What effect (increase, decrease, no effect) did the LCNRV rule have on the cash flow for 2014? What will be the long-term effect on cash flow (increase, decrease, no effect)? Computations are not necessary.

P8–9 **Evaluating the Effects of Manufacturing Changes on the Inventory Turnover Ratio and Cash Flows from Operating Activities**

LO6

H. T. Tan and Company has been operating for five years as an electronics component manufacturer specializing in cell phone components. During this period, it has experienced rapid growth in sales revenue and inventory. Mr. Tan and his associates have hired you as the company's first corporate controller. You have put into place new purchasing and manufacturing procedures that are expected to reduce inventories by approximately one-third by year-end. You have gathered the following data related to the changes (in thousands):

Item	Beginning of Year	End of Year (projected)
Inventory	$495,700	$304,310
		Current Year (projected)
Cost of sales		$7,008,984

Required:

1. Compute the inventory turnover ratio based on two different assumptions:

   a. Those presented in the preceding table (a decrease in the balance in inventory).

   b. No change from the beginning of the year in the inventory balance.

2. Compute the effect of the projected change in the balance in inventory on cash flow from operating activities for the year (show the sign and amount of the effect).

3. On the basis of the preceding analysis, write a brief memo explaining how an increase in inventory turnover can result in an increase in cash flow from operating activities. Also explain how this increase can benefit the company.

P8–10   **(Appendix 8A) Recording Sales and Purchases with Cash Discounts and Returns** (AP8–5)
Campus Stop Inc. is a student co-op. On January 1, 2014, the beginning inventory was $150,000, the trade receivables balance was $4,000, and the allowance for doubtful accounts had a credit balance of $800. Campus Stop uses a perpetual inventory system and records inventory purchases by using the gross method.

The following transactions (summarized) occurred during 2014:

a. Sold merchandise for $275,000 cash; the cost of sales is $137,500.

b. Received merchandise returned by customers as unsatisfactory and paid a cash refund of $1,600; the returned merchandise had cost $800.

c. Purchased merchandise from vendors on credit, terms 3/10, n/30, as follows:

   i. August Supply Company, invoice price, $5,000.

   ii. Other vendors, invoice price, $120,000.

d. Purchased equipment for use in store for cash, $2,200.

e. Purchased office supplies for future use in the store; paid cash, $700.

f. Paid freight on merchandise purchased, $400 cash.

g. Paid trade payables in full during the period as follows:

   i. Paid August Supply Company after the discount period, $5,000.

   ii. Paid other vendors within the discount period, $116,400.

Required:
Prepare journal entries for each of the preceding transactions.

ALTERNATE PROBLEMS

LO2

eXcel

AP8–1   **Analyzing and Interpreting the Effects of Inventory Errors** (P8–2)
The statements of earnings for four consecutive years for Colca Company reflected the following summarized amounts:

	2016	2015	2014	2013
Sales revenue	$58,000	$62,000	$51,000	$50,000
Cost of sales	37,000	43,000	35,000	32,500
Gross profit	21,000	19,000	16,000	17,500
Operating expenses	12,000	14,000	12,000	10,000
Pretax earnings	$ 9,000	$ 5,000	$ 4,000	$ 7,500

Subsequent to the development of these amounts, it has been determined that the physical inventory taken on December 31, 2014, was understated by $3,000.

Required:

1. Revise the statements of earnings to reflect the correct amounts, taking into consideration the inventory error.

2. Compute the gross profit percentage for each year (*a*) before the correction and (*b*) after the correction. Do the results lend confidence to your corrected amounts? Explain.

3. What effect would the error have had on the income tax expense, assuming an average tax rate of 30 percent?

AP8–2 Analyzing the Effects of Three Alternative Inventory Methods (P8–3)   ■ LO3, 4

Yared Company uses a periodic inventory system. The company's accounting records for the most popular item in inventory showed the following details:

Transaction	Units	Unit Cost
Beginning Inventory, January 1, 2015	1,800	$2.50
Transactions during 2015:		
a. Purchase, January 30	2,500	3.10
b. Sale, March 14 ($5 each)	(1,450)	
c. Purchase, May 1	1,200	4.00
d. Sale, August 31 ($5 each)	(1,900)	

Required:

Compute (a) the cost of goods available for sale during 2015, (b) the cost of ending inventory at December 31, 2015, and (c) the cost of sales for 2015, under each of the following inventory costing methods (show computations and round to the nearest dollar):

1. Weighted-average cost.
2. FIFO.
3. Specific identification, assuming that the company is permitted to use it and that two-fifths of the units sold on March 14, 2015, were selected from the beginning inventory and three-fifths from the purchase of January 30, 2015. Assume that the sale of August 31, 2015, was selected from the remainder of the beginning inventory, with the balance from the purchase of May 1, 2015.

As a shareholder, which of these three methods would you prefer?

AP8–3 Evaluating the Effects of Inventory Costing Methods on Financial Statement Elements (P8–6)   ■ LO4

The Sportex Company, a diversified distribution outlet for sporting goods, purchases cartons of tennis balls from the Ball Corporation and markets the balls under the Sportex name. Purchases and sales data for January 2016, the first month of operations, are provided below:

Date	Transaction	Number of Cartons	Total Cost	Amount of Invoice
January 2	Purchase	800	$16,000	
January 5	Sale	500		$20,000
January 19	Purchase	600	13,200	
January 21	Sale	700		29,200
January 29	Purchase	500	11,000	

Sportex uses a perpetual inventory system.

Required:

1. Compute the cost of sales in January 2016 by using the FIFO method.
2. Compute the cost of ending inventory at January 31, 2016, assuming that Sportex uses the weighted-average cost method. (Round your calculation of the average cost to the nearest cent.)
3. Would the computations you made in (1) and (2) change if the company used a periodic inventory system? Explain.

AP8–4 Evaluating the Effects of Inventory Costing Methods on Financial Statement Elements (P8–7)   ■ LO4

The following details were extracted on November 30, 2014, from the records of Seema Company for a specific product:

Date	Quantity	Unit Cost	Unit Sale Price
Beginning inventory, January 1	300	$ 9	
Purchase, February 10	400	10	
Sale, April 7	300	9	$15
Purchase, August 20	300	11	
Sale, November 29	350	10	16

On December 21, 2014, Seema sold 200 units to a customer at $18 per unit. Assume that the company uses a periodic inventory system and that its fiscal year ends on December 31, 2014.

Required:

1. Which inventory costing method does Seema use? Explain.

2. Prepare the journal entries to record the purchase transaction on August 20 and the sale transaction on December 21, assuming that both are cash transactions.

3. Compute the inventory turnover ratio during 2014, and briefly explain what the amount means.

4. Assume that the demand for this product slowed down during December 2014, and its net realizable value dropped to $9.5 per unit at December 31, 2014. Seema reports its ending inventory at the LCNRV. Prepare the journal entry that should be recorded at December 31, 2014.

5. Compute the cost of sales for 2014, assuming for this part only that Seema uses a perpetual inventory system and the weighted-average cost method.

AP8–5   **(Appendix 8A) Recording Sales and Purchases with Cash Discounts and Returns** (P8–10)
The following transactions were selected from those occurring during the month of January 2014 for Dan's Store Inc. A wide variety of goods is offered for sale. Credit sales are extended to a few select customers; the usual credit terms are n/EOM (end of the month). The cost of sales is always one-half of the gross sales price.

a. Sales to customers:
Cash, $228,000
Credit, $72,000

b. Unsatisfactory merchandise returned by customers:
Cash, $3,000
Credit, $2,000

c. Purchased merchandise from vendors on credit; terms 2/10, n/30:
  i. Amount billed by Amy Supply Company, $4,000
  ii. Amount billed by other vendors, $68,000

d. Paid freight on merchandise purchased, $1,500 cash

e. Collections on trade receivables, $36,000

f. Paid trade payables in full during the period as follows:
  i. Amy Supply Company after the discount period, $4,000
  ii. Paid other vendors within the discount period, $66,640

g. Paid $1,000 for two new laptop computers for the office

Required:
Prepare journal entries for these transactions, assuming that a perpetual inventory system is used. Record inventory purchases by using the gross method.

CASES AND PROJECTS

FINDING AND INTERPRETING FINANCIAL INFORMATION

■ **LO1, 3**   **CP8–1**   **Finding Financial Information**

RONA Inc.

Go to *Connect* for the financial statements of RONA Inc.

1. How much inventory does the company own at the end of the current year?

2. Estimate the amount of inventory that the company purchased during the current year. (*Hint:* Use the cost of sales equation.)

3. What method does the company use to determine the cost of its inventory?

4. Compute the inventory turnover ratio for the current year. What does an inventory turnover ratio tell you?

5. What was the change in inventory? How did it affect net cash provided by operating activities for the current year?

CP8–2 Finding Financial Information

Refer to the financial statements of Canadian Tire Corporation given in Appendix A at the end of this book.

1. What method does the company use to determine the cost of its inventory?

2. Did the company write down its inventory at year-end? If so, what is the amount of the write-down?

3. Compute Canadian Tire's inventory turnover ratio for the year ended December 29, 2012. What does this ratio tell you?

4. If the company overstated ending inventory by $10 million for the year ended December 29, 2012, what would be the correct value for earnings before income taxes?

■ LO1, 3, 6

Canadian Tire
Corporation

CP8–3 Comparing Companies within an industry

Refer to the financial statements of Canadian Tire Corporation (Appendix A) and RONA Inc. (on *Connect*) and the Industry Ratio Report (Appendix B on *Connect*).

Required:

1. Compute the inventory turnover ratio for both companies for the current year. What would you infer from the difference?

2. Compare the inventory turnover ratio for both companies to the industry average. Are these two companies doing better or worse than the industry average in turning over their inventory?

■ LO6

Canadian Tire
Corporation

RONA Inc.

FINANCIAL REPORTING AND ANALYSIS CASES

CP8–4 Review of Business Operations and Preparation of a Correct Statement of Earnings (A Comprehensive and Challenging Case)[9]

It is July 15, 2014. You, a junior accountant at a small accounting firm, go over your notes from your afternoon meeting with Marco Douga. Marco came to your office looking for help with his business, Marco's Professional Print Shop Ltd. (MPP). Marco is the owner-manager of MPP, a copy and print shop located in Newville. He recently approached a bank for a loan.

At his last meeting with the bank, the bank manager indicated that the loan is almost approved and told Marco that he needed to examine MPP's 2013 financial statements. In your file, you have the following information:

Exhibit I: Summary notes of the discussion with Marco Douga.
Exhibit II: Statement of earnings for the years ended December 31, 2013 and 2012, prepared by the client.

Your supervisor is eager to see a draft statement of earnings for the year ended December 31, 2013, based on the information you have thus far.

Required:

1. Identify any areas of concern that you may have about the operation of the business, particularly the proper accounting for revenue and expenses, and the control of operations.

2. Prepare a revised statement of earnings based on the information that you gathered during your meeting with Marco.

3. Identify the weaknesses in MPP's internal control of operations. What changes would you recommend? Explain.

EXHIBIT I

Summary Notes of the Discussion with Marco Douga

MPP provides copying and small print job services from a single location close to a university. The business was organized in January 2012 to meet the needs of companies, the university, and students in the area. At the time, there were no copying businesses in the area, and Marco saw this as an opportunity to become his own boss after many years of working as a mechanic for the local bus company.

Marco re-mortgaged his home for $55,000. This money was invested in the share capital of MPP. He also borrowed money from relatives to get the business started. With the money, Marco was able to purchase the computers, printers, copiers, and scanners needed to provide the full range of quality services that he thought his customers would need. Most of the equipment he purchased was used, which greatly reduced start-up costs.

(continued)

He also purchased the furniture and fixtures needed to set up a functional and attractive place for the business. As of December 31, 2013, MPP still owed Marco's relatives $100,000. Marco personally paid $3,800 interest for each of the last two years on the additional mortgage on his home. MPP now needs a loan for two reasons. First, some of Marco's relatives want their loans repaid. Since the business is now on its way, Marco thinks MPP can repay some of the money it owes. Second, Marco would like to upgrade some of MPP's equipment and obtain some additional pieces of equipment.

In addition to providing copying and printing services, MPP sells a variety of stationery and office products, and provides assistance in designing documents and other printed materials. MPP operates long hours to provide high-quality customer service, as well as to complete customer orders. More than one person has to be on duty at all times to ensure that production can be done while customers are being served, and so that pick-ups from and deliveries to customers can be made. Marco tries to be in the store as much as possible, but he is not able to be there all the time. His wife, Carla, works in the store about 15 hours per week. The store is operated by employees only (when neither Marco nor his wife is present) for about 25 hours per week, mostly at non-peak times.

Marco spends a lot of time trying to attract new customers. He regularly visits businesses in the area to meet the decision makers, often treating them to an evening out or a meal. About 40 percent of the advertising and promotion budget goes toward this type of activity. The remaining money is spent on advertising in community newspapers, sponsorship of various community activities, and printing and delivering flyers to businesses in the vicinity.

Marco is satisfied with the performance of his business. He thinks that it has grown nicely since its inception and anticipates that it will be profitable soon. Carla performs MPP's accounting and prepares a yearly statement of earnings, but she has little training in accounting.

Customers can pay by cash or credit card, or MPP will provide credit to any customers who ask. About 25 percent of MPP's business is for cash, 25 percent is on credit cards, and the remainder is on credit offered by MPP. MPP asks customers to pay within 10 days, but often they do not. When a sale is completed, it is rung up on the cash register. When Marco and Carla are in the store, they are the only ones who operate the register. Marco admits that, because he is in too much of a hurry, he sometimes puts the cash in his pocket rather than take the time to ring up the sale. Having cash in hand allows him to pay his babysitter and other personal expenses. Though it was hard for him to be certain, Marco estimated that transactions worth about $10,000 each year have been handled in this way. When Marco and Carla are out of the store, the cash is controlled by one of the employees. That employee is required to lock up for the day, count the cash in the register, and then lock the cash in a drawer in Marco's office. Marco has a lot of confidence in his employees, most of whom are students attending university and working part-time to make money.

Carla records the revenue by adding up the deposits made to the company's bank account during the year. Amounts owed by customers are recorded at the time of delivery, on a specially designated sheet of paper kept by the cash register. As cash is received, the related balance on the list is reduced. The accounts receivable balance on December 31 is the total amount on the list on that date. On December 31, 2013, there was $16,200 on the list and on December 31, 2012, the amount was $11,505. When Carla prepared the statement of earnings, she included a bad debt expense of $1,955 in 2012 and $2,754 in 2013, the amounts being estimated at 17 percent of the accounts receivable balance.

Marco obtained a corporate credit card on which he makes MPP's purchases. Items purchased on the credit card are expensed in the year as long as a statement is received from the credit card company before Carla prepares the year-end statement of earnings. If the statement comes in after that time, the expenses will get picked up the following year. Marco sometimes makes personal purchases on the corporate credit card if he thinks he is too close to his credit limit on his personal credit card. Marco estimates that he charged about $4,000 of personal expenses to the corporate credit card in each of the last two years. In addition, Marco has taken about $25,000 in cash each year from the business for personal reasons. Carla included these amounts in the payments to employees item on the statement of earnings.

MPP maintains supplies of paper, toner, bindings, and other materials used to meet customers' printing and photocopying needs. In addition, there is an inventory of merchandise that MPP sells to customers. Marco determines what he needs for inventory by doing a visual check of the storeroom every few days. When he needs particular items, he calls the suppliers, who are usually able to deliver the goods within a few days. On occasion, Marco has to go to a large business supply store, because he has run out of needed stock before the supplier can deliver the goods, and he pays for these purchases with the corporate credit card. Carla determines the cost of merchandise sold during a year by adding up the amounts on the invoices received from the suppliers.

The amount of inventory on hand at the end of each year is counted so that Marco can get a clear idea of what he has on hand. Marco was told that management needed the inventory value on December 31, 2013, and 2012. He determined the value of the inventory by using the list of what was in the stockroom on December 31 and by applying prices from the most recent supplier price lists. On December 31, 2013, MPP had inventory of $12,222, and on December 31, 2012, the balance was $8,200.

Marco pays suppliers' invoices in full as soon as they are received. Marco explained that he is afraid to miss a payment because suppliers may stop supplying. He figures that paying the bills as soon as they are received is the best way of avoiding the problem.

Employees are paid minimum wage. Since it is easier for Carla, employees are paid their gross earnings by cheque at the end of each week.

EXHIBIT II

Statement of earnings supplied by the client

MARCO'S PROFESSIONAL PRINT SHOP LTD.
STATEMENT OF EARNINGS
For the year ended December 31

	2013	2012
Sales	$360,547	$ 260,034
Cost of merchandise sold	124,984	96,212
Selling, general, and administrative	42,204	35,249
Payments to employees	90,099	83,740
Computers, printers, copiers, and scanners	10,000	85,000
Furniture and fixtures	—	15,000
Advertising and promotion	34,727	29,503
Utilities	18,300	17,900
Interest on loans from relatives	5,000	5,000
Bank charges	2,000	1,500
Rent	22,000	22,000
Bad debt expense	2,754	1,955
Other expenses	16,618	12,444
	368,686	405,503
Net loss	$ (8,139)	$(145,469)

CP8–5 **Using Financial Reports: Analyzing Inventory and Gross Profit for a Seasonal Business**

■ LO6

Danier Leather Inc.

Danier Leather Inc. manufactures and sells high-quality, fashionable leather clothing and accessories. The company's business is seasonal, as are most retail businesses. Historically, more than 40 percent of the company's total annual sales have been generated during its second fiscal quarter (October–December), which includes the holiday selling season. The company's results of operations depend significantly upon the sales generated during this period. A variety of factors affect sales, including fashion trends, competition, economic conditions, the timing of merchandise releases and promotional events, changes in merchandise assortment, success of marketing programs, cross-border shopping, and weather conditions, among others. The following table provides selected financial information for two recent years. All amounts are in thousands:

Time Period	Net Sales	Cost of Sales	Ending Inventory
Fiscal year 2010			$26,539
First quarter 2011	$ 23,427	$11,161	36,413
Second quarter 2011	61,442	25,500	41,163
Third quarter 2011	46,039	22,827	31,138
Fourth quarter 2011	26,713	11,845	28,964
Fiscal year 2011	157,621	71,333	28,964
First quarter 2012	22,091	10,401	39,775
Second quarter 2012	59,487	26,328	36,789
Third quarter 2012	39,131	20,364	28,383
Fourth quarter 2012	27,510	14,420	24,891
Fiscal year 2012	148,219	71,513	24,891

Required:

1. Compute the gross profit and the inventory turnover ratio for fiscal years 2011 and 2012.
2. Compute the company's gross profit for each quarter. What does the seasonal pattern of the gross profit reveal?
3. Is there a seasonal pattern in inventory balances? Would Danier's choice of fiscal year-end affect the inventory turnover ratio computed in (1)? Explain.
4. Re-compute Danier's inventory turnover ratios for 2012 based on the average of the quarterly balances of ending inventory instead of the annual balances. Is there a significant difference between this ratio and the ratio computed in (1)? Explain.

■ LO2, 3, 6   **CP8–6**   **Using Financial Reports: Analyzing Reported Information**

Alimentation
Couche-Tard

Alimentation Couche-Tard is the second-largest convenience store operator in North America. It has more than 9,000 outlets: Couche-Tard in Québec; Mac's in central and western Canada; and Circle K in the United States. The following table includes selected information from its financial statements (amounts in millions of U.S. dollars):

	Year Ended April 29, 2012	Year Ended April 24, 2011	Year Ended April 26, 2010
Revenues	22,997.5	18,550.4	15,781.1
Cost of sales	20,028.4	15,804.7	13,334.5
Earnings before income taxes	603.9	490.4	368.6
Income tax expense	146.3	121.2	114.7
Trade receivables	375.2	315.5	252.7
Inventories	543.9	526.0	469.9
Trade payables	812.7	701.7	618.2

Required:

1. Compute the following amounts for each of the fiscal years 2011 and 2012:

   a. Collections from customers.

   b. Purchases of merchandise from suppliers.

   c. Payments to suppliers.

   d. The trade receivables turnover ratio and the average collection period.

   e. The inventory turnover ratio and the average period to sell inventory.

   f. The average period for conversion of inventories into cash.

2. The company uses the indirect method to report its cash flows from operations. How would the changes in trade receivables, inventory, and trade payables be reported in the operating activities section of its statement of cash flows for 2012?

3. In the notes to its financial statements, the company states that the cost of merchandise in its distribution centres is determined according to the FIFO method. Would you expect the company's net earnings to increase or decrease if it used the weighted-average costing method instead of FIFO? Explain.

4. Assume that the company purchased canned products from a local supplier on April 26, 2012, with terms F.O.B. shipping point. The merchandise, at a cost of $1.4 million, had not arrived at the company's warehouse until April 30, and was not included in the inventory count at year-end. What effect would this error have on the company's net earnings for 2012? Show calculations.

■ LO2, 3, 6   **CP8–7**   **Using Financial Reports: Analyzing Reported Information**

Geox S.p.A.

Geox S.p.A. is an Italy-based company active in the footwear and apparel manufacturing industry, which includes classic, casual, and sports footwear, as well as apparel for men, women, and children. The company's products are sold in more than 70 countries worldwide through a widespread distribution network. Geox prepares its financial statements in accordance with IFRS. The following table includes selected information from its financial statements (amounts in millions of euros):

	2012	2011	2010
Net sales	807.6	887.3	850.1
Cost of sales	410.5	478.1	435.1
Earnings before income taxes	20.0	82.5	93.4
Income tax expense	7.7	28.0	32.2
Trade receivables	145.5	154.2	124.5
Inventories	209.2	196.6	172.1
Trade payables	162.6	133.0	117.8

Required:

1. Compute the following amounts for each of the fiscal years 2011 and 2012:

   a. Collections from customers.

   b. Purchases of merchandise from suppliers. Assume for simplicity that the company buys its products from other manufacturers.

   c. Payments to suppliers.

   d. Trade receivables turnover ratio and the average collection period.

   e. Inventory turnover ratio and the average period to sell inventory.

   f. Average period for conversion of inventories into cash.

2. The company uses the indirect method to report its cash flows from operations. How would the changes in trade receivables, inventory, and trade payables be reported in the operating activities section of its statement of cash flows for 2012?

3. In the notes to its financial statements, the company states that the cost of merchandise is determined by using the weighted-average costing method. Would you expect the company's net earnings to increase or decrease if it used FIFO instead of weighted-average cost? Explain.

4. Assume that the company purchased goods from a supplier in Asia with terms F.O.B. destination. These goods, which cost €1.2 million, were shipped on December 24, 2012, but had not arrived by December 31. The company's accountant included the cost of these goods in inventory at year-end. Is that an error? If so, what effect would this error have on the company's net earnings for 2012? Show calculations.

CRITICAL THINKING CASES

CP8–8 Evaluating the Use of a Perpetual Inventory System to Control Theft

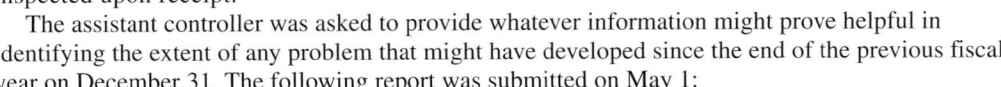

The president of National Wholesalers suspects that employees are stealing several items of merchandise, particularly items that are small enough to hide in clothing. The president's suspicions resulted from complaints made in April by several retailers who claimed that shortages were frequently found when orders of financial and programmable calculators were inspected upon receipt.

The assistant controller was asked to provide whatever information might prove helpful in identifying the extent of any problem that might have developed since the end of the previous fiscal year on December 31. The following report was submitted on May 1:

	Financial Calculators	Programmable Calculators
Number of units in inventory on December 31, per physical count	19,600	7,600
Cost per unit	$ 8.40	$ 29.25
Number of units purchased since January 1:		
January	4,200	1,400
February	3,600	3,100
March	5,100	2,700
April	2,700	1,800
Total	15,600	9,000
Average cost per unit of purchases since January 1	$ 8.40	$ 30.00
Average gross profit percentage on merchandise billed to retailers	30%	25%
Sales recorded from January 1 to April 30	$343,200	$496,400
Number of units physically counted in the warehouse on April 30	6,400	3,900

Required:

1. Compute the number of units of each type of merchandise that are unaccounted for on May 1. The company uses a periodic inventory system and the weighted-average inventory costing method.

2. Determine the monetary value of the apparent loss.

3. Assuming that the apparent loss realized during the period January 1–April 30 is representative of the loss that might be realized on these two items during an entire year, would you recommend that (*a*) a new inventory system be installed in the warehouse at an annual cost of $4,000 to maintain perpetual inventory records of these two items of merchandise and (*b*) a quarterly physical inventory count of these items be implemented at an additional cost of $1,000 per quarterly count? Show supporting computations.

■ **LO2**

Caterpillar Inc.

CP8–9 **Evaluating an Acquisition: Effect of Inventory Valuation on Earnings and Management Bonuses**

Caterpillar Inc. is the largest manufacturer of construction equipment in the world. In the course of growing its business, the company often purchased other companies. ERA Mining Machinery Limited (Siwei) was one such purchase. In June 2012, Caterpillar paid US$653.4 million, including US$475 million in cash, for all of Siwei's shares. Often when companies such as Caterpillar acquire other companies, they pay a premium over the fair value of the net assets acquired. The premium is called goodwill and the goodwill, associated with the Siwei acquisition was reported by Caterpillar at US$625 million.

By November 2012, Caterpillar disclosed its concerns regarding accounting fraud and, in particular, the misrepresentation of the value of inventory reported by Siwei. Siwei undertook improper cost allocation and revenue recognition methods as well, leading to an overstatement of net earnings as well as assets, including an overstatement of inventory by US$17 million. Caterpillar discovered the discrepancy following a physical inventory count after it had purchased Siwei. Caterpillar's chief financial officer noted publicly that a physical count was not a normal part of due diligence. This led some observers to conclude that in China, a physical inventory count should become part of the due diligence process.

The fraud appears to have been deliberate and occurred over several years. Siwei manufactures hydraulic roof supports to prevent the roofs of coal mines from collapsing. Caterpillar announced a write-down of US$580 million in the value of Siwei, which affected its earnings for the fourth quarter of 2012.

Caterpillar conducted its own internal investigation and subsequently dismissed all the senior management at Siwei, replacing them with management personnel from Caterpillar. Deloitte and Ernst & Young were the auditors acting for Caterpillar during the acquisition of Siwei, and RSM Nelson Wheeler of Hong Kong was Siwei's auditor.

The chief executive officer of Caterpillar, Mr. Doug Oberhelman, has taken full responsibility for the current situation. The company is considering what steps it should take to recover losses and enforce accountability on those responsible for the alleged fraud.

Required:

A number of news articles have been written about this alleged fraud. Access some of these articles to answer the following questions.

1. As a new staff member at Caterpillar Inc.'s auditing firm, you are assigned to write a memo on the effect of the overstatement of the value of inventory. Illustrate this effect with the use of adjusting entries to the appropriate financial statement accounts. Assume that Caterpillar is subject to an income tax rate of 30 percent.

2. Assume that both the CFO and the CEO of Caterpillar receive cash bonuses based on net earnings at the end of the year. What effect, if any, did the write-down of US$580 million have on the net earnings of Caterpillar Inc.? What effect, if any, did the write-down have on the share price?

FINANCIAL REPORTING AND ANALYSIS TEAM PROJECT

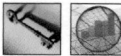

■ **LO4**

CP8–10 **Team Project: Analyzing Inventories**

As a team, select an industry to analyze. A list of companies classified by industry can be obtained by accessing **www.fpinfomart.ca** and then choosing "Companies by Industry." You can also find a list of industries and companies within each industry via **http://ca.finance.yahoo.com/investing** (click on "Order Annual Reports" under "Tools"). Each team member should acquire the annual report for one publicly traded company in the industry, with each member selecting a different company. (Library files, the SEDAR service at **www.sedar.com**, and the company website are good sources.)

Required:

On an individual basis, each team member should then write a short report answering the following questions about the selected company. Discuss any patterns across the companies that you as a team observe. Then, as a group, write a short report comparing and contrasting your companies.

1. If your company lists inventories on its statement of financial position, what percentage is this asset of total assets for each of the last three years? If your company does not list inventories, discuss why this is so.

2. If your company lists inventories, what inventory costing method does it use? What do you think motivated this choice?

3. Perform a ratio analysis:

   a. What does the inventory turnover ratio measure in general?

   b. If your company reports inventories, compute the ratio for the last three years.

   c. What do your results suggest about the company?

   d. If available, find the industry ratio for the most recent year, compare it to your results, and discuss why you believe your company differs or is similar to the industry ratio.

4. What is the effect of the change in inventories on cash flows from operations for the most recent year; that is, did the change increase or decrease operating cash flows? Explain your answer.

SOLUTIONS TO SELF-STUDY QUIZZES

Self-Study Quiz 8-1

1. $$BI + P - EI = COS$$
   $$(200 \times \$200) + P - (175 \times \$200) = 300 \times \$200$$
   $$P = \$55,000$$

2.

Net sales	$90,000
Cost of sales	60,000
Gross profit	$30,000

Self-Study Quiz 8-2

1.

	With Inventory Error 2015	With Inventory Error 2014	Without Inventory Error 2015	Without Inventory Error 2014
SARLOS LTD. STATEMENTS OF EARNINGS For the Years Ended December 31				
Sales	$600,000	$500,000	$600,000	$500,000
Cost of sales	350,000	300,000	340,000	310,000
Gross profit	250,000	200,000	260,000	190,000
Selling, general, and administrative expenses	120,000	100,000	120,000	100,000
Earnings before income tax	130,000	100,000	140,000	90,000
Income tax expense (at 40%)	52,000	40,000	56,000	36,000
Net earnings	$ 78,000	$ 60,000	$ 84,000	$ 54,000

2. The combined net earnings for both 2014 and 2015 is $138,000. The effects of the inventory error at the end of 2014 cancel out after two years. The 2014 error would not affect the financial statements for 2016.

Self-Study Quiz 8-3

1. FIFO cost of sales $= (10 \times \$10) + (5 \times \$11) = \$155$

   $$\text{Average cost} = \frac{\$100 + \$55 + \$65}{10 + 5 + 5} = \$11$$

   Weighted average cost of sales $= 15 \times \$11 = \$165$

	FIFO	Weighted Average
Sales revenue (15 × $20)	$300	$300
Cost of sales	155	165
Gross profit	145	135
Other expenses	100	100
Pretax earnings	45	35

2. The weighted-average cost would be recommended because it produces lower pretax earnings and lower taxes. The FIFO method would be recommended if the company's objective is to report higher net earnings.

Self-Study Quiz 8-4

1.

Year	2012	2011	2010	2009	2008
Average inventory	$26,927.5	$27,751.5	$23,792	$24,224.5	$27,982.5
Inventory turnover	2.65	2.57	3.25	3.66	3.12

These ratios show that efficiency in managing inventory improved in 2009 but decreased afterwards.

2. Both the ending inventory and the cost of sales will decrease by $1,000, but the rate of decrease of cost of sales, the numerator (= $1,000 ÷ $71,513 = 0.014), is much smaller than the decrease in the denominator, ending inventory (= $1,000 ÷ $24,891 = 0.040). This will cause the inventory turnover ratio to increase.

$$\text{Inventory turnover ratio} = \frac{\$70,513}{(\$28,964 + \$23,891) \div 2} = 2.67$$

3. A decrease in trade payables would have decreased cash flow from operations because Danier Leather would have paid its vendors more than purchases made on account during the period.

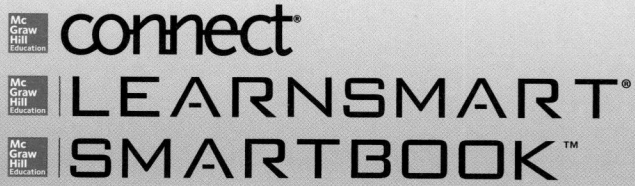

connect

LEARNSMART®

SMARTBOOK™

For more information on the resources available from McGraw-Hill Ryerson, go to www.mcgrawhill.ca/he/solutions.

Reporting and Interpreting Property, Plant, and Equipment; Natural Resources; and Intangibles

After studying this chapter, you should be able to do the following:

FOCUS COMPANY: **WestJet Airlines**

MANAGING EARNINGS THROUGH CONTROL OF PRODUCTIVE CAPACITY

WestJet Airlines (**www.westjet.com**), Canada's second-largest airline, has provided low-fare, friendly service to customers since its first flight took off in 1996. Clive Beddoe, along with a small team of Calgary entrepreneurs, started up WestJet with 220 employees and three Boeing 737-200 aircraft serving five destinations. By the end of 2012, the company employed over 9,000 people, had 100 aircraft and served 81 destinations in North America, Central America, and the Caribbean. WestJet plans to expand its fleet to 155 aircraft by 2018, including Bombardier's Q400 aircraft to provide a regional service between small cities. This investment in new aircraft allows WestJet to operate one of the youngest and most fuel-efficient fleets of any large North American commercial airline and illustrates one way of responding to environmental concerns.

WestJet is a capital-intensive company, with more than $1.986 million in property and equipment reported on its statement of financial position at December 31, 2012, representing 53 percent of its total assets. In fiscal year 2012, WestJet spent $218 million on aircraft additions, compared to approximately $61 million in 2011. WestJet's expansion plan is part of a long-term strategy of controlled growth, financed by a combination of debt, equity, and cash generated from its operations.

Since the demand for air travel is seasonal, with peak demand occurring during specific times of the year, planning for optimal productive capacity in the airline industry is very difficult. WestJet's managers must determine how many aircraft are needed in which cities at what points in time to fill all seats demanded. Otherwise, the company loses revenue (not enough seats to meet demand) or has higher costs (too many seats unfilled and unpaid for).

UNDERSTANDING THE BUSINESS

Running a business such as an airline, a resource extraction and processing organization, or a pharmaceutical company means acquiring adequate property, plant facilities, and equipment that will provide the capacity to serve the customers' current and future needs. Capital-intensive companies must pay large sums for their capacity, with the expectation of regaining that money over time, plus all operating costs and a reasonable profit. This explains why property, plant, and equipment of this type are referred to as either long-lived assets or fixed assets. For any airline, the aircraft, spare engines and parts, hangars, flight simulators, buildings, and equipment are all fixed assets. In comparison, resource extraction, processing, and distribution companies require the property (land) from which to extract raw resources, the plant facilities to process raw materials into refined products, and a distribution system to bring the refined products to the point of sale.

Pharmaceutical and biotechnology companies, however, require the property, plant, and equipment to conduct research and manufacture their products, but, more important, they require the know-how to discover and apply scientific information. Technology companies are similar in that the capacity to invent, develop, and successfully install communication systems relies heavily on intellectual capital. In these two industries, patents provide evidence that the knowledge expected to provide long-term benefit to the company has legal protection for a limited period of time. The most prominent assets on the statements of financial position of companies in these industries are usually intangible assets such as licences, brand names, and patents. The most valuable knowledge, however, may not be patented, because of the legal time limit to the protection provided, but kept secret from competitors indefinitely through strong confidentiality agreements.

One of the major challenges facing managers of most businesses is forecasting the level of long-lived productive capacity they will need to produce forecasted revenue streams. On the one hand, if managers underestimate the level of capacity needed in the future, the company will not be able to produce goods or services that are in demand and will miss the opportunity to earn revenue. On the other hand, if managers overestimate the productive capacity needed, the company will incur excessive costs that will reduce its profitability.

The airline industry provides an outstanding example of the difficulty associated with planning for and analyzing the capacity to produce service revenue. If an aircraft destined for Toronto takes off from Calgary with empty seats, the economic value associated with those seats is lost for that flight. There is obviously no way to sell the seat to a customer after the aircraft has left the gate. Unlike a manufacturer, an airline cannot place seats in inventory for use on future flights.

Likewise, if a large number of people want to board a flight, the airline must turn away some customers if seats are not available. You might be willing to buy a television set from Sears even if you are told that it is out of stock and there will be a one-week delay in delivery. But you probably won't fly home for a holiday on an airline that would have you wait one week because no seats were available on its flights when you wanted to fly. You would simply pick another airline or choose a different mode of transportation.

The battle for passengers in the airline industry is fought in terms of property, plant, and equipment. Passengers want convenient schedules (which require a large number of aircraft), and they want to fly in new, modern aircraft. Because airlines have such a large investment in equipment with no opportunity to hold unused seats in inventory, they work hard to fill aircraft to capacity for each flight.

While each flight generates revenue, it also creates wear and tear on the equipment, no matter how many seats are filled. Conceptually, WestJet's managers understand that this wear and tear means the cash flow from using this aircraft in future time periods will be lower than the cash flow currently experienced. In pricing an airline ticket for a specific flight, WestJet's management includes an amount to cover this daily wear and tear, which is part of the cost of operating an aircraft. The wear and tear is estimated and recorded as annual depreciation expense. WestJet estimates that the lifetime of an aircraft is 20 years, during which the company expects to recover the acquisition cost of the aircraft; to recover the related maintenance, operating, and financing costs; and to turn a profit.

In summary, issues related to property, plant, and equipment have a pervasive impact on a company in terms of strategy, pricing decisions, and profitability. Business managers devote considerable time to planning optimal levels of productive capacity that are adequate to meeting expected future demand. Accountants estimate and report the cost of using these assets throughout their productive lives, taking into consideration applicable income tax laws and regulations, and financial analysts closely review financial statements to determine the impact of management decisions on the company's profitability and financial condition.

This chapter is organized according to the life cycle of long-lived assets—acquisition, use, and disposal. First, we will discuss the measuring and reporting issues related to land, buildings, and equipment. Then we will discuss the measurement and reporting issues for natural resources and intangible assets. Among the issues we will discuss are maintaining, using, and disposing of property and equipment over time, and measuring and reporting assets considered impaired in their ability to generate future cash flows.

ORGANIZATION OF THE CHAPTER

Acquisition and Maintenance of Property, Plant, and Equipment	**Use, Impairment, and Disposal of Property, Plant, and Equipment**	**Natural Resources and Intangible Assets**
• Classification of Long-Lived Assets • Fixed Asset Turnover Ratio • Measuring and Recording Acquisition Cost • Various Acquisition Methods • Repairs, Maintenance, and Betterments	• Depreciation Concepts • Alternative Depreciation Methods • Changes in Depreciation Estimates • Managers' Selection among Accounting Alternatives • Measuring Asset Impairment • Disposal of Property, Plant, and Equipment	• Acquisition and Depletion of Natural Resources • Acquisition and Amortization of Intangible Assets • Examples of Intangible Assets

ACQUISITION AND MAINTENANCE OF PROPERTY, PLANT, AND EQUIPMENT

LO1

Define, classify, and explain the nature of long-lived assets, and interpret the fixed asset turnover ratio.

Exhibit 9.1 shows the asset section of WestJet's statement of financial position at December 31, 2012. More than half of WestJet's total assets are property and equipment. The company's annual report contains additional information about the acquisition cost of property and equipment owned or controlled by WestJet, and related depreciation; the amount of new investment in equipment during the year; and the amount of equipment that was sold or retired, as well as details of other long-lived assets with probable long-lived benefits. Let us begin by classifying these long-lived assets.

Classification of Long-Lived Assets

Accountants use the terms **long-lived assets**, long-term assets, or capital assets to identify property, plant, equipment, and intangible properties held for production, rental to others, or administrative purposes, as well as the development, construction,

LONG-LIVED (or **LONG-TERM** or **CAPITAL) ASSETS** are tangible or intangible resources owned by a business and used in its operations to produce benefits over several years.

Exhibit **9.1**

WestJet Airlines Asset Section of the Statement of Financial Position

REAL-WORLD EXCERPT

WestJet Airlines Ltd.

ANNUAL REPORT

WESTJET AIRLINES LTD.
Consolidated Statement of Financial Position
December 31, 2012 and 2011
(in thousands of dollars)

	Note	2012	2011
Assets			
Current assets:			
Cash and cash equivalents	5	$1,408,199	$1,243,605
Restricted cash	6	51,623	48,341
Accounts receivable	20	37,576	34,122
Prepaid expenses, deposits and other	20	101,802	66,936
Inventory	20	35,595	31,695
		1,634,795	1,424,699
Non-current assets:			
Property and equipment	7	1,985,599	1,911,227
Intangible assets	8	50,808	33,793
Other	20	75,413	103,959
Total assets		$3,746,615	$3,473,678

Source: WestJet Airlines Ltd., Annual Report 2012.

maintenance, or repair of other assets. Long-lived assets are acquired, constructed, or developed for use on a continuing basis. They are not normally sold to generate revenue, although the normal course of business for real estate companies is the purchase and sale of long-lived assets such as land and buildings. Long-lived assets can be tangible or intangible and have the following characteristics:

TANGIBLE ASSETS have physical substance.

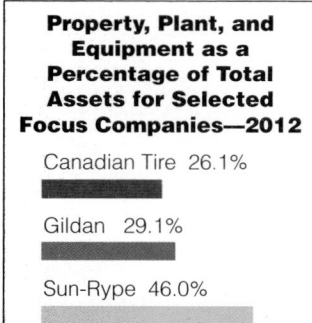

Property, Plant, and Equipment as a Percentage of Total Assets for Selected Focus Companies—2012

Canadian Tire 26.1%

Gildan 29.1%

Sun-Rype 46.0%

1. **Tangible assets** (or fixed assets) can be touched because they have physical substance. This classification is most often called *property, plant, and equipment*. The four kinds of tangible assets held for use in operations are as follows:

   a. *Land*, which is reported on the statement of financial position as a separate item if it has a material value. Unlike aircraft or patents on pharmaceutical products, land does not become obsolete; therefore, it is never depreciated. It may, however, be impaired in value.

   b. *Buildings, fixtures,* and *equipment*, which are reported as a separate item on the statement of financial position or in the notes. WestJet reports the details of such assets in Note 7, separating aircraft, spare engines, buildings, ground property and equipment, leasehold improvements, and assets under finance lease.

   c. *Biological assets*, which are living animals or plants such as sheep, dairy cattle, pigs, bushes, vines, and fruit trees. For example, Andrew Peller Limited, which produces wine, reports the grapevines controlled by the company as biological assets.

   d. *Natural resources*, which include mineral deposits such as gold or diamonds, oil wells, and reserves. Corporations such as Barrick Gold, Lucara Diamond Corp., and Suncor Energy Inc. extract natural resources.

INTANGIBLE ASSETS have property ownership rights but not physical substance.

2. **Intangible assets** have no physical substance. Historically, they were called "intangibles and other nothings." WestJet's intangible assets include computer software and landing rights—which give the airline the exclusive right for departure and landing at specific time periods. Intangible assets frequently arise from intellectual effort and are known as *intellectual property*. Examples include copyrights, patents, licences, trademarks, software, franchises, and subscription lists.

FIXED ASSET TURNOVER RATIO	KEY RATIO ANALYSIS 

ANALYTICAL QUESTION → How effectively is management utilizing its property, plant, and equipment to generate revenues?

RATIO AND COMPARISONS → The fixed asset turnover ratio is useful in answering this question. It is computed as follows:

$$\text{Fixed Asset Turnover Ratio} = \frac{\text{Net Sales (or operating revenues)}}{\text{Average Net Fixed Assets*}}$$

*[Beginning + Ending Balances of Property, Plant, and Equipment (net of accumulated depreciation)] ÷ 2

The 2012 ratio for WestJet is

$$\frac{\$3,427,409}{(\$1,911,227 + \$1,985,599) \div 2} = 1.76 \text{ times}$$

Comparisons over Time			Comparisons with Competitors	
WestJet Airlines			Southwest Airlines	Ryanair
2010	2011	2012	2012	2012
1.27	1.57	1.76	1.37	0.99

INTERPRETATIONS

In General → The fixed asset turnover ratio measures the sales dollars generated by each dollar of fixed assets used. A high ratio normally suggests effective management. An increasing ratio over time signals more efficient use of fixed asset use. Creditors and security analysts use this ratio to assess a company's effectiveness at generating sales from its long-lived assets.

Focus Company Analysis → WestJet's fixed asset turnover ratio has increased from 2010 to 2012, indicating a more efficient use of fixed assets. The fleet renewal at WestJet through 2012 appears to have improved its service to passengers and increased its net sales. When compared to two other companies in the industry, WestJet appears to be more efficient at utilizing its fixed assets than both Southwest Airlines and Ryanair. WestJet can further improve on its ratio by increasing its revenues from flights, either by increasing the number of flights or by increasing the number of paying passengers for existing flights.

A Few Cautions → A lower or declining ratio may indicate that a company is expanding (by acquiring additional productive assets) in anticipation of higher sales in the future. An increasing ratio could also signal that a firm has cut back on capital expenditures because it anticipates a downturn in business. As a consequence, appropriate interpretation of the fixed asset turnover ratio requires an investigation of related activities.

SELECTED FOCUS COMPANIES' FIXED ASSET TURNOVER RATIOS—2012

BCE   1.03

Gildan   3.49

Danier Leather   10.08

Measuring and Recording Acquisition Cost

LO2

Apply the cost principle to measure the acquisition and maintenance of property, plant, and equipment.

The *cost principle* requires that all reasonable and necessary costs incurred in acquiring a long-lived asset, placing it in its operational setting, and preparing it for use should be recorded in a designated asset account. We say that the costs are *capitalized* when they are recorded as assets instead of as expenses in the current period. These costs, including any sales taxes, legal fees, transportation costs, and installation costs, are added to the purchase price of the asset. Special discounts and interest charges associated with the purchase should not, however, be included in the cost of the asset. Interest charges should be reported as interest expense.

In addition to purchasing buildings and equipment, a company may acquire undeveloped land, typically with the intent to build a new factory or office building. When a company purchases land, all of the incidental costs paid by the purchaser, such as title fees, sales commissions, legal fees, title insurance, delinquent taxes, and surveying fees, should be included in its cost. Because land is not subject to depreciation, it must be recorded as a separate asset.

Sometimes a company purchases an old building or used machinery for use in its business operations. Renovation and repair costs incurred by the purchaser prior to the asset's use should be included as a part of its cost.

Assume that WestJet purchased one new Q400 aircraft from Bombardier on January 1, 2014 (the beginning of WestJet's 2014 fiscal year), for a list price of $27.5 million. Also assume that Bombardier offered WestJet a discount of $800,000 for signing the purchase agreement. This means that the price of a new airplane to WestJet is $26.7 million. In addition, WestJet paid $300,000 to have the airplane delivered and $1,000,000 to prepare the airplane for use. The amount recorded for the purchase, called the **acquisition cost**, is the net cash amount paid or, when non-cash assets are used up as payment, the fair market value of the asset given or asset received, whichever can be more clearly determined (called the *cash-equivalent price*). WestJet would calculate the acquisition cost of the aircraft as follows:

> The ACQUISITION COST is the net cash-equivalent amount paid or to be paid for the asset.

Invoice price	$ 27,500,000
Deduct: Discount from Bombardier	800,000
Net cash invoice price	26,700,000
Add: Transportation charges paid by WestJet	300,000
Preparation costs paid by WestJet	1,000,000
Cost of the aircraft (added to the asset account)	$28,000,000

Various Acquisition Methods

For Cash   Assuming that WestJet paid cash for the aircraft and related transportation and preparation costs, the transaction is recorded as follows:

Aircraft (A)	28,000,000	
Cash (A)		28,000,000

Assets		=	Liabilities	+	Shareholders' Equity
Aircraft	+28,000,000				
Cash	−28,000,000				

It might seem unusual for WestJet to pay cash to purchase new assets that cost $28 million, but this is often the case. When it acquires productive assets, a company may pay with cash that was either generated from operations or cash that was recently borrowed. Notice that WestJet's cash balance at December 31, 2012, exceeds $1.4 billion. It also is possible for the seller to finance the purchase on credit.

For Debt   Now let us assume that WestJet signed a note payable for the aircraft and paid cash for the transportation and preparation costs. WestJet would record the following journal entry:

Aircraft (A)	28,000,000	
Cash (A)		1,300,000
Note payable (L)		26,700,000

Assets		=	Liabilities		+	Shareholders' Equity
Aircraft	+28,000,000		Note payable	+26,700,000		
Cash	−1,300,000					

For Equity (or Other Non-cash Consideration)   Any non-cash consideration, such as a company's common shares or a right given by the company to the seller to purchase the company's goods or services at a special price, might be part of the transaction. When a non-cash consideration is included in the purchase of an asset, the cash-equivalent cost (fair market value of the asset given or received) is determined.

Assume that WestJet gave Bombardier 1,000,000 of its common shares, with a market value of $23 per share (the approximate stock price on the date of the transaction), and paid the balance in cash, including cash for the transportation and preparation costs. The journal entry and transaction effects follow:

Aircraft (A)	28,000,000	
Cash (A)		5,000,000
Common shares (SE)		23,000,000

Assets		=	Liabilities	+	Shareholders' Equity	
Aircraft	+28,000,000				Common shares	+23,000,000
Cash	−5,000,000					

By Construction In some cases, a company may construct an asset for use instead of buying it from a manufacturer. The acquisition cost of this self-constructed asset will include all direct and indirect costs of construction, including interest on any loans obtained to construct the asset. As soon as the asset is available for use, the accumulated construction costs will be depreciated over its productive life. The amount of interest that is included in the cost of the construction is called **capitalized interest**, which reduces the company's total interest expense every year until the facility is ready for use. Once the construction of the facility is completed, any interest costs on construction loans, however, must be expensed. The complex computation of interest capitalization is discussed in other accounting courses.

For example, in 2009, WestJet completed the construction of its new head office in Calgary, which the company refers to as its Campus facility. Because the company had the asset built for its own use, the cost includes necessary costs of construction such as labour and materials, as well as overhead costs directly attributable to the construction activity. The costs also include the interest expense incurred during the construction period, based on the amount of funds invested in the construction of the Campus. WestJet added the interest incurred to the other construction costs of the new building until it was ready for use in operations.

Capitalizing labour, materials, and a portion of interest expense increases assets, decreases expenses, and increases net earnings. Let us assume the new Campus cost WestJet $600,000 in labour costs, $1,300,000 in materials and supplies, as well as interest expense of $100,000 incurred during the construction project. WestJet would record the following journal entry:

> **CAPITALIZED INTEREST** represents interest on borrowed funds directly attributable to construction until the asset is ready for its intended use.

Building (A)	2,000,000	
Cash (A).		2,000,000

Assets		=	Liabilities	+	Shareholders' Equity
Building	+2,000,000				
Cash	−2,000,000				

WestJet described its policy on capitalized interest in Note 1 to its financial statements:

REAL-WORLD EXCERPT

WestJet Airlines Ltd.

ANNUAL REPORT

NOTES TO CONSOLIDATED FINANCIAL STATEMENTS

1. Summary of Significant Accounting Policies

o) Borrowing costs

Interest and other borrowing costs are capitalized to a qualifying asset provided they are directly attributable to the acquisition, construction or production of the qualifying asset. For specific borrowings, any investment income on the temporary investment of borrowed funds is offset against the capitalized borrowing costs.

Source: WestJet Airlines Ltd., Annual Report 2012.

In 2012, WestJet recorded $46,887,000 of interest related to aircraft financing, but it did not capitalize any interest.

As a Basket Purchase of Assets   When several long-lived assets, such as land, building, and equipment, are acquired in a single transaction and for a single lump sum, known as a **basket purchase**, the cost of each asset must be measured and recorded separately. This is true because land is not depreciated but buildings and equipment are, although at different rates. The purchase price must be apportioned among the land, the building, and the equipment, on a rational basis.

A **BASKET PURCHASE** is an acquisition of two or more assets in a single transaction for a single lump sum.

Accountants use current market values of the acquired assets on the date of acquisition to apportion the single lump sum to the various assets in the basket. Assume that WestJet paid $3,000,000 cash to purchase a building and the land on which the building is located. As the current market values of the building and land were not known, a professional appraisal was obtained. This appraisal, totalling $3,150,000, indicated the following estimated market values: $1,890,000 for the building and $1,260,000 for the land. The total purchase price is then apportioned on the basis of relative market values as follows:

Building	Land
$\dfrac{\text{Market value}}{\text{Total market value}} = \dfrac{\$1,890,000}{\$3,150,000} = 60\%$	$\dfrac{\text{Market value}}{\text{Total market value}} = \dfrac{\$1,260,000}{\$3,150,000} = 40\%$
60% × $3,000,000 Total cost = $1,800,000	40% × $3,000,000 Total cost = $1,200,000

The cost of the building is determined by multiplying the total cost of $3,000,000 by the ratio of the market value of the building to the total market value ($1,890,000 ÷ $3,150,000 = 60 percent). Similarly, the cost of the land is determined by multiplying the total cost by the ratio of the market value of the land to the total market value ($1,260,000 ÷ $3,150,000 = 40 percent). Assuming that WestJet purchases the assets with cash, the journal entry and effects are as follows:

Land (A)	1,200,000	
Building (A)	1,800,000	
Cash (A)		3,000,000

Assets		=	Liabilities	+	Shareholders' Equity
Land	+1,200,000				
Building	+1,800,000				
Cash	−3,000,000				

PAUSE FOR FEEDBACK

In general, all necessary and reasonable costs to prepare the asset for its intended use are part of the cost of the asset. Assets can be acquired with cash, with debt, or with the company's shares (at market value). Before you move on, complete the following questions to test your understanding of this concept.

SELF-STUDY **QUIZ 9-1**

McDonald's Corporation

In a recent year, McDonald's Corporation purchased buildings and equipment priced at $1.8 billion. Assume that the company also paid $8 million for transportation costs, $1.3 million for installation and preparation of the buildings and equipment before use, and $100,000 in maintenance contracts to cover repairs to the buildings and equipment during use.

1. Compute the acquisition cost for the buildings and equipment.

2. For each situation below, indicate the effects of this acquisition on the following financial statement categories. Use "+" for increase and "−" for decrease, and indicate the accounts and amounts:

	Assets	Liabilities	Shareholders' Equity
a. Paid 30 percent in cash and signed a note payable for the balance.			
b. Issued 10 million shares at a market price of $105 per share and paid the balance in cash.			

After you complete your answers, check them with the solutions at the end of the chapter.

Repairs, Maintenance, and Betterments

Most assets require substantial expenditures during their useful lives to maintain or enhance their productive capacity. These expenditures include cash outlays for ordinary repairs and maintenance, major repairs, replacements, and additions. Remember that the terms *expenditure* and *expense* are not synonymous. An expenditure is the payment of money to acquire goods or services. These goods and services may be recorded as either assets or expenses, depending on whether they benefit future periods or only the current period. Expenditures that are made after an asset is acquired are classified as follows:

1. **Ordinary repairs and maintenance**, or **revenue expenditures**—expenditures that maintain the productive capacity of the asset during the current accounting period only. These cash outlays are recorded as *expenses* in the current period. Ordinary repairs and maintenance are expenditures for the normal maintenance and upkeep of long-lived assets. These expenditures are recurring in nature, involve relatively small amounts at each occurrence, and do not directly lengthen the useful life of the asset.

   In the case of WestJet, the most significant component of its revenue expenditures is the routine maintenance work on aircraft engines, landing gear, airframes and other aircraft equipment. Although the cost of individual ordinary repairs is relatively small, in the aggregate these expenditures can be substantial. In 2012, WestJet reported $154.4 million for maintenance expenses on its consolidated statement of earnings.

2. **Extraordinary repairs** and **betterments**—expenditures that increase the productive life, operating efficiency, or capacity of the asset. These **capital expenditures**, which provide benefits to the company over a number of accounting periods, are added to the appropriate *asset* accounts. They occur infrequently, involve large amounts of money, and increase an asset's economic usefulness in the future through either increased efficiency or longer life. Examples include additions, complete reconditioning, and major overhauls and replacements, such as the complete replacement of an engine on an aircraft.

   An example of a betterment is WestJet's installation of blended winglets on its aircraft to improve the aerodynamic performance and handling design of the 737-800s. From a maintenance perspective, winglets help aircraft achieve better climb performance that allows lower thrust settings, which extends engine life and reduces costs. The aircraft itself uses less fuel, helping WestJet implement its greener air strategy.

ORDINARY REPAIRS AND MAINTENANCE are expenditures for normal operating upkeep of long-lived assets.

REVENUE EXPENDITURES maintain the productive capacity of the asset during the current accounting period only and are recorded as expenses.

EXTRAORDINARY REPAIRS are infrequent expenditures that increase the asset's economic usefulness in the future.

BETTERMENTS are costs incurred to enhance the productive or service potential of a long-lived asset.

CAPITAL EXPENDITURES increase the productive life, operating efficiency, or capacity of the asset and are recorded as increases in asset accounts, not as expenses.

In many cases, no clear line distinguishes capital expenditures (assets) from revenue expenditures (expenses). In these situations, accountants must exercise professional judgment and make subjective decisions. Many managers prefer to classify an item as a capital expenditure for financial reporting, because it reduces expenses and increases net earnings for the period. Of course, most managers prefer to classify the expenditure as a deductible expense on the income tax return, to pay lower taxes in the current period. Because the decision to capitalize or expense is subjective, auditors closely review the items reported as capital and revenue expenditures.

To avoid spending too much time on classifying capital and revenue expenditures, some companies develop simple policies that govern the accounting for these expenditures. For example, one large computer company expenses all individual items that cost less than $1,000. These policies are acceptable because immaterial (relatively small dollar) amounts will not affect users' decisions when analyzing financial statements.

A QUESTION OF ACCOUNTABILITY

LIVENT: HIDING HUNDREDS OF MILLIONS IN EXPENSES THROUGH CAPITALIZATION

When expenditures that should be recorded as current-period expenses are improperly capitalized as part of the cost of an asset, the effects on the financial statements can be enormous. In one of the largest Canadian accounting frauds in history, Livent inflated its net earnings and cash flows from operations by hundreds of millions of dollars in just such a scheme. This fraud turned Livent's actual losses into earnings. For example, in 1997 an actual $8 million loss was reported as net earnings of $4.3 million. Charges were initially brought in 1999 in the United States after the former chief financial officer informed a new manager of the fraud. The founders, Myron Gottlieb and Garth Drabinsky, were finally convicted and sentenced for forgery and fraud in February 2009.

The forgery pertained primarily to invoices of an engineering firm, which actually did fulfill its contractual obligations to construct the sets for Livent's productions. In essence, Livent reported expenses incurred to prepare for the production of its musicals on Broadway as if they were long-lived assets. These false additions to long-lived assets were then depreciated and a fraction of their total cost reported on the statement of earnings as depreciation expense, instead of their full cost. In combination, the accounting statements were materially misleading and overstated the financial health of Livent.

PAUSE FOR FEEDBACK

A corporation maintains and improves on the ability of its long-lived assets to generate future benefits in a variety of ways: repairing or maintaining (expensed in current period) or adding to or improving (capitalized as part of the cost of the asset).

SELF-STUDY QUIZ 9-2

A building that originally cost $400,000 has been used over the past 10 years and needs continuous maintenance and repairs. Indicate whether each of the following expenditures should be expensed in the current period or capitalized as part of the cost of the asset.

	EXPENSE OR CAPITALIZE?
1. Major replacement of electrical wiring throughout the building.	_____
2. Repairs to the front door of the building.	_____
3. Annual cleaning of the filters on the building's air conditioning system.	_____
4. Significant repairs due to damage from an unusual flood.	_____

After you complete your answers, check them with the solutions at the end of the chapter.

USE, IMPAIRMENT, AND DISPOSAL OF PROPERTY, PLANT, AND EQUIPMENT

LO³

Apply various depreciation methods as assets are held and used over time.

Depreciation Concepts

All long-lived assets, such as aircraft purchased by WestJet, have limited useful lives, except land. Long-lived assets represent the prepaid cost of a bundle of future services or benefits. A portion of an asset's acquisition cost must be allocated as an expense to the periods in which revenue is earned as a result of its use. WestJet earns revenue when it provides air travel service and incurs an expense when using its aircraft to generate the revenue.

The term used to identify and allocate the acquisition cost of using buildings and equipment that generate revenue over time is depreciation. Thus, **depreciation** is the process of allocating the acquisition cost of buildings and equipment over their productive lives by using a systematic and rational method.[1]

Students are often confused about the concept of depreciation as accountants define it. In accounting, depreciation is a process of *cost allocation*, not a process of determining an asset's current market value or worth. Depreciation is not a cash expense but a distribution of the acquisition cost over the same time period in which the asset is expected to generate revenue. When an asset is depreciated, the amount remaining on the statement of financial position *does not represent its current market value*. Under the cost principle, the cost of a long-lived asset is recorded at its current market value only on the acquisition date. At subsequent dates, the undepreciated cost is not measured on a market value basis. WestJet reported in its statement of earnings a depreciation and amortization expense of $185,401,000 for the year 2012. The journal entry and transaction effects, including the contra-asset account (XA), follow:

DEPRECIATION is the process of allocating the acquisition cost of buildings and equipment over their useful lives by using a systematic and rational method.

| Depreciation expense (E) . . . . | 185,401,000 | |
| Accumulated depreciation (XA) . . . . | | 185,401,000 |

Assets	=	Liabilities	+	Shareholders' Equity
Accumulated depreciation (XA) −185,401,000				Depreciation expense (E) −185,401,000

The periodic depreciation expenses throughout the asset's useful life are accumulated in the contra-asset account Accumulated Depreciation and deducted from the related asset's acquisition cost. The acquisition cost minus accumulated depreciation and any write-downs in asset value is called the **carrying amount** or **book value** and appears on the statement of financial position. In addition, companies like WestJet disclose information about the long-lived assets they own or control, and the related accumulated depreciation, in a note to the financial statements.

The **CARRYING AMOUNT** (or **BOOK VALUE**) is the acquisition cost of an asset less accumulated depreciation and any write-downs in asset value.

NOTES TO CONSOLIDATED FINANCIAL STATEMENTS
7. Property and Equipment

2012	Cost	Accumulated Depreciation	Net Book Value
Aircraft	2,605,277	(1,127,889)	1,477,388
Ground property and equipment	136,167	(79,052)	57,115
Spare engines and rotables	146,422	(44,713)	101,709
Deposits on aircraft	208,602	–	208,602
Buildings	135,924	(20,025)	115,899
Leasehold improvements	16,538	(5,536)	11,002
Assets under finance leases	821	(821)	–
Assets under development	13,884	–	13,884
	3,263,635	(1,278,036)	1,985,599

2011	Cost	Accumulated Depreciation	Net Book Value
Aircraft	2,510,811	(996,178)	1,514,633
Ground property and equipment	130,543	(70,880)	59,663
Spare engines and rotables	130,675	(40,259)	90,416
Deposits on aircraft	110,245	–	110,245
Buildings	135,822	(16,586)	119,236
Leasehold improvements	15,462	(4,107)	11,355
Assets under finance leases	4,221	(1,116)	3,105
Assets under development	2,574	–	2,574
	3,040,353	(1,129,126)	1,911,227

Source: WestJet Airlines Ltd., Annual Report 2012.

FINANCIAL ANALYSIS

CARRYING AMOUNT AS AN APPROXIMATION OF REMAINING LIFE

Carrying Amount/ Original Cost—2012

Ryanair 82%

Southwest Airlines 65%

WestJet 57%

Some analysts compare the carrying amount of assets to their original cost as an approximation of their remaining life. If the carrying amount of an asset is 100 percent of its cost, it is a new asset; if the carrying amount is 25 percent of its cost, the asset has about 25 percent of its estimated life remaining. In WestJet's case, the carrying amount of its aircraft is approximately 57 percent of the original cost. This compares with 65 percent for Southwest Airlines and 82 percent for Ryanair. This comparison suggests that, of the three companies, WestJet's aircraft have the shortest life remaining relative to their estimated useful lives.

Based on the information WestJet provided in its Note 1 (j) and Note 7, the carrying amount for aircraft can be used to estimate the asset's remaining useful life. You simply compute the ratio of carrying amount to acquisition cost, and multiply this by the asset's estimated useful life. Consider, for example, WestJet's aircraft.

$$\frac{\text{Carrying Amount}}{\text{Acquisition Cost}} \times \text{Estimated Useful Life} = \frac{\$1,477,388}{\$2,605,277} \times 20 = 11.3 \text{ years}$$

The useful life of WestJet's important assets can be analyzed in this manner, and comparisons can be made to other companies in the industry. This is, however, only a rough approximation, because the carrying amount of long-lived assets depends on the estimates of useful life and residual value, as well as the specific depreciation method used.

The calculation of depreciation expense requires three amounts for each depreciable asset:

1. Acquisition cost.
2. *Estimated* useful life to the company.
3. *Estimated* residual (or salvage) value at the end of the asset's useful life to the company.

Two of these three amounts are estimates. Therefore, *depreciation expense is an estimate.*

Estimated useful life represents management's estimate of the asset's useful *economic life* to the company, rather than of its total economic life to all potential users. The asset's expected physical life is often longer than the company intends to use the asset. Economic life may be expressed in terms of years or units of capacity, such as the number of hours a machine is expected to operate or units it can produce. WestJet plans to use its aircraft over a period of 20 years, whereas its buildings are expected to last for 40 years. The subsequent owner of the aircraft would use an estimated useful life based on its own policies.

The determination of estimated useful life of a long-lived asset must conform to the *continuity assumption.* This assumption holds that the business will continue to pursue its commercial objectives and will not liquidate in the foreseeable future. In Note 1 to its financial statements, WestJet, as do other companies, discloses the useful lives of its long-lived assets and the methods used to depreciate them. We will use the same estimates in our illustrations, where appropriate:

> **ESTIMATED USEFUL LIFE** is the expected service life of an asset to the current owner.

REAL-WORLD EXCERPT

WestJet Airlines Ltd.
ANNUAL REPORT

NOTES TO CONSOLIDATED FINANCIAL STATEMENTS

1. Summary of Significant Accounting Policies

(j) Property and equipment:

Property and equipment is stated at cost and depreciated to its estimated residual value. Assets under capital lease are initially recorded at the present value of minimum lease payments at the inception of the lease.

Asset Class	Basis	Rate
Aircraft, net of estimated residual value	Straight-line	20 years
Engine, airframe, and landing gear overhaul	Straight-line	8 to 15 years
Live satellite television included in aircraft	Straight-line	10 years/Term of lease
Ground property and equipment	Straight-line	5 to 25 years
Spare engines and parts, net of estimated residual value	Straight-line	20 years
Buildings	Straight-line	40 years
Leasehold improvements	Straight-line	5 years/Term of lease
Assets under finance leases	Straight-line	Term of lease

Estimated residual values of the Corporation's aircraft range between $4 million and $6 million per aircraft. Spare engines have a residual value equal to 10% of the original purchase price. Residual values, where applicable, are reviewed annually against prevailing market rates at the consolidated statement of financial position date.

Major overhaul expenditures are capitalized and depreciated over the expected life between overhauls. All other costs relating to the maintenance of fleet assets are charged to the consolidated statement of earnings on consumption or as incurred.

Rotable assets are purchased, depreciated, and disposed of on a pooled basis. When parts are purchased, the cost is added to the pool and depreciated over its useful life of 20 years. The cost to repair rotable parts is recognized in maintenance expense as incurred.

Source: WestJet Airlines Ltd., Annual Report 2012.

Residual (or **salvage**) **value** represents management's estimate of the amount the company expects to recover upon disposal of the asset at the end of its estimated useful life. The residual value may be the estimated value of the asset as salvage or scrap, or its expected value if sold to another user.

> **RESIDUAL (or SALVAGE) VALUE** is the estimated amount to be recovered, less disposal costs, at the end of the estimated useful life of an asset.

Residual value is the estimated amount to be recovered, less any estimated costs of dismantling, disposal, and sale. In many cases, disposal costs may approximately equal the gross residual value. Therefore, many depreciable assets are assumed to have no residual value. In the case of aircraft owned by WestJet, the company uses third-party industry market valuations, recommendations from the aircraft manufacturer, and actual experience to estimate useful life and expected residual value. WestJet explains that revisions will arise from changes to both market prices of used aircraft and utilization of the aircraft.

FINANCIAL ANALYSIS

DIFFERENCES IN ESTIMATED LIVES WITHIN A SINGLE INDUSTRY

Notes to actual financial statements of companies in the airline industry reveal the following estimates for estimated lives of flight equipment:

Company	Estimated Life (in years)	Residual Value
Lufthansa Group	12	15 percent of cost
Emirates Airlines	15	10 percent of cost
JetBlue Airways	25	20 percent of cost
Southwest Airlines	23–25	0–15 percent of cost

The differences in estimated lives may be attributable to a number of factors, such as type of aircraft used by each company, equipment replacement plans, differences in operations, and the degree of management prudence in setting its accounting policies. In addition, given the same type of aircraft, companies that plan to use the equipment over fewer years may estimate higher residual values than do companies that plan to use the equipment longer.

Differences in estimated lives and residual values of assets used by specific companies can have a significant impact on a comparison of the profitability of the competing companies. Analysts must be certain that they identify the causes for the differences in depreciable lives.

Individual items of property, plant, and equipment may include various significant parts that have different useful lives. For this reason, IFRS require that companies allocate the acquisition cost of each item of property, plant, and equipment to its component parts, and that each significant part be depreciated separately over its useful life.[2] An aircraft, the airframe, the engines, and the landing gear may have different useful lives. It is therefore appropriate to allocate specific costs to these aircraft components and depreciate them separately. This is known as componentization of assets:

REAL-WORLD EXCERPT

WestJet Airlines Ltd.

ANNUAL REPORT

NOTES TO CONSOLIDATED FINANCIAL STATEMENTS

1. Summary of Significant Accounting Policies
(s) Critical accounting judgments and estimates
(i) Componentization
The componentization of the Corporation's assets, namely aircraft, are based on management's judgment of what components constitute a significant cost in relation to the total cost of an asset and whether these components have similar or dissimilar patterns of consumption and useful lives for purposes of calculating depreciation and amortization.
Source: WestJet Airlines Ltd., Annual Report 2012.

Alternative Depreciation Methods

Accountants agree that there is no single best method of depreciation, because the cost of using long-lived assets to generate revenue differs significantly among companies. Thus, managers may choose from different acceptable depreciation methods.

Exhibit **9.2**

Illustrative Data for Computing Depreciation under Alternative Methods

WESTJET AIRLINES

Acquisition cost of aircraft, purchased on January 1, 2014	$28,000,000
Estimated useful life (in years)	20
Estimated residual value	$6,000,000
Estimated useful life (in flights)	40,000 flights
Actual flights in Year: 2014 2,100 flights	
Year: 2015 1,950 flights	
Year: 2016 2,050 flights	

Their decision should reflect the anticipated reduction in future cash flow as a result of the wear and tear from using the asset over time. Once selected, the depreciation method should be applied consistently over time to enhance comparability of financial information to users. We will discuss the three most common depreciation methods:

1. Straight-line

2. Units-of-production

3. Declining (or diminishing) balance

The hypothetical data shown in Exhibit 9.2 will be used to illustrate each of the three methods of calculating depreciation expense for one Q400 aircraft purchased on January 1, 2014.[3]

Straight-Line Method   More companies, including WestJet, use straight-line depreciation in their financial statements than all other methods combined. Under **straight-line depreciation**, an equal portion of an asset's depreciable cost is allocated to each accounting period over its estimated useful life. The formula to estimate annual depreciation expense follows:

STRAIGHT-LINE DEPRECIATION is the method that allocates the cost of an asset in equal periodic amounts over its useful life.

Straight-Line Formula

Depreciable Cost   **Straight-Line Rate**

(Cost − Residual Value) × 1/Useful Life = Depreciation Expense

In this formula, "cost minus residual value" is the amount to be depreciated, also called *depreciable cost*. The term "1 ÷ useful life" is the straight-line rate. Using the data provided in Exhibit 9.2, the depreciation expense is computed as follows:

($28,000,000 − $6,000,000) × 1/20 = $1,100,000

Amount for the adjusting entry: reported on the statement of earnings (closed at year-end)

Balance in the contra-asset account after the adjusting entry

Cost less accumulated depreciation: reported on the statement of financial position

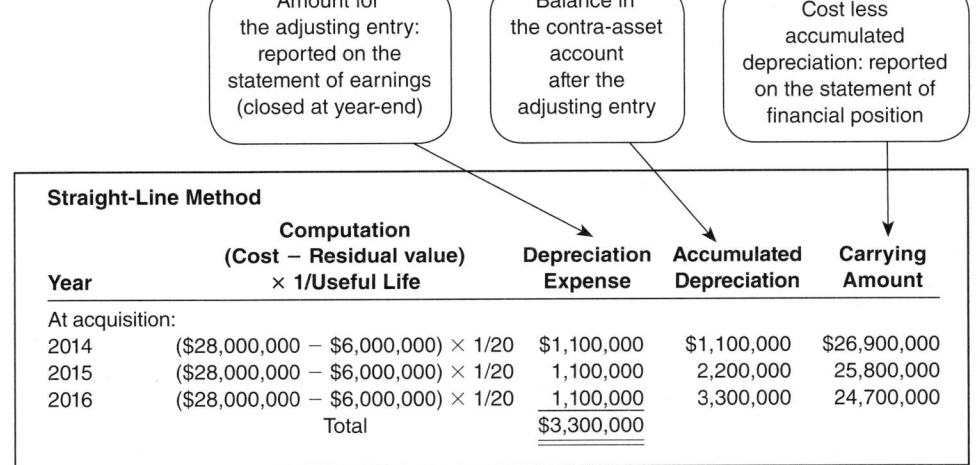

Straight-Line Method

Year	Computation (Cost − Residual value) × 1/Useful Life	Depreciation Expense	Accumulated Depreciation	Carrying Amount
At acquisition:				
2014	($28,000,000 − $6,000,000) × 1/20	$1,100,000	$1,100,000	$26,900,000
2015	($28,000,000 − $6,000,000) × 1/20	1,100,000	2,200,000	25,800,000
2016	($28,000,000 − $6,000,000) × 1/20	1,100,000	3,300,000	24,700,000
	Total	$3,300,000		

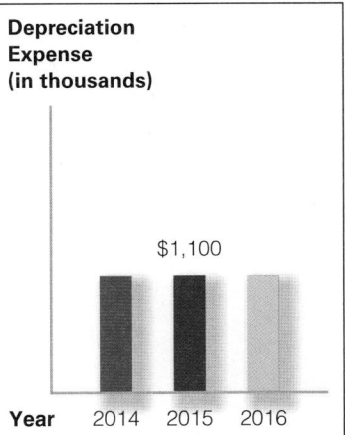

Depreciation Expense (in thousands)

$1,100

Year   2014   2015   2016

Notice that

- Depreciation expense is a constant amount for each year.
- Accumulated depreciation increases by an equal amount each year.
- Carrying amount decreases by the same amount each year until it equals the estimated residual value.

This is the reason for the name *straight-line method*. Notice, too, that the adjusting entry can be prepared from this schedule, and the effects on the statement of earnings and ending balance on the statement of financial position are known. WestJet uses the straight-line method for all of its long-lived assets. Most companies in the airline industry use the straight-line method. Depreciation expense, accumulated depreciation, and carrying amount decrease systematically from period to period at a constant rate each year. The depreciation expense is said to be a *fixed expense* because it is constant each year, regardless of the actual air miles flown by the aircraft.

UNITS-OF-PRODUCTION DEPRECIATION is a method to allocate the cost of an asset over its useful life based on the relation of its periodic output to its total estimated output.

Units-of-Production (Activity) Method   Assume WestJet uses the **units-of-production depreciation** method, which allocates the cost of an asset over its useful life based on the relation of its periodic output to its total estimated output. The formula to estimate annual depreciation expense under this method follows:

Units-of-Production Formula

Depreciation Rate per Unit

$$\underbrace{\frac{(\text{Cost} - \text{Residual Value})}{\text{Estimated Total Production}}} \times \frac{\text{Actual}}{\text{Production}} = \text{Depreciation Expense}$$

Dividing the depreciable amount by the estimated total production yields the depreciation rate per unit of production (or activity), which is then multiplied by the actual annual production (or activity) to determine depreciation expense. Using the information in Exhibit 9.2, the computation of the depreciation rate per unit follows:

$$\frac{\$28,000,000 - \$6,000,000}{40,000 \text{ flights}} = \$550 \text{ per flight}$$

For every flight, WestJet would record depreciation expense of $550. The depreciation schedule for the years 2014, 2015, and 2016 under the units-of-production method follows:

Depreciation Expense (in thousands)

$1,155 $1,073 $1,128

Year   2014   2015   2016

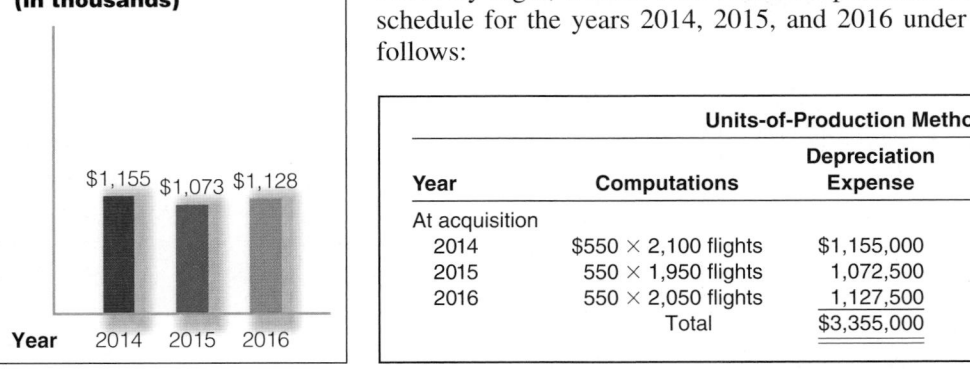

Units-of-Production Method				
Year	Computations	Depreciation Expense	Accumulated Depreciation	Carrying Amount
At acquisition				$28,000,000
2014	$550 × 2,100 flights	$1,155,000	$1,155,000	26,845,000
2015	550 × 1,950 flights	1,072,500	2,227,500	25,772,500
2016	550 × 2,050 flights	1,127,500	3,355,000	24,645,000
	Total	$3,355,000		

When the units-of-production method is used, depreciation expense is said to be a *variable expense* because it varies directly with production or use. The carrying amount and the amount of accumulated depreciation will also fluctuate from year to year.

You might wonder what happens if the total estimated productive output differs from actual output. Remember that the estimate is management's best guess of total output. If any difference occurs at the end of the asset's life, the final adjusting entry to depreciation expense should be for the amount needed to cause the asset's carrying amount to equal the asset's estimated residual value.

The units-of-production method is based on an estimate of an asset's total productive capacity or output that is difficult to determine. This is another example of the degree of subjectivity inherent in accounting.

Declining-Balance Method If the asset is considered to be more efficient or productive in its earliest years, with a levelling off in later years, managers might choose the **declining-balance depreciation** method to reflect a sharper reduction in the economic benefits (cash flow) expected to be derived from the asset in the earlier rather than later years. This is called *accelerated depreciation*. Special equipment acquired to produce a patented drug is an example. The drug faces little or no competition in its early years. Therefore, the producer can demand a higher price and derive more benefits from the equipment. In later years, as products mimicking the benefits of the drug are developed and brought to market, the asset's economic benefits will drop because of competition. Finally, when the drug is no longer protected by the patent, manufacturers of generic products can flood the market at very low prices. While the therapeutic benefits of the drug will not change, the economic benefits to the pharmaceutical company will be relatively low. Hence, a declining-balance method is used to better reflect the decline of economic benefits over time.

> **DECLINING-BALANCE DEPRECIATION** is the method that allocates the cost of an asset over its useful life based on a multiple of the straight-line rate (often two times).

The relationship between accelerated depreciation expense, repair expense, and the total expense of using the asset is shown in Exhibit 9.3. Although accelerated methods are seldom used for financial reporting purposes, the method that is used more frequently than others is the declining-balance method.

Declining-balance depreciation is based on multiplying the asset's carrying amount by a fixed rate that exceeds the straight-line (SL) rate. The rate is often double (two times) the SL rate and is called the *double-declining-balance rate*. For example, if the estimated useful life of an asset is 10 years and the SL rate is 10 percent ($1 \div 10$), then the declining-balance rate is 20 percent ($2 \times$ the SL rate of 10 percent). Other typical acceleration rates are 1.5 times and 1.75 times. The double-declining-balance (DDB) rate is adopted most frequently by companies utilizing the accelerated method, and will be used in our illustration.

To calculate depreciation expense under the double-declining-balance method, the carrying amount of the asset is multiplied by the DDB rate as follows:

Double-Declining-Balance Formula

Carrying Amount

Declining-Balance Rate

$$(\text{Cost} - \text{Accumulated Depreciation}) \times \frac{2}{\text{Useful Life}} = \text{Depreciation Expense}$$

Exhibit **9.3**

The Relationship among Depreciation Expense, Repair Expense, and Total Expense

There are two important differences between this method and the others described previously:

- Notice that accumulated depreciation, not residual value, is included in the formula. Since accumulated depreciation increases each year, carrying amount (cost − accumulated depreciation) decreases. The DDB rate is applied to a lower carrying amount each year, resulting in a decline in depreciation expense over time.
- An asset's carrying amount cannot be depreciated below residual value. Therefore, if the annual computation reduces carrying amount below residual value, a lower amount of depreciation expense must be recorded so that carrying amount equals residual value. No additional depreciation expense is computed in subsequent years.

Computation of DDB depreciation expense is illustrated using the data given in Exhibit 9.2 (amounts in thousands of dollars):

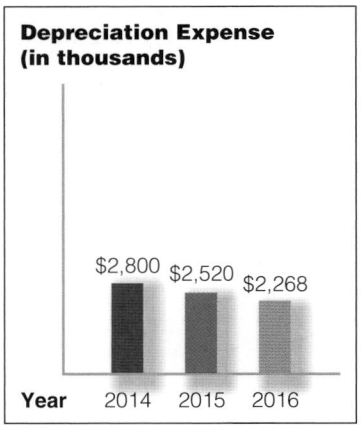

Depreciation Expense (in thousands)

$2,800 $2,520 $2,268

Year   2014   2015   2016

Double-Declining-Balance Method				
Year	**Computation (Cost − Accumulated Depreciation) × 1/Useful Life**	**Depreciation Expense**	**Accumulated Depreciation**	**Carrying Amount**
At acquisition:				$28,000,000
2014	($28,000,000 − $0) × 2/20	$2,800,000	$2,800,000	25,200,000
2015	($28,000,000 − $2,800,000) × 2/20	2,520,000	5,320,000	22,680,000
2016	($28,000,000 − $5,320,000) × 2/20	2,268,000	7,588,000	20,412,000
	Total	$ 7,588,000		

The calculated depreciation expense for this asset differs depending upon the depreciation method used. Using the straight-line method, the annual expense is $1,100,000 each year of the aircraft's 20-year useful life. Using the units-of-production method, annual depreciation expense varies each year from a low of $1,072,500 in 2015 to a high of $1,155,000 in 2014. Finally, using the double-declining-balance method, depreciation expense declines every year from $2,800,000 in 2014 to $2,268,000 in 2016. This, in part, explains why an analyst must be careful when using the carrying amount to estimate the remaining useful life of an asset. Using our example, we obtain different estimates for the remaining useful life for the same aircraft after three years, depending on the depreciation method used:

Depreciation Method	Estimated Remaining Useful Life
Straight-line	($24,700,000/$28,000,000) × 20 = 17.64 years or approximately 18 years
Units-of-production	($24,645,000/$28,000,000) × 20 = 17.60 years or approximately 18 years
Double-declining-balance	($20,412,000/$28,000,000) × 20 = 14.58 years or approximately 15 years

This example illustrates why care must be taken to read the notes to the financial statements of any company and identify the accounting policies it uses before comparing its financial results to those of other companies.

The depreciation method that is selected by management informs external users of management's expectation of the pattern of economic benefits that the company will derive from the asset over time. Companies will use different depreciation methods for different types of assets. For example, Norbord Inc., a Canadian manufacturer of wood-based panels used in housing construction, uses different depreciation methods for buildings and production equipment:

> **2. SIGNIFICANT ACCOUNTING POLICIES:**
>
> **(g) Property, Plant and Equipment**
> Property, plant and equipment are recorded at cost less accumulated depreciation. Property and plant includes land and buildings. Buildings are depreciated on a straight-line basis over 20 to 40 years. Production equipment is depreciated using the units-of-production basis. This method amortizes the cost of equipment over the estimated units to be produced during its estimated useful life, which ranges from 10 to 25 years. When parts of an item of property, plant and equipment have different useful lives, they are accounted for as separate items (major components) of property, plant and equipment. The rates of depreciation are intended to fully depreciate manufacturing and non-manufacturing assets over their useful lives. These periods are assessed at least annually to ensure that they continue to approximate the useful lives of the related assets.
>
> *Source:* Norbord Inc., Annual Report 2012.

As this note indicates, companies may use different depreciation methods for different classes of assets. They are expected to apply the same methods to those assets to maintain comparability of information over time.

In the previous illustration, we assumed that the aircraft was purchased at the beginning of the year. In reality, however, companies purchase assets at any date during the year, which complicates the computation of depreciation expense for the first year of acquisition. For practical purposes, acquisitions made during the year are depreciated in a convenient manner during the asset's first year of operation. Depreciation expense can be computed for the number of months the asset is actually in use, or it can be computed for half a year using the half-year convention.

For example, if WestJet acquired the aircraft on October 1, 2014, instead of January 1, 2014, the annual straight-line depreciation expense could be pro-rated by determining the monthly depreciation expense and multiplying the monthly depreciation by the number of months WestJet flew this aircraft during 2014 (three months in this case):

$$\text{Depreciation expense} = (\$1,100,000 \div 12) \times 3 \text{ months} = \$275,000$$

Alternatively, companies that acquire many long-lived assets during the year may use the half-year rule, which implies that similar long-lived assets, such as office equipment, that are acquired at different dates throughout the year can be assumed to have been purchased around the middle of the year. Thus, all the office equipment acquired during the fiscal year is depreciated for half a year at the end of the year of acquisition. This practical rule is acceptable as long as the amount of depreciation expense for the year is not materially misstated.

In Summary The following table summarizes the three depreciation methods and computations for each method. Exhibit 9.4 shows graphically the differences in depreciation expense over time for each method.

Method	Computation	Depreciation Expense
Straight-line	$(\text{Cost} - \text{Residual value}) \times \dfrac{1}{\text{Useful life}}$	Equal amounts each year
Units-of-production	$\dfrac{(\text{Cost} - \text{Residual value})}{\text{Estimated total production}} \times \text{Annual production}$	Varying amounts based on production level
Double-declining-balance	$(\text{Cost} - \text{Accumulated depreciation}) \times \dfrac{2}{\text{Useful life}}$	Declining amounts over time

Exhibit **9.4**

Differences in Depreciation
Methods over Time

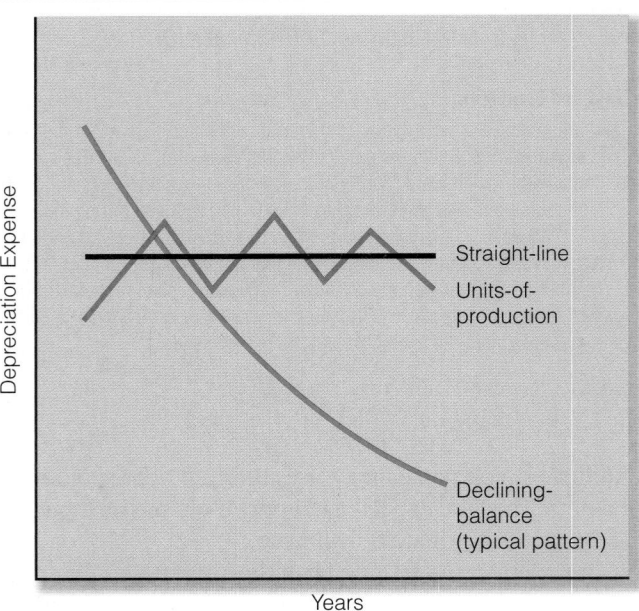

**FINANCIAL
ANALYSIS**

IMPACT OF ALTERNATIVE DEPRECIATION METHODS

Assume that you are analyzing two companies that are identical except that one uses accelerated depreciation and the other uses the straight-line method. Which company would you
expect to report higher net earnings? Actually, the question is tricky; you cannot say for certain which company's net earnings would be higher.

The accelerated methods report higher depreciation expense and, therefore, lower net
earnings during the early years of the life of an asset. In later years, this effect reverses.
Therefore, companies that use accelerated depreciation report lower depreciation expense
and higher net earnings during the later years of an asset's life compared to those using the
straight-line method. The graph in Exhibit 9.4 shows the pattern of depreciation over the life of
an asset for the straight-line and declining-balance methods discussed in this chapter. When
the curve for the accelerated method falls below the curve for the straight-line method, the
accelerated method produces higher net earnings than the straight-line method. The total
depreciation of the asset over its useful life should be the same for each method.

The depreciation method that a company uses to allocate the cost of an asset over
time should faithfully represent the economic decline in the ability of the asset to generate economic benefits in the future. Furthermore, the chosen method should be used
consistently from one period to the next. Users of financial statements must understand
that differences in depreciation methods rather than real economic differences can cause
significant variations in reported net earnings. For example, the Japanese company Sony
Corporation changed its depreciation method for property, plant, and equipment for fiscal year 2013 from the declining-balance method the straight-line method, because the
company "believes that the straight-line method better reflects the pattern of consumption
of the estimated future benefits to be derived from those assets being depreciated and
provides a better matching of costs and revenues over the assets' estimated useful lives."[4]
This change in depreciation methods resulted in a decrease in depreciation expense
and an increase in net earnings. This change in the depreciation method coincided with

Sony's reporting of net losses for fiscal years 2012 and 2013. The decrease in deprecia-tion expense reduced the net loss for fiscal year 2013, although the effect of the change is relatively small (approximately 3 percent of the total amount of depreciation and amortiza-tion expense).

PAUSE FOR
FEEDBACK

Three cost allocation methods are discussed in this section:

- Straight-line: (Cost − Residual value) × 1/Useful life
- Units-of-production: [(Cost − Residual value)/Estimated total production] × Annual production
- Double-declining-balance: (Cost − Accumulated depreciation) × 2/Useful life

Practise these methods using the following information.

SELF-STUDY **QUIZ 9-3**

Assume that WestJet acquired new computer equipment at a cost of $240,000. The equipment has an estimated life of six years (and an estimated operating life of 50,000 hours) with an estimated residual value of $30,000. Determine the depreciation expense for the first full year under each of the following methods:

1. Straight-line
2. Double-declining-balance
3. Units-of-production (assuming the equipment ran for 8,000 hours in the first year)

After you complete your answers, check them with the solutions at the end of the chapter.

Changes in Depreciation Estimates

Depreciation is based on two estimates—useful life and residual value. These estimates are made at the time a depreciable asset is acquired. As experience with the asset accu-mulates, one or both of these initial estimates may have to be revised to more faithfully represent the economic effect of using the asset in operations. In addition, extraordi-nary repairs and betterments may be added to the original acquisition cost at some time during the asset's use. When it is clear that either estimate should be revised to a mate-rial degree or the asset's cost has been changed, the undepreciated asset balance (less any residual value at that date) should be apportioned over the remaining estimated life from the current year into the future. This is called a *change in estimate.*

To compute the new depreciation expense resulting from a change in estimate for any of the depreciation methods described in this chapter, substitute the carry-ing amount for the original acquisition cost, the new residual value for the original amount, and the estimated remaining useful life for the original estimated useful life. As an illustration, the computation using the straight-line method is as follows.

Assume the following for an aircraft owned by WestJet:

Cost of aircraft when acquired	$28,000,000
Estimated useful life	20 years
Estimated residual value	$6,000,000
Accumulated depreciation through year 5	
($28,000,000 − $6,000,000) × 1/20 = $1,100,000 per year	
× 5 years	
= $5,500,000	

Shortly after the start of year 6, WestJet changed the initial estimated useful life to 25 years and lowered the estimated residual value to $4,000,000. At the end of year 6, the computation of the new amount for depreciation expense is as follows:

Acquisition cost	$28,000,000
Less: Accumulated depreciation (years 1–5)	5,500,000
Carrying amount	$22,500,000
Less: New residual value	4,000,000
New depreciable amount	$18,500,000
Annual depreciation based on remaining life:	
$18,500,000 ÷ 20 years (25 − 5 years) =	$ 925,000 per year

Companies may also change depreciation methods (e.g., from declining-balance to straight-line), although such change requires significantly more disclosure since the comparability of information over time is compromised. Changes in accounting estimates and depreciation methods should be made only when the new estimate or accounting method "better measures" the periodic net earnings of the business.

PAUSE FOR FEEDBACK

When management changes an estimate used in a depreciation computation, the carrying amount of the asset at the time of the change minus any expected residual value is allocated over the remaining life of the asset. Before you move on, practise the depreciation computation using the following information.

SELF-STUDY QUIZ 9-4

Assume that WestJet Airlines owned a service truck that originally cost $100,000. When purchased, the truck had an estimated useful life of 10 years, with no residual value. After operating the truck for five years, WestJet determined that the remaining life was only two more years. Based on this change in estimate, what amount of annual depreciation should be recorded over the remaining life of the asset? WestJet uses the straight-line method.

After you complete your answer, check it with the solution at the end of the chapter.

Managers' Selection among Accounting Alternatives

Financial Reporting   For financial reporting purposes, corporate managers must select the depreciation method that provides the best matching of revenues and expenses for any given asset. If the asset is expected to provide benefits evenly over time, then the straight-line method is preferred. Managers also find this method easy to use and explain. If no other method provides improved faithful representation, then the straight-line method is selected. Also, during the early years of an asset's life, the straight-line method reports higher net earnings than the accelerated methods do. For these reasons, the straight-line method is by far the most common.

However, certain assets produce more revenue in their early lives because they are more efficient then than in later years. In this case, managers select an accelerated method to allocate cost. In addition, as the asset ages, repair costs are likely to increase. Thus, the total of the depreciation expense and repair expense for any given period is likely to provide a nearly constant amount of expenses each period.

In addition to selecting a method of depreciation subsequent to the acquisition of property, plant, and equipment, managers must decide if they wish to measure these assets at historical cost (adjusted for depreciation) or to revalue them to their fair value at the end of the fiscal year. The primary argument in favour of revaluation is that the historical cost of an asset purchased 15 or 20 years ago is not meaningful because of the impact of inflation. For example, most people would not compare the original purchase price of a house acquired in 1984 to the purchase price for the identical house next door acquired in 2014, because the price of houses has changed dramatically between those years. A primary argument against the revaluation of property, plant, and equipment is the lack of objectivity involved in estimating an asset's current cost. Consequently, most companies use the cost method for financial reporting purposes.

Tax Reporting   WestJet Airlines, like most public companies, must prepare two sets of reports. One set is prepared under IFRS for reporting to shareholders. The other set is prepared to determine the company's tax obligation and is computed in conformity with the tax rules enacted by the tax authorities of the country where the company has been legally established. Canadian corporations must compute their tax obligations in accordance with the *Income Tax Act*. The reason that the two sets of rules are different is simple: the objectives of financial reporting and tax reporting differ:

Financial Reporting (IFRS)	Tax Reporting
The objective of financial reporting is to provide financial information about the reporting entity that is useful to existing and potential investors, lenders, and other creditors in making decisions about providing resources to the entity.	The objective of the *Income Tax Act* is to raise sufficient revenues to pay for the expenditures of the federal government, with many provisions designed to encourage certain behaviours that are thought to benefit society (e.g., contributions to charities are tax-deductible to encourage people to support worthy programs).

It is easy to understand why two sets of accounting reports are permitted, but perhaps the more interesting aspect concerns the reason why managers incur the extra cost of preparing two sets of reports. In some cases, differences between the *Income Tax Act* and IFRS leave the manager no choice but to have separate reports. In other cases, the explanation is an economic one, called the *least and the latest rule*. In general, taxpayers want to pay the lowest amount of tax that is legally permitted at the latest possible date. If you had the choice of paying $100,000 to the federal government at the end of this year or at the end of next year, you would choose the end of next year. By doing so, you would be able to invest the $100,000 saved for an extra year and earn a return on the investment.

By complying with the requirements of the *Income Tax Act*, corporations can defer (delay) paying millions and sometimes billions of dollars in taxes. The following companies, which prepare their financial statements in compliance with IFRS, reported material amounts of deferred tax obligations in a recent year. The deferral of payment of income tax to future years was in large part due to differences between the depreciation methods used for financial reporting versus tax reporting:

Company	Deferred Tax Liabilities Due to Applying Different Depreciation Methods
WestJet Airlines Ltd.	$ 357 million
Canadian National Railway Company	5,555 million
Suncor Energy Inc.	10,463 million

The depreciation methods discussed in the previous section are not acceptable for federal income tax reporting. One objective of domestic tax law is to provide an incentive for existing Canadian companies to invest in modern property, plant, and equipment in order to retain their global competitiveness. Governments around the world also compete to attract production facilities by using their tax laws to support their domestic economic growth. More production usually means more employment for Canadians, and economic growth.

Corporations that are subject to taxation in Canada must apply capital cost allowance (CCA) to tangible assets, as determined by the schedules provided by the tax authorities. The CCA schedules must be used to calculate the maximum annual expense used in computing taxable income according to the tax rules and regulations. These schedules classify capital assets into different classes and stipulate the maximum CCA rate (a declining-balance rate) for each class. For example, aircraft is currently Class 9, with a CCA rate of 25 percent per year.

CCA does not attempt to match the cost of an asset with the revenue it produces over its useful life, in conformity with the matching process. Instead, CCA provides for accelerated depreciation of an asset over a period that is usually much shorter than the asset's estimated useful life. Because CCA is based on an accelerated method, the high expense reported under CCA reduces a corporation's taxable income more in the early years of a long-lived asset than in later years. For example, the straight-line depreciation expense related to the Q400 aircraft is $1,100,000 for 2014, but the corresponding CCA will be $7,000,000 ($28,000,000 × 25 percent), of which half may be deducted in the first year the asset is acquired. The difference between the CCA deduction of $3,500,000 and the depreciation expense of $1,100,000 reduces taxable income by $2,400,000. This will reduce the amount of income tax payable, leaving WestJet with more cash available to finance its growth. Chapter 10 provides further discussion on this topic.

A QUESTION OF ACCOUNTABILITY

TWO SETS OF REPORTS

When they first learn that companies prepare two sets of reports, some people question the ethics or the legality of the practice. In reality, *it is both legal and ethical to prepare separate reports for tax and financial reporting purposes. However, these reports must reflect the same transactions.* The amounts reported for tax purposes are essentially adjustments to amounts recorded in the accounting system for financial reporting purposes. Understating revenues or overstating expenses on a tax return can result in financial penalties and/or imprisonment. Accountants who aid tax evaders can also be fined or imprisoned, and can lose their professional licences.

INTERNATIONAL PERSPECTIVE

DEPRECIATION METHODS IN OTHER COUNTRIES

With the severe and extreme economic contraction in 2008 and 2009, many countries worldwide relaxed either their accounting or their tax regulations in an effort to stimulate their domestic economies. Austria, for example, has permitted accelerated depreciation up to 30 percent of either acquisition or construction costs for property, plant, and equipment, such as aircraft, for assets acquired in 2009 and 2010, while the United States enacted the *American Recovery and Reinvestment Act of 2009*, extending a 50 percent acceleration provision to include properties placed into service in 2009 as well as those already available for 2008.

While accounting methods have remain unchanged, tax regulations in some countries have changed to reduce the cash burden of tax payments on capital-intensive industries and stimulate investment in new long-lived assets. The economic goal is to sustain economic growth and retain jobs. When users of financial statements for airlines compare reported net earnings for companies operating in these three countries, knowing the income tax regimes are comparable is as important as knowing the accounting methods are comparable as well.

Measuring Asset Impairment

LO4

Explain the effect of asset impairment on the financial statements.

Canadian corporations are required to review the carrying amount of their tangible and intangible assets for possible impairment. Assets can have different values that are used for different purposes. Historical acquisition costs are essential for verifiability of past transactions. These costs are then adjusted for systematic depreciation over their useful lives. However, adjusted historical costs are not relevant for investment decisions that rely on expectations of future cash flows. Consequently, investors and creditors may be interested in the asset's *fair value*, which reflects the amount at which an asset can be bought or sold between two knowledgeable, willing parties in an arm's-length transaction. However, companies usually acquire long-lived assets for use in their production processes, and not for resale to others. Therefore, a long-lived asset has *value in use*, which is measured as the present value (or current cash equivalent) of future cash flows expected to be derived from use of the asset over time.

Subsequent to acquisition, the economic benefits or future cash flows associated with assets do change for a variety of reasons. Adverse changes to future benefits may be triggered, for example, by reduced market price for the asset, contraction in the economy, ongoing evidence of operating cash flow losses, and technological obsolescence. Consequently, assets should then be assessed for possible impairment.

Impairment occurs when events or changed circumstances cause the carrying amount of these assets to exceed their recoverable amount, which is the higher of its value in use and its fair value less costs to sell:

If Carrying amount > Recoverable amount, then the asset is impaired.

A simple illustration will help in understanding how this concept is applied. Assume that WestJet has an old aircraft that is still in good working condition. This aircraft has a carrying amount of $15 million. Because of an economic downturn, its current market price has dropped to $13 million, and the company will incur $0.5 million in costs to sell this aircraft to an interested buyer. At the same time, the value in use of the aircraft or current cash equivalent of future net cash flows expected to be derived from using it is $14 million. In this case, the test for impairment indicates that this aircraft is impaired by $1 million, which is determined as follows:

Fair value less costs to sell	$12.5 million
Value in use	14 million
Recoverable amount (= Value in use)	14 million
Carrying amount	15 million

Since the carrying amount exceeds the recoverable amount, the aircraft is impaired by $1 million, the difference between these two values. If the aircraft's value in use is greater than $15 million, then the aircraft is not impaired and there is no need, in this case, to determine the aircraft's fair value less costs to sell.

Fair values can be determined based on quoted market prices. If there is no current market price, then fair values can be based on prices of similar assets for which a recent transaction occurred, on an arm's-length appraisal value, or by using specific valuation techniques.

In the previous example, the recoverable amount was determined for one asset—an aircraft. Sometimes, however, an asset does not generate cash inflows that are largely independent from other assets or groups of assets. In this case, the asset would be grouped with other assets that would form a cash-generating unit. The recoverable amount would then be determined for the cash-generating unit as a whole instead of the individual assets to which it belongs.

Although WestJet reported no impairment losses to its property, plant, and equipment, let us assume that a review of WestJet's aircraft indicated that an asset group of aircraft has a carrying amount of $132 million. The value in use of this asset group was estimated at $120 million, and fair value less costs to sell was estimated at $125 million by using published sources of market prices of used aircraft as well as third-party bids. These aircraft are therefore impaired because their recoverable amount, $125 million, is lower than their carrying amount. The following journal entry would be recorded:

Loss due to impairment of assets (SE)	7,000,000	
Aircraft (A)		7,000,000

Assets		=	Liabilities	+	Shareholders' Equity	
Aircraft	−7,000,000				Loss due to impairment	−7,000,000

An impairment loss recognized in a prior period can be reversed in the future if there has been a change in the estimates used to determine the asset's recoverable amount since the impairment loss was recognized. In this case, the increased carrying amount of the asset shall not exceed the carrying amount that would have been determined (net of depreciation) had no impairment loss been recognized for the asset in prior years.

Companies that recognize impairment losses or reversal of prior impairment losses are required to disclose in the notes to their financial statements specific details about each material impairment loss recognized or reversed during the period, either for an individual asset or for a cash-generating unit. The disclosures include the nature of the asset or the cash-generating unit, the events and circumstances that led to the recognition or reversal of the impairment loss, the amount of the impairment loss recognized or reversed, and the methods used to determine the recoverable amount.

For example, in 2012, Suncor Energy reported in great detail the sources of restructuring and impairment charges, including impairment of $1.487 billion on the Voyageur upgrader project in its Oil Sands business:

REAL-WORLD EXCERPT

Suncor Energy Inc.

ANNUAL REPORT

MANAGEMENT'S DISCUSSION AND ANALYSIS

Operating Earnings Adjustments

In 2012, the company recorded after-tax impairments (net of reversals), write-offs and provisions of $2.176 billion. Given Suncor's view of the challenging economic outlook for the Voyageur upgrader project, at December 31, 2012, Suncor performed an impairment test. Based on an assessment of expected future net cash flows, the company recorded an after-tax impairment charge of $1.487 billion. Due to political unrest and international sanctions against Syria, Suncor recorded an after-tax impairment (net of reversals) and write-offs for assets in Syria of $517 million. Additional impairments in 2012 included after-tax impairment charges of $65 million to reflect future development uncertainty relating to certain exploration assets in East Coast Canada and North America Onshore, and an after-tax impairment charge of $63 million for certain North America Onshore properties due to a decline in price forecasts. In addition, the company recorded an after-tax provision of $44 million in North America Onshore relating to future commitments for unutilized pipeline capacity.

Source: Suncor Energy, Annual Report 2012.

The complex nature of testing for asset impairment is covered in advanced accounting courses.

Disposal of Property, Plant, and Equipment

LO⁵

Analyze the disposal of property, plant, and equipment.

In some cases, a business may *voluntarily* decide not to hold a long-lived asset for its entire life. The company may drop a product from its line and no longer need the equipment that was used to produce the product, or managers may want to replace a machine with a more efficient one. These disposals include sale, trade-in, and retirement. When WestJet disposes of an old aircraft, it may sell it to a cargo airline or regional airline. A business may also dispose of an asset *involuntarily* as a result of a casualty, such as a storm, fire, or accident.

Disposals of long-lived assets seldom occur on the last day of the accounting period. Therefore, depreciation must be updated to the date of disposal. The disposal of a depreciable asset usually requires two entries:

1. An adjusting entry to update the depreciation expense and accumulated depreciation accounts.

2. An entry to record the disposal. The cost of the asset and any accumulated depreciation at the date of disposal must be removed from the accounts. The difference between any resources received on disposal of an asset and its carrying amount at the date of disposal is a gain or loss on disposal of the asset. This gain (or loss) is revenue (or expense) from "peripheral or incidental" activities rather than from normal operations. Gains and losses from disposals are usually shown separately on the statement of earnings after earnings from operations.

Assume that at the end of 2013 WestJet sold an aircraft that was no longer needed because of the elimination of service to a small city. The original cost of the aircraft was $2.6 million. The unrecorded depreciation expense for the year was $71,000.[5] The aircraft was sold for $1.9 million in cash and had accumulated depreciation of $224,000 at the beginning of 2013. The loss on the sale of this aircraft is $405,000, calculated as follows:

Cash received		$1,900,000
Original cost	$2,600,000	
Less: Accumulated depreciation	295,000	
Carrying amount		2,305,000
Loss on disposal		$ (405,000)

The entries and effects of the transaction on the date of the sale are as follows:

1. Depreciation expense (E)	71,000	
Accumulated depreciation—Aircraft (XA)		71,000
2. Cash (A)	1,900,000	
Accumulated depreciation—Aircraft (XA)	295,000	
Loss on sale of asset (SE)	405,000	
Aircraft (A).		2,600,000

Assets		=	Liabilities	+	Shareholders' Equity	
1. Accumulated depreciation	−71,000				1. Depreciation expense	−71,000
2. Cash	+1,900,000				2. Loss on sale of asset	−405,000
Accumulated depreciation	+ 295,000					
Aircraft	− 2,600,000					

A gain or loss on disposal occurs because (1) depreciation expense is based on estimates that may differ from actual experience and (2) depreciation is based on original cost, not current market value. Because the gain or loss on disposal is not part of the continuing operating activities of a company, it is usually shown as a separate line item on the statement of earnings. In 2012, for example, WestJet sold property and equipment and reported a net gain of $469,000 as a separate item on its consolidated statement of earnings.

PAUSE FOR FEEDBACK

When disposing of a long-lived asset, a company must first record depreciation expense for usage of the asset since the last time it was recorded. Then, the asset at cost, and its related accumulated depreciation, are eliminated. The difference between the cash received, if any, and the carrying amount of the asset is either a gain or a loss on disposal.

SELF-STUDY QUIZ 9-5

Now let us assume the same facts as above, except that the aircraft was sold for $2,500,000 cash. Prepare the two entries on the date of the sale.

1. Update the depreciation expense for the year.

2. Record the sale.

After you complete your answers, check them with the solutions at the end of the chapter.

Companies may also trade in an old asset in exchange for a new asset and pay cash to cover the difference in the assets' values. Let us assume that an old vehicle, originally acquired at $20,000 with $16,000 of accumulated depreciation, has a fair market value of $3,000. The company exchanges this vehicle in partial payment for computer hardware and pays an additional amount of $1,600 in cash. This trade-in transaction includes a non-cash consideration. Hence, the computer hardware is recorded at its fair market value, unless the fair market value of the old vehicle is more objectively determinable. Notice that the carrying amount of the vehicle is $4,000 and the total payment for the computer hardware is $4,600, which is equal to the fair market value of the vehicle plus the cash consideration. Assuming that the fair market value of the vehicle is more objectively determinable, the journal entry and effects of the trade-in transaction are as follows:[6]

Computer hardware (A)	4,600	
Accumulated depreciation—Vehicle (XA)	16,000	
Loss on disposal of assets (SE)	1,000	
Vehicle (A)		20,000
Cash (A)		1,600

In certain situations, the company may dispose of an old, unusable asset if it cannot sell it to another party. The abandonment or retirement of an asset results in a loss that is equal to the asset's carrying amount. The journal entry to record the retirement of an asset is similar to the case of a sale or a trade-in, except that the cash account is not affected.

NATURAL RESOURCES AND INTANGIBLE ASSETS

Acquisition and Depletion of Natural Resources

You may be familiar with some large companies that develop raw materials and products from **natural resources**, assets that occur in nature, such as oil, diamonds, gold, and iron ore (e.g., Suncor Energy Inc., Barrick Gold Corporation). These resources are often called *wasting assets* because they are depleted (i.e., physically used up). Companies that develop natural resources are critical to the economy because they produce such essential items as lumber for construction and fuel for heating and transportation. Such companies attract considerable public attention because of the significant effect they can have on the environment.

It may surprise you to know that, in Canada, natural resource companies do not own the land from which they extract oil or minerals. They acquire mineral rights from the government to explore, develop, and extract minerals from the land, but they do not own the land itself. When the rights to explore and develop natural resources are acquired, they are recorded in conformity with the cost principle. The land remains the common property of Canadians. This is one reason why concerned citizens often read financial statements from companies involved in mineral exploration, development, and extraction to determine the amount of money spent to protect and remediate any damage done to the environment.

Through exploration, the company estimates the value of the resources extracted and sold throughout their productive lives. The quantity of resources in the reserve is carefully surveyed by using sophisticated geological engineering methods. The initial reserve value is then **depleted** or allocated on a systematic and rational basis to match the expected revenue generated from the sale of the resources.[7]

Often these companies keep the reserve value separate from other property, plant, and equipment values incurred, because the companies may have to construct special roads and erect housing, buildings, and facilities in remote locations to extract the resources. When the site is put into production, these accumulated costs will be depreciated over the productive life of the site. Thus, natural resource companies amortize the acquisition costs of intangible mineral rights, deplete their reserve values, and depreciate exploration and development costs as well as self-constructed extraction facilities.

Suncor Energy Inc. is a well-known participant in the development of the Athabasca oil sands. It is a global company, identified as an integrated petroleum explorer, developer, and refiner. The company depletes the acquisition cost of oil and gas reserves by using the units-of-production method. The company values the barrels of oil and cubic feet of natural gas in the reserves by using an estimate of proved, proved developed, and undeveloped reserves.

LO6

Apply measurement and reporting concepts for natural resources and intangible assets.

NATURAL RESOURCES are assets that occur in nature, such as mineral deposits, timber, oil, and gas.

DEPLETION is the systematic and rational allocation of the cost of a natural resource over the period of exploitation.

REAL-WORLD EXCERPT

Suncor Energy Inc.
ANNUAL REPORT

---

3. SUMMARY OF SIGNIFICANT ACCOUNTING POLICIES

(h) Depreciation, Depletion and Amortization

Exploration and evaluation assets are not subject to depreciation, depletion and amortization, with the exception of certain exploration assets. Once transferred to Property, Plant and Equipment and commercial production commences, these costs are depleted on a unit-of-production basis over proved developed reserves with the exception of property acquisition costs which are depleted over proved reserves.

Capital expenditures associated with significant development projects are not depleted until assets are substantially complete and ready for their intended use.

Costs to develop oil and gas properties, and costs of dedicated infrastructure, such as wellhead equipment, offshore platforms and subsea structures, are depleted on a unit-of-production basis over proved developed reserves. A portion of these costs may not be depleted if they relate to undeveloped reserves.

Major components of Property, Plant and Equipment are depreciated on a straight-line basis over their expected useful lives.

Source: Suncor Energy Inc., Annual Report 2012.

Assume that the depletion of one of Suncor Energy's proved and developed oil reserves is $6,000,000 for the current year. The journal entry to record the depletion of reserves, and the transaction effects are as follows:

Oil inventory (A)...	6,000,000	
Oil reserves (A)..		6,000,000
(or Accumulated depletion XA)........................		

Assets		=	Liabilities	+	Shareholders' Equity
Oil inventory	+6,000,000				
Oil reserves	−6,000,000				
(or Accumulated depletion)					

Note that the amount of the natural resource that is depleted is capitalized as inventory, not expensed. When the inventory is sold, the cost of sales is then included as an expense on the statement of earnings.

A *depletion rate* is computed by dividing the total acquisition and development cost (less any estimated residual value, which is rare) by the estimated units that can be withdrawn economically from the resource. The depletion rate is multiplied each period by the actual number of units withdrawn during the accounting period. This procedure is the same as the units-of-production method of calculating depreciation.

When buildings and similar improvements are acquired for the development and exploitation of a natural resource, they should be recorded in separate asset accounts and depreciated—not depleted. Their estimated useful lives cannot be longer than the time needed to exploit the natural resource, unless they have a significant use after the source is depleted.

Acquisition and Amortization of Intangible Assets

Intangible assets are increasingly important resources for organizations. An intangible asset has value because of certain rights and privileges conferred by law on its owner. An intangible asset has no material or physical substance. Examples include mineral rights to explore and develop land, landing rights for timeslots at airports, patents, trademarks, and licences. Intangible assets are usually evidenced by a legal document. The growth in the importance of intangible assets has resulted from the tremendous expansion in computer information systems and Web technologies. In fact, many lawyers specialize in finding potential targets for patent infringement lawsuits for their clients.

Intangible assets are recorded at historical cost only if they are purchased. If an intangible asset is developed internally, the cost of development is normally recorded as an expense. Upon acquisition of intangible assets, managers determine whether the separate intangibles have definite or indefinite lives.

AMORTIZATION is the systematic and rational allocation of the acquisition cost of an intangible asset over its useful life.

Definite Life   The cost of an intangible with a definite life is allocated on a straight-line basis each period over its useful life in a process called **amortization** that is similar to depreciation and depletion. However, most companies do not estimate a residual value for their intangible assets. Let us assume a company purchases a patent for $800,000 and intends to uses it for 20 years. The adjusting entry to record $40,000 in patent amortization expense ($800,000 ÷ 20 years) is as follows:

Patent amortization expense (E)...........................	40,000	
Patent (A) (or Accumulated amortization XA)		40,000

Amortization expense is included on the statement of earnings, and the intangible assets are reported at cost less accumulated amortization on the statement of financial position.

Indefinite Life   Intangible assets with indefinite lives are *not amortized*. Instead, these assets are to be tested at least annually for possible impairment, and the asset's carrying amount is written down (decreased) to its recoverable amount if impaired. The two-step process is similar to that used for other long-lived assets, including intangibles with definite lives.

Let us assume a company purchases for $120,000 cash a copyright that is expected to have an indefinite life. At the end of the current year, management determines that the fair value of the copyright is $90,000. The $30,000 loss ($120,000 carrying amount less $90,000 fair value) is recorded as follows:

Loss due to impairment (SE).................................	30,000	
Copyright (A)		30,000

Examples of Intangible Assets

Many Canadian companies disclose information about goodwill and other intangible assets in their annual reports. These intangibles include broadcast rights, publishing rights, trademarks, patents, licences, customer lists, franchises, and purchased research and development. For example, WestJet provided the following details on its intangible assets of $50.8 million in the notes to its 2012 annual report:

REAL-WORLD EXCERPT

WestJet Airlines Ltd.

ANNUAL REPORT

NOTES TO CONSOLIDATED FINANCIAL STATEMENTS

8. Intangible assets

December 31, 2012	Cost	Accumulated amortization	Net book value
Software	54,519	(35,549)	18,970
Landing Rights	17,782	(521)	17,261
Other	4,956	–	4,956
Assets under development	9,621	–	9,621
	86,878	(36,070)	50,808

Source: WestJet Airlines Ltd., Annual Report 2012.

Goodwill   By far, the most frequently reported intangible asset is **goodwill (cost in excess of net assets acquired)**. The term *goodwill*, as used by most businesspeople, means the favourable reputation that a company has with its customers. Goodwill arises from factors such as customer confidence, reputation for good service and quality products, and financial standing. For example, WestJet's promise to deliver no-frills, friendly, reliable transportation combines factors that produce customer loyalty and repeated travel. From its first day of operations, a successful business continuously builds its own goodwill through a combination of factors that cannot be sold separately. In this context, goodwill is said to be internally generated and is not reported as an asset.

The only way to report goodwill as an asset is to purchase another business. Often, the purchase price of a business exceeds the fair market value of all of the identifiable assets owned by the business minus all of the identifiable liabilities owed to others. Why would a company pay more to acquire a business as a whole than it would pay if it bought the assets individually? The answer is to obtain its goodwill. It may be easy for a company to buy a fleet of aircraft, but it would not generate the same level of revenue flying the same routes as if it acquired the goodwill associated with WestJet's brand name.

For accounting purposes, goodwill is defined as the difference between the purchase price of a company as a whole and the fair market value of its net assets (all identifiable assets minus all identifiable liabilities):

For accounting purposes, GOODWILL (COST IN EXCESS OF NET ASSETS ACQUIRED) is the excess of the purchase price of a business over the market value of its identifiable assets and liabilities.

Purchase price
− Fair market value of identifiable assets and liabilities
Goodwill to be reported

In many acquisitions, the amount recorded as goodwill can be very large. For example, CGI Group Inc., a leading provider of information technology and business solutions, has completed several acquisitions over the years. The company reported an amount of $5,820 million for goodwill as at September 30, 2012, representing 55.7 percent of its total assets at that time.

Companies that reported goodwill related to acquisitions prior to July 1, 2001, were required to amortize it over an estimated useful life (not to exceed 40 years) by using the straight-line method. IFRS consider goodwill to have an indefinite life, but any subsequent impairment in its value should be written down. This leads to the recognition of a loss that is reported as a separate item on the statement of earnings in the year the impairment occurs.

A **TRADEMARK** is an exclusive legal right to use a special name, image, or slogan.

Trademarks   A **trademark** is an exclusive legal right to use a name, image, or slogan identified with a product or a company. For example, banks such as the Bank of Montreal, auto manufacturers such as Toyota and General Motors, and fast-food restaurant chains such as Pizza Hut have familiar trademarks. Trademarks are protected by law when they are registered at the Canadian Intellectual Property Office of Industry Canada. The protection of a trademark provides the registered holder with exclusive rights to the trademark and can be renewed every 15 years throughout its life. Trademarks are often some of the most valuable assets that a company can own, but they are rarely seen on statements of financial position. The reason is simple: intangible assets are not recorded unless they are purchased. Companies often spend millions of dollars developing trademarks, but these expenditures are recorded as expenses and not capitalized. Purchased trademarks that have definite lives are amortized on a straight-line basis over their estimated useful life, up to a maximum period of 40 years.

A **PATENT** is granted by the federal government for an invention; it is an exclusive right given to the owner to use, manufacture, and sell the subject of the patent.

Patents   A **patent** is an exclusive right granted by the Canadian Intellectual Property Office of Industry Canada for a period of 20 years. It is typically granted to a person who invents a new product or discovers a new process. The patent enables the owner to use, manufacture, and sell both the subject of the patent and the patent itself. Without the protection of a patent, inventors would likely be unwilling to develop new products. The patent prevents a competitor from simply copying a new invention or discovery until the inventor has had a period of time to earn an economic return on the new product.

A patent that is *purchased* is recorded at cost. An *internally developed* patent is recorded at only its registration and legal cost because IFRS require the immediate expensing of research and development costs. Development costs can, however, be capitalized if specific conditions are satisfied. In conformity with the matching process, the cost of a patent must be amortized over the shorter of its economic life and its remaining legal life.

Eastman Kodak Company, a pioneer in the photography business, has developed many patents since it was formed in 1889. These internally developed patents have been quite valuable to the company, but they are not reported as assets on its statements of financial position. In February 2013, the company sold its digital imaging patents for approximately US$530 million in order to reduce its debt. These patents were not reported on the company's statements of financial position because their valuation would have been subjective in the absence of an exchange transaction or an active market for such patents.

A **COPYRIGHT** is the exclusive right to publish, use, and sell a literary, musical, or artistic work.

Copyrights   **Copyright** protection is also granted by the Canadian Intellectual Property Office. It gives the owner the exclusive right to publish, use, and sell a literary, musical, or artistic piece of work for a period not exceeding 50 years after the author's death. The book that you are reading has a copyright to protect the publisher and the authors. It is illegal, for example, for an instructor to copy several chapters from this book and hand them out in class. The same principles, guidelines, and procedures used in accounting for the cost of patents are also used for copyrights.

Franchises A **franchise** is a contractual right to sell certain products or services, use certain trademarks, or perform activities in a geographical region. Franchises may be granted by either the government or other businesses for a specified period and purpose. A city may grant one company a franchise to distribute gas to homes for heating purposes, or a company may sell franchises, such as the right for a local outlet to operate a Quiznos restaurant. Franchise agreements are contracts that can have a variety of provisions. They usually require an investment by the franchisee; therefore, they should be accounted for as intangible assets. The life of the franchise agreement depends on the contract. It may be for a single year or an indefinite period.

A FRANCHISE is a contractual right to sell certain products or services, use certain trademarks, or perform activities in a geographical region.

Tim Hortons, for example, had over 4,200 restaurants at December 31, 2012. The company's franchisees operate under several types of licence agreements. A typical franchise term for a standard restaurant is 10 years, with possible renewal periods. In Canada, franchisees who lease land and/or buildings from the company are required to pay a royalty of 4.5 percent of the weekly gross sales of the restaurant in addition to monthly royalty payments for advertising and rental costs.

Technology The number of companies reporting a **technology** intangible asset has increased significantly in recent years. Computer software and Web development costs are becoming increasingly significant as companies modernize their processes and make greater use of advances in information and communication technology. For example, internally developed and externally acquired software represented about 30 percent of the carrying amount of goodwill and intangibles reported by Canadian Tire Corporation as at December 31, 2012.

TECHNOLOGY includes costs for computer software and Web development.

Licences and Operating Rights **Licences and operating rights** are typically obtained through agreements with governmental units or agencies and permit the holders to use public property in performing their services. For airline companies, the operating rights are authorized landing slots that are regulated by the government and are in limited supply at many airports. They are intangible assets that can be bought and sold by the airlines. Other types of licences that grant permission to companies include airwaves for radio and television broadcasts, and land for cable and telephone lines.

LICENCES AND OPERATING RIGHTS, obtained through agreements with governmental units and agencies, permit owners to use public property in performing their services.

Research and Development Expense—Not an Intangible Asset If an intangible asset is developed internally, the cost of research is recorded as an expense. When a company can demonstrate that technical and commercial feasibility of the resulting product or service has been established, then development costs can be deferred and amortized over the lifetime of the commercialized product. For example, Bombardier, a Canadian manufacturer of planes and trains, capitalized in 2012 an amount of $1,565 million in development expenditures related to its aerospace program tooling:

REAL-WORLD EXCERPT

Bombardier

ANNUAL REPORT

NOTES TO THE CONSOLIDATED FINANCIAL STATEMENTS

2. Summary of Significant Accounting Policies
Intangible assets
Internally generated intangible assets include development costs (mostly aircraft prototype design and testing costs) and internally developed or modified application software. These costs are capitalized when certain criteria for deferral such as proven technical feasibility are met. The costs of internally generated intangible assets include the cost of materials, direct labour, manufacturing overheads and borrowing costs.
Source: Bombardier Inc., Annual Report 2012.

LEASEHOLDS are rights granted to a lessee under a lease contract.

Leaseholds   A **leasehold** is the right granted in a contract called a *lease* to use a specific asset. Leasing is a common type of business contract. For a consideration called *rent*, the owner (lessor) extends to another party (lessee) certain rights to use specified property. Leases may vary from simple arrangements, such as the month-to-month (*operating*) lease of an office or the daily rental of an automobile, to long-lived (*capital*) leases having complex contractual arrangements.

Lessees sometimes make significant improvements to a leased property when they enter into a long-term lease agreement. A company that agrees to lease office space on a 15-year lease may install new fixtures or move walls to make the space more useful. These improvements are called *leasehold improvements* and are recorded as an asset by the lessee despite the fact that the lessor usually owns the leasehold improvements at the end of the lease term. The cost of leasehold improvements should be amortized over the estimated useful life of the related improvements or the remaining life of the lease, whichever is shorter.

FOCUS ON CASH FLOWS — PRODUCTIVE ASSETS AND DEPRECIATION

LO7

Explain the impact on cash flows of the acquisition, use, and disposal of long-lived assets.

Effect on Statement of Cash Flows

The indirect method for preparing the operating activities section of the statement of cash flows involves reconciling net earnings (reported on the statement of earnings) to cash flows from operations. This means that, among other adjustments, (1) revenues and expenses that do not affect cash and (2) gains and losses that relate to investing or financing activities (not operations) should be eliminated. When depreciation is recorded, no cash payment is made (i.e., there is no credit to Cash). Since depreciation expense (a non-cash expense) is subtracted from revenues in calculating net earnings, it must be added back to net earnings to eliminate its effect.

Gains and losses on disposal of long-lived assets represent the difference between cash proceeds and the carrying amount of the assets disposed of. Hence, gains and losses are non-cash amounts that do not relate to operating activities, but they are included in the computation of net earnings. Therefore, gains are subtracted from net earnings and losses are added to net earnings in the computation of cash flow from operations.

Effect on Statement of Cash Flows

IN GENERAL → Acquiring, selling, and depreciating long-lived assets affect a company's cash flows as indicated in the following table:

SELECTED FOCUS COMPANY COMPARISONS: PERCENTAGE OF DEPRECIATION AND AMORTIZATION TO CASH FLOWS FROM OPERATIONS—2012

Canadian Tire Corporation   45.1%

Gildan Activewear Inc.   43.0%

Thompson Reuters Corporation   64.6%

	Effect on Cash Flows
Operating activities (indirect method)	
Net earnings	$xxx
Adjusted for:	
Depreciation expense	+
Gains on disposal of long-lived assets	−
Losses on disposal of long-lived assets	+
Losses due to asset impairment write downs	+
Investing activities	
Purchase of long-lived assets	−
Sale of long-lived assets	+

Exhibit **9.5**
WestJet Statement of Cash Flows

REAL-WORLD EXCERPT

WestJet Airlines Ltd.
ANNUAL REPORT

Consolidated Statement of Cash Flows
For the years ended December 31
(in thousands of Canadian dollars)

	2012	2011
Operating activities:		
Net earnings	$242,392	$148,702
Items not involving cash:		
Depreciation and amortization	185,401	174,751
Change in long-term maintenance provisions	34,426	38,522
Loss (gain) on disposal of property and equipment	(469)	54
Other adjustments (summarized)	259,884	204,431
	721,634	**566,460**
Investing activities:		
Aircraft additions	(218,116)	(61,265)
Other property and equipment and intangible additions	(51,191)	(57,108)
	$(269,307)	$(118,373)

Source: WestJet Airlines Ltd., Annual Report 2012.

FOCUS COMPANY ANALYSIS → Exhibit 9.5 shows a condensed version of WestJet's statement of cash flows prepared using the indirect method. Buying and selling long-lived assets are investing activities. In 2012, WestJet used $269,307,000 in cash to purchase aircraft and other property and equipment. Since selling long-lived assets is not an operating activity, any gains (losses) on sale of long-lived assets that are included in net earnings are deducted from (added to) net earnings in the operating activities section to eliminate the effect of the sale. Unless they are large, these gain and loss adjustments are normally not specifically highlighted on the statement of cash flows. WestJet reports a gain of $469,000 on its statement of cash flows for 2012.

Finally, in capital-intensive industries such as airlines, depreciation and amortization expense is a significant non-cash expense. In WestJet's case, depreciation and amortization expense is the single largest adjustment to net earnings in determining cash flows from operations. It was 30.8 percent of operating cash flows in 2011 but dropped to 25.7 percent in 2012.

A MISINTERPRETATION

FINANCIAL
ANALYSIS

Some analysts misinterpret the meaning of a non-cash expense and often say that "cash is provided by depreciation." Although depreciation is added in the operating section of the statement of cash flows, *depreciation is not a source of cash*. Cash from operations can be provided only by selling goods and services. A company with a large amount of depreciation expense does not generate more cash compared with a company that reports a small amount of depreciation expense, assuming that they are exactly the same in every other respect. While depreciation expense reduces the amount of reported net earnings for a company, it does not reduce the amount of cash generated by the company, because it is a non-cash expense. Remember that the effects of recording depreciation are a reduction in shareholders' equity and in long-lived assets, not in cash. That is why, on the statement of cash flows, depreciation expense is added back to net earnings (on an accrual basis) to compute cash flows from operations (net earnings on a cash basis).

Although depreciation is a non-cash expense, the *depreciation method used for tax purposes can affect a company's cash flows*. For tax purposes, the Income Tax Act requires companies to use a capital cost allowance (CCA), a form of depreciation based on the declining-balance method. The higher the amount of CCA reported by a company for tax purposes, the lower the taxable income and the income taxes it must pay. Because taxes must be paid in cash, a reduction in the tax obligation of a company reduces the company's cash outflows.

The maximum deduction for CCA for each class of assets is based on rates specified by the Canada Revenue Agency, but corporations may choose to deduct lower amounts for CCA during periods of losses or low earnings before taxes, and postpone CCA deductions to future years to minimize their income tax obligations.

ACCOUNTING STANDARDS
FOR PRIVATE ENTERPRISES

Accounting standards for private enterprises differ from IFRS in two main areas: (1) measurement of property, plant, and equipment and (2) measurement of impairment losses.

Financial Reporting Issue	IFRS	ASPE
Measurement of property, plant, and equipment	Canadian publicly accountable enterprises may use either the cost model or the revaluation model to measure property, plant, and equipment subsequent to acquisition. Increases in fair value are recorded if the revaluation model is used. However, most companies use the cost model.	The cost model must be used to report property, plant, and equipment, and increases in their fair values are not recorded.
Measurement of impairment of long-lived assets	The asset's carrying amount is compared to its recoverable amount (the higher of the asset's value in use and its fair value less costs to sell) to determine if an impairment has occurred.	The asset's carrying amount is compared to its fair value less costs to sell to determine if impairment occurred.
	An impairment loss can be reversed if the asset's recoverable amount subsequently increases.	An impairment loss cannot be reversed if the asset's fair value subsequently increases.
	Impairment testing is required for each reporting date.	Impairment testing is required only if impairment is suspected.

DEMONSTRATION **CASE**

Diversified Industries has been operating for a number of years. It started as a residential construction company. In recent years, it expanded into heavy construction, ready-mix concrete, sand and gravel, construction supplies, and earth-moving services.

The following transactions were selected from those completed during 2014. They focus on the primary issues discussed in this chapter.

2014

January 1	Management decided to buy a building that was about 10 years old. The location was excellent, and there was adequate parking. The company bought the building and the land on which it was situated for $305,000. It paid $100,000 in cash and signed a mortgage note payable for the rest. A reliable appraiser provided the following market values: land, $132,300, and building, $182,700.
January 12	Paid renovation costs on the building of $38,100, prior to use.
June 19	Bought a third location for a gravel pit (designated No. 3) for $50,000 cash. The location had been carefully surveyed. It was estimated that 100,000 cubic metres of gravel could be removed from the deposit.
July 10	Paid $1,200 for ordinary repairs on the building.
August 1	Paid $10,000 for costs of preparing the new gravel pit for exploitation.
Dec. 31	Year-end adjustments:

  a. The building will be depreciated on a straight-line basis over an estimated useful life of 30 years. The estimated residual value is $35,000.
  b. During 2014, 12,000 cubic metres of gravel were removed from gravel pit No. 3 and sold.
  c. The company owns a patent right that is used in operations. On January 1, 2014, the patent account had a balance of $3,300. The patent has an estimated remaining useful life of six years (including 2014).
  d. At the beginning of the year, the company owned equipment with a cost of $650,000 and a carrying amount of $500,000. The equipment is being depreciated by using the double-declining-balance method, with a useful life of 20 years with no residual value.
  e. At year-end, the company identified a piece of old excavation equipment with a cost of $156,000 and remaining carrying amount of $120,000. Due to its smaller size and lack of safety features, the old equipment has limited use. The company reviewed the asset for possible impairment of value. The equipment has a fair value of $40,000.

Required:

1. Indicate the accounts affected and the amount and direction (+ for increase and − for decrease) of the effect for each of the preceding events on the basic accounting equation. Use the following headings:

Date	Assets	=	Liabilities	+	Shareholders' Equity

2. Record the adjusting journal entries based on the information for December 31([a] and [b] only).

3. Show the December 31, 2014, statement of financial position classifications and amount for each of the following items:

   Property, plant, and equipment—land, building, equipment, and gravel pit

   Intangible asset—patent

4. Assuming that the company had sales of $1,000,000 for the year and a carrying amount of $500,000 for property, plant, and equipment at the beginning of the year, compute the fixed asset turnover ratio. Explain its meaning.

We strongly recommend that you prepare your own answers to these requirements and then check your answers with the following solution.

SUGGESTED **SOLUTION**

Date	Assets			Liabilities		Shareholders' Equity	
Jan. 1 (1)	Cash Land Building	−100,000 +128,100 +176,900		Note payable	+205,000		
Jan. 12 (2)	Cash Building	−38,100 +38,100					
June 19 (3)	Cash Gravel pit No. 3	−50,000 +50,000					
July 10 (4)	Cash	−1,200				Repairs expense	−1,200
Aug. 1 (5)	Cash Gravel pit No. 3	−10,000 +10,000					
Dec. 31 *a* (6)	Accumulated depreciation	−6,000				Depreciation expense	−6,000
Dec. 31 *b* (7)	Gravel pit No. 3 Gravel inventory	−7,200 +7,200					
Dec. 31 *c* (8)	Patent	−550				Amortization expense	−550
Dec. 31 *d* (9)	Accumulated depreciation	−50,000				Depreciation expense	−50,000
Dec. 31 *e* (10)	Equipment	−80,000				Loss due to asset impairment	−80,000

(1)

	Land		Building		Total
Market	$132,300	+	$182,700	=	$315,000
Percentage of total	42%	+	58%	=	100%
Cost	$128,100	+	$176,900	=	$305,000

(2)   Capitalize the expenditure of $38,100 because it is necessary to prepare the asset for use.

(3)   This is a natural resource.

(4)   This is an ordinary repair (revenue expenditure) that should be expensed.

(5)   Capitalize the expenditure of $10,000 because it is necessary to prepare the asset for use.

(6)   **Cost of building**

Initial payment	$176,900
Repairs prior to use	38,100
Acquisition cost	$215,000

Straight-line depreciation

Depreciation = ($215,000 − $35,000)/30 years
= $6,000 annually

(7)   **Cost of gravel pit**

Initial payment	$50,000
Preparation costs	10,000
Acquisition cost	$60,000

Units-of-production depletion

Depletion rate = $60,000/100,000
= $0.60 per cubic metre
Depletion amount = 12,000 × $0.60 = $7,200

(8)   **Straight-line depreciation**

Unamortized cost of patent	$3,300
Remaining useful life	÷ 6 years
	$ 550

(9)   **Double-declining-balance depreciation**

Annual depreciation = $500,000 (carrying amount) × 2/20 = $50,000

(10) **Asset impairment**

Carrying amount of old equipment	$120,000
Fair value	− 40,000
Loss due to impairment	$ 80,000

2. Adjusting entries December 31, 2014:

    a. Depreciation expense, building (E)   6,000

         Accumulated depreciation (XA)   6,000

    b. Gravel inventory (A)   7,200

         Gravel pit No. 3 (A)   7,200

3. Statement of financial position, December 31, 2014:

Assets		
Property, plant, and equipment		
Land		$128,100
Building	$215,000	
Less: Accumulated depreciation	6,000	209,000
Equipment ($650,000 − $80,000)	570,000	
Less: Accumulated depreciation ($150,000 + $50,000)	200,000	370,000
Gravel pit		52,800
Total		759,900
Intangible asset		
Patent ($3,300 − $550)		2,750

4. Fixed asset turnover ratio:

$$\frac{\text{Net Sales}}{\text{Average Net Fixed Assets}} = \frac{\$1,000,000}{(\$500,000 + \$759,9900) \div 2} = 1.59$$

This construction company is capital intensive. The fixed asset turnover ratio measures the company's efficiency at using its investment in property, plant, and equipment to generate sales.

CHAPTER **TAKE-AWAYS**

1. **Define, classify, and explain the nature of long-lived assets, and interpret the fixed asset turnover ratio.**
   a. Non-current assets are those that a business retains for long periods of time, for use in the course of normal operations rather than for sale. They may be divided into tangible assets (land, buildings, equipment, natural resources) and intangible assets (including goodwill, patents, and franchises).
   b. The cost allocation method utilized affects the amount of net property, plant, and equipment that is used in the computation of the fixed asset turnover ratio. Accelerated methods reduce book value and increase the turnover ratio.

2. **Apply the cost principle to measure the acquisition and maintenance of property, plant, and equipment.**
   The acquisition cost of property, plant, and equipment is the cash-equivalent purchase price plus all reasonable and necessary expenditures made to acquire and prepare the asset for its intended use. These assets may be acquired by using cash, debt, or equity, or through self-construction. Expenditures made after the asset is in use are either capital expenditures or revenue expenditures:
   a. Capital expenditures provide benefits for one or more accounting periods beyond the current period. Amounts are debited to the appropriate asset accounts and depreciated or depleted over their useful lives.
   b. Revenue expenditures provide benefits during the current accounting period only. Amounts are debited to appropriate current expense accounts when the expenses are incurred.

3. **Apply various depreciation methods as assets are held and used over time.**
   Cost allocation methods: In conformity with the matching process, cost (less any estimated residual value) is allocated to periodic expense over the periods benefited. Because of depreciation, the carrying amount of an asset declines over time and net earnings is reduced by the amount of the expense. Common depreciation methods include straight-line (a constant amount

over time), units-of-production (a variable amount over time), and double-declining-balance (a decreasing amount over time).
- Depreciation—buildings and equipment
- Depletion—natural resources
- Amortization—intangibles

4. **Explain the effect of asset impairment on the financial statements.**
   When events or changes in circumstances reduce the estimated future cash flows of long-lived assets below their carrying amounts, the carrying amounts should be written down (by recording a loss) to the fair value of the assets.

5. **Analyze the disposal of property, plant, and equipment.**
   When assets are disposed of through sale or abandonment,
   - Record additional depreciation since the last adjustment was made.
   - Remove the cost of the old asset and its related accumulated depreciation or depletion.
   - Recognize the cash proceeds.
   - Recognize any gains or losses when the asset's carrying amount is not equal to the cash received.

6. **Apply measurement and reporting concepts for natural resources and intangible assets.**
   The cost principle should be applied in recording the acquisition of natural resources and intangible assets. Natural resources should be depleted (usually by the units-of-production method) with the amount of the depletion expense usually capitalized to an inventory account. Intangibles with definite useful lives are amortized by using the straight-line method. Intangibles with indefinite useful lives, including goodwill, are not amortized, but are reviewed at least annually for impairment. Intangibles are reported at their carrying amount on the statement of financial position.

7. **Explain the impact on cash flows of the acquisition, use, and disposal of long-lived assets.**
   Depreciation expense is a non-cash expense that has no effect on cash. It is added back to net earnings on the statement of cash flows to determine cash from operations. Acquiring and disposing of long-lived assets are investing activities.

   In the previous chapters, we discussed business and accounting issues related to the assets a company holds. In Chapters 10, 11, and 12, we shift our focus to the other side of the statement of financial position to see how managers finance the operations of their business and the acquisition of productive assets. We discuss various types of liabilities in Chapters 10 and 11 and examine owners' equity in Chapter 12.

KEY **RATIO**

The fixed asset turnover ratio measures how efficiently a company utilizes its investment in property, plant, and equipment over time. The company's ratio can be compared to the ratio of its competitors. It is computed as follows):

$$\text{Fixed Asset Turnover Ratio} = \frac{\text{Net Sales (or operating revenues)}}{\text{Average Net Fixed Assets}}$$

FINDING **FINANCIAL INFORMATION**

STATEMENT OF FINANCIAL POSITION	STATEMENT OF EARNINGS
Under Long-Lived Assets	**Under Operating Expenses**
Property, plant, and equipment (net of accumulated depreciation)	Depreciation, amortization, and depletion expense *or* as part of
Natural resources (net of accumulated depletion)	Selling, general, and administrative expenses and
Intangibles (net of accumulated amortization)	Cost of sales (with the amount of depreciation expense disclosed in a note)

STATEMENT OF CASH FLOWS
Under Operating Activities (indirect method)
Net earnings
+ Depreciation and amortization expense
− Gains on sales of assets
+ Losses on sales of assets
Under Investing Activities
+ Sales of assets for cash
− Purchases of assets for cash

NOTES
Under Summary of Significant Accounting Policies
  Description of management's choice of
  depreciation methods, including useful
  lives, and the amount of annual depreciation
  expense, if not listed on the statement of
  earnings
Under a Separate Footnote
  If not specified on the statement of financial position,
  a listing of the major classifications of long-lived
  assets at cost and the balance in accumulated
  depreciation, amortization, and depletion

GLOSSARY

Review key terms and definitions on *Connect*.

QUESTIONS

1. Define *long-lived assets*. Why are they considered a "bundle of future services"?
2. How is the fixed asset turnover ratio computed? Explain its meaning.
3. What are the classifications of long-lived assets? Explain each.
4. Relate the cost principle to accounting for long-lived assets. Under the cost principle, what amounts should usually be included in the acquisition cost of a long-lived asset?
5. Describe the relationship between the matching process and accounting for long-lived assets.
6. What is a basket purchase? What measurement problem does it pose?
7. Distinguish between
    a. Capital expenditures and revenue expenditures. How is each accounted for?
    b. Ordinary and extraordinary repairs. How is each accounted for?
8. Distinguish between depreciation and depletion.
9. In computing depreciation, three values must be known or estimated; identify and explain the nature of each.
10. Estimated useful life and residual value of a long-lived asset relate to the current owner or user rather than all potential users. Explain this statement.
11. What type of depreciation expense pattern is provided under each of the following methods? When is the use of each method appropriate?
    a. Straight-line
    b. Units-of-production
    c. Double-declining-balance
12. Over what period should an addition to an existing long-lived asset be depreciated? Explain.
13. What is an asset impairment? How is it accounted for?
14. Define *intangible asset*. What period should be used to amortize an intangible asset?
15. Define *goodwill*. When is it appropriate to record goodwill as an intangible asset?
16. Explain how research and development expenditures should be accounted for.
17. Why is depreciation expense added to net earnings on the statement of cash flows when using the indirect method of reporting cash flow from operations?

EXERCISES

E9–1 Classifying Long-Lived Assets and Related Cost Allocation Concepts ■ **LO1**
For each of the following long-lived assets, indicate its nature and related cost allocation concept. Use the following symbols:

	Nature		Cost Allocation Concept
L	Land	DP	Depletion
B	Building	A	Amortization
E	Equipment	D	Depreciation
NR	Natural resource	NO	No cost allocation
I	Intangible	O	Other

Asset	Nature	Cost Allocation Concept	Asset	Nature	Cost Allocation Concept
(1) Copyright	_____	_____	(6) Operating licence	_____	_____
(2) Land held for use	_____	_____	(7) Land held for sale	_____	_____
(3) Warehouse	_____	_____	(8) Delivery vans	_____	_____
(4) Oil well	_____	_____	(9) Timber tract	_____	_____
(5) New engine for old machine	_____	_____	(10) Production plant	_____	_____

LO1

Ballard Power
Systems Inc.

E9–2   Preparing a Partial Classified Statement of Financial Position

The following is a list of account titles and amounts (in thousands) reported by Ballard Power Systems Inc., a leading developer and manufacturer of fuel cells, an alternative power source for automobiles:

Raw materials	$ 8,353	Work in progress	$ 1,820
Leasehold improvements	7,518	Accumulated amortization—Intangibles	41,194
Prepaid expenses	934	Fuel cell technology	43,443
Trade receivables	17,164	Cash and cash equivalents	20,316
Finished goods	3,441	Computer equipment	6,339
Furniture and fixtures	741	Building	15,846
Land	1,220	Short-term investments	25,878
Other long-term assets	1,126	Production and test equipment	47,460
Goodwill	48,106	Accumulated depreciation—	
		Property, plant, and equipment	48,399

Required:

Prepare the asset section of the statement of financial position for Ballard Power Systems Inc., classifying the assets into current assets and noncurrent assets.

LO2

E9–3   Identifying Capital and Revenue Expenditures

For each of the following items, enter the correct letter to the left to show the type of expenditure. Use the following:

Type of Expenditure
C Capital expenditure   R Revenue expenditure   N Neither

Transactions

_____ (1) Paid $400 for ordinary repairs.
_____ (2) Paid $6,000 for extraordinary repairs.
_____ (3) Paid cash, $20,000, for addition to old building.
_____ (4) Paid for routine maintenance, $200, on credit.
_____ (5) Purchased a machine, $7,000; signed a long-term note.
_____ (6) Paid $2,000 for organization costs.
_____ (7) Paid one-year insurance premium in advance, $900.
_____ (8) Purchased a patent, $4,300 cash.
_____ (9) Paid $10,000 for monthly salaries.
_____ (10) Paid cash dividends, $20,000.

LO1

E9–4   Computing and Evaluating the Fixed Asset Turnover Ratio

The following information was reported by Cutter's Air Cargo Service for 2012:

Net fixed assets (beginning of year)	$1,900,000
Net fixed assets (end of year)	2,300,000
Net sales	3,300,000
Net earnings	1,600,000

Compute the company's fixed asset turnover ratio for the year. What can you say about Cutter's ratio when compared with WestJet's ratio for 2012, as computed in the chapter?

E9–5   Computing and Interpreting the Fixed Asset Turnover Ratio from a Financial Analyst's Perspective

■ LO1

Apple Inc.

The following data were disclosed in the annual reports of Apple Inc., which designs, manufactures, and markets mobile communication and media devices, personal computers, and portable digital music players. Its products include Mac, iPod, iPhone, and iPad, among others.

(in millions of US dollars)	2012	2011	2010	2009	2008
Net sales	$156,508	$108,249	$65,225	$42,905	$37,491
Net property, plant, and equipment	15,452	7,777	4,768	2,954	2,455

Required:

1. Compute Apple's fixed asset turnover ratio for the four years 2009 through 2012.
2. How might a financial analyst interpret the results?

E9–6   Determining Financial Statement Effects of Acquisition of Several Assets in a Basket Purchase

■ LO2

Kline Corporation acquired additional land and a building that included several pieces of equipment for $600,000. The acquisition was settled as follows: cash, $120,000; issuance of Kline's common shares, $120,000; and signing of a long-term note, $360,000. An appraiser estimated the market values to be $200,000 for the land, $500,000 for the building, and $100,000 for the equipment. Indicate the accounts affected and the amount and direction (+ for increase and − for decrease) of the effect of this acquisition on the accounting equation. Use the following headings:

Assets	=	Liabilities	+	Shareholders' Equity

E9–7   Computing and Recording Cost and Depreciation of Assets in a Basket Purchase (Straight-Line Depreciation)

■ LO2, 3

Zeidler Company bought a building and the land on which the building is located for a total cash price of $356,000. The company paid transfer costs of $4,000. Renovation costs on the building were $46,000. An independent appraiser provided market values for the land, $100,000, and building, $300,000 before renovation.

Required:

1. Apportion the cost of the property on the basis of the appraised values. Show computations.
2. Prepare the journal entry to record the purchase of the building and land, including all expenditures. Assume that all transactions were for cash and that all purchases occurred at the start of the year.
3. Compute depreciation of the building at the end of one year, using the straight-line method. Assume an estimated useful life of 12 years and an estimated residual value of $28,000.
4. What would be the carrying amount of the property (building and land) at the end of year 2?

E9–8   Determining Financial Statement Effects of an Asset Acquisition and Depreciation (Straight-Line Depreciation)

■ LO2, 3

The following transactions related to a machine purchased by Vicario Company in 2015:

March	1	Purchased the machine at an invoice price of $10,000; paid $8,000 cash and signed a note for the balance, payable on October 1, 2015 with annual interest at a rate of 6 percent.
March	3	Paid freight of $250.
March	5	Paid installation costs of $475.
October	1	Paid the balance due plus the related interest.
December 31		Recorded straight-line depreciation on the machine based on an estimated useful life of 10 years and an estimated residual value of $1,725.

Required (round all amounts to the nearest dollar):

1. Indicate the accounts affected and the amount and direction (+ for increase and − for decrease) of the effect of each transaction (March 1, 3, 5, and October 1) on the accounting equation. Use the following headings:

Date	Assets	=	Liabilities	+	Shareholders' Equity

2. Compute the acquisition cost of the machine.

3. Compute the depreciation expense to be reported for 2015.

4. What is the impact on the cost of the machine of the interest paid on the note? Under what circumstances can interest expense be included in an asset's acquisition cost?

5. What would be the carrying amount of the machine at the end of 2016?

LO1, 2

ACE Aviation
Holdings

E9–9   **Evaluating the Impact of Capitalized Interest on Cash Flows and the Fixed Asset Turnover Ratio from an Analyst's Perspective**

You are a financial analyst charged with evaluating the asset efficiency of companies in the airline industry. The financial statements for Air Canada include the following note:

U) INTEREST CAPITALIZED

Borrowing costs are expensed as incurred, except for interest attributable to the acquisition, construction, or production of an asset that necessarily takes a substantial period of time to get ready for its intended use, in which case they are capitalized as part of the cost of that asset. Capitalization of borrowing costs commences when expenditures for the asset and borrowing costs are being incurred and the activities to prepare the asset for its intended use are in progress. Borrowing costs are capitalized up to the date when the project is completed and the related asset is available for its intended use.

Required:

1. Assume that Air Canada followed this policy for a major construction project this year. What is the direction of the effect of Air Canada's policy on the following? Use + for increase, − for decrease, and NE for no effect.

   a. Cash flows

   b. Fixed asset turnover ratio

2. Normally, how would your answer to (1*b*) affect your evaluation of Air Canada's effectiveness in utilizing property, plant, and equipment?

3. If the fixed asset turnover ratio changes because of interest capitalization, does this change indicate a real change in efficiency? Why or why not?

LO3

E9–10   **Recording Depreciation and Repairs (Straight-Line Depreciation), and Determining Financial Statement Effects**

Stacey Company operates a small manufacturing facility as a supplement to its regular service activities. At the beginning of 2015, an asset account for the company showed the following balances:

Manufacturing equipment	$100,000
Accumulated depreciation through 2014	54,000

In early January 2015, the following expenditures were incurred for repairs and maintenance:

Routine maintenance and repairs on the equipment	$ 1,000
Major overhaul of the equipment	12,000

The equipment is being depreciated on a straight-line basis over an estimated life of 15 years, with a $10,000 estimated residual value. The company's fiscal year ends on December 31.

Required:

1. Calculate the depreciation expense for the manufacturing equipment for 2014.

2. Prepare the journal entries to record the two expenditures that occurred during 2015.

3. Prepare the adjusting entry at December 31, 2015, to record the depreciation of the manufacturing equipment, assuming no change in the estimated life or residual value of the equipment. Show computations.

4. Indicate the accounts affected, amounts, and direction (+ for increase and − for decrease) of the effects of the journal entries you prepared for (1) to (3) on the accounting equation. Use the following headings:

Date	Assets	=	Liabilities	+	Shareholders' Equity

E9–11 Computing Depreciation under Alternative Methods ■ LO3

Purity Ice Cream Company bought a new ice cream maker at the beginning of the year at a cost of $10,000. The estimated useful life was four years, and the residual value was $1,000. Assume that the estimated productive life of the machine was 9,000 hours. Actual annual usage was 3,600 hours in year 1; 2,700 hours in year 2; 1,800 hours in year 3; and 900 hours in year 4.

Required:

1. Complete a separate depreciation schedule for each of the alternative methods. Round your computations to the nearest dollar.

   a. Straight-line

   b. Units-of-production

   c. Double-declining-balance

Method: _____		Depreciation Expense	Accumulated Depreciation	Carrying Amount
Year	Computation			
At acquisition				
1				
2				
Etc.				

2. Assuming that the machine was used directly in the production of one of the products that the company manufactures and sells, what factors might management consider in selecting a preferable depreciation method in conformity with the matching process?

E9–12 Computing Depreciation under Alternative Methods ■ LO3

Sterling Steel Company purchased a new stamping machine at the beginning of the year at a cost of $580,000. The estimated residual value was $60,000. Assume that the estimated useful life was five years and the estimated productive life of the machine was 260,000 units. Actual annual production was as follows:

Year	1	2	3	4	5
Units	73,000	62,000	30,000	53,000	42,000

Required:

1. Complete a separate depreciation schedule for each of the alternative methods. Round your computations to the nearest dollar.

   a. Straight-line

   b. Units-of-production

   c. Double-declining-balance

Method: _____		Depreciation Expense	Accumulated Depreciation	Carrying Amount
Year	Computation			
At acquisition				
1				
2				
Etc.				

2. Assuming that the machine was used directly in the production of one of the products that the company manufactures and sells, what factors might management consider in selecting a preferable depreciation method in conformity with the matching process?

■ **LO3**

E9–13

Ford Motor Company

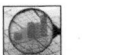

Explaining Depreciation Policy

An annual report for Ford Motor Company contained the following note:

> **Significant Accounting Policies**
>
> **Depreciation of Property, Plant, and Equipment.** Property and equipment are stated at cost and depreciated primarily using the straight-line method over the estimated useful life of the asset. Useful lives range from 3 years to 36 years. The estimated useful lives generally are 14.5 years for machinery and equipment and 30 years for buildings and land improvements. Special tools placed in service beginning in 1999 are depreciated using the units-of-production method over the expected vehicle model cycle life. Maintenance, repairs, and rearrangement costs are expensed as incurred.

Required:

Why do you think the company changed its depreciation method for special tools acquired in 1999 and subsequent years?

■ **LO3**

E9–14

FedEx Corporation

Interpreting Management's Choice of Different Depreciation Methods for Tax and Financial Reporting

An annual report for FedEx Corporation included the following information:

> For financial reporting purposes, we record depreciation and amortization of property and equipment on a straight-line basis over the asset's service life or the related lease term. For income tax purposes, depreciation is generally computed using accelerated methods when applicable.

Required:

Explain why FedEx uses different methods of depreciation for financial reporting and tax purposes.

■ **LO3, 7**

E9–15

Computing Depreciation and Carrying Amount for Two Years by Using Alternative Depreciation Methods, and Interpreting the Impact on Cash Flows

Schrade Company bought a machine for $96,000 cash. The estimated useful life was four years, and the estimated residual value was $6,000. Assume that the estimated useful life is 120,000 units. Units actually produced were 43,000 in year 1 and 45,000 in year 2.

Required:

1. Determine the appropriate amounts to complete the following schedule. Show computations, and round to the nearest dollar.

Method of Depreciation	Depreciation Expense for		Carrying Amount at the End of	
	Year 1	Year 2	Year 1	Year 2
Straight-line				
Units-of-production				
Double-declining-balance				

2. Which method would result in the lowest earnings per share for year 1? For year 2?
3. Which method would result in the highest amount of cash outflows in year 1? Why?
4. Indicate the effects of (*a*) acquiring the machine and (*b*) recording annual depreciation on the operating and investing activities on the statement of cash flows for year 1. Assume that straight-line depreciation is used.

■ **LO4**

E9–16

Identifying Asset Impairment

For each of the following scenarios, indicate whether an asset has been impaired (Y for yes and N for no) and, if so, the amount of loss that should be recorded.

	Carrying Amount	Value in Use	Fair Value Less Costs to Sell	Is Asset Impaired?	If So, Amount of Loss
a. Machine	$ 15,500	$ 10,000	$ 8,500		
b. Copyright	31,000	41,000	39,900		
c. Factory building	58,000	26,000	29,000		
d. Building	227,000	237,000	210,000		

E9–17 Inferring Asset Impairment and Disposal of Assets
■ LO4, 5

Danier Leather Inc. is a Canadian company that designs, manufactures, and markets quality leather and suede products for both women and men. The following note and information were reported in a recent annual report:

Danier Leather Inc.

Note 3—SIGNIFICANT ACCOUNTING POLICIES

Impairment of non-financial assets

Property and equipment and computer software with finite lives are tested for impairment when events or changes in circumstances indicate that the carrying amount may not be recoverable at the financial position date. For purposes of measuring recoverable amounts, assets are grouped at the lowest levels for which there are separately identifiable cash flows (cash-generating units or CGUs), which is at the individual store level for the Company. The recoverable amount is the greater of an asset's fair value less costs to sell and value in use (being the present value of the expected future cash flows of the relevant asset or CGU). An impairment loss is recognized for the amount by which the asset's carrying amount exceeds its recoverable amount. The Company evaluates impairment losses for potential reversals when events or circumstances warrant such consideration.

	Dollars in thousands
Cost of property, plant, and equipment (beginning of year)	$43,742
Cost of property, plant, and equipment (end of year)	42,846
Additions to property, plant, and equipment during the year	3,974
Accumulated depreciation and impairment losses (beginning of year)	29,338
Accumulated depreciation and impairment losses (end of year)	27,834
Depreciation expense during the year	3,300
Cost of equipment sold during the year	4,870
Accumulated depreciation on equipment sold	4,870
Cash received on equipment sold	65

Required:

1. Reconstruct the journal entry for the disposal of equipment during the year.

2. Compute the amount of property, plant, and equipment that Danier Leather wrote off as impaired during the year. Danier records impairment losses as adjustments to accumulated depreciation. (*Hint:* Set up T-accounts.)

E9–18 Recording the Disposal of an Asset and Financial Statement Effects
■ LO5

FedEx Corporation is a global leader in express distribution. It has the world's largest fleet of all-cargo aircraft and thousands of vehicles and trailers to pick up and deliver packages. Assume that FedEx sold a small delivery truck that had been used in the business for three years. The records of the company reflect the following:

FedEx Corporation.

Delivery truck	$38,000
Accumulated depreciation	23,000

Required:

1. Prepare the journal entry to record the disposal of the truck and the related transaction effects, assuming that the sales price was (*a*) $15,000; (*b*) $15,600; (*c*) $14,600.

2. Based on the three preceding situations, explain the effects of the disposal of an asset on financial statements.

■ LO5   **E9–19**   **Recording the Disposal of an Asset at Three Different Sale Prices**

Marriott International

Marriott International is a worldwide operator and franchisor of hotels and related lodging facilities totalling over $1.4 billion in property and equipment. It also develops, operates, and markets time-share properties totalling nearly $2 billion. Assume that Marriott replaced furniture that had been used in the business for five years. The records of the company reflected the following regarding the sale of the existing furniture:

| Furniture (cost) | $6,000,000 |
| Accumulated depreciation | 5,500,000 |

Required:

1. Prepare the journal entry for the disposal of the furniture, assuming that it was sold for
   a. $500,000 cash
   b. $1,600,000 cash
   c. $400,000 cash
2. Based on the three preceding situations, explain the effects of the disposal of an asset.

■ LO5   **E9–20**   **Inferring Asset Age and Recording Accidental Loss on a Long-Lived Asset (Straight-Line Depreciation)**

On January 1, 2015, the records of Smita Corporation showed the following:

| Truck (estimated residual value, $3,000) | $18,000 |
| Accumulated depreciation (straight line, two years) | 6,000 |

On September 30, 2015, the delivery truck was a total loss as a result of an accident. As the truck was insured, the company collected $7,600 cash from the insurance company on October 5, 2015.

Required:

1. Based on the data given, compute the estimated useful life of the truck.
2. Prepare all journal entries to record the events that occurred on September 30 and October 5, 2015, and the related adjustments to the accounts. Show computations.

■ LO6   **E9–21**   **Computing the Acquisition and Depletion of a Natural Resource**

Freeport-McMoRan
Copper & Gold Inc.

Freeport-McMoRan Copper & Gold Inc. is a natural resources company involved in the exploration, development, and extraction of natural resources, with the majority of its resources in Indonesia. Annual revenues exceed $21 billion. Assume that in February 2014, Freeport-McMoRan paid $7,000,000 for a mineral deposit in Bali. During March, it spent $740,000 in preparing the deposit for exploitation. It was estimated that 9,000,000 cubic yards could be extracted economically. During 2014, 720,000 cubic yards was extracted and sold. During January 2015, the company spent another $60,000 for additional developmental work. After conclusion of the latest work, the estimated remaining recovery was increased to 12,200,000 cubic yards over the remaining life. During 2015, 600,000 cubic yards was extracted.

Required:

1. Compute the acquisition cost of the deposit in 2014.
2. Compute the depletion expense for 2014.
3. Compute the carrying amount of the deposit after payment of the January 2015 developmental costs.
4. Compute the depletion expense for 2015.
5. Prepare the journal entries to record the acquisition of the deposit in 2014 and the depletion expense for 2014.

■ LO6   **E9–22**   **Computing Goodwill and Patents**

Elizabeth Pie Company has been in business for 30 years and has developed a large group of loyal restaurant customers. Vaclav's Foods made an offer to buy Elizabeth Pie Company for $5,000,000. The carrying amount of Elizabeth Pie's recorded assets and liabilities on the date of the offer is $4,400,000, with a market value of $4,600,000. Elizabeth Pie holds a patent for a pie crust–fluting machine that the company invented (the patent, with a market value of $200,000, was never recorded by Elizabeth Pie because it was developed internally). The company estimates goodwill from loyal customers to be $300,000 (also never recorded by the company). Should Elizabeth Pie Company management accept Vaclav's Foods' offer of $5,000,000? If so, compute the amount of goodwill that Vaclav's Foods should record on the date of the purchase.

E9–23 Computing and Reporting the Acquisition and Amortization of Four Different Intangible Assets

■ LO6

Wyatt Company had four intangible assets at the end of 2015 (end of the fiscal year):

a. Computer software and Web development technology purchased on January 1, 2015, for $70,000. The technology is expected to have a useful life of four years.

b. A patent purchased from R. Jay on January 1, 2015, for a cash cost of $6,000. Jay had registered the patent with the Canadian Intellectual Property Office seven years earlier on January 1, 2008. The cost of the patent is amortized over its legal life.

c. A lease on some property for a five-year term beginning January 1, 2015. The company immediately spent $7,800 cash for long-lived improvements (estimated useful life, eight years; no residual value). At the termination of the lease, there will be no recovery of these improvements.

d. A trademark that was internally developed and registered with the Canadian government for $13,000 on November 1, 2014. Management decided that the trademark has an indefinite life.

Required:

1. What is the acquisition cost of each intangible asset?
2. Compute the amortization of each intangible asset at December 31, 2015. The company does not use contra accounts.
3. Show how these assets and any related expenses should be reported on the statement of financial position at December 31, 2015, and on the statement of earnings for 2015.

E9–24 Recording Rent Paid in Advance, Leasehold Improvements, Periodic Rent, and Related Amortization

■ LO6

Tim Hortons Inc.

Tim Hortons Inc. is Canada's leading chain of quick-service restaurants, offering a variety of coffees, donuts, and other baked goods. Assume that Tim Hortons planned to open a new store on St. George Street near the University of Toronto and obtained a 15-year lease starting January 1, 2015. Although a serviceable building was on the property, the company had to build an additional structure for storage. The 15-year lease required an $18,000 cash advance payment plus cash payments of $5,000 per month during occupancy. During January 2015, the company spent $90,000 cash to build the structure. The new structure has an estimated life of 18 years with no residual value.

Required:

1. Prepare the journal entries for the company to record the payment of the $18,000 advance on January 1, 2015, and the first monthly rental.
2. Prepare the journal entry to record the construction of the new structure.
3. Prepare any adjusting entries required at December 31, 2015, the end of the company's fiscal year, with respect to (a) the advance payment and (b) the new structure. Assume that straight-line depreciation is used. Show computations.
4. Compute the total expense resulting from the lease for 2015.

E9–25 Finding Financial Information as a Potential Investor

■ LO1, 2, 3, 4, 5, 6, 7

You are considering investing the cash gifts you received for graduation in shares of various companies. You visit the websites of major companies, searching for relevant information.

Required:

For each of the following, indicate where you would locate the information in an annual report. (*Hint:* The information may be in more than one location.)

1. The detail on major classifications of long-lived assets.
2. The accounting method(s) used for financial reporting purposes.
3. Whether the company has had any capital expenditures for the year.
4. The net amount of property, plant, and equipment.
5. Policies on amortizing intangibles.
6. Depreciation expense.
7. Any significant gains or losses on disposals of long-lived assets.

8. Accumulated depreciation of property, plant, and equipment at the end of the last fiscal year.

9. The amount of assets written off as impaired during the year.

■ LO2, 3   **E9–26**   **Recording and Explaining Depreciation, Extraordinary Repairs, and Changes in Estimated Useful Life and Residual Value (Straight-Line Depreciation)**

The records of Luci Company reflected the following details for Machine A at December 31, 2015, the end of the company's fiscal year:

Cost when acquired	$30,000
Accumulated depreciation	10,200

During January 2016, the machine was renovated at a cost of $15,500. As a result, the estimated life increased from five years to eight years and the residual value increased from $4,500 to $6,500. The company uses straight-line depreciation.

Required:

1. Prepare the journal entry to record the renovation.

2. How old was the machine at the end of 2015?

3. Prepare the adjusting entry at the end of 2016 to record straight-line depreciation for the year.

4. Explain the rationale for your entries in (1) and (3).

■ LO3   **E9–27**   **Computing the Effect of a Change in Useful Life and Residual Value on Financial Statements and Cash Flows (Straight-Line Depreciation)**

Dustin Company owns the office building occupied by its administrative office. The office building was reflected in the accounts at the end of last year as follows:

Acquisition cost	$330,000
Accumulated depreciation (based on straight-line depreciation, an estimated life of 50 years, and a residual value of $30,000)	78,000

Following a careful study, management decided in January of this year that the total estimated useful life should be changed to 30 years (instead of 50) and the residual value reduced to $22,500 (from $30,000). The depreciation method will not change.

Required:

1. Compute the annual depreciation expense prior to the change in estimates.

2. Compute the annual depreciation expense after the change in estimates.

3. What will be the net effect of changing the estimates on the statement of financial position, net earnings, and cash flows for the year?

■ connect **PROBLEMS**

■ LO3   **P9–1**   **Understanding the Nature of Depreciation**

At the beginning of his first year at university, Georgio Labos bought a used combination colour television and stereo system for $960. He estimates that these two items will be almost worthless by the time he graduates in four years and plans to abandon them then.

Required:

1. Assume that Georgio expects to receive four years of entertainment services for the $960. What is the book value of these items after one year? Use straight-line depreciation with no residual value.

2. The university's academic year lasts a total of 30 weeks, from early September to late April. Georgio does not take the TV and stereo system with him on vacations. During the academic year, he participates in many activities, so he averages three hours per week of watching television and listening to music. What is the average cost per hour of use? (Ignore costs of electricity and repairs.)

3. Georgio is disturbed by the answer to (2). He complains to a friend that this amount exceeds the hourly cost of going to the movies on specific days of the week. His friend suggests that he could lower the average cost by leaving the TV set on whenever he goes to class. Georgio attends classes for 12 hours per week. Comment on this suggestion.

4. After owning the TV set and stereo system for one year, Georgio became curious about the price he could get for selling these items. He discovered that the most he could receive is $600. He does not plan to sell them but the information distresses him. What amount should he associate with the TV set and stereo system after one year? Explain.

P9–2 Determining the Acquisition Cost and the Financial Statement Effects of Depreciation, Extraordinary Repairs, and Asset Disposal (AP9–1)   ■ LO1, 2, 3, 5

On January 2, 2012, Athol Company bought a machine for use in operations. The machine has an estimated useful life of eight years and an estimated residual value of $2,600. The company provided the following information:

a. Invoice price of the machine, $82,000.

b. Freight paid by the vendor per sales agreement, $1,000.

c. Installation costs, $2,400 cash.

d. Cost of cleaning up the supplies, boxes, and other garbage that remained after the installation of the machine, $100 cash.

e. Payment of the machine's price was made as follows:

January 2:
• Issued 2,000 common shares of Athol Company at $3.50 per share.
• Signed a $45,000 note payable due April 16, 2012, plus 8 percent interest.
• Balance of the invoice price to be paid in cash. The invoice allows for a 2 percent cash discount if the cash payment is made by January 11.

    January 15:   Paid the balance of the invoice price in cash.

    April 16:   Paid the note payable and interest in cash.

f. On June 30, 2014, the company completed the replacement of a major part of the machine that cost $18,575. This expenditure is expected to reduce the machine's operating costs, increase its estimated useful life by two years, and increase its estimated residual value to $2,000.

g. Assume that on October 1, 2019, the company decided to replace the machine with a newer, more efficient model. It then sold the machine to Sako Ltd. on that date for $30,000 cash.

Required:

1. Compute the acquisition cost of the machine, and explain the basis for including certain costs in the determination of the machine's acquisition cost.

2. Indicate the accounts affected, amounts, and direction (+ for increase and – for decrease) of the effects of the purchase and subsequent cash payments on the accounting equation. Use the following headings:

Date	Assets	=	Liabilities	+	Shareholders' Equity

3. Prepare the journal entries to record the purchase of the machine and subsequent cash payments on January 15 and April 16, 2012.

4. Compute the depreciation expense for each of the years 2012, 2013, and 2014, assuming the company's fiscal year ends on December 31. Use the straight-line depreciation method.

5. Prepare the journal entry to record the sale of the machine on October 1, 2019. (*Hint:* First determine the balance of the accumulated depreciation account on that date.)

P9–3 Analyzing the Effects of Repairs, a Betterment, and Depreciation (AP9–2)   ■ LO2, 3

A recent annual report for Swifty Air Cargo Company states the following:

Property, Plant, and Equipment

Expenditures for major additions, improvements, flight equipment modifications, and specific equipment overhaul costs are capitalized when such costs are determined to extend the useful life of the asset or are part of acquiring the asset. Maintenance and repairs are charged to expense as incurred.

Assume that Swifty made extensive repairs on an existing building and added a new section. The building is a garage and repair facility for delivery trucks that serve the local area. The existing building originally cost $820,000, and by the end of 2013, it was half depreciated on the basis of a useful life of 20 years and no residual value. Assume straight-line depreciation was used. During 2014, the following expenditures related to the building were made:

a. Ordinary repairs and maintenance expenditures for the year, $17,000 paid in cash.

b. Extensive and major repairs to the roof of the building, $120,000 paid in cash. These repairs were completed on December 31, 2014.

c. The new section, completed on December 31, 2014, at a cost of $230,000 paid in cash, has an estimated useful life of nine years and no residual value.

Required:

1. Applying the policies of Swifty, complete the following schedule, indicating the effects of the preceding expenditures. If there is no effect on an account, write N on the line (amounts in thousands):

	Building	Accumulated Depreciation	Depreciation Expense	Repairs Expense	Cash
Balance January 1, 2014	$820,000	$410,000			
Depreciation for 2014		_____	_____		_____
Balance prior to expenditures	820,000	_____	_____		
Expenditure a	_____	_____	_____	_____	_____
Expenditure b	_____	_____	_____	_____	_____
Expenditure c	_____	_____	_____	_____	_____
Balance December 31, 2014	_____	_____	_____	_____	_____

2. What was the carrying amount of the building at December 31, 2014?

3. Compute the depreciation expense for 2015, assuming no additional capital expenditures on this building in 2015.

4. Explain the effect of depreciation on cash flows.

■ LO2, 3

eXcel

P9–4 **Computing a Basket Purchase Allocation, and Recording Depreciation under Three Alternative Methods** (AP9–3)

At the beginning of the year, Wong's Martial Arts Centre bought three used fitness machines from Hangar Inc. for a total cash price of $38,000. Transportation costs on the machines were $2,000. The machines were immediately overhauled and installed, and started operating. The machines were different; therefore, each had to be recorded separately in the accounts. An appraiser was requested to estimate their market value at the date of purchase (prior to the overhaul and installation). The carrying amounts shown on Hangar's books are also available. The carrying amounts, appraisal results, installation costs, and renovation expenditures follow:

	Machine A	Machine B	Machine C
Carrying amount—Hangar	$8,000	$29,000	$6,000
Appraisal value	9,500	32,000	8,500
Installation costs	300	500	200
Renovation costs prior to use	2,000	400	600

By the end of the first year, each machine had been operating 8,000 hours.

Required:

1. Compute the cost of each machine by making a supportable allocation of the total cost to the three machines. Explain the rationale for the allocation basis used.

2. Prepare the entry to record depreciation expense at the end of year 1, assuming the following:

	Estimates		
Machine	Life	Residual Value	Depreciation Method
A	5	$1,500	Straight-line
B	40,000 hours	900	Units-of-production
C	4	2,000	Double-declining-balance

P9–5 **Inferring Depreciation Amounts, and Determining the Effects of a Depreciation Error on Key Ratios** (AP9–4)

Bauer Performance Sports Ltd. is a leading developer and manufacturer of ice hockey, roller hockey, and lacrosse equipment as well as related apparel. The following information was reported in Note 14 to the company's financial statements for fiscal year 2012 (in thousands of dollars):

	2012	2011
Machinery and equipment	$ 5,423	$ 5,177
Data processing equipment	2,945	1,332
Furniture and fixtures	3,570	2,248
Leasehold improvements	2,846	3,822
Construction in progress	240	1,270
	15,024	13,849
Less: Accumulated depreciation	(7,480)	(6,800)
	$ 7,544	$ 7,049

Required:

1. Assuming that Bauer did not sell any property, plant, and equipment in 2012, what was the amount of depreciation expense recorded in 2012?

2. Assume that Bauer failed to record depreciation in 2012. Indicate the effect of the error (i.e., overstated or understated) on the following ratios: (*a*) earnings per share, (*b*) fixed asset turnover ratio, (*c*) current ratio, and (*d*) return on equity. Computations are not required.

P9–6 **Evaluating the Effect of Alternative Depreciation Methods on Key Ratios from an Analyst's Perspective**

Bombardier Inc. is one of the largest manufacturers of planes and trains in the world. The company's long-lived assets exceed $9 billion. As a result, depreciation is a significant item on Bombardier's statement of earnings. You are a financial analyst for Bombardier and have been asked to determine the impact of alternative depreciation methods. For your analysis, you have been asked to compare methods based on a machine that cost $106,000. The estimated useful life is 13 years, and the estimated residual value is $2,000. The machine has an estimated useful life in productive output of 200,000 units. Actual output was 20,000 in year 1 and 16,000 in year 2.

Required:

1. For years 1 and 2 only, prepare a separate depreciation schedule for each of the following alternative methods. Round your computations to the nearest dollar.
   a. Straight-line
   b. Units-of-production
   c. Double-declining-balance

Method: _____				
Year	Computation	Depreciation Expense	Accumulated Depreciation	Carrying Amount
At acquisition				
1				
2				

2. Evaluate each method in terms of its effect on cash flow, fixed asset turnover ratio, and earnings per share (EPS). Assuming that Bombardier is most interested in reducing taxes and maintaining a high EPS for year 1, which method of depreciation would you recommend to management? Would your recommendation change for year 2? Why or why not?

P9–7 **Inferring Asset Age, and Determining Financial Statement Effects of a Long-Lived Asset Disposal (A Challenging Problem)** (AP9–5)

Mattel Inc. is the leading toy maker in the world. The company's revenues exceed $6 billion. In the toy business, it is very difficult to determine the life expectancy of a product. Products that children love one year may sit on the shelf the following year. As a result, companies in the toy business often sell productive assets that are no longer needed. Assume that on December 31, 2014, the end of the company's fiscal year, Mattel's records showed the following data about a machine that was no longer needed to make a toy that was popular last year:

Machine, original cost	$104,000
Accumulated depreciation	55,000*
*Based on an estimated useful life of eight years, a residual value of $16,000, and straight-line depreciation.	

On April 1, 2015, the machine was sold for $52,000 cash.

Required:

1. How old was the machine on January 1, 2015? Show computations.
2. Indicate the effect (i.e., the amount and direction, increase or decrease) of the sale of the machine on April 1, 2015, on the following (ignore income taxes):
   a. Total assets.
   b. Net earnings.
   c. Cash flows (by each section of the statement: operating, investing, and financing activities).

LO5, 7   **P9–8**   **Inferring Activities Affecting Property, Plant, and Equipment from Notes to the Financial Statements, and Analyzing the Impact of Depreciation on Cash Flows** (AP9–6)

Singapore Airlines

Singapore Airlines reported the following information in the notes to a recent annual report (in Singapore dollars):

SINGAPORE AIRLINES

Notes to the Accounts

21. Property, plant, and equipment (in $ million)

	Beginning of Year	Additions	Disposals/ Transfers	End of Year
Cost				
Aircraft	$19,610.8	$ 94.9	$ 476.5	$19,229.2
Other property, plant, and equipment (summarized)	4,614.9	1,550.9	1,959.8	4,206.0
Accumulated depreciation				
Aircraft	8,498.9	1,433.3	1,727.2	8,205.0
Other fixed assets (summarized)	1,849.2	155.2	155.6	1,848.8

Singapore Airlines also reported the following cash flow details:

Cash Flow from Operating Activities (in $ million)

	The Company	
	Current Year	Prior Year
Earnings before income taxes	$ 448.2	$1,419.0
Adjustments for:		
Depreciation of property, plant, and equipment	1,588.5	1,671.7
Loss (Gain) on disposal of property, plant, and equipment	1.4	(103.3)
Other adjustments (summarized)	(119.6)	(7.2)
Net cash provided by operating activities	$1,918.5	$2,980.2

Required:

1. Reconstruct the information in Note 21 into T-accounts for property, plant, and equipment and accumulated depreciation:

Property, Plant, and Equipment		Accumulated Depreciation	
Beg. balance			Beg. balance
Acquisitions	Disposals/transfers	Disposals/transfers	Depreciation expense
End. balance			End. balance

2. Compute the amount of cash the company received for disposals and transfers. Show computations.

3. Compute the percentage of depreciation expense to cash flows from operations. How do you interpret this percentage?

P9–9 Recording and Interpreting the Disposal of Three Long-Lived Assets (AP9–7)

During 2015, Côté Company disposed of three different assets. On January 1, 2015, prior to the disposal of the assets, the accounts reflected the following:

Asset	Original Cost	Residual Value	Estimated Life	Accumulated Depreciation (straight-line)
Machine A	$20,000	$2,000	8 years	$13,500 (6 years)
Machine B	41,000	4,000	10 years	29,600 (8 years)
Machine C	75,000	3,000	12 years	60,000 (10 years)

The machines were disposed of in the following ways:

a. Machine A: Sold on January 1, 2015, for $7,200 cash.

b. Machine B: Sold on April 1, 2015, for $8,500; received cash, $2,500, and a note receivable for $6,000, due on March 31, 2016, plus 6 percent interest.

c. Machine C: Suffered irreparable damage from an accident on July 2, 2015. On July 10, 2015, a salvage company removed the machine immediately at no cost. The machine was insured, and $18,000 cash was collected from the insurance company.

Required:

1. Prepare all journal entries related to the disposal of each machine in 2015.

2. Explain the accounting rationale for the way that you recorded each disposal.

P9–10 Determining Financial Statement Effects of Activities Related to Various Long-Lived Assets (AP9–8)

BSP Company completed the following transactions during fiscal year 2014:

January	1	Purchased a patent for $28,000 cash, with an estimated useful life of seven years.
April	1	Purchased the assets (not detailed) of another business for $164,000 cash, including $10,000 for goodwill. The company assumed no liabilities. Goodwill has an indefinite life.
October	15	Paid $5,500 for regular maintenance and ordinary repairs.
December 31		Constructed a storage shed on land leased from D. Heald at a cost of $15,600. The lease will expire in three years. (Amounts spent to enhance leased property are capitalized as intangible assets called leasehold improvements.)
December 31		Sold Machine A for $6,000 cash. The machine was purchased on January 1, 2011, for $25,000. It had a useful life of five years and a residual value of $5,000. Its accumulated depreciation totalled $12,000 as at December 31, 2013.
December 31		Paid $5,200 for a complete reconditioning of Machine B, which was acquired on January 1, 2013, for $31,000. The machine had a useful life of 15 years and a residual value of $7,000.

The company uses the straight-line method of depreciation and amortization.

Required:

1. Indicate the accounts affected, amounts, and direction of the effects (+ for increase, − for decrease, and NE for no effect) of each transaction on the accounting equation. Use the following structure:

Date	Assets	=	Liabilities	+	Shareholders' Equity

2. Compute the amount of depreciation expense for Machine B to be recorded at December 31, 2015, the company's year-end.

P9–11 Computing Goodwill from the Purchase of a Business and Related Amortization (AP9–9)

Lassonde Industries Inc. is a North American leader in the development, manufacture, and sale of innovative and distinctive lines of fruit and vegetable juices and drinks marketed under recognized brands such as Everfresh, Fairlee, Flavür, Fruité, Graves, Oasis, and Rougemont.

Lassonde Industries Inc.

The notes to the company's financial statements for 2011 indicate that it acquired the outstanding shares of Clement Pappas Company on August 12, 2011. The purchase price was $395,287,000 and the fair market value of identifiable assets acquired and liabilities assumed are as follows (in thousands of dollars):

Current assets	$ 86,169
Property, plant, and equipment	85,200
Intangible assets	134,146
Current liabilities	(25,453)
Finance lease obligations	(940)

Required:

1. Compute the amount of goodwill resulting from the purchase.

2. Compute the adjustments that Lassonde Industries would make at the end of its fiscal year, December 31, 2012, for depreciation and amortization of all the long-lived assets it acquired. The intangible assets include four major categories that have different useful lives as follows:

Intangible Asset	Acquisition Cost	Estimated Useful Life
Client relationships	$64,484	15 years
Trademarks and trade name	49,547	20 years
Technologies and certifications	19,819	10 years
Non-compete agreements	296	5 years

Assume that all the acquired long-lived assets have no residual value and that property, plant, and equipment have an estimated useful life of 10 years. The company does not amortize goodwill.

■ LO6   **P9–12**   **Determining the Financial Statement Effects of the Acquisition and Amortization of Intangibles**

Figg Company, with a fiscal year ending December 31, acquired three intangible assets during 2015. For each of the following transactions, indicate the accounts affected and the amounts and direction of the effects (+ for increase, − for decrease, and N for no effect) on the accounting equation. Use the following headings:

Date	Assets	=	Liabilities	+	Shareholders' Equity

a. On January 1, 2015, the company purchased a patent from Ullrich Ltd. for $6,000 cash. Ullrich had developed the patent and registered it with the Canadian Intellectual Property Office on January 1, 2010.

b. On January 1, 2015, the company purchased a copyright for a total cash cost of $12,000; the remaining legal life was 25 years. Company executives estimated that the copyright would have no value by the end of 20 years.

c. The company purchased another company in January 2015 at a cash cost of $130,000. Included in the purchase price was $30,000 for goodwill; the balance was for plant, equipment, and fixtures (no liabilities were assumed).

d. On December 31, 2015, the company amortized the patent over its remaining legal life.

e. On December 31, 2015, the company amortized the copyright over the appropriate period.

■ LO4, 6   **P9–13**   **Computing Amortization, Carrying Amount, and Asset Impairment Related to Different Intangible Assets** (AP9–10)

Havel Company has five different intangible assets to be accounted for and reported on the financial statements. Management is concerned about the amortization of the cost of each of these intangibles. Facts about each intangible follow:

a. *Patent.* The company purchased a patent at a cash cost of $54,600 on January 1, 2015. The patent had a legal life of 20 years from the date of registration with the Canadian Intellectual Property Office, which was January 1, 2011. It is amortized over its remaining legal life.

b. *Copyright.* On January 1, 2015, the company purchased a copyright for $22,500 cash. The legal life remaining from that date is 30 years. It is estimated that the copyrighted item will have no value by the end of 25 years.

c. *Franchise.* The company obtained a franchise from McKerma Company to make and distribute a special item. It obtained the franchise on January 1, 2015, at a cash cost of $14,400 for a 12-year period.

d. *Licence.* On January 1, 2014, the company secured a licence from the city to operate a special service for a period of five years. Total cash expended to obtain the licence was $14,000.

e. *Goodwill.* The company started business in January 2013 by purchasing another business for a cash lump sum of $400,000. Included in the purchase price was $60,000 for goodwill. Company executives stated that "the goodwill is an important long-lived asset to us." It has an indefinite life.

Required:

1. Compute the amount of amortization that should be recorded for each intangible asset at the end of the fiscal year, December 31, 2015.
2. Compute the carrying amount of each intangible asset on December 31, 2016.
3. Assume that on January 2, 2017, the copyrighted item was impaired in its ability to continue to produce strong revenues. The other intangible assets were not affected. Havel estimated that the copyright will be able to produce future cash flows of $18,000. The fair value of the copyright is determined to be $16,000. Compute the amount, if any, of the impairment loss to be recorded.

P9–14 Analyzing and Recording Entries Related to a Change in Estimated Life and Residual Value   ■ LO3
Rungano Corporation is a global publisher of magazines, books, and music, as well as video   e**X**cel
collections, and it is one of the world's leading direct-mail marketers. Many direct-mail marketers use high-speed Didde press equipment to print their advertisements. These presses can cost more than $1 million. Assume that Rungano owns a Didde press acquired at an original cost of $1,200,000. It is being depreciated on a straight-line basis over a 20-year estimated useful life and has a $150,000 estimated residual value. At the end of 2015, the press had been depreciated for eight years. In January 2016, a decision was made, on the basis of improved maintenance procedures, that a total estimated useful life of 25 years and a residual value of $219,000 would be more realistic. The fiscal year ends December 31.

Required:

1. Compute (*a*) the amount of depreciation expense recorded in 2015 and (*b*) the carrying amount of the printing press at the end of 2015.
2. Compute the amount of depreciation that should be recorded in 2016. Show computations.
3. Prepare the adjusting entry to record depreciation expense at December 31, 2016.

ALTERNATE PROBLEMS

AP9–1 Determining the Acquisition Cost and the Financial Statement Effects of Depreciation,   ■ LO1, 2, 3, 5
Extraordinary Repairs, and Asset Disposal (P9–2)
On July 1, 2012, the Fitzgerald Corp. bought a machine for use in operations. The machine has an estimated useful life of six years and an estimated residual value of $2,500. The company provided the following information:

a. Invoice price of the machine, $60,000.

b. Freight paid by the vendor per sales agreement, $650.

c. Installation costs, $2,500 cash.

d. Payment of the machine's price was made as follows:

   July 1:
   • Fitzgerald Corp. issued 2,000 common shares at $5 per share.
   • Signed an interest-bearing note for the balance of the invoice price, payable on September 1, 2012, plus 9 percent interest.

October 1: Paid the note payable and related interest in cash.

e. On June 30, 2015, the company completed the replacement of a major part of the machine that cost $11,500. This expenditure is expected to reduce the machine's operating costs and increase its estimated useful life by two years. At the same time, the machine's estimated residual value was reduced to $2,000.

f. Assume that on July 1, 2019, the company decided to dispose of the machine by selling it to Ayad Inc. on that date for $16,000 cash.

Required:

1. Compute the acquisition cost of the machine, and explain the basis for including certain costs in the determination of the machine's acquisition cost.

2. Indicate the accounts affected and the amounts and direction (+ for increase and – for decrease) of the effects of the purchase and subsequent cash payment on the accounting equation. Use the following headings:

Date	Assets	=	Liabilities	+	Shareholders' Equity

3. Prepare the journal entries to record the purchase of the machine and subsequent cash payments on September 1, 2012.

4. Compute the depreciation expense for each of the years 2012 and 2015, assuming the company's fiscal year ends on December 31. Use the straight-line depreciation method.

5. Prepare the journal entry to record the sale of the machine on July 1, 2019. (*Hint:* First determine the balance of the Accumulated Depreciation account on that date.)

■ **LO2, 3**   **AP9–2**   **Analyzing the Effects of Repairs, a Betterment, and Depreciation** (AP9–3)

AMERCO

A recent annual report for AMERCO, the holding company for U-Haul International Inc., included the following note:

> **Property, Plant, and Equipment**
>
> Property, plant, and equipment are stated at cost. Interest costs incurred during the initial construction of buildings or rental equipment are considered part of the cost. Depreciation is computed for financial reporting purposes principally using the straight-line method over the following estimated useful lives: rental equipment 2–20 years, building and non-rental equipment 3–55 years. Major overhauls to rental equipment are capitalized and are depreciated over the estimated period benefited. Routine maintenance costs are charged to operating expense as they are incurred.

AMERCO subsidiaries own property, plant, and equipment that provide offices for U-Haul and that are utilized in the manufacture, repair, and rental of U-Haul equipment. Assume that AMERCO made extensive repairs on an existing building and added a new wing. The building is a garage and repair facility for rental trucks that serve the Vancouver area. The existing building originally cost $460,000, and by December 31, 2014 (5 years), it was one-quarter depreciated on the basis of a 20-year estimated useful life and no residual value. Assume straight-line depreciation, computed to the nearest month. During 2015, the following expenditures related to the building were made:

a. Ordinary repairs and maintenance expenditures for the year, $10,000 paid in cash.

b. Extensive and major repairs to the roof of the building, $34,000 paid in cash. These repairs were completed on June 30, 2015.

c. The new wing was completed on June 30, 2015, at a cash cost of $173,000. By itself, the wing had an estimated useful life of 15 years and no residual value. The company intends to sell the building and wing at the end of the building's useful life.

Required:

1. Applying the policies of AMERCO, complete the following schedule, indicating the effects of the preceding expenditures. If there is no effect on an account, write N on the line:

	Building	Accumulated Depreciation	Depreciation Expense	Repairs Expense	Cash
Balance, January 1, 2015	$460,000	$115,000			
Depreciation January 1–June 30		_____	_____		_____
Balance prior to expenditures	460,000	_____	_____		
Expenditure *a*	_____	_____	_____	_____	_____
Expenditure *b*	_____	_____	_____	_____	_____
Expenditure *c*	_____	_____	_____	_____	_____
Depreciation July 1–December 31:					
Existing building		_____	_____	_____	_____
Major repairs and betterments		_____	_____	_____	_____
Balance, December 31, 2015	_____	_____	_____	_____	_____

2. What was the carrying amount of the building on December 31, 2015?
3. Explain the effect of depreciation on cash flows.

AP9–3 **Computing a Basket Purchase Allocation, and Recording Depreciation under Three Alternative Methods (P9–4)**   ■ LO2, 3

At the beginning of the year, Labinski Inc. bought three used machines from Dumas Corporation for a total cash price of $62,000. Transportation costs on the machines were $3,000. The machines were immediately overhauled and installed, and started operating. The machines were different; therefore, each had to be recorded separately in the accounts. An appraiser was requested to estimate their market value at the date of purchase (prior to the overhaul and installation). The carrying amounts shown on Dumas's books are also available. The carrying amounts, appraisal results, installation costs, and renovation expenditures follow:

	Machine A	Machine B	Machine C
Carrying amount—Dumas	$10,500	$28,000	$26,000
Appraisal value	11,500	32,000	28,500
Installation costs	800	1,100	1,100
Renovation costs prior to use	600	1,400	1,600

By the end of the first year, each machine had been operating 7,000 hours.

Required:

1. Compute the cost of each machine by making a supportable allocation of the total cost to the three machines (round your calculations to two decimal places). Explain the rationale for the allocation basis used.
2. Prepare the entry to record depreciation expense at the end of year 1, assuming the following:

	Estimates		
Machine	Life	Residual Value	Depreciation Method
A	4	$1,000	Straight-line
B	35,000 hours	2,000	Units-of-production
C	5	1,500	Double-declining-balance

AP9–4 **Inferring Depreciation Amounts, and Determining the Effects of a Depreciation Error on Key Ratios (P9–5)**   ■ LO1, 3

Gildan Activewear Inc.

Gildan Activewear Inc. is a Canadian vertically integrated manufacturer and marketer of quality branded basic family apparel, including T-shirts, fleece, sport shirts, socks, and underwear. The following information was reported in Note 9 to the company's financial statements for fiscal year 2012:

	September 30, 2012	October 2, 2011
Land	$ 38,936	$ 35,113
Buildings and improvements	231,032	194,530
Manufacturing equipment	532,341	464,886
Other equipment	96,624	91,853
Assets not yet utilized in operations	11,769	47,547
	910,702	833,929
Less accumulated depreciation	358,265	283,605
Carrying amount	$552,437	$550,324

Required:

1. Assuming that Gildan did not have any asset impairment losses and did not sell any property, plant, and equipment in fiscal year 2012, what was the amount of depreciation expense recorded in 2012?
2. Assume that Gildan failed to record depreciation in 2012. Indicate the effect of the error (i.e., overstated or understated) on the following: (*a*) earnings per share, (*b*) fixed asset turnover ratio, (*c*) current ratio, and (*d*) return on equity. Computations are not required.

LO5, 7   **AP9–5**   **Inferring Asset Age, and Determining Financial Statement Effects of a Long-Lived Asset**

Hasbro Inc.

Disposal (A Challenging Problem) (P9–7)

Hasbro Inc. designs, manufactures, and markets high-quality toys, games, and infant products. The company's revenues exceed $4.0 billion. In the toy business, it is very difficult to determine the life expectancy of a product. Products that children love one year may sit on the shelf the following year. As a result, companies in the toy business often sell productive assets that are no longer needed. Assume that on December 31, 2014, the end of the company's fiscal year, Hasbro's records showed the following data about a machine that was no longer needed to make a toy that was popular last year:

Machine, original cost	$214,000
Accumulated depreciation	128,000*

*Based on an estimated useful life of six years, a residual value of $22,000, and straight-line depreciation.

On July 1, 2015, the machine was sold for $76,000 cash.

Required:

1. How old was the machine on January 1, 2015? Show computations.
2. Indicate the effect (i.e., the amount and direction—increase or decrease) of the sale of the machine on July 1, 2015, on
   a. Total assets.
   b. Net earnings.
   c. Cash flows (for each section of the statement: operating, investing, and financing activities).

LO5, 7   **AP9–6**   **Inferring Activities Affecting Fixed Assets from Notes to the Financial Statements, and**

Cathay Pacific Airways

Analyzing the Impact of Depreciation on Cash Flows (P9–8)

Cathay Pacific Airways reported the following information in the notes to the financial statements of its 2012 annual report (in millions of Hong Kong dollars):

CATHAY PACIFIC AIRWAYS

Notes to the Accounts

10. Fixed Assets

	Acquisition Cost	Accumulated Depreciation
Balance, January 1, 2012	$130,668	$57,170
Additional acquisitions	20,177	
Depreciation expense		6,617
Disposals	(6,275)	(4,195)
Other changes (summarized)	(2,199)	(1,499)
Balance, December 31, 2012	$142,371	$58,093

Cathay Pacific also reported the following cash flow details:

Cash Flow from Operating Activities (in millions of HK dollars)		
	2012	2011
Earnings from operations	$1,788	$ 5,500
Adjustments for:		
Depreciation	6,617	6,127
Loss on disposal of fixed assets, net	101	159
Other adjustments (summarized)	733	3,607
Cash generated from operations	$9,239	$15,393

Required:

1. Reconstruct the information in Note 12 into T-accounts for fixed assets and accumulated depreciation:

Fixed Assets			Accumulated Depreciation	
Beg. balance				Beg. balance
Acquisitions	Disposals	Disposals		Depreciation expense
End. balance				End. balance

2. Compute the amount of cash the company received for disposals during 2012. Show computations.
3. Compute the percentage of depreciation expense to cash flows from operations for 2012. How do you interpret this percentage?

AP9–7 Recording and Interpreting the Disposal of Three Long-Lived Assets (P9–9)   ■ LO3, 5

During 2015, Callaway Company disposed of three different assets. On January 1, 2015, prior to the disposal of the assets, the accounts reflected the following:

Asset	Original Cost	Residual Value	Estimated Life	Accumulated Depreciation (straight-line)
Machine A	$24,000	$2,000	5 years	$17,600 (4 years)
Machine B	16,500	5,000	10 years	8,050 (7 years)
Machine C	59,200	3,200	14 years	48,000 (12 years)

The machines were disposed of in the following ways:

a. Machine A: Sold on January 1, 2015, for $6,250 cash.

b. Machine B: Sold on July 1, 2015, for $9,500; received cash, $4,500, and a $5,000 interest-bearing (10 percent) note receivable due at the end of 12 months.

c. Machine C: Suffered irreparable damage from an accident on October 2, 2015. On October 10, 2015, a salvage company removed the machine immediately at a cost of $500. The machine was insured, and $11,500 cash was collected from the insurance company.

Required:

1. Prepare all journal entries related to the disposal of each machine.
2. Explain the accounting rationale for the way that you recorded each disposal.

AP9–8 Determining Financial Statement Effects of Activities Related to Various Long-Lived Assets (P9–10)   ■ LO3, 5

Zhou Corporation completed the following transactions during fiscal year 2016:

| January | 1 | Purchased a license for $7,200 cash with an estimated useful life of four years. |
| January | 1 | Repaved the parking lot of the building leased from H. Lane for $17,800. The lease will expire in 10 years, but the estimated useful life of the parking lot is five years with no residual value. (Amounts spent to enhance leased property are capitalized as intangible assets called leasehold improvements.) |

July	1	Purchased another business for $120,000 cash. The transaction included $115,000 for the assets and $24,000 for the liabilities assumed by Zhou. The remainder was goodwill with an indefinite life.
November 30		Paid $6,700 for ordinary repairs and regular maintenance of the building.
December 31		Sold Machine A for $6,000 cash. The machine was acquired for $21,500 on January 1, 2013, and had a useful life of four years and a residual value of $3,500. Its accumulated depreciation totalled $13,500 at December 31, 2015.
December 31		Paid $7,000 for a complete reconditioning of Machine B, which was acquired on July 1, 2012, for $18,000. By December 31, 2015, accumulated depreciation totalled $7,000. Zhou expected to use the machine for eight years and then sell it for $2,000 at the end of its useful life.

The company uses the straight-line method of depreciation and amortization.

Required:

1. For each of these transactions, indicate the accounts affected and the amounts and direction of the effects (+ for increase and − for decrease) on the accounting equation. Use the following structure:

Date	Assets	=	Liabilities	+	Shareholders' Equity

2. Compute the amount of depreciation and amortization expense for Machine B to be recorded at December 31, 2017, the company's year-end.

■ LO6   **AP9–9**   **Computing Goodwill from the Purchase of a Business and Related Amortization** (P9–11)

The notes to a recent annual report from Weebok Corporation included the following:

Business Acquisitions

During the current year, the company acquired the assets of Sport Shoes Inc.

Assume that Weebok acquired Sport Shoes on January 2, 2014. Weebok acquired the name of the company and all of its assets, except cash, for $450,000 cash. Weebok did not assume the liabilities. On January 2, 2014, the statement of financial position of Sport Shoes reflected the following carrying amounts, and an independent appraiser estimated the following market values for the assets:

January 2, 2014	Carrying Amount	Market Value
Trade receivables, net	$ 45,000	$ 45,000
Inventory	220,000	210,000
Property, plant, and equipment, net	32,000	60,000
Other assets	3,000	10,000
Total assets	$300,000	
Liabilities	$ 60,000	
Shareholders' equity	240,000	
Total liabilities and shareholders' equity	$300,000	

Required:

1. Compute the amount of goodwill resulting from the purchase. (*Hint:* Assets are purchased at market value, which is their cost at the date of acquisition.)

2. Compute the adjustments that Weebok would make at the end of its fiscal year, December 31, 2014, for depreciation of all long-lived assets (straight-line), assuming an estimated remaining useful life of 15 years and no residual value. The company does not amortize goodwill.

■ LO4, 6   **AP9–10**   **Computing Amortization, Carrying Amount, and Asset Impairment Related to Different Intangible Assets** (P9–13)

Theriault Corporation has five different intangible assets to be accounted for and reported on the financial statements. The management is concerned about the amortization of the cost of each of these intangibles. Facts about each intangible follow:

a. *Patent.* The company purchased a patent at a cash cost of $18,600 on January 1, 2015. The patent had a legal life of 20 years from the date of registration with the Canadian Intellectual Property Office, which was January 1, 2013. It is amortized over its remaining legal life.

b. *Copyright.* On January 1, 2015, the company purchased a copyright for $24,750 cash. The legal life remaining from that date is 30 years. It is estimated that the copyrighted item will have no value by the end of 15 years.

c. *Franchise.* The company obtained a franchise from Farrell Company to make and distribute a special item. It obtained the franchise on January 1, 2015, at a cash cost of $19,200 for a 12-year period.

d. *Licence.* On January 1, 2014, the company secured a licence from the city to operate a special service for a period of seven years. Total cash expended to obtain the licence was $21,000.

e. *Goodwill.* The company started business in January 2013 by purchasing another business for a cash lump sum of $650,000. The purchase price included $75,000 for goodwill. Company executives stated that "the goodwill is an important long-lived asset to us." It has an indefinite life.

Required:

1. Compute the amount of amortization expense that should be recorded for each intangible asset at the end of the fiscal year, December 31, 2015.
2. Compute the carrying amount of each intangible asset on January 1, 2018.
3. Assume that on January 2, 2018, the franchise was impaired in its ability to continue to produce strong revenues. The other intangible assets were not affected. Theriault estimated that the franchise will be able to produce future cash flows of $16,500, with a fair value of $15,000. Compute the amount, if any, of the impairment loss to be recorded.

CASES AND PROJECTS

FINDING AND INTERPRETING FINANCIAL INFORMATION

CP9–1 Finding Financial Information

Go to *Connect* for the financial statements of RONA Inc.

■ **LO1, 3**

RONA Inc.

Required:

Answer each of the following questions and indicate where you located the information to answer the question. (*Hint:* Use the notes to the financial statements for some of these questions.)

1. What method(s) of depreciation of property, plant, and equipment and amortization of intangible assets does the company use?
2. What types of property, plant, and equipment does RONA own or control as at December 30, 2012?
3. What types of intangible assets does RONA own as at December 30, 2012?
4. What is the amount of accumulated depreciation on the company's buildings as at December 30, 2012?
5. For depreciation purposes, what is the estimated useful life of the computer hardware? How old is the computer hardware, on average?
6. What amount of depreciation and amortization expense was reported for the 2012 fiscal year?
7. Did RONA acquire any businesses during fiscal year 2012? If so, what was the total cost of acquisition and what percentage of that cost was attributed to goodwill?
8. What is the fixed asset turnover ratio for the 2012 fiscal year? What does it suggest?

CP9–2 Finding Financial Information

Refer to the financial statements and accompanying notes of Canadian Tire Corporation given in Appendix A at the end of this book.

■ **LO1, 3**

Canadian Tire Corporation

Required:

Answer each of the following questions and indicate where you located the information to answer the question. (*Hint:* Use the notes to the financial statements for some of these questions.)

1. How much did the company spend on property and equipment (capital expenditures) in fiscal 2012?
2. What is the estimated useful life of leasehold improvements for depreciation purposes?
3. What was the historical cost of fixtures and equipment held by the company at the end of the 2012 fiscal year?

4. What proportion of the cost of buildings has been depreciated as at December 29, 2012? Is it possible to estimate how old the buildings are, on average?

5. What amount of depreciation of property, plant, and equipment and amortization of intangible assets was reported as an expense for the 2012 fiscal year?

6. What is the company's fixed asset turnover ratio for fiscal 2012? What does it suggest?

CP9–3

Canadian Tire
Corporation vs.
RONA Inc.

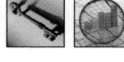

Comparing Companies within an Industry

Refer to the financial statements of Canadian Tire Corporation (Appendix A) and RONA Inc. (on *Connect*) and the Industry Ratio Report (Appendix B on *Connect*).

Required:

1. Compute the ratio of property, plant, and equipment (net) to total assets, for both companies each year. Why might the companies' ratios differ?

2. Compute the percentage of the gross amount of property, plant, and equipment that has been depreciated for each company for the most recent year. Why do you think the percentages differ?

3. Compute the fixed asset turnover ratio for the most recent year presented for both companies. Which has the higher efficiency in using assets? Why?

4. Compare the fixed asset turnover ratio for both companies to the industry average. Are these companies doing better or worse than the industry average in asset efficiency?

FINANCIAL REPORTING AND ANALYSIS CASES

CP9–4

Broadening Financial Research Skills: Identifying Competitors in an Industry

Reuters provides lists of industries and the competitors in each at **http://www.reuters.com**.

Required:

Access the Reuters website and identify three competitors for the following industries:

1. Airline
2. Consumer electronics
3. Food processing
4. Footwear

CP9–5

Papa John's
International

Using Financial Reports: Analyzing the Age of Assets

Papa John's International is a major pizza chain. At December 31, 2012, there were 4,163 pizzerias in 35 countries, including 73 restaurants in Canada. A note to a recent annual report for Papa John's International contained the following information (in thousands of US dollars):

	2012	2011
Land	$ 32,776	$ 32,735
Buildings and improvements	86,219	85,907
Leasehold improvements	96,652	90,855
Equipment and other	249,055	231,059
Construction in progress	23,262	5,159
	487,964	445,715
Less accumulated depreciation and amortization	(291,303)	(263,805)
Net property and equipment	$196,661	$181,910

Source: Papa John's International, Annual Report 2012, Form 10-K.

Depreciation and amortization expense (in thousands of dollars) charged to operations was $32,798 in the current year and $32,681 in the previous year. Depreciation is generally computed by using the straight-line method for financial reporting purposes.

Required:

1. What is your best estimate of the average expected life for Papa John's depreciable assets?
2. What is your best estimate of the average age of Papa John's depreciable assets?

■ LO1, 3, 6, 7

CanWest Global
Communications
Corp.

CP9–6 Using Financial Reports: Analyzing Fixed Asset Turnover Ratio and Cash Flows

CanWest Global Communications Corp. is a diversified Canadian communications and media company, providing consumers with broadband cable television, high-speed Internet, home phone, telecommunications, and satellite direct-to-home services. CanWest was acquired by Shaw Communications Inc. in 2010. Selected data from a recent annual report are as follows (in millions of dollars):

Property, plant and equipment, and intangibles	Current Year	Prior Year
From the consolidated statement of financial position and notes		
Property, plant, and equipment, net	$3,242	$3,200
Intangible assets with indefinite lives	7,622	7,599
Intangible assets with finite lives, net	469	419
From the consolidated statement of earnings		
Revenue	$4,988	$4,741
From the consolidated statement of cash flows		
Net earnings for the year	$ 761	$ 470
Adjustments:		
Depreciation of property, plant, and equipment	643	604
Amortization of intangible assets	447	405
Other adjustments, net	(534)	(238)
Cash provided by operations	$1,317	$1,241
From the notes to the financial statements		
Accumulated depreciation on property and equipment	$2,967	$2,963

Required:

1. Compute the cost of the property, plant, and equipment at the end of the current year. Explain your answer.
2. What is your best estimate of the average expected life of CanWest's property, plant, and equipment? What was the approximate age of the property, plant, and equipment at the end of the current year? Assume that CanWest uses straight-line depreciation.
3. Compute the fixed asset turnover ratio for the current year. Explain your results.
4. Compute an estimate of the amortization expense of intangible assets with finite lives for the next year.
5. On the consolidated statement of cash flows, why are the depreciation and amortization amounts added to net earnings for the year?

CRITICAL THINKING CASES

■ LO1, 3

WestJet Airlines Ltd.

CP9–7 Making a Decision as a Financial Analyst: Interpreting the Impact of the Capitalization of Interest on an Accounting Ratio

The capitalization of interest associated with self-constructed assets was discussed in this chapter. A recent annual report for WestJet Airlines Ltd. disclosed the following information concerning capitalization of interest:

> **1. Significant accounting policies (continued):**
>
> **(o) Borrowing costs:**
> Interest and other borrowing costs are capitalized to a qualifying asset provided they are directly attributable to the acquisition, construction or production of the qualifying asset. For specific borrowings, any investment income on the temporary investment of borrowed funds is offset against the capitalized borrowing costs.

Assume that WestJet capitalized interest in the amount of $500,000 and disclosed $2.2 million of interest expense in its statement of earnings for the year. One useful accounting ratio is the interest coverage ratio (earnings before interest and taxes divided by interest expense).

Required:

1. Explain why an analyst would calculate this ratio.
2. Did WestJet include the $500,000 in the reported interest expense of $2.2 million? If not, should an analyst include it when calculating the interest coverage ratio? Explain.

■ **LO3, 7**   **CP9–8**   **Evaluating an Ethical Dilemma: Analyzing an Accounting Change**

Norbord Inc.

The interim report for the fourth quarter of 2009 for Norbord Inc. included the following information:

Note 2. Changes in Accounting Policies and Significant Accounting Estimates

Property, Plant, and Equipment

. . . The Company had utilized the straight line method of depreciation for production equipment, which allocates cost equally to each period. In a period of fluctuating production levels, the straight line depreciation method does not result in rational allocation of the cost of equipment to production. Consequently, effective March 29, 2009, the Company changed to the unit of production depreciation method for its production assets. This method allocates the equipment costs to the actual units produced based on estimated annual capacity over the remaining useful life of the assets. The impact of this change has been applied prospectively as a change in an estimate, and it resulted in a $12 million reduction in depreciation expense in 2009.

Required:

1. What was the stated reason for the change in depreciation method? What other factors do you think management considered when it decided to make this accounting change?
2. Do you think this is an ethical decision?
3. Who were affected by the change, and how were they benefited or harmed?
4. What impact did this change have on cash flows for Norbord?
5. As an investor, how would you react to the fact that Norbord's depreciation expense will decrease by $12 million?

■ **LO1, 2**   **CP9–9**   **Evaluating an Ethical Dilemma: A Real-Life Example**

Assume you work as a staff member in a large accounting department for a multinational public company. Your job requires you to review documents relating to the company's equipment purchases. Upon verifying that purchases are properly approved, you prepare journal entries to record the equipment purchases in the accounting system. Typically, you handle equipment purchases costing $100,000 or less.

This morning, you were contacted by the executive assistant to the chief financial officer (CFO). She says that the CFO has asked to see you immediately in his office. Although your boss's boss has attended a few meetings where the CFO was present, you have never met the CFO during your three years with the company. Needless to say, you are anxious about the meeting.

Upon entering the CFO's office, you are warmly greeted with a smile and friendly handshake. The CFO compliments you on the great work that you have been doing for the company. You soon feel a little more comfortable, particularly when the CFO mentions that he has a special project for you. He states that he and the CEO have negotiated significant new arrangements with the company's equipment suppliers, which require the company to make advance payments for equipment to be purchased in the future. The CFO says that, for various reasons that he did not want to discuss, he will be processing the payments through the operating division of the company rather than the equipment accounting group. Given that the payments will be made through the operating division, they will initially be classified as operating expenses of the company. He indicates that clearly these advance payments for property and equipment should be recorded as assets, so he will be contacting you at the end of every quarter to make an adjusting journal entry to capitalize the amounts inappropriately classified as operating expenses. He advises you that a new account, called Prepaid Equipment, has been established for this purpose. He quickly wraps up the meeting by telling you that it is important that you not talk about the special project with anyone. You assume he doesn't want others to become jealous of your new important responsibility.

A few weeks later, at the end of the first quarter, you receive a voicemail from the CFO stating, "The adjustment that we discussed is $771,000,000 for this quarter." Before deleting the message, you replay it to make sure you heard it right. Your company generates over $8 billion in revenues and incurs $6 billion in operating expenses every quarter, but you have never made a journal entry for that much money. So, just to be sure there is not a mistake, you send an e-mail to the CFO confirming the amount. He phones you back immediately to abruptly inform you, "There's no mistake. That's the number." Feeling embarrassed that you may have annoyed the CFO, you quietly make the adjusting journal entry.

For each of the remaining three quarters in that year and for the first quarter in the following year, you continue to make these end-of-quarter adjustments. The "magic number," as the CFO liked to call it, was $560,000,000 for Q2, $742,745,000 for Q3, $941,000,000 for Q4, and $818,204,000 for Q1 of the following year. During this time, you have had several meetings and lunches with the CFO where he provides you the magic number, sometimes supported with nothing more than a Post-it note with the number written on it. He frequently compliments you on your good work and promises that you will soon be in line for a big promotion.

Despite the CFO's compliments and promises, you are growing increasingly uncomfortable with the journal entries that you have been making. Typically, whenever an ordinary equipment purchase involves an advance payment, the purchase is completed a few weeks later. At that time, the amount of the advance is removed from an Equipment Deposit account and transferred to the appropriate equipment account. This has not been the case with the CFO's special project. Instead, the Prepaid Equipment account has continued to grow, now standing at over $3.8 billion. There has been no discussion about how or when this balance will be reduced, and no depreciation has been recorded for it.

Just as you begin to reflect on the effect the adjustments have had on your company's fixed assets, operating expenses, and earnings from operations, you receive a call from the vice-president for internal audit. She needs to talk with you this afternoon about "a peculiar trend in the company's fixed asset turnover ratio and some suspicious journal entries that you have been making."

Required:

1. Complete the following table to determine what the company's accounting records would have looked like had you not made the journal entries as part of the CFO's special project. Comment on how the decision to capitalize amounts, which were initially recorded as operating expenses, has affected the level of earnings from operations in each quarter.

(amounts in millions of U.S. dollars)	Q1 Year 1 (March 31) With Entries	Q1 Year 1 (March 31) Without Entries	Q2 Year 1 (June 30) With Entries	Q2 Year 1 (June 30) Without Entries	Q3 Year 1 (September 30) With Entries	Q3 Year 1 (September 30) Without Entries	Q4 Year 1 (December 31) With Entries	Q4 Year 1 (December 31) Without Entries	Q1 Year 2 (March 31) With Entries	Q1 Year 2 (March 31) Without Entries
Property and equipment, net	$38,614	$	$35,982	$	$38,151	$	$38,809	$	$39,155	$
Sales revenues	8,825	8,825	8,910	8,910	8,966	8,966	8,478	8,478	8,120	8,120
Operating expenses	7,628		8,526		7,786		7,725		7,277	
Earnings from operations	1,197		384		1,180		753		843	

2. Using the publicly reported numbers (which include the special journal entries that you recorded), compute the fixed asset turnover ratio (rounded to two decimal places) for the periods ended Q2–Q4 of year 1 and Q1 of year 2. What does the trend in this ratio suggest to you? Is this consistent with the changes in earnings from operations reported by the company?

3. Before your meeting with the vice-president for internal audit, you think about the above computations and the variety of peculiar circumstances surrounding the "special project" for the CFO. What in particular might have raised your suspicion about the real nature of your work?

4. Your meeting with internal audit was short and unpleasant. The vice-president indicated that she had discussed her findings with the CFO before meeting with you. The CFO claimed that he too had noticed the peculiar trend in the fixed asset turnover ratio, but that he had not had a chance to investigate it further. He urged internal audit to get to the bottom of things, suggesting that perhaps someone might be making unapproved journal entries. Internal audit had identified you as the source of the journal entries and had been unable to find any documents that approved or substantiated the entries. She ended the meeting by advising you to find a good lawyer. Given your current circumstances, describe how you would have acted earlier had you been able to foresee where it might lead you.

5. In the real case on which this one is based, the internal auditors agonized over the question of whether they had actually uncovered a fraud or whether they were jumping to the wrong conclusion. The *Wall Street Journal* mentioned this on October 30, 2002, by stating, "it was clear . . . that their findings would be devastating for the company. They worried about whether their revelations would result in layoffs. Plus, they feared that they would somehow end up being blamed for the mess." Beyond the personal consequences mentioned in this quote, describe other potential ways in which the findings of the internal auditors would likely be devastating for the publicly traded company and those associated with it.

WorldCom Verizon   *Epilogue:* This case is based on a fraud committed at WorldCom (now called Verizon). The case draws its numbers, the nature of the unsupported journal entries, and the CFO's role in carrying out the fraud from a report issued by WorldCom's bankruptcy examiner. Year 1 in this case was actually 2001 and year 2 was 2002. This case excludes other fraudulent activities that contributed to WorldCom's $11 billion fraud. The 63-year-old CEO was sentenced to 25 years in prison for planning and executing the biggest fraud in the history of American business. The CFO, who cooperated in the investigation of the CEO, was sentenced to five years in prison.

FINANCIAL REPORTING AND ANALYSIS TEAM PROJECT

LO3, 7   CP9–10

Team Project: Analyzing Long-Lived Assets

As a team, select an industry to analyze. A list of companies classified by industry can be obtained by accessing **www.fpinfomart.ca** and then choosing "Companies by Industry." You can also find a list of industries and companies within each industry via **http://ca.finance.yahoo.com/investing** (click on "Order Annual Reports" under "Tools").

Each group member should acquire the annual report for a different publicly traded company in the industry. (Library files, the SEDAR service at **www.sedar.com**, and the company's website are good sources.)

Required:

On an individual basis, each team member should then write a short report answering the following questions about the selected company. Discuss any patterns across the companies that you as a team observe. Then, as a group, write a short report comparing and contrasting your companies.

1. List the accounts and amounts of the company's long-lived assets (land, buildings, equipment, intangible assets, natural resources, and other).
   a. What is the percentage of each to total assets?
   b. What do the results of your analysis suggest about the strategy your company has followed with respect to investing in long-lived assets?
2. What cost allocation method(s) and estimates does the company use for each type of long-lived asset?
3. Compute the approximate average remaining useful life of property, plant, and equipment overall.
4. What does the company disclose regarding asset impairment? What was its impairment loss, if any, in the most recent year?
5. Perform a ratio analysis:
   a. What does the fixed asset turnover ratio measure in general?
   b. Compute the ratio for the last three years.
   c. What do your results suggest about the company?
   d. If available, find the industry ratio for the most recent year, compare it to your results, and discuss why you believe your company differs from or is similar to the industry ratio.
6. What was the effect of depreciation expense on cash flows from operating activities? Compute the ratio of depreciation expense to cash flows from operating activities for each of the past three years.
7. Refer to the statement of cash flows and identify the capital expenditures that the company made over the last three years. Did the company sell any long-lived assets?

SOLUTIONS TO SELF-STUDY QUIZZES

Self-Study Quiz 9-1

1. (Amounts in thousands)

Property, Plant, and Equipment (PPE)	
Acquisition cost	$1,800,000
Transportation	8,000
Installation	1,300
Total	$1,809,300

The maintenance contracts are not necessary for making the assets ready for use and therefore are not included in the acquisition cost.

2. (Amounts in thousands)

	Assets	Liabilities		Shareholders' Equity	
a. PPE	+ 1,809,300	Note payable	+ 1,266,510		
Cash	− 542,790				
b. PPE	+ 1,809,300			Share capital	+ 1,050,000
Cash	− 759,300				

Self-Study Quiz 9-2

1. Capitalize
2. Expense
3. Expense
4. Capitalize

Self-Study Quiz 9-3

1. ($240,000 − $30,000) × 1/6 = $35,000
2. ($240,000 − 0) × 2/6 = $80,000
3. [($240,000 − $30,000) ÷ 50,000] × 8,000 = $33,600

Self-Study Quiz 9-4

$50,000 (carrying amount after 5 years) ÷ 2 years (remaining life) = $25,000 depreciation expense per year.

Self-Study Quiz 9-5

1. Depreciation expense (E)	71,000	
Accumulated depreciation—aircraft (XA) ...		71,000
2. Cash (A)	2,500,000	
Accumulated depreciation—aircraft (XA)	295,000	
Gain on sale of asset (+Gain, +SE)		195,000
Aircraft (A)		2,600,000

Reporting and Interpreting Current Liabilities

After studying this chapter, you should be able to do the following:

LEARNING OBJECTIVES

LO1 Define, measure, and report current liabilities.

LO2 Compute and interpret the quick ratio.

LO3 Compute and interpret the trade payables turnover ratio.

LO4 Report notes payable, and explain the time value of money.

LO5 Report contingent liabilities and commitments.

LO6 Explain the importance of working capital and its impact on cash flows.

FOCUS COMPANY: **Bauer Performance Sports**

MANAGING CAPITAL STRUCTURE

Bauer Performance Sports Ltd. (www.bauerperformancesports.com) is a publicly traded company on the Toronto Stock Exchange (TSX) whose affiliates are leaders in the development, design, manufacture, marketing, and distribution of hockey, roller hockey, and lacrosse equipment and related apparel. Founded in Kitchener, Ontario, in 1927, Bauer Hockey designed the first ice skate with the blade attached to the boot in 1933. Bauer Hockey was acquired by Nike Inc. in 1995 and then split into an independent company in 2008; Bauer Performance Sports Ltd. (Bauer Hockey's parent company) began trading on the TSX on March 10, 2011. Bauer's products are sold in over 45 countries through a global distribution network of more than 3,700 retailers. Products are manufactured in facilities located worldwide.

The company has stated that 90 percent of all players in the National Hockey League (NHL) wore at least one piece of Bauer hockey equipment during the 2011–12 season. It is a brand leader in every product category, from helmets to hockey sticks, with a global market share exceeding 50 percent. It is a successful company that increased its sales from US$220 million for fiscal year 2008 to US$375 million for fiscal year 2012.

In addition to operating activities, management must focus on a number of critical financing activities to ensure that the company remains profitable and is able to generate sufficient resources to meet its goals. The financing activities for Bauer generate funds to serve two important purposes: (1) to finance the current operating activities of the business and (2) to acquire long-lived assets that permit the company to grow in the future.

UNDERSTANDING THE BUSINESS

Businesses finance the acquisition of their assets from two sources: funds supplied by creditors (debt) and funds provided by owners (equity). The mixture of debt and equity used by a business to finance its short- and long-term operating requirements is called its **capital structure**. In addition to selecting a capital structure, management can select from a variety of sources when borrowing money, as illustrated in the liabilities section of the statement of financial position of Bauer in Exhibit 10.1.

In deciding how best to finance its projects, Bauer's management must consider two key factors: the financial risk associated with the source of financing and the return to shareholders on their investment in the company. From the firm's perspective, debt capital is riskier than equity, because interest and principal payments on debt are legal obligations that must be paid. If a company cannot meet a required debt payment because of a temporary cash shortage, creditors may force the company into bankruptcy and require the sale of assets to satisfy the debt obligations. As with any business transaction, borrowers and lenders attempt to negotiate the most favourable terms possible. Managers devote considerable effort to analyzing alternative funding arrangements.

In contrast, dividend payments to shareholders are not legal obligations until declared by the board of directors. Therefore, equity offers lower financial risk to the issuing corporation. While companies may suspend or reduce the amount of dividends during periods of financial difficulty, they may not suspend the payment of principal and interest owed to creditors without negative consequences.

Companies that include debt in their capital structure must also make strategic decisions concerning the proper balance between short-term and long-term debt. To evaluate a company's capital structure, financial analysts calculate a number of accounting ratios. In this chapter, we primarily discuss current (short-term) liabilities, as well as some important accounting ratios. We will also introduce present value concepts in Appendix 10B. In the next chapter, we discuss special types of long-term debt.

CAPITAL STRUCTURE is the mixture of debt and equity that finances the short- and long-term operating requirements of a company.

BAUER PERFORMANCE SPORTS LTD.
Consolidated Statements of Financial Position (Partial)
(in thousands of U.S. dollars)

	May 31, 2012	May 31, 2011
Liabilities		
Current liabilities		
Debt (Note 17)	$ 9,195	$ 27,721
Trade and other payables	24,126	33,519
Accrued liabilities (Note 18)	27,387	24,017
Provisions (Note 19)	1,735	819
Income taxes payable	551	629
Current portion of other liabilities (Note 20, 25)	416	7,752
Total current liabilities	**63,410**	**94,457**
Non-current liabilities		
Debt (Note 17)	126,927	120,948
Provisions (Note 19)	429	580
Retirement benefit obligations (Note 20)	5,348	5,283
Other non-current liabilities (Note 21, 25)	16	5,375
Total non-current liabilities	**132,720**	**132,186**
Total liabilities	**$196,130**	**$226,643**

Source: Bauer Performance Sports Ltd., Annual Report 2012.

Exhibit **10.1**
Liabilities of Bauer Performance Sports Ltd.

REAL-WORLD EXCERPT

Bauer Performance Sports Ltd.

ANNUAL REPORT

ORGANIZATION OF THE CHAPTER

Liabilities Defined and Classified	Current Liabilities	Contingent Liabilities and Commitments	Working Capital Management

| • Quick Ratio | • Trade Payables
• Trade Payables Turnover Ratio
• Accrued Liabilities
• Notes Payable
• Current Portion of Long-Term Debt
• Deferred Revenues
• Provisions Reported on the Statement of Financial Position | | |

Supplemental material:

Appendix 10A: Deferred Income Tax Assets and Liabilities

Appendix 10B: Present Value Concepts

Appendix 10C: Present Value Tables

Appendix 10D: Present Value Computations Using Excel (on *Connect*)

Appendix 10E: Future Value Concepts (on *Connect*)

LO¹

Define, measure, and report current liabilities.

LIABILITIES are debts or obligations arising from past transactions that will be paid with assets or services.

LIABILITIES DEFINED AND CLASSIFIED

Most people have a reasonable understanding of the definition of the word *liability*. Accountants formally define **liabilities** as debts or obligations arising from an entity's past transactions that will be paid with assets or services. As Exhibit 10.1 shows, Bauer reported current and non-current liabilities of US$196,130,000 at May 31, 2012. Bauer has borrowed money in the past from creditors and purchased goods and services on credit (past transactions), promising its creditors to pay cash (an asset) at some point in the future, based on the terms of its debt agreements.

When a liability is first recorded, it is measured in terms of its current cash equivalent, which is the cash amount that a creditor would accept to settle the liability immediately. Although Bauer had current and non-current debt of US$136,122,000 as at May 31, 2012, it will repay much more than that, because the company must also pay interest on the debt. Interest payable in the future is not included in the amount of the liability because it accrues and becomes a liability with the passage of time. For fiscal year 2012, the company reported US$9,029,000 of interest expense in the notes to its financial statements, but it paid US$7,388,000 as reported on its statement of cash flows. The difference of US$1,641,000 represents a liability that must be paid in the future.

Like most businesses, Bauer has several kinds of liabilities and a wide range of creditors. The list of liabilities on the statement of financial position differs from one company to the next, because different operating activities result in different types of liabilities. The liability section of Bauer's statement of financial position begins with the caption "Current liabilities." **Current liabilities** are defined as short-term obligations that will be paid within the current operating cycle of the business or within one year of the statement of financial position date, whichever is longer. Because most companies have an operating cycle that is shorter than one year, current liabilities can normally be defined simply as liabilities that are due within one year. Non-current liabilities include all other liabilities.

CURRENT LIABILITIES are short-term obligations that will be paid within the normal operating cycle or one year, whichever is longer.

Information about current liabilities is very important to managers and analysts because these obligations must be paid in the near future. Companies that do not settle their current obligations in a timely manner quickly find that suppliers of goods and services may not be prepared to grant them credit for their purchases, and may be forced to seek short-term financing through banks. Analysts say that a company has **liquidity** if it has the ability to pay its current obligations. A number of financial ratios are useful in evaluating liquidity, including the current ratio (discussed in Chapter 2) and the quick ratio. The quick ratio is a conservative measure of liquidity, comparing only the most liquid assets (cash, short-term investments, and net receivables) to current liabilities. In contrast, the current ratio includes all current assets in the numerator of the ratio.

LIQUIDITY is the ability to pay current obligations.

QUICK RATIO

KEY RATIO ANALYSIS

ANALYTICAL QUESTION → Does the company currently have the resources to pay its short-term debt?

RATIO AND COMPARISONS → Analysts use the *quick ratio* as an indicator of the amount of quick assets (cash, short-term investments, and net receivables) available to satisfy current liabilities. It is computed as follows:

LO²

Compute and interpret the quick ratio.

Quick Ratio = Quick Assets ÷ Current Liabilities

The 2012 ratio for Bauer Performance Sports Ltd. is

US$108,589,000 ÷ US$63,410,000 = 1.71

Comparisons over Time			Comparisons with Competitors	
Bauer			**Nike**	**Adidas***
2010	**2011**	**2012**	**2012**	**2011**
1.16	1.07	1.71	1.82	0.73

*The fiscal years of both Bauer and Nike end on May 31, whereas that of Adidas ends on December 31. The ratio for Adidas is based on fiscal year 2011 instead of 2012, because it includes seven months of 2011 compared to five months of 2012.

INTERPRETATIONS

In General → A high ratio normally suggests good liquidity, but too high a ratio suggests inefficient use of resources. Many strong companies use sophisticated management techniques to minimize funds invested in current assets, and as a result, have quick ratios that are very low.

Focus Company Analysis → Bauer's quick ratio for 2012 indicates that the company has US$1.71 to pay each US$1.00 in current liabilities. The increase in the quick ratio from 2010 to 2012 is the result of an increase in net receivables due to a higher level of sales. In comparison to Bauer's ratio, Nike's ratio is slightly higher but Adidas's is much lower.

A Few Cautions → The quick ratio may be a misleading measure of liquidity because it can be influenced by small variations in the flow of transactions. The repayment of a large bank loan could have a big impact on the ratio. Analysts recognize that managers can manipulate the quick ratio by engaging in particular types of transactions just before the close of the fiscal year. For example, the quick ratio can be improved by paying creditors immediately prior to the preparation of financial statements.

PAUSE FOR FEEDBACK

Companies incur current liabilities that require settlement within a short period of time. These liabilities are usually settled through cash payments. The quick ratio indicates whether quick assets are sufficient to pay current liabilities. Before you move on, complete the following questions to test your understanding of this ratio.

Liabilities are very important from an analytical perspective because they affect a company's future cash flows and risk characteristics. Current liabilities are usually grouped according to type of creditor, separating liabilities owed to trade suppliers and other creditors (trade and other payables) from those owed to banks (short-term borrowings), providers of services (accrued liabilities), governments (taxes payable), and others. For many types of liabilities, the amount of the debt is determined based on contractual agreements between the company and suppliers of goods, services, or funds. Most of these liabilities are recorded as they occur during the accounting period, as in the case of trade payables for merchandise purchases, loans from banks, and notes payable to creditors. However, specific liabilities that can be determined with accuracy, such as salaries payable and interest payable, require accrual through adjusting entries at the end of the accounting period prior to the preparation of financial statements.

For other types of liabilities, the exact amounts will not be known with certainty until a future event, but they must be estimated and recorded if they relate to transactions that occurred during the accounting period. For example, a liability for a product warranty will not be known until the repair work is carried out in the future. But the matching process requires that warranty costs be recognized as an expense during the same period in which the product was sold. Because these costs and the related liability are not known, they must be estimated based on past experience or some reasonable basis and recorded through adjusting entries. Most often, the estimate of future warranty costs is based on a percentage of net sales.

In particular cases, it may not be possible to provide a reasonable estimate of a potential future liability that is contingent on a future event. Relevant information about contingent liabilities must therefore be disclosed in notes to the financial statements.

CURRENT LIABILITIES

Many current liabilities have a direct relationship to the operating activities of a business. In other words, specific operating activities are financed, in part, by a related current liability. Some examples from Bauer's annual report (Exhibit 10.1) are as follows:

Operating Activity		Current Liability
Purchase hockey apparel	→	Trade payables
Advertise company products in various media	→	Accrued liabilities
Service performed by employees	→	Accrued liabilities
Provide warranty on products sold	→	Provisions

By understanding the relationship between operating activities and current liabilities, an analyst can easily explain changes in the various current liability accounts.

We will now discuss the current liability accounts that are found on most statements of financial position.

Trade Payables

Most companies do not produce all the goods and services they use in their basic operations. Instead, they purchase goods and services from other businesses. Typically, these transactions are made on credit, with cash payments occurring after the goods and services have been provided. As a result, these transactions create *trade payables*, also called trade accounts payable.

For many companies, trade credit is a relatively inexpensive way to finance the purchase of inventory, because interest does not normally accrue on trade payables. As an incentive to encourage more sales, some vendors may offer very generous credit terms that may allow the buyer to resell merchandise and collect cash before payment must be made to the original vendor. For example, Apple Inc. maintains an efficient cash management system by collecting cash from its credit customers before it pays its trade suppliers. In fiscal year 2012, Apple collected cash from customers within 19 days, on average, but waited 74 days to pay its trade suppliers.

Some managers may be tempted to delay payment to suppliers for as long as possible to conserve cash. Normally, this strategy is not advisable. Most successful companies develop positive working relationships with their suppliers to ensure that they receive quality goods and services. Managers can destroy good supplier relationships if they are slow to pay. In addition, financial analysts become concerned if a business does not meet its obligations to trade creditors on a timely basis because delayed payment often indicates that the company is experiencing financial difficulties. Both managers and analysts use the trade payables turnover ratio to evaluate effectiveness in managing payables.

TRADE PAYABLES TURNOVER RATIO

KEY RATIO
ANALYSIS

ANALYTICAL QUESTION → How efficient is management at meeting its obligations to suppliers?

RATIO AND COMPARISONS → The *trade payables turnover ratio* is a measure of how quickly management is paying trade creditors. Analysts use this ratio as a measure of liquidity. It is computed as follows:

LO3

Compute and interpret the trade payables turnover ratio.

Trade Payables Turnover Ratio = Cost of Sales ÷ Average Net Trade Payables

The 2012 ratio for Bauer Performance Sports Ltd. is

US$232,121 ÷ US$28,822.5* = 8.05

*(US$33,519 + US$24,126) ÷ 2 = US$28,822.5

In reality, the numerator of this ratio should be net credit purchases, not cost of sales. Because credit purchases are not usually reported in financial statements, we use total purchases of merchandise inventory as a rough approximation, assuming that all purchases are made on credit. For merchandising companies, we compute purchases by adjusting the cost of sales for the change in inventory during the period as follows:[1]

Purchases = Cost of Sales + Ending Inventory − Beginning Inventory

For Bauer, purchases for fiscal year 2012 equal US$225,099, and the trade payables turnover ratio for 2012 would have decreased to 7.81 if the amount of purchases was substituted for cost of sales in the numerator. The decrease in the ratio from 8.05 to 7.81 is not significant. For most companies, inventories do not change significantly over time; hence, the cost of sales can be used instead of purchases in computing this ratio.

Comparisons over Time				Comparisons with Competitors	
Bauer				**Nike**	**Adidas**
2010	**2011**	**2012**		**2012**	**2011**
8.55	7.47	8.05		8.93	16.76

If Bauer's trade payables are turned over 8.05 times per year or 365 days, how many days would be needed, on average, to turn these payables once? This is known as the *average age of payables* and is computed by dividing 8.05 into 365 days:

$$\text{Average Age of Payables} = 365 \div \text{Average Trade Payables}$$

Bauer's average age of payables for 2012 is

$$\text{365 Days} \div 8.05 = \text{45.3 Days}$$

INTERPRETATIONS

In General → A high turnover ratio normally suggests that a company is paying its suppliers in a timely manner.

Focus Company Analysis → The trade payables turnover ratio for Bauer has decreased over the past three years, from 8.55 in 2010 to 8.05 in 2012. Bauer's 2012 ratio is lower than those of its competitors, which may indicate that Bauer is more aggressive than both Nike and Adidas in its cash management policy. By conserving cash (with slower payments to suppliers), the company is able to minimize the amount of money it must borrow and pay back with interest.

A Few Cautions → The trade payables turnover ratio is an average associated with all trade payables. The ratio might not reflect reality if a company pays some creditors on time but is late with others. The ratio is also subject to manipulation. Managers could be late with payments to creditors during the entire year but catch up at year-end so that the ratio is at an acceptable level. As our focus company analysis indicates, a low ratio can indicate either liquidity problems (i.e., the company is not able to generate sufficient cash to meet its obligations) or aggressive cash management (i.e., the company maintains only the minimum amount of cash necessary to support its operating activities). The first is a problem; the second is a strength. Analysts would have to study other factors, such as the quick ratio and the amount of cash flows generated from operating activities, to determine which is the case.

Accrued Liabilities

ACCRUED LIABILITIES are expenses that have been incurred but have not been paid at the end of the accounting period.

In many situations, a business incurs an expense in one accounting period and makes cash payment for the expense in a subsequent period. **Accrued liabilities** are expenses that have been incurred before the end of an accounting period but have not yet been paid. These expenses include such items as employee salaries and wages, rent, interest, and income taxes. They are recorded as adjusting entries at year-end.

Income Taxes Payable   Like individuals, corporations must pay tax at the appropriate federal and provincial rates on income from active business operations, property income, and capital gains arising from the sale of assets. Federal income tax rates change over time because of changes in governmental tax policies, and provincial income tax rates vary across Canadian provinces. In general, the combined corporate income tax rate is in the range of 30 to 35 percent.

Bauer reported an income tax expense of US$13,122,000 for 2012, as shown in the following excerpt from its consolidated statement of income:

BAUER PERFORMANCE SPORTS LTD.
Consolidated Statement of Income
For the Years Ended May 31

(in thousands of U.S. dollars)	2012	2011
Income before income tax expense	43,305	796
Income taxes (Note 16)	(13,122)	(366)
Net income	30,183	430
Excerpt from Note 16—Income Taxes		
Current	(414)	394
Deferred	13,536	(28)
Income taxes reported on the statement of income	13,122	366

Source: Bauer Performance Sports Ltd., Annual Report 2012.

Notice that the income tax expense for each year has two components: a current portion and a deferred portion. The current portion is payable within prescribed time limits, but the deferred portion arises because of differences between the accounting rules used for financial reporting and the tax rules corporations must use to determine their taxable income, as explained in Chapter 9.[2]

Taxes Other than Income Taxes In addition to paying taxes on income, companies are often required to collect and pay other types of taxes and fees, depending on the specific industry and geographical location in which they operate. These taxes add to the cost of producing and selling goods and services and are eventually passed on to customers through higher sales prices.[3] Typically, the prices of goods and services are increased by the federal Goods and Services Tax (GST), currently set at 5 percent, and a Provincial Sales Tax (PST) that varies between 0 and 10 percent, depending on the province, or a combined federal and provincial sales tax called the Harmonized Sales Tax (HST).[4]

The GST and PST, or HST, amounts are added to the sales price, collected from customers, and then remitted to the federal and provincial governments. In this respect, the seller acts as an intermediary between the customer and the federal and provincial governments and facilitates the collection of sales taxes from customers. When a company sells goods and services, the applicable sales taxes, if any, are added to the sales price, but they are not revenue for the seller. The sales taxes collected from customers represent liabilities that are remitted periodically (monthly or quarterly) to the respective governments. For example, if Bauer had a retail outlet in British Columbia and sold apparel to a customer for $40, the total cash paid by the customer includes a GST of $2.00 ($40 × 5%) and a PST of $2.80 ($40 × 7%). The journal entry to record this transaction, and the transaction effects, are as follows:

Cash (A)	44.80	
Sales revenue (R)		40.00
GST payable (L)		2.00
PST payable (L)		2.80

Assets		=	Liabilities		+	Shareholders' Equity	
Cash	+44.80		GST payable	+2.00		Sales revenue	+40.00
			PST payable	+2.80			

All of the GST and PST collected from customers is accumulated in these two liability accounts and then remitted to the federal and provincial governments on a monthly or quarterly basis. The unpaid amounts at year-end are included in current liabilities.

PAUSE FOR FEEDBACK

Customers are required to pay sales taxes on most of the goods and services they acquire. They pay these taxes to the companies that sell these goods and services. Companies serve as agents of the federal and provincial governments in collecting these taxes and then remitting them to the government authorities. Before you move on, complete the following question to test your understanding of sales taxes.

SELF-STUDY QUIZ 10-2

Assume that the sale of apparel for $40 cash was made in a Bauer store located in Toronto, where sales of apparel are subject to a harmonized sales tax of 13 percent. Prepare the journal entry to record the sale transaction.

After you complete your answer, check it with the solution at the end of the chapter.

Payroll Liabilities   At the end of each accounting period, employees will usually have earned salaries that have not been paid. Unpaid salaries may be reported as a separate item or as part of accrued liabilities, as is the case with Bauer. In addition to reporting salaries that have been earned but are unpaid, companies must also report the cost of unpaid benefits, which include retirement programs, vacation time, employment insurance, health insurance, and many others. Employers must also remit income tax and other social benefit contributions on behalf of their employees to the appropriate government agencies. While we will look at only the three largest deductions for most people, reporting is similar for each type of payroll tax.

Employee Deductions   Federal and provincial laws require the employer to deduct an appropriate amount of income tax each period from the gross earnings of each employee. Employee income tax is usually the largest amount withheld from wages and salaries by the employer. The amount of income tax withheld from the employee's salary is recorded by the employer as a current liability between the date of deduction and the date on which the amount held is remitted to the government. If you have been employed and received a pay cheque, you have probably noticed that additional amounts were deducted from your gross earnings for Employment Insurance (EI); for contributions to the Canada Pension Plan (CPP), or Quebec Pension Plan (QPP) in the province of Quebec; for future retirement benefits; for health insurance; and for other contributions that you and your employer must remit to the appropriate agencies.

In general, employers match the employee's CPP remittance, but they are required by Canada Revenue Agency to pay $1.40 for every $1.00 remitted by the employee for EI. Other deductions, such as union dues and workers' compensation, depend on the terms of employment and will result in a future obligation for the employer to remit these amounts to the legal recipient. In total, the employer's share of contributions remitted by a corporation on behalf of its employees to other parties can add up to 20 percent of the employee's gross earnings.

Compensation expense for employee services includes all funds earned by the employee as well as funds that must be paid to others on behalf of employees (i.e., benefits). To illustrate, let us assume that Bauer's Canadian operations accumulated the following information in their detailed payroll records for the first two weeks of January 2014:

Salaries and wages earned	$1,800,000
Income taxes withheld	450,000
CPP contributions	71,000
EI contributions	35,000

The entry to record the payroll and employee deductions, and the related transaction effects, follow:

Compensation expense (E)			1,800,000	
Liability for income taxes withheld (L)				450,000
CPP payable (L)				71,000
EI payable (L)				35,000
Cash (A)				1,244,000

Assets		=	Liabilities		+	Shareholders' Equity	
Cash	−1,244,000		Liability for income taxes withheld	+450,000		Compensation expense	−1,800,000
			CPP payable	+71,000			
			EI payable	+35,000			

The employer must also contribute an equal amount of CPP contributions and 1.40 times the employees' contributions to EI. The second entry records the taxes that employers must pay from their own funds:

Compensation expense (E)			120,000	
CPP payable (L)				71,000
EI payable (L)				49,000

Assets		=	Liabilities		+	Shareholders' Equity	
			CPP payable	+71,000		Compensation expense	−120,000
			EI payable	+49,000			

The compensation expense ($1,800,000 + $120,000) includes salaries and wages earned, as well as the employer's share of CPP and EI contributions. The cash paid to employees ($1,244,000) is less than the total amount earned ($1,800,000) because the employer must withhold both income taxes ($450,000) and the employees' share of CPP and EI contributions ($106,000). The CPP and EI payable reflect both the employees' share and the employer's share.

The current liabilities of Bauer include US$27,387,000 in accrued liabilities. The various items that make up this amount are disclosed in Note 18 to the company's financial statements for 2012.

REAL-WORLD EXCERPT

Bauer Performance Sports Ltd.

ANNUAL REPORT

18. ACCRUED LIABILITIES

Accrued liabilities include the following:

(thousands of U.S. dollars)	May 31, 2012	May 31, 2011
Accrued payroll and related costs, excluding taxes	$12,437	$10,637
Accrued advertising and volume rebate	6,086	5,392
Accrued legal fees	1,068	463
Accrued endorsements and royalties	966	595
Customer credit balances	407	2,176
Acquisition contingent consideration	2,228	−
Other	4,195	4,754
Total	$27,387	$24,017

Source: Bauer Performance Sports Ltd., Annual Report 2012.

Notes Payable

LO4

Report notes payable, and explain the time value of money.

Most companies need to borrow money to finance their operations. When a company borrows money, a formal written contract is usually prepared. Obligations supported by these written notes are typically called *notes payable*. A note payable

The **TIME VALUE OF MONEY** is interest that is associated with the use of money over time.

specifies the amount borrowed, the date by which it must be paid, and the interest rate associated with the borrowing.

Creditors are willing to lend cash because they will earn interest as compensation for giving up the use of their money for a period. This simple concept, called the **time value of money**, is interest that is associated with the use of money over time. The longer the borrowed money is held, the larger is the dollar amount of interest expense. Interest at a given interest rate on a two-year loan is more than interest on a one-year loan. To the *borrower*, interest is an expense; to the *creditor*, interest is revenue.

To calculate interest, three variables must be considered: (1) the principal (i.e., the cash that was borrowed), (2) the annual interest rate, and (3) the time period for the loan. The interest formula is

$$\textbf{Interest} = \textbf{Principal} \times \textbf{Annual Interest Rate} \times \textbf{Time}$$

To illustrate the accounting for a note payable, assume that on November 1, 2014, Bauer borrowed US$100,000 cash on a one-year, 6 percent note payable. The interest is payable on April 30, 2015, and October 31, 2015. The principal is payable at the maturity date of the note, October 31, 2015. The note is recorded in the accounts as follows:

Cash (A)			100,000	
Note payable, short term (L)				100,000

Assets	=	Liabilities	+	Shareholders' Equity
Cash +100,000		Notes payable +100,000		

Interest on this note is incurred as long as the debt is outstanding. Interest expense is recorded when it is incurred rather than when the cash is actually paid. Because the company uses the money for two months during 2014, it records interest expense in 2014 for two months, even though cash is not paid until April 30.

The computation of interest expense for 2014 is as follows:

$$\textbf{Interest} = \textbf{Principal} \times \textbf{Annual Interest Rate} \times \textbf{Time}$$

$$\textbf{Interest} = \textbf{US\$100,000} \times \textbf{6\%} \times \textbf{2/12} = \textbf{US\$1,000}$$

Note that interest expense is calculated for a specific accounting period, which varies from one month up to one year. The entry to record interest expense on December 31, 2014, is as follows:

Interest expense (E)			1,000	
Interest payable (L)				1,000

Assets	=	Liabilities	+	Shareholders' Equity
		Interest payable +1,000		Interest expense −1,000

On April 30, 2015, Bauer would pay US$3,000 in interest, which includes the US$1,000 accrued and reported in 2014, plus the US$2,000 interest accrued in the first four months of 2015. The following journal entry would be made:

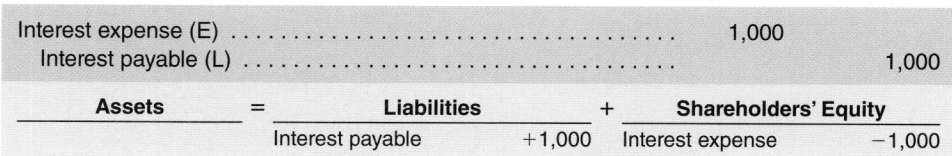

Interest expense (E)			2,000	
Interest payable (L)			1,000	
Cash (A)				3,000

Assets	=	Liabilities	+	Shareholders' Equity
Cash −3,000		Interest payable −1,000		Interest expense −2,000

When a company borrows money from a creditor, it must pay interest on the amount borrowed. Interest is incurred over time, and the amount payable depends on the amount borrowed, the interest rate, and how long the loan was outstanding. Before you move on, complete the following questions to test your understanding of this concept.

SELF-STUDY QUIZ 10-3

In the previous example, we assumed that the US$100,000 note payable by Bauer required payment of interest on April 30 and October 31. Assume that the note required payment of interest on January 31 and July 31.

1. What adjusting entry should Bauer make at May 31, 2015, the end of its fiscal year?

2. What entry should the company make on July 31, 2015?

3. What entry should the company make on January 31, 2016?

After you complete your answers, check them with the solutions at the end of the chapter.

Current Portion of Long-Term Debt

The distinction between current and long-term debt is important for both managers and analysts. Because current debt must be paid within the next year, companies must have sufficient cash to repay currently maturing debt. To provide accurate information concerning current liabilities, a company must reclassify long-term debt within a year of its maturity date as a current liability. Assume that Bauer signed a note payable of US$5 million on June 1, 2013. Repayment is required on May 31, 2016. The statements of financial position at May 31, 2014 and 2015, would report the following:

May 31, 2014

Non-current liabilities	
Note payable	US$5,000,000

May 31, 2015

Current liabilities	
Current portion of long-term note	US$5,000,000

An example of this type of disclosure can be seen in Exhibit 10.1. Notice that Bauer reported US$9,195,000 as the current portion of debt at May 31, 2012. This portion is payable in full during fiscal year 2013. In some cases, companies will refinance debt when it comes due rather than pay out cash currently on hand.

Deferred Revenues

In most business transactions, cash is paid after the product or service has been delivered. In some cases, cash is paid before delivery. You have probably bought a gift card from a store and given it to a friend for a special occasion. The card seller collects money from you before your friend uses the gift card. When a company collects cash before the related revenue has been earned, the cash received represents **deferred revenue**.

For example, Sears Canada Inc., which offers a broad range of merchandise from apparel and home fashions to appliances through many department stores and online, also sells extended warranty services on the products it sells. Should the product break down, Sears will provide repair services within its contractual obligations. More frequently, however, the product will function properly and no service is required. Sears initially

DEFERRED REVENUES are revenues that have been collected but not earned; they are liabilities until the goods or services are provided.

defers revenue from selling extended warranties and then recognizes revenue from the sale of extended warranties gradually over the duration of the contracts or when the service is completed. Sears included the following details in a recent annual report:

NOTES TO THE CONSOLIDATED FINANCIAL STATEMENTS

13. Deferred revenue

The components of deferred revenue were as follows:

	Fiscal Year Ended	
(in millions of Canadian dollars):	**February 2, 2013**	**January 28, 2012**
Arising from extended warranty service contracts[i]	$151.5	$144.6
Arising from unshipped sales[ii]	60.9	65.7
Arising from customer loyalty program[iii]	37.7	41.3
Arising from gift card issuances[iv]	25.5	29.1
Arising from vendor partnership agreements[v]	6.5	9.7
Other[vi]	6.1	6.8
Total deferred revenue	$288.2	$297.2
Current	$197.5	$208.0
Non-current	90.7	89.2
Total deferred revenue	$288.2	$297.2

The following explanations describe the Company's deferred revenue:

(i) Deferred revenue arising from the sale of extended warranty service contracts, which provide coverage for product repair services over the term of the contracts.

(ii) Deferred revenue arising from the sale of merchandise which has not yet been delivered to or picked up by the customer. The revenue is recognized once the merchandise is delivered to the customer.

(iii) Deferred revenue arising from the Company's Sears Club loyalty program.

(iv) Deferred revenue arising from the purchase of gift cards by customers that have not yet been redeemed for merchandise. At redemption of the gift card, the revenue is recognized.

(v) Deferred revenue arising from multi-element partnership agreements with vendors. The revenue is recognized in accordance with the terms of the agreements.

(vi) Other includes deferred revenue for goods that have not yet been fully delivered or services not yet rendered. The revenue is recognized when the goods have been delivered or by reference to the stage of completion of the service.

Source: Sears Canada Inc., Annual Report 2012. Used with the permission of Sears Canada Inc.

Deferred revenue is reported as a liability because cash has been collected but the related revenue has not been earned by the end of the accounting period. The obligation to provide the services or goods in the future still exists. These obligations are classified as current or long term, depending on when they must be settled.

The information disclosed in this note indicates that Sears has engaged in transactions that resulted in different types of deferred revenue.

Assume that Sears signed new extended warranty contracts for appliances sold during 2012 and received $81.6 million from customers in advance. The journal entry to record the deferred revenue for these contracts, and related transaction effects, follow:

Cash (A)	81.6	
Deferred extended warranty revenue (L)		81.6

Assets		=	Liabilities	+	Shareholders' Equity
Cash	+81.6		Deferred extended warranty revenue +81.6		

As time passes, Sears earns a portion of the deferred revenue on the new contracts as well as part of the deferred revenue recorded in previous accounting periods.

Assuming that a total of $74.7 million was earned during 2012, the entry to record the earned revenue would be as follows:

Deferred extended warranty revenue (L)	74.7	
Revenue from extended warranties (R)		74.7

Gift cards and prepaid cards have become popular ways of selling merchandise or service for future delivery. These cards are usually purchased as gifts to others for special occasions. When a store sells a gift card, the amount received is a liability until the store delivers merchandise or service in the future. When the recipient of the gift card presents it to the store for redemption, the amount redeemed is recorded as revenue, the deferred revenue account is reduced, and the cost of merchandise given or service rendered is recorded as an expense. Sears sells gift cards throughout the fiscal year, particularly during the end-of-year holiday shopping season. The information disclosed in Note 13 to its annual report for fiscal year 2012 indicates that gift cards worth $25.5 million had not been redeemed by February 2, 2013, but would likely be presented for redemption within a short period of time.

Provisions Reported on the Statement of Financial Position

The liabilities discussed so far reflect specific amounts to be paid to identifiable parties by certain dates. When either the amount or the timing of the liability is uncertain, it is referred to as a **provision**. A provision must be recognized when the following conditions are met: (1) an entity has a present obligation as a result of a past event, (2) it is probable that cash or other assets will be required to settle the obligation, and (3) a reliable estimate can be made of the amount of the obligation. For example, an estimated liability is created when a company offers a warranty with the products it sells. The cost of providing repair work must be estimated and recorded as a liability (and expense) in the period in which the product is sold. Most companies quickly refund money for any defective products that they sell. The following disclosures from Bauer's annual report provide additional information about its provisions, including warranty liabilities:

A PROVISION is a liability of uncertain timing or amount.

REAL-WORLD EXCERPT

Bauer Performance Sports Ltd.
ANNUAL REPORT

NOTES TO CONSOLIDATED FINANCIAL STATEMENTS

4.6 Provisions

Provisions for warranty costs, product recall, restructuring, and onerous contracts are recognized when the Company has a legal or constructive obligation as a result of a past event, it is more likely than not that an outflow of economic benefits will be required to settle the obligation, and the amount can be reliably estimated.

Where the effect of the time value of money is material, the future cash flows expected to be required to settle the obligation are measured at the present value discounted using a current pre-tax rate that reflects the risks specific to the liability. The increase in the provision due to the passage of time is reflected as interest expense.

Warranty provisions, which are recognized when the underlying products are sold, represent the estimated cost of fulfilling the obligation of the Company's general warranty policy in which it warrants its products against manufacturing defects and workmanship. Warranties range from thirty days up to one year from the date sold to the consumer, depending on the type of product. In determining the amount of the provision, the Company considers historical levels of claims, warranty terms and the estimated sell-through to the end consumer.

Product recall provision is recognized when the Company has an obligation to recall a product. The provision represents the estimate of claims expected from consumers and customers and legal and administrative costs.

A provision for restructuring is recognized when the Company has approved a detailed and formal restructuring plan and the restructuring either has commenced or has been announced publicly. Future operating losses are not provided for.

Onerous contracts are contracts where the unavoidable cost of meeting the obligations under the contract exceeds the economic benefit expected to be received under it. A provision is recognized at the lower of the net present value of the cash flows required to fulfill the contract or the cost of settling the obligation.

(*continued*)

19. Provisions

	Warranty	Product recall	Other	Total
Balance May 31, 2011	$ 638	$ 30	$ 731	$ 1,399
Additions	5,405	172	157	5,734
Reversals	–	–	–	–
Utilizations	(4,490)	(189)	(202)	(4,881)
Exchange differences	(52)	–	(36)	(88)
Balance May 31, 2012	$ 1,501	$ 13	$ 650	$ 2,164
Current	$ 1,501	$ 13	$ 221	$ 1,735
Non-current	–	–	429	429
Balance May 31, 2012	$ 1,501	$ 13	$ 650	$ 2,164

Source: Bauer Performance Sports Ltd., Annual Report 2012.

Bauer determines its warranty liability based on number of units sold, historical and anticipated rates of warranty claims on those units, and cost per claim to satisfy Bauer's warranty obligation. Bauer's estimate of the warranty expenses incurrent in fiscal year 2012 as a result of the period's sales is US5,405,000. The journal entry to record the estimated liability at year-end follows:

Warranty expense (E)	5,405,000	
Provision for product warranty (L)		5,405,000

Assets	=	Liabilities		+	Shareholders' Equity	
		Provision for product warranty	+5,405,000		Warranty expense	−5,405,000

When the company receives units that require repair under the warranty, its employees repair the defective product, replace component parts as needed, and return the units to customers. The costs Bauer incurred during fiscal year 2012 to satisfy its warranty obligations total US$4,490,000. Bauer refers to this amount as "utilizations" of the warranty. It is recorded as follows:

Provision for product warranty (L)	4,490,000	
Cash (A)		4,490,000

This journal entry assumes that Bauer paid cash to satisfy the warranty. If the product is exchanged for another one, then the Inventories account is credited instead of Cash. The warranty expense is not affected by the costs incurred under the warranty because the warranty expense is recognized separately, based on the volume of sales made during the fiscal year.

In addition to estimated liabilities for warranties, provisions are usually made for legal and tax disputes that arise in the ordinary course of business; closing of stores or specific operations; and restructuring of production, sales, or administrative structures. Information on provisions for items such as store closures helps potential and existing creditors, investors, and analysts to understand the implications of these liabilities.

A QUESTION OF ACCOUNTABILITY

OVERSTATEMENT OF LIABILITIES AND MANAGEMENT INCENTIVES

The amount of liabilities that companies are expected to pay in the future is not always known with certainty. As we indicated above, estimates of potential liabilities are often made when companies accrue expenses associated with specific accounting periods. The methods of estimating such expenses and liabilities often lead to imprecise amounts of future payments.

The imprecise nature of the estimation process leads to either an overstatement or an understatement of the correct amount of the liability. An overstatement of expenses leads to an understatement of net earnings in the estimation period, and a subsequent overstatement of net earnings in the next accounting period. Occasionally, managers may rely on the inaccurate nature of estimated liabilities to manipulate net earnings in ways that serve their self-interests. For example, the key executives of Nortel, which was one of the top global makers of telecommunication equipment in North America, overstated accrued liabilities during the years 2000 to 2002. In the first quarter of 2003, Nortel's executives reduced the overstated accrued liabilities, which had the effect of turning a loss for that quarter into a net earnings figure. Since the compensation of key executives was related to the company's financial performance, the key executives, who decided to reduce the balance of accrued liabilities in order to increase net earnings, received bonus payments from the company because the reported net earnings figure was sufficiently large to cause a distribution of bonuses to key management personnel. When such an action was later uncovered by auditors, the company's board of directors fired the three top executives who had overall responsibility for the company's financial statements.

CONTINGENT LIABILITIES AND COMMITMENTS

LO5
Report contingent liabilities and commitments.

Most students have an intuition about contingent liabilities. If you believe that failure to study may lead to failing a course, then you understand the concept of contingent liability. The actual failure in a course will be a liability because the student will incur additional costs for repeating the course. A student may not know, however, whether he or she failed the course until the final grade has been reported, but students know that it is possible to fail the course if they do not study. Their actions prior to the final assessment and subsequent reporting of their grades may lead to failure and additional costs, which makes the failure to study a contingent liability.

Each of the liabilities that we have discussed is reported on the statement of financial position with a specific monetary value because each involves the *probable* future sacrifice of economic benefits. Some transactions or events create only a possible (but not probable) future sacrifice of economic benefits. These situations create contingent liabilities, which are possible liabilities that arise from past events and whose existence will be confirmed only by the occurrence or non-occurrence of one or more uncertain future events not entirely under the control of the company. In some cases, it is not probable that cash of other assets will be required to settle the obligation, or the amount of the obligation cannot be measured with sufficient reliability.[5] A **contingent liability** is a possible liability that is created as a result of a past event, and may or may not become a recorded liability, depending on future events.

A **CONTINGENT LIABILITY** is a possible liability that is created as a result of a past event; it is not an effective liability until some future event occurs.

Contingent Liability Examples

Lawsuits   Environmental problems   Tax disputes

Whether a situation produces a provision or a contingent liability depends on two factors: the probability of the future economic sacrifice and the ability of management to estimate the amount of the liability reliably. The following table illustrates the various possibilities when a past event has resulted in a present obligation or a possible obligation that depends on whether specific future events occur or not:

Level of certainty of the present or possible obligation	Should a liability be recognized?	Disclosure requirements
There is a present obligation that probably requires an outflow of resources.		
1. The amount of the liability can be estimated reliably.	A provision must be recognized.	Disclosure of the provision is required.
2. The amount of the liability cannot be estimated reliably.	No provision shall be recognized.	Disclosure is required for the contingency.
There is either a present or a possible obligation that may, but probably will not, require an outflow of resources.	No provision shall be recognized.	Disclosure is required for the contingency.
There is either a present or a possible obligation where the likelihood of an outflow of resources is remote.	No provision shall be recognized.	Disclosure is not required.

The notes to Bauer's financial statements include a note that specifies the type of contingencies that the company may face in the future. The excerpt below provides a list of contingencies that are typical for many companies:

REAL-WORLD EXCERPT

Bauer Performance Sports Ltd.

ANNUAL REPORT

NOTES TO CONSOLIDATED FINANCIAL STATEMENTS

26. COMMITMENTS AND CONTINGENCIES

. . .

Contingencies

. . .

In the ordinary course of its business, the Company is involved in various legal proceedings involving contractual and employment relationships, product liability claims, trademark rights, and a variety of other matters. The Company does not believe there are any pending legal proceedings that will have a material impact on the Company's financial position or results of operations.

Source: Bauer Performance Sports Ltd., Annual Report 2012.

Bauer reported not only its contingent liabilities but also its commitments to pay specific amounts in the future. Commitments reflect contractual agreements to enter into transactions with other parties. Commitments to buy or sell goods and services or to make specific payments are not normally recorded in the accounting system, as long as there is no exchange transaction. Commitments to pay or receive cash are relevant to financial statement users and help them in predicting the company's future cash flows.

The commitments reported by Bauer are specific to companies in this industry and focus on endorsement contracts. Companies such as Bauer, Nike, and Adidas sign multi-year contracts with high-profile athletes such as Henrik Lundqvist, featured on the cover of Bauer's 2012 annual report. The company uses endorsements to promote its products and capture greater market share but is well aware that athletic performance can falter due to strikes and injury. For this reason, Bauer's commitments depend on athletic performance in the future.

REAL-WORLD EXCERPT

Bauer Performance Sports Ltd.

ANNUAL REPORT

NOTES TO CONSOLIDATED FINANCIAL STATEMENTS

26. COMMITMENTS AND CONTINGENCIES

Commitments

The Company enters into endorsement contracts[1] with athletes and sports teams. Amounts of commitments under endorsement contracts are as follows:

	May 31, 2012	May 31, 2011
Less than one year	$3,809	$2,222
Between one and five years	4,151	2,651
More than five years	67	20
Total	$8,027	$4,893

[1]The amounts listed for endorsement contracts represent approximate amounts of base compensation and minimum guaranteed royalty fees the Company is obligated to pay athlete and sport team endorsers of the Company's products. Actual payments under some contracts may be higher than the amounts listed as these contracts provide for bonuses to be paid to the endorsers based upon athletic achievements and/or royalties on product sales in future periods. Actual payments under some contracts may also be lower as these contracts include provisions for reduced payments if athletic performance declines in future periods. In addition to the cash payments, the Company is obligated to furnish the endorsers with products for their use. It is not possible to determine how much the Company will spend on this product on an annual basis as the contracts do not stipulate a specific amount of cash to be spent on the product. The amount of product provided to the endorsers will depend on many factors including general playing conditions, the number of sporting events in which they participate, and the Company's decisions regarding product and marketing initiatives. In addition, the costs to design, develop, source, and purchase the products furnished to the endorsers are incurred over a period of time and are not necessarily tracked separately from similar costs incurred for products sold to customers.

At May 31, 2012, the Company had commitments to purchase inventory of $61,200 and non-inventory of $791.

Source: Bauer Performance Sports Ltd., Annual Report 2012.

WORKING CAPITAL MANAGEMENT

LO6

Explain the importance of working capital and its impact on cash flows.

Working capital is defined as the difference between current assets and current liabilities. It is important to both managers and financial analysts because it has a significant impact on the health and profitability of a company.

WORKING CAPITAL is the difference between current assets and current liabilities.

The working capital accounts are actively managed to achieve a balance between costs and benefits. On the one hand, if a business has too little working capital, it runs the risk of not being able to meet its obligations to creditors. On the other hand, too much working capital may tie up resources in unproductive assets and incur additional costs. Excess inventory, for example, ties up funds that could be invested more profitably elsewhere in the business and incurs additional costs associated with storage and deterioration.

Changes in working capital accounts are also important to managers and analysts because they have a direct impact on the cash flows from operating activities reported on the statement of cash flows.

WORKING CAPITAL AND CASH FLOWS

FOCUS ON
CASH FLOWS

Many working capital accounts have a direct relationship to income-producing activities. Trade receivables, for example, are related to sales revenue: trade receivables increase when sales are made on credit. Cash is collected when the customer pays the bill. Similarly, trade payables increase when an expense is incurred without a cash payment. A cash outflow occurs when the account is paid. Changes in working capital accounts that are related to income-producing activities must be considered when computing cash flows from operating activities.

EFFECT ON THE STATEMENT OF CASH FLOWS

In General → On the statement of cash flows, the net earnings figure is adjusted (under the indirect method) to compute cash flows from operating activities. As explained in Chapter 5, changes in working capital accounts (other than cash) affect cash flows from operations as shown in the following table:

	Effect on Cash Flows
Operating activities (indirect method)	
Net earnings	$xxx
Adjusted for:	
Decreases in current assets* or increases in current liabilities	+
Increases in current assets* or decreases in current liabilities	−
*Other than cash	

Focus Company Analysis → A segment of Bauer's Consolidated Statement of Cash Flows for fiscal year 2012, prepared using the indirect method, follows:

BAUER PERFORMANCE SPORTS LTD.
Consolidated Statement of Cash Flows
(in thousands of U.S. dollars)

	May 31, 2012	May 31, 2011
Operating activities:		
Net income	$ 30,183	$ 430
Adjustments to net income:		
Share-based payment expense (Note 23)	1,318	1,354
Depreciation and amortization	5,470	6,433
Finance costs (Note 11)	16,416	31,281
Finance income (Note 11)	(14,514)	(3,962)
Income tax expense (Note 16)	13,122	366
Bad debt expense (Note 6)	698	377
Loss (gain) on disposal of assets	57	(38)
Loss on early extinguishment of debt (Note 17)	–	2,220
Increase (decrease) in changes in assets and liabilities (excluding the effect of acquisitions):		
Trade and other receivables	(18,076)	(13,243)
Inventories	4,430	(35,336)
Other assets	(2,498)	(1,534)
Trade and other payables	(8,397)	15,776
Accrued and other liabilities	(3,749)	(1,261)
Cash from operating activities	24,460	2,863
Interest paid	(7,388)	(11,865)
Income taxes paid	(2,564)	(3,115)
Income tax refunds received	2,644	252
Net cash from (used in) operating activities	$ 17,152	$(11,865)

Source: Bauer Performance Sports Ltd., Annual Report 2012.

Recall from our previous discussions of the statement of cash flows that revenues and expenses reported on the statement of earnings include both cash and non-cash components, and that changes in working capital accounts (other than cash and cash equivalents) reflect non-cash revenues and expenses during the accounting period. The disclosed information shows that changes in non-cash working capital items decreased cash flows from operating activities by US$28,290,000 in 2012 and US$35,598,000 in 2011. The changes in working capital items help users evaluate how well Bauer is managing the sources and uses of its operating cash flows.

Note also that, instead of adjusting net earnings (net income) for the non-cash components of finance costs and income tax expense, both the finance costs and income tax expense are added back to net earnings, and then the amounts paid for interest and income taxes are deducted from net earnings while income tax refunds received is added to net earnings. Similarly, finance income is deducted from net earnings because the entire amount is non-cash income reflecting unrealized gain on financial assets.

ACCOUNTING STANDARDS FOR PRIVATE ENTERPRISES

Accounting standards for private enterprises do not differ much from IFRS in reporting the common types of current liabilities. Two notable differences in the standards relate to recognition of contingent liabilities and accounting for income taxes.

Financial Reporting Issue	IFRS	ASPE
Recognition of contingent liabilities	A contingent liability is recognized if the occurrence of the future event is both *probable* and measurable. An event is probable if it more likely to occur than not. This leads to the recognition of more contingent liabilities than under ASPE.	A contingent liability is recognized if the occurrence of the future event is both *likely* (that is, highly probable) and measurable.
Accounting for income taxes	Canadian publicly accountable enterprises are required to report both the current and deferred portions of the income taxes that result from differences between IFRS and income tax laws.	Users of the financial statements of Canadian private enterprises remain unconvinced of the incremental value of information conveyed by deferred income taxes. For this reason, Canadian private enterprises may report an income tax expense that simply equals the income tax payable.

DEMONSTRATION CASE

Hull Construction completed several transactions during the year. In each case, decide if a liability should be recorded and, if so, determine the amount. Assume the current date is December 31, 2014. Review Appendix 10A before determining the amount of the liabilities in transactions 5 and 6.

1. Employees earned salaries of $100,000 that have not been paid. This amount included $30,000 of employee income taxes withheld, $4,500 in contributions to the Canada Pension Plan, and $1,500 in Employment Insurance contributions.

2. The company borrowed $100,000 on June 30 at an annual interest rate of 7 percent. No payments associated with this loan have been made.

3. A customer made a $75,000 down payment on a construction project. Work will begin next month.

4. The company lost a lawsuit for $250,000 but plans to appeal.

5. On December 31, 2014, a bank lent money to Hull. The company agreed to repay the bank $100,000 on December 31, 2015. The bank charges an annual interest rate of 5 percent.

6. The company signed a loan agreement that requires it to pay $50,000 per year for 20 years. The annual interest rate is 8 percent.

We strongly recommend that you prepare your own answers to these requirements and then check your answers with the following solution.

SUGGESTED **SOLUTION**

1. Four liability accounts should be increased: liability for income taxes withheld, $30,000; CPP payable, $9,000 ($4,500 + $4,500); EI payable, $3,600 ($1,500 + $1,500 × 1.40); and salaries payable, $64,000 ($100,000 − $30,000 − $4,500 − $1,500).

2. The amount borrowed ($100,000) should be recorded as a liability on June 30. In addition, interest accrued but not paid should be recorded as a liability at year-end. This amount is $100,000 × 7% × 6/12 = $3,500.

3. The customer deposit ($75,000) is a liability until work is performed and the related revenue earned.

4. Most likely, the $250,000 should be recorded as a liability, unless the grounds for appeal significantly reduce the probability that the $250,000 will eventually be paid.

5. A liability should be recorded for the present value of the obligation. The amount is determined by using the present value factor from Table 10C.1 for $n = 1$, $i = 5\%$: $100,000 × 0.9524 = $95,240.

6. A liability should be recorded for the present value of the obligation. The amount is determined by using the present value factor from Table 10C.2 for $n = 20$, $i = 8\%$: $50,000 × 9.8181 = $490,905.

APPENDIX 10A: DEFERRED INCOME TAX ASSETS AND LIABILITIES

In previous chapters, we made simplifying assumptions concerning income tax expense. We often provided the amount of income tax expense (e.g., $100,000) and prepared a journal entry similar to the following:

| Income tax expense (E) | 100,000 | |
| Income tax payable (L) | | 100,000 |

Assets	=	Liabilities	+	Shareholders' Equity
		Income tax payable +100,000		Income tax expense −100,000

However, separate rules govern the preparation of financial statements (IFRS) and tax returns (*Income Tax Act*). Specifically, some types of revenue are exempt from tax while other types of expenses are not deductible in computing taxable income. These *permanent differences* do not cause much complication in accounting for income taxes. However, *temporary differences* of the following types result in complex accounting:

1. Product warranty costs that are recognized as a liability and an expense for financial reporting purposes when the related products are sold, but are deductible for tax purposes only when payments under the warranty are made.

2. Long-lived assets, including development costs, which are usually depreciated by using the straight-line method for financial reporting purposes, but are depreciated on an accelerated basis (capital cost allowance; CCA) for tax purposes.

The differences between depreciation expense and CCA are by far the most common source of temporary differences, which disappear over the long run. Assuming the corporation is a going concern, a specific long-lived asset will eventually be unable to generate further benefits to the corporation and will be fully depreciated. Similarly, the cost of this asset would have been deducted over the years as CCA for tax purposes. So the main issue is timing of the recognition of revenues and expenses for financial reporting versus tax purposes. These temporary differences cause the income tax expense (which is based on earnings before taxes reported on the statement of earnings) to be different from the income tax payable (which is based on taxable income computed on the income tax return).

This difference creates an interesting accounting problem: should the tax liability reported on the statement of financial position be the amount of income taxes currently payable based on the tax return, or should the liability include deferred tax effects that exist because of differences between IFRS and the income tax rules? Accountants have resolved this issue by recording the "economic" liability, which includes income taxes currently payable, adjusted for the effects of temporary differences between IFRS and the income tax rules.

The difference between the amounts of income tax expense and income taxes payable is called *deferred income tax*. Deferred income tax items exist because of temporary differences caused by reporting revenues and expenses on a company's statement of earnings in conformity with IFRS, and on the tax return in accordance with the *Income Tax Act*. In practice, deferred income taxes can be either assets (such as taxes related to cash collected from a customer, which is taxable before it is reported as a revenue on the statement of earnings) or liabilities (such as taxes related to depreciation and amortization, reported on the tax return on an accelerated basis and on the statement of earnings on a straight-line basis).

To illustrate, let us consider one item that gives rise to deferred income taxes. Assume that a Canadian company uses straight-line depreciation for its financial statements and CCA for its tax return. As a result, it reports lower income on its tax return than on its statement of earnings, because CCA reported on the tax return exceeds depreciation expense reported on the statement of earnings. Assume that the company computed income taxes payable of $8,000,000 based on the numbers reported on the tax return, and reported income tax expense of $10,000,000 on its statement of earnings. The company records its tax obligation as follows:

Income tax expense (E) 10,000,000
    Deferred income taxes (L) 2,000,000
    Income tax payable (L) 8,000,000

Assets	=	Liabilities		+	Shareholders' Equity	
		Deferred income taxes	+2,000,000		Income tax expense	−10,000,000
		Income tax payable	+8,000,000			

The deferred income tax amount is settled when the difference between CCA and depreciation expense "reverses" in the future. This happens when the CCA recorded on the tax return becomes lower than the straight-line depreciation reported on the statement of earnings (remember from Chapter 9 that declining depreciation, such as CCA, causes higher depreciation expense than straight-line depreciation in the early years of an asset's life and lower depreciation in the later years). When a temporary difference reverses, the deferred income tax amount is reduced.

In reality, although temporary differences reverse in theory, new temporary differences are created as companies purchase new long-lived assets, offsetting the reversing differences. Consequently, the deferred income tax liabilities reported by most companies may not result in significant cash outflows in the foreseeable future.

As indicated earlier, the deferred income tax liability arises primarily from differences between depreciation expense and CCA. What if companies used CCA for reporting purposes instead of straight-line depreciation? In this case, most of the temporary differences would disappear and the deferred income tax asset or liability would be reduced to a relatively small amount, thus reducing the significance of this item on the statements of financial position of most companies. However, the use of CCA for financial reporting purposes increases the depreciation expense, thus reducing net earnings. Managers may not favour this outcome if it affects their remuneration and the market value of the company's shares, even though the use of CCA instead of straight-line depreciation does not affect cash outflows for income tax purposes.

Bauer, which has its main offices in Canada and the United States, with smaller offices in Germany, Finland, Sweden, and Taiwan, computes its current income tax payable in conformity with Canadian tax rules and uses IFRS to report its net earnings. The following excerpts from the company's financial statement notes illustrate its tax-related disclosures:

NOTES TO CONSOLIDATED FINANCIAL STATEMENTS

4.14 Income tax

Income tax expense comprises current and deferred income tax. Current tax and deferred income tax is recognized through profit or loss except to the extent that it relates to a business combination, or items recognized directly in equity or in other comprehensive income. Current tax is the expected tax payable or receivable on the taxable income or loss for the period, using tax rates enacted or substantively enacted at the reporting date, and any adjustment to tax payable in respect of previous years.

Deferred income tax is recognized in respect of temporary differences between the carrying amounts of assets and liabilities for financial reporting purposes and the amounts used for taxation purposes.

. . .

In determining the amount of current and deferred tax the Company takes into account the impact of uncertain tax positions and whether additional taxes and interest may be due. The Company believes that its accruals for tax liabilities are adequate for all open tax years based on its assessment of many factors, including interpretations of tax law and prior experience. This assessment relies on estimates and assumptions and may involve a series of judgments about future events. New information may become available that causes the Company to change its judgments regarding the adequacy of existing tax liabilities; such changes to tax liabilities will impact tax expense in the period the determination is made.

Deferred income tax is measured at the tax rates that are expected to be applied to temporary differences when they reverse, based on the laws that have been enacted or substantively enacted by the reporting date.

. . .

A deferred income tax asset is recognized for unused tax losses, tax credits and deductible temporary differences, to the extent that it is probable that future taxable profits will be available against which they can be utilized. Deferred income tax assets are reviewed at each reporting date and are reduced to the extent that it is no longer probable that the related tax benefit will be realized.

Source: Bauer Performance Sports Ltd., Annual Report 2012.

Exhibit 10.2 shows Bauer's tax-related note disclosures for 2012. The disclosures include the current and deferred components of the income tax expense for 2012, as well as a listing of the items that caused temporary differences between financial reporting and income tax reporting and resulted in net deferred income tax assets. The items that resulted in temporary differences include allowance for doubtful accounts; property, plant, and equipment; intangibles; and deferred research expenses, among others.

Exhibit **10.2**

NOTES TO CONSOLIDATED FINANCIAL STATEMENTS

16. INCOME TAXES

The expense for income taxes consists of the following:

	Year ended May 31, 2012	Year ended May 31, 2011
Tax recognized in profit or loss:		
Current tax expense (benefit):		
Current year	$ 500	$ 394
Adjustment for prior years	(914)	−
Total	(414)	394
Tax recognized in profit or loss:		
Deferred tax expense (benefit):		
Origination and reversal of temporary differences	15,428	(264)
Change in enacted rates	(1,892)	236
Total	13,536	(28)
Total tax recognized in profit or loss	13,122	$ 366
Tax benefit recognized directly in equity:		
Share-based compensation	1,803	1,228
Total	$ 1,803	$1,228
Tax benefit recognized in other comprehensive income:		
Defined benefit plans	$ 117	$ 114

(continued)

The change in enacted tax rates is due primarily to the graduated decrease in the Canadian statutory federal and Quebec provincial rates enacted on June 30, 2010 for years 2010 through 2015 and the adjustment of the deferred tax assets to the appropriate tax rates.

. . .

Deferred income tax assets are recognized only to the extent that it is probable that taxable profit will be available against which the deductible temporary differences or tax losses can be utilized. The tax effect of temporary differences and carryforwards, which give rise to net deferred income tax assets, consists of the following:

	Year ended May 31, 2012	Year ended May 31, 2011
Allowance for doubtful accounts	$ 1,379	$ 1,330
Inventory	1,781	1,654
Accrued expenses	3,432	2,807
Net operating loss carryforwards	2,918	15,981
Share-based compensation and defined benefit plans	5,858	4,595
Property, plant and equipment	(1,972)	(1,023)
Intangible assets	467	625
Deferred research expenses	1,750	1,103
Investment tax credit carryforwards	1,322	806
Other	(512)	(583)
Total deferred income tax assets	$16,423	$27,295

Source: Bauer Performance Sports Ltd., Annual Report 2012.

APPENDIX 10B: PRESENT VALUE CONCEPTS

The concept of *present value* (PV) is based on the time value of money. It provides a foundation for measuring and reporting long-term notes and bonds. **Present value** is the current cash equivalent of an amount to be received in the future, or a future amount discounted for compound interest. Quite simply, money received today is worth more than money to be received one year from today (or at any other future date) because it can be used to earn interest. If you invest $1,000 today at 4 percent, you will have $1,040 in one year. In contrast, if you receive $1,000 one year from today, you will lose the opportunity to earn the $40 interest revenue. The difference between the $1,000 and the $1,040 is interest that can be earned during the year.

In one of your mathematics courses, you have probably already solved some problems involving the time value of money. In the typical problem, you were told a certain dollar amount had been deposited in a savings account earning a specific rate of interest. You were asked to determine the dollar amount that would be in the savings account after a certain number of years. In this appendix, we will show you how to solve problems that are the opposite of the ones you have worked with. In present value problems, you are told a dollar amount to be received in the future (such as the balance of a savings account after five years) and asked to determine the present value of the amount (the amount that must be deposited in the savings account today).

The value of money changes over time because money can earn interest. With a present value problem, you know the dollar amount of a cash flow that will occur in the future and need to determine its value now. The opposite situation occurs when you know the dollar amount of a cash flow that occurs today and need to determine its value at some point in the future. These problems are called *future value* problems. **Future value** is the sum to which an amount will increase as a result of compound interest. The following illustrates the basic difference between present value and future value problems:

PRESENT VALUE is the current cash equivalent of an amount to be received in the future, or a future amount discounted for compound interest.

FUTURE VALUE is the sum to which an amount will increase as a result of compound interest.

	Now	Future
Present value	?	$1,000
Future value	$1,000	?

Present and future value problems may involve two types of cash flow: a single payment or an annuity (a series of cash payments).[6] Thus, four different situations are related to the time value of money:

1. Present value of a single payment
2. Future value of a single payment
3. Present value of an annuity
4. Future value of an annuity

Present value problems involving single amounts and annuities are discussed below. Future value problems are covered in an online appendix to this chapter (Appendix 10E on *Connect*).

Present Value of a Single Amount

The present value of a single amount is the amount of cash you are willing to accept today in lieu of a cash receipt at some date in the future. You might be offered the opportunity to invest in a debt instrument paying you $10,000 in 10 years. Before you decided whether to invest, you would want to determine the present value of the instrument. Graphically, the present value of $1 due at the end of the third period with an interest rate of 4 percent can be represented as follows:

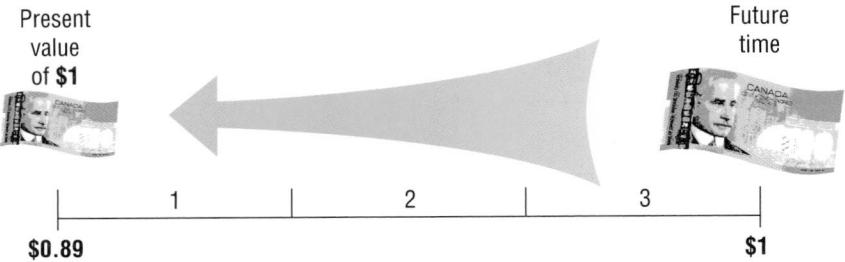

To compute the present value of an amount to be received in the future, we subtract interest that is earned over time from the amount to be received in the future. For example, if you place $100 in a savings account that earns 2 percent, you will have $102 at the end of a year. In a present value problem, you are told that you have $102 at the end of the year and must compute the amount to be deposited at the beginning of the year. To solve this type of problem, you must discount the amount to be received in the future at interest rate i for n periods. The formula to compute the present value of a single amount is

$$\text{Present Value} = \frac{1}{(1+i)^n} \times \text{Amount}$$

The formula is not difficult to use, but most analysts use calculators, Excel, or present value tables for computations. We will illustrate how to use present value tables. Assume that today is January 1, 2014, and you have the opportunity to receive $1,000 cash on December 31, 2016. At an interest rate of 4 percent per year, how much is the $1,000 payment worth to you on January 1, 2014? You could discount the amount year by year,[7] but it is easier to use Table 10C.1 in Appendix 10C, "Present Value of $1." For $i = 4\%$, $n = 3$, we find that the present value of $1 is 0.8890. The present value of $1,000 to be received at the end of three years can be computed as follows:

From Table 10C.1,
$i = 4\%$
$n = 3$

→ **$1,000 × 0.8890 = $889.00**

Learning how to compute a present value amount is not difficult, but it is more important that you understand what it means. The $889.00 is the amount that you would pay to have the right to receive $1,000 at the end of three years, assuming an interest rate of 4 percent. Conceptually, you would be indifferent about having $889.00

today and receiving $1,000 in three years, because you can use financial institutions to convert dollars from the present to the future and vice versa. If you had $889.00 today but preferred $1,000 in three years, you could simply deposit the money into a savings account that paid annual interest at 4 percent and it would grow to $1,000 in three years. Alternatively, if you had a contract that promised you $1,000 in three years, you could sell it to an investor for $889.00 cash today because it would permit the investor to earn the difference in interest.

PAUSE FOR **FEEDBACK**

There are two types of payments when you compute present values. So far, we have discussed single payments. In the next section, we will discuss annuities. Before you move on, complete the following questions to test your understanding of these concepts.

SELF-STUDY **QUIZ 10-4**

1. If the interest rate in a present value problem increases from 4 percent to 5 percent, will the present value increase or decrease? Explain.

2. What is the present value of $10,000 to be received 10 years from now if the interest rate is 6 percent compounded annually?

After you complete your answers, check them with the solution at the end of this chapter.

Present Value of an Annuity

Many business problems involve multiple cash payments over a number of periods instead of a single payment. An **annuity** is a series of consecutive payments characterized by

1. An equal dollar amount each interest period.

2. Interest periods of equal length (year, half-year, quarter, or month).

3. An equal interest rate each interest period.

An **ANNUITY** is a series of equal amounts of cash that are paid or received at equally distant points in time.

Examples of annuities include monthly payments on an automobile or a home loan, annual contributions to a savings account, and monthly retirement benefits.

The present value of an annuity is the value now of a series of equal amounts to be received (or paid) each period for some specified number of periods in the future. It is computed by discounting each of the equal periodic amounts. A good example of this type of problem is a retirement program that offers the retiree a monthly income after retirement. The present value of an annuity of $1 for three periods at 4 percent may be represented graphically as follows:

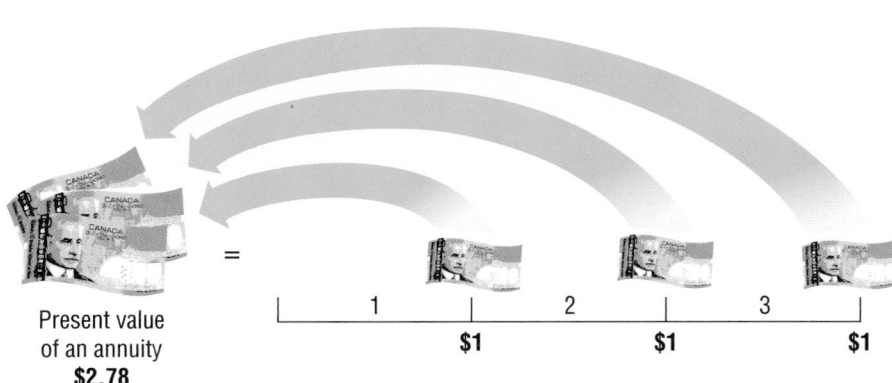

Present value
of an annuity
$2.78

1   2   3

$1 $1 $1

Assume you are to receive $1,000 cash on each December 31, 2014, 2015, and 2016. How much would the sum of these three $1,000 future amounts be worth on January 1, 2014, assuming an interest rate of 4 percent per year? We could use Table 10C.1 in Appendix 10C to calculate the present value as follows:

			Factor from Table 10C.1		
Year	Amount		Appendix 10C, $i = 4\%$		Present Value
1	$1,000	×	0.9615 ($n = 1$)	=	$ 961.50
2	$1,000	×	0.9246 ($n = 2$)	=	924.60
3	$1,000	×	0.8890 ($n = 3$)	=	889.00
			Total present value	=	$2,775.10

We can compute the present value of this annuity more easily, however, by using Table 10C.2 in Appendix 10C as follows:

From Table 10C.2,
$i = 4\%$
$n = 3$

$$\$1,000 \times 2.7751 = \$2,775.10$$

Exhibit 10.3 provides a graphical illustration of the present value computations discussed above.

Interest Rates and Interest Periods The preceding illustrations assumed annual periods for compounding and discounting. Although interest rates are almost always quoted on an annual basis, most interest-compounding periods encountered in business are less than one year (semi-annually or quarterly). When interest periods are less than a year, the values of n and i must be restated to be consistent with the length of the interest period.

To illustrate, 4 percent interest compounded annually for five years requires use of $n = 5$ and $i = 4\%$. If compounding is quarterly, the interest period is one-quarter of a year (i.e., four periods per year), and the quarterly interest rate is one-quarter of the annual rate (i.e., 1 percent per quarter). Therefore, 4 percent interest compounded quarterly for five years requires use of $n = 20$ and $i = 1\%$.

Exhibit **10.3**

Overview of Present Value Computations

Table No.	Designation	Definition and Graphic Representation	Table Formula
10C.1	**Present value of $1,000 ($p$)** $n = 3$ $i = 4\%$	The present value (now) of $1,000 due n periods hence, discounted at interest rate i per period. This is simply a future amount with compound interest subtracted from it.	$\dfrac{1}{(1+i)^n}$

Present value of $1,000

| $889.00 | | | $1,000 |

| 10C.2 | **Present value of annuity of $1,000* ($p$)** $n = 3$ $i = 4\%$ | The present value (now) of n periodic payments of $1,000 each to be received (or paid) each period, discounted at interest rate i per period. The first payment is at the end of the first period. | $\dfrac{1 - \dfrac{1}{(1+i)^n}}{i}$ |

Present value of n payments of $1,000

| $2,775.10 | $1,000 | $1,000 | $1,000 |

*Notice that these are ordinary annuities; that is, they are often called *end-of-period annuities*. Thus, the table values for *p*, the present value, are at the beginning of the period of the first payment. Annuities due assume the opposite; that is, they are *beginning-of-period annuities*. Ordinary annuity values can be converted into annuities due simply by multiplication of (1 + *i*).

TRUTH IN ADVERTISING

A QUESTION
OF ACCOUNTABILITY

A number of advertisements in newspapers, in magazines, on television, and on the Internet can easily be misinterpreted if the consumer does not understand present value concepts. We discuss two examples.

Most car companies offer seasonal promotions with special financing incentives. A car dealer may advertise 1.9 percent interest on car loans when banks are charging 6 percent. Typically, the lower interest rate is not a special incentive because the dealer simply charges a higher price for cars that the dealership finances. It may be better to borrow from the bank and "pay cash" at the dealership to negotiate a lower price. Customers should use the present value concepts illustrated in this chapter to compare financing alternatives.

Another misleading advertisement is one that promises a chance to become an instant millionaire. The fine print discloses that the winner will receive $25,000 for 40 years, which is $1,000,000 (40 × $25,000), but the present value of this annuity at 8 percent is only $298,000. Most winners are happy to get the money, but they are not really millionaires.

Some consumer advocates criticize businesses that use these types of advertisements. They argue that consumers should not have to study present value concepts to understand advertisements. Some of these criticisms may be valid, but the quality of information contained in advertisements that include interest rates has improved during the past few years.

Accounting Applications of Present Values

Many business transactions require the use of present value concepts. We illustrate two such cases so that you can test your understanding of these concepts:

Case A On January 1, 2014, Nesca Corp. bought some new equipment. The company signed a note and agreed to pay $200,000 for the equipment on December 31, 2015. The market interest rate for this note was 6 percent. The $200,000 represents the cash-equivalent price of the equipment and the interest that will be earned for two years.

1. How should the accountant record the purchase?

   Answer: This case requires application of the present value of a single amount. In conformity with the cost principle, the cost of the equipment is its current cash-equivalent price, which is the present value of the future payment. The problem can be shown graphically as follows:

January 1, 2014	December 31, 2014	December 31, 2015
?		$200,000

The present value of the $200,000 is computed as follows:

$$\$200,000 \times 0.8900 = \$178,000 \longleftarrow$$

From Table 10C.1,
$i = 6\%$
$n = 2$

Therefore, the journal entry is as follows:

Equipment (A)	178,000	
Note payable (L)		178,000

Assets	=	Liabilities	+	Shareholders' Equity
Equipment +178,000		Note payable +178,000		

Some companies prefer to record the following journal entry:

Equipment (A)	178,000	
Discount on notes payable (XL)	22,000	
Note payable (L)		200,000

Assets	=	Liabilities	+	Shareholders' Equity
Equipment +178,000		Note payable +200,000		
		Discount −22,000		

The discount account is a contra-liability account that represents the interest that will accrue on the note over its life.

2. What journal entry should be made at the end of the first and second years for interest expense?

Answer: The following schedule shows the computation of interest expense for the two years.

Date	Interest Expense Unpaid Balance × 6%	Unpaid Balance of Note Payable
January 1, 2014		$178,000
December 31, 2014	$178,000 × 6% = $10,680	188,680
December 31, 2015	188,680 × 6% = 11,320*	200,000

*The exact computation is $11,320.80, which is rounded down to $11,320 to ensure that the unpaid balance of the note does not exceed $200,000.

Each year's interest expense is recorded in an adjusting entry as follows:

Dec. 31, 2014 Interest expense (E)	10,680	
Note payable (L)		10,680

Assets	=	Liabilities	+	Shareholders' Equity
		Note payable +10,680		Interest Expense −10,680

Dec. 31, 2015 Interest expense (E)	11,320	
Note payable (L)		11,320

Assets	=	Liabilities	+	Shareholders' Equity
		Note payable +11,320		Interest Expense −11,320

Notice that interest of $10,680 accrued during 2014 but was not paid. It is therefore added to the balance of the note payable account. This interest amount has itself earned interest during 2015.

3. What journal entry should be made on December 31, 2015, to record the payment of the debt?

Answer: At this date, the amount to be paid is the note payable balance, which is the same as the maturity amount on the due date. The journal entry to record full payment of the debt follows:

Note payable (L)	200,000	
Cash (A)		200,000

Assets	=	Liabilities	+	Shareholders' Equity
Cash −200,000		Note payable −200,000		

Case B   On January 1, 2014, Nesca bought new research equipment. The company elected to finance the purchase with a note payable to be paid in three equal annual instalments of $146,886. Each instalment includes principal plus interest on the unpaid balance at 5 percent per year. The annual instalments are due on December 31, 2014, 2015, and 2016. This problem can be shown graphically as follows:

January 1, 2014	December 31, 2014	December 31, 2015	December 31, 2016
?	$146,886	$146,886	$146,886

1. What is the amount of the note?

   Answer: The note is the present value of each instalment payment, $i = 5\%$ and $n = 3$. This is an annuity because payment is made in three equal instalments. The amount of the note is computed as follows:

$$\$146,886 \times 2.7232 = \$400,000 \longleftarrow$$

From Table 10C.2, $i = 5\%$ $n = 3$

   The acquisition is recorded as follows:

   Research equipment (A) 400,000
       Note payable (L) 400,000

Assets	=	Liabilities	+	Shareholders' Equity
Research equipment +400,000		Note payable +400,000		

2. What was the total amount of interest expense in dollars?

   Answer:

$$\$146,886 \times 3 - \$400,000 = \$40,658$$

3. Prepare a debt payment schedule that shows the entry for each payment and the effect on interest expense and the unpaid amount of principal each period.

   Answer:

		Debt Payment Schedule		
Date	Cash Payment (Credit)	Interest Expense (Unpaid Principal × 5%) (Debit)	Decrease in Principal (Debit)	Unpaid Principal
1/1/2014				$400,000
31/12/2014	$146,886	$400,000 × 5% = $ 20,000	$126,886[a]	273,114[b]
31/12/2015	146,886	273,114 × 5% = $ 13,656	133,230	139,884
31/12/2016	146,886	139,884 × 5% = $ 7,002*	139,884	0
Total	$440,658	$ 40,658*	$400,000	

   *To accommodate rounding error.
   Computations: [a]$146,886 − $20,000 = $126,886
       [b]$400,000 − $126,886 = $273,114

   Notice in the debt payment schedule that, for each successive payment, the payment on principal increases and interest expense decreases. This effect occurs because the interest each period is based on a lower amount of the unpaid principal. When an annuity is involved, schedules such as this one are often useful analytical tools.

4. What journal entry should be made at the end of each year to record the payments on this note?

   Answer:

   Dec. 31, 2014 Note payable (L) 126,886
              Interest expense (E) 20,000
              Cash (A) 146,886

Assets	=	Liabilities	+	Shareholders' Equity
Cash −146,886		Note payable −126,886		Interest expense −20,000

   Dec. 31, 2015 Note payable (L) 133,230
              Interest expense (E) 13,656
              Cash (A) 146,886

Assets	=	Liabilities	+	Shareholders' Equity
Cash −146,886		Note payable −133,230		Interest expense −13,656

Dec. 31, 2016 Note payable (L)	139,884	
Interest expense (E)	7,002	
Cash (A)		146,886

Assets		=	Liabilities		+	Shareholders' Equity	
Cash	−146,886		Note payable	−139,884		Interest expense	−7,002

APPENDIX 10C: PRESENT VALUE TABLES

Table 10C.1
Present Value of $1, $p = 1/(1 + i)^n$

Periods	1.5%	1.75%	2%	2.25%	2.5%	2.75%	3%	3.25%	3.5%
1	0.9852	0.9828	0.9804	0.9780	0.9756	0.9732	0.9709	0.9685	0.9662
2	0.9707	0.9659	0.9612	0.9565	0.9518	0.9472	0.9426	0.9380	0.9335
3	0.9563	0.9493	0.9423	0.9354	0.9286	0.9218	0.9151	0.9085	0.9019
4	0.9422	0.9330	0.9238	0.9148	0.9060	0.8972	0.8885	0.8799	0.8714
5	0.9283	0.9169	0.9057	0.8947	0.8839	0.8732	0.8626	0.8522	0.8420
6	0.9145	0.9011	0.8880	0.8750	0.8623	0.8498	0.8375	0.8254	0.8135
7	0.9010	0.8856	0.8706	0.8558	0.8413	0.8270	0.8131	0.7994	0.7860
8	0.8877	0.8704	0.8535	0.8369	0.8207	0.8049	0.7894	0.7742	0.7594
9	0.8746	0.8554	0.8368	0.8185	0.8007	0.7834	0.7664	0.7499	0.7337
10	0.8617	0.8407	0.8203	0.8005	0.7812	0.7624	0.7441	0.7263	0.7089
11	0.8489	0.8263	0.8043	0.7829	0.7621	0.7420	0.7224	0.7034	0.6849
12	0.8364	0.8121	0.7885	0.7657	0.7436	0.7221	0.7014	0.6813	0.6618
13	0.8240	0.7981	0.7730	0.7488	0.7254	0.7028	0.6810	0.6598	0.6394
14	0.8118	0.7844	0.7579	0.7323	0.7077	0.6840	0.6611	0.6391	0.6178
15	0.7999	0.7709	0.7430	0.7162	0.6905	0.6657	0.6419	0.6189	0.5969
16	0.7880	0.7576	0.7284	0.7005	0.6736	0.6479	0.6232	0.5995	0.5767
17	0.7764	0.7446	0.7142	0.6851	0.6572	0.6305	0.6050	0.5806	0.5572
18	0.7649	0.7318	0.7002	0.6700	0.6412	0.6137	0.5874	0.5623	0.5384
19	0.7536	0.7192	0.6864	0.6552	0.6255	0.5972	0.5703	0.5446	0.5202
20	0.7425	0.7068	0.6730	0.6408	0.6103	0.5813	0.5537	0.5275	0.5026
30	0.6398	0.5942	0.5521	0.5130	0.4767	0.4431	0.4120	0.3831	0.3563
40	0.5513	0.4996	0.4529	0.4106	0.3724	0.3379	0.3066	0.2782	0.2526
50	0.4750	0.4200	0.3715	0.3287	0.2909	0.2576	0.2281	0.2021	0.1791
Periods	**3.75%**	**4%**	**4.5%**	**5%**	**6%**	**7%**	**8%**	**9%**	**10%**
1	0.9639	0.9615	0.9569	0.9524	0.9434	0.9346	0.9259	0.9174	0.9091
2	0.9290	0.9246	0.9157	0.9070	0.8900	0.8734	0.8573	0.8417	0.8264
3	0.8954	0.8890	0.8763	0.8638	0.8396	0.8163	0.7938	0.7722	0.7513
4	0.8631	0.8548	0.8386	0.8227	0.7921	0.7629	0.7350	0.7084	0.6830
5	0.8319	0.8219	0.8025	0.7835	0.7473	0.7130	0.6806	0.6499	0.6209
6	0.8018	0.7903	0.7679	0.7462	0.7050	0.6663	0.6302	0.5963	0.5645
7	0.7728	0.7599	0.7348	0.7107	0.6651	0.6227	0.5835	0.5470	0.5132
8	0.7449	0.7307	0.7032	0.6768	0.6274	0.5820	0.5403	0.5019	0.4665
9	0.7180	0.7026	0.6729	0.6446	0.5919	0.5439	0.5002	0.4604	0.4241
10	0.6920	0.6756	0.6439	0.6139	0.5584	0.5083	0.4632	0.4224	0.3855
11	0.6670	0.6496	0.6162	0.5847	0.5268	0.4751	0.4289	0.3875	0.3505
12	0.6429	0.6246	0.5897	0.5568	0.4970	0.4440	0.3971	0.3555	0.3186
13	0.6197	0.6006	0.5643	0.5303	0.4688	0.4150	0.3677	0.3262	0.2897
14	0.5973	0.5775	0.5400	0.5051	0.4423	0.3878	0.3405	0.2992	0.2633
15	0.5757	0.5553	0.5167	0.4810	0.4173	0.3624	0.3152	0.2745	0.2394
16	0.5549	0.5339	0.4945	0.4581	0.3936	0.3387	0.2919	0.2519	0.2176
17	0.5348	0.5134	0.4732	0.4363	0.3714	0.3166	0.2703	0.2311	0.1978
18	0.5155	0.4936	0.4528	0.4155	0.3503	0.2959	0.2502	0.2120	0.1799
19	0.4969	0.4746	0.4333	0.3957	0.3305	0.2765	0.2317	0.1945	0.1635
20	0.4789	0.4564	0.4146	0.3769	0.3118	0.2584	0.2145	0.1784	0.1486
30	0.3314	0.3083	0.2670	0.2314	0.1741	0.1314	0.0994	0.0754	0.0573
40	0.2293	0.2083	0.1719	0.1420	0.0972	0.0668	0.0460	0.0318	0.0221
50	0.1587	0.1407	0.1107	0.0872	0.0543	0.0339	0.0213	0.0134	0.0085

Table 10C.2
Present Value of Annuity of $1, p = [1 - 1/(1 + i)^n]/i$

Periods*	1.5%	1.75%	2%	2.25%	2.5%	2.75%	3%	3.25%	3.5%
1	0.9852	0.9828	0.9804	0.9780	0.9756	0.9732	0.9709	0.9685	0.9662
2	1.9559	1.9487	1.9416	1.9345	1.9274	1.9204	1.9135	1.9066	1.8997
3	2.9122	2.8980	2.8839	2.8699	2.8560	2.8423	2.8286	2.8151	2.8016
4	3.8544	3.8309	3.8077	3.7847	3.7620	3.7394	3.7171	3.6950	3.6731
5	4.7826	4.7479	4.7135	4.6795	4.6458	4.6126	4.5797	4.5472	4.5151
6	5.6972	5.6490	5.6014	5.5545	5.5081	5.4624	5.4172	5.3726	5.3286
7	6.5982	6.5346	6.4720	6.4102	6.3494	6.2894	6.2303	6.1720	6.1145
8	7.4859	7.4051	7.3255	7.2472	7.1701	7.0943	7.0197	6.9462	6.8740
9	8.3605	8.2605	8.1622	8.0657	7.9709	7.8777	7.7861	7.6961	7.6077
10	9.2222	9.1012	8.9826	8.8662	8.7521	8.6401	8.5302	8.4224	8.3166
11	10.0711	9.9275	9.7868	9.6491	9.5142	9.3821	9.2526	9.1258	9.0016
12	10.9075	10.7395	10.5753	10.4148	10.2578	10.1042	9.9540	9.8071	9.6633
13	11.7315	11.5376	11.3484	11.1636	10.9832	10.8070	10.6350	10.4669	10.3027
14	12.5434	12.3220	12.1062	11.8959	11.6909	11.4910	11.2961	11.1060	10.9205
15	13.3432	13.0929	12.8493	12.6122	12.3814	12.1567	11.9379	11.7249	11.5174
16	14.1313	13.8505	13.5777	13.3126	13.0550	12.8046	12.5611	12.3244	12.0941
17	14.9076	14.5951	14.2919	13.9977	13.7122	13.4351	13.1661	12.9049	12.6513
18	15.6726	15.3269	14.9920	14.6677	14.3534	14.0488	13.7535	13.4673	13.1897
19	16.4262	16.0461	15.6785	15.3229	14.9789	14.6460	14.3238	14.0119	13.7098
20	17.1686	16.7529	16.3514	15.9637	15.5892	15.2273	14.8775	14.5393	14.2124
30	24.0158	23.1858	22.3965	21.6453	20.9303	20.2493	19.6004	18.9819	18.3920
40	29.9158	28.5942	27.3555	26.1935	25.1028	24.0781	23.1148	22.2084	21.3551
50	34.9997	33.1412	31.4236	29.8344	28.3623	26.9972	25.7298	24.5518	23.4556

Periods*	3.75%	4%	4.5%	5%	6%	7%	8%	9%	10%
1	0.9639	0.9615	0.9569	0.9524	0.9434	0.9346	0.9259	0.9174	0.9091
2	1.8929	1.8861	1.8727	1.8594	1.8334	1.8080	1.7833	1.7591	1.7355
3	2.7883	2.7751	2.7490	2.7232	2.6730	2.6243	2.5771	2.5313	2.4869
4	3.6514	3.6299	3.5875	3.5460	3.4651	3.3872	3.3121	3.2397	3.1699
5	4.4833	4.4518	4.3900	4.3295	4.2124	4.1002	3.9927	3.8897	3.7908
6	5.2851	5.2421	5.1579	5.0757	4.9173	4.7665	4.6229	4.4859	4.3553
7	6.0579	6.0021	5.8927	5.7864	5.5824	5.3893	5.2064	5.0330	4.8684
8	6.8028	6.7327	6.5959	6.4632	6.2098	5.9713	5.7466	5.5348	5.3349
9	7.5208	7.4353	7.2688	7.1078	6.8017	6.5152	6.2469	5.9952	5.7590
10	8.2128	8.1109	7.9127	7.7217	7.3601	7.0236	6.7101	6.4177	6.1446
11	8.8798	8.7605	8.5289	8.3064	7.8869	7.4987	7.1390	6.8052	6.4951
12	9.5227	9.3851	9.1186	8.8633	8.3838	7.9427	7.5361	7.1607	6.8137
13	10.1424	9.9856	9.6829	9.3936	8.8527	8.3577	7.9038	7.4869	7.1034
14	10.7396	10.5631	10.2228	9.8986	9.2950	8.7455	8.2442	7.7862	7.3667
15	11.3153	11.1184	10.7395	10.3797	9.7122	9.1079	8.5595	8.0607	7.6061
16	11.8702	11.6523	11.2340	10.8378	10.1059	9.4466	8.8514	8.3126	7.8237
17	12.4050	12.1657	11.7072	11.2741	10.4773	9.7632	9.1216	8.5436	8.0216
18	12.9205	12.6593	12.1600	11.6896	10.8276	10.0591	9.3719	8.7556	8.2014
19	13.4173	13.1339	12.5933	12.0853	11.1581	10.3356	9.6036	8.9501	8.3649
20	13.8962	13.5903	13.0079	12.4622	11.4699	10.5940	9.8181	9.1285	8.5136
30	17.8292	17.2920	16.2889	15.3725	13.7648	12.4090	11.2578	10.2737	9.4269
40	20.5510	19.7928	18.4016	17.1591	15.0463	13.3317	11.9246	10.7574	9.7791
50	22.4345	21.4822	19.7620	18.2559	15.7619	13.8007	12.2335	10.9617	9.9148

*There is one payment each period.

Available on *Connect*: APPENDIX 10D: PRESENT VALUE COMPUTATIONS USING EXCEL

Available on *Connect*: APPENDIX 10E: FUTURE VALUE CONCEPTS

CHAPTER **TAKE-AWAYS**

1. **Define, measure, and report current liabilities.**
   Strictly speaking, accountants define liabilities as obligations arising from past transactions that will be settled in the future by some transfer or use of assets or provision of services. They are classified on the statement of financial position as either current or non-current. Current liabilities are short-term obligations that will be paid within the normal operating cycle of the business or within one year of the statement of financial position date, whichever is longer. Non-current liabilities are all obligations not classified as current.

2. **Compute and interpret the quick ratio.**
   The quick ratio is a comparison of the most liquid or quick assets (cash, short-term investments, and net receivables) to current liabilities. Analysts use this ratio to assess the liquidity of a company.

3. **Compute and interpret the trade payables turnover ratio.**
   This ratio is computed by dividing cost of sales by average trade payables. It shows how quickly management is paying its trade creditors and is considered to be a measure of liquidity.

4. **Report notes payable, and explain the time value of money.**
   A note payable specifies the amount borrowed, when it must be repaid, and the interest rate associated with the debt. Accountants must report the debt and the interest as it accrues. The time value of money refers to the fact that interest accrues on borrowed money with the passage of time.

5. **Report contingent liabilities and commitments.**
   A contingency is a possible liability that has arisen as a result of a past event. Such contingencies are disclosed in a note if it is not probable that cash or other assets will be required to settle the obligation, or if the amount of the obligation cannot be measured with sufficient reliability. A commitment is a contractual agreement to enter into a transaction with another party in the future.

6. **Explain the impact of changes in current liabilities on cash flows.**
   Changes in trade payables and accrued liabilities affect cash flows from operating activities. Cash flows are increased when trade payables and accrued liabilities increase, and vice versa.

In this chapter, we focused on current liabilities and introduced present value concepts. In the next chapter, we will discuss non-current liabilities in the context of the capital structure of the company.

KEY **RATIOS**

The quick ratio measures the ability of a company to pay its current obligations. It is computed as follows:

$$\text{Quick Ratio} = \frac{\text{Quick Assets}}{\text{Current Liabilities}}$$

The trade payables turnover ratio and its companion average age of payables are measures of how quickly a company pays its creditors. They are computed as follows:

$$\text{Trade Payables Turnover Ratio} = \frac{\text{Cost of Sales}}{\text{Average Net Trade Payables}}$$

$$\text{Average Age of Payables} = \frac{365}{\text{Trade Payables Turnover Ratio}}$$

FINDING **FINANCIAL INFORMATION**

STATEMENT OF FINANCIAL POSITION

Under Current Liabilities

Liabilities listed by account title, such as
Trade payables
Accrued liabilities
Notes payable
Deferred income taxes

Under Non-current Liabilities

Liabilities listed by account title, such as
Long-term debt
Deferred income taxes

STATEMENT OF EARNINGS

Liabilities are shown only on the statement of financial position, never on the statement of earnings. Transactions affecting liabilities often affect a statement of earnings account. For example, accrued salary compensation affects a statement of earnings account (Compensation expense) and a statement of financial position account (Salaries payable).

STATEMENT OF CASH FLOWS

Under Operating Activities (indirect method)

Net earnings
+ Increases in most current liabilities
− Decreases in most current liabilities

NOTES

Under Summary of Significant Accounting Policies

Description of pertinent information concerning the accounting treatment of liabilities. Normally, there is minimal information.

Under a Separate Note

If not listed on the statement of financial position, a listing of the major classifications of liabilities with information about maturities and interest rates appears in a note. Information about contingent liabilities is reported in the notes.

GLOSSARY

Review key terms and definitions on *Connect*.

QUESTIONS

1. Define *liability*. Differentiate between a current liability and a non-current liability.
2. How can external parties be informed about the liabilities of a business?
3. Liabilities are measured and reported at their current cash-equivalent amount. Explain.
4. A *liability* is a known obligation of either a definite or an estimated amount. Explain.
5. Define *working capital*. How is it computed?
6. What is the quick ratio? How is it related to the classification of liabilities?
7. Define *accrued liability*. What type of entry usually reflects an accrued liability?
8. Define *deferred revenue*. Why is it a liability?
9. Define *note payable*. What other liability is associated with a note payable? Explain.
10. Define *provisions*. How do they differ from other liabilities?
11. What is a contingent liability? How is a contingent liability reported?
12. Compute interest expense for the following note: face value, $4,000; 12 percent interest; date of note, April 1, 2014. Assume that the fiscal year ends on December 31, 2014.
13. Explain the concept of the time value of money.
14. (Appendix 10B) Explain the basic difference between future value and present value.
15. (Appendix 10B) What is an annuity?

connect EXERCISES

LO1   **E10–1**   **Identifying Current Liabilities**

A current liability is a short-term obligation that is normally expected to be settled within one year. For each of the following events and transactions that occurred in November 2014, indicate the title of the current liability account that is affected and the amount that would be reported on a statement of financial position prepared on December 31, 2014. If an event does not result in a current liability, explain why.

   a. A customer purchases a ticket from WestJet Airlines for $470 cash to travel in January 2015. Answer from WestJet's standpoint.

   b. Hall Construction Company signs a contract with a customer for the construction of a new $500,000 warehouse. At the signing, Hall receives a cheque for $50,000 as a deposit on the future construction. Answer from Hall's standpoint.

   c. On November 1, 2014, a bank lends $10,000 to a company. The loan carries a 9 percent annual interest rate, and the principal and interest are due in a lump sum on October 31, 2015. Answer from the company's standpoint.

   d. A popular ski magazine company receives a total of $1,800 from subscribers on December 31, the last day of its fiscal year. The subscriptions begin in the next fiscal year. Answer from the magazine company's standpoint.

   e. On November 20, the campus bookstore receives 500 accounting textbooks at a cost of $70 each. The terms indicate that payment is due within 30 days of delivery. Answer from the bookstore's standpoint.

   f. Ziegler Company, a farm equipment company, receives its phone bill at the end of January 2015 for $230 for January calls. The bill has not been paid to date.

LO1, 2   **E10–2**   **Computing Shareholders' Equity and Working Capital; Explaining the Quick Ratio and Working Capital**

Dumont Corporation is preparing its 2014 statement of financial position. The company records show the following related amounts at the end of the fiscal year, December 31, 2014:

Cash	$ 25,000	Liability for withholding taxes	$ 6,000
Short-term investments	54,000	Deferred rent revenue	14,000
Trade receivables	147,000	Bonds payable (due in 15 years)	180,000
Inventories	110,000	Wages payable	14,000
Prepayments	2,000	Property taxes payable	6,000
Non-current assets	296,200	Note payable (6%; due in 6 months)	24,000
Notes payable (8%, due in 5 years)	30,000	Interest payable	3,200
Trade payables	119,000	Shareholders' equity	200,000
Income taxes payable	28,000		

Required:

   1. Compute (*a*) the amount of working capital and (*b*) the quick ratio (show computations). Why is working capital important to management? How do financial analysts use the quick ratio?

   2. Would your computations be different if the company reported $250,000 worth of contingent liabilities in the notes to its financial statements? Explain.

LO2   **E10–3**   **Analyzing the Impact of Transactions on Liquidity**

API Ltd. has a quick ratio of 0.80 and working capital in the amount of $1,240,000. For each of the following transactions, determine whether the quick ratio and working capital will increase, decrease, or remain the same.

   a. Paid trade payables in the amount of $50,000.

   b. Recorded accrued salaries in the amount of $100,000.

   c. Borrowed $250,000 from the bank, to be repaid in 90 days.

   d. Purchased $20,000 of new inventory on credit.

E10–4 Recording Payroll Costs with Discussion   ▪ LO1

Matyas Company completed the salary and wage payroll for April 2014. The payroll provided the following details:

Salaries and wages earned	$224,000
Employee income taxes withheld	55,000
CPP contributions*	11,100
EI contributions†	4,000
Union dues withheld	3,000
Insurance premiums withheld	1,000

*$11,100 each for employer and employees.
†Employment Insurance, employees' share.

Required:

1. Prepare the journal entry to record the payroll for April, including employee deductions.
2. Prepare the journal entry to record the employer's additional payroll expenses.
3. Prepare a combined journal entry to show the payment of amounts owed to governmental agencies and other organizations.
4. What was the total compensation expense for the company? Explain. What percentage of the payroll was take-home pay? From the employers' perspective, does an economic difference between the cost of salaries and the cost of benefits exist? From the employees' perspective, does a difference exist?

E10–5 Computing Payroll Costs; Discussion of Labour Costs   ▪ LO1

Riverside Ltd. has completed the payroll for January 2015, reflecting the following data:

Salaries and wages earned	$69,000
Employee income taxes withheld	16,900
CPP contributions*	3,415
EI contributions†	1,242
Union dues withheld	1,200

*$3,415 each for employer and employee.
†Employment Insurance, employees' share.

Required:

1. What amount of additional compensation expense must be paid by the company? What was the amount of the employees' take-home pay?
2. List the liabilities that are reported on the company's statement of financial position at January 31, 2015. The employees' take-home pay was paid on that day.
3. Would employers react differently to a 4 percent increase in the employer's share of CPP than to a 4 percent increase in the basic level of salaries? Would financial analysts react differently?

E10–6 Recording a Note Payable through Its Time to Maturity with Discussion of Management Strategy   ▪ LO1, 4

Many businesses borrow money during periods of increased business activity to finance inventory and trade receivables. Sears Canada Inc. is one of Canada's largest general merchandise retailers. Each year, Sears Canada builds up its inventory to meet the needs of December holiday shoppers. A large portion of these holiday sales are on credit. As a result, Sears Canada often collects cash from the sales several months after the December holidays. Assume that on November 1, 2014, Sears Canada borrowed $4.5 million cash from the bank for working capital purposes and signed an interest-bearing note due in six months. The interest rate was 5 percent per annum, payable at maturity. Assume that the fiscal year of Sears Canada ends on December 31.

Sears Canada Inc.

Required:

1. Prepare the journal entry to record the note on November 1, 2014.
2. Prepare any adjusting entry required at December 31, 2014.
3. Prepare the journal entry to record payment of the note and interest on the maturity date, April 30, 2015.
4. If Sears Canada needs extra cash for every December holiday season, should management borrow money on a long-term basis to avoid the necessity of negotiating a new short-term loan each year?

■ **LO1, 4**   **E10–7**   **Determining Financial Statement Effects of Transactions Involving Notes Payable**

Sears Canada Inc.

Refer to the previous exercise.

Required:
Determine the financial statement effects for each of the following transactions: (*a*) issuance of the note on November 1, 2014, (*b*) impact of the adjusting entry at December 31, 2014, and (*c*) the payment of the note and interest on April 30, 2015. Indicate the accounts affected, amounts, and direction of the effects (+ for increases and − for decreases) on the accounting equation. Use the following headings:

Date	Assets	=	Liabilities	+	Shareholders' Equity

■ **LO1**   **E10–8**   **Reporting Warranty Liability**

Gonzales Co. provides warranties for many of its products. Its estimated warranty liability account had a balance of $140,800 at January 1, 2014. Based on an analysis of warranty claims during the past several years, the warranty expense for 2014 was established at 0.4 percent of sales. During 2014, the actual cost of servicing products under warranty was $64,400, and sales were $14,400,000.

Required:
1. Compute the warranty expense that should appear on the company's statement of earnings for the year ended December 31, 2014.
2. What amount will be reported in the estimated warranty liability account on the statement of financial position as at December 31, 2014?

■ **LO1**   **E10–9**   **Reporting Warranty Liabilities**

Amster Corp. produces and sells a single product that requires considerable servicing and adjustment during the first two years after sale. The company offers a warranty for two years covering most service requirements. The product's price ranges from $900 to $1,200, depending on the particular model produced. Warranty work costs $100 per product, regardless of the model. This amount has been quite stable for several years. Most of the warranty work occurs between the 6th and the 18th month after sale. The company's sales have been expanding, from approximately 9,000 units in 2009 to approximately 12,000 units in 2014.

Required:
How should Amster Corp. account for warranty costs, and how should the information be reported on its financial statements?

■ **LO1, 2, 6**   **E10–10**   **Determining the Impact of Transactions, Including Analysis of Cash Flows**

Diego Company sells a wide range of goods through two retail stores operating in adjoining cities. Most purchases of goods for resale are on account. Occasionally, a short-term note payable is used to obtain cash for current use. The following transactions were selected from those occurring during 2015:

a. On January 10, 2015, purchased merchandise on credit, $36,000; the company uses a perpetual inventory system.

b. On March 1, 2015, borrowed $200,000 cash from the bank and signed an interest-bearing note payable at the end of one year, with an annual interest rate of 4 percent payable at maturity.

c. On April 5, 2015, sold merchandise on credit, $67,800; this amount included GST of $3,000 and PST of $4,800. The cost of sales represents 70 percent of the sales invoice.

Required:
1. Describe the financial statement effects of these transactions. Indicate the accounts affected and the amounts and direction of the effects (+ for increases and − for decreases) on the accounting equation. Use the following headings:

Date	Assets	=	Liabilities	+	Shareholders' Equity

2. What amount of cash is paid on the maturity date of the note?
3. Discuss the impact of each transaction on Diego's cash flows.
4. Discuss the impact of each transaction on the quick ratio. Assume that the quick ratio is greater than 1.0 before considering each transaction.

E10–11 Reporting Contingent Liabilities

LO5

Buzz Coffee Shops is famous for its large servings of hot coffee. After a famous case involving McDonald's, the lawyer for Buzz warned management (during 2011) that it could be sued if someone were to spill hot coffee and be burned: "With the temperature of your coffee, I can guarantee it's just a matter of time before you're sued for $1,000,000." Unfortunately, in 2013, the prediction came true when a customer filed suit. The case went to trial in 2014, and the jury awarded the customer $400,000 in damages, which the company immediately appealed. During 2015, the customer and the company settled their dispute for $150,000. What is the proper reporting each year of the events related to this liability?

E10–12 (Appendix 10A) Computing Deferred Income Tax: One Temporary Difference, with Discussion

The comparative statements of earnings of Martin Corporation for fiscal years 2014 and 2015 showed the following summarized pretax data:

	2014	2015
Sales revenue	$55,000	$63,000
Expenses (excluding income tax)	39,000	43,000
Pretax earnings	$16,000	$20,000

The expenses in 2014 included an amount of $4,000 that was deductible for tax purposes in 2015. The average income tax rate was 32 percent. Taxable income from the income tax returns was $20,000 for 2014 and $16,000 for 2015.

Required:

1. For each year, compute (*a*) the income taxes payable and (*b*) the deferred income tax. Is the deferred income tax a liability or an asset? Explain.

2. Show what amounts related to income taxes should be reported each year on the statement of earnings and the statement of financial position. Assume that the income tax is paid on March 1 of the next year.

3. Explain why income tax expense is not simply the amount of cash paid during the year.

E10–13 (Appendix 10A) Recording Deferred Income Tax: One Temporary Difference; Discussion of Management Strategy

The comparative statement of earnings for Chung Corporation for fiscal years 2013 and 2014 provided the following summarized pretax data:

	2013	2014
Revenue	$75,000	$82,000
Expenses (excluding income tax)	54,000	58,000
Pretax earnings	$21,000	$24,000

The expenses for 2014 included an amount of $3,000 that was deductible only on the 2013 income tax return. The average income tax rate was 30 percent. Taxable income shown in the tax returns was $18,000 for 2013 and $27,000 for 2014.

Required:

1. For each year, compute (*a*) the income taxes payable and (*b*) the deferred income tax. Is the deferred income tax a liability or an asset? Explain.

2. Prepare the journal entry for each year to record the income taxes payable, the deferred income tax, and the income tax expense.

3. Show the tax-related amounts that should be reported each year on the statement of earnings and the statement of financial position. Assume that income tax is paid on March 1 of the next year.

4. Why would management want to incur the cost of preparing separate tax and financial accounting reports to defer the payment of taxes?

E10–14   **(Appendix 10A) Computing and Reporting Deferred Income Tax: Depreciation**
Amber Corporation reported the following summarized pretax data at the end of each year:

Statement of Earnings for the Year	2013	2014	2015
Revenues	$170,000	$182,000	$195,000
Expenses (including depreciation*)	122,000	126,000	130,000
Pretax earnings	$ 48,000	$ 56,000	$ 65,000

*Straight-line depreciation expense on a machine purchased January 1, 2013, for $75,000. The machine has a three-year estimated life and no residual value. The company used capital cost allowance on the income tax return as follows: 2013, $37,500; 2014, $25,000; and 2015, $12,500. The average income tax rate is 28 percent for each of the three years.

Taxable income from the income tax return was as follows: 2013, $32,000; 2014, $56,000; and 2015, $85,000.

Required:

1. For each year, compute (*a*) the income taxes payable and (*b*) the deferred income tax. Is the deferred income tax a liability or an asset? Explain.

2. Show the tax-related amounts that should be reported each year on the statement of earnings and the statement of financial position.

E10–15   **(Appendix 10B) Computing Present Values**
On January 1, 2014, Shannon Company completed the following transactions (assume a 10 percent annual interest rate):

a. Bought a delivery truck and agreed to pay $50,000 at the end of three years.

b. Rented an office building and was given the option of paying $10,000 at the end of each of the next three years or paying $28,000 immediately.

Required (show computations and round to the nearest dollar):

1. In (*a*), what is the cost of the truck that should be recorded at the time of purchase?

2. In (*b*), which option for the office building should the company select?

E10–16   **(Appendix 10B) Computing the Value of an Asset Based on Present Value**
Quetario Company is considering purchasing a machine that would save the company $13,500 in cash per year for six years, at the end of which the machine would be retired with no residual value. The firm wishes to earn a minimum return of 8 percent, compounded annually, on any such investment. Assume that the cash savings occur at year-end, and ignore income taxes.

Required:

1. What is the maximum amount that the firm should be willing to pay for this machine? Show your computations.

2. Would the maximum amount be different if the machine is expected to have a residual value of $4,000 at the end of six years? Explain.

3. As an alternative to the scenario in (2), the company could buy a machine that had no residual value and offered no cost savings for the first five years, but this machine would offer cost savings of $113,561 at the end of the sixth year. If the company can buy only one machine, which one should it be? Defend your answer.

E10–17   **(Appendix 10B) Reporting a Mortgage Note**
On January 1, 2015, Wong Corporation signed a mortgage note for $5,000,000 at 8 percent for a term of five years. Mortgage payments are made semi-annually on June 30 and on December 31. Each mortgage payment is a blend of interest on the unpaid amount and a partial repayment of the principal loan.

Required:

1. Compute the amount of each mortgage payment.

2. Record the mortgage payments on June 30, 2015, and December 31, 2015.

3. What is the current portion of the mortgage at December 31, 2015? What portion of the mortgage would appear as long-term debt on the statement of financial position at that same date?

P10–1 Recording and Reporting Current Liabilities with Discussion of the Effects on the Quick Ratio (AP10–1)

LO1, 2

Dumax Company completed the following transactions during 2015. The company's fiscal year ends on December 31, 2015.

Jan.	2	Paid accrued interest in the amount of $52,000.
Apr.	30	Borrowed $550,000 from Commerce Bank; signed a 12-month, 6 percent interest-bearing note.
May	20	Sold merchandise for $6,000 cash plus harmonized sales tax at 14 percent, and realized a gross profit of 40 percent of sales.
June	3	Purchased merchandise for resale at a cost of $75,800; terms 2/10, n/30.
July	5	Paid the invoice received on June 3.
Aug.	31	Signed a contract to provide security service to a small apartment complex and collected $6,840 of fees for six months in advance, including HST at the rate of 14 percent. (Record the collection in a way that will not require an adjusting entry at year-end.)
Dec.	31	Reclassified a long-term debt in the amount of $100,000 to a current liability.
	31	Determined that salary and wages earned but not yet paid on December 31 totalled $85,000. Ignore payroll taxes.
	31	Recorded income tax expense for the year in the amount of $125,000. The current income taxes payable were $93,000.

Required:

1. Prepare journal entries to record each of these transactions, assuming that a perpetual inventory system is used.
2. Prepare all adjusting and reclassification entries required on December 31, 2015.
3. Show how all of the current liabilities arising from these transactions are reported on the statement of financial position at December 31, 2015.
4. For each transaction and entry, state whether the quick ratio is increased, decreased, or remains unchanged. Assume that the quick ratio is less than 1.0 prior to each transaction.

P10–2 Determining Financial Effects of Transactions Affecting Current Liabilities with Discussion of Cash Flow Effects (AP10–2)

LO1, 6

Refer to the previous problem.

Required:

1. For each transaction (including adjusting entries) listed in the previous problem, indicate the accounts affected, amounts, and direction of the effects (+ for increases and − for decreases) on the accounting equation. Use the following headings:

Date	Assets	=	Liabilities	+	Shareholders' Equity

2. For each transaction and related adjusting entry, state whether cash flow from operating activities is increased, decreased, or unchanged.

P10–3 Recording and Reporting Accrued Liabilities and Deferred Revenue and Financial Statement Effects with Discussion

LO1

During 2015, Riverside Company completed the following two transactions. The company's fiscal year ends on December 31.

a. Paid and recorded wages of $130,000 during 2015; however, at the end of December 2015, wages of $1,300 for three days are unpaid and unrecorded because the next weekly pay day is January 6, 2016.

b. Rented office space to another party and collected $3,000 on December 10, 2015. The rent collected was for 30 days from December 12, 2015, through January 10, 2016, and was credited in full to rent revenue.

Required:

1. Prepare (*a*) the adjusting entry required on December 31, 2015, and (*b*) the journal entry on January 6, 2016, to record the payment of any unpaid wages from December 2015.
2. Prepare (*a*) the journal entry for the collection of rent on December 10, 2015, and (*b*) the adjusting entry on December 31, 2015.

3. Determine the financial statement effects for each of the journal entries you prepared in (1) and (2). Indicate the accounts affected, amounts, and direction of the effects (+ for increases and − for decreases) on the accounting equation. Use the following headings:

Date	Assets	=	Liabilities	+	Shareholders' Equity

4. Show how the liabilities related to these transactions should be reported on the company's statement of financial position at December 31, 2015.

5. Explain why the accrual method of accounting provides more relevant information to financial analysts than the cash method.

■ **LO1, 2, 4**   **P10–4**   **Determining Financial Statement Effects of Various Liabilities** (AP10–3)

Dell Inc.

1. Dell Inc. is a leading technology company that offers a broad range of product categories, including mobility products, desktop PCs, software and peripherals, servers and networking, and storage. Its annual report contained the following note:

> *Warranty*—We record warranty liabilities at the time of sale for the estimated costs that may be incurred under the terms of the limited warranty. . . . The specific warranty terms and conditions vary depending upon the product sold and the country in which we do business, but generally include technical support, parts, and labor over a period ranging from one to three years. Factors that affect our warranty liability include the number of installed units currently under warranty, historical and anticipated rates of warranty claims on those units, and cost per claim to satisfy our warranty obligation.

Required:
Assume that estimated warranty costs for 2013 were $1 billion and that the warranty work was performed during 2014. Describe the financial statement effects for each year.

The Walt Disney Company

2. Walt Disney is a well-recognized brand in the entertainment industry, with products ranging from broadcast media to parks and resorts. The following note is from its annual report:

> **Walt Disney**
>
> **Revenue Recognition**
>
> Revenues from advance theme park ticket sales are recognized when the tickets are used. For non-expiring, multi-year tickets, we recognize revenue over a three-year time period based on estimated usage, which is derived from historical usage patterns.

Required:
Assume that Disney collected $120 million in 2013 for multi-year tickets that will be used in future years. For 2014, the company estimates that 70 percent of the tickets will be used, and the remaining 30 percent will be used in 2015. Describe the financial statement effects for each year.

Brunswick Corporation

3. Brunswick Corporation is a multinational company that manufactures and sells marine and recreational products. Its annual report contained the following information:

> **Litigation**
>
> A jury awarded $44.4 million in damages in a suit brought by Independent Boat Builders Inc., a buying group of boat manufacturers and its 22 members. Under the antitrust laws, the damage award has been tripled, and the plaintiffs will be entitled to their attorney's fees and interest.
>
> The Company has filed an appeal contending the verdict was erroneous as a matter of law, both as to liability and damages.

Required:
How should Brunswick report this litigation in its financial statements?

Shoppers Drug Mart Corporation

4. A recent annual report for Shoppers Drug Mart Corporation (acquired by Loblaw Companies Limited in 2013) included quick assets of $574.2 million and current liabilities of $2,335 million. Based on the quick ratio, do you think that Shoppers Drug Mart is experiencing financial difficulty?

5. Alcoa is involved in the mining and manufacturing of aluminum. Its products can become an advanced alloy for the wing of a Boeing 787 or a common, recyclable Coca-Cola can. The annual report for Alcoa stated the following:

Alcoa

Environmental Expenditures

Liabilities are recorded when remediation costs are probable and the costs can be reasonably estimated.

Required:

In your own words, explain Alcoa's accounting policy for environmental expenditures. What is the justification for this policy?

P10–5 Recording and Reporting Product Warranties

Bombardier Inc. specializes in manufacturing transportation products (aircraft, railway equipment, snowmobiles, and watercraft). The company offers warranties on all of its products. Note 2 to Bombardier's financial statements for fiscal year 2011 stated the following:

■ **LO1**

Bombardier Inc.

Product warranties typically range from one to five years, except for aircraft and bogie structural warranties that extend up to 20 years.

Selected information from Bombardier's annual reports follows (amounts in millions of U.S. dollars):

	2012	2011	2010
Revenues	16,768	18,347	17,892
Provision for product warranties at year-end	966	1,073	1,120

During fiscal year 2012, Bombardier paid $365 million to customers in exchange for returned products under the warranty.

Required:

1. Compute the amount of warranty expense for fiscal year 2012.
2. Prepare journal entries to record both the warranty expense for the year and the payments made under the warranty.
3. Compute the ratio of the warranty liability to revenues for the three years. Has the ratio increased or decreased during the three-year period?
4. Based on the limited information available about the warranty expense and payments in 2012, should Bombardier increase the balance of the warranty liability in future years? Explain.

P10–6 Defining and Analyzing Changes in Current Liabilities (AP10–4)

Dell Inc. sells computer products as well as extended-warranty services on the products it sells, a common practice in the electronics industry. Should the product break down, Dell will provide repair services within its contractual obligations. More frequently, however, the product will function properly and no service is required. Dell initially defers revenue from selling extended warranties. Revenue from the sale of extended warranties is recognized gradually over the duration of the contracts or when the service is completed. Dell included the following note disclosures in a recent annual report:

■ **LO1**

Dell Inc.

NOTE 1: SUMMARY OF SIGNIFICANT ACCOUNTING POLICIES

Standard Warranty Liabilities—Dell records warranty liabilities for its standard limited warranty at the time of sale for the estimated costs that may be incurred under its limited warranty. The liability for standard warranties is included in accrued and other current and other non-current liabilities on the Consolidated Statements of Financial Position. The specific warranty terms and conditions vary depending upon the product sold and the country in which Dell does business, but generally includes technical support, parts, and labor over a period ranging from one to three years. Factors that affect Dell's warranty liability include the number of installed units currently under warranty, historical and anticipated rates of warranty claims on those units, and cost per claim to satisfy Dell's warranty obligation.

. . .

Deferred Revenue—Deferred revenue represents amounts received in advance for extended warranty services, amounts due or received from customers under a legally binding commitment prior to services being rendered, deferred revenue related to Dell-owned software offerings, as well as other deferred revenue. . . .

NOTE 9—WARRANTY AND DEFERRED EXTENDED WARRANTY REVENUE

Dell records liabilities for its standard limited warranties at the time of sale for the estimated costs that may be incurred. . . . Revenue from the sale of extended warranties is recognized over the term of the contract or when the service is completed, and the costs associated with these contracts are recognized as incurred. . . . Changes in Dell's liabilities for standard limited warranties and deferred services revenue related to extended warranties are presented in the following tables for the periods indicated:

	Fiscal Year Ended		
	Feb. 1, 2013	Feb. 3, 2012	Jan. 28, 2011
	(in millions)		
Warranty liability:			
Warranty liability at beginning of period	888	895	912
Costs accrued for new warranty contracts	992	1,025	1,046
Service obligations honored	(1,118)	(1,032)	(1,063)
Warranty liability at end of period	762	888	895

	Fiscal Year Ended		
	Feb. 1, 2013	Feb. 3, 2012	Jan. 28, 2011
	(in millions)		
Deferred extended warranty revenue:			
Deferred extended warranty revenue at beginning of period	7,002	6,416	5,910
Revenue deferred for new extended warranties	4,130	4,301	3,877
Revenue recognized	(4,029)	(3,715)	(3,371)
Deferred extended warranty revenue at end of period	7,103	7,002	6,416

Source: Dell Inc., Annual Report 2013, Form 10K.

Required:

1. Prepare the journal entries to record the transactions related to the changes to the warranty liability during fiscal year 2013.
2. Prepare the journal entries to record the transactions related to the changes to the deferred extended warranty revenue during fiscal year 2013.
3. Dell reported net revenues of $56,940, $62,071, and $61,494 for fiscal years 2013, 2012, and 2011, respectively. Compute the ratio of the warranty expense to net revenues for the three years. Has the ratio increased or decreased during the three-year period? Provide possible reasons for the changes in the ratio.
4. Based on the limited information available about the warranty expense and settlements during these three years, should Dell reduce the ratio of the warranty expense to net revenues in future years? Explain.

■ LO1   **P10–7**   **Determining Financial Statement Effects of Deferred Revenues**

A. Deferred revenues—customer deposits

Eastern Brewing Company (EBC) distributes its products in an aluminum keg. Customers are charged a deposit of $25 per keg, and deposits received from customers are recorded in the keg deposits account.

Required:

1. Where on the statement of financial position will the keg deposits account be found? Explain.
2. A production specialist who works for EBC estimates that 50 kegs for which deposits were received during the year will never be returned. How would the deposits related to these 50 kegs be reflected in the company's financial statements?

B. Deferred revenues—rent

On September 1, 2014, Noreen Ltd. collected $72,000 in cash from its tenant as an advance rent payment on its store location. The six-month lease period ends on February 28, 2015, at which time the lease contract may be renewed. Noreen's fiscal year ends on December 31.

Required:

1. Prepare journal entries to record the collection of rent on September 1, 2014, and the related adjustment for the amount of rent earned during 2014.

2. If the amount received on September 1, 2014, had covered a period of 18 months, how should Noreen report the deferred rent amount on its statement of financial position as at December 31, 2014?

C. Deferred revenues—subscription fees

Tremblay Inc. publishes a monthly newsletter for retail marketing managers and requires its subscribers to pay $60 in advance for a one-year subscription. During the month of April 2015, Tremblay Inc. sold 150 one-year subscriptions and received payments in advance from all new subscribers. Only 90 of the new subscribers paid their fees in time to receive the April newsletter. The other subscribers received the newsletter in May.

Required:

Prepare journal entries to record the subscription fees received in advance during April 2015, and the related adjusting entry to recognize the subscription revenue earned during April 2015.

P10–8 **Defining and Analyzing Changes in Current Liabilities** (AP10–5)

■ LO1

Leon's Furniture Limited is one of Canada's largest home furnishing retailers, with a network of 75 stores selling a wide range of furniture, major appliances and home electronics. The company reported the following items in its statement of financial position dated December 31, 2012 (in thousands of Canadian dollars):

Leon's Furniture Limited

	December 31, 2012	December 31, 2011
Current liabilities		
Trade and other payables	$73,542	$86,357
Customers' deposits	20,386	19,157
Dividends payable	7,055	17,457
Deferred warranty plan revenue	14,743	16,152

Required:

1. Define each of the current liabilities and identify the types of transactions that cause each liability to change (increase, decrease).

2. The company reported that $7,594 of deferred warranty plan revenue was earned during fiscal year 2012. Determine the amount that was collected in advance from customers during 2012, and prepare the related journal entry.

3. The company's board of directors declared dividends of $28,047 during 2012. Prepare the journal entries to record the declaration and payment of dividends during 2012.

P10–9 **Making a Decision as Chief Financial Officer: Contingent Liabilities**

■ LO1, 5

For each of the following situations, determine whether the company should (*a*) report a liability on the statement of financial position, (*b*) disclose a contingent liability, or (*c*) not report the situation. Justify and explain your conclusions.

1. An automobile company introduces a new car. Past experience demonstrates that lawsuits will be filed as soon as the new model is involved in any accidents. The company can be certain that at least one jury will award damages to people injured in an accident.

2. A research scientist determines that your company's bestselling product may infringe on another company's patent. If the other company discovers the infringement and files a lawsuit, your company could lose millions of dollars.

3. As part of land development for a new housing project, your company has polluted a natural lake. Under provincial law, you must clean up the lake once you complete the development. The development project will take five to eight years to complete. Current estimates indicate that it will cost $2 to $3 million to clean up the lake.

4. Your company has just been notified that it lost a product liability lawsuit for $1 million that it plans to appeal. Management is confident that the company will win on appeal, but the lawyers believe that it will lose.

5. A key customer is unhappy with the quality of a major construction project. The company believes that the customer is being unreasonable but, to maintain goodwill, has decided to do $250,000 in repairs next year.

■ LO2, 3   **P10–10**   **Analyzing and Interpreting the Quick Ratio and the Trade Payables Turnover Ratio** (AP10–6)

Clearwater Seafoods Inc.

Clearwater Seafoods Inc. is a leader in the global seafood market. Its main operations include harvesting, processing, distribution, and marketing of seafood products primarily in Canada, the United States, Europe, and Asia. Selected financial statement information for the company over the four-year period 2009–2012 is presented below (amounts in thousands of Canadian dollars):

	2012	2011	2010	2009
Quick assets	$ 84,935	$ 51,444	$ 44,480	$ 38,321
Current liabilities	64,169	86,614	78,531	132,547
Cost of sales	276,190	263,220	234,854	240,215
Trade payables	44,633	40,767	33,327	31,604
Increase (decrease) in inventories	(9,846)	14,238	(8,534)	(1,413)

Required:

1. Compute the quick ratio for each of the four years, and comment on the four-year trend of the ratio.

2. Compute the trade payables turnover ratio and the average age of payables for the years 2010–2012. Did the company's management of its trade payables improve over time? Explain.

3. In computing the trade payables turnover ratio, it is preferable to use purchases instead of cost of sales in the numerator. Re-compute the ratio for each of the years 2010–2012 using purchases in the numerator. Do the new ratios differ significantly from those computed in (2)? Explain.

■ LO6   **P10–11**   **Determining Cash Flow Effects** (AP10–7)

For each of the following transactions, determine whether cash flows from operating activities will increase, decrease, or remain the same:

a. Purchased merchandise on credit.

b. Paid a trade payable.

c. Accrued payroll for the month but did not pay it.

d. Borrowed money from the bank. The term of the note is 90 days.

e. Reclassified a long-term note as a current liability.

f. Paid accrued interest expense.

g. Recorded a liability based on a pending lawsuit.

h. Paid back the bank for money borrowed in (*d*), along with related interest.

i. Collected cash from a customer for services that will be performed in the next accounting period.

j. Paid GST to the federal government. The amount was previously collected from customers.

P10–12   **(Appendix 10A) Recording and Reporting Deferred Income Tax: Depreciation** (AP10–8)

At December 31, 2014, the records of Pearson Corporation provided the following information:

Statement of Earnings	
Revenues	$160,000
Depreciation expense (straight line)	(11,000)
Other expenses (excluding income tax)	(90,000)
Earnings before income taxes	$ 59,000

Additional information is as follows:

a. Revenues include $20,000 interest on tax-free municipal bonds.

b. Depreciation expense relates to equipment acquired on January 1, 2014, at a cost of $44,000, with no salvage value and an estimated useful life of four years.

c. The accelerated depreciation (capital cost allowance) used on the tax return is as follows: 2014, $17,600; 2015, $13,200; 2016, $8,800; and 2017, $4,400.

d. The company is subject to an income tax rate of 30 percent. Assume that 85 percent of the income tax liability is paid in the year incurred.

e. The income tax return for 2014 shows a taxable income of $32,400.

Required:

1. Compute the income taxes payable and the deferred income tax for 2014. Is the deferred income tax a liability or an asset? Explain.

2. Prepare the journal entry to record income taxes for 2014.

3. Show how the tax-related amounts should be reported on the statement of earnings for 2014 and the statement of financial position at December 31, 2014.

P10–13 **(Appendix 10B) Comparing Options by Using Present Value Concepts (AP10–9)**
After hearing a knock at your front door, you are surprised to see the Prize Patrol from a large, well-known magazine subscription company. It has arrived with the good news that you are the big winner, having won $20 million. Later, after consulting with a lawyer, you discover that you have three options: (1) you can receive $1 million per year for the next 20 years (starting one year from now), (2) you can have $8 million today, or (3) you can have $2 million today and receive $700,000 for each of the next 20 years. Your investment adviser tells you that it is reasonable to expect to earn 5 percent annual compound interest on investments. Which option do you prefer? What factors influenced your decision?

P10–14 **(Appendix 10B) Computing Equal Periodic Debt Payments, and Completing a Schedule (AP10–10)**
On January 1, 2014, you bought a new Toyota automobile for $30,000. You made a $5,000 cash down payment and signed a $25,000 note, payable in four equal instalments on each December 31, the first payment to be made on December 31, 2014. The interest rate is 8 percent per year on the unpaid balance. Each payment will include payment on principal plus the interest.

Required:

1. Compute the amount of the equal payments that you must make.

2. What is the total amount of interest that you will pay during the four years?

3. Complete the following schedule:

Debt Payment Schedule				
Date	Cash Payment	Interest Expense	Decrease in Principal	Unpaid Principal
1/1/2014				
31/12/2014				
31/12/2015				
31/12/2016				
31/12/2017				
Totals				

4. Explain why the amount of interest expense decreases each year.

5. To reduce the total amount of interest paid on this note, you considered the possibility of making equal payments every three months (four payments per year). Compute the amount of the equal payments that you must make, and the amount of interest that will be saved over the life of the note.

P10–15 **(Appendix 10B) Computing Amounts for a Debt Fund with Journal Entries**
On December 31, 2013, Post Company decided to invest a sufficient amount of cash to pay the principal amount of a $160,000 debt due on December 31, 2016. The company will make four equal annual deposits on December 31 of the years 2013 through 2016. The fund will earn 7 percent compound annual interest, which will be added to the balance at each year-end. The fund trustee will pay the loan principal (to the creditor) upon receipt of the last fund deposit. The company's fiscal year ends on December 31. The four annual deposits have a present value of $122,064 on December 31, 2013.

Required (show computations and round to the nearest dollar):

1. How much cash must be deposited each December 31?

2. What amount of interest will be earned on the four deposits until December 31, 2016?

3. How much interest revenue will the fund earn each year?

4. Prepare journal entries for the company to record the following transactions:

   a. The first deposit on December 31, 2013.

   b. The deposit at December 31, 2014, and interest revenue for 2014.

   c. The payment of the debt on December 31, 2016.

5. Show how the effect of the fund will be reported on the income statement for 2014 and the statement of financial position at December 31, 2014.

ALTERNATE PROBLEMS

■ LO1, 2, 6   **AP10–1**   **Recording and Reporting Current Liabilities with Discussion of the Effects on the Quick Ratio** (P10–1)

Computek Ltd. completed the following transactions during 2015. The company's fiscal year ends on December 31, 2015.

Jan.   8   Purchased on account merchandise for resale at a cost of $14,500, with terms 2/10, n/30. The company uses a periodic inventory system.

    19   Paid the invoice received on January 8.

Mar. 10   Sold merchandise on credit for a total amount of $11,300, which included GST at 5 percent and PST at 8 percent of the sales amount.

Apr.   1   Borrowed $35,000 from the bank for general use; signed a 12-month, 6 percent interest-bearing note.

June   3   Purchased merchandise for resale at a cost of $16,420.

July   5   Paid the invoice received on June 3.

Aug.   1   Rented a small office in a building owned by the company and collected $6,000 for six months' rent in advance. Ignore sales taxes. (Record the collection in a way that will not require an adjusting entry at year-end.)

Dec. 20   Received a $100 refundable deposit from a customer as a guarantee to return a large trailer "borrowed" for 30 days.

    31   Determined that wages earned but not yet paid on December 31 amounted to $9,500. Ignore payroll taxes.

Required:

1. Prepare the journal entry for each of these transactions.
2. Prepare the adjusting entry (entries) required on December 31, 2015.
3. Show how all of the liabilities arising from these transactions are reported on the statement of financial position at December 31, 2015.
4. For each transaction and related adjusting entry, state whether the quick ratio increases, decreases, or remains the same. Assume that the quick ratio is less than 1.0 before considering each transaction.

■ LO1, 6   **AP10–2**   **Determining Financial Effects of Transactions Affecting Current Liabilities with Discussion of Cash Flow Effects** (P10–2)

Refer to the previous problem.

Required:

1. For each transaction (including adjusting and reclassification entries), indicate the accounts affected, amounts, and direction of the effects (+ for increases and − for decreases) on the accounting equation. Use the following headings:

Date	Assets	=	Liabilities	+	Shareholders' Equity

2. For each transaction, state whether cash flow from operating activities is increased, decreased, or unchanged.

■ LO1, 2   **AP10–3**   **Determining Financial Statement Effects of Various Liabilities** (P10–4)

Ford Motor Company

1. Ford Motor Company is one of the world's largest companies, with annual sales of cars and trucks in excess of $120 billion. Its annual report contained the following note:

Warranties

Estimated warranty costs are accrued for at the time the vehicle is sold to a dealer. Estimates for warranty costs are made based primarily on historical warranty claim experience.

Required:

This year, Ford reported claims amounting to $4.0 billion and accrued expenses for warranties in the amount of $3.9 billion. Describe the financial statement effects for this year.

2. Carnival Cruise Lines operates cruise ships in Alaska, the Caribbean, the South Pacific, and the Mediterranean. Some cruises are brief; others can last for several weeks. The company does more than $1 billion in cruise business each year. The following note is from its annual report:

Required:

In your own words, explain how deferred revenue is reported on the statement of financial position for Carnival. Assume that Carnival collected $15 million in 2014 for cruises that will be completed in the following year. Of that amount, $3 million was related to cruises of 10 or fewer nights that were not complete; $7 million to cruises of more than 10 nights that, on average, were 60 percent complete; and $5 million was related to cruises that had not yet begun. What is the amount of deferred revenue that should be reported on the 2014 statement of financial position?

3. An annual report for Exxon Mobil Corporation reported a quick ratio of 0.45. For the previous year, the ratio was 0.70. Based on this information, do you think that Exxon Mobil is experiencing financial difficulty? What other information would you want to consider in making this evaluation?

4. Brunswick Corporation is a multinational company that manufactures and sells marine and recreational products. Its annual report contained the following information:

Required:

In your own words, explain Brunswick's accounting policy for environmental expenditures. What is the justification for this policy?

AP10–4 Recording and Reporting Warranty Liabilities (P10–6)

■ **LO1**

International Business Machines (IBM) is a leading provider of computer products and services. The company is known for its hardware products but has focused on providing information technology services in recent years. IBM provides standard warranties with the sale of its products. The company's note on significant accounting policies is as follows:

In addition, IBM offers its customers an option to purchase extended warranties. Revenue from extended warranty contracts, for which the company is obligated to perform, is recorded as deferred revenue income and subsequently recognized on a straight-line basis over the delivery period.

Selected information related to warranties provided by IBM follows (in millions of U.S. dollars):

	2012	2011	2010
Net revenues	$104,507	$106,916	$99,870
Standard warranty liability, end of year	394	407	375
Settlements made during the year	392	420	418
Extended warranty deferred revenue, end of year	606	636	670
Additions to extended warranty deferred revenue during the year	268	314	329

Required:

1. Compute the amount of warranty expense for 2011 and 2012.

2. Prepare journal entries to record both the warranty expense for 2012 and the payments made under the warranty during the year.

3. Compute the ratio of the warranty expense to net revenues for the three years. Assume that the warranty expense is $477 for 2010. Has the ratio increased or decreased during the three-year period? Provide possible reasons for the changes in the ratio.

4. Based on the limited information available about the warranty expense and settlements during these three years, should IBM reduce the ratio of the warranty expense to net sales in future years? Explain.

5. Compute the extended warranty revenue recognized during 2011 and 2012, and prepare the journal entry to record the revenue recognized in 2012.

◼ LO1   **AP10–5**   **Defining and Analyzing Changes in Current Liabilities** (P10–8)

Danier Leather Inc.

Danier Leather Inc. is one of North America's leading designers, manufacturers, and retailers of quality leather and suede for both women and men. The company reported the following items in its statement of financial position dated June 30, 2012, and related note disclosures (in thousands of Canadian dollars):

	June 30, 2012	June 25, 2011
Current liabilities		
Payables and accruals	$10,161	$11,024
Deferred revenue	1,463	1,489
Sales return provision (Note 10)	124	47
Income taxes payable	—	278

Note 10. Sales Return Provision:

The provision for sales returns primarily relates to customer returns of unworn and undamaged purchases for a full refund within the time period provided by Danier's return policy, which is generally 14 days after the purchase date. Since the time period of the provision is of relatively short duration, all of the provision is classified as current. The following transactions occurred during the years ended June 30, 2012, and June 25, 2011, with respect to the sales return provision:

	June 30, 2012	June 25, 2011
Beginning of period	$ 47	$ —
Amount provided during the period	1,799	1,687
Released during the period	(1,722)	(1,640)
End of period	$ 124	$ 47

Required:

1. Define each of the current liabilities and identify the types of transactions that cause each liability to change (increase, decrease).

2. Assume that the company received $17,365 from customers in advance of delivering them the products they ordered. Determine the amount of deferred revenue that the company earned during fiscal year 2012, and prepare the related journal entries to record the transactions that affected the deferred revenue account.

3. Prepare the journal entries to record the transactions that affected the provision for sales returns account during 2012.

◼ LO2, 3   **AP10–6**   **Analyzing and Interpreting the Quick Ratio and the Trade Payables Turnover Ratio** (P10–10)

Potash Corporation of Saskatchewan

Potash Corporation of Saskatchewan is the world's largest fertilizer company, producing the three primary crop nutrients potash, phosphate and nitrogen. Potash Corp. is a major player in meeting the growing challenge of feeding the world, and has operations and business interests in seven countries. Selected financial statement information for this company over the most recent four-year period is shown below (in millions of U.S. dollars):

	2012	2011	2010	2009
Quick assets	$1,651	$1,625	$1,471	$1,599
Current liabilities	1,851	2,194	3,144	1,598
Cost of sales	4,023	3,933	3,361	2,643
Trade payables	623	578	592	509

Required:

1. Compute the quick ratio for each of the four years, and comment on the four-year trend of the ratio.

2. Compute the trade payables turnover ratio and the average age of payables for the years 2010–2012. Did the company improve on its management of trade payables? Explain.

AP10–7 Determining Cash Flow Effects (P10–11)

For each of the following transactions, determine whether cash flows from operating activities will increase, decrease, or remain the same:

a. Purchased merchandise for cash.

b. Paid salaries and wages for the last month of the previous accounting period.

c. Paid PST to the provincial government, based on collections from customers.

d. Borrowed money from the bank. The term of the note is two years.

e. Withheld CPP contributions from employees' pay cheques and immediately paid these to the government.

f. Recorded accrued interest expense.

g. Paid cash as a result of losing a lawsuit. A liability had been recorded.

h. Paid salaries and wages for the current month.

i. Performed services for a customer who had paid for them in the previous accounting period.

AP10–8 (Appendix 10A) Recording and Reporting Deferred Income Taxes: Two Temporary Differences (P10–12)

The records of Calib Corporation provided the following summarized data for 2014 and 2015:

Year-End December 31		
	2014	**2015**
Statement of Earnings		
Revenues	$210,000	$218,000
Expenses (excluding income tax)	130,000	133,000
Earnings before income taxes	$ 80,000	$ 85,000

a. Calib is subject to an income tax rate of 35 percent. Assume that 80 percent of the income taxes payable are paid in the current year and 20 percent on February 28 of the next year.

b. The temporary differences resulted from the following:

i. The 2015 expenses include an amount of $8,000 that must be deducted only in the 2014 tax return.

ii. The 2015 revenues include an amount of $6,000 that was taxable only in 2016.

c. The taxable income shown in the tax returns was $72,000 for 2014 and $87,000 for 2015.

Required:

1. For each year, compute (*a*) the income taxes payable and (*b*) the deferred income taxes. Identify whether the deferred income tax amounts are assets or liabilities. Explain.

2. Prepare the journal entry for each year to record income taxes payable, deferred income taxes, and income tax expense.

3. Show the tax-related amounts that should be reported each year on the statement of earnings and the statement of financial position.

4. As a financial analyst, would you evaluate differently a deferred income tax liability compared with income taxes currently payable?

AP10–9 (Appendix 10B) Comparing Options by Using Present Value Concepts (P10–13)

After completing a long and successful career as senior vice-president for a large bank, you are preparing for retirement. After visiting the human resources office, you have found that you have several retirement options: (1) you can receive an immediate cash payment of $7,000,000, (2) you can receive $600,000 per year for life (you have a life expectancy of 20 years), or (3) you can receive $600,000 per year for 10 years and then $700,000 per year for life (this option is intended to give you some protection against inflation). You have determined that you can earn 5 percent compounded annually on your investments. Which option do you prefer and why?

AP10–10   **(Appendix 10B) Computing Equal Periodic Debt Payments, and Completing a Schedule with Journal Entries (P10–14)**

On January 1, 2014, Ontario Company sold a new machine to Canada Company for $70,000. Canada Company made a cash down payment of $20,000 and signed a $50,000, 8 percent note for the balance due. The note is payable in three equal instalments due on December 31, 2014, 2015, and 2016. Each payment includes principal plus interest on the unpaid balance. Canada Company recorded the purchase as follows:

Jan.1, 2014		
Machinery	70,000	
Cash		20,000
Note payable		50,000

Required (show computations and round to the nearest dollar):

1. What is the amount of the equal annual payments that Canada Company must make?
2. What is the total interest on the note over the three years?
3. Complete the following debt payment schedule:

Debt Payment Schedule				
Date	Cash Payment	Interest Expense	Decrease in Principal	Unpaid Principal
1/1/2014				
31/12/2014				
31/12/2015				
31/12/2016				
Total				

4. Prepare the journal entry for each of the three payments.
5. Explain why interest expense decreased in amount each year.

CASES AND PROJECTS

FINDING AND INTERPRETING FINANCIAL INFORMATION

LO1, 3, 4   **CP10–1**   **Finding Financial Information**

Canadian Tire Corporation

Refer to the financial statements of Canadian Tire Corporation in Appendix A of this book.

Required:

1. Does Canadian Tire report income taxes payable as a separate account on its statement of financial position at the end of the current year? If not, where would this account be included on Canadian Tire's statement of financial position?
2. How did changes in trade and other payables affect cash flows from operating activities in the current year?
3. What is the amount of non-current liabilities at the end of the current year?
4. What amounts of deferred income tax assets and liabilities are reported on the statement of financial position at the end of the current year?
5. Does the company disclose information on contingent liabilities?

LO1, 4   **CP10–2**   **Finding Financial Information**

RONA Inc.

Go to *Connect* for the financial statements of RONA Inc.

Required:

1. What is the amount of trade and other payables at the end of the current year?
2. How did changes in trade and other payables affect cash flows from operating activities in the current year?
3. The dividends payable account decreased by $269,000 during the current year. How much did RONA pay in dividends to its shareholders during the current year?

4. What is the amount of non-current borrowings at the end of the current year?

5. Does the company have any contingent liabilities?

CP10–3 Comparing Companies within an Industry

Refer to the financial statements of Canadian Tire Corporation (Appendix A) and RONA Inc. (*Connect*), and the Industry Ratio Report (Appendix B on *Connect*).

■ **LO2, 3**

Canadian Tire vs. RONA

Required:

1. Compute the quick ratio for each company for each year shown in the financial statements.

2. Compare the most recent quick ratio for each company to the industry average from the Industry Ratio Report. Based solely on the quick ratio, are these companies more or less liquid than the average company in their industry?

3. Compute the trade payables turnover ratio for each company for each year.

4. Using this information and any other data from the annual report, write a brief assessment of the liquidity of the two companies.

FINANCIAL REPORTING AND ANALYSIS CASES

CP10–4 Explaining a Note: Accrued Liability for a Frequent Flyer Program

Most major airlines have frequent flyer programs that permit passengers to earn free tickets based on the number of reward miles they have flown. A Southwest Airlines annual report contained the following note:

■ **LO1**

Southwest Airlines

> **Frequent Flyer Awards**
>
> The Company records a liability for the estimated incremental cost of providing free travel under its (and AirTran's) frequent flyer program for all amounts earned from flight activity that are expected to be redeemed for future travel. The estimated incremental cost includes direct passenger costs such as fuel, food, and other operational costs, but does not include any contribution to overhead or profit.

Required:

1. What cost measures other than incremental cost could Southwest use?

2. What account should Southwest debit when it accrues this liability?

CP10–5 Using Financial Reports: Evaluating Cash Management

Maple Leaf Foods Inc. is one of Canada's largest meat processors. It produces fresh and processed pork and poultry products under the Maple Leaf and Schneiders brands. Selected financial information is presented below for the period 2009–2012 (in millions of dollars):

■ **LO2, 3**

Maple Leaf Foods Inc.

	2012	2011	2010	2009
Net Sales	$4,865	$4,894	$4,968	$5,222
Net trade receivables	71	134	109	372
Inventories	302	293	277	298
Cost of sales	4,097	4,126	4,219	4,487
Trade payables	447	482	476	633

Required:

1. Compute the following ratios for each of the years 2010–2012:

   a. Trade payables turnover

   b. Inventory turnover

   c. Trade receivables turnover

2. One of the measures of a company's effectiveness in utilizing cash resources is the cash conversion cycle, which is the difference between the average number of days needed to convert inventory to cash and the average number of days to pay trade suppliers. Compute the cash conversion cycle for each of the years 2010–2012. Did the company improve on its management of cash? Explain.

CRITICAL THINKING CASES

LO1, 2   **CP10–6**   **Making Decisions as a Manager: Liquidity**

In some cases, a manager can engage in transactions that improve the appearance of financial reports without affecting the underlying economic reality. In this chapter, we discussed the importance of liquidity as measured by the quick ratio and working capital. For each of the following transactions, (*i*) determine whether reported liquidity, as measured by the quick ratio and working capital, is improved and (*ii*) state whether you believe that the fundamental liquidity of the company has been improved. Assume that the company has positive working capital and a quick ratio of 0.5 immediately prior to each transaction.

  a.   Borrowed $1 million from the bank, payable in 90 days.

  b.   Borrowed $10 million with a long-term note, payable in five years.

  c.   Reclassified the current portion of long-term debt as long term as a result of a new agreement with the bank that guarantees the company's ability to refinance the debt when it matures.

  d.   Paid $100,000 of the company's trade payables.

  e.   Entered into a borrowing agreement that allows the company to borrow up to $10 million when needed.

  f.   Required all employees to take accrued vacation to reduce its liability for vacation compensation.

LO2   **CP10–7**   **Evaluating an Ethical Dilemma: Managing Reported Results**

The president of a regional wholesale distribution company planned to borrow a significant amount of money from the bank at the beginning of the next fiscal year. He knew that the bank placed a heavy emphasis on the liquidity of potential borrowers. To improve the company's quick ratio, the president told his employees to stop shipping new merchandise to customers and to stop accepting merchandise from suppliers for the last three weeks of the fiscal year. Is this behaviour ethical? Would your answer be different if the president had been concerned about reported net earnings and asked all of the employees to work overtime to ship out merchandise that had been ordered at the end of the year?

FINANCIAL REPORTING AND ANALYSIS TEAM PROJECT

LO1, 2, 3, 4   **CP10–8**   **Team Project: Examining an Annual Report**

As a team, select an industry to analyze. A list of companies classified by industry can be obtained by accessing **www.fpinfomart.ca** and then choosing "Companies by Industry." You can also find a list of industries and companies within each industry via **http://ca.finance.yahoo.com/investing** (click on "Order Annual Reports" under "Tools").

Each group member should acquire the annual report for a different publicly traded company in the industry. (Library files, the SEDAR service at **www.sedar.com**, and the company's website are good sources.)

Required:
On an individual basis, each team member should then write a short report answering the following questions about the selected company. Discuss any patterns across the companies that you as a team observe. Then, as a group, write a short report comparing and contrasting your companies.

1. List the accounts and amounts of the company's current liabilities for the last three years.

   a. What is the percentage of each to the respective year's total liabilities?

   b. What do the results of your analysis suggest about the strategy your company has followed with respect to borrowed funds overall and over time?

2. What, if any, contingent liabilities are reported by the company for the most recent year, and what is your assessment of the risk of each after reading the note(s)?

3. Perform a ratio analysis:

   a. What does the quick ratio measure in general?

   b. Compute the ratio for the last three years.

   c. What do your results suggest about the company?

   d. If available, find the industry ratio for the most recent year, compare it to your results, and discuss why you believe the ratio for your company differs from or is similar to the industry ratio.

4. Perform another ratio analysis:

   a. What does the trade payables turnover ratio measure in general?

   b. Compute the ratio for the last three years.

   c. What do your results suggest about the company?

   d. If available, find the industry ratio for the most recent year, compare it to your results, and discuss why you believe the ratio for your company differs from or is similar to the industry ratio.

5. What is the effect of the change in trade payables on cash flows from operating activities for the most recent year; that is, did the change increase or decrease operating cash flows? Explain your answer.

SOLUTIONS TO SELF-STUDY QUIZZES

Self-Study Quiz 10-1

Effect on quick ratio:

1. Decrease, because the current liabilities will increase but the quick assets will remain the same

2. Increase, because cash will increase but current liabilities will not change

3. Increase, because the relative decrease in current liabilities is greater than the relative decrease in quick assets

4. No change, because this transaction affects only *non-current* assets and *non-current* liabilities

Self-Study Quiz 10-2

Cash	45.20	
Sales revenue		40.00
HST payable		5.20

Self-Study Quiz 10-3

1.

Interest expense	2,000	
Interest payable		2,000

2.

Interest expense	1,000	
Interest payable	2,000	
Cash		3,000

3.

Interest expense	3,000	
Cash		3,000

Self-Study Quiz 10-4

1. The present value will decrease. With a higher interest rate, more interest will accumulate over time, so the initial amount needed at the start will be smaller because the interest component will be larger.

2. $10,000 \times 0.5584 = \$5,584$

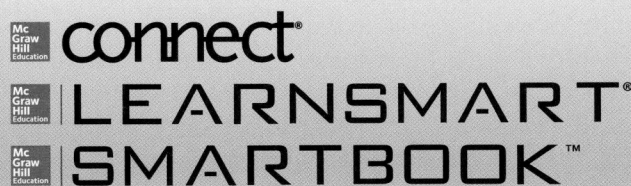

C H A P T E R

11

Reporting and Interpreting Non-current Liabilities

After studying this chapter, you should be able to do the following:

BCE

BCE Inc. 2012 Annual Report

Today just got better.

FOCUS COMPANY: **Bell Canada Enterprises (BCE)**

FINANCING GROWTH WITH LONG-TERM DEBT

Bell Canada Enterprises (BCE) Inc. (www.bce.ca) is Canada's largest communications company. The core business of BCE is delivering wired or wireless telecommunication services across any screen the customer chooses, from smartphone to television. For example, BCE's wireless network can now serve 97 percent of Canada's population, carrying more than one billion text messages per week. It is also a multi-media delivery service for sports TV, such as TSN and RDS; live news content from CTV and MTV; and on-demand entertainment from the Comedy Network, Discovery Channel, and BNN.

BCE has invested in its broadband networks, which supply customers with data across the worldwide web for residential customers, business-to-business markets, and government. BCE has followed a strategy of integration, beginning with the $3.2 billion acquisition of CTV in 2011 and the creation of Bell Media. It recently became a joint owner of Maple Leaf Sports and Entertainment, which owns not only sports teams but also stadiums, such as the Air Canada Centre and Maple Leaf Square condominium and commercial complex.

The communications industry is a capital-intensive industry. In 2012, BCE spent over $3.5 billion on investments in both tangible and intangible assets. Management of capital-intensive businesses faces a number of challenges. Large investments must be made based on estimates of customer demand many years into the future. If management does not make sufficient investments, customers will be lost to other companies. If an over-investment is made, money will be tied up in assets that do not generate revenue, and earnings will suffer.

In addition to deciding upon the proper level of investment in long-lived assets, management must decide on the optimal mix of sources of financing for those assets. BCE finances its investments in long-lived assets from three sources: internally generated funds, investments by owners, and borrowings from long-term creditors.

UNDERSTANDING THE BUSINESS

Non-current liabilities include all of the entity's obligations that are not classified as current liabilities, such as long-term notes and bonds payable. Typically, a non-current liability will require payment more than one year in the future. These obligations may be created by borrowing money, or they may result from other activities.

BCE reports its non-current liabilities on the statement of financial position, after current liabilities, as shown in Exhibit 11.1. Details of the long-term debt, deferred tax liabilities, post-employment benefit obligations, and other non-current liabilities are disclosed separately and explained in the notes.

In Chapter 10, we introduced the term *capital structure*, the mix of debt and equity that is used to finance a company's growth. Almost all companies employ some debt in their capital structure. In this chapter, the main focus is on long-term debt, which simply reflects a contractual obligation whereby the borrower receives cash or other assets in exchange for a promise to pay the lender a fixed or determinable amount of money at a specific date in the future.

The use of long-term debt offers significant advantages to companies such as BCE:

1. *Shareholders maintain control.* Debt does not dilute ownership and control of the company, because debtholders participate neither in the management of operations nor in the eventual distribution of retained earnings to shareholders.

2. *Interest expense is tax deductible.* The deductibility of interest for tax purposes reduces the net cost of borrowing. This is an advantage compared to dividends paid on shares that are not tax deductible.

3. *The impact on earnings is positive.* Money can often be borrowed at a low interest rate and invested at a higher rate. Assume that Maple Leaf Sports and Entertainment owns a store selling apparel with logos of Toronto's sports teams on it.

NON-CURRENT LIABILITIES are all of the entity's obligations not classified as current liabilities.

Exhibit **11.1**
Non-current Liabilities

REAL-WORLD EXCERPT

BCE Inc.

ANNUAL REPORT

CONSOLIDATED STATEMENTS OF FINANCIAL POSITION
As at December 31

(in millions of Canadian dollars)	Note	2012	2011
LIABILITIES			
Current Liabilities			
Trade payable and other liabilities	17	$ 3,915	$ 4,077
Interest payable		128	134
Dividends payable		453	415
Current tax liabilities		113	47
Debt due within one year	18	2,136	2,106
Total current liabilities		6,745	6,779
Non-current liabilities			
Long-term debt	19	13,886	12,721
Deferred tax liabilities		8,761	881
Post-employment benefit obligations	20	3,422	2,719
Other non-current liabilities	21	1,429	1,561
Total non-current liabilities		19,498	17,882
Total liabilities		$26,243	$24,661

Source: BCE Inc., Annual Report 2012.

The company has shareholders' equity of $500,000 invested in the store and generates $100,000 in earnings before interest and taxes per year. Management plans to open a new store that will also cost $500,000 and generate $100,000 in earnings before interest and taxes per year. Should management issue new shares or borrow the money at an interest rate of 8 percent? The following analysis for both stores shows that the use of debt will increase the return to the owners:

	Option 1 Equity	Option 2 Debt
Earnings before interest and income taxes	$ 200,000	$200,000
Interest expense	-0-	40,000
	200,000	160,000
Income tax expense (at 35%)	70,000	56,000
Net earnings	$ 130,000	$104,000
Owners' equity	$1,000,000	$500,000
Return on equity (net earnings/owners' equity)	13%	20.8%

Unfortunately, long-term debt carries higher risk than equity. The following are the major disadvantages associated with issuing long-term debt:

1. *Risk of bankruptcy.* Interest payments to the debtholders must be made each period whether the corporation generates net earnings or incurs a loss.

2. *Negative impact on cash flows.* Debt must be repaid at a specific time in the future. Management must be able to generate sufficient cash to repay the debt or have the ability to refinance it.

Sound business practice requires maintaining an appropriate balance between debt and equity capital.

The types of long-term debt available to a company of BCE's size are not available to students and professors, or even to small and medium-sized corporations. Because of its size and the predictability of its revenue, BCE can borrow from a single lender or it may issue debt to many lenders. Single-lender debt is typically in the form of a note or a mortgage note, whereas multiple-lender debt is typically in the form of a debenture or a bond.

In this chapter, we examine BCE's issuance of bonds and study the accounting rules governing the recording and reporting of long-term debt. We also describe other typical non-current liabilities and examine how the reported debt and supplementary disclosures are used by analysts to make informed judgments about investment and/ or credit risk.

ORGANIZATION OF THE CHAPTER

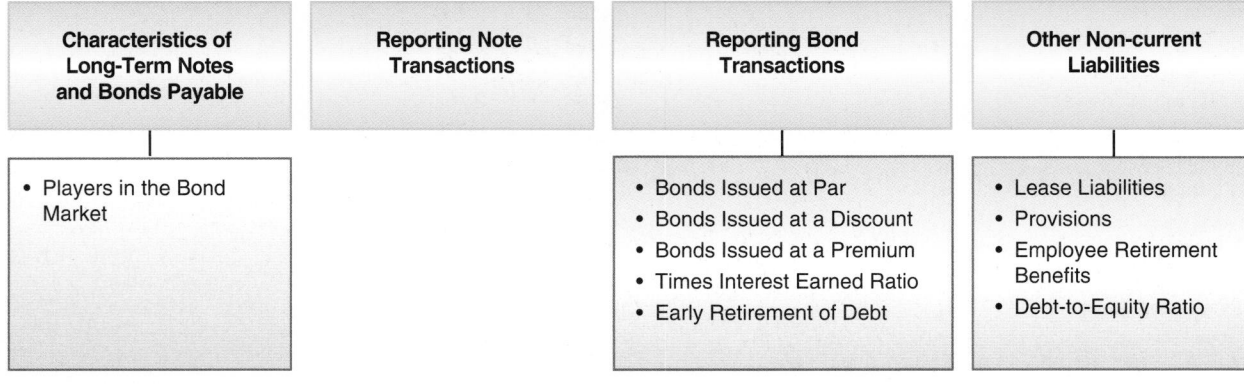

Characteristics of Long-Term Notes and Bonds Payable	Reporting Note Transactions	Reporting Bond Transactions	Other Non-current Liabilities
• Players in the Bond Market		• Bonds Issued at Par • Bonds Issued at a Discount • Bonds Issued at a Premium • Times Interest Earned Ratio • Early Retirement of Debt	• Lease Liabilities • Provisions • Employee Retirement Benefits • Debt-to-Equity Ratio

Supplemental material:
Appendix 11A: Reporting Interest Expense on Bonds by Using the Straight-Line Amortization Method

CHARACTERISTICS OF LONG-TERM NOTES AND BONDS PAYABLE

LO1

Describe the characteristics of long-term notes and bonds payable.

Companies can raise long-term debt directly from a number of financial service organizations, including banks, insurance companies, and pension fund companies. Raising debt from one of these organizations is known as *private placement*. This type of debt is often called a *note payable*, which is a written promise to pay a stated sum of money at one or more specified future dates, called the *maturity date(s)*.

In many cases, a company's need for debt capital exceeds the financial capability of any single creditor. In these situations, the company may issue publicly traded debt called *bonds*. The bonds can be traded in established markets that provide bondholders with liquidity (i.e., the ability to sell the bond and receive cash quickly). BCE borrows billions of dollars or other currencies in long-term debt to develop and provide communications services to its various customers reliably and quickly at a cost they are willing to pay. In exchange for the borrowed money, BCE signs debt agreements in the form of loans, notes, or mortgage notes with banks and other institutional lenders. Loans and notes are often for terms of five years or less, while mortgage terms can exceed 25 years.

Lenders often protect their interests by requesting that the debt be secured rather than unsecured. If you have a credit card, a student loan, or perhaps an automobile loan, you may have read the terms of the debt contract, which indicate whether or not the debt is secured. In the case of a personal credit card, the debt is unsecured, which means that if a debtor fails to make the required payment, or *defaults*, the lender cannot repossess any specific asset of the cardholder. In the case of a large, personal long-term loan, such as an automobile loan, lenders will insist on the right to repossess the automobile in the event of default. Repossession allows the lender to sell the automobile and recover all or part of the unpaid loan.

Corporations such as BCE can secure their notes and bonds payable by using revenue, inventory, property, equipment, and buildings. Secured debt provides the creditor with the right to foreclose on the debt and repossess the assets, or collateral, pledged by the company as security should the company violate the terms of its debt contract. BCE has disclosed information concerning its long-term debt, as shown in Exhibit 11.2. The note lists the different types of notes and bonds that BCE's

	Note	Weighted Average Interest Rate	Maturity	December 31, 2012	December 31, 2011
Bell Canada					
Debentures					
1997 trust indenture		4.77%	2014–2035	$ 7,350	$ 6,850
1976 trust indenture		9.59%	2014–2054	1,250	1,250
Subordinated debentures		8.21%	2026–2031	275	275
Finance leases		7.12%	2013–2047	2,272	1,898
Other				227	266
Total - Bell Canada				11,374	10,539
CTV Specialty Television Inc.					
Notes		6.08%	2014	300	300
Finance leases		3.72%	2014–2017	15	6
Total - CTV Specialty Television Inc.				315	306
Bell Aliant					
Debentures, notes and bonds		5.40%	2013–2037	2,632	2,636
Finance leases and other		4.40%	2013–2037	58	55
Total - Bell Aliant				2,690	2,691
Total debt				14,379	13,536
Net unamortized premium/discount				51	63
Unamortized debt issuance costs				(41)	(43)
Less: Amount due within one year	18			(503)	(835)
Total long-term debt				$13,886	$12,721

Exhibit **11.2**
Note 19: Long-Term Debt

REAL-WORLD EXCERPT

BCE Inc.

ANNUAL REPORT

Exhibit **11.2**
(*continued*)

Restrictions

Some of the debt agreements:

- require us to meet specific financial ratios
- impose covenants, maintenance tests and new issue tests
- require us to make an offer to repurchase certain series of debentures upon the occurrence of a change of control event as defined in the relevant debt agreements.

We are in compliance with all conditions and restrictions.

BELL CANADA

All outstanding debentures are issued under trust indentures and are unsecured. All debentures are issued in series and certain series are redeemable at Bell Canada's option prior to maturity at the prices, times and conditions specified in each series.

On February 11, 2013, Bell Canada redeemed early its 10.0% Series EA debentures, issued under its 1976 trust indenture, having an outstanding principal amount of $150 million which was due on June 15, 2014. We incurred a $17 million charge for the premium costs on early redemption which will be included in Other income.

On June 18, 2012, Bell Canada issued 3.35% Series M-25 debentures under its 1997 trust indenture, with a principal amount of $1 billion, which mature on June 18, 2019.

On December 15, 2011, Bell Canada repaid upon maturity its 6.90% Series M-12 debentures under its 1997 trust indenture, with an outstanding principal amount of $250 million.

On May 19, 2011, Bell Canada issued 3.65% Series M-23 debentures under its 1997 trust indenture, with a principal amount of $500 million, which mature on May 19, 2016, and 4.95% Series M-24 debentures under its 1997 trust indenture, with a principal amount of $500 million, which mature on May 19, 2021.

On March 16, 2011, Bell Canada issued 4.40% Series M-22 debentures under its 1997 trust indenture, with a principal amount of $1 billion, which mature on March 16, 2018.

Finance Leases

A new satellite was placed in service on June 15, 2012. In the second quarter of 2012, Bell Canada recorded a finance lease obligation of $476 million and an asset of $572 million, including $96 million of capitalized launch and setup costs.

CTV SPECIALTY TELEVISION INC.

The CTV Specialty Television Inc. (CTV Specialty) notes and revolving credit facility are secured by all present and future assets of CTV Specialty and its wholly-owned subsidiaries. At December 31, 2012, the carrying value of CTV Specialty assets exceeded the amounts owing.

BELL ALIANT

All outstanding debentures, notes and bonds are issued under trust indentures and are unsecured with the exception of Télébec, Limited Partnership's debentures of $100 million, which are secured by a mortgage on a property located in the province of Québec. All debentures, notes and bonds are issued in series and certain series are redeemable at Bell Aliant's option prior to maturity at the prices, times and conditions specified in each series.

On April 26, 2011, Bell Aliant issued 4.88% medium-term notes, with a principal amount of $300 million, which mature on April 26, 2018. The net proceeds were used to partially redeem early its 4.72% medium-term notes with a principal amount of $300 million. The remaining outstanding principal amount of $105 million was redeemed on September 26, 2011. We incurred a $4 million charge for the premium cost of early redemption which is included in Other income.

Source: BCE Inc., Annual Report 2012.

The BOND PRINCIPAL is the amount payable at the maturity of the bond. It is also the basis for computing periodic cash interest payments.

PAR VALUE and FACE AMOUNT are other names for bond principal or the maturity value of a bond.

The STATED RATE is the rate of interest per period specified in the bond contract.

subsidiaries have issued in the past. After studying this chapter, you will understand the terms used in the note related to long-term debt, particularly the accounting and financial issues associated with bonds.

All debentures and subordinated debentures have been issued in Canadian dollars and bear a fixed rate of interest.

A bond usually requires the payment of interest over its life, with the repayment of principal on the maturity date. The **bond principal** is (1) the amount payable at the maturity date and (2) the basis for computing periodic cash interest payments. The principal also is called the **par value**, **face amount**, or *maturity value*. All bonds have a par value, which is the amount that will be paid when the bond matures. For most Canadian bonds, the par value is $1,000, but it can be any amount.

A bond always specifies the **stated rate** of interest and the timing of periodic cash interest payments, usually annually or semi-annually. Each periodic interest payment is equal to the principal times the stated interest rate. The selling price of a bond does not affect the periodic cash payment of interest. For example, a $1,000,

6-percent bond always pays cash interest of $60 on an annual basis or $30 on a semi-annual basis.

Different types of bonds have different characteristics, primarily because individual creditors have different types of risk and return preferences. A retired person, for example, may be willing to receive a lower interest rate in return for greater security. This type of creditor might want a mortgage bond that pledges a specific asset as security if the company is unable to repay the bond. Another creditor might be willing to accept higher risk with a low interest rate and an unsecured status if the company provides the opportunity to convert the bond into common shares at some point in the future. Companies design bond features that are attractive to different groups of creditors, just as automobile manufacturers try to design cars that appeal to different groups of consumers. Important types of bonds are shown in the illustration below:

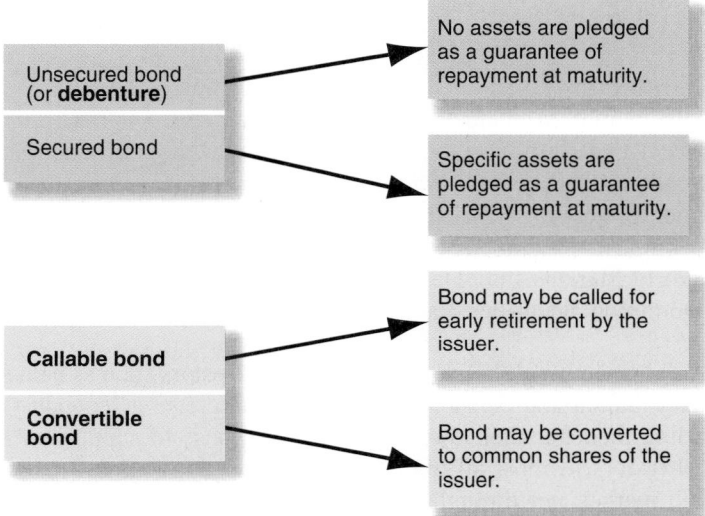

A **DEBENTURE** is an unsecured bond; no assets are specifically pledged to guarantee repayment.

CALLABLE BONDS may be called for early retirement at the option of the issuer.

CONVERTIBLE BONDS may be converted to other securities of the issuer (usually common shares).

Companies such as BCE often need to build research and communication facilities to implement the most up-to-date high-speed communications services. One possibility is for BCE to finance the project by issuing bonds that are secured by the assets that will be in place once the project is finished. Another possibility is to issue bonds secured by the amount of revenues expected from the completed project. The company could also issue debentures that are unsecured, depending on how much risk the debenture holders are willing to take.

When a company decides to issue new bonds, it prepares a bond, or trust, **indenture** (bond contract) that specifies the legal provisions of the bonds. These provisions include the maturity date, rate of interest to be paid, date of each interest payment, and any conversion privileges. The indenture also contains covenants designed to protect the creditors. Typical covenants include limitations on new debt that the company might issue in the future, limitations on the payment of dividends, and required minimum levels of certain accounting ratios, such as the current ratio. Managers prefer covenants that are less restrictive because they may limit the company's future actions. Creditors, however, prefer more restrictive covenants that reduce the risk of losing their investment. As with any business transaction, the final result is achieved through a process of negotiation.

An **INDENTURE** is a bond contract that specifies the legal provisions of a bond issue.

Bond covenants are usually reported in the notes to the financial statements. For example, the note disclosures in Exhibit 11.2 indicate that some of the debt agreements that either BCE or its subsidiaries have signed require BCE to meet specific financial ratios.

The disclosures in Exhibit 11.2 also provide specific information about the characteristics of the bonds, debentures, and notes issued by BCE and its subsidiaries.

For example, all outstanding debentures of Bell Canada are unsecured. They are issued in series, and certain series are redeemable at Bell Canada's option prior to maturity at the prices, times, and conditions specified in each series. In contrast, the notes issued by CTV Specialty Television Inc. are secured by all present and future assets of CTV Specialty and its subsidiaries. The bond issuer also prepares a prospectus, which is a legal document given to potential bond investors. The prospectus describes the company, the bond, and how the proceeds of the bond will be used.[1]

A **BOND CERTIFICATE** is the bond document that each bondholder receives.

A **TRUSTEE** is an independent party appointed to represent the bondholders.

When a bond is issued, the investor receives a **bond certificate**. All of the bond certificates for a single bond issue are identical. The face of each certificate shows the same maturity date, interest rate, interest dates, and other provisions. An independent party, called the **trustee**, is usually appointed to represent the bondholders. A trustee's duties are to ascertain whether the issuing company fulfills all of the provisions of the bond indenture.

Players in the Bond Market

Most companies work with an underwriter that either buys the entire issue of bonds and then resells them to individual creditors (called a *firm commitment underwriter*), or an underwriter that simply sells the bonds or notes without any obligation to purchase them (called a *best efforts underwriter*). It is not uncommon for companies to use several underwriters to sell a large bond issue. For example, Canadian underwriters that help companies sell notes, debentures, and bonds include BMO Nesbitt Burns Inc., CIBC World Markets Inc., Desjardins Securities Inc., National Bank Financial Inc., RBC Dominion Securities Inc., Scotia Capital Inc., and TD Securities Inc., among others.

Bond dealers typically sell bonds to institutional investors such as banks, insurance companies, and mutual and pension funds. They also create a secondary market for bonds by trading them for their own account in response to supply and demand by institutional investors. Almost all trades occur by telephone, known as an over-the-counter (OTC) market, not through a formal bond exchange. The market for bonds exceeds, by far, the value of stocks traded on a typical day because of the high value of each trade. A bond trade of $200 million would not be unusual in this market.[2]

Because of the complexities associated with bonds, several agencies exist to evaluate the probability that a bond issuer will not be able to meet the requirements specified in the indenture. This risk is called *default risk*. In general, the higher the risk of default, the higher will be the interest rate required to successfully persuade investors to purchase the bond, and the more restrictive will be the covenants protecting the bondholder. Dominion Bond Rating Service (DBRS), Moody's Investor Services Inc. (Moody's), Fitch Inc., and Standard and Poor's Rating Services (S&P) each assesses the default risk for every issue of corporate debentures and bonds.[3] Their ratings range from investment grade (low default risk) to extremely speculative junk bonds (high default risk). If it becomes apparent that there has been a change in default risk for any debt already issued, each rating service will issue a public bulletin that upgrades or downgrades the credit rating, along with reasons for the change.[4]

Bond prices change for two main reasons: changes in creditworthiness of the bond issuer and changes in market interest rates. The company's creditworthiness depends on the operating, investing, and financing decisions made by management. However, interest rates are not within the control of corporations but depend on the supply and demand for money. The most important interest rate is the rate at which the federal government can borrow money for the long term. This is the benchmark, risk-free rate of return on bonds, because purchasers believe that the federal government will never fail to repay, or default, on its debts. The interest rates of all other debt instruments are established relative to this risk-free rate. The difference between the interest rate on debt instruments and the risk-free rate is called the *spread*. The size of the spread depends upon the perceived additional risk that the company will default on either its interest or principal payments on the debt.

REPORTING NOTE TRANSACTIONS

LO²

Report notes payable and related interest expense.

BCE borrows billions of dollars in long-term debt to develop technologies that will expand its business and allow it to successfully compete against other companies. When individual lenders, such as a bank, are willing to provide the required amount of money at a reasonable interest rate and repayment conditions, BCE signs a loan, a note, or a mortgage note and receives the necessary funds to purchase specific assets. For example, in Exhibit 11.2, the explanatory note related to the debenture, notes, and bonds issued by Bell Aliant, a subsidiary of BCE, indicates that Bell Aliant issued on April 26, 2011, 4.88 percent medium-term notes with a principal amount of $300 million that is payable on April 26, 2018.

The terms of a debt agreement are negotiated between the lender and the borrower and depend on the size of the debt and the creditworthiness of the borrower. The debt contract specifies the interest rate on the debt and the dates of payment of both interest and principal. In the case of notes payable, the lender and the borrower may agree that the principal will be paid at a specific date in the future (the maturity date), plus annual or semi-annual interest payments. Alternatively, they may agree that equal portions of the principal are payable annually along with interest on the debt, or that equal payments covering both principal and interest (i.e., *blended* payments) will be made periodically until the principal is fully paid at the maturity date.

In the following illustration, we assume that on January 1, 2014, a company borrowed $100,000 from a local bank, to be repaid over a period of five years, plus interest at the rate of 6 percent per year. We consider three possible repayment schedules:

1. Payment of the principal on December 31, 2018, with interest payable annually on December 31.

2. Payment of one-fifth of the principal annually on December 31, with interest payable annually on that date.

3. Payment of five equal annual amounts that include both principal and interest each December 31.

Exhibit 11.3 shows the computation of the payments of principal and interest on an annual basis under each of the three alternatives. Notice that the company pays the largest amount of interest under option 1 because the principal is not repaid until the end of year 5. Under both options 2 and 3, interest expense decreases over time because part of the principal is paid every year.

PAUSE FOR FEEDBACK STOP

Companies that borrow money from creditors make different arrangements to repay the amount borrowed and related interest. Exhibit 11.3 shows three different alternatives for repayment of debt. Study this exhibit carefully before attempting the self-study quiz.

SELF-STUDY QUIZ 11-1

Refer to Exhibit 11.3, option 3, and answer the following requirements:

1. Prepare the journal entry to record the payment at December 31, 2016. Show the effects of this transaction on the accounting equation.

2. Assume that the company agreed to repay the loan of $100,000 in ten semi-annual equal payments instead of five equal annual payments. Compute the amount of the semi-annual payment and the total interest payable over the five-year period. (*Hint:* Use $i = 3\%$ [6% ÷ 2] and $n = 10$ [5 years × 2] to compute the semi-annual payment.)

3. Explain why the total amount of interest is lower than $18,699, the amount that is shown in Exhibit 11.3.

After you complete your answers, check them with the solutions at the end of the chapter.

EXHIBIT **11.3**

Note Repayment Schedule

Date	Cash Payment (Credit)	Interest Expense: Unpaid Principal × 6% (Debit)	Payment of Principal (Debit)	Carrying Amount (Unpaid Balance)
Option 1: Principal paid at the maturity date; interest paid annually on December 31				
1/1/2014				$100,000
31/12/2014	$ 6,000	$ 6,000	–0–	100,000
31/12/2015	6,000	6,000	–0–	100,000
31/12/2016	6,000	6,000	–0–	100,000
31/12/2017	6,000	6,000	–0–	100,000
31/12/2018	106,000	6,000	$100,000	–0–
	$130,000	$30,000	$100,000	
Option 2: Interest and one-fifth of the principal paid annually on December 31				
1/1/2014				$100,000
31/12/2014	$ 26,000	$ 6,000	$ 20,000	80,000
31/12/2015	24,800	4,800	20,000	60,000
31/12/2016	23,600	3,600	20,000	40,000
31/12/2017	22,400	2,400	20,000	20,000
31/12/2018	21,200	1,200	20,000	–0–
	$118,000	$18,000	$100,000	
Option 3: Equal amounts including both principal and interest paid annually on December 31				
1/1/2014				$100,000
31/12/2014	$ 23,739*	$ 6,000	$ 17,739	82,261
31/12/2015	23,739	4,936	18,803	63,458
31/12/2016	23,739	3,807	19,932	43,526
31/12/2017	23,739	2,612	21,127	22,399
31/12/2018	23,739	1,344	22,399†	–0–
	$118,695	$18,699	$100,000	

*The $100,000 represents the present value of an annuity of five payments at an interest rate of 6 percent:
Annuity × $P_{i=6\%, n=5}$ (Table 10C.2, Appendix 10C, 4.2124) = $100,000
Annuity = $100,000 ÷ 4.2124 = $23,739.40, rounded down to $23,739 for simplicity
†A difference of $4 is due to rounding down the annuity payments over the five years.

In the previous illustration, we assumed that the company borrowed $100,000 on January 1, 2014, and paid interest and/or principal at the end of the fiscal year. In practice, however, companies borrow money or incur debt whenever the need arises during the year. In this case, the interest expense that is not paid by the end of the fiscal year should be accrued and reported as interest payable (or accrued liability) on the statement of financial position.

Repayment schedules such as Exhibit 11.3 are useful in that they allow the borrower to predict the cash flows needed for principal and interest payments on an annual basis and permit the accountant to compute the interest expense that should be recognized periodically, as well as the reduction of the note payable, if applicable. The schedule also allows for the splitting of the long-term debt between the current and long-term portions for the purposes of classifying and reporting the debt on the statement of financial position. For example, under option 3, the remaining principal of $43,526 at December 31, 2016, would be split into two amounts: $21,127, which is reported as the current portion of long-term debt (payable within one year), and $22,399, which is reported as long-term debt.

To assist financial statement users in assessing a company's financial position and future cash flow commitments on its existing long-term debt, companies are required to disclose the total amount of expected payments in each of the next five years to meet scheduled repayments of the principal amount of the debt. BCE provided such details in the management discussion and analysis (MD&A) section of its annual report.

MANAGEMENT DISCUSSION AND ANALYSIS

Contractual Obligations

The following table is a summary of our contractual obligations at December 31, 2012, that are due in each of the next five years and thereafter.

(in millions of dollars)	2013	2014	2015	2016	2017	Thereafter	Total
Debt	116	1,877	1,377	1,217	1,149	6,298	12,034
Notes payable and bank advances	698	—	—	—	—	—	698
Minimum future lease payments under finance leases	548	431	267	236	235	1,837	3,554
Loan secured by trade receivables	935	—	—	—	—	—	935
Interest payable on long-term debt, notes payable, bank advances and loan secured by trade receivables	687	595	532	471	419	4,627	7,331
Net interest receipts on derivatives	(28)	(25)	(24)	(22)	(11)	—	(110)
MLSE financial liability	—	—	—	—	135	—	135
Operating leases	229	201	176	139	107	489	1,341
Commitments for property, plant and equipment, and intangible assets	166	28	10	14	—	—	218
Purchase obligations	1,628	1,300	1,149	384	275	923	5,659
Proposed acquisition of Astral (1)	3,553	—	—	—	—	—	3,553
Total	8,532	4,407	3,487	2,439	2,309	14,174	35,348

Source: BCE Inc., Annual Report 2012.

REAL-WORLD EXCERPT

BCE Inc.

ANNUAL REPORT

REPORTING BOND TRANSACTIONS

LO3

Report bonds payable and interest expense for bonds sold at par, at a discount, or at a premium.

Exhibit 11.2 shows that Bell Aliant has issued debentures, notes, and bonds for a total face value of $2,636 million as at December 31, 2012. Each bond indenture specifies two types of cash payments:

1. *Principal.* This is usually a single payment made when the bond matures. It is also called the *par* or *face value.*

2. *Cash interest payments.* These payments are computed by multiplying the principal amount times the interest rate, called the **coupon rate**, or contract or stated rate, of interest stated in the bond contract. The bond contract specifies whether these payments are made quarterly, semi-annually, or annually.

The **COUPON RATE** is the stated rate of interest on bonds.

Neither the company nor the underwriter determines the price at which the bonds sell. Instead, the market determines the current cash equivalent of future interest and principal payments by using present value concepts covered in Chapter 10. To determine the present value of the bond, compute the present value of the principal (a single payment) and the present value of the interest payments (an annuity) and add the two amounts.

Creditors demand a certain rate of interest to compensate them for the risks related to bonds, called the **market interest rate** (also known as the **yield**, or **effective-interest rate**). Because the market rate is the interest rate on a debt when it is incurred, it should be used in computing the present value of the bond.

The **MARKET INTEREST RATE** is the current rate of interest on a debt when incurred; also called the **YIELD** or **EFFECTIVE-INTEREST RATE**.

The present value of a bond may be the same as par, above par (**bond premium**), or below par (**bond discount**). If the stated and the market interest rates are the same, a bond sells at par. If a bond pays a stated interest rate that is lower than the market rate that creditors demand, they will not buy it unless its price is reduced (i.e., a discount must be provided). If a bond pays a stated rate that is higher than the market rate that creditors demand, they will be willing to pay a premium to buy it.

The **BOND PREMIUM** is the difference between the selling price and par when the bond is sold for more than par.

This relationship can be shown graphically as follows:[5]

The **BOND DISCOUNT** is the difference between the selling price and par when the bond is sold for less than par.

Bond Contract	Market Rate	Bond Price
Coupon interest rate is 6%	4%	Premium
	6%	Par
	8%	Discount

Basically, corporations and creditors are indifferent to whether a bond is issued at par, at a discount, or at a premium, because bonds are always priced to provide the market rate of interest. To illustrate, consider a corporation that issues three separate bonds on the same day. The bonds are exactly the same except that one has a stated interest rate of 6 percent, another 7 percent, and a third 8 percent. If the market rate of interest was 7 percent, the first would be issued at a discount, the second at par, and the third at a premium, but a creditor who bought any one of the bonds would earn the market interest rate of 7 percent:

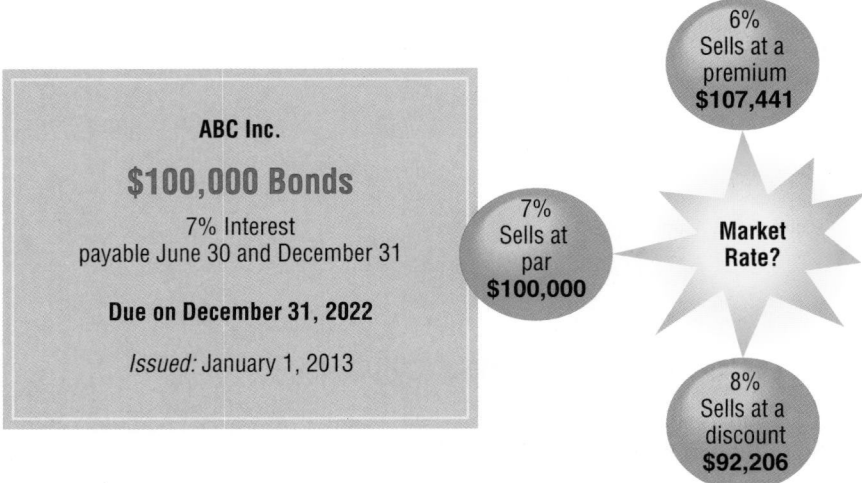

FINANCIAL ANALYSIS

BOND INFORMATION FROM THE BUSINESS PRESS

Bond prices are reported each day in the business press based on transactions that occurred in the market on the previous trading day. The following is typical of the information you will find:

Bond	Coupon	Maturity Date	July 15, 2013		July 16, 2013	
			Bid $	Yield %	Bid $	Yield %
Bell Canada	4.40	March 16, 2018	106.35	2.93	106.59	2.88
Manulife Financial	5.06	December 15, 2036	97.40	5.25	97.45	5.25

Source: http://www.financialpost.com/markets/data/bonds-canadian.html.

Bell Canada's bond, highlighted above, has a coupon rate of 4.40 percent and will mature on March 16, 2018. The bond's yield was 2.93 percent on July 15, 2013, and its price was 106.35 percent of its par value, or $1,063.50. Market conditions caused the yield to decrease to 2.88 percent the following day, but the coupon rate remains fixed at 4.40 percent. As the yield decreased relative to the fixed coupon rate, the price increased from $106.35 on July 15, 2013, to $106.59 on July 16, 2013, which illustrates the inverse relationship between the yield and the bond price.

Bell Canada's bond sold on July 15, 2013, at a premium because the market rate demanded by buyers is lower than the coupon rate offered by the company. In comparison, Manulife's bond sold at a discount of 2.6 percent of its face value on the same date because it offers a coupon rate of 5.06 percent that is lower than the market interest rate of 5.25 percent. Notice that the yields for these bonds are significantly different because of the specific characteristics of these bonds that affect their riskiness.

Changes in the daily bond prices do not affect the company's financial statements. For financial reporting purposes, the company uses the interest rates that existed when the bonds were first sold to the public. Subsequent changes do not affect the company's accounting for the bonds.

PAUSE FOR **FEEDBACK** STOP

Your study of bonds will be easier if you understand the terminology that has been introduced in this chapter. Let us review some of those terms.

SELF-STUDY **QUIZ 11-2**

Define the following:

1. Market interest rate. Identify synonyms for *market interest rate*.
2. Coupon interest rate. Identify synonyms for *coupon interest rate*.
3. Bond discount.
4. Bond premium.

After you complete your answers, check them with the solutions at the end of the chapter.

Bonds Issued at Par

Bonds sell at their par value when buyers are willing to invest in them at the interest rate stated on the bond. To illustrate, let us assume that on January 1, 2013, Mobile Services Corporation (MSC), a hypothetical Canadian company, issued 6 percent bonds with a par value of $400,000 and received $400,000 in cash (which means that the bonds sold at par). The bonds were dated to start earning interest on January 1, 2013, and will pay interest each June 30 and December 31. The bonds mature in 10 years, on December 31, 2022.

The amount of money a corporation receives when it sells bonds is the present value of the future cash flows associated with them. When MSC issued its bonds, it agreed to make two types of payments in the future: a single payment of $400,000 when the bond matures in 10 years and an annuity of $12,000 payable twice each year for 10 years. The bond payments can be shown graphically as follows:

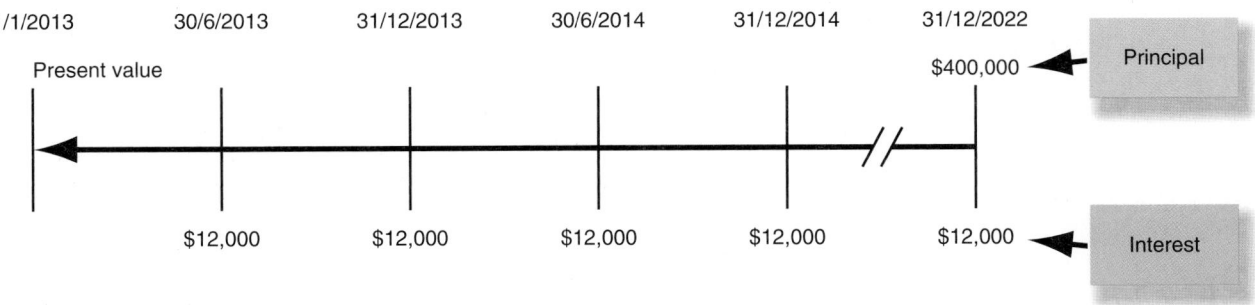

The present value of the bond payments can be computed with the tables contained in Appendix 10C by using the factor for 20 periods and an interest rate of 3 percent (6 percent ÷ 2):

	Present Value
a. Single payment: $400,000 × 0.5537	$221,480
b. Annuity: $12,000 × 14.8775	178,520*
Issue price of MSC's bonds	$400,000
*Rounded	

When the effective rate of interest equals the stated rate of interest, the present value of the future cash flows associated with a bond always equals the bond's par value.

Remember that a bond's selling price is determined by the present value of its future cash flows, not the par value. On the date of issue, bond liabilities are recorded at the present value of future cash flows as follows:

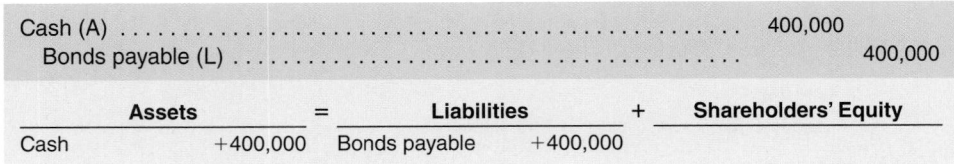

| Cash (A) .... | 400,000 | |
| Bonds payable (L) .... | | 400,000 |

Assets	=	Liabilities	+	Shareholders' Equity
Cash	+400,000	Bonds payable	+400,000	

Reporting Interest Expense on Bonds Issued at Par The creditors who bought the bonds did so with the expectation that they would earn interest over the life of the bond. MSC will pay interest at 3 percent (i.e., 6 percent per year) on the par value of the bonds each June 30 and December 31 until the bond's maturity date. The amount of interest each period will be $12,000 (3% × $400,000). The entry to record the interest payments follows:

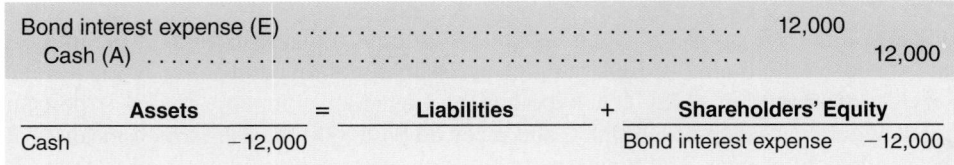

| Bond interest expense (E) .... | 12,000 | |
| Cash (A) .... | | 12,000 |

Assets	=	Liabilities	+	Shareholders' Equity	
Cash	−12,000			Bond interest expense	−12,000

Bond interest payment dates rarely coincide with the last day of a company's fiscal year. Interest expense incurred but not paid must be accrued with an adjusting entry. If MSC's fiscal year ended on May 31, the company would accrue interest for five months and record interest expense and interest payable.

PAUSE FOR FEEDBACK

Calculation of the present value of the principal and interest payments is straightforward. Practise the mechanics of computing the present value of a bond issue before moving on.

SELF-STUDY QUIZ 11-3

Assume that MSC issued $100,000 bonds that will mature in 10 years. The bonds pay interest at the end of each year at an annual rate of 4 percent. They were sold when the market rate was 4 percent. Determine the selling price of the bonds.

After you complete your answer, check it with the solution at the end of the chapter.

Bonds Issued at a Discount

Bonds sell at a discount when the market rate of interest demanded by the buyers is higher than the stated interest rate offered by the issuer. Assume that the market rate of interest was 8 percent when MSC sold its bonds (which have a par value of $400,000). The bonds have a stated rate of 6 percent, payable semi-annually, which is less than the market rate on that date. Therefore, the bonds sold at a *discount*. This usually occurs when the market rate of interest increases after the company determines the coupon rate on the bonds.

To compute the issue price of the bonds, we need to compute the present value of the future cash flows specified on the bond. As in the previous example, the number of periods is 20, but we must use an interest rate of 4 percent (8 percent ÷ 2), which is the market rate of interest. Thus, the issue price of MSC's bonds is computed as follows:

	Present Value
a. Principal: $400,000 × 0.4564	$182,560
b. Interest: $12,000 × 13.5903	163,084
Issue (sale) price of MSC's bonds	$345,644*
*Discount: $400,000 − $345,644 = $54,356	

The cash price of the bonds issued by MSC is $345,644. Some people refer to this price as 86.4, which means that the bonds were sold at 86.4 percent of their par value ($345,644 ÷ $400,000).

When a bond is sold at a discount, the bonds payable account is credited for the par value, and the discount is recorded as a debit to discount on bonds payable. The issuance of MSC's bonds at a discount is recorded as follows:[6]

Cash (A)	345,644	
Discount on bonds payable (XL)	54,356	
Bonds payable (L)		400,000

Assets		=	Liabilities		+ Shareholders' Equity
Cash	+345,644		Bonds payable	+400,000	
			Discount on bonds payable	−54,356	

Note that the discount is recorded in a separate contra-liability account (discount on bonds payable) as a debit. The statement of financial position reports the bonds payable at their carrying amount, which is their maturity amount less any unamortized discount. MSC, like most companies, does not separately disclose the amount of unamortized discount (or premium) when the amount is small relative to other amounts reported on the statement of financial position.

Although MSC received only $345,644 when it sold the bonds, it must repay $400,000 when the bonds mature. This extra cash that must be paid is an adjustment to the interest payments, ensuring that creditors earn the market rate of interest on the bonds. To compute the interest expense, the borrower apportions or amortizes the bond discount to each semi-annual interest period as an increase to the interest payment. Therefore, the amortization of bond discount is an increase in bond interest expense. Canadian publicly accountable enterprises are required to use the effective-interest method to amortize bond discount or premium. An alternative method, straight-line amortization, which may be used by Canadian private enterprises, is discussed in Appendix 11A.

BCE uses the effective-interest method to amortize any discount or premium on its long-term debt:

NOTES TO CONSOLIDATED FINANCIAL STATEMENTS

Note 2. Significant Accounting Policies

Other financial liabilities
Other financial liabilities, which include trade payables and accruals, compensation payable, obligations imposed by the Canadian Radio-television and Telecommunications Commission (CRTC), interest payable and long-term debt are recorded at amortized cost using the effective-interest method.

Cost of Issuing Debt and Equity
The cost of issuing debt is included as part of long-term debt and is accounted for at amortized cost using the effective-interest method.

Source: BCE Inc., Annual Report 2012.

Exhibit 11.2 lists all the outstanding long-term debt issued by BCE, Bell Canada, CTV, and Bell Aliant. Some of these bonds, debentures, and notes were sold at a discount while others were sold at a premium. The net unamortized premium or discount on long-term debt amounted to $51 million at December 31, 2012.

The **EFFECTIVE-INTEREST METHOD** amortizes a bond discount or premium on the basis of the effective-interest rate.

Reporting Interest Expense on Bonds Issued at a Discount by Using Effective-Interest Amortization   Under the **effective-interest method**, interest expense for a bond is computed by multiplying the current unpaid balance (or carrying amount) by the market rate of interest that existed on the date the bonds were sold. The periodic amortization of a bond discount or premium is then calculated as the difference between interest expense and the amount of cash paid or accrued. This process can be summarized as follows:

Step 1: Compute interest expense:

$$\text{Internet Expense} = \text{Unpaid Balance} \times \text{Effective Interest Rate} \times n/12$$
$$n = \text{Number of Months in Each Interest Period}$$

Step 2: Compute the amortization amount:

Amortization of Bond Discount = Interest Expense − Interest Paid (or accrued)

The first interest payment on MSC's bonds is on June 30, 2013. Interest expense at the end of the first six months is calculated by multiplying the unpaid balance of the debt by the market rate of interest for six months ($345,644 × 8% × 6/12 = $13,826). This represents the amount of interest revenue that bondholders expected to earn on their investment during this six-month period when they decided to purchase the bonds. The amount of cash paid is calculated by multiplying the principal by the stated rate of interest for six months ($400,000 × 6% × 6/12 = $12,000). The difference between the interest expense and the cash paid (or accrued) is the amount of discount that has been amortized ($13,826 − $12,000 = $1,826).

The journal entry to record the periodic interest expense is as follows:

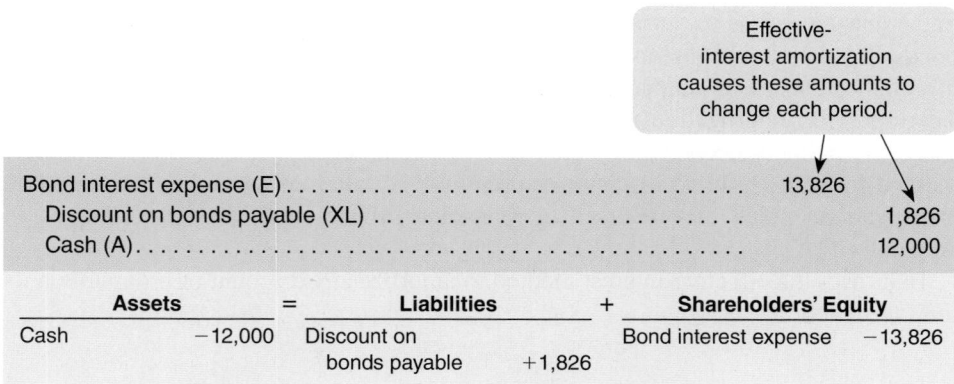

Effective-interest amortization causes these amounts to change each period.

Bond interest expense (E)		13,826	
Discount on bonds payable (XL)			1,826
Cash (A)			12,000

Assets		=	Liabilities		+	Shareholders' Equity	
Cash	−12,000		Discount on bonds payable	+1,826		Bond interest expense	−13,826

Each period, the amortization of the bond discount increases the bond's carrying amount (or unpaid balance). The amortization of bond discount can be thought of as interest that was earned by the bondholders but not paid to them. During the first six months of 2013, the bondholders earned interest of $13,826 but received only $12,000 in cash. The additional $1,826 was added to the carrying amount of the bond and will be paid when the bond matures.

Interest expense for the second half of 2013 is calculated by multiplying the carrying amount on June 30, 2013, by the market rate of interest for six months ($347,470 × 8% × 6/12 = $13,899). The amortization of the bond discount in the second period is $1,899:

Bond interest expense (E)	13,899	
Discount on bonds payable (XL)		1,899
Cash (A).		12,000

Assets	=	Liabilities	+	Shareholders' Equity	
Cash	−12,000	Discount on bonds payable	+1,899	Bond interest expense	−13,899

Notice that interest expense for the second half of 2013 is greater than the amount for the first six months of the year. This is logical, because MSC effectively borrowed more money during the second half of the year (i.e., the $1,826 unpaid interest). Interest expense increases each year during the life of the bond, because the amortized bond discount reflects unpaid interest on an increasing amount. This process can be illustrated with the amortization schedule shown below for the first two years and the last year of the bond's life:

Amortization Schedule: Bond Discount (Effective Interest)				
Date	**(a)** Interest to Be Paid [$400,000 × 3%]	**(b)** Interest Expense [4% × (d) Carrying Amount, Beginning of Period]	**(c)** Amortization [(b) − (a)]	**(d)** Carrying Amount [Beginning Carrying Amount + (c)]
1/1/2013				$345,644
30/6/2013	$12,000	$13,826	$1,826	347,470
31/12/2013	12,000	13,899	1,899	349,369
30/6/2014	12,000	13,975	1,975	351,344
31/12/2014	12,000	14,054	2,054	353,398
.	.	.	.	.
.	.	.	.	.
30/6/2022	12,000	15,699	3,699	396,164
31/12/2022	12,000	15,836*	3,836	400,000
*The interest expense of $15,847 was rounded down by $11 so that the carrying amount does not exceed $400,000.				

Interest expense (column b) is computed by multiplying the market rate of interest by the carrying amount at the beginning of the period (column d). Amortization is computed by subtracting interest paid (column a) from interest expense (column b). The carrying amount (column d) is computed by adding amortization of bond discount (column c) to the carrying amount at the beginning of the period.

Bonds payable are reported on the statement of financial position at their carrying amount—that is, the maturity amount less any unamortized bond discount (or plus any unamortized bond premium). The carrying amount reflects the present value of remaining payments using the effective-interest rate at the date of issue. It increases over time as the amortized bond discount is added to the initial bond issue price. At the maturity date of the bonds, the unamortized discount (i.e., the balance in the discount on bonds payable account) is zero. At that time, the maturity value of the bonds and the carrying amount are the same (i.e., $400,000).

PAUSE FOR FEEDBACK

We have computed interest expense using the effective-interest method of amortization and determined the carrying amount of the bond after each interest payment date. Practise these computations before moving on.

SELF-STUDY QUIZ 11-4

Assume that MSC issued $100,000 bonds that will mature in 10 years. The bonds pay interest twice each year at an annual rate of 7 percent. They were sold when the market rate was 8 percent.

1. What amount of interest expense would be reported at the end of the first year?
2. What is the carrying amount of the bonds at the end of the first year?

After you complete your answers, check them with the solutions at the end of the chapter.

Bonds are recorded at the present value of their future cash flows using an interest rate determined by the market on the date the bonds were sold. The accounting for the bonds is not affected by subsequent changes in the market rate of interest. This interest rate is based on the terms of the debt issue and the risk characteristics of the debt.

FINANCIAL
ANALYSIS

ZERO COUPON BONDS

So far, we have discussed common bonds that are issued by many corporations. For a number of reasons, corporations may issue bonds with unusual features. The concepts you have learned will help you understand these bonds. For example, a corporation might issue a bond that does not pay periodic cash interest. These bonds are often called zero coupon bonds. Why would an investor buy a bond that did not pay interest? Our discussion of bond discounts has probably given you a good idea of the answer. The coupon interest rate on a bond can be virtually any rate and the price of the bond will be adjusted so that investors earn the market rate of interest. A bond with a zero coupon interest rate is simply a deeply discounted bond that will sell for substantially less than its maturity value.

Let us use the $400,000 MSC bond to illustrate a zero coupon rate. Assume that the market rate of interest is 6.5 percent and the bond pays no cash interest. The bond matures in 10 years. The selling price of the bond is the present value of the maturity amount, because no other cash payments will be made over the life of the bond. We can compute the present value with the tables in Appendix 10C, using the present value factor for 20 periods and an interest rate of 3.25 percent, assuming semi-annual compounding:

	Present Value
Single payment: $400,000 × 0.5275	$211,000

Accounting for a zero coupon bond is not different from accounting for other bonds sold at a discount. However, the amount of the discount is much larger.

Bonds Issued at a Premium

Bonds sell at a premium when the market rate of interest is lower than the stated interest rate. Assume that the market rate of interest is 4 percent while MSC's bonds pay interest of 6 percent semi-annually. In this case, the bonds sell at a premium. The issue price for MSC's bonds is computed as follows:

	Present Value
a. Principal: $400,000 × 0.6730	$269,200
b. Interest: $12,000 × 16.3514	196,217
Issue (sale) price of MSC's bonds	$465,417

When a bond is sold at a premium, the bonds payable account is credited for the par value, and the premium is recorded as a credit to premium on bonds payable, an adjunct-liability account. The issuance of MSC's bonds at a premium is recorded as follows:

Cash (A)	465,417	
Premium on bonds payable (L)		65,417
Bonds payable (L)		400,000

Assets	=	Liabilities	+	Shareholders' Equity
Cash +465,417		Premium on		
		bonds payable +65,417		
		Bonds payable +400,000		

The carrying amount of the bond is the sum of the balances of the two accounts, premium on bonds payable and bonds payable, or $465,417.

Reporting Interest Expense on Bonds Issued at a Premium by Using Effective-Interest Amortization

The effective-interest method is basically the same for a discount or a premium. In either case, interest expense for a bond is computed by multiplying the carrying amount (i.e., the unpaid balance) by the market rate of interest on the date the bonds were sold. The periodic amortization of a bond premium or discount is then calculated as the difference between interest expense and the amount of cash paid or accrued.

The first interest payment on MSC's bonds is made on June 30, 2013. The interest expense at the end of the first six months is calculated by multiplying the unpaid balance of the debt by the market rate of interest for six months ($465,417 \times 4\% \times 6/12 = \$9,308$). It also represents the interest revenue that bondholders expected to earn on their investment during this six-month period when they decided to purchase the bonds. The amount of cash paid is calculated by multiplying the principal by the stated rate of interest for six months ($400,000 \times 6\% \times 6/12 = \$12,000$). The difference between the interest expense and the cash paid (or accrued) is the amount of premium that has been amortized ($12,000 - \$9,308 = \$2,692$). Thus, the amount of cash paid to bondholders includes two components: interest expense of $9,308, reflecting interest revenue to the bondholders for the first six-month period, and an amortized premium of $2,692, representing a partial payment of the premium that bondholders paid initially when they purchased the bonds.

The payment of interest on the bonds is recorded as follows:

Bond interest expense (E)	9,308	
Premium on bonds payable (L)	2,692	
Cash (A)		12,000

Assets	=	Liabilities	+	Shareholders' Equity
Cash −12,000		Premium on		Bond interest expense −9,308
		bonds payable −2,692		

The basic difference between effective-interest amortization of a bond discount and a bond premium is that the amortization of a discount *increases* the carrying amount of the liability and the amortization of a premium *reduces* it. The following schedule illustrates amortization of the bond premium for the first two years and the last year of the bond's life:

	(a) Interest to Be Paid [$400,000 × 3%]	(b) Interest Expense [2% × (d) Carrying Amount, Beginning of Period]	(c) Amortization [(a) − (b)]	(d) Carrying Amount [Beginning Carrying Amount − (c)]
Date				
1/1/2013				$465,417
30/6/2013	$12,000	$9,308	$2,692	462,725
31/12/2013	12,000	9,255	2,745	459,980
30/6/2014	12,000	9,200	2,800	457,179
31/12/2014	12,000	9,144	2,856	454,323
.	.	.	.	.
.	.	.	.	.
30/6/2022	12,000	8,156	3,844	403,938
31/12/2022	12,000	8,063*	3,937	400,000

Amortization Schedule: Bond Premium (Effective Interest)

* The interest expense of $8,079 was rounded down by $16 so that the carrying amount does not exceed $400,000.

Interest expense (column b) is computed by multiplying the market rate of interest by the carrying amount at the beginning of the period (column d). Amortization is computed by subtracting interest expense (column b) from interest paid (column a). The carrying amount (column d) is computed by subtracting amortization of bond premium (column c) from the carrying amount at the beginning of the period.

In summary, interest expense changes each accounting period as the effective amount of the liability changes. As in the case of a bond discount, the carrying amount of the bonds reflects the present value of remaining payments using the effective-interest rate at the date of issue.

PAUSE FOR FEEDBACK

The use of an amortization schedule facilitates the computation of interest expense, amortization of the premium on bonds payable, and the carrying amount of the bonds over the bond's life. Practise these computations before moving on.

SELF-STUDY QUIZ 11-5

Refer to the amortization schedule above and answer the following requirements:

1. Complete the schedule for three additional semi-annual payments of interest until June 30, 2016.

2. Compute the unpaid balance of the bonds at June 30, 2016. Can you think of another way of computing this balance? If so, show your computations.

After you complete your answers, check them with the solutions at the end of the chapter.

Interest expense is reported on the statement of earnings. Because interest is related to financing activities rather than operating activities, it is normally not included in operating expenses on the statement of earnings. Instead, interest expense is reported as a deduction from Earnings from Operations. BCE Inc. reports interest expense of $865 million for 2012, as shown in Exhibit 11.4.

Exhibit **11.4**

Consolidated Statement of Earnings

REAL-WORLD EXCERPT

BCE Inc.

ANNUAL REPORT

Consolidated Income Statement For the Year Ended December 31

(in millions of Canadian dollars)	NOTE	2012	2011
...			
Earnings before finance costs and income taxes		4,362	3,959
Finance costs			
Interest expense	6	(865)	(842)
Interest on employee benefit obligations	20	(958)	(984)
Expected return on pension assets	20	1,069	1,032
Other income	7	270	129
Earnings before income taxes		3,878	3,294
Income taxes	8	(825)	(720)
Net earnings		3,053	2,574

Source: BCE Inc., Annual Report 2012.

Interest payments are legal obligations for the borrower; therefore, financial analysts, investors, and creditors want to be certain that a business is generating sufficient resources to meet its obligations. The times interest earned ratio is useful when making this assessment.

TIMES INTEREST EARNED RATIO

KEY RATIO ANALYSIS

ANALYTICAL QUESTION → Is the company generating sufficient resources (added value) from its profit-making activities to meet its current obligations associated with debt?

RATIO AND COMPARISONS → The times interest earned ratio is helpful in answering this question. It is computed as follows:

$$\text{Times Interest Earned Ratio} = \frac{\text{Net Earnings} + \text{Interest Expense} + \text{Income Tax Expense}}{\text{Interest Expense}}$$

The 2012 ratio for the BCE Inc. is

$$\frac{\$3,053 + \$865 + \$825}{\$865} = 5.48$$

LO4

Compute and interpret the times interest earned ratio.

Comparisons over Time				Comparisons with Competitors	
BCE				Rogers Communications	TELUS
2010	2011	2012		2012	2012
5.12	5.13	5.48		4.40	6.00

INTERPRETATIONS

In General → A high ratio is viewed more favourably than a low ratio. Basically, the ratio shows the amount of earnings before interest and income tax that is generated relative to interest expense. A high ratio shows an extra margin of protection in case profitability deteriorates. Analysts are particularly interested in a company's ability to meet its required interest payments, because failure to do so could result in bankruptcy.

Focus Company Analysis → In 2012, BCE's profit-making activities generated $5.48 for each $1.00 of interest expense. BCE's net earnings could fall substantially before the company would appear to have trouble meeting its interest obligations with resources generated by normal operations. BCE's ability to repay its creditors improved slightly in 2012 relative to the previous two years. Its ratio is in line with the ratios of competing companies.

A Few Cautions → The times interest earned ratio is often misleading for new or rapidly growing companies that tend to invest considerable resources to build capacity for future operations. In such cases, the times interest earned ratio will reflect significant amounts of interest expense associated with the new capacity but not the earnings that will be generated with the new capacity. Analysts should consider the company's long-term strategy when using this ratio. While this ratio is widely used, some analysts prefer to compare interest expense to the amount of cash that a company can generate, because creditors cannot be paid with "net earnings" that are generated. The cash coverage ratio addresses this concern and is discussed in Chapter 13.

LO⁵

Report the early retirement of bonds.

Early Retirement of Debt

Bonds are normally issued for long periods, such as 20 or 30 years. As mentioned earlier, bondholders who need cash prior to the maturity date can simply sell the bonds to another investor. This transaction does not affect the books of the company that issued the bonds.

As mentioned earlier, each bond issue has characteristics specified in the bond indenture. The issuing company often adds special characteristics to a bond to make it more attractive to investors, who normally have a large number of investment alternatives from which to select.

RETRACTABLE BONDS may be turned in for early retirement at the option of the bondholder.

Bonds sometimes offer different features with respect to early retirement. Callable (redeemable) bonds may be called for early retirement at the option of the issuer. **Retractable bonds** may be turned in for early retirement at the option of the bondholder. Convertible bonds may be converted to other securities of the issuer (usually common shares) at the option of the bondholder. These features are normally present for debt issues that are marketable.

Assume that MSC's bonds are redeemable. Typically, the bond indenture would include a call premium for redeemable bonds.

Assume that the $400,000 face-value bonds that were issued by MSC on January 1, 2013, at a discount in the previous illustration were called by the company on December 31, 2018, at 101 percent of par, four years before their maturity. The company's decision to call these bonds is typically made when the market rate of interest decreases to the point where the market value of the bonds exceeds the call price. MSC would issue new bonds that pay a lower interest rate than the outstanding bonds, thus saving on interest payments.

If the market rate of interest drops to 4 percent, then MSC can issue new bonds that pay interest of 4 percent instead of 6 percent. Semi-annual interest payments would then be reduced from $12,000 to $8,000 ($400,000 × 0.02). The cash savings of $4,000 every six months is equivalent to $29,302 ($4,000 × 7.3255[7]) at December 31, 2018. Redemption of the bonds requires MSC to pay a premium of $4,000 ($400,000 × 0.01), but it saves the company $29,302. It is therefore a sound economic decision.

However, the early retirement of these bonds would result in an accounting loss that equals the difference between the redemption amount and the carrying amount of the bonds. At December 31, 2018, the carrying amount of the bond is $373,072, representing the present value of the remaining future principal and interest payments.[8] This amount is then compared to the redemption amount of $404,000 ($400,000 × 1.01), resulting in a loss of $30,928. The company's accountants would make the following journal entry to record the bond redemption:

Bonds payable (L)	400,000	
Loss on redemption of bonds (SE)	30,928	
Discount on bonds payable (XL)		26,928
Cash (A)		404,000

Assets		=	Liabilities		+	Shareholders' Equity	
Cash	−404,000		Bonds payable	−400,000		Loss on redemption of bonds	−30,928
			Discount on bonds payable	+26,927			

The bond redemption results in an economic gain but also in an accounting loss, because the carrying amount of the bonds is not adjusted over time to reflect changes in the market value of these bonds.

In some cases, a company may elect to retire debt early by purchasing it on the open market, just as an investor would. This approach is necessary when the bonds do not have a call feature. It might also be an attractive approach if the price of the bonds fell after the date of issue. What could cause the price of a bond to fall? The most common cause is a rise in interest rates. As you may have noticed during our discussion of present value concepts, bond prices move in the opposite direction of interest rates. If interest rates go up, bond prices fall, and vice versa. When interest rates go up, a company wanting to retire a bond before maturity may find that buying the bond on the open market is less expensive than paying a call premium.

When interest rates increase, the market value of the bonds decreases, and the redemption or repurchase of the bonds in the open market results in a gain. The gain increases the company's net earnings, which reflects positively on the performance of management. However, if the company needs to reissue bonds at a higher interest rate, then the gain on redemption or repurchase of the bonds is misleading, because the company will need to make higher interest payments on the refinanced debt. In contrast, when interest rates decrease, the refinancing of long-term debt by retiring old debt and issuing new debt will result in a loss on debt retirement, but it will reduce the amount of periodic interest payments. Hence, management may be inclined to retire debt prematurely in order to show improved financial performance, but this decision may affect cash flows negatively in the future.

BORROWING IN FOREIGN CURRENCIES

INTERNATIONAL PERSPECTIVE

Many corporations with foreign operations elect to finance those operations with foreign debt to lessen the exchange rate risk. This type of risk exists because the relative value of each nation's currency varies virtually on a daily basis due to various economic factors. As this book is being written, the U.S. dollar is worth approximately $1.0264. A year earlier, it was worth $0.9992. A Canadian company that owed debt denominated in U.S. dollars would experience a loss from this increase in the value of the U.S. dollar relative to the value of the Canadian dollar.

A Canadian corporation that conducts business operations in the United States might decide to borrow money in U.S. dollars to finance its operations. If it has operations in Europe, it may borrow in euros to finance its European operations. The cash flows from the business will be in euros, which can be used to pay off the debt, which is in euros. If the business generated cash flows in euros but paid off debt in Canadian dollars, it would be exposed to exchange rate risk because the value of the Canadian dollar fluctuates relative to the euro.

Bombardier Inc. is a world leader in the transportation industry, producing planes, trains, and public transit cars, with manufacturing facilities in many countries. To finance its investments and operations, Bombardier borrows money in Canadian dollars, U.S. dollars, and euros. A summary of the long-term debt denominated in foreign currencies follows:

Currency	Amount Borrowed in Foreign Currency	Equivalent Amount in Canadian Dollars at December 31, 2012
U.S. dollar	2,412 million	2,612 million
Euro	1,565 million	2,345 million

The bonds denominated in the various currencies had to be translated to Canadian dollars at exchange rates in effect on December 31, 2012, before the amounts could be added together and reported on the statement of financial position at that date.

For reporting purposes, accountants must convert, or translate, foreign debt into a single currency. Conversion rates for all major currencies are published in most newspapers and on the Internet. To illustrate foreign currency translation, assume that Bombardier borrowed US$1 million. For reporting purposes, the accountant must use the conversion rate at December 31, 2012, which was USD 1 = CAD 1.0051. The equivalent of the US$1,000,000 debt is CAD$1,005,100 (US$1,000,000 × 1.0051). As you can see, the Canadian dollar equivalent of foreign debt will change if the conversion rate changes, even when no additional borrowings or repayments occur. Changes in conversion rates result in foreign exchange gains or losses that are covered in advanced accounting courses.

Borrowing in foreign currencies gives rise to foreign exchange risk, whereby a decrease in the value of the Canadian dollar relative to the foreign currency would require a larger amount of Canadian dollars to settle the foreign debt. The reverse is true if the Canadian dollar appreciates relative to foreign currency. A variety of risk reduction techniques can be undertaken by Bombardier to limit the potential increase in Canadian dollars it may have to pay. These include currency forwards, futures, swaps, and options, which are different types of financial instruments. Accounting for financial instruments is taught in advanced accounting courses.

OTHER NON-CURRENT LIABILITIES

LO⁶

Describe other non-current liabilities.

In addition to long-term debt, companies report a number of other non-current liabilities that result from their operating, investing, and financing activities. Typical non-current liabilities are lease obligations, asset retirement obligations, accrued retirement benefits liability, and deferred income taxes (covered in Appendix 10A).

Lease Liabilities

Companies often lease rather than purchase assets. For example, renting extra delivery trucks during a busy period is more economical than owning them if they are not needed during the rest of the year. When a company leases an asset on a short-term basis, the agreement, called an **operating lease**, does not transfer substantially the risks and rewards of ownership from the lessor to the lessee. No liability is recorded when an operating lease is created. Instead, a company records rent expense as it uses the asset. Assume that on December 15, 2014, a company signed an operating lease contract to rent five large trucks during January 2015. No liability is recorded in 2014. Rent expense is recorded during January 2015 as the trucks are actually used.

An **OPERATING LEASE** does not transfer substantially all the risks and rewards of ownership from the lessor to the lessee.

For a number of reasons, a company may prefer to lease an asset on a long-term basis rather than purchase it. If control of the leased asset has been transferred to the lessee along with the risks and rewards of ownership, then the lease is called a **finance lease**, regardless of the contractual form of the obligation the two parties signed. In essence, a finance lease contract represents the purchase and financing of an asset even though it is legally a lease agreement. Unlike an operating lease, finance leases are accounted for as if an asset has been purchased, by recording an asset and a liability.

A **FINANCE LEASE** transfers substantially all the risks and rewards of ownership from the lessor to the lessee.

Because of the significant differences in accounting for operating and finance leases, guidelines have been established to distinguish between them. A finance lease would normally satisfy one or more of the following situations:[9]

- Ownership of the asset is transferred to the lessee at the end of the lease term.
- The lease contract provides the lessee with an option to purchase the asset in the future at a price that is expected to be sufficiently lower than its fair market value at the time the option becomes exercisable.
- The lease term is for the major part of the asset's economic life even if title is not transferred.

- The present value of the minimum lease payments is substantially all of the fair value of the leased asset when the lease is signed.
- The leased assets are of such a specialized nature that only the lessee can use them without major modifications.

The accounting for leases as finance leases reflects the economic substance of the transaction, which is in essence a purchase of an asset with long-term financing, rather than the legal form of the commitment to make specific payments in the future. As a result, the financial statements should faithfully represent the economic nature of the transaction. If managers have a choice of recording a lease as operating or finance, most would prefer to record it as an operating lease. By doing so, the company is able to report less debt on its statement of financial position.

In contrast, the accounting for finance leases requires reporting a non-current liability, thereby increasing the debt-to-equity ratio (discussed later in this chapter). Furthermore, the current portion of the lease liability increases current liabilities, reduces working capital, and lowers the current ratio. Companies avoid these undesirable consequences if finance leases are accounted for as operating leases. It is important to note, however, that the cash outflows are not affected by the classification of leases. Many financial analysts are concerned that companies can avoid reporting debt associated with finance leases by structuring the lease agreement in a manner that meets the requirements for recording it as an operating lease.[10]

To record a finance lease, it is necessary to determine the current cash equivalent of the required lease payments. Assume that BCE signs a lease for new telecommunications equipment. The accountant has determined that the lease is a finance lease with a current cash equivalent of $25 million. Once the lease is signed, the transaction is recorded in a manner similar to the actual purchase of telecommunications equipment:

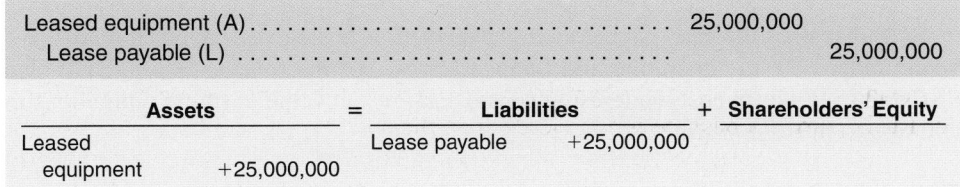

Leased equipment (A). 25,000,000
    Lease payable (L) 25,000,000

Assets	=	Liabilities	+	Shareholders' Equity
Leased equipment +25,000,000		Lease payable +25,000,000		

BCE Inc. leases assets for use in its operations. Some of the lease contracts are accounted for as finance leases, while others qualify as operating leases, as disclosed in the following excerpts from the notes to the financial statements:

REAL-WORLD EXCERPT

BCE Inc.

ANNUAL REPORT

NOTES

2. Significant Accounting Policies
Leases

Leases of property, plant, and equipment are recognized as finance leases when we obtain substantially all the risks and rewards of ownership of the underlying assets. At the inception of the lease, we record an asset together with a corresponding long-term liability at the lower of the fair value of the leased asset or the present value of the minimum lease payments. If there is reasonable certainty that the lease transfers ownership of the asset to us by the end of the lease term, the asset is amortized over its useful life. Otherwise, the asset is amortized over the shorter of its useful life and the lease term and the liability is measured at amortized cost using the effective interest method.

All other leases are classified as operating leases. Lease payments are expensed on a straight-line basis over the term of the lease.

Source: BCE Inc., Annual Report 2012.

NOTES

12. PROPERTY, PLANT, AND EQUIPMENT

Finance Leases

BCE's significant finance leases are for satellites and office premises. The office leases have a typical lease term of 15 years. The leases for satellites, used to provide programming to our Bell TV customers, have lease terms ranging from 12 to 15 years. The satellite leases are non-cancellable.

. . .

The following table provides a reconciliation of our minimum future lease payments to the present value of our finance lease obligations.

December 31, 2012	2013	2014	2015	2016	2017	Thereafter	Total
Minimum future lease payments	548	431	267	236	235	1,837	3,554
Less							
Future finance costs	(162)	(147)	(134)	(125)	(116)	(525)	(1,209)
Present value of future lease obligations	386	284	133	111	119	1,312	2,345

25. COMMITMENTS AND CONTINGENCIES

Commitments

The following table is a summary of our contractual obligations at December 31, 2012, that are due in each of the next five years and thereafter.

December 31, 2012	2013	2014	2015	2016	2017	Thereafter	Total
Operating leases	229	201	176	139	107	489	1,341

. . .

BCE's significant operating leases are for office premises and retail outlets with lease terms ranging from 1 to 30 years. These leases are non-cancellable and are renewable at the end of the lease period. Rental expense relating to operating leases was $269 million in 2012 and $253 million in 2011.

Source: BCE Inc., Annual Report 2012.

BCE discloses the cash payments it is expected to make over each of the next five years under both the operating and finance leases. For the finance leases, BCE also discloses the finance costs (interest expense) and present value of future obligations in addition to the cash payments.

Provisions

In Chapter 10, we indicated that companies establish provisions when either the amount or the timing of the liability is uncertain. In many cases, companies make investing or operating decisions resulting in future obligations that may not be determinable with accuracy, particularly if the amount of the obligation is dependent on the timing of future events. Examples include restructuring of the company's operations; legal disputes; and the dismantlement, removal, and restoration of property, plant, and equipment.

Employee Retirement Benefits

Most employers provide retirement programs for their employees. In a *defined contribution* program, the employer makes cash payments to an investment fund. When employees retire, they are entitled to a portion of the fund. If the investment strategy of the fund is successful, the retirement income for the employees will be larger. If the strategy is not successful, it will be lower. In other words, the employees bear the risk associated with the investments in the plan. The employer's only obligation is to make the required annual payments to the fund, which are recorded as pension expense.

Other employers offer *defined benefit* programs. Under these programs, an employee's retirement benefits are based on a percentage of his or her pay at retirement or a certain amount of money for each year of employment. In these cases, the amount of pension expense that must be accrued each year is the change in the current cash value of the employee's retirement package. The current cash value changes each year for a variety of reasons. For example, it changes (1) as employees get closer to receiving benefits, (2) as employees' retirement benefits increase because of higher pay or longer service, or (3) if the employees' life expectancies change. The company must report a pension liability based on any portion of the current cash value of the retirement program that has not actually been funded. For example, if the company transferred $8 million to the pension fund manager but the current cash value of the pension program was $10 million, the company would report a $2 million pension liability on its statement of financial position.

For many corporations, especially those with unionized workforces, the financial obligation associated with defined benefit retirement programs can be very large, because the risk associated with investments in the pension plan is borne by the employer, which must cover any shortfall between the investment income and the payments to retirees. For this reason, companies have been moving away from defined benefit pension plans in favour of defined contribution pension plans.

In addition to defined benefit or defined contribution pensions plans, employers may offer other post-employment benefits to their employees, such as healthcare benefits and life insurance benefits for some employees. In recent years, employer-provided healthcare benefits have been the subject of much discussion. These have often been referred to in the financial press as legacy costs. As more people retire and live longer, these legacy costs will increase. Moreover, large companies pay for a portion of their employees' post-retirement health insurance costs. The issue arises because these potential future payments are recorded as an expense in the current accounting period.

The cost of these future benefits must be estimated and recorded as an expense in the periods when the employees perform services. The recording of future healthcare costs for retired employees is an excellent example of the use of estimates in accounting. Imagine the difficulty of estimating future healthcare costs when you do not know how long employees will live or how healthy they will be during their lives.

BCE offers its employees both defined benefit and defined contribution pension plans. In addition, it provides healthcare and life insurance benefits to some employees during retirement. Because defined benefit plans are costly to employers, new BCE employees can generally participate only in defined contribution plans. In 2012, the pension and other employment benefit plans cost BCE $269 million, and its post-employment benefit obligations amounted to $3,422 million at December 31, 2012, as reported in Exhibit 11.1.

Accounting for retirement benefits is a complex topic that is discussed in detail in subsequent accounting courses. We introduce the topic at this point as another example of the application of the matching process, which requires that expenses be recorded in the year in which the benefit is received. The benefit in this case is the work performed by the employees, and all costs incurred to compensate employees for their work must be recorded regardless of the timing of pension payments. This accounting procedure also avoids creating improper incentives for managers. If the future cost of retirement benefits was not included in the period in which work was performed, managers might have the incentive to offer employees increases in their retirement benefits instead of increases in their salaries. In this manner, managers could understate the true cost of employee services and make their companies appear more profitable.

DEBT-TO-EQUITY RATIO

KEY RATIO ANALYSIS

LO7

Compute and interpret the debt-to-equity ratio.

Companies raise large amounts of money to acquire additional assets by issuing shares to investors and borrowing funds from creditors. These additional assets are used to generate more earnings. However, since debt must be repaid, taking on increasing amounts of debt carries increased risk. The debt-to-equity ratio provides one measure for analysts to examine the company's financing strategy.

ANALYTICAL QUESTION → As an investor who must decide whether or not to buy shares, it is important to know how much of the company's assets is financed by creditors and how much is financed by owners. The debt-to-equity ratio is used to assess the debt capacity of a business. It is computed as follows:

$$\text{Debt-to-Equity Ratio} = \frac{\text{Total Liabilities}}{\text{Shareholders' Equity}}$$

The 2012 ratio for BCE is

$$\frac{\$24,667}{\$14,759} = 1.78$$

RATIO AND COMPARISONS

Comparisons over Time			Comparisons with Competitors	
BCE			**Rogers Communications**	**TELUS**
2010	**2011**	**2012**	**2012**	**2012**
2.53	1.67	1.78	4.21	1.66

INTERPRETATIONS

In General → The debt-to-equity ratio indicates how much debt has been used to finance the company's acquisition of assets relative to equity financing that is supplied by shareholders. A high ratio normally suggests that a company relies heavily on funds provided by creditors. Managers use the ratio to decide whether they should finance any additional acquisitions by using debt. Creditors use this ratio to assess the risk that a company may not be able to meet its financial obligations during a business downturn. Investors use it to assess the level of financial risk associated with the expected cash flows from their investment (dividends and appreciation in share value).

Focus Company Analysis → The debt-to-equity ratio for BCE decreased in 2011 relative to 2010, and increased slightly in 2012. BCE recognized massive impairment losses in the past resulting from overpayment for acquisitions. The asset write-down resulted in a significant deficit, which is being reduced over time as the company continues to report net earnings year after year. It is also important to note that BCE's ratio is in line with TELUS's ratio, but significantly better than Rogers' ratio.

A Few Cautions → The debt-to-equity ratio tells only part of the story with respect to risks associated with debt. The ratio is a good indication of debt capacity, but it does not help the investor understand whether the company's operations can support the amount of debt that it has. Remember that debt carries with it the obligation to make cash payments for interest and principal. As a result, most investors would evaluate the debt-to-equity ratio within the context of the amount of cash the company is able to generate from operating activities.

PAUSE FOR FEEDBACK

We learned how to compute two ratios: the times interest earned ratio and the debt-to-equity ratio. Check your understanding of these ratios before you move on.

SELF-STUDY QUIZ 11-6

Which company has a higher level of risk: a company with a high debt-to-equity ratio and a high interest coverage ratio or a company with a low debt-to-equity ratio and a low interest coverage ratio?

After you have completed your answer, check it with the solution at the end of the chapter.

FINANCING ACTIVITIES ON THE STATEMENT OF CASH FLOWS

BONDS PAYABLE

The issuance of long-term debt is reported as a cash inflow from financing activities. The repayment of principal is reported as an outflow from financing activities. As noted in Chapter 5, interest paid may be reported in either the operating or the financing section of the statement of cash flows.

LO8

Explain how financing activities are reported on the statement of cash flows.

EFFECT ON STATEMENT OF CASH FLOWS

In General → As we saw in Chapter 10, transactions involving short-term creditors (e.g., trade payables) affect working capital and are, therefore, reported in the operating activities section of the statement of cash flows. Cash received from long-term creditors is reported as an inflow from financing activities. Cash payments made to long-term creditors are reported as outflows from financing activities. Examples are shown in the following table:

Financing Activity	Effect on Cash Flows
Issuance of bonds	+
Debt retirement	−
Repayment of bond principal upon maturity	−

Focus Company Analysis → A segment of BCE's statements of cash flows for the years 2011 and 2012 follows:

Consolidated cash flow statement for the year ended 31 December 2012			
In millions of Canadian dollars	Note	2012	2011
Cash flows used in financing activities			
Increase in notes payable and bank advances		$ 377	$ 30
Reduction in securitized trade receivables		(15)	(318)
Issue of long-term debt		1,055	2,314
Repayment of long-term debt		(946)	(2,350)
Issue of common shares		39	152
Issue of preferred shares	23	280	345
Issue of equity securities by subsidiaries to non-controlling interest		11	403
Repurchase of common shares	23	(107)	(143)
Cash dividends paid on common shares		(1,683)	(1,520)
Cash dividends paid on preferred shares		(133)	(118)
Cash dividends/distributions paid by subsidiaries to non-controlling interest		(340)	(315)
Other financing activities		(45)	(61)
Cash flows used in financing activities		$(1,507)	$(1,581)

Source: BCE Inc., Annual Report 2012.

SELECTED FOCUS COMPANY COMPARISONS: CASH FLOWS FROM FINANCING ACTIVITIES (IN MILLIONS OF DOLLARS)—2012

WestJet Airlines	−288
Gildan Activewear	−69
Canadian Tire	247

REAL-WORLD EXCERPT

BCE Inc.

ANNUAL REPORT

In 2012, the company raised a substantial amount of long-term debt ($1,055 million). It also reduced its long-term debt by $946 million. Repayments of long-term debt are made when the debt matures or when a company decides to redeem the outstanding debt prematurely in order to take advantage of lower interest rates.

Analysts are particularly interested in the financing activities section of the statement of cash flows because it provides important insights about the future capital structure for the company. Rapidly growing companies typically report significant amounts of funds in this section of the statement.

ACCOUNTING STANDARDS
FOR PRIVATE ENTERPRISES

The accounting standards for private enterprises differ from IFRS in measuring and reporting specific types of long-term debt.

Financial Reporting Issue	IFRS	ASPE
Measurement of long-term debt	Canadian publicly accountable enterprises generally measure their long-term debt at amortized cost, but they are required to use the effective-interest method of amortization.	Canadian private enterprises generally measure their long-term debt at amortized cost. They may use the effective-interest method or the simpler straight-line method to amortize any discount or premium on debt issuance, particularly if the two methods do not usually produce significant differences in the carrying amounts of long-term debt.
Classification of redeemable long-term debt	Publicly accountable enterprises must classify such debt as a current liability.	If long-term bonds, debentures, or notes become redeemable (callable) as a result of a violation of a debt covenant, a private enterprise may continue to classify the debt as long term if the enterprise succeeds in renegotiating the debt agreement prior to releasing its financial statements.
Classification of finance leases	The criteria for classification of finance leases allow for some flexibility in implementation.	ASPE provide guidance as to the minimum percentages that constitute a major portion of the economic life of the leased asset (75%) or a substantial portion of the fair value of a leased asset (90%).

DEMONSTRATION CASE

To raise funds to build a new plant, Reed Company management issued bonds. The bond indenture specified the following:

> Par value of the bonds ($1,000 bonds): $600,000
> Date of issue: February 1, 2014; due in 10 years on January 31, 2024
> Stated interest rate: 6.5 percent per annum, payable semi-annually on July 31 and January 31

The market interest rate was 6 percent when the bonds were sold on February 1, 2014. The fiscal year for Reed Company ends on December 31.

Required:

1. How much cash did Reed Company receive from the sale of the bonds on February 1, 2014? Show your computations.

2. Prepare the journal entry on February 1, 2014, to record the sale and issuance of the bonds payable.

3. Prepare the journal entry for the payment of interest and amortization of the premium for the first interest payment on July 31, 2014. The company uses the effective-interest method.

4. Prepare the adjusting entry required on December 31, 2014, the end of the fiscal year.

5. Prepare the journal entry to record the second interest payment and the amortization of the premium on January 31, 2015.

6. Show how bond interest expense and bonds payable are reported on the financial statements at December 31, 2014.

We strongly recommend that you prepare your own answers to these requirements and then check your answers with the following solution.

SUGGESTED **SOLUTION**

1. The sale price of the bonds is the present value of future payments:

Principal $600,000 × 0.5537 (Table 10C.1, *n* = 20, *i* = 3): $332,220
Interest ($600,000 × 6.5% × 1/2) × 14.8775 (Table 10C.2, *n* = 20, *i* = 3):   290,111
                                        $622,331

2. February 1, 2014 (issuance date):

Cash (A)	622,331	
Premium on bonds payable (L)		22,331
Bonds payable (L)		600,000
To record sale of bonds payable.		

3. July 31, 2014 (first interest payment date):

Bond interest expense (E) ($622,331 × 3%)	18,670	
Premium on bonds payable (L)	830	
Cash (A) ($600,000 × 3.25%)		19,500
To record payment of semi-annual interest.		

4. December 31, 2014 (end of the accounting period):

Bond interest expense (E) [($622,331 − $830) × 6% × 5/12]	15,538	
Premium on bonds payable (L)	712	
Bond interest payable (L) ($600,000 × 6.5% × 5/12)		16,250
Adjusting entry for five months' interest accrued plus amortization of the premium, August 1 to December 31, 2014.		

5. January 31, 2015 (second interest date):

Bond interest payable (L)	16,250	
Bond interest expense (E) [($622,331 − $830) × 6% × 1/12]	3,108	
Premium on bonds payable (L)	142	
Cash (A)		19,500
To record payment of semi-annual interest.		

6. Interest expense reported on the 2014 statement of earnings should be for 11 months, February 1 through December 31. Interest expense, per these entries, is $18,670 + $15,538 = $34,208.

Statement of Earnings for 2014:

Interest expense	$ 34,208

Statement of Financial Position, December 31, 2014:

Non-current liabilities:

Bonds payable, 6% (due January 31, 2024)	$600,000
Add unamortized premium*	20,789
	$620,789

*$22,331 − ($830 + $712) = $20,789

APPENDIX 11A: REPORTING INTEREST EXPENSE ON BONDS BY USING THE STRAIGHT-LINE AMORTIZATION METHOD

While the effective-interest method is the preferred method to amortize bond discount or premium, Canadian private enterprises may use **straight-line amortization**, which allocates an equal amount to each interest period, because it is relatively easy to compute the required numbers. You may wonder why private enterprises are permitted to use a method that is not conceptually correct. The answer is *materiality*. Private

STRAIGHT-LINE AMORTIZATION of a bond discount or premium is a simplified method that allocates an equal amount to each interest period.

enterprises are permitted to use the straight-line method because the amortized discounts or premiums that result from the two methods are normally not materially different. We use the examples in the chapter to illustrate the amortization of a bond discount as well as of a bond premium.

Bonds Issued at a Discount Refer to the illustration in the chapter, in which MSC's $400,000 bond issue was sold at a discount of $54,356. To amortize the bond discount over the life of MSC's bonds by using straight-line amortization, an equal amount is allocated to each interest period. MSC's bonds have 20 six-month interest periods. Therefore, the amount amortized on each semi-annual interest date is $2,718 ($54,356 ÷ 20 periods). This amount is added to the interest paid ($12,000) to compute interest expense for the period ($14,718).

The journal entry to record the interest payment each period is as follows:

Bond interest expense (E)	14,718	
Discount on bonds payable (XL)		2,718
Cash (A)		12,000

Assets		=	Liabilities		+	Shareholders' Equity	
Cash	−12,000		Discount on bonds payable	+2,718		Bond interest expense	−14,718

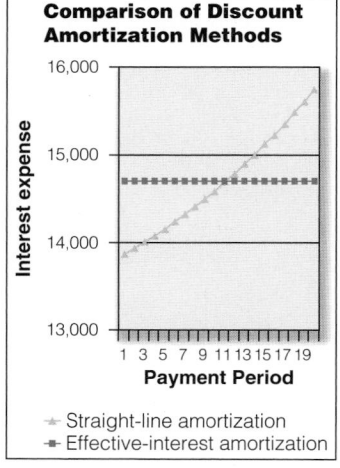

Comparison of Discount Amortization Methods

Interest expense (y-axis): 13,000 / 14,000 / 15,000 / 16,000
Payment Period (x-axis): 1 3 5 7 9 11 13 15 17 19

→ Straight-line amortization
→ Effective-interest amortization

Bonds payable are reported on the statement of financial position at their carrying amount—that is, the maturity amount less any unamortized bond discount (or plus any unamortized bond premium). At June 30, 2013, the carrying amount of MSC's bonds is more than the original issue price. The carrying amount increases to $348,362 ($345,644 + $2,718) because of the amortization of the discount. In each interest period, the carrying amount of the bonds increases by $2,718 because the unamortized discount decreases by $2,718. At the maturity date of the bonds, the unamortized discount (i.e., the balance in the discount on bonds payable account) is zero. At that time, the maturity amount of the bonds and the carrying amount are the same (i.e., $400,000). The process can be seen in the following amortization schedule, which shows the first two years and the last year of the bond's life. Compare it to the amortization schedule based on the effective-interest method:

	(a) Interest to Be Paid [$400,000 × 3%]	(b) Interest Expense [(a) + (c)]	(c) Amortization [$54,356 ÷ 20 periods]	(d) Carrying Amount [Beginning Carrying Amount + (c)]
Amortization Schedule: Bond Discount (Straight Line)				
Date				
1/1/2013				$345,644
30/6/2013	$12,000	$14,718	$2,718	348,361
31/12/2013	12,000	14,718	2,718	351,079
30/6/2014	12,000	14,718	2,718	353,797
31/12/2014	12,000	14,718	2,718	356,515
.	.	.	.	.
.	.	.	.	.
30/6/2022	12,000	14,718	2,718	397,282
31/12/2022	12,000	14,718	2,718	400,000

Under the straight-line method, interest expense remains constant over the life of the bond, but it increases when the effective-interest method is used. The graph in the margin above illustrates these differences. However, both methods amortize the same historic discount and do not reflect current market values.

PAUSE FOR
FEEDBACK

We have computed interest expense using the straight-line method of amortization of the bond discount and determined the carrying amount of the bond after each interest payment date. Practise these computations before moving on.

SELF-STUDY QUIZ 11-7

Assume that MSC issued $100,000 bonds that will mature in 10 years. The bonds pay interest twice each year at an annual rate of 7 percent. They were sold when the market rate was 8 percent.

1. Determine the selling price of the bonds.

2. What amount of interest was paid at the end of the first year?

3. What amount of interest expense would be reported at the end of the first year using straight-line amortization of bond discount?

After you complete your answers, check them with the solutions at the end of the chapter.

Bonds Issued at a Premium   Refer to the illustration in the chapter, in which MSC's $400,000 bond issue was sold at a premium of $65,417. The premium recorded by MSC must be apportioned to each of the 20 interest periods. Using the straight-line method, the premium that is amortized in each semi-annual interest period is $3,271 ($65,417 ÷ 20 periods). This amount is subtracted from the interest payment ($12,000) to calculate the interest expense ($8,729). Thus, amortization of the bond premium decreases interest expense.

The payment of interest on the bonds is recorded as follows:

Bond interest expense (E)	8,729	
Premium on bonds payable (L)	3,271	
Cash (A)		12,000

Assets		=	Liabilities		+	Shareholders' Equity	
Cash	−12,000		Premium on bonds payable	−3,271		Bond interest expense	−8,729

Notice that the $12,000 cash paid each period includes $8,729 interest expense and $3,271 premium amortization. Thus, the cash payment to the investors includes the current interest they have earned, plus a return of part of the premium they paid when they bought the bonds.

The carrying amount of the bonds is the amount in the bonds payable account plus any unamortized premium. On June 30, 2013, the carrying amount of the bonds is $462,146 ($400,000 + $65,417 − $3,271). A partial amortization schedule follows:

	(a) Interest to Be Paid [$400,000 × 2%]	(b) Interest Expense [(a) − (c)]	(c) Amortization [$65,417 ÷ 20 periods]	(d) Carrying Amount [Beginning Carrying Amount − (c)]
Date				
1/1/2013				$465,417
30/6/2013	$12,000	8,729	3,271	462,146
31/12/2013	12,000	8,729	3,271	458,875
30/6/2014	12,000	8,729	3,271	455,604
31/12/2014	12,000	8,729	3,271	452,333
.	.	.	.	.
.	.	.	.	.
30/6/2022	12,000	8,729	3,271	403,271
31/12/2022	12,000	8,729	3,271	400,000

Amortization Schedule: Bond Premium (Straight Line)

Exhibit **11.5**

Amortization of Bond Discount and
Premium Compared—Straight-Line
Amortization

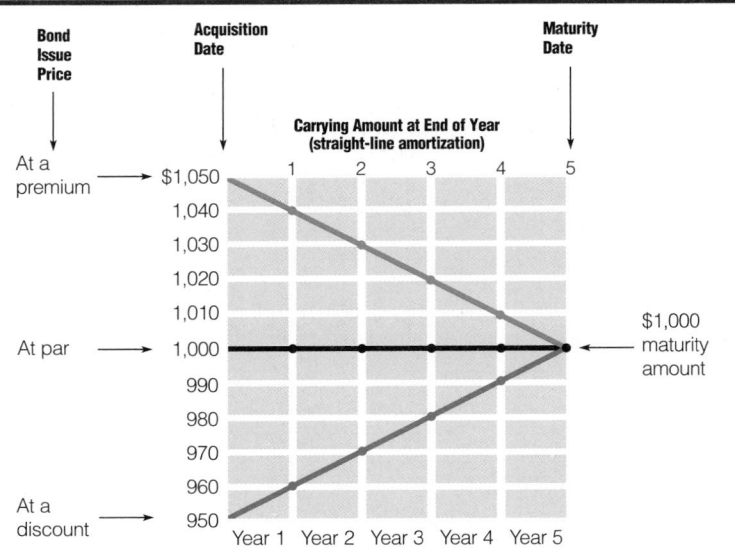

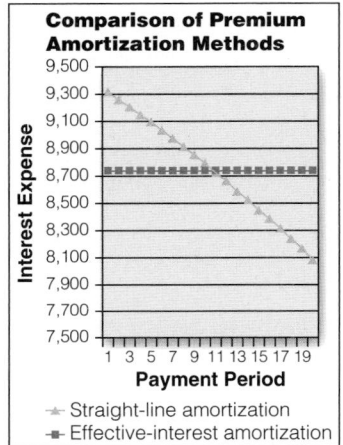

Comparison of Premium Amortization Methods

Interest Expense

— Straight-line amortization
— Effective-interest amortization

At the maturity date, after the last interest payment, the bond premium is fully amortized, and the maturity amount equals the carrying amount of the bonds. When the bonds are paid off in full, the same entry will be made whether the bond was originally sold at par, at a discount, or at a premium. Exhibit 11.5 compares the effects of the amortization of bond discount and bond premium on a $1,000 bond.

Under the straight-line method, interest expense remains constant over the life of the bond, but it decreases when the effective-interest method is used. The graph in the margin illustrates these differences.

PAUSE FOR FEEDBACK

We have computed interest expense using the straight-line method of amortization of the bond premium. Prastise these computations before moving on.

SELF-STUDY **QUIZ 11-8**

Assume that MSC issued $100,000 bonds that will mature in 10 years. The bonds pay interest twice each year at an annual rate of 9 percent. They were sold when the market rate was 8 percent.

1. Determine the selling price of the bonds.
2. What amount of interest was paid at the end of the first year?
3. What amount of interest expense would be reported at the end of the first year using straight-line amortization?

After you complete your answers, check them with the solutions at the end of the chapter.

CHAPTER **TAKE-AWAYS**

1. **Describe the characteristics of long-term notes and bonds payable.**
    Long-term notes and bonds payable have a number of characteristics designed to meet the needs of the issuing corporation and the creditor.

    Corporations use debt to raise long-term capital. Long-term debt offers a number of advantages compared to equity, including financial leverage, the tax deductibility of interest, and the fact that control of the company is not diluted. Long-term debt carries additional risk because interest and principal payments are not discretionary.

2. **Report notes payable and related interest expense.**

   A note or mortgage payable requires periodic payment of interest and repayment of the principal amount. The principal is typically repaid in blended payments of both principal and interest over the life of the note. The interest portion of the payment should be separated from the principal repayment for proper recording of the interest and the reduction of the liability.

3. **Report bonds payable and interest expense for bonds sold at par, at a discount, or at a premium.**

   Three types of events must be recorded over the life of a typical bond: (1) the receipt of cash when the bond is first sold, (2) the periodic payment of interest, and (3) the repayment of principal upon the maturity of the bond.

   Bonds are sold at a discount whenever the coupon interest rate is less than the market rate of interest. A discount is the difference between the par value of the bond and its selling price. The discount is recorded as a contra liability when the bond is sold and is amortized over the life of the bond as an adjustment to interest payment.

   Bonds are sold at a premium whenever the coupon interest rate is higher than the market rate of interest. A premium is the difference between the selling price of the bond and its par value. The premium is recorded as a liability when the bond is sold and is amortized over the life of the bond as an adjustment to interest payment.

4. **Compute and interpret the times interest earned ratio.**

   This ratio measures the ability of a company to meet its interest obligations with resources from its profit-making activities. The ratio is computed by comparing interest expense to earnings before interest expense and income taxes.

5. **Report the early retirement of bonds.**

   A corporation may retire bonds before their maturity date. The difference between the carrying amount and the amount paid to retire the bonds is reported as a gain or a loss, depending on the circumstances.

6. **Describe other non-current liabilities.**

   In addition to long-term debt, companies report a number of other non-current liabilities that result from their operating, investing, and financing activities. Typical non-current liabilities include lease obligations, provisions, retirement benefit obligations, and deferred income taxes.

7. **Compute and interpret the debt-to-equity ratio.**

   The debt-to-equity ratio (total liabilities ÷ shareholders' equity) measures the relationship between total liabilities and the shareholders' capital that finances the assets. The higher the ratio, the more debt is used to finance assets. As the ratio (and thus debt) increases, risk increases.

8. **Explain how financing activities are reported on the statement of cash flows.**

   Cash flows associated with transactions involving long-term creditors are reported in the financing activities section of the statement of cash flows. Interest paid may be reported in either the operating activities section or the financing activities section.

The capital structure of a business is made up of funds supplied by both the creditors and the owners. In this chapter, we discussed the role of bonds payable in the capital structure of a business. In the next chapter, we will discuss shareholders' equity.

KEY **RATIOS**

The times interest earned ratio measures a company's ability to generate resources from current operations to meet its interest obligations. The computation of this ratio follows:

$$\text{Times Interest Earned} = \frac{\text{Net Earnings} + \text{Interest Expense} + \text{Income Tax Expense}}{\text{Interest Expense}}$$

The debt-to-equity ratio measures the relationship between liabilities and the shareholders' capital that finances the assets. The higher the ratio, the more debt is assumed by the company to finance assets. The ratio is computed as follows:

$$\text{Debt-to-Equity Ratio} = \frac{\text{Total Liabilities}}{\text{Shareholders' Equity}}$$

FINDING **FINANCIAL INFORMATION**

STATEMENT OF FINANCIAL POSITION

Under Current Liabilities

Notes, bonds, and debentures are normally listed as non-current liabilities. An exception occurs when these liabilities are within one year of maturity. Such debts are reported as current liabilities with the following title:

Current portion of long-term debt

Under Non-current Liabilities

Notes, bonds, and debentures are listed under a variety of titles, depending on the characteristics of the debt. Titles include

Notes payable

Bonds payable

Debentures

Financial liabilities

STATEMENT OF CASH FLOWS

Under Financing Activities

+ Cash inflows from long-term creditors
− Cash outflows to long-term creditors (including interest paid)

Under Operating Activities

Interest paid if classified as an operating activity

STATEMENT OF EARNINGS

Interest expense associated with long-term debt is reported on the statement of earnings. Most companies report interest expense as part of finance costs in a separate category on the statement of earnings.

NOTES

Under Summary of Significant Accounting Policies

Description of pertinent information concerning the accounting treatment of liabilities. Normally, there is minimal information. Some companies report the method used to amortize bond discounts and premiums.

Under a Separate Note

Most companies include a separate note called "Long-term debt" that reports information about each major debt issue, including amount and interest rate. The note may also provide detail concerning debt characteristics and covenants.

■ connect **GLOSSARY**

Review key terms and definitions on *Connect*.

QUESTIONS

1. What are the primary characteristics of a bond? For what purposes are bonds usually issued?
2. What is the difference between a bond indenture and a bond certificate?
3. Differentiate secured debt from unsecured debt.
4. Differentiate among redeemable, retractable, and convertible bonds.
5. From the perspective of the issuer, what are some advantages of using debt instead of issuing shares?
6. As the tax rate increases, the net cost of borrowing money decreases. Explain.
7. At the date of issuance, bonds are recorded at their current cash-equivalent amount. Explain.
8. What is the nature of the discount and premium on bonds payable? Explain.
9. What is the difference between the stated interest rate and the effective-interest rate on a bond?
10. Differentiate between the stated and effective rates of interest on a bond sold (*a*) at par, (*b*) at a discount, and (*c*) at a premium.
11. What is the carrying amount of a bond payable?
12. If a company issues a bond at a discount, will interest expense each period be more or less than the cash payment for interest? If another company issues a bond at a premium, will interest expense be more or less than the cash payment for interest? Is your answer to either question affected by the method used to amortize the discount or premium?
13. (Appendix 11A) Explain the basic difference between the straight-line and effective-interest methods of amortizing bond discount or premium. Explain when the straight-line method may be used.

EXERCISES

E11–1 Bond Terminology: Fill in the Blanks

LO1

1. The _____ is the amount (*a*) payable at the maturity of the bond and (*b*) on which the periodic cash interest payments are computed.

2. _____ is another name for bond principal, or the maturity amount for a bond.

3. The _____ is the rate of cash interest per period stated in the bond contract.

4. A _____ is an unsecured bond; no assets are specifically pledged to guarantee repayment.

5. _____ may be called for early retirement at the option of the issuer.

6. _____ may be converted to other securities of the issuer (usually common shares).

E11–2 Determining Financial Statement Effects for Long-Term Note and First Interest Payment, with Premium

LO1, 3

Grocery Corporation sold $500,000, 7 percent notes on January 1, 2014, at a market rate of 8 percent. The notes were dated January 1, 2014, with interest to be paid each December 31; they mature 10 years from January 1, 2014. Use effective-interest amortization.

Required:

1. How are the financial statements affected by the issuance of the notes? Describe the impact on the debt-to-equity and times interest earned ratios, if any.

2. How are the financial statements affected by the payment of interest on December 31? Describe the impact on the debt-to-equity and times interest earned ratios, if any.

3. Show how the interest expense, interest payment, and notes payable should be reported on the financial statements for 2014.

E11–3 Explaining Why Debt Is Sold at a Discount

LO1

Shaw Communications Inc.

A recent annual report of Shaw Communications Inc. contained the following note:

> **10. LONG-TERM DEBT**
>
> On December 7, 2010, the Company issued $500,000,000 senior notes at a rate of 5.50% due December 7, 2020. The effective rate is 5.55% due to the discount on the issuance.

After reading this note, one student asked why Shaw didn't simply sell the notes for an effective yield of 5.55 percent and avoid having to account for a very small discount over the life of the notes. Prepare a written response to this question.

E11–4 Explaining Bond Features

LO3

Carnival Corporation

Carnival Corporation is a global cruise company and one of the largest vacation companies in the world. The notes to its financial statements for 2009 include the following:

> **CONVERTIBLE NOTES**
>
> At November 30, 2009, Carnival Corporation's 2% convertible notes ("2% Notes") are convertible into 15.2 million shares of Carnival Corporation common stock. The 2% Notes are convertible at a conversion price of $39.14 per share, subject to adjustment, during any fiscal quarter for which the closing price of the Carnival Corporation common stock is greater than $43.05 per share for a defined duration of time in the preceding fiscal quarter. The conditions for conversion of the 2% Notes were not satisfied during 2009 and 2008. Only a nominal amount of our 2% Notes have been converted since their issuance in 2000.
>
> On April 15, 2011, the 2% note holders may require us to repurchase all or a portion of the 2% Notes at their face values plus any unpaid accrued interest. In addition, we currently may redeem all or a portion of the outstanding 2% Notes at their face value plus any unpaid accrued interest, subject to the note holders' right to convert. Upon conversion, redemption or repurchase of the 2% Notes, we may choose to deliver Carnival Corporation common stock, cash or a combination of cash and common stock with a total value equal to the value of the consideration otherwise deliverable.
>
> *Source:* Carnival Corporation, Annual Report 2009.

Required:

1. Explain the various features of these notes.
2. When the notes were issued, interest rates were much higher than the 2 percent offered by the company. Why would an investor accept such a low interest rate?

Trans-Canada
Pipelines

E11–5   **Interpreting Information Reported in the Business Press**

The business press reported the following information concerning a bond issued by Trans-Canada Pipelines:

Bonds	Coupon	Maturity	Bid $	Yield %
Trans-Canada Pipelines	8.05	February 17, 2039	149.81	4.69

Required:

1. Explain the meaning of the reported information. If you bought Trans-Canada Pipelines bonds with $10,000 face value, how much would you pay (based on the information reported above)?
2. Assume that the bond was originally sold at par. What impact would the increase in value have on the financial statements for Trans-Canada Pipelines?

The Walt Disney
Company

E11–6   **Explaining an International Transaction**

A Walt Disney annual report contained the following note:

> The Company issued 100 billion (approximately $920 million) of Japanese yen bonds through a public offering in Japan. The bonds are senior, unsecured debt obligations of the Company, which mature in June 2019. Interest on the bonds is payable semi-annually at a fixed interest rate of 5% per year through maturity. The bonds provide for principal payments in dollars and interest payment in Japanese yen.

Required:

1. Describe how this bond would be reported on the statement of financial position.
2. Explain why you think management borrowed money in this manner.

E11–7   **Analyzing Financial Ratios**

You have just started your first job as a financial analyst for a large investment company. Your boss, a senior analyst, has finished a detailed report evaluating bonds issued by two different companies. She stopped by your desk and asked for help: "I have compared two ratios for the companies and found something interesting." She went on to explain that the debt-to-equity ratio for Applied Technologies Inc. is much lower than the industry average and that the one for Innovative Solutions Inc. is much higher. On the other hand, the times interest earned ratio for Applied Technologies is much higher than the industry average, and the ratio for Innovative Solutions is much lower. Your boss then asked you to explain what the ratios indicate about the two companies so that she could include the explanation in her report. How would you respond to your boss?

E11–8   **Comparing Different Options to Repay a Note Payable**

On October 1, 2014, Rocco Inc. purchased new equipment for $50,000 and was considering three different options for payment of this amount:

1. Pay the full amount on September 30, 2018, along with annual interest, payable each September 30.
2. Pay one quarter of this amount each September 30 along with the interest that would have accrued on the unpaid amount until that date.
3. Pay four equal annual instalments that include both interest and a partial repayment of the full amount, starting on September 30, 2015.

The equipment vendor would charge Rocco an annual interest rate of 5 percent for any of the three options.

Required:

Which of these three options would result in the lowest amount of interest payments over the four years? Support your answer with computations.

E11–9 **Computing the Issue Price of a Note Payable**

On January 1, 2014, Kaizen Corporation issued a $500 million note that matures in 10 years. The note has a stated interest rate of 6 percent. When the note was issued, the market rate was 6 percent. The note pays interest twice per year, on June 30 and December 31. At what price was the note issued?

E11–10 **Computing the Issue Price of a Bond with Analysis of Net Earnings and Cash Flow Effects**

Imai Company issued a $1-million bond that matures in five years. The bond has a 9 percent coupon rate. When the bond was issued, the market rate was 8 percent. The bond pays interest twice per year, on June 30 and December 31. Record the issuance of the bond on June 30. Was the bond issued at a discount or at a premium? How will the discount or premium affect future net earnings and future cash flows?

E11–11 **Computing Issue Prices of Bonds for Three Cases**

Thompson Corporation is planning to issue $100,000, five-year, 6 percent bonds. Interest is payable semi-annually each June 30 and December 31. All of the bonds will be sold on July 1, 2014; they mature on June 30, 2019.

Required:

Compute the issue (sale) price on July 1, 2014, if the yield is (*a*) 6 percent, (*b*) 5 percent, and (*c*) 7 percent. Show computations.

E11–12 **Recording Bond Issue and First Interest Payment with Premium (Effective-Interest Amortization)**

On January 1, 2015, Bochini Corporation sold a $10 million, 8.25 percent bond issue. The bonds were dated January 1, 2015, had a yield of 8 percent, pay interest each December 31, and mature 10 years from the date of issue.

Required:

1. Prepare the journal entry to record the issuance of the bonds.
2. Prepare the journal entry to record the interest payment on December 31, 2015. Use effective-interest amortization.
3. Show how the bond interest expense and the bonds payable should be reported on the annual financial statements for 2015.

E11–13 **Determining Financial Statement Balance with the Effective-Interest Amortization of a Bond Discount**

Eagle Corporation issued $10,000,000, 6.5 percent bonds dated April 1, 2015. The market rate of interest was 7 percent, with interest paid each March 31. The bonds mature in three years, on March 31, 2018. Eagle's fiscal year ends on December 31.

Required:

1. What was the issue price of these bonds?
2. Compute the bond interest expense for fiscal year 2015. The company uses the effective-interest method of amortization.
3. Show how the bonds should be reported on the statement of financial position at December 31, 2015.
4. What amount of interest expense will be recorded on March 31, 2016? Is this amount different from the amount of cash that is paid? If so, why?

E11–14 **Analyzing a Bond Amortization Schedule: Reporting Bonds Payable**

Stein Corporation issued a $1,000 bond on January 1, 2014. The bond specified an interest rate of 9 percent payable at the end of each year. The bond matures at the end of 2016. It was sold at a market rate of 11 percent per year. The following schedule was completed:

	Cash Paid	Interest Expense	Amortization	Carrying Amount
January 1, 2014 (issuance)				$ 951
End of year 2014	?	$105	$15	966
End of year 2015	?	106	16	982
End of year 2016	?	108	18	1,000

Required:

1. What was the bond's issue price?
2. Did the bond sell at a discount or a premium? How much was the premium or discount?

3. What amount of cash was paid each year for bond interest?

4. What amount of interest expense should be shown each year on the statement of earnings?

5. What amount(s) should be shown on the statement of financial position for bonds payable at each year-end? (For 2016, show the balance just before repayment of the bond.)

6. What method of amortization was used?

7. Show how the following amounts were computed for 2015: (*a*) $106, (*b*) $16, and (*c*) $982.

8. Is the method of amortization that was used preferable? Explain why.

■ **LO3**   **E11–15**   **Preparing a Debt Payment Schedule with the Effective-Interest Method of Amortization, and Determining Reported Amounts**
Shuttle Company issued $1,000,000, three-year, 5 percent bonds on January 1, 2013. The bond interest is paid each December 31. The bond was sold to yield 4 percent.

Required:

1. Complete a bond payment schedule. Use the effective-interest method.

2. What amounts will be reported on the financial statements (statement of financial position, statement of earnings, and statement of cash flows) for 2013, 2014, and 2015?

■ **LO5**   **E11–16**   **Reporting the Retirement of a Bond with Discount**
The Nair Company issued a $5 million bond at a discount five years ago. The current carrying amount of the bond is $4.75 million. The company now has excess cash and decides to retire the bond. The bond is callable at 101 percent of its face value.

Required:
Prepare the journal entry to record the retirement of the bond.

■ **LO8**   **E11–17**   **Determining Effects on the Statement of Cash Flows**
The effects of specific events that occur over the life of a bond are reported on the statement of cash flows. Determine whether each of the following events affects the statement of cash flows. If so, describe the impact and specify where the effect is reported on the statement.

1. A $1,000,000 bond is issued at a discount in 2013. The carrying amount of the bond reported on the statement of financial position on that date is $985,000, before any amortization of bond discount.

2. At year-end, accrued interest amounts to $50,000, and $1,000 of the bond discount is amortized by using the effective-interest method.

3. Early in 2014, the accrued interest is paid. At the same time, $8,000 of interest that accrued in 2014 is paid.

■ **LO6**   **E11–18**   **Evaluating Lease Alternatives**
As the new vice-president for consumer products at Acme Manufacturing, you are attending a meeting to discuss a serious problem associated with delivering merchandise to customers. Bob Vargas, director of logistics, summarized the problem, saying, "It's easy to understand; we just don't have enough delivery trucks given our recent growth." Barb Belini from the accounting department responded, "Maybe it's easy to understand, but it's impossible to do anything. Because of Bay Street's concern about the amount of debt on our statement of financial position, we're under a freeze and can't borrow money to acquire new assets. There's nothing we can do."

On the way back to your office after the meeting, your assistant offers a suggestion, "Why don't we just lease the trucks we need? That way we can get the assets we want without having to record a liability on the statement of financial position."

How would you respond to this suggestion?

■ **LO6**   **E11–19**   **Reporting a Liability**

McDonald's Corporation

McDonald's Corporation is one of the world's most popular fast-food restaurants, offering good food at convenient locations. Effective management of its properties is a key to its success. McDonald's both owns and leases property, as the following note in a recent annual report indicates:

> The Company owns and leases real estate primarily in connection with its restaurant business. The Company identifies and develops sites that offer convenience to customers and long-term sales and profit potential to the Company. The Company generally owns the land and building or secures long-term leases for restaurant sites, which ensures long-term occupancy rights and helps control related costs.

Required:
Should McDonald's report finance leases on its statement of financial position? Explain. If the obligation should be reported as a liability, how should the amount be measured?

E11–20 **Reporting Retirement Benefits and Effect on the Debt-to-Equity Ratio**

LO6, 7

Sears Canada Inc.

Sears Canada Inc. offers Canadian consumers a diverse array of shopping options, with department and specialty stores, a comprehensive website, and a broad range of home-related services. At February 2, 2013, Sears had approximately 35,000 associates (or employees) helping customers through their personal shopping and catalogue ordering. The company's annual report for 2012 included the following information:

NOTES TO CONSOLIDATED FINANCIAL STATEMENTS

20. Retirement benefit plans

The Company currently maintains a defined benefit registered pension plan and a defined contribution registered pension plan which covers eligible, regular full-time associates as well as some of its part-time associates. The defined benefit plan provides pensions based on length of service and final average earnings. . . .

In July 2008, the Company amended its pension plan and introduced a defined contribution component. The defined benefit component continues to accrue benefits related to future compensation increases although no further service credit is earned. In addition, the Company no longer provides medical, dental and life insurance benefits at retirement for associates who had not achieved the eligibility criteria for these non-pension post-retirement benefits as at December 31, 2008.

Source: Sears Canada Inc., Annual Report 2012.

In addition, a note to the company's financial statements indicates that it adopted changes to its accounting for retirement benefit obligations pursuant to an amendment to IAS 19.

The company's statements of financial position at February 2, 2013, and January 28, 2012, include the following information (in millions of dollars):

	February 2, 2013	January 28, 2012	
		Amounts Restated in 2012 Annual Report	Amounts Reported in 2011 Annual Report
Total assets	$2,479.1	$2,730.7	$2,834.4
Shareholders' equity	1,076.4	1,092.0	1,460.3
Retirement benefit liability	415.7	452.3	144.1

Required:

1. Compare and contrast defined benefit and defined contribution pension plans.

2. What change did Sears introduce to its employee retirement program in July 2008? What is the main reason for this change? Explain.

3. Compute and interpret the debt-to-equity ratio using the amounts reported in the 2011 annual report.

4. Sears adopted the amendments to IAS 19 (Employee Benefits) in the first quarter of 2012 and adjusted its assets and liabilities as at January 28, 2012, accordingly. The adjustments resulted in a significant decrease in shareholders' equity due primarily to the increase in the retirement benefit liability. Compute the debt-to-equity ratio based on the restated amounts at January 28, 2012. Do you think Sears management would have made these adjustments voluntarily? Explain.

E11–21 **Reporting a Liability, with Discussion**

LO6

Air Canada

An annual report for Air Canada contained the following information:

---

9. PENSION AND OTHER BENEFIT LIABILITIES

The Corporation maintains several defined benefit and defined contribution plans providing pension, other post-retirement and post-employment benefits to its employees and former employees for whom the related pension assets and liabilities have not yet been settled.

. . .

The other employee benefits include health, life, and disability. These benefits consist of both post-employment and post-retirement benefits. The post-employment benefits relate to disability benefits available to eligible active employees, while the post-retirement benefits are comprised of health care and life insurance benefits available to eligible retired employees.

Required:

Should Air Canada report a liability for these benefits on its statement of financial position? Explain.

LO1, 3   **E11–22**   **(Appendix 11A) Computing the Issue Price of a Bond, with Discussion**

Charger Corporation issued a $250,000 bond that matures in five years. The bond has a stated interest rate of 8 percent and pays interest on February 1, May 1, August 1, and November 1. When the bond was issued, the market rate of interest was 12 percent. Record the issuance of the bond on February 1. Also record the payment of interest on May 1 and August 1. Use the straight-line method for amortization of any discount or premium. Explain why someone would buy a bond that did not pay the market rate of interest.

LO3   **E11–23**   **(Appendix 11A) Recording Bond Issue and First Interest Payment with Discount (Straight-Line Amortization)**

On January 1, 2015, Seton Corporation sold a $10,000,000, 5.5 percent bond issue. The bonds were dated January 1, 2015, had a yield of 6 percent, pay interest each December 31, and mature 10 years from January 1, 2015.

Required:

1. Prepare the journal entry to record the issuance of the bonds.
2. Prepare the journal entry to record the interest payment on December 31, 2015. Use straight-line amortization.
3. Show how the bond interest expense and the bonds payable should be reported on the financial statements for 2015.

LO3   **E11–24**   **(Appendix 11A) Recording Bond Issue: Entries for Issuance and Interest**

Northland Corporation had $400,000, 10-year bonds outstanding on December 31, 2014 (end of the fiscal year). Interest is payable each December 31. The bonds were issued (sold) on January 1, 2014. The 2014 annual financial statements showed the following:

Statement of earnings	
Bond interest expense (straight-line amortization)	$ 33,200
Statement of financial position	
Bonds payable (net liability)	389,200

Required (show computations):

1. What was the issue price of the bonds? Prepare the journal entry to record the issuance of the bonds on January 1, 2014.
2. What was the coupon rate on the bonds? Prepare the entry to record interest expense for 2014.

LO3, 4, 7   **E11–25**   **(Appendix 11A) Determining Financial Statement Effects of Long-Term Debt and Related Interest**

Chamandy Corporation issued a $25,000,000, 7 percent note on July 1, 2015, at a market rate of 6 percent. The note was dated July 1, 2015, with interest to be paid each June 30. The note matures in 10 years. The company's fiscal year ends on December 31.

Required:

1. How are the financial statements affected by the issuance of the note? Describe the impact on the debt-to-equity and the times interest earned ratios, if any.
2. How are the financial statements affected by the payment of interest on June 30, 2015? Describe the impact on the debt-to-equity and the times interest earned ratios, if any.
3. Show how the interest expense and the note payable should be reported on the December 31, 2015, annual financial statements. Use the straight-line method to amortize any discount or premium.

▇connect PROBLEMS

LO1, 3   **P11–1**   **Recording Issuance of Note and Computation of Interest (AP11–1)**

Rogers Communications Inc.

Rogers Communications Inc. is a diversified Canadian communications and media company engaged in wireless, cable, and media communications. On March 15, 2013, Rogers sold notes with the following specifications:

Principal amount	$500 million
Maturity date	March 15, 2023
Issue price	99.845% of principal amount
Coupon rate	3.00%
Effective interest rate	3.018%
Interest payment dates	March 15 and September 15

Required:

1. Prepare a journal entry to record the sale of these notes on March 15, 2013.

2. Prepare the journal entry to record the payment of interest and amortization of the discount on September 15, 2013. The company uses the effective-interest method of amortization.

3. Compute the interest expense that accrued from September 15, 2013, to December 31, 2013, the end of Rogers' fiscal year, and prepare the adjusting journal entry on December 31, 2013, to record interest expense and amortization of the discount on the notes.

4. Show the amounts that should be reported on Rogers' financial statements for 2013.

5. Compute the total amount of interest expense over the life of the notes.

6. After looking at the issue price, a student asked why Rogers did not simply sell the notes at 100 percent of the principal amount instead of selling them at a discount. How would you respond to this question?

P11–2 Recording Bond Issuance and Interest Payment with Explanation of Bond Premium and Discussion of Management Strategy (AP11–2)

■ LO3, 4, 7

On March 1, 2014, Catalin Corporation issued $40 million in bonds that mature in 10 years. The bonds have a stated interest rate of 5.8 percent and pay interest on March 1 and September 1. When the bonds were sold, the market rate of interest was 6 percent. Catalin uses the effective-interest method. By December 31, 2014, the market interest rate had increased to 6.5 percent.

Required:

1. Record the issuance of the bond on March 1, 2014.

2. Compute the present value of the difference between the interest paid each six months ($40 million × 5.8% × 6/12 = $1.16 million) and the interest demanded by the market ($40 million × 6% × 6/12 = $1.2 million). Use the market rate of interest and the 10-year life of the bond in your present value computation. What does this amount represent? Explain.

3. Record the payment of interest on September 1, 2014.

4. Record the adjusting entry for accrued interest on December 31, 2014.

5. Why does interest expense change each year when the effective-interest method is used?

6. Compute the present value of Catalin's bonds, assuming that they had a 7-year life instead of a 10-year life. Compare this amount to the carrying amount of the bond at March 1, 2017. What does this comparison demonstrate?

7. Determine the impact of these transactions at year-end on the debt-to-equity ratio and the times interest earned ratio.

P11–3 Recording Bond Issuance and Interest Payments (Effective-Interest Method) (AP11–3)

■ LO3

eXcel

Nordic Company issued bonds with the following provisions:

Maturity value: $60,000,000
Interest: 7.9 percent per annum payable semi-annually each June 30 and December 31
Terms: Bonds dated January 1, 2014, due five years from that date
The company's fiscal year ends on December 31. The bonds were sold on January 1, 2014, at a yield of 8 percent.

Required:

1. Compute the issue (sale) price of the bonds (show computations).

2. Prepare the journal entry to record the issuance of the bonds.

3. Prepare the journal entries at the following dates: June 30, 2014; December 31, 2014; and June 30, 2015. Use the effective-interest method to amortize bond discount or premium.

4. How much interest expense would be reported on the statement of earnings for 2014? Show how the liability related to the bonds should be reported on the statement of financial position at December 31, 2014.

P11–4 Completing an Amortization Schedule (Effective-Interest Amortization)

■ LO3

Berj Corporation issued bonds and received cash in full for the issue price. The bonds were dated and issued on January 1, 2013. The coupon rate was payable at the end of each year. The bonds mature at the end of four years. The following schedule has been partially completed (amounts in thousands):

Date	Cash Paid	Interest Expense	Amortization	Carrying Amount
January 1, 2013				$6,101
End of year 2013	$450	$427	$23	6,078
End of year 2014	450	?	?	6,053
End of year 2015	450	?	?	?
End of year 2016	450	?	?	6,000

Required:

1. Complete the amortization schedule.
2. What was the maturity amount of the bonds?
3. How much cash was received at the date of issuance (sale) of the bonds?
4. What was the amount of discount or premium on the bond?
5. How much cash will be disbursed for interest each period and in total for the full life of the bond issue?
6. What method of amortization is being used? Explain.
7. What is the coupon rate of interest?
8. What is the effective rate of interest?
9. What amount of interest expense should be reported on the statement of earnings each year?
10. Show how the bonds should be reported on the statement of financial position at the end of each year (show the last year immediately before repayment of the bonds).

■ LO5

P11–5   **Understanding the Early Retirement of Debt** (AP11–4)

CM Entertainment Inc. owns and operates movie theatres. The company sold 6.5 percent bonds for $105,000,000 and used the cash proceeds to retire bonds with a face value of $100,000,000 with a coupon rate of 8 percent. At that time, the old bonds had a carrying amount of $99,547,000.

Required:

1. Why did the company issue new bonds to retire the old bonds?
2. Prepare the journal entries to record the issuance of the new bonds and the early retirement of the old bonds.
3. How should CM Entertainment report the gain or loss on retirement of the old bonds?

■ LO2

P11–6   **Computing Equal Periodic Debt Payments, and Completing a Schedule** (AP11–5)

On June 1, 2014, you bought a new sports car for $60,000. You made a $10,000 cash down payment and signed a $50,000 note, payable in four equal instalments on each June 1, with the first payment to be made on June 1, 2015. The interest rate is 6 percent per year on the unpaid balance. Each payment will include payment on principal plus interest.

Required:

1. Compute the amount of the equal payments that you must make.
2. What is the total amount of interest that you will pay during the four years?
3. Complete the following schedule:

		Debt Payment Schedule		
			Decrease in	
Date	Cash Payment	Interest Expense	Principal	Unpaid Principal
1/6/2014				
1/6/2015				
1/6/2016				
1/6/2017				
1/6/2018				
Totals				

4. Explain why the amount of interest expense decreases each year.

5. To reduce the total amount of interest paid on this note, you considered the possibility of making equal payments every three months (four payments per year). Compute the amount of the equal payments that you must make and the amount of interest that will be saved over the life of the note.

P11–7 Computing Equal Periodic Debt Payments, and Completing a Schedule

Lassonde Industries Inc. develops, manufactures and markets a wide range of fruit and vegetable juices and drinks as well as specialty food products, such as fondue broths and sauces, soups, sauces and gravies, pestos, and sauces for pasta and pizza. It also produces apple cider and wine-based beverages.

Lassonde Industries Inc.

The company's long-term debt includes the following obligations:

Long-Term Debt	As at Dec. 31, 2012	As at Dec. 31, 2011
	(In thousands of dollars)	
1. Obligation related to the acquisition of equipment, 5.5%, payable starting in December 2010 in eight equal annual blended instalments of $262,212 through 2017.	$1,120	$1,310
2. Obligation under a finance lease for distribution equipment, 9.7%, payable starting in November 2011 in 11 equal semi-annual blended instalments of $44,998, through November 2016.	293	350

Required:

1. Assume that the equipment related to the first obligation was acquired on January 1, 2010, and that the first payment of $262,212 was made on December 31, 2010. Verify that the carrying amount reported by the company as at December 31, 2012, represents the present value of the remaining annual payments. (Note: Tables 10C.1 and 10C.2 in Chapter 10 do not include the 5.5 percent interest rate. Use Microsoft Excel or a calculator to compute the present value of future payments.)

2. How much interest will the company pay as part of the five remaining instalments on the 5.5 percent obligation? (*Hint:* You may find it helpful to prepare a schedule similar to Exhibit 11.3, option 3.)

3. Prepare the journal entry to record payment of the instalment on December 31, 2013.

4. Assume that the obligation under the finance lease was signed on June 1, 2011, and that the first semi-annual instalment was made on November 30, 2011. Verify that the carrying amount reported by the company as at December 31, 2012, represents the present value of the remaining semi-annual payments. Use a calculator or Microsoft Excel to compute the present value of future payments.

P11–8 (Appendix 11A) Comparing Bonds Issued at Par, Discount, and Premium

Sikes Corporation, whose fiscal year ends on December 31, issued the following bonds:

Date of bonds: January 1, 2015
Maturity amount and date: $10 million due in 10 years (December 31, 2024)
Interest: 5 percent per annum payable each December 31
Date of sale: January 1, 2015

Required:

1. Provide the following amounts to be reported on the 2015 financial statements (use straight-line amortization and show amounts in thousands):

	Issued at Par	at 96	at 102
	Case A	Case B	Case C
a. Interest expense	$	$	$
b. Bonds payable			
c. Unamortized premium or discount			
d. Carrying amount of bonds			
e. Stated rate of interest			
f. Cash paid for interest			

2. For each of cases B and C, explain why interest expense is different from cash paid for interest.

3. Assume that you are an investment adviser and a retired person has written to you asking, "Why should I buy a bond at a premium when I can find one at a discount? Isn't that stupid? It's like paying the list price for a car instead of negotiating a discount." Write a brief letter in response to the question.

■ LO3

e**X**cel

P11–9   **(Appendix 11A) Completing a Schedule Comparing Bonds Issued at Par, Discount, and Premium (AP11–6)**

Quartz Corporation sold a $50 million, 7 percent bond issue on January 1, 2015. The bonds pay interest each December 31 and mature 10 years from January 1, 2015. For comparative study and analysis, assume three independent selling scenarios: case A, bonds sold at par; case B, bonds sold at 98; case C, bonds sold at 102. Use straight-line amortization and disregard income tax unless specifically required.

Required:

1. Complete the following schedule to analyze the differences among the three cases.

	Case A (Par)	Case B (at 98)	Case C (at 102)
a. Cash inflow at the date of issue (sale)			
b. Total cash outflow through the maturity date			
c. Net cash outflow = total interest expense over the life of the bonds			
d. Total interest expense, net of income tax (25 percent)			
Statement of earnings for 2015			
e. Bond interest expense			
Statement of financial position at December 31, 2015, non-current liabilities			
f. Bonds payable, 7 percent			
g. Unamortized discount			
h. Unamortized premium			
i. Net liability			

2. For each case, explain why the amounts in items (*c*), (*d*), and (*e*) of (1) are the same or different.

■ LO3

 e**X**cel

P11–10   **(Appendix 11A) Computing Amounts for Bond Issue, and Comparing Amortization Methods (AP11–7)**

Dektronik Corporation manufactures electrical test equipment. The company's board of directors authorized a bond issue on January 1, 2013, with the following terms:

Maturity (par) value: $800,000
Interest: 7.5 percent per annum payable each December 31
Maturity date: December 31, 2017
Effective-interest rate when sold: 8 percent

Required:

1. Compute the bond issue price. Explain why both the stated and effective-interest rates are used in this computation.

2. Assume that the company used the straight-line method to amortize the discount or premium on the bond issue. Compute the following amounts for each year (2013–2017):

   a. Cash payment for bond interest.

   b. Amortization of bond discount or premium.

   c. Bond interest expense.

   d. Carrying amount of the bond.

   e. Interest expense as a percentage of the carrying amount at the beginning of the year.

   The straight-line method is theoretically deficient when interest expense is related to the carrying amount of the debt. Explain.

3. Assume instead that the company used the effective-interest method to amortize the discount or premium. Prepare an effective-interest bond amortization schedule similar to the one in the text. The effective-interest method provides a constant interest rate when interest expense is related to the carrying amount (unpaid balance). Explain by referring to the bond amortization schedule.

4. Which method should the company use to amortize the bond discount or premium? As a financial analyst, would you prefer one method over the other? If so, why?

ALTERNATE PROBLEMS

AP11–1 Recording Issuance of Note and Computation of Interest (P11–1)

Shaw Communications Inc. is a diversified Canadian communications company that provides cable television, Internet, digital phone, telecommunications, and satellite direct-to-home services to more than 3 million customers. On February 17, 2011, the company sold long-term notes with the following specifications:

LO1, 3

Shaw Communications Inc.

Principal amount	$400 million
Maturity date	November 9, 2039
Issue price	97.379% of principal amount
Coupon rate	6.75%
Effective interest rate	6.961%
Interest payment dates	May 9 and November 9

Because the company pays semi-annual interest of $13,500,000, it collected from the investors in these notes an amount representing interest that accrued for 99 days, from November 9, 2010, to February 17, 2011. This amount was repaid to the investors on May 9, 2011, as part of the semi-annual payment. For interest computations, assume that the year consists of 360 days.

Required:

1. Prepare the journal entries to record the sales of the notes on February 17, 2011.

2. Prepare the journal entries to record the payments of interest and amortization of the discount on May 9 and November 9, 2011. The company uses the effective-interest method to amortize the discount.

3. Compute the interest expense that accrued from November 9, 2011, to December 31, 2011, the end of Shaw's fiscal year, and prepare the adjusting journal entries on December 31, 2011, to record interest expense and amortization of the discount on the notes.

4. Show the amounts that should be reported on Shaw's financial statements for 2011.

5. Compute the total amount of interest expense over the life of the notes.

6. After looking at the issue price, a student asked why the management of Shaw Communications did not simply sell the notes at 100 percent of the principal amount instead of selling them at a discount. How would you respond to this question?

AP11–2 Using the Effective-Interest Method with Explanation of Bond Premium and Discussion of Management Strategy (P11–2)

LO3

On March 1, 2015, Carter Corporation issued $15,000,000 in bonds that mature in 10 years. The bonds have a coupon rate of 6.3 percent and pay interest on March 1 and September 1. When the bonds were sold, the market rate of interest was 6 percent. Carter uses the effective-interest method to amortize bond discount or premium. By December 31, 2015, the market interest rate had increased to 7 percent.

Required:

1. Record the issuance of the bond on March 1, 2015.

2. Compute the present value of the difference between the interest paid each six months ($472,500) and the interest demanded by the market ($15 million $\times$ 6% $\times$ 6/12 = $450,000). Use the

market rate of interest and the 10-year life of the bond in your present value computation. What does this amount represent? Explain.

3. Record the payment of interest on September 1, 2015.

4. Record the adjusting entry for accrued interest on December 31, 2015.

5. Why does interest expense change each year when the effective-interest method is used?

6. Compute the present value of Carter's bonds, assuming that they had a 7-year life instead of a 10-year life. Compare this amount to the carrying amount of the bond at March 1, 2018. What does this comparison demonstrate?

7. Determine the impact of the transactions at year-end on the debt-to-equity ratio and the times interest earned ratio.

■ LO3

eXcel

AP11–3 **Computing the Issue Price of Bonds, and Recording Issuance and Interest Payments** (P11–3)

Jaymar Company issued bonds with the following provisions:

Maturity value: $100,000,000
Interest: 8.1 percent per annum payable semi-annually each June 30 and December 31
Terms: Bonds dated January 1, 2015, due 10 years from that date
The company's fiscal year ends on December 31. The bonds were sold on January 1, 2015, at a yield of 8 percent.

Required:

1. Compute the issue (sale) price of the bonds. Show computations.

2. Prepare the journal entry to record the issuance of the bonds.

3. Prepare the journal entries at the following dates: June 30, 2015; December 31, 2015; and June 30, 2016. Use the effective-interest method to amortize bond discount or premium.

4. How much interest expense would be reported on the statement of earnings for 2015? Show how the liability related to the bonds should be reported on the statement of financial position at December 31, 2015.

■ LO1, 5

Thomson Reuters
Corporation

AP11–4 **Understanding the Difference between Carrying Amount and Market Value** (P11–5)

Thomson Reuters Corporation is the world's leading source of electronic information and services to businesses and professionals in various fields, such as media, financial services, tax and accounting, and healthcare and science. The company's annual report for 2012 indicates that the carrying amount of long-term debt is $7,231 million, but its fair value is $8,170 million. The fair value of debt is estimated based on either quoted market prices for similar issues or current rates offered to the company for debt of the same maturity.

Required:

What is meant by "fair value"? Explain why there is a difference between the carrying amount and the fair value of the long-term debt for Thomson Reuters. Assume that Thomson Reuters decided to retire all of its long-term debt for cash (a very unlikely event). Prepare the journal entry to record the transaction.

■ LO2

eXcel

AP11–5 **Computing Equal Periodic Debt Payments, and Completing a Schedule with Journal Entries** (P11–6)

On January 1, 2014, Ontario Company sold a new machine to Canada Company for $70,000. Canada Company made a cash down payment of $20,000 and signed a $50,000, 8 percent note for the balance due. The note is payable in three equal instalments due on December 31, 2014, 2015, and 2016. Each payment includes principal plus interest on the unpaid balance. Canada Company recorded the purchase as follows:

January 1, 2014		
Machinery	70,000	
Cash		20,000
Note payable		50,000

Required (show computations and round to the nearest dollar):

1. What is the amount of the equal annual payments that Canada Company must make?

2. What is the total interest on the note over the three years?

3. Complete the following debt payment schedule:

Debt Payment Schedule				
Date	Cash Payment	Interest Expense	Decrease in Principal	Unpaid Principal
1/1/2014				
31/12/2014				
31/12/2015				
31/12/2016				
Total				

4. Prepare the journal entries for each of the three payments.
5. Explain why interest expense decreased in amount each year.

AP11–6 (Appendix 11A) **Completing a Schedule That Involves a Comprehensive Review of the Issuance of Bonds at Par, Discount, and Premium, Including Cash Flows** (P11–9)

■ LO3, 8

On January 1, 2013, Ontec Corporation sold and issued $100 million, five-year, 10 percent bonds. The bond interest is payable annually each December 31. Assume three separate and independent selling scenarios: case A, bonds sold at par; case B, bonds sold at 90; and case C, bonds sold at 110.

Required:

1. Complete a schedule similar to the following for each separate case, assuming straight-line amortization of discount and premium. Disregard income tax. Show all dollar amounts in millions.

	At Start of 2013	At End of 2013	At End of 2014	At End of 2015	At End of 2016	At End of 2017 Prior to Payment of Principal	Payment of Principal
Case A: sold at par (100)	$	$	$	$	$	$	$
Cash inflow							
Cash outflow							
Interest expense on statement of earnings							
Carrying amount on statement of financial position							
Case B: sold at a discount (90)							
Cash inflow							
Cash outflow							
Interest expense on statement of earnings							
Carrying amount on statement of financial position							
Case C: sold at a premium (110)							
Cash inflow							
Cash outflow							
Interest expense on statement of earnings							
Carrying amount on statement of financial position							

2. For each separate case, calculate the following:
   a. Total cash outflow.
   b. Total cash inflow.
   c. Net cash outflow.
   d. Total interest expense over the life of the bonds.
3. *a.* Explain why the net cash outflows differ among the three cases.
   b. For each case, explain why the net cash outflow is the same as total interest expense.

AP11–7 (Appendix 11A) **Straight-Line versus Effective-Interest Methods of Amortizing Bond Discount, with Discussion** (P11–10)

■ LO3

Canadian Products Corporation manufactures office equipment and supplies. The company authorized a bond issue on January 1, 2013, with the following terms:

Maturity (par) value: $120,000,000
Interest: 7.9 percent per annum payable each December 31

Maturity date: December 31, 2017

Effective-interest rate when sold: 8 percent

Required:

1. Compute the bond issue price. Explain why both the stated and effective-interest rates are used in this computation.

2. Prepare the entry to record this bond issue.

3. Assume that the company used the straight-line method to amortize the discount or premium on the bond issue. Compute the following amounts for each year (2013–2017):

    a. Interest paid.

    b. Amortization of bond discount or premium.

    c. Bond interest expense.

    d. Carrying amount of the bond.

    e. Interest expense as a percentage of the carrying amount at the beginning of the year.

    The straight-line method is theoretically deficient when interest expense is related to the carrying amount of the debt. Explain.

4. Assume instead that the company used the effective-interest method to amortize the discount or premium. Prepare an effective-interest bond amortization schedule similar to the one in the text. The effective-interest method provides a constant interest rate when interest expense is related to the net liability. Explain by referring to the bond amortization schedule.

5. Which method should the company use to amortize the bond discount or premium? As a financial analyst, would you prefer one method over the other? If so, why?

CASES AND PROJECTS

FINDING AND INTERPRETING FINANCIAL INFORMATION

■ LO3, 7, 8   **CP11–1**   **Finding Financial Information**

Canadian Tire
Corporation

Refer to the financial statements of Canadian Tire Corporation given in Appendix A of this book.

Required:

1. How much did the company report for finance costs, and how much cash was paid for interest during the year ended December 29, 2012? Where did you find the information?

2. Review the company's note on long-term debt, and identify the different types of debt that the company has issued in the past, as well as the characteristics of the various debt issues.

3. Does the company report other long-term liabilities? If so, identify these liabilities.

■ LO3, 7, 8   **CP11–2**   **Finding Financial Information**

RONA Inc.

Go to *Connect* for the financial statements of RONA Inc.

Required:

1. How much cash was paid for interest during the year ended December 30, 2012?

2. Review the company's note on long-term debt. Does the company provide details about its debt issues? If so, identify the characteristics of one of the debt issues.

3. Describe the company's established arrangements, if any, that permit it to borrow money if needed.

4. Does the company report other non-current liabilities? If so, identify these liabilities.

■ LO1, 4, 6   **CP11–3**   **Comparing Companies**

Canadian Tire
Corporation vs.
RONA Inc.

Refer to the financial statements of Canadian Tire Corporation (Appendix A) and RONA Inc. (on *Connect*).

Required:

1. Examine the statements of cash flows for both companies. What are the primary sources of cash flows for both companies for fiscal year 2012?

2. Two financial ratios (the debt-to-equity ratio and the times interest earned ratio) are discussed in this chapter. Compute these ratios for both companies for fiscal year 2012. Are they relevant for these companies? Explain.

FINANCIAL REPORTING AND ANALYSIS CASES

CP11–4 Analyzing the Use of Debt

■ LO1

Cricket Corporation's financial statements for 2014 showed the following:

Statement of Earnings	
Revenues	$300,000
Expenses	(198,000)
Interest expense	(2,000)
Pretax earnings	100,000
Income tax (30%)	(30,000)
Net earnings	$ 70,000
Statement of Financial Position	
Assets	$300,000
Liabilities (average interest rate, 10%)	20,000
Share capital	200,000
Retained earnings	80,000
	$300,000

Notice that the company had a debt of only $20,000 compared with share capital of $200,000. A consultant recommended the following: debt, $100,000 (at 10 percent) instead of $20,000, and share capital of $120,000 (12,000 shares) instead of $200,000 (20,000 shares). That is, the company should finance the business with more debt and less owner contribution.

Required (round to the nearest percent):

1. You have been asked to develop a comparison between (*a*) the actual results and (*b*) the results based on the consultant's recommendation. To do this, you decided to develop the following schedule:

Item	Actual Results for 2014	Results with an $80,000 Increase in Debt and an $80,000 Decrease in Equity
a. Total debt		
b. Total assets		
c. Total shareholders' equity		
d. Interest expense		
e. Net earnings		
f. Return on total assets		
g. Earnings available to shareholders:		
(1) Amount		
(2) Per share		
(3) Return on shareholders' equity		

2. Based on the completed schedule in (1), provide a comparative analysis and interpretation of the actual results and the consultant's recommendation.

CP11–5 International Financing

■ LO1

Access the website of Bombardier Inc. at **www.bombardier.ca**, and retrieve the most recent annual report. The note related to long-term debt discloses that Bombardier has borrowed money in a currency other than the Canadian dollar. Write a brief memo explaining why the company borrowed money in a foreign currency.

CRITICAL THINKING CASES

CP11–6 Making a Decision as a Financial Analyst

■ LO1

You are working for a large mutual fund company as a financial analyst. You have been asked to review two competitive companies in the same industry. Both have similar cash flows and net earnings, but one has no debt in its capital structure while the other has a debt-to-equity ratio of 1.2. Based on this limited information, which company would you prefer? Justify your conclusion. Would your preference be influenced by the companies' industry?

■ LO1   **CP11–7**   **Evaluating an Ethical Dilemma**

You work for a small company considering investing in a new Internet business. Financial projections suggest that the company will be able to earn in excess of $20 million per year on an investment of $100 million. The company president suggests borrowing the money by issuing bonds that will carry a 7 percent interest rate. He says, "This is better than printing money! We won't have to invest a penny of our own money, and we get to keep $13 million per year after we pay interest to the bondholders." As you think about the proposed transaction, you feel a little uncomfortable about taking advantage of the creditors in this fashion. You feel that it must be wrong to earn such a high return by using money that belongs to other people. Is this an ethical business transaction?

■ LO1   **CP11–8**   **Evaluating an Ethical Dilemma**

Many retired people invest a significant portion of their money in bonds of corporations because of the relatively low level of risk. During the 1980s, significant inflation caused some interest rates to rise to as high as 15 percent. Retired people who bought bonds that paid only 6 percent continued to earn at the lower rate. During the 1990s, inflation subsided and interest rates declined. Many corporations took advantage of call options on bonds and refinanced high interest rate debt with low interest rate debt. In your judgment, is it ethical for corporations to continue paying low interest rates when rates increase but to call bonds when rates decrease?

■ LO1   **CP11–9**   **Evaluating an Ethical Dilemma**

Assume that you are a portfolio manager for a large insurance company. The majority of the money you manage is from retired schoolteachers who depend on the income you earn on their investments. You have invested a significant amount of money in the bonds of a large corporation and have just received a call from the company's president explaining that it is unable to meet its current interest obligations because of deteriorating business operations related to increased international competition. The president has a recovery plan that will take at least two years. During that time, the company will not be able to pay interest on the bonds, and, she admits, if the plan does not work, bondholders will probably lose more than half of their money. As a creditor, you can force the company into immediate bankruptcy and probably get back at least 90 percent of the bondholders' money. You also know that your decision will cause at least 10,000 people to lose their jobs if the company ceases operations. Given only these two options, what should you do?

FINANCIAL REPORTING AND ANALYSIS TEAM PROJECT

■ LO 1, 3, 4, 7, 8

CP11–10

Team Project: Examining an Annual Report

As a team, select an industry to analyze. A list of companies classified by industry can be obtained by accessing **www.fpinfomart.ca** and then choosing "Companies by Industry." You can also find a list of industries and companies within each industry via **http://ca.finance.yahoo.com/investing** (click on "Order Annual Reports" under "Tools").

Each group member should acquire the annual report for a different publicly traded company in the industry. (Library files, the SEDAR service at **www.sedar.com**, and the company's website are good sources.)

Required:

On an individual basis, each team member should then write a short report answering the following questions about the selected company. Discuss any patterns across the companies that you, as a team, observe. Then, as a group, write a short report comparing and contrasting your companies.

1. Has your company issued any long-term bonds or notes? If so, read the related note and list any unusual features (e.g., callable, convertible, secured by specific collateral).

2. If your company issued any bonds, were they issued at either a premium or a discount? If so, does the company use the straight-line or effective-interest amortization method?

3. Perform a ratio analysis:
   a. What does the times interest earned ratio measure, in general?
   b. Compute the ratio for the last three years.
   c. What do your results suggest about the company?
   d. If available, find the industry ratio for the most recent year, compare it with your results, and discuss why you believe your company differs from or is similar to the industry ratio.

4. Ratio analysis:
   a. What does the debt-to-equity ratio measure, in general?
   b. Compute the ratio for the last three years.

c. What do your results suggest about the company?

d. If available, find the industry ratio for the most recent year, compare it with your results, and discuss why you believe your company differs from or is similar to the industry ratio.

5. During the recent year, how much cash did the company receive on issuing debt? How much did it pay on debt principal? What does management suggest were the reasons for issuing and/or repaying debt during the year?

SOLUTIONS TO SELF-STUDY QUIZZES

Self-Study Quiz 11-1

1.

Note payable (L)	19,932	
Interest expense (E)	3,807	
Cash (A)		23,739

Assets		=	Liabilities		+	Shareholders' Equity	
Cash	−23,739		Note payable	−19,932		Interest expense	−3,807

2. Annuity $\times$ P$_{i=3\%, n=10}$ (Table 10C.2, Appendix 10C, 8.5302) = $100,000

Annuity = $100,000 ÷ 8.5302 = $11,723.05

Total amount of annuity payments = $11,723.05 $\times$ 10 semi-annual periods = $117,230.50

Total interest paid over the five-year period = $117,230.50 − $100,000 = $17,230.50

3. The total interest paid in this case is lower than $18,699 because a portion of the principal amount is paid every six months instead of once per year. This allows the borrower to save on interest on the remaining unpaid portion of the principal.

Self-Study Quiz 11-2

1. The market rate is the interest rate demanded by creditors. It is the rate used in the present value computations to discount future cash flows. The market interest rate is also called yield, or effective-interest rate.

2. The coupon interest rate is the stated rate on the bonds. It is also called stated rate and contract rate.

3. A bond that sells for less than par is sold at a discount. This occurs when the stated rate is lower than the market rate.

4. A bond that sells for more than par is sold at a premium. This occurs when the coupon rate is higher than the market rate.

Self-Study Quiz 11-3

Principal:	$100,000	$\times$	0.6756	=	$67,560
Interest:	4,000	$\times$	8.1109	=	32,444
					$100,004

The additional $4 is due to rounding errors.

Self-Study Quiz 11-4

1.

Principal:	$100,000	$\times$	0.4564	=	$45,640
Interest:	3,500	$\times$	13.5903	=	47,566
					$93,206

Interest expense, first semi-annual period = $93,206 $\times$ (0.08 ÷ 2) = $3,728

Amortization of bond discount = $3,728 − $3,500 = $228

Carrying amount, end of first semi-annual period = $93,206 + $228 = $93,434

Interest expense, second semi-annual period = $93,434 $\times$ (0.08 ÷ 2) = $3,737

Interest expense for the first year = $3,728 + $3,737 = $7,465

2. Carrying amount, end of second semi-annual period = $93,434 + $228 = $93,662

Self-Study Quiz 11-5

1.

Date	(a) Interest to Be Paid ($400,000 × 3%)	(b) Interest Expense (2% × Carrying Amount, Beginning of Period)	(c) Amortization (a) − (b)	(d) Carrying Amount
Amortization Schedule: Bond Premium (effective interest)				
31/12/2014				$454,323
30/6/2015	$12,000	$9,086	$2,914	451,409
31/12/2015	12,000	9,028	2,972	448,437
30/6/2016	12,000	8,969	3,031	445,406

2. The carrying amount at June 30, 2016, is $445,406. This amount is the unpaid balance of the bonds and represents the present value of the remaining payments using the market rate of interest when the bonds were issued. At June 30, 2016, there are 13 interest payments remaining and the principal of the bonds. Their present value is

$$\text{Present value} = \$400,000 \times 0.7730 \text{ (Table 10C.1, Appendix 10C)}$$
$$+ \$12,000 \times 11.3484 \text{ (Table 10C.2, Appendix 10C)}$$
$$= \$445,380 \text{ (The difference of \$26 is due to rounding.)}$$

Self-Study Quiz 11-6

A company can be forced into bankruptcy if it does not meet its interest obligations to creditors. Many successful companies borrow very large amounts of money without creating unreasonable risk, because they generate sufficient funds from normal operations to meet their obligations. Even a small amount of debt can be a problem if a company does not generate funds to meet current interest obligations. Usually, the company with a high interest coverage ratio (even if it has a high debt-to-equity ratio) is viewed as being less risky than one with a low interest coverage ratio.

Self-Study Quiz 11-7

1. Principal: $100,000 ×   0.4564 = $45,640
   Interest: $ 3,500 × 13.5903 =   47,566
                                         $93,206

2. Interest paid = $100,000 × 0.07 = $7,000

3. Interest expense = Interest payment + Amortization of bond discount = $7,000 + $6,794/10 = $7,679.40

Self-Study Quiz 11-8

1. Principal: $100,000 ×   0.4564 = $ 45,640
   Interest: $4,500 × 13.5903 =   61,156
                                         $106,796

2. Interest paid = $100,000 × 0.09 = $9,000

3. Interest expense = Interest payment − Amortization of bond premium = $9,000 − $6,796/10 = $8,320.40

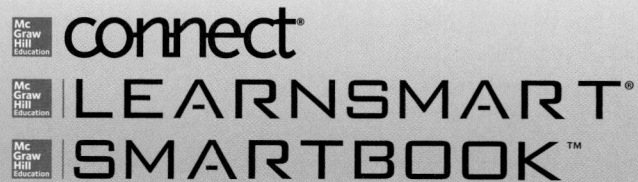

Reporting and Interpreting Shareholders' Equity

After studying this chapter, you should be able to do the following:

LO1 Explain the role of share capital in the capital structure of a corporation.

LO2 Analyze the earnings per share ratio.

LO3 Describe the characteristics of common shares, and analyze transactions affecting common shares.

LO4 Discuss dividends, and analyze related transactions.

LO5 Analyze the dividend yield ratio.

LO6 Discuss the purpose of stock dividends, stock splits, and report transactions.

LO7 Describe the characteristics of preferred shares, and analyze transactions affecting preferred shares.

LO8 Measure and report changes in shareholders' equity.

LO9 Discuss the impact of share capital transactions on cash flows.

FOCUS COMPANY: **BCE INC.**

FINANCING CORPORATE GROWTH WITH CAPITAL SUPPLIED BY OWNERS

Bell Canada Enterprises Inc. (BCE) (www.bce.ca) is Canada's largest communications company. It provides voice, data, and image communications services to millions of global customers. BCE has achieved its current size and profitability through investments in and acquisitions of companies such as CTV and Maple Leaf Sports and Entertainment. But the business continues to change rapidly as customers demand different and more services at a price competitive with U.S. providers.

In order to continue to thrive and grow, BCE has announced its intention of improving household service, investing in expanding its broadband access to all of BCE's services on any screen the customer chooses. The company closely manages its statement of financial position and, in particular, its capital structure—that is, the proportion of debt and equity used to finance its growth. BCE wants to ensure a strong credit profile in order both to encourage new investment and to increase the dividends paid to its shareholders.

In Chapters 10 and 11, we discussed the role of liabilities in the capital structure of a company. In this chapter, we study both the role that shareholders' equity plays in building a successful business and strategies that managers use to maximize shareholders' wealth.

UNDERSTANDING THE BUSINESS

To some people, the words *corporation* and *business* are almost synonymous. You have probably heard friends refer to a career in business as "the corporate world." Equating business and corporations is understandable, because corporations are the dominant form of business organization in terms of volume of operations. If you were to write the names of 50 familiar companies on a piece of paper, probably all of them would be corporations.

The popularity of the corporate form can be attributed to a critical advantage that corporations have over sole proprietorships and partnerships. They can raise large amounts of capital because both large and small investors can easily participate in their ownership. This ease of participation is related to three important factors:

- Shares can be purchased in small amounts. You could buy a single share of BCE for approximately $43 at the time of writing this chapter and become one of the owners of this company.
- Ownership interest can easily be transferred through the sale of shares on established markets, such as the Toronto Stock Exchange (TSX).
- Stock ownership provides investors with limited liability.[1]

Many Canadians own shares, either directly or indirectly through a mutual fund or pension program. Share ownership offers them the opportunity to earn higher returns than they otherwise could on deposits to bank accounts or investments in corporate bonds. Unfortunately, share ownership also involves higher risk of loss of the investment in shares. The proper balance between risk and the expected return on an investment depends on individual preferences.

BCE's statement of financial position at December 31, 2012, reports total equity of $14,725 million, as indicated in Exhibit 12.1. For most corporations, shareholders' equity includes two primary sources:

1. *Contributed capital*, which reflects the amount invested by shareholders. Contributed capital has two distinct components: (*a*) amounts initially received from the sale of shares and (*b*) contributed surplus that reflects contributions made by shareholders in excess of the amounts credited to share capital accounts. The contributed capital accounts for BCE are preferred shares, common shares, and contributed surplus.

2. *Retained earnings* generated by the profit-making activities of the company. This is the cumulative amount of net earnings earned since the corporation's organization, less the cumulative amount of dividends paid by the corporation since organization.[2]

Most companies generate a significant portion of their shareholders' equity from retained earnings rather than from capital raised through the sale of shares. In the case of BCE, Exhibit 12.1 shows a negative amount, a deficit, which suggests that BCE has not been a profitable company. We will address this interesting issue as well as other details in Exhibit 12.1 later in this chapter.

Exhibit 12.2 reports the changes that occurred to the various components of shareholders' equity during fiscal year 2012. This exhibit looks fairly complicated, but the main changes that took place in 2012 relate to issuance of preferred and common shares, repurchase of shares, and distribution of dividends. We will refer to this exhibit for specific transactions throughout the chapter.

SELECTED FOCUS COMPANY COMPARISONS: RETAINED EARNINGS AS A PERCENTAGE OF SHAREHOLDERS' EQUITY—2012

WestJet Airlines Ltd. 53.9%

Sun-Rype Products 61.4%

Danier Leather 75.6%

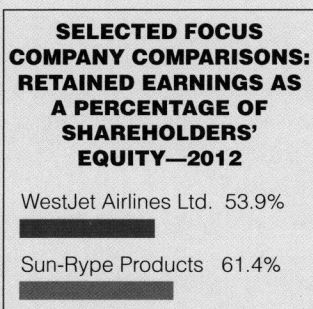

Exhibit **12.1**

Shareholders' Equity Sections of Consolidated Statements of Financial Position

REAL-WORLD EXCERPT

BCE Inc.

ANNUAL REPORT

CONSOLIDATED STATEMENTS OF FINANCIAL POSITION (PARTIAL) SHAREHOLDERS' EQUITY At December 31			
(in millions of Canadian dollars)	Note	2012	2010
Equity attributable to owners of the parent			
Preferred shares	23	$ 3,395	$ 3,115
Common shares	23	13,611	13,566
Shares subject to cancellation	23	–	(50)
Contributed surplus	23	2,557	2,527
Accumulated other comprehensive income (loss)		(6)	5
Retained earnings (deficit)		(5,682)	(5,385)
Total equity attributable to owners of the parent		13,875	13,778
Non-controlling interest		850	981
Total equity		$14,725	$14,759

Source: BCE Inc., Annual Report 2012.

Exhibit **12.2**

Consolidated Statements of Changes in Equity

CONSOLIDATED STATEMENTS OF CHANGES IN EQUITY
ATTRIBUTED TO BCE SHAREHOLDERS

For the Year Ended December 31, 2012 (In millions of Canadian dollars)	Note	Preferred Shares	Common Shares	Subject to Cancellation	Contributed Surplus	Accumulated Other Comprehensive Income	Deficit	Total	Non-controlling Interest	Total Equity
Balance at January 1, 2012		3,115	13,566	(50)	2,527	5	(5,385)	13,778	981	14,759
Net earnings		–	–	–	–	–	2,763	2,763	290	3,053
Other comprehensive (loss) income		–	–	–	–	(11)	(1,138)	(1,149)	(89)	(1,238)
Comprehensive (loss) income		–	–	–	–	(11)	1,625	1,614	201	1,815
Preferred shares issued	23	280	–	–	–	–	(3)	277	–	277
Common shares issued under stock option plan	23	–	43	–	(4)	–	–	39	–	39
Common shares issued under employee savings plan	23	–	48	–	–	–	–	48	–	48
Common shares repurchased and cancelled	23	–	(46)	–	(3)	–	(58)	(107)	–	(107)
Common shares subject to cancellation	23	–	–	50	–	–	–	50	–	50
Other share-based payments		–	–	–	37	–	(3)	34	5	39
Dividends declared on BCE common and preferred shares		–	–	–	–	–	(1,858)	(1,858)	–	(1,858)
Dividends declared by subsidiaries to non-controlling interest		–	–	–	–	–	–	–	(348)	(348)
Equity securities issued by subsidiaries to non-controlling interest		–	–	–	–	–	–	–	11	11
Balance at December 31, 2012		3,395	13,611	–	2,557	(6)	(5,682)	13,875	850	14,725

Source: BCE Inc., Annual Report 2012.

REAL-WORLD EXCERPT

BCE Inc.

ANNUAL REPORT

ORGANIZATION OF THE CHAPTER

Ownership of a Corporation
- Benefits of Share Ownership
- Authorized, Issued, and Outstanding Shares
- Earnings per Share Ratio

Common Share Transactions
- No Par Value and Par Value Shares
- Initial Sale of Shares
- Sale of Shares in Secondary Markets
- Shares Issued for Non-cash Assets or Services
- Shares Issued for Employee Compensation
- Repurchase of Shares

Dividends on Common Shares
- Dividend Yield Ratio

Stock Dividends and Stock Splits
- Stock Dividends
- Stock Splits

Preferred Shares
- Special Features of Preferred Shares
- Dividends on Preferred Shares

Measuring and Reporting Changes in Shareholders' Equity
- Retained Earnings
- Accumulated Other Comprehensive Income (Loss)

Accounting and Reporting for Unincorporated Businesses

Supplemental material:

Appendix 12A: Accounting for Owners' Equity for Sole Proprietorships and Partnerships

OWNERSHIP OF A CORPORATION

The corporation is the only business form that the law recognizes as a separate entity. As a distinct entity, the corporation enjoys a continuous existence, separate and apart from its owners. It may own assets, incur liabilities, expand and contract in size, sue others, be sued, and enter into contracts independent of the shareholders.

To protect everyone's rights, both the creation and governance of corporations are tightly regulated by law. Corporations are created by making application to the federal government or a provincial government. The Canada Business Corporations Act (CBCA) outlines all of the legal requirements of federal incorporation (**www.laws. justice.gc.ca**).

To create a corporation, an application for a charter must be submitted to the appropriate government authorities. The application must specify the name of the corporation, the purpose (type of business), the types and number of shares authorized, and a minimum amount of capital that the owners must invest at the date of organization. Upon approval of the application, the government issues a charter, sometimes called the *articles of incorporation*. Each corporation is governed by a board of directors elected by the shareholders.

LO¹

Explain the role of share capital in the capital structure of a corporation.

Benefits of Share Ownership

When you invest in a corporation, you are known as a *shareholder* or *stockholder*. As a shareholder, you receive shares that you can subsequently sell on established stock exchanges without affecting the corporation.

Owners of common shares receive the following benefits:

1. **A voice in management.** They may vote at the shareholders' meeting (or by proxy) on major issues concerning management of the corporation.[3]
2. **Dividends.** They receive a proportionate share of the distribution of the corporation's net earnings.
3. **Residual claim.** They may receive a proportionate share of the distribution of remaining assets upon the liquidation of the company.

Owners, unlike creditors, are able to vote at the annual shareholders' meeting. The following notice of the annual and special meeting of shareholders was sent to all shareholders of BCE in March 2013.

REAL-WORLD EXCERPT

BCE Inc.

NOTICE OF SHAREHOLDERS'
ANNUAL MEETING

NOTICE OF 2013 ANNUAL GENERAL SHAREHOLDER MEETING

You are invited to our Annual General Shareholder Meeting

TIME AND DATE
Thursday, May 9, 2013, 9:30 a.m. (Eastern time)

PLACE
TIFF Bell Lightbox, Reitman Square, 350 King Street West, Toronto, Ontario, in Cinema 1

WEBCAST
If you cannot attend the Meeting in person, you can view a live webcast on our website at **www.bce.ca**. The webcast will also be archived on our website for viewing at your convenience for a period of up to two weeks after the meeting.

WHAT THE MEETING WILL COVER
We will be covering five items at the meeting:

1. receiving financial statements
2. electing directors
3. appointing auditors
4. considering an advisory (non-binding) resolution on executive compensation
5. considering the shareholder proposals described in Schedule A.

The meeting may also consider other business that properly comes before it.

VOTING BY PROXY IS THE EASIEST WAY TO VOTE

Shareholders have a choice of voting by proxy on the Internet, by telephone, by fax, or by mail using their proxy form or voting instruction form, as the case may be, or in person at the meeting. Please refer to your proxy form or your voting instruction form, as the case may be, or to the section entitled *About Voting Your Shares* for more information on the voting methods available to you. **If you elect to vote on the Internet or by telephone, you do not need to return your proxy form or voting instruction form.**

ELECTRONIC DELIVERY

Non-registered shareholders who requested a copy of proxy materials and all registered shareholders will receive a printed copy of proxy materials by mail.

We encourage shareholders to sign up to receive BCE's corporate information electronically. You can choose to receive all of our corporate documents electronically, such as future circulars and annual reports. We will send you an e-mail telling you when they are available on our website.

To sign up, go to our website at **www.bce.ca**, click on the banner "2013 Annual General Shareholder Meeting" and then on the "Sign up for electronic delivery" link.

If you do not sign up for this service, we will continue to send you these documents by mail, unless you tell us otherwise on your proxy form or voting instruction form.

Source: BCE Inc., Notice of 2013 Annual General Shareholder Meeting and Management Proxy Circular.

The notice of the annual meeting was accompanied by a *management information* (or *proxy*) *circular* that contained several pages of information concerning the people who were nominated to be members of the board of directors. Since most owners do not actually attend the annual meeting, the notice included a proxy card, which is similar to an absentee ballot. Each owner may complete the proxy and mail it to the company, which will include it in the votes at the annual meeting.

Shareholders have ultimate authority in a corporation, as shown in Exhibit 12.3. The board of directors and, indirectly, all the employees are accountable to the shareholders. The organizational structure shown in Exhibit 12.3 is typical of most corporations, but the specific structure depends on the nature of the company's business.

Exhibit **12.3**

Typical Organizational Structure of a Corporation

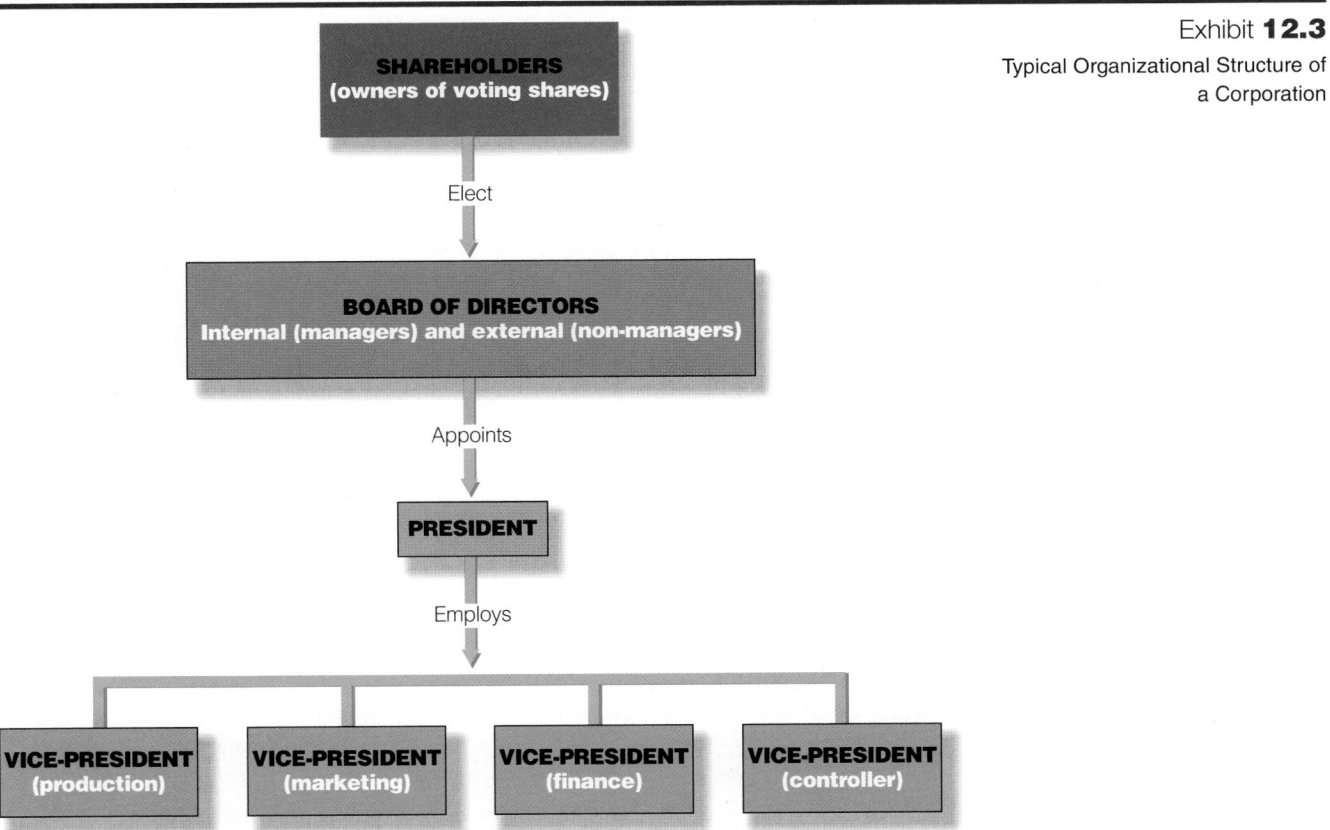

Authorized, Issued, and Outstanding Shares

The **AUTHORIZED NUMBER OF SHARES** is the maximum number of shares that a corporation can issue, as specified in the charter.

The term **ISSUED SHARES** refers to the number of shares that have been issued.

The term **OUTSTANDING SHARES** refers to the total number of shares that are owned by shareholders on any particular date.

When a corporation is created, its corporate charter specifies the type and maximum number of shares that it can sell to the public. This maximum is called the **authorized number of shares**. Typically, the corporate charter authorizes a larger number of shares than the corporation expects to issue initially. This strategy provides future flexibility for the issuance of additional shares without the need to amend the charter. In the case of BCE, the number of authorized common shares is unlimited.

The number of **issued shares** and the number of **outstanding shares**—that is, the total number of shares that are owned by shareholders on any particular date—are determined by the corporation's equity transactions. For BCE, the numbers of issued shares and outstanding shares are the same; at December 31, 2012, this number was 775.4 million. The number of issued shares may differ from the number of outstanding shares if the company has bought back some of its shares from shareholders. If a corporation needs to sell more shares than its charter authorizes, it must seek permission from the current shareholders to modify the charter.

Exhibit 12.4 defines and illustrates the terms usually used in relation to corporate shares.

Exhibit **12.4**

Authorized, Issued, and Outstanding Shares

Definitions	Illustrations	
Authorized number of shares:		
The maximum number of shares that can be issued, as specified in the charter of the corporation.	The charter specifies "an unlimited number of common shares."	
Issued number of shares:		
The total number of shares that the corporation has issued to date.	To date, XYZ Corporation has sold and issued 30,000 common shares.	
Unissued number of shares:		
The number of authorized shares that have never been issued to date.	Authorized shares	100,000
	Issued shares	(30,000)
	Unissued shares	70,000
Treasury shares:*		
Shares that have been issued to investors and then reacquired by the issuing corporation.	To date, XYZ Corporation has repurchased 1,000 previously issued shares.	
Outstanding number of shares:		
The number of shares currently owned by shareholders—that is, the number of shares authorized, minus the total number of unissued shares, minus the number of treasury shares.	Authorized shares	100,000
	Treasury shares	(1,000)
	Unissued shares	(70,000)
	Outstanding shares	29,000

*Notice that when treasury shares are held, the number of shares issued and the number outstanding differ by the number of treasury shares held (treasury shares are included in "issued" but not in "outstanding").

KEY RATIO ANALYSIS

EARNINGS PER SHARE RATIO

LO²

Analyze the earnings per share ratio.

ANALYTICAL QUESTION → How profitable is a company?

RATIO AND COMPARISONS → The *earnings per share* (EPS) is a measure of the return on investment that is based on the number of shares outstanding instead of the dollar amounts reported on the statement of financial position. In simple situations, it is computed as follows:

$$\text{Earnings per Share} = \frac{\text{Net Earnings Available to Common Shareholders}}{\text{Average Number of Common Shares Outstanding}}$$

The 2012 ratio for BCE is

$$\frac{\$2,624}{774.0} = \$3.39$$

Comparisons over Time				Comparisons with Competitors	
BCE				Rogers Communications	TELUS
2010	2011	2012		2012	2012
$2.74	$2.88	$3.39		$3.28	$0.89

INTERPRETATIONS

In General → All analysts and investors are interested in a company's earnings. You have probably seen newspaper headlines announcing a company's earnings. Notice that those news stories normally report EPS. The reason is simple. Numbers are much easier to compare on a per share basis. For example, in 2012, BCE reported $2,624 million of earnings attributable to common shareholders compared to $2,221 million in 2011. If we make that comparison on a per share basis, EPS increased from $2.88 to $3.39, an increase of 17.7 percent that takes into consideration the change in the number of common shares outstanding during the year.

Focus Company Analysis → BCE has a strategy of growth and reinvestment of earnings. Analysts are watching EPS to be sure the company will achieve its strategy. BCE's EPS increased from $2.74 in 2010 to $3.39 in 2012. Its EPS in 2012 exceeds the EPS figures of its competitors. However, comparison of the EPS figures for the three companies may not be very informative as a measure of profitability of shareholders' investments in these companies. The reason is simple: shares of different companies are likely to have different prices, which makes EPS comparisons less meaningful than other measures of profitability.

A Few Cautions → While EPS is an effective and widely used measure of profitability, it can be misleading if there are significant differences in the market values of the shares being compared. Two companies earning $1.50 per share might appear to be comparable, but if shares in one company cost $10 while shares of the other cost $175, they are not comparable. For example, BCE's stock price was $42.6 at December 31, 2012. But the stock price of Rogers Communications was $45.2 at that date, even though BCE has a higher EPS figure. Obviously, investors expect a large EPS number for companies with higher stock prices.

COMMON SHARE TRANSACTIONS

Corporations issue two types of shares: common shares and preferred shares. All corporations issue common shares, while only some issue preferred shares, which grant preferences that the common shares do not have. In this section, we discuss common shares, and in a subsequent section we discuss preferred shares.

Common shares are the basic voting shares issued by a corporation. They are often called the *residual equity* because they rank after the preferred shares for dividend and asset distribution upon liquidation of the corporation. The dividend rate for common shares is determined by the board of directors based on the company's profitability, unlike the dividend rate on preferred shares, which is determined by contract. When the company is not profitable, the board may cut or eliminate dividends on common shares, but in most cases it cannot reduce preferred dividends.

COMMON SHARES are the basic voting shares issued by a corporation; called *residual equity* because they rank after preferred shares for dividend and liquidation distributions.

No Par Value and Par Value Shares

Par value is the nominal value per share established in the charter of a corporation. It has no relationship to the market value per share. The CBCA and most provincial corporation acts prohibit the issuance of par value shares. The few Canadian companies that still have par value shares outstanding issued them before the CBCA was amended in 1985. For this reason, the remainder of this chapter focuses on **no par value shares**, which do not have an amount per share specified in the corporate charter. In contrast, most U.S. corporations issue par value shares.

PAR VALUE is the nominal value per share specified in the charter; it serves as the basis for legal capital.

NO PAR VALUE SHARES are shares that have no par value specified in the corporate charter.

The original purpose of requiring corporations to specify a par value per share was to establish a minimum permanent amount of capital that the owners could not withdraw as long as the corporation existed. Thus, owners could not withdraw all of their capital in anticipation of a bankruptcy, which would leave creditors with an empty corporate shell. This permanent amount of capital is called **legal capital**. The requirement that shares not be issued for less than their par value often resulted in par values that were too small to be effectively meaningful. This notion of legal capital has lost its significance over time, because the par values of shares have been set at very low amounts by issuing corporations. In contrast, when a corporation issues no par value shares, the legal capital is the initial amount received from shareholders.

BCE's corporate charter authorizes the issue of no par value common shares. However, its preferred shares have a stated value upon which the dividend payments are based. This stated value has no relationship to the market value of the preferred shares.

Initial Sale of Shares

Two names are applied to transactions involving the initial sale of a company's shares to the public. An *initial public offering*, or *IPO*, involves the very first sale of a company's shares to the public (i.e., when the company first "goes public"). You have probably heard the story of Facebook, for example, whose shares decreased dramatically in value after it issued its IPO. While investors sometimes earn significant returns on IPOs, they also take significant risks. Once the shares of a company are traded on established markets, additional sales of new shares to the public are called *seasoned new issues* or *secondary share offerings*.

As was the case with debt (discussed in Chapter 11), most companies use an underwriter to assist in the sale of shares. The underwriter is usually an investment bank that acts as an intermediary between the corporation and the investors. The underwriter advises the corporation on matters concerning the sale and is directly involved in the sale of shares to the public.

Most sales of shares to the public are cash transactions. To illustrate accounting for an initial sale of shares, assume that BCE sold 100,000 common shares for $45 per share. The company records the following journal entry:

Cash (A) (100,000 × $45)	4,500,000	
Common shares (SE)		4,500,000

Assets	=	Liabilities	+	Shareholders' Equity	
Cash +4,500,000				Common shares	+4,500,000

In 2012, BCE issued new shares for $43 million, as shown in Exhibit 12.2. These shares were issued on exercise of stock options, as explained later in the chapter.

Sale of Shares in Secondary Markets

When a company sells shares to the public, the transaction is between the issuing corporation and the buyer. Subsequent to the initial sale, investors can sell shares to other investors without directly affecting the corporation. For example, if investor Eric Mortisson sold 1,000 of BCE's common shares to Jennifer Hussein, BCE does not record a journal entry on its books. Eric received cash for the shares he sold, and Jennifer received shares for the cash she paid. BCE itself did not receive or pay anything because of this transaction.

Each business day, the financial information service providers, such as bloomberg .com, reuters.com, finance.yahoo.com, and money.msn.com, report the results of thousands of transactions between investors in the secondary markets, where trading of shares takes place. These markets include the Toronto Stock Exchange (TSX) and TSX Venture Exchange (in Canada); the New York Stock Exchange (NYSE), American Stock Exchange, and NASDAQ (in the United States); and similar markets in other countries.

Managers of corporations follow very closely the movements in the price of their company's shares. Shareholders expect to earn money on their investment from both dividends and increases in the share (or stock) price. In many instances, senior management has been replaced because of poor performance of the shares in the secondary markets. Although managers watch the share price on a daily basis, it is important to remember that the transactions between investors do not directly affect the company's financial statements.

GOING PUBLIC

FINANCIAL ANALYSIS

As noted earlier, an IPO is the first sale of shares to the public. Prior to that sale, the company is a private company. A company might want to go public for one of two common reasons. In some cases, for the company to grow and meet consumer demand, it must expand its productive capacity. The need for new capital may be beyond the capability of the private owners. By going public, the company can raise the funds needed to expand.

In other cases, the company may not need significant funds, but the current owners may want to create a market for its shares. Often, selling shares is difficult if the company is not listed on a major stock exchange. By going public, a company can increase the marketability of its shares.

IPOs often create a lot of interest among investors. Some good opportunities are available to earn excellent returns by investing in growing companies. Substantial risk is also associated with many IPOs.

In recent years, much interest has surrounded Internet companies that have gone public. For example, Google Inc., which operates one of the most popular search engines, had an IPO of its shares at an initial price of $85. Since the IPO in August 2004, Google's share price increased significantly, reaching $806 by March 2013 because of investors' expectations of the company's future profitability.

There are countless stories of people in their twenties and thirties who have become instant millionaires after the IPO of a new Internet company. Less well publicized, however, are the stories of individuals who have lost money investing in shares of new and unproven businesses.

Shares Issued for Non-cash Assets or Services

Small companies are playing an increasingly important role in the North American economy. Often, they are private enterprises that account for a large percentage of the new jobs that have been created in the past decade. Many of today's corporate giants were small start-up companies just a few years ago. Companies such as Dell, Microsoft, Amazon.com, and Google Inc. began, literally, as basement operations in the homes of their founders.

One feature common to all start-up companies is a shortage of cash. Because these companies often cannot afford to pay cash for needed assets and services, they sometimes issue shares to people who can supply these assets and services. Many executives, for instance, will join start-up companies for very low salaries because they also earn compensation in the form of common shares. An executive who was granted Google shares during its early days would be very wealthy today.

When a company issues shares to acquire assets or services, the acquired items are recorded at the *market value* of the shares issued at the date of the transaction in accordance with the *cost principle*. If the market value of the shares issued cannot be determined, the market value of the consideration received should be used.

To illustrate, assume that during its early years of operation, BCE was unable to pay cash for needed legal services. The company issued 10,000 shares to a law firm when a share was selling for $15. At that time, the company recorded the following journal entry:

| Legal fees (E) | 150,000 | |
| Common shares (SE) | | 150,000 |

Assets	=	Liabilities	+	Shareholders' Equity	
				Legal fees	−150,000
				Common shares	+150,000

Notice that the value of the legal services received is assumed to be the same as the value of the shares that were issued. This assumption is reasonable because two independent parties usually keep negotiating a deal until the value of what is given up equals the value of what is received.

Shares Issued for Employee Compensation

One of the advantages of the corporate form is the possibility to separate the management of a business from its ownership. This separation can also be a disadvantage because some managers may not act in the best interests of shareholders. This problem can be overcome in a number of ways. Compensation packages can be developed to reward managers for meeting goals that are important to shareholders. Another strategy is to offer managers *stock options*, which permit them to buy shares at a fixed price.

The holder of a stock option has an interest in a company's performance in the same manner as a shareholder. Stock option plans have become an increasingly common form of compensation over the past few years. However, the excessive use of stock options as a form of compensating key executives led the executives of some companies to manipulate reported financial information in an effort to increase the share price, allowing them to benefit by buying shares at a fixed price and selling them at a higher price for a profit.

The BCE annual report provides the following disclosures with respect to its future contractual obligations related to stock options:

NOTES TO CONSOLIDATED FINANCIAL STATEMENTS

Note 24. Share-based Payments
The following table summarizes BCE's outstanding stock options at December 31, 2012 and 2011.

	Note	2012 Number of Options	2012 Weighted Average Exercise Price ($)	2011 Number of Options	2011 Weighted Average Exercise Price ($)
Outstanding, January 1		4,027,309	$33	8,491,226	$32
Granted		2,681,201	$40	2,443,954	$36
Exercised (1)	23	(1,296,962)	$30	(5,090,918)	$30
Expired		(4,850)	$28	(1,604,969)	$40
Forfeited		(96,342)	$37	(211,984)	$35
Outstanding, December 31		5,310,356	$37	4,027,309	$33
Exercisable, December 31		420,822	$30	1,725,634	$30

(1) The weighted average share price for options exercised was $42 and $38 in 2012 and 2011, respectively.

Source: BCE Inc., Annual Report 2012.

The options issued by BCE specify that shares could be bought at a predetermined exercise price. Granting a stock option is a form of compensation even if the exercise price and the current share price are the same.

Stock options are a widely used form of executive compensation. Most companies offer them with an exercise price equal to the current market price per share. For example, assume that BCE granted a key employee options to purchase a total of 10,000 common shares in the future at an average price of $30, which equals the market price per share on the date of the grant. The option holder would benefit from the stock option in a few years if the market price per share exceeded $30, presumably because the increase in BCE's market value would be partially attributed to the employee's managerial skills. Undoubtedly, the difference between the increased market price and the exercise price of $30 is a form of taxable compensation to the employee. Exhibit 12.2 shows that BCE issued common shares for $43 million on exercise of stock options during 2012.

When the options are exercised, BCE receives $30 per common share, while it could have obtained a higher price if it sold the same shares in the market to other investors. Clearly, the exercise of employee stock options entails a cost to BCE that should be measured and reported. The more interesting issue, however, is whether BCE incurs a cost at the time of granting the options. In general, a fair value of the options can be estimated by using specific valuation methods and then compared with the exercise price to determine the additional compensation expense for the period.

In 2012, BCE granted its key employees 2,681,201 stock options at a weighted-average exercise price of $40 per share, and 1,296,962 stock options were exercised by employees during that year. A total of 4,850 stock options expired during 2012 because the exercise price of $28 exceeded the market price per share, so the stock option holders could not benefit from them prior to the expiry date of the stock options. Comparatively, in 2011 a total of 1,604,969 stock options expired because the exercise price was set at a much higher price ($40).

The measurement and reporting of the cost of stock options has been hotly debated by accounting standard setters and company executives. Many companies rely on stock options to compensate their employees and key executives, especially in the technology, energy, and gold mining sectors. Companies in these sectors have lobbied against reporting the cost of stock options as an expense on the statement of earnings, because it lowers their net earnings, and may even turn net earnings into losses.

Canadian companies must estimate and report compensation expense associated with stock options. The specific procedures to compute the compensation expense are covered in intermediate accounting courses.

Repurchase of Shares

A corporation may want to purchase its own shares from existing shareholders for a number of reasons. One common reason is to increase the market price per share and the EPS that result from the reduction in the number of outstanding shares.

Most Canadian companies cancel their shares when they buy them back from shareholders. When shares are cancelled, the appropriate share capital account is reduced by an amount that reflects the average issuance price per share. If the purchase price is less than the average issuance price, the difference is credited to contributed surplus. For example, if BCE purchases 50,000 common shares in the open market at $30 per share and the average price of the previously issued common shares is $34,[4] the journal entry and the transaction effects will be as follows:

Common shares (SE) (50,000 × $34)	1,700,000	
Cash (A)		1,500,000
Contributed surplus (SE)		200,000

Assets		=	Liabilities	+	Shareholders' Equity	
Cash	−1,500,000				Common shares	−1,700,000
					Contributed surplus	+200,000

Repurchases of shares at prices lower than the average issue price do not result in profit for the issuing company because they are capital transactions, not operating transactions. Companies profit from buying and selling shares issued by other companies, but not their own shares.[5]

Assume further that BCE subsequently purchased 50,000 of its own common shares when the price per share was $40. In this case, the excess of the purchase price over the issuance price is $6 per share for a total of $300,000. This difference is debited first to contributed surplus to the extent of $200,000 (the account balance), and the remaining amount of $100,000 is debited to retained earnings. The retained earnings account is reduced, because the excess of the purchase price over the contribution made previously by shareholders reflects the company's profitable operations, which resulted in net earnings and caused an increase in share price. Hence, the $100,000 is viewed as a distribution of accumulated net earnings, or retained earnings, to shareholders who sold their shares to the company. The journal entry and the transaction effects follow:

Common shares (SE) (50,000 × $34)	1,700,000	
Contributed surplus (SE)	200,000	
Retained earnings (SE)	100,000	
Cash (A)		2,000,000

Assets		=	Liabilities	+	Shareholders' Equity	
Cash	−2,000,000				Common shares	−1,700,000
					Contributed surplus	−200,000
					Retained earnings	−100,000

Contributed surplus related to one class of shares, such as common shares, can be used only for share transactions involving the same class of shares.

The disclosures in Exhibit 12.2 show that BCE repurchased and cancelled common shares in 2012. The share repurchase transactions resulted in cash payment of $107 million with reductions of $46 million in the common shares account, a reduction of $3 million in the contributed surplus account, and a reduction of $58 million in the retained earnings account (increase in deficit).

PAUSE FOR FEEDBACK

We have looked at several transactions involving the sale and repurchase of common shares. In the next section, we will discuss dividends. Before you move on, complete the following questions to test your understanding of share repurchase transactions.

SELF-STUDY QUIZ 12-1

BCE's annual report for 2011 included the following statement:

In December 2011, BCE repurchased and cancelled a total of 3,500,466 common shares for a total cost of $143 million. Of the total cost, $61 million represents stated capital and $4 million represents the reduction of the contributed surplus attributable to these common shares. The remaining $78 million was charged to the deficit.

1. Use the information above to reconstruct the journal entry to record the repurchase transaction.

2. Compute the average issuance price of BCE's common shares prior to the repurchase transaction.

After you complete your answers, check them with the solutions at the end of the chapter.

DIVIDENDS ON COMMON SHARES

LO⁴

Discuss dividends, and analyze related transactions.

Investors buy common shares because they expect a return on their investment. This return can come in two forms: appreciation of the share price, and dividends. Some investors prefer to buy shares that pay little or no dividends, because companies that reinvest the majority of their earnings tend to increase their future earnings potential, along with their stock price. Wealthy investors in high tax brackets prefer to receive their return on equity investments in the form of higher stock prices, because capital gains may be taxed at a lower rate than dividend income. Other investors, such as retired people who need a steady income, prefer to receive their return on an investment in the form of dividends. These people often seek shares that will pay very high dividends, such as shares of utility companies.

A corporation does not have a legal obligation to pay dividends. While creditors can force a company into bankruptcy if it does not meet required interest payments on debt, shareholders do not have a similar right if a corporation is unable to pay dividends. Although a corporation does not have a legal obligation to pay a dividend, a liability is created when the board of directors approves (i.e., declares) a dividend.

Without a qualifier, the term *dividend* means a cash dividend, but dividends can also be paid in assets other than cash or by issuing additional shares. The most common type of dividend is a cash dividend.

A dividend declaration by BCE's board of directors includes three important dates:

1. The **declaration date** is the date on which the board of directors officially approved the dividend. As soon as it makes the declaration, it creates a dividend liability.

2. The **date of record** follows the declaration; it is the date on which the corporation prepares the list of current shareholders, based on its shareholder records. The dividend is payable only to those names listed on the record date. No journal entry is made on this date.

3. The **payment date** is the date on which the cash is disbursed to pay the dividend liability. It follows the date of record as specified in the dividend announcement.

The **DECLARATION DATE** is the date on which the board of directors officially approves a dividend.

The **DATE OF RECORD** is the date on which the corporation prepares the list of current shareholders as shown on its records; dividends can be paid only to the shareholders who own shares on that date.

The **PAYMENT DATE** is the date on which a cash dividend is paid to the shareholders of record.

BCE pays cash dividends on its outstanding common shares on a quarterly basis. The quarterly dividend on common shares is often increased when the company's profitability increases. For example, BCE increased its dividend per common share from $0.34 in 1998 to $0.5825 in 2013. In some cases, however, a corporation may reduce or even suspend dividend payment to common shareholders if its financial situation deteriorates. BCE provides details of the quarterly dividends on its preferred and common shares on its website. For example, details related to the cash dividends on common shares declared during 2012 are as follows:

REAL-WORLD EXCERPT

BCE Inc.

DIVIDEND INFORMATION

Date of Declaration	Date of Record	Date of Payment	Amount of Dividend
February 8, 2012	March 15, 2012	April 15, 2012	$0.5425
May 3, 2012	June 15, 2012	July 15, 2012	0.5425
August 7, 2012	September 14, 2012	October 15, 2012	0.5675
October 31, 2012	December 14, 2012	January 15, 2013	0.5675

Source: **www.bce.ca/investors/dividendinfo/dividenddates/.**

For instructional purposes, the time lag between the date of declaration and the date of payment may be ignored because it does not pose any substantive issues. When all three dates fall in the same accounting period, a single entry on the date of payment may be made in practice, for purely practical reasons.

Assume, for simplicity, that BCE had 775 million common shares outstanding on October 31, 2012. The total amount of cash dividends paid on January 15, 2013, is therefore $439,812,500.

The declaration of dividends creates a liability on October 31, 2012, that is recorded as follows:

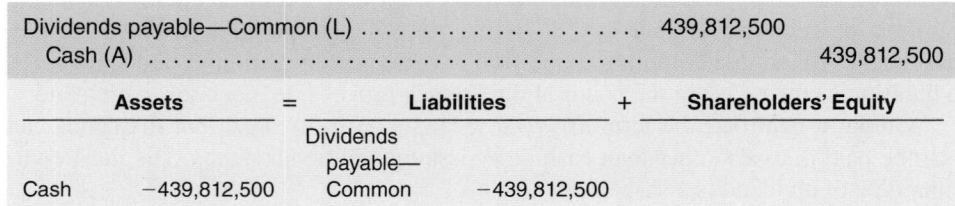

| Dividends declared—Common (SE) | ..... | 439,812,500 | | | |
| Dividend payable—Common (L) | ..... | | | 439,812,500 | |

Assets	=	Liabilities	+	Shareholders' Equity
		Dividends payable— Common +439,812,500		Dividends declared— Common −439,812,500

The payment of the dividends on common shares on January 15, 2013, is recorded as follows:

| Dividends payable—Common (L) | ..... | 439,812,500 | | | |
| Cash (A) | ..... | | | 439,812,500 | |

Assets	=	Liabilities	+	Shareholders' Equity
Cash −439,812,500		Dividends payable— Common −439,812,500		

Notice that the declaration and payment of a cash dividend have two impacts: they reduce assets (cash) and shareholders' equity (retained earnings) by the same amount. This observation explains the two fundamental requirements for the payment of a cash dividend:

1. *Sufficient retained earnings.* The corporation must have accumulated a sufficient amount of retained earnings to cover the amount of the dividend. Incorporation laws often limit cash dividends to the balance in the retained earnings account. BCE reports a deficit instead of retained earnings in its statement of financial position, as shown in Exhibit 12.2, yet it has declared cash dividends to its shareholders during 2012. How it that possible? According to section 42 of the CBCA, a corporation may declare and pay dividends if payment of the dividend does not place the company into a position that would prevent it from paying its liabilities as they become due. BCE's statement of financial position at December 31, 2012, shows that the carrying amount of its assets far exceeds the carrying amount of its liabilities. In addition, BCE's statement of cash flows shows that the company generated $5.5 billion from operating activities in 2012. BCE's liquidity position allowed its board of directors to declare and pay dividends even though its retained earnings account has a debit balance.

2. *Sufficient cash.* The corporation must have access to sufficient cash to pay the dividend and to meet the operating needs of the business. The mere fact that the retained earnings account has a large credit balance does not mean that the board of directors can declare and pay a cash dividend. The cash generated in the past by earnings represented in the retained earnings account may have been expended to acquire inventory, buy operational assets, and pay liabilities. Consequently, no necessary relationship exists between the balance of retained earnings and the balance of cash on any particular date. Quite simply, retained earnings is not cash.

Exhibit 12.2 indicates that BCE declared dividends on preferred and common shares for a total amount of $1,858 million in 2012, which is less than the net earnings for 2012.

The company has established a dividend reinvestment plan that allows shareholders to receive additional common shares instead of cash dividends. It also encourages its employees to purchase BCE common shares through an employee savings plan, whereby employees can use a percentage of their salaries to buy BCE common shares through regular payroll deductions.

IMPACT OF DIVIDENDS ON SHARE PRICE

FINANCIAL ANALYSIS

When a company declares a dividend, it is important to establish which shareholders receive the dividend. For this reason, the stock exchanges set an *ex-dividend date*, which is normally two business days before the date of record, to make certain that dividend cheques are sent to the right people. If you buy shares before the ex-dividend date, you receive the dividend. If you buy the shares on the ex-dividend date or later, the previous shareholder receives the dividend. While this date is important in understanding dividends, it has no accounting implications.

If you follow share prices, you will notice that the price of a company's common share often falls on the ex-dividend date. The reason is simple. On that date, the share is worth less because it no longer includes the right to receive the next dividend.

PAUSE FOR **FEEDBACK**

One of the reasons that investors buy common shares is to earn dividends. We have looked at dividends paid in cash. In the next section, we will look at dividends paid in shares. Before you move on, complete the following questions to test your understanding of cash dividends.

SELF-STUDY **QUIZ 12-2**

The board of directors of BCE Inc. declared on November 6, 2013, a quarterly dividend of $0.5825 per common share, payable on January 15, 2014, to shareholders of record on December 16, 2013. Assume that BCE had 750 million common shares outstanding on the declaration date. Answer the following questions concerning this dividend:

1. On which date is a liability created?

2. On which date does a cash outflow occur?

3. Prepare the journal entry to record the payment of the dividend.

4. What are the three fundamental requirements for the payment of a dividend?

After you complete your answers, check them with the solutions at the end of this chapter.

Because of the importance of dividends to many investors, analysts often compute the dividend yield ratio to evaluate a corporation's dividend policy.

DIVIDEND YIELD RATIO

KEY RATIO **ANALYSIS**

ANALYTICAL QUESTION → Investors in common shares expect to earn a return on their investment. A portion of this return comes in the form of dividends. How much do investors earn on their investment based on dividends?

RATIO AND COMPARISONS → The *dividend yield ratio* is a measure of the percentage return that shareholders earn from the dividends they receive. Potential investors often use this ratio to help select among alternative investment opportunities. In 2012, BCE declared two quarterly dividends of $0.5425 per share and two quarterly dividends of $0.5675 per share, for a total of $2.22 per share. The ratio is computed as follows:

LO5

Analyze the dividend yield ratio.

$$\text{Dividend Yield Ratio} = \frac{\text{Dividends per Share}}{\text{Market Price per Share}}$$

The 2012 ratio for BCE is

$$\frac{\$2.22}{\$42.63} = 0.052 \text{ or } 5.2\%$$

Comparisons over Time			Comparisons with Competitors	
BCE			Rogers Communications	TELUS
2010	2011	2012	2012	2012
5.1%	4.8%	5.2%	3.5%	3.8%

INTERPRETATIONS

In General → Investors in common shares earn a return from dividends and capital appreciation (increases in the market price of the shares they own). Growth-oriented companies often pay out very small amounts of dividends and rely on increases in their market price to provide a return to investors. Others pay out large dividends but have more stable market prices. Each type of share appeals to different types of investors with different risk and return preferences.

Focus Company Analysis → During the three years 2010 through 2012, BCE distributed annual dividends of $1.785, $2.045, and $2.22 per share, respectively. Its share price was $35.34, $42.47, and $42.63 on December 31, 2010, 2011, and 2012, respectively. BCE's dividend yield is relatively stable over the three-year period, and higher than those of Rogers Communications and TELUS.

A Few Cautions → Remember that the dividend yield ratio tells only part of the return on investment story. Often, potential capital appreciation is a much more important consideration. When analyzing changes in the ratio, it is important to understand the cause. For example, a company might pay out $2 per share in dividends each year. If the market price of its shares is $100 per share, the yield is 2 percent. If the market price per share falls to $25 the following year and the company continues to pay out $2 per share in dividends, the dividend yield ratio will "improve" to 8 percent. Most analysts would not interpret this change as being favourable.

LO6

Discuss the purpose of stock dividends, stock splits, and report transactions.

STOCK DIVIDENDS AND STOCK SPLITS

Stock Dividends

A **stock dividend** is a distribution of additional shares of a corporation's own share capital to its shareholders on a pro rata basis, at no cost to the shareholder. Stock dividends usually consist of additional common shares issued to the holders of common shares. The term "pro rata basis" means that each shareholder receives additional shares equal to the percentage of shares already held. A shareholder with 10 percent of the outstanding shares receives 10 percent of any additional shares issued as a stock dividend.

A **STOCK DIVIDEND** is a distribution of additional shares of a corporation's own equity.

The term "stock dividend" is sometimes misused in annual reports and news articles. A recent *Wall Street Journal* headline announced that a particular company had just declared a "stock dividend." A close reading of the article revealed that the company had declared a cash dividend on the shares.

The value of a stock dividend is the subject of much debate. In reality, a stock dividend has no economic value. All shareholders receive a pro rata distribution of shares, which means that each shareholder owns exactly the same portion of the company as before. The value of an investment is determined by the percentage of the company that is owned, not the number of shares that are held. If you get change for a dollar coin, you are not wealthier because you hold *four* quarters instead of only *one* dollar coin. Similarly, if you own 10 percent of a company, you are not wealthier simply because the company declares a stock dividend and gives you (and all other shareholders) more shares.

At this point, you may still wonder why having extra shares does not make an investor wealthier. The reason is simple: the stock market reacts immediately when a stock dividend is issued, and the share price falls proportionally. Theoretically, if the share price was $60 before a stock dividend, normally (in the absence of events affecting the company) the price will fall to $30 if the number of shares is doubled. Thus, an investor could own 100 shares worth $6,000 before the stock dividend (100 × $60) and 200 shares worth $6,000 after the stock dividend (200 × $30).

In reality, the fall in price is not exactly proportional to the number of new shares that are issued. In some cases, the stock dividend makes the stock more attractive to new investors. Many investors prefer to buy shares in round lots, which are multiples of 100 shares.

An investor with $10,000 might not buy a share selling for $150 because she cannot afford to buy 100 shares. She might buy the share, however, if the price is less than $100 as a result of a stock dividend. In other cases, stock dividends are accompanied by an announcement of increases in cash dividends, which are attractive to some investors.

When a common stock dividend occurs, the company must transfer from retained earnings an additional amount into the common shares account to reflect the additional shares that have been issued. The amount transferred should reflect the fair market value per share at the declaration date, as recommended in the CBCA.

For small stock dividends that are less than 20–25 percent of the outstanding shares, the amount transferred from the retained earnings account to the common shares account is based on the market price per share at the date of declaration. If the company declared a cash dividend instead of a stock dividend, and the shareholders used the cash they received to buy additional shares, the shareholders would be paying the market price to acquire additional shares. This assumption is valid if the stock dividend is relatively small, so that it will not cause a significant change in the market price. For larger stock dividends, the market price per share will drop significantly, so it will not be an appropriate basis for transferring an amount from retained earnings to common shares. In this case, the amount transferred is based on the average issue price per share. In either situation, the stock dividend does not change total shareholders' equity. It changes only the balances of specific shareholders' equity accounts.

Let us assume that a company declared on July 25, 2014, a 10 percent stock dividend on common shares to be issued on August 25, 2014, to shareholders of record on August 10, 2014. The company had 100,000 shares outstanding, and the market price per share was $20 on the date of declaration. The declaration of the stock dividend requires the following journal entry on July 25, 2014:

Dividends declared—Common (SE) (100,000 × 10% × $20)	200,000	
Stock dividend to be issued (SE)		200,000

Assets	=	Liabilities	+	Shareholders' Equity	
				Dividends declared—Common	−200,000
				Stock dividend to be issued	+200,000

The equity account Stock Dividend to Be Issued is credited, instead of the Common Shares account, until the shares are issued. The issuance and distribution of the additional shares on August 25, 2014, is recorded as follows:

Stock dividend to be issued (SE)	200,000	
Common shares (SE)		200,000

Assets	=	Liabilities	+	Shareholders' Equity	
				Stock dividend to be issued	−200,000
				Common shares	+200,000

If the company had declared a 50 percent stock dividend, the average price received for issuing all of the common shares would be used instead of the market price per share as a basis for the reduction of retained earnings. If the average issue price per share is $15, the Dividends Declared—Common account would be reduced by $750,000 (100,000 × 50% × $15) and the Common Shares account would be increased by the same amount.

Stock Splits

Stock splits are *not* dividends. They are similar to a stock dividend but are quite different in terms of their impact on the shareholders' equity accounts. In a **stock split**, the *total* number of authorized, issued, and outstanding shares is increased by a specified number, such as a 2-for-1 split. In this instance, each share held is called in, and two new shares are issued in its place.

A STOCK SPLIT is an increase in the total number of authorized shares by a specified ratio; it does not decrease retained earnings.

BCE has had three stock splits over the years. A 4-for-1 split occurred on October 4, 1948, followed by a 3-for-1 split on April 26, 1979. The last split was a 2-for-1, executed on May 14, 1997. In summary, a common share issued prior to October 4, 1948, has already split into 24 shares. If these stock splits did not occur, BCE's share price would have been $1,044 at the time of writing this book.

In both a stock dividend and a stock split, the shareholder receives more shares but does not pay to acquire the additional shares. A stock dividend requires a journal entry; a stock split does not require one but is disclosed in the notes to the financial statements. The comparative effects of a stock dividend versus a stock split may be summarized as follows:

Shareholders' Equity	Before	After a 100% Stock Dividend	After a 2-for-1 Stock Split
Contributed capital			
Number of shares outstanding	30,000	60,000	60,000
Issue price per share	$ 10	$ 10	$ 5
Common shares	300,000	600,000	300,000
Retained earnings	650,000	350,000	650,000
Total shareholders' equity	$950,000	$950,000	$950,000

PAUSE FOR FEEDBACK

We have concluded our discussion of common shares by looking at stock dividends and stock splits. In the next section, we will examine preferred shares. Before you move on, complete the following questions to test your understanding of stock dividends.

SELF-STUDY QUIZ 12-3

Barton Corporation issued 100,000 new common shares as a result of a stock dividend when the market value was $30 per share. The average issue price is $10 per share.

1. Record this transaction, assuming that it was a small stock dividend.

2. Record this transaction, assuming that it was a large stock dividend.

3. What journal entry is required if the transaction is a stock split?

After you complete your answers, check them with the solutions at the end of the chapter.

LO7

Describe the characteristics of preferred shares, and analyze transactions affecting preferred shares.

PREFERRED SHARES are shares that have specified rights over common shares.

PREFERRED SHARES

In addition to common shares, some corporations issue *preferred shares*. **Preferred shares** differ from common shares because of a number of rights granted to the preferred shareholders. The most significant differences are as follows:

- **Preferred shares do not grant voting rights.** As a result, they do not appeal to investors who want some control over the operations of the corporation. Indeed, this is one of the main reasons some corporations issue preferred shares to raise equity capital. Preferred shares permit them to raise funds without diluting common shareholders' control of the company.

- **Preferred shares are less risky than common shares.** Preferred shareholders have a priority over common shareholders for the receipt of dividends and in the distribution of assets if the corporation goes out of business. Usually a specified amount per share must be paid to preferred shareholders upon dissolution before any remaining assets can be distributed to the common shareholders.

- **Preferred shares typically have a fixed dividend rate.** Preferred shares typically have no par value but, unlike common shares, they often carry a nominal value called the *stated value*. BCE's preferred shares have a stated value of $25 per share. Most preferred shares have fixed dividend rates or amounts per share. The fixed dividend is attractive to certain investors who want a stable income from their investment.

Special Features of Preferred Shares

Some corporations issue **convertible preferred shares**, which provide preferred shareholders the option to exchange their preferred shares for a different series of preferred shares or common shares of the corporation. The terms of the conversion specify the conversion dates and a conversion ratio.

The classification of preferred shares as equity or debt depends upon the terms of the preferred equity issue. Preferred shares may be *redeemable* or *callable* at some future date at the option of the issuing corporation. Corporations are unlikely to redeem preferred shares if conditions are financially unfavourable to the company. Such redeemable shares are classified as equity, because the issuing corporation can choose not to redeem the shares. However, preferred shares that have fixed redemption dates are classified as debt, because the issuing corporation has a future financial liability. Moreover, dividends on these shares are treated as expenses, much like the interest expense related to long-term debt.

Some preferred share issues are *retractable* at the option of the shareholder. In that case, preferred shareholders have the right to receive the redemption price from the corporation at a specific future date. Thus, retractable preferred shares represent a contractual obligation to deliver cash or another financial asset at a future date under conditions that may be unfavourable to the issuing corporation. Consequently, retractable preferred shares are classified as debt.

The notes to BCE's consolidated financial statements for 2012 provide a considerable amount of detail regarding its preferred shares.

CONVERTIBLE PREFERRED SHARES are preferred shares that are convertible to common shares at the option of the holder.

REAL-WORLD EXCERPT

BCE Inc.

ANNUAL REPORT

NOTE 23: SHARE CAPITAL

Preferred Shares

BCE Inc.'s articles of amalgamation provide for an unlimited number of First Preferred Shares and Second Preferred Shares, all without par value. The terms set out in the articles authorize BCE's directors to issue the shares in one or more series and to set the number of shares and conditions for each series.

The following table is a summary of the principal terms of BCE Inc.'s First Preferred Shares. There were no Second Preferred Shares issued and outstanding at December 31, 2012. BCE Inc.'s articles of amalgamation, as amended, describe the terms and conditions of these shares in detail.

						Number of Shares		At December 31	
Series	Annual Dividend Rate	Convertible Into	Conversion Date	Redemption Date	Redemption Price	Authorized	Issued and Outstanding	2012	2011
Q	floating	Series R	December 1, 2015	At any time	$25.50	8,000,000	—	—	—
R	4.49%	Series Q	December 1, 2015	December 1, 2015	$25.00	8,000,000	8,000,000	200	200
S	floating	Series T	November 1, 2016	At any time	$25.50	8,000,000	3,606,225	90	90
T	3.393%	Series S	November 1, 2016	November 1, 2016	$25.00	8,000,000	4,393,775	110	110
Y	floating	Series Z	December 1, 2017	At any time	$25.50	10,000,000	8,772,468	219	203
Z	3.152%	Series Y	December 1, 2017	December 1, 2017	$25.00	10,000,000	1,227,532	31	47
AA	3.45%	Series AB	September 1, 2017	September 1, 2017	$25.00	20,000,000	10,144,302	259	257
AB	floating	Series AA	September 1, 2017	At any time	$25.50	20,000,000	9,855,698	251	253
AC	4.60%	Series AD	March 1, 2013	March 1, 2013	$25.00	20,000,000	9,244,555	236	236
AD	floating	Series AC	March 1, 2013	At any time	$25.50	20,000,000	10,755,445	274	274
AE	floating	Series AF	February 1, 2015	At any time	$25.50	24,000,000	1,422,900	36	36
AF	4.541%	Series AE	February 1, 2015	February 1, 2015	$25.00	24,000,000	14,577,100	364	364
AG	4.50%	Series AH	May 1, 2016	May 1, 2016	$25.00	22,000,000	10,841,056	271	271
AH	floating	Series AG	May 1, 2016	At any time	$25.50	22,000,000	3,158,944	79	79
AI	4.15%	Series AJ	August 1, 2016	August 1, 2016	$25.00	22,000,000	10,754,990	269	269
AJ	floating	Series AI	August 1, 2016	At any time	$25.50	22,000,000	3,245,010	81	81
AK	4.15%	Series AL	December 31, 2016	December 31, 2016	$25.00	25,000,000	13,800,000	625	345
AL	floating	Series AK	December 31, 2021			25,000,000			
								3,395	3,115

Source: BCE Inc., Annual Report 2012.

BCE has also disclosed details of the specific features of each series of preferred shares. All of its outstanding preferred shares at December 31, 2012, are non-voting, except under special circumstances, when the holders are entitled to one vote per share. Holders of Series R, T, Z, AA, AC, AF, AG, AI, and AK shares are entitled to fixed cumulative quarterly dividends, which are reset every five years, whereas holders of Series S, Y, AB, AD, AE, AH, AJ and AL shares are entitled to floating adjustable cumulative monthly dividends with a floating dividend rate that is calculated every month. All of these preferred shares are convertible at the holder's option into another associated series of preferred shares on a one-for-one basis. In addition, BCE may redeem each of the preferred shares in the first series above at $25.00 per share on the applicable redemption date and every five years after that date, whereas each preferred share in the second series may be redeemed at any time at $25.50 per share.[6]

PAUSE FOR FEEDBACK

We have listed the various types of preferred shares that BCE Inc. has issued over time. Each series of preferred shares has specific characteristics. In the next section, we will discuss dividend preferred shares. Before you move on, complete the following questions to test your understanding of preferred shares.

SELF-STUDY QUIZ 12-4

Refer to the previous table showing a summary of BCE's preferred shares, and answer the following questions related to Preferred Shares, Series AC.

1. What is the total amount of dividends payable on Series AC per year?
2. What is meant by *redemption date*?
3. What is the earliest date that BCE can redeem its Series AC shares?

After you complete your answers, check them with the solutions at the end of the chapter.

Dividends on Preferred Shares

Investors who purchase preferred shares give up certain advantages that are available to investors in common shares. Generally, preferred shareholders do not have the right to vote at the annual meeting, nor do they share in increased earnings if the company becomes more profitable. To compensate these investors, preferred shares offer a dividend preference. The two most common dividend preferences are

1. Current dividend preference and
2. Cumulative dividend preference.

Current Dividend Preference   Preferred shares always carry a **current dividend preference**, which requires that the current preferred dividend be paid before any dividends are paid on the common shares. When the current dividend preference has been met and there are no other preferences, dividends can then be paid to the common shareholders.

Declared dividends must be allocated between the preferred and common shares. First, dividends are allocated to the preferred shares, and then the remainder of the total dividend is allocated to the common shares. Exhibit 12.5 illustrates the allocation of the current dividend preference under three different assumptions concerning the total amount of dividends to be paid.

Cumulative Dividend Preference   The **cumulative dividend preference** states that if all or a part of the current dividend is not paid in full, the unpaid amount, known as **dividends in arrears**, must be paid before any common dividends can be paid. Of

CURRENT DIVIDEND PREFERENCE is the feature of preferred shares that grants preferred shareholders priority for dividends over common shareholders.

CUMULATIVE DIVIDEND PREFERENCE is the feature of preferred shares that requires specified current dividends not paid in full to accumulate for every year in which they are not paid. These cumulative preferred dividends must be paid before any common dividends can be paid.

DIVIDENDS IN ARREARS are dividends on cumulative preferred shares that have not been declared in prior years.

Exhibit **12.5**
Dividends on Preferred Shares:
Current Dividend Preference Only

Preferred shares outstanding, $1.20; 2,000 shares.
Common shares outstanding, 5,000 shares.
Allocation of dividends between preferred and common shares assuming current dividend preference only:

Assumptions	Total Dividends Paid	$1.20 Preferred Shares (2,000 shares)*	Common Shares (5,000 shares)
No. 1	$ 2,000	$2,000	0
No. 2	3,000	2,400	$ 600
No. 3	18,000	2,400	15,600

*Preferred dividends = 2,000 × $1.20 = $2,400

Exhibit **12.5**
Dividends on Preferred Shares:
Current Dividend Preference Only

Exhibit **12.6**
Dividends on Preferred Shares:
Cumulative Dividend Preference

Preferred shares outstanding, $1.20; 2,000 shares.
Common shares outstanding, 5,000 shares.
Dividends are in arrears for the two preceding years.
Allocation of dividends between preferred and common shares, assuming cumulative preference:

Assumptions (dividends in arrears, 2 years)	Total Dividends Paid	$1.20 Preferred Shares (2,000 shares)*	Common Shares (5,000 shares)
No. 1	$ 2,400	$2,400	0
No. 2	7,200	7,200	0
No. 3	8,000	7,200	$ 800
No. 4	30,000	7,200	22,800

*Current dividend preference, 2,000 × $1.20 = $2,400; dividends in arrears preference, $2,400 × 2 years = $4,800; and current dividend preference plus dividends in arrears = $7,200.

course, if the preferred shares are non-cumulative, dividends cannot be in arrears; any dividends that are not declared are lost permanently by the preferred shareholders. Because preferred shareholders are not willing to accept this unfavourable feature, preferred shares are usually cumulative.

The allocation of dividends between cumulative preferred shares and common shares is illustrated in Exhibit 12.6 under four different assumptions concerning the total amount of dividends to be paid. Notice that the dividends in arrears are paid first; then the current dividend preference is paid; and, finally, the remainder is paid to the common shareholders.

In 2012, BCE declared a total amount of $1,858 million in dividends on preferred shares, as disclosed in Exhibit 12.2.

MEASURING AND REPORTING CHANGES IN SHAREHOLDERS' EQUITY

LO8

Measure and report changes in shareholders' equity.

Exhibit 12.2 discloses the balances of the various components of BCE's shareholders' equity at January 1, 2012, and December 31, 2012, as well as the changes that occurred to each component over these two years. While we provided explanations for many changes that occurred in 2012, two components of shareholders' equity deserve further discussion: retained earnings and accumulated other comprehensive income (loss).

Retained Earnings

Retained earnings represent net earnings less dividends that have been declared since the first day of the company's operations. Most companies report retained earnings on their statements of financial position. In BCE's case, its retained earnings turned into a deficit in 2003 after a massive write-off of the value of BCE's investments in other companies. Its deficit of $5,830 million on December 31, 2003, was reduced each year and reached $1,299 million by December 31, 2009. However, the transition from using Canadian generally accepted accounting principles to IFRS caused a reduction in the carrying amounts of BCE's assets and an increase in its liabilities, with a net decrease in shareholders' equity that increased the deficit from $1,299 million to $7,508 million as at January 1, 2010, but it was later reduced to $5,682 million by December 31, 2012. The gradual reduction of this deficit will allow BCE to report retained earnings in future years.

Under rare circumstances, you may see a statement that includes an adjustment to the beginning balance of retained earnings resulting from a correction of a material accounting error that occurred in the financial statements of a prior period.

If an accounting error from a previous period is corrected by making an adjustment to the current statement of earnings, net earnings for the current period will be improperly measured. To avoid this problem, the financial statements of the prior period in which the error occurred are restated to reflect the correction of the error. The nature of the prior-period error should be disclosed along with the effect of the correction on each financial statement item that is affected by the error. To the extent that prior-period errors affect specific statement of earnings items, retained earnings of the prior period will also be affected.

Adjustments to the financial statements of prior periods should also be made if the entity changes its accounting policies, such as a change from the FIFO method of inventory valuation to the weighted-average cost method, or when companies are required to adopt new accounting standards. In these cases, the entity adjusts the opening balance of each affected component of equity, including retained earnings.

A QUESTION OF ACCOUNTABILITY

PROPER ACCOUNTING FOR PRIOR-PERIOD ERRORS

Adjustments related to errors made in prior periods should not affect the current-period earnings, particularly when compensation of key management personnel is tied to measures of profitability, such as net earnings. In the case of Nortel, which was one of the top global makers of telecommunications equipment in North America, provisions were made for such items as inventory write-downs and contract disputes that lacked proper justification. These provisions, which reflected overstated expenses, were reversed in a subsequent accounting period. The excessive amount of the reversed provisions turned the net loss of one accounting period into a net earnings figure that was sufficiently large to trigger payment of bonuses to key management personnel. This inaccurate accounting for the effect of prior errors was subsequently discovered, and key management personnel were accused of management fraud. The reversal of the erroneous provisions should have been reported as an adjustment to the earnings of prior periods and should not have affected the current period's earnings. Had the accounting been done properly, bonuses would not have been paid to key management personnel and accusations of management fraud could have been avoided.

Accumulated Other Comprehensive Income (Loss)

IFRS require Canadian publicly accountable enterprises to report accumulated other comprehensive income (loss). As explained in Chapter 6, this equity item reflects the financial effect of events that cause changes in shareholders' equity, other than investments by shareholders or distributions to shareholders. Such changes in equity result from unrealized gains or losses related to the valuation of specific assets and liabilities at fair value. For BCE, these changes, shown in Exhibit 12.2, include such items as unrealized gains or losses on available-for-sale assets, unrealized gains or losses on derivatives transactions that are designated as cash flow hedges, and unrealized gains or losses on translating the financial statements of companies that have operations in other countries but are controlled by the Canadian reporting entity. The unrealized gains and losses resulting from these changes are not reported on the statement of earnings because they have not been realized yet. Measurement of the unrealized gains and losses related to these and similar items is fairly complex and is covered in intermediate and advanced accounting courses.

RESTRICTIONS ON THE PAYMENT OF DIVIDENDS

FINANCIAL
ANALYSIS

Two common constraints on the ability of a corporation to pay dividends are the existence of debt covenants and preferred stock dividends in arrears. For additional security, some creditors include a debt covenant that limits the amount of dividends a corporation can pay. These debt covenants often include a limit on borrowing and require a minimum balance of cash or working capital. If debt covenants are violated, the creditor can demand immediate repayment of the debt. The disclosure principle requires disclosure of debt covenants, typically in a separate note to the financial statements.

The existence of dividends in arrears on preferred shares can also limit a company's ability to pay dividends to its common shareholders and can affect a company's future cash flows. Dividends are never an actual liability until the board of directors declares them. Hence, dividends in arrears are not reported on the statement of financial position but are disclosed in the notes to the statements. The following note from Lone Star Industries is typical if a company has dividends in arrears:

> The total of dividends in arrears on the $13.50 preferred shares at the end of the year was $11,670,000. The aggregate amount of such dividends must be paid before any dividends are paid on common shares.

REAL-WORLD EXCERPT

Lone Star Industries

ANNUAL REPORT

Analysts are particularly interested in information concerning these restrictions because of the impact they have on the company's dividend policy.

FINANCING ACTIVITIES

FOCUS ON
CASH FLOWS

Transactions involving share capital have a direct impact on the capital structure of a business. Because of the importance of these transactions, they are reported in a separate section of the statement called "cash flows from financing activities." Examples of cash flows associated with share capital are included in the statements of cash flows for BCE shown in Exhibit 12.7. Remember that shares issued in exchange for assets do not impact cash flow and are disclosed in a note to the statement of cash flows.

LO⁹

Discuss the impact of share capital transactions on cash flows.

EFFECT ON STATEMENT OF CASH FLOWS

IN GENERAL → Cash received from owners is reported as an inflow. Cash paid to owners is reported as an outflow. Examples are shown in the following table:

Financing activities	Effect on Cash Flows
Issuance of shares	+
Repurchase of shares	−
Payment of cash dividends	−

FOCUS COMPANY ANALYSIS → BCE has issued both preferred and common shares during 2012. The company repurchased common shares for cancellation during 2012, and paid dividends on both common and preferred shares during the year.

SELECTED FOCUS COMPANY COMPARISONS: CASH FLOWS FROM FINANCING ACTIVITIES—2012

(in millions)

Sun-Rype	−$12.9
WestJet Airlines Ltd.	−$288.1
Thomson Reuters	−US$1,551

Exhibit **12.7**

Excerpt from Statements of Cash Flows for BCE Inc.

REAL-WORLD EXCERPT

BCE Inc.

ANNUAL REPORT

CONSOLIDATED STATEMENTS OF CASH FLOWS
For the Years Ended December 31

(in $ millions)	Note	2012	2011
Cash flows used in financing activities			
(Decrease) increase in notes payable and bank advances		377	30
Reduction in securitized trade receivables		(15)	(318)
Issue of long-term debt		1,055	2,314
Repayment of long-term debt		(946)	(2,350)
Issue of common shares		39	152
Issue of preferred shares	23	280	345
Issue of equity securities by subsidiaries to non-controlling interest		11	403
Repurchase of common shares	23	(107)	(143)
Cash dividends paid on common shares		(1,683)	(1,520)
Cash dividends paid on preferred shares		(133)	(118)
Cash dividends/distributions paid by subsidiaries to non-controlling interest		(340)	(315)
Other financing activities		(45)	(61)
Cash flows used in financing activities		(1,507)	(1,581)

Source: BCE Inc., Annual Report 2012.

ACCOUNTING AND REPORTING FOR UNINCORPORATED BUSINESSES

In this book, we emphasize the corporate form of business because it plays a dominant role in our economy. In fact, there are three forms of business organizations: corporations, sole proprietorships, and partnerships. As we have seen in this chapter, a corporation is a legal entity, separate and distinct from its owners. It can enter into contracts in its own name, it can be sued, and it is taxed as a separate entity. A *sole proprietorship* is an unincorporated business owned by one individual. If you started a lawn care business in the summer by yourself, it would be a sole proprietorship. It is not necessary to file any legal papers to create a proprietorship. A *partnership* is an unincorporated business owned by two or more people. Again, it is not necessary to file legal papers to create a partnership, but it is certainly a good idea to have a lawyer draw up a contract between the partners.

Neither partnerships nor proprietorships are separate legal entities. As a result, owners may be directly sued and are individually taxed on the earnings of the business.

The fundamentals of accounting and reporting for unincorporated businesses are the same as for a corporation, except for shareholders' equity. Typical account structures for the three forms of business organizations are outlined in Exhibit 12.8.

Accounting for sole proprietorships and partnerships is discussed in Appendix 12A.

Exhibit **12.8**

Comparative Account Structure among Types of Business Entities

Typical Account Structure

Corporation (Shareholders' Equity)	Sole Proprietorship (Owner's Equity)	Partnership (Partners' Equity)
Share capital, contributed surplus	Doe, capital	Able, capital; Baker, capital
Retained earnings	Not used	Not used
Dividends paid	Doe, drawings	Able, drawings; Baker, drawings
Revenues, expenses, gains, and losses	Same	Same
Assets and liabilities	Same	Same

ACCOUNTING STANDARDS FOR PRIVATE ENTERPRISES

Canadian private enterprises do not issue shares to the public. To finance their growth, most private enterprises turn to banks and other creditors as sources of financing. Because the external users of financial statements prepared by private enterprises are primarily creditors, the Canadian accounting standards for private enterprises have been simplified relative to IFRS. The main differences in accounting standards related to the equity section of the statement of financial position are summarized below:

Financial Reporting Issue	IFRS	ASPE
Reporting of changes in equity	Canadian publicly accountable enterprises are required to prepare a statement of changes in equity that includes the changes in all equity accounts.	Canadian private enterprises prepare a statement of retained earnings and disclose all other changes in equity in the notes to their financial statements.
Measurement of share-based compensation expense	Publicly accountable enterprises must use specific valuation models to measure share-based compensation expense.	Canadian private enterprises are permitted to use a simplified valuation model to measure the value of share-based compensation because of the difficulty in determining a fair value for shares that have no public market.
Reporting of EPS	Publicly accountable enterprises must report EPS on the statement of earnings.	Canadian private enterprises are not required to report EPS because external users do not believe this information is useful. Users, in particular creditors, are most interested in cash flows from operating activities.

DEMONSTRATION CASE

This case focuses on the organization and operations for the first year of Mera Corporation, which was organized on January 2, 2014. The laws specify that the legal capital for no par value shares is the full amount of the shares. The corporation was organized by 10 local entrepreneurs for the purpose of operating a business to sell various supplies to hotels. The charter authorized the following share capital:

- Common shares, no par value, unlimited number of shares.
- Preferred shares, 5 percent, $25 par value, 10,000 shares (cumulative, non-convertible, and non-voting; liquidation value, $26).

The following summarized transactions, selected from 2014, were completed during the months indicated:

a. January 5   Sold a total of 7,500 shares of no par value common shares to the 10 entrepreneurs for cash at $52 per share. Credit the common shares account for the total issue amount.

b. February 1   Sold 7,560 preferred shares at $25 per share; cash collected in full.

c. March 10   Purchased land for a store site and made full payment by issuing 400 preferred shares. Early construction of the store is planned. Debit Land (store site). The preferred share is selling at $25 per share.

d. April 15   Paid $2,000 cash for organization costs. Debit the intangible asset account Organization Costs.

e. May 25   Issued 40 preferred shares to A. B. Cain in full payment of legal services rendered in connection with organization of the corporation. Assume that the preferred share is selling regularly at $25 per share. Debit organization costs.

f. June 10   Sold 500 no par value common shares for cash to C. B. Abel at $54 per share.

g. November 30   The company's board of directors declared the annual dividends on the preferred shares, and a dividend of $0.50 per common share. The dividends are payable on December 20 to shareholders of record at December 15.

h. December 20   Paid the declared dividends on preferred and common shares.

i. December 31   Purchased equipment for $600,000; paid cash. No depreciation expense should be recorded in 2014.

j. December 31   Borrowed $20,000 cash from the City Bank on a one-year, interest-bearing note. Interest is payable at a 12 percent rate at maturity.

k. December 31   Calculated the following for the year: gross revenues, $129,300; expenses, $98,000, including corporation income tax but excluding amortization of organization costs. Assume that these summarized revenue and expense transactions involved cash. Because the equipment and the bank loan transactions were on December 31, no related adjusting entries at the end of 2014 are needed.

l. December 31   Decided that a reasonable amortization period for organization costs, starting as of January 1, 2014, is 10 years. This intangible asset must be amortized to expense.

Required:

1. Prepare appropriate journal entries, with a brief explanation, for each of these transactions.

2. Prepare the required adjusting entry for 2014 to amortize organization costs.

3. Prepare appropriate closing entries at December 31, 2014.

4. Prepare a statement of financial position for Mera Corporation at December 31, 2014. Emphasize full disclosure of shareholders' equity.

5. Assume that, instead of issuing common shares in January for $390,000, the company issued shares for $260,000 and borrowed an amount of $130,000 from its bank, signing a note, payable on December 31, 2016. Interest on the note is 10 percent, payable on December 31 of each year. Is borrowing from the bank more beneficial to the common shareholders, compared with issuing additional common shares? Explain. For the purpose of this analysis, use an income tax rate of 40 percent.

We strongly recommend that you prepare your own answers to these requirements, and then check your answers with the following solution.

SUGGESTED **SOLUTION**

1. Journal entries:

a. January 5   Cash (A)   390,000
                 Common shares (SE)   390,000
                 Sale of no par value common shares
                 ($52 × 7,500 shares = $390,000).

b. February 1   Cash (A)   189,000
                 Preferred shares, 5% (SE)   189,000
                 Sale of preferred shares ($25 × 7,560 shares = $189,000).

c. March 10   Land (A)   10,000
                 Preferred shares, 5% (SE)   10,000
                 Purchased land for future store site; paid in full by issuance
                 of 400 preferred shares ($25 × 400 shares = $10,000).

d. April 15   Organization costs (A)   2,000
                 Cash (A)   2,000
                 Paid organization costs.

e. May 25   Organization costs (A)   1,000
                 Preferred shares 5% (SE)   1,000
                 Organization costs (legal services) paid by issuance of
                 40 preferred shares. The implied market value is $25 × 40
                 shares = $1,000.

f. June 10   Cash (A)   27,000
                 Common shares (500 shares) (SE)   27,000
                 Sold 500 no par value common shares ($54 × 500 shares = $27,000).

g. November 30   Dividends declared—Preferred (SE) 10,000
                  Dividends declared—Common (SE) 4,000
                      Dividends payable—Preferred (L) 10,000
                      Dividends payable—Common (L) 4,000
                  Declaration of the annual dividend on preferred shares
                  (8,000 × $25 × 0.05) and a dividend of $0.50 per common share.

h. December 20   Dividends payable—Preferred (L) 10,000
                  Dividends payable—Common (L) 4,000
                      Cash (A) 14,000
                  Payment of the declared dividends.

i. December 31   Equipment (A) 600,000
                      Cash (A) 600,000
                  Purchased equipment.

j. December 31   Cash (A) 20,000
                      Note payable (L) 20,000
                  Borrowed cash and signed a one-year, 12 percent interest-bearing note.

k. December 31   Cash (A) 129,300
                      Revenues (E) 129,300
                  Expenses (E) 98,000
                      Cash (A) 98,000
                  To record summarized revenues and expenses.

2. December 31   Expenses (E) 300
                      Organization costs (A) 300
                  Adjusting entry to amortize organization costs for one year
                  [($2,000 + $1,000) ÷ 10 years = $300].

3. Closing entries:
   December 31   Revenues (R) 129,300
                      Income summary 129,300
                  Income summary 98,300
                      Expenses ($98,000 + $300) (E) 98,300
                  Income summary 31,000
                      Retained earnings (SE) 31,000

4. Statement of Financial Position:

MERA CORPORATION
Statement of Financial Position at December 31, 2014

Assets

Current assets

Cash		$ 41,300

Tangible assets

Land	$ 10,000	
Equipment (no depreciation assumed in the problem)	600,000	610,000

Intangible assets

Organization costs (cost, $3,000 less amortization, $300)		2,700
Total assets		$654,000

Liabilities

Current liabilities

Note payable, 12%		$ 20,000

Shareholders' Equity

Contributed capital

Preferred shares, 5% (par value $25; authorized 10,000 shares, issued and outstanding 8,000 shares)	$200,000	
Common shares (no par value; authorized unlimited, issued, and outstanding 8,000 shares)	417,000	
Total contributed capital	617,000	
Retained earnings	17,000	
Total shareholders' equity		634,000
Total liabilities and shareholders' equity		$654,000

5. Interest on the loan equals $13,000 ($130,000 × 10%) for 2014. This expense will reduce the income tax expense by $5,200 ($13,000 × 40%). The net earnings of $31,000 will then be reduced by $7,800 ($13,000 − $5,200) for a revised net earnings of $23,200. Net earnings available to common shareholders equals $13,200 after deducting $10,000 of dividends on preferred shares. The return on common shareholders' equity therefore equals 4.7 percent ($13,200 ÷ $278,100, which is the average common shareholders' equity = [$260,000 + ($260,000 + $270,000 + $13,200 − $4,000)]/2).

Without the $130,000 loan, the return on common shareholders' equity is 5.1 percent ([$31,000 − $10,000]/[($390,000 + $434,000*)/2]). This shows that borrowing an amount of $130,000 at 10 percent is not preferable to issuing additional common shares in this particular case.

*$390,000 + $27,000 + $31,000 − $14,000

APPENDIX 12A: ACCOUNTING FOR OWNERS' EQUITY FOR SOLE PROPRIETORSHIPS AND PARTNERSHIPS

Proprietorships and partnerships are private enterprises that do not issue shares for sale to the public. They normally report their financial information in accordance with the accounting standards for private enterprises. These standards are less complicated than the IFRS that publicly accountable enterprises must use. For example, private enterprises are not required to report other comprehensive income.

The use of accounting standards for private enterprises does not mean, however, that the standards are less rigorous than those used by publicly accountable enterprises. This simplified set of standards makes the preparation and audit of financial statements affordable for smaller business entities. All of the principles, such as economic substance over form and the excess of benefit over cost, guided the production of these standards.

Owner's Equity for a Sole Proprietorship

A sole proprietorship is an unincorporated business owned by one person. Only two owner's equity accounts are needed: a capital account for the proprietor (J. Doe, capital) and a drawing (or withdrawal) account for the proprietor (J. Doe, drawings).

The capital account of a sole proprietorship serves two purposes: to record investments by the owner and to accumulate periodic net earnings or loss. The drawing account is used to record the owner's withdrawals of cash or other assets from the business. The drawing account is closed to the capital account at the end of each accounting period. The capital account reflects the cumulative total of all investments by the owner, plus all earnings of the entity, less all withdrawals of resources from the entity by the owner.

In most respects, the accounting for a sole proprietorship is the same as for a corporation. Exhibit 12.9 presents the recording of selected transactions and the owner's equity section of the statement of financial position of Doe Retail Store to illustrate the accounting for owner's equity for a sole proprietorship.

Exhibit **12.9**	**Selected Transactions during 2014**
Accounting for Owner's Equity for a Sole Proprietorship	**January 1, 2014**

J. Doe started a retail store by investing $150,000 of personal savings. The journal entry for the business is as follows:

Cash (A) 150,000
   J. Doe, capital (OE) 150,000

Assets		=	**Liabilities**	+	**Owner's Equity**	
Cash	+150,000				J. Doe, capital	+150,000

During 2014

Exhibit **12.9**

(Continued)

Each month during the year, Doe withdrew $1,000 cash from the business for personal living expenses. Accordingly, the following journal entry was made each month:

| J. Doe, drawings (OE) .... | 1,000 | |
| Cash (A) .... | | 1,000 |

Assets	=	Liabilities	+	Owner's Equity	
Cash	−1,000			J. Doe, drawings	−1,000

Note: At December 31, 2014, after the last withdrawal, the drawings account will reflect a debit balance of $12,000.

December 31, 2014

The store's operations for the year resulted in revenues of $128,000 and expenses of $110,000. The revenue and expense accounts are closed to the capital account at the end of the year. The closing entry follows:

Individual revenue accounts (R)	128,000	
Individual expense accounts (E)		110,000
J. Doe, capital (OE)		18,000

Assets	=	Liabilities	+	Owner's Equity	
				Revenues	−128,000
				Expenses	+110,000
				J. Doe, capital	+18,000

December 31, 2014

The journal entry required to close the drawings account follows:

| J. Doe, capital (OE) .... | 12,000 | |
| J. Doe, drawings (OE) .... | | 12,000 |

Assets	=	Liabilities	+	Owner's Equity	
				J. Doe, capital	−12,000
				J. Doe, drawings	+12,000

Statement of Financial Position, December 31, 2014 (partial)

Owner's equity	
J. Doe, capital, January 1, 2014	$150,000
Add: Net earnings for 2014	18,000
Total	168,000
Deduct: Withdrawals for 2014	(12,000)
J. Doe, capital, December 31, 2014	$156,000

A sole proprietorship does not pay income taxes. Therefore, its financial statements do not reflect income tax expense or income taxes payable. Instead, the net earnings of a sole proprietorship are taxed when it is included on the owner's personal income tax return. Because an employer/employee contractual relationship cannot exist with only one party involved, a "salary" to the owner is not recognized as an expense of a sole proprietorship. The owner's salary is accounted for as a distribution of net earnings (i.e., a withdrawal).

Owners' Equity for a Partnership

Small businesses and professionals such as accountants, doctors, and lawyers may use the partnership form of business. It is formed by two or more persons reaching mutual agreement about the terms of the partnership. The law does not require an application for a charter as it does in the case of a corporation. Instead, the agreement between the partners constitutes a legally enforceable partnership contract. The agreement should specify matters such as division of net earnings, management responsibilities, transfer or sale of partnership interests, disposition of assets upon liquidation, and procedures to be followed in case of the death of a partner. If the partnership agreement does not specify these matters, the applicable provincial laws are binding.

The primary advantages of a partnership are (1) ease of formation, (2) complete control by the partners, and (3) lack of income taxes on the business itself. The primary disadvantage is the unlimited liability of each partner for the partnership's liabilities. If the partnership does not have sufficient assets to satisfy outstanding debt, its creditors can seize the partners' personal assets.

As with a sole proprietorship, accounting for transactions undertaken by a partnership follows the same underlying fundamentals as any other form of business organization, except for those entries that directly affect owners' equity.

Accounting for partners' equity follows the same pattern as illustrated earlier for a sole proprietorship, except that separate partner capital and drawings accounts must be established for each partner. Investments by each partner are credited to the partner's capital account, and withdrawals from the partnership by each partner are debited to the respective drawings accounts. The net earnings for a partnership are divided between the partners in the profit ratio specified in the partnership agreement, and credited to each partner's account. The respective drawings accounts are closed to the partner capital accounts. After the closing process, each partner's capital account reflects the cumulative total of all investments of that individual partner, plus the partner's share of all partnership earnings, less all the partner's withdrawals.

Exhibit 12.10 presents selected journal entries and partial financial statements for AB Partnership to illustrate the accounting for the distribution of net earnings and partners' equity.

Exhibit **12.10**	**Selected Transactions during 2014**
Accounting for Partners' Equity	**January 1, 2014**

A. Able and B. Baker organized AB Partnership on this date. Able contributed $60,000 and Baker $40,000 cash to the partnership and agreed to divide profit (and loss) 60% and 40%, respectively. The journal entry for the business to record the investment follows:

Cash (A)	100,000	
A. Able, capital (OE)		60,000
B. Baker, capital (OE)		40,000

Assets		=	**Liabilities**	+	**Owner's Equity**	
Cash	+100,000				A. Able, capital	+60,000
					B. Baker, capital	+40,000

During 2014

The partners agreed that Able would withdraw $1,000 and Baker $650 per month in cash. Accordingly, the following journal entry for the withdrawals was made each month:

A. Able, drawings (OE)	1,000	
B. Baker, drawings (OE)	650	
Cash (A)		1,650

Assets		=	**Liabilities**	+	**Owner's Equity**	
Cash	−1,650				A. Able, drawings	−1,000
					B. Baker, drawings	−650

December 31, 2014

Exhibit **12.10**

(continued)

Assume that the normal closing entries for the revenue ($150,000) and expense accounts ($120,000) resulted in net earnings of $30,000 that was distributed between the two partners. The closing entry is as follows:

Individual revenue accounts (R) 150,000	
Individual expense accounts (E)	120,000
A. Able, capital (OE)	18,000
B. Baker, capital (OE)	12,000

Assets	=	Liabilities	+	Owner's Equity	
				Revenues	−150,000
				Expenses	+120,000
				A. Able, capital	+18,000
				B. Baker, capital	+12,000

Net earnings are divided as follows:

A. Able, $30,000 × 60%	$18,000
B. Baker, $30,000 × 40%	12,000
Total	$30,000

December 31, 2014

The journal entry required to close the drawings accounts follows:

A. Able, capital (OE) 12,000	
B. Baker, capital (OE) 7,800	
A. Able, drawings (OE)	12,000
B. Baker, drawings (OE)	7,800

Assets	=	Liabilities	+	Owner's Equity	
				A. Able, capital	−12,000
				B. Baker, capital	−7,800
				A. Able, drawings	+12,000
				B. Baker, drawings	+7,800

A separate statement of partners' capital, similar to the following, is customarily prepared to supplement the statement of financial position:

AB PARTNERSHIP
Statement of Partners' Capital
For the Year Ended December 31, 2014

	A. Able	B. Baker	Total
Investment, January 1, 2014	$60,000	$40,000	$100,000
Add: Additional investments during the year	-0-	-0-	-0-
Net earnings for the year	18,000	12,000	30,000
Totals	78,000	52,000	130,000
Deduct: Drawings during the year	(12,000)	(7,800)	(19,800)
Partners' equity, December 31, 2014	$66,000	$44,200	$110,200

The financial statements of a partnership follow the same format as those for a corporation, except that (1) the statement of earnings includes an additional section titled distribution of net earnings, (2) the partners' equity section of the statement of financial position is detailed for each partner, (3) a partnership has no income tax expense because partnerships do not pay income tax (each partner must report his or her share of the partnership net earnings on his or her individual tax return), and (4) salaries paid to partners are not recorded as expense but are treated as a distribution of net earnings (withdrawals).

CHAPTER **TAKE-AWAYS**

1. **Explain the role of share capital in the capital structure of a corporation.**

   The law recognizes corporations as separate legal entities. Owners invest in a corporation and receive shares that can be traded on established stock exchanges. Shares provide a number of rights, including the right to receive dividends.

2. **Analyze the earnings per share ratio.**

   The EPS ratio facilitates the comparison of a company's earnings over time or with other companies' earnings at a single point in time. By expressing earnings on a per share basis, differences in the size of companies become less important.

3. **Describe the characteristics of common shares, and analyze transactions affecting common shares.**

   A common share is the basic voting share issued by a corporation. Usually it has no par value, but par value shares can also be issued. Preferred shares are issued by some corporations. These shares contain some special rights and may appeal to certain investors.

   A number of key transactions involve share capital: (1) initial sale of shares, (2) cash dividends, (3) stock dividends and stock splits, and (4) repurchase of shares. Each is illustrated in this chapter.

4. **Discuss dividends, and analyze related transactions.**

   The return associated with an investment in shares comes from two sources: appreciation of share price and dividends. Dividends are recorded as a liability when they are declared by the board of directors (i.e., on the date of declaration). The liability is satisfied when the dividends are paid (i.e., on the date of payment).

5. **Analyze the dividend yield ratio.**

   The dividend yield ratio measures the percentage of return on investment from dividends. For most companies, the return associated with dividends is very small.

6. **Discuss the purpose of stock dividends, stock splits, and report transactions.**

   Stock dividends are distributions of a company's shares to existing shareholders on a pro rata basis. The transaction involves transferring an additional amount into the common shares account from the retained earnings account. A stock split also involves the distribution of additional shares to shareholders, but no additional amount is transferred into the common shares account from the retained earnings account.

7. **Describe the characteristics of preferred shares, and analyze transactions affecting preferred shares.**

   Preferred shares provide investors certain advantages, including dividend preferences and a preference on asset distributions in the event the corporation is liquidated.

8. **Measure and report changes in shareholders' equity.**

   The shareholders' equity section of the statement of financial position is affected by many changes that occur over time. These changes are reported in a separate statement of changes in equity that discloses a summary of the effects of transactions and events that affected the various components of equity, including share capital, contributed surplus, retained earnings, and accumulated other comprehensive income (loss).

9. **Discuss the impact of share capital transactions on cash flows.**

   Both inflows (e.g., issuance of share capital) and outflows (e.g., repurchase of shares) are reported in the financing activities section of the statement of cash flows. The payment of dividends is reported as an outflow in this section.

Throughout the preceding chapters, we emphasized the conceptual basis of accounting. An understanding of the rationale underlying accounting is important for both preparers and users of financial statements. In Chapter 13, we bring together our discussion of the major users of financial statements and how they analyze and use them. We discuss and illustrate many widely used analytical techniques discussed in earlier chapters, as well as additional techniques. As you study Chapter 13, you will see that an understanding of accounting rules and concepts is essential for effective analysis of financial statements.

KEY **RATIOS**

The earnings per share ratio states the net earnings of a corporation on a per common share basis. The ratio is computed as follows:

$$\text{Earnings per Share} = \frac{\text{Net Earnings Available to Common Shareholders}}{\text{Average Number of Common Shares Outstanding}}$$

The dividend yield ratio measures the dividend return on the current share price. The ratio is computed as follows:

$$\text{Dividend Yield Ratio} = \frac{\text{Dividends per Share}}{\text{Market Price per Share}}$$

FINDING **FINANCIAL INFORMATION**

STATEMENT OF FINANCIAL POSITION

Under Current Liabilities
Dividends, once declared by the board of directors, are reported as a liability (usually current).

Under Non-current Liabilities
Transactions involving share capital do not usually generate non-current liabilities.

Under Shareholders' Equity
Typical accounts include
Preferred shares
Common shares
Contributed surplus
Retained earnings
Accumulated other comprehensive income (loss)

STATEMENT OF EARNINGS

Share capital is never shown on the statement of earnings. Dividends are not an expense. They are a distribution of net earnings and are, therefore, not reported on the statement of earnings.

STATEMENT OF CASH FLOWS

Under Financing Activities
+ Cash inflows from initial sale of shares
− Cash outflows for dividends
− Cash outflows for repurchase of shares

STATEMENT OF CHANGES IN SHAREHOLDERS' EQUITY

This statement reports detailed information concerning shareholders' equity, including
(1) amounts in each equity account,
(2) number of shares outstanding, and
(3) impact of transactions such as declaration of dividends and repurchase of shares.

NOTES

Under Summary of Significant Accounting Policies
Usually, very little information concerning share capital is provided in this summary.

Under a Separate Note
Most companies report information about their stock option plans and information about major transactions such as stock dividends. A historical summary of dividends paid per share is typically provided.

GLOSSARY

Review key terms and definitions on *Connect*.

QUESTIONS

1. Define *corporation* and identify its primary advantages.
2. What is the charter of a corporation?
3. Explain each of the following terms: (*a*) *authorized shares*, (*b*) *issued shares*, and (*c*) *outstanding shares*.

4. Name three rights of shareholders. Which of these is most important in your mind? Why?
5. Differentiate between common shares and preferred shares.
6. Explain the distinction between par value shares and no par value shares.
7. What are the usual characteristics of preferred shares?
8. What are the two basic sources of shareholders' equity? Explain each.
9. Shareholders' equity is accounted for by source. What does *source* mean?
10. What are the two basic requirements to support the declaration of a cash dividend? What are the effects of a cash dividend on assets and shareholders' equity?
11. Differentiate between cumulative and non-cumulative preferred shares.
12. Define *stock dividend*. How does it differ from a cash dividend?
13. What are the primary purposes of issuing a stock dividend?
14. Identify and explain the three important dates with respect to dividends.
15. Define *retained earnings*. What are the primary components of retained earnings at the end of each period?
16. Define *prior-period errors*. How are they reported?
17. Define *accumulated other comprehensive income (loss)*. Why is it a separate component of shareholders' equity?
18. Your parents have just retired and have asked you for some financial advice. They have decided to invest $100,000 in a company very similar to BCE Inc. The company has issued both common and preferred shares. What factors would you consider in giving them advice? Which type of shares would you recommend?

connect EXERCISES

LO1, 3, 7   **E12–1**   **Determining the Effects of the Issuance of Common and Preferred Shares**

Kelly Incorporated was issued a charter on January 15, 2014, that authorized the following share capital:

    Common shares, no par value, 100,000 shares.

    Preferred shares, $1.50, no par value, 5,000 shares. (*Note:* $1.50 is the dividend rate.)

During 2014, the following selected transactions occurred:

a. Issued 20,000 common shares at $18 cash per share.

b. Issued 3,000 preferred shares at $25 cash per share.

At the end of 2014, the company's net earnings equalled $40,000.

Required:

1. Prepare the shareholders' equity section of the statement of financial position at December 31, 2014.
2. Assume that you are a common shareholder. If Kelly needed additional capital, would you prefer to have it issue additional common or preferred shares? Explain.

LO2, 8   **E12–2**   **Reporting Shareholders' Equity**

The financial statements of Planet Media Inc. included the following selected information at December 31, 2015:

Common shares	$1,600,000
Retained earnings	900,000
Net earnings	1,000,000
Dividends declared	800,000

The common shares were sold at $20 per share.

Required:

1. What was the amount of retained earnings at the beginning of 2015?
2. Compute EPS.
3. Prepare the shareholders' equity section of the company's statement of financial position at December 31, 2015.

E12–3 Reporting Shareholders' Equity, and Determining Dividend Policy　　　　　■ LO1, 3
Sampson Corporation was organized in 2014 to operate a financial consulting business. The charter authorized the issue of 12,000 common shares. During the first year, the following selected transactions were completed:

a. Issued 6,000 common shares for cash at $22 per share.

b. Issued 600 common shares for a piece of land to be used for a facilities site; construction began immediately. Assume that the market price per share was $22 on the date of issuance. Debit the land account.

c. Issued 1,000 common shares for cash at $23 per share.

d. At year-end, the statement of earnings showed a loss of $7,000. Because a loss was incurred, no income tax expense was recorded.

Required:

1. Prepare the journal entry required for each of these transactions.
2. Prepare the shareholders' equity section as it should be reported on the statement of financial position at year-end, December 31, 2014.
3. Can Sampson pay dividends at year-end? Explain.

E12–4 Determining the Effects of Transactions on Shareholders' Equity　　　　　■ LO1, 3, 7
Quick Fix-it Corporation was organized in January 2015 to operate several car repair businesses in a large metropolitan area. The charter issued by the government authorized the following no par value shares:

    Common shares, 200,000 shares

    Preferred shares, 50,000 shares

During January and February 2015, the following transactions were completed:

a. Collected $80,000 cash from shareholders and issued 4,000 common shares.

b. Issued 2,000 preferred shares at $25 per share; collected the cash.

c. Issued 500 common shares to a new investor at $25 per share; collected the cash.

The company's operations resulted in net earnings of $40,000 for 2015. The board of directors declared cash dividends of $25,000 that were paid in December 2015. The preferred shares have a dividend rate of $1 per share.

Required:

1. Prepare the shareholders' equity section of the statement of financial position at December 31, 2015.
2. Why would an investor prefer to buy a preferred share rather than a common share?
3. Is it ethical to sell shares to outsiders at a higher price than the amount paid by the organizers?

E12–5 Recording Shareholders' Equity Transactions, Including Non-cash Consideration　　■ LO1, 3
Teacher Corporation obtained a charter at the start of 2014 that authorized 50,000 no par value common shares and 40,000, $1, no par value preferred shares. The corporation was organized by four individuals who "reserved" 51 percent of the common shares for themselves. The remaining shares were to be sold to other individuals at $50 per share on a cash basis. During 2014, the following selected transactions occurred:

a. Collected $25 per share cash from three of the organizers and received two adjoining lots of land from the fourth organizer. Issued 3,000 common shares to each of the four organizers and received title to the land.

b. Issued 6,000 common shares to an investor at $50 cash per share.

c. Issued 8,000 preferred shares at $25 cash per share.

d. At the end of 2014, the accounts reflected net earnings of $42,000.

Required:

1. Prepare the journal entries to record each of these transactions.
2. Write a brief memo to explain the basis that you used to determine the cost of the land.
3. Is it ethical to sell shares to outsiders at a higher price than the amount paid by the organizers?

LO1, 4, 5   **E12–6**   **Determining the Ending Balance of Retained Earnings, and Evaluating Dividend Policy**

The following account balances were selected from the records of Blake Corporation at December 31, 2014, after all adjusting entries were completed:

Common shares (no par value; authorized 100,000 shares, issued 34,000 shares)	$680,000
Contributed surplus	163,000
Dividends declared in 2014	18,000
Retained earnings, January 1, 2014	75,000
Correction of prior-period accounting error (a debit, net of income tax)	8,000
Income summary for 2014 (credit balance)	28,000

The stock price was $22.63 per share on that date.

Required:

1. Identify the amounts that would be reported in the retained earnings column of the statement of changes in equity for 2014.
2. Prepare the shareholders' equity section of the statement of financial position at December 31, 2014.
3. Compute and evaluate the dividend yield ratio.

LO4, 6   **E12–7**   **Analyzing the Impact of Dividend Policy**

McDonald and Associates is a small manufacturer of electronic connections for local area networks. Consider three independent situations.

Case 1: McDonald increases its cash dividends by 50 percent, but no other changes occur in the company's operations.

Case 2: The company's net earnings and cash flows increase by 50 percent, but this does not change its dividends.

Case 3: McDonald issues a 50 percent stock dividend, but no other changes occur.

Required:

1. How do you think each situation would affect the company's stock price?
2. If the company changed its accounting policies and reported higher net earnings, would the change have an impact on the stock price?

LO4   **E12–8**   **Computing Dividends on Preferred Shares, and Analyzing Differences**

The records of Hoffman Company reflected the following balances in the shareholders' equity accounts at December 31, 2014:

Common shares, no par value, 40,000 shares outstanding	$800,000
Preferred shares, $2, no par value, 6,000 shares outstanding	150,000
Retained earnings	235,000

On September 1, 2015, the board of directors was considering the distribution of a $62,000 cash dividend. No dividends were paid during 2013 and 2014. You have been asked to determine dividend amounts under two independent assumptions (show computations):

a. The preferred shares are non-cumulative.

b. The preferred shares are cumulative.

Required:

1. Determine the total amounts that would be paid to the preferred shareholders and to the common shareholders under the two independent assumptions.
2. Write a brief memo to explain why the dividend per common share was less under the second assumption.
3. Why would an investor buy Hoffman's common shares instead of its preferred shares if they pay a lower dividend per share? Explain. The market prices of the preferred and common shares were $25 and $40, respectively, on September 1, 2015.

LO4, 6   **E12–9**   **Determining the Impact of Dividends**

Average Corporation has the following shares outstanding at the end of 2013:

Preferred shares, $3, no par value; 8,000 outstanding shares

Common shares, no par value; 30,000 outstanding shares

On October 1, 2014, the board of directors declared dividends as follows:

Preferred shares: Full dividend amount, payable December 20, 2014

Common shares: 10 percent common stock dividend (i.e., one additional share for each 10 held), issuable December 20, 2014

On December 20, 2014, the market prices were $50 per preferred share and $32 per common share.

Required:

Explain the effect of each of the dividends on the assets, liabilities, and shareholders' equity of the company at each of the specified dates.

E12–10 **Recording the Payment of Dividends**

Sun Life Financial Inc. disclosed the following information in a press release:

■ **LO4**

Sun Life Financial Inc.

> **TORONTO – (May 8, 2013) –** The Board of Directors of Sun Life Financial Inc. (TSX: SLF) (NYSE: SLF) today announced a quarterly dividend of $0.36 per common share, payable June 28, 2013, to shareholders of record at the close of business on May 29, 2013. This is the same amount as paid in the previous quarter.
>
> The Board also announced that the following quarterly dividends on its Class A Non-Cumulative Preferred Shares are payable on June 28, 2013, to shareholders of record at the close of business on May 29, 2013:
>
> | | |
> |---|---|
> | Series 1 | $0.296875 per share |
> | Series 2 | $0.30 per share |
> | Series 3 | $0.278125 per share |
> | Series 4 | $0.278125 per share |
> | Series 5 | $0.28125 per share |
> | Series 6R | $0.375 per share |
> | Series 8R | $0.271875 per share |
> | Series 10R | $0.24375 per share |
> | Series 12R | $0.26563 per share |

Required:

1. Prepare the journal entries to record the declaration and payment of dividends to common shareholders. Assume that there were 590 million common shares outstanding on May 8, 2013.

2. Prepare the journal entries to record the declaration and payment of dividends to the holders of 8 million Series 10R preferred shares.

3. All the preferred shares were issued on different dates between 2005 and 2011 at $25 per share. Why does Sun Life pay different dividend amounts for the different series?

E12–11 **Analyzing Stock Dividends**

On December 31, 2015, the shareholders' equity section of the statement of financial position of R & B Corporation reflected the following:

■ **LO6**

Common shares (no par value, authorized 60,000 shares, outstanding 30,000 shares)	$360,000
Contributed surplus	12,000
Retained earnings	175,000
Accumulated other comprehensive income	28,000

On February 1, 2016, the board of directors declared a 10 percent stock dividend to be issued April 30, 2016. The market value per share was $18 on the declaration date.

Required:

1. For comparative purposes, prepare the shareholders' equity section of the statement of financial position (*a*) before the stock dividend and (*b*) after the stock dividend. (*Hint:* Use two columns for this requirement.)

2. Explain the effects of this stock dividend on the company's assets, liabilities, and shareholders' equity.

■ LO6   **E12–12**   **Analyzing Stock Dividends**

At the beginning of 2015, the shareholders' equity section of the statement of financial position of Ponti Corporation reflected the following:

Common shares, no par value, authorized unlimited number of shares, issued and outstanding 36,000 shares	$360,000
Retained earnings	750,000

On February 1, 2015, the board of directors declared a 100 percent stock dividend to be issued on April 30, 2015. The price per common share was $18 on February 1, 2015.

Required:

1. For comparative purposes, prepare the shareholders' equity section of the statement of financial position (*a*) before the stock dividend and (*b*) after the stock dividend. (*Hint:* Use two columns to show amounts for this requirement.)
2. Explain the effects of this stock dividend on assets, liabilities, and shareholders' equity.

■ LO6   **E12–13**   **Determining the Impact of Stock Dividends and Stock Splits**

Milano Tools Inc. announced a 100 percent stock dividend.

Required:

1. Determine the impact (increase, decrease, no change) of this dividend on the following:
   a. Total assets.
   b. Total liabilities.
   c. Common shares.
   d. Total shareholders' equity.
   e. Market value per common share.
2. Now assume that the company announced a 2-for-1 stock split. Determine the impact of the stock split on the five items above. Explain why the accounting for stock dividends differs from that of the stock split.

■ LO4   **E12–14**   **Evaluating Dividend Policy**

H&R Block

H&R Block is a well-known name, especially during income tax time each year. The company serves more than 25 million taxpayers in more than 10,000 offices in Canada, Australia, England, and the United States. The company's news releases for 2013 contained the following announcement:

> **H&R Block Announces Quarterly Cash Dividend**
>
> KANSAS CITY, MO — (MARKETWIRE) — 03/06/13 — H&R Block, Inc. (NYSE: HRB), the world's largest consumer tax services provider, today announced that its Board of Directors declared a quarterly cash dividend of 20 cents per share, payable April 1, 2013, to shareholders of record as of March 18, 2013.
>
> *Source:* H&R Block News Release.

The following day, March 7, 2013, the Company announced a loss from continuing operations of US$17 million for the third fiscal quarter ending on January 31, 2013.

Required:

1. Explain why H&R Block can pay dividends despite the loss that it announced for the previous quarter.
2. What factors did the board of directors consider when it declared the dividends?

■ LO3   **E12–15**   **Analyzing the Repurchase of Shares**

Dorel Industries Inc.

Dorel Industries Inc. manufactures and markets juvenile products, bicycles, and a wide assortment of both domestically produced and imported furniture products, principally within North America. The company's annual report for 2012 included the following information (dollar amounts are in thousands):

From the beginning of the year to April 3, 2012, the date of its expiry, the Company repurchased under its previous normal course issuer bid ("NCIB") a total of 47,100 Class "B" Subordinate Voting Shares for a cash consideration of $1,207. The excess of the shares' repurchase value over their carrying amount ($913) was charged to retained earnings as share repurchase premiums. On April 2, 2012, the Company announced that it had decided to implement a new normal course issuer bid (the "2012 NCIB"). As approved by the TSX, under the 2012 NCIB, the Company is entitled to repurchase for cancellation up to 850,000 Class "B" Subordinate Voting Shares during the period of April 4, 2012, to April 3, 2013, or until such earlier time as the bid is completed or terminated at the option of the Company. Any shares the Company purchases under the 2012 NCIB will be purchased on the open market plus brokerage fees through the facilities of the TSX at the prevailing market price at the time of the transaction. Shares acquired under the 2012 NCIB will be cancelled. In accordance with the 2012 NCIB, the Company repurchased during the period ended December 30, 2012, a total of 629,000 Class "B" Subordinate Voting Shares for a cash consideration of $16,605. The excess of the shares' repurchase value over their carrying amount ($12,679) was charged to retained earnings as share repurchase premiums.

Source: Dorel Industries Inc., Annual Report 2012.

Required:

1. Determine the average issuance price per Class "B" Subordinate Voting Share.
2. Determine the impact of this transaction on the financial statements.
3. Why do you think the board decided to repurchase the company's shares?
4. What impact will this purchase have on Dorel's future dividend obligations?

E12–16 Repurchase of Shares

■ LO3

Danier Leather Inc. manufactures and retails leather products, earning international recognition as a leader in leather and suede design. The company's annual report for the fiscal year ended June 30, 2012, included the following (all amounts are in thousands):

Danier Leather Inc.

(d) Normal course issuer bids

During the past several years, the Company has received approval from the TSX to commence various normal course issuer bids ("NCIBs"). On May 5, 2011, the Company received approval from the TSX to commence its fifth normal course issuer bid (the "2011 NCIB"). The 2011 NCIB permitted the Company to acquire up to 176,440 Subordinate Voting Shares, representing approximately 5% of the Company's issued and outstanding Subordinate Voting Shares at the date of acceptance of the notice of intention in respect of the 2011 NCIB filed with the TSX during the period from May 9, 2011, to May 8, 2012, or such earlier date as the Company may have completed its purchases under the 2011 NCIB. The 2011 NCIB expired on May 8, 2012, without being renewed. During the fourth quarter of fiscal 2011 and the first quarter of fiscal 2012, the Company repurchased an aggregate of 125,000 Subordinate Voting Shares for cancellation at a weighted average price of $11.44.

The following Subordinate Voting Shares were repurchased for cancellation under the NCIBs in effect during year ended June 30, 2012, and June 25, 2011, respectively:

	June 30, 2012	June 25, 2011
Number of shares repurchased under NCIBs	50,000	75,000
Amount charged to share capital	$ 219	$ 329
Amount charged to retained earnings representing the excess over the average paid-in value	311	571
Total cash consideration	$ 530	$ 900

Source: Danier Leather Inc., Annual Report 2012.

Required:

1. What was the average price that the company paid to repurchase shares in fiscal year 2012?
2. Prepare the journal entry to record a summary of the 2012 repurchase transactions.

■ LO1, 4, 6   **P12–1**   **Finding Missing Amounts** (AP12–1)

At December 31, 2014, the records of Nortech Corporation provided the following selected and incomplete data:

> Common shares, no par value
>   Shares authorized, 200,000
>   Shares issued,___?___; issue price $17 per share; cash collected in full, $2,125,000
> Net earnings for 2014, $118,000
> Dividends declared and paid during 2014, $75,000
> Prior-period error, correction of 2013 accounting error, $9,000 (a credit, net of income tax)
> Retained earnings balance, January 1, 2014, $155,000

Required:

1. Complete the following tabulation:

   Shares authorized, _____.

   Shares issued, _____.

   Shares outstanding, _____.

2. EPS, $ _____.

3. Dividend paid per common share, $ _____.

4. The prior-period error should be reported on the _____ as an addition to _____ (or a deduction from _____).

5. The amount of retained earnings available for dividends on January 1, 2014, was $ _____.

6. Assume that the board of directors voted a 100 percent stock split (the number of shares will double). After the stock split, the average issue price per share will be $_____ and the number of outstanding shares will be _____.

7. Assume that the company declared a 100 percent stock dividend instead of the 100 percent stock split. Compare and contrast the stock dividend and the stock split with regard to their effects on shareholders' equity components.

■ LO1, 3   **P12–2**   **Recording Transactions Affecting Shareholders' Equity** (AP12–2)

King Corporation began operations in January 2015. The charter authorized the following share capital:

   Preferred shares: 5 percent, $25 par value, authorized 40,000 shares.

   Common shares: no par value, authorized 100,000 shares.

During 2015, the following transactions occurred in the order given:

a. Issued 20,000 common shares to each of the three organizers. Collected $9 cash per share from two of the organizers, and received a plot of land with a small building on it in full payment for the shares of the third organizer and issued the shares immediately. Assume that 30 percent of the non-cash payment received applies to the building.

b. Sold 6,000 preferred shares at $25 per share. Collected the cash and issued the shares immediately.

c. Sold 2,000 preferred shares at $25 and 2,000 common shares at $12 per share. Collected the cash and issued the shares immediately.

d. The operating results at the end of 2015 were as follows:

Revenues	$330,000
Expenses, including income taxes	240,000

Required:

1. Prepare the journal entries to record each of these transactions and to close the accounts.

2. Write a brief memo explaining how you determined the cost of the land and the building in the first journal entry.

3. Prepare the shareholders' equity section of the statement of financial position for King Corporation as at December 31, 2015.

P12–3   Preparing the Shareholders' Equity Section after Selected Transactions (AP12–3)   ▌LO1, 3, 4, 6

Eddie Edwards Limited, a public company, was formed on January 2, 2014, with the following authorized capital structure:

> Preferred shares: No par value, $1.00 per share quarterly cumulative dividend, callable at 103, 100,000 shares
>
> Common shares: Unlimited number of shares

The following selected transactions occurred during the first six months of operations:

January 2	Issued 100,000 common shares in exchange for land and building with a combined appraised value of $2,200,000. Sixty percent of the acquisition cost is attributable to the building.
January 3	Issued 50,000 preferred shares for $1,250,000 cash.
April 1	Declared the quarterly cash dividend on the preferred shares, payable on April 25.
April 10	Declared and distributed a 5 percent common stock dividend on all outstanding common shares as of March 31. The market price of the common shares on March 31 was $24 per share.
April 25	Paid the preferred dividend that was declared on April 1.

Required:

1. Prepare journal entries to record the above transactions.
2. Prepare the shareholders' equity section of the statement of financial position for Eddie Edwards Limited as at June 30, 2014. Assume that the company recorded net earnings of $500,000 for its first six months.

P12–4   Comparing Stock and Cash Dividends (AP12–4)   ▌LO4, 6

Calgate Company had the following shares outstanding and retained earnings at December 31, 2014:   e**X**cel

Preferred shares, 4% (par value $25; outstanding, 10,000 shares)	$250,000
Common shares (outstanding, 30,000 shares)	600,000
Retained earnings	281,000

The board of directors is considering the distribution of a cash dividend to the two groups of shareholders. No dividends were declared during 2012 or 2013. Three independent cases are assumed:

Case A: The preferred shares are non-cumulative; the total amount of dividends is $51,000.

Case B: The preferred shares are cumulative; the total amount of dividends is $60,000.

Case C: Same as case B, except the amount is $96,000.

Required:

1. Compute the amount of dividends, in total and per share, that would be payable to each class of shareholders for each case. Show computations.
2. Assume that the company issued a 10 percent common stock dividend on the outstanding common shares when the market value per share was $24. Complete the following comparative schedule for common shares only, including explanation of the differences.

	Amount of Dollar Increase (Decrease)	
Item	Cash Dividend—Case C	Stock Dividend
Assets	$_____	$_____
Liabilities	$_____	$_____
Shareholders' equity	$_____	$_____

P12–5   Analyzing Dividend Policy   ▌LO4

Dana and David, two young financial analysts, were reviewing financial statements for Smart
Phone Limited (SPL), a manufacturer of wireless mobile communication devices. Dana noted that the company did not report any dividends in the financing activity section of the statement of cash flows and said, "I have heard that SPL is one of the best performing companies. If it's so good, I wonder why it isn't paying any dividends." David wasn't convinced that Dana was looking in the right place for dividends but didn't say anything.

Dana continued the discussion and noted, "Sales are up by nearly 50 percent over the previous two years. While net earnings are up over $600 million compared to last year, cash flow from operating activities increased by nearly $1,500 million compared to the previous year."

At that point, David noted that the statement of cash flows reported that the company had repurchased nearly $800 million in common shares. He commented, "No wonder it can't pay dividends. With cash flows being used to repurchase shares, the board is probably reluctant to oblige itself to dividends."

Required:

1. Correct any misstatements that either Dana or David made. Explain.
2. Which of the factors presented in the case help you understand the company's dividend policy?

■ **LO4**   **P12–6**   **Determining the Financial Statement Effects of Dividends**

Uno Company has outstanding 52,000 common shares and 25,000, $2, preferred shares. On December 1, 2014, the board of directors voted to distribute a $2 cash dividend per preferred share and a 5 percent common stock dividend on the common shares. At the date of declaration, the common share was selling at $40 and the preferred share at $25. The dividends are to be paid, or issued, on February 15, 2015. The company's fiscal year ends on December 31.

Required:

Explain the comparative effects of the two dividends on the assets, liabilities, and shareholders' equity (*a*) through December 31, 2014, (*b*) on February 15, 2015, and (*c*) overall from December 1, 2014, through February 15, 2015. A schedule similar to the following might be helpful:

	Comparative Effects Explained	
	Cash Dividend on Preferred	**Stock Dividend on Common**
Item		
1. Through December 31, 2014: Assets, etc.		

■ **LO4, 6**   **P12–7**   **Recording Dividends**

RBC Financial Group

RBC Financial Group provides personal and commercial banking, wealth management services, insurance, corporate and investment banking, and transaction processing services on a global basis. On March 3, 2006, a press release announced the following:

> Royal Bank of Canada (RY: TSX, NYSE, SWX) today announced that its Board of Directors has declared a stock dividend, which has the same effect as a two-for-one split of its common shares.
>
> RBC's last stock dividend was paid on October 5, 2000.
>
> The Board of Directors today also declared a quarterly common share cash dividend of $0.72 per share, which represents $0.36 per share on a post-stock dividend basis. This dividend of $0.36 per share is payable on May 24, 2006, to common shareholders of record on April 25, 2006.

Required:

1. Prepare any journal entries that RBC Financial should make as the result of information in the preceding report. Assume that the company has 1.3 million shares outstanding with a market value of $47 per share and an average issue price of $5.60.
2. What factors did the board of directors consider in making this decision?

■ **LO8**   **P12–8**   **Determining the Balance of Retained Earnings, and Preparing the Shareholders' Equity Section**

The annual report of Prodimax Ltd. for fiscal year 2014 included the financial statements for fiscal year 2013, which were restated to reflect the effects of a fraudulent action by a former employee. The restated financial statements included the following items and their account balances:

Share capital	$ 7,375	
Retained earnings, beginning of year	74,494	
Net earnings	8,467	
Dividends declared	3,108	
Effect of prior-period error	593	Debit balance

Required:

1. Determine the balance of retained earnings for the year ending October 31, 2013, and prepare the shareholders' equity section of the statement of financial position as at October 31, 2013.

2. The company provided the following explanation for the prior-period error. Use the amounts shown in the "Adjustment" column below to reconstruct the journal entry that was prepared to record the effect of the alleged fraud on the identified financial statement accounts:

PRIOR-PERIOD ERROR

During fiscal 2014, management uncovered evidence of a misappropriation of certain assets (related to an alleged fraud by a former non-executive employee). As a result, management determined that certain costs, which previously had been included in the cost of inventories, should have been expensed. In addition, certain costs previously included in cost of goods sold have been reclassified as unusual items. Accordingly, the consolidated financial statements for the fiscal year ended October 31, 2013, have been restated as follows from the amounts previously reported:

	As Previously Reported	Adjustment	As Restated
Cost of sales	$96,660	$(1,058)	$95,602
Unusual items	—	1,173	1,173
Income tax expense	4,730	(44)	4,686
Net earnings	8,538	(71)	8,467
Inventories	62,045	(1,072)	60,973
Income taxes recoverable	693	408	1,101
Retained earnings as at October 31, 2013	79,924	(664)	79,260
Retained earnings as at October 31, 2012	74,494	(593)	73,901

P12–9 **Determining the Balance of Retained Earnings, and Preparing the Statement of Changes in Equity (AP12–5)**

■ LO8

Thomson Reuters Corporation

The consolidated statements of changes in equity of Thomson Reuters Corporation for fiscal years 2012 and 2011 included the following items and their account balances at December 31, 2012 and 2011 (in millions of U.S. dollars). This list shows the balances of the various components of shareholders' equity at the beginning of each year, and changes that affected these components during the year. These changes are presented in a random order:

	2012	2011
Share capital, beginning of year	10,134	10,077
Contributed surplus, beginning of year	154	207
Retained earnings, beginning of year	7,633	10,158
Accumulated other comprehensive income (loss), beginning of year	(1,516)	(1,480)
Shares issued under stock compensation plan	101	113
Net earnings (loss)	1,836	(1,652)
Shares issued under dividend reinvestment plan	38	74
Other comprehensive income (loss), net	(21)	(36)
Dividends declared	1,062	1,037
Contributed surplus—stock compensation plans	16	(53)
Shares purchased for cancellation	72	130
Excess of purchase price over carrying value of shares repurchased and cancelled	96	196

Required:

Prepare a statement of changes in equity for fiscal years 2012 and 2011, similar to the statement that appears in Exhibit 12.2. Include the following headings: Share Capital, Contributed Surplus, Retained Earnings, and Accumulated Other Comprehensive Income.

■ LO3

P12–10

Canadian Tire
Corporation

Analyzing the Repurchase of Shares (AP12–6)

Canadian Tire Corporation offers a range of retail goods and services, including general merchandise, apparel, sporting goods, petroleum, and financial services. Its annual report for fiscal year 2012 included the following:

28. Share Capital

During 2012 and 2011, the Company issued and repurchased Class A Non-Voting Shares. The net excess of the issue price over the repurchase price results in contributed surplus. The net excess of the repurchase price over the issue price is allocated first to contributed surplus, with any remainder allocated to retained earnings.

The following transactions occurred with respect to Class A Non-Voting Shares during 2012:

(C$ in millions)	Number	$
Shares outstanding at beginning of the year	78,020,208	710.3
Issued		
Dividend reinvestment plan	69,545	4.6
Stock option plan	200	–
Employee profit sharing plan	59,078	4.1
Dealer profit sharing plans	54,724	3.7
Repurchased	(483,354)	(33.1)
Excess of issue price over repurchase price	–	(1.8)
Shares outstanding at end of the year	77,720,401	$687.8

Since 1988, the Company has followed an anti-dilution policy. The Company repurchases shares to substantially offset the dilutive effects of issuing Class A Non-Voting Shares pursuant to various corporate programs and in 2012 the Company purchased an additional 299,806 Class A Non-Voting Shares.

Conditions of Class A Non-Voting Shares and Common Shares

The holders of Class A Non-Voting Shares are entitled to receive a preferential cumulative dividend at the rate of $0.01 per share per annum. After payment of preferential cumulative dividends at the rate of $0.01 per share per annum on each of the Class A Non-Voting Shares with respect to the current year and each preceding year and payment of a non-cumulative dividend on each of the Common Shares with respect to the current year at the same rate, the holders of the Class A Non-Voting Shares and the Common Shares are entitled to further dividends declared and paid in equal amounts per share without preference or distinction or priority of one share over another.

. . .

Required:

1. Why do you think Canadian Tire's board of directors decided to repurchase the company's Class A non-voting shares?
2. Prepare the journal entry to record a summary of the repurchase transactions.
3. Compute the repurchase price and weighted-average issuance price of the repurchased Class A shares. Explain why the difference between the repurchase price and the issuance price is not recorded as a gain on repurchase of shares.
4. Assume that Canadian Tire had 3,423,366 common shares and 77,720,401 Class A non-voting shares when the board of directors declared that a total of $28.5 million will be paid as dividends to both classes of shares. Assume further that Canadian Tire did not declare dividends in 2010 and 2011. Allocate the total amount of dividends between the two classes of shares.

■ LO1

P12–11

eXcel

(Appendix 12A) Comparing Owners' Equity Sections for Alternative Forms of Organization

Assume for each of the following independent cases that the accounting period for NewBiz ends on December 31, 2015, and that the income summary account at that date reflected a debit balance (loss) of $20,000:

Case A: Assume that NewBiz is a *sole proprietorship* owned by Proprietor A. Prior to the closing entries, the capital account reflected a credit balance of $50,000 and the drawings account a balance of $8,000.

Case B: Assume that NewBiz is a *partnership* owned by Partner A and Partner B. Prior to the closing entries, the owners' equity accounts reflected the following balances: A, capital, $40,000; B, capital, $38,000; A, drawings, $5,000; and B, drawings, $9,000. Net earnings and losses are divided equally.

Case C: Assume that NewBiz is a *corporation*. Prior to the closing entries, the shareholders' equity accounts showed the following: share capital, authorized 30,000 shares, outstanding 15,000 shares, $150,000; contributed surplus, $5,000; retained earnings, $65,000.

Required:

1. Prepare all of the closing entries indicated at December 31, 2015, for each of the three separate cases.
2. Show for each case how the owners' equity section of the statement of financial position would appear at December 31, 2015.

ALTERNATE PROBLEMS

AP12–1 Finding Missing Amounts (P12–1)   ■ LO1, 4, 6

At December 31, 2015, the records of Kozmetsky Corporation provided the following selected and incomplete data:

> Common shares, no par value
>   Shares authorized, unlimited
>   Shares issued, ____?____; issue price $10 per share
> Net earnings for 2015, $4,800,000
>   Common shares account, $2,000,000
> Dividends declared and paid during 2015, $2 per share
> Retained earnings balance, January 1, 2015, $71,900,000

Required:

1. Complete the following tabulation:
   Shares issued, _____.
   Shares outstanding, _____.
2. EPS, $_____.
3. Total dividends paid on common shares during 2015, $_____.
4. Assume that the board of directors voted a 100 percent stock split (the number of shares will double). After the stock split, the average issue price per share will be $_____ and the number of outstanding shares will be _____.
5. Disregard the stock split assumed in (4). Assume instead that a 10 percent stock dividend was declared and issued when the market price of the common shares was $91. Explain how the shareholders' equity will change.

AP12–2 Recording Transactions Affecting Shareholders' Equity (P12–2)   ■ LO1, 3

Peterson Company was granted a charter that authorized the following share capital:
   Preferred shares: 8 percent, par value $25, 20,000 shares
   Common shares: No par value, 100,000 shares

During the first year, 2014, the following selected transactions occurred in the order given:

a. Sold 30,000 common shares at $35 cash per share and 5,000 preferred shares at $25 cash per share. Collected cash and issued the shares immediately.

b. Issued 2,000 preferred shares as full payment for a plot of land to be used as a future plant site. Assume that the share was selling at $25.

c. Declared and paid the quarterly cash dividend on the preferred shares.

d. At December 31, 2014, the income summary account has a credit balance of $76,000.

Required:

1. Prepare the journal entries to record each of these transactions.
2. Explain the economic difference between acquiring an asset for cash and acquiring it by issuing shares. Is it "better" to acquire a new asset without having to give up another asset?

■ **LO1, 3, 4**   **AP12–3**   **Preparing the Shareholders' Equity Section after Selected Transactions** (P12–3)

The shareholders' equity accounts of Gennar Inc. at January 2, 2014, are as follows:

Preferred shares, no par value, cumulative, 4,000 shares issued	$ 200,000
Common shares, no par value, 125,000 shares issued	2,500,000
Retained earnings	1,600,000

The following transactions occurred during the year:

March 10	Purchased a building for $3,000,000. The seller agreed to receive 20,000 preferred shares and 15,000 common shares of Gennar in exchange for the building. The preferred shares were trading in the market at $50 per share on that day.
July 1	Declared a semi-annual cash dividend of $1.00 per common share and the required amount of dividends on preferred shares, payable on August 1, 2014, to shareholders of record on July 21, 2014. The annual dividend of $2 per preferred share had not been paid in either 2013 or 2014.
August 1	Paid the cash dividend declared on July 1 to both common and preferred shareholders.
December 31	Determined that net earnings for the year were $385,000.

Required:

1. Prepare journal entries to record the above transactions.
2. Prepare the shareholders' equity section of Gennar's statement of financial position as at December 31, 2014.

■ **LO4, 6**   **AP12–4**   **Comparing Stock and Cash Dividends** (P12–4)

Ritz Company had the following shares outstanding and retained earnings at December 31, 2015:

Preferred shares, 8% (par value $25; outstanding, 9,000 shares)	$225,000
Common shares (outstanding, 5,000 shares)	800,000
Retained earnings	720,000

The board of directors is considering the distribution of a cash dividend to the two groups of shareholders. No dividends were declared during 2013 or 2014. Three independent cases are assumed:

Case A: The preferred shares are non-cumulative; the total amount of dividends is $25,000.

Case B: The preferred shares are cumulative; the total amount of dividends is $36,000.

Case C: Same as case B, except the amount is $77,500.

Required:

1. Compute the amount of dividends, in total and per share, payable to each class of shareholders for each case. Show computations.
2. Assume that the company issued a 10 percent common stock dividend on the outstanding common shares when the market value per share was $47. Complete the following comparative schedule for common shares only, including an explanation of the differences.

	Amount of Dollar Increase (decrease)	
Item	**Cash Dividend—Case C**	**Stock Dividend**
Assets	$_____	$_____
Liabilities	$_____	$_____
Shareholders' equity	$_____	$_____

■ **LO8**   **AP12–5**   **Determining the Balance of Retained Earnings, and Preparing the Statement of Changes in Equity** (P12–9)

Alimentation
Couche-Tard Inc.

The consolidated statements of changes in equity of Alimentation Couche-Tard Inc. for fiscal years 2012 and 2011 included the following items and their account balances at April 29, 2012, and April 24, 2011 (in millions of Canadian dollars). This list shows the balances of the various components of shareholders' equity at the beginning of each year, and the changes that affected these components during the year. These changes are presented in a random order:

	2012	2011
Share capital, beginning of year	$ 323.8	$ 319.5
Contributed surplus, beginning of year	19.3	20.4
Retained earnings, beginning of year	1,596.3	1,319.7
Accumulated other comprehensive income, beginning of year	40.0	0.4
Stock option–based compensation expense	0.4	1.1
Net earnings	457.6	369.2
Other comprehensive income (loss), net	(31.1)	39.6
Dividends declared	49.8	32.8
Initial fair value of stock options exercised	1.8	2.2
Cash received on exercise of options	19.2	11.4
Repurchase and cancellation of shares	23.8	9.3
Excess of acquisition cost over book value of Class A multiple voting shares and Class B subordinate voting shares repurchased and cancelled	177.3	59.8

Required:

1. Compute the balance of retained earnings at April 29, 2012.

2. Prepare a statement of changes in equity for fiscal years 2012 and 2011, similar to the statement that appears in Exhibit 12.2.

AP12–6 Analyzing the Repurchase of Shares (P12–10)

■ LO3

Jean Coutu Group

The Jean Coutu Group operates a network of franchised stores in Canada, located in the provinces of Québec, New Brunswick, and Ontario under the banners of PJC Jean Coutu, PJC Clinique, PJC Santé, and PJC Santé Beauté, and employs more than 17,000 people. Its annual report for fiscal year 2012 included the following:

23. Capital Stock

. . .

Changes that occurred in capital stock are presented as follows:

	2012 Shares		2011 Shares	
	(in millions)	$	(in millions)	$
Class A subordinate voting shares				
Outstanding shares, beginning of year	115.4	614.4	118.9	654.8
Exercise of exchange privilege	—	—	3.0	—
Repurchased and cancelled	(10.4)	(55.5)	(6.8)	(35.1)
Repurchased and not cancelled	—	—	—	(1.5)
Stock options exercised	0.1	0.8	—	0.2
Outstanding shares, end of year	104.8	559.7	115.4	614.4

a) Normal course issuer bid

For the years ended March 3, 2012 and February 26, 2011, the Corporation repurchased 10,400,000 and 6,819,900 Class A subordinate voting shares at an average price of $11.93 and $9.23 per share for a total consideration of $124.1 million and $63.0 million including related costs, respectively. Amounts of $68.6 million and $26.4 million representing the excess of the purchase price over the carrying value of the repurchased shares were included in retained earnings for the years ended March 3, 2012 and February 26, 2011, respectively. The shares repurchased during fiscal year ended March 3, 2012 were cancelled during this period. The shares repurchased during fiscal year ended February 26, 2011 were cancelled during this period, except for 287,200 shares that were cancelled after February 26, 2011.

Required:

1. Why do you think Jean Coutu's board of directors decided to repurchase the company's shares?

2. Prepare the journal entry to record a summary of the repurchase transactions.

3. Compute the weighted-average issuance price per common share when the shares were repurchased, and explain why Jean Coutu paid a much higher price for repurchasing its own shares.

4. What impact will this transaction have on Jean Coutu's future dividend obligations?

CASES AND PROJECTS

FINDING AND INTERPRETING FINANCIAL INFORMATION

■ LO1, 3, 4   **CP12–1**   **Finding Financial Information**

Canadian Tire
Corporation

Refer to the financial statements of Canadian Tire Corporation given in Appendix A of this book.

Required:

1. Identify the types of shares that Canadian Tire is authorized to issue, and their characteristics. Do all types of shares have the same voting rights? If not, explain why.

2. Did the company repurchase shares during 2012? If so, how many shares were repurchased? Reconstruct a summary journal entry to record the share repurchase transactions.

3. Does the company provide stock options to senior executives? If so, describe the plan that is currently in effect. How many stock options were granted in 2012, and how many were exercised during the same year? What was the compensation expense related to the stock option plan for 2012?

4. Identify all the cash flows related to issuance of shares, repurchase of shares, and payment of dividends during fiscal year 2012.

5. The company declared dividends on the different types of outstanding shares during 2012. How much cash did the company pay in 2012 in dividends? Why is this amount different from the dividends declared by the board of directors?

6. Has the company ever issued a stock dividend or declared a stock split? If so, describe the procedure. (*Hint:* Access the following link for details: **http://corp.canadiantire.ca/EN/ Investors/Pages/FAQs.aspx**.)

■ LO1, 3, 4   **CP12–2**   **Finding Financial Information**

RONA Inc.

Go to *Connect* for the financial statements of RONA Inc.

Required:

1. Identify the types of shares that RONA is authorized to issue, and their characteristics. Do all types of shares have the same voting rights? If not, explain why.

2. Does the company have any treasury shares at December 30, 2012? If so, how many shares?

3. Did the company repurchase shares during 2012? If so, how many shares were repurchased? Reconstruct the journal entry to record the share repurchase transactions.

4. Does the company provide stock options to senior executives? If so, describe the plan that is currently in effect. How many stock options were granted in 2012, and how many were exercised during the same year? What was the compensation expense related to the stock option plan for 2012?

5. Identify all the cash flows related to issuance of shares, repurchase of shares, and payment of dividends during fiscal year 2012.

6. The company declared dividends on both preferred and common shares during 2012. How much cash did the company pay in 2012 in dividends to common shareholders? Why is this amount different from the dividends declared by the board of directors?

■ LO4, 5, 6   **CP12–3**   **Comparing Companies within an Industry**

Canadian Tire
Corporation vs.
RONA Inc.

Refer to the financial statements of Canadian Tire Corporation (Appendix A) and RONA Inc. (on *Connect*) and the Industry Ratio Report (Appendix B on *Connect*).

Required:

1. Canadian Tire Corporation split its stock in the past. Describe the impact that the split would have on the market value of the stock compared to a company that did not split its stock. Why do some companies elect to split their stock?

2. Calculate the dividend yield ratios for Canadian Tire (assume a market price of $69 per share) and RONA (assume a market price of $10.5 per share) for the most recent reporting year.

3. Why would an investor choose to invest in a corporation whose board of directors does not declare and pay dividends?

4. Using the information from the following table, compare the dividend-related industry average ratios for the retailing industry to the media industry and the utilities industry. What type of investor would be interested in buying shares in a utility instead of a retailing company? Why?

DIVIDEND RATIOS FOR VARIOUS INDUSTRIES		
Industry	**Example Company**	**Dividend Yield**
Media	Cineplex Inc.	2.56%
Retailing	RONA Inc.	1.50%
Utilities	ATCO Ltd.	5.35%

FINANCIAL REPORTING AND ANALYSIS CASES

CP12–4 Finding Information Missing from an Annual Report

Procter & Gamble is a multi-billion dollar company that sells a variety of consumer products, such as Mr. Clean, Cheer, Crest, Vicks, Scope, Pringles, Folgers, Vidal Sassoon, and Zest. The company's annual report contained the following information (in millions except per share data):

a. Retained earnings at June 30, 2012, totalled $75,349.

b. Net earnings for the year ended June 30, 2012, was $10,756.

c. The number of common shares outstanding at June 30, 2012, was 4,008.4 shares.

d. Dividends declared on common shares equalled $2.14 per share.

Required:

1. Compute the total amount of dividends declared by the company.

2. A shareholder observed that P&G has a sizeable amount of retained earnings and wondered why the company accumulated this amount instead of distributing it to its shareholders. Write a brief memo to explain why earnings have been retained by the company.

3. Compute the company's EPS, assuming that P&G had not issued preferred shares. Is EPS a useful measure of performance? Explain.

CP12–5 Characteristics of Preferred Shares

Power Financial Corporation is a Canadian diversified international management company that holds interests, directly or indirectly, in companies that are active in the financial services industry in Canada, the United States, and Europe. The company's 2012 annual report included the following information about specific issues of preferred shares:

> **20. Share Capital**
>
> In the second quarter of 2010, the Corporation issued 11,200,000 4.40% Non-Cumulative 5-Year Rate Reset First Preferred Shares, Series P for cash proceeds of $280 million. The 4.40% Non-Cumulative First Preferred Shares, Series P are entitled to fixed non-cumulative preferential cash dividends at a rate equal to $1.10 per share per annum. On January 31, 2016, and on January 31 every five years thereafter, the Corporation may redeem for cash the Series P First Preferred Shares in whole or in part, at the Corporation's option, at $25.00 per share plus all declared and unpaid dividends to the date fixed for redemption, or the Series P First Preferred Shares are convertible to Non-Cumulative Floating Rate First Preferred Shares, Series Q, at the option of the holders on January 31, 2016, or on January 31 every five years thereafter. Transaction costs incurred in connection with the Series P First Preferred Shares of $8 million were charged to retained earnings.

Required:

1. Identify the various characteristics of these preferred shares.

2. Based on the characteristics of these shares, should they be classified as debt or equity? Explain.

CP12–6 Analyzing Dividend Policy

Walmart has been one of the most successful retail companies in history with steady growth in earnings over the past eight years. The following information was extracted from the company's annual reports. The market price is an average of the highest and lowest price for the year. Dividends and net income are in millions of U.S. dollars:

	2012*	2011	2010	2009	2008	2007	2006	2005
Dividends	$ 4,437	$ 5,048	$ 4,217	$ 3,746	$ 3,586	$ 2,802	$ 2,511	$ 2,214
Net income (net earnings)	16,999	15,959	14,335	13,346	12,075	11,284	11,231	10,267
Dividends per common share	1.59	1.46	1.21	0.95	0.88	0.67	0.60	0.52
Market price per share	69.95	56.49	53.40	46.92	48.73	47.23	48.00	56.19
Dividend yield	2.27%	2.58%	2.27%	2.02%	1.81%	1.42%	1.25%	0.93%

*Walmart's fiscal year starts on February 1 and ends on January 31. The information under this column refers essentially to fiscal year 2013 (February 1, 2012–January 31, 2013). It is labelled as 2012 because this period includes 11 months in 2012.

Assume that you are a financial analyst preparing a forecast of Walmart's operating results for fiscal year 2014. Because of a number of factors, you believe that net earnings for 2014 will be in the range of $17,000 million to $17,500 million. To complete your financial forecast, you now need to estimate the total amount of dividends that Walmart will pay.

Required:

1. Based on the information above, describe the dividend policy of Walmart, and estimate the dividends that the company will pay in 2014. (*Hint:* The ratio of dividends to net earnings, called the *dividend payout ratio*, may provide useful information about the company's dividend policy.)

2. Walmart's board of directors has increased dividends per share continuously over the past eight years. What is your expectation of dividends per share for fiscal year 2014? Justify your answer.

3. The dividend yield has also increased steadily over the past eight years. What should be the market price per share for the dividend yield to reach 2.50 percent, assuming a dividend of $1.84 per share? Explain.

CRITICAL THINKING CASES

LO5, 6 **CP12–7** **Evaluating an Ethical Dilemma**

You are a member of the board of directors of a large company that has been in business for more than 100 years. The company is proud of the fact that it has paid dividends every year that it has been in business. Because of this stability, many retired people have invested large portions of their savings in the company's common stock. Unfortunately, the company has struggled for the past few years as it tries to introduce new products and is considering not paying a dividend this year. The president wants to skip the dividend in order to have more cash to invest in product development, saying, "If we don't invest this money now, we won't get these products to market in time to save the company. I don't want to risk thousands of jobs." One of the most senior board members speaks next: "If we don't pay the dividend, thousands of retirees will be thrown into financial distress. Even if you don't care about them, you have to recognize our stock price will crash when they all sell." The company treasurer proposes this alternative: "Let's skip the cash dividend and pay a stock dividend. We can still say we've had a dividend every year." The entire board now turns to you for your opinion. What should the company do?

LO4 **CP12–8** **Evaluating an Ethical Dilemma**

You are the president of a very successful Internet company that has had a remarkably profitable year. You have determined that the company has more than $10 million in cash generated by operating activities not needed in the business. You are thinking about paying it out to shareholders as a special dividend. You discuss the idea with your vice-president, who reacts angrily to your suggestion, declaring, "Our stock price has gone up by 200 percent in the last year alone. What more do we have to do for the owners? The people who really earned that money are the employees who have been working 12 hours a day, six or seven days a week to make the company successful. Most of them didn't even take vacations last year. I say we have to pay out bonuses and nothing extra for the shareholders." As president, you know that you are hired by the board of directors, which is elected by the shareholders. What is your responsibility to both groups? To which group would you give the $10 million?

FINANCIAL REPORTING AND ANALYSIS TEAM PROJECT

LO1, 3, 4, 7 **CP12–9** **Team Project: Examining an Annual Report**

As a team, select an industry to analyze. A list of companies classified by industry can be obtained by accessing **www.fpinfomart.ca** and then choosing "Companies by Industry." You can also find a list of industries and companies within each industry via **http://ca.finance.yahoo.com/investing** (click on "Order Annual Reports" under "Tools").

Each group member should acquire the annual report for a different publicly traded company in the industry. (Library files, the SEDAR service at **www.sedar.com**, and the company's website are good sources.)

Required:

On an individual basis, each team member should then write a short report answering the following questions about the selected company. Discuss any patterns across the companies that you as a team observe. Then, as a team, write a short report comparing and contrasting your companies.

1. *a.* List the accounts and amounts of the company's shareholders' equity.

   b. From the notes to financial statements, identify any unusual features in the contributed capital accounts (e.g., convertible preferred, non-voting common), if any.

2. Identify the cash flows related to share capital transactions. You will need to refer to the statement of cash flows.

    a. If new shares were issued during the year, what was the average price per share at the time of issuance?

    b. Reconstruct the journal entry for the issuance of shares.

3. What type of dividends did the company declare during the year? How much was paid in cash?

SOLUTIONS TO SELF-STUDY QUIZZES

Self-Study Quiz 12-1

1.

Common shares	61	
Contributed surplus	4	
Deficit	78	
Cash		143

2. Average issuance price = ($61,000,000 + $4,000,000)/3,500,466 = $18.57

Self-Study Quiz 12-2

1. The liability is created on the declaration date, November 6, 2013.

2. The cash outflow occurs on the payment date, January 15, 2014.

3.

Dividends payable	436,875,000	
Cash		436,875,000

    (750,000,000 × $0.5825)

4. The fundamental requirements are availability of retained earnings, declaration by the board of directors, and availability of cash. However, if a corporation reports a deficit, it may declare and pay dividends if payment of the dividend does not place the company into a position that would prevent it from paying its liabilities as they become due.

Self-Study Quiz 12-3

1.

Retained earnings	3,000,000	
Common shares		3,000,000

2.

Retained earnings	1,000,000	
Common shares		1,000,000

3. No journal entry is required in the case of a stock split.

Self-Study Quiz 12-4

1. Total annual dividends = Number of shares × Dividend per share

                     = 9,244,555 × ($25 × 4.60%) = $10,631,238

2. The redemption date is the earliest date when BCE can call Series AC back from shareholders and pay them $25.00 per share.

3. The earliest redemption date is March 1, 2013.

Analyzing Financial Statements

After studying this chapter, you should be able to do the following:

LEARNING
OBJECTIVES

LO1 Explain how a company's business strategy affects financial analysis.

LO2 Discuss how analysts use financial statements.

LO3 Compute and interpret component percentages.

LO4 Compute and interpret profitability ratios.

LO5 Compute and interpret liquidity ratios.

LO6 Compute and interpret solvency ratios.

LO7 Compute and interpret market test ratios.

FOCUS COMPANY: **Canadian Tire Corporation, Limited**

FINANCIAL ANALYSIS: BRINGING IT ALL TOGETHER

The history of Canadian Tire Corporation, Limited (**www.canadiantire.ca**), is an unusual success story. Founded in 1923 by two brothers, John W. and Alfred J. Billes, in Toronto, Canadian Tire has become one of Canada's most-shopped-at general retailers, with nearly 1,700 retail and gasoline outlets across Canada offering automotive and hardware products, sporting goods, clothes for work or play, convenient gas bars, and everything needed for the home. Canadian Tire's financial statements are presented in Exhibit 13.1.

Canadian Tire operates businesses that offer a wide variety of products and services. These include Canadian Tire Financial Services Limited, Canadian Tire Bank, Canadian Tire Real Estate Limited, FGL Sports Ltd., and Mark's Work Warehouse Ltd. Canadian Tire and its subsidiaries employed more than 68,000 full-time and part-time employees as of December 31, 2012. Canadian Tire's net revenues grew at an average rate of 6.9 percent per year during the 10-year period 2003–2012, and its earnings grew at an average annual rate of 9.5 percent during the same period.

Financial analysts evaluate Canadian Tire's historical performance to determine whether they should recommend that their clients purchase its shares. The analysts want some reasonable assurance that the company will continue to thrive, causing the company's share price to increase, and thereby benefiting their clients. Two analysts looking at the same company, however, may arrive at different conclusions, depending in part on the investors' investment objectives: growth or safety. Some analysts may reject Canadian Tire because it is too risky relative to other investment opportunities, whereas others may recommend the investment because Canadian Tire has grown quickly relative to the risk in its business.

As you analyze Canadian Tire's financial results, it is important to remember that any analysis is understood in the context of what an investor wants to accomplish. Your analysis, in itself, will present neither a good nor a bad picture of Canadian Tire's performance. This assessment must be made in the context of not only the investor's goals but also the industry's performance and the economic environment.

Would you want to buy shares in Canadian Tire? To make a rational decision, you want to consider more factors than just the company's rapid growth in profitability and the recommendation of a financial analyst. The information contained in Canadian Tire's financial statements and the analytical tools discussed in this chapter provide an important basis to help you decide whether to invest in Canadian Tire shares.

CANADIAN TIRE CORPORATION, LIMITED Consolidated Balance Sheets		
(C$ in millions)	December 29, 2012*	December 31, 2011
ASSETS		
Current Assets:		
Cash and cash equivalents (Note 9)	$ 1,015.5	$ 325.8
Short-term investments (Note 10)	168.9	196.4
Trade and other receivables (Note 11)	750.6	829.3
Loans receivable (Note 12)	4,265.7	4,081.7
Merchandise inventories	1,503.3	1,448.6
Prepaid expenses and deposits	39.1	44.3
Assets classified as held for sale (Note 13)	5.5	30.5
Total current assets	7,748.6	6,956.6
Long-term receivables and other assets (Note 14)	681.2	668.9
Long-term investments	182.7	128.2
Goodwill and intangible assets (Note 15)	1,089.9	1,110.0
Investment property (Note 16)	95.1	72.4
Property and equipment (Note 17)	3,343.5	3,365.9
Deferred income taxes (Note 18)	40.4	36.8
Total assets	**$13,181.4**	**$12,338.8**
LIABILITIES		
Current Liabilities:		
Bank indebtedness (Note 9)	$ 86.0	$ 124.8
Deposits (Note 19)	1,311.0	1,182.3
Trade and other payables (Note 20)	1,631.3	1,640.9
Provisions (Note 21)	185.8	191.9
Short-term borrowings (Note 23)	118.9	352.6
Loans payable (Note 24)	623.7	628.7
Income taxes payable	5.5	3.9
Current portion of long-term debt (Note 25)	661.9	27.9
Total current liabilities	4,624.1	4,153.0
Long-term provisions (Note 21)	54.8	55.1
Long-term debt (Note 25)	2,336.0	2,347.7
Long-term deposits (Note 19)	1,111.8	1,102.2
Deferred income taxes (Note 18)	77.7	66.1
Other long-term liabilities (Note 26)	213.4	205.7
Total liabilities	8,417.8	7,929.8
SHAREHOLDERS' EQUITY		
Share capital (Note 28)	688.0	710.5
Contributed surplus	2.9	1.1
Accumulated other comprehensive income (loss)	(1.7)	11.0
Retained earnings	4,074.4	3,686.4
Total shareholders' equity	4,763.6	4,409.0
Total liabilities and shareholders' equity	**$13,181.4**	**$12,338.8**

The related notes form an integral part of these consolidated financial statements.

*The fiscal year of Canadian Tire consists of a 52- or 53-week period ending on the Saturday closest to December 31.

Source: Canadian Tire Corporation, Limited, Annual Report 2012.

Exhibit **13.1**
Canadian Tire Financial Statements

REAL-WORLD EXCERPT

Canadian Tire

ANNUAL REPORT

Exhibit **13.1**
(*continued*)

CANADIAN TIRE CORPORATION, LIMITED
Consolidated Statements of Income

	For the years ended	
(C$ in millions, except per share amounts)	December 29, 2012	December 31, 2011
Revenue (Note 31)	$ 11,427.2	$ 10,387.1
Cost of producing revenue (Note 32)	(7,929.3)	(7,326.4)
Gross profit	3,497.9	3,060.7
Other income	5.7	18.4
Operating expenses		
Distribution costs	(356.2)	(368.7)
Sales and marketing expenses	(1,636.4)	(1,307.9)
Administrative expenses	(707.6)	(640.4)
Total operating expenses (Note 33)	(2,700.2)	(2,317.0)
Operating income	803.4	762.1
Finance income	18.1	23.0
Finance costs	(144.3)	(155.2)
Net finance costs (Note 34)	(126.2)	(132.2)
Income before income taxes	677.2	629.9
Income taxes (Note 35)	(178.0)	(162.9)
Net income	$ 499.2	$ 467.0
Basic earnings per share	$ 6.13	$ 5.73
Diluted earnings per share	$ 6.10	$ 5.71
Weighted average number of Common and Class A Non-Voting Shares outstanding (Note 29):		
Basic	81,435,218	81,447,398
Diluted	81,805,594	81,803,786

The related notes form an integral part of these consolidated financial statements.
Source: Canadian Tire Corporation, Limited, Annual Report 2012.

CANADIAN TIRE CORPORATION, LIMITED
Consolidated Statements of Cash Flows

	For the years ended	
(C$ in millions, except per share amounts)	December 29, 2012	December 31, 2011
Cash generated from (used for):		
Operating activities		
Net income	$ 499.2	$ 467.0
Adjustments for:		
Gross impairment loss on loans receivable (Note 12)	323.7	352.0
Depreciation on property and equipment and investment property (Note 33)	248.9	229.8
Income tax expense	178.0	162.9
Net finance costs	126.2	132.2
Amortization of intangible assets (Note 33)	86.2	66.3
Changes in fair value of derivative instruments	(7.7)	(3.1)
Deferred income taxes	16.5	(6.4)
Other	13.7	9.8
Gain on revaluation of shares (Note 8)	–	(10.4)
	1,484.7	1,400.1
Changes in working capital and other (Note 36)	(434.0)	219.6
Cash generated from operating activities before interest and income taxes	1,050.7	1,619.7
Interest paid	(155.3)	(176.6)
Interest received	8.9	26.1
Income taxes paid	(161.3)	(63.7)
Cash generated from operating activities	743.0	1,405.5

Exhibit **13.1**

(*continued*)

CANADIAN TIRE CORPORATION, LIMITED

Consolidated Statements of Cash Flows

(C$ in millions, except per share amounts)	For the years ended	
	December 29, 2012	December 31, 2011
Investing activities		
Acquisition of FGL Sports (Note 8)	–	(739.9)
Acquisition of short-term investments	(264.0)	(334.8)
Acquisition of long-term investments	(130.0)	(123.1)
Additions to property and equipment and investment property	(222.3)	(230.5)
Additions to intangible assets	(64.3)	(128.9)
Long-term receivables and other assets	17.6	(3.2)
Proceeds from the disposition of long-term investments	4.7	18.1
Proceeds from the maturity and disposition of short-term investments	360.7	364.0
Proceeds on disposition of property and equipment, investment property and assets held for sale	45.0	21.0
Other	(8.9)	(4.1)
Cash used for investing activities	(261.5)	(1,161.4)
Financing activities		
Net (repayment) issuance of short-term borrowings	(233.7)	10.1
Issuance of loans payable	235.3	129.3
Repayment of loans payable	(240.3)	(187.6)
Issuance of share capital (Note 28)	12.4	11.6
Repurchase of share capital (Note 28)	(33.1)	(11.9)
Issuance of long-term debt	637.4	–
Repayment of long-term debt and finance lease liabilities	(30.1)	(355.6)
Dividends paid	(97.7)	(89.6)
Payment of transaction costs related to long-term debt	(3.2)	–
Cash generated from (used for) financing activities	247.0	(493.7)
Cash generated (used) in the year	728.5	(249.6)
Cash and cash equivalents, net of bank indebtedness, beginning of year	201.0	450.9
Effect of exchange rate fluctuations on cash held	–	(0.3)
Cash and cash equivalents, net of bank indebtedness, end of year (Note 9)	$ 929.5	$ 201.0

The related notes form an integral part of these consolidated financial statements.
Source: Canadian Tire Corporation, Limited, Annual Report 2012.

UNDERSTANDING THE BUSINESS

Companies spend billions of dollars each year preparing, auditing, and publishing their financial statements. These statements are then mailed to current and prospective investors. Most companies also make financial information available to investors on the Internet. Canadian Tire has a particularly interesting website that contains current financial statements, recent news articles about the company, and a variety of other relevant information.

The reason that Canadian Tire and other companies spend so much money providing information to investors is simple: financial statements help people make better economic decisions. Two broad groups of people use financial statements. One group is the management of the business; it relies on accounting data to make important operating decisions, such as the pricing of products or expansion of productive capacity. The second group is the external decision makers, who rely on accounting information to make important investment and credit decisions. In fact, the conceptual framework unequivocally states that the objective of financial reporting is to communicate information primarily to meet the needs of external decision makers, including present and potential owners, investment analysts, and creditors.

Users of financial statements are interested in three types of information:

1. *Information about past performance.* Information concerning items such as net earnings, sales volume, cash flows, and return earned on the investment helps people assess the success of the business and the effectiveness of its management. Such information also helps the decision maker compare one company with others.

2. *Information about the present condition of a business.* This type of information helps answer the following questions. What types of assets are owned? How much debt does the business owe, and when is it due? What is its cash position? What are its EPS, return on investment, and debt-to-equity ratios? What is the inventory position? Answers to these and similar questions help people assess the successes and failures of the past. More important, they provide information that is useful in assessing the cash flow and earnings potentials of the business.

3. *Information about the future performance of the business.* Decision makers select from among several alternative courses of action. Because all decisions are future oriented, financial statements based on historical cost are not an ideal basis upon which to forecast future performance. Investors are most interested in risk and the potential rewards for accepting risk. In general, as risk in the business environment increases, investors demand higher future returns on their investments to compensate them for that increased risk. Investors prefer to earn maximum return for minimum risk when choosing companies in which to invest.

Reliable accounting measures of past performance are one source of information upon which investors base their assessments of risk and potential return. Analysis of reliable measures indicating financial trends for each company is therefore very important. If investors can reasonably assume that important business factors will in the future be very similar to the current situation, then a reliable historical trend is often a satisfactory basis upon which to predict future financial performance. For example, the recent sales and earnings trends of a business are usually good indicators of what might be expected in the future. In other words, investors must know where the company has been in order to predict where it is likely to go.

ORGANIZATION OF THE CHAPTER

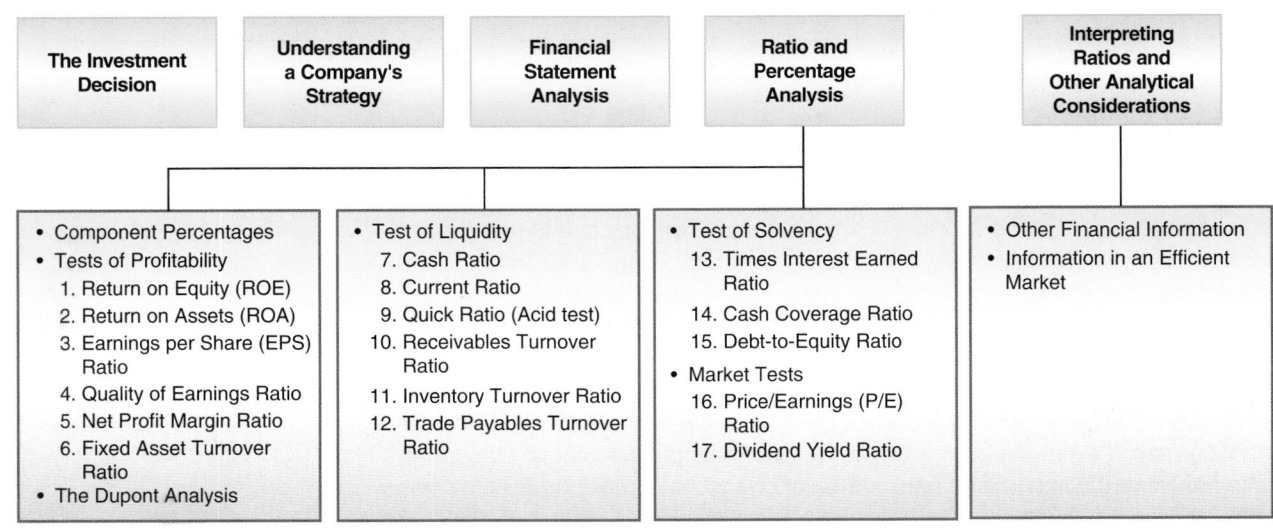

Supplemental material:
Appendix 13A: Expanding the Dupont Model—The Scott Formula (on *Connect*)

THE INVESTMENT DECISION

Of the people who use financial statements, current and potential investors are perhaps the single largest group. They often rely on the advice of professional analysts who develop recommendations on widely held stocks, such as Canadian Tire stock. Most individual investors use analysts' reports, tracking their recommendations. As this book was being written, professional analysts issued the following investment recommendations for Canadian Tire:

Analyst Ratings: Canadian Tire	Current Month	Last Month	Two Months Ago	Three Months Ago
1—Buy	2	2	1	1
2—Outperform	7	8	8	8
3—Hold	2	2	3	3
4—Underperform	0	0	0	0
5—Sell	0	0	0	0

Source: www.reuters.com/finance/stocks/analyst?symbol5CTCa.TO. Accessed September 18, 2013.

What do these recommendations mean? Analysts are information intermediaries who interpret audited financial information and advise their clients on whether they should buy, hold, or sell shares. It is clear that analysts reach different conclusions despite access to the same set of financial information. Notice also that analysts' recommendations shift over time as new information is released and actual performance becomes observable.

Analysts are expected to have a good understanding of financial statements and the standards that imbue these reports with both relevance and faithful representation. They may disagree, however, on how to interpret the results of their analyses of a company's past performance. Analysts' differing opinions affect their predictions of the future operating performance to the extent that their analyses of a company's past performance are relevant to formulating their predictions. The level of disagreement among financial analysts shows that financial statement analysis is part art and part science.

In addition to analyzing a company's financial statements, analysts consider other factors that might affect the future operating performance of the company and its financial situation. These include global, economic, and industry factors that are not controllable by the company, and management's ability to adapt its business plans in response to the uncertainties and risks associated with these uncontrollable factors. Management success at containing the effects of uncontrollable risks and managing in the face of uncertainties plays a role in analysts' predictions of the future economic health of a specific company. Regardless of how careful an analyst is, however, the truth about predictions is that they often prove to be inaccurate.

When considering an investment in shares, the investor should evaluate the future net earnings and growth potential of the business on the basis of three factors:

1. *Economy-wide factors.* The overall health of the economy has a direct impact on the performance of an individual business. Prudent investors must consider data such as the unemployment rate, the general inflation rate, and changes in interest rates. For example, increases in interest rates often slow economic growth because consumers are less willing to buy merchandise on credit when interest rates are high. Furthermore, companies that wish to expand their operations will find it too expensive to borrow funds.

2. *Industry factors.* Certain events have a major impact on each company within an industry but have only a minor impact on other companies outside the industry. For example, a major drought will be devastating for food-related industries but will have no effect on the electronics industry.

3. *Individual company factors.* To properly analyze a company, you should learn as much as you can about it. Good analysts do not rely solely on the information

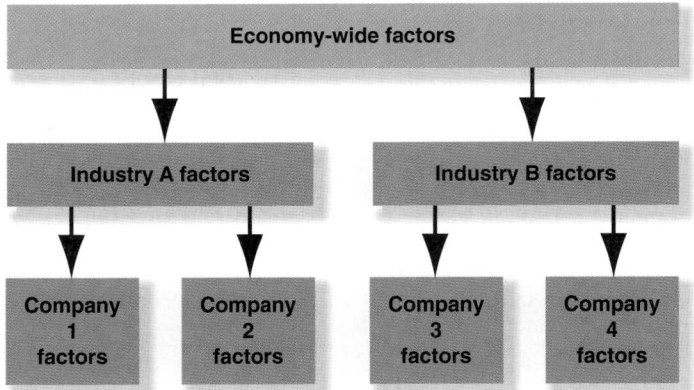

contained in the financial statements. They visit the company, buy its products, and read about it in the business press. For example, if you evaluate McDonald's, it is equally important to assess the quality of its statement of financial position and the quality of its McChicken sandwich.

Besides considering these factors, investors should understand a company's business strategy when evaluating its financial statements. Before discussing analytical techniques, we will show you how business strategy affects financial statement analysis.

LO¹

Explain how a company's business strategy affects financial analysis.

UNDERSTANDING A COMPANY'S STRATEGY

Financial statement analysis involves more than just "crunching numbers." Before you start looking at numbers, you should know what you are looking for. While financial statements report on transactions, each of these transactions is the result of a company's operating decisions as it implements its business strategy.

A useful starting point for financial statement analysis is the return on equity (ROE) or *DuPont model*. The DuPont model helps us analyze the profitability of a business and demonstrates that a variety of strategies can result in high levels of profitability. The model follows:

Businesses can earn a high rate of return for the owners (i.e., a high ROE) by following different strategies. There are two fundamental strategies:

1. *Product differentiation.* Under this strategy, companies offer products with unique benefits, such as high quality or unusual features or style. These unique benefits allow a company to charge higher prices. In general, higher prices result in higher profit margins, which lead to higher returns on equity (as shown in the DuPont model).

2. *Cost advantage.* Under this strategy, companies attempt to operate more efficiently than their competitors, allowing them to offer lower prices to attract customers. The efficient use of resources is captured in the total asset turnover ratio, and as the ROE model illustrates, a high total asset turnover ratio leads to higher return on investment.

You can probably think of a number of companies that have followed one of these two basic strategies:

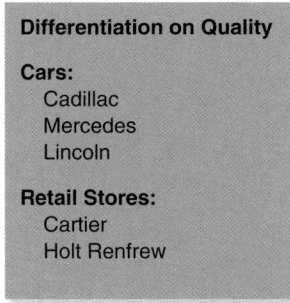

Differentiation on Quality

Cars:
Cadillac
Mercedes
Lincoln

Retail Stores:
Cartier
Holt Renfrew

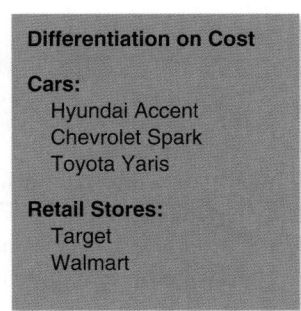

Differentiation on Cost

Cars:
Hyundai Accent
Chevrolet Spark
Toyota Yaris

Retail Stores:
Target
Walmart

The best place to start your analysis is with a solid understanding of a company's business strategy. To evaluate how a company is doing, you must know what managers are trying to do. You can learn a lot about a company's strategy by reading its complete annual report, especially the letter from the president. It also is useful to read articles about the company in the business press.

Canadian Tire's business strategy is described in its annual report as follows:

5.0 Strategic objectives

5.1 Strategic objectives and initiatives

While meeting the needs of the jobs and joys of everyday living in Canada, the Company has focused its retail businesses and financial services business to support growth and productivity improvements in order to achieve the five-year financial aspirations outlined in 2010 (see section 5.2 for financial aspirations). Underlying the growth and productivity initiatives in 2012 were four strategic objectives that are key to sustained future growth:

1. **Strengthen core retail**
   Achieve growth in CTR through a customer-centric approach

2. **Align all business units to reinforce the core**
   Operate as "one company"

3. **Build a high-performing organization**
   Establish a corporate culture of continuous improvement

4. **Create new platforms for growth**
   Identify and evaluate new growth opportunities

Source: Canadian Tire Corporation, Limited, Annual Report 2012.

This strategy has several implications for our analysis of Canadian Tire:

1. Productivity is critical. Canadian Tire must be able to generate more earnings per square metre of retail space to improve net earnings and the return on invested capital.

2. To increase sales as it opens new stores, Canadian Tire must stick to what it has done best in order to enhance in-store customer experience, which will improve customer loyalty and increase repeated sales.

3. Profitability arises from prudent investment of scarce capital and cost control, which provide economies of scale even when volume decreases.

With these implications in mind, we can attach more meaning to the information contained in Canadian Tire's financial statements.

As the preceding discussion indicates, a company can take different actions to try to affect each of the ratios in the DuPont model. To understand the impact of these actions, financial analysts disaggregate each of the ratios into more detailed ratios. For example, the total asset turnover ratio is further disaggregated into turnover ratios for specific assets such as trade receivables, inventory, and fixed assets. We have developed our understanding of these ratios in previous chapters, but we will bring them together in the next few sections as part of a comprehensive review of ratio analysis.

LO²

Discuss how analysts use financial statements.

FINANCIAL STATEMENT ANALYSIS

Analyzing financial data without a basis of comparison is impossible. For example, would you be impressed with a company that earned $1 million last year? You are probably thinking, "It depends." Earnings of $1 million might be very good for a company that lost money the year before, but not good for a company that earned $500 million during the previous year. It might be good for a small company but not good for a very large company. And, it might be good if all the other companies in the industry lost money, but not good if they all earned much more.

As you can see from this simple example, financial results cannot be evaluated in isolation. To properly analyze the information reported in financial statements, you must develop appropriate comparisons. The task of finding appropriate benchmarks requires judgment and is not always an easy task. For this reason, financial analysis is a sophisticated skill, not a mechanical process.

There are two types of benchmarks for making financial comparisons: time series and comparisons with other companies.

1. *Time series analysis.* In this type of analysis, information for a single company is compared over time. For example, a key measure of performance for a retail company is the change in sales volume each year for its existing stores. The time series chart below shows that Canadian Tire was able to achieve sales growth in existing stores in most of the years during the period 2001–2012:[1]

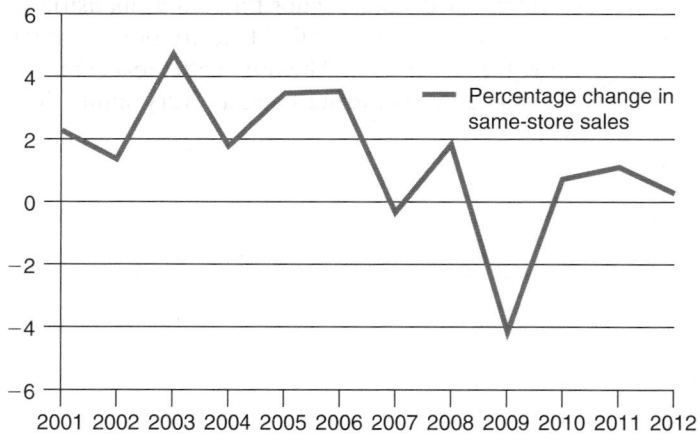

2. *Comparison with similar companies.* Financial results are often affected by industry- and economy-wide factors. By comparing a company with another one in the same line of business, an analyst can obtain better insight into its performance. For example, the comparison of profit margin (net earnings as a percentage of sales) for 2012 and the change in sales for Canadian Tire, RONA, and Richelieu Hardware from the previous year shows that Canadian Tire had the highest increase in sales, but Richelieu Hardware reported a higher profit margin ratio. While Canadian Tire was able to increase its sales, it appears that Richelieu Hardware was more effective at controlling its expenses relative to the increase in its sales:

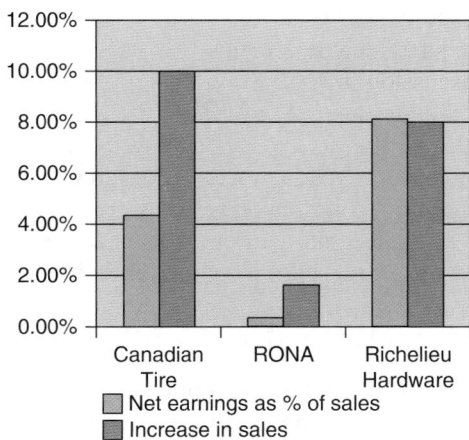

Finding comparable companies is often very difficult. Canadian Tire's products include auto parts and petroleum products, which are not sold by either RONA or Richelieu Hardware. No single retailer competes directly with Canadian Tire across the wide variety of products and services that the company offers.

Care must be exercised when selecting comparable companies from the same basic industry. Days Inn, Four Seasons, Hilton, Holiday Inn, and Marriott are all in the hotel industry, but not all could be considered comparable companies for the purpose of financial analysis. These hotels offer different levels of quality and appeal to different types of customers.

The governments of the United States, Canada, and Mexico developed the North American Industry Classification System for use in reporting economic data. The system assigns a specific industry code to each corporation, based on its business operations. Analysts often use these six-digit codes to identify companies that have similar business operations. Financial information services, such as Standard & Poor's, provide averages for many common accounting ratios for various industries as defined by the industrial classification codes. Because of the diversity of companies included in each industry classification, these data should be used with great care. For this reason, some analysts prefer to compare two companies that are very similar instead of using industry-wide comparisons.

RATIO AND PERCENTAGE ANALYSES

All financial analysts use **ratio analysis**, or **percentage analysis**, when they review companies. A ratio or percentage expresses the proportional relationship between two different amounts, allowing for easy comparisons. Assessing a company's profitability is difficult if you know only that it had net earnings of $500,000. Comparing net earnings to other numbers, such as shareholders' equity, provides additional insights. If shareholders' equity is $5 million, the relationship of net earnings to shareholder investment is $500,000 ÷ $5,000,000 = 10 percent. This measure indicates a different level of performance than would be the case if shareholders' equity were $50 million. Ratio analysis condenses the large volume of raw financial data and helps decision makers identify significant relationships and make meaningful comparisons between companies.

Ratios may be computed by using amounts in one statement, such as the statement of earnings, or in two different statements, such as the statement of earnings and the statement of financial position. In addition, amounts on a single statement may be expressed as a percentage of a base amount.

RATIO (PERCENTAGE) ANALYSIS is an analytical tool designed to identify significant relationships; it measures the proportional relationship between two financial statement amounts.

A **COMPONENT PERCENTAGE**
expresses each item on a
particular financial statement as
a percentage of a single base
amount.

Component Percentages

Analysts often compute **component percentages**, which express each item on a financial statement as a percentage of a single *base amount*, the denominator of the ratio. To compute component percentages for the statement of earnings, the base amount is net sales revenue. Each expense is expressed as a percentage of net sales revenue. On the statement of financial position, the base amount is total assets; each element of the statement of financial position is divided by total assets. This is also known as creating a common-size financial statement.

Discerning important relationships and trends in Canadian Tire's statement of earnings shown in Exhibit 13.1 is difficult without using component percentages. Net earnings increased by 6.9 percent between 2011 and 2012, which appears to be good; but it is difficult for an analyst to evaluate the operating efficiency of Canadian Tire based on the reported numbers on the statement of earnings.

Exhibit 13.2 shows a component percentage analysis for Canadian Tire's statement of earnings (from Exhibit 13.1). One additional year, 2010, is presented for comparative purposes.[2] If you simply reviewed the dollar amounts on the statement of earnings, you might be concerned about several significant differences. For example, sales and marketing expenses increased by $328.5 million between 2011 and 2012. Is this increase reasonable, relative to the increase in sales? Should you be concerned, as an analyst? The component percentage indicates that sales and marketing expenses actually increased slightly as a percentage of sales revenue during that period. In other words, sales and marketing expenses have increased in proportion to sales revenue.

The component analysis for Canadian Tire shown in Exhibit 13.2 helps highlight several additional issues:

1. Net earnings (net income) increased from $444.20 million in 2010 to $499.2 million in 2012. However, profit margin decreased during the same period from 4.8 percent to 4.4 percent, indicating that expenses increased at a faster rate than sales revenue.
2. Some of the changes in percentages may seem immaterial, but they involve very significant amounts of money. The decrease in the ratio of distribution costs as a percentage of sales from 3.5 percent in 2011 to 3.1 percent in 2012 represents $12.5 million.
3. The gross profit as a percentage of sales increased between 2010 and 2012. The company attributes this increase to a focused effort to rebalance sales and margins at its Canadian Tire Retail unit, reduced promotional activity at Mark's compared to 2011, and the impact of synergies realized through the acquisition of FGL Sports, as well as improvement in the margin rate in its Financial Services business due to an improvement in net write-offs.

Exhibit **13.2**

Component Percentages for
Canadian Tire

	Component Percentages		
Statement of Earnings	**2012**	**2011**	**2010**
Revenue (Note 31)	100.0%	100.0%	100.0%
Cost of producing revenue	69.4	70.5	69.7
Gross profit	30.6	29.5	30.3
Other income	0.0	0.2	0.0
Operating expenses			
Distribution costs	3.1	3.5	3.2
Sales and marketing expenses	14.3	12.6	11.8
Administrative expenses	6.2	6.2	7.4
Total operating expenses	23.6	22.3	22.5
Operating income	7.0	7.4	7.8
Finance income	(0.2)	(0.2)	(0.4)
Finance costs	1.3	1.5	1.8
Net finance costs	1.1	1.3	1.4
Income before income taxes	5.9	6.1	6.4
Income taxes	1.5	1.6	1.6
Net income	4.4	4.5	4.8

4. Significant stability in all of the statement of earnings relationships indicates a well-run company. Notice that most of the individual statement of earnings items changed by less than 1.5 percentage points over a three-year period, except for sales and marketing expenses. The more stable these relationships are over a long time period, particularly during economic turbulence, the more confidence analysts will have in their predictions of the company's future, based on relationships among the various elements of the company's financial statements.

Exhibit 13.3, similar to Exhibit 13.2, shows a component percentage analysis for Canadian Tire's statement of financial position covering a period of four years. If you simply reviewed the dollar amounts on the statement of earnings, you might be

	Component Percentages				Exhibit **13.3**
Statement of Financial Position	**2012**	**2011**	**2010**	**2009**	Component Percentages for
ASSETS					Canadian Tire
Current Assets:					
Cash and cash equivalents	7.7	2.6	5.1	7.8	
Short-term investments	1.3	1.6	1.8	0.5	
Trade and other receivables	5.7	6.7	6.1	7.5	
Loans receivable	32.3	33.1	36.7	35.1	
Merchandise inventories	11.4	11.7	8.2	8.2	
Income taxes recoverable	0.0	0.0	0.9	0.8	
Prepaid expenses and deposits	0.3	0.4	0.3	0.4	
Assets classified as held for sale	0.0	0.3	0.2	0.1	
Total current assets	58.8	56.4	59.3	60.4	
Long-term receivables and other assets	5.1	5.4	6.6	7.0	
Long-term investments	1.4	1.0	0.7	0.4	
Goodwill and intangible assets	8.3	9.0	3.3	2.9	
Investment property	0.7	0.6	0.6	0.6	
Property and equipment	25.4	27.3	29.3	28.1	
Deferred income taxes	0.3	0.3	0.3	0.4	
Total assets	100.0	100.0	100.0	100.0	
LIABILITIES					
Current Liabilities:					
Bank indebtedness	0.7	1.0	1.1	0.7	
Deposits	9.9	9.6	5.6	7.6	
Trade and other payables	12.4	13.3	10.7	10.5	
Provisions	1.4	1.6	1.8	1.9	
Short-term borrowings	0.9	2.9	0.9	1.4	
Loans payable	4.7	5.1	6.2	6.6	
Income taxes payable	0.0	0.0	—	—	
Current portion of long-term debt	5.0	0.2	3.2	6.1	
Total current liabilities	35.1	33.7	29.4	34.8	
Long-term provisions	0.4	0.4	0.2	0.2	
Long-term debt	17.7	19.0	21.4	21.4	
Long-term deposits	8.4	8.9	11.4	10.5	
Deferred income taxes	0.6	0.5	—	—	
Other long-term liabilities	1.6	1.7	1.2	1.1	
Total liabilities	63.9	64.3	63.8	68.1	
SHAREHOLDERS' EQUITY					
Share capital	5.2	5.8	6.4	6.3	
Contributed surplus	0.02	0.01	0.0	0.0	
Accumulated other comprehensive income (loss)	0.01	0.1	(0.3)	(0.4)	
Retained earnings	30.9	29.9	30.1	26.0	
Total shareholders' equity	36.1	35.7	36.2	31.9	
Total liabilities and shareholders' equity	100.0	100.0	100.0	100.0	

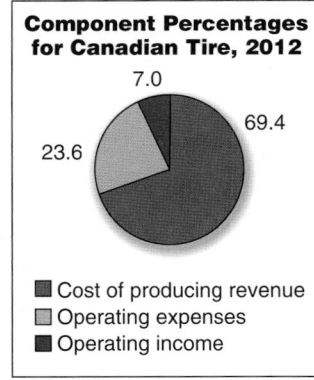

Component Percentages for Canadian Tire, 2012

7.0

69.4

23.6

■ Cost of producing revenue
□ Operating expenses
■ Operating income

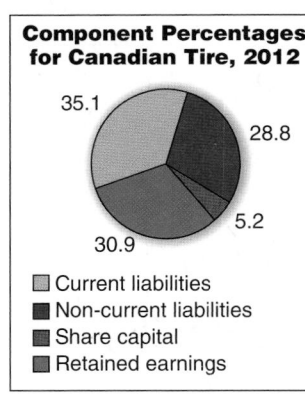

Component Percentages for Canadian Tire, 2012

35.1

28.8

5.2

30.9

□ Current liabilities
■ Non-current liabilities
■ Share capital
■ Retained earnings

concerned about several significant differences. For example, total liabilities increased by $488.0 million between 2011 and 2012. Is this increase reasonable, relative to the increase in assets during 2012? Should you be concerned, as an analyst? The component percentage indicates that total liabilities actually decreased slightly as a percentage of total assets. In other words, total liabilities have decreased proportionally to total assets.

The component analysis for Canadian Tire shown in Exhibit 13.3 provides several additional insights:

1. Receivables and merchandise inventories represent approximately 50 percent of the total assets, and this percentage has been relatively stable over time.

2. Total liabilities have declined slightly over the past few years but are relatively stable. They make up about 65 percent of the financing of total assets.

3. The various percentages indicate generally that the financial situation of Canadian Tire is relatively stable over time despite significant changes in the dollar value of certain elements of the statement of financial position.

Many analysts use graphics software in their study of financial results. Graphic representation is especially useful when communicating findings during meetings or in printed form. A graphic summary of key 2012 data from Exhibits 13.2 and 13.3 is shown in the margin.

In addition to component percentages, analysts use ratios to compare related items from the financial statements. Of the many ratios that can be computed from a single set of financial statements, analysts use only those that are relevant to the analysis of a given situation. Comparing cost of sales to property, plant, and equipment is never useful because these items have no natural relationship. Instead, an analyst will often compute certain widely used ratios and then decide which additional ratios are relevant to the particular decision. For example, research and development costs as a percentage of sales is not a commonly used ratio, but it is useful when analyzing companies that depend on new products, such as pharmaceutical or technology firms.

When you compute ratios, remember a basic fact about financial statements: statement of financial position amounts relate to an instant in time, and statement of earnings amounts relate to a specified period. Therefore, when a statement of earnings amount is compared with a statement of financial position amount, you should express the statement of financial position amount as an average of the beginning and ending balances. In practice, many analysts simply use the ending statement of financial position amount. This approach is appropriate only if no significant changes have occurred in statement of financial position amounts. For consistency, we always use average amounts.

Financial statement analysis is a process that requires judgment. Not all ratios are relevant to the analysis of a given situation. We will discuss several ratios that are appropriate to most situations. They can be grouped into the five categories shown in Exhibit 13.4.

Tests of Profitability

Profitability is a primary measure of the overall success of a company. Indeed, it is necessary for a company's survival. Investors and creditors prefer a single measure of profitability that is meaningful in all situations. Unfortunately, no single measure can be devised to meet this comprehensive need. Several **tests of profitability** focus on measuring the adequacy of net earnings by comparing it to other items reported on the financial statements.

1. Return on Equity (ROE)   *Return on equity* (also called *return on owners' investment*) relates net earnings to the investment made by the owners. It reflects the simple fact that investors expect to earn more money if they invest more money. Two investments that

Exhibit **13.4**
Widely Used Accounting Ratios

Ratio

Tests of Profitability		Basic Computation
1. Return on equity (ROE)	Chapter 4	$\dfrac{\text{Net Earnings}}{\text{Average Shareholders' Equity}}$
2. Return on assets (ROA)	Chapter 3	$\dfrac{\text{Net Earnings} + \text{Interest Expense (net of tax)}}{\text{Average Total Assets}}$
Financial leverage percentage	Chapter 13	Return on Equity − Return on Assets
3. Earnings per share (EPS) ratio	Chapter 12	$\dfrac{\text{Net Earnings Available to Common Shareholders}}{\substack{\text{Average Number of} \\ \text{Common Shares Outstanding}}}$
4. Quality of earnings	Chapter 5	$\dfrac{\text{Cash Flows from Operating Activities}}{\text{Net Earnings}}$
5. Net profit margin ratio	Chapter 4	$\dfrac{\text{Net Earnings}}{\text{Net Sales}}$
6. Fixed asset turnover ratio	Chapter 9	$\dfrac{\text{Net Sales}}{\text{Average Net Fixed Assets}}$

Tests of Liquidity

7. Cash ratio	Chapter 13	$\dfrac{\text{Cash} + \text{Cash Equivalents}}{\text{Current Liabilities}}$
8. Current ratio	Chapter 2	$\dfrac{\text{Current Assets}}{\text{Current Liabilities}}$
9. Quick ratio	Chapter 10	$\dfrac{\text{Quick Assets}}{\text{Current Liabilities}}$
10. Receivables turnover ratio	Chapter 7	$\dfrac{\text{Net Credit Sales}}{\text{Average Net Trade Receivables}}$
11. Inventory turnover ratio	Chapter 8	$\dfrac{\text{Cost of Sales}}{\text{Average Inventory}}$
12. Trade payables turnover ratio	Chapter 10	$\dfrac{\text{Cost of Sales}}{\text{Average Net Trade Payables}}$

Tests of Solvency

13. Times interest earned ratio	Chapter 11	$\dfrac{\text{Net Earnings} + \text{Interest Expense} + \text{Income Tax Expense}}{\text{Interest Expense}}$
14. Cash coverage ratio	Chapter 13	$\dfrac{\substack{\text{Cash Flows from Operating Activities} \\ \text{(before Interest and Taxes)}}}{\text{Interest Paid}}$
15. Debt-to-equity ratio	Chapter 11	$\dfrac{\text{Total Liabilities}}{\text{Shareholders' Equity}}$

Market Tests

16. Price/earnings ratio	Chapter 13	$\dfrac{\text{Current Market Price per Share}}{\text{Earnings per Share}}$
17. Dividend yield ratio	Chapter 12	$\dfrac{\text{Dividends per Share}}{\text{Market Price per Share}}$

Note: Most of these ratios have been discussed in previous chapters. The specific chapter appears next to the ratio.

offer a return of $10,000 are not comparable if one requires an investment of $100,000 and the other requires an investment of $250,000. The ROE is computed as follows:[3]

$$\text{Return on Equity} = \frac{\text{Net Earnings}}{\text{Average Shareholders' Equity}}$$

$$\text{Canadian Tire, 2012} = \frac{\$499.2}{\$4,586.3^*} = 10.9\%$$

*($4,409.0 + $4,763.6) ÷ 2

Canadian Tire earned 10.9 percent on the owners' investment. Was that return high or low? We can answer this question by comparing Canadian Tire's ROE with the ratios of similar companies. The ROEs for two of Canadian Tire's competitors, RONA and Richelieu Hardware, are 1 percent and 16.9 percent, respectively.

Clearly, Canadian Tire produced a better ROE than RONA but lags behind Richelieu Hardware.

We gain additional insight by examining Canadian Tire's ROE over time:

	2012	2011	2010
ROE	10.9	11.1	11.6

This comparison shows that Canadian Tire's performance, as measured by ROE, declined slightly over the three years, primarily because of increased operating expenses.

2. Return on Assets (ROA) Another test of profitability compares net earnings to the total assets (i.e., total investment) used to generate the net earnings. Many analysts consider the *return on assets* (ROA) to be a better measure of management's ability to utilize assets effectively, because it is not affected by the way in which the assets were financed. For example, the ROE could be very large for a company that has a large amount of debt compared to a company that earned the same return based on the same amount of assets but borrowed less money. The ROE measures profitability from the perspective of the shareholders, whereas the ROA takes into consideration the resources contributed by both shareholders and creditors. For this reason, the return to shareholders, net earnings, is augmented by the return to creditors, which is interest expense. Interest expense is measured net of income tax, because it represents the net cost of the funds provided by creditors to the corporation.[4]

The ROA is computed as follows:

$$\text{Return on Assets} = \frac{\text{Net Earnings} + \text{Interest Expense}^5 \text{ (net of tax)}}{\text{Average Total Assets}}$$

$$\text{Canadian Tire, 2012} = \frac{\$499.2 + \$144.3 \times (1 - 0.263^*)}{\$12,760.1^\dagger} = 4.7\%$$

*Income tax rate = Income tax expense ÷ Earnings before income taxes = $178.0 ÷ $677.2 = 0.263
†($12,338.8 + $13,181.4) ÷ 2

Canadian Tire earned 4.7 percent on the total resources it used during the year. Canadian Tire achieved a better return on assets than RONA (1.2%) but did not utilize its assets as effectively as Richelieu Hardware (13.7%).

Financial Leverage Percentage The *financial leverage percentage* measures the advantage or disadvantage that occurs when a company's ROE differs from its ROA (i.e., ROE − ROA ≠ 0). In the DuPont model discussed earlier in this chapter, financial leverage was defined as the proportion of assets acquired with funds supplied by owners. The financial leverage percentage measures a related but different concept. It describes the relationship between the ROE and the ROA.

Return on Equity for Selected Industries—2012

Paper and forest products 1.8%

Gold 7.9%

Retailing 14.4%

Telecommunications services 18.4%

Leverage is positive when the rate of return on a company's assets exceeds the average after-tax interest rate on its borrowed funds. Basically, the company borrows at one rate and earns a higher rate of return on its investments. Most companies have positive leverage.

Financial leverage percentage can be measured by comparing the two return on investment ratios as follows:

$$\textbf{Financial Leverage Percentage = Return on Equity − Return on Assets}$$
$$\textbf{Canadian Tire, 2012} = 10.9\% − 4.7\% = 6.2\%$$

When a company is able to borrow funds at an after-tax interest rate and invest those funds to earn a higher after-tax rate of return, the difference benefits the owners. The notes to Canadian Tire's annual report indicate that the company has borrowed money at rates ranging from 2.394 percent to 6.32 percent, with a weighted-average interest rate of 4.54 percent before tax. This cost of debt would be reduced to 3.34 6 percent [= 4.54% × (1 − 0.263)]. The borrowed money is invested in assets earning 4.7 percent. The difference between the income earned on the money it has borrowed and the interest it has paid to creditors is available for Canadian Tire's shareholders. This benefit of financial leverage is the primary reason that most companies obtain a significant amount of their resources from creditors rather than from the sale of shares. Notice that financial leverage can be enhanced either by investing effectively (i.e., earning a high return on investment) or by borrowing effectively (i.e., paying a low rate of interest).

A negative financial leverage percentage means that ROE has decreased relative to ROA or that ROA has increased relative to ROE. ROE decreases when net earnings decrease, signalling a deterioration in the company's profitability, or when equity increases through the issuance of additional shares. An inflow of cash from a new equity issue may indicate that the company is entering a growth phase that is expected to increase net earnings. Another possibility is that ROA may have increased substantially relative to ROE because of an increase in after-tax interest expense and in the cost of debt financing. Without careful interpretation of relevant information available on a specific company, investors cannot accurately interpret a decrease in ROE as either good news or bad news.

In general, if a decrease in ROE signals future growth despite a temporarily negative financial leverage percentage, investors may not be too alarmed by negative leverage. If, however, an increase in ROA is the result of borrowing at high interest rates, investors could well interpret negative leverage as reflecting bad news. It is, therefore, important for investors to be cautious when interpreting any increase or decrease in ratios.

Canadian Tire's financial leverage percentage is higher than RONA's (−0.2 percent) but significantly lower than the ratio of Richelieu Hardware (13.3 percent).

3. Earnings per Share Ratio *Earnings per share* (EPS) is a measure of the return on investment that is based on the number of shares outstanding instead of the dollar amounts reported on the statement of financial position. In simple situations, EPS is computed as follows:

$$\textbf{Earnings per Share Ratio} = \frac{\textbf{Net Earnings Available to Common Shareholders}}{\textbf{Average Number of Common Shares Outstanding}}$$

$$\textbf{Canadian Tire, 2012} = \frac{\$499.2}{81.4*} = \$6.13$$

*Reported on the statement of earnings.

This computation of EPS is based on information reported on the statement of earnings. The additional complexities in the computation of EPS are discussed in advanced accounting courses.

EPS is probably the single most widely watched ratio. Companies' announcements of their net earnings each quarter during the fiscal year are normally reported in the business press. The following news story by Reuters concerning Canadian Tire's earnings results for the fourth quarter of 2012 illustrates the importance of EPS:

Canadian Tire profit dips on restructuring, acquisition costs

Feb 21 (Reuters)—Diversified retailer Canadian Tire Corp reported a slightly lower fourth-quarter profit as a result of restructuring charges and costs related to its acquisition of FGL Sports in August 2011.

Net income fell to C$163.1 million ($160.7 million), or C$2.00 per share, in the second quarter, from C$166.3 million, or C$2.03 per share, a year earlier. It took a restructuring charge of C$19.6 million during the quarter.

Canadian Tire, one of Canada's biggest and best-known retailers, had announced a number of executive departures in the quarter to cut costs.

Revenue rose 1 percent to C$3.16 billion. Sales in its flagship Canadian Tire banner fell 2 percent to C$1.55 billion.

. . .

The company said adjusted fourth-quarter profit rose 2.8 percent on better performance in its credit card business.

Shares of the Toronto-based company, which has a market value C$5.58 billion, were down 1 percent at C$67.55 in early Thursday trade on the Toronto Stock Exchange.

Source: **www.reuters.com/article/2013/02/21/canadiantire-results-idUSL4N0BL5BU20130221? type=companyNews**. Accessed March 2, 2013.

4. Quality of Earnings Ratio   Most financial analysts are concerned about the quality of a company's earnings because the use of some accounting procedures can result in higher earnings reports. For example, a company that uses short estimated lives for non-current assets will report lower earnings than will a similar company that uses longer estimated lives. One method of evaluating the quality of a company's earnings is to compare its reported earnings to its cash flows from operating activities, as follows:

$$\text{Quality of Earnings Ratio} = \frac{\text{Cash Flows from Operating Activities}}{\text{Net Earnings}}$$

$$\text{Canadian Tire, 2012} = \frac{\$743}{\$499.2} = 1.49$$

A quality of earnings ratio higher than 1 is considered to indicate higher-quality earnings, because each dollar of net earnings is supported by at least one dollar of cash flow. Recall that net earnings include both cash and non-cash components that result from accrual of revenues and expenses that will affect cash in future accounting periods. A ratio below 1 indicates that accruals represent a significant portion of net earnings, which suggests that earnings are of lower quality than if the ratio exceeded 1. Richelieu Hardware had a quality of earnings ratio of 0.99, but RONA's ratio is −4.25 because of net cash outflow for operating activities.

5. Net Profit Margin Ratio   The *net profit margin ratio* measures the percentage of each sales dollar, on average, that represents net earnings. It is computed as follows:

$$\text{Net Profit Margin Ratio} = \frac{\text{Net Earnings}}{\text{Net Sales}}$$

$$\text{Canadian Tire, 2012} = \frac{\$499.2}{\$11,427.2} = 4.4\%$$

During 2012, each dollar of Canadian Tire's sales generated 4.4 cents of net earnings. Care must be used in analyzing the net profit margin ratio because it does not consider the amount of resources employed (i.e., total investment) to generate net earnings. For example, the hypothetical statements of earnings of Canadian Tire and Richelieu Hardware might show the following:

	Richelieu Hardware	Canadian Tire
a. Sales revenue	$500,000	$150,000
b. Net earnings	25,000	7,500
c. Net profit margin ratio (b ÷ a)	5%	5%
d. Total investment	$250,000	$125,000
e. Return on total investment* (b ÷ d)	10%	6%
*Assuming no interest expense.		

In this example, both companies reported the same profit margin (5 percent). Richelieu Hardware, however, appears to be performing much better, because it is earning a 10 percent return on the total investment versus the 6 percent earned by Canadian Tire. The profit margin percentages do not reflect the effect of the $250,000 total investment in Richelieu Hardware compared to the $125,000 total investment in Canadian Tire. Thus, the net profit margin ratio omits one of the two important factors that should be used in evaluating return on the investment.

It is very difficult to compare profit margins for companies in different industries. For example, profit margins are low in the food industry, but they are high in the jewellery business. Both types of businesses can be quite profitable, however, because a high sales volume can compensate for a low profit margin. Grocery stores have low profit margins but generate a large sales volume from their relatively inexpensive stores and inventory. Although jewellery stores generate more net earnings from each sales dollar, they require a large investment in luxury stores and very expensive inventory.

The trade-off between profit margin and sales volume can be stated in very simple terms: would you prefer to have 5 percent of $1,000,000 or 10 percent of $100,000? As you can see, a larger percentage is not always better.

The operating strength of Canadian Tire (4.4 percent) is short of Richelieu Hardware's operating performance (8.1 percent), and both are stronger than RONA (0.4 percent) when you compare their net profit margin ratios for 2012.

6. Fixed Asset Turnover Ratio   Another measure of operating efficiency is the fixed asset turnover ratio, which compares sales volume with a company's investment in fixed assets. The term *fixed assets* is synonymous with *property, plant, and equipment*. The ratio is computed as follows:

$$\text{Fixed Asset Turnover Ratio} = \frac{\text{Net Sales}}{\text{Average Net Fixed Assets}}$$

$$\text{Canadian Tire, 2012} = \frac{\$11,427.2}{\$3,354.7^*} = 3.41$$

*($3,365.9 + $3,343.5) ÷ 2

The fixed asset turnover ratio for Canadian Tire is lower than the ratios for both RONA (5.79) and Richelieu Hardware (23.3). In simple terms, this means that both RONA and Richelieu Hardware have a competitive advantage over Canadian Tire in terms of their ability to effectively utilize fixed assets to generate revenue. For each dollar that Canadian Tire invested in property, plant, and equipment, it was able to earn $3.41 in sales revenue, while RONA earned $5.79 and Richelieu Hardware earned $23.3.

The fixed asset turnover ratio is widely used to analyze capital-intensive companies, such as airlines and electric utilities. For companies that have large amounts of inventory and trade receivables, analysts often prefer to use the total asset turnover ratio, which is based on total assets rather than fixed assets:

$$\text{Total Asset Turnover Ratio} = \frac{\text{Net Sales}}{\text{Average Total Assets}}$$

$$\text{Canadian Tire, 2012} = \frac{\$11,427.2}{\$12,760.1^*} = 0.90$$

*($12,338.8 + $13,181.4) ÷ 2

In 2012, Canadian Tire was able to generate $0.90 in revenue for each dollar invested in the company's assets. This ratio does not compare favourably to the ratio of either RONA (1.75) or Richelieu Hardware (1.69).

As we showed with the ROE model earlier in this chapter, one strategy to improve ROE is to generate more revenue from the company's assets. Many analysts consider this type of improvement to be an important indication of the quality of the company's management.

PAUSE FOR FEEDBACK

We have discussed several measures of profitability. Next we will discuss tests of liquidity. Before you move on, complete the following questions to test your understanding of these ratios.

SELF-STUDY QUIZ 13-1

Dollarama Inc. reported the following data in a recent annual report (in millions of dollars):

	Current Year	Last Year
Net earnings	$ 173.5	
Net sales	1,602.8	
Interest expense (net of tax)	14.3	
Shareholders' equity	894.9	$ 731.2
Total assets	1,407.7	1,311.1

1. Compute the following ratios:
   a. Return on equity
   b. Return on assets
   c. Net profit margin
2. Does the company use debt effectively to generate returns to shareholders? Explain.

After you complete your answers, check them with the solutions at the end of this chapter.

The Dupont Analysis

Exhibit 13.5 shows a decomposition of Canadian Tire's ROE, which was presented earlier. This analysis shows the sources of the change in ROE and can provide useful insights into Canadian Tire's business strategy.

Exhibit 13.5 shows a decrease in profit margin for fiscal years 2011 and 2012. The component percentages (see Exhibit 13.2) suggest that this decrease was caused mainly by an increase in the cost of sales (cost of producing revenue) in 2011 and an increase in sales and marketing expenses in 2012 that outpaced the increase in revenues for these years. The company improved on its utilization of assets to generate revenue, but its financial leverage decreased in 2011 and increased slightly in 2012. The increase in the total asset turnover ratio was not significant enough to offset the decreases in the other two components of the DuPont model.[6] This decomposition of the ROE highlights the areas that require further analysis in order to increase the return on shareholders' equity.

	Fiscal Year Ended		
	December 29, 2012	**December 31, 2011**	**January 1, 2011**
ROE Components			
Net earnings	$ 499.2	$ 467.0	$ 444.2
Net sales	11,427.2	10,387.1	9,213.1
Average total assets	12,760.1	11,693.7	11,227.9
Average shareholders' equity	4,586.3	4,207.0	3,824.0
DuPont model			
Net earnings/Net sales	0.044	0.045	0.048
× Net sales/Avg. total assets	0.896	0.888	0.821
× Avg. total assets/ Avg. shareholders' equity	2.782	2.780	2.936
= Net earnings/Avg. shareholders' equity	0.109	0.111	0.116

Exhibit **13.5**

Canadian Tire ROE Decomposition

PAUSE FOR FEEDBACK STOP

We used ROE analysis in Exhibit 13.5 to understand how Canadian Tire's ROE had changed over the fiscal years 2010–2012. This type of analysis is often called *time series analysis*. ROE analysis can also be used to explain why a company has an ROE that is different from its competitors' at a single point in time. This type of analysis is called *cross-sectional analysis*. Before you move on, complete the following analysis to test your understanding of the DuPont model.

SELF-STUDY QUIZ 13-2

Google Inc. and Yahoo Inc. both supply Internet search services. Both companies have developed reputations for good service. The following is an analysis of their ROEs for a recent year. Using the DuPont analysis, explain how Google produced its higher ROE.

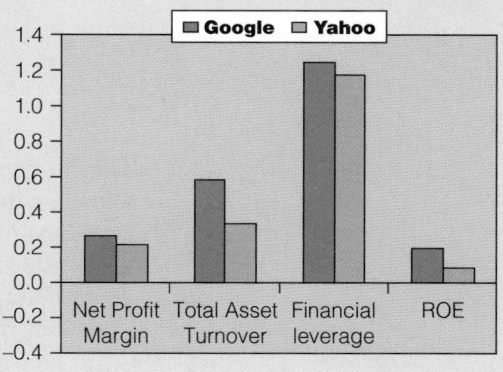

DuPont model	Google	Yahoo
Net earnings/Net sales	0.257	0.213
× Net sales/Avg. total assets	0.581	0.335
× Avg. total assets/Avg. shareholders' equity	1.249	1.180
= Net earnings/Avg. shareholders' equity	0.187	0.084

After you complete your answer, check it with the solution at the end of this chapter.

Tests of Liquidity

Liquidity refers to a company's ability to meet its currently maturing debts. **Tests of liquidity** focus on the relationship between current assets and current liabilities and measure a company's ability to meet its currently maturing obligations. A company's ability to pay its current liabilities is an important factor in evaluating its short-term financial strength. For example, a company that does not have cash available to pay for purchases on a timely basis will lose its cash discounts and run the risk of having its credit discontinued by vendors. Three ratios are used to measure liquidity: cash ratio, current ratio, and quick ratio.

LO⁵

Compute and interpret liquidity ratios.

TESTS OF LIQUIDITY are ratios that measure a company's ability to meet its currently maturing obligations.

7. Cash Ratio   Cash is the lifeblood of a business. Without cash, a company cannot pay employees or meet obligations to its creditors. Even a profitable business will fail without sufficient cash. One measure of the adequacy of available cash, called the *cash ratio*, is computed as follows:

$$\text{Cash Ratio} = \frac{\text{Cash} + \text{Cash Equivalents}}{\text{Current Liabilities}}$$

$$\text{Canadian Tire, 2012} = \frac{\$1,015.5}{\$4,624.1} = 0.22$$

Analysts often use this ratio to compare similar companies. Both Canadian Tire and Richelieu Hardware (0.92) have ratios that exceed RONA's ratio (0.04), indicating that RONA has a smaller cash reserve compared to current liabilities.

Would analysts be concerned about a low cash ratio for Canadian Tire? Probably not, because there are other factors to consider. The statement of financial position for Canadian Tire shows that the company has a sizeable portfolio of loans receivable that can be sold to a financial institution for cash should the company need to pay current liabilities. Most analysts believe that the cash ratio should not be too high, because holding excess cash is usually uneconomical. It is far better to invest the cash in productive assets or reduce debt.

Some analysts do not use this ratio because it is very sensitive to small events. The collection of a large trade receivable, for example, would have a significant positive effect on the cash ratio. The current ratio and the quick ratio are much less sensitive to the timing of cash collections from customers.

8. Current Ratio   The *current ratio* measures the relationship between current assets and current liabilities at a specific date. It is computed as follows:

$$\text{Current Ratio} = \frac{\text{Current Assets}}{\text{Current Liabilities}}$$

$$\text{Canadian Tire, 2012} = \frac{\$7,748.6}{\$4,624.1} = 1.68$$

The current ratio measures the cushion of working capital that companies maintain to allow for the inevitable unevenness in the flow of funds through the working capital accounts. At the end of 2012, Canadian Tire had $1.68 in current assets for each $1 of liabilities. Most analysts would judge the ratio to be very strong, given Canadian Tire's ability to generate cash. By comparison, RONA has a higher ratio (2.42) than Canadian Tire's and a lower ratio than Richelieu Hardware's (4.56).

To properly use the current ratio, analysts must understand the nature of a company's business. Many manufacturing companies have developed sophisticated systems to minimize the amount of inventory they must hold. These systems, called *just-in-time inventory*, are designed so that an inventory item will arrive just as it is needed. While these systems work well in manufacturing processes, they do not work as well in retailing. Customers expect to find merchandise when they want it, and it has proven difficult to precisely forecast consumer behaviour. As a result, most retailers have comparatively large current ratios because they must carry large inventories. Most companies use a systems approach to inventory management that improves on the distribution of merchandise throughout their supply chains. For example, Canadian Tire has implemented state-of-the-art and innovative technologies, including dimensioner technology; voice pick technology; and automated guided vehicle technology, which replaces traditional human-operated forklifts. These processes allow improved transportation, simplified order processing at suppliers, and reduced lead time for identification of the products needed by specific stores to replenish inventories.

Analysts consider a current ratio of 2 to be financially conservative. Indeed, most companies have current ratios that are below 2. The optimal level for a current ratio depends on the business environment in which a company operates. If cash flows are predictable and stable, as they are for a utility company, the current ratio can even be lower than 1. For a business with highly variable cash flows, such as an airline, a ratio exceeding 1 may be desirable.

Analysts become concerned if a company's current ratio is high compared to those of other companies. A firm is operating inefficiently when it ties up too much money in inventory or trade receivables. There is no reason, for instance, for a Canadian Tire store to hold 1,000 tires in stock if it sells only 100 tires a month.

9. Quick (Acid Test) Ratio The *quick ratio* is a more stringent test of short-term liquidity than the current ratio. The quick ratio compares quick assets, defined as *cash and near-cash assets*, to current liabilities. Quick assets include cash, short-term investments, and trade receivables (net of the allowance for doubtful accounts). Inventories are omitted from quick assets because of the uncertainty of the timing of cash flows from their sale. Prepayments are also excluded from quick assets. Thus, the quick, or acid test, ratio is a more severe test of liquidity than the current ratio. It is computed as follows:

$$\text{Quick Ratio} = \frac{\text{Quick Assets}}{\text{Current Liabilities}}$$

$$\text{Canadian Tire, 2012} = \frac{\$6,200.7}{\$4,624.1} = 1.34$$

The quick ratio is a measure of the safety margin that is available to meet a company's current liabilities. Canadian Tire has $1.34 in cash and near-cash assets for every $1 in current liabilities. This value is relatively high because Canadian Tire carries a relatively large amount of credit card receivables that resulted from customers' use of Canadian Tire's credit card. Richelieu Hardware has a larger ratio of 2.28, but RONA's ratio of 0.74 is smaller.

Current Ratio for Selected Industries—2012

Telecommunications services 0.64

Paper and forest products 2.60

Pharmaceuticals 3.51

Software 3.89

Metals and mining 6.68

Biotechnology 7.83

PAUSE FOR FEEDBACK STOP

We have discussed three measures of liquidity: the cash ratio, the current ratio, and the quick ratio. Next we will discuss additional measures of liquidity. Before you move on, complete the following question to test your understanding of these ratios.

SELF-STUDY QUIZ 13-3

The current ratios for six industries appear in the margin at the top of this page. The following quick ratios, presented in random order, pertain to the same six industries:

	Industries					
	1	2	3	4	5	6
Quick ratio	2.83	0.52	3.62	1.24	6.79	5.11

Two of these six industries are software and biotechnology. Identify the ratio associated with each of these two industries. On average, the quick assets for the software industry represent over 90 percent of the industry's current assets.

After you complete your answer, check it with the solution at the end of this chapter.

10. Receivables Turnover Ratio   Trade receivables are closely related to both short-term liquidity and operating efficiency. A company that can quickly collect cash from its customers has good liquidity and does not needlessly tie up funds in unproductive assets. The receivables turnover ratio is computed as follows:

$$\text{Receivables Turnover Ratio} = \frac{\text{Net Credit Sales*}}{\text{Average Net Trade Receivables}}$$

$$\text{Canadian Tire, 2012} = \frac{\$11,427.2}{\$4,902.8^{\dagger}} = 2.33$$

*Since the amount of net credit sales is normally not reported separately, most analysts use net sales in this equation.

†($4,827.7 + $4,977.9) ÷ 2

This ratio is called a *turnover* because it reflects how many times the trade receivables were recorded and collected, and then new receivables recorded again during the period (i.e., turned over). Receivables turnover expresses the relationship of the average balance in trade receivables to the transactions (i.e., credit sales) that created those receivables. This ratio measures the effectiveness of the company's credit granting and collection activities. A high receivables turnover ratio suggests effective collection activities. Granting credit to poor credit risks and making ineffective collection efforts cause this ratio to be low. A very low ratio is obviously a problem, but a very high ratio can also be troublesome because it suggests an overly stringent credit policy that could cause lost sales and net earnings.

The receivables turnover ratio is often converted to a time basis known as the *average age of trade receivables*. The computation is as follows:

$$\text{Average Age of Receivables} = \frac{\text{Days in a Year}}{\text{Receivables Turnover Ratio}}$$

$$\text{Canadian Tire, 2012} = \frac{365}{2.33} = 157 \text{ days}$$

The effectiveness of credit and collection activities is sometimes judged by the general rule that the average collection period should not exceed 1.5 times the credit terms. For example, if the credit terms require payment in 30 days, the average collection period should not exceed 45 days (i.e., not more than 15 days past due). Like all rules, this one has many exceptions.

When you evaluate financial statements, you should always think about the reasonableness of the numbers you compute. We computed the average age of receivables for Canadian Tire as 157 days, more than five months. Is that number reasonable? To entice customers to buy products from their stores, companies often use special promotions offering interest-free credit for 90 to 180 days on large purchases made on the credit cards they issue to their customers. For example, Canadian Tire offers deferred payments for six months on any Canadian Tire store purchase over $200. This is why Canadian Tire refers to its credit card receivables as loans receivable, since they are essentially interest-free short-term loans to customers. Given this fact, an average collection period of 159 days seems reasonable for Canadian Tire.

In contrast, the average collection periods for RONA and Richelieu Hardware are 27.4 days and 54.2 days, respectively. Do these average collection periods seem reasonable? Probably not. Because we did not know each company's credit sales, we used total sales as an approximation. Think about the last time you watched a customer buying merchandise on credit in a retail store. Most customers use a bank credit card such as MasterCard or Visa. From the seller's perspective, a sales transaction involving a bank credit card is recorded in virtually the same manner as a cash sale. A credit sale involving a credit card does not create a trade receivable on the seller's books. Instead, the trade receivable is recorded on the books of the credit card company.

11. Inventory Turnover Ratio Like the receivables turnover ratio, the *inventory turnover ratio* is a measure of both liquidity and operating efficiency. It reflects the relationship of inventory to the volume of sales during the period. It is computed as follows:

$$\text{Inventory Turnover Ratio} = \frac{\text{Cost of Sales}}{\text{Average Inventory}}$$

$$\text{Canadian Tire, 2012} = \frac{\$7,929.3}{\$1,475.95*} = 5.37 \text{ times}$$

*($1,448.6 + $1,503.3) ÷ 2

Because a company normally realizes profit each time the inventory is sold, an increase in the ratio is usually favourable. If the ratio is too high, however, it may be an indication that sales were lost because desired items were not in stock. The cost of a lost sale is often much higher than the lost profit. When a business is out of stock on an item desired by a customer, the individual will often go to a competitor to find it. That visit may help the competitor establish a business relationship with the customer. Thus, the cost of being out of stock may be all future profits of a lost customer.

On average, Canadian Tire's inventory was acquired and sold to customers five times during the year. The inventory turnover ratio is critical for companies that have adopted Canadian Tire's business strategy. They want to be able to offer the customer the right product when it is needed at a price that beats the competition. If Canadian Tire does not effectively manage its inventory levels, it will incur extra costs that must be passed on to the customer. Canadian Tire has a higher inventory turnover ratio than both RONA (4.10) and Richelieu Hardware (4.02).

Inventory turnover ratios vary significantly from one industry to the next. Companies in the food industry (grocery stores and restaurants) have high inventory turnover ratios because their inventory is subject to rapid deterioration in quality. Companies that sell expensive merchandise (automobiles and high-fashion clothes) have much lower ratios because sales of these items are infrequent but customers want to have a selection to choose from when they do buy.

The inventory turnover ratio is often converted to a time basis called the *average days' supply in inventory*. The computation is as follows:

$$\text{Average Day's Supply in Inventory} = \frac{\text{Days in Year}}{\text{Inventory Turnover Ratio}}$$

$$\text{Canadian Tire, 2012} = \frac{365}{5.37} = 68 \text{ days}$$

12. Trade Payables Turnover Ratio The *trade payables turnover ratio* evaluates the company's effectiveness in managing payables to trade creditors. It is computed as follows:

$$\text{Trade Payables Turnover Ratio} = \frac{\text{Cost of Sales}}{\text{Average Net Trade Payables}}$$

In reality, the numerator of this ratio should be net credit purchases, not cost of sales. Because credit purchases are not usually reported in financial statements, we use total purchases of merchandise inventory as a rough approximation, assuming that all purchases are made on credit. For merchandising companies, we compute purchases by adjusting the cost of sales for the change in inventory during the period as follows:[7]

Purchases = Cost of Sales + Ending Inventory − Beginning Inventory

For Canadian Tire, purchases for fiscal year 2012 equal $7,984 million ($7,929.3 + $1,503.3 − $1,448.6). For most companies, inventories do not change significantly over time. In fact, Canadian Tire's inventories increased by 3.8 percent in 2012; hence, the cost of sales represents a reasonable approximation of the cost of purchases and can be used instead of purchases in computing this ratio.

The computation of the trade payables turnover ratio for Canadian Tire follows:

$$\text{Canadian Tire, 2012} = \frac{\$7,929.3}{\$1,503.95^*} = 5.27 \text{ times}$$

*($1,509.2 + $1,498.7) ÷ 2

This ratio reflects how many times the trade payables were recorded and paid, and then new payables recorded again during the period. The trade payables turnover ratio expresses the relationship of the average balance in trade payables to the purchase transactions that created those payables. Usually, a low ratio raises questions concerning a company's liquidity. It could also reflect aggressive cash management. By conserving cash with slow payments to trade suppliers, the company minimizes the amount of money it must borrow, and the related interest. The trade payables turnover ratio is often converted to a time basis known as the *average age of payables*. The computation is as follows:

$$\text{Average Age of Payables} = \frac{\text{Days in a Year}}{\text{Trade Payables Turnover Ratio}}$$

$$\text{Canadian Tire, 2012} = \frac{365}{5.27} = 69.3 \text{ days}$$

The trade payables turnover ratio can be subject to manipulation. Managers may delay payment to creditors during the entire year but catch up at year-end so that the ratio is at an acceptable level. The trade payables turnover ratios of RONA (7.31) and Richelieu Hardware (9.31) indicate that they pay their trade suppliers faster than Canadian Tire. Their average ages of payables are 49.9 days and 39.2 days, respectively.

Using Ratios to Analyze the Operating Cycle   In Chapter 3, we introduced the concept of the operating cycle, which is the time it takes for a company to pay cash to its suppliers, sell goods to its customers, and collect cash from its customers. Analysts are interested in the operating cycle because it helps them evaluate a company's cash needs and is a good indicator of management efficiency.

The operating cycle for most companies involves three distinct phases: acquisition of inventory, sale of inventory, and collection of cash from customers. We have discussed three ratios that are helpful in evaluating a company's operating cycle. They are the trade payables turnover ratio, the inventory turnover ratio, and the receivables turnover ratio. Each of these ratios measures the number of days it takes to complete an operating activity. The lengths of the component parts for Canadian Tire's operating cycle are as follows:

Ratio	Operating Activity	Time
Trade payables turnover ratio	Purchase of inventory	69 days
Inventory turnover ratio	Sale of inventory	68 days
Receivables turnover ratio	Collection of cash from customers	157 days

The component parts of the operating cycle help us understand the cash needs of the company. Canadian Tire, on average, pays for its inventory 69.3 days after it receives it. It takes, on average, 225 days (68 + 157) for Canadian Tire to sell the inventory and collect cash from customers. Therefore, Canadian Tire must invest cash in its operating activities for nearly 156 days between the time it pays its vendors and the time it collects from its customers. Companies prefer to minimize the time between paying vendors and collecting cash from customers, because it frees up cash for other productive purposes. Canadian Tire could reduce this time by increasing the inventory turnover or changing its credit policy to speed up collection from customers, but that may cause a decrease in sales.

Companies that sell products over the Internet may not need to stock merchandise for long periods. In fact, Dell Inc. disclosed in its annual report for fiscal 2012 that its cash conversion cycle was −36 days during that year, indicating that Dell paid suppliers, on average, 36 days after it sold its products and collected from customers. While Canadian Tire needs money to finance the purchase of inventory, Dell has relied on suppliers to provide the necessary financing.

PAUSE FOR
FEEDBACK

We have discussed several measures of liquidity. Next we will discuss tests of solvency. Before you move on, complete the following questions to test your understanding of these measures.

SELF-STUDY QUIZ 13-4

Dollarama Inc. reported the following data in a recent annual report (in millions of dollars):

Cash and short-term investments	$ 70.3
Trade receivables	1.8
Inventories	315.9
Other current assets	8.4
Current liabilities	142.8

Compute the following ratios:

1. Current ratio.
2. Quick ratio.
3. Cash ratio.

After you complete your answers, check them with the solutions at the end of this chapter.

Tests of Solvency

Solvency refers to a company's ability to meet its long-term obligations. **Tests of solvency**, which are measures of a company's ability to meet these obligations, include the times interest earned, cash coverage, and debt-to-equity ratios.

13. Times Interest Earned Ratio Interest payments are a definite obligation of the borrowing company. If a company fails to make required interest payments, creditors may force it into bankruptcy. Because of the importance of interest payments, analysts often compute a ratio called the *times interest earned ratio*:

$$\text{Times Interest Earned Ratio} = \frac{\text{Net Earnings} + \text{Interest Expense} + \text{Income Tax Expense}}{\text{Interest Expense}}$$

$$\text{Canadian Tire, 2012} = \frac{\$499.2 + \$144.3 + \$178.0}{\$144.3} = 5.69 \text{ times}$$

LO6

Compute and interpret solvency ratios.

TESTS OF SOLVENCY are ratios that measure a company's ability to meet its long-term obligations.

This ratio compares the earnings that a company generated during one period, before deducting interest and income tax expenses, to its interest expense for the same period. It represents a margin of protection for the creditors. In 2012, Canadian Tire generated nearly $5.7 in earnings before interest and taxes for each $1 of interest expense, a ratio that indicates a secure position for creditors. Canadian Tire's ratio is higher than that of RONA (2.27). The ratio could not be computed for Richelieu Hardware; its interest expense appears to be negligible as it was not disclosed separately.

Some analysts prefer to calculate this ratio based on all contractually required payments, including principal payments and rent obligations under lease contracts. Other analysts believe that this ratio is flawed, because interest expense and other obligations are paid in cash, not with net earnings. These analysts prefer to use the *cash coverage ratio*.

14. Cash Coverage Ratio Given the importance of cash flows and required interest payments, it is easy to understand why many analysts use the *cash coverage ratio*. It is computed as follows:

$$\text{Cash Coverage Ratio} = \frac{\text{Cash Flows from Operating Activities before Interest and Taxes}}{\text{Interest Paid (from statement of cash flows)}}$$

$$\text{Canadian Tire, 2012} = \frac{\$1,050.7}{\$155.3} = 6.77 \text{ times}$$

The cash coverage ratio compares the cash generated with the cash obligations of the period. Analysts are concerned about a company's ability to make required interest payments. The cash coverage ratio for Canadian Tire shows that the company generated $6.77 in cash from operations for every $1 of interest paid, which is good coverage. Canadian Tire's cash coverage ratio is lower than RONA's (7.86), and Richelieu Hardware's ratio cannot be calculated. Note that the numerator and the denominator of the cash coverage ratio use *interest paid and income taxes paid* from the statement of cash flows instead of *interest expense and income taxes expense* from the statement of earnings. Accrued interest and interest payments are normally similar in amount, but are not always the same.

15. Debt-to-Equity Ratio The *debt-to-equity ratio* expresses a company's debt as a proportion of its shareholders' equity.[8] It is computed as follows:

$$\text{Debt-to-Equity Ratio} = \frac{\text{Total Liabilities}}{\text{Shareholders' Equity}}$$

$$\text{Canadian Tire, 2012} = \frac{\$8,417.8}{\$4,763.6} = 1.77$$

> **Debt-to-Equity Ratio for Selected Industries—2012**
>
> Gold 0.17
>
> Software 0.21
>
> Retailing 0.36
>
> Paper and forest products 0.79
>
> Telecommunications services 1.21

In 2012, for each $1 of shareholders' equity, Canadian Tire had $1.77 of liabilities. By comparison, RONA and Richelieu Hardware's debt-to-equity ratios were 0.49 and 0.22, respectively.

Debt is risky for a company because specific interest payments must be made even if the company has not generated sufficient net earnings. In contrast, dividends are always at the company's discretion and are not legally enforceable until they are declared by the board of directors. Thus, equity capital is usually considered much less risky than debt.

Despite the risk associated with debt, most companies obtain significant amounts of resources from creditors because of the advantages of financial leverage discussed earlier. In addition, interest paid is a deductible expense on the corporate income tax return. In selecting a capital structure, a company must balance the higher returns available through leverage against the higher risk associated with debt. Because of the importance of this risk–return relationship, most analysts consider the debt-to-equity ratio to be a key part of any company evaluation.

Market Tests

Several ratios, often called **market tests**, relate the current market price per share to the return that accrues to investors. Many analysts prefer these ratios because they are based on the current value of an owner's investment in a company.

16. Price/Earnings (P/E) Ratio The *price/earnings (P/E) ratio* measures the relationship between the current market price per share and its EPS. Recently, when the price of a Canadian Tire common share was $69.11, EPS was $6.13, as calculated earlier. The P/E ratio for the company is computed as follows:

$$\text{Price/Earnings Ratio} = \frac{\textbf{Current Market Price per Share}}{\textbf{Earnings per Share}}$$

$$\text{Canadian Tire, 2012} = \frac{\$69.11}{\$6.13} = \textbf{11.3}$$

The P/E ratio indicates that Canadian Tire's shares were selling at a price that was 11.3 times its EPS. The P/E ratio reflects the stock market's assessment of the company's future business performance. A high ratio indicates that the market expects earnings to grow rapidly. Canadian Tire's P/E ratio is reasonable but it is lower than the ratios of its competitors. RONA's P/E ratio is 149.3, indicating that investors expect its earnings of $0.07 per share to grow significantly in the future. The P/E ratio of Richelieu Hardware (15.5) is also higher than that of Canadian Tire.

Sometimes the components of the P/E ratio are inverted, giving the *capitalization rate*, a rate at which the stock market is apparently capitalizing the current earnings. The capitalization rate for Canadian Tire is $6.13 ÷ $69.11 = 8.8 percent.

In economic terms, the share price is related to the present value of the company's future earnings. Thus, a company that expects to increase its earnings in the future is worth more than one that cannot grow its earnings (assuming other factors are the same). But while a high P/E ratio and good growth prospects are considered favourable, there are risks. When a company with a high P/E ratio does not meet the level of earnings expected by the market, the negative impact on its share price can be dramatic.

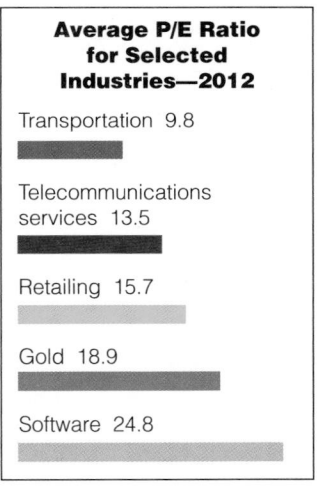

Average P/E Ratio for Selected Industries—2012

Transportation 9.8

Telecommunications services 13.5

Retailing 15.7

Gold 18.9

Software 24.8

17. Dividend Yield Ratio When investors buy shares, they expect returns from two sources: dividend income and price appreciation. The *dividend yield ratio* measures the relationship between the dividend per share paid to shareholders and the current market price per share. Canadian Tire paid a dividend of $1.25 per share when the market price per share was $69.11. Its dividend yield ratio is computed as follows:

$$\text{Dividend Yield Ratio} = \frac{\textbf{Dividend per Share}}{\textbf{Market Price per Share}}$$

$$\text{Canadian Tire, 2012} = \frac{\$1.25}{\$69.11} = \textbf{1.8\%}$$

The dividend yield ratio for shares of most companies is not high compared with returns on alternative investments. Investors may accept low dividend yields if they expect that the price of a company's shares will increase while they own it. Clearly, investors who bought Canadian Tire's common shares did so with the expectation that their price would increase. In contrast, companies with low growth potential tend to offer much higher dividend yields than do companies with high growth potential. These latter companies usually appeal to retired investors who need current income rather than future growth potential.

The dividend yields for both RONA (1.3 percent) and Richelieu Hardware (1.4 percent) are lower than that for Canadian Tire. The chart in the margin shows dividend yields for a selection of companies.

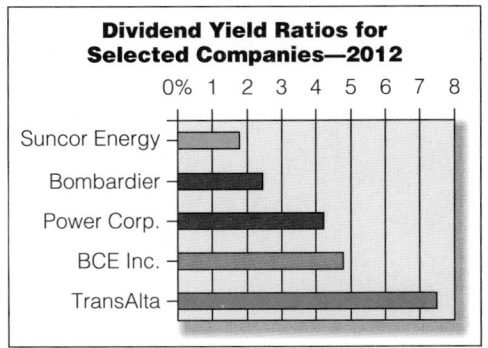

Dividend Yield Ratios for Selected Companies—2012

0% 1 2 3 4 5 6 7 8

Suncor Energy
Bombardier
Power Corp.
BCE Inc.
TransAlta

We have discussed several measures of solvency and two market tests. Next we will discuss important analytical considerations. Before you move on, complete the following questions to test your understanding of these measures.

SELF-STUDY QUIZ 13-5

Dollarama Inc. reported the following data in a recent annual report (in millions of dollars):

Total liabilities	$522.20
Shareholders' equity	931.50
Earnings before interest and taxes	315.90
Interest expense	10.80
Earnings per share	2.35
Share price at year-end	43.25

Compute the following ratios:

1. Debt-to-equity
2. Times interest earned ratio
3. P/E ratio

After you complete your answers, check them with the solutions at the end of this chapter.

INTERPRETING RATIOS AND OTHER ANALYTICAL CONSIDERATIONS

Except for EPS, the computation of financial ratios has not been standardized by the accounting profession or security analysts. Thus, users of financial statements should compute the various ratios in accordance with their decision objectives. Before using ratios computed by others, the analyst should determine the computational approach that was used.

Ratios can best be interpreted only by comparing them to other ratios or to some threshold value. For example, a very low current ratio may indicate an inability to meet maturing debts, and a very high current ratio may indicate an unprofitable use of funds. Furthermore, an optimal ratio for one company may not be optimal for another. Comparisons of ratios for different companies are appropriate only if the companies are indeed comparable in terms of industry, nature of operations, size, and accounting policies.

Because ratios are based on the aggregation of information, they may obscure underlying factors that are of interest to the analyst. For example, a current ratio that is considered optimal may obscure a short-term liquidity problem if the company has a very large amount of inventory but a minimal amount of cash with which to pay debts as they mature. Careful analysis can uncover this type of problem.

In other cases, analysis cannot uncover obscured problems. For example, consolidated statements include financial information about the parent and its subsidiaries. The parent company may have a high current ratio and the subsidiary a low ratio. When the statements are consolidated, the current ratio may fall within an acceptable range. The fact that the subsidiary could have a serious liquidity problem is obscured in this case.

	Years before Bankruptcy					
	5	**4**	**3**	**2**	**1**	Exhibit **13.6**
Current ratio	1.20	0.91	0.74	0.60	0.49	Selected Financial Ratios for
Debt-to-equity ratio	2.03	2.45	4.88	15.67	N/A*	Braniff International

*In the year before bankruptcy, Braniff reported negative owners' equity as a result of a large net loss that produced a negative balance in retained earnings. Total liabilities exceeded total assets.

Despite limitations, ratio analysis is a useful analytical tool. For instance, financial ratios are effective for predicting bankruptcy. Exhibit 13.6 gives the current and debt-to-equity ratios for Braniff International Corporation (an airline company in the United States) for each year before it filed for bankruptcy. Notice the deterioration of these ratios each year. Analysts who studied the financial ratios were probably not surprised by Braniff's bankruptcy. After selling many of its assets and undergoing a complete financial restructuring, Braniff was able to resume limited flight operations but was forced to file for bankruptcy for a second time after additional financial difficulty.

Financial statements provide information to all investors, both sophisticated and unsophisticated. However, users who understand basic accounting principles and terminology are able to more effectively analyze the information in the financial statements. For example, unsophisticated users who do not understand the cost principle might believe that assets are reported on the statement of financial position at their fair market value. Interpreting accounting numbers without an understanding of the concepts that were used to develop them is impossible.

In analyzing different companies, you will find that they rarely use exactly the same accounting policies. Comparisons among companies are appropriate only if the analyst who is making them understands the impact of various accounting alternatives. For example, one company may be prudent in selecting accounting alternatives such as declining depreciation, while another may use profit-maximizing alternatives such as straight-line depreciation. Those who do not understand the different effects of accounting methods are very likely to misinterpret financial results. Perhaps the most important first step in analyzing financial statements is a review of the company's accounting policies, which are disclosed in a note to the statements.

Other Financial Information

The ratios we have discussed are useful for most analytical purposes. Because each company is different, you must exercise professional judgment when you conduct each financial analysis. To illustrate, let us look at some special factors that might affect our analysis of Canadian Tire.

1. *Rapid growth.* Growth in total sales volume does not always indicate that a company is successful. Sales volume from new stores may obscure the fact that existing stores are not meeting customer needs and are experiencing declining sales. In robust economic times, the retail industry often undertakes long-term expansion plans, which rapidly become unprofitable if the economy slows. For example, Canadian Tire's earnings releases report that the company posted same-store sales increases ranging from 1.4 percent to 4.7 percent between 2001 and 2006, but with the economic recession, this growth slowed down or changed to decreases in comparable store sales between 2007 and 2012. Nevertheless, the management of Canadian Tire continued to report net earnings throughout this turbulent period.

2. *Uneconomical expansion.* Some growth-oriented companies open stores in less than desirable locations if good locations cannot be found. These poor locations can cause the company's average productivity to decline. One measure of productivity in the retail industry is sales volume per square foot of selling space. For The Home Depot, which is a competitor in the home renovation industry, productivity

increased from 2002 to 2005; it then declined from 2006 to 2009 before showing signs of improvement in later years. In response to economic hard times that started in 2008, The Home Depot has considerably decreased its new store openings in an effort to improve its productivity:

Year	Sales per Square Foot
2012	$319
2011	299
2010	288
2009	279
2008	298
2007	332
2006	358
2005	377
2004	375
2003	371
2002	370

3. *Subjective factors.* Remember that some vital information about a company is not contained in the annual report. The best way to evaluate Canadian Tire's innovation by introducing new products, programs, and services to customers is to visit its stores and those of competitors.

As these examples illustrate, no single approach can be used to analyze all companies. Furthermore, an effective analyst will look beyond the information contained in an annual report.

A QUESTION OF ACCOUNTABILITY   INSIDER INFORMATION

Financial statements are an important source of information for investors. Announcement of an unexpected earnings increase or decrease can cause a substantial movement in the price of a company's shares.

A company's accountants are often aware of important financial information before it is made available to the public. This is called *insider information*. Some people may be tempted to buy or sell shares based on insider information, but to do so is a serious criminal offence. Securities commissions have brought charges against a number of individuals who traded on insider information. Their conviction resulted in large fines and time served in jail.

In some cases, it may be difficult to determine whether something is insider information. For example, an individual may simply overhear a comment made in the company elevator by two executives. A well-respected Wall Street investment banker gave good advice when dealing with such situations: "If you are not sure if something is right or wrong, apply the newspaper headline test. Ask yourself how you would feel to have your family and friends read about what you had done in the newspaper." Interestingly, many people who spent time in jail and lost small fortunes in fines because of insider trading convictions say that the most difficult part of the process was telling their families.

To uphold the highest ethical standard, many public accounting firms have rules that prevent members of their professional staff from investing in companies that the firm audits. These rules are designed to ensure that the company's auditors cannot be tempted to engage in insider trading and to maintain independence from the audited firm.

Information in an Efficient Market

Considerable research has been done on the way in which stock markets react to new information. Much of this evidence supports the view that the markets react very quickly to new information in an unbiased manner (i.e., the market does not systematically overreact or underreact to new information). A market that reacts to information in this manner is called an *efficient market*. In an **efficient market**, the price of a security fully reflects all publicly available information.

It is not surprising that the stock markets react quickly to new information. Many professional investors manage stock portfolios valued in the hundreds of millions of dollars. These investors have a large financial incentive to discover new information about a company and trade quickly based on that information.

The research on efficient markets has important implications for financial analysis. It is probably not beneficial to study old information (e.g., an annual report that was released six months earlier) in an effort to identify an undervalued stock. In an efficient market, the price of the stock reflects all of the information contained in the report shortly after it was released. Furthermore, a company cannot manipulate the price of its stock by manipulating its accounting policy. The market should be able to differentiate between a company with increasing earnings because of improved productivity and one that has increased its earnings by changing from prudent to liberal accounting policies.

EFFICIENT MARKETS are securities markets in which prices fully reflect all publicly available information.

ACCOUNTING STANDARDS FOR PRIVATE ENTERPRISES

As we noted in previous chapters, the Accounting Standards for Canadian Private Enterprises differ from IFRS with respect to measurement and reporting of specific elements of financial statements, even though both sets of standards are derived from the same conceptual framework for accounting. When analyzing financial statements, users should be aware of the measurement rules that underlie the values reported on these statements, particularly if comparisons are being made between private enterprises and publicly accountable enterprises that use different sets of financial reporting standards.

Appendix 13A: Expanding the Dupont Model— The Scott Formula (Online)

CHAPTER **TAKE-AWAYS**

1. **Explain how a company's business strategy affects financial analysis.**
   In simple terms, a business strategy establishes the objectives a business is trying to achieve. Performance is best evaluated by comparing the financial results to the objectives that the business was working to achieve. In other words, an understanding of a company's strategy provides the context for conducting financial statement analysis.

2. **Discuss how analysts use financial statements.**
   Analysts use financial statements to understand present conditions and past performance, as well as to predict future performance. Financial statements provide important information to help users understand and evaluate corporate strategy. The data reported on statements can be used for either time series analysis (evaluating a single company over time) or in comparison with similar companies at a single point in time. Most analysts compute component percentages and ratios when using statements.

3. **Compute and interpret component percentages.**

   To compute component percentages for the statement of earnings, the base amount is net sales revenue. Each expense is expressed as a percentage of net sales revenue. On the statement of financial position, the base amount is total assets; the balance of each account is divided by total assets. Component percentages are evaluated by comparing them over time for a single company or by comparing them with percentages for similar companies.

4. **Compute and interpret profitability ratios.**

   Several tests of profitability focus on measuring the adequacy of net earnings by comparing it to other items reported on the financial statements. Exhibit 13.4 lists these ratios and shows how to compute them. Profitability ratios are evaluated by comparing them over time for a single company or by comparing them with ratios for similar companies.

5. **Compute and interpret liquidity ratios.**

   Tests of liquidity measure a company's ability to meet its current maturing debt. Exhibit 13.4 lists these ratios and shows how to compute them. Liquidity ratios are evaluated by comparing them over time for a single company or by comparing them with ratios for similar companies.

6. **Compute and interpret solvency ratios.**

   Solvency ratios measure a company's ability to meet its long-term obligations. Exhibit 13.4 lists these ratios and shows how to compute them. Solvency ratios are evaluated by comparing them over time for a single company or by comparing them with ratios for similar companies.

7. **Compute and interpret market test ratios.**

   Market test ratios relate the current price per share to the return that accrues to investors. Exhibit 13.4 lists these ratios and shows how to compute them. Market test ratios are evaluated by comparing them over time for a single company or by comparing them with ratios for similar companies.

FINDING **FINANCIAL INFORMATION**

STATEMENT OF FINANCIAL POSITION

Analysts use information reported on the statement of financial position to compute many ratios. Most analysts use an average of the beginning and ending amounts for statement of financial position accounts when the ratio calculation also includes an amount reported on the statement of earnings.

STATEMENT OF EARNINGS

EPS is the only ratio that is required to be reported on the financial statements. It is usually reported at the bottom of the statement of earnings.

STATEMENT OF CASH FLOWS

Some ratios use amounts reported on this statement.

STATEMENT OF CHANGES IN EQUITY

Ratios are not reported on this statement.

NOTES

Under Summary of Significant Accounting Policies

This note has no information pertaining directly to ratios, but it is important to understand differences in accounting policies if you are comparing two companies.

Under a Separate Note

Most companies include a 5-year or a 10-year financial summary as a separate note. This summary includes data for significant financial statement items, some accounting ratios, and non-accounting information.

■ connect **GLOSSARY**

Review key terms and definitions on *Connect.*

QUESTIONS

1. What are three fundamental uses of external financial statements by decision makers?
2. What are some of the primary items on financial statements about which creditors are usually concerned?
3. Why are the notes to the financial statements important to decision makers?
4. What is the primary purpose of comparative financial statements?
5. Why are statement users interested in financial summaries covering several years? What is the primary limitation of a 5-year or a 10-year financial summary?
6. What is ratio analysis? Why is it useful?
7. What are component percentages? Why are they useful?
8. Explain the two concepts of return on investment.
9. What is financial leverage? How is it measured as a percentage?
10. Is profit margin a useful measure of profitability? Explain.
11. Compare and contrast the current ratio and the quick ratio.
12. What does the debt-to-equity ratio reflect?
13. What are market tests?
14. Identify three factors that limit the effectiveness of ratio analysis.
15. Dimitri Company has prepared draft financial results now being reviewed by the accountants. You notice that the financial leverage percentage is negative. You also note that the current ratio is 2.4 and the quick ratio is 3.7. You remember that these financial relationships are unusual. Does either imply that a mistake has been made? Explain.

EXERCISES

connect

E13–1 Preparing a Schedule by Using Component Percentages

■ LO3

Alimentation Couche-Tard Inc. is a leading convenience store operator in Canada, with Couche-Tard stores in Québec and Mac's stores in central and western Canada. It also operates Circle K shops in the United States. Complete the component percentage analysis on the company's statement of earnings that follows. Discuss the insights provided by this analysis:

Alimentation Couche-Tard Inc.

CONSOLIDATED STATEMENTS OF EARNINGS
For the years ended April 29, 2012, April 24, 2011, and April 25, 2010
(in millions of U.S. dollars (Note 2), except per share amounts)

	2012	2011	2010
	$	$	$
Revenues	22,997.5	18,550.4	16,439.6
Cost of sales	20,028.4	15,804.7	13,886.3
Gross profit	2,969.1	2,745.7	2,553.3
Operating, selling, administrative, and general expenses	2,151.7	2,028.9	1,906.7
Depreciation and amortization of property and equipment and other assets	239.8	213.7	204.5
	2,391.5	2,242.6	2,111.2
Operating income	577.6	503.1	442.1
Share of earnings of joint venture accounted for using the equity method	21.6	16.9	–0–
Net financial (revenues) expenses	(4.7)	29.6	29.9
Earnings before income taxes	603.9	490.4	412.2
Income taxes	146.3	121.2	109.3
Net earnings	457.6	369.2	302.9

E13–2 Analyzing the Impact of Selected Transactions on the Current Ratio

■ LO5

Current assets for JC Inc. totalled $54,000, and the current ratio was 1.8. Assume that the following transactions were completed: (1) purchased merchandise for $6,000 on short-term credit and (2) purchased a delivery truck for $20,000—paid $4,000 cash and signed a two-year interest-bearing note for the balance.

Required:
Compute the current ratio after each transaction.

LO5

Procter & Gamble

E13–3 **Analyzing the Impact of Selected Transactions on Trade Receivables and Inventory Turnover**

Procter & Gamble is a multinational corporation that manufactures and markets many products that are probably in your home. Last year, sales for the company were $83,680 (all amounts in millions). The annual report did not disclose the amount of credit sales, so we will assume that 30 percent of sales were on credit. The average gross margin rate was 50 percent on sales. Account balances follow:

	Beginning	Ending
Trade receivables (net)	$6,068	$6,275
Inventory	6,721	7,379

Required:
Compute the turnover ratios for the trade receivables and inventory, the average age of receivables, and the average days' supply of inventory.

LO4, 5

E13–4 **Analyzing the Impact of Specific Events on Selected Ratios**

Consider the following two independent situations:

1. A manufacturer reported an inventory turnover ratio of 8.6 during 2013. During 2014, management introduced a new inventory control system that was expected to reduce average inventory levels by 25 percent without affecting sales volume. Given these circumstances, would you expect the inventory turnover ratio to increase or decrease during 2014? Explain.

2. Lexis Corporation is considering changing its inventory method from FIFO to weighted average and wants to determine the impact on selected accounting ratios. In general, what would be the impact of this change on the following ratios, assuming that prices have been increasing over time: net profit margin ratio, fixed asset turnover ratio, current ratio, and quick ratio?

LO4

Nokia Corporation

E13–5 **Computing Financial Leverage**

Nokia Corporation is a global leader in providing integrated communications and electronic solutions for businesses. Its financial statements reported the following at year-end (in millions of euros):

Average total assets	€35,738
Average total debt (2% interest)	20,989
Net earnings (average tax rate 30%)	260

Required:
Compute the financial leverage percentage. Was it positive or negative?

LO5

E13–6 **Analyzing the Impact of Selected Transactions on the Current Ratio**

Current assets for GK Company totalled $100,000, and the current ratio was 1.5. Assume that the following transactions were completed: (1) paid $6,000 for merchandise purchased on short-term credit, (2) purchased a delivery truck for $20,000 cash, (3) wrote off a bad trade receivable for $1,000, and (4) paid previously declared dividends in the amount of $20,000.

Required:
Compute the current ratio after each transaction.

LO3

Dollarama

E13–7 **Inferring Financial Information**

Dollarama is the leading dollar store operator in Canada with over 800 locations in all provinces. In a recent year, the company reported average inventories of $287.6 million and an inventory turnover ratio of 3.49. Average total fixed assets were $162.5 million, and the fixed asset turnover ratio was 9.86. Determine the gross profit for Dollarama.

LO5

E13–8 **Computing Selected Ratios**

Sales for the year for RK Ltd. were $1,500,000, of which one-half was on credit. The average gross margin rate was 40 percent on sales. Account balances follow:

	Beginning	Ending
Trade receivables (net)	$150,000	$180,000
Inventory	150,000	90,000

Required:
Compute and comment on the turnover ratios for the trade receivables and inventory, the average age of receivables, and the average days' supply of inventory.

E13–9   Analyzing the Impact of Selected Transactions on the Current Ratio

Current assets for Clarke Inc. totalled $1,000,000, the current ratio was 2.0, and the company uses the periodic inventory method. Assume that the following transactions were completed: (1) sold $26,000 in merchandise on account, (2) declared but did not pay dividends of $40,000, (3) paid rent in advance in the amount of $24,000, (4) paid previously declared dividends in the amount of $40,000, (5) collected a trade receivable in the amount of $20,000, and (6) reclassified $90,000 of long-term debt as a short-term liability.

Required:
Compute the current ratio after each transaction.

E13–10   Computing Liquidity Ratios

■ **LO5**

Cintas

Cintas designs, manufactures, and implements corporate identity uniform programs that it rents or sells to customers throughout the United States and Canada. The company's stock is traded on the NASDAQ and has provided investors with significant ROEs over the past few years. Selected information from the company's statement of financial position follows. The company reported revenue of $4,102,000 and cost of sales of $2,363,392 for fiscal year 2012:

CINTAS Statement of Financial Position		
(amounts in thousands)	2012	2011
Cash and cash equivalents	$339,825	$438,106
Short-term investments	—	87,220
Trade receivables, less allowance of $17,017 ($17,057)	450,861	429,131
Inventories, net	251,205	249,658
Prepayments	24,704	23,481
Trade payables	94,840	110,279
Accrued compensation and related liabilities	91,214	79,834
Income taxes, current	22,188	33,542
Long-term debt due within one year	225,636	1,335

Required:
Compute the current ratio, quick ratio, inventory turnover ratio, and receivables turnover ratio (assuming that 60 percent of sales was on credit) for 2012, and comment on the liquidity position of the company.

E13–11   Determining the Impact of Selected Transactions on Measures of Solvency

■ **LO6**

Three commonly used measures of solvency are the debt-to-equity ratio, the times interest earned ratio, and the cash coverage ratio. For each of the following transactions, determine whether the measure will increase, decrease, or not change. Assume that all ratios are higher than 1.

a. Issued shares in exchange for equipment for $500,000.

b. Issued bonds at par for $1 million cash.

c. Previously declared dividends are paid in cash.

d. Accrued interest expense is recorded.

e. A customer pays money on his trade receivable.

E13–12   Using Financial Information to Identify Mystery Companies

■ **LO3, 4, 5, 6**

The following selected financial data pertain to four unidentified companies:

a. Retail fur store.

b. Advertising agency.

c. Wholesale candy company.

d. Car manufacturer.

	Company			
	1	**2**	**3**	**4**
Statement of Financial Position Data				
(component percentage)				
Cash	3.5	4.7	8.2	11.7
Trade receivables	16.9	28.9	16.8	51.9
Inventory	46.8	35.6	57.3	4.8
Property, plant, and equipment	18.3	21.7	7.6	18.7
Statement of Earnings Data				
(component percentage)				
Gross profit	22.0	22.5	44.8	N/A*
Net earnings before taxes	2.1	0.7	1.2	3.2
Selected Ratios				
Current ratio	1.3	1.5	1.6	1.2
Inventory turnover ratio	3.6	9.8	1.5	N/A
Debt-to-equity ratio	2.6	2.6	3.2	3.2
*N/A = Not applicable				

Required:
Match each company with its financial information. Support your choices.

■ LO3, 4, 5, 6   **E13–13**   **Using Financial Information to Identify Mystery Companies**
The following selected financial data pertain to four unidentified companies:

a. Travel agency.

b. Hotel.

c. Meat packer.

d. Drug company.

	Company			
	1	**2**	**3**	**4**
Statement of Financial Position Data				
(component percentage)				
Cash	7.3	21.6	6.1	11.3
Trade receivables	28.2	39.7	3.2	22.9
Inventory	21.6	0.6	1.8	27.5
Property, plant, and equipment	32.1	18.0	74.6	25.1
Statement of Earnings Data				
(component percentage)				
Gross profit	15.3	N/A*	N/A	43.4
Earnings before income taxes	1.7	3.2	2.4	6.9
Selected Ratios				
Current ratio	1.5	1.2	0.6	1.9
Inventory turnover ratio	27.4	N/A	N/A	3.3
Debt-to-equity ratio	1.7	2.2	5.7	1.3
*N/A = Not applicable				

Required:
Match each company with its financial information. Support your choices.

■ LO3, 4, 5, 6   **E13–14**   **Using Financial Information to Identify Mystery Companies**
The following selected financial data pertain to four unidentified companies:

a. Cable TV company.

b. Grocery store.

c. Accounting firm.

d. Retail jewellery store.

	Company			
	1	**2**	**3**	**4**
Statement of Financial Position Data				
(component percentage)				
Cash	5.1	8.8	6.3	10.4
Trade receivables	13.1	41.5	13.8	4.9
Inventory	4.6	3.6	65.1	35.8
Property, plant, and equipment	53.1	23.0	8.8	35.7
Statement of Earnings Data				
(component percentage)				
Gross profit	N/A*	N/A	45.2	22.5
Earnings before income taxes	0.3	16.0	3.9	1.5
Selected Ratios				
Current ratio	0.7	2.2	1.9	1.4
Inventory turnover	N/A	N/A	1.4	15.5
Debt-to-equity	2.5	0.9	1.7	2.3
*N/A = Not applicable				

Required:
Match each company with its financial information. Support your choices.

E13–15 Using Financial Information to Identify Mystery Companies   ■ LO3, 4, 5, 6
The following selected financial data pertain to four unidentified companies:

a. Full-line department store.

b. Wholesale fish company.

c. Automobile dealership (new and used cars).

d. Restaurant.

	Company			
	1	**2**	**3**	**4**
Statement of Financial Position Data				
(component percentage)				
Cash	11.6	6.6	5.4	7.1
Trade receivables	4.6	18.9	8.8	35.6
Inventory	7.0	45.8	65.7	26.0
Property, plant, and equipment	56.0	20.3	10.1	21.9
Statement of Earnings Data				
(component percentage)				
Gross profit	56.7	36.4	14.1	15.8
Earnings before income taxes	2.7	1.4	1.1	0.9
Selected Ratios				
Current ratio	0.7	2.1	1.2	1.3
Inventory turnover ratio	30.0	3.5	5.6	16.7
Debt-to-equity ratio	3.3	1.8	3.8	3.1

Required:
Match each company with its financial information. Support your choices.

E13–16 Inferring Information from the DuPont Model   ■ LO1
In this chapter, we discussed the DuPont model. Using that framework, find the missing amount in each case below:

Case 1: ROE is 10 percent, net earnings are $300,000, total asset turnover ratio is 5, and net sales are $1,000,000. What is the amount of average shareholders' equity?

Case 2: Net earnings are $440,000, net sales are $8,000,000, average shareholders' equity is $2,000,000, ROE is 22 percent, and total asset turnover ratio is 8. What is the amount of average total assets?

Case 3: ROE is 15 percent, net profit margin ratio is 10 percent, total asset turnover ratio is 5, and average total assets are $1,000,000. What is the amount of average shareholders' equity?

Case 4: Net earnings are $150,000, ROE is 15 percent, total asset turnover ratio is 5, net sales are $1,000,000, and financial leverage is 2. What is the amount of average total assets?

▉ connect **PROBLEMS**

▉ **LO3**

eXcel

P13–1 **Analyzing Comparative Financial Statements by Using Percentages** (AP13–1)
The comparative financial statements prepared at December 31, 2014, for Goldfish Company showed the following summarized data:

	2014	2013
Statement of Earnings		
Sales revenue	$195,000*	$165,000
Cost of sales	120,000	100,000
Gross margin	75,000	65,000
Operating expenses and interest expense	60,000	53,000
Earnings before income taxes	15,000	12,000
Income tax expense	4,000	3,000
Net earnings	$ 11,000	$ 9,000
Statement of Financial Position		
Cash	$ 4,000	$ 8,000
Trade receivables (net)	15,000	18,000
Inventory	40,000	35,000
Property, plant, and equipment (net)	45,000	38,000
	$104,000	$ 99,000
Current liabilities (no interest)	$ 16,000	$ 19,000
Non-current liabilities (10% interest)	45,000	39,000
Common shares (6,000 shares)	30,000	30,000
Retained earnings†	13,000	11,000
	$104,000	$ 99,000

*One-third was credit sales.
†During 2014, cash dividends amounting to $9,000 were declared and paid.

Required:

1. Complete the following columns for each item in the preceding comparative financial statements:

Increase (Decrease) 2014 over 2013	
Amount	Percentage

2. Answer the following:
   a. By what amount did working capital change?
   b. What was the percentage change in the average income tax rate?
   c. What was the amount of cash inflow from revenues for 2014?
   d. What was the percentage change for the average markup realized on sales?

▉ **LO3, 4, 5, 6** **P13–2** **Analyzing Comparative Financial Statements by Using Percentages and Selected Ratios** (AP13–2)
Use the data given in P13–1 for Goldfish Company.

Required:

1. Present component percentages for 2014 only.
2. Answer the following for 2014:
   a. What was the average percentage markup on sales?
   b. What was the average income tax rate?
   c. Compute the net profit margin ratio. Was it a good or poor indicator of performance? Explain.

d. What percentage of total resources was invested in property, plant, and equipment?

e. Compute the debt-to-equity ratio. Does it look good or bad? Explain.

f. What was the ROA?

g. What was the ROE?

h. Compute the financial leverage percentage. Did borrowing from creditors benefit shareholders? Explain.

P13–3 Analyzing Ratios (AP13–3)

Sears Canada Inc. and Canadian Tire Corporation are two giants of the Canadian retail industry. Both offer full lines of moderately priced merchandise. Annual sales for Sears total $4.3 billion. Canadian Tire is somewhat larger, with $11 billion in revenues. Compare the two companies as potential investments based on the following ratios:

■ LO4, 5, 6, 7

Sears Canada Inc. and Canadian Tire Corporation

Ratio	Sears Canada	Canadian Tire
P/E	13.3	14.0
Net profit margin ratio	4.5%	3.9%
Quick ratio	1.02	1.54
Current ratio	1.8	1.99
Debt-to-equity	1.05	1.38
ROE	14.9%	9.2%
ROA	7.6%	5.2%
Dividend yield	0%	0%
EPS	$2.18	$4.10
Price per share at year-end	$29.0	$57.5
Dividends per share	$0	$0.84

P13–4 Analyzing a Financial Statement by Using Several Ratios

Summer Corporation has just completed its comparative statements for the year ended December 31, 2015. At this point, certain analytical and interpretive procedures are to be undertaken. The completed statements (summarized) are as follows:

■ LO4, 5, 6, 7

e**X**cel

	2015	2014
Statement of Earnings		
Sales revenue	$960,000[a]	$840,000[a]
Cost of sales	540,000	460,000
Gross margin	420,000	380,000
Operating expenses (including interest on bonds)	342,000	336,000
Pretax earnings	78,000	44,000
Income tax expense	24,000	12,000
Net earnings	$ 54,000	$ 32,000
Statement of Financial Position		
Cash	$ 13,600	$ 7,800
Trade receivables (net)	84,000	56,000
Merchandise inventory	50,000	40,000
Prepayments	400	200
Property, plant, and equipment (net)	260,000	240,000
	$408,000	$344,000
Trade payables	$ 34,000	$ 36,000
Income taxes payable	2,000	4,000
Bonds payable (5% interest rate)	140,000[b]	100,000
Common shares (40,000 shares)	200,000[c]	200,000
Retained earnings	32,000[d]	4,000
	$408,000	$344,000

[a]Credit sales totalled 40 percent of total sales.

[b]$40,000 of bonds were issued on January 2, 2015.

[c]The market price of the stock at the end of 2015 was $18 per share.

[d]During 2015, the company declared and paid a cash dividend of $26,000.

Required:

1. Compute appropriate ratios for 2015 and explain the meaning of each.
2. Answer the following for 2015:

    a. Evaluate the financial leverage percentage. Explain its meaning by using the computed amount(s).

    b. Evaluate the net profit margin ratio and explain how a shareholder might use it.

    c. Explain to a shareholder why the current ratio and the quick ratio are different. Do you observe any liquidity problems? Explain.

    d. Assuming that credit terms are 1/10, n/30, do you perceive an unfavourable situation for the company related to credit sales? Explain.

    e. By how much should the balance of trade receivables decrease if the company wishes to reduce its average collection period to 30 days?

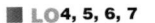 **LO4, 5, 6, 7**   **P13–5**   **Comparing Alternative Investment Opportunities** (AP13–4)

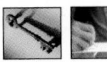 The 2014 financial statements for Armstrong and Blair companies are summarized below:

 e**X**cel

	Armstrong Company	Blair Company
Statement of Financial Position		
Cash	$ 17,500	$ 11,000
Trade receivables (net)	20,000	15,000
Inventory	50,000	20,000
Property, plant, and equipment (net)	70,000	200,000
Other non-current assets	42,500	154,000
Total assets	$200,000	$400,000
Current liabilities	$ 50,000	$ 25,000
Long-term debt (10%)	30,000	35,000
Share capital	75,000	250,000
Contributed surplus	15,000	55,000
Retained earnings	30,000	35,000
Total liabilities and shareholders' equity	$200,000	$400,000
Statement of Earnings		
Sales revenue (1/3 on credit)	$225,000	$405,000
Cost of sales	(122,500)	(202,500)
Expenses (including interest and income tax)	(80,000)	(157,500)
Net earnings	$ 22,500	$ 45,000

Selected data from the 2013 statements follows:

Trade receivables (net)	$ 10,000	$ 20,000
Inventory	46,000	24,000
Long-term debt	30,000	35,000
Other data:		
Share price at end of 2014	$ 18	$ 15
Income tax rate	30%	30%
Dividends declared and paid in 2014	$ 18,000	$ 75,000
Number of common shares during 2014	7,500	25,000

    The companies are in the same line of business and are direct competitors in a large metropolitan area. Both have been in business approximately 10 years, and each has had steady growth. The management of each has a different viewpoint in many respects. Blair Company is more conservative, and as its president said, "We avoid what we consider to be undue risk." Neither company is publicly held. Armstrong Company has an annual audit by an independent auditor, but Blair Company does not.

Required:

1. Complete a schedule that reflects a ratio analysis of each company. Compute the ratios discussed in the chapter. Use ending balances if average balances are not available.

2. A client of yours has the opportunity to buy 10 percent of the shares in one or the other company at the share prices given. Based on the data given, prepare a comparative written evaluation of the ratio analyses (and any other available information) and give your recommended choice with supporting explanation.

P13–6 Analyzing the Impact of Alternative Inventory Methods on Selected Ratios

LO4, 5, 6

Company A uses the FIFO method to cost inventory, and Company B uses the weighted-average method. The two companies are exactly alike except for the difference in inventory costing methods. Costs of inventory items for both companies have been rising steadily in recent years, and each company has increased its inventory each year. Each company has paid its tax liability in full for the current year (and all previous years), and each company uses the same accounting methods for both financial reporting and income tax reporting, except for inventory valuation.

Required:

Identify which company will report the higher amount for each of the following ratios. If this is not possible, explain why.

1. Current ratio.
2. Quick ratio.
3. Debt-to-equity ratio.
4. ROE.
5. EPS.

P13–7 Analyzing Financial Statements by Using Appropriate Ratios (AP13–5)

LO4, 5, 6, 7

Sun-Rype Products Ltd. manufactures and markets a variety of fruit juices and fruit snacks, such as Fruit to Go, Squiggles, and FruitSource snack bars. Its products are sold in grocery stores, wholesalers, and drug stores. The following information was reported in a recent annual report:

Sun-Rype Products Ltd.

eXcel

SUN-RYPE PRODUCTS LTD.
Consolidated Statement of Comprehensive Income
For the years ended December 31
(in thousands of Canadian dollars, unless otherwise stated)

	2012	2011
Net sales (Note 15)	$152,795	$147,529
Cost of sales (Note 6)	(125,474)	(126,311)
Gross profit	27,321	21,218
Sales and marketing expenses	(11,699)	$(14,721)
Distribution expenses	(6,813)	(7,352)
General and administrative expenses	(5,987)	(6,410)
Loss on disposal of property, plant, and equipment	—	(57)
Results from operating activities	2,822	(7,322)
Finance costs (Note 17)	(708)	(714)
Income (loss) before income taxes	2,114	(8,036)
Income tax recovery (expense)	(847)	2,349
Net income (loss) for the year	1,267	(5,687)
Other comprehensive income (loss)		
Foreign currency translation differences for foreign operations	(13)	(53)
Total comprehensive income (loss) for the year	$ 1,254	$ (5,740)
Basic and diluted earnings (loss) per share (Note 14) *(in dollars)*	$ 0.12	$ (0.53)

SUN-RYPE PRODUCTS LTD.
Consolidated Statement of Financial Position
(in thousands of Canadian dollars)

	December 31, 2012	December 31, 2011
Assets		
Current assets		
Cash	$ 4,227	$ 571
Trade and other receivables (Note 5)	14,047	13,672
Income taxes recoverable	446	2,244
Inventories (Note 6)	29,149	31,794
Prepaid expenses	502	579
Total current assets	48,371	48,860
Non-current assets		
Property, plant, and equipment (Note 7)	42,041	46,195
Goodwill (Note 8)	1,061	1,084
Total non-current assets	43,102	47,279
Total assets	91,473	96,139
Liabilities		
Current liabilities		
Trade and other payables (Note 9)	25,672	19,479
Provisions (Note 10)	1,687	1,297
Income taxes payable	116	–
Loans and borrowings (Note 11)	3,646	12,926
Total current liabilities	31,121	33,702
Non-current liabilities		
Loans and borrowings (Note 11)	8,781	12,636
Deferred tax liabilities (Note 12)	4,035	3,422
Total non-current liabilities	12,816	16,058
Total liabilities	43,937	49,760
Equity		
Share capital (Note 13)	17,697	17,724
Contributed surplus	724	794
Retained earnings	29,181	27,914
Accumulated other comprehensive loss	(66)	(53)
Total equity	47,536	46,379
Total liabilities and equity	$91,473	$96,139

SUN-RYPE PRODUCTS LTD.
Consolidated Statement of Cash Flows
For the Years ended December 31
(in thousands of Canadian dollars)

	2012	2011
Cash Flows from Operating Activities		
Net income (loss) for the year	$ 1,267	$ (5,687)
Adjustments for:		
Depreciation	5,166	4,745
Impairment loss	164	293
Loss on disposal of property, plant, and equipment	–	57
Unrealized foreign exchange loss (gain)	69	(552)
Interest expense	826	608
Income tax expense (recovery)	847	(2,349)
	8,339	(2,885)

(continued)

	2012	2011
Change in trade and other receivables	(324)	890
Change in inventories	2,510	(6,122)
Change in prepayments	73	(125)
Change in trade and other payables	6,077	1,865
Change in provisions	397	651
Cash generated from operating activities	17,072	(5,726)
Interest paid	(826)	(608)
Income tax paid	1,690	(276)
Net cash from (used in) operating activities	17,936	(6,610)
Cash flows from investing activities		
Business acquisitions	–	(9,087)
Acquisition of property, plant, and equipment	(1,418)	(3,929)
Net cash used in investing activities	(1,418)	(13,016)
Cash flows from financing activities		
Advances of loans and borrowings	1,502	18,551
Repayment of loans and borrowings	(14,264)	(1,282)
Repurchase of own shares	(97)	–
Net cash from financing activities	(12,859)	17,269
Net increase (decrease) in cash	3,659	(2,357)
Cash position, beginning of year	571	2,928
Effect of exchange rate changes on cash	(3)	–
Cash position, end of year	$ 4,227	$ 571

Source: Sun-Rype Products Ltd., Annual Report 2012.

Additional information related to 2010 at year-end is as follows:

Shareholders' equity	$52,119
Total assets	82,318
Property, plant, and equipment	39,719
Trade and other receivables	14,260
Inventories	24,961
Trade and other payables	18,061

The market price per share was $6.23 at December 31, 2011, and $6.10 at December 31, 2012.

Required:

1. For Sun-Rype's past two years, compute the ratios discussed in this chapter. If there is insufficient information, describe what is missing and explain what you would do.

2. Assume that you work in the loan department of City Bank, and you are evaluating an application from Sun-Rype for a two-year loan of $10 million to purchase the shares of another competing company. What specific ratios would you consider in your evaluation, and would you lend Sun-Rype the requested amount?

P13–8 Analyzing an Investment by Comparing Selected Ratios (AP13–6)

■ LO5, 6, 7

You have the opportunity to invest $10,000 in one of two companies from a single industry. The only information you have follows. The word *high* refers to the top third of the industry, *average* is the middle third, and *low* is the bottom third. Which company would you select? Write a brief report justifying your recommendation.

Ratio	Company A	Company B
Current	High	Average
Quick	Low	Average
Debt-to-equity	High	Average
Inventory turnover	Low	Average
P/E	Low	Average
Dividend yield	High	Average

LO5, 6, 7   **P13–9**   **Analyzing an Investment by Comparing Selected Ratios** (AP13–7)

You have the opportunity to invest $10,000 in one of two companies from a single industry. The only information you have is shown below. The word *high* refers to the top third of the industry, *average* is the middle third, and *low* is the bottom third. Which company would you select? Write a brief report justifying your recommendation.

Ratio	Company A	Company B
Current	Low	Average
Quick	Average	Average
Debt-to-equity	Low	Average
Inventory turnover	High	Average
P/E	High	Average
Dividend yield	Low	Average

LO3–7   **P13–10**   **Analyzing Financial Statements by Using Appropriate Ratios**

Morksen Corp. has enjoyed modest success in penetrating the personal electronic devices market since it began operations a few years ago. A new line of devices introduced recently has been well received by customers. However, the company president, who is knowledgeable about electronics but not accounting, is concerned about the future of the company.

   Although the company has a line of credit with the local bank, it currently needs cash to continue operations. The bank wants more information before it extends the company's credit line. The president has asked you, as the company's chief accountant, to evaluate the company's performance by using appropriate financial statement analysis, and to recommend possible courses of action for the company. In particular, the president wants to know how the company can obtain additional cash. Summary financial statements for the past three years are available below.

Required:

1. Evaluate the company's performance and its financial condition for the past two years. Select six appropriate ratios to analyze the company's profitability, liquidity, and solvency for 2013 and 2014, and explain to the company's president the meaning of each ratio you calculate.

2. Based on your analysis of the ratios that you computed in (1), what recommendation would you make to the president for obtaining additional cash?

MORKSEN CORP.			
Consolidated Statements of Earnings			
For the Years Ended December 31			
(in thousands of dollars)	2014	2013	2012
Sales	$64,000	$56,000	$46,800
Cost of sales	50,000	43,000	36,000
Gross profit	14,000	13,000	10,800
Operating expenses before interest and income taxes	8,000	7,400	6,620
Interest expense	1,780	1,220	–
Earnings before income taxes	4,220	4,380	4,180
Income tax expense	1,900	2,040	1,940
Net earnings	$ 2,320	$ 2,340	$ 2,240

MORKSEN CORP.
Consolidated Statements of Financial Position
At December 31

(in thousands of dollars)	2014	2013	2012
Assets			
Current assets			
Cash	$ 380	$ 480	$ 1,000
Short-term investments	740	740	740
Trade receivables	10,880	8,400	5,140
Merchandise inventory	16,660	10,060	7,220
Total current assets	28,660	19,680	14,100
Property, plant, and equipment			
Land	4,000	4,000	2,000
Buildings and equipment	26,000	26,000	18,000
	30,000	30,000	20,000
Less: accumulated depreciation	8,940	7,440	5,760
Net property, plant, and equipment	21,060	22,560	14,240
Total assets	$49,720	$42,240	$28,340
Liabilities and Shareholders' Equity			
Current liabilities			
Bank loan	$16,500	$11,400	$ –
Trade payables	6,000	4,300	2,880
Other liabilities	1,640	1,600	1,500
Income tax payable	960	1,040	1,000
Total current liabilities	25,100	18,340	5,380
Shareholders' equity			
Common shares	20,000	20,000	20,000
Retained earnings	4,140	3,520	2,640
Other comprehensive income	480	380	320
Total shareholders' equity	24,620	23,900	22,960
Total liabilities and shareholders' equity	$49,720	$42,240	$28,340

ALTERNATE PROBLEMS

AP13–1 Analyzing Financial Statements by Using Ratios and Percentage Changes (P13–1)   ■ LO1

Taber Company has just prepared the following comparative annual financial statements for 2015:

TABER COMPANY
Comparative Statement of Earnings
For the Years Ended December 31

	2015	2014
Sales revenue (one-half on credit)	$110,000	$100,000
Cost of sales	52,000	49,000
Gross margin	58,000	51,000
Expenses (including $4,000 interest expense each year)	40,000	37,000
Pretax earnings	18,000	14,000
Income tax expense (30%)	5,400	4,200
Net earnings	$ 12,600	$ 9,800

TABER COMPANY
Comparative Statement of Financial Position
At December 31, 2015 and 2014

	2015	2014
Assets		
Cash	$ 49,500	$ 18,000
Trade receivables (net; terms 1/10, n/30)	37,000	32,000
Inventory	25,000	38,000
Property, plant, and equipment (net)	95,000	105,000
Total assets	$206,500	$193,000
Liabilities		
Trade payables	$ 42,000	$ 35,000
Income taxes payable	1,000	500
Note payable, long-term	40,000	40,000
Shareholders' equity		
Share capital (9,000 shares)	90,000	90,000
Retained earnings	34,900	25,400
Other comprehensive income (loss)	(1,400)	2,100
Total liabilities and shareholders' equity	$206,500	$193,000

Required (round percentages and ratios to two decimal places):

1. For 2015, compute the tests of (*a*) profitability, (*b*) liquidity, (*c*) solvency, and (*d*) market. Assume that the quoted price of the stock was $23 per share for 2015. Dividends declared and paid during 2015 were $5,200.

2. Answer the following for 2015:

   a. Compute the percentage changes in sales, net earnings, cash, inventory, and debt.

   b. What is the pretax interest rate on the note payable?

3. Identify at least two problems facing the company that are suggested by your responses to (1) and (2).

■ **LO3, 4, 5**   **AP13–2**   **Using Ratios to Analyze Several Years of Financial Data (P13–2)**

The following information was contained in the annual financial statements of Pine Company, which started business January 1, 2013 (assume account balances only in cash and share capital on this date; all amounts are in thousands of dollars):

	2013	2014	2015	2016
Trade receivables (net; terms n/30)	$11	$12	$18	$ 24
Merchandise inventory	12	14	20	30
Net sales (three-fourths on credit)	44	66	80	100
Cost of sales	28	40	55	62
Net earnings (loss)	(8)	5	12	11

Required (show computations and round to two decimal places):

1. Complete the following tabulation:

Items	2013	2014	2015	2016
a. Profit margin—percentage				
b. Gross profit percentage				
c. Expenses as percentage of sales, excluding cost of sales				
d. Inventory turnover ratio				
e. Days' supply in inventory				
f. Receivables turnover ratio				
g. Average collection period				

2. Evaluate the results of the related ratios *a*, *b*, and *c* to identify the favourable or unfavourable factors. Give your recommendations to improve the company's operations.

3. Evaluate the results of the last four ratios (*d*, *e*, *f*, and *g*), and identify any favourable or unfavourable factors. Give your recommendations to improve the company's operations.

AP13–3 Analyzing Ratios (P13–3)

■ LO4, 7

Coca-Cola and PepsiCo

Coke and Pepsi are well-known international brands. Coca-Cola sells more than $46 billion worth of beverages each year, while annual sales of Pepsi products exceed $65 billion. Compare the two companies as potential investments based on the following ratios:

Ratio	Coca-Cola	PepsiCo
P/E ratio	19.3	17.8
Gross profit percentage	64.2	53.5
Net profit margin ratio	22.0%	13.7%
Quick ratio	0.7	0.5
Current ratio	1.3	1.4
Debt-to-equity ratio	0.9	1.3
ROE	29.5%	39.8%
ROA	15.9%	16.4%
Dividend yield	2.9%	2.9%

AP13–4 Comparing Loan Requests from Two Companies by Using Several Ratios (P13–5)

■ LO4, 5, 6, 7

eXcel

The 2014 financial statements for Rand and Tand companies are summarized below:

	Rand Company	Tand Company
Statement of Financial Position		
Cash	$ 25,000	$ 45,000
Trade receivables (net)	55,000	5,000
Inventory	110,000	25,000
Property, plant, and equipment (net)	550,000	160,000
Other assets	140,000	57,000
Total assets	$ 880,000	$ 292,000
Current liabilities	$ 120,000	$ 15,000
Long-term debt (12%)	190,000	55,000
Share capital	480,000	210,000
Contributed surplus	50,000	4,000
Retained earnings	38,000	7,000
Other comprehensive income	2,000	1,000
Total liabilities and shareholders' equity	$ 880,000	$ 292,000
Statement of Earnings		
Sales revenue (on credit)	(½) $ 800,000	(¼) $ 280,000
Cost of sales	(480,000)	(150,000)
Expenses (including interest and income tax)	(240,000)	(95,000)
Net earnings	$ 80,000	$ 35,000
Selected Data from the 2013 Statements		
Trade receivables, net	$ 47,000	$ 11,000
Long-term debt (12%)	190,000	55,000
Inventory	95,000	38,000
Other Data		
Share price at end of 2014	$ 14.00	$ 11.00
Income tax rate	30%	30%
Dividends declared and paid in 2014	$ 20,000	$ 9,000
Number of common shares during 2014	24,000	10,500

These two companies are in the same line of business and in the same province but in different cities. Each company has been in operation for about 10 years. Rand Company is audited by a national accounting firm; Tand Company is audited by a local accounting firm. Both companies received an unqualified opinion (i.e., the independent auditors found nothing wrong) on the financial statements. Rand Company wants to borrow $75,000 cash, and Tand Company needs $30,000. The loans will be for a two-year period and are needed for working capital purposes.

Required:

1. Complete a schedule that reflects a ratio analysis of each company. Compute the ratios discussed in the chapter.
2. Assume that you work in the loans department of a local bank. You have been asked to analyze the situation and recommend which loan is preferable. Based on the data given, your analysis prepared in (1), and any other information, give your choice and provide a supporting explanation.

■ LO3, 4, 5, 6, 7 **AP13–5**

Lassonde Industries Inc.

e**X**cel

Analyzing Financial Statements by Using Appropriate Ratios (P13–7)

Lassonde Industries Inc. manufactures and sells fruit and vegetable juices and drinks, as well as specialty food products under such brand names as Oasis, Fruité, Fairlee, and Canadian Club. The company's products are distributed to wholesalers, supermarkets, and food service providers. The following information was reported in a recent annual report:

LASSONDE INDUSTRIES INC.
Consolidated Statement of Income
For the Years ended December 31
(in thousands of Canadian dollars)

	Dec. 31 2012	Dec. 31 2011
Sales	$1,022,218	$760,258
Cost of sales	743,387	548,876
Selling and administrative expenses	194,584	151,035
(Gains) losses on capital assets	(1,269)	–
	936,702	699,911
Operating profit	85,516	60,347
Financial expenses	24,055	13,928
Other (gains) losses	2,949	33
Profit before income taxes	58,512	46,386
Income tax expense	13,482	11,804
Profit	45,030	34,582
Attributable to:		
Company shareholders	43,946	34,471
Non-controlling interest	1,084	111
	$ 45,030	$ 34,582
Basic and diluted earnings per share (in $)	$ 6.29	$ 5.12
Weighted average number of shares outstanding (in thousands)	6,988	6,729

LASSONDE INDUSTRIES INC.
Consolidated Statement of Financial Position
For the Years Ended December 31
(in thousands of Canadian dollars)

	2012	2011
Assets		
Current		
Cash and cash equivalent	$ 22,186	–
Accounts receivable	103,792	$96,999
Inventories	162,065	166,708
Investment	2,079	2,036
Other current assets	10,272	16,157
Non-current assets held for sale	–	605
Derivative instruments	1,039	4,137
	301,433	286,642
Property, plant, and equipment	238,894	237,486
Other intangible assets	129,940	141,008
Net defined benefit asset	4,082	1,069
Deferred tax assets	–	3,284
Other long-term assets	697	922
Goodwill	124,982	127,630
	$800,028	$798,041
Liabilities		
Current		
Bank overdraft	–	7,987
Bank indebtedness	–	15,710
Accounts payable and accrued liabilities	133,575	117,858
Other current liabilities	749	550
Derivative instruments	2,966	228
Current portion of long-term debt	12,750	6,835
	150,040	149,168
Derivative instruments	1,563	612
Net defined benefit liability	598	634
Long-term debt	282,456	312,451
Deferred tax liabilities	19,015	17,918
Other long-term liabilities	38,151	38,007
	491,823	518,790
Shareholders' equity		
Capital, reserves, and retained earnings attributable to the Company shareholders	290,891	262,661
Non-controlling interest	17,314	16,590
	308,205	279,251
	$800,028	$798,041

LASSONDE INDUSTRIES INC.
Consolidated Statement of Cash Flows
For the Years Ended December 31
(in thousands of Canadian dollars) (audited)

	2012	2011
Operating Activities		
Profit	$45,030	$ 34,582
Adjustments for:		
Income tax expense	13,482	11,804
Interest income and expense	22,746	12,051
Depreciation and amortization	31,622	23,073
Change in fair value of financial instruments	3,896	1,948
Change in net defined benefit asset/liability	(5,259)	(5,907)
Gain on disposal of property, plant, and equipment	(1,269)	–
Impairment losses on property, plant, and equipment	138	–
Other (gains) losses	(3)	49
Unrealized foreign exchange gains	(74)	(308)
	110,309	77,292
Change in non-cash operating working capital items	22,680	(7,573)
Taxes received	887	283
Taxes paid	(11,183)	(14,497)
Interest received	208	593
Interest paid	(21,131)	(10,260)
Settlements of derivative financial instruments	(567)	–
Unearned discounts	297	–
	101,500	45,838
Financing activities		
Change in bank indebtedness	(15,710)	15,710
Change in long-term debt related to the operating line of credit	(10,038)	9,018
Increase in long-term debt	450	227,749
Repayment of long-term debt	(12,662)	(8,240)
Dividends paid on Class A shares	(3,978)	(3,601)
Dividends paid on Class B shares	(4,615)	(4,465)
Proceeds from the issuance of Class A shares	–	30,196
Repurchase of Class A shares	–	(58)
Investment of the non-controlling interest	–	15,918
Increase in other long-term liability	–	35,774
	(46,553)	318,001
Investing activities		
Consideration transferred on business combination, net of acquired cash on hand	–	(392,910)
Acquisition of an investment	(43)	(36)
Acquisition of property, plant, and equipment	(25,432)	(19,322)
Acquisition of other intangible assets	(1,647)	(279)
Proceeds from the disposal of property, plant, and equipment	2,255	106
	(24,867)	(412,441)
Increase (decrease) in cash equivalents	30,080	(48,602)
Cash and equivalent at beginning	(7,987)	40,937
Impact of exchange rate changes on cash and cash equivalent	93	(322)
Cash and cash equivalent at end	$22,186	$ (7,987)

Additional cash flow information is presented in Note 27.

Source: Lassonde Industries Inc., Annual Report 2012.

Additional information related to 2010 at year end is as follows:

Shareholders' equity	$200,846
Total assets	368,858
Property, plant, and equipment	149,843
Accounts receivable	57,934
Inventories	91,833
Accounts payable and accrued liabilities	65,996

The company declared and paid a dividend of $1.23 per share during fiscal year 2012 and $1.19 per share during fiscal year 2011. The market price per share was $64.00 at December 31, 2011, and $75.52 at December 31, 2012.

Required:

1. Compute the ratios discussed in this chapter for the last two years. If there is insufficient information, describe what is missing and explain what you would do.

2. Assume the role of an investment adviser. A client of yours has the opportunity to invest $1 million in shares of international companies. Prepare a written evaluation of relevant ratios and indicate whether you would recommend to your client that the $1 million be invested in the shares of Lassonde Industries.

AP13–6 **Analyzing an Investment by Comparing Selected Ratios** (P13–8)

■ LO6, 7

You have the opportunity to invest $10,000 in one of two companies from a single industry. The only information you have is shown below. The word *high* refers to the top third of the industry, *average* is the middle third, and *low* is the bottom third. Which company would you select? Write a brief report justifying your recommendation.

Ratio	Company A	Company B
EPS	High	Low
ROA	Low	High
Debt-to-equity	High	Average
Current	Low	Average
P/E	Low	High
Dividend yield	High	Average

AP13–7 **Analyzing an Investment by Comparing Selected Ratios** (P13–9)

■ LO4, 5, 6, 7

You have the opportunity to invest $10,000 in one of two companies from a single industry. The only information you have follows. The word *high* refers to the top third of the industry, *average* is the middle third, and *low* is the bottom third. Which company would you select? Write a brief report justifying your recommendation.

Ratio	Company A	Company B
ROA	High	Average
Net profit margin	High	Low
Financial leverage	High	Low
Current	Low	High
P/E	High	Average
Debt-to-equity	High	Low

CASES AND PROJECTS

FINDING AND INTERPRETING FINANCIAL INFORMATION

■ **LO**4, 5, 6, 7   **CP13–1**   **Analyzing Financial Statements**

Canadian Tire
Corporation

Refer to the financial statements of Canadian Tire Corporation given in Appendix A of this book. From the list of ratios that were discussed in this chapter, select and compute the ratios that will help you evaluate the company's operations for fiscal year 2012. Assume a market price of $70 per share.

■ **LO**4, 5, 6, 7   **CP13–2**   **Analyzing Financial Statements**

RONA Inc.

Go to *Connect* for the financial statements of RONA Inc. From the list of ratios that were discussed in this chapter, select and compute the ratios that will help you evaluate the company's operations for fiscal year 2012. Assume a market price of $12 per share.

■ **LO**4, 5, 6, 7   **CP13–3**   **Comparing Companies within an Industry**

Canadian Tire
Corporation

RONA Inc.

Refer to the financial statements of Canadian Tire Corporation (Appendix A), to *Connect* for the financial statements of RONA Inc., and to the Industry Ratio Report (Appendix B on *Connect*). Compute the following ratios for fiscal year 2012: ROE, EPS, net profit margin, current ratio, inventory turnover, debt-to-equity, P/E, and dividend yield. Assume the stock price is $70 for Canadian Tire Corporation and $12 for RONA Inc. Compare the ratios for each company to the industry average ratios.

FINANCIAL REPORTING AND ANALYSIS CASE

■ **LO**1   **CP13–4**   **Interpreting Financial Results Based on Corporate Strategy**

In this chapter, we discussed the importance of analyzing financial results based on an understanding of the company's business strategy. Using the DuPont model, we illustrated how different strategies could earn high returns for investors. Assume that two companies in the same industry adopt fundamentally different strategies. One manufactures high-quality consumer electronics. Its products employ state-of-the-art technology, and the company offers a high level of customer service both before and after the sale. The other company emphasizes low cost with good performance. Its products utilize well-established technology but are never innovative. Customers buy these products at large, self-service warehouses and are expected to install the products by using information contained in printed brochures. Which of the ratios discussed in this chapter would you expect to differ for these companies as a result of their different business strategies?

CRITICAL THINKING CASES

■ **LO**4, 5, 6, 7   **CP13–5**   **Analyzing the Impact of Alternative Depreciation Methods on Ratio Analysis**

Speedy Company uses the double-declining-balance method to depreciate its property, plant, and equipment, and Turtle Company uses the straight-line method. Both companies use declining-balance depreciation for income tax purposes. The two companies are exactly alike except for the difference in depreciation methods.

Required:

1. Identify the financial ratios discussed in this chapter that are likely to be affected by the difference in depreciation methods.
2. Which company will report the higher amount for each ratio that you have identified? If you cannot be certain, explain why.

■ **LO**4, 5   **CP13–6**   **Analyzing the Impact of Alternative Accounting Methods on Ratios**

The ratios computed for Canadian Tire in this chapter are compared with those of RONA Inc. and Richelieu Hardware Ltd. The comparison of ratios across these three companies assumes that they use the same accounting methods in reporting the various elements of their financial statements.

Required:

1. Access the annual reports of the three companies through their respective websites and identify the method(s) each company uses
   a. to depreciate its property, plant and equipment, and
   b. to value its inventory at year-end.
2. Are the methods used by these companies similar or different? Explain.
3. If two of these companies used different accounting methods, what impact would the different methods have on the following ratios:
   a. Net profit margin.
   b. ROE.
   c. Current ratio.
   d. Debt-to-equity.

CP13–7 Evaluating an Ethical Dilemma

■ LO4

Bianca Company requested a sizeable loan from Provincial Bank to acquire a large tract of land for future expansion. Bianca reported current assets of $1,900,000 ($430,000 in cash) and current liabilities of $1,075,000. Provincial denied the loan request for a number of reasons, including the fact that the current ratio was below 2. When Bianca was informed of the loan denial, the controller of the company immediately paid $420,000 that was owed to several trade creditors. The controller then asked Provincial to reconsider the loan application. Based on these abbreviated facts, would you recommend that Provincial approve the loan request? Why? Are the controller's actions ethical?

FINANCIAL REPORTING AND ANALYSIS TEAM PROJECT

CP13–8 Team Project: Examining an Annual Report

■ LO1, 3, 4, 5, 6, 7

As a team, select an industry to analyze. A list of companies classified by industry can be obtained by accessing **www.fpinfomart.ca** and then choosing "Companies by Industry." You can also find a list of industries and companies within each industry via **http://ca.finance.yahoo.com/investing** (click on "Order Annual Reports" under "Tools").

Using a Web browser, each team member should acquire the annual report for one publicly traded company in an industry, with each member selecting a different company. (Library files, the SEDAR service at **www.sedar.com**, and the company website are good resources.)

Required:

On an individual basis, each team member should write a short report providing the following information about the selected company. Discuss any patterns across the companies that you as a team observe. Then, as a team, write a short report comparing and contrasting your companies.

Compute and interpret each of the ratios discussed in this chapter. The most frequently used sections will be the financial statements. Also, you may want to review the notes, the summary of financial information (usually for the past 5 to 10 years), and management's discussion and analysis.

SOLUTIONS TO SELF-STUDY QUIZZES

Self-Study Quiz 13-1

1. a. ROE = Net Earnings/Average Shareholders' Equity = $173.5/[($731.2 + $894.9)/2] = 0.213 or 21.3%
   b. ROA = (Net Earnings + Interest Expense, net of tax)/Average Total Assets
      = ($173.5 + $14.3)/[($1,311.1 + $1,407.7)/2] = 0.138 or 13.8%
   c. Profit margin = Net Earnings/Net Sales = $173.5/$1,602.80 = 0.108 or 10.8%
2. The company uses debt effectively to generate return to shareholders. Its ROE exceeds its ROA.

Self-Study Quiz 13-2

Google's profit margin ratio is higher than that of Yahoo, and its total asset turnover ratio is also significantly higher than Yahoo's. Google is more efficient at controlling costs relative to revenue. Its financial leverage percentage is slightly higher than Yahoo's. Overall, Google has a faster total asset turnover ratio, higher net profit margin ratio, and higher leverage, which explains why its ROE is twice as high as Yahoo's.

Self-Study Quiz 13-3

The quick ratio should be lower than the current ratio, because the numerator of the quick ratio includes only part of the current assets. The quick ratio of 6.79 is greater than the current ratios of five of the six industries, so it cannot be associated with any of these five industries. Consequently, this quick ratio must be associated with the biotechnology industry. Since the quick assets for the software industry exceed 90 percent of its current assets, the quick ratio of this industry must be 3.61, because this ratio is the only one that exceeds 90 percent of the related current ratio.

Self-Study Quiz 13-4

1. Current ratio = Current Assets/Current Liabilities = \$396.4/\$142.8 = 2.77
2. Quick ratio = Quick Assets/Current Liabilities = \$72.1/\$142.8 = 0.50
3. Cash ratio = (Cash + Cash Equivalents)/Current Liabilities = \$70.3/\$142.8 = 0.49

Self-Study Quiz 13-5

1. Debt-to-Equity Ratio = Total Liabilities/Shareholders' Equity
   = \$522.2/\$931.5 = 0.56

2. Times Interest Earned Ratio = Earnings before Interest and Taxes/Interest Expense
   = \$315.9/\$10.8 = 29.25 times

3. P/E ratio = Market Price/Earnings per Share = \$43.25/\$2.35 = 18.40

**FINANCIAL STATEMENTS OF THE CANADIAN TIRE
CORPORATION, LIMITED**

This appendix includes the financial statements of the Canadian Tire Corporation,
Limited, for 2012, and selected notes to these financial statements. Notes 4, 5, 7, 13, 27,
29, 35, 37, 38, 40, and 41, and sections of notes 2, 6, and 12, were omitted because of
space limitations. The complete set of the Canadian Tire Corporation's financial statements and related notes are available on *Connect.*

2012 Financial
Statements

Consolidated Financial
Statements
of the Canadian Tire Corporation, Limited

Management's Responsibility for Financial Statements

The management of Canadian Tire Corporation, Limited is responsible for the accompanying consolidated financial statements and all other information in the Annual Report. The financial statements have been prepared by management in accordance with International Financial Reporting Standards, which recognize the necessity of relying on some best estimates and informed judgements. All financial information in the Annual Report is consistent with the consolidated financial statements.

To discharge its responsibilities for financial reporting and safeguarding of assets, management depends on the Company's systems of internal accounting control. These systems are designed to provide reasonable assurance that the financial records are reliable and form a proper basis for the timely and accurate preparation of financial statements. Management meets the objectives of internal accounting control on a cost effective basis through the prudent selection and training of personnel, adoption and communication of appropriate policies, and employment of an internal audit program.

The Board of Directors oversees management's responsibilities for the consolidated financial statements primarily through the activities of its Audit Committee, which is composed solely of directors who are neither officers nor employees of the Company. This Committee meets with management and the Company's independent auditors, Deloitte LLP, to review the consolidated financial statements and recommend approval by the Board of Directors. The Audit Committee is also responsible for making recommendations with respect to the appointment of and for approving remuneration and the terms of engagement of the Company's auditors. The Audit Committee also meets with the auditors, without the presence of management, to discuss the results of their audit, their opinion on internal accounting controls, and the quality of financial reporting.

The consolidated financial statements have been audited by Deloitte LLP, who were appointed by shareholder vote at the annual shareholders' meeting. Their report is presented below.

Stephen G. Wetmore
President and
Chief Executive Officer
February 21, 2013

Dean McCann
Chief Financial Officer and
Executive Vice-President, Finance

Independent Auditor's Report

To the Shareholders of Canadian Tire Corporation, Limited

We have audited the accompanying consolidated financial statements of Canadian Tire Corporation, Limited, which comprise the consolidated balance sheets as at December 29, 2012 and December 31, 2011, and the consolidated statements of income, consolidated statements of comprehensive income, consolidated statements of changes in shareholders' equity and consolidated statements of cash flows for the years ended December 29, 2012 and December 31, 2011, and a summary of significant accounting policies and other explanatory information.

Management's Responsibility for the Consolidated Financial Statements

Management is responsible for the preparation and fair presentation of these consolidated financial statements in accordance with International Financial Reporting Standards, and for such internal control as management determines is necessary to enable the preparation of consolidated financial statements that are free from material misstatement, whether due to fraud or error.

Auditor's Responsibility

Our responsibility is to express an opinion on these consolidated financial statements based on our audits. We conducted our audits in accordance with Canadian generally accepted auditing standards. Those standards require that we comply with ethical requirements and plan and perform the audit to obtain reasonable assurance about whether the consolidated financial statements are free from material misstatement.

An audit involves performing procedures to obtain audit evidence about the amounts and disclosures in the consolidated financial statements. The procedures selected depend on the auditor's judgment, including the assessment of the risks of material misstatement of the consolidated financial statements, whether due to fraud or error. In making those risk assessments, the auditor considers internal control relevant to the entity's preparation and fair presentation of the consolidated financial statements in order to design audit procedures that are appropriate in the circumstances, but not for the purpose of expressing an opinion on the effectiveness of the entity's internal control. An audit also includes evaluating the appropriateness of accounting policies used and the reasonableness of accounting estimates made by management, as well as evaluating the overall presentation of the consolidated financial statements.

We believe that the audit evidence we have obtained in our audits is sufficient and appropriate to provide a basis for our audit opinion.

Opinion

In our opinion, the consolidated financial statements present fairly, in all material respects, the financial position of Canadian Tire Corporation, Limited as at December 29, 2012 and December 31, 2011, and its financial performance and its cash flows for the years then ended in accordance with International Financial Reporting Standards.

Deloitte LLP

Chartered Accountants
Licensed Public Accountants

February 21, 2013
Toronto, Ontario

Consolidated Balance Sheets

As at (C$ in millions)	December 29, 2012	December 31, 2011
ASSETS		
Cash and cash equivalents (Note 9)	$ 1,015.5	$ 325.8
Short-term investments (Note 10)	168.9	196.4
Trade and other receivables (Note 11)	750.6	829.3
Loans receivable (Note 12)	4,265.7	4,081.7
Merchandise inventories	1,503.3	1,448.6
Prepaid expenses and deposits	39.1	44.3
Assets classified as held for sale (Note 13)	5.5	30.5
Total current assets	**7,748.6**	**6,956.6**
Long-term receivables and other assets (Note 14)	681.2	668.9
Long-term investments	182.7	128.2
Goodwill and intangible assets (Note 15)	1,089.9	1,110.0
Investment property (Note 16)	95.1	72.4
Property and equipment (Note 17)	3,343.5	3,365.9
Deferred income taxes (Note 18)	40.4	36.8
Total assets	**$ 13,181.4**	**$ 12,338.8**
LIABILITIES		
Bank indebtedness (Note 9)	$ 86.0	$ 124.8
Deposits (Note 19)	1,311.0	1,182.3
Trade and other payables (Note 20)	1,631.3	1,640.9
Provisions (Note 21)	185.8	191.9
Short-term borrowings (Note 23)	118.9	352.6
Loans payable (Note 24)	623.7	628.7
Income taxes payable	5.5	3.9
Current portion of long-term debt (Note 25)	661.9	27.9
Total current liabilities	**4,624.1**	**4,153.0**
Long-term provisions (Note 21)	54.8	55.1
Long-term debt (Note 25)	2,336.0	2,347.7
Long-term deposits (Note 19)	1,111.8	1,102.2
Deferred income taxes (Note 18)	77.7	66.1
Other long-term liabilities (Note 26)	213.4	205.7
Total liabilities	**8,417.8**	**7,929.8**
SHAREHOLDERS' EQUITY		
Share capital (Note 28)	688.0	710.5
Contributed surplus	2.9	1.1
Accumulated other comprehensive income (loss)	(1.7)	11.0
Retained earnings	4,074.4	3,686.4
Total shareholders' equity	**4,763.6**	**4,409.0**
Total liabilities and shareholders' equity	**$ 13,181.4**	**$ 12,338.8**

The related notes form an integral part of these consolidated financial statements.

Maureen J. Sabia
Director

Graham W. Savage
Director

Consolidated Statements of Income

For the years ended
(C$ in millions, except per share amounts)

	December 29, 2012	December 31, 2011
		(Note 41)
Revenue (Note 31)	$ 11,427.2	$ 10,387.1
Cost of producing revenue (Note 32)	(7,929.3)	(7,326.4)
Gross margin	3,497.9	3,060.7
Other income	5.7	18.4
Operating expenses		
Distribution costs	(356.2)	(368.7)
Sales and marketing expenses	(1,636.4)	(1,307.9)
Administrative expenses	(707.6)	(640.4)
Total operating expenses (Note 33)	(2,700.2)	(2,317.0)
Operating income	803.4	762.1
Finance income	18.1	23.0
Finance costs	(144.3)	(155.2)
Net finance costs (Note 34)	(126.2)	(132.2)
Income before income taxes	677.2	629.9
Income taxes (Note 35)	(178.0)	(162.9)
Net income	$ 499.2	$ 467.0
Basic earnings per share	$ 6.13	$ 5.73
Diluted earnings per share	$ 6.10	$ 5.71
Weighted average number of Common and Class A Non-Voting Shares outstanding (Note 29):		
Basic	81,435,218	81,447,398
Diluted	81,805,594	81,803,786

The related notes form an integral part of these consolidated financial statements.

Consolidated Statements of Comprehensive Income

For the years ended
(C$ in millions)

	December 29, 2012	December 31, 2011
Net income	$ 499.2	$ 467.0
Other comprehensive income (loss)		
Derivatives designated as cash flow hedges:		
(Losses) gains, net of tax of $7.8 (2011 – $0.4)	(21.0)	0.8
Reclassification of losses to non-financial asset, net of tax of $3.5 (2011 – $15.6)	9.7	40.0
Reclassification of (gains) losses to income, net of tax of $nil (2011 – $0.4)	(0.1)	1.0
Available-for-sale financial assets:		
Gains, net of tax of $0.2 (2011 – $3.5)	0.3	8.9
Reclassification of gains to income, net of tax of $0.6 (2011 – $2.9)	(1.6)	(7.4)
Actuarial adjustments, net of tax of $3.9 (2011 – $4.9) (Note 27)	(9.5)	(14.2)
Total other comprehensive income (loss)	(22.2)	29.1
Total comprehensive income	$ 477.0	$ 496.1

The related notes form an integral part of these consolidated financial statements.

Consolidated Statements of Cash Flows

For the years ended (C$ in millions)	December 29, 2012	December 31, 2011
		(Note 41)
Cash generated from (used for):		
Operating activities		
Net income	$ 499.2	$ 467.0
Adjustments for:		
Gross impairment loss on loans receivable (Note 12)	323.7	352.0
Depreciation on property and equipment and investment property (Note 33)	248.9	229.8
Income tax expense	178.0	162.9
Net finance costs	126.2	132.2
Amortization of intangible assets (Note 33)	86.2	66.3
Changes in fair value of derivative instruments	(7.7)	(3.1)
Deferred income taxes	16.5	(6.4)
Other	13.7	9.8
Gain on revaluation of shares (Note 8)	–	(10.4)
	1,484.7	1,400.1
Changes in working capital and other (Note 36)	(434.0)	219.6
Cash generated from operating activities before interest and income taxes	1,050.7	1,619.7
Interest paid	(155.3)	(176.6)
Interest received	8.9	26.1
Income taxes paid	(161.3)	(63.7)
Cash generated from operating activities	743.0	1,405.5
Investing activities		
Acquisition of FGL Sports (Note 8)	–	(739.9)
Acquisition of short-term investments	(264.0)	(334.8)
Acquisition of long-term investments	(130.0)	(123.1)
Additions to property and equipment and investment property	(222.3)	(230.5)
Additions to intangible assets	(64.3)	(128.9)
Long-term receivables and other assets	17.6	(3.2)
Proceeds from the disposition of long-term investments	4.7	18.1
Proceeds from the maturity and disposition of short-term investments	360.7	364.0
Proceeds on disposition of property and equipment, investment property and assets held for sale	45.0	21.0
Other	(8.9)	(4.1)
Cash used for investing activities	(261.5)	(1,161.4)
Financing activities		
Net (repayment) issuance of short-term borrowings	(233.7)	10.1
Issuance of loans payable	235.3	129.3
Repayment of loans payable	(240.3)	(187.6)
Issuance of share capital (Note 28)	12.4	11.6
Repurchase of share capital (Note 28)	(33.1)	(11.9)
Issuance of long-term debt	637.4	–
Repayment of long-term debt and finance lease liabilities	(30.1)	(355.6)
Dividends paid	(97.7)	(89.6)
Payment of transaction costs related to long-term debt	(3.2)	–
Cash generated from (used for) financing activities	247.0	(493.7)
Cash generated (used) in the year	728.5	(249.6)
Cash and cash equivalents, net of bank indebtedness, beginning of year	201.0	450.9
Effect of exchange rate fluctuations on cash held	–	(0.3)
Cash and cash equivalents, net of bank indebtedness, end of year (Note 9)	$ 929.5	$ 201.0

The related notes form an integral part of these consolidated financial statements.

Consolidated Statements of Changes in Shareholders' Equity

(C$ in millions)	Share capital	Contributed surplus	Cash flow hedges	Fair value changes in available-for-sale financial assets	Total accumulated other comprehensive income (loss)	Retained earnings	Total shareholders' equity
Balance at December 31, 2011	$ 710.5	$ 1.1	$ 9.4	$ 1.6	$ 11.0	$ 3,686.4	$ 4,409.0
Total comprehensive income							
Net income						499.2	499.2
Other comprehensive income (loss)							
Derivatives designated as cash flow hedges:							
Losses, net of tax of $7.8			(21.0)		(21.0)		(21.0)
Reclassification of losses to non-financial asset,							
net of tax of $3.5			9.7		9.7		9.7
Reclassification of gains to income,							
net of tax of $nil			(0.1)		(0.1)		(0.1)
Available-for-sale financial assets:							
Gains, net of tax of $0.2				0.3	0.3		0.3
Reclassification of gains to income,							
net of tax of $0.6				(1.6)	(1.6)		(1.6)
Actuarial adjustments, net of tax of $3.9						(9.5)	(9.5)
Total other comprehensive (loss)	–	–	(11.4)	(1.3)	(12.7)	(9.5)	(22.2)
Total comprehensive income (loss)	–	–	(11.4)	(1.3)	(12.7)	489.7	477.0
Contributions by and distributions to shareholders							
Issue of Class A Non-Voting Shares (Note 28)	12.4				–		12.4
Repurchase of Class A Non-Voting Shares (Note 28)	(33.1)				–		(33.1)
Excess of issue price over repurchase price (Note 28)	(1.8)	1.8			–		–
Dividends					–	(101.7)	(101.7)
Total contributions by and distributions to shareholders	(22.5)	1.8	–	–	–	(101.7)	(122.4)
Balance at December 29, 2012	$ 688.0	$ 2.9	$ (2.0)	$ 0.3	$ (1.7)	$ 4,074.4	$ 4,763.6
Balance at January 1, 2011	$ 711.6	$ 0.3	$ (32.4)	$ 0.1	$ (32.3)	$ 3,325.3	$ 4,004.9
Total comprehensive income							
Net income						467.0	467.0
Other comprehensive income (loss)							
Derivatives designated as cash flow hedges:							
Gains, net of tax of $0.4			0.8		0.8		0.8
Reclassification of losses to non-financial asset,							
net of tax of $15.6			40.0		40.0		40.0
Reclassification of losses to income,							
net of tax of $0.4			1.0		1.0		1.0
Available-for-sale financial assets:							
Gains, net of tax of $3.5				8.9	8.9		8.9
Reclassification of gains to income, net of tax of $2.9				(7.4)	(7.4)		(7.4)
Actuarial adjustments, net of tax of $4.9						(14.2)	(14.2)
Total other comprehensive income (loss)	–	–	41.8	1.5	43.3	(14.2)	29.1
Total comprehensive income	–	–	41.8	1.5	43.3	452.8	496.1
Contributions by and distributions to shareholders							
Issue of Class A Non-Voting Shares (Note 28)	11.6				–		11.6
Repurchase of Class A Non-Voting Shares (Note 28)	(11.9)				–		(11.9)
Excess of issue price over repurchase price (Note 28)	(0.8)	0.8			–		–
Dividends					–	(91.7)	(91.7)
Total contributions by and distributions to shareholders	(1.1)	0.8	–	–	–	(91.7)	(92.0)
Balance at December 31, 2011	$ 710.5	$ 1.1	$ 9.4	$ 1.6	$ 11.0	$ 3,686.4	$ 4,409.0

The related notes form an integral part of these consolidated financial statements.

1. The Company and its operations

Canadian Tire Corporation, Limited is a Canadian public company primarily domiciled in Canada. Its registered office is located at 2180 Yonge Street, Toronto, Ontario, M4P 2V8, Canada. It is listed on the Toronto Stock Exchange (TSX – CTC, CTC.A). Canadian Tire Corporation, Limited and entities it controls are together referred to in these consolidated financial statements as "the Company".

The Company is comprised of two main business operations that offer a range of retail goods and services, including general merchandise, apparel, sporting goods, petroleum and financial services. Details of its two reportable operating segments, Retail and Financial Services, are provided in Note 7. The Company acquired FGL Sports Ltd. (formerly The Forzani Group Ltd.) ("FGL Sports") on August 18, 2011. The operations of FGL Sports are included in the Company's results from operations and financial position commencing August 19, 2011.

2. Basis of preparation

Fiscal year

The fiscal year of the Company consists of a 52- or 53-week period ending on the Saturday closest to December 31. The fiscal years for the consolidated financial statements and notes presented for 2012 and 2011 are the 52-week period ended December 29, 2012, and the 52-week period ended December 31, 2011, respectively.

Statement of compliance

These consolidated financial statements have been prepared in accordance with International Financial Reporting Standards (IFRS) and using the accounting policies described herein.

These consolidated financial statements were authorized for issuance by the Company's Board of Directors on February 21, 2013.

Basis of presentation

These consolidated financial statements have been prepared on the historical cost basis, except for the following items, which are measured at fair value:

• financial instruments at fair value through profit or loss;
• derivative financial instruments;
• available-for-sale financial assets;
• liabilities for share-based payment plans; and
• initial recognition of assets acquired and liabilities assumed in business combinations.

In addition, the post-employment defined benefit obligation is recorded at its discounted present value.

Functional and presentation currency

These consolidated financial statements are presented in Canadian dollars ("C$"), the Company's functional currency ("the functional currency"). All financial information is presented in millions, except per share amounts, which are presented in whole dollars, and the number of shares or the weighted average number of shares, which are presented in whole numbers.

Use of estimates and judgments

The preparation of these consolidated financial statements in accordance with IFRS requires management to make judgments, estimates and assumptions that affect the application of accounting policies and the reported amounts of assets and liabilities and disclosures of contingent assets and liabilities at the date of these consolidated financial statements and the reported amounts of revenue and expenses during the reporting periods. Actual results may differ from estimates made in these consolidated financial statements.

Judgment is used mainly in determining whether a balance or transaction should be recognized in the consolidated financial statements. Estimates and assumptions are used mainly in determining the measurement of recognized transactions and balances. However, judgment and estimates are often interrelated.

Judgments, estimates and assumptions are continually evaluated and are based on historical experience and other factors, including expectations of future events that are believed to be reasonable under the circumstances. Revisions to accounting estimates are recognized in the period in which the estimates are revised and in future periods affected.

Management has applied judgment in its assessment of the appropriateness of consolidation of entities; the classification of leases and financial instruments; the recognition of tax losses and provisions; the determination of cash generating units (CGUs); the identification of investment property; the identification of the indicators of impairment for property and equipment, investment property and intangible assets; and the allocation of purchase price adjustments on business combinations.

Estimates are used when determining the useful lives of property and equipment, investment property and intangible assets for the purposes of depreciation and amortization; when accounting for and measuring items such as inventory, customer loyalty programs, deferred revenue, income and other taxes, provisions and purchase price adjustments on business combinations; when making assumptions underlying actuarial determination of post-employment benefits; when measuring certain fair values, including those related to the valuation of business combinations, share-based payments and financial instruments; when testing goodwill, intangible assets with indefinite useful lives and other assets for impairment; and when updating models used in the determination of allowances on loans receivable. The allowances on loans receivable are based on historical customer payment experience as described in Note 3; future customer behaviour may be affected by a number of factors, including changes in interest and unemployment rates and program design changes.

New standards implemented
Deferred taxes – recovery of underlying assets
In December 2010, the IASB amended IAS 12 – *Income Taxes* ("IAS 12"), introducing an exception to the general measurement requirements of IAS 12. Investment property measured at fair value is exempt from the general measurement requirements of IAS 12. The amendment was effective for annual periods beginning on or after January 1, 2012. This amendment did not have an impact on the Company as its investment property is not measured at fair value.

Financial instruments: Disclosures
In October 2010, the IASB amended IFRS 7 – *Financial Instruments: Disclosures* ("IFRS 7"), which requires additional disclosures on transferred financial assets. The amendment was applicable prospectively for annual periods beginning on or after July 1, 2011. The additional disclosures on transferred financial assets are provided in Note 12.

3. Significant accounting policies

The accounting policies set out below have been applied consistently to all periods presented in these consolidated financial statements and have been applied consistently throughout the Company.

Basis of consolidation
These consolidated financial statements include the accounts of Canadian Tire Corporation, Limited and entities it controls. Control exists when Canadian Tire Corporation, Limited has the power, directly or indirectly, to govern the financial and operating policies of an entity/arrangement so as to obtain benefit from its activities. The significant entities controlled by Canadian Tire Corporation, Limited are identified in Note 40.

The results of certain subsidiaries that have different year-ends have been included in these consolidated financial statements for the 52 weeks ended December 29, 2012, and for the 52 weeks ended December 31, 2011. The year-end of Canadian Tire Financial Services Limited ("Financial Services") is December 31.

Special purpose entities (SPEs)
A number of SPEs are consolidated without the Company having direct or indirect shareholdings in these entities. An SPE is consolidated if, based on the evaluation of the substance of its relationship with the Company, including consideration of the Company's exposure to the SPE's risks and rewards, the Company concludes that it controls the SPE. SPEs were established under terms that impose strict limitations on the decision-making powers of the SPEs' management. As a result, in such instances, since either the Company receives the majority of the benefits related to the SPEs' operations and net assets, the Company is exposed to risks related to the SPEs' activities or the Company obtains the majority of the residual or ownership risk related to the SPEs, these SPEs are deemed to be controlled by the Company.

Business combinations
The Company applies the acquisition method in accounting for business combinations.

The Company measures goodwill as the difference between the fair value of the consideration transferred, including the recognized amount of any non-controlling interest in the acquiree, and the net recognized amount (generally fair value) of the identifiable assets acquired and liabilities assumed, all measured as at the acquisition date.

Consideration transferred includes the fair value of the assets transferred (including cash), liabilities incurred by the Company on behalf of the acquiree, the fair value of any contingent consideration and equity interests issued by the Company.

Where a business combination is achieved in stages, previously held interests in the acquired entity are remeasured to fair value at the acquisition date, which is the date control is obtained, and the resulting gain or loss, if any, is recognized in net income. Amounts arising from interests in the acquiree prior to the acquisition date that have previously been recognized in OCI are reclassified to net income.

Transaction costs that the Company incurs in connection with a business combination are expensed in the period as incurred.

Foreign currency translation

Transactions in foreign currencies are translated into Canadian dollars at rates in effect at the date of the transaction. Monetary assets and liabilities in foreign currencies are translated into Canadian dollars at the closing exchange rate at the balance sheet date. Non-monetary items that are measured in terms of historical cost are translated into Canadian dollars at the exchange rate at the date of the original transaction. Non-monetary assets and liabilities that are measured at fair value are translated into Canadian dollars at the exchange rate at the date that the fair value is determined. Exchange gains or losses arising from translations are recorded in other income or cost of producing revenue in the consolidated statements of income.

Financial instruments

Recognition and measurement

Financial assets and financial liabilities, including derivatives, are recognized in the consolidated balance sheets when the Company becomes a party to the contractual provisions of a financial instrument or non-financial derivative contract. All financial instruments are required to be measured at fair value on initial recognition. Subsequent measurement of these assets and liabilities is based on either fair value or amortized cost using the effective interest method, depending upon their classification.

Transaction costs that are directly attributable to the acquisition or issue of financial assets and financial liabilities (other than financial assets and financial liabilities classified as fair value through profit or loss (FVTPL) are added to or deducted from the fair value of the financial assets or financial liabilities, as appropriate, on initial recognition. Transaction costs directly attributable to the acquisition of financial assets or financial liabilities classified as FVTPL are recognized immediately in net income.

The Company classifies financial instruments, at the time of initial recognition, according to their characteristics and management's choices and intentions related thereto for the purposes of ongoing measurement. Classification choices for financial assets include a) FVTPL, b) held to maturity, c) available for sale and d) loans and receivables. Classification choices for financial liabilities include a) FVTPL and b) other liabilities.

The Company's financial assets and financial liabilities are generally classified and measured as follows:

Asset/Liability	Category	Measurement
Cash and cash equivalents	Loans and receivables	Amortized cost
Short-term investments	Available for sale[1]	Fair value
Trade and other receivables	Loans and receivables	Amortized cost
Loans receivable	Loans and receivables	Amortized cost
Deposits (recorded in prepaid expenses and deposits)	Loans and receivables	Amortized cost
Long-term receivables and other assets	Loans and receivables	Amortized cost
Long-term investments	Available for sale[2]	Fair value
Bank indebtedness	Other liabilities	Amortized cost
Deposits	Other liabilities	Amortized cost
Trade and other payables	Other liabilities	Amortized cost
Short-term borrowings	Other liabilities	Amortized cost
Loans payable	Other liabilities	Amortized cost
Long-term debt	Other liabilities	Amortized cost

[1] Certain short-term investments are classified as FVTPL.
[2] Certain long-term investments are classified as FVTPL.

Financial instruments at fair value through profit or loss

Financial instruments are classified as FVTPL when the financial instrument is either held for trading or designated as such upon initial recognition. Financial assets are classified as held for trading if acquired principally for the purpose of selling in the near future or if part of an identified portfolio of financial instruments that the Company manages together and has a recent actual pattern of short-term profit-making. Derivatives are also categorized as held for trading unless they are designated as hedges.

Financial instruments classified as FVTPL are measured at fair value, with changes in fair value recorded in net income in the period in which they arise.

Held to maturity

Debt instruments are classified as held to maturity if the Company has the positive intent and ability to hold the instruments to maturity. Subsequent to initial recognition, held-to-maturity financial assets are measured at amortized cost using the effective interest method, less any impairment losses.

Available for sale

Financial assets classified as available for sale are measured at fair value with changes in fair value recognized in OCI until realized through disposal or other than temporary impairment. Dividend income from available-for-sale financial assets is recognized in net income when the Company's right to receive payments is established. Interest income on available-for-sale financial assets, calculated using the effective interest method, is recognized in net income.

Loans and receivables

Loans and receivables are financial assets with fixed or determinable payments that are not quoted in an active market. Subsequent to initial recognition, loans and receivables are measured at amortized cost using the effective interest method, less any impairment, with gains and losses recognized in net income in the period that the asset is derecognized or impaired.

Other liabilities

Subsequent to initial recognition, other financial liabilities are measured at amortized cost using the effective interest method with gains and losses recognized in net income in the period that the liability is derecognized.

Derecognition of financial instruments

A financial asset is derecognized when the contractual rights to the cash flows from the asset expire or when the Company transfers the financial asset to another party without retaining control or substantially all the risks and rewards of ownership of the asset. Any interest in transferred financial assets that is created or retained by the Company is recognized as a separate asset or liability.

A financial liability is derecognized when its contractual obligations are discharged, are cancelled or expire.

Derivative financial instruments

The Company enters into various derivative financial instruments as part of the Company's strategy to manage its foreign currency and interest rate exposures. The Company also enters into equity derivative contracts to hedge certain future share-based payment expenses. The Company does not hold or issue derivative financial instruments for trading purposes.

All derivative financial instruments, including derivatives that are embedded in financial or non-financial contracts that are not closely related to the host contracts, are measured at fair value. The gain or loss that results from remeasurement at each reporting period is recognized in net income immediately unless the derivative is designated and effective as a hedging instrument, in which event the timing of the recognition in net income depends on the nature of the hedge relationship.

Embedded derivatives

Embedded derivatives (elements of contracts whose cash flows move independently from the host contract) are required to be separated and measured at their respective fair values unless certain criteria are met. The Company does not have any significant embedded derivatives in contracts that require separate accounting and disclosure.

Hedge accounting

Where hedge accounting can be applied, certain criteria are documented at the inception of the derivative contract and updated at each reporting date.

Fair-value hedges

For fair-value hedges, the carrying amount of the hedged item is adjusted for changes in fair value attributable to the hedged risk, and this adjustment is recognized in net income immediately. Changes in the fair value of the hedged item, to the extent that the hedging relationship is effective, are offset by changes in the fair value of the hedging derivative, which are also included in net income. When hedge accounting is discontinued, the carrying amount of the hedged item is no longer adjusted and the cumulative fair-value adjustments to the carrying amount of the hedged item are amortized to net income over the remaining term of the hedged item using the effective interest method.

Cash flow hedges

For cash flow hedges, the effective portion of the changes in the fair value of the hedging derivative, net of taxes, is recognized in OCI, while the ineffective and unhedged portions are recognized immediately in net income. Amounts recorded in accumulated other comprehensive income (AOCI) are reclassified to net income in the periods when the hedged item affects net income. However, when a forecasted transaction that is hedged results in the recognition of a non-financial asset or liability, the gains and losses previously recognized in AOCI are reclassified from AOCI and included in the initial measurement of the cost of the non-financial asset or liability.

When hedge accounting is discontinued, the amounts previously recognized in AOCI are reclassified to net income during the periods when the variability in the cash flows of the hedged item affects net income. Gains and losses on derivatives are reclassified immediately to net income when the hedged item is sold or terminated early. If hedge accounting is discontinued due to the hedged item no longer being expected to occur, the amount previously recognized in AOCI is reclassified immediately to net income.

The Company enters into foreign currency contracts to hedge the exposure to foreign currency risk on the future payment of foreign-currency-denominated inventory purchases. The changes in fair value of these contracts are included in OCI to the extent the hedges continue to be effective, excluding the time value component of foreign exchange options, which is included in net income. Once the inventory is received, the Company reclassifies the related AOCI amount to merchandise inventories. Subsequent changes in the fair value of the foreign exchange contracts are recorded in net income as they occur.

Cash and cash equivalents

Cash and cash equivalents are defined as cash plus highly liquid and rated certificates of deposit or commercial paper with an original term to maturity of three months or less.

Short-term investments

Short-term investments are investments in highly liquid and rated certificates of deposit, commercial paper or other securities, primarily Canadian and United States government securities and notes of other creditworthy parties, with an original term to maturity of more than three months and remaining term to maturity of less than one year.

Trade and other receivables

The allowance for impairment of trade and other receivables is established when there is objective evidence that the Company will not be able to collect all amounts due according to the original terms of the receivables. Significant financial difficulties of the debtor, probability that the debtor will enter bankruptcy or financial reorganization, and default or delinquency in payments are considered indicators that the trade receivable is impaired. The amount of the allowance is calculated as the difference between the asset's carrying amount and the present value of estimated future cash flows, discounted at the original effective interest rate. The carrying amount of the asset is reduced through the use of an allowance account, and the amount of the loss is recognized in administrative expenses in the consolidated statements of income. When a trade receivable is uncollectible, it is written off against the allowance account. Subsequent recoveries of amounts previously written off are recognized as a recovery in administrative expenses in the consolidated statements of income.

Loans receivable

Credit card, personal and line of credit loans

Credit card, personal and line of credit loans are recognized when cash is advanced to the borrower. They are derecognized when either the borrower repays its obligations, the loans are sold or written off or substantially all of the risks and rewards of ownership are transferred.

Losses for impaired loans are recognized when there is objective evidence that impairment of the loans has occurred. Impairment allowances are calculated on individual loans and on groups of loans assessed collectively. Impairment losses are recorded in cost of producing revenue in the consolidated statements of income. The carrying amount of impaired loans in the consolidated balance sheets is reduced through the use of impairment allowance accounts. Losses expected from future events are not recognized.

All individually significant loans receivable are assessed for specific impairment. All individually significant loans receivable found not to be specifically impaired are then collectively assessed for any impairment that might be incurred but not yet identified. Loans receivable that are not individually significant are collectively assessed for impairment by grouping together loans receivable with similar risk characteristics.

The Company uses a roll rate methodology. This methodology employs statistical analysis of historical data and experience of delinquency and default to estimate the amount of loans that will eventually be written off as a result of events occurring before the reporting date, with certain adjustments for other relevant circumstances influencing the recoverability of the loans receivable. The estimated loss is the difference between the present value of the expected future cash flows, discounted at the original effective interest rate of the portfolio, and the carrying amount of the portfolio. Default rates, loss rates and the expected timing of future recoveries are regularly benchmarked against actual outcomes to ensure that they remain appropriate.

Dealer loans

Loans to Associate Dealers ("Dealers"), independent third-party operators of Canadian Tire Retail stores, are initially measured at fair value plus directly attributable transaction costs and are subsequently measured at their amortized cost using the effective interest method, less an allowance for impairment, if any.

Merchandise inventories

Merchandise inventories are carried at the lower of cost or net realizable value.

Cash consideration received from vendors is recognized as a reduction to the cost of related inventory unless the cash consideration received is either a reimbursement of incremental costs incurred by the Company or a payment for assets or services delivered to the vendor.

The cost of merchandise inventories are determined based on weighted average cost and includes costs incurred in bringing the merchandise inventories to their present location and condition. All inventories are finished goods.

Net realizable value is the estimated selling price of inventory during the normal course of business less estimated selling expenses.

Long-term investments

Investments in highly liquid and rated certificates of deposit, commercial paper or other securities with a remaining term to maturity of greater than one year are classified as long-term investments.

The Company's exposure to credit, currency and interest rate risks related to other investments is disclosed in Note 6.

Intangible assets

Goodwill

Goodwill represents the excess of the cost of an acquisition over the fair value of the Company's share of the identifiable assets acquired and liabilities assumed in a business combination. Goodwill is measured at cost less impairment and is not amortized.

Intangible assets

Intangible assets with finite useful lives are measured at cost and are amortized on a straight-line basis over their estimated useful lives, generally up to a period of five years. The estimated useful lives and amortization methods are reviewed annually with the effect of any changes in estimate being accounted for on a prospective basis.

Intangible assets with indefinite useful lives are measured at cost less impairment and are not amortized. Expenditures on research activities are expensed as incurred.

Investment property

Investment property is property held to earn rental income or for appreciation of capital or both. The Company has determined that properties it provides to its Dealers, franchisees and agents are not investment property as these relate to the Company's operating activities. This was determined based on certain criteria such as whether the Company provides significant ancillary services to the lessees of the property. The Company includes property that it leases out to third parties (other than Dealers, franchisees or agents) in investment property.

Investment property is measured in the same manner as property and equipment.

Property and equipment

Property and equipment are measured at cost less accumulated depreciation and any accumulated impairment. Land is measured at cost less any accumulated impairment. Properties in the course of construction are measured at cost less any accumulated impairment losses. The cost of an item of property or equipment comprises costs that can be directly attributed to its acquisition and initial estimates of the cost of dismantling and removing the item and restoring the site on which it is located.

Buildings, fixtures and equipment are depreciated on a declining balance method to their residual value over their estimated useful lives. The estimated useful lives, amortization method and residual values are reviewed annually with the effect of any changes in estimate being accounted for on a prospective basis.

Leasehold improvements and lease inducements are amortized on a straight-line basis over the terms of the respective leases.

Assets held under finance leases are depreciated on the same basis as owned assets or, where shorter, over the terms of the respective leases.

Depreciation and amortization rates are as follows:

Asset category	Depreciation rate/term
Buildings	4–20%
Fixtures and equipment (Including software intangible assets)	5–40%
Leasehold improvements	Shorter of term of lease or estimated useful life
Assets under finance lease	Shorter of term of lease or estimated useful life

Leased assets

Leases are classified as finance leases whenever the terms of the lease transfer substantially all the risks and rewards of ownership to the lessee. All other leases are classified as operating leases.

Lessor

When the Company is the lessor in an operating lease, rental income and licence fees are recognized in net income on a straight-line basis over the term of the lease.

Lessee

When the Company is the lessee in an operating lease, rent payments are charged to net income on a straight-line basis over the term of the lease.

Assets under finance leases are recognized as assets of the Company at their fair value or, if lower, at the present value of the minimum lease payments, each determined at the inception of the lease. The corresponding liability is included in the consolidated balance sheets as a finance lease obligation. Lease payments are apportioned between finance costs and reduction of the lease obligations so as to achieve a constant rate of interest on the remaining balance of the liability.

Sale and leaseback

The accounting treatment of a sale and leaseback transaction depends upon the substance of the transaction and whether the sale is made at the asset's fair value.

For sale and finance leasebacks, any gain or loss from the sale is deferred and amortized over the lease term. For sale and operating leasebacks, the assets are sold at fair value and, accordingly, the gain or loss from the sale is recognized immediately in net income.

Impairment of assets

The carrying amounts of property and equipment, investment property and intangible assets with finite useful lives are reviewed at the end of each reporting period to determine whether there are any indicators of impairment. If any such indicators exist, then the recoverable amount of the asset is estimated. Goodwill and intangible assets with indefinite useful lives and intangible assets not yet available for use are not amortized but are tested for impairment at least annually or whenever there is an indicator that the asset may be impaired.

Cash generating units

When it is not possible to estimate the recoverable amount of an individual asset, the Company estimates the recoverable amount of the CGU to which the asset belongs. The CGU corresponds to the smallest identifiable group of assets whose continuing use generates cash inflows that are largely independent of the cash inflows from other assets or groups of assets. The Company has determined that its Retail CGUs comprise individual stores or groups of stores within a geographic market.

Goodwill is allocated to each of the CGUs (or groups of CGUs) expected to benefit from the synergies of the combination. Goodwill acquired in a business combination is allocated to groups of CGUs according to the level at which management monitors that goodwill. Intangible assets with indefinite useful lives are allocated to the CGU to which they relate. Any impairment loss is allocated first to reduce the carrying amount of any goodwill allocated to the CGU and then to the other assets of the CGU pro rata based on the carrying amount of each asset in the CGU.

Determining the recoverable amount

An impairment loss is recognized when the carrying amount of an asset, or of the CGU to which it belongs, exceeds the recoverable amount. The recoverable amount of an asset or CGU is defined as the higher of its fair value less costs to sell (FVLCS) and its value in use (VIU).

In assessing VIU, the estimated future cash flows are discounted to their present value. Cash flows are discounted using a weighted average cost of capital before tax, plus a risk premium specific to each line of business. The Company estimates cash flows before taxes based on the most recent actual results or budgets. Cash flows are then extrapolated over a period of up to five years, taking into account a terminal value calculated by discounting the final year in perpetuity. The growth rate applied to the terminal values is based on the Bank of Canada's target growth rate or a growth rate specific to the individual item being tested based on management's estimate.

Recording impairments and reversal of impairments

Impairments and reversals of impairments are recognized in other income in the consolidated statements of income. Impairments of goodwill cannot be reversed. Impairments of other assets recognized in prior periods are assessed at the end of each reporting period to determine if the indicators of impairment have reversed or no longer exist. An impairment is reversed if the estimated recoverable amount exceeds the carrying amount. The increased carrying amount of an asset attributable to a reversal of impairment may not exceed the carrying amount that would have been determined had no impairment been recognized in prior periods.

Assets classified as held for sale

Non-current assets and disposal groups are classified as assets held for sale when their carrying amount is to be recovered principally through a sale transaction rather than through continuing use. This condition is regarded as met only when the sale is highly probable and the asset (or disposal group) is available for immediate sale in its present condition. Management must be committed to the sale, and it should be expected to qualify for recognition as a completed sale within one year from the date of classification. Assets (and disposal groups) classified as held for sale are measured at the lower of the carrying amount or FVLCS.

Borrowing costs

Borrowing costs directly attributable to the acquisition or construction of a qualifying asset are capitalized. Qualifying assets are those that require a minimum of three months to prepare for their intended use. All other borrowing costs are recognized in cost of producing revenue and in finance costs in the consolidated statements of income in the period in which they occur.

Employee benefits

Short-term benefits

Short-term employee benefit obligations are measured on an undiscounted basis and are expensed as the related service is provided.

The Company recognizes a liability and an expense for short-term benefits such as bonuses, profit-sharing and stock purchases if the Company has a present legal obligation or constructive obligation to pay this amount as a result of past service provided by the employee and the obligation can be estimated reasonably.

Post-employment benefits

The Company provides certain health care, dental care, life insurance and other benefits but not pensions for certain retired employees pursuant to Company policy. The Company accrues the cost of these employee benefits over the periods in which the employees earn the benefits. The cost of employee benefits earned by employees is actuarially determined using the projected benefit method pro-rated on length of service and management's best estimate of salary escalation, retirement ages of employees, employee turnover and expected health and dental care costs. The costs are discounted at a rate that is based on market rates as at the measurement date. Actuarial gains and losses are immediately recorded in OCI.

The Company also provides post-employment benefits with respect to a Deferred Profit Sharing Plan (DPSP).

Other long-term employee benefits include:

Termination benefits

Termination benefits are payable when employment is terminated by the Company before the normal retirement date or whenever an employee accepts voluntary redundancy in exchange for these benefits. The Company recognizes a provision for termination benefits when it is demonstrably committed to either terminating the employment of current employees according to a detailed formal plan without possibility of withdrawal or providing termination benefits as a result of an offer made to encourage voluntary redundancy.

Share-based payments

Stock options with tandem stock appreciation rights (stock options) are granted with a feature that enables the employee to exercise the stock option or receive a cash payment equal to the difference between the market price of the Company's Class A Non-Voting Shares as at the exercise date and the exercise price of the stock option. These stock options are considered to be compound instruments. The fair value of compound instruments is measured at each reporting date, taking into account the terms and conditions on which the rights to cash or equity instruments are granted. As the fair value of the settlement in cash is the same as the fair value of the settlement as a traditional stock option, the fair value of the stock option is the same as the fair value of the debt component. The corresponding expense and liability are recognized over the respective vesting period.

The fair value of the amount payable to employees in respect of share unit plans, which are settled in cash, is recorded as a liability over the period that the employees unconditionally become entitled to payment. The fair value of the liability is remeasured at each reporting date with the change in the liability being recognized in administrative expenses in the consolidated statements of income.

Insurance reserve

Included in trade and other payables is an insurance reserve that consists of an amount determined from loss reports and individual cases and an amount, based on past experience, for losses incurred but not reported. These estimates are continually reviewed and are subject to the impact of future changes in such factors as claim severity and frequency. While management believes that the amount is adequate, the ultimate liability may be in excess of or less than the amounts provided, and any adjustment will be reflected in the periods in which they become known. The Company uses actuarial valuations in determining its reserve for outstanding losses and loss-related expenses using an appropriate reserving methodology for each line of business. The Company does not discount its liabilities for unpaid claims.

Provisions

A provision is recognized if, as a result of a past event, the Company has a present legal or constructive obligation that can be estimated reliably and it is probable that an outflow of economic benefits will be required to settle the obligation. The amount recognized as a provision is the best estimate of the consideration required to settle the present obligation at the end of the reporting period, taking into account risks and uncertainty of cash flows. Where the effect of discounting is material, provisions are determined by discounting the expected future cash flows at a pre-tax rate that reflects current market assessments of the time value of money and the risks specific to the liability.

Sales and warranty returns

Accruals for sales and warranty returns are estimated on the basis of historical returns and are recorded so as to allocate them to the same period the corresponding revenue is recognized. These accruals are reviewed regularly and updated to reflect management's best estimate; however, actual returns could vary from these estimates.

Site restoration and decommissioning

Legal or constructive obligations associated with the removal of underground fuel storage tanks and site remediation costs on the retirement of certain property and equipment and with the termination of certain lease agreements are recognized in the period in which they are incurred when it is probable that an outflow of resources embodying economic benefits will be required and a reasonable estimate of the amount of the obligation can be made. The obligations are initially measured at the Company's best estimate, using an expected value approach, and are discounted to present value.

Onerous contracts

A provision for onerous contracts is recognized when the expected benefits to be derived by the Company from a contract are lower than the unavoidable costs of meeting its obligations under the contract. The provision is measured at the present value of the lower of the expected cost of terminating the contract or the expected net cost of continuing with the contract.

Customer loyalty

Provisions for the fair value of loyalty program redemptions are estimated on the basis of historical redemptions. The provisions are reviewed regularly and updated to reflect management's best estimate; however, actual redemptions could vary from these estimates.

Restructuring

A provision for restructuring is recognized when the Company has approved a detailed and formal restructuring plan and the restructuring has either commenced or has been announced publicly. The measurement of a restructuring provision includes only direct costs arising from the restructuring, rather than ongoing activities and future operating losses of the entity.

Long-term debt

Long-term debt is classified as current when the Company expects to settle the liability in its normal operating cycle, it holds the liability primarily for the purpose of trading or the liability is due to be settled within 12 months after the date of the consolidated balance sheets.

Share capital

Shares issued by the Company are recorded at the value of proceeds received. Repurchased shares are removed from equity. No gain or loss is recognized in net income on the purchase, sale, issue or cancellation of the Company's shares.

Dividends

Dividend distributions to the Company's shareholders are recognized as a liability in the consolidated balance sheets in the period in which the dividends are approved by the Company's Board of Directors.

Revenue

The Company recognizes revenue when the amount can be reliably measured, when it is probable that future economic benefits will flow to the entity and when specific criteria have been met for each of the Company's activities as described below.

Sale of goods

Revenue from the sale of goods includes merchandise sold to Dealers and to Mark's Work Wearhouse Ltd. ("Mark's"), PartSource and FGL Sports franchisees; the sale of gasoline through agents; and the sale of goods by Mark's, PartSource and FGL Sports corporate-owned stores. This revenue is recognized when the goods are delivered, less an estimate for the sales and warranty returns. Revenue from the sale of goods is measured at the fair value of the consideration received less an appropriate deduction for actual and expected returns, discounts, rebates and warranty and loyalty program costs, net of sales taxes.

Sales and warranty returns

If there is any uncertainty regarding the right of a customer to return goods, no revenue is recognized until the uncertainty is resolved. However, in the case of warranties, if warranty claims can be reasonably estimated, revenue is then recorded for the net amount.

Customer loyalty programs

Loyalty award credits issued as part of a sales transaction relating to the Company's Gas Advantage, Cash Advantage and Sport Chek MasterCard Rewards credit card programs result in revenue being deferred until the loyalty award is redeemed by the customer. The portion of the revenue that is deferred is the fair value of the award. The fair value of the award takes into account the amount for which the award credits could be sold separately, less the proportion of the award credits that are not expected to be redeemed by customers.

Interest income on loans receivable

Interest income includes interest charged on loans receivable and fees that are an integral part of the effective interest rate on financial instruments, such as annual credit card fees. Interest income on financial assets that are classified as loans and receivable is determined using the effective interest method.

Services rendered

Service revenue includes Roadside Assistance Club membership revenue; Home Services revenue; insurance premiums and reinsurance revenue; extended warranty contract fees; merchant, interchange and processing fees; cash advance fees; foreign exchange fees; and service charges on the loans receivable of the Financial Services operating segment, as well as Mark's clothing alteration revenue. Service revenue is recognized according to the contractual provisions of the arrangement, which is generally when the service is provided or over the contractual period.

Merchant, interchange and processing fees, cash advance fees and foreign exchange fees on credit card transactions are recognized as revenue at the time transactions are completed. Revenue from separately priced extended warranty contracts is recorded on a straight-line basis over the term of the contracts. Revenue from Home Services is recognized when the work order is complete.

Reinsurance premiums are recorded on an accrual basis and are included in net income on a pro rata basis over the life of the insurance contract, with the unearned portion deferred in the consolidated balance sheets. Premiums that are subject to adjustment are estimated based on available information. Any variances from the estimates are recorded in the periods in which they become known.

Royalties and licence fees

Royalties and licence fees include licence fees from petroleum agents and Dealers and royalties from Mark's and FGL Sports franchisees. Royalties and licence fee revenues are recognized as they are earned in accordance with the substance of the relevant agreement and are measured on an accrual basis.

Rental income

Rental income from operating leases where the Company is the lessor is recognized on a straight-line basis over the terms of the respective leases.

Vendor rebates

The Company records cash consideration received from vendors as a reduction in the price of vendors' products and recognizes it as a reduction to the cost of related inventory or, if the related inventory has been sold, to the cost of producing revenue. Certain exceptions apply where the cash consideration received is either a reimbursement of incremental costs incurred by the Company or a payment for assets or services delivered to the vendor, in which case the cost is reflected as a reduction in operating expenses.

The Company recognizes rebates that are at the vendor's discretion when the vendor either pays the rebates or agrees to pay them and payment is considered probable and is reasonably estimable.

Finance income and costs

Finance income comprises interest income on funds invested (including available-for-sale financial assets). Interest income is recognized as it accrues using the effective interest method.

Finance costs comprises interest expense on borrowings (including borrowings related to the Dealer Loan Program), unwinding of the discount on provisions and impairment recognized on financial assets. Interest on deposits is recorded in cost of producing revenue in the consolidated statements of income.

Income taxes

The income tax expense for the year comprises current and deferred tax. Income tax expense is recognized in net income except to the extent that it relates to items recognized either in OCI or directly in equity. In this case, the income tax expense is recognized in OCI or in equity, respectively.

The income tax expense is calculated on the basis of the tax laws enacted or substantively enacted at the date of the consolidated balance sheets in the countries where the Company operates and generates taxable income.

Deferred income tax is recognized using the liability method on unused tax losses, unused tax credits and temporary differences arising between the tax bases of assets and liabilities and their carrying amounts in these consolidated financial statements. However, deferred income tax is not accounted for if it arises from initial recognition of goodwill or initial recognition of an asset or liability in a transaction other than a business combination that at the time of the transaction affects neither accounting nor taxable income. Deferred income tax is determined using tax rates (and laws) that have been enacted or substantively enacted at the date of the consolidated balance sheets and are expected to apply when the related deferred income tax asset is realized or the deferred income tax liability is settled.

Deferred income tax assets are recognized only to the extent that it is probable that future taxable income will be available against which the temporary differences can be utilized. Deferred income tax liabilities are provided on temporary differences arising on investments in subsidiaries and associates, except where the timing of the reversal of the temporary difference is controlled by the Company and it is probable that the temporary difference will not reverse in the foreseeable future.

Earnings per share

Basic earnings per share is calculated by dividing the net income attributable to Common and Class A Non-Voting shareholders of the Company by the weighted average number of Common and Class A Non-Voting shares outstanding during the reporting period. Diluted earnings per share is calculated by adjusting the net income attributable to shareholders and the weighted average number of shares outstanding for the effects of all dilutive potential equity instruments, which comprise employee stock options.

Operating segments

An operating segment is a component of the Company that engages in business activities from which it may earn revenues and incur expenses, including revenues and expenses that relate to transactions with any of the Company's other operations, and for which discrete financial information is available. Segment operating results are reviewed regularly by the Company's CEO to make decisions about resources to be allocated to the segment and to assess the segment's performance.

6. Financial risk management

6.1 Overview

The Company has exposure to the following risks from its use of financial instruments:
• credit risk;
• liquidity risk; and
• market risk (including foreign currency and interest rate risk).

This note presents information about the Company's exposure to each of the above risks and the Company's objectives, policies and processes for measuring and managing risk. Further quantitative disclosures are included throughout these consolidated financial statements and notes thereto.

6.2 Risk management framework

The Company's financial risk management policies are established to identify and analyze the risks faced by the Company, to set acceptable risk tolerance limits and controls and to monitor risks and adherence to limits. The financial risk management policies and systems are reviewed regularly to ensure they remain consistent with the objectives and risk tolerance acceptable to the Company and current market trends and conditions. The Company, through its training and management standards and procedures, aims to uphold a disciplined and constructive control environment in which all employees understand their roles and obligations.

6.3 Credit risk

Credit risk is the risk of financial loss to the Company if a customer or counterparty to a financial instrument fails to meet its contractual obligations and arises principally from the Company's credit card customers, Dealer network, investment securities and financial derivative instrument counterparties.

The Company's maximum exposure to credit risk, over and above amounts recognized in the consolidated balance sheets, include the following:

(C$ in millions)	2012	2011[1]
Undrawn loan commitments	$ 10,135.1	$ 10,682.1
Guarantees	632.1	562.8
Total	$ 10,767.2	$ 11,244.9

[1] The prior period's figure has been restated to correspond to the current-year presentation. Undrawn loan commitments were previously defined to include credit card accounts with zero credit limit and accounts with status prohibiting purchases. The definition was changed in the current year to exclude these accounts. As result of the change in definition, prior-year undrawn loan commitments have been reduced by $6,874.4 million. Guarantees were previously defined to include the amounts outstanding as at the balance sheet date for which the Company is the indemnifier. The definition was changed in the current year to include the maximum amount that could be drawn and indemnified by the Company. As a result of the change in definition, prior-year guarantees have been increased by $274.9 million.

6.3.1 Trade and other receivables

Trade and other receivables are primarily from Dealers and franchisees spread across Canada, a large and geographically dispersed group who, individually, generally comprise less than one per cent of the total balance outstanding.

6.3.2 Loans and mortgages receivable

The carrying amount of loans and mortgages receivable includes secured mortgage loans of $67.1 million (2011 – $68.9 million) as well as loans to Dealers totalling $629.7 million (2011 – $634.9 million) that are secured by the assets of the respective Dealer corporations. Consequently, the Company's exposure to loans receivable credit risk resides at Franchise Trust and at the Bank.

Credit risk at the Bank is influenced mainly by the individual characteristics of each credit card customer. Concentration of credit risk exists if a number of customers are engaged in similar activities, are located in the same geographic region or have similar economic characteristics such that their ability to meet contractual obligations could be similarly affected by changes in economic, political or other conditions. Concentrations of credit risk indicate a related sensitivity of the Bank's performance to developments affecting a particular counterparty, industry or geographic location. The Bank uses sophisticated credit scoring models, monitoring technology and collection modelling techniques to implement and manage strategies, policies and limits that are designed to control risk. Loans receivable are generated by a large and geographically dispersed group of customers. Current credit exposure is limited to the loss that would be incurred if all of the Bank's counterparties were to default at the same time.

The Bank maintains comprehensive procedures and information systems to effectively monitor and control the characteristics and quality of its credit portfolio. To ensure the Bank's credit granting, documentation and collection processes are followed correctly, the Bank maintains the following:

- a credit rating system that defines risk-rating criteria and rates all credits individually according to those criteria;
- portfolio characteristic monitoring;
- credit review processes; and
- independent inspections of its credit portfolio to ensure compliance.

6.3.3 Allowance for credit losses and past due amounts

In determining the recoverability of a loan receivable, the Company considers any change in the credit quality of the loan receivable from the date credit was initially granted up to the end of the reporting period. The concentration of credit risk is limited due to the customer base being large and unrelated.

The Company's allowances for credit losses are maintained at levels that are considered adequate to absorb future credit losses.

A continuity of the Company's allowances for trade and other receivables is as follows:

	Trade and other receivables	
(C$ in millions)	2012	2011
Balance, beginning of year	$ 12.2	$ 7.7
Net additions (reversals)	1.4	4.5
Balance, end of year	$ 13.6	$ 12.2

A continuity of the Company's allowances for loans receivable is as follows:

	Loans receivable[1,2]	
(C$ in millions)	2012	2011
Balance, beginning of year	$ 118.7	$ 117.7
Impairments for credit losses	265.6	302.0
Recoveries	58.1	50.0
Writeoffs	(331.7)	(351.0)
Balance, end of year	$ 110.7	$ 118.7

[1] Loans include credit card loans, personal loans and line of credit loans.
[2] No allowances for credit losses have been made with respect to Franchise Trust and FGL Sports loans receivable.

The Company's aging of the trade and other receivables and loans receivable that are past due, but not impaired, is as follows:

	2012			2011		
(C$ in millions)	1–90 days	> 90 days	Total	1–90 days	> 90 days	Total
Trade and other receivables	$ 13.5	$ 14.5	$ 28.0	$ 27.0	$ 14.1	$ 41.1
Loans receivable[1]	76.6	52.7	129.3	94.0	69.2	163.2
Total	$ 90.1	$ 67.2	$ 157.3	$ 121.0	$ 83.3	$ 204.3

[1] No past due loans for Franchise Trust and FGL Sports.

A loan is considered past due when the counterparty has not made a payment by the contractual due date. Credit card and line of credit loan balances are written off when a payment is 180 days in arrears. Line of credit loans are considered impaired when a payment is over 90 days in arrears and are written off when a payment is 180 days in arrears. Personal loans are considered impaired when a payment is over 90 days in arrears and are written off when a payment is 365 days in arrears. No collateral is held against loans receivable.

8. Business combinations

8.1 Acquisition of FGL Sports

The Company acquired control of FGL Sports on August 18, 2011, through its approximately 97 per cent ownership of the issued and outstanding Class "A" shares ("the Common shares") of FGL Sports that were acquired on and prior to August 18, 2011. The Company acquired the remaining Common shares of FGL Sports on August 25, 2011.

FGL Sports is a Canadian retailer of sporting goods offering a comprehensive assortment of brand-name and private-label products operating stores from coast to coast under the following corporate and franchise banners: Sport Chek, Sports Experts, Intersport, Atmosphere, the TechShop, Nevada Bob's Golf, Hockey Experts, Sport Mart, National Sports, Athletes World, S3 and Fitness Source.

The acquisition of FGL Sports increased the Company's operation in the Sporting Goods category of its retail operating segment. A significant portion of FGL Sports sales are in athletic apparel and footwear, with the balance of sales in sporting hard goods that complement the Company's existing assortment of sporting goods. The acquisition of retail banners like Sport Chek and Sports Experts is thus a natural extension of the Company's sporting goods business.

For the year ended December 31, 2011, FGL Sports contributed revenue of $645.6 million and net income of $29.4 million to the Company's results.

FGL Sports recorded $32.6 million of capital expenditures during the 19 weeks from the date of acquisition to December 31, 2011.

8.1.1 Consideration transferred

The acquisition date fair value of consideration transferred is as follows:

(C$ in millions)	
Cash	$ 765.2
Fair value of previously held interests	35.4
Total consideration transferred	$ 800.6

8.1.2 Fair value of identifiable assets acquired and liabilities assumed as at acquisition date

The fair value of identifiable assets acquired and liabilities assumed as at the acquisition date are as follows:

(C$ in millions)	
Cash and cash equivalents	$ 25.3
Trade and other receivables[1]	111.1
Loans receivable	0.8
Merchandise inventories	455.9
Income taxes recoverable	3.4
Prepaid expenses and deposits	11.1
Long-term receivables and other assets	4.9
Intangible assets	382.3
Property and equipment	155.1
Trade and other payables	(288.9)
Short-term borrowings	(241.9)
Provisions	(31.0)
Deferred income taxes	(58.2)
Other long-term liabilities	(37.7)
Total net identifiable assets	$ 492.2

[1] Gross trade and other receivables acquired is $112.4 million, of which $1.3 million was expected to be uncollectible as at the acquisition date.

8.1.3 Goodwill arising on acquisition of FGL Sports

Goodwill was recognized as a result of the acquisition as follows:

(C$ in millions)	
Total consideration transferred	$ 800.6
Less: Total net identifiable assets	492.2
Goodwill	$ 308.4

The goodwill recognized on acquisition of FGL Sports is attributable mainly to the expected future growth potential from the expanded customer base of FGL Sports banners and brands and the network of stores which are predominantly mall-based and provide access to the 18–35-year-old customer segment.

None of the goodwill recognized is expected to be deductible for income tax purposes.

For the year ended December 31, 2011, the Company incurred acquisition-related costs of $12.1 million relating to external legal fees, consulting fees and due diligence costs. These costs are included in administrative expenses in the consolidated statements of income.

For the year ended December 31, 2011, a pre-tax gain of $10.4 million was recognized relating to the Company's previously held interest in FGL Sports prior to the acquisition date. The gain is recognized in other income in the consolidated statements of income and is included as part of the fair value of previously held interests included in the total consideration transferred, noted in the table above.

The impact of the acquisition on the consolidated statements of cash flows for the year ended December 31, 2011, is as follows:

(C$ in millions)	
Total consideration transferred	$ 765.2
Cash and cash equivalents acquired	(25.3)
Acquisition of FGL Sports	$ 739.9

8.2 Other acquisitions

During the year ended December 29, 2012, the Company acquired three franchise operations for total consideration of $6.9 million, of which $2.6 million was in the form of a promissory note payable. The fair value of identifiable assets acquired and liabilities assumed includes $0.1 million in trade and other receivables, $2.5 million in inventory, $4.2 million in intangible assets, $0.4 million in property and equipment and $0.3 million in liabilities. The purpose of these acquisitions is to convert franchise businesses into corporate stores.

The Company acquired control of Golden Viking Sports on July 1, 2012, through its 100 per cent ownership of the issued and outstanding shares for total consideration of $2.4 million, net of cash and cash equivalents acquired. The fair value of identifiable assets acquired and liabilities assumed includes $1.4 million in trade and other receivables, $3.8 million in inventory, $0.6 million in prepaid expenses and deposits, $4.2 million in liabilities and $0.1 million in deferred income taxes liability. In addition, $0.9 million in goodwill was recognized as a result of this acquisition. The purpose of this acquisition is to grow the Company's wholesale business, especially in the U.S.

During the year ended December 31, 2011, the Company acquired three franchise operations for total consideration of $7.7 million, of which $3.3 million was in the form of promissory notes payable. The fair value of identifiable assets acquired includes $3.6 million in intangible assets and $0.3 million in property and equipment. In addition, $0.5 million in goodwill was recognized as a result of these acquisitions. The purpose of these acquisitions is to convert franchise businesses into corporate stores.

9. Cash and cash equivalents

Cash and cash equivalents comprise of the following:

(C$ in millions)	2012	2011
Cash	$ 40.5	$ 79.6
Cash equivalents	533.6	233.4
Restricted cash and cash equivalents[1]	441.4	12.8
Total cash and cash equivalents	1,015.5	325.8
Bank indebtedness	(86.0)	(124.8)
Cash and cash equivalents, net of bank indebtedness	$ 929.5	$ 201.0

[1] Relates to GCCT and is restricted for the purposes of paying out note holders and additional funding costs.

10. Short-term investments

(C$ in millions)	2012	2011
Unrestricted short-term investments	$ 167.3	$ 195.4
Restricted short-term investments[1]	1.6	1.0
	$ 168.9	$ 196.4

[1] Relates to GCCT and is restricted for the purposes of paying out note holders and additional funding costs.

11. Trade and other receivables

(C$ in millions)	2012	2011
Trade and other receivables	$ 743.6	$ 800.9
Derivatives	6.5	15.8
Total financial assets (Note 37)	750.1	816.7
Other	0.5	12.6
	$ 750.6	$ 829.3

Trade and other receivables are primarily receivables from Dealers, vendors, franchisees and agents.

Receivables from Dealers are in the normal course of business, including cost-sharing and financing arrangements. The average credit period on sales of goods is between one and 90 days. Interest (ranging from 0.0 per cent to prime plus 5.0 per cent) is charged on amounts past due.

Receivables from vendors are on account of rebate and commercial discounts receivable from vendors.

The Company's exposures to credit risks and impairment losses related to trade and other receivables are disclosed in Note 6.3.

12. Loans receivable

Quantitative information about the Company's loans receivable portfolio is as follows:

(C$ in millions)	Total principal amount of receivables[1]		Average balance[1]	
	2012	2011	2012	2011
Credit card loans	$ 4,234.3	$ 4,026.8	$ 3,979.5	$ 3,900.5
Line of credit loans	7.5	8.8	8.2	10.0
Personal loans [2]	0.5	3.3	1.6	6.4
Total Financial Services' loans receivable	4,242.3	4,038.9	$ 3,989.3	$ 3,916.9
Dealer loans [3]	623.7	628.7		
Other loans	7.7	8.8		
Total loans receivable	4,873.7	4,676.4		
Less: long-term portion [4]	608.0	594.7		
Current portion of loans receivable	$ 4,265.7	$ 4,081.7		

[1] Amounts shown are net of allowance for loan impairment.
[2] Personal loans are unsecured loans that are provided to qualified existing credit card holders for terms of one to five years. Personal loans have fixed monthly payments of principal and interest; however, the personal loans can be repaid at any time without penalty.
[3] Dealer loans issued by Franchise Trust (Note 24).
[4] The long-term portion of loans receivable is included in long-term receivables and other assets and includes Dealer loans of $601.5 million (2011 – $587.5 million).

The gross impairment loss on loans receivable for the year ended December 29, 2012, was $323.7 million (2011 – $352.0 million). Recoveries of bad debts for the year ended December 29, 2012, were $58.1 million (2011 – $50.0 million).

For the year ended December 29, 2012, the amount of cash received from interest earned on credit cards and loans was $669.6 million (2011 – $655.3 million).

14. Long-term receivables and other assets

(C$ in millions)	2012	2011
Loans receivable (Note 12)	$ 608.0	$ 594.7
Mortgages receivable	61.1	63.9
Derivatives	4.4	4.4
Other receivables	1.9	1.6
Total financial assets (Note 37)	675.4	664.6
Other	5.8	4.3
	$ 681.2	$ 668.9

Mortgages receivable

The Company has a long-term mortgage receivable with an interest rate of 12 per cent and repayment of principal until 2016.

15. Goodwill and intangible assets

The following table presents the changes in cost and accumulated amortization and impairment of the Company's intangible assets:

2012

| (C$ in millions) | Indefinite-life intangible assets and goodwill | | Finite-life intangible assets | | |
	Goodwill	Other intangibles	Software	Other intangibles	Total
Cost					
Balance, beginning of year	$ 377.6	$ 380.9	$ 847.0	$ 22.4	$ 1,627.9
Additions internally developed	–	–	64.7	–	64.7
Additions linked to business combinations	0.9	4.2	–	–	5.1
Other additions	–	0.2	1.4	–	1.6
Disposals/retirements	–	–	(3.0)	(0.2)	(3.2)
Other movements and transfers	–	(0.3)	–	0.3	–
Balance, end of year	$ 378.5	$ 385.0	$ 910.1	$ 22.5	$ 1,696.1
Accumulated depreciation and impairment					
Balance, beginning of year	$ –	$ –	$ (516.4)	$ (1.5)	$ (517.9)
Amortization for year	–	–	(83.9)	(2.3)	(86.2)
Impairment losses	(1.6)	–	(0.9)	–	(2.5)
Disposals/retirements	–	–	2.4	–	2.4
Other	–	–	–	(2.0)	(2.0)
Balance, end of year	$ (1.6)	$ –	$ (598.8)	$ (5.8)	$ (606.2)
Net carrying amount, end of year	$ 376.9	$ 385.0	$ 311.3	$ 16.7	$ 1,089.9

2011

| (C$ in millions) | Indefinite-life intangible assets and goodwill | | Finite-life intangible assets | | |
	Goodwill	Other intangibles	Software	Other intangibles	Total
Cost					
Balance, beginning of year	$ 68.7	$ 60.4	$ 688.1	$ –	$ 817.2
Additions internally developed	–	0.4	125.0	–	125.4
Additions related to business combinations	308.9	320.1	43.4	22.4	694.8
Disposals/retirements	–	–	(9.5)	–	(9.5)
Balance, end of year	$ 377.6	$ 380.9	$ 847.0	$ 22.4	$ 1,627.9
Accumulated depreciation and impairment					
Balance, beginning of year	$ –	$ –	$ (455.8)	$ –	$ (455.8)
Amortization for year	–	–	(64.8)	(1.5)	(66.3)
Disposals/retirements	–	–	4.2	–	4.2
Balance, end of year	$ –	$ –	$ (516.4)	$ (1.5)	$ (517.9)
Net carrying amount, end of year	$ 377.6	$ 380.9	$ 330.6	$ 20.9	$ 1,110.0

The following table presents the details of the Company's goodwill:

(C$ in millions)	2012	2011
FGL Sports	$ 309.3	$ 308.4
Mark's	52.2	52.2
CTR	15.4	17.0
Total	$ 376.9	$ 377.6

The following table presents the details of the Company's indefinite-life other intangible assets:

(C$ in millions)	2012	2011
FGL Sports corporate banners	$ 184.4	$ 184.4
FGL Sports franchise banners	77.9	77.9
FGL Sports private-label brands	7.2	7.2
FGL Sports franchise agreements	46.7	46.9
Mark's store banner	46.0	46.0
Mark's franchise locations	16.2	12.1
Mark's private-label brands	4.0	4.0
Mark's franchise agreements	2.0	2.0
Other trademarks	0.6	0.4
Total	$ 385.0	$ 380.9

The following table presents the details of the Company's finite-life other intangible assets:

(C$ in millions)	2012	2011
FGL Sports customer relationships	$ 7.6	$ 9.6
FGL Sports private-label brands	0.5	0.6
FGL Sports off-market leases	8.6	10.7
Total	$ 16.7	$ 20.9

FGL Sports corporate and franchise banners represent legal trademarks of the Company and have expiry dates ranging from 2018 to 2023. Mark's store banners ("Mark's Work Wearhouse/L'Équipeur") represent legal trademarks of the Company and expire in 2021. FGL Sports and Mark's private-label brands have legal expiry dates. The Company currently has no approved plans to change its store banners, other than those announced, and intends to continue to renew all trademarks and private-label brands at each expiry date indefinitely. The Company expects these assets to generate cash flows in perpetuity. Therefore, these intangible assets are considered to have indefinite useful lives. FGL Sports franchise agreements, Mark's franchise locations, and Mark's franchise agreements have expiry dates with options to renew or have indefinite lives. The Company's intention is to renew these agreements at each renewal date indefinitely, and the Company expects the franchise agreements and franchise locations will generate cash flows in perpetuity. Therefore, these assets are considered to have indefinite useful lives.

Other finite-life intangible assets include FGL Sports customer relationships, certain private-label brands and off-market leases that the Company has assessed as having limited life terms. These assets are being amortized over a term of five years.

The amount of borrowing costs capitalized in 2012 was $1.7 million (2011 – $1.7 million). The capitalization rate used to determine the amount of borrowing costs capitalized during the year was 5.7 per cent (2011 – 5.7 per cent).

The amount of research and development expenditures recognized as an expense in 2012 was $6.7 million (2011 – $4.4 million).

Amortization expense of finite-life intangible assets is included in distribution costs, sales and marketing expenses and administrative expenses in the consolidated statements of income.

Impairment of intangible assets and subsequent reversal
The Company performed its annual impairment test of goodwill and indefinite-life intangible assets using the following key rates:

	FGL Sports	Mark's	CTR
Discount rate (pre-tax)	10.9%	10.9%	10.9–12.3%
Growth rate	2.0%	2.0%	2.0–3.0%

During the year ended December 29, 2012, the Company recorded an impairment on software intangibles of $0.9 million (2011 – $nil) as part of its banner rationalization plan at FGL Sports. In addition, the Company recorded $1.6 million (2011 – $nil) of impairment on goodwill related to the purchase of Retail stores. These impairments pertain to the Company's Retail operating segment and are reported in other income in the consolidated statements of income. There were no reversals of impairment recorded in 2012 and 2011.

For all other goodwill and intangible assets, the estimated recoverable amount exceeded the carrying amount. There is no reasonable possible change in assumptions that would cause the carrying amount to exceed the recoverable amount.

Capital commitments

The Company has no commitments for the acquisition of intangible assets (2011 – $nil).

16. Investment property

The following table presents the changes in the cost and accumulated depreciation and impairment on the Company's investment property:

(C$ in millions)	2012	2011
Cost		
Balance, beginning of year	$ 90.7	$ 84.8
Additions	19.3	6.6
Disposals/retirements	(0.2)	(0.2)
Reclassified from held for sale	17.9	–
Other movements and transfers	(1.7)	(0.5)
Balance, end of year	$ 126.0	$ 90.7
Accumulated depreciation and impairment		
Balance, beginning of year	$ (18.3)	$ (16.2)
Depreciation for the year	(2.7)	(2.6)
Impairment	(0.7)	–
Reversals of impairment	1.4	1.1
Reclassified from held for sale	(9.3)	–
Other movements and transfers	(1.3)	(0.6)
Balance, end of year	$ (30.9)	$ (18.3)
Net carrying amount, end of year	$ 95.1	$ 72.4

The investment property generated rental income of $10.1 million (2011 – $9.3 million).

Direct operating expenses (including repairs and maintenance) arising from investment property recognized in net income were $5.0 million (2011 – $4.0 million).

The Company determines the fair value of each commercial property by applying a pre-tax capitalization rate to the rental income for the current leases. The capitalization rate ranged from 5.25 per cent to 11.0 per cent (2011 – 5.0 per cent to 11.0 per cent). The cash flows are for a term of five years, including a terminal value. The Company has real estate management expertise that is used to perform the valuation of investment property. As such, a valuation has not been performed by an independent valuation specialist. The estimated fair value of investment property was $198.7 million (2011 – $138.6 million).

Impairment of investment property and subsequent reversal

During the year ended December 29, 2012, the Company recorded reversal of impairment of $1.4 million (2011 – $1.1 million) on properties where it was determined that the FVLCS exceeded their carrying amount. The Company recorded impairment of $0.7 million (2011 – $nil) on properties where the FVLCS is less than their carrying amount. These properties pertain to the Company's Retail operating segment. The impairment and reversal of impairment are reported in other income in the consolidated statements of income.

Capital commitments

The Company has no commitments for the acquisition of investment property (2011 – $nil).

17. Property and equipment

The following table presents the changes in the cost and accumulated depreciation and impairment on the Company's property and equipment:

(C$ in millions)	Land	Buildings	Fixtures and equipment	Leasehold improvements	Assets under finance lease	Construction in progress	2012 Total
Cost							
Balance, beginning of year	$ 750.2	$ 2,589.6	$ 826.0	$ 712.5	$ 267.4	$ 137.0	$ 5,282.7
Additions	5.3	24.5	62.5	33.0	12.1	111.8	249.2
Additions related to business combinations	–	–	0.4	–	–	–	0.4
Disposals/retirements	(1.3)	(3.3)	(26.6)	(4.7)	(8.6)	–	(44.5)
Classified as held for sale	(9.9)	(15.2)	(0.3)	(0.3)	–	0.6	(25.1)
Other movements and transfers	–	88.1	18.4	37.7	2.3	(147.1)	(0.6)
Balance, end of year	$ 744.3	$ 2,683.7	$ 880.4	$ 778.2	$ 273.2	$ 102.3	$ 5,462.1
Accumulated depreciation and impairment							
Balance, beginning of year	$ (1.4)	$ (1,014.8)	$ (545.6)	$ (216.5)	$ (138.5)	$ –	$ (1,916.8)
Additions	–	(96.6)	(71.9)	(55.1)	(22.6)	–	(246.2)
Impairment	0.1	(1.0)	(2.1)	(4.4)	–	–	(7.4)
Disposals/retirements	(0.1)	1.9	24.3	4.0	8.6	–	38.7
Classified as held for sale	1.3	7.7	0.1	0.5	(0.2)	–	9.4
Other movements and transfers	–	(0.1)	3.8	–	–	–	3.7
Balance, end of year	$ (0.1)	$ (1,102.9)	$ (591.4)	$ (271.5)	$ (152.7)	$ –	$ (2,118.6)
Net carrying amount, end of year	$ 744.2	$ 1,580.8	$ 289.0	$ 506.7	$ 120.5	$ 102.3	$ 3,343.5

(C$ in millions)	Land	Buildings	Fixtures and equipment	Leasehold improvements	Assets under finance lease	Construction in progress	2011 Total
Cost							
Balance, beginning of year	$ 751.8	$ 2,522.0	$ 747.5	$ 548.5	$ 262.2	$ 129.0	$ 4,961.0
Additions	3.6	73.0	68.8	70.9	9.7	6.7	232.7
Additions related to business combinations	9.1	19.7	27.3	97.3	–	2.0	155.4
Disposals/retirements	(0.1)	(1.5)	(16.9)	(4.0)	(2.2)	(0.1)	(24.8)
Classified as held for sale	(11.4)	(25.3)	–	–	–	–	(36.7)
Other movements and transfers	(2.8)	1.7	(0.7)	(0.2)	(2.3)	(0.6)	(4.9)
Balance, end of year	$ 750.2	$ 2,589.6	$ 826.0	$ 712.5	$ 267.4	$ 137.0	$ 5,282.7
Accumulated depreciation and impairment							
Balance, beginning of year	$ (3.2)	$ (937.3)	$ (492.4)	$ (181.3)	$ (114.8)	$ –	$ (1,729.0)
Additions	–	(95.0)	(67.5)	(38.7)	(26.0)	–	(227.2)
Impairment	(1.3)	(0.3)	–	–	–	–	(1.6)
Disposals/retirements	0.1	1.1	14.0	3.8	2.1	–	21.1
Classified as held for sale	–	13.9	–	–	–	–	13.9
Other movements and transfers	3.0	2.8	0.3	(0.3)	0.2	–	6.0
Balance, end of year	$ (1.4)	$ (1,014.8)	$ (545.6)	$ (216.5)	$ (138.5)	$ –	$ (1,916.8)
Net carrying amount, end of year	$ 748.8	$ 1,574.8	$ 280.4	$ 496.0	$ 128.9	$ 137.0	$ 3,365.9

The Company capitalized borrowing costs of $2.1 million (2011 – $4.1 million) on indebtedness related to property and equipment under construction. The rate used to determine the amount of borrowing costs capitalized during the year was 5.7% (2011 – 5.7%).

The carrying amount of assets under finance leases at December 29, 2012, comprises of $58.7 million (2011 – $68.8 million) in buildings and $61.8 million (2011 – $60.1 million) in fixtures and equipment.

The carrying amount of property and equipment whose title was restricted is $nil (2011 – $nil).

The amount of compensation from third parties included in net income for property and equipment that was impaired, lost or given up was $0.1 million (2011 – $0.4 million).

Impairment of property and equipment and subsequent reversal

During the year ended December 29, 2012, the Company recorded impairment of $7.4 million (2011 – $1.6 million), related primarily to its banner rationalization plan at FGL Sports. The impairment pertains to the Company's Retail operating segment and is reported in other income in the consolidated statements of income. There was no reversal of impairment in 2012 or 2011.

Capital commitments

The Company has commitments of approximately $28.5 million at December 29, 2012 for the acquisition of property and equipment (2011 – $39.8 million).

18. Deferred income tax assets and liabilities

The tax-effected unused tax losses and temporary differences that result in deferred tax assets (liabilities) and the amount of deferred taxes recognized in the net income or equity are as follows:

					2012
(C$ in millions)	Balance, beginning of year	Recognized in net income	Recognized in other comprehensive income	Acquired in business combination	Balance, end of year
Reserves and deferred income	$ 103.5	$ 0.8	$ –	$ –	$ 104.3
Property and equipment	(52.6)	(3.2)	–	–	(55.8)
Intangible assets	(135.1)	(7.2)	–	–	(142.3)
Employee benefits	27.6	1.9	3.9	–	33.4
Financial instruments	(4.0)	–	4.7	–	0.7
Finance lease assets and obligations	11.6	0.2	–	–	11.8
Site restoration and decommissioning	2.8	0.3	–	–	3.1
Deferred items	1.0	(0.9)	–	–	0.1
Inventory	(2.0)	2.3	–	(0.1)	0.2
Non-capital loss	17.9	(10.0)	–	–	7.9
Other	–	(0.7)	–	–	(0.7)
Net deferred tax asset (liability)[1]	$ (29.3)	$ (16.5)	$ 8.6	$ (0.1)	$ (37.3)

					2011
(C$ in millions)	Balance, beginning of year	Recognized in net income	Recognized in other comprehensive income	Acquired in business combination	Balance, end of year
Reserves and deferred income	$ 77.9	$ 8.6	$ –	$ 17.0	$ 103.5
Property and equipment	(50.3)	(2.3)	–	–	(52.6)
Intangible assets	(43.4)	(2.9)	–	(88.8)	(135.1)
Employee benefits	21.9	0.8	4.9	–	27.6
Financial instruments	13.0	–	(17.0)	–	(4.0)
Finance lease assets and obligations	11.8	(0.2)	–	–	11.6
Site restoration and decommissioning	2.6	0.2	–	–	2.8
Deferred items	(0.3)	(0.2)	–	1.5	1.0
Inventory	–	3.6	–	(5.6)	(2.0)
Non-capital loss	–	0.1	–	17.8	17.9
Other	1.4	(1.3)	–	(0.1)	–
Net deferred tax asset (liability)[2]	$ 34.6	$ 6.4	$ (12.1)	$ (58.2)	$ (29.3)

[1] Includes the net amount of deferred tax assets of $40.4 million and deferred tax liabilities of $77.7 million.
[2] Includes the net amount of deferred tax assets of $36.8 million and deferred tax liabilities of $66.1 million.

No deferred tax is recognized on the unremitted earnings of non-Canadian subsidiaries to the extent that the Company is able to control the timing of the reversal of the temporary difference, and it is probable that it will not reverse in the foreseeable future. The taxable temporary difference in respect of the amount of undistributed earnings of non-Canadian subsidiaries was approximately $132.7 million at December 29, 2012 (2011 – $125.3 million).

19. Deposits

Deposits consist of broker deposits and retail deposits.

Cash from broker deposits is raised through sales of GICs through brokers rather than directly to the retail customer. Broker deposits are offered for varying terms ranging from 30 days to five years, and all issued GICs are non-redeemable prior to maturity (except in certain rare circumstances). Total short-term and long-term broker deposits outstanding at December 29, 2012, were $1,579.7 million (2011 – $1,597.4 million).

Retail deposits consist of HIS deposits, retail GICs and TFSA deposits. Total retail deposits outstanding at December 29, 2012, were $843.1 million (2011 – $687.1 million).

Repayment requirements

(C$ in millions)

2013	$ 505.1
2014	420.2
2015	235.3
2016	143.0
2017	313.3
Current and long-term broker and retail deposits	1,616.9
High-interest savings accounts	813.4
Total[1]	$ 2,430.3

[1] The carrying amount of deposits as of December 29, 2012 is net of $7.5 million of GIC broker discount fees (2011 – $6.1 million).

Effective rates of interest

	2012	2011
GIC deposits	3.73%	3.86%
HIS account deposits	1.90%	2.06%

20. Trade and other payables

(C$ in millions)	2012	2011
Trade payables and accrued liabilities	$ 1,498.7	$ 1,509.2
Derivatives	13.1	2.8
Total financial liabilities (Note 37)	1,511.8	1,512.0
Deferred revenue	41.2	39.5
Insurance reserve	13.8	12.9
Other	64.5	76.5
	$ 1,631.3	$ 1,640.9

Deferred revenue consists mainly of unearned insurance premiums, unearned roadside assistance revenue and unearned revenue related to gift certificates and gift cards.

Other consists of sales taxes payable.

The average credit period on trade payables is five to 90 days (2011 – five to 90 days).

21. Provisions

The following table presents the changes to the Company's provisions:

(C$ in millions)	Sales and warranty returns	Site restoration and decommissioning	Onerous contracts	Customer loyalty	Other	2012 Total
Balance, beginning of year	$ 113.2	$ 26.8	$ 7.1	$ 68.1	$ 31.8	$ 247.0
Charges, net of reversals	242.8	11.5	0.4	112.8	1.0	368.5
Utilizations	(245.7)	(5.0)	(2.8)	(107.7)	(16.0)	(377.2)
Unwinding of discount	1.0	0.4	–	–	–	1.4
Change in discount rate	–	0.9	–	–	–	0.9
Balance, end of year	$ 111.3	$ 34.6	$ 4.7	$ 73.2	$ 16.8	$ 240.6
Less: Current provisions	108.6	7.3	1.5	66.1	2.3	185.8
Long-term provisions	$ 2.7	$ 27.3	$ 3.2	$ 7.1	$ 14.5	$ 54.8

Sales and warranty returns

The provision for sales and warranty returns relates to the Company's obligation to stores within its Dealer network for defective goods in their current inventories and defective goods sold to customers throughout its store operations that have yet to be returned, as well as after sales and service for replacement parts.

Site restoration and decommissioning

In the normal course of business, the Company leases property and has a legal or constructive obligation to return the sites to their original or agreed-upon state at the end of the lease term.

Onerous contracts

The Company recognizes a provision for onerous lease contracts on premises that are no longer being used due to store closures.

Customer loyalty

The Company maintains a provision related to its loyalty programs, including paper-based Canadian Tire 'Money' issued at Petroleum gas bars and to Dealers and Electronic Canadian Tire 'Money' on-the-Card issued whenever consumers make a Canadian Tire Options MasterCard purchase. In addition, the Company is testing a new loyalty program called Canadian Tire 'Money' Advantage. All forms of loyalty can be redeemed only at the Canadian Tire Retail stores for merchandise at the option of the consumer.

An obligation arises from the above customer loyalty program when the Dealers pay the Company to acquire paper-based Canadian Tire 'Money' because the Dealers retain the right to return Canadian Tire 'Money' to the Company for refund in cash. An obligation also arises when the Company issues electronic-based Canadian Tire 'Money' on-the-Card or Canadian Tire 'Money' Advantage. These obligations are measured at fair value by reference to the fair value of the awards for which they could be redeemed based on the estimated probability of their redemption and are expensed to sales and marketing expenses in the consolidated statements of income.

Other

Other provisions include liabilities for severance under restructuring arrangements, the cost of legal issues that have not yet been settled and other claims. The amount and timing of when the Company expects to discharge these liabilities are uncertain and are based on the Company's best estimates.

22. Contingencies

Legal matters

The Company and certain of its subsidiaries are party to a number of legal proceedings. The Company has determined that each such proceeding constitutes a routine legal matter incidental to the business conducted by the Company and that the ultimate disposition of the proceedings will not have a material effect on its consolidated net income, cash flows or financial position.

The Bank is the subject of two class action proceedings regarding allegations that certain fees charged on the Bank-issued credit cards are not permitted under the Quebec Consumer Protection Act. The Bank has determined that it has a solid defense to both actions on the basis that banking and cost of borrowing disclosure are matters of exclusive federal jurisdiction. Accordingly, no provision has been made for amounts, if any, that would be payable in the event of an adverse outcome. If the court rules against the Company, the total aggregate exposure would be approximately $26.2 million at December 29, 2012.

23. Short-term borrowings

Short-term borrowings include commercial paper notes and bank line of credit borrowings. The commercial paper notes are short-term notes issued with varying original maturities of one year or less, typically 90 days or less, at interest rates fixed at the time of each renewal. Short-term borrowings may bear interest payable at maturity or be sold at a discount and mature at face value. Commercial paper notes issued by the Company are recorded at amortized cost.

24. Loans payable

Franchise Trust, an SPE, is a legal entity sponsored by a third-party bank that originates loans to Dealers. Loans payable are the loans that Franchise Trust has incurred to fund the loans to Dealers. These loans are not direct legal liabilities of the Company but have been consolidated in the accounts of the Company as the Company effectively controls the silo of Franchise Trust containing the Dealer loan program.

Loans payable, which are initially recognized at fair value and are subsequently measured at amortized cost, are due within one year.

25. Long-term debt

Long-term debt includes the following:

	2012		2011	
(C$ in millions)	Face value	Carrying amount	Face value	Carrying amount
Senior notes[1]				
Series 2006-2, 4.405%, May 20, 2014	$ 238.7	$ 238.7	$ 238.7	$ 238.7
Series 2008-1, 5.027%, February 20, 2013	600.0	599.5	600.0	598.3
Series 2010-1, 3.158%, November 20, 2015	250.0	249.0	250.0	248.8
Series 2012-1, 2.807%, May 20, 2017	200.0	199.0	–	–
Series 2012-2, 2.394%, October 20, 2017	400.0	398.0	–	–
Subordinated notes[1]				
Series 2006-2, 4.765%, May 20, 2014	13.9	13.9	13.9	13.9
Series 2008-1, 6.027%, February 20, 2013	34.9	34.9	34.9	34.8
Series 2010-1, 4.128%, November 20, 2015	14.6	14.6	14.6	14.5
Series 2012-1, 3.827%, May 20, 2017	11.6	11.6	–	–
Series 2012-2, 3.174%, October 20, 2017	23.3	23.3	–	–
Medium-term notes				
4.95% due June 1, 2015	300.0	299.6	300.0	299.4
5.65% due June 1, 2016	200.0	198.9	200.0	198.6
6.25% due April 13, 2028	150.0	149.4	150.0	149.4
6.32% due February 24, 2034	200.0	199.1	200.0	199.1
5.61% due September 4, 2035	200.0	199.2	200.0	199.2
Finance lease obligations	166.6	166.6	176.4	176.4
Promissory note	2.6	2.6	4.5	4.5
Total debt	$ 3,006.2	$ 2,997.9	$ 2,383.0	$ 2,375.6
Current	$ 661.9	$ 661.9	$ 27.9	$ 27.9
Non-current	2,344.3	2,336.0	2,355.1	2,347.7
Total debt	$ 3,006.2	$ 2,997.9	$ 2,383.0	$ 2,375.6

[1] Senior and subordinated notes are those of GCCT.

The carrying amount of long-term debt is net of debt issuance costs of $7.7 million (2011 – $6.6 million) and the benefit on the effective portion of the fair value hedges of $0.6 million (2011 – benefit of $0.8 million).

Senior and subordinated notes

Asset-backed series senior and subordinated notes issued by the Company are recorded at amortized cost using the effective interest method.

Subject to the payment of certain priority amounts, the series senior notes have recourse on a priority basis to the related series ownership interest. The series subordinated notes have recourse to the related series ownership interests on a subordinated basis to the series senior notes in terms of the priority of payment of principal and, in some circumstances, interest. The series notes, together with certain other permitted obligations of GCCT, are secured by the assets of GCCT. The entitlement of note holders and other parties to such assets is governed by the priority and payment provisions set forth in the GCCT Indenture and the related series supplements under which these series of notes were issued.

Repayment of the principal of the series 2006-2, 2008-1, 2010-1, 2012-1 and 2012-2 notes is scheduled to commence and be completed on the expected repayment dates indicated in the preceding table. Following repayment of principal owing, and in some circumstances interest, under the series senior notes, collections distributed to GCCT in respect of the related ownership interests will be applied to pay principal owing under series subordinated notes.

Principal repayments may commence earlier than these scheduled commencement dates if certain events occur, including:

• the Bank failing to make required distributions to GCCT or failing to meet covenant or other contractual terms;
• the performance of the receivables failing to achieve set criteria; and
• insufficient receivables in the pool.

None of these events occurred in the year ended December 29, 2012.

Medium-term notes

Medium-term notes are unsecured and are redeemable by the Company, in whole or in part, at any time, at the greater of par or a formula price based upon interest rates at the time of redemption.

Finance lease obligations

Finance leases relate to distribution centres, fixtures and equipment. The Company generally has the option to renew such leases or purchase the leased assets at the conclusion of the lease term. During 2012, interest rates on finance leases ranged from 0.81 per cent to 12.75 per cent. Remaining terms at December 29, 2012, were one to 169 months.

Finance lease obligations are payable as follows:

| | 2012 | | | | | 2011 |
| | Future minimum lease | | Present value of minimum lease | Future minimum lease | | Present value of minimum lease |
(C$ in millions)	payments	Interest	payments	payments	Interest	payments
Due in less than one year	$ 34.5	$ 9.6	$ 24.9	$ 33.9	$ 10.3	$ 23.6
Due between one year and two years	25.8	8.6	17.2	30.1	9.4	20.7
Due between two years and three years	23.3	7.8	15.5	23.1	8.5	14.6
Due between three years and four years	18.9	7.0	11.9	21.0	7.7	13.3
Due between four years and five years	15.2	6.4	8.8	18.3	7.0	11.3
More than five years	118.5	30.2	88.3	129.7	36.8	92.9
	$ 236.2	$ 69.6	$ 166.6	$ 256.1	$ 79.7	$ 176.4

Promissory notes

Promissory notes were issued as part of store acquisitions (Note 8.2). These notes are non-interest-bearing.

Debt covenants

The Company has provided covenants to certain of its lenders. The Company was in compliance with all of its covenants as at December 29, 2012.

26. Other long-term liabilities

(C$ in millions)	2012	2011
Employee benefits (Note 27)	$ 125.9	$ 108.6
Deferred gains	24.2	27.0
Deferred revenue	18.3	20.3
Derivatives (Note 37)	0.2	3.9
Other	44.8	45.9
	$ 213.4	$ 205.7

Deferred gains relate to the sale and leaseback of certain distribution centres. The deferred gains are amortized over the terms of the leases.

28. Share capital

(C$ in millions)	2012	2011
Authorized		
3,423,366 Common Shares		
100,000,000 Class A Non-Voting Shares		
Issued		
3,423,366 Common Shares (2011 – 3,423,366)	$ 0.2	$ 0.2
77,720,401 Class A Non-Voting Shares (2011 – 78,020,208)	687.8	710.3
	$ 688.0	$ 710.5

All issued shares are fully paid. The Company does not hold any of its Common or Class A Non-Voting Shares. Neither the Common nor Class A Non-Voting Shares have a par value.

During 2012 and 2011, the Company issued and repurchased Class A Non-Voting Shares. The net excess of the issue price over the repurchase price results in contributed surplus. The net excess of the repurchase price over the issue price is allocated first to contributed surplus, with any remainder allocated to retained earnings.

The following transactions occurred with respect to Class A Non-Voting Shares during 2012 and 2011:

(C$ in millions)	2012		2011	
	Number	$	Number	$
Shares outstanding at beginning of the year	78,020,208	$ 710.3	78,020,007	$ 711.4
Issued				
Dividend reinvestment plan	69,545	4.6	71,604	4.3
Stock option plan	200	–	1,200	–
Employee Profit Sharing Plan	59,078	4.1	59,491	3.6
Dealer profit sharing plans	54,724	3.7	59,302	3.7
Repurchased	(483,354)	(33.1)	(191,396)	(11.9)
Excess of issue price over repurchase price	–	(1.8)	–	(0.8)
Shares outstanding at end of the year	77,720,401	$ 687.8	78,020,208	$ 710.3

Since 1988 the Company has followed an anti-dilution policy. The Company repurchases shares to substantially offset the dilutive effects of issuing Class A Non-Voting Shares pursuant to various corporate programs and in 2012 the Company purchased an additional 299,806 Class A Non-Voting Shares.

Conditions of Class A Non-Voting Shares and Common Shares

The holders of Class A Non-Voting Shares are entitled to receive a preferential cumulative dividend at the rate of $0.01 per share per annum. After payment of preferential cumulative dividends at the rate of $0.01 per share per annum on each of the Class A Non-Voting Shares with respect to the current year and each preceding year and payment of a non-cumulative dividend on each of the Common Shares with respect to the current year at the same rate, the holders of the Class A Non-Voting Shares and the Common Shares are entitled to further dividends declared and paid in equal amounts per share without preference or distinction or priority of one share over another.

In the event of the liquidation, dissolution or winding-up of the Company, all of the property of the Company available for distribution to the holders of the Class A Non-Voting Shares and the Common Shares shall be paid or distributed equally, share for share, to the holders of the Class A Non-Voting Shares and to the holders of the Common Shares without preference or distinction or priority of one share over another.

The holders of Class A Non-Voting Shares are entitled to receive notice of and to attend all meetings of the shareholders; however, except as provided by the *Business Corporations Act* (Ontario) and as hereinafter noted, they are not entitled to vote at those meetings. Holders of Class A Non-Voting Shares, voting separately as a class, are entitled to elect the greater of (i) three Directors or (ii) one-fifth of the total number of the Company's Directors.

The holders of Common Shares are entitled to receive notice of, to attend and to have one vote for each Common Share held at all meetings of holders of Common Shares, subject only to the restriction on the right to elect those directors who are elected by the holders of Class A Non-Voting Shares as set out above.

Common Shares can be converted, at any time and at the option of each holder of Common Shares, into Class A Non-Voting Shares on a share-for-share basis. The authorized number of shares of either class cannot be increased without the approval of the holders of at least two-thirds of the shares of each class represented and voted at a meeting of the shareholders called for the purpose of considering such an increase. Neither the Class A Non-Voting Shares nor the Common Shares can be changed by way of subdivision, consolidation, reclassification, exchange or otherwise unless at the same time the other class of shares is also changed in the same manner and in the same proportion.

Should an offer to purchase Common Shares be made to all or substantially all of the holders of Common Shares (other than an offer to purchase both Class A Non-Voting Shares and Common Shares at the same price and on the same terms and conditions) and should a majority of the Common Shares then issued and outstanding be tendered and taken up pursuant to such offer, the Class A Non-Voting Shares shall thereupon be entitled to one vote per share at all meetings of the shareholders and thereafter the Class A Non-Voting Shares shall be designated as Class A Shares.

The foregoing is a summary of certain of the conditions attached to the Class A Non-Voting Shares of the Company and reference should be made to the Company's articles for a full statement of such conditions.

As of December 29, 2012, the Company had dividends declared and payable to holders of Class A Non-Voting Shares and Common Shares of $28.5 million (2011 – $24.5 million) at a rate of $0.35 per share (2011 – $0.30).

On February 21, 2013 the Company's Board of Directors declared a dividend of $0.35 per share payable on June 1, 2013 to shareholders of record as of April 30, 2013.

Dividends per share declared were $1.25 in 2012 (2011 – $1.125).

30. Share-based payments

The Company's share-based payment plans are described below. There were no cancellations or significant modifications to any of the plans during 2012.

Stock options

The Company has granted stock options to certain employees that enable such employees to exercise their stock options and subscribe for Class A Non-Voting Shares or receive a cash payment equal to the difference between the market price of the Company's Class A Non-Voting Shares as at the exercise date and the exercise price of the stock option. The exercise price of each option equals the weighted average closing price of Class A Non-Voting Shares on the Toronto Stock Exchange for the 10-day period preceding the date of grant. Stock options granted prior to 2006 generally vested on a graduated basis over a four-year period and are exercisable over a term of 10 years. Stock options granted in 2006 and 2007 vested on a graduated basis over a three-year period and are exercisable over a term of seven years. Stock options granted from 2008 to 2011 generally vest on the third anniversary of their grant and are exercisable over a term of seven years. Stock options granted in 2012 generally vest on a graduated basis over three-year period and are exercisable over a term of seven years. At December 29, 2012, approximately 2.4 million Class A Non-Voting Shares were issuable under the stock option plan.

Compensation expense, net of hedging arrangements, recorded for stock options for the year ended December 29, 2012, was $9.5 million (2011 – $6.0 million).

Stock option transactions during 2012 and 2011 were as follows:

	2012		2011	
	Number of options	Weighted average exercise price	Number of options	Weighted average exercise price
Outstanding at beginning of year	2,563,916	$ 55.22	2,280,374	$ 53.49
Granted	742,802	63.76	433,804	62.30
Exercised and surrendered	(744,620)	44.31	(68,511)	34.59
Forfeited	(155,715)	64.81	(81,651)	61.68
Expired	–	–	(100)	21.03
Outstanding at end of year	2,406,383	$ 60.62	2,563,916	$ 55.22
Stock options exercisable at end of year	876,505		975,809	

[1] The weighted average market price of the Company's shares when the options were exercised in 2012 was $67.28 (2011 – $63.95).

The following table summarizes information about stock options outstanding and exercisable at December 29, 2012:

	Options outstanding			Options exercisable	
Range of exercise prices	Number of outstanding options	Weighted average remaining contractual life[1]	Weighted average exercise price	Number exercisable at December 29 2012	Weighted average exercise price
$ 66.04 to 82.42	313,109	1.59	$ 71.89	290,965	$ 72.28
63.67 to 64.82	783,291	5.36	63.83	109,978	64.82
62.30 to 63.42	637,771	3.98	62.72	256,035	63.34
44.52 to 56.71	490,420	4.14	53.40	37,735	52.32
29.63 to 40.04	181,792	3.02	39.48	181,792	39.48
$ 29.63 to 82.42	2,406,383	4.08	$ 60.62	876,505	$ 61.07

[1] Weighted average remaining contractual life is expressed in years.

Performance share unit plans

The Company grants performance share units (PSUs) to certain employees. Each PSU entitles the participant to receive a cash payment in an amount equal to the weighted average closing price of Class A Non-Voting Shares traded on the Toronto Stock Exchange during the 10-day period commencing on the first business day after the last day of the performance period, multiplied by a factor determined by specific performance-based criteria. The performance period of each plan is approximately three years from the date of issuance. Compensation expense, net of hedging arrangements, recorded for these PSUs for the year ended December 29, 2012, was $20.1 million (2011 – $15.3 million).

Deferred share unit plans

Directors

The Company offers a Deferred Share Unit Plan (DSUP) for members of the Board of Directors. Under this plan, each director may elect to receive all or a percentage of his or her annual compensation, which is paid quarterly, in the form of notional Class A Non-Voting Shares of the Company called deferred share units (DSUs). The issue price of each DSU is equal to the weighted average share price at which Class A Non-Voting Shares of the Company trade on the Toronto Stock Exchange during the 10-day period prior to the last day of the calendar quarter in which the DSU is issued. The DSU account of each director includes the value of dividends, if any, as if reinvested in additional DSUs. The director is not permitted to convert DSUs into cash until retirement. The value of the DSUs when converted to cash will be equivalent to the market value of the Class A Non-Voting Shares at the time the conversion takes place pursuant to the DSUP details. Compensation expense (recovery) recorded for the year ended December 29, 2012, was $0.4 million (2011 – ($0.1) million).

Executives

The Company also offers a DPSP for certain executives. Under this plan, executives may elect to receive all or a percentage of their annual bonus in the form of DSUs. The issue price of each DSU is equal to the weighted average share price at which Class A Non-Voting Shares of the Company trade on the Toronto Stock Exchange during the five business days prior to the tenth business day following the release of the Company's financial statements for the year in respect of which the annual bonus was earned. The DSU account for each employee includes the value of dividends, if any, as if reinvested in additional DSUs. The executive is not permitted to convert DSUs into cash until his or her departure from the Company. The value of the DSUs when converted to cash will be equivalent to the market value of the Class A Non-Voting Shares at the time the conversion takes place pursuant to the DSUP details. Compensation expense recorded for the year ended December 29, 2012, was $0.1 million (2011 – $nil).

The fair value of stock options and PSUs was determined using the Black-Scholes option pricing model with the following inputs:

	2012		2011	
	Stock options	**PSUs**	Stock options	PSUs
Share price at end of year (C$)	**$ 69.11**	**$ 69.11**	$ 65.90	$ 65.90
Weighted average exercise price (C$)[1]	**$ 60.53**	**N/A**	$ 54.78	N/A
Expected remaining life (years)	**3.3**	**1.2**	3.2	1.0
Expected dividends	**2.3%**	**3.1%**	1.9%	3.2%
Expected volatility	**25.2%**	**19.8%**	25.3%	21.9%
Risk-free interest rate	**1.5%**	**1.3%**	1.3%	1.2%

[1] Reflects expected forfeitures.

The expense recognized for share-based compensation is summarized as follows:

(C$ in millions)	2012	2011
Expense arising from share-based payment transactions	**$ 34.2**	$ 18.9
Effect of hedging arrangements	**(4.1)**	2.3
Total expense included in net income	**$ 30.1**	$ 21.2

The total carrying amount of liabilities for share-based payment transactions at December 29, 2012, was $66.0 million (2011 – $72.8 million).

The intrinsic value of the liability for vested benefits at December 29, 2012, was $13.9 million (2011 – $12.9 million).

31. Revenue

(C$ in millions)	2012	2011
Sale of goods	**$ 10,005.8**	$ 8,997.6
Interest income on loans receivable	**707.2**	697.2
Services rendered	**361.3**	354.7
Royalties and licence fees	**340.3**	325.9
Rental income	**12.6**	11.7
	$ 11,427.2	$ 10,387.1

Major customers

The Company does not have reliance on any one customer.

32. Cost of producing revenue

(C$ in millions)	2012	2011
Inventory cost of sales	$ 7,545.3	$ 6,916.7
Net impairment loss on loans receivable	261.2	296.2
Finance costs on deposits	72.5	70.1
Other	50.3	43.4
	$ 7,929.3	$ 7,326.4

Inventory writedowns as a result of net realizable value being lower than cost, recognized in the year ended December 29, 2012 were $82.6 million (2011 – $73.3 million).

Inventory writedowns recognized in previous periods and reversed in the year ended December 29, 2012 were $17.3 million (2011 – $23.9 million). The reversal of writedowns was the result of actual losses being lower than previously estimated.

The writedowns and reversals are included in inventory cost of sales.

33. Operating expenses by nature

(C$ in millions)	2012	2011
Personnel expenses	$ 987.9	$ 817.4
Occupancy	571.6	438.4
Marketing and advertising	341.0	317.1
Depreciation of property and equipment and investment property	248.9	229.8
Amortization of intangible assets	86.2	66.3
Other	464.6	448.0
	$ 2,700.2	$ 2,317.0

34. Finance income and finance costs

(C$ in millions)	2012	2011
Finance income[1]		
Tax instalments	$ 0.1	$ 3.6
Mortgages	8.2	7.4
Short- and long-term investments	8.4	9.9
Other	1.4	2.1
Total finance income	$ 18.1	$ 23.0
Finance costs[1]		
Subordinated and senior notes[2]	$ 57.4	$ 63.9
Medium-term notes[3]	59.2	59.2
Loans payable	13.5	17.1
Finance leases	10.9	11.4
Short-term borrowings	3.1	4.4
Other	4.0	5.0
	148.1	161.0
Less: Capitalized borrowing costs	3.8	5.8
Total finance costs	$ 144.3	$ 155.2
Net finance costs	$ 126.2	$ 132.2

[1] The presentation of the components of finance income and finance costs has changed. The prior period's figures have been restated to correspond to the current-year presentation.

[2] Relates to GCCT and includes $1.7 million of amortization of debt issuance costs (2011 – $0.2 million).

[3] Includes $0.4 million of amortization of debt issuance costs (2011 – $0.4 million).

36. Notes to the consolidated statements of cash flows

Changes in working capital and other comprise the following:

(C$ in millions)	2012	2011
Trade and other receivables	$ 77.4	$ (31.4)
Loans receivable	(521.7)	(318.5)
Merchandise inventories	(41.5)	(88.9)
Income taxes	(15.1)	7.3
Prepaid expenses and deposits	5.8	4.4
Deposits	134.7	401.1
Trade and other payables	(65.3)	242.1
Provisions	(8.4)	(9.7)
Long-term provisions	(8.0)	0.2
Deferred revenue	(2.2)	15.7
Employee benefits	10.3	(2.7)
Changes in working capital and other	$ (434.0)	$ 219.6

Supplementary information

During the year ended December 29, 2012, the Company acquired property and equipment and investment property at an aggregate cost of $268.5 million (2011 – $239.3 million) and intangible assets at an aggregate cost of $66.3 million (2011 – $125.4 million).

The amount related to property and equipment and investment property acquired that is included in trade and other payables at December 29, 2012, is $47.6 million (2011 – $25.1 million). The amount related to intangible assets that is included in trade and other payables at December 29, 2012, is $5.4 million (2011 – $4.8 million).

Also included in the property and equipment, investment property and intangible assets acquired are non-cash items relating to finance leases, asset retirement obligations and capitalized interest in the amount of $25.1 million (2011 – $13.1 million).

39. Guarantees and commitments

Guarantees

In the normal course of business, the Company enters into numerous agreements that may contain features that meet the definition of a guarantee. A guarantee is defined to be a contract (including an indemnity) that contingently requires the Company to make payments to the guaranteed party based on (i) changes in an underlying interest rate, foreign exchange rate, equity or commodity instrument, index or other variable that is related to an asset, a liability or an equity security of the counterparty; (ii) failure of another party to perform under an obligating agreement; or (iii) failure of a third party to pay its indebtedness when due.

The Company has provided the following significant guarantees and other commitments to third parties:

Standby letters of credit and performance guarantees

Franchise Trust, a legal entity sponsored by a third-party bank, originates loans to Dealers for their purchase of inventory and fixed assets. While Franchise Trust is consolidated as part of these financial statements, the Company has arranged for several major Canadian banks to provide standby letters of credit to Franchise Trust to support the credit quality of the Dealer loan portfolio. The banks may also draw against the standby letters of credit to cover any shortfalls in certain related fees owing to it. In any case where a draw is made against the standby letters of credit, the Company has agreed to reimburse the banks issuing the standby letters of credit for the amount so drawn. In the unlikely event that all the standby letters of credit had been fully drawn simultaneously, the maximum payment by the Company under this reimbursement obligation would have been $164.0 million at December 29, 2012 (2011 – $137.2 million). The Company has not recorded any liability for these amounts due to the credit quality of the Dealer loans and to the nature of the underlying collateral represented by the inventory and fixed assets of the borrowing Dealers.

Business and property dispositions

In connection with agreements for the sale of all or a part of a business or property and in addition to indemnifications relating to failure to perform covenants and breach of representations and warranties, the Company has agreed to indemnify the purchasers against claims from its past conduct, including environmental remediation. Typically, the term and amount of such indemnification will be determined by the parties in the agreements. The nature of these indemnification agreements prevents the Company from estimating the maximum potential liability it would be required to pay to counterparties. Historically, the Company has not made any significant indemnification payments under such agreements, and no amount has been accrued in the consolidated financial statements with respect to these indemnification agreements.

Lease agreements

The Company has entered into agreements with certain of its lessors that guarantee the lease payments of certain sublessees of its facilities to lessors. Generally, these lease agreements relate to facilities the Company has vacated prior to the end of the term of its lease. These lease agreements require the Company to make lease payments throughout the lease term if the sublessee fails to make the scheduled payments. These lease agreements have expiration dates through January 2016. The Company has also guaranteed leases on certain franchise stores in the event the franchisees are unable to meet their remaining lease commitments. These lease agreements have expiration dates through January 2016. The maximum amount that the Company may be required to pay under these agreements was $6.2 million (2011 – $6.9 million), except for six lease agreements for which the maximum amount cannot be reasonably estimated. In addition, the Company could be required to make payments for percentage rents, realty taxes and common area costs. No amount has been accrued in the consolidated financial statements with respect to these lease agreements.

Third-party-debt agreements

The Company has guaranteed the debt of certain Dealers. These third-party debt agreements require the Company to make payments if the Dealer fails to make scheduled debt payments. The majority of these third-party debt agreements have expiration dates extending to January 26, 2013. The maximum amount that the Company may be required to pay under these debt agreements was $50.0 million (2011 – $50.0 million), of which $40.3 million (2011 – $38.8 million) was issued at December 29, 2012. No amount has been accrued in the consolidated financial statements with respect to these debt agreements.

Indemnification of lenders and agents under credit facilities

In the ordinary course of business, the Company has agreed to indemnify its lenders under various credit facilities against costs or losses resulting from changes in laws and regulations that would increase the lenders' costs and from any legal action brought against the lenders related to the use of the loan proceeds. These indemnifications generally extend for the term of the credit facilities and do not provide any limit on the maximum potential liability. Historically, the Company has not made any significant indemnification payments under such agreements, and no amount has been accrued in the consolidated financial statements with respect to these indemnification agreements.

Other indemnification commitments

In the ordinary course of business, the Company provides other additional indemnification commitments to counterparties in transactions such as leasing transactions, service arrangements, investment banking agreements, securitization agreements, indemnification of trustees under indentures for outstanding public debt, director and officer indemnification agreements, escrow agreements, price escalation clauses, sales of assets (other than dispositions of businesses discussed above) and the arrangements with Franchise Trust discussed above. These additional indemnification agreements require the Company to compensate the counterparties for certain amounts and costs incurred, including costs resulting from changes in laws and regulations (including tax legislation) or as a result of litigation claims or statutory sanctions that may be suffered by a counterparty as a consequence of the transaction. The terms of these additional indemnification agreements vary based on the contract and do not provide any limit on the maximum potential liability. Historically, the Company has not made any significant payments under such additional indemnifications, and no amount has been accrued in the consolidated financial statements with respect to these additional indemnification commitments.

Other commitments

As at December 29, 2012, the Company had other commitments. The Company has not recognized any liability relating to these commitments:

The Company has obtained documentary and standby letters of credit aggregating $24.0 million (2011 – $25.8 million) relating to the importation of merchandise inventories and to facilitate various real estate activities.

The Company has entered into agreements to buy back franchise-owned merchandise inventory should the banks foreclose on any of the franchisees. The terms of the guarantees range from less than a year to the lifetime of the particular underlying franchise agreement. The Company's maximum exposure as at December 29, 2012 was $70.0 million (2011 – $69.9 million).

The Company has committed to pay $9.2 million (2011 – $9.2 million) for various commitments and contingent liabilities, including a customs bond and the obligation to buy back two franchise stores.

The Company has committed to pay $41.4 million (2011 – $68.4 million) in total to third parties for credit card processing and information technology services mainly in support of the Company's credit card and retail banking services for periods up to 2017.

Endnotes

CHAPTER 1

1. Some companies refer to this statement as a "balance sheet," a title that was commonly used prior to the adoption of IFRS in Canada.
2. A corporation is a business that is incorporated under the federal or provincial laws. The owners are called shareholders or stockholders. Ownership is represented by shares of capital that can usually be bought and sold freely. The corporation operates as a separate legal entity, separate and apart from its owners. The shareholders enjoy limited liability; that is, they are liable for the debts of the corporation only to the extent of their investments. Appendix 1A discusses forms of ownership in more detail.
3. Many companies refer to this measure as "net income," while others prefer to use the term "profit." The three terms—net earnings, net income, and profit—are synonymous. We use net earnings because it is consistent with other terms used in financial statements, such as earnings per share and retained earnings.
4. The title "statement of earnings" is more commonly used than "income statement" by Canadian publicly accountable enterprises. Another title, "statement of operations," is also used by some companies. The three titles are synonymous.
5. A detailed version of the statement of changes in equity is discussed in Chapter 6.
6. Retained earnings decrease when expenses exceed revenues, resulting in a loss. The complete process of declaring and paying dividends is discussed in Chapter 12.
7. Sun-Rype did not declare dividends in 2012, but we assume that it did for illustrative purposes only.
8. Alternative ways to present cash flows from operating activities are discussed in Chapter 5.
9. The basic financial statements and related notes are part of more elaborate documents called annual reports that are produced by public companies. Annual reports are normally split into two sections. The first is non-financial and usually includes a letter to shareholders from the chairperson of the company's board of directors and the chief executive officer; descriptions of the company's management philosophy, products, and successes (and occasionally failures); exciting prospects and challenges for the future; and beautiful photographs of products, facilities, and personnel.

    The second section includes the core of the report. The principal components of this financial section include summarized financial data for five or ten years, management's discussion and analysis of the company's financial condition and results of operations, four financial statements and related notes, auditor's report, recent stock price information, a summary of quarterly financial data, and a list of directors and officers of the company.
10. The IASB's website (www.ifrs.org) provides more details about the process of producing IFRS.
11. Legally, this is enforced by the OSC through National Instrument 52-109—Certification of Disclosure in Issuers' Annual and Interim Filings. Chief executive and chief financial officers must sign a legal document with every financial report filed with the OSC. That document certifies that the CEO and CFO have designed or supervised the design of a financial data collection and reporting system that will result in financial statements free of material misstatement and fraud. This is an assurance of the quality of financial information disclosed by companies listed on Canadian stock exchanges.
12. A typical audit report for Canadian public companies consists of the auditor's responsibility and opinion.
13. Updates of the status of discussions in various jurisdictions are available from CPA Canada at www.cpacanada.ca.
14. Refer to CPA Canada (www.cpacanada.ca) for details of the educational and experience requirements.
15. The Auditing and Assurance Standards Board (AASB) of the Canadian Institute of Chartered Accountants sets standards for auditing of public companies. The AASB has recently produced new Canadian Auditing Standards that are essentially the International Standards on Auditing issued by the International Auditing and Assurance Standards Board.
16. Chartered Professional Accountants of Canada (2012). *The Chartered Professional Accountant Competency Map*, p. 8. Accessible through CPA Canada's website, www.cpacanada.ca.
17. Not-for-profit organizations and pension plans are subject to different sets of accounting standards. The accounting standards applicable to the various types of organizations are compiled in different parts of the *CICA Handbook*. Part I of the *Handbook* includes IFRS. Part II includes accounting standards for private enterprises.
18. Refer to the following website for more details about the types of services and skills that should be provided by accountants in the future: www.accountemps.com/WhatCanadianEmployersSeek.

CHAPTER 2

1. International Accounting Standards Committee (1989). *Framework for the Preparation and Presentation of Financial Statements*. Adopted by the International Accounting Standards Board, 2001.
2. International Accounting Standards Board (2010). *Conceptual Framework for Financial Reporting 2010*.
3. *Ibid.*
4. A more detailed discussion of these qualitative characteristics is presented in Chapter 6.
5. The basic rules for consolidation of financial statements are covered in Chapter 14 (on *Connect*).
6. From this concept, accountants have developed what is known as the double-entry system of recordkeeping.
7. Contracts of this nature that are likely to result in significant future liabilities must be noted in the financial statements as commitments.

CHAPTER 3

1. In addition to the audited annual statements, most businesses prepare quarterly financial statements (also known as *interim reports* covering a three-month period) for external users. The securities commissions require publicly accountable enterprises to do so.
2. Another common format, *single step*, reorganizes all accounts on the multiple-step format. All revenues are listed

together and all expenses except taxes are listed together. The expenses subtotal is then subtracted from the revenue subtotal to arrive at earnings before income taxes, the same subtotal as on the multiple-step statement. For example, Sun-Rype's statement of earnings is presented in Exhibit 1.3 in Chapter 1 using the single-step format. Many companies use some variation of the single-step and multiple-step formats.

3. All amounts in this chapter are in thousands of Canadian dollars, except where noted otherwise.

4. Sales discounts, returns, and allowances are covered in Chapter 7.

5. Further discussion of classification of expenses by nature is provided in Chapter 6.

6. International Accounting Standards Board, 2009. *International Accounting Standard 18, Revenue*, paragraph 14. A joint project between the IASB and the Financial Accounting Standards Board on *Revenue from Contracts with Customers* was initiated in 2010 and is expected to result in a new international financial reporting standard. Companies that prepare IFRS-based financial reports are expected to implement the new standard for reporting periods beginning after December 15, 2017.

7. Further discussion of the application of the revenue principle to special circumstances is provided in Chapter 7.

8. International Accounting Standards Board. *International Financial Reporting Standard 8, Operating Segments*, requires publicly traded companies to disclose specific information about their operating segments, products and services, geographical areas in which they operate, and major customers to enable users of their financial statements to evaluate the nature and financial effects of the business activities in which they engage and the economic environments in which they operate.

9. Interest received may be classified as investing cash flow because it is a return on investments. Alternatively, it may be classified as operating cash flow because it enters into the determination of net earnings or net loss. We classified it as an investing activity for this illustration.

CHAPTER 4

1. A firm's fiscal year does not have to conform to the calendar year (January 1 to December 31). Some companies choose a fiscal year that ends on a date that is more convenient than December 31 to prepare its financial statements. For example, a retail company may choose a fiscal year that ends on January 31, after the busy shopping period during the holiday season. In some cases, companies choose a fiscal year-end that is defined as "the last Saturday of the month" or "the Sunday closest to the end of the month," which results in financial information covering 52 weeks in some years and 53 weeks in other years.

2. Errors in a trial balance may also occur in a manual record-keeping system when wrong accounts and/or amounts are posted from correct journal entries. If the two columns are not equal, errors have occurred in one or more of the following:

- In preparing journal entries when debits do not equal credits.
- In posting the correct monetary effects of transactions from the journal entry to the ledger.
- In computing ending balances in accounts.
- In copying ending balances in the ledger to the trial balance.

These errors can be traced and should be corrected before adjusting the records.

3. Companies can choose fiscal periods other than actual month-ends, and financial statements can cover different accounting periods (month, quarter, or year). Adjusting entries may be prepared monthly, quarterly, and/or annually to ensure that proper amounts are included on the financial reports presented to external users.

4. Sun-Rype reports combine trade receivables and other receivables into one element titled "Trade and other receivables" on its statement of financial position. The transactions affecting trade receivables in this illustration are posted to the trade receivables account, which is a component of trade and other receivables.

5. Valuation of property, plant, and equipment is discussed in Chapters 6 and 9.

6. The computation of interest is relatively simple. Interest = Amount borrowed $\times$ Annual interest rate $\times$ Time. For this example, interest has accrued for 10 months, from March 1 to December 31, 2014. The amount accrued is computed as follows: $300,000 \times 0.06 \times (10 \text{ months} \div 12) = \$15,000$. Interest computations are covered in more detail in Chapter 10.

7. In fact, a bank employee was able to accumulate a large sum of money by altering a computer program to round off amounts of exchange transactions to the nearest cent and by transferring the fractional amounts to a specific account under his control. Even though the amounts involved per transaction were very small, the volume of banking transactions resulted in the accumulation of a relatively large amount. Fortunately, the employee's fraud was detected a few years later and an appropriate penalty was imposed on him.

8. For a discussion and illustration of the use of a worksheet for end-of-period adjustments, refer to Appendix C on *Connect*.

9. If there are preferred dividends (discussed in Chapter 12), the amount is subtracted from net earnings in the numerator. Outstanding shares are those that are currently held by the shareholders.

CHAPTER 5

1. Original maturity means original maturity to the entity holding the investment. For example, both a three-month Treasury bill and a three-year Treasury note purchased three months from maturity qualify as cash equivalents. A Treasury note purchased three years ago, however, does not become a cash equivalent when its remaining maturity is three months.

2. Amortization refers to the allocation of the cost of intangible assets (such as computer software) over their useful lives. It is similar to depreciation of property, plant, and equipment.

3. Danier Leather did not declare dividends during fiscal year 2012. It is assumed that it declared and paid dividends to shareholders for illustrative purposes.

4. Certain non-current assets, such as long-term receivables from customers, and non-current liabilities, such as post-retirement obligations to employees, are considered to be operating items. These items are covered in other accounting courses.

5. Examples of the accounts excluded are dividends payable, short-term borrowing (or bank indebtedness), and current portion of long-term debt (representing long-term debt with an original term longer than one year that is due within one year of the statement date).

6. Adding back depreciation and amortization to net earnings does not mean that this expense is a source of cash. In fact, depreciation and amortization are the result of a process of allocating the cost of assets over time, regardless of the timing of payment for the assets.

7. Gains and losses on sales of equipment and investments are dealt with in a similar manner and are discussed in Appendix 5A. Other similar additions and subtractions are discussed in other accounting courses.

8. Certain non-current assets, such as long-term receivables from customers, and non-current liabilities, such as post-retirement obligations to employees, are considered to be operating items. These items are covered in other accounting courses.

9. The amount of cash collected from customers is the same, regardless of the mix of cash sales and credit sales. To be sure, assume that sales are 20 percent cash and 80 percent on account, and compute the amount of cash collected from customers during the period.

10. When a loss is reported, a more negative ratio indicates greater ability to finance the company from operations, which was the case for Danier Leather in 2009.

11. An alternative definition that does not subtract dividends but adds interest after tax is often called the free cash flow of the firm. Other variations of this definition are sometimes reported by companies in the management discussion and analysis sections of their annual reports.

12. This description was simplified to eliminate discussion of stock options.

13. We assume, for simplicity, that the amount paid to repurchase the shares is the same amount received when the shares were issued.

14. Danier Leather did not declare dividends during fiscal year 2012, but, for illustrative purposes, we assumed that it did.

15. The disposal of assets and the resulting gains or losses are discussed in detail in Chapter 9.

16. We assume that all sales are made on account. However, the amount of cash collected from customers is the same, regardless of the mix of cash and credit sales. To be sure, assume that sales are 20 percent cash and 80 percent on account, and compute the amount of cash collected from customers during the period. You can use other percentages as well.

17. We assume that all purchases are made on account. However, the amount of cash paid to suppliers is the same regardless of the mix of cash and credit purchases. To be sure, assume that purchases are 10 percent cash and 90 percent on account, and compute the amount of cash paid to suppliers during the period. You can use other percentages as well.

CHAPTER 6

1. A brief history of both companies is available on the company's website, **http://thomsonreuters.com/about/company_history**.

2. Details of Thomson Reuters' corporate governance structure and activities can be found at **http://ir.thomsonreuters.com/phoenix.zhtml?c=76540&p=irol-govHighlights**.

3. The most prominent of these regulators is the Ontario Securities Commission (OSC). The OSC staff review company reports for compliance with their standards, investigate irregularities, and punish violators. Many OSC investigations are reported in the business press, such as the *National Post* or *The Globe and Mail*. The OSC also publishes this information online each month at **http://www.osc.gov.on.ca/en/SecuritiesLaw_bulletin_index.htm**.

4. In some cases, the auditor may not be satisfied that the company's financial statements are in compliance with IFRS. A qualified opinion is then issued if the company's management is not willing to modify the financial reports as per the auditor's recommendation. If the exceptions to IFRS are very serious, then the auditor may issue an adverse opinion, if the company's management cannot be persuaded to rectify the problems to avoid such an opinion. In extreme cases, the auditor may deny the issuance of an opinion if insufficient information is available to express an opinion. These latter types of opinions are rarely issued by auditors.

5. Canadian companies that have shares traded on U.S. stock exchanges can file SEC forms electronically with EDGAR (Electronic Data Gathering and Retrieval), a site sponsored by the SEC.

6. To look at SEDAR, just type the address on your Web browser. Select French or English, depending on your preference, and then select Company Profiles, followed by the letter of the alphabet that corresponds to the first letter of the company's name. You will then see a list of companies that includes the selected company. Many of the financial statement examples used in this book were downloaded from this website.

7. Debentures are debt securities that are not secured with specific collateral (no specific assets are pledged as security for the debt). Bonds are normally secured by specific collateral, such as investments in shares of other companies. Chapter 11 provides more details about bonds and debentures.

8. U.S., Canadian, and international companies that have shares trading on U.S. securities exchange markets are required to file a number of reports with the SEC. These forms for U.S. companies include Form 10-K, an annual report that provides a detailed description of the business and more detailed schedules concerning various figures reported in the annual financial statements, and Form 10-Q, which is essentially a quarterly report to shareholders. Canadian companies listed in the United States typically file their annual reports with the SEC on Form 40-F, and they furnish their quarterly reports, press releases, and other periodic disclosures on Form 6-K.

9. These qualitative characteristics are discussed in Chapter 3, Qualitative Characteristics of Useful Financial Information, of *The Conceptual Framework for Financial Reporting* 2010, IASB (September 2010). This framework has been incorporated in Part I of the *CICA Handbook—Accounting*.

10. In the original conceptual frameworks produced by the FASB and the IASB, verifiability was considered a

component of reliability, which also encompassed accuracy and freedom from bias. In the revised conceptual framework, reliability has been replaced with faithful representation as the second fundamental qualitative characteristic. A critical review of the primary qualitative characteristics and their relative significance for performance evaluation and investment and credit decisions is provided in Patricia C. O'Brien, "Changing the Concepts to Justify the Standards," *Accounting Perspectives* 8, No. 4 (2009): 263–275, and in Patricia C. O'Brien and William R. Scott, "Contracting Theory," *CA Magazine* 145, No. 3 (2012): 44–46.

11. To help users better understand the contents of its financial reports, IBM includes on its website (**www.ibm.com/investor/help**) a glossary of terms and provides basic explanations of the information contained in financial statements.

12. Canadian Securities Administrators, "National Instrument 52-109 Certification of Disclosure in Issuers' Annual and Interim Filings (NI 52-109)" (October 2008). Accessed June 14, 2013, from the OSC website, **www.osc.gov.on.ca/en/home.htm**.

13. The expenses that are deducted from revenue to obtain operating profit can alternatively be classified in accordance with the main elements of the costs of production and sale—namely, the cost of raw materials and consumables used, changes in inventories of finished products and work in progress, employee benefit costs, and depreciation and amortization expenses. For example, the Danish company ECCO Sko A/S, which produces and markets footwear products worldwide, classifies its operating expenses by nature (see, for example, page 54 of its 2011 annual report at **http://www.ecco.com/en-XI/Media-Center/~/media/Files/Pdf/Annual%20reports/ECCO_ANNUAL_REPORT_2011.pdf**).

14. International Accounting Standards Board, *International Financial Reporting Standard 13—Fair Value Measurement*, (May 2011): para. 9.

15. An excellent review of fair value accounting of financial assets and liabilities, and its role in the 2007–2009 financial crisis, is provided in M. Magnan, "Fair Value Accounting and the Financial Crisis: Messenger or Contributor?" *Accounting Perspectives* 8, No. 3 (2009): 189–213. In another article in the same journal, A. R. Abdel-Khalik argues that historical cost information is essential in evaluating management's stewardship of the economic resources entrusted to them, stating that fair value accounting does not provide information for this purpose. See A. R. Abdel-Khalik, "Fair Value Accounting and Stewardship," *Accounting Perspectives* 9, No. 4 (2010): 253–269.

CHAPTER 7

1. Gildan uses U.S. dollars as a reporting currency because a significant portion of its revenues, expenses, assets, and liabilities are denominated in U.S. dollars.

2. Gildan does not generally collect from customers using credit cards, and it does not generally offer sales discounts for early payment of trade accounts receivable. However, we assume, for illustrative purposes, that Gildan accepts credit cards as payments for products sold, and offers sales discounts to customers who purchase its products on account and then pay the amount due within a specific period.

3. In 2013, the International Accounting Standards Board (IASB) issued a new International Financial Reporting Standard titled "Revenue from Contracts with Customers" that clarifies the principles for recognizing revenue. The new standard supersedes both IAS 11 (Construction Contracts) and IAS 18 (Revenue). The new standard will affect, among other things, how revenue is recognized for royalties arising from licensing of intellectual property and how revenue should be allocated to each component of a bundle of products and services. Individuals who have purchased mobile devices usually sign service contracts that extend beyond one year. The customer typically pays for the purchased handset and future services that are bundled together into one lump sum, which must be split into different amounts to be recognized over time as revenue is earned. Canadian publicly accountable enterprises are expected to apply the provisions of the new standard for fiscal years beginning after December 15, 2017.

4. Some retail businesses, such as Canadian Tire, issue their own cards and avoid credit card discounts when customers use the store's credit card to pay for their purchases.

5. It is important not to confuse a cash discount with a trade discount. Vendors sometimes use a trade discount for quoting sales prices; the sales price is the list or printed catalogue price less the trade discount. For example, an item may be quoted at $10 per unit, subject to a 20 percent trade discount, on orders of 100 units or more; thus, the price for the large order is $8 per unit. Similarly, the price on a slow-moving product line can be lowered simply by increasing the trade discount. Sales revenue should always be recorded net of trade discounts. Manufacturers also offer discounts for early order and shipment to help manage production flows.

6. We use the gross method in all examples in this textbook. Some companies use the alternative net method, which records sales revenue after deducting the amount of the cash discount. Since the choice of method has little effect on the financial statements, discussion of this method is left for other accounting courses.

7. Alternatively, Gildan might offer the customer a $200 allowance to keep the wrong-colour T-shirts. If the customer accepts the offer, Gildan would report $200 as sales returns and allowances.

8. Sales discounts and credit card discounts may also be reported as expenses on the statement of earnings.

9. This assumes that all sales are on account.

10. Internal control is defined as the "process designed, implemented and maintained by those charged with governance, management and other personnel to provide reasonable assurance about the achievement of an entity's objectives with regard to reliability of financial reporting, effectiveness and efficiency of operations, and compliance with applicable laws and regulations." *CICA Assurance Handbook*, Part 1, Glossary of Terms.

11. Canadian Securities Administrators, "National Instrument 52-109, Certification of Disclosure in Issuers' Annual and Interim Filings" (August 2008).

12. PricewaterhouseCoopers, "The Global Economics Crimes Survey." November 2011. The report is accessible through PwC's website, **www.pwc.com/gx/en/economic-crime-**

survey/index.jhtml. Interested readers may also wish to consult another report by PwC, "Securing the bottom line: Canadian retail security survey 2012" (available at **http:// www.pwc.com/en_CA/ca/retail-consumer/publications/ pwc-security-survey-2012-10-29-en.pdf**), and two other reports on occupational fraud: Association of Certified Fraud Examiners (ACFE), "The 2012 Report to the Nations on Occupational Fraud and Abuse," Austin, TX (available at **www.acfe.com/rttn.aspx**), and Association of Certified Fraud Examiners and Dominic Peltier-Rivest, "Detecting Occupational Fraud in Canada: A Study of Its Victims and Perpetrators (available at **www.acfe.com/uploadedFiles/ ACFE_Website/Content/documents/rttn-canadian.pdf**).

13. These codes vary among banks.
14. International Accounting Standards Board, *International Accounting Standard 11—Construction Contracts*: para. 22.
15. Other measures of completion include surveys of work performed or completion of a physical proportion of the contract work. See IAS 11, para. 30.
16. The difference between the expected cost and the actual cost of construction, which did not occur in this simple example, creates additional accounting problems.
17. International Accounting Standards Board, *International Accounting Standard 18—Revenue:* paras. 20 and 26.

CHAPTER 8

1. Tax reports often differ from the statements prepared for shareholders and other external users.
2. Although Danier Leather produces and sells a wide variety of leather garments and accessories, we focus our attention on a specific type of product to illustrate the main concepts of inventory costing. Danier Leather attributes a nine-digit style number to each type of jacket. The number 101 does not refer to any specific style.
3. Many companies, such as Gildan Activewear Inc., provide product information to their current and potential customers. The website **www.mygildan.com/gildan-retriever/search** allows Gildan's customers to find out how many units of each product are available at each location that distributes its products in Canada, the United States, Mexico, Europe, or the Asia-Pacific region.
4. A fourth method—last-in, first-out (LIFO)—is accepted in the United States but is prohibited under IAS 2—Inventories.
5. Notice that the simple average of the unit costs is $210 [($200 + $210 + $220)/3], but the weighted average is $210.40, because the latter considers the number of units purchased at each unit cost. Beware of using a simple average.
6. As indicated in Chapter 6, corporate governance is no longer at the discretion of managers if an important corporate goal is to retain the company's listing on a stock exchange, such as the Toronto Stock Exchange (TSX). Corporate governance is a matter of full compliance with the laws and the regulations of the country in which companies have listed their shares. Companies such as Suncor Energy Inc. are listed on both the TSX and the New York Stock Exchange (NYSE). In the United States, Suncor Energy's internal control system and quality of financial disclosure must comply with Sarbanes-Oxley Act sections 303 (similar to Canada's NI 52-209) and 404, requiring that Suncor Energy have a third-party audit of the design and implementation of its internal control system. The penalties for

non-compliance can be in the millions of dollars for both companies and their executives. The reward to managers who act in the best interests of the shareholders is not only a reputation for ethical behaviour but also avoidance of significant financial penalties, and sometimes of jail.

7. The loss could be debited to a separate account, such as loss due to write-down of inventory, which is closed to cost of sales at the end of the accounting period.
8. IAS 2 states that in some cases it may be appropriate to group similar or related items. This may occur when "items of inventory relating to the same product line that have similar purposes or end uses, are produced and marketed in the same geographical area, and cannot be practicably evaluated separately from other items in that product line." (para. 29)
9. Adapted with permission from Canadian Institute of Chartered Accountants, *Filling the GAAP to IFRS: Teaching Supplements for Canada's Accounting Academics, CD3—Questions and Answers Pack,* 2008. Toronto: CICA. Any changes to the original material are the sole responsibility of the author and have not been reviewed or endorsed by the CICA.

CHAPTER 9

1. The term "depletion" most often refers to the allocation of the acquisition cost of natural resources, while the term "amortization" is often used in reference to the allocation of the acquisition cost of intangible assets. These terms are discussed later in this chapter.
2. International Accounting Standard Board, *International Accounting Standard 16—Property, Plant and Equipment*: paras. 43–47.
3. Most of the examples that we discuss in this chapter assume that assets were acquired on the first day of the year and depreciated for the entire year. In practice, assets are purchased at various times during the year. Most companies adopt a policy to cover partial-year depreciation, such as "to the nearest full month" or "half year in the year of acquisition."
4. Sony Corporation, Annual Report 2012.
5. Sale of the aircraft during the year requires updating the accumulated depreciation account to the date of sale by computing depreciation for a fraction of the year. The depreciation expense could be based on the number of months of depreciation, or 50 percent of the annual depreciation if the company uses the half-year rule.
6. The same analysis applies when a company exchanges an old asset for a new asset of the same kind, such as an old vehicle for a newer model.
7. Consistent with the procedure for recording depreciation, an accumulated depletion account may be used. In practice, most companies credit the asset account directly for the periodic depletion. This procedure is also typically used for intangible assets, which are discussed in the next section.

CHAPTER 10

1. For manufacturing companies, the purchases consist primarily of raw materials used in the production of finished goods. The computation of raw materials purchased is discussed in cost accounting courses.
2. Appendix 10A provides further details on the current and deferred components of income tax expense.

3. To highlight the relative significance of the taxes and fees imposed on the airline industry, WestJet Airlines offered to sell one-way tickets for $3 on flights between Calgary and Edmonton on June 30, 2002. However, the price of a $6 return ticket quickly rose to $89.27 when all of the applicable fees and taxes were added! See P. Fitzpatrick, "WestJet Launches $3 Ticket Protest," *National Post* (Financial Post), June 21, 2002: FP1.

4. The provinces of New Brunswick, Newfoundland and Labrador, Nova Scotia, Ontario, and Prince Edward Island have harmonized sales taxes. The provinces of British Columbia, Manitoba, Quebec, and Saskatchewan have separate provincial sales taxes. The province of Alberta, and the three territories—Northwest Territories, Nunavut, and Yukon—do not have provincial sales taxes. At the time of writing this text, sales taxes ranged from a GST rate of 5 percent in Alberta and the three territories to an HST rate of 15 percent in Nova Scotia.

5. International Accounting Standards Board, *International Accounting Standard 37—Provisions, Contingent Liabilities and Contingent Assets*: para. 10.

6. Present value and future value problems involve cash flows. The basic concepts are the same for cash inflows (receipts) and cash outflows (payments). No fundamental differences exist between present value and future value calculations for cash payments versus cash receipts.

7. The detailed discounting is as follows:

Periods	Interest for the Year	Present Value*
1.	$1,000.00 − ($1,000.00 × 1/1.04) = $38.46	$1,000.00 − $38.46 = $961.54
2.	$ 961.54 − ($ 961.54 × 1/1.04) = $36.98	$ 961.54 − $36.98 = $924.56
3.	$ 924.56 − ($ 924.56 × 1/1.04) = $35.56†	$ 924.56 − $35.56 = $889.00

*Verifiable in Table 10C.1.
†Adjusted for rounding.

CHAPTER 11

1. An example of a prospectus issued by Bell Canada is available on the SEDAR system (www.sedar.com). Access the website, search for Bell Canada under "B," view the documents filed by the company, and select "Prospectus supplement—English," dated June 19, 2012.

2. Further details about the bond market are available at www.investinginbonds.com.

3. Standard & Poor's (S&P) has a useful website at www.standardandpoors.com for those interested in learning about the credit ratings used by this credit rating agency.

4. The details of how default risk is rated vary slightly from one agency to another. You can view a sample of these descriptions in detail at www.dbrs.com.

5. The difference between the coupon interest rate and the market interest rate is often very small, usually a fraction of 1 percent, when the bonds are sold. Companies try to sell their bonds at prices close to their par value. However, the market rate of interest continuously changes as a result of such factors as inflation expectations and the level of business activity. It is, therefore, virtually impossible to issue a bond at a point when the coupon rate and the market rate are exactly the same.

6. Alternatively, the bonds payable account could be credited for $345,644, thus eliminating the need to use the discount on bonds payable account. In this case, the bonds payable account is credited periodically for the amount of interest expense that is not paid or accrued (which equals the amortized discount).

7. From Table 10C.2, Chapter 10, the present value of an annuity of $1 discounted at 2 percent for 8 periods.

8. The carrying amount is the present value of the remaining cash payments (eight interest payments and the principal amount), which equals $400,000 × 0.7307 + $12,000 × 6.7327 or $373,072.

9. International Accounting Standards Board, *International Accounting Standard 17, Leases* (2009): para. 10.

10. The current standard related to lease accounting (IAS 17) has been criticized because the distinction between operating leases and finance leases and the reporting of leases in financial statements does not always provide a faithful representation of leasing arrangements. For this reason, a new international financial reporting standard, which was in the final preparation stage when this text was written, will practically eliminate the distinction between operating and finance leases and require the lessees to report the leased property as an asset and the corresponding lease payments as liabilities on their statements of financial position.

CHAPTER 12

1. If a corporation becomes insolvent, creditors have recourse for their claims only to the corporation's assets. Thus, shareholders stand to lose only their equity in the corporation. In the case of a partnership or sole proprietorship, creditors have recourse to the owners' personal assets if the assets of the business are insufficient to meet its debts.

2. Publicly accountable enterprises are required to report a third component of equity called accumulated other comprehensive income (loss). We discuss this component briefly later in this chapter.

3. A voting proxy is written authority by a shareholder that gives another party the right to vote the shareholder's shares in the annual meeting of the shareholders. Typically, proxies are solicited by and given to the president of the corporation.

4. The average issue price per share equals the balance of the common shares account divided by the number of common shares outstanding.

5. Assume that a company issues shares at $10 per share and then buys them back from some shareholders at $9 per share. If the difference of $1 is treated as profit, then the company will have to pay income tax, causing a reduction in cash. If it continues with similar transactions, then it will pay income taxes on earnings that did not result from operating transactions. The decrease in cash causes a decrease in the company's assets, which depresses the company's market value and causes further deterioration in the share price. No one would want to invest in such a company. Earnings are generated from operating activities, not capital transactions.

6. Further details about each series of BCE's preferred shares are available on its website at www.bce.ca/en/investors/preferredshares/.

CHAPTER 13

1. The percentage change in sales for existing stores is computed as follows:

$$\text{Percentage change} = \left[\frac{\text{Sale}_{\text{Current Year}} - \text{Sale}_{\text{Previous Year}}}{\text{Sale}_{\text{Previous Year}}} \times 100 \right]$$

Similar percentage changes can be computed for various elements of financial statements.

2. Component percentages could be presented for a longer period of time. We have limited the statement of earnings items to three years because Canadian publicly accountable enterprises adopted IFRS for fiscal years starting on January 1, 2011, with comparative figures for 2010. Financial statement information from previous years is based on Canadian generally accepted accounting principles (GAAP). For some financial statement items, Canadian GAAP and IFRS result in different reported values for the same item because of differences in the measurement and financial reporting standards. For example, finance costs were reported at $64.1 million under GAAP for fiscal year 2010 and represented 0.7 percent of the sales revenue for that year ($8,980.9 million). However, finance costs were reported by Canadian Tire as $168.1 million under IFRS for the same year and represented 1.8 percent of the revised amount of sales revenue ($9,213.1 million).

3. The figures for Canadian Tire used throughout the following ratio examples are taken from the financial statements in Exhibit 13.1.

4. To illustrate the net cost of using debt, assume that a company earned $100 in revenue and incurred $70 in operating expenses. Consider two scenarios: (1) the company uses long-term debt that cost $10 in interest expense and (2) the company does not use debt:

	Debt Financing	Equity Financing
Earnings before interest and taxes	$30	$30
Interest expense	(10)	0
Earnings before income taxes	$20	$30
Income tax expense (@40 percent)	(8)	(12)
Net earnings	$12	$18

The deduction of interest expense from earnings before interest and taxes reduced the income tax expense from $12 to $8, and net earnings decreased by only $6. Therefore, the net cost of using debt in this case is $6, or $10 × (1 × 0.4, the tax rate).

5. IFRS require companies to report interest expense and other financing-related expenses as "finance costs" on the statement of earnings. Details of the finance costs are typically reported in a note to the financial statements. The finance costs of Canadian Tire are, essentially, interest expense.

6. An expanded version of the DuPont model is provided by the Scott formula. Interested readers are referred to Appendix 13A on *Connect* for a detailed application of the Scott formula to the financial statements of Canadian Tire Corporation, Limited.

7. For manufacturing companies, the purchases consist primarily of raw materials used in the production of finished goods. The computation of raw materials purchased is discussed in cost accounting courses.

8. Alternatively, the relationship between debt and owners' equity may be calculated with the following ratio:

$$\frac{\text{Total Liabilities to}}{\text{Total Equities}} = \frac{\text{Total Liabilities}}{\text{Total Liabilities and Shareholders' Equity}}$$

$$\text{Canadian Tire, 2012} = \frac{\$8,417.8}{\$13,181.4} = 63.9\%$$

This ratio is one of those readily available through the component percentage analysis in Exhibit 13.3.

CHAPTER 1
Financial data in this chapter have been reproduced with permission from Sun-Rype Products Ltd.
Page 1: © Danny Meldung/Photo Affairs, Inc. Products provided by Sun-Rype Products Ltd.

CHAPTER 2
Financial data in this chapter have been reproduced with permission from Sun-Rype Products Ltd.
Page 43: Courtesy of Sun-Rype Products Ltd.

CHAPTER 3
Financial data in this chapter have been reproduced with permission from Sun-Rype Products Ltd.
Page 104: Courtesy of Sun-Rype Products Ltd.

CHAPTER 4
Financial data in this chapter have been reproduced with permission from Sun-Rype Products Ltd.
Page 163: Courtesy of Sun-Rype Products Ltd.

CHAPTER 5
Financial data in this chapter have been reproduced with permission from Danier Leather Inc.
Page 233: © Danier Leather Inc.

CHAPTER 6
Financial data in this chapter have been reproduced with permission from Thomson Reuters.
Page 291: © Idealink Photography/Alamy

CHAPTER 7
Financial data in this chapter have been reproduced with permission from Gildan Activewear Inc.
Page 344: © Gildan Activewear Inc. 2013

CHAPTER 8
Financial data in this chapter have been reproduced with permission from Danier Leather Inc.
Page 409: Courtesy of Danier Leather Inc.

CHAPTER 9
Financial data in this chapter have been reproduced with permission from WestJet Airlines Ltd.
Page 465: © WestJet Airlines Ltd.

CHAPTER 10
Financial data in this chapter have been reproduced with permission from Bauer Performance Sports Ltd.
Page 534: © RICK MADONIK/TORONTO STAR/GetStock.com

CHAPTER 11
Financial data in this chapter have been reproduced with permission from BCE Inc.
Page 588: Source: BCE Inc., Annual Report 2012

CHAPTER 12
Financial data in this chapter have been reproduced with permission from BCE Inc.
Page 641: Courtesy of BCE Inc.

CHAPTER 13
Financial data in this chapter have been reproduced with permission from Home Depot.
Page 692: © Canadian Tire Corporation Limited

CHAPTER 14 (online)
Financial data in this chapter have been reproduced with permission from Empire Company Limited.
Opener: Sobeys Inc.

Index